Footprint story

It was 1921

Ireland had just been partitioned, the British miners were striking for more pay and the federation of British industry had an idea. Exports were booming in South America – how about a handbook for businessmen trading in that far away continent? The Anglo-South American Handbook was born that year, written by W Koebel, the most prolific writer on Latin America of his day.

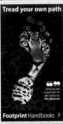

1924

Two editions later the book was 'privatized' and in 1924, in the hands of Royal Mail, the steamship company for South America, it became The South American Handbook, subtitled 'South America in a nutshell'. This annual publication became the 'bible' for generations of travellers to South America and remains so to this day. In the early days travel was by sea and the Handbook gave all the details needed for the long voyage from Europe. What to wear for dinner; how to arrange a cricket match with the Cable & Wireless staff on the Cape Verde Islands and a full account of the journey from Liverpool up the Amazon to Manaus: 5898 miles without changing cabin!

1939

As the continent opened up, the South American Handbook reported the new Pan Am flying boat services, and the fortnightly airship service from Rio to Europe on the Graf Zeppelin. For reasons still unclear but with extraordinary determination, the annual editions continued through the Second World War.

1970s

Many more people discovered South America and the backpacking trail started to develop. All the while the Handbook was gathering fans, including literary vagabonds such as Paul Theroux and Graham Greene (who once sent some updates addressed to "The publishers of the best travel guide in the world, Bath, England").

1990s

During the 1990s the company set about developing a new travel guide series using this legendary title as the flagship. By 1997 there were over a dozen guides in the series and the Footprint imprint was launched.

2000s

The series grew quickly and there were soon Footprint travel guides covering more than 150 countries. In 2004, Footprint launched its first thematic guide: *Surfing Europe*, packed with colour photographs, maps and charts. This was followed by further thematic guides such as *Diving the World, Snowboarding the World, Body and Soul escapes, Travel with Kids and European City Breaks*.

2010

Today we continue the traditions of the last 89 years that have served legions of travellers so well. We believe that these help to make Footprint guides different. Our policy is to use authors who are genuine experts who write for independent travellers; people possessing a spirit of adventure, looking to get off the beaten track.

Argentina Handbook

Lucy E Cousins

Argentina is immense, intense and dramatic. Wherever you go, the contrasts are breathtaking. From the dry deserts of the north to the frozen landscapes of the south, you will never get bored in Argentina. The behemoth capital Buenos Aires is reminiscent of a sophisticated modern European city: life races past the grand baroque building at dizzying speeds, and there are hip bars and chic boutiques dotted around the city; but step into a *milonga* and the mysterious rituals of the tango belong to a previous century.

At one end of the country the mighty Iguazú Falls thunder through lush jungle filled with electric-blue butterflies, and crumbling mission ruins lie undisturbed among the trees and vines. At the other, silent glaciers stretch endlessly before you, until they shatter with a roar and a splash into a milky turquoise-blue lagoon; world-class ski resorts overlook dark brooding lakes and forests that turn auburn in the autumn; and the serene Beagle Channel meets Argentina's most southerly city, the windy and rugged Ushuaia, used by many as a jump-off point for the wilds of Antarctica.

And in between? Infinite space. Drive the desolate Ruta 40 through the lonely expanse of Patagonia and the only sign of life will be a couple of condors and a thousand prehistoric handprints on a cave wall. Yet throughout the country, from dusty Salta to freezing Patagonia, the Argentine people are generous, friendly and always approachable, ensuring that this is a place you'll want to return to.

This page Gauchos herd sheep by Lago Argentino on the Patagonian grasslands.
Previous page Accordion player in La Boca district of Buenos Aires.

PARAGUAY

Río Pilcomayo

4 Purmamarca
Jujuy
Santa Rosa
de Tastil
Salta

Río Bermejo

Formosa

Puerto **5**
Iguazú

Mount
Llullaillaco
(6739m)

Cafayate

Río Salado

Resistencia

Río Alto Paraná

6

Ojos de
Salado
(6864m)

Tucumán

Corrientes

Posadas

7

Bonete
(6759m)

Santiago
del Estero

BRAZIL

Catamarca

Mercedes

La Rioja

Río Dulce

Pacific
Ocean

Mercedario
(6770m)

San Juan

Laguna
Mar
Chiquito

2 Córdoba

Río Paraná

Santa Fe
Paraná

URUGUAY

Aconcagua
(6959m)

3

Mendoza

Río Uruguay

Rosario

Tupungato
(6635m)

San Luis

Río Cuarto

BUENOS
AIRES

1

CHILE

San Rafael

La Plata

Río de
la Plata

Chascomús

Santa Rosa

Tandil

Pinamar

Tromen
(3978m)

Bahía
Blanca

Mar del Plata

Río Colorado

Neuquén

Río Neuquén

Río Limay

Lanín
(3768m)

San Martín
de los Andes

Río Negro

Lago Nahuel
Huapi

Viedma

Tronador
(3478m)

Bariloche
El Bolsón

Puerto
Madryn

8 Esquel

Gaiman

Trelew

9

Río Chubut

Atlantic
Ocean

Comodoro
Rivadavia

Lago
Buenos
Aires

Río Deseado

Perito
Moreno

Puerto
Deseado

Lago San
Martín

Puerto
San Julián

11 El Chaltén

Fitz Roy
(3405m)

Lago Viedma

10 El Calafate

Lago Argentino

Falkland Islands/
Islas Malvinas

Río Gallegos

Puerto
Natales

Darwin

Punta
Arenas

Río Grande

Tierra del Fuego

12

CHILE

Ushuaia

N

200 km
200 miles

Argentina highlights

See colour maps at back of book

1 San Telmo, the oldest and most atmospheric district in Buenos Aires. ▶▶ page 82.

2 Córdoba, less hectic than Buenos Aires and just as vibrant; and don't forget a visit to the Jesuit *estancias* nearby. ▶▶ page 176.

3 Aconcagua, the highest peak on the continent, only for the fit and super motivated. ▶▶ page 248.

4 Quebrada de Humahuaca, stunning multi-coloured gorges of terracotta with ancient oasis villages. ▶▶ page 323.

5 Iguazú Falls, the spectacular sight of 275 waterfalls converging on one spot. ▶▶ page 362.

6 Quiet San Ignacio, with the ruins of a Jesuit mission at its heart. ▶▶ page 382.

7 Esteros del Iberá, a birdwatcher's heaven and floating islands in paradise. ▶▶ page 393.

8 Virgin forest, hanging glaciers and perfect hikes in Los Alerces National Park. ▶▶ page 523.

9 Basking whales, penguin colonies and harems of sea lions on the glorious beaches of Península Valdés. ▶▶page 543.

10 Perito Moreno Glacier, the world's only advancing and retreating glacier. ▶▶ page 587.

11 Trekking heaven around the stunning granite peak of Cerro Fitz Roy. ▶▶ page 588.

12 Estancia Harberton, pioneer life on the serene Beagle Channel, Tierra del Fuego. ▶▶ page 651.

Clockwise from top

Cerro Fitz Roy.

Córdoba city.

Perito Moreno Glacier.

Aconcagua.

San Telmo district, Buenos Aires.

Opposite page top Quebrada de Humahuaca.

Opposite page bottom Península Valdés.

Clockwise from top

Parque Nacional Los Alerces.

Estancia Harberton.

San Ignacio.

Esteros del Iberá.

Opposite page Iguazú Falls.

Festivals

Festival de la Empanada
Each September the *empanada* festival in Tucumán brings together the best *empanada* chefs in the country. There are cooking displays, music and of course the fiercely contested 'best *empanada*' competition. The region generally produces spicy *empanadas* with golden pastry. Don't eat for a week beforehand so you'll have room to fit in as much as you can. Book bus tickets and accommodation early as this festival is popular with tourists and locals.

Fiesta de la Tradición
To celebrate the culture and lifestyle of the Argentine gauchos, each November the population of San Antonio de Areco, a small town near Buenos Aires, swells as people arrive from far afield to attend the Fiesta de la Tradición. There are horse-riding displays, live music, stalls selling gaucho clothes and metal-work, and gaucho-inspired artwork is on show. The festival concludes on 10 November with the Día de la Tradición which pays homage to José Hernández who wrote the epic gaucho poem *Martín Fierro*.

Festival de la Luz
The Festival de la Luz (Festival of Light), each August and September in Buenos Aires, is a collaboration of more than 34 photography festivals around the world. All over the city, free exhibitions, events, conferences and workshops are held, and even the smallest of art galleries participate. It is a true celebration of the photographic arts. Look in newspapers for events.

Fiesta Nacional de la Cereza
Situated just off the Ruta 40 in an oasis on the shores of Lago Buenos Aires, Los Antiguos is usually a sleepy country town. But come January and with the Fiesta Nacional de la Cereza (Cherry Festival), now nearing the ripe old age of 20, the hotels fill up, the streets crowd with cars and people from all over Argentina come to enjoy the local

produce. There are stalls selling fruit, including cherries, and local crafts. Over the three days of the festival the streets are never empty. Each night there are fireworks and at the end of the festival a Cherry Queen is chosen, attracting crowds of up to 30,000 people.

Oktoberfest

Attractive Villa General Belgrano in Córdoba keeps up the Oktoberfest tradition every year when the small German-style village turns into a mosh pit of beer lovers. Local beer halls fill up quickly and accommodation is really hard to find. Come for the party atmosphere and the mix of people. Don't come for a peaceful weekend away. The locally brewed beers are always a favourite.

Vendimia wine festival

The Vendimia wine festival in Mendoza lasts from January right through to the first weeks of March, and involves huge flamboyant parades day and night featuring floats carrying the 17 candidates for Harvest Queen. Some 200,000 people usually attend this event. The festival also promotes local growers and their products, as well as national musicians and artists. This festival has been celebrated for nearly 70 years and it attracts more and more people every year.

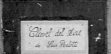

Contents

Contents

Footprint features

Essentials

Planning your trip

Deciding what regions, cities and attractions to visit whilst travelling in Argentina will be hard as it offers such diverse geography: snow, desert, lakes and an endless coastline. Whatever you do, allow more time than you think you'll need. Unless you have unlimited time and money, you probably have to accept from the start that you can't see it all. Distances are huge, and it's time consuming to get around. There are daily flights to all the major destinations but most go via Buenos Aires, so travelling between the north and the south, for example, will take a full day out of your itinerary. Although there are few trains in Argentina, there is an efficient and extensive network of long-distance buses, which even offer complimentary hot meals. So rather than just ticking places off your list on a relentless itinerary, allow at least a couple of days free in each place if you can, and don't try to do too much. It's much more satisfying to explore one area in real depth than to dart about all over the country in one week.

Where to go

Buenos Aires is a great first port of call, whether you want to see the football, try tango or shop till you drop. Chic Palermo Viejo is the place for cool restaurants and new design, San Telmo with its cobbled streets is one of the oldest neighbourhoods, and the delta river system just north of the city is a calm retreat of houses on stilts. From there you can head south to the wilds of Patagonia. Whether escaping like Butch and Sundance, or seeking freedom like the Welsh pioneers, you'll find a liberating expanse of nothing. Head east to Puerto Madryn for amazing marine life or travel the solitary Ruta 40 in Ernesto 'Che' Guevara's tyre tracks. From windy El Calafate, cross an iceberg-strewn lake for breathtaking views of the southern ice field, and later attempt an ice trek on Glacier Perito Moreno. Further south, Tierra del Fuego offers the ultimate wilderness and, as you take a boat trip along the Beagle Channel, you'll feel like a true explorer. From there you can follow the Argentine Andes northwards as they stretch along a wonderland of snow-capped mountains, dotted with lakes and lagoons of all shades of blue. Start at picturesque Bariloche: chalet-style hotels, chocolate shops and a backdrop of peaks, where you could hike for a week without getting bored. A little way along the Seven Lakes Drive is the upmarket San Martín de los Andes or smaller Villa La Angostura. Hide out in an *estancia* to ride the wild lands, or go whitewater rafting into Chile. Discover quiet Villa Pehuenia, set amidst forests of silent monkey puzzle trees, or fish for giant trout at Junín de los Andes. Head south to laid-back El Bolsón for superb hiking along crystalline rivers, catch the *Old Patagonian Express* into the hills, or hike into the pristine forests of Los Alerces. The northwest is another Argentina, of rich indigenous culture and ancient civilizations, with ruined cities at Quilmes, Las Pailas, El Shinkal and Tastil. Explore the Quebrada de Humahuaca, a vast red gorge dotted with quaint oasis villages near the border with Bolivia, or the timeless Valles Calchaquíes, where high-altitude wine is grown in dramatic rugged landscapes. Colourful Salta's colonial splendour contrasts perfectly with the culture of the *puna*, where Pachamama festivities are a glimpse of another time. Admire the colonial churches and Jesuit missions of Córdoba or, for wine lovers, Mendoza has superb bodegas stretching out to a backdrop of the Andes, and excellent hiking for serious mountaineers. Finally the lush northwest, which boasts the country's star attraction: Iguazú Falls. Constant and stunning, the falls should not be missed. Heading

Packing for Argentina

You'll be able to buy most things you're likely to need once you're in Argentina, and at cheaper prices than at home in most cases (except imported goods, which are prohibitively expensive). Scan all documents, your passport and flight ticket, and email them to yourself and a friend in case there's an emergency. Carry a photocopy of your passport at all times.

Buy as big a memory card for your camera as you can afford. There are plenty of places in all towns that will download your photos onto CD and wipe the card, but you'll take many more photos than you think in any given day. Make sure you download your photos as often as possible so that if you lose your camera you won't lose all your photos too. A word of advice for long bus journeys: carry small packs of tissues

(available at the *kiosko* in the terminal) for toilet roll, and water for teeth brushing, since toilets on buses can be quite an adventure.

Along with your usual clothes, camera and diary, consider bringing: a light waterproof jacket, comfortable walking shoes or boots, a lightweight fleece top, a smartish set of clothes (for the occasional night at a good hotel or restaurant), a money pouch (worn under your clothes, particularly in Buenos Aires), a padlock (if you're planning to stay in hostels), suncream, insect repellent, sunglasses, a torch or Maglite (useful for walking around remote, unlit villages at night) and a folding knife (handy for picnics, but remember not to carry it in hand luggage on the plane). See page 22 for a list of trekking equipment.

south, explore the Jesuit mission ruins hidden by the thick jungle, or relax in a lodge in the Esteros del Iberá wetlands, a paradise for birds.

One week

With just one week in the country, it is best to limit your itinerary. The essentials for any trip are the bright lights of Buenos Aires and the stunning Iguazú Falls. To experience Buenos Aires, see a tango show, watch some football and perhaps do a little shopping, you need a minimum of three days. Then take an overnight bus (16 hours), or a more expensive but much shorter flight, to Iguazú Falls. Two days is sufficient to see both the Argentine and Brazilian sides of the falls, or better still allow two days to explore the larger Argentine park. Then, returning to Buenos Aires, the more budget conscious could spend the weekend in the fantastic Hostelling International (HI) hostel in the delta system just north of Buenos Aires. Alternatively, spend a night at one of the grandiose *estancias* close to the capital, where you can ride horses, play sports, swim or just relax in the sun. Those with a little more money could fly down to El Calafate in Patagonia to experience the immensity of the Perito Moreno Glacier for two days. Spend a whole day staring at the 60-m-high ice walls from the wooden walkways on the peninsula, then return to a luxury spa and complete the trip with a full-body massage.

Two weeks

Two weeks allows you to see a lot more, but will require a non-stop itinerary. Enjoy fast-paced Buenos Aires in all its glory for three packed days before flying or taking an overnight bus to Iguazú Falls. After two days exploring the walkways and waterfalls, fly via Buenos Aires to either El Calafate (at its best from November to March) or Salta (preferably

May to October when the heat isn't unbearable). In El Calafate, once you have spent a day at the Perito Moreno Glacier, catch the four-hour bus to El Chaltén to enjoy the relatively easy four-day hikes into the mountains. Relax at night in one of the cosy hotels and visit the lively restaurants in this small tourist town. Otherwise, skip El Chaltén and head across the border to Puerto Natales in Chile. From there, hire your camping equipment and head off on the 'W' circuit of the spectacular Torres del Paine National Park.

In the cooler months (from May to October) when El Chaltén and Torres del Paine close, head north to Salta: the cultural capital of Argentina. Salta is host to a wealth of impeccable colonial architecture, the exhilarating Tren a las Nubes (one of the highest trains in the world), and a rich culinary tradition (try the spicy *empanadas*). Don't forget to visit the nearby vineyards in Cafayate for a day as well.

Hire a car or catch the local buses up to Quebrada de Humahuaca in the north, an ancient rock formation with astounding colours, connecting a string of little villages, including Tilcara, Humahuaca and Purmamarca. Stay at the fantastic HI hostel in Tilcara for priceless views, or head to exclusive Purmamarca for a luxury resort. Fly back to Buenos Aires and spend one last night drinking local wine and eating *dulce de leche* pancakes.

Three or four weeks

A month is the ideal amount of time to spend in Argentina, but three weeks is a good compromise, giving you enough time to get a feel for the country's extraordinary contrasts. With a month, start in Buenos Aires before heading up to the Iguazú Falls for two days. Then the best option is to fly south to El Calafate to visit the Perito Moreno Glacier (don't miss the glacier ice trek). From November to March head over to El Chaltén (four hours) for a few days' hiking, or cross the border to trek the Torres del Paine National Park in Chile. In the cooler months (April to October), you can still visit the glacier in El Calafate but just make sure you have enough warm clothes! From there, fly to Ushuaia to see the 'End of the World'. You could visit a local *estancia*, take a tour on the Beagle Channel or visit one of the world's most southerly ski fields.

Next, head north. From El Calafate take the Ruta 40 to Bariloche stopping off at the Cueva de las Manos: incredibly preserved prehistoric cave paintings in the middle of nowhere. From Ushuaia, take a flight to Bariloche. The next few days should be spent either hiring a car or catching the fantastic local buses around the Lake District: from hippy El Bolsón with its home-made jams, to the 2000-year-old trees of the Alerces National Park, from the serene lakeside setting of San Martín de Los Andes, to the bright red bark of the Arrayanes National Park. There is plenty here to keep you busy. Camp, stay at the wonderful hostels or splurge on boutique lodges. Moving on, head further north by bus to Mendoza to visit the nearby vineyards and do a winery tour, before travelling to Córdoba to marvel at the colonial architecture and the restored Jesuit missions. Finally, make your way up to Salta in the north to try the food, experience the Andean culture and visit the stunning Quebrada de Humahuaca, staying in one of the little adobe-built hotels in Tilcara or Humahuaca, before heading back to Buenos Aires for your final night.

When to go

Argentina is an appealing destination for warm, sunny holidays in the middle of the northern hemisphere winter though, since the country covers such a vast area, there is somewhere to visit at any time of year. The southern hemisphere summer is from

December to March, spring is from mid-September to November, autumn is from March to May and winter from June to August.

Before you look at when to go, start thinking about what you would like to see. Generally speaking, November to April is the best time for travelling to Mendoza, San Juan, Córdoba, Patagonia and Ushuaia. Trekking trails are open and national parks are at their prettiest. For the rest of the country, namely Salta, Jujuy, Tucumán, Corrientes and Iguazú Falls, May to October is best as temperatures tend to be cooler, and there is less rain. Exceptions are the marine reserve at Península Valdés, which has different seasons for different animals, and also the ski season at the various resorts, which is from about June to mid-October, depending on the climate.

Buenos Aires city is wonderful any time of year but is at its best in spring and autumn, when the weather is sunny and mild. The city can be hot and humid in the height of summer, with temperatures over 40°C and humidity at 80%. If you come in summer, consider spending a night in the delta or on an *estancia*, to cool down.

What to do

Birdwatching

It comes as no surprise in a country so rich in untouched natural habitats that the birdlife is extraordinary, and extremely varied. From the wealth of seabirds at Península Valdés to the colourful species in the subtropical rainforest near the Iguazú Falls, from the marshlands of Esteros del Iberá or the Chaco savannah to the Lake District and the mountainous interior of Tierra del Fuego, there are marvellous opportunities to spot birds. At least 980 of the 2926 species of birds registered in South America exist in Argentina and, in many places, with easy access. There are specialist tours led by expert guides in most areas; see the travelling text for details.

ⓘ All Patagonia, www.allpatagonia.com, runs birdwatching trips in Patagonia and Tierra del Fuego. In the northeast, contact Daniel Samay of Explorador Expediciones, www.rainforestevt.com.ar, and in the Lake District, Angel Fernández, T02944-524609, T011-15609799, and Daniel Feinstein, T/F02944-442259. An excellent British-based tour operator that can arrange birdwatching trips is Select Latin America, T020-7407 1478, www.selectlatinamerica.co.uk.

Climbing

The Andes offer great climbing opportunities. Among the most popular peaks are Aconcagua, in Mendoza province, Pissis in Catamarca, and Lanín and Tronador, reached from the Lake District. The northern part of Los Glaciares National Park, around El Chaltén, has some spectacular peaks with very difficult mountaineering. Climbing clubs can be found in Mendoza, Bariloche, Esquel, Junín de los Andes, Ushuaia and other cities, and in some places equipment can be hired. ⓘ Club Andino, www.caba.org.ar.

Fishing

Argentina offers some of the world's finest fishing, in beautiful virgin landscape, and with good accommodation. In the Lake District, there's world-renowned fly fishing for trout (rainbow, brown and brook); and for chinook or landlocked salmon. The centre is around Junín de los Andes and Bariloche, in rivers Quilquihue, Chimehuín, Collón-Curá, Meliquina and Caleufú, and Lakes Traful, Gutiérrez, Mascardi, Cholila, Futalaufquén (in Los Alerces National Park), Falkner, Villarino; Huechulafquén, Paimún, Epulafquén, Tromen (all in Lanín National Park); and, in the far north, Quillén. In the Lake District, the season lasts usually from November to April.

In Tierra del Fuego, huge brown trout can be fished from Río Grande and Lago Fagnano, while over the border in Chilean Tierra del Fuego, Lago Blanco is fast becoming popular. In the northeast, *sorubim* and giant *pacu* can be fished at the confluence of rivers Paraná and Paraguay, as well as *dorado*, known for its challenging fight. The closed season in this area is November to January. On the Atlantic coast, San Blas is famous for shark fishing, for bacota shark and bull shark weighing up to 130 kg, while all along the coast, there's good sea fishing. Fishing can also be found in other parts of the country and is offered by many *estancias*. *Pejerrey*, *corvina* and *pescadilla* can be found in large quantities along the coast of Buenos Aires province, and many of the reservoirs of the Central Sierras, the West and Northwest are well stocked.

All rivers are 'catch and release', and to fish anywhere in Argentina you need a permit costing US$5 per day, US$15 per week, US$50 per year. It certainly makes sense to do some research before you arrive, to find the right area for the kind of fishing you want to do.

ⓘ **Fly Fishing Association of Argentina**, T011-4773 0821, for fishing licences. In Patagonia, there's assistance from the **National Parks Administration**, T011-4311 8853/0303.

Horse riding

In a country that boasts the top 10 polo players in the world, the tradition of horse treks and horse riding is alive and strong. Offered all through the country, from Salta in the north to El Calafate in the south, horse-riding tours, or *cabalgatas,* vary in length, and in quality. Generally speaking, if you visit an *estancia* or working farm that offers horse riding you'll find healthy horses, huge expanses of land and the wind whistling through your hair. If you go with adventure tourism agencies, you may have an English-speaking guide more suited to beginners. Choose the best option to suit your level of experience. One of the most challenging and spectacular horse treks traces the path that General San Martín and his soldiers took across the Andes near San Juan. Reaching up to 4000 m, and scaling the cliff edge, the five-day ride uses donkeys due to the harsh terrain.

ⓘ www.estanciasargentinas.com and www.estanciasdebsas.com.ar will help locate *estancias* that offer horse riding.

Skiing

The skiing season runs from mid-June to mid-October, but dates vary between resorts. The country's best and deservedly famous is Las Leñas, south of Mendoza, due to its long, varied and challenging pistes, its spectacular setting, superb accommodation, and also for having a dedicated snowboarding area. It's also the most expensive resort, so if you're looking for a cheaper option in the same area, consider Los Penitentes, a more modest but friendly resort. There's good skiing all along the Lake District, with the biggest centre at Cerro Catedral, near Bariloche. This is a huge resort with scope for cross-country skiing and snowboarding, and the advantages of a major town with excellent hotels and services. Nearby, the smaller but upmarket resorts of Cerro Bayo at Villa la Angostura and Cerro Chapelco at San Martín de los Andes have even more beautiful settings and cater for families. La Hoya, near Esquel, is much cheaper with a laid-back family feel. And at the end of the world, in Ushuaia, there's great cross-country and downhill skiing at Cerro Castor. Details of all of these resorts are given in the text, together with websites.

ⓘ www.welcomeargentina.com/ski and www.allaboutar.com/sports_skiing.htm are useful for general information on all resorts.

Tango

What was once the dance of immigrants from the Buenos Aires dockyards is now one of the most internationally recognizable aspects of Argentine culture. At the turn of the 19th century, the tango was seen as a dance practised by the lower classes in the streets and in brothels. And it wasn't until Argentine sailors brought it to Europe through French ports that it started to become acceptable in polite society in Buenos Aires. A little later, in 1913, Europe was officially in the grips of a tango craze. In London, the Waldorf Hotel introduced Tango Teas in the same vein as the French *Thés Dansants*, and Selfridges held a successful Tango Ball. In Paris, women's fashion was influenced by the dance, and shops sold tango stockings, tango hats and tango shoes. Even silent film star Rudolph Valentino danced it on-screen in 1921. Around this time, famous tango singer Carlos Gardel (whose name and face you'll see throughout Buenos Aires) toured South America as well as Paris, Barcelona, Madrid and New York. The so-called Golden Era for tango was from the 1930s to 1955 when a military coup ousted the president. From then onwards until the early 1980s, tango was in decline. It was ignored and even persecuted during the military dictatorship. Young people no longer wanted to dance it, and nearly two generations of Argentines grew up without learning it. However, after years of neglect, the Argentine people have re-embraced the dance at all levels. Women and men in their 40s and 50s are returning to the *milongas* or dancehalls to learn the steps, while their sons and daughters are listening to the new wave of tango music called *tango electrónica*. One more influence is fuelling this vibrant resurgence; the hundreds of tourists from around the world who arrive every year anxious to learn, practise and live the dance. A recent movement, which is causing a small sensation, is gay tango, known as Tango Queer. Several gay *milongas* have started up and there is a constant stream of dancers eager to learn the sexy steps. Each year in August, Buenos Aires hosts a tango festival, which boasts the best international and local dancers, free displays, classes and the sale of all things tango.

Useful websites

www.welcomeargentina.com/tango/lugares.html For an overview of tango shows available.

www.tangodata.gov.ar Fantastic government website listing *milongas*, classes and shows.

www.festivaldetango.gov.ar Everything you'll need to know about the annual Buenos Aires tango festival.

www.festivaltangoqueer.com.ar Official website for the Queer Tango Festival in Buenos Aires.

www.history-of-tango.com A comprehensive look at the history of the dance.

www.la2x4.gov.ar Website for tango radio station.

Trekking → *Visit www.parquesnacionales.gov.ar for more detailed information.*

The whole of the west of the country, along the mountains of the Andes, offers superb opportunities for trekking. The Lake District in summer is the most rewarding because there are so many spectacular landscapes to explore within easy reach of the centres of Bariloche, El Bolsón and San Martín de los Andes. The national parks here are well set up for walkers, with good information and basic maps available, and *refugios* and campsites convenient for accommodation on longer hikes. However, it's worth exploring the lesser-known extremes of the lakes, at Pehuenia in the north, with wonderful walks among the araucaria trees, and at Parque Nacional Los Alerces, with trekking into the virgin forest. All these walks are described in detail in the relevant areas. The season for walking is December to April.

The mountainous region to the west of Mendoza, around Aconcagua, offers good and challenging trekking, as well as further north in the Cordón del Plata in San Juan, where oasis villages in the valley are good bases for several peaks around Mercedario. Altitude sickness (see Health, page 45) can be a problem in these areas, and you should allow time in your schedule for adjustment. Further north, in Salta and Jujuy, there's a complete contrast of landscape. The *puna* to the west is dramatic desert, dropping to the arid and rocky mountainous landscape in the Quebrada de Humahuaca and, continuing east, there are cloudforests. It's possible to walk through all three zones in a single extended expedition, though you'd need to go with a guide. Throughout the area there are attractive villages to use as bases for day walks. In the northeast, there are a few good walks in the national park of the Iguazú Falls, and many more good places to walk in the provinces to the south. The centre of the country, in the sierras around Córdoba, are good for day walks, especially in the Traslasierra. In Patagonia, there are petrified forests and caves with pre-historic handprints to walk to, as well as the remoter reaches of Parque Nacional Perito Moreno. The most dramatic trekking is in the south of Patagonia, whether in the mountains around Mount Fitz Roy or ice trekking on the glaciers themselves in Parque Nacional Los Glaciares. And near Ushuaia, there are unforgettable views from peaks in the Parque Nacional Tierra del Fuego, along the shores of the Beagle Channel and from wilder peaks in mountains behind the town.

These are the highlights, but wherever you go in Argentina, you can find somewhere to trek. The spaces are wide open and there really are no limits.

Shops in large towns in Argentina stock clothes and camping supplies, but the following are things to consider taking. **Clothing**: a warm hat (wool or man-made fibre), wicking thermal underwear, T-shirts/shirts, trousers (quick-drying and preferably windproof), warm (wool or fleece) jumper/jacket (preferably two), gloves, waterproof jacket and overtrousers (preferably Gore-Tex), shorts, walking boots and socks, change of footwear or flip-flops. **Camping gear**: tent (capable of withstanding high winds), sleeping mat (closed cell, Karrimat, or inflatable, Thermarest), sleeping bag (three-season minimum), sleeping bag liner, stove and spare parts, fuel, matches and lighter, cooking and eating utensils, pan scrubber, survival bag. **Food**: take supplies for at least two days more than you plan to use; tea, coffee, sugar, dried milk, porridge, dried fruit, honey, soup, pasta, rice, soya (TVP), fresh fruit and vegetables, bread, cheese, crackers, biscuits, chocolate, salt, pepper, other herbs and spices, cooking oil. **Miscellaneous**: map and compass, torch and spare batteries, pen and notebook, Swiss army knife, sunglasses, sun cream, lip salve and insect repellent, first-aid kit, water bottle and towel.

Hikers have little to fear from the animal kingdom apart from insects, and robbery and assault are very rare. You are more of a threat to the environment than vice versa.

Note It's best not to go hiking alone, as hiking areas in Argentina are generally far less visited than those in Europe, and if you twist an ankle, it might be a long time before someone finds you. So try to join up with other people, and always register with *guardaparques* (rangers) before you set off.

Whitewater rafting
There are some good whitewater-rafting runs in Mendoza province, near the provincial capital and near San Rafael and Malargüe. In the Lake District there are possibilities in the Lanín, Nahuel Huapi and Los Alerces national parks.

Getting there

Air

Flights from Europe

There are flights to Buenos Aires from London, Amsterdam, Barcelona, Madrid, Frankfurt, Paris, Milan, Rome and Zurich with **Aerolíneas Argentinas** ① *1st floor, 22 Conduit St, London, W1S 2XR, T020-7290 7887, www.aerolineas.com*, and other European carriers. From Britain, only **British Airways** goes direct to Buenos Aires, and has been repeatedly recommended for comfort and service.

Flights from North America and Canada

Aerolíneas Argentinas and other South American and North American airlines fly from Miami, New York, Washington, Los Angeles, San Francisco, Atlanta, New Orleans, Dallas and Chicago. **Canadian Air International** and **Lan Chile** fly from Toronto and Montreal.

Flights from Australasia and South Africa

Aerolíneas Argentinas, Lan Chile and **Qantas** fly from Sydney (Australia), via Auckland, New Zealand (except Qantas who now have direct flights), two or three times a week. **Malaysia Airlines** fly twice a week from Kuala Lumpur to Buenos Aires, via Johannesburg, and **South African Airways** fly four times a week from Johannesburg, via Sao Paulo.

Flights from Latin America

Aerolíneas Argentinas and other carriers fly between Buenos Aires and all the South American capitals, plus Santa Cruz and Cochabamba in Bolivia and Guayaquil in Ecuador. Several flights between Buenos Aires, Rio de Janeiro and São Paulo stopover in Porto Alegre, Florianópolis and Curitiba. There are also flights from Belo Horizonte, Salvador, Recife and Fortaleza, Havana, Mexico City and Cancún.

General tips

Check your baggage allowance as airlines vary widely. The limit is usually 20-32 kg per person for economy class; strictly enforced with extortionate charges for excess baggage. For internal flights in Argentina, the baggage limit with **Aerolíneas Argentinas** is now 15 kg, and they are extremely inflexible, also charging wildly for excess. This means you will either have to leave some things in your hotel in Buenos Aires, or consider limiting your baggage to 15 kg when you leave home.

Airport information

All flights from outside Argentina, apart from those from neighbouring countries, arrive at Ezeiza International Airport (officially known as Ministro Pistarini), situated 35 km southwest of Buenos Aires (for detailed information including transport to Buenos Aires, see page 62). All internal flights as well as some flights to or from neighbouring countries come to Jorge Newbery Airport, generally known as Aeroparque, situated 4 km north of the centre of Buenos Aires on the bank of the Río de la Plata (see page 62 for details). Most provincial airports have a desk offering tourist information, banking facilities and a *confitería* (cafeteria) as well as car hire. There are usually minibus services into the city and taxis are available. For details of airport tax, see page 51.

Entry fee

Argentina recently joined Brazil, Chile and Bolivia in charging an 'Entry Request Fee'. Unlike Chile, which charges fees only from the citizens of the USA, Argentina is requesting payment from all citizens of Australia, Canada and the US. Fees for the citizens of above-mentioned countries are:

Australia – US$100, Canada – US$70 (single entry), United States – US$140. Payments are made at the airport and can be made in US dollars, Argentine pesos, by credit cards or traveller's cheque. Although it is not specified, the fees are in theory valid for the life of the passport, except in the case of Canadian citizens who have to pay each time they enter Argentina. **Note** This process has caused queue times to lengthen, so allow more time when booking onward travel.

Prices and discounts

Fares vary considerably from airline to airline, so it's worth checking with an agency for the best deal for when you want to travel. The cheap-seat allocation will sell out quickly in holiday periods. The busiest seasons for travelling to Argentina are 7 December to 15 January, Easter, and 1 July to 10 September, when you should book as far ahead as possible. There might be special offers available from February to May and September to November. Fares usually fall into one month, three month or yearly fare categories, and it's more expensive the longer you want to stay. Return dates must be booked when the ticket is bought, but most airlines will let you change the date for a penalty of around US$100. With student (or under 26) fares, some airlines are flexible on the age limit, others strict, and usually these tickets are the most flexible, though they're not always the cheapest available.

Discount flight agents

Using the web to book flights, hotels and other services directly is becoming increasingly popular and you can get some good deals. Be aware, though, that cutting out the travel agents is denying yourself the knowledge and experience that they can give, not just in terms of the best flights to suit your itinerary, but also advice on documents, insurance, safety, routes and lodging. A reputable agent will also be bonded to give you some protection if arrangements collapse while you are travelling.

UK and Ireland
Journey Latin America, 12-13 Heathfield Terrace, London, W4 4JE, T020-8747 8315, and 12 St Ann's Sq, Manchester, M2 7HW, www.journeylatinamerica.co.uk. Leading specialist for tailor-made holidays in Latin America, running escorted tours throughout the region. They also offer a wide range of flight options.

STA Travel, 86 Old Brompton Rd, London, SW7 3LH, T0871-2300040, www.statravel.co.uk. Branches throughout the UK and many university campuses. Specialists in low-cost student/youth flights and tours. Good for student IDs and insurance.
Trailfinders, 194 Kensington High St, London, W8 7RG, T08450585858, www.trailfinders.com. 18 branches in London and throughout the UK. Also one in Dublin and 5 travel centres in Australia.

North America
Air Brokers International, 323 Geary St, Suite 411, San Francisco, CA 94102, T01-800-883 3273, www.airbrokers.com. Consolidator and specialist on RTW and Circle Pacific tickets.
Discount Airfares Worldwide On-Line, www.etn.nl/discount.htm. A hub of consolidator and discount agent links.
STA Travel, 5900 Wilshire Blvd, Suite 2110, Los Angeles, CA 90036, T1-800-781 4040,

www.sta-travel.com. Also branches in
New York, San Francisco, Boston, Miami,
Chicago, Seattle and Washington DC.
Travel CUTS, 187 College St, Toronto,
ON, M5T 1P7, T1-800-592 2887,
www.travelcuts.com. Specialist in student
discount fares, IDs and other travel services.
Also has branches in other Canadian cities.
Travelocity, www.travelocity.com.
Online consolidator.

Australia and New Zealand
Flight Centres, 82 Elizabeth St, Sydney,
T133133, www.flightcentre.com.au; 205 Queen
St, Auckland, T0800-243544, www.flightcentre.
co.nz. Branches in other towns and cities.
STA Travel, 702 Harris St, Sydney, T134782,
www.sta travel.com.au.
Travel.com.au, 80 Clarence St, Sydney,
T02-929 01500, www.travel.com.au.

Road

There are many entry points from neighbouring countries, and with good long-distance
bus services, this is a convenient way of entering Argentina if you're travelling around.

The main routes are as follows: in the west from Santiago (Chile) to Mendoza; in the
northwest from Villazón (Bolivia) to Jujuy and Salta; in the northeast from Asunción
(Paraguay) to Resistencia, from Encarnación (Paraguay) to Posadas, and from Foz do Iguazú
(Brazil) to Puerto Iguazú; in the Lake District by boat and bus from Puerto Montt (Chile) to
Bariloche; in Patagonia by road from Puerto Natales (Chile) to El Calafate or by road and ferry
crossings from Tierra del Fuego to Río Gallegos and El Calafate. There are also three road
crossings from Uruguay via bridges over the Río Uruguay, as well several ferry crossings, the
most important of which are from Montevideo and Colonia de Sacramento to Buenos Aires.
For more information on border crossing, see the boxes in individual chapters.

Sea

It's possible to cruise to Argentina and there are some luxurious options available, as
well as more basic freight travel options. Contact a specialist agency, such as Strand
Travel in London, www.strandtravel.co.uk, or www.cruise-locators.com, who have
information on all cruise lines.

Getting around

Air

There are plenty of internal flights from Buenos Aires to all over Argentina with two airlines:
Aerolíneas Argentinas and **Lan Chile**. There are some flights between cities without having
to return to Buenos Aires, such as Córdoba and Salta, El Calafate and Ushuaia – more in high
season. Aerolíneas Argentinas charges different fees for locals and foreigners. As a
foreigner, you need to book domestic tickets online on their 'international sites' (choose the
country of your residency). You can only make a reservation online, you can't pay for it.
However, the ticket has to be purchased over the phone within 24 hours, otherwise the
reservation gets cancelled. Calling can be stressful, especially if the line is bad. After all this,
you will be asked to reconfirm 48 hours before your flight. There are two solutions: wait to
book your internal flights with a travel agent in Argentina or switch to **LAN** (www.lan.com)
which has online purchasing. The army airline **LADE**, www.lade.com.ar, provides a weekly

service connecting towns in Patagonia, useful to avoid going via Buenos Aires – but these are booked up ahead of time.

All internal flights are fully booked way in advance for travel in December and January, Easter, and in July. Flights to El Calafate, Ushuaia, Bariloche and Puerto Iguazú are particularly booked up, and if travelling during these periods, consider booking at least your first internal flight before you leave home. Outside busy periods, it's usually possible to book internal flights with just a few days' notice, though note that flights to Ushuaia are always heavily booked. It's wise to leave some flexibility in your schedule to allow for bad weather, which may delay flights in the south, at El Calafate and Ushuaia. Meals are rarely served on internal flights, though you'll get a hot drink and a cake.

Airpasses

Airpasses allow you to pre-book between three to six internal flights at a discount, as long as your international flight is also with that company. Airpasses are no longer the cheapest way of getting around, and can be very restricting since you have to book all dates when you book your international ticket. You'll probably find it easier to book internal flights separately. But check with the airlines directly, in case they have a promotion: **LAN**, from within Chile T+600-526 2000, from within Argentina T0810-999 9525, www.lan.com; **Aerolíneas Argentinas**, T0845-601 1915, from within Argentina T0800-222 86527, www.aerolineas.com.

The following are the current cheapest available fares, one way, from Buenos Aires to: Bariloche (two hours) US$215, Salta (two hours) US$189, El Calafate (3¼ hours) US$156, Iguazú (two hours) US$156, Trelew (two hours) US$146, Ushuaia (four hours) US$165. Other useful routes for connecting popular destinations without having to return to Buenos Aires: Trelew to El Calafate US$170, Ushuaia to El Calafate US$165, El Calafate to Bariloche US$240.

Road

Bus

This enormous country is connected by a network of efficient long-distance buses, which are by far the cheapest way of getting around, as well as being more environmentally friendly than plane travel. They are safe and comfortable, and long journeys are travelled overnight, which saves time, as long as you can sleep. There are three levels of service: *común*, which offers little comfort for overnight buses, and with lots of stops (*intermedio*); *semi-cama*, with a slightly reclining seat; and *coche-cama*, where seats recline (some almost completely flat) and there are few stops and hot food served. On *semi-cama* and *coche-cama* services videos will be shown (usually action movies, very loud, just as you're about to go to sleep), and meals will be provided. This might be anything from a *sandwich de miga* (very soft white bread with a slice of cheese and ham) to a full meal, with wine and a pudding. There will also be a toilet on board (of dubious cleanliness), and the bus will usually stop somewhere en route for toilets and food. The difference in price between the services is often small, and *coche-cama* is most definitely worth the extra for a good night's sleep. It's a good idea to bring with you on long bus journeys: water, both to drink and for brushing your teeth, as the water in the toilet usually runs out; tissues or toilet roll; fruit or snacks, and a sandwich. Whatever you do, avoid being downstairs as although the larger chairs are down there, they are right next to the toilet and the main door both of which are in constant use throughout the night. If the cold air doesn't wake you up as the bus doors open at 0300, the smell from the toilet will. Ask the bus company to order you a vegetarian meal, if you want one, at least 24 hours before the scheduled departure.

Local buses are to be recommended too: since many Argentines rely on public transport, buses run to small villages and places in mountains, steppe or *puna*. Services are less frequent, but worth waiting for, to get off the beaten track and completely away from other tourists. Information on frequency and prices is given in the text where possible, but services may change, so it's worth ringing the bus terminal to check.

Bus companies may give a 20% discount if you show an international student card (or ISIC card), and this may also be available to teachers and university professors if they provide proof of employment. Note that discounts aren't usually available December to March. You can request the seat you want when you book; on old buses, seats at the back can be intolerably noisy with air conditioning (take a jumper in summer, since the air conditioning can be fierce). Make sure your seat number is on your ticket. Luggage is safely stored in a large hold at the back of the bus, and you'll be given a numbered ticket to reclaim it on arrival. It's always a good idea to lock your bags. *Maleteros* take the bags off the bus, and expect a small tip – 50 centavos or a peso is fine (many Argentines refuse to pay).

Bus company websites, www.andesmar.com.ar and www.viabariloche.com.ar, are useful for route planning across Argentina. Another great site to help you plan your journey is www.plataforma10.com. You can check bus prices and times, and can also book tickets for buses all over Argentina.

Car

It's worth hiring a car if there are several of you, for more freedom to explore the remoter reaches of the country, where buses and tours may not yet have been established. Go carefully though: distances are huge, and road surfaces in rural places are often earth (*tierra*) or gravel (*ripio*), so allow plenty of time – 60 kph is the maximum speed for cars on *ripio*. Apart from the unreliability of the gravel surface, there are unpredictable potholes and rocks in the road, and swerving at speed is inevitably dangerous. Check the vehicle carefully with the hire company for scratches and cracks in the windscreen before you set off, so that you won't be blamed for them on your return. With the exception of roads around Buenos Aires, there's little traffic and roads are single lane in each direction. Service stations for fuel, toilets, water and food are much further apart than in Europe and the United States so always carry water and keep the tank full. Be aware that most Argentines don't use their indicator when they overtake (which they do often), and they use their horn frequently.

Car hire Renting a car costs from US$50 to US$100 a day, depending how big a car you want, and how much mileage (kilometrage) is included: discounts might be offered for longer periods. Busy tourist places are more expensive than quieter towns, but small towns have fewer cars for hire. For most roads, even *ripio*, a conventional car will be fine, but if you're planning to head off into the *puna*, jungle, or remote parts of Patagonia such as the Ruta 40, consider hiring a four-wheel-drive vehicle (4WD). These may be *camionetas* in Argentina – small trucks, high off the ground, and with space at the back, useful for storing luggage and bicycles. Diesel (*gasoil*) cars are much cheaper to run than petrol (*nafta*), although the diesel can sometimes be hard to get. Make sure that insurance is included, and note that the insurance excess (what you'll have to pay if there's an accident) is extremely high in Argentina, because tourists have a history of turning cars over on *ripio* roads.

Driving in Argentina

Roads Only 29% of Argentina's roads are paved. Most main roads are rather narrow but roadside services are good. To avoid flying stones on gravel and dirt roads, don't follow trucks too closely, overtake with plenty of room, and pull over and slow down for oncoming vehicles. You'll find that most people won't use their indicator or brakes regularly, and the horn frequently. Most main roads have private tolls about every 100 km, US$0.20-1.50. Unprivatized secondary roads are generally poor. Internal checkpoints prevent food, vegetable and meat products from entering Patagonia, Mendoza, San Juan, Catamarca, Tucumán, Salta and Jujuy provinces.

Road safety All motorists are required to carry two warning triangles, a fire extinguisher, a tow rope or chain, and a first-aid kit. The handbrake must be fully operative and seat belts must be worn. Headlights must be on during the day in Buenos Aires province.

Documents Full car documentation must be carried (including an invoice for the most recently paid insurance premium) together with your international driving licence.

Organizations Automóvil Club Argentino (ACA), Av Libertador Gen San Martín 1850, Buenos Aires, T011-4808 4000 or T0800-888 9888, www.aca.org.ar, has a travel-documents service, car service facilities and road maps. Foreign automobile clubs with reciprocity with ACA are allowed to use facilities and discounts (with a membership card). ACA accommodation comprises: Motel, Hostería, Hotel, and Unidad Turística, and they also organize campsites. All have meal facilities of some kind.

Car hire The minimum age for renting a car is usually 25, and a credit card is required. Prices range from US$50-100 a day, with the highest prices in Patagonia. In tourist centres such as Salta, Bariloche or Mendoza it may be easier and cheaper to hire a taxi for the day.

Fuel Petrol/gasoline (*nafta*) costs on average US$0.75 a litre and US$0.55 for diesel. Cars are being converted to *gas natural comprimido* (GNC), which costs around 25% cheaper than *nafta* but filling stations are further away.

You'll need a credit card to hire a car, since companies take a print of the card as their guarantee, instead of a deposit. You'll be required to show a drivers' licence (just the plastic bit of a British licence) and minimum age for renting is 25 (private arrangements may be possible). You must ensure that the renting agency gives you ownership papers of the vehicle, which have to be shown at police and military checks, and if you plan to take the car over a border into Chile or Bolivia, for example, you must let the hire company know, as they'll need to arrange special papers for you to show, and the car must have the number plate etched on its windows. The multinational car hire companies (**Hertz, Avis**) are represented all over Argentina, along with Brazilian company **Localiza**, who are very reliable. Local companies may be cheaper, but check the vehicles carefully. Details of car hire companies are given in the Transport sections throughout the book.

Security Car theft has become common in Buenos Aires, much less so in the rest of the country, but park the car in busy well-lit places, where possible throughout the country. Always remove all belongings and leave the empty glove compartment open when the car is unattended to reduce temptation. In tourist areas, street children will offer to guard your car, worth 50 centavos, or outside restaurant areas in cities, there may be a man guarding cars for a peso. It's worth paying, though doesn't guarantee anything.

Cycling

If you have the time, cycling offers you one of the most rewarding ways to explore Argentina. You can get to all of the out-of-the-way places, and enjoy some exhilarating rides, especially in the Andes – anywhere between Salta to El Calafate, with some breathtaking and hair-raising rides in the Lake District in between. Travelling by bike gives you the chance to travel at your own pace and meet people who are not normally in contact with tourists. There's little traffic on the roads in much of the country, which are wide enough to let trucks pass with ease in most places. The challenges are the enormous distances, the fact that there are few places to stop for food and drink in much of the country, and the lack of shade.

Main roads are paved, apart from the famous Ruta 40 in its southern half, and many roads into rural areas, which are gravel. For these, a mountain bike is advisable. Bring a comprehensive tool kit and spares. Bike shops are few and far between, although there are excellent shops in the Lake District, for example. Consider hiring bikes here if you just want some gentle riding for a few days or so. It goes without saying that you'll need tough waterproof panniers and clothing.

Useful tips Wind, not hills, will be your biggest enemy cycling in Argentina. Try to make the best use of the mornings when wind is lowest. In parts of Patagonia there can be gusting winds of 80 kph around the clock at some times of year, whereas in other areas there can be none. Take care to avoid dehydration by drinking regularly, and carry the basic food staples (sugar, salt, dried milk, tea, coffee, porridge oats, raisins, dried soups, etc) and supplement these with whatever local foods can be found in the markets.

Always camp out of sight of a road. Remember that thieves are attracted to towns and cities, so when sightseeing, try to leave your bicycle with someone, such as a café owner. However, don't take unnecessary risks; always see that your bicycle is secure (most hotels will allow bikes to be kept in rooms). All over Argentina, the dogs are famous for barking at bikes and some can be vicious; carry a stick or some small stones to frighten them off. There's little traffic on most roads, but make yourself conspicuous by wearing bright clothing and for protection wear a helmet.

Train

The British built a fine network of railways all over the country, which gradually fell into decline through the second half of the 20th century, and were dealt the final blow by handing over control to the provinces in 1994. Few provinces had the resources to run trains and now the few tracks operating run freight trains only.

The only passenger services are within the area of Gran Buenos Aires, to Tigre with **Tren de la Costa**, T011-47326343, and an efficient service from Buenos Aires Constitución station south through the Pampas to the coast: via Chascomús to Mar del Plata, Necochea and Tandil, run by **Ferrobaires**, T011 43040038. There are only two long-distance train lines. One is: from Buenos Aires to Tucumán with **TUFESA**: long, uncomfortable, and not recommended. The other is from Viedma (on the east coast, south of Bahía Blanca) to Bariloche in the Lake District, a more comfortable overnight service which also takes cars.

In Viedma, T02920-422130, in Bariloche, T02944-423172, www.trenpatagonico-sa.com.ar. The only other train services are the tourist **Tren a las Nubes**, www.trenalasnubes.com.ar, which runs from Salta up to San Antonio de los Cobres in the *puna*, and the narrow gauge railway from Esquel in Patagonia, **La Trochita** (made famous by Paul Theroux as the *Old Patagonian Express*), http://latrochita.org.ar.

Maps

Several road maps are available, including those of the **ACA** (the most up to date), the **Firestone** road atlas and the **Automapa**, www.automapa.com.ar (regional maps, Michelin-style, high quality). The bigger cities in Argentina have just been added to Google Maps, so this will help with directions, though remember to ask a local as well, to make sure you are heading through an OK part of town.

Topographical maps are issued by the **Instituto Geográfico Militar** ① *Av Cabildo 381, Buenos Aires, T011-45765578 (1 block from Subte Ministro Carranza, Line D, or take bus 152), Mon-Fri 0800-1300, www.igm.gov.ar.* 1:500,000 sheets cost US$3 each; better coverage of 1:100,000 and 1:250,000, but no city plans. For walkers, the *Sendas y Bosques* (Walks and Forests) series are 1:200,000, laminated and easy to read, with good books containing English summaries, www.guiasendasybosques.com.ar, are recommended.

Sleeping

Hotels and guesthouses may display a star rating, but this doesn't necessarily match international standards. Many more expensive hotels charge different prices for *extranjeros* (non-Argentines) in US$, which is unavoidable since a passport is required as proof of residency. If you pay in cash (pesos) you may get a reduction. Room tax (VAT) is 21% and is not always included in the price (ask when you check in). All hotels will store luggage for a day, and most have English-speaking staff. For upmarket chain hotels throughout Argentina contact **N/A Town & Country Hotels**, www.newage-hotels.com. For hostels, see **Hostelling International Argentina** ① *Florida 835, T011-4511-8723, www.hostels.org.ar, Mon-Fri 0900-1830*, which offers discounts to card-holders at their 70 hostels throughout Argentina, long-distance buses and backpacker tours. An HI card in Argentina costs US$16. For a complete listing of sleeping options, see www.welcomeargentina.com.

Hotels, hosterías, residenciales and hospedajes
The standard of accommodation in Argentina is generally good, and although prices have risen in the last two years, good hotels are generally very good value for visitors. You'll find that most cities and tourist towns list hotels and *hosterías* as separate: this is no reflection on quality or comfort, but simply on size: a *hostería* has fewer than 20 rooms. Both hotels and *hosterías* will have rooms with private bathrooms (usually showers rather than bath tubs, which you'll find only in the more expensive establishments). Prices often rise in high summer (January to February), at Easter and in July. During public holidays or high season you should always book ahead. A few of the more expensive hotels in Buenos Aires and major tourist centres such as Puerto Madryn, Bariloche and El Calafate charge foreigners higher prices than Argentines, which can be very frustrating, though there's little you can do about it. If you're given a price in US dollars, ask if there's a reduction if you pay in pesos and in cash. Most places now accept credit cards, but check before you

Accommodation tips

Hotels

- Sometimes hotels offer cheaper deals through their websites: always check there first.
- Before you book have a look at where the hotel is located. Sometimes, such as in El Calafate, there are some fabulous hotels but they are quite a distance out of town and without a car you won't enjoy your stay quite so much.
- Note that most hotels, even the five-star hotels, do not provide tea and coffee making services, nor do they always have minibars.
- Some good websites for luxury hotels are www.tenriverstenlakes.com, www.designsuites.com, and www.newage-hotels.com (all in English).

Hostels

- Check your hostel with the description in this guidebook, speak to other travellers or search websites like www.hostelz.com and www.tripadvisor.com, as some hostels look much better on their websites than in real life.
- In Patagonia most hostels either don't have cutlery in the kitchen or require a deposit to use it. Best to buy your own set and guard it with your life.
- In the North, the linen provided by some hostels can be old and thin. If you can, buy a pillow case and sleeping bag liner that can act as a set of sheets if need be. And don't forget the obvious things, such as a padlock, flip-flops for the shower and an indelible pen to mark your food in the kitchen.
- Some good websites for hostels are www.latinbackpackers.com, www.hostels.com, and www.hihostels.com (all in English).

come. It's worth booking your first few nights' accommodation before you arrive, and most hotels have an email address on their websites (provided in the Listings sections throughout the book) so that you can make contact before setting off.

Estancias These are the large farms and cattle ranches found all over the country, many of them now open to tourists, and offering a marvellous insight into Argentine life. Most are extremely comfortable places to stay, and offer wonderful horse riding and other activities such as birdwatching and walking, in addition to the authentic experience of life on the land. They can be pricey but meals, drinks, transfers and activities are included. It will certainly be the most memorable part of your stay.

There's a whole spectrum of *estancias* from a simple dwelling on the edge of a pristine lake in the Patagonian wilderness to a Loire-style chateau in the Pampas. You'll certainly be treated to the traditional *asado*, meat cooked over an open fire, and most impressively, *asado al palo*, where the animal is speared on a cross-shaped stick and roasted to perfection.

Gauchos still work the land on horseback in their traditional outfit of *bombachas* (baggy trousers, comfortable for spending hours on horseback), *trensa* (a wide leather belt with silver clasps), a poncho (in the northwest), a *pañuelo* (neckerchief), a *boina* (beret) and on the feet *alpargatas* (simple cotton shoes).

Estancias can be pricier than hotels, but some are accessible even to travellers on a budget, at least for a day visit. *Día de campo* (day on the farm) is offered by lots of *estancias*, a full day of horse riding, or a ride in a horse-drawn carriage, an *asado* lunch, and then often other farm activities, or time to relax in the peaceful grounds. Overnight stays costs from US$50 for two in the most humble places to US$250 per person for the most luxurious.

Though *estancias* are found throughout rural Argentina, they vary enormously in style and activities. In the province of Buenos Aires you will find *estancias* covering thousands of hectares of flat grassland with large herds of cattle and windpumps to extract water; horse riding will certainly be offered and perhaps cattle-mustering, at La Luisa and Palantelén for example. Some of the finest buildings are in this area, such as Dos Talas and La Porteña. In Patagonia there are giant sheep *estancias* overlooking glaciers, mountains and lakes, such as *estancias* **Maipú**, **Helsingfors** or **Alma Gaucha**. There are *estancias* on Tierra del Fuego, full of the history of the early pioneers who built them (**Viamonte** and **Harberton**), while on the mainland nearby, **Estancia Monte Dinero** has a colony of Magellanic penguins on its doorstep. There's more wildlife close at hand in the *estancias* on Península Valdés. And in Salta, there are colonial-style *fincas*, whose land includes jungly cloudforest with marvellous horse riding.

The most distinctive or representative *estancias* are mentioned in the text, but for more information see: www.turismo.gov.ar (in English), the national tourist website with all *estancias* listed; www.caminodelgaucho.com.ar, an excellent organization which can arrange stays in the Pampas *estancias*; www.estanciasdesantacruz.com, a helpful agency which arranges *estancia* stays in Santa Cruz and the south, including transport. A useful book *Tursimo en Estancias y Hosterías* is produced by **Tierra Buena**, www.guiatierrabuena.com.ar. You can of course contact *estancias* directly, and reserve, ideally with a couple of weeks' notice.

Cabañas These are a great option if you have transport and there are at least two of you. They are self-catering cottages, cabins or apartments, usually in rural areas, and often in superb locations, such as the Lake District. They're tremendously popular among Argentine holidaymakers, who tend to travel in large groups of friends, or of several families together, and as a result the best *cabañas* are well-equipped and comfortable. They can be very economical too, especially for groups of four or more, but are feasible even for two, with considerable reductions off-season. If you're travelling by public transport, *cabañas* are generally more difficult to get to, but ask the tourist office if there are any within walking or taxi distance. Throughout the Lake District, *cabañas* are plentiful and competitively priced.

Camping Organized campsites are referred to in the text immediately after hotel listings for each town. Camping is very popular in Argentina (except in Buenos Aires) and there are many superbly situated sites, most with good services, whether municipal or private. There are many quieter, family orientated places, but if you want a livelier time, look for a campsite (often by the beaches) with younger people, where there's likely to be partying until the small hours. Camping is allowed at the side of major highways and in all national parks (except at Iguazú Falls), but in Patagonia strong winds can make camping very difficult. Wherever you camp, pack your rubbish and put out fires with earth and water. Fires are not allowed in many national parks because of the serious risk of forest fires. It's a good idea to carry insect repellent.

If taking a cooker, the most frequent recommendation is a multi-fuel stove that will burn unleaded petrol or, if that is not available, kerosene or white fuel. Alcohol-burning stoves are reliable but slow and you have to carry a lot of fuel. Fuel can usually be found at chemists/pharmacies. Gas cylinders and bottles are usually exchangeable, but if not can be recharged; specify whether you use butane or propane. Gas canisters are not always available. White gas (*bencina blanca*) is readily available in hardware shops (*ferreterías*).

Eating and drinking

Asado and parrillas
Not for vegetarians! The great classic meal throughout the country is the *asado* – beef or lamb cooked expertly over an open fire. This ritual is far more than a barbecue, and with luck you'll be invited to sample an *asado* at a friend's home or *estancia* to see how it's done traditionally. *Al asador* is the way meat is cooked in the country, with a whole cow splayed out on a cross-shaped stick, stuck into the ground at an angle over the fire beneath. And in the *parrilla* restaurants, found all over Argentina, cuts of meat are grilled over an open fire in much the same way. You can order any cuts from the range as individual meals, but if you order *parrillada* (usually for two or more people), you'll be brought a selection from the following cuts: *achuras* – offal; *chorizos* – sausages including *morcilla* (British black pudding or blood sausage); *tira de asado* – ribs; *vacío* – flank; *bife ancho* – entrecote; *lomito* – sirloin; *bife de chorizo* – rump steak; *bife de lomo* – fillet steak. You can ask for '*cocido*' to have your meat well-done, '*a punto*' for medium, and '*jugoso*' for rare. Typical accompaniments are *papas fritas* (chips), salad and the spicy *chimichurri* sauce made from oil, chilli pepper, salt, garlic and vinegar.

Other typically Argentine meals → See also menu reader, page 707.
Other Argentine dishes to try include the *puchero*, a meat stew; *bife a caballo*, steak topped with a fried egg; *choripán*, a roll with a chorizo inside (similar to a hot dog, but better). *Puchero de gallina* is chicken, sausage, maize, potatoes and squash cooked together. *Milanesas*, breaded, boneless chicken or veal, are found everywhere and good value. Good snacks are *lomitos*, a juicy slice of steak in a sandwich; and *tostados*, delicate toasted cheese and tomato sandwiches, often made from the soft crustless *pan de miga*.

Italian influences
It might seem that when Argentines aren't eating meat, they're eating pizza. Italian immigration has left a fine legacy in thin crispy pizzas available from even the humblest pizza joint, adapted to the Argentine palate with some unusual toppings. *Palmitos* are tasty, slightly crunchy hearts of palm, usually tinned, and a popular Argentine delicacy,

Eating price codes

🍴🍴🍴 over US$12	🍴🍴 US$7-12	🍴 under US$7

Prices refer to the cost of a two-course meal for one person, excluding drinks or service charge. Note that most restaurants charge '*cubierto*' which is a cover charge and pays for things like bread and service. These charges can range from between US$1 and US$3 depending on where you are eating and are generally per peson. All charges should be clearly labelled on the bottom of the menu. It is normal to tip about 10% of the meal.

though they're in short supply and the whole plant has to be sacrificed for one heart. They're often accompanied on a pizza with the truly unspeakable *salsa golf*, a lurid mixture of tomato ketchup and mayonnaise. You'll probably prefer excellent provolone or roquefort cheeses on your pizza – both Argentine and delicious. Fresh pasta is widely available, bought ready to cook from dedicated shops. Raviolis are filled with ricotta, *verduras* (spinach), or *cuatro quesos* (four cheeses), and with a variety of sauces. These are a good option for vegetarians, who need not go hungry in this land of meat. Most restaurants have *pasta casero* – home-made pasta – and sauces without meat, such as *fileto* (tomato sauce) or pesto. *Ñoquis* (gnocchi), potato dumplings normally served with tomato sauce, are cheap and delicious (traditionally eaten on the 29th of the month).

Vegetarian
Vegetables in Argentina are cheap, of excellent quality, many of them organic, and available fresh in *verdulerías* (vegetable shops) all over towns. Look out for *acelga*, a large-leafed chard with a strong flavour, often used to fill pasta, or *tarta de verduras*, vegetable pies, which you can buy everywhere, fresh and very good. Butternut squash, *zapallo*, is used to good effect in *tartas* and in filled pasta. Salads are quite safe to eat in restaurants, and fresh, although not wildly imaginative. Only in remote areas in the northwest of the country should you be wary of salads, since the water here is not reliable. In most large towns there are vegetarian restaurants, and don't forget the wonderful vegetarian *empanadas* such as cheese and onion, spinach or mushroom (see below). Vegetarians must specify: '*No como carne, ni jamón, ni pollo*' ('I don't eat meat, or ham, or chicken') since many Argentines think that vegetarians will eat chicken or ham, and will certainly not take it seriously that you want to avoid all meat products.

Regional specialities
The Argentine speciality *empanadas* are tasty small semicircular pastry pies traditionally filled with meat, but now widely available filled with cheese, *acelga* (chard) or corn. They originate in Salta and Tucumán, where you'll still find the best examples, but can be found all over the country as a starter in a *parrilla*, or ordered by the dozen to be delivered at home with drinks among friends.

Northwest Around Salta and Jujuy you'll find *humitas*, parcels of sweetcorn and onions, steamed in the corn husk, superb, and *tamales*, balls of cornflour filled with beef and onion, and similarly wrapped in corn husk leaves to be steamed. The other speciality of the region is *locro* – a thick stew made of maize, white beans, beef, sausages, pumpkin and herbs. Good fish is served in many areas of the country and along the east coast you'll always be offered *merluza* (hake), *lenguado* (sole), and often salmon as well.

Atlantic coast If you go to Puerto Madryn or the Atlantic coast near Mar del Plata, then seafood is a must: *arroz con mariscos* is similar to paella and absolutely delicious. There will often be *ostras* (oysters) and *centolla* (king crab) on the menu too.

Lake District The *trucha* (trout) is very good and is best served grilled, but as with all Argentine fish you'll be offered a bewildering range of sauces, such as roquefort, which rather drown the flavour. Also try the smoked trout and the wild boar. Berries are very good here in summer, with raspberries and strawberries abundant and flavoursome, particularly around El Bolsón. And in Puehuenia, you must try the pine nuts of the monkey puzzle trees: sacred food to the Mapuche people.

Northeast In the northeast, there are some superb river fish to try: *pacú* is a large, firm fleshed fish with lots of bones, but very tasty. The other great speciality is *surubí*, a kind of catfish, particularly good cooked delicately in banana leaves.

Desserts

Argentines have a sweet tooth, and are passionate about *dulce de leche* – milk and sugar evaporated to a pale, soft caramel, and found on all cakes, pastries, and even for breakfast. If you like this, you'll be delighted by *facturas* and other pastries, stuffed with *dulce de leche*, jams of various kinds, and sweet cream fillings. *Helado* (ice cream) is really excellent in Argentina, and for US$3 in any *heladería*, you'll get two flavours, from a huge range, piled up high on a tiny cone; an unmissable treat. Jauja (El Bolsón) and Persicco (Buenos Aires) are the best makes. Other popular desserts are *dulce de batata*, a hard, dense, sweet potato jam, so thick you can carve it; *dulce de membrillo* (quince preserve); *dulce de zapallo* (pumpkin in syrup). All are eaten with cheese. The most loved of all is *flan*, which is not a flan at all but crème caramel, often served on a pool of caramelized sugar, and *dulce de leche*. Every Argentine loves *alfajores*, soft maize-flour biscuits filled with *dulce de leche* or apricot jam, and then coated with chocolate, especially if they're the Havanna brand. Croissants (*media lunas*) come in two varieties: *de grasa* (savoury, made with beef fat) and *dulce* (sweet and fluffy). These will often be your only breakfast since Argentines are not keen on eating first thing in the morning (maybe because they've only just had dinner!), and only supply the huge buffet-style 'American Breakfast' in international hotels to please tourists.

Drink

The great Argentine drink, which you must try if invited, is *mate* (see box, opposite). A kind of green tea made from dried *yerba* leaves, drunk from a cup or seasoned gourd through a silver perforated straw, it is shared by a group of friends or work colleagues as a daily social ritual. The local **beers**, mainly lager-type, are excellent: Quilmes is the best seller, but look out for home-made beers from microbreweries in the lakes, especially around El Bolsón. **Spirits** are relatively cheap, other than those that are imported; there are cheap drinkable Argentine gins and whiskeys. Clericó is a white wine **sangría** drunk in summer and you'll see lots of Argentine males drink the green liquor *Fernet* with cola. It tastes like medicine but is very popular. It is best not to drink the **tap water**; in the main cities it's safe, but often heavily chlorinated. Never drink tap water in the northwest,

The *mate* ritual

Mate (pronounced *mattay*) is the essential Argentine drink. All over the country, whenever groups of Argentines get together, they share a *mate*. It's an essential part of your trip to Argentina that you give it a go, at least once. It's a bitter green tea made from the leaves of the *yerba mate* plant, *ilex paraguaiensis*, and is mildly stimulating, less so than caffeine, and effective at ridding the body of toxins as well as being mildly laxative and diuretic. It was encouraged by the Jesuits as an alternative to alcohol, and grown in their plantations in the northeast of Argentina.

The *mate* container is traditionally made from a hollowed gourd, but can be made of wood or tin. There are also ornate varieties made to traditional gaucho patterns by the best silversmiths.

Dried *yerba* leaves are placed in the *mate* to just over half full, and then the whole container is shaken upside down using a hand to prevent spillage. This makes sure that any excess powder is removed from the leaves before drinking. Hot water is added to create the infusion, which is then sipped through the *bombilla*, a perforated metal straw. One person in the group acts as *cebador*, trickling fresh hot water into the *mate*, having the first sip (which is the most bitter) and passing it to each person in turn to sip. The water must be at 80-82°C (just as the kettle starts to 'sing') and generally *mate* is drunk *amargo* – without sugar. But add a little if it's your first time, as the drink is slightly bitter. When you've had enough, simply say *gracias* as you hand the *mate* back to the *cebador*, and you'll be missed out on the next round.

If you're invited to drink *mate* on your visit to Argentina, always accept, as it's rude not to, and then keep trying: it might take a few attempts before you actually like the stuff. To share a *mate* is to be part of a very special Argentine custom, and you'll delight your hosts by giving it a go.

---

where it is notoriously poor. Many Argentines mix soda water with their wine (even red wine) as a refreshing drink.

Wines   Argentine wines are excellent and drinkable throughout the price range, which starts at US$2.50 a bottle. Red grape varieties of Malbe, Merlot, Syrah, Cabernet Sauvignon, and the white Torrontés are particularly recommended; try brands Lurton, Norton, Bianchi, Trapiche or Etchart in any restaurant. Good sparkling wines include the *brut nature* of Navarro Correas, whose Los Arboles Cabernet Sauvignon is an excellent red wine, and Norton's Cosecha Especial. See Mendoza, page 231, and Salta, page 284, for more details.

Eating out

The siesta is observed nearly everywhere but Buenos Aires and some of the larger cities. At around 1700, many people go to a *confitería* for *merienda* – tea, sandwiches and cakes. Restaurants rarely open before 2100 and most people turn up at around 2230, often later. Dinner usually begins at 2200 or 2230; Argentines like to eat out, and usually bring babies and children along, however late it is. If you're invited to someone's house for dinner, don't expect to eat before 2300, so have a few *facturas* at 1700, the Argentine *merienda*, to keep you going.

If you're on a tight budget, ask for the *menú fijo* (set-price menu), usually good value, also try *tenedor libre* restaurants – eat all you want for a fixed price. Markets usually have cheap food. Food in supermarkets is cheap and good quality.

Entertainment

Argentines, of whatever age, are generally extremely sociable and love to party. This means that even small towns have a selection of bars catering for varied tastes, plenty of live music and somewhere to dance, even if they are not the chic clubs you might be used to in Western urban cities. The point of going out here is to meet and chat rather than drink yourself under the table, and alcohol is consumed in moderation. Argentines are amazed at the quantities of alcohol that some tourists put away. If invited to an Argentine house party, a cake or *masitas* (a box of little pastries) will be just as much appreciated as a bottle of wine.

Dancing → *For further information, see Music, page 687.*

Argentines eat dinner at 2300, and then go for a drink at around 2400, so the dancing usually starts at around 0300, and goes on till 0600 or 0700. *Boliches* can mean anything from a bar with dancing, found in most country towns, to a disco on the outskirts, a taxi ride away from the centre. In Buenos Aires, there's a good range of clubs, playing the whole range from tango, salsa, and other Latin American dance music, to electronica. Elsewhere in Argentina nightclubs play a more conventional mixture of North American (lots of 80s classics) and Latin American pop with a bit of Argentine *rock nacional* thrown in, though you'll find a more varied scene in bigger cities like Córdoba, Rosario and Mendoza. **Tango** classes are popular all over the country, and especially in Buenos Aires, where *milongas* are incredibly trendy: a class followed by a few hours of dancing. Even if you're a complete novice, it's worth trying at least one class to get a feel for the steps; being whisked around the floor by an experienced dancer is quite a thrill even if you haven't a clue what to do with your legs.

Music → *For further information, see page 687*

Live music is everywhere in Argentina, with bands playing Latin American pop or jazz in bars even in small cities. The indigenous music is *folclore*, which varies widely throughout the country. Traditional gaucho music around the Pampas includes *payadores*: witty duels with guitars for two singers, much loved by Argentines, but bewildering if your Spanish is limited to menus and directions. The northwest has the country's most stirring *folclore*, where you should seek out *peñas* to see live bands playing fabulous *zambas* and *chacareras*. The rhythms are infectious, the singing passionate, and Argentine audiences can't resist joining in. Even tourist-oriented *peñas* can be atmospheric, but try to find out where the locals go, like **La Casona del Molino** in Salta. Most cities have *peñas*, and you'll often see some great bands at the gaucho **Day of Tradition** festivals (mid-November) throughout Argentina and at local town fiestas.

Festivals and events

The main holiday period is January to March when all Argentine schoolchildren are on holiday and most families go away for a few weeks up to two months. All popular tourist destinations become extremely busy at this time, with foreign visitors adding to the crowds, particularly in Bariloche, El Calafate and Ushuaia. You should book transport and accommodation ahead. You'll find that most of Buenos Aires' residents leave town for the whole of January. The richest go to Punta del Este in Uruguay and the beaches in Brazil, everyone else heads to Mar del Plata and the rest of the coast. During Easter week, and the winter school holidays throughout July, hotels may also fill up fast, particularly in the ski resorts. No one works on the national holidays, and these are often long weekends, with a resulting surge of people to popular holiday places.

1 Jan New Year's Day (public holiday).
Mar/Apr Good Friday and Easter weekend (public holiday).
1 May Labour Day (public holiday).
25 May May Revolution of 1810 (public holiday).
10 Jun Malvinas Day (public holiday). Best not to announce it if you are British around this day.
20 Jun Flag Day (public holiday).
9 Jul Independence Day (public holiday).
17 Aug Anniversary of San Martín's death (public holiday).
12 Oct Columbus Day (public holiday).

10 Nov Día de la Tradición. There are gaucho parades throughout Argentina on the days leading up to this festival, with fabulous displays of horsemanship, gaucho games, enormous *asados* and traditional music. It's worth seeing the festivities in any small town.
25 Dec Christmas Day. Banks are closed and there are limited bus services on 25 and 31 Dec.
30 Dec (not 31 because so many offices in centre are closed). There is a ticker-tape tradition in downtown Buenos Aires: paper falls from the sky and the crowds stuff passing cars and buses with long streamers.

Shopping

Best buys

Shopping in Argentina is relatively cheap for visitors from Western Europe and the USA since the devaluation of the peso in 2002, although inflation is a problem. Argentine fashion and leather goods are particularly good value; shoes, sunglasses and outdoor gear too are very reasonably priced, and if you have a free afternoon in Buenos Aires, it might be worth considering buying your holiday clothes here when you arrive: head straight for Palermo Viejo.

Tax free shopping is relatively easy and it's worth following this simple procedure to get the IVA (VAT) returned to you at the airport as you leave the country: shop at places displaying the Global Refund TAX FREE sign. Before you pay, ask for the TAX FREE refund form. The shop must fill this out for you as you pay. Keep this form, in the envelope they'll give you, together with your receipt. At the airport, after security, and before passport control, look out for the TAX FREE kiosk. Hand them all your TAX FREE envelopes, with the receipts, and they will give them the customs stamp. Then once you've gone through passport control, look for the TAX FREE Refund Desk, also called Assist Card, where your stamped forms will be taken, and the tax will be refunded either in cash or to your credit card. Not all shops offer this service; the ones that do usually have a sign up. See www.globalrefund.com, for more information, or in Argentina call T011-43422413.

Argentine specialities

In Buenos Aires, leather is the best buy, with many shops selling fine leather jackets, coats and trousers, as well as beautifully made bags and shoes. With a mixture of Italian influenced design, and a flavour of the old gaucho leather-working traditions, there's a strong emerging Argentine style.

Handicrafts, *artesanía*, are available all over the country, but vary from region to region. Traditional gaucho handicrafts include woven or plaited leather belts of excellent quality, as well as key rings and other pieces made of silver. These are small and distinctive and make excellent gifts. Look out, too, for the traditional baggy gaucho trousers, *bombachas*, comfortable for days in the saddle, and ranging from cheap sturdy cotton to smart versions with elaborate tucks.

Take home a *mate*, the hollowed gourd, often decorated, and the silver *bombilla* that goes with it, for drinking the national drink. In the northwest there are beautifully made woven items: brightly coloured rugs, or saddle mats, and the country's best ponchos. Look out for the hand-dyed and woven ponchos, instead of the mass-produced variety, available in smaller rural areas, or in the fine handicrafts market at Salta or Catamarca. There are the deep red Güemes versions or soft fine ponchos made of *vicuña* (a local cousin of the llama), usually in natural colours. In markets all over the northwest, you'll find llama wool jumpers, hats and socks, and brightly coloured woven bags, Bolivian influenced, but typical of the *puna* region. There are also fine carved wooden pieces. In the Lake District too, there's lots of woodwork, and weavings of a different kind, from the Mapuche peoples, with distinctive black and white patterns. Smoked fish and meat, and delicious home-made jams from *sauco* (elderberry) or *frambuesa* (raspberry) are among the local delicacies. In the northeast, there are Guaraní handicrafts such as bows and arrows. Argentina's national stone, the fleshy pink and marbled rhodochrosite, is mined in the northwest, but available all over Buenos Aires too, worked into fine jewellery, and less subtle paperweights and ashtrays.

Responsible travel

Sustainable or ecotourism is not just about looking after the physical environment, but can involve a consideration of the impact of tourism on the local community. There are several *estancias* now committed to generating their own energy, organic farming, and taking care of their community of employees so that the profits of tourism are fairly distributed. These include: Los Potreros, Córdoba; Colomé winery, Valles Salchaquíes, Salta; Estancia Santa Anita, Salta; Estancia Huechahue, Junín de los Andes; Portal de Piedra jungle lodge, Jujuy; Estancia Peuma Hue, Bariloche; and Yacutinga Jungle Lodge, Iguazú. In Argentina access to certain areas of pristine wilderness is restricted by controls over the number of visitors. Having a low-impact policy over these wilderness regions means that, although only few visitors can enjoy them, their environment is protected from damage or over-use.

In northwest Argentina, where tourism has boomed in the last few years, the impact on local communities is particularly devastating. The provincial governments cheerfully

How big is your footprint?

• Where possible choose a destination, tour operator or hotel with a proven ethical and environmental commitment – if in doubt, ask.

• Use water and electricity carefully – travellers may receive preferential supply while the needs of local communities are overlooked.

• Learn about local etiquette and culture – consider local norms and behaviour and dress appropriately for local cultures and situations.

• Always ask before taking photographs or videos of people.

• Spend money on locally produced (rather than imported) goods and services, buy directly from the producer or from a 'fair trade' shop, and use

common sense when bargaining – the few dollars you save may be a week's salary to others.

• Consider staying in local accommodation rather than foreign-owned hotels – the economic benefits for host communities are far greater, and there are more opportunities to learn about local culture.

• Protect wildlife and other natural resources – don't buy souvenirs or goods unless they are clearly sustainably produced and are not protected under CITES legislation.

• Make a voluntary contribution to Climate Care, www.co2.org, to help counteract the pollution caused by tax-free fuel on your flight.

exploit the colourful local culture while sharing little of the profit. So rather than taking a tour with those flashy companies based in Salta city, seek out local indigenous guides in the towns and villages you visit, in places like Cachi and San Antonio de los Cobres, Tilcara and Santa Rosa de Tastil. You'll have a far richer experience and make real contact with Andean and Puna culture, their histories and traditions.

Essentials A-Z

Accident and emergency

Police T101. **Medical** T107.

If robbed or attacked, call the tourist police, Comisaría del Turista, Av Corrientes 436, Buenos Aires, T011-4346 5748 (24 hrs) or T0800-999 5000 (English spoken), turista@policiafederal.gov.ar. Note that you will most likely not get your stolen goods back, but a police report is essential for your insurance claim.

Begging

There is increasingly more begging in larger cities, where you will be asked for *una moneda* (some change). On trains and sometimes buses you'll see and hear people telling their stories and asking for help. A lot of people were left financially vulnerable after the 2001 economic crash and many were reduced to living on the streets and begging. Although not all Argentines give to beggars, they are universally polite and apologetic to them. So whether you decide to give or not, make sure you are just as polite as the Argentines in your conduct.

Children

Travel with children will most definitely bring you into closer contact with Argentine families and individuals, and you may find officials tend to be more amenable where children are concerned. Everyone will be delighted if your child knows a little Spanish.

Travelling with children in Argentina is potentially safe, easy and a great adventure. The country is full of wonders that children can enjoy, and Argentine people are extremely affectionate to children. There's a real feeling here that children are part of society, not to be sent to be bed at 2000,

and are often seen running around restaurants at 2300, or out with their parents in the evenings. This means that many family restaurants have play zones for kids with a climbing frame or soft play area, usually within sight of your table. And if you'd rather dine without your children, more expensive hotels provide a baby-sitter service. For more information see *Travel with Kids* by William Gray (Footprint).

Accommodation
Hotel accommodation in Argentina is good value for families; most places have rooms for 3, 4 or even 5 people, or 2 rooms with a connecting door. Many quite modest hotels have a suite, with 2 rooms and a bathroom, for families. If you're happy to be self-catering, look out for *cabañas* all over rural areas, like the Lake District, see page 32 for more information. Prices start at around US$42 per night for a basic *cabaña* sleeping 4, US$65 in tourist areas where they're usually spacious and can be extremely luxurious.

Food
Food is easy in Argentina, since most dishes aren't strongly seasoned, and easy meals like pasta, pizza and salads are of a high standard and available everywhere. The meat is lean and portions are huge, so that if you order a steak in a restaurant there will generally be enough for you and a child (or 2 hungry children). However, children's meals are offered at most restaurants, and many establishments have high chairs. Argentine children tend to drink fizzy drinks, but freshly squeezed orange juice is widely available, and it's best to order mineral water. If your children have special dietary needs, it's worth learning the Spanish to explain.

Transport
For most tourist attractions, there are cheaper prices for children. However, on

all long-distance buses you pay a fare for each seat, and there are no half-fares if the children occupy a seat each. For shorter trips it is cheaper, if less comfortable, to seat small children on your knee. For long bus journeys, it's a good idea to bring water, fruit and biscuits, since the food provided may not be to your children's taste. There are toilets on all long-distance buses, and these are definitely improving, but they may not be clean or have water and toilet paper, so bring tissues. All bus stations have a *kiosko*, selling drinks, snacks and tissues. Bring games and perhaps music for them to listen to as the videos shown on most buses are generally action movies, not suitable for under 12s. On sightseeing tours you could try and bargain for a family rate – often children can go free. All civil airlines charge half for children under 12 but some military services don't have half-fares, or have younger age limits.

Customs and duty free

You can buy duty-free goods on arrival at Ezeiza Airport, though the shops are small and pricey, and you can also buy products on the boats to Uruguay.

No duties are charged on clothing, personal effects or toiletries. Cameras, laptops, binoculars, mp3 players and other things that a tourist normally carries are duty-free if they have been used and only 1 of each article is carried. This is also true of scientific and professional instruments for personal use. Travellers may only bring in new personal goods up to a value of US$300 (US$100 from neighbouring countries). The duty and tax payable amounts to 50% of the item's cost. At the airport, make sure you have the baggage claim tag (usually stuck to your ticket or boarding card), as these are inspected at the exit from the customs inspection area. 2 litres of alcoholic drink, 400 cigarettes and 50 cigars are also allowed in duty-free. For tourists originating from neighbouring

countries the quantities allowed are 1 litre of alcoholic drink, 200 cigarettes and 20 cigars.

If you have packages sent to Argentina, the green customs label should not be used unless the contents are of real value and you expect to pay duty. For such things as books or samples use the white label if available. A heavy tax is imposed on packages sent to Argentina by courier.

Global Refund

Some products give you the option to get the tax back on them, see page 38. The IVA (VAT) is usually 13.70% of the product's cost. For further information see **Global Refund Argentina**, Paraguay 755, floor 8, T011-5238 1976, taxfree@ar.globalrefund.com.ar.

Disabled travellers

Facilities for the disabled in Argentina are sorely lacking. Wheelchair users won't find many ramps or even lowered curbs, although this is improving in Buenos Aires; pavements tend to be shoddy and broken even in big cities. Only a few upmarket hotels have been fully adapted for wheelchair use, although many more modern hotels are fine for those with limited mobility. The best way to assess this is to ring or email the hotel in advance. Argentines generally go out of their way to help you, making up for poor facilities with kindness and generosity. Tourist sites aren't generally well adapted for disabled visitors, with limited access for the physically disabled, particularly at archaeological sites. However, many museums have ramps or lifts, and some offer special guided tours for the visually impaired, and signed tours for the hearing-impaired. Iguazú Falls has good access for wheelchair users or those with walking difficulties, along sturdy modern walkways with no steps, right up to the falls. Getting close to glacier Perito Moreno is not easy. Speaking Spanish is obviously a great help, and travelling with a companion is advisable.

Some travel companies specialize in holidays tailor-made for the individual's level of disability.

Books
You might like to read *Nothing Ventured* by Alison Walsh (Harper Collins), which gives personal accounts of worldwide journeys by disabled travellers, plus advice and listings.

Contacts
Other useful contacts include **Directions Unlimited**, New York; and **Mobility International USA**, Twin Peaks Press, Vancouver, Canada.

Websites
Disability Action Group, www.disabilityaction.org. Information on independent travel.
Global Access Disabled Network, www.globalaccessnews.com.
Royal Association for Disability and Rehabilitation, www.radar.org.uk.
Society for Accessible Travel and Hospitality, www.sath.org. Lots of advice on how to travel with specific disabilities.

Other useful sites include: www.access-able.com; www.gimponthego.com; www.justargentina.org/argentina/argentina-disabled-travellers.asp; www.makoa.org/travel.htm.

Dress

Argentines of whatever class tend to dress neatly and take care to be clean and tidy so it's much appreciated if you do the same. In the 'interior', particularly outside Buenos Aires, people are more conservative and will tend to judge you by the way you dress. Buying clothing locally can help you to look less like a tourist – clothes are cheap in Argentina in comparison with Western Europe and America.

Drugs

Users of drugs, even of soft ones, without medical prescription should be particularly careful, as Argentina imposes heavy penalties – up to 10 years' imprisonment – for even possession of such substances, and tends to make little distinction between marijuana and hard drugs. The planting of drugs on travellers, by traffickers or the police, is not unknown. If offered drugs on the street, make no response at all and keep walking.

Note that people who roll their own cigarettes are often suspected of carrying drugs and can be subjected to intensive searches. It is advisable to stick to commercial brands of cigarettes.

Electricity

220 volts AC (and 110 too in some hotels), 50 cycles. European Continental-type plugs in old buildings, Australian 3-pin flat-type in the new. Adaptors can be purchased locally for either type (ie from new 3-pin to old 2-pin and vice versa). Best to bring a universal adapter for British 3-pin plugs, as these are not available in Argentina.

Embassies and consulates

Visit www.mrecic.gov.ar, for a full list of embassies.

Gay and lesbian travellers

Argentina is fast becoming one of the most popular gay destinations in the world and there is enough happening in the capital to keep you busy for a few weeks. New gay hotels are opening, gay clubs are booming and there is a range of gay-orientated travel agencies to help you plan your stay. However, in the interior of the country, away from Buenos Aires, you might encounter homophobia; being openly demonstrative in public will certainly raise eyebrows everywhere apart from the hipper places in Buenos Aires. The tourist office produces a handy leaflet with a map showing gay friendly bars, pubs, saunas, health centres and wine bars, and change is gradually reaching government levels as well. Discrimination on the grounds of sexual orientation was banned in 1996, and in 2005 Argentina was the first South American country to legalize same-sex marriages.

Accommodation
There are plenty of gay-friendly hotels, see www.Gmaps360.com, for recommendations in Buenos Aires and Mar del Plata. For exclusively gay accommodation we recommend the **Axel Hotel**; **Big House Guest House**; and **Lugar Gay de Buenos Aires**, all in the San Telmo area of Buenos Aires, see page 90.

Clubs
There are many gay-friendly and gay-exclusive clubs. See www.theronda.com.ar, for more details, and page 97 for listings.

Publications
The 2 best publications are bi-monthly: *Gmaps* (www.Gmaps360.com.ar) and the *Ronda* (www.theronda.com.ar), both found in coffee shops, hotels and gyms around the city. *Gmaps* also produce a free **G-Card** (www.Gcard.com.ar) which gives you discounts, free passes, and extra services in a range of places. Order one and have it sent to your hotel.

Useful websites
www.gay.com Directory for gay life in Argentina.
www.gaytravel.com Excellent site with information on gay travel.
www.gaytravel.co.uk Good online travel agent offering good deals and gay hotels.
www.nexo.org A useful site for gay information within Argentina (Spanish only).
www.thegayguide.com.ar For travel tips on bars in Buenos Aires.

Greetings

Argentines are extremely courteous and friendly people, and start every interaction, no matter how small, with a greeting. You'll be welcomed in shops and ticket offices too. Take the time to respond with a smile and a *Buenos días* or *Hola* in return. Argentines are sociable people, and haven't yet lost the art of passing the time of day – you'll be considered a bit abrupt if you don't too. As you leave, say *Chau* (bye) or *Hasta luego* (see you later). Strangers are generally treated with great kindness and generosity and your warmth in return will be greatly appreciated.

If you're introduced to new people or friends, you'll be kissed, once, on the right cheek as you say hello and goodbye. This sometimes goes for men to men too, if they're friends (although it's more of a touching of cheeks than a kiss). In a business or official context, Argentines tend to be formal, and very polite.

Health

See your GP or travel clinic at least 6 weeks before departure for general advice on travel risks and vaccinations. Try phoning a specialist travel clinic if your own doctor is unfamiliar with health conditions in Argentina. Make sure you have sufficient medical travel insurance, get a dental check, know your own blood group and if you suffer a long-term condition such as diabetes or epilepsy, obtain a Medic Alert bracelet/necklace (www.medicalert.co.uk). If you wear glasses, take a copy of your prescription.

Vaccinations and anti-malarials
Vaccinations for tetanus, hepatitis A, typhoid, yellow fever and, following the 2009 outbreak, influenza A (H1N1) are commonly recommended for Argentina. Sometimes advised are vaccines for hepatitis B and rabies. The final decision, however, should be based on a consultation with your GP or

travel clinic. You should also confirm your primary courses and boosters are up to date.

Malaria is a substantial risk in parts of north and northeastern Argentina. Specialist advice should be taken on the best anti-malarials to use.

Health risks

The most common cause of travellers' **diarrhoea** is from eating contaminated food. Be wary of salads (what were they washed in, who handled them), re-heated foods or food that has been left out in the sun having been cooked earlier in the day. There is a simple adage that says wash it, peel it, boil it or forget it. It is also standard advice to be careful with water and ice. Ask yourself where the water came from. If you have any doubts then boil it or filter and treat it. Tap water in the major cities is in theory safe to drink but it may be advisable to err on the side of caution and drink only bottled or boiled water. Avoid having ice in drinks unless you trust that it is from a reliable source. There are many filter/ treatment devices now available on the market. Swimming in sea or river water that has been contaminated by sewage can also be a cause; ask locally if it is safe. Diarrhoea may be also caused by viruses, bacteria (such as E-coli), protozoal (such as giardia), salmonella and cholera. It may be accompanied by vomiting or by severe abdominal pain. Any kind of diarrhoea responds well to the replacement of water and salts. Sachets of rehydration salts can be bought in most chemists and can be dissolved in boiled water. If the symptoms persist, consult a doctor.

Travelling in high altitudes can bring on **altitude sickness**. On reaching heights above 3000 m, the heart may start pounding and the traveller may experience shortness of breath. Smokers and those with underlying heart or lung disease are often hardest hit. Take it easy for the first few days, rest and drink plenty of water – you will feel better soon. It is essential to get acclimatized before undertaking long treks or arduous activities.

Mosquitoes are more of a nuisance than a serious hazard but some, of course, are carriers of serious diseases such as **malaria**, so it is sensible to avoid being bitten as much as possible. Sleep off the ground and use a mosquito net and some kind of insecticide. Mosquito coils release insecticide as they burn and are available in many shops, as are tablets of insecticide, which are placed on a heated mat plugged into a wall socket.

If you get sick

Contact your embassy or consulate for a list of doctors and dentists who speak your language, or at least some English. Doctors and health facilities in major cities are also listed in the Directory sections of this book. Good-quality healthcare is available in the larger centres of Argentina but it can be expensive, especially hospitalization. Make sure you have adequate insurance (see below).

Useful websites

www.btha.org British Travel Health Association.
www.cdc.gov US government site that gives excellent advice on travel health and details of disease outbreaks.
www.fco.gov.uk British Foreign and Commonwealth Office travel site has useful information on each country, people, climate and a list of UK embassies/consulates.
www.fitfortravel.scot.nhs.uk A-Z of vaccine/health advice for each country.
www.numberonehealth.co.uk Travel screening services, vaccine and travel health advice, email/SMS text vaccine reminders and screens returned travellers for tropical diseases.

Insurance

Insurance is strongly recommended and policies are very reasonable. If you have financial restraints the most important aspect of any insurance policy is medical care and repatriation. Ideally you want to make sure you are covered for personal items too. Read the small print *before* heading off so you are aware of what is covered and what is not, what is required to submit a claim and what to do in the event of an emergency.

Internet

The best way to keep in touch is undoubtedly by email. Telephone is expensive in Argentina so all Argentines have adapted rapidly to internet, with broadband widely available even in small towns, many of them also offering Skype. Most *locutorios* (phone centres) also have internet, and there are dedicated centres on almost every block in town. Prices vary, the more expensive in more remote towns from around US$0.80 to US$2 per hr.

Language

→ *See Footnotes, page 702, for a list of useful words and phrases, and page 707 for the menu reader.*
Your experience in Argentina will be completely transformed if you can learn even a little of the language before you arrive. Spanish is the first language, with a few variations and a distinctive pronunciation. In areas popular with tourists, you'll find some people speak English and perhaps French or Italian, but since much of the pleasure of Argentina is in getting off the beaten track, you'll often find yourself in situations where only Spanish is spoken. Argentines are welcoming and curious, and they're very likely to strike up conversation on a bus, shop or in a queue for the cinema. They're also incredibly hospitable and your attempts to speak Spanish will be enormously appreciated.

If you have a few weeks before you arrive, try and learn a few basic phrases, useful verbs and numbers. If you're reading this on the plane, it's not too late to get a grasp of basic introductions, food and directions.

Argentine Spanish sounds like no other. The main difference is that in words with 'll'

and 'y', the sound is pronounced like a soft 'j' sound, as in 'beige'. The 'd' sound is usually omitted in words ending in 'd' or '-ado', and 's' sounds are often omitted altogether at the ends of words. And in the north and west of the country, you'll hear the normal rolled 'r' sound replaced by a hybrid 'r j' put together. Grammatically, the big change is that the Spanish 'tú' is replaced by 'vos' which is also used almost universally instead of 'usted', unless you're speaking to someone much older or higher in status. In the conjunction of verbs, the accent is on the last syllable (eg vos, tenés, podés). In the north and northwest, though, the Spanish is more akin to that spoken in the rest of Latin America. In Buenos Aires, you might hear the odd word of lunfardo, Italian-oriented slang.

Language schools

Large cities all offer Spanish-language classes, see individual chapters for recommendations. If you would like to arrange your classes before you arrive, as well as your accommodation, try one of the following organizations:

Academia Buenos Aires, Hipólito Yrigoyen 571, 4th floor, Buenos Aires, T011-4345 5954, www.academiabuenosaires.com. Spanish classes in Buenos Aires and Mendoza.

Amerispan, 1334 Walnut St, 6th floor, Philadelphia PA 19107, USA, T0800-879 6640, www.amerispan.com. North American company offering Spanish immersion programmes, educational tours, and volunteer and internship positions in Buenos Aires, Córdoba and Mendoza. Also programmes for younger people.

Expanish, Viamonte 927, 1st floor, T011-4322 0011, www.expanish.com. Buenos Aires-based agency that can organize packages including accommodation, excursions and classes in Buenos Aires, and Patagonia in Argentina, as well as in Peru, Ecuador and Chile. Highly recommended.

Spanish Abroad, 5112 N, 40th St, Suite 101, Phoenix, AZ 85018, T1-888-722 7623, www.spanishabroad.com. Spanish classes in Buenos Aires and Córdoba.

Media

Newspapers

The national daily papers are La Nación, a broadsheet, intelligent and well written (www.lanacion.com.ar); and Clarín, more accessible, also a broadsheet (www.clarin.com.ar). Both these papers have good websites and excellent Sunday papers with informative travel sections. Other daily national papers are La Prensa, La Razón, and the left wing Página-12, always refreshing for a different perspective. There's a daily paper in English, the Buenos Aires Herald (www.buenosairesherald.com), which gives a brief digest of world news, as well as Argentine news. Magazines you might like to look at include: Noticias, news and culture; Gente, a kind of Hello! for Argentina; El Gráfico, a good sports magazine, and particularly Lugares. This glossy monthly travel magazine has superb photography and is a very useful resource for travel tips and ideas of where to go, often with English translation at the back. Issues are themed; the northwest, the lakes, etc, and previous issues are often available from kioskos too. For information in English on what is going on around the country, see www.theargenaindependent.com.

Few foreign-language newspapers are available outside Buenos Aires, but to keep in touch with world news, websites of your own favourite newspaper are invaluable. Many hotels have cable TV in the rooms, but rarely have any English news channels.

Money → US$1 = Arg $3.93, £1 = Arg $5.99, €1 = Arg $5.10, AUS$1 = Arg $3.41 (Jul 2010).

Currency

The unit of currency is the Argentine peso (Arg $), divided into 100 centavos. Peso notes in circulation are 2, 5, 10, 20, 50 and 100. Coins in circulation are 5, 10, 25 and 50 centavos and 1 peso. Most major towns have exchange places (casas de cambio), and exchange rates are quoted in major newspapers daily. Also see www.xe.com, for up-to-date rates. There is a severe shortage of coins in Argentina, and you will find that hardly anyone can break large notes. Use them in supermarkets, restaurants and hotels, and take out odd amounts from the bank like $190 pesos instead of $200 pesos.

Cost of travelling

Argentina's economy has picked up since the 2001 economic crisis, but prices have risen steeply, particularly for hotels and tourist services. Nevertheless, you'll still find Argentina a very economical country to travel around.

You can find comfortable accommodation with a private bathroom and breakfast for around US$50 for 2 people, while a good dinner in the average restaurant will be around US$10-15 per person. Prices are much cheaper away from the main touristy areas: El Calafate, Ushuaia and Buenos Aires can be particularly pricey. For travellers on a budget, hostels usually cost US$10-13 per person in a shared dorm. Cheap breakfasts can be found in any ordinary café for around US$4, and there are cheap set meals for lunchtime at many restaurants, costing around US$7, US$8 in Buenos Aires. Camping costs vary widely, but expect to pay no more than US$3-6 per tent – usually less. Long-distance bus travel on major routes is very cheap, and it's well worth splashing out an extra 20% for *coche cama* service on overnight journeys.

Credit and debit cards

By far the easiest way to get cash while you're in Argentina is to use a credit card at an ATM (*cajero automático*). These can be found in every town or city (with the notable exception of El Chaltén in the south) and most accept all major cards, with Visa and MasterCard being the most widely accepted in small places. The rate of exchange is that which applies at the moment the money is withdrawn and commission is usually around 2-3%, but check with your credit card company before leaving home. Note that Argentine ATMs give you your cash and receipt before the card is returned: don't walk away without the card, as many travellers are reported to have done. Credit cards are now accepted almost everywhere as payment but you will need to show your passport together with the card. It's a good idea to carry cash to pay in cheaper shops, restaurants and hotels, and some places will give a discount for cash. Note that when taking money out of the ATM, Banelco machines have a limit of $320 pesos per withdrawal and $1000 pesos per day. Link machines permit more than that, $600 pesos, and $1200 pesos per day. This can be very frustrating so try paying for hotels and tours on credit card if you can. MasterCard emergency number is T0800-555 0507 and Visa is T0800-32222.

Traveller's cheques

There's little point in carrying traveller's cheques in Argentina since there are exchange facilities only in big towns, and commission is very high: usually 10%. A passport is essential and you may have to show proof of purchase, so transactions can take a long time. Traveller's cheques also attract thieves and though you can of course arrange a refund, the process will hold up your travel plans. Far better to bring your debit card and withdraw money from ATMs.

Transfers

Transfers are almost impossible: money can be transferred between banks but you'll need to find out which local bank is related to your own (normally none) and give all the relevant information with the routing codes. Allow 2-3 days; cash is usually paid in pesos and is subject to tax. For Western Union in Argentina, T011-4322-7774.

Opening hours

Business hours Banks, government offices and businesses are usually open Mon-Fri 0800-1300 in summer, and Mon-Fri 1000-1500 in winter. Some businesses open again in the evening, 1700-2000. **Cafés and restaurants:** cafés are busy from 2400. Restaurants are open for lunch 1230-1500, dinner 2100-2400. **Nightclubs:** open at 2400, but usually only get busy around 0200. **Post offices:** often open *corrido* – don't close for lunch or siesta. **Shops:** in Buenos Aires most are open 0900-1800. Elsewhere, everything closes for siesta 1300-1700.

Police

Whereas Europeans and North Americans are accustomed to law enforcement on a systematic basis, enforcement in Argentina is more of a sporadic affair. Many people feel that the police are corrupt and unreliable due to incredibly low pay, and there are reports that they sometimes work with local thieves to turn a blind eye to muggings. In fact, they are usually courteous, and will be helpful to tourists.

Post

Be aware that mail sent to Argentina may not arrive or may arrive late. Sending mail home is not a problem, it is cheap and efficient. Letters from Argentina take 10-14 days to get to Europe and the USA. Rates for letters up to 20 g to Europe and USA, US$1.80, up to 150 g, US$10. Post can be sent from the *correo* (post office) or from private postal service *Oca*, through any shop displaying the purple sign. The post service is reliable, but for assured delivery, register everything.

Small parcels of up to 2 kg can be sent from all post offices. Larger parcels must be sent from the town's main post office, where your parcel will be examined by customs to make sure that the contents

are as stated on your customs form, and taken to *Encomiendas Internacionales* for posting. Any local *correo* can tell you where to go. Customs usually open in the morning only. Having parcels sent to Argentina incurs a customs tax, which depends on the value of the package, and all incoming packages are opened by customs. If when you are in Buenos Aires you are sent anything large or electronic, it will get stopped at Ezeiza International Airport Customs, you will then have to go there, wade through paperwork for about 2 hrs and then possibly pay a duty tax. Try to avoid being sent anything really valuable. Poste restante is available in every town's main post office, fee US$1.50.

Safety

Relatively speaking, Buenos Aires is one of the safest cities in South America, and Argentina as a whole is an easy and safe place to travel, but that doesn't mean you need to drop your guard altogether. There are a few simple things you can do to avoid being a victim of crime.

Fake money

There is a big problem with fake notes in Argentina. The best way to tell if your money is not a fake is to look for the following 3 things. the green numbers showing the value of the note (on the left hand top corner) should shine, or shimmer; if you hold the note up to the sky you should see a watermark; lastly there should be a continuous line from the top of the note to the bottom about ¾ of the way along (also when held up to the light). The most common fake notes are $100 pesos, $20 pesos and $10 pesos. Some taxi drivers reportedly circulate fakes late at night with drunk passengers, or you may be given them back in change in markets and fairs. Check the notes thoroughly before walking away. Try to break large notes in hostels/hotels or supermarkets to avoid being given a fake in change.

Places to avoid

In most towns the train and bus stations should be avoided late at night and early in the morning. If you arrive at that time, try to arrange for your hotel or hostel to pick you up. If you can, in Buenos Aires and when you are travelling, visit the bus station to buy your tickets the day before so you can find out where the platform is and where you need to go. Also watch your belongings being stowed in the boot of the bus, and keep the ticket you'll be given since you'll need it to claim your luggage on arrival.

Precautions

Some general tips are: don't walk along the street with your map or guidebook in hand – check where you are going beforehand and duck into shops to have a quick look at your map. In cafés make sure you have your handbag on your lap or your backpack strap around your ankles. Try not to wear clothes that stand out, and certainly don't wear expensive rings, watches or jewellery that shines. Remember that the people around you don't know that you bought that watch for US$10 second hand – to them it looks expensive. Always catch Radio Taxis ask at your hostel/hotel the best taxi company to use and their direct number. When in a taxi, if possible lock the doors, or ask the driver to.

And finally, just remember the golden rules: store your money and credit cards in small amounts in different places in your luggage; scan and email yourself copies of your passport, visas and insurance forms; and keep an eye on the news or newspapers to be aware of what is happening in the country that you are travelling in.

If you are the victim of a **sexual assault**, you are advised in the first instance to contact a doctor (this can be your home doctor if you prefer). You will need tests to determine whether you have contracted any sexually transmitted diseases; you may also need advice on post-coital contraception. You should also contact your embassy, where consular staff are very willing to help in cases of assault. For more advice see www. dailystrength. org and www.rapecrisis.org.uk.

Scams

Be aware of scams. There are 2 favoured scams in use. One is that someone will discreetly spill a liquid on you, then a 'helpful stranger' will draw your attention to it and offer to help you clean it off. Meanwhile someone else has raided your pockets or run off with your bags. If someone does point out something on your clothes, keep walking until you see a coffee shop and clean up there. The second scam involves someone driving past you on a motorbike, ripping your bag off your shoulders, and driving away off into the sunset. To avoid this, wear your bag with the strap over your head and one shoulder and keep your bag on the opposite side of your body to the street. If travelling with a laptop, don't use a computer bag. Buy a satchel or handbag big enough to carry it in.

Taxis

Always take Radio Taxis. Ask your hostel or hotel for a reputable company and call them whenever you need a taxi. They generally take only around 10 mins to come. Always lock the doors in the taxi as taxi doors have reportedly been opened at traffic intersections when the car is stationary.

Student travellers

If you're in full-time education, you're entitled to an International Student Identity Card (ISIC), www.isic.org, available from student travel offices and agencies. This gives you special prices on transport, cultural events and a variety of other concessions and services. All student cards must carry a photograph. Some hostel chains also give ISIC card discounts. See **Hostelling International**, www.hostels.org.ar.

Asatej, Paraguay 523, 2nd floor, Buenos Aires, T011-5218 6556, www.asatej.com. Helpful Argentine Youth and Student Travel Organization, which runs a Student Flight Centre, Florida 835, p 3, oficina 320, T011-4114 7600, Mon-Fri 0900-1900 (and 5 other branches in BA: Belgrano, Montserrat, Palermo, Recoleta, Caballito). Sells flights, including cheap 1-way flights, hires cars and arranges accommodation, and group and individual tours to places in Argentina. Information for all South America, noticeboard for travellers, ISIC cards sold (giving extensive discounts; Argentine ISIC guide available here), English and French spoken. Also runs **Red Argentino de Alojamiento Para Jovenes** (affiliated to HI) and the **Asatej Travel Store**, at the same office, selling wide range of travel goods.

Oviajes, Uruguay 385, p 6, Buenos Aires, T011-43716137, Lavalle 477, p 1, and also at Echeverría 2498 p 1, Buenos Aires, T011-4785 7840, www.oviajes.com.ar. Offers travel facilities, ticket sales, information and issues Hostels of Americas, Nomads and Hostels of Europe, ISIC, ITIC and G0 25 cards, aimed at students, teachers and independent travellers.

South American Explorers clubhouse, Chile 557, San Telmo, www.saexplorers.org/clubhouses/buenosaires, Mon-Fri 0930-1700 and Sat 0930-1300. A new clubhouse. Friendly English, European and American staff offer really knowledgeable advice and it's a comfortable gathering place for travellers. Events and Spanish conversation classes held weekly, English library, book swap and luggage storage. Highly recommended. Join their free newsletter mailing on the website.

TIJE, San Martín 640, p 6, Buenos Aires, T011-4326 2036 or branches at Paraguay 1178, p 7, Buenos Aires, T011-5218 2800 and Zabala 1736, p 1, Buenos Aires, T011-4770 9500, www.tije.com, and at STB (STA representative), Viamonte 577, p 3, Buenos Aires, T011-5217 2727, www.stb.com.ar. Cheap fares.

YMCA (Central), Reconquista 439, Buenos Aires, T011-4311 4785.

YWCA, Tucumán 844, Buenos Aires, T011-4322 1550.

Tax

Airport tax

US$28 to be paid on all international flights exiting the country, except to Montevideo from Aeroparque Airport, which is subject to US$14 tax. Airport tax can be prepaid, and you should check if it's included in your ticket when you book. Internal flights are subject to US$12, included in your ticket everywhere but the airport at El Calafate, where you must pay in pesos. When in transit from one international flight to another, you may be obliged to pass through immigration and customs, have your passport stamped and be made to pay an airport tax on departure. There is a 5% tax on the purchase of air tickets. There is now an entry fee for Argentina, see page 24.

VAT

21%; VAT is not levied on medicines, books and some foodstuffs.

Telephone → Country code +54.

Ringing: equal tones with long pauses. Engaged: equal tones with equal pauses.

Phoning in Argentina is made very easy by the abundance of *locutorios* – phone centres with private booths where you can talk for as long as you like, and pay afterwards, the price appearing on a small screen in your booth. There's no need for change or phonecards, and *locutorios* often have internet, photocopying and fax services.

An alternative to *locutorios* is to buy a phonecard and use it from your hostel or hotel. 2 good brands are **Argentina Global** and **Hable Mas**, available from *kioskos* and *locutorios* for 5 or 10 pesos. Dial the free 0800 number on the card, and a code (which you scratch the card to reveal), and you can phone anywhere in the world. For US$3 you can talk for 1 hr internationally. Call from your hotel/hostel, as it only is the cost of a local call. These can sometimes be used in *locutorios* too, though the rates are higher, and sometimes from your hotel room, ask reception. Otherwise Skype, www.skpye. com, is the cheapest way to keep in touch.

Time

GMT -3.

Tipping

10% in restaurants and cafés. Porters and ushers are usually tipped. Tipping isn't obligatory, but it is appreciated.

Tour operators

If the choices available in Argentina are overwhelming, and you have little time to spend, or if you're not keen on travelling alone, it's worth considering booking a package with a specialist tour operator. Whether you choose an adventurous expedition, or a more sedate trip; a bespoke journey just for you, or a group holiday, these companies work with agents on the ground who will book all your transport and accommodation, so that you can just enjoy the experience. UK and Australian travellers are advised to choose a tour operator from **LATA**, the Latin American Travel Association, www.lata.org, which is also a useful source of country information.

In the UK
Abercrombie and Kent, Dorland House, 20 Regent St, London, SW1Y 4PH, T 0845-618 2200, www.abercrombiekent.co.uk. Upmarket tailor-made travel.
Andean Trails, The Clockhouse, Bonnington Mill Business Centre, 72 Newhaven Rd, Edinburgh, EH6 4JG, T0131-467 7086, www.andeantrails.co.uk.

Audley Travel, New Mill, New Mill Lane, Witney, Oxfordshire, OX29 9SX, T01993-838 000, www.audleytravel.com. High-quality tailor-made travel, including the Northwest, Lake District and Patagonia. Good on the ground knowledge. Recommended.

Austral Tours, 20 Upper Tachbrook St, London, SW1V 1SH, T020-7233 5384, www.latinamerica.co.uk. Good tailor-made tours, combining Argentina and Chile, the Lake District and the wine regions. *Estancia* stays, cultural trips and places off the beaten track.

Cazenove and Loyd, 9 Imperial Studios, 3-11 Imperial Rd, London, SW6 2AG, T020-7384 2332, www.cazloyd.com.

Cox and Kings, Gordon House, 10 Greencoat Pl, London, SW1P 1PH, T020-7873 5000, www.coxandkings.co.uk.

Discover the World, Arctic House, 8 Bolters Lane, Banstead, Surrey, SM7 2AR, T01737-214 250, www.discover-the-world.co.uk.

Dragoman, Camp Green, Debenham, Suffolk, IP14 6LA, T01728-861133, www.dragoman.co.uk.

Explore, Nelson House, 55 Victoria Rd, Farnborough, Hampshire, GU14 7PA, T0845-013 1537, www.explore.co.uk. Quality small-group trips, especially in Patagonia. Also offers family adventures, or with a focus on culture, wildlife or trekking.

Journey Latin America, 12-13 Heathfield Terrace, London, W4 4JE, T020-8747 8315, www.journeylatinamerica. co.uk. Deservedly well regarded, this excellent long-established company runs adventure tours, escorted groups and tailor-made tours to Argentina and other destinations in South America. Also cheap flights and expert advice. Well organized and very professional. Recommended.

Last Frontiers, The Mill, Quainton Rd, Waddesdon, Bucks, HP18 0LP, T01296-653000, www.lastfrontiers.com. Excellent company offering top-quality tailor-made trips all over Argentina, including superb wine tours, trips combining Iguazú and Salta, trips to the Esteros del Iberá, and horse riding in Patagonia and Córdoba. By far the best company for *estancia* stays; a real in-depth knowledge of Argentina. Highly recommended.

Select Latin America, 3.51 Canterbury Court, 1-3 Brixton Rd, Kennington Park Business Centre, London, SW9 6DE, T020-7407 1478, www.selectlatinamerica. co.uk. Specializing in tailor-made and small-group tours with a cultural or natural history emphasis, this is a friendly small company with some good itineraries, including birdwatching in the Los Esteros del Iberá, Antarctica, R40 and their speciality: the Galápagos.

Steppes Travel, Travel House, 51 Castle St, Cirencester, GL7 1QD, T01285-880980, www.steppestravel.co.uk. Tailor-made and group itineraries throughout Argentina and Latin America.

Trips Worldwide, 14 Frederick Pl, Clifton, Bristol, BS8 1AS, T0800-0111 945, www.tripsworldwide.co.uk. Tailor made itineraries and trips.

Specialist tour operators

There are many more specialized tour operators, offering specialist trips for birdwatching and horse riding. Below is just a selection.

Adventures Abroad, T0114-247 3400, www.adventures-abroad.com. Impressive company running superb and imaginative tours for small groups to Patagonia, Iguazú and Puerto Madryn, the glaciers and Ushuaia. Great itineraries.

Exodus, Grange Mills, Weir Rd, London SW12 0NE, T020-8675 5550, www.exodus.co.uk. Excellent, well-run trekking and climbing tours of Patagonia and Chile, including Torres del Paine, cycling in the Lake District, Antarctica and a great tour following in Shackleton's footsteps.

Naturetrek, Cheriton Mill, Cheriton, Alresford, Hampshire, SO24 0NG, T01962-733051, www.naturetrek.co.uk. Small group birdwatching tours, fixed departure.

STA Travel, offices worldwide, www.sta travel.co.uk/.com. Cheap flights, and sell Dragoman's trip which includes Argentina.

Trailfinders, 194 Kensington High St, London, W8 7RG, T0845-058 5858, www.trailfinders.com. Reliable for cheap flights and tours.

In North America

Argentina For Less, 7201 Wood Hollow Dr, Austin, TX 78731, USA, T1-877-661 6989, T+44-203-002 0571 (UK), www.argentina forless.com. Progressive tourism company with a focus solely on Latin America. US-based but with local offices and operations.

Discover Latin America, 6205 Blue Lagoon Dr, Suite310, Miami, Florida 33126, T305-266 5827, www.discoverlatinamerica.com.

ExpeditionTrips.com, 6553 California Av SW, Seattle, WA 98136, T1877-412 8527, www.expeditiontrips.com.

Worldwide Horseback Riding Adventures, PO Box 807, 10 Stalnaker St, Dubois, Wyoming 82513, toll free T0800-545 0019, www.riding tours.com. US-based horse-riding company.

In South America

Exprinter Viajes, San Martín 170, 1st floor, Buenos Aires, Argetina, T0054-11-4341 6600, www.exprinterviajes.com.ar.

Navimag, Navierra Magallanes SA, Angelmó 2187, Puerto Montt, Chile, T0056-2-442 3120, www.navimag.com.

Say Hueque, Viamonte 749, 6th floor, Buenos Aires, Argentina, T0054-11-51992517/20, www.sayhueque.com. Travel agency for independent travellers (English spoken). Offers trips all over the country.

South America Adventure Travel, Global Encounters, JA Cabrera 4423/29, Buenos Aires, Argentina, T512-592 3877 (US or international), T877-275 4957 (US toll free), www.southamericaa dventure.travel. With offices throughout South America, they specialize in quality, budget adventure tours.

Gay and lesbian

Calu Travel Service, Paraguay 946, Buenos Aires, Argentina, T011-4325 5477, www.calutravel.com.ar. Lots of travel services and access to the only gay beach in the country at Mar del Plata.

Pride Travel, Paraguay 523, 2nd floor, Buenos Aires, Argentina, T011-5218 6556, www.pride-travel.com. The city's own gay travel agency, often recommended, which organizes tours and trips, nights out in Buenos Aires, and travel advice for the rest of the country.

Also try **BueGay**, www.buegay.com.ar; **StepGay**, www.stepgay.com; and **Free Attitude**, www.freeattitude.com.ar, for help in planning your trip.

Tourist information

There are tourist information offices in all provincial capitals, in major tourist destinations and many bus terminals/airports in popular destinations. Infrastructure varies across the country, but they can usually give you a town map and sometimes a list of accommodation, as well as the tours, sights and festivals in the area. Staff in more popular tourist areas usually speak at least some English (and sometimes French, German, Italian) and are usually helpful. Opening hours are long – typically 0800-2000 in summer but may close at weekends. All bus terminals have an office (often signed *Informes*) with bus information.

Information

Administración de Parques Nacionales, Santa Fe 690, opposite Plaza San Martín, Buenos Aires, T011-4311 0303, Mon-Fri 1000-1700. Has leaflets on national parks.
Aves Argentinas/AOP (a BirdLife International partner), 25 de Mayo 749, p 2, Buenos Aires, T011-4312 8958. Information on birdwatching and specialist tours, good library open Wed and Fri 1500-2000 (closed Jan).

Tourist offices

Loads of information on Argentina is now available on the internet, much of it reasonably up-to-date and in English. Most provinces in Argentina have their own website and it's useful to have a look before you travel for inspiration and information. Each province has a tourist office, **Casa de Provincia**, in Buenos Aires, Mon-Fri 1000-1630/1730. The following regional websites are recommended:
Buenos Aires Province, Av Callao 237, T011-4371 7046, www.casaprov.gba.gov.ar. Also www.bue.gov.ar.
Catamarca, Av Córdoba 2080, T/F03833-4374 6891, www.catamarca.gov.ar.
Chaco, Av Callao 322, T03722-4372 5209, www.chaco.gov.ar.
Chubut, Sarmiento 1172, T02965-4302 2009, www.chubut.gov.ar.
Córdoba, Av Callao 332, T0351-4373 4277, www.cba.gov.ar. Also www.cordobatrip.com.
Corrientes, San Martín 333, p 4, T/F03783-4394 2808, www.corrientes.gov.ar.
Formosa, Hipólito Yrigoyen 1429, T03717-4381 2037, www.casadeformosa.gov.ar.
Jujuy, Av Santa Fe 967, T0388-4393 6096, www.casadejujuy.gov.ar, www.turismo.jujuy.gov.ar.
La Pampa, Suipacha 346, T011-4326 1145, www.turismolapampa.gov.ar.
La Rioja, Av Callao 745, T03822-4815 1929, www.larioja.gov.ar/turismo.
Mar del Plata, Av Corrientes 1660, local 16, T0223-4384 5658, www.mardelplata.gov.ar.
Mendoza, Av Callao 445, T0261-4374 1105, www.mendoza.gov.ar. Also www.turismo.mendoza.gov.ar, www.mendoza.com.ar and www.welcometomendoza.com.ar.
Misiones, Santa Fe 989, T03752-4322 1097, www.misiones.gov.ar.
Municipalidad de la Costa, B Mitre 737, www.lacostaturismo.com.ar.
Neuquén, Maipú 48, T0299-4343 2324, www.neuquen.gov.ar.
Río Negro, Tucumán 1916, www.rionegro tur.com.ar.

Salta, Diagonal Norte 933, T0387-4326 2456, www.turismosalta.gov.ar.

San Antonio de Areco, www.sanantoniode areco.com/turismo.

San Juan, Sarmiento 1251, T02646-4382 9241, www.sanjuan.gov.ar.

San Luis, Azcuénaga 1083, T02652-5778 1621, www.sanluis.gov.ar.

Santa Cruz, 25 de Mayo 279, www.epatagonia.gov.ar.

Santa Fe, Montevideo 373, p 2, T0342-5811 4327.

Santiago del Estero, Florida 274, T0385-4326 9418, www.sde.gov.ar.

Tierra del Fuego, Sarmiento 745, www.tierradelfuego.org.ar.

Tucumán, Suipacha 140, T0381-4322 0010, www.tucumanturismo.gov.ar.

For tourist information on **Patagonia**, see www.patagonia.com.ar, www.patagonia-argentina.com or www.patagonia-chile.com. For Patagonia and bookings for cheap accommodation and youth hostels, contact **Asatej**, see student travellers on page 50.

Websites

www.alojar.com.ar Accommodation search engine and tourist information in Spanish.

www.buenosairesherald.com *Buenos Aires Herald*, English-language daily.

www.expat-connection.com Expat group in Buenos Aires which organizes events.

www.getsouth.com A fantastic site filled with accommodation and tour recommendations, as well as discounts and travel advice. Highly recommended.

www.infobae.com An Argentine online newspaper, in Spanish.

www.livinginargentina.com Online magazine about Argentine culture and travel destinations.

www.mercotour.com Information on travel and other matters in Argentina, Uruguay, Chile and Brazil, in Spanish, English and Portuguese.

www.meteonet.com.ar Useful website for forecasts and weather satellite images.

www.museosargentinos.org.ar/museos Argentina's museums.

www.responsibletravel.org A great website for people interested in responsible travel (also see www.travelersphilanthropy.org).

www.saexplorers.org/clubhouses/buenos aires/ Argentina page of this non-profit organization that offers services such as luggage storage, travel information, discounts and events.

www.streema.com Site that enables you to listen to radio stations all over the world.

www.tageblatt.com.ar *Argentinisches Tageblatt*, German-language weekly, very informative.

www.welcomeargentina.com Information for the whole country, in several languages.

Vaccinations

No vaccination certificates are required for entry. For further details, see Health, page 44.

Visas and immigration

Visas on entry

Passports are not required by citizens of neighbouring countries who hold identity cards issued by their own governments. Visas are not necessary for US citizens, British citizens and nationals of other Western European countries, plus Australia, Barbados, Bolivia, Brazil, Canada, Chile, Colombia, Costa Rica, Croatia, Czech Republic, Dominican Republic, Ecuador, El Salvador, Guatemala, Haiti, Honduras, Hungary, Israel, Jamaica, Japan, Malaysia, Mexico, New Zealand, Nicaragua, Panama, Paraguay, Peru, Poland, Singapore, Slovenia, South Africa, Turkey, Uruguay and Venezuela. Visitors from these countries are given a tourist card on entry and may stay for 3 months. There is an entry fee, however, for details see page 24.

For visitors from all other countries, there are 3 types of visa: a business 'temporary' visa (US$35, valid 1 year), a tourist visa (US$35 approximately, fees may change), and a transit visa. Tourist visas are usually valid for 3 months and are multiple entry.

Visa extensions and renewals

All visitors can renew their tourist visas for another 3 months by going in person to the National Directorate of Migration, Antártida Argentina 1365, Buenos Aires, T011-4312 8663 (ring first to check opening times), and paying a fee of US$35: ask for *Prorrogas de Permanencia*. No renewals are given after the expiry date. Alternatively, for a 90-day extension of your stay in Argentina, just leave the country at any land border, and you'll get another 3 month tourist visa stamped in your passport on return. Alternatively, you can forego all the paper-work by paying a US$45 fine at a border immigration post (queues are shorter than in Buenos Aires, but still allow 30 mins). The most popular way of renewing your visa from Buenos Aires is to spend the day in Uruguay, which is only 45 mins away by boat.

Advice and tips

All visitors are advised to carry their passports at all times, and it is illegal not to have identification handy. In practice, though, this is not advisable. Photocopy your passport twice, carry 1 copy, and scan your passport and email it to yourself for emergencies. You'll often be asked for your passport number, when checking into hotels and if paying by credit card, so learn it off by heart. The police like searching backpackers at border points: remain calm – this is a normal procedure. If you are staying in the country for several weeks, it may be worthwhile registering at your embassy or consulate. This will help if your passport is stolen as the process of replacing it is simplified and speeded up

Weights and measures

The metric system is used in Argentina.

Women travellers

Single women might attract surprise – *¿Estás sola?* Are you travelling alone? – but this is rather because Argentines are such sociable people and love to travel in groups, than because it's dangerous. Argentine men can't seem to help paying women attention, and you may hear the traditional *piropo* as you walk past: a compliment, usually fairly unimaginative, and nothing to cause offence. Just ignore it and walk on. Men are generally respectful of a woman travelling alone, and won't make improper suggestions, but just in case here are some tips: Wear a ring on your wedding finger, and carry a photograph of '*mi marido*', your 'husband'. By saying that your 'husband' is close at hand, you may dissuade an aspiring suitor. Argentine men are famously charming and persistent chatters up, so firmly discourage any unwanted contact and be aware of any signals that might be interpreted as encouragement. If politeness fails, don't feel bad about showing offence and leaving.

Do not walk alone around Buenos Aires in quiet areas or at night. When accepting a social invitation, make sure that someone knows the address you're going to and the time you left. And if you don't know your hosts well, a good ploy is to ask if you can bring a friend, even if you've no intention of doing so, to check the intentions of whoever's inviting you. Wherever you are, try to act with confidence, and walk as though you know where you are going, even if you don't. Someone who looks lost is more likely to attract unwanted attention. Do not disclose to strangers where you are staying. When you set out, err on the side of caution until your instincts have adjusted to the customs of a new culture. Always ask the hotel, the restaurant or your hosts to call you a **Radio Taxi** as these are usually much safer and regulated closely.

Book accommodation ahead so that when you arrive in a new town you can take a taxi straight to your hotel or hostel and avoid looking lost and vulnerable at bus stations. Many hotels or hostels are open 24 hrs, but if you arrive in the early morning, it's safest to wait in the bus station *confitería*, where there are usually people around, than to venture into the centre.

Women should be aware that tampons are quite hard to find in Argentina and it may be best to bring a supply. In most chemists and supermarkets tampons are generally held behind the counter and you'll need to ask for them (pronounced, roughly the same in Spanish, *tampón*). Tampons and towels must never be flushed, whether in a private home or hotel. Carry a supply of plastic bags in case bins aren't provided.

For more advice for women travellers see www.womenstravelclub.com and www.travellingwomen.blogspot.com.

Working in Argentina

Foreigners can't work in Argentina without a work permit which you'll only get with an official job (or if you are from New Zealand as you can apply for a 12-month working visa). At a time of high unemployment, it's hard to find work and you might consider it unfair to take work away from Argentines. The exception to this is teaching English, and it's possible to pick up work with a school, even if you don't have any qualifications. But you will be paid more if you have a TEFL certificate (Teaching English as a Foreign Language) and experience. Otherwise, private lessons are always an option, but they pay very poorly, currently around US$5-6 per hr. Jobs in schools are advertised in the English-language newspaper, the *Buenos Aires Herald*; www.craigslist.com; the *South American Explorers* free newsletter, www.saexplorers.org; and in the schools themselves.

EBC, www.ebc-tefl-course.com, offer a comprehensive 4-week TEFL training course that is highly recommended. Most graduates walk away with a job already organized.

If you are intent on trying to obtain a work visa speak to **Immigration**, Antártida Argentina 1365, Buenos Aires, T011-4312 8663. A good level of Spanish is essential.

Contents

Footprint features

At a glance

⊖ **Getting around** Cheap and frequent buses, trains and relatively affordable taxis. Some areas like Palermo, Recoleta and San Telmo are best on foot.

⊜ **Time required** At least 1 week to see the sites, go to a tango show and enjoy a day trip.

◑ **Weather** Dec-Mar can be quite hot and humid, May-Aug can be windy, cold and rainy.

⊗ **When not to go** May-Aug when the winds can be ferocious, or Mar when the torrential rains can wash the streets away.

Buenos Aires

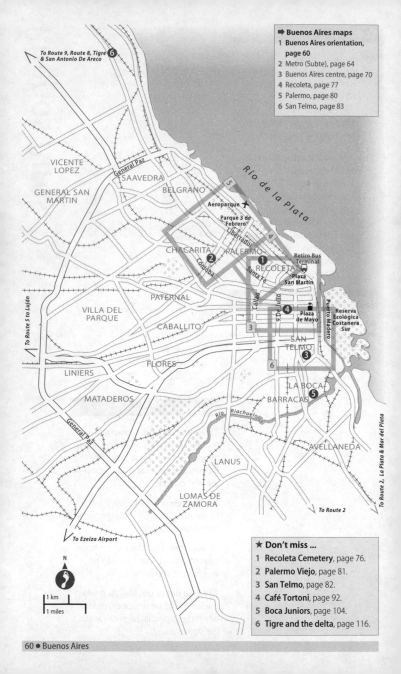

➡ Buenos Aires maps
1 Buenos Aires orientation,
  page 60
2 Metro (Subte), page 64
3 Buenos Aires centre, page 70
4 Recoleta, page 77
5 Palermo, page 80
6 San Telmo, page 83

To Route 9, Route 8, Tigre & San Antonio De Areco 6

VICENTE LOPEZ

TSAAVEDRA

GENERAL SAN MARTIN

BELGRANO

General Paz

Río de la Plata

Aeroparque ✈

Parque 3 de Febrero

Libertador

CHACARITA

PALERMO

RECOLETA

2

1

Retiro Bus Terminal

Plaza San Martín

Córdoba

Santa Fe

Callao

9 de Julio

PATERNAL

VILLA DEL PARQUE

CABALLITO

4

Plaza de Mayo

3

Puerto Madero

Reserva Ecológica Costanera Sur

To Route 5 to Luján

FLORES

SAN TELMO

3

6

LINIERS

LA BOCA

BARRACAS

5

MATADEROS

General Paz

Río Riachuelo

AVELLANEDA

To Route 2, La Plata & Mar del Plata

LANUS

LOMAS DE ZAMORA

To Route 2

To Ezeiza Airport

N

1 km
1 miles

★ Don't miss ...
1 Recoleta Cemetery, page 76.
2 Palermo Viejo, page 81.
3 San Telmo, page 82.
4 Café Tortoni, page 92.
5 Boca Juniors, page 104.
6 Tigre and the delta, page 116.

Buenos Aires is one of the world's great cities: grand baroque buildings to rival Paris, theatres and cinemas to rival London, and restaurants, shops and bars to rival New York. But the atmosphere is uniquely Argentine, from the steak sizzling on your plate in a crowded *parrilla* to the tango being danced in the romantic *milongas*.

The city seethes with life and history. Once you've marvelled at the grand Casa Rosada (government house) where Perón addressed his people in Plaza de Mayo, and sipped espresso at Borges' old haunt, Café Tortoni, head to the cemetery in swish Recoleta where Evita is buried amid stunning art galleries and buzzing cafés. Take a long stroll around charming Palermo Viejo, with its enticing cobbled streets full of chic bars and little designer shops. Or explore beautifully crumbling San Telmo, the oldest part of the city, for its Sunday antique market where tango dancers passionately entwine among the fading crystal and 1920s tea sets.

Buenos Aires' nightlife is legendary and starts late. You'll have time for your first tango class at a *milonga*, before tucking into *piquant empanadas*, a huge steak and a glass of fine Argentina Malbec at around 2300. Superb restaurants abound; wander around the renovated docks at Puerto Madero, try the trendy eateries of Las Cañitas or the hip hangouts of Palermo Viejo. Or combine the pleasures of fine food and a dazzling tango show.

But if the city's thrills become too intense, take a train up the coast to the pretty colonial suburb of San Isidro or take a boat through the lush jungly delta, where you can hide away in a cabin, or retreat to a luxury *estancia* until you're ready for your next round of shopping, eating and dancing.

While there's plenty to keep you entertained in Buenos Aires for a week at least, there are great places to escape to for a day or two within easy striking distance. These include the calm rural *estancias*, the Tigre (river delta) and the cowboy towns.

Ins and outs → *Colour map 4, B5. Phone code 011. Population 2,776,138 (Greater Buenos Aires 12,046,799).*

Getting there

Air Buenos Aires has two airports: **Ezeiza** (officially Ministro Pistarini) ① *T011-5480 6111, www.aa2000.com.ar*, for international flights and domestic flights to El Calafate and Ushuaia in high season, 35 km southwest of the centre; and **Aeroparque Jorge Newberry** ① *T011-4514 1515, www.aa2000.com.ar*, for domestic flights and **Aerolíneas Argentinas** and *puna* flights to Montevideo and Punta del Este, just to the north of Palermo, Avenida Costanera R Obligado.

A display in **Ezeiza** immigration shows choices and prices of transport into the city. The safest way to get between airports, or to get to town from **Ezeiza**, is the efficient bus service run by **Manuel Tienda León** ① *T011-4315 5115, www.tiendaleon.com.ar*, which links Ezeiza with the centre, and hotels (leaving every 30 minutes, charging US$11.50 for the 90-minute journey and US$1 more for transfers to central hotels). They can also organize transfers to Mar del Plata, Santa Fe, La Plata and Rosario. You can pay in pesos, dollars, euros, with credit or debit cards, or book online (return ticket is cheaper). Alternatively, take a reliable Radio Taxi (such as **Pidalo Taxis**, T011-4956 1200), 45 minutes, US$36 – make sure you pay for your taxi inside or just outside the airport at the little booth and wait in the queue. Don't be tempted to just jump in the closest taxis, for security sake. Alternatively you can take a *remise* taxi – these have a fixed fare, and can be booked from a desk at the airport, and charge US$35. There is a local public transport bus which takes between 1½ and two hours and costs US$0.50, but it isn't advisable late at night or early in the morning. **Manuel Tienda León** is the most reliable company, and has a clearly visible desk by Arrivals.

Aeroparque, the largely domestic airport, is 4 km north of the city centre, right on the riverside, just 15 minutes' drive from anywhere in the centre of town. Manuel Tienda León buses leave every hour from 0900 to 2000 and at 2130, and charge US$4.50 for the 30-minute journey to Retiro, with onward connections to hostels/hotels. *Remises* charge US$6.50 and ordinary taxis US$6. Again, Manuel Tienda León is the most reliable company. Their office in town is near Retiro train station and from here you can order a Radio Taxi. Ask them about their transfer service to hotels in the centre of town. There's a left luggage office here and a phone and banks with ATMs are a block away.

Bus Buses connect Buenos Aires with towns all over Argentina and neighbouring countries, and arrive at **Retiro bus terminal** ① *Ramos Mejía and Antártida Argentina, T011-4310 0700*, about five blocks north of Plaza San Martín. Always take a Radio Taxi to the terminal, and take a *remise* taxi from the terminal into town, since the area is insalubrious, and ordinary taxis here are not reliable. There are two recommended *remise* taxi companies on the main platform as you get off the bus: **Remises Via** T011-4777 8888 and **Premium Radio Taxi**, T011-4983 6666. Go to the kiosk, pay the fixed fare for your journey and your driver will take you down to his car. If you decide to take a Radio Taxi, quote your hotel phone number and tell the company where to pick you up – for example at Puente 3, arriba (bridge 3, upper level) – as there are five such bridges leading from the arrivals level.

Car Driving in Buenos Aires is no problem if you have eyes in the back of your head, two sets of hands and nerves of steel. For more details on car hire, see Essentials, page 27.

Ferry There's a ferry port at Puerto Madero, where boats arrive from Uruguay. For more detailed information, see Transport, page 108.

Remise taxi *Remises* charge a fixed fare and are operated by Transfer Express and Manuel Tienda León (there is a counter at Ezeiza). The journey to the centre from Ezeiza costs US$35 and from Aeroparque, US$6.50. Transfer Express operates on-request *remise* taxis, vans and minibuses from both airports to any point in town and between them.

Taxi Taxis from Ezeiza to the centre charge US$36 (plus US$1.50 toll), but do not have a good reputation for security, and you'll have to bargain. Far better to take a *remise* taxi, see above.

Train Next to the bus terminal is **Retiro railway station**, serving the suburbs and a few provincial stations such as Rosario and Tigre, with only one long-distance train to Tucumán.

Private transfer Most upmarket hotels will offer a transfer, but you can also organize your own for not much more than a taxi (US$36-40). They will meet your flight, and wait if it's delayed. Recommended is Oscar Carrizo from Remis Executive Transfer, T011-1550 360188 (T+54 911 5036 0188 if calling internationally), o_carrizo@hotmail.com. Contact him with your arrival/departure flight information, first and last name, number of people, and the address of where you're going to or being picked up from. He only speaks Spanish but is very friendly and very trustworthy.

Getting around
Colectivo There is a good network of buses – *colectivos* – covering a very wide radius; frequent, efficient and very fast (hang on tight). The basic fare is US$0.30, or US$0.50 to the suburbs, and you can only pay with coins which you drop into a machine behind the driver. Check that your destination appears on the bus stop, and in the little card in the driver's window, since each number has several routes. Useful guides *Guía T*, US$1.50 and *Lumi*, US$1.80 available at news-stands and *kioskos*, give the routes of all buses. A cheap tour of the city can be had by taking the No 29 bus in La Boca – El Caminito, all the way through to the posh residential suburb of Belgrano (the bus goes further but this trip will have already taken you at least an hour). You will pass by colonial houses in San Telmo, the Casa Rosada, the wonderful buildings of the Tribunales, the bustle of Marcelo T Alvear and Avenida Santa Fe with its nearby shops, trendy Palermo. Take your leave in Belgrano near *Subte* stop Juramento and catch the quick and efficient *Subte* back to the city.

Subte (Metro) The best way to get around the city, the *Subte* is fast, clean and safe (though late at night it's best to take a taxi). There are six lines, labelled 'A' to 'E', and line 'H'. A, B, D, E and H run under the major avenues linking the outer parts of the city to the centre. The fifth line, 'C', links Plaza Constitución with the Retiro railway station and provides connections with all the other lines. Note that in the centre, three stations – 9 de Julio (Line 'D'), Diagonal Norte (Line 'C') and Carlos Pellegrini (Line 'B') – are linked by pedestrian tunnels. A single fare is US$0.30, payable in pesos only at the ticket booth, or you can buy a *Subte* Card (www.subtecard.com.ar) which can also be used to pay at some shops. If you are only visiting for a few days it isn't worth the hassle; instead buy a card of 10 rides – interchangeable with friends. Trains run Monday to Saturday 0500-2250 and Sunday 0800-2200. Although it is relatively safe, be extra careful at night. Free maps are available from *Subte* stations and the tourist office.

Taxi Taxis are painted yellow and black, and carry 'Taxi' flags, but for security they should rarely be hailed on the street. Taxis are the notorious weak link in the city's security, and you should always phone a Radio Taxi, since you're guaranteed that they're with a registered company; some 'Radio Taxis' you see on the street are false. Call one of the numbers listed on page 108, give your address and a taxi will pick you up in five of 10 minutes. You may need to give a phone number for reference – use your hotel number. Alternatively, ask your hotel before you leave for the day which taxi company they use, as these will be reliable, and then you can always call that company when you're out, giving the hotel name as a reference. Fares are shown in pesos. The meter starts at US$1.20 when the flag goes down; make sure it isn't running when you get in. A fixed rate of US$0.09 for every 200 m or one-minute wait is charged thereafter. A charge is sometimes made for each piece of hand baggage (ask first). Alternatively, *remise* taxis (private cars) charge a fixed rate to anywhere in town, and are very reliable, though can work out more expensive for short journeys. **Remises Vía** ① *T011-4777 8888*, is recommended, particularly from Retiro bus station. *Remise* taxis operate all over the city; they are run from an office, have no meter but charge

② Metro (Subte)

→ Buenos Aires maps
1 Buenos Aires orientation, page 60
2 **Metro (Subte), page 64**
3 Buenos Aires centre, page 70
4 Recoleta, page 77
5 Palermo, page 80
6 San Telmo, page 83

Metro Lines
A
B
C
D
E
H

N
Not to scale

fixed prices, which can be cheaper than regular taxis. About a 10% tip is expected. For more detailed transport information, see page 107.

Tourist information

Tourist offices The **national office** ① *Av Santa Fe 883, T011-4312 2232, T011-4312 5550, www.turismo.gov.ar, Mon-Fri 0900-1700*, provides maps and literature covering the whole country. There are kiosks at both **airports** (in the Aerolíneas Argentinas section of the domestic airport T011-4771 0104), daily 0800-2000. There are **city-run tourist kiosks** at ① *Florida 100, junction with Roque Sáenz Peña*; in **Recoleta** ① *Av Quintana 596, junction with Ortiz*; in **Puerto Madero** ① *Dock 4*; in **San Telmo** ① *Defensa 1250*; and at **Retiro bus station** (ground floor). For free tourist information call T0800-555 0016 (Mon-Fri 0900-1700) or for assistance anywhere in the city, call T0800-999 5000 (24 hours).

For **city information** ① *T011-4313 0187, Mon-Fri 0730-1800, Sat-Sun 1000-1800, www.bue.gov.ar, a great site in Spanish, English and Portuguese*. Free guided tours are usually organized by the city authorities: free leaflet from city-run offices. Audio guided tours in several languages are available for 12 different itineraries by downloading mp3 files and maps from www.bue.gov.ar. **Tango Information Centre** ① *1st floor at Galerías Pacífico, Sarmiento 1551, T011-4373 2823*, is a very helpful, privately run tourist office.

South American Explorers ① *BA Clubhouse, currently moving to a new address, check the website for details or call T011-4307 1309, T011-3475 8200, www.saexplorers.org, baclub@saexplorers.org, Skype SAEBuenosAires, Mon-Fri 0930-1700, Sat-Sun 0930-1300*, offers knowledgeable advice and the clubhouse is a comfortable gathering place for travellers. For more information, see page 51.

Information Good guides to bus and subway routes are *Guía T, Lumi, Peuser* and *Filcar* (usually covering the city and Greater Buenos Aires in two separate editions), US$1-9, available at news-stands (*kioskos*). Also handy is Auto Mapa's pocket-size *Plano* of the federal capital, or the more detailed *City Map* covering La Boca to Palermo, both available at news-stands, US$4, otherwise it's easy to get free maps of the city centre from most hotels. *Buenos Aires Day & Night* is a free bi-monthly tourist magazine with useful information and a downtown map available together with similar publications at tourist kiosks and hotels. *Bainsider* (www.bainsidermag.com) is a fantastic resource magazine for getting to know the city (US$1.50 in *kioskos*). Their website is full of useful information. Also free fortnightly online newspaper *Argentina Independent* (www.argentinaindependent.com) in English will be helpful. *La Nación* newspaper has a Sunday tourism section (very informative). On

Friday, the youth section of rival newspaper *Clarín (Sí)* lists free entertainments. Search Clarín's website (www.clarin.com) for the up-to-date page on entertainment; look at '*Sección Espectáculos*' (in Spanish). *Página 12* has a youth supplement on Thursdays called *NO*. The *Buenos Aires Herald* publishes *Get Out* on Friday, listing entertainment. Information on what's on is available at www.buenosairesherald.com (both newspaper and website are in English). Also see www.whatsupbuenosaires.com for detailed listings (in English) of events, DJs, art exhibitions and basically anything that is going on in the capital. There are countless free publications found in cafés which also have information. There are a few wonderful blogs (in English) as well: www.baires.elsur.org (for an expat's view of the city); www.goodmorningba.com (for forums); www.movingtoargentina.typepad.com (for advice on moving to the city); and www.argentinepost.com (for up-to-date information and news about the country).

Orientation

The city of Buenos Aires is situated just inland from the docks on the south bank of the Río de la Plata. The formal city centre is around **Plaza de Mayo**, where the historical **Cabildo** faces the florid pink presidential palace, the **Casa Rosada**, from whose balcony presidents have appealed to their people, and where the people have historically come to protest. From here, the broad Parisian-style boulevard of the **Avenida de Mayo** leads to the seat of government at the wonderfully imposing **Congreso de la Nación**, lined with marvellous buildings from the city's own belle époque, including the theatrical **Café Tortoni** ⓘ *www.cafetortoni.com.ar*, built in 1858 and frequented by Argentine writer Jorges Luis Borges. Halfway, it crosses the widest street in the world, the 18 lanes of roaring **Avenida 9 de Julio**, a main artery leading south, with its mighty central obelisk and the splendid Teatro Colón (which has recently undergone a multi-million dollar makeover).

The main shopping streets are found north of Plaza de Mayo, along the popular pedestrianized **Florida**, which leads to the elegant and leafy Plaza San Martín. This central area is easy to walk around and you can buy everything from chic leather bags to cheap CDs, with lots of banks, internet cafés and *locutorios* (phone centres).

Just west of the centre, crossing Avenida 9 de Julio, is the smart upmarket suburb or *barrio* of **Recoleta** where wealthy *Porteños* (Buenos Aires' residents) live in large apartment blocks with doormen and gold door handles; you'll find most of the city's finest museums here, as well as the famous **Recoleta Cemetery**, where Evita Perón was finally buried. Just outside the cemetery, there's a busy craft market at weekends, innumerable cafés and bars, and the chic **Buenos Aires Design**, an upmarket shopping centre filled with exclusive products. Further north still, via the elegant green parks of **Palermo**, with its zoo, wonderfully shaped planetarium and botanical garden, is the fabulous *barrio* of **Palermo Viejo**. This is *the* place to hang out in Buenos Aires, and a relaxing place to shop, as you stroll leafy cobbled streets past 1920s buildings and browse in cool designer clothes and interiors shops. The whole area is alive with bars and excellent restaurants, and there are fabulous places to stay in Palermo Viejo, and neighbouring Palermo Soho too, making it possible to avoid the city centre altogether if you want a quieter visit.

Puerto Madero has become the most popular place to eat close to the centre, with busy upmarket restaurants and luxury hotels filling the handsome brick warehouses on the stylishly renovated docks area. This is a good place to go for an early evening drink, and to stroll past old sailing ships and painted cranes. Further south, the green spaces of the **Costanera Sur** are busy in summer with *Porteños* relaxing, groups of friends sipping *mate* or barbecuing steak. Here there's a **Reserva Ecológica** where you could retreat for some inner city wildlife, and walk or cycle for a couple of hours. Just inland, the city's most atmospheric *barrio* is irresistible **San Telmo**, once the city's centre, with narrow streets where cafés and antique markets are tucked away in the attractively crumbling 1900s buildings. Now the area is a lively and bohemian artistic centre with a popular market in the quaint Plaza Dorrego and along the cobbled street of Defensa on Sundays, where tango is danced for tourists among stalls selling silver, plates and bric-a-brac. Nightlife is lively here, but you'll also want to explore the city's tasty restaurants in Recoleta, Palermo, or the Las Cañitas area in between the two.

Street layout

Streets are organized on a regular grid pattern, with blocks numbered in groups of one hundred. It's easy to find an address, since street numbers start from the dock side/the river rising from east to west, and north/south streets are numbered starting from Avenida Rivadavia, one block north of Avenida de Mayo, and rise in both directions. Juan D Perón used to be called Cangallo, and Scalabrini Ortiz used to be Canning (the old names are sometimes still referred to). Avenida Roque Sáenz Peña and Avenida Julio A Roca are commonly referred to as Diagonal Norte and Diagonal Sur respectively.

Background

Buenos Aires was officially founded in 1536 by Pedro de Mendoza acting on orders from his Spanish King. A small fort was built (most researchers place the fort closer to modern day San Isidro north of the current-day city), and a small band of settlers were left to eke out a living. The settlement failed after a few precious years and it was left up to Juan de Garay (who has a street named after him in San Telmo, it was in fact the first official street of the city) 40 odd years later, in 1580, to found – for the second time – the city he named Ciudad de la Santísima Trinidad y Puerto de Nuestra Señora del Buen Ayre. Not surprisingly, the name in its entirety, didn't stick. It was shortened to Santa María del Buen Aire, then shortened again to simply Buenos Aires.

However, in present day Buenos Aires nothing remains of this early settlement, which also didn't take off as a city for some 200 years. It has none of the colonial splendour of Salta (in the northwest of Argentina), because while Salta was by that time a busy administrative centre on the main trade route for silver and mules from the main Spanish colony of Alto Perú, Santa María del Buen Aire, the city of the 'good winds', was left to fester, her port used only for a roaring trade in contraband. Later on Jesuits came and built schools, churches and the country's first university in what is now San Telmo, a legacy left in the wonderful Manzana de las Luces, which you can still explore today.

In 1776 Buenos Aires became Viceroyalty of the Río de la Plata area, putting it firmly on the map for trade, and the city's strategic position on this estuary brought wealth and progress. Two invasions by the British for control of the port in 1806 and 1807 were quickly quelled but sparked a surge for independence in the burgeoning Argentine nation. There is a street in San Telmo called Defensa that marks the limit of where the British soldiers reached, when residents were ordered by the army, lacking in weapons, to pour boiling oil from the building tops to stop the invasion. Hence the name Defensa – defence. After separating from Spain in 1816, Buenos Aires became its new capital, giving the *Porteños* a further sense of pride.

By 1914, Buenos Aires was rightfully regarded as the most important city in South America. The wealth generated from the vast fertile Pampas, inhabited by the immigrants from Europe was manifested in the flamboyant architecture you see in Teatro Colón, Avenida de Mayo and the palaces of Recoleta. Massive waves of immigration from Italy and Spain had arrived in Buenos Aires in the late 19th century, creating the characteristic Argentine identity, and the language described most accurately as Spanish spoken by Italians. The tango was born in the port areas of the city, music filled with nostalgia for the places left behind, and currently enjoying a revival among 20-somethings, who fill the *milongas*, breathing new passion into old steps. Now, nearly a third of the country's 36 million inhabitants live in Gran Buenos Aires, in the sprawling conurbation that stretches west from the smart areas of Palermo, Martínez, and upmarket San Isidro, to the poorer Avellaneda and La Matanza. Shanty towns, called *villas*, surround the city and the most famous Villa 31 can be seen behind Retiro bus station in the centre, which you will see if you catch any long distance bus. It is all part of the colourful stew of Buenos Aires' life. It is truly one of the world's great cities, and a fine start to your trip to Argentina.

City centre

Plaza de Mayo

This broad open plaza is both the historic heart of the city, and its centre of power, since it's surrounded by some of the city's most important public buildings. Just behind the Plaza de Mayo were the city's original docks, where Argentina's wealth was built on exporting meat and leather from the Pampas. All the country's powers are gathered nearby, and the Plaza remains the symbolic political centre of the city. Most famously, there's pink Casa de Gobierno or **Casa Rosada** ①*Bolívar 65, T011-4334 1782, tours Sun 1400-1800, guided tours 1500 and 1630, free,* which lies on the east side, looking out towards the Río Plata, and contains the offices of the president of the Argentine Republic. The changing of the guards takes place every two hours from 0700-1900.

The decision to paint the seat of government pink resulted from President Sarmiento's (1868-1874) desire to symbolize national unity by blending the colours of the rival factions that had fought each other for much of the 19th century: the Federalists (red) and the Unitarians (white). The colour itself was originally derived from a mixture of lime and ox blood and fat, to render the surface impermeable. The Plaza has been the site of many historic events: Perón and Evita frequently appeared on its balcony before the masses gathered on the plaza, at one point the military (opposed to Perón) bombed it, and when the economy crumbled in December 2001, angry crowds of *cacerolazas* (including middle-class ladies banging their *cazerolas*, or saucepans) demonstrated outside, together with angry mobs. Since 1977, the Mothers and now, Grandmothers, of the Plaza de Mayo (*Madres y Abuelas de la Plaza de Mayo*), www.madres.org, have marched in silent remembrance of their children who disappeared during the 'Dirty War' (see box, page 674). Every Thursday at 1530, they march anti-clockwise around the central monument with photos of their disappeared loved-ones pinned to their chests. It is a moving sight. On the plaza, there are statues of General Belgrano in front of the Casa Rosada and of Columbus, behind the Casa Rosada in the Parque Colón. The guided tours of the Casa de Gobierno allow you to see its statuary and the rich furnishing of its halls and its libraries.

Opposite the Casa Rosada, on the west side of the plaza, is the white-columned **Cabildo**, which has been rebuilt several times since the original structure was erected in the 18th century; most recently the façade in 1940. Inside, where the movement for independence from Spain was first planned, is the **Museo del Cabildo y la Revolución** ① *Bolívar 65, T011-4334 1782, Tue-Fri 1030-1700, Sun 1130-1800, US$1,* which has just been renovated. Inside is worth a visit, especially for the paintings of old Buenos Aires, the documents and maps recording the May 1810 revolution, and memorabilia of the British attacks, as well as Jesuit art. In the patio is a café and stalls selling handicrafts (Thursday-Friday 1100-1800).

Many of the centre's most important buildings date from after 1776 when Buenos Aires underwent a big change, becoming the capital of the new viceroyalty and the official port. The **Catedral Metropolitana** ① *Rivadavia 437, T011-4331 2845, Mon-Fri 0800-1900, Sat-Sun 0900-1930, guided visits Sat and Sun at 1630 (San Martín's mausoleum and crypt) and 1315 (religious art), and daily at 1530 (temple and crypt), Mass held daily, check for times*, on the north side of the plaza, lies on the site of the first church in Buenos Aires, built in 1580. The current structure was built in French neoclassical style between 1758 and 1807, and inside, in the right-hand aisle, guarded by soldiers in fancy uniforms, is the imposing tomb of General José de San Martín (1778-1850), Argentina's greatest hero who liberated the country from the Spanish.

Just east of the cathedral, the **Banco de la Nación** is regarded as one of the great works of the famous architect Alejandro Bustillo (who designed the wonderful **Hotel Llao Llao** in Bariloche). Built in 1940-1955, its central hall is topped by a marble dome 50 m in diameter. Take in all these buildings, and you become aware that the banks, political and religious institutions, together with the military headquarters opposite, are all gathered in one potent place. No wonder then that people always come here to demonstrate.

Downtown: La City

Just north of Plaza de Mayo, between 25 de Mayo and the pedestrianized Florida, lies the main banking district known as La City, with some handsome buildings to admire. The **Banco de Boston** ① *Florida 99 and Av RS Peña*, dates from 1924, and while there are no guided visits, you can walk inside during banking hours to appreciate its lavish ceiling and marble interior (no cameras allowed). There's also the marvellous art-deco **Banco de la Provincia de Buenos Aires**, at San Martín 137, built in 1940, and the **Bolsa de Comercio**, at 25 de Mayo and Sarmiento, which dates from 1916 and houses the stock exchange, but visits aren't permitted. The **Banco Hipotecario** (formerly the Bank of London and South America), corner Reconquista and B Mitre, was designed by SEPRA (Santiago Sánchez Elia, Federico Peralta Ramos, and Alfredo Agostini). It was completed in 1963, in bold 'brutalist' design. You can visit during banking hours.

The **Basílica Nuestra Señora de La Merced** ① *J D Perón and Reconquista 207, Mon-Fri 0800-1800*, founded in 1604 and rebuilt 1760-1769, was used as a command post in 1807 by Argentine troops resisting the British invasion. Its highly decorated interior has an altar with an 18th-century wooden figure of Christ, the work of indigenous carvers from Misiones, and it has one of the few fine carillons of bells in Buenos Aires. A craft fair is held on Thursday and Friday 1100-1900. Next door, at Reconquista 269, is the **Convento de la Merced**, originally built in 1601 but reconstructed in the 18th and 19th centuries with a peaceful courtyard in its cloisters.

There are a few rather dry museums here, purely for historians: **Museo Numismático Dr José Evaristo Uriburu**, in the Banco Central library, tells the history of the country through its currency; **Museo y Biblioteca Mitre** ① *San Martín 336, T011-4394 8240, www.museomitre.gov.ar, Mon-Fri 1400-1730 (library and archives only on Wed), US$1.50*, preserves intact the colonial-style home of President Bartolomé Mitre (1862-1868). More interesting and accessible is the bizarre **Museo de la Policía Federal** ① *San Martín 353, floors 8 and 9, T011-4394 6857, Tue-Fri 1400-1800, closed Jan and Feb*, which portrays the

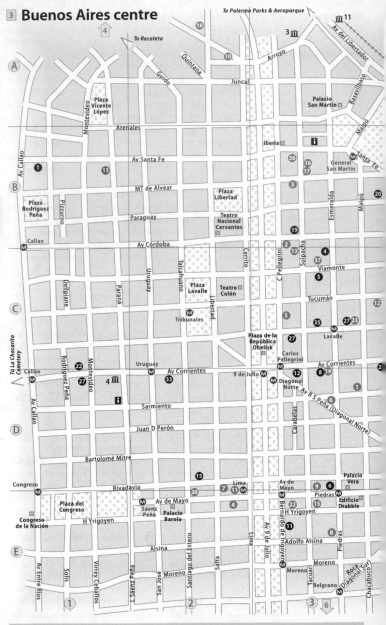

To Palermo Parks & Aeroparque

To Recoleta

Quintana

Guido

Arroyo

Av del Libertador

Juncal

Palacio
San Martín

Plaza
Vicente
López

Arenales

Montevideo

Pizzurno

Av Santa Fe

Iberia

General
San Martín

Av Callao

MT de Alvear

Plaza
Rodríguez
Peña

Plaza
Libertad

Esmeralda

Maipú

Paraguay

Teatro
Nacional
Cervantes

Callao

Av Córdoba

Delpiane

Cerrito

Suipacha

Uruguay

Paraná

Talcahuano

Libertad

Plaza
Lavalle

Teatro
Colón

Viamonte

Tucumán

Tribunales

Carlos
Pellegrini

Lavalle

Rodríguez Peña

Montevideo

Plaza de la
República
Obelisk

To La Chacarita
Cemetery

Callao

Uruguay

Av Corrientes

9 de Julio

Diagonal
Norte

Av Corrientes

Av R S Peña (Diagonal Norte)

Av Callao

Sarmiento

Carabelas

Juan D Perón

Bartolomé Mitre

Palacio
Vera

Congreso

Rivadavia

Av de
Mayo

Lima

Piedras

Edificio
Drabble

Plaza del
Congreso

Av de Mayo

Sáenz
Peña

Palacio
Barolo

Bernardo de Irigoyen

H Yrigoyen

Congreso
de la Nación

H Yrigoyen

Adolfo Alsina

Piedras

Alsina

Av 9 de Julio

Moreno

Av Entre Ríos

Solís

Virrey Cebalos

L Sáenz Peña

San José

Santiago del Estero

Salta

Lima

Tacuari

Belgrano

Moreno

Roca (Diagonal Sur)

Chacabuco

200 metres
200 yards

Sleeping
About Baires Hostel **2** B3
Alvear Palace **10** A2
BA Stop **7** D2
Bisonte Palace **3** B3
Casa Calma **17** B3
Castelar **4** E2
06 Central **1** D3
Clan House **8** E3
725 Continental **6** D3
Dolmen **16** B3
Four Seasons **18** A2
Frossard **12** C4
Goya **13** C3
Hispano **9** D3
Hostel Suites
  Obelisco **19** D3
Lime House **11** D2
Marbella **20** E2
Marriott Plaza **21** B4
Milhouse Hostel **22** E3
Moreno **14** E4
NH City **26** E4
O'Rei **23** C3
Panamericano **5** C3
Plaza San Martín
  Suites **36** B3
Portal Del Sur **15** F3
V&S **37** C3
Waldorf **38** B4

Eating
Broccolino **4** C3
Café Tortoni **6** D3
California Burrito
  Company **2** C4
Club Español **11** E3
Confitería Ideal **12** D3
Dadá **3** B4
El Gato Negro **22** C1
El Palacio de la Papa
  Frita **27** C3/D1
El Querandí **28** E4
Empire Bar **30** B4

Gianni's **5** C3
Güerrín **33** D2
La Casona del Nonno **35** C3
La Chacra **19** B3
La Madeleine **1** B1
Las Cuartetas **8** D3
Morizono **48** B4
Pura Vida **14** C4
Rocket **15** D2
Sorrento **25** C4
Tancat **20** B4

Bars & clubs
Druid In **7** B4
La Cigale **23** B4
Le Bar **9** C4
Milion **13** B1

Museums
Casa de Gobierno
  (Casa Rosada) **1** D5
Centro Cultural San Martín,
  Museo de Arte Moderno
  & Teatro Municipal
  San Martín **4** D1
Museo de Arte
  Hispanoamericano
  Isaac Fernández
  Blanco **3** A3
Museo de la Ciudad **5** E4
Museo de la Policía
  Federal **13** D4
Museo del Cabildo
  y la Revolución **6** E4
Museo Etnográfico
  JB Ambrosetti **8** E4
Museo Nacional
  Ferroviario **11** A3
Museo Numismático
  Dr José Evaristo
  Uriburu **12** D4
Museo y Biblioteca
  Mitre **10** D4

fascinating history of crime in the city, and includes a gruesome forensic section, definitely not for the squeamish. Information on museums can be found at www.museosargentinos.org.ar (in English).

South of Plaza de Mayo

To the southwest of the Plaza de Mayo, towards San Telmo, there is an entire block of buildings built by the Jesuits between 1622 and 1767, called the **Manzana de las Luces** (Enlightenment Square) – bounded by streets Moreno, Alsina, Perú and Bolívar. The former Jesuit church of **San Ignacio de Loyola** (see below for tours), begun in 1664, is the oldest colonial building in Buenos Aires and the best example of the baroque architecture introduced by the Jesuits (renovated in the 18th and 19th centuries), with splendid golden naves dating from 1710-1734 (www.manzanadelasluces.gov.ar). Also in this block are the **Colegio Nacional de Buenos Aires** ① *Bolívar 263, T011-4331 0734, www.cnba.uba.ar*, formerly the Jesuits' Colegio Máximo in the 18th century, and now the city's most prestigious secondary school. Below these buildings are **18th-century tunnels** ① *T011-4342 4655*. These are thought to have been used by the Jesuits for escape or for smuggling contraband from the port. For centuries the whole block was the centre of intellectual activity, and although little remains to see today, the history is fascinating. All **guided tours** ① *from Perú 272, Mon-Fri 1500, Sat-Sun 1500, 1630, 1800 (Mon 1300 free tour) in Spanish (in English by prior arrangement), arrive 15 mins before tour, US$2*, explore the tunnels; only weekend tours include San Ignacio and Colegio Nacional.

Museo de la Ciudad ① *Alsina 412, T011-4343 2123, www.museos.buenosaires.gov.ar/ciudad.htm, Mon-Sun, 1100-1900, US$1, free on Mon and Wed,* is worth visiting for an insight into 19th-century Buenos Aires life. The historical house includes a 1900s chemist's shop, Farmacia La Estrella, and has a permanent exhibition covering social history and popular culture, with special exhibitions on daily life in Buenos Aires. The **Church of San Francisco** ① *Alsina and Defensa, Mon-Fri 0700-1300, 1500-1900, guided visits Tue 1530 and 1630, Sat 1630 and 1730,* was built by the Franciscan Order in 1730-1754 and given a new façade in 1911 in German baroque style. There's a fine baroque pulpit and the chapel of San Roque.

Argentina has a rich heritage from numerous indigenous groups that inhabited the country before the Spanish arrived, and their history is well-charted in the anthropological museum **Museo Etnográfico J B Ambrosetti** ① *1 block south of the San Francisco church at Moreno 350, T011-4345 8196, www.museoetnografico.filo.uba.ar, Tue-Fri 1300-1900, Sat-Sun 1500-1900 (closed in Jan), US$0.70, guided visits Sat-Sun 1600.* Displays are limited, but very well laid out, and include some fascinating treasures, such as Inca textiles and ceramics, and Bolivian and Mapuche silverwork, all in an attractive building dating from 1880.

One block further south at Defensa and Belgrano, the **Church of Santo Domingo**, ① *Mon-Fri 0900-1300, Sun 1000-1200, no tours offered,* was founded in 1751. During the British attack on Buenos Aires in 1806 some of the British soldiers took refuge in the church and it was bombarded by local forces. Look out for the huge wooden cannon balls embedded in the towers on the outside: fakes, sadly. The British flags inside are worth seeing, and General Belgrano, a major figure in Argentine independence, is buried here.

Avenida de Mayo to Congreso

From Plaza de Mayo, take a stroll down this broad leafy avenue which links the Casa Rosada to the **Congress** building to the west. The avenue was built between 1889 and 1894, inspired by the grand design of Paris, and filled with elaborate French baroque and art nouveau buildings. At Perú and Avenida de Mayo is the **Subte station Perú**, furnished

Jorge Luis Borges

More than any writer, Borges has most vividly captured the spirit of Buenos Aires. Born in the city in 1899, he was obsessed with the myths and realities of Argentina and its culture, and by the wealth of literature from world classics. His entirely original blend of these two different worlds has made him the most influential figure in Argentine literary culture, with a worldwide reputation. In 1914, Borges travelled with his family to live in Switzerland and Spain, where he added Latin, French and German to his already fluent English (he had an English grandmother). He started to write, and became involved with the Ultraísmo literary movement, which scorned the mannerism and opulence of Modernismo for a style that embraced shocking imagery and free verse, which Borges described as 'avoiding ornamental artefacts'. Borges became an active member of the literary avant garde when he returned to Buenos Aires in 1921, and in the following few years, he contributed regularly to literary magazines, publishing seven books of poetry and essays that established his lifelong obsessions: a view of life from the margins, and a fascination with authorship and individual consciousness.

From 1933, Borges was Literary Editor of the Newspaper Crítica, where he published his Historia Universal de la Infamia (A Universal History of Infamy) in 1935, establishing a style somewhere between the non-fictional essay and the fictional short story. In the late 1930s he published a series of significant essays and short stories collections, including El Jardín de Senderos que se Bifurcan (The Garden of Forking Paths), in 1931, with one of his most famous stories, El Sur (The South). In 1944 Borges published arguably the most important series of stories in the history of Latin American literature, the great Ficciones (Fictions), which overturned conventions of realism while exploring the nature of literature itself, together with philosophy and metaphysics. El Aleph followed in 1949, and his most important essays, Otras Inquisiciones (Other Inquisitions) in 1952. A masterful storyteller, Borges never wrote more than a few pages, and was never tempted by the novel form, insisting that more could be explored in a few elliptical, highly suggestive and poetic lines than in hundred of pages of dull realist prose.

The late 1940s brought him almost total blindness due to glaucoma, and a running dispute with the Perón regime. Borges' work was overlooked in Europe and the USA until the late 1960s, by which time he was completely blind, and wrote mainly poetry, a form that he could compose in his head. The worldwide popularity of his fiction led him to publish two further books of short stories later in life, El Informe de Brodie (Dr Brodie's Report, 1970), and El Libro de Arena (The Book of Sand, 1975). In his final years, he travelled the world with his companion María Kodama, whom he married. He died in Geneva, of liver cancer, in June 1986.

by the Museo de la Ciudad to resemble its original state, with posters and furniture of the time. You'll need to buy a US$0.30 ticket to have a look, or take a train.

Along the avenue west from here, you'll see the splendid French style **Casa de la Cultura** at number 575, home of the newspaper La Prensa, which is topped with bronze statues. At No 702 is the fine Parisian-style **Edificio Drabble**, and at No 769, the elegant **Palacio Vera**, from 1910. Argentina's most celebrated writer, Jorge Luis Borges, was fond of the many cafés that once filled Avenida de Mayo, of which **Café Tortoni** ① *www.cafetortoni.com.ar*, at No 825, is the most famous in Buenos Aires and the haunt of many illustrious writers, artists and poets since 1858. Its high ceilings with ornate plaster work and art nouveau stained glass, tall columns and elegant mirrors plunge you straight back into another era. It's an atmospheric place for coffee, but particularly wonderful for the poetry recitals, tango and live music, which are still performed here in the evenings. There are also plenty of places nearby for a quick lunch, and lots of cheap hotels.

Continuing west over Avenida 9 de Julio, there's the superb 1928 **Hotel Castelar** ① *www.castelarhotel.com.ar*, at No 1152, still open (see Sleeping, page 86), and retaining its former glory, as is the beautiful art nouveau **Hotel Chile**, at No 1297. At the western end of the avenue is the astounding **Palacio Barola** ① *No 1370, www.pbarolo.com.ar, guided tours Mon and Thu 1400 and 1800, book tours in English, US$8, T011-1550 279 035, barolotours@gmail.com*, built by a textile magnate in 1923 with architectural details inspired by the Italian poet Dante. Avenida de Mayo culminates on the **Plaza del Congreso**, with the **congress building** ① *T011-4953 3081, ext 3885 for guided visits, Mon, Tue Thu, Fri 1100, 1700, 1900*, in Italian academic style, housing the country's government.

Plaza San Martín and Retiro

Ten blocks north of the Plaza de Mayo, and just south of **Retiro station**, is the splendid Plaza San Martín, on a hill originally marking the northern limit of the city. It has since been designed by Argentina's famous landscape architect Charles Thays, and is filled with luxuriant mature palms and plane trees. It is popular with runners in the early morning, as well as office workers at lunchtimes. At the western corner is an equestrian **statue of San Martín** (1862), and at the northern end of the plaza is the **Malvinas memorial** with elaborately dressed guards and an eternal flame to those who fell in the Falklands/ Malvinas War, 1982.

Around the plaza are several elegant mansions, among them the **Palacio San Martín**, designed in 1909 in French academic style for the wealthy Anchorena family, and now occupied by the Ministry of Foreign Affairs. Most striking is the elegant art deco **Edificio Kavanagh**, east of the plaza, which was the tallest building in South America when completed in 1936. Behind it is the **Basilica del Santísimo Sacramento** (1916), the church favoured by wealthy *Porteños*.

The **Plaza de la Fuerza Aérea**, northeast of Plaza San Martín, was until 1982 called the Plaza Británica; in the centre is a clock tower presented by British and Anglo-Argentine residents in 1916, still known as the Torre de los Ingleses.

Three blocks northwest of Plaza San Martín is one of the city's most delightful museums, the **Museo de Arte Hispanoamericano Isaac Fernández Blanco** ① *Suipacha 1422, www.museofernandezblanco.buenosaires.gob.ar, Tue-Fri, 1400-1900, Sat and Sun 1100-1900, US$0.30, Thu free, closed Jan, for guided visits in English or French, T011-4327 0228, guided tours in Spanish Sat, Sun 1600*. Housed in a beautiful 1920s neo-colonial mansion with tiled Spanish-style gardens, it contains a fascinating collection of colonial art, with fine Cuzqueño school paintings, and dazzling ornate silverware from Alto Perú and Río de la Plata. There are also temporary exhibitions of Latin American art. Highly recommended.

North of Plaza San Martín is **Retiro railway station**, really three separate terminals. The area is not safe to walk around, but if you're catching a train, drop in to see the oldest and finest of these, the **Mitre**, dating from 1908, a classical construction with an atmospheric interior, and a fantastic refurbished 1900s *confitería* with the original bar and high wooden ceilings – a great place for a coffee. Behind the station is the **Museo Nacional Ferroviario** ① *accessed from Av del Libertador 405, T011 4318 3343, Mon-Fri 1030-1600, free*, which contains locomotives, machinery and documents on the history of Argentine railways.

Avenida 9 de Julio is the world's widest thoroughfare, with nine lanes of traffic in each direction, leading south to Plaza de la Constitución and routes south of the city. It's crossed by the major streets of Avenida de Mayo and Córdoba, and at the junction with Corrientes is the city's famous landmark, a 67-m-tall **obelisk** constructed in 1936, commemorating the 400th anniversary of the city's founding, where football fans traditionally congregate in crowds to celebrate a victory. The city's main shopping street Avenida Santa Fe starts at Plaza San Martín and crosses Avenida 9 de Julio before heading through Retiro and Recoleta to Palermo. It's a huge stretch of shops, but the most well known brands are to be found between Talcahuano and Avenida Pueyrredon.

Four blocks west of the obelisk, you can see art exhibitions, go to the theatre and learn tango at the **Centro Cultural General San Martín** ① *Av Corrientes 1530, www.ccgsm. gov.ar, www.ccgsh.gov.ar, museum US$0.80, Wed free*. It's a rather austere 1970s concrete building, but it houses good photography exhibitions, the Teatro Municipal San Martín (www.teatrosanmartin.com.ar) and a salon of the Museo Municipal de Arte Moderno. There's also a tango information desk at the entrance.

Teatro Colón

① *Main entrance on Libertad, between Tucumán and Viamonte, T011-4378 7132, T011-4378 7133, www.teatrocolon.org.ar. The theatre is over 100 years old and has recently reopened after a multi-million dollar overhaul, just in time for the country's bicentennial in 2010. If you have time, try to see a performance or contact the theatre to do a backstage tour, prices and times not released at time of printing.*

On Avenida 9 de Julio, a block north of the obelisk, Teatro Colón is one of the world's greatest opera houses and one of the city's finest buildings. It opened in 1908 and is an extraordinary testimony to the country's former wealth. Behind the classical façade, the opulent foyer is decorated with three kinds of marble brought from Europe, a Parisian stained glass dome in the roof, and a Venetian-tiled mosaic floor. The perfectly preserved auditorium is French baroque style, from the chandelier in the ceiling (which conceals a chamber where singers or musicians can be hidden to produce music from the heavens) to the French gilded lights and red velvet curtains. It has an almost perfect acoustic, due to the horseshoe shape and the mix of marble and soft fabrics, and an immense stage, 35 m deep. Workshops and rehearsal spaces lie underneath the Avenida 9 de Julio itself, and there are stores of costumes, including 22,000 pairs of shoes.

Puerto Madero

East of the city centre at Puerto Madero, the 19th-century docks have been successfully transformed into an attractive area with lots of good restaurants, cafés, bars and upmarket hotels among the modern developments of offices, shops, housing and even a university campus. It's a good place for a walk, among the tall brick buildings and along the docks, with their cranes and winches now freshly painted. Restaurants are mostly found along the waterside of the old warehouses lining Avenida Alicia M de Justo from the northern end of Dique 4, where you'll find a helpful **tourist information** kiosk in a glass construction under one of the cranes.

Walking south, there are a couple of interesting ships to look at. By Dique 3, there's the **Fragata Presidente Sarmiento** ① *Av Dávila and Perón, T011-4334 9386, daily 0900-2000,*

US$1, free for children under 5, which was the Argentine flagship from 1899 to 1938, and is now a museum. Walking further south, in Dique 1, Avenida Juan de Garay, is the **Corbeta Uruguay**, the sailing ship that rescued Otto Nordenskjold's Antarctic expedition in 1903. Also over Dique 3 is the striking harp-like bridge, the **Puente de la Mujer** (Bridge of Women), suspended by cables from a single arm.

Costanera Sur

Buenos Aires has an extraordinary green space right at the heart of the city and on the waterfront. At the southernmost end of Dique 1, cross the pivoting bridge (level with Brazil Street) to the broad avenue of the Costanera Sur. This pleasant wide avenue used to run east of the docks, a fashionable promenade by the waterside in the early 20th century. Now it's separated from the river by the wide splay of land created in a 1970s landfill project, now enjoying a revival, with many restaurants open along the boulevard at night, and it's a pleasant place to walk by day. There's a wonderfully sensuous marble fountain designed by famous Tucumán sculptress Lola Mora, **Las Nereidas**, at the southernmost entrance to the **Reserva Ecológica** ⓘ *entrances at Av Tristán Achával Rodríguez 1550 (take Estados Unidos east from San Telmo), T011-4315 1320, for pedestrians and bikes only, Tue-Sun 0800-1800, in summer closes at 1900, free, bus No 2 passes next to the southern entrance*, where there are more than 200 species of birds, including the curve-billed reed hunter. Free guided tours are available at weekends, 1030 and 1530 (daily in summer), from the administration next to the southern entrance, but much can be seen from the road before then (binoculars useful). Also free nocturnal visits every month on the Friday closest to the full moon (book Monday before, T011-4893 1588). It is a 30-minute walk from the entrance to the river shore, taking about three hours to walk the whole perimeter. In summer it is very hot with little shade. For details (birdwatching, in particular) contact **Aves Argentinas/AOP** (see Tourist information, page 55).

Recoleta

The area of Recoleta is known as Barrio Norte, the chic place to live in the centre of the capital. Stretching west from Plaza San Martín, beyond Avenida 9 de Julio, Recoleta became a fashionable residential area when wealthy families started to move here from the crowded city centre after a yellow fever outbreak in 1871. Many of its French-style mansions date from the turn of the 20th century, and there are smart apartment blocks with marble entrances in leafy streets, making for a pleasant stroll around the many cafés, art galleries and museums. At its heart is the **Plaza de la Recoleta** by the **Recoleta Cemetery**. Running down its southeastern side is Ortiz, lined with cafés and *confiterías* ranging from the refined and traditional to touristy eateries, most with tables outside. Overhead are the branches of the **gran gomero**, a rubber tree, whose limbs are supported on crutches. At weekends, the **Plaza Francia** is filled with an art and craft market from 1100 until 1800, when the whole place is lively, with street artists and performers.

Recoleta is famous for its cemetery, where Eva Perón is buried, along with other illustrious figures from Argentina's history. **Cementerio de la Recoleta** ⓘ *entrance at Junín 1790, www.cementeriorecoleta.com.ar, not far from Museo de Bellas Artes (see below), T011-4804 7040, www.mnba.org.ar, Tue-Fri 1230-2030, Sat and Sun 0930-2030*, is like a miniature city, its narrow streets weaving between imposing family mausoleums built in every imaginable architectural style, a vast congregation of stone angels on their roofs. To negotiate this enormous labyrinth, a guided tour is recommended, but at the very least you'll want to see Evita Perón's tomb, lying in the Duarte family mausoleum. To find it from the entrance, walk straight ahead to the first tree-filled plaza, turn left, and where this avenue meets a main avenue (go just beyond the Turriata tomb), turn right and then take the third passage on the left.

The former Jesuit church of **El Pilar**, next to the cemetery, is a beautiful example of colonial architecture dating from 1732, restored in 1930. There are stunning 18th-century gold altarpieces made in Alto Peru, and a fine wooden image of San Pedro de Alcántara, attributed to the famous 17th-century Spanish sculptor Alonso Cano, preserved in a side chapel on the left. Downstairs is an interesting small museum of religious art, from whose windows you have a good view of the cemetery next door.

The **Centro Cultural Recoleta** ① *Junín 1930, www.centroculturalrecoleta.org, Tue-Fri 1400-2100, Sat, Sun, holidays 1000-2100, T011-4803 0358*, alongside the Recoleta cemetery, occupying the cloisters of a former monastery, has constantly changing exhibitions of contemporary local art by young artists. Next door, the **Buenos Aires Design Centre** ① *www.designrecoleta.com.ar*, has stylish homewares by contemporary Argentine designers. There are also lots of good restaurants here, some with views over

4 Recoleta

▲ To Río de la Plata

200 metres
200 yards

Sleeping 🛏
Alvear Palace 1
Art Hotel 4
Four Seasons 3
Palacio Duhau-Park
  Hyatt 2
Trip Recoleta 5

Eating 🍴
Café Victoria 7
Clásica y Moderna 1
Como en Casa 2
El Sanjuanino 8
La Madeleine 11
Lola 12
Rodi Bar 13
Sirop 14
Tandoor 3

Bars & clubs 🍸
Buller Brewing Company 6
Casa Bar 4
El Living 5
Milion 15
Shamrock 9

the nearby plazas from their open terraces, recommended for an evening drink at sunset. In **Plaza San Martín de Tours** next door, there are more huge gomera trees with their extraordinary sinuous roots, and here you're likely to spot one of Buenos Aires' legendary dog walkers, managing an unfeasible 20 or so dogs without tangling their leads. There's a **tourist information booth** ⓘ *T011-4804 5667*, at Ayacuco 1958. **Village Recoleta** ⓘ *T011-4805 2220*, on Vicente López and Junín, houses a multiplex cinema, with a fantastic bookshop and cafés at its entrance.

Recoleta museums

Most of the city's great museums are collected together in Recoleta, where the wide and fast avenue **Avenida del Libertador** runs north from Recoleta towards Palermo, past further parks and squares as well as several major museums. Of these the undoubted star is **Museo de Arte Latinoamericano de Buenos Aires** (MALBA) ⓘ *Av Figueroa Alcorta 3415, T011-4808 6500, www.malba.org.ar, Wed-Mon 1200-2000 (Wed free till 2100), US$1.30, free for ISIC holders, cinema tickets US$4, book in advance*, opened in 2001 to house a permanent collection of Latin American art, and temporary exhibitions. The minimalist building may strike you as rather stark, but the works inside are full of passion – powerful, humorous and moving pieces, very accessible and highly recommended. There's also an elegant café serving delicious food and cakes, and a cinema showing well-chosen art house films, as well as Argentine classics. If you've time for only one museum, make it this one.

For a taste of older Argentine art, visit the **Museo de Bellas Artes** ⓘ *Av del Libertador 1473, T011-4803 0802, www.mnba.org.ar, Tue-Fri 1230-1930, Sat-Sun 0930-1930, guided tours Tue-Sun 1600, 1700, 1800, tours for children in summer Tue-Fri 1100, 1700, Sat-Sun 1600, free.* There's a fairly ordinary survey of European works, but some particularly good post-Impressionist paintings and fine Rodin sculptures. Best of all though, there is a varied collection of Argentine 19th- and 20th-century paintings, sculpture and wooden carvings.

The **Biblioteca Nacional** (National Library) ⓘ *Av del Libertador 1600 and Agüero 2502, T011-4806 6155, www.bn.gov.ar, Mon-Fri 0900-2100, Sat and Sun 1200-1900, closed Jan, excellent guided tours (Spanish) daily 1600 from main entrance, for tours in other languages contact in advance*, is a huge cube standing on four sturdy legs in an attractive garden with a bust of Eva Perón. Only a fraction of its stock of about 1.8 million volumes and 10,000 manuscripts is available, but it's open to visitors, and worth a look to enjoy one of the frequent exhibitions and recitals.

The fabulous **Museo Nacional de Arte Decorativo** ⓘ *Av del Libertador 1902, www.mnad.org.ar, daily 1400-1900, T011-4802 6606, US$0.90, ½-price to ISIC holders, guided tours Wed, Thu, Fri 1630*, is housed in a fabulously elegant building and contains collections of painting, furniture, porcelain, crystal and sculpture. It also hosts classical music concerts on Wednesdays and Thursdays. The French style mansion is worth seeing on it's own, and there is a lovely café outside in the garden.

Offering a real insight into the Argentine soul, the **Museo de Arte Popular José Hernández** ⓘ *Av Libertador 2373, T011-4802 7294, Wed-Sun 1300-1900, US$0.50, free Sun, closed in Feb*, is named after the writer of Argentina's famous epic poem *Martín Fierro*, and contains one of the most complete collections of folkloric art in the country. There are plenty of gaucho artefacts: ornate silver *mates*, wonderful plaited leather *talebartería* and decorated silver stirrups, together with pre-Hispanic artefacts, and paintings from the Cuzco school. There is also a handicrafts shop and library.

Palermo

Palermo is Buenos Aires' most colourful area, growing in recent years from a peaceful residential *barrio* to a seriously hip and chic place to eat, shop and party.

Palermo parks

Palermo was originally named after Giovanni Domenico Palermo who transformed these lands into productive orchards and vineyards in the 17th century. President De Rosas built a sumptuous mansion, **La Quinta**, here in the early 19th century, and Palermo's great parks were established by Sarmiento and designed by Argentina's most famous landscape designer, Charles Thays, in the early 20th century. It remains a sought-after residential area for middle-class *Porteños*, and the wonderful parks are the most popular inner-city green space at weekends. Best not to go at night as they turn into an unofficial 'red-light' district.

Of this series of parks, the **Parque Tres de Febrero** ① *Mon-Fri 0800-1800, Sat and Sun 0800-2000 in winter, daily 0800-2000*, is the largest, with lakes and a really beautiful rose garden, especially in spring time when the displays are particularly abundant and fragrant. Also in the park is the **Museo de Arte Moderno Eduardo Sivori** ① *T011- 4774 9452, www.museosivori.org.ar, Tue-Fri 1200-2000 (winter 1800), Sat and Sun 1000-2000 (winter 1800), US$0.60, Sat and Wed free*, where you can immerse yourself in a fine collection of Argentine art, with 19th- and 20th-century paintings, engravings, tapestries and sculptures. South of here is the beautifully harmonious **Japanese garden** ① *T011-4804 4922, www.jardinjapones.org.ar, daily 1000-1800, US$1.50, guided visits Sat 1500, 1600*, with huge koi to feed, and little bridges over ornate streams, a charming place to walk and delightful for children. There's also a good café with Japanese dishes available among the usual menu, and also the **Japanese-Argentine Cultural Centre** where you can learn flower arranging, tea ceremony and origami. To the east of both of these is the wonderful alien spaceship-like building of the **planetarium** ① *T011-4771 9393, www.planetario.gov.ar, museum Mon-Fri 1000-1500, free, fantastic planetarium shows (in Spanish), US$2.50*, with several impressive meteorites from Campo del Cielo at its entrance. The **Jardín Zoológico, Las Heras and Sarmiento** ① *T011-4011 9900, www.zoobuenos aires.com.ar, daily 1000-1900, guided visits available, US$6, children under 13 free*, west of the Japanese gardens, has a decent collection of animals, in spacious surroundings, and an even more impressive collection of buildings of all kinds of styles, in grounds landscaped by Charles Thays. The llamas and guanacos are particularly appealing, especially if you don't get to see them in their native habitats elsewhere in the country.

The **Municipal Botanical Gardens** ① *west of the zoo at Santa Fe 2951, daily 0800-1800, free*, form one of the most appealing parts of the parks, despite being a little unkempt. Thays designed the gardens in 1902, and its different areas represent various regions of Argentina with characteristic specimens; particularly interesting are the trees native to the different provinces. North of the zoo are the showgrounds of the **Sociedad Rural Argentina** ① *entrance is from Plaza Italia (take Subte, line D)*, where the Annual Livestock Exhibition, known as Exposición Rural, is staged in July/August, providing interesting insights into Argentine society, not to mention truck loads of livestock, horses and roosters on display.

Further north is the 45,000-seater Palermo race track, **Hipódromo Argentino** ① *T011-4777 9001, www.palermo.com.ar*, where races are held on average 10 days per month; it's well worth a visit even for non-racegoers. Nearby are the **Municipal Golf Club**, **Buenos Aires Lawn Tennis Club**, riding clubs and polo field, and the **Club de Gimnasia y**

5 Palermo

Las Cañitas

→ **Buenos Aires maps**
1 Buenos Aires orientation, page 60
2 Metro (Subte), page 64
3 Buenos Aires centre, page 70
4 Recoleta, page 77
5 Palermo, page 80
6 San Telmo, page 83

Sleeping 🛏
Bait **15**
Bo Bo **4**
Casa Alfaro **6**
Casa Esmeralda **14**
Che Lulu **5**
Costa Rica **12**
Cypress In **7**
Five Cool Rooms **3**
Glu **17**
Home **8**
Hostel Suites Palermo **18**
Krista **9**

Legado Mítico **11**
Malabia House **1**
Solar Soler **10**
Tango Backpackers Hostel **2**
Vida Baires **16**
Zentrum Boutique Hostel **13**

Eating 🍴
Baez **9**
Bar 6 **30**
Bio **14**
B-Blue **5**
Cabernet **18**

Campo Bravo **12**
Cluny **31**
De la Ostia **10**
Dominga **20**
Eh! Santino **15**
El Diamante **21**
El Manto **22**
El Preferido de Palermo **13**
Eterna Cadencia **23**
Garum **24**
Janio **25**
Krishna **1**
La Cabrera **2**

Mark's Deli **26**
Miranda **27**
Morelia **8**
Novecento **11**
Olsen **3**
Omm **28**
Omm Carnes **29**
Persicco **17**
Social Paraíso **7**
Un' Altra Volta **4**

Carlos Gardel

To this day there is still a lot of controversy about the origins of Argentina's favourite performer. Most people argue that Gardel, the legendary singer whose name is virtually synonymous with tango, was born in 1890 in Toulouse, France, to Berthe Gardés and an unknown father. To avoid social stigma, his mother decided to emigrate to the Abasto market area of Buenos Aires when her son was just two years old, and it was partly these humble beginnings that helped him to become an icon for poor *Porteños*.

Just as the exact origin of tango itself is something of a mystery, Gardel's formative years around the city are obscure, until around 1912 when he began his artistic career in earnest, performing as one half of the duo Gardel-Razzano. He began his recording career with Columbia with a recording of 15 traditional songs, but it was with his rendition of *Mi Noche Triste* (My Sorrowful Night) in 1917, that his mellifluous voice became known. As *tango-canción* became popular –

the song rather than just a musical accompaniment to the dance – Gardel's career took off, and by the early 1920s he was singing entirely within this new genre, and achieving success as far afield as Madrid.

Gardel became a solo artist in 1925 and with his charm and natural machismo was the very epitome of tango both in Argentina and, following his tours to Europe, around the world. Between 1933 and 1935, he was based in New York, starring in numerous Spanish-speaking films, and the English language *The Tango on Broadway* in 1934. On 24 June 1935, while on a tour of South America, his plane from Bogotá to Cali crashed into another on the ground while taking off. Gardel was killed instantly, he was only 45. Gardel had recorded some 900 songs during his relatively short career, and the brilliance of his voice, the way he represented the spirit of the Río de la Plata to his fans at home, and the untimely nature of his dramatic death ensured the endurance of his popularity.

Esgrima (Athletic and Fencing Club). The parks are bordered to the north by Aeroparque (Jorge Newbery Airport), the city's domestic airport.

Palermo Viejo

The most atmospheric, and oldest, part of Palermo can be found in the quadrant between the Córdoba and Santa Fe, south of Juan B Justo and north of Avenida Scalabrini Ortiz. This area is also known as **Palermo Soho** (the two names are interchangeable), supposedly because of similarities with SoHo in New York, rather than London. You'll also hear people mention **Palermo Hollywood**, which is on the other side of the railway tracks and Avenida Juan B Justo which bisects the area. There are fewer shops in this part, and it's so-called because of the number of TV and film companies based here, but there are lots of restaurants and bars, so it's worth exploring. The whole of Palermo is a very seductive place, with its cobbled streets lined with trees, tall bohemian houses bedecked with flowers and plants, and leafy plazas. It's become a very fashionable place to live, but it's even more popular among young *Porteños* shopping for contemporary clothing and interiors, and drinking in chic bars in the evenings. There's no *Subte* station in the middle of Palermo, but there are three stations within five blocks or so, along Avenida Santa Fe, and there are buses which pass close by. A taxi from San Telmo to Palermo costs about US$8.

To start exploring, take the *Subte* (Line D) to either Scalabrini Ortiz, Plaza Italia or Palermo stations (depending on where you want to start). Walk up towards **Plaza Palermo Viejo** also called **Plaza Armenia** or to Plaza Serrano officially called **Plaza Cortázar**, named after Argentina's famous novelist and writer, whose novel *Rayuela* (Hopscotch) is set around here. These two plazas are both surrounded by cafés and bars, and in the four blocks between are all the clothing and accessories shops you could ever need (see Shopping, page 101, for more details). Meander up **Malabia**, and then around streets **Costa Rica**, **El Salvador** and **Honduras**, with detours along Armenia and Guruchaga when some boutique catches your eye. For a list of recommended clothes shops, see page 102. Even if you loathe shopping, Palermo Viejo will appeal since the whole area is wide open and relaxed, and it retains the quiet atmosphere of a residential district.

For bars and restaurants, you can wander further afield and stray onto the other side of Juan B Justo, though note that you can only cross the railway tracks at Honduras, Paraguay and Santa Fe. Alternatively, take a Radio Taxi from the centre of town straight to one of the restaurants recommended in this guide, and wander the nearby blocks to lap up the atmosphere and satisfy yourself there's nowhere you fancy more. So many new restaurants have opened up in the last few years that you'll be spoilt for choice. Palermo is a great place for meeting in the evenings, with bars and restaurants attracting lively crowds of trendy locals as well as increasing numbers of tourists. On the northwestern edge of Palermo, separated from the main area by yet another railway line, is **Las Cañitas**, a hugely popular area of restaurants centred around **Báez**.

South of the centre

San Telmo

The city's most atmospheric *barrio* is also its oldest. San Telmo starts south of the Plaza de Mayo, and is built along a slope which was once the old beach of the Río de la Plata. Formerly one of the wealthiest areas of the city, it was abandoned by the rich during a serious outbreak of yellow fever in 1871, and so was never modernized or destroyed for rebuilding like much of the rest of the city. San Telmo is one of the few areas where buildings have survived from the mid-19th century, crumbling and largely unchanged, so it's a delightful place to stroll and explore the artists' studios and small museums hidden away in its narrow streets, with plenty of cafés and shops selling antiques, records, handmade shoes, second-hand books and crafts of all kinds. In the last couple of years, new boutiques, design shops and chic bars (and hotels) have been opening up in newly renovated old houses in San Telmo and moving out towards Montserrat too, similar to those in Palermo Viejo.

A quiet place to meander during the week, the *barrio* comes alive on Sundays when there's an antiques and bric-a-brac market held in the central **Plaza Dorrego**, a small square enclosed by charming old houses. This is a good place to start exploring, after enjoying the free tango demonstrations that take place near the plaza on Sundays 1000-1800, and sometimes during the week as well. Behind the plaza, on Carlos Calvo (entrances on Bolívar, Estados Unidos and Defensa too), there's a wonderful indoor fruit market – **Mercado de San Telmo** built in 1897, which also has some antiques and vintage clothes. Walk south along Defensa, filled with street musicians on Sundays, many of them excellent, and pop into the artists' studios, antique shops and cafés that line the street. Just a block from the plaza is the white stuccoed church of **San Pedro González Telmo** ① *Humerto Primero, T011-4361 1168, Mon-Sat 0830-1200, 16-1900, guided tours Sun at*

1500, 1600, free. Begun by the Jesuits in 1734, but only finished in 1931, it's a wonderful confection of styles with ornate baroque columns and Spanish-style tiles.

One block further south, in an old tobacco warehouse, the **Museo de Arte Moderno de Buenos Aires** ① *San Juan 350, T011-4361 1121, www.museos.buenosaires.gov.ar/mam.htm,*

6 San Telmo

To Plaza de la República

Belgrano
Av Belgrano
Venezuela
Santo Domingo
Piedras
Tacuarí
México
Chile
Defensa
Av Paseo Colón
Av Ingeniero J Luis Huergo
Azopardo
Bolívar
El Viejo Almacén
Av Independencia
Independencia
Estados Unidos
Mercado de San Telmo
Dr Giuffra
Carlos Calvo
Chacabuco
Plaza Dorrego
San Pedro González Telmo
Humberto 1°
Museo de Arte Moderno de Buenos Aires
Av San Juan
Autopista 25 de Mayo
Cochabamba
Av Juan de Garay
Brasil
Av Caseros
Museo Histórico Nacional
Parque Lezama
Plaza Constitución
Constitución Station
Finochietto
To La Boca
PUERTO MADERO
To Ezeiza Airport
To Costanera Sur
To Plaza de Mayo
Alicia Moreau de Justo
Aristóbulo Brown

200 metres
200 yards

Sleeping
1890 8
América del Sur 9
Axel 17
Casa Bolívar 10
Circus 12
Dandi Royal 5
El Hostal de Granados 3
Four 11
Garden House Art Factory Hostel 10
Hostel-Inn Buenos Aires 1
Hostel-Inn Tango 7
La Casita de San Telmo 4

La Cayetana Historic House 16
Lugar Gay de Buenos Aires 19
Mansión Vitraux 20
Ostinatto 13
Ribera Sur 14
Sandanzas 6
Telmho 15
The Cocker 2

Eating
Bar Británico 16
Brasserie Petanque 4
Café San Juan 9
Defensa al Sur 1
El Desnivel 3
El Hipopótamo 2

La Brigada 5
La Trastienda 7
La Vinería de Gualterio Bolívar 6
Los Lobos 8
Nonna Bianca 10
Pride Café 11

Bars & clubs
70 Living 17
Bar Dorrego 18
Gibralter 13
La Puerta Roja 14
La Resistencia 15
Plan B 19
Seddon 12

which is currently closed for renovations, houses good visiting exhibitions of contemporary international and Argentine art. Due to re-open in 2011.

At the end of Defensa is **Parque Lezama** ① *Defensa and Brasil, Sat and Sun 1000-2000*, originally one of the most beautiful parks in the city, but now a little run down, and not a safe place to wander at night. According to tradition, Pedro de Mendoza founded the city on this spot in 1535, and there's an imposing statue to him in the centre of the park. Also on this corner you'll find the famous **Bar Británico** which has been open almost continuously since 1960. It has featured in films (including *The Motorcycle Diaries*) and was an institution in the suburb, but has been refurbished by new owners. It is still open 24 hours and is a good place to have a coffee and watch the world go by. On the west side of the park is the **Museo Histórico Nacional** ① *Defensa 1600, T011-4307 1182, Wed-Sun 1100-1800, US$0.50, guided tours Sat-Sun 1530*, which presents the history of the city and of Argentina through the key historical figures and events, with some impressive artefacts, portraits and war paintings, particularly of San Martín. Unfortunately, there's currently little information available in English.

There is an ever-growing number of restaurants along Defensa, many of them cheap and lively places to eat, and several venues offering tango shows. The best is the historical **El Viejo Almacén** ① *Independencia and Balcarce, T011-4307 7388, www.viejoalmacen. com, open daily, dinner from 2000, show 2200, US$70 with all drinks, dinner and show US$105, show only US$58*, started by celebrated tango singer Edmundo Rivero in the late 1960s. Here the city's finest tango dancers demonstrate their extraordinary skills in a small, atmospheric theatre, with excellent live music and singing from some of the great names of tango. Highly recommended. There are plenty of good restaurants sprinkled through San Telmo, and lots of hostels are here too.

La Boca

East of the Plaza de Mayo, behind the Casa Rosada, a broad avenue, Paseo Colón, runs south towards the old port district of La Boca, where the polluted Riachuelo river flows into the Plata. An area of heavy Italian immigration in the early 1900s, La Boca is known for the brightly painted blue, yellow and lime green zinc façades of its houses, a tradition brought over by Genoese immigrants who painted their homes with the leftover paint from ships. It's a much-touted tourist destination, but very disappointing in reality. There is nothing authentic left of the area, and just one block of brightly painted houses to see on pedestrianized **El Caminito**, put there, somewhat cynically, by the Buenos Aires tourist board. El Caminito leads west from the little triangular plaza **La Vuelta de Rocha**, and this street is in fact the only place you're allowed to visit in La Boca, since policemen are permanently stationed there to stop tourists from straying further. This is because the area is apparently rife with petty crime and tourist muggings are a common occurrence. There's a small arcade of artists' workshops and a couple of cafés in the **Centro Cultural de los Artistas**, with tango dancers, street entertainers and touristy souvenir shops. You might be tempted to stray from this touristy area and find the 'real' La Boca: don't. The surrounding streets are notorious for crime, you will almost certainly be a very obvious target, and in any case, the Riachuelo river is far from picturesque, with its distinctive rotting smell. To reach La Boca from the centre, phone for a Radio Taxi, US$5 from downtown (see Ins and outs, page 62) and call from the *locutorio* in Centro Cultural for a taxi to take you home. Police are on hand in the Vuelta de Rocha to help and advise tourists. There is a freephone number to contact the **tourist police office** ① *T0800-999 5000, staff speak English and other European languages.*

The real attractions here are two fine museums: La Boca really owes its fame to the artist Benito Quinquela Martín (1890-1977) who painted its ships, docks and workers all his life, and whose vivid and colourful paintings can be seen in the **Museo de Bellas Artes Benito Quinquela** ① *Pedro de Mendoza 1835, T011-4301 1080, Tue-Sun 1030-1730, closed Jan, US$0.40.* The artist lived here for many years, and you can also see his own extensive collection of paintings by Argentine artists, and sculpture on a roof terrace with wonderful views over the whole port, revealing the marginalized poverty behind the coloured zinc façades. There's more contemporary art a block away in the **Fundacíon Proa** ① *Av Pedro de Mendoza 1929, T011-4104 1000, www.proa.org, Tue-Sun 1100-1900, guided visits Tue-Fri 1700, Sat and Sun 1500 and 1700, US$1.50,* a modern space opened in 1996 behind the ornate Italianate façade of a 1908 warehouse, showing temporary exhibitions of Argentine, Latin American and international contemporary art. Check the press for details. The roof terrace here is also great, and a nightclub venue.

La Boca is home to one of the country's great football teams, **Boca Juniors** (see page 104), and the area is especially rowdy when they're playing at home. Football is one of the great Argentine experiences, and the easiest way to go to a match is as part of a group arranged with a company such as **Tangol** (see Tour operators, page 106). Aficionados of the beautiful game will be entertained by the **Museo de la Pasión Boquense** ① *Brandsen 805, T011-4362 1100, daily 1000-1800 (times change if a match is on).* US$6.50, or US$9 for museum entry and a stadium tour (yes, you'll see Maradona's personal box).

◉ Buenos Aires listings

For Sleeping and Eating price codes and other relevant information, see Essentials pages 30-36.

● Sleeping

In the current economic climate, some hotels are offering discounts for multi-night stays, so it is worth checking out several hotels to get the cheapest deal. The tourist offices at both airports can book hotels, and if you pay in pesos, you can sometimes get further discounts.

City centre and Recoleta *p68, maps p70 and p77*
LL 725 Continental, Av Roque Saenz Peña 725, T011-4131 6000, www.725continental. com. Modern design business hotel in the centre. Wonderful bar, stunning roof-top pool, gym with a view. Very chic.
LL Alvear Palace, Av Alvear 1891, T/F011-4808 2100, www.alvearpalace.com. The height of elegance, an impeccably preserved 1930s Recoleta palace, taking you back in time to Buenos Aires' wealthy heyday. A marble foyer, with Louis XV-style chairs and

an orangery where you can take tea with superb patisseries (US$15). Recommended.
LL Casa Calma, Suipacha 1015, T011-5199 2800, www.casacalma.com.ar. Despite its downtown setting this sleek, yet homely luxury boutique hotel has managed to create a relaxing haven with rainforest music in the hallways, a wellness centre and an honesty bar.
LL Four Seasons, Posadas 1086, T011-4321 1200, www.fourseasons.com/buenosaires. A modern palace decorated in traditional style, offering sumptuous luxury in an exclusive atmosphere. Spacious public areas, adorned with paintings and flowers, chic, lavishly decorated rooms, and 7 suites in **La Mansión** where Madonna filmed *Evita* and numerous famous guests have enjoyed the residence, pool and health club.
LL Marriott Plaza, Florida 1005, T011-4318 3000, www.marriottplaza.com.ar. With a superb location overlooking Plaza San Martín, this is the city's most historic hotel, built in Parisian style in 1909, and retaining period elegance in the public rooms and bedrooms,

which are charming and luxurious. A pool and fitness centre, excellent restaurant, the Plaza Grill, and very good service throughout.
LL Palacio Duhau-Park Hyatt, Av Alvear 1661, T011-51711234, www.buenosaires. park.hyatt.com. Refurbished aristocratic mansion in the heart of Recoleta, with wonderful gardens and a great terrace for enjoying an evening cocktail.
L-AL Panamericano, Carlos Pellegrini 551, T011-4348 5000, www.panamericano news.com. Smart and modern city hotel, with luxurious and tasteful rooms, a lovely covered rooftop pool with a million dollar view of Av 9 de Julio, and superb restaurant, Tomo 1. Excellent service too.
AL Art Hotel, Azcuénaga 1268, T011-4821 4744, www.arthotel.com.ar. Great location on a quiet street in Recoleta and handy for the *Subte* and shopping in Santa Fe, this is a reliable and comfortable little hotel with small, neat, well-equipped rooms, and good breakfasts. It's a pricey option but made worthwhile by the great service from all the multilingual staff who go out of their way to make your stay comfortable. Free internet. Recommended.
AL Bisonte Palace, Marcelo T de Alvear 902, T011-43284751, www.hotelesbisonte.com. A delightful old place, with calm entrance foyer, which remains gracious thanks to charming and courteous staff. The rooms are modern and spacious, breakfast is ample, and it is in a good location.
AL Dolmen, Suipacha 1079, T011-4315 7117, www.hoteldolmen.com.ar. In a good location, this hotel has a spacious entrance lobby, with a calm relaxing atmosphere, good professional service, comfortable modern well-designed rooms, and a little pool.
AL La Cayetana Historic House, México 1330, T011-43832230, www.lacayetana hotel.com.ar. This fabulous 1820s restored house has 11 suites set off a lovely courtyard. Each room is individually designed, there is Wi-Fi, buffet breakfast and parking. Located

a little out of the centre in the quiet suburb of Monserrat. Recommended.
AL Moreno, 376 Moreno, T011-6091 2000, www.morenobuenosaires.com. Decorated in dark, rich tones this hotel is the best value in its category. Large rooms, some with a view over the nearby basilica, and only 150 m to Plaza de Mayo. Jacuzzi, gym and chic bar. Recommended.
AL NH City Hotel, Bolívar 160, T011-4121 6464, www.nh-hoteles.com. Very chic, with perfect minimalist design for a discerning younger clientele, this is one of 8 in the Spanish-owned chain in central Buenos Aires (see the website for the others), with beautifully designed modern interiors in a 1930s building off Plaza de Mayo, and luxurious rooms. Small rooftop pool, good restaurant.
AL-A Castelar, Av de Mayo 1152, T011-4383 5000, www.castelarhotel.com.ar. Wonderfully elegant 1920s hotel which retains all the original features in the grand entrance and bar. Cosy bedrooms (some a bit too cosy), helpful staff, and excellent value. Ask if there's going to be a party, though, as it can be very noisy. Also a spa with Turkish baths and massage. Recommended.
AL-A Plaza San Martín Suites, Suipacha 1092, T011-43284740, www.plazasan martin.com.ar. Neat modern self-contained apartments, comfortable and attractively decorated, with lounge and little kitchen, so that you can relax in privacy, right in the city centre, with all the services of a hotel. Sauna, gym, room service. Good value.
A Waldorf, Paraguay 450, T011-312 2071, www.waldorf-hotel.com.ar. Welcoming staff and a comfortable mixture of traditional and modern in this centrally located hotel. Good value, with a buffet breakfast, English spoken. Recommended.
B Frossard, Tucumán 686, T011-4322 1811, www.hotelfrossard.com.ar. A lovely old 1940s building with high ceilings and the original

doors, attractively modernized, and though the rooms are small, the staff are welcoming. This is good value and near Florida.

B Goya, Suipacha 748, T011-4322 9269, www.goyahotel.com.ar. A range of rooms offered in this friendly, welcoming and central place, worth paying for the superior rooms (**A**), though all are comfortable and well maintained. Good breakfast, English spoken.

B Hispano, Av De Mayo 861, T011-4345 2020, www.hhispano.com.ar. This hotel has been welcoming budget travellers since the 1950s. Rooms are plain but comfortable, set around a light courtyard, with a section of garden to enjoy. Only 3 blocks from the Casa Rosada, and 2 from the busy pedestrianized Florida.

B Marbella, Av de Mayo 1261, T/F011-4383 3573, www.hotelmarbella.com.ar. Modernized and central, though quiet. Breakfast included, English, French, Italian, Portuguese and German spoken. Highly recommended.

B-C The Clan House, Alsina 817, T011-4331 4448, www.bedandbreakfastclan.com.ar. This wonderful B&B has 17 brightly coloured, modern rooms, and offers buffet breakfast, Wi-Fi and a small but lovely terrace. Recommended.

D O'Rel, Lavalle 733, T011-4393 7186, www.hotelorei.com.ar. Slightly cheaper without bath, central, simple but comfortable, spotless, laundry facilities, helpful staff.

Hostels

D Hostel Downtown, Callao 341, San Nicolás, T011-4372 8898, www.laroccahostel.com. English-speaking staff, breakfast included and free Wi-Fi.

E pp Hostel Suites Obelisco, Av Corrientes 830, T011-4328 4040, www.hostelsuites. com. Top-notch hostel, with bright new furnishings and friendly staff. Great facilities, tourist info desk and lots of organized activities. They will organize a free transfer from Ezeiza international airport if you book more than 1 night. Dorms and doubles (**C**) available. HI discount.

E pp Milhouse Hostel, H Yrigoyen 959, T011-4383 9383, www.milhousehostel.com. This hostel, set in a fantastic 1890 building, is for travellers who want to make friends and party. It's lots of fun and very lively so be prepared. Tours can be booked from the reception.

E pp Portal del Sur, Hipólito Yrigoyen 855, T0114342 2821, www.portaldelsurba.com.ar. Nice dorms and especially lovely double (**B**) and single rooms available. Converted 19th-century building, with 4 storeys of private rooms. Recommended for single travellers.

E pp Trip Recoleta, Vincente López 2180, T011-4807 8726, www.triprecoleta.com.ar. New, spotless dorms and doubles (**B**) decorated in a chic modern style, right next to the Recoleta cemetery and many popular bars and cafés. Wi-Fi and nice terrace.

E pp **V&S**, Viamonte 887, T011-4322 0994, www.hostelclub.com. Attractive double rooms with bath (**B**). This is one of the city's best-loved hostels, central and beautifully run by friendly English-speaking staff, there's a welcoming little café and place to sit, a tiny kitchen, internet access and lots of tours arranged, plus tango nights, etc. Good place to meet people. Highly recommended.

E-F pp **About Baires Hostel**, Viamonte 982, T011-4328 4616, www.aboutbaireshostel. com. Located in a lovely building, this hostel is only a short walk to the centre, shopping street Av Santa Fe and the Obelisco. Same-sex dorms are available (**F**), as are double rooms (**C**). Prices include breakfast.

F pp **06Central**, Maipú 306, T011-5219 0052, www.06centralhostel.com. A few metres from the Obelisco and the theatre street of Corrientes, this hostel offers simple, clean, spacious dorms, and nicely decorated doubles (**C**). Kitchen, cosy communal area.

F pp **BA Stop**, Rivadavia 1194, T011-4382 7406, www.bastop.com. Set in a converted 1900s corner block, the walls are covered in fun murals, and the communal areas are inviting. Pool table and buffet breakfast. May be a little noisy as it is right in the middle of the city.

F pp **Lime House**, Lima 11, T011-4383 4561, www.limehouse.com.ar. Fun, lively hostel that organizes bar nights and has a residents-only bar in the reception. Located on busy 9 de Julio so some rooms may be noisy especially those close to the reception/bar and pool table, but the staff and the welcoming atmosphere makes this a fun place to stay. Doubles (**E**) available.

Puerto Madero p75

LL Faena Hotel + Universe, Martha Salotti 445, Dique 2, T011-4010 9000, www.faena hotelanduniverse.com. One of the best hotels in the world, this is where the rich and famous stay. Lush, red drapery fills the lobby and the luxury rooms. Stylish swimming pool, extensive gym and glove-wearing men who open doors for you. If you can't afford to stay

here, which is most of us, see a tango show or have a drink in the bar at least.

LL Hilton, Av Macacha Güemes 351, Puerto Madero, T011-4891 0000, www.hilton.com. A modern business hotel built in the revamped docks area with views of the Costanera Sur, and with plenty of restaurants nearby, this has neat functional rooms, the El Faro restaurant, a health club and pool.

Palermo p79, map p80

LL Legado Mítico, Gurruchaga 1848, T011-4833 1300, www.legadomitico.com. Stylishly designed small hotel with 11 beautiful rooms all subtly thematic. Named after Argentine cultural legends such as Victoria Ocampo, Ernesto Guevara and Jorge Luis Borges, they use local designs, products and art works. Pure luxury. Highly recommended.

LL The Glu Hotel, Godoy Cruz 1733, T011-4831 4646, www.thegluhotel.com. Right in the heart of trendy Palermo, a stone's throw from the markets at Plaza Serrano, this hotel is new, modern and recommended. Its huge rooms have all the mod-cons and the roof-top jacuzzi is exactly what you'll need after a long day shopping in the surrounding boutiques.

LL-AL Bo Bo, Guatemala 4882, Palermo Viejo, T011-4774 0505, www.bobohotel.com. Very chic and one of the most welcoming places to stay in Palermo. Bo Bo has just 7 rooms, designed around different themes, though all are warm, elegant and minimalist, with stylish bathrooms (some with disabled access). There's also an excellent restaurant (††) and bar, relaxing places in the evening, with lots of dark wood and smart tables, serving very classy food. Great service from friendly staff, who all speak English. Recommended.

LL-AL Home, Honduras 5860, T011-4778 1008, www.homebuenosaires.com. Another trendy boutique hotel, this one in Palermo Hollywood, with bold 1950s-inspired textiles and minimalist concrete floors, creating a funky vibrant urban chic feel. Just a handful of minimalist rooms around a bar serving light snacks (soup, salads and tapas). Small pool and space to sunbathe at the back. A good place to hang out in the evenings.

AL Craft Hip Hotel, Nicaragua 4583, T011-4833 0060, www.crafthotel.com. With a running theme of white in its 10 rooms, this hotel is a real find. Right on Plaza Armenia and close to shops, bars and restaurants, the rooms are small but imaginatively done out with flatscreen TVs, ipods, Wi-Fi and there is an extremely welcoming roof-top terrace.

AL Five Cool Rooms, Honduras 4742, T011-5235 5555, www.fivebuenosaires.com. Too cool for its own good perhaps, the style here is brutal concrete with lots of black wood in the spacious rooms, all with king-size beds and bathrooms. There's a living room with DVDs to watch and internet. There's a terrace upstairs too. It's a bit over priced, but the staff are efficient and speak fluent English.

AL Krista, Bonpland 1665, T011-4771 4697, www.kristahotel.com.ar. A delightful surprise: this intimate boutique hotel is hidden behind the plain façade of an elegant townhouse, once owned by Perón's doctor. In Palermo Hollywood, so well-placed for restaurants. It's a very appealing place to stay, and good value with its comfortable, calm, individually designed spacious rooms, all with simple bathrooms and smart bedlinen. Wi-Fi, wheelchair access. A real gem. Recommended.

AL Malabia House, Malabia 1555, Palermo Viejo, T011-4833 2410, www.malabiahouse. com.ar. An elegant B&B in a tastefully converted old house, with 15 light and airy individually designed bedrooms in white and pale green, and lovely calm sitting rooms. Great breakfast. This was the original Palermo boutique hotel, and while it's not the cheapest of the options available, and always booked in advance, it's recommended as a reliable and welcoming option.

A Cypress In, Costa Rica 4828, Palermo Viejo, T011 4833 5834, www.cypressin.com. This cosy, compact B&B offers 8 neat rooms on 2 floors, decorated in pleasing stark modern style, in a centrally located house, where the staff are very friendly. Stylish, small

sitting and dining area, and outside patio. Charming. Very good value. Recommended.

A Hotel Costa Rica, Costa Rica 4137/39, T011-4864 7390, www.hotelcostarica.com.ar. Small boutique hotel, with minimalist design and a bright, welcoming air. Lovely terrace to sunbathe on. 3 blocks from Plaza Palermo Viejo with its restaurants and boutiques.

A Solar Soler, Soler 5676, T011-4776 3065, www.solarsoler.com.ar. Very homely and extremely welcoming B&B in a great location in an old town house in Palermo Hollywood. Recommended for its excellent service and charming multilingual staff. All rooms have bathrooms (ask for the quiet ones at the back), there's free internet and the breakfasts are good. Recommended.

A-B Vida Baires, Gallo 1483, T011-4827 0750, www.vidabaires.com.ar. Located in the residential section of Palermo, close to shops and public transport, this French-style building has been converted into a lovely boutique hotel with 7 clean, light and attractive rooms. Lovely original features and friendly welcome.

B Casa Alfaro, Gurruchaga 2155, T011- 4831 0517. Homely rustic style in this converted old house, with exposed brick walls, red stone floors and lots of woven rugs. A variety of rooms for 2-4, some with bathrooms, and quieter rooms at the back, where there's a lovely little garden. The whole place is clean and neat, and the owner speaks English.

B-C Che Lulu, Emilio Zola 5185, T011-4772 0289, www.chelulu.com. Some double rooms and more hostel-style accommodation (**E**) in this friendly, rambling, laid-back house along a quaint quiet street just a few blocks from Palermo *Subte*. Not luxurious but great value and very welcoming. Often recommended.

Hostels

C Hostel Palermo, Córdoba 3874, T011-4866 6423, www.laroccavip.com. Breakfast included, free Wi-Fi, rooftop terrace. Singles, doubles and dorms.

E pp Hostel Suites Palermo, Charcas 4752, T011-4773 0806, www.hostelsuitespalermo. com. Located at the busy end of Palermo, near the zoo, this hostel is warm and welcoming, and is only a short walk to the closet *Subte* stop. Dorms and private rooms (**C**). HI discount.

E pp **Zentrum Boutique Hostel**, Costa Rica 4520, T011-4833 9518, www.zentrumhostel. com.ar. More a boutique hotel with some dorm beds, this hostel is located in a renovated townhouse using stylish, modern designs. Double rooms without bathroom (**B**) and with bathroom (**A**) are highly recommended. Enjoy the wonderful wooden terrace to watch the sun go down.

F pp **Bait**, El Salvador 5115, T011-4774 3088, www.baitba.com. Small, friendly and located 3 blocks from the main plaza. Rooms are simply decorated, and there is a small private bar upstairs which serves snacks and cold beer.

F pp **Casa Esmeralda**, Honduras 5765, T011-4772 2446, www.casaesmeralda.com.ar. Laid-back, dorms and doubles (**C**), neat garden with hammocks and fishpond. Sebastián, owner of trendy bars **La Cigale** and **Zanzibar**, offers basic comfort with great charm.

F pp **Tango Backpackers Hostel**, Paraguay 4601, T011-4776 6871, www.tangobp.com. Well situated to enjoy Palermo's nightlife, this is a friendly hostel with shared rooms and doubles (**D**), all the usual facilities plus its own restaurant. HI discount.

San Telmo *p82, map p83*

LL Axel Hotel, Venezuela 649, T011-4136 9393, www.axelhotels.com. Stunning gay hotel with 5 floors of stylishly designed rooms, each floor with a cosy living area. Rooftop pool and gourmet restaurant top it off. Recommended.

LL Mansion Vitraux, Carlos Calvo 369, T011-4300 6886, www.mansionvitraux.com. A stylish luxury hotel with only 12 well-designed rooms, nightly wine tastings and gourmet food. Small dipping pool.

L-AL Dandi Royal, Piedras 922, T011-4307 7623, www.hotelmansiondandiroyal.com. Perfectly restored 1900s house with stunningly elegant entrance hall and some beautiful rooms all decorated in the original

style, with luxurious bathrooms. Interesting location between San Telmo and Congreso, and the added benefit of tango classes downstairs. Charming welcome from English-speaking staff, small pool and much better value than most of the boutique hotels.

AL-A 1890 Hotel, Salta 1074, T011-4304 8798, www.1890hotel.com.ar. Located just outside San Telmo, this fabulous boutique hotel has 6 rooms all decorated in a modern and attractive way with a/c, heating and wonderful bathrooms. The building itself is a renovated 19th-century house and there is a tranquil patio for relaxing.

AL-A Casa Bolívar, Finochietto 524, T011-4300 3619, www.casabolivar.com. Each room in this wonderful hotel has a different theme, from Oriental, to Pop, to art deco, and they all have a kitchenette and modern bathrooms. Serving breakfast, but no other meals, this is a good longer-term option.

AL-A Ribera Sur, Paseo Colón 1145, between San Juan and Humberto 1, www.riberasur hotel.com.ar. Slightly strange location on a busy 8-lane road on the limit of San Telmo, but inside, this hotel offers a peaceful oasis in shades of grey and white. Chic rooms, great bar downstairs and a tiny pool.

AL-A The Cocker, Av Garay 458, T011-4362 8451, www.thecocker.com. In the heart of the antiques district, this art nouveau house has been cleverly and tastefully restored. It now offers a perfect urban retreat with stylish suites, a cosy, light living room and delightful roof terraces and gardens. Recommended.

A Telmho, Defensa 1086, T011-4116 5467, www.telmho-hotel.com.ar. Smartly decorated doubles with huge beds and windows that open up onto the famous Plaza Dorrego. See the market from the wonderful roof garden. Flatscreen TVs, new modern bathrooms and helpful staff.

A La Casita de San Telmo, Cochabamba 286 T011-4307 5073, www.lacasitadesan telmo.com. A restored 1840s house, 7 rooms, most of which open onto a garden with a beautiful fig tree. The owners are tango fans. Rooms are rented by the day, week or month.

A-B Lugar Gay de Buenos Aires, Defensa 1120, T011-4300 4747, www.lugargay.com.ar. A men-only gay B&B with 8 comfortable rooms. There is a video room and jacuzzi, and it is located a stone's throw from Plaza Dorrego.
A-B The Four, Carlos Calvo 535, T011-4362 1729, www.thefourhotel.com. In the heart of San Telmo this 1930s building has been converted into a lovely B&B with 6 rooms named after the years of important events in the neighbourhood. Appealing terrace, as well as welcoming staff. Recommended.
C Garden House Art Factory, Piedras 545, T011-4343 1463, www.artfactory ba.com.ar. Watch the sun set from the terrace and bar of this upmarket place. Dorms available (**E**).

Hostels

E pp **América del Sur**, Chacabuco 718, T011-4300 5525, www.americahostel.com.ar. Large, newly purpose-built hostel with hotel-like double rooms (**A**) and a fantastic terrace. New facilities throughout and a great location.
E pp **Circus**, Chacabuco 1020, T011-4878 7786, www.hostelcircus.com. New 'luxury' hostel with clean and stylish rooms, new fittings throughout the tastefully renovated building, and even a small heated swimming pool. Doubles (**B**) available.
F pp **El Hostal de Granados**, Chile 374, T011-4362 5600, www.hostaldegranados. com.ar. Small, well-equipped rooms in an interesting building on a popular street with bars and restaurants, lots of light, for 2 (**C**) to 4, with bath, breakfast included, kitchen, free internet, laundry service, discounts for longer stays.
F pp **Hostel-Inn Tango**, Piedras 680, T011-4300 5764, and **Hostel-Inn Buenos Aires**, Humberto Primero 820, T011-4300 7992, www.hostel-inn.com. Both well-organized hostels in old renovated houses, popular, lively, lots of activities and facilities such as internet, transfers, Spanish lessons. Breakfast included. 20% discount for HI card holders and 10% off long-distance buses.
F pp **Ostinatto**, Chile 680, T011-4362 9639, www.ostinatto.com.ar. Converted 5-level 1920s building, which has a huge open-plan kitchen, spacious dorms, a multi-use dance room where Spanish lessons are held and, best of all, a roof terrace where low-costs meals are served. Doubles (**B**) with or without a bathroom are also available. Located in a quiet but central street. Recommended.
F pp **Sandanzas**, Balcarce 1351, T011-4300 7375, www.sandanzas.com.ar. Arty budget hostel run by a group of friends who've created an original and welcoming space, small but with a nice, light, airy feel. Lounge and patio, internet, kitchen, breakfast. Also double rooms (**D**) with own bath.

Apartments/self-catering

If you are staying for more than a few days it will be more cost effective to rent an apartment. That way you can cook your own meals and perhaps share with friends. Apartments cost from US$40 per night, see www.craigslist.com (Argentina pages).
Bahouse, T011-4815 7602, www.bahouse.com. ar. Very good furnished flats. Well located in Retiro, Recoleta, Belgrano, Palermo and centre.
ByT Argentina, T011-4878 5000, www.byt argentina.com. Accommodation in residences and with host families; also furnished flats.
Casa 34, Av Rivadavia 550, 4th floor, T011-4342 5686, www.casa34.com. Helpful, with a big range.
Tu Casa Argentina, Esmeralda 980 2B, T011-4312 4127, www.tucasargentina.com. Furnished flats by the day, week or month; from about US$400 per month.

❼ Eating

Eating out in Buenos Aires is one of the city's great pleasures, with a huge variety of restaurants from the chic to the cheap, and lots of eclectic and exotic choices alongside the inevitable *parrilla* restaurant where you can eat the legendary huge Argentine steak, grilled to perfection over a wood fire. Argentines are very sociable and love to eat out, so if a restaurant is full, it's usually a good sign. Remember, though, that they'll usually start eating between 2130 and 2230. If in doubt, head for Puerto Madero, where there are lots of good mid-range places serving international as well as local cuisine. There are good deals at lunchtime in many restaurants where the *menú del día* costs US$4-7 for 2 courses and coffee. The following list gives only those restaurants easily accessible for people staying in the city centre. Wherever you're staying, take a Radio Taxi to Palermo or Las Cañitas for a wide range of excellent restaurants all within strolling distance. For more information on the gastronomy of Buenos Aires see these helpful websites: www.guiaoleo.com.ar, restaurant guide in Spanish and English; www.vidalbuzzi.com.ar, great guide in Spanish. 2 fantastic food-orientated blogs written in English are: www.saltshaker.net, by chef Dan Perlman who also runs a highly recommended private restaurant in his house, see website for details; and www.buenosairesfoodies.com.

City centre *p68, map p70*

¶¶¶ La Chacra, Av Córdoba 941 (just off 9 de Julio). A superb traditional *parrilla* with excellent steaks brought sizzling to your table, impeccable old-fashioned service and a lively buzzing atmosphere.

¶¶¶ Morizono, Reconquista 899. Japanese sushi and sashami, as well as other dishes.

¶¶¶ Sorrento Corrientes 668 (just off Florida). Intimate, elegant atmosphere, with dark wood, nicely lit tables, serving traditional menu with good fish dishes and steak.

¶¶ Broccolino, Esmeralda 776. Good Italian food, very popular, try *pechuguitas*.

¶¶ Club Español, Bernardo de Irigoyen 180 (on Av 9 de Julio, near Av de Mayo). Faded splendour in this fine old Spanish social club serving excellent seafood.

¶¶ Dadá, San Martín 941. Both a restaurant and bar, and great for gourmet lunches such as prawn salad. Great eclectic decoration.

¶¶ El Palacio de la Papa Frita, Lavalle 735 and 954, Av Corrientes 1620. Great traditional place for a filling feed, with a large menu and quite atmospheric, despite the bright lighting.

¶¶ El Querandí, Perú 302 and Moreno. Good food in an intimate atmosphere in this historical place that was opened in the 1920s. Also a popular café, well known for its Gin Fizz, and as a tango venue.

¶¶ Empire Bar, Tres Sargentos 427. Serves slightly expensive but good Thai food in a tasteful atmosphere.

¶¶ Rocket, Rivadavia 1285, Mon-Fri. British-style restaurant serving food such as curry and fish pie.

¶¶ Tancat, Paraguay 645. Really authentic Basque food and delicious dishes from other Spanish regions. Recommended.

¶ California Burrito Company, Lavalle 441, www.californiaburritoco.com, Mon-Fri. Huge Tex-Mex burritos, Corona beers, Margaritas, cheap tacos Tue nights. Highly recommended.

¶ Gianni´s, Viamonte 834 and 25 de Mayo 757, daily 0900-1700. The set menu is an ideal lunch option, served in a renovated old house. Risottos and salads are very good.

¶ Güerrín, Av Corrientes 1368. A Buenos Aires institution, serving incredibly cheap and filling slabs of pizza and *fainá* (chickpea polenta) which you eat standing up at a zinc bar. If you eat at a table you miss out on the colourful local life. Wonderful.

¶ La Casona del Nonno, Lavalle 827. Popular with tourists for its cheap set-price menu, Italian-style food, cheap pastas and *parrilla*.

¶ Las Cuartetas, Av Corrientes 838. Local pizza institution open early to very very late, with fantastic cheap pizzas and 1970s-style furniture. Highly recommended.

¶ Pura Vida, Reconquista 516, www.pura vidabuenosaires.com, Mon-Fri. Use all natural ingredients in their salads, juices, sandwiches, wraps and soups. Recommended. There's also a branch in Recoleta.

Tea rooms, café-bars and ice-cream parlours

Café Tortoni, Av de Mayo 825-9, www.cafe tortoni.com.ar. This famous Buenos Aires café has been the elegant haunt of artists and writers for over 150 years: Carlos Gardel sang here and Borges was a regular. It's self-conscious of its tourist status these days, but still atmospheric, with marble columns, stained-glass ceilings, old leather chairs and photographs of its famous clientele on the walls. Excellent coffee and cakes, and good tea, all rather pricey, but worth a visit for the interesting *peña* evenings of poetry and music, and jazz and tango.

Clásica y Moderna, Av Callao 892. One of the city's most welcoming cafés, with a bookshop at the back. Lots of brick and wood, this has a great atmosphere and is good from breakfast right through to drinks at night, with live music Thu to Sat. Highly recommended.

Como en Casa, Riobamba 1239. Set in a lovely building with a black and white tiled courtyard with a small fountain. Gourmet salads, sandwiches and amazing cakes. Try the brie and sun-dried tomato pizzetta.

Confitería Ideal, Suipacha 384. One of the most atmospheric cafés in the city. Wonderfully old-fashioned 1930s interior, almost untouched, serving coffee and excellent cakes, good service. Upstairs, tango is taught in the afternoons and there's tango dancing at a *milonga* here afterwards, from 2200. Highly recommended.

El Gato Negro, Av Corrientes 1669. A lovely old traditional café serving a wide choice of coffees and teas, and good cakes. You can also buy a big range of spices here.

Puerto Madero *p75*

The revamped docks area is an attractive place to eat and to stroll along the waterfront before dinner. There are good places here, generally in stylish interiors and with good service. Can be a little overpriced.

₸₸₸ Asia de Cuba, Perina Dealessi 750, www.asiadecuba.com.ar. Stunning restaurant serving Asian-influenced dishes. Very attentive staff.

₸₸₸ El Bistro + Cava, Martha Salotti 445, inside the **Faena + Universe Hotel**. Expensive but exquisite food with an experienced wine sommelier to assist in your choices. Highly recommended.

₸₸₸ El Clan, Olga Cossettini 1501, www.el-clan.com.ar. Chandeliers, long curtains and shiny cutlery. Try the grilled salmon or the home-made pasta.

₸₸₸ La Parolaccia, Nos 1052 and 1170. Excellent pasta and Italian-style dishes (seafood is the speciality at No 1170), executive lunch US$8 Mon-Fri, popular.

₸₸₸-₸₸ i Fresh Market, Azucena Villaflor and Olga Cossettini. Fresh fruits and vegetables served in the most varied ways in this small, trendy restaurant and deli, from breakfast to dinner.

₸₸ La Parolaccia, 2 sister restaurants: a general bistro at Alicia Moreau de Justo No 1052, and the best seafood restaurant in Puerto Madero, at No 1160, serving fresh and deliciously cooked seafood in a lively brasserie atmosphere. Both places are very stylish, and very popular with *Porteños*. Bargain lunches during the week and superb pastas. Recommended.

Recoleta and Barrio Norte *p76, map p77*

₸₸₸ Lola, Roberto M Ortiz 1805. Well known for superb pasta dishes, lamb and fish. Recommended.

₸₸₸ Sirop, Pasaje del Correo, V López 1661, T011-4813 5900. Delightful chic design, delicious French-inspired food, superb patisseries too. Highly recommended.

₸₸₸ Tandoor, La Prida 1293. Indian restaurant with seriously spicy food. Great service but slightly expensive. Recommended.

₸₸ El Sanjuanino, Posadas 1515. Atmospheric place offering the best of Argentina's dishes from the northwest: *humitas*, *tamale* and *empanadas*, as well as unusual game dishes.

₸₸ Rodi Bar, Vicente López 1900. Excellent *bife* and other dishes in this typical *bodegón*. A welcoming and unpretentious place.

₸ La Madeleine, Av Santa Fe 1726, open 24 hrs. Great for cheap pasta in a bright and cheerful atmosphere. Recommended.

Tea rooms and ice-cream parlours

Alvear Palace, Av Alvear 1891, T011-4808 2949. Afternoon tea served in the garden restaurant, **L'Orangerie**. 3-tier cake stands filled with cucumber sandwiches and wonderful cakes. Highly recommended. Book ahead.

Café Victoria, Roberto M Ortiz 1865. Wonderful, old-fashioned café, popular with perfectly coiffed ladies sipping tea in a refined atmosphere. Great cakes.

Palermo p79, map p80

There are lots of chic restaurants and bars in Palermo Viejo, Palermo Hollywood and the Las Cañitas district (see below). It's a sprawling area, and lovely to walk around in the evenings. Take a taxi to one of these restaurants and walk around once you're in the area before deciding where to eat.

Palermo has lots of good cafés opposite the park, and there is fabulous ice cream at **Un' Altra Volta**, Av del Libertador 3060, T011-4805 1818.

Cabernet, Jorge Luis Borges 1757, T011-4831 3071. The smoked salmon and caviar blinis starter here is unmissable. Dine outside in the elegant terrace, fragrant with jasmine, and heated in winter, or in the more traditional clubby interior in this traditional *chorizo* house, given a cosmopolitan twist with purple walls. Sophisticated, traditional cuisine, a great wine list and good service. Worth the price for a special dinner.

Cluny, El Salvador 4618, T011-4831 7176. A great place for lunch, the menu is as stylish as the black and cream surroundings. Excellent home-made bread. The fish and pasta sauces are made up of exquisite combinations of flavours. One of Palermo's classiest restaurants, whether you dine in the bistro at the back, or chic white armchairs in the middle. Friendly staff, mellow music. Recommended.

Dominga, Honduras 5618, T011-4771 4443, www.domingarestaurant.com. Open evenings only. Elegant, excellent food from a short but creative menu, professional service, good wine list, ideal for a romantic meal or treat.

El Manto, Costa Rica 5801, T011-4774 2409, Mon-Sat lunch and dinner. The usual chic concrete look, but the food is exceptional: delicious Armenian dishes cooked by a real Armenian chef, in this spacious relaxed restaurant. Friendly service. Good for a quiet evening.

Janio, Malabia 1805, T011-4833 6540. With a great position overlooking Plaza Palermo Viejo and a lovely upstairs terrace, this was one of the fist Palermo restaurants. Open from breakfast until the early hours, this is a lively, laid-back place for lunch, with a good fixed-price menu, and more sophisticated Argentine cuisine in the evenings. A great place to meet for a drink.

Bar 6, Armenia 1676 T011-4833 6807, Mon-Sat. One of the best chic, modern bars. Serves food in laid-back spacious surroundings, with bare concrete, bold colours and sofas upstairs for relaxing on. Excellent lunches, friendly atmosphere, good for a drink in the evening. Recommended.

B-Blue, Armenia 1692, www.b-blue.com.ar. A trendy café with loads of healthy vegetarian food. Recommended. Wi-Fi.

Bio, Humboldt 2199, T011-4774 3880. Open daily, but closed Mon for dinner. Situated on a sunny corner where you can sit outside, Bio servces delicious gourmet organic food. Fresh lime green decor and a friendly atmosphere.

El Diamante, Malabia 1688, 1st floor, T011-4831 5735, Mon-Sat. Great loud music in this cosy restaurant and bar with a terrace upstairs for a party atmosphere, gay-friendly.

El Preferido de Palermo, Borges and Guatemala, T011-4778 7101. Very popular *bodegón* serving both Argentine and Spanish-style dishes.

Eterna Cadencia, Honduras 5574, T011-4774 4100, Tue-Sun 0900-2400. A real find, a great little café in a fabulous small bookshop with a wonderful selection of English classics and contemporary literature. Beautifully designed high ceilinged rooms with comfortable sofas at the back. Great for a light lunch.

Garum, Malabia 1721, T011-4831 6203. Elegant restaurant and wine bar in an imaginatively redesigned old house. Wine tastings and good Mediterranean food. Spacious rooms decorated with contemporary art exhibitions.

Krishna, Malabia 1833. A small, intimate place serving very good Indian-flavoured vegetarian dishes.

La Cabrera, Cabrera 5127/5099, www.parrillalacabrera.com.ar. You can't make reservations for this amazing *parrilla*, but they will offer you sparkling wine while you wait. The wait however shouldn't be too long as they now have 2 restaurants virtually next to each other. Fantastic for food and pasta. Huge portions.

Mark's Deli, El Salvador 4701. Fabulous café/restaurant serving goodies such as huge salads, overflowing sandwiches and juices. Recommended.

Miranda, Costa Rica and Fitz Roy, T011-4771 4255. Traditional *parrilla* in hip surroundings, with simple rustic design and a lively atmosphere in the evenings. Also offers pasta and a good wine list. Lunch is good value.

Olsen, Gorriti 5870. Recommended Swedish-style restaurant with delicate food, great cocktails and a relaxing terrace outside.

Omm, Honduras 5656, T011-4774 4224. Hip, cosy wine and tapas bar with great wines and good food. Open daily from 1800, happy hour from 1800-2100. Sister restaurant Omm Carnes, Costa Rica 5198, T011-4773 0954, for steak and meat dishes in a similarly trendy environment, open daily from 1100 but closed for dinner on Sun.

Social Paraíso, Honduras 5182. A real find for a great lunch. Simple, delicious dishes served in a relaxed, chic atmosphere in this friendly place run by art collectors. Groovy paintings on the walls and a lovely little patio hidden at the back. Good fish and tasty salads. Recommended.

Persicco, Salguero and Cabello, Maure and Migueletes and Av Rivadavia 4933. Branches in upmarket areas, but most convenient is **Salguero** (near Alto Palermo shopping centre), Salguero 2591 y Cabello. 'The best

ice cream in the world.' You haven't tasted ice cream until you've had Persicco's mascarpone, or their *flan de dulce de leche*. Exquisite chocolate flavours, fruity ice creams, sorbets and even coffee. Also offer a delivery service, T0810-333 7377, and free Wi-Fi.

Las Cañitas

Northeast of Palermo Hollywood, separated from it by a railway track, this has developed into a popular little area for eating, with a huge number of restaurants packed into a few blocks along Báez. Most open at around 2000, and also for lunch at weekends:

Báez, next door to **Morelia**. Very trendy, with lots of orange neon, serving sophisticated Italian-style food, including the delicious goat's cheese ravioli.

Campo Bravo, Báez and Arevalo. A stylish, minimalist place serving superb steaks and vegetables on the *parrilla* in a friendly atmosphere. Popular and recommended.

De la Ostia, Báez 212. A small and chic bistro for tapas and Spanish-style food, with a good atmosphere.

Eh! Santino, Báez 194. A trendy small restaurant for Italian-style food and drinks. Dark and cosy with lots of mirrors.

Morelia, Báez 260. Cooks superb pizzas on the *parrilla* or in wood ovens, and has a lovely roof terrace for summer.

Novecento. Across the road from **De la Ostia** is a lively French-style bistro, stylish but unpretentious. Serves good fish dishes among other things on the broad menu.

San Telmo *p82, map p83*

There are plenty of restaurants along Defensa and in the surrounding streets, and new places are opening all the time.

Defensa Al Sur, Defensa 1338, T011-4300 8017. Converted old shopfront, housing one of the poshest restaurants in the area. Wonderful wines and a modern twist on local dishes. Recommended.

La Brigada, Estados Unidos 465, T011-4361 5557. The best choice for *parrilla* in San Telmo, this is a really superb and atmospheric *parrilla*, serving excellent Argentine cuisine and wines in a cosy, buzzing atmosphere. Very popular and not cheap, but highly recommended. Always reserve in advance.

Ψ Brasserie Pétanque, Defensa y México, T011-4342 7930. Very good French cuisine at affordable prices and set lunch Mon-Fri. It's an appealing little place, a tasteful combination of Paris and Buenos Aires.

Ψ Café San Juan, Av San Juan 450, T011-4300 1112. Not a café but a very small *bodegón* – looking just like a typical *restaurant de barrio* (local dive) but with an excellent cook. A short menu includes delicious *tapas de salmón*. It's very popular so book ahead.

Ψ La Vinería de Gualterio Bolívar, Bolívar 865, T011-4361 4709. Serving tiny portions of tapas-like dishes which are delicious, this small restaurant also boasts efficient staff and an extensive wine list. Recommended.

Ψ Los Lobos, corner of Estados Unidos and Balcarce. Attractive restaurant, simply designed, serving modern fare such as spinach and camembert omelette. Good for lunch.

Ψ Bar Británico, Brasil and Defensa 399, T11-43612107. Open 24 hrs, with a long and impressive history behind it. Worth the walk to soak up the atmosphere over lunch.

Ψ El Desnivel, Defensa 855. Popular for cheap and basic food, packed at weekends.

Ψ La Trastienda, Balcarce 460. Theatre café with lots of live events. Also serves meals and drinks from breakfast till dinner, great music. A relaxed place to hang out with an arty crowd. Recommended.

Ψ Pride Cafe, corner of Balcarce and Giuffra. Wonderful sandwiches, juices, salads and great brownies. Lots of magazines to read.

Ψ El Hipopótamo, Brasil and Defensa (on Parque Lezama). A typical *bodegón*, popular with families. Argentine menu and huge portions. The service is rather slow.

Ψ Nonna Bianca, Estados Unidos 425. Great ice cream, as well as an internet café.

◑ Bars and clubs

Generally it is not worth going to clubs before 0230 at weekends. Dress is usually smart, and you can be charged anything from US$10-15 sometimes including a drink. Most gay clubs charge US$10 entry on the door.

City centre *p68, map p70*
Bars
See also under Live music, below.
Druid In, Reconquista 1040. Live music weekly, English spoken.
La Cigale, 25 de Mayo 722. A popular place after office hrs that's usually crowded by 2400. Very good music, recommended for its Tue evenings with guest DJs.
Le Bar, Tucumán 422. Busy, 2-level cocktail bar which attracts the after office crowd and is a great unpretentious place to chill out.

Recoleta *p76, map p77*
Bars
Buller Brewing Company, Roberto M Ortiz 1827. Happy hour till 2100.
Casa Bar, Rodríguez Peña 1150. Offering beers from all over the world, this restored French mansion is a good place to watch international sports matches. Affordable food deals.
Milion, Paraná 1048. A French-style residence with lots of space, sitting areas, cushions and tables in the sumptuous halls. It has also a garden and serves very good drinks. A mixed clientele, between 25 and 40 years old. Recommended Fri after midnight.
The Shamrock, Rodríguez Peña 1220. Irish-run, popular, expensive Guinness, happy hour for ISIC card holders.

Clubs
El Living, Marcelo T de Alvear 1540, T011-4811 4730. As small, cosy and relaxed as a living room gets, playing 1980s music amongst others.

Palermo *p79, map p80*
Bars
878, Thames 878. From the outside this doesn't look like a bar, but knock on the door after 2400 and you'll be invited inside to a cosy red room filled with people. Recommended.
Bangalore Pub, Humboldt 1416, and Niceto Vega. Great English pub serving wonderful mojitos and wraps. Also serve curries.
Carnal, Niceto Vega 5511 and Humboldt. Busy roof terrace that is great in summer, with good music and a bar downstairs.
Congo, Honduras 5329. Huge bar which extends to a large beer garden at the back. Interesting crowd and a good range of cocktails. Men usually have to pay a US$6 cover charge redeemable for drinks.
Mundo Bizarro, Serrano 1222 and Córdoba. This hugely popular bar gets its name from bizarre films shown on a big screen. People usually come here for dinner first (food is American-style), then they stay all night. DJ on Fri and Sat; 1960s and 1980s music the rest of the week. 20- to 35-year-old crowd.
Sugar, Costa Rica 4619. Welcoming bar with lots of red and wood to make it feel cosy. Cheapest beer and drinks in Palermo. Happy hour every night. Friendly crowd.

Clubs
Club 69 (at Niceto Club), Niceto Vega 5510, T011-4779 9396, www.nicetoclub.com, or www.club69.com.ar. On Thu for a 20-something crowd, good music with live shows, packed after 0200.
Mint, Av Costanera Norte and Sarmiento (in Punta Carrasco). On Sat, Latin and electronic music. Mostly 20-somethings. Attractive terrace on the river.
Pacha, Av Costanera Norte and Pampa, www.pachabuenosaires.com. A big place, upmarket feel, 20- to 30-year-olds, electronic music.

Gay bars and clubs
Bach Bar, Cabrera 4390, www.bach-bar.com. ar. Friendly lesbian bar in Palermo Viejo.

Sitges, Av Córdoba 4119, T011-4861 2763, www.sitgesonline.com.ar. Gay and lesbian bar, near Amerika.

San Telmo *p82, map p83*
Bars
A great way to visit some of the best bars is to join a pub crawl. A good company to contact is Pub Crawl BA (www.pubcrawlba.com) who run pub crawls every week. It's a good way to make friends and have a safe night out.
70 Living, Defensa 714. Good terrace with well-made cocktails, and a great atmosphere with DJs spinning smooth beats.
Bar Dorrego, Humberto Primo and Defensa. This bar/café has a fantastic atmosphere and waiters inside, and you can also sit in the plaza outside. Good for late-night coffees or beers.
Bar Seddon, corner of Defensa and Chile. Wonderful traditional bar open till late with live music on Fri nights. Candles, high ceilings, as well as black and white tiles on the floor. Recommended.
Gibraltar, Perú 895. Small British pub with a tiny beer garden, a pool table and happy hour at 1800-2000 each night. Popular with tourists and locals alike, it is best to go either really early at 1800 or late about 0130. Try the green curry or the pie.
La Puerta Roja, Chacabuco 733. No sign outside but ring the doorbell and climb the marble stairs. Stylishly designed bar serving pints, great food (wraps and curries) and open till late. Recommended.
La Resistencia, Defensa and Independencia. Local hangout that serves cheap beer and plays lots of rock music. A fun night out and a chance to speak some Spanish.
Plan B, Brasil 444, a short walk from Plaza Dorrego. This alternative bar doesn't look much from the outside but it is actually a converted house, with high ceilings, peeling paint and friendly hosts. You can bring your own music, and there is a pool table.

Clubs
Museum, Perú between Chile and México. Absolutely huge club, which packs out on

Wed 'After Office' nights, from 2100 until about 0200.

Gay bars and clubs
Amerika, Gascón 1040, Almagro, T011-4865 4416, www.ameri-k.com.ar. The largest gay club which draws over 2000 party-goers spread over 3 floors.

🎨 Entertainment

Details of most events are given in the 'Espectáculos' section of newspapers, *La Nación* and *Clarín*, the *Buenos Aires Herald* (English) on Fri, and the helpful www.whatsupbuenosaires.com.

Cinemas
The selection of films shown in Buenos Aires is excellent, ranging from new Hollywood releases to Argentine and world cinema; details are listed daily in all main newspapers. Films are shown uncensored and in the original language, with most foreign films subtitled rather than dubbed into Spanish: only children's films are dubbed. Check this before buying tickets though. Tickets are best booked in the early afternoon to ensure good seats (average price US$5.50, more expensive at weekends and as much as US$6.50 on Sat night; there are discounts on Wed and for 1st show daily, but other discounts depend on the cinema). Most shopping malls have cinemas and these tend to show more mainstream Hollywood movies, but you can find recent European or non-Hollywood films elsewhere, mostly in the Atlas chain of cinemas: **Arteplex**, Av Cabildo 2829, T011-4781 6500, Belgrano; **Cineduplex**, Av Rivadavia 5050, T011-4902 5682; and **Lorca**, Av Corrientes 1428. Old movies, classics, curiosities and experimental cinema are shown at **MALBA art gallery**, Av Figueroa Alcorta 3415, T011-4808 6500, and at **Sala Leopoldo Lugones** (Teatro San Martín), Av Corrientes 1530, 10th floor, T011-4371 0111. Most Argentinian movies are shown at

Complejo Tita Merello, Suipacha 442, T011-4322 1195, and at **Gaumont**, Av Rivadavia 1635, T011-4371 3050.

For what's on in all cinemas throughout Buenos Aires, see any daily paper or websites such as www.lanacion.com.ar, www.buenosairesherald.com, or www.terra.com.ar. Independent foreign and national films are shown during the **Festival de Cine Independiente**, held every Apr.

Cultural events and activities
Centro Cultural Borges, Galerías Pacífico, Viamonte and San Martín, www.ccborges.org.ar. Music and dance concerts, special exhibitions, some offer student discounts.
Centro Cultural Recoleta, Junín 1930, next to the Recoleta cemetery, www.centro culturalrecoleta.org. Many free activities.
Ciudad Cultural Konex, Sarmiento 3131, Abasto, www.ciudadculturalkonex.org. A fantastic converted industrial site, the most popular event is the Fiesta la Bomba de Tiempo, US$4 – a passionate drum and beat show that starts at midnight. Highly recommended.
Fundación Proa, Av Pedro de Mendoza 1929, www.proa.org. Contemporary art in La Boca.
Luna Park stadium, Bouchard 465, www.lunapark.com.ar. Pop/jazz concerts, sports events, ballet and musicals.
Palais de Glace, Posadas 1725, www.palaisdeglace.org. Temporary art exhibitions, especially photography and other cultural events.
Teatro Colón, www.teatrocolon.org.ar. Newly renovated and bursting with great events. See the website for details.
Teatro San Martín, Corrientes 1530, www.teatrosanmartin.com.ar. Organizes cultural activities, many free, including concerts. 50% ISIC discount for Thu, Fri and Sun events (only in advance at 4th floor, Mon-Fri). The theatre's **Sala Leopoldo Lugones** shows international classic films, daily, US$2.

Live music

La Peña del Colorado, Güemes 3657, T011-4822 1038. Argentinean *folclore* music played live in this atmospheric and cheerful place, where regional food is served. Recommended.

La Trastienda, Balcarce 460. This popular venue attracts a mixed crowd for very different types of music.

Maluco Beleza, Sarmiento 1728. Live Brazilian dance music.

Mítico Argentino Humberto, Primo 489. In the heart of San Telmo, see local bands. Although it is tourist-central around Plaza Dorrego, you'll rub shoulders with lots of Argentines as well.

ND Ateneo, Paraguay 918. A small theatre for a great variety of Latin American music.

Niccto, Niccto Vega 5510 (Palermo Hollywood district) and **La Cigale**, 25 de Mayo 722, T011-4312 8275.

Jazz

Café Tortoni, Av de Mayo 825, T011-4342 4328, www.cafetortoni.com.ar. Features the Fénix Jazz Band (Dixieland), Sat 2300.

La Revuelta, Alvarez Thomas 1368, T011-4553 5530. Live jazz, bossa nova and tango.

Notorious, Av Callao 966, T011-4813 6888, www.notorious.com.ar. Music shop and live music.

Thelonious, Salguero 1884, T011-4829 1562. Atmospheric jazz bar serving snacks and good cocktails.

Tango

There are basically 2 ways to enjoy Buenos Aires' wonderfully sensuous and passionate dance: watch superb tango at a show, or learn to dance at a class and then try your new steps at a *milonga* (tango club). Tango may seem impossibly complicated, but it's the key to the Argentine psyche, and you haven't experienced the dance unless you've tried it on the dance floor.

There is a tango information desk at the Centro Cultural San Martín, Sarmiento 1551, T011-4373 2829, daily 1400-2100, and a useful website: www.tangoguia.com. Look out for the latest leaflet listing tango classes and *milongas*, *Passionate Buenos Aires*, produced by the city tourist board, and available from tourist information kiosks.

Tango shows

This is the way to see tango dancing at its best. Most shows pride themselves on a very high level of dancing, and although they're not cheap, this could be the highlight of your visit.

Bar Sur, Estados Unidos 299, T011-4362 6086. 2000-0300, US$60 including all-you-can-eat pizza, drinks extra. Good fun, and the public sometimes join the professional dancers.

Café Tortoni, see cafés above. Daily tango shows from 2030, US$12.

El Cabaret at Faena Hotel and Universe, Martha Salotti 445, T011-4010 9200. A glamorous and sensual show, charting tango's evolution, daily at 2030.

El Querandí, Perú 302, T011-5199 1770. Elaborate tango show restaurant, daily, dinner 2030, show at 2215, US$100 for both, including a transfer from your hotel.

El Viejo Almacén, Independencia and Balcarce, T011-4307 7388. The best place of all. Daily, with dinner from 2030, show at 2200, US$105 with all included, or US$58 show only (recommended). Very impressive dancing from the city's best dancers, excellent live band and great singing from some of tango's great names. Highly recommended.

La Esquina de Carlos Gardel, Carlos Gardel 3200, T011-4867 6363, www.esquinacarlos gardel.com.ar. Dinner at 2030 and show at 2215, US$108 for both, US$76 show only. Recommended.

La Ventana, Balcarce 431, T011-4331 0217. Daily dinner from 2000 (dinner and show US$100) or show with 2 drinks, 2200, US$55. Touristy but very good, and the only show to include some of Argentina's traditional *folclore* music.

Piazzolla Tango, Florida 165 (basement), Galería Güemes, T011-4344 8200, www. piazzollatango.com. A beautifully restored belle époque hall hosts a smart tango show; dinner at 2045 (dinner and show US$98), show at 2215 (show only US$53).

Tangol, Florida 971, p 1, T011-4312 7276, www.tangol.com, see also Tour operators, page 106. Run trips to tango shows.

Milongas and tango classes

Milongas are extremely popular among younger *Porteños*, since tango underwent a revival a few years ago. You can take a class and get a good feel for the music, before the dancing starts a couple of hours later. Both traditional tango and *milonga* (a more cheerful style of music with a faster rhythm) are played, and venues occasionally have live orchestras. Cost is usually around US$4, and even complete beginners are welcome. Tango classes are also given all over the city, but you might find *milongas* more fun, and they're better places to meet people.

Central Cultural Torquato Tasso, Defensa 1575, T011-4307 6506. Daily evening classes, dancing Sun at 2100. English spoken.

Confitería Ideal, Suipacha 384, T011-5265 8069. Dancing Mon, Wed, Sat and Sun. Daily classes from 1500.

Dandi, Piedras 936, T011-4361 3537, www.mansiondandiroyal.com. Excellent teaching with Noelia and Nahuel or Rodolfo and Irma. Mon, Tue, Fri 1900, Wed 1800, Sat 1700, Sun 1930, 2200.

La Catedral, Sarmiento 4006. A wonderful old church hall, with eclectic furniture and a wonderful restaurant. Lessons start at 2100, and then it turns into a milonga after 2230. US$4 entrance fee includes both. Sometimes there are singing and tango performances as well. Don't be put off by the plain frontage.

La Viruta, Armenia 1366, Palermo Viejo, T011-4774 6357, www.lavirutatango.com. Most popular among a young trendy crowd. Wed, 2300, Fri and Sat 2400. Classes Wed 2130, Thu 2000 (includes tango and *milonga* lessons), Fri and Sat 2230, Sun 2000 (includes *milonga* and tango lessons).

Porteño y Bailarín, Riobamba 345, T011-4932 5452, www.porteybailarin.com.ar. Tue and Sun class 2100, dancing 2300.

Theatre

About 20 commercial theatres play all year, and there are many amateur theatres, with a theatre festival at the end of May. The main theatre street is Av Corrientes which has miles and miles of side-by-side theatres. Check out *La Nación* for theatre times. You are advised to book early for a seat at a concert, ballet or opera. Tickets for most popular shows (including rock and pop concerts) are sold also through **Entrada Plus**, T011-4324 1010; **Ticketek**, T011-5237 7200, www.ticketek. com.ar. See www.alternativa teatral.com, or www.mundoteatral.com.ar. For listings, see www.terra.com.ar, www.lanacion.com, www.buenosairesherald.com.

The following includes the main theatres, almost all of them in the centre. **Beckett Teatro**, Guardia Vieja 3556, T011-4867 5185; **Broadway**, Av Corrientes 1155, T011-4381 1180; **Centro Cultural Borges**, Viamonte and San Martín, T011-5555 5359; **Centro Cultural de la Cooperación**, Av Corrientes 1543, T011-5077 8077; **Ciudad Cultural Konex**, Sarmiento 3131, T011-5237 7200, www.ciudadculturalkonex.org; **Coliseo**, Marcelo T de Alvear 1125, T011-4816 3789; **El Nacional**, Av Corrientes 960, T011-4326 4218; **General San Martín**, Av Corrientes 1530, T0800-333 5254; **La Plaza**, Av Corrientes 1660, T011-6320 5350; **Liceo**, Rivadavia and Paraná, T011-4381 5745; **Lola Membrives**, Av Corrientes 1280, T011-4381 0076; **Maipo**, Esmeralda 443, T011-4322 4882; **Multiteatro**, Av Corrientes 1283, T011-4382 9140; **Nacional Cervantes**, Libertad 815, T011- 4816 4224; **Opera**, Av Corrientes 860, T011-4326 1335; **Payró**, San Martín 766, T011-4312 5922; **Regina**, Av Santa Fe 1235, T011-4812 5470; Teatro Colón, www.teatrocolon.org.ar. **Teatro del Globo**, Marcelo T de Alvear 1155, T011-4816 3307; **Teatro del Pueblo**, Av Roque Sáenz Peña 943, T011-4326 3606.

O Shopping

Contemporary Argentine design is excellent, with fashionable cuts and fabrics which would hold their own in London or Milan but at a third of the price. Argentine designers make the most of the superb quality leather for jackets, shoes and bags, ranging from the funky to the classic and traditional.

Palermo is the best place for chic little boutiques and some well-known international names, with shops spread out through pleasant leafy streets with lots of cafés (see below for details). For the major names, head straight to **Patio Bullrich**, an upmarket indoor shopping mall. In the centre of town, the main shopping streets are the pedestrianized **Florida**, stretching south from Plaza San Martín, and the whole of **Santa Fe**, from Av 9 de Julio to Av Pueyrredon, though some blocks are more upmarket than others, and there are some obviously cheaper zones. Palermo is so full of boutiques and chic interiors shops you will be spoilt for choice, and it's hard to know where to start. The 2 main shopping streets to head for, then, are **Honduras** and **El Salvador**, between Malabia and Serrano, with more options further south on Gorriti and along Costa Rica.

To get the tax back on purchases, see Essentials, page 38.

Antiques
There are many high quality antiques for sale around Recoleta: a stroll along the streets around Callao and Quintana will yield some great buys. For cheaper antiques, and second-hand bric-a-brac, San Telmo is the place. The market on Sun is a good place to start, but on other days all the shops along Defensa are still open, and it's worth searching around for bargains. China, glass, rugs, old silver *mates*, clothes and jewellery are among the goodies you can pick up. **Pasaje de la Defensa**, Defensa 1179. A beautifully restored 1880s house containing small shops.

Books
You'll find most bookshops along Florida, Av Corrientes or Av Santa Fe, and in shopping malls. Second hand and discount bookshops are mostly along Av Corrientes and Av de Mayo. Rare books are sold in several specialized stores in the Microcentro (the area enclosed by Suipacha, Esmeralda, Tucumán and Paraguay). The main chains of bookshops to look for, usually selling a small selection of foreign books, are: **Cúspide**, with several branches on Florida, Av Corrientes and some malls, and the biggest and most interesting store at Village Recoleta, Vicente López and Junín; **Distal**, Florida 738 and more branches on Florida and Av Corrientes; **Yenny-El Ateneo**, in all shopping malls, also sell music. The biggest store is on Av Santa Fe 1860 set in an amazing old theatre, it is one of the best bookshops in South American, there is café where the stage should be, and it extends 3 floors up.

For a larger selection of books in English, try the following:
Eterna Cadencia, Honduras 5574, T011-4774 4100. Great bookshop with excellent selection of novels in English: classics, contemporary fiction and translations of Spanish and Argentine authors. Highly recommended for its café too.
Crack Up, Costa Rica 4767, T011-4831 3502. Funky, open-plan bookshop and café that extends to the street. Open Mon-Wed till 2230, and till the early hrs the rest of the week.
Walrus Books, Estados Unidos 617, T011-4300 713. Shop in San Telmo with second-hand books in English, including Latin American authors. Good children's section.

You can also try **ABC**, Maipú 866; **Joyce, Proust & Co**, Tucumán 1545 p 1 A, also sells books in other European languages; **Kel**, Marcelo T de Alvear 1369; **Librería Rodríguez**, Sarmiento 835; **LOLA**, Viamonte 976, Mon-Fri 1200-1830, small publishers specializing in Latin America natural history, also sell used and rare editions, most in English.

Foreign newspapers are available from news-stands on Florida, in Recoleta and the kiosk at Corrientes and Maipú.

Camping equipment
Angel Baraldo, Av Belgrano 270, www.baraldo.com.ar. Imported and Argentine stock.
Buenos Aires Sports, Panamericana and Paraná, Martínez (Shopping Unicenter, 2nd level). Good equipment.
Cacique Camping, Esteban Echeverría 3360, Munro, T011-47624475, caciquenet@ciudad.com.ar. Clothing and equipment.
Camping Center, Esmeralda 945, www.camping-center.com.ar. Good selection of outdoor sports gear and equipment.
Ecrin, Mendoza 1679, T011-4784 4799, www.ecrin.com.ar. Sells imported climbing equipment.
Fugate (no sign), Gascón 238 (off Rivadavia 4000 block), T011-4982 0203. Also repairs equipment.
Jorge Gallo, Liniers 1522, Tigre, T011-4731 0323. For GPS repair service.
Montagne, Florida 719, Paraná 834, www.montagenoutdoors.com.ar. Good selection of outdoor sports gear and equipment.
Outside Mountain Equipment, Otero 172 (Chacarita), T011-4856 6204, www.outside.com.ar.

Camping gas available at: **Britam**, B Mitre 1111; **El Pescador**, Paraguay and Libertad; **Todo Gas**, Sarmiento 1540.

Clothes and accessories
The following can all be found in Palermo.

Men's clothes and accessories
Airborn, Gurruchaga 1770. Informal and more formal clothes.
Balthazar, Gorriti 5131. Smart men's clothes and accessories.
Etiqueta Negra, www.etiquetanegra.us. An Argentine clothing label that produces classic styles with a twist. Find them at all shopping malls.
Il Reve, Gurruchaga 1867. Smart, well-tailored and original menswear.

Postman, Armenia 1555. Great leather postman's bags and wallets.
Sartori, Gurruchaga 1538. Shoes with a baseball/camper feel.

Women's clothes and accessories
Caro Cuore, Armenia 1535. Great underwear, alluring and beautifully designed, and much cheaper than in Europe. Vast, calm shop where the staff are really helpful.
Colombas, Jorge Luis Borges 2029. Fabulous handmade jewellery, eclectic, hippy and very original styles, as well as lovely chic hand-knitted jumpers.
Elementos, El Salvador 4817. Soft minimalist suede and leather bags.
Josefina Ferroni, Armenia 1471. Chic shoes.
María Blizniuk, Costa Rica and Borges. Lovely feminine designs, cute shoes too.
Mariana Dappianno, Honduras 4932. Interesting and elegant designer, novel textiles.
Mariano Toledo, Armenia 1564, www.marianotoledo.com. Very elegant, unusual and feminine modern designs, innovative fabrics and cuts. See website for inspiration.
Nueveveinticinco (925), Honduras 4808, www.nueveveinticinco.com.ar. Fabulous jewellery shop where the owners create wonderful contemporary designs around stunning rocks of all kinds, and also to your specifications. Incredible value.
Rapsodia, El Salvador 4757. Great range of this best selling eclectic brand of eccentric clothes. Wonderful jeans and helpful staff who rush around and get your size.
Renzo Rainero, Gurruchaga and Honduras. High-quality leather and interesting designs.
Uma, Honduras 5225. Stylish and contemporary leather.

Handicrafts
Alhué, Juncal 1625. Very good indigenous-style crafts.
Art Petrus, Florida 969, and **Hotel Panamericano** at Carlos Pellegrini.

Arte y Esperanza, Balcarce 234. Excellent little shop selling an impressive range of indigenous crafts from all over Argentina, particularly the northwest. Chaguar bags, masks and weavings. Ethical owners give most of the profits back to the communities who make the goods. Standard is high and prices are reasonable. Highly recommended.
El Boyero, Galería Larreta, Florida 953. High quality silver, leather, wood work and other typical Argentine handicrafts.
Martín Fierro, Santa Fe 992. Good handicrafts, stonework, etc. Recommended.
Plata Nativa, Galería del Sol, Florida 860, local 41, www.platanativa.com. For Latin American folk handicrafts.

Interiors
There are fabulous interior design shops throughout Palermo, of which just a couple are mentioned, since it's assumed you won't be able to take much home with you. Look out for the free shopping guides which list the Palermo shops and show them on a map.
Arte Étnico Argentino, El Salvador 4600. Great collection of indigenous art from all over Argentina. High quality and reasonable prices, given that they're a little higher than you'd pay in the place of origin. Weavings, especially, are superb.
Calma Chicha, Honduras 4925, and a smaller branch at Defensa and Guiffra in San Telmo, www.calmachicha.com. The name means calm before the storm, and this is the 1 place you should browse in for gifts to bring home. Wonderful minimalist cowhide postman's bags and wallets, seats and table mats – or buy an entire cowhide! Also loads of chic kitsch, like the 'Hand of God' flick books that endlessly replay Maradona's immortal moment, plus tin *mates* and cute toys.

Leather
As you'd expect from all the cattle Argentina produces, leather is cheap and of very high quality here.

Aida, Galería de la Flor, shop 30, Florida 670. Here you can have a leather jacket made to measure in the same day.
Campanera Dalla Fontana, Reconquista 735. A leather factory producing fast, efficient and reasonably priced made-to-measure clothes.
Casa López, Marcelo T de Alvear 640/658. The most traditional and finest leather shop, expensive but worth it.
Galería del Caminante, Florida 844. A variety of good shops with leather goods, arts and crafts, souvenirs, etc.
Prüne, Florida 963, and in many shopping centres. Fashionable designs for bags, boots and shoes. Lots of choice, reasonably priced.
Uma, in shopping malls and at Honduras 5225 (Palermo Viejo). The trendiest of all.
  Quality inexpensive leather goods are available at **All Horses**, Suipacha 1350; and at **La Curtiembre**, Juncal 1173, Paraguay 670.

Markets
Markets can be found all over Buenos Aires, since many plazas and parks have fairs at weekends where you can find almost the same kind of handicrafts everywhere. The following are recommended for something different:
Feria de las Artes, on Defensa, around Alsina, Fri 1200-1700. A few stalls selling crafts.
Feria de Mataderos, Av de los Corrales 6436, T011-4687 1949, www.feriademataderos. com.ar, Sun 1100-2000. Traditional gaucho crafts and games. See Around Buenos Aires, page 114, for more about Mataderos.
Mercado de las Luces, in the Manzana de las Luces, Perú and Alsina, Mon-Fri 1100-1900, Sun 1400-1900. Handicrafts.
Parque Centenario, Díaz Vélez and L Marechal. Sat market, with local crafts and good, cheap hand-made clothes.
Parque Rivadavia, Rivadavia 4900. Books and magazines, daily; records, toys, stamps and coins, Sun 0900-1300.
Plaza Dorrego, San Telmo. A wonderfully atmospheric market for souvenirs, antiques and some curious bric-a-brac. Free tango performances and live music, Sun 1300-2000.

Plaza Italia, Santa Fe and Uriarte (Palermo). Second-hand textbooks and magazines are sold daily; handicrafts market on Sat 1200-2000, Sun 1000-2000.
Recoleta, just outside the cemetery. At weekends, a huge craft market is held, with lots of street performers and food on sale too. Recommended.

Shopping malls

Alcorta, Salguero 3172. Massive mall with everything, plus supermarkets and some cheaper shops. Hard to reach without a car though.
Alto Palermo, Av Santa Fe and Coronel Díaz. Nearest *Subte* opposite Bulnes, Line D. Great for all the main clothes chain stores, and about 10 blocks' walk from Palermo's boutiques.
Galerias Pacificos, corner of Florida and Córdoba, nearest *Subte* Plaza San Martín on Line C, Mon-Sat 1000-2100, Sun 2100-2100. Has a good range of everything and a food court in the basement.
Patio Bullrich, Posadas 1245, nearest *Subte* 8 blocks from Plaza San Martín, Line C. The city's most upmarket mall, with all the international designer names and the best Argentine designers too. Also valet parking, taxi service and small food court in very elegant surroundings.
Unicenter, Paraná 3745, Martínez, www.unicenter.com.ar, no *Subte* anywhere near but you can take the No 60 bus from the city for about an hr or take a taxi, US$9. Has everything you could possibly imagine in one overwhelming place. Take a flask of brandy, this is the biggest shopping centre in South America.

▲ Activities and tours

Bicycle hire and tours
La Bicicleta Naranja, Pasaje Giuffra 308, San Telmo, www.labibibletanajanja.com.ar. Bike hire and bike tours to all parts of the city, 4-5 hrs.

Lan&Kramer Bike Tours, T011-4311 5199, www.biketours.com.ar. Starts daily at 0930 and 1400 next to the monument of San Martín (Plaza San Martín), 3½- to 4-hr cycle tours to the south or the north of the city; also to San Isidro and Tigre, 4½-5 hrs, and rent bikes at Florida 868,14H.
Urban biking, Moliere 2801 (Villa Devoto) T011-45684321, www.urbanbiking.com. 4-hr cycle tours starting next to the English clock tower in Retiro, light lunch included, also night city tours, and day tours to San Isidro and Tigre. They also rent bikes and organize cycle tours in the Pampas.

Boat trips
Barbacharters, T011-4824 3366. Boat trips and fishing in the delta and Tigre areas.
Smile on Sea, T011-155 018 8662 (mob), www.smileonsea.com. 2-hr boat trips off Buenos Aires coast in the day and at sunset, leaving from Puerto Madero on 32-ft sailing boats (up to 5 passengers). Also 8-hr trips to San Isidro and delta and longer holidays along the Uruguayan coast.

Cricket
Cricket is played Nov-Mar. More information at **Asociación de Cricket Argentino**, Paraguay 1270, T011-4816 3569.

Football and rugby
Football season is Mar-Jul, Aug-Dec, matches on Sun and sometimes on Wed, Fri or Sat.
Fans of the beautiful game should see **Boca Juniors**, matches every 2nd Sun 1500-1900 at their stadium, **La Bombonera**, Brandsen 805, La Boca, www.bocajuniors. com.ar. Cheapest tickets US$7. For details of the museum, see page 85. Try to see the murals along Av Almirante Brown. Take buses 29, 33, 53, 64, 86, 152, 168; along Av Patricios buses 10, 39, 93. Do not take a bus if travelling alone: call a Radio Taxi. Or you could walk. Their arch-rivals are the slightly upmarket **River Plate**, www.carp.org.ar, and they also have a museum near the stadium, daily 1000-1900, www.museoriver.com.

To reach the stadium and the museum take bus No 29 from centre going north.

Rugby season Apr-Oct/Nov. See also **Tangol** under Tour operators, page 106.

Golf

Those wishing to play at the private golf clubs should bring handicap certificate and make telephone booking. There are about a dozen clubs. Weekend play possible with a member. Some hotels may be able to arrange. **Campo de Golf de la Ciudad** in Palermo, open to anyone. For information contact, **Asociación Argentina de Golf**, T011-4325 1113.

Helicopter rides

Patagonia Chopper, www.patagonia chopper.com.ar. Helitours of Buenos Aires and its surroundings, 15-45 mins.

Horse racing and horse riding

At **Hipódromo Argentino de Palermo**, a large, modern racecourse, popular throughout the year; and at San Isidro. Riding schools at both courses.
Turismo Feeling, San Martín 969, p 9, T011-4313 5533, www.feelingturismo.com.ar. Excellent and reliable horseback trips in the Andes, and adventure tourism.

Motor racing

There are stock racing and Formula 3 competitions Mar-Dec, and drag racing year round, Fri evenings at the **Oscar Alfredo Gálvez Autodrome**, Av Coronel Roca and Av General Paz, T011-4605 3333, www.autodromoba.com.ar.

Polo

Argentina has the top polo players in the world. The high handicap season is Sep-Dec, but it is played all year round (low season is May-Aug). A visit to the national finals at Palermo in Nov and Dec is recommended. For information, **Asociación Argentina de Polo**, T011-4777 6444, www.aapolo.com.

Swimming

Public baths near Aeroparque, **Punta Carrasco**, and **Parque Norte**, both popular. **Club de Amigos**, Av Figueroa Alcorta and Av Sarmiento, T011-4801 1213, open all year round.

Tour operators

An excellent way of seeing Buenos Aires and its surroundings is on a 3-hr tour, especially for those travelling alone, or concerned about security. Longer tours might include dinner and a tango show, or a trip to an *estancia* (farm or ranch), with excellent food. Bookable through most travel agents.
Argentina Excepcion, Juncal 4455, Floor 5, 'A', T011-4772 6620, www.argentina-excepcion. com. A friendly French/Argentine-owned agency that offers individually tailored holidays around Argentina. They also offer themed holidays: fishing, golf, tango and trekking.
ATI, Esmeralda 567, T011-5217 9030, www.ativiajes.com. Mainly group travel, very efficient, many branches.

BAT, Buenos Aires Tur, Lavalle 1444, office 10, T011-4371 2304, www.buenosaires tur.com. City tours twice daily; Tigre and delta, daily, 6 hrs.

Buenos Aires Vision, Esmeralda 356 p 8, T011-4394 4682, www.buenosaires-vision. com.ar. City tours, Tigre and delta, tango (cheaper without dinner) and Fiesta Gaucha.

Cicerones de Buenos Aires, J J Biedma 883, T011-4330 0800, www.cicerones.org.ar. Non-profit organization offering volunteer greeting/guiding service for visitors to the city. Free, safe and different.

Class Adventure Travel, JA Cabrera 4423/29, C1414, T011-4833 8400, USA T1-877-240 4770 (Toll Free), UK T020-7096 1259, international T001-512 535 2536, www.cat-travel.com. Dutch-owned and run, with 10 years of experience. Excellent for tailor-made travel solutions throughout the continent. CAT has offices in several South American countries.

Cultour, www.cultour.com.ar. A highly recommended walking tour of the city, 3-4 hrs led by a group of charming Argentine history/tourism graduates. In English and Spanish.

Ecole del Sur Travel, Av Rivadavia 1479, p 1B, T011- 4383 1026, www.ecoledelsur.com. Organizes tours, packages and accommodation.

Eternautas, Av Julio A Roca 584, p 7, T011-5031 9916/15 4173 1078, www.eternautas. com. Historical, cultural and artistic tours of the city and Pampas guided in English, French or Spanish by historians and other social scientists from the University of Buenos Aires. Flexible and highly recommended.

Eves Turismo, Tucumán 702, T011-4393 6151, www.eves.com. Helpful and efficient, recommended for flights.

Exprinter, Sáenz Peña 615, p 7 office 101, T011-4393 4160, Galería Güemes, www.exprinterviajes.com.ar. Especially their 5-day, 4-night tour to Iguazú and San Ignacio Miní.

Flyer, Reconquista 617, p 8, T011-4313 8224, www.flyer.com.ar. English, Dutch, German spoken. Recommended, especially for *estancias*, fishing, polo and motor-home rental.

HI Travel Argentina, Florida 835, T011-4511 8723, www.hitravel.com.ar.

Nomads Community Travel Agency, Lima 11, CP1073, T011-5218 3059, www.comunidadnomade.com.ar. Tailor-made trips around Buenos Aires, the surrounding area and throughout Argentina.

Pride Travel, Paraguay 523 p 2, T011-5218 6556, www.pride-travel.com. The best choice for gay and lesbian travellers in Argentina; they also rent apartments.

Say Hueque, Viamonte 749, p 6, of 1, T011-5199 2517/20, and in Palermo at Guatemala 4845, p1 of 4, T011-4775 7862, www.sayhueque.com. Good-value tours for independent travellers in Argentina. Friendly, English-speaking staff. Specializes in trips to Patagonia, Iguazú and Mendoza.

Tangol, Florida 971, ground floor, local 31, T011-4312 7276, www.tangol.com. Friendly, independent travel agency specializing in

football and tango. Also offers city tours, various sports, such as polo and paragliding, trips to ranches, plane and bus tickets, and accommodation. Overland trips to Patagonia, Sep-Apr. English spoken. Special deals for students. A reliable and dynamic company. Recommended.

Transhumans Voyages, Av Córdoba 966, T011-1567 316591, www.transhumans voyages.info. A great company that promotes responsible tourism. They organize trips to the Northeast, Northwest, around Buenos Aires and in Patagonia based on cultural experiences and respecting the environment. A portion of the cost of your holiday goes toward environmental education in schools in rural Argentina. Highly recommended.

⊖ Transport

Air

For airport details, see page 62; for flight information, see Essentials, pages 23 and 25.

Ezeiza has 2 terminals: 'A' for all airlines except **Aerolíneas Argentinas**, which uses 'B'. 'A' has a very modern check-in hall. There are duty free shops (expensive), exchange facilities (**Banco de la Nación; Banco Piano; Global Exchange**) and ATMs (Visa and MasterCard), post office (open 0800-2000), Secure Bag US$10, and a left luggage office (US$2 per piece). There is a **Devolución IVA/Tax Free** desk (return of VAT). *Locutorios* with limited internet access. For more information see www.aa2000.com.ar.

Aeroparque terminal is divided into 2 sections, 'A' for all arrivals and **Aerolíneas Argentinas** and LAN check-in desks, 'B' for **Puna** and **LADE** check-in desks. On the 1st floor there is a *patio de comidas* (a food court), several shops and the airport tax counter. At the airport you'll find tourist information, car rental, bus companies, bank, ATMs, exchange facilities, post office, public phones, Secure Bag (US$10 per piece) and luggage deposit (between sections A-B at the information point), US$4 per

piece a day. For more information see www.aa2000.com.ar.

Airport bus

There is an airport bus service run by **Manuel Tienda León**, Av Madero 1299 and San Martín, behind Sheraton Hotel in Retiro, T011-4315 5115, www.tiendaleon.com. Buses run to **Ezeiza**: 0400, 0500, every 30 mins from 0600-2100, then 2200 and 2230 (try to be 15 mins early), US$11.50, 50-min journey, and then onto the domestic airport Aeroparque, US$4.50, another 25 mins. **Manuel Tienda León** buses to **Aeroparque** leave every hr from 0710-0255, 20-mins, US$4.50. They can also organize transfers to Mar del Plata, Santa Fe, La Plata and Rosario, from both airports. You can buy your ticket online or at the airport.

Airline offices

Aerolíneas Argentinas (AR) and **Austral**, Perú 2, Av Leandro N Alem 1134 and Av Cabildo 2900, T0810-2228 6527. **Air France-KLM**, San Martín 344 p 23, T011-4317 4700. **Alitalia**, Suipacha 1111, T011-4310 9999. **American Airlines**, Av Santa Fe 881, T011-4318 1111, Av Pueyrredón 1997 and branches in Belgrano and Acassuso. **Avianca**, Carlos Pellegrini 1163 p 4, T011-4394 5990. **British Airways**, Viamonte 570, T011-4320 6600. **Copa**, Carlos Pellegrini 989 p 2, T0810-222 2672. **Cubana**, Sarmiento 552 p 11, T011-4325 0691. **Delta**, Reconquista 737, T0800-666 0133. **Iberia**, Carlos Pellegrini, 1163, T011-4131 1000. **LAB**, Carlos Pellegrini 141, T011-4323 1900. **Lan Chile**, Cerrito 886 and Paraguay, T0810-999 9526. **Líneas Aéreas del Estado (LADE)**, Perú 710, T011-5129 9000, Aeroparque T011-4514 1524. **Lufthansa**, M T Alvear 590, p 6, T011-4319 0600. **Malaysia Airlines**, Suipacha 1111 p 14, T011-431 26971. **Mexicana**, Av Córdoba 1131. **Puna**, Florida 1, T011-4342 7000. **TAM**, Cerrito 1030, T011-4819 4800. **United Airlines**, Av Madero 900, T0810-777 8648. **Varig**, Av Córdoba 972, p 4, T011-4329 9211.

Road
Bus
When leaving Buenos Aires by bus it is best to visit the terminal the day before to buy your ticket and familiarize yourself with the area and where the platforms are, so when you return laden with luggage you know exactly where to go. To get to the bus station, take a Radio Taxi, catch a local bus (nearly all of them stop at the train station nearby), or take the *Subte* Line C and follow the signs to the bus station (not recommended late at night or early in the morning).

Note that buses get heavily booked up Dec-Mar, especially at weekends. All long-distance buses arrive at the Retiro bus terminal at Ramos Mejía and Av Antártida Argentina. For Retiro terminal enquiries, T011-4310 0700. Long-distance bus tickets can now be booked by telephone or through the internet using a credit card.

The biggest bus companies are: **Andesmar**, T011-4313 3717, www.andesmar.com; **Chevallier**, T011-4000 5255, www.nuevachevallier.com.ar; **Flecha Bus** T011-4000 5200, www.flechabus.com.ar; **Vía Bariloche** T011-4315 7700, www.via bariloche.com.ar. A great site to help you plan your journey is www.plataforma10.com. You can check bus prices and times, and can also book tickets for buses all over Argentina.

The terminal is on 3 floors. Departures are displayed on screens. Ticket offices are on the upper floor, but there are hundreds of them so you'll need to consult the list of companies and their office numbers at the top of the escalator. They're organized by regions of the country, and each region is colour-coded. There are left-luggage lockers, requiring tokens from kiosks, US$2.50. Large baggage should be left at *guarda equipaje* on the lower floor. The service of luggage porters is supposed to be free. **Buenos Aires city tourist information** is at desk 83 on the upper floor. Bus information is at the Ramos Mejía entrance on the middle floor.

Car hire
Avis, Cerrito 1527, T011-4326 5542, www.avis.com.ar; **Budget**, San Martín 1225, T011-4314 7773, www.budget.com.ar, ISIC and GO 25 discount; **Hertz**, Paraguay 1138, T011-4816 8001, www.hertzargentina.com.ar.

Taxis
Pidalo: T011-4956 1200; **Radio Taxi Sur**, T011-4638 2000; **Radio Taxi 5 Minutos**, T011-4523 1200; **Radio Taxi Diez**, T011-4585 5007; **Radio Taxi Premium**, T011-4374 6666.

Sea
The *Buenos Aires Herald* (English-language daily) notes all shipping movements.

Ferry
To **Montevideo** and **Colonia del Sacramento** from Terminal Dársena Norte, Av Antártida Argentina 821 (2 blocks from Av Córdoba and Alem), **Buquebus**, T011-4316 6500, www.buquebus.com (tickets from Terminal or from offices at Av Córdoba 879 and Posadas 1452). Direct to **Montevideo**, 1-4 a day, 3 hrs, US$82 tourist class (return, vehicles US$88, motorcycles US$68, bus connection to Punta del Este US$11 extra).

To Uruguay As Colonia is in Uruguay and you will need to exit Argentina before you board the ferry. To **Colonia**, services by 2 companies, **Buquebus**, 2-3 ferry services a day, 3 hrs, US$51 return, with bus connection to Montevideo (US$10 extra), motorcycles US$25, cars US$41. **Ferrylíneas Sea Cat** www.seacatcolonia.com, operates a cheaper fast service to Colonia from the same terminal, 1-3 daily, 1 hr, US$53 tourist class (return), vehicles US$61, motorcycles US$36 with bus connection to Punta del Este (US$9 extra). There is a new company called **Colonia Express**, www.coloniaexpress.com, which also runs cheaper trips to Uruguay. They leave from a bit further along the port, offer competitive rates and have a much smaller, slightly faster boat, US$40 return. Their cheapest deals are on Wed. Catch a taxi from town (US$5). Don't forget your passport.

Rail

There are 4 main terminals: **Retiro** (3 lines: Mitre, Belgrano, San Martín in separate buildings), **Constitución**, **Once**, **Federico Lacroze**.

Almost the only passenger trains in Argentina today are Buenos Aires commuter trains, and locals feel they're in pretty bad condition, with the exception of the semi-decent Mitre line to Tigre. There are only a few long-distance services, all very shoddy, and not to be considered as a serious alternative to long-distance bus or air travel.

Tickets are checked before boarding and on the train, and are collected at the end of the journey (so don't lose your ticket!); urban and suburban fares are charged according different sections of each line. For information contact the companies directly: **Ferrobaires**, T011-4304 0028, www.ferrobaires.gba.gov.ar; **Ferrovías**, T011-4511 8833; **Metropolitano**, T0800-1223 58736, www.metropolitano. com.ar; **Metrovías**, T011-4555 1616, www.metrovias.com.ar; **TBA**, T011-4317 4407, www.tbanet.com.ar; **Trenes Especiales**, T011-4551 1634.

Retiro

Retiro station runs 3 different lines in separate buildings: train information T011-4311 8704.
Mitre line Run by TBA, services to all the suburbs, though you're most likely to use it to get to Tigre if you want an alternative to the tourist Tren de la Costa. Urban and suburban services to **Belgrano**, **Mitre** (connection to Tren de la Costa, see below), **Olivos**, **San Isidro**, **Tigre** (see below), Capilla del Señor (connection at Victoria, US$1), **Escobar** and **Zárate** (connection at Villa Ballester, US$1). Long-distance services to **Rosario Norte**, 1 weekly on Fri evening, 6 hrs, US$10.50 (return); to **Tucumán** via Rosario, Mon and Fri, 2100, returning Mon and Thu 1000, 26 hrs, US$33.50 sleeper, US$18 pullman, US$11.50 1st (service run by NOA Ferrocarriles, T011-4893 2244)
Belgrano line For trains to the northwestern suburbs (Villa Rosa), run by Ferrovías, T011-4511 8833.

San Martín line Run by Metropolitano. Urban and suburban services to **Palermo**, **Chacarita**, **Devoto**, **Hurlingham** and **Pilar**. Long-distance services to **Junín**, daily, 5 hrs, US$4.50.

Constitución

Train information T011-4304 0028. Like the terminals of Retiro, it is best not to hang around Constitución longer than you need to. Train and bus stations are favourites of scam artists and pickpockets.
Roca line Run by **Metropolitano**, see above). Urban and suburban services to **La Plata**, US$1.20; **Ezeiza** (the suburb NOT the airport), US$0.35; **Ranelagh**, US$0.27; and **Quilmes**, US$0.20. Long-distance services (run by **Ferrobaires**, T011-4304 0028/3165): to **Bahía Blanca**, 5 weekly, 12½ hrs, US$14; to **Mar del Plata** daily in summer, book ahead, 5 hrs US$12; to **Pinamar**, 2 weekly, 6 hrs US$7; to **Miramar**, in summer only, daily, 7 hrs, US$7; to **Tandil**, weekly, 7½ hrs, US$8; to **Quequén**, 2 weekly, 12 hrs, US$7-13.

Federico Lacroze Urquiza

Train line information, and **Metro headquarters**, run by Metrovías, T0800-555 1616 or T011-4555 1616, www.metrovias.com.ar. Suburban services to General Lemos, and long-distance services to Posadas, run by Trenes Especiales.

Once

Train information, T011-4861 0043. **Once** train station is notorious for petty crime. Best to avoid it if you can.
Once Sarmiento line Run by TBA, see above. Urban and suburban services to **Caballito**; **Flores**; **Merlo**; **Luján** (connection at Moreno) US$0.60; **Mercedes**, US$1.20; and **Lobos**. Long-distance services to **Santa Rosa** and **General Pico** can be seasonally interrupted by floods. A fast service runs daily between **Puerto Madero** (station at Av Alicia Moreau de Justo and Perón) and **Castelar**.

O Directory

Banks

ATMs are widespread throughout the city. Note that most tourists find they have a limit of US$300 a day, and that they need to take this out in 3 US$100 transactions from the ATM. This has nothing to do with your bank, it is a limit that Argentine banks impose (look for Link ATMs as they are most reliable). Don't contact your bank about this, they have no control over it. The financial district lies within a small area north of Plaza de Mayo, between Rivadavia, 25 de Mayo, Av Corrientes and Florida. In non-central areas you'll find banks/ATMs along the main avenues. Banks are open Mon-Fri 1000-1500. Most banks charge commission especially on TCs (as much as US$10). US dollar bills are often scanned electronically for forgeries.

American Express offices are at Arenales 707 and Maipú, by Plaza San Martín, T011-4310 3000 or T0810-555 2639, www.americanexpress.com, where you can apply for a card, get financial services and change Amex TCs (1000-1500 only, T0810-444 2437, no commission into US$ or pesos). No commission either at Banco de la Provincia de Buenos Aires, several branches, or at Banco Columbia, Perón 350. Citibank, B Mitre 502, T0810-444 2484, changes only Citicorps TCs, no commission, branch at Florida 199. General MasterCard office, Perú 151, T011-4348 7000, www.mastercard.com.ar, 0930-1800. Visa, Corrientes 1437 p 2, T011-4379 3400, www.visa.com.ar. Currency exchange Casas de cambio include Banco Piano, San Martín 345, T011-4321 9200 (has exchange facility at Ezeiza airport, 0500-2400), www.banco piano.com.ar, changes all TCs (commission 2%); Eves, Tucumán 702; Forex, Marcelo T de Alvear 540, T011-4311 5543; Banco Ciudad at Av Córdoba 675 branch is open to tourists (providing passport) for exchange currency and TCs, Mon 1000-1800, Tue-Fri 1000-1700,

Sat-Sun 1100-1800. **Lost or stolen cards** MasterCard, T0800-555 0507; Visa T011-4379 3333 (T0810-666 3368, from outside BA). **Money transfers** Western Union branches in *Correo Argentino* post offices (for transfers within Argentina) and at Av Córdoba 975 (for all transfers), T0800-800 3030.

Cultural centres

Alliance Française, Córdoba 946, T011-4322 0068, www.alianzafrancesa.org.ar, French library, temporary film and art exhibitions; Biblioteca Centro Lincoln, Maipú 672, T011-5382 1536, www.bcl.edu.ar, Mon-Wed 1000-2000, Thu and Fri 1000-1800 (Jan and Feb Mon-Fri 1300-1900), library (borrowing for members only), English/US newspapers; British Arts Centre (BAC), Suipacha 1333, T011-4393 6941, www.britishartscentre. org.ar, English plays and films, music concerts and photography exhibitions (closed Jan); British Council, Marcelo T. de Alvear 590, p 4, T011-4311 9814, Mon-Thu 0830-1700, Fri 0830-1330; Goethe Institut, Corrientes 319/43, T011-4311 8964, German library, Mon, Tue, Thu 1230-1930, Fri 1230-1600, closed Jan, newspapers, free German films shown, cultural programmes, German-language courses, in the same building, upstairs, is the German Club, Corrientes 327; Instituto Cultural Argentino Norteamericano (ICANA), Maipú 672, T011-5382 1500, www.icana.org.ar.

Embassies and consulates

All open Mon-Fri unless stated otherwise. Australia, Villanueva 1400 and Zabala, T011-4779 3500, www.argentina.embassy. gov.au, daily 0830-1100, ticket queuing system, take bus 29 along Av Luis María Campos to Zabala; Belgium, Defensa 113 p 8, T011-4331 0066, 0800-1300, www.diplomatie.be/buenosaires/; Bolivia, Consulate, Alsina 1886, T011-4381 4171, www.embajadade bolivia. com.ar, 0830-1530, visa while you wait or a month wait (depending on the country of origin), tourist bureau; **Brazil**, Consulate, Pellegrini 1363, p 5, T011-4515 6500, www.conbrasil. org.ar, 1000-1300, tourist visa takes at least 48 hrs, US$100; **Canada**, Tagle 2828, T011-4808 1000, www.canadainternational. gc.ca/argentina-argentine, Mon-Thu 0830-1230, 1330-1730, tourist visa Mon-Thu 0845-1130; **Chile**, Consulate, San Martín 439, p 9, T011-4394 6582, www.embajadadechile.com.ar/embajada. asp, 0900-1330; **Denmark**, Consulate, Alem 1074, p 9, T011-4312 6901, www.dinamarca.net, Mon-Thu 0930-1200; **France**, Santa Fe 846, p 4, T011-4312 2409, www.consulatfrance.int.ar, 0900-1230, 1400-1600 (by appointment); **Germany**, Villanueva 1055, T011-4778 2500, www.embajada-alemana.org.ar, 0830-1100; **Ireland**, Av Del Libertador 1068 p 6, T011-5787 0801, www.embassyof ireland.org.ar, 0900-1300, 1400-1530; **Italy**, consulate at Marcelo T de Alvear 1125/49, T011-4816 6133/36, www.consbuenosaires. esterl.it, Mon, Tue, Thu, Fri 0800-1100; **Netherlands**, Olga Cossentini 831 p 3, Puerto Madero, T011- 4338 0050, www.embajadaholanda.int.ar, Mon-Thu 0900-1300, Fri 0900-1230; **New Zealand**, Pellegrini 1427 p 5, T011-4328 0747, www.nzembassy.com/argentina, Mon-Thu 0900 1300, 1400-1730, Fri 0900-1300; **Norway**, Esmeralda 909, p 3 B, T011-4312 2204, www.noruega.org.ar, 0930-1400; **Spain**, Consulate, Guido 1760, T011-4811 0070, www.mae.es/consulados/buenosaires, 0815-1430; **Sweden**, Tacuarí 147 p 6, T011-4329 0800, www.swedenabroad.com/ buenosaires, 1000-1200; **Switzerland**, Santa Fe 846, p10, T011-4311 6491, www.eda.admin.ch/buenosaires, 0900-1200; **UK**, Luis Agote 2412 (near corner Pueyrredón and Guido), T011-4808 2200 (call T011-15-5114 1036, for emergencies only out of normal office hours), http://ukin argentina.fco.gov.uk/en/, 0900-1300 (Jan-Feb 0900-1200); **Uruguay**, Consulate,

Av Las Heras 1907, T011-4807 3045, www.embajadadeluruguay. com.ar, 0930-1730, visa takes up to 72 hrs; **US Embassy and Consulate General**, Colombia 4300, T011-5777 4533 (for emergencies involving US citizens, call T011-5777 4354 or T011-5777 4873 after office hours), http://argentina.usembassy.gov/.

Emergencies
Central Police Station: Moreno 1550, Virrey Cevallos 362, T011-4370 5911/5800 (emergency, T101 from any phone, free). See page 41 for **Comisaría del Turista** (tourist police).

Internet
Prices range from US$0.50-US$1.50 per hr, shop around. Most *locutorios* (phone offices) have internet access.

Language schools
There are many good Spanish teachers and schools, for advice contact South American Explorers, www.saexplorers.org, for their recommendations.

Private teachers
Cristina Gioveni, T011-156 859 3434, www. sffi.com.ar, or cristinagioveni@yahoo.com.ar, lessons either at her office or at the your place, group and 1-to-1 lessons available and take a taster class for free; **Ezequiel Cerioni**, www.bahabla.com, ezequielcerioni@ gmail.com, qualified, will visit your house or you can go to his, is entertaining and often recommended; **Gisela Giunti**, J.E. Uriburu 541, 6th Floor 'A', T011-155 626 0162, www.giselagiunti.com, offers personalized, private classes for individuals or small groups, competitive rates, great reviews and highly recommended.

Schools
Academia Buenos Aires, Hipólito Yrigoyen 571, 4th floor, T011-4345 5954, www.academiabuenosaires.com, slightly

more expensive classes than most, but high attention to detail and great teachers, also offers a recommended school in Montevideo, Uruguay, www.academiauruguay.com; **All-Spanish**, Talcahuano 77, p 1, T011-4381 3914, www.all-spanish.com.ar, good reports; **Amauta Spanish School**, Frederico Lacroze 2129, T011-4777 2130, www.amautaspanishschool.org, individual lessons or small groups, also has a school in Bariloche; **Argentina I.L.E.E**, T011-4782 7173, www.argentinailee.com, recommended by individuals and organizations alike, also have schools in Córdoba and Bariloche; **Ecole del SurTravel**, Av Rivadavia 1479, p 1, department B, T011-4383 1026, www.ecoledelsur.com. A language school that also organizes tours, packages and accommodation. **Elebaires**, Av de Mayo 1370, office 10, 3rd floor, T011-4371 3149, www.elebaires.com.ar,

small school with focused classes, also offers 1-to-1 lessons and excursions, recommended; **Español Andando**, T011-5278 9886, www.espanol-andando.com, offers a different approach to classes, recommended, courses run for a week, and each day you will meet your fellow students and your teacher in a different part of the city and learn how the locals say it; **Expanish**, Viamonte 927, 1st floor, T011-4322 0011, www.expanish.com, well-organized Spanish courses which can involve excursions, accommodation and Spanish lessons in sister schools in Lima, Peru and Chile, highly recommended; **IBL (International Bureau of Language)**, Florida 165, 3rd floor, T011-4331 4250, www.ibl.com.ar, group and 1-to-1 lessons, all levels; **Universidad de Buenos Aires**, 25 de Mayo 221, T011-4334 7512, www.idiomas.filo.uba.ar, offers cheap, coherent courses, including summer intensive courses.

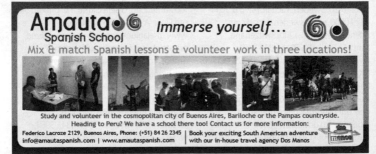

Medical services
Urgent medical service For free municipal ambulance service to an emergency hospital department (day and night) **Casualty ward, Sala de guardia,** T107, or T011-4923 1051/58 (SAME).

Inoculations If not provided, buy the vaccines in **Laboratorio Biol,** Uriburu 153, T011-4953 7215, or in larger chemists. Many chemists have signs indicating that they give injections and any hospital with an infectology department will give hepatitis A. **Dirección de Sanidad de Fronteras y Terminales de Transporte,** Ing Huergo 690, T011-4343 1190, Mon 1400-1500, Tue-Wed 1100-1200, Thu and Fri 1600-1700 (bus 20 from Retiro), no appointment required, yellow fever only, take passport; **Hospital Rivadavia,** Av Las Heras 2670, T011-4809 2000, Mon-Fri, 0700-1300 (bus 10, 37, 59, 60, 62, 92, 93 or 102 from Plaza Constitución); **Travel Medicine Service (Centros Médicos Stamboulian),** 25 de Mayo 464, T011-4311 3000, French 3085, T011-5236 7772, also in Belgrano and Flores, private health advice for travellers and inoculations centre.

Public hospital British Hospital, Perdriel 74, T011-4309 6400, www.hospitalbritanico. org.ar, US$42 a visit, first-aid centre (*centros asistenciales*); **German Hospital,** Av Pueyrredón 1640, between Beruti and Juncal, T011-4827 7000, www.hospitalale man.com.ar, first-aid centre; **Hospital Argerich,** Almte Brown corner of Pi and Margall 750, T011-4121 0700; **Hospital Juan A Fernández,** Cerviño and Bulnes, T011-4808 2600, good medical attention.

Dental treatment Carroll Forest, Vuelta de Obligado 1551 (Belgrano), T011-4781 9037, info@carroll-forest.com.ar, excellent dental treatment centre; **Dental Argentina,** T011-4828 0821, www.dental-argentina.com.ar.

Post offices
Correo Central, Correos Argentinos, Sarmiento and Alem, T011-4891 9191, www.correoargentino.com.ar, Mon-Fri, 0800-2000, Sat 1000-1300, poste restante (only to/from domestic destinations) on ground floor (US$0.90 per letter), philatelic section Mon-Fri 1000-1700, T011-5550 5176; **Centro Postal Internacional,** for all parcels over 2 kg for mailing internationally, at Av Comodoro Py and Antártida Argentina, near Retiro station, helpful, many languages spoken, packaging materials available, Mon-Fri 1000-1700; **DHL,** T0810-222 2345, www.dhl.com.ar; **FedEx,** T0810-333 3339, www.fedex.com; **Post office,** Montevideo 1408 near Plaza V López, also at Santa Fe 945 and many others, friendly staff, Spanish only; UPS, T0800-222 2877, www.ups.com.

Telephone
International and local calls, internet and fax from phone offices (*locutorios* or *telecentros*), of which there are many in the city centre. For more information, see Essentials A-Z, page 51.

Visas
Migraciones: (Immigration), Antártida Argentina 1355, edificio 4, T011-4317 0200, daily 0730-1330, www.migraciones.gov.ar (visas extended mornings only). See also Essentials, page 56.

Around Buenos Aires

If you don't relish the frenzy of a big city, especially at the end of a trip exploring some of the widest landscapes on earth, you'll be relieved to know there are calm rural estancias (cattle farms), the fascinating Tigre river delta, and cowboy towns which celebrate an authentic gaucho culture – all within an hour or two of Buenos Aires.

Mataderos is on the western edge of the city, and worth visiting only on Sundays, when it's the site of a wonderful market, with displays of gaucho horsemanship. The air is filled with the smoky aroma of grilling steak on asados, and there's even tango dancing. If gaucho culture intrigues you, it's worth setting out for the impeccably preserved 1900s gaucho towns of San Antonio de Areco, to the west of the city, or Chascomus in the south (handy for Ezeiza International Airport). There are lots of grand estancias near both towns, where you can try horse riding or simply lap up the luxury. Details on these places are in the next chapter, Buenos Aires Province.

Closer at hand, the two most popular destinations for day trips are north of the city along the coast of the Río de la Plata, easily reached by train from the city. San Isidro is a beautiful old colonial suburb where you can find huge luxury residential mansions, a wonderful church on the plaza and a ring of smart shops in the charming old quarter, making it a pleasant place to stroll around, especially at weekends when the craft market is on. Also appealing is the Tigre river delta which is a maze of overgrown waterways that can be explored by boat or local ferry. Find a waterfont restaurant, or a romantic boutique hotel on stilts hidden away up a lazy river and spend a few days relaxing.

Finally, you could take a boat trip across the Río de la Plata to the quaint Portuguese colonial town of Colonia del Sacramento (which is in Uruguay). Stroll around the antique buildings on this quiet peninsula, or hire a bike: there's nothing much to do here except eat and gaze at the views, but the architecture is very appealing and there's an amazing sense of calm. After the constant bustle of Buenos Aires, Colonia is a welcome retreat. ▸▸ For listings, see pages 121-124.

Mataderos

On the western edge of the city in an area where historically cattle were slaughtered, there is now a popular market, the **Feria de Mataderos** ⓘ *Lisandro de la Torre and Av de los Corrales, www.feriademataderos.com.ar, every Sun and holidays from 1100, Sat 1800-2400 in summer.* Take *Subte* E to the end of the line and then a taxi (US$4), or if there's a group of you, take buses 36, 92, 97, 126, 141. A Radio Taxi all the way will cost US$12. It's a long way out of the centre (about two hours by bus), but worth it to see this fair of Argentine handicrafts and traditional artwork, with music and dance festivals, demonstrations of gaucho horsemanship skills, typical regional food, and games such as *pato*, a game played on horseback, originally with a duck, and *carrera de sortijas* where players on horseback have to spear a ring on a string with their lance. Nearby is the **Museo de los Corrales** ⓘ *Av de los Corrales 6436, T011-4687 1949, Sun 1300-1900.*

San Isidro → *For listings, see pages 121-124. Colour map 4, B5.*

Just to the north of Buenos Aires city, 22 km away, San Isidro is an attractive small town with a lovely setting on the coast, easily reached by the **Tren de La Costa** (see below) or local train from Retiro, Mitre station (US$0.75). It's an appealing place to come for an afternoon, for a stroll along the historical old quarter by the river, or to shop in the converted old railway station. This is the most sought-after residential area in greater

Buenos Aires, and there are lots of bars and places to eat along the coast, with pretty green spaces for walking or relaxing. The **tourist information office** ① *just off the central plaza Mitre, at Ituzaingo 608, on the corner with Av del Libertador, T011-4512 3209, www.sanisidro.gov.ar*, is staffed by extremely helpful bilingual staff.

Start your tour of San Isidro at the Tren de la Costa train station, nicely renovated, and now housing shops where you can pick up good handicrafts as well as clothes and accessories. Walk up into the pretty main **Plaza Mitre**, filled with shady mature trees and fragrant flowers in summer, and where there is a handicrafts market every weekend. From here, have a look at the old Municipal buildings, before walking along Beccar Varela Street to look at the aristocratic houses. This was historically the site of country houses for the aristocracy in the late 19th century, and there are a number of fine colonial buildings including several country houses (*quintas*). **Quinta Pueyrredón** houses the Museo Pueyrredón, containing artefacts from the life of General Juan Martín Pueyrredón. The main shopping street, with lots of *locutorios* and places you can download and print photos, as well as conventional shops, is **Belgrano**, between Avenida del Libertador and Avenida Centenario, the busy main road into Buenos Aires city.

The **Ribera**, the area by the coast stretching southeast of the centre, is green and peaceful, with plenty of park areas where you can sit gazing out at the great view of the Río de la Plata. There are marinas for yachts and windsurfing, and the **Club Náutico San Isidro**, reached from Mitre. There are also plenty of places to eat along here as this is a popular upmarket nightspot for *Porteños*, all along the coast road southeast of the centre of San Isidro from Primera Junta southeast to Paraná. It's worth strolling onto the viewpoint from the Mirador de Roque Sáenz Peña for the views over to Buenos Aires. Further southeast, there's a small nature reserve right on the Río de la Plata, the **Reserva Ecológica Municipal**, *T011-4747 6179, 0900-1900, guided visit at 1700 in summer; 0900-1800, guided visits Sat-Sun 1600 in winter, free entry*, which hosts an impressive array of birdlife, with over 200 species. Access is from the coast road, Camino de la Ribera, via Vicente López.

An interesting country house to visit is the French-inspired **Villa Ocampo** ① *1011-4807 4428, Thu-Sun 1230-1800, US$3, students US$2.* Built in 1891, this beautiful house with galleried verandas and attractive gardens was the home of the famous Argentine writer Victoria Ocampo, where she frequently entertained illustrious visitors from Argentina's literary world. Take a taxi as this is 10 blocks north of the centre. Ask the tourist office for precise directions.

San Isidro is most famous for the **Hipódromo San Isidro**, its magnificent turf racecourse. Built in 1935, this immense racecourse is one of the best known in South America. Races are run every Wednesday, and some Saturdays or Sundays from 1500-2000. Beyond the compact town centre, the residential area is huge and sprawling, and is *the* place to live if you're a wealthy *Porteño*. Naturally, nearby is where you find Argentina's biggest shopping mall, the disarmingly immense **Unicenter Shopping**, at Paraná and the Ruta Panamericana, see page 104. Don't even attempt to get there by bus: take a taxi, ask the driver to collect you at a predetermined time and allow at least half a day. All the main brands are here, as well as a good range of restaurants in the Patio de Comidas.

Tren de la Costa → *T011-4002 6000.*

One of Argentina's most comfortable trains is this tourist service that whisks visitors from Maipú station in the Vicente López area of Buenos Aires all the way to Tigre, via some of the most picturesque spots on the coast of the Río de la Plata. To get to Maipú, take a normal (TBA) commuter train from Retiro in the centre of Buenos Aires and change at Maipú for the Tren de la Costa. San Isidro is the most appealing place to stop on your way to Tigre, but you could also try Borges station, for the pleasant residential area of Olivos, with its waterfront filled with millionaires' homes, and Barrancas, where you can hire rollerblades and bikes, and visit the second-hand market. You can get off and on as many times as you like for the fixed single ticket price of US$2.10. Trains leave every 20 minutes, Monday to Thursday 0710-2300, Friday 0710-2400, Saturday and Sunday 0830-0010. Buses to Tren de la Costa are No 60 from Constitución, Nos 19 or 71 from Once, and No 152 from the centre. For those on a tight budget, you can also reach Tigre by taking the TBA train all the way from Retiro for US$0.45 (55 minutes). Trains leave every seven minutes Monday to Friday, or every 15 minutes Saturday and Sunday. It takes 35 minutes to reach San Isidro from Maipú, and 60 minutes to reach Tigre.

Tigre → For listings, see pages 121-124. Colour map 4, B5.

Tigre is deservedly the city's most popular weekend destination: a town based on the edge of the magnificent river delta of the Río Paraná, some 32 km northwest of the city. The delta is a maze of waterways and hundreds of islands, formed by the accumulation of sediment brought down by the mighty Paraná river that runs from the border with Brazil down to the Río de la Plata, slicing between the First and Second sections of the delta. The delta is a natural paradise, mostly wild and untouched, the lush, jungly banks of the islands making picturesque settings for quaint wooden holiday homes on stilts, the odd boutique hotel, and restaurants hidden miles away from the noise of the city and reached only by boat. In fact, some 3000 people live on the delta islands, and since there are no paths or bridges, the only way to get around is by boat, which is how services such as supermarkets, banks and libraries are brought to the islanders. Tigre is the perfect place to cool down on a hot afternoon in summer, and even if you only come for a few hours, you can take one of the regular motor launches for a 60- or 90-minute tour of the nearby rivers for a pleasurable introduction to this watery world. If a tour isn't your thing, just catch the local 1920s-style wooden ferries to a point along the river to explore. Most people stop at Tres Bocas (45 minutes each way), as there are three restaurants to choose from. A return journey will cost around US$4: just wait at the little wharf until a boat comes past – every 10 minutes or so – and wave until they see you. With more time, hire a kayak to see the wonderfully overgrown expanses at more leisure, or try rowing or canoeing. There are many houses you can rent by the night on the islands (from around US$45, 20% more at weekends), reached by the regular motor launch bus service and visited by a mobile food shop. You could hide away here for a night or two on a romantic retreat; it's a peaceful place to escape to. All houses have electricity and phone, but bring drinking water and sunscreen.

There are lots of restaurants scattered throughout the delta, and also *recreos* – little resorts with facilities such as swimming pools and tennis courts, as well as waterfront bars and restaurants. One of these is **El Alcazar**, just 10 minutes' boat journey from Tigre, with tennis and volleyball, by a sandy beach, where you can bring your own steaks to barbecue on the *parrilla* grills. Tigre itself has a funfair and an excellent fruit and handicrafts market; a short walk from the centre, along Mitre and turn right at the Delta station. The amusement park, **Parque de Diversiones** ① *Fri-Sun only*, is immediately on your left, with the Casino next door in a soulless concrete building. The fruit market, **Puerto de Frutos** ① *daily 1100-2000*, is four blocks further along on the left, on Sarmiento. There's a fairly drab town centre with everything you might need, but the riverside area is the most picturesque, and here you'll find one excellent hotel, **Villa Julia**, which also serves superb food (see Sleeping, page 121). Tigre is a great place to visit any time of the year, with a mild climate even in winter, but note that it's quietest midweek: in summer it gets very busy at weekends, though the festive atmosphere is very appealing in itself. Regattas are held in November and March. Remember to bring a hat and insect repellent in summer.

Tigre can be reached by bus from Constitución (bus No 60): the 60 'bajo' takes a little longer than the 60 'alto' but is more interesting for sightseeing. Tigre is also easily reached on the Tren de la Costa (see above) and you should get off at Estación Fluvial, not Delta. The direct train from Retiro station, Buenos Aires (TBA Mitre section) terminates at the Tigre station, which is different to that of the Tren de la Costa (it is more central and you can see the ferry terminal from the entrance). The journey takes 60 minutes and costs US$0.75; make sure you stay on the train until it reaches the last stop. Alternatively, you can take the train to Bartolomé Mitre and change at the Maipú station (the stations are linked) for the Tren de la Costa. There is an excellent **tourist office** ⓘ *next to Estación Fluvial, at Mitre 305, www.tigre.gov.ar, T011-4512 4497, daily 1000-1800*, with helpful English-speaking staff who can show you the huge folder of houses to rent by the night (complete with photographs) and advise you of boat/bus times to reach them. There's one excellent hotel in Tigre itself, and some average hotels among the delta islands, with a gorgeous boutique hotel, **La Pascuala** (see Sleeping, page 121) in the Second Section, on the other side of the Río Paraná.

Before you take a boat trip, have a stroll along the riverside, the path parallel to Lavalle that leads to Paseo Victorica. You'll pass several rowing clubs, some of them in palatial old buildings, such as the British Rowing Club of 1873, the Buenos Aires Rowing Club, and the Italian Club, as well as the Tudor-style half-timbered Club Regata opposite. The main tourist centre is around the old railway station, **Estación Fluvial**, the large old building, now tastefully restored, with souvenir shops, a McDonald's, and many companies selling boat trips: **Sturla** ⓘ *T011-4731 1300*, is one of the most reliable, offering a 90-minute trip for US$7. Boats leave from the quayside just by the Estación Fluvial, and you can take your pick from big catamarans or smaller wooden boats. The tour guides on all boats speak English and give an informative tour.

There's one museum in Tigre, the **Museo Naval de la Nación** ⓘ *Paseo Victoria 602, T011-4749 0608, Mon-Thu 0830-1230, Fri 0800-1730, Sat-Sun 1000-1830, US$0.60*, which covers the origins and development of the Argentine navy, with lots of model ships. There are also relics of the Falklands/Malvinas War on display outside. You might also be interested in the **Municipal Art Gallery** ⓘ *Paseo Victoria 972, T011-4512 4528, museo dearte@tigre.gov.ar, Mon-Fri 0900-1900, Sat-Sun 1200-1900, US$1.50*, a 10-minute walk along the river and housed in the newly restored Tigre Hotel from 1909 – a wonderfully ornate building with many chandeliers. On show are mainly 20th-century works of art detailing the river and its inhabitants. In the delta there is a small museum based around the house of Sarmiento – one of Argentina's most famous presidents. You'll see it from the river, it is a huge glass enclosure with a small wooden house inside like a big fish bowl. You can ask the ferry driver to drop you off there.

Isla Martín García → *For listings, see pages 121-124. Colour map 4, B5.*

Situated in the Río de la Plata just off the Uruguayan coast and some 45 km north of Buenos Aires, Martín García is now a provincial nature reserve and one of the best excursions from Buenos Aires, with many trails through the cane brakes, trees and rocky outcrops, and interesting birds and flowers.

This was the site of Juan Díaz de Solís' landfall in 1516, and the island's strategic position has given it a chequered history. It was used for quarantining immigrants from Europe, and then as a prison: four 20th-century Argentine presidents have been detained here, including Juan Perón, and in 1914 British sailors were interned here, as were

Colonia del Sacramento

Río de la Plata

Sleeping
Don Antonio Posada **10**
El Viajero **20**
Español **5**
Esperanza **6**
Hostal de los Poetas **2**
Hostel Colonial **7**
Italiano **8**

Plaza Mayor **12**
Posada de la Flor **11**
Posada del Angel **13**
Posada del Gobernador **14**
Posada del Río **15**
Posada del Virrey **16**
Posada Manuel
de Lobo **17**

Radisson Colonia
de Sacramento &
Restaurant Del Carmen **1**
Romi **18**
Royal **19**

survivors from the *Graf Spee* in the Second World War (see box, page 204). Evidence ranges from stone-quarries used for building the older churches of Buenos Aires to four gun batteries and a *faro* (lighthouse) dating from 1890. The **Museo Histórico** in the former *pulpería* houses a display of artefacts, documents and photos. Wildlife is varied, particularly around the edges of the island, and includes laurels, ceibo and several species of orchid. Over 200 species of birds visit the island. Take insect repellent.

There are four weekly boat trips which run from Tigre at 0900, returning 2030, taking three hours. Prices are around US$47 including a light lunch, *asado* and guide (US$99 per person including weekend overnight at inn, full board). Reservations can be made through **Cacciola** ① *Florida 520, 1st floor, Office 113, T011-4393 6100, www.cacciolaviajes.com*, who also handle bookings for the inn and restaurant on the island.

Colonia del Sacramento

→ *For listings, see pages 121-124. Colour map 4, B6.*

A Portuguese colonial town on the east bank of the Río de la Plata, Colonia del Sacramento is a very popular destination for excursions from Buenos Aires. The **airport** is 17 km out of town along Route 1; for a taxi to Colonia, buy a ticket in the building next to arrivals, US$2.50. The modern town, with a population of 22,000, which extends along a bay, is charming and lively with neat, leafy streets. The small historic neighbourhood is particularly interesting because there is so much well-preserved colonial architecture There is a pleasant Plaza 25 de Agosto and a grand Intendencia Municipal (Méndez and Avenida General Flores, the main street). The best beach is Playa Ferrando, 2 km to the east (buses from General Flores every two hours). There are regular sea and air connections with Buenos Aires and a free port. Colonia del Sacramento is in Uruguay. Remember to take your passport with you. There are no transport taxes although you will be subject to immigration formalities if you travel further into Uruguay.

Eating ⑦
Blanco y Negro 10
Club Colonia 2
El Asador 14
El Drugstore
 & Viejo Barrio 4
El Torreón 11
La Amistad 8
La Bodeguita 12
Lo de Renata 1
Mercosur 5
Mesón de la Plaza 9
Pulpería Los Faroles 6
Yacht Club 7

The **tourist office** ① *Flores and Rivera, T+598 (0)52-23700, Mon-Fri 0900-1900, Sat and Sun 0900-1900,* has good maps of the Barrio Histórico. There is also a tourist office at the passenger terminal by the dock.

Sights → *Phone code +598-(0)52.*

With its narrow streets (wander around Calle de los Suspiros), colonial buildings and reconstructed city walls, the Barrio Histórico has been declared Patrimonio Cultural de la Humanidad by UNESCO. The **Plaza Mayor** (Plaza 25 de Mayo) is especially picturesque. At its eastern end is the **Puerta del Campo**, the restored city gate and drawbridge. On the south side is the **Museo Portugués**; see also the narrow Calle de los Suspiros, nearby. At the western end of the Plaza are the **Museo Municipal** in the former house of Almirante Brown (with indigenous archaeology, historical items, palaeontology and natural history), the **Casa Nacarello** next door, the **Casa del Virrey**, and the ruins of the **Convento de San Francisco** (1695), to which is attached the *faro* (lighthouse) built in 1857 (free, but a tip or donation is appreciated). Entry to the museums in this historic quarter is by combined ticket bought from Museo Municipal: US$2.50, opening hours tend to be 1100-1730 every day.

Just north of the Plaza Mayor a narrow street, the Calle Misiones de los Tapes, leads east to the river. At its further end is the tiny **Museo del Azulejo** housed in the Casa Portuguesa. Two blocks north of here is the Calle Playa which runs east to the Plaza Manuel Lobo/Plaza de Armas, on the northern side of which is the **Iglesia Matriz**, on Vasconcellos, the oldest church in Uruguay. Though destroyed and rebuilt several times, the altar dates from the 16th century. Free concerts are held each Friday during the summer months on the church grounds. Two blocks north of the church, on the northern edge of the old city, are the fortifications of the **Bastión del Carmen**; just east of it is the **Teatro Bastión del Carmen**. One block south of the Bastión, at San José and España, is the **Museo Español**, formerly the house of General Mitre. Hire a buggy or a bicycle and explore, then pick a restaurant and peacefully soak up the sun, eat a huge lunch and enjoy a cold drink. Wonderful.

Estancias near Buenos Aires

Many of the province's finest *estancias* can be visited relatively easily from Buenos Aires, either to spend a day (*día de campo*) or longer. *Día de campo* usually includes horse riding, or riding in a horse-drawn carriage over the *estancia*'s lands, followed by lunch. This is usually a traditional *asado*, often cooked outside with half a cow speared over an open fire: quite a spectacle and absolutely delicious. In the afternoon you may be treated to demonstrations of farm life, music and dancing from the region, or you might just choose to walk in the beautiful grounds of the *estancia*, read under a tree or swim in the pool. To really appreciate the luxury or peace of an *estancia*, an overnight stay is recommended. Most places are still run as working farms by their owners, who will welcome you personally, and staying with them gives you a unique insight into Argentine rural life and history. Several good websites with details of *estancias* are: www. turismo.gov.ar, www.caminodelgaucho.com.ar, and www.raturestancias.com.ar.

There are many *estancias* grouped around the attractive towns of **San Antonio de Areco** (see page 129), **Chascomús** (see page 136) and **Dolores** (see page 136), all listed under Buenos Aires Province.

For Sleeping and Eating price codes and other relevant information, see Essentials pages 30-36.

⊜ Sleeping

San Isidro p114

L Del Casco, Av Libertador 16, 170, T/F011-4732 3993, www.hoteldelcasco.com.ar. Perfectly situated gracious colonial-style country house built in 1892, now beautifully converted. The bedrooms are huge and tastefully decorated, with old furniture and luxurious bathrooms. The service, from the young bilingual staff, is excellent, and the breakfasts are enormous. All highly recommended. A peaceful alternative for exploring the city.
A Posada de San Isidro Apart Hotel, Maipú 66, T011-4732 1221, www.posadasanisidro.com.ar. Pleasant, modern functional rooms in a new building, offering impeccable and good value self-catering accommodation. Small pool, breakfast available, handy for the main line train station.

Tigre p116

LL-L La Pascuala, 'la segunda sección', 1 hr by motor launch, arrange with reception, T011-4378 0982, www.lapascuala.com. One of Argentina's most delightful places to stay, this is an exclusive and intimate boutique hotel hidden far away from civilization in the wild further reaches of the Second Section of the Tigre delta. The hotel consists of 15 individual suite-lodges on stilts, connected by wooden walkways, each with a huge and luxurious bedroom with its own veranda looking over the river, and an immense bathroom, all beautifully designed for maximum calm and relaxation, equipped with everything you could possibly need. The price is high, but all meals, wine and afternoon tea are included, and the service is top notch. Highly recommended.
LL-L Villa Julia, Paseo Victorica 800, T011-4749 0642, www.villajuliaresort.com.ar. This beautiful villa, built in 1906 on the waterfront,

has now been tastefully converted into a chic little boutique hotel with just 9 rooms. There are superb views from the upper rooms, and all are decorated in the original style of the hotel, with very comfortable beds. Many of the bathrooms have the original furniture and pretty art nouveau tiles. The sitting room downstairs is calm and elegant, and the peaceful dining room is a really special place for dinner with a small but imaginative menu. Open to non-residents too.
L-AL Rumbo 90 Delta Lodge and Spa, in the eastern area of the delta, 45 mins by launch from Tigre, T011-155 843 9454, www.rumbo90.com.ar. In a glorious natural setting, with 40 ha of rainforest to wander around in, this is a comfortable hotel, bedrooms have smart bathrooms with jacuzzi and there is a spa offering facial treatments. Not as luxurious as **La Pascuala**, but a lovely setting.

Hostels

B Marco Polo Náutico, Paraná de las Palmas and Cruz Colorada, T011-4728 0395, www.marcopoloinnnautico.com. A wonderful retreat in the middle of the delta reached by a local ferry. Spacious doubles and triples available. A little pricey but a lovely place to relax for a few days. Kayaking, swimming pool, beach, pool tables and bar.
E Tigre Hostel, Av del Libertador 190, T011-4749 4034, www.tigrehostel.com.ar. A lovely river house in the heart of Tigre itself, close to shops and the boat station. Stunning double (**C**) and triple bedrooms, with a cosy living room in which to while away the afternoons. Recommended.

Camping

C TAMET Tigre Delta, Río Luján y Abra Vieja, T011-4728 0396, www.tamet.com.ar. Clean, 3-ha park with hot showers, *hostería* doubles with bath also available (including breakfast). Table tennis, volleyball, canoes, restaurant and basic cooking facilities.

Isla Martín García *p117*
C Hostería Martín García, owned by
Cacciola. US$7 per person for hostel
accommodation with private bath. US$6 per
person with shared bathroom. For bungalow
rental, T0315-24546.

Camping
Martín García, T011-4728 10808.

Colonia del Sacramento *p119, map p118*
AL Radisson Colonia De Sacramento,
Washington Barbot 283, T+598 (0)52-
30460, www.radissoncolonia.com. Fantastic
location overlooking the quiet jetty. Stylish
restaurant with fabulous views over the river.
A Don Antonio Posada, Ituzaingó 232, T+598
(0)52-25344, www.posadadon antonio.com.
1870 building, buffet breakfast, a/c, TV,
garden, pool, internet, Wi-Fi, excellent.
A Esperanza, Gral Flores 237, T+598
(0)52- 22922, www.hotelesperanzaspa.
com. Charming, with sauna, heated pool
and treatments.
A Italiano, Intendente Suárez 105, T+598
(0)52-27878. With or without bath, good
restaurant, heated pool. Recommended.
A Plaza Mayor, del Comercio 111, T/F+598
(0)52-23193, www.posadaplazamayor.
com/Ingles. Lovely, English spoken.
A Posada del Angel, Washington Barbot 59,
T+598 (0)52-24602, www.posadadelangel.net.
Expect a warm welcome at this small hotel
with pool, set on a quiet street close to the
historic quarter.
A Posada del Gobernador, 18 de Julio 205,
T+598 (0)52-23018, www.delgobernador.com.
Breakfast included, charming. Recommended.
A Posada Manuel de Lobo, Ituzaingó 160,
T+598 (0)52-22463, www.posadamanuel
delobo.com. Built in 1850. Large rooms,
huge baths, parking, some smaller rooms,
nice breakfast area inside and out.

A Posada del Virrey, España 217, T+598
(0)52-22223, www.posadadelvirrey.com.
Large rooms, some with view over bay
(cheaper with small bathroom and no
balcony), with breakfast. Recommended.
A Royal, General Flores 340, T+598 (0)52-
22169, www.hotelroyalcolonia.com.
Shabby lobby but pleasant rooms, some
with Río de la Plata views, with breakfast,
comfortable, good restaurant, pool, noisy a/c
but recommended.
A-B Posada de la Flor, Ituzaingó 268, T+598
(0)52-30794, www.posada-delaflor.com. At
the quiet end of C Ituzaingó, next to the river
and to the Barrio Histórico, simply decorated
rooms on a charming patio and roof terrace
with river views.
C Hostal de los Poetas, Mangarelli 675,
T/F+598 (0)52-25457. With bath, quiet,
pleasant. Recommended but far from
the centre.
C Hotel Romi, Rivera 236, T+598 (0)52-
30456, www.hotelromi.com.uy. Central, all
rooms have private bathrooms. Parking.

Hostels
E pp El Viajero, Washington Barbot 164,
T+598 (0)52-22683, www.elviajero
colonia.com. Small, friendly hostel with
a/c and Wi-Fi. Some doubles (**B**).
E pp Hostel Colonial, General Flores
440, T+598 (0)52-30347, www.hihostels.
com. Central, but noisy hostel with free bike
hire and Wi-Fi. Some doubles (**D**).
F pp Español, Manuel Lobo 377, T+598
(0)52-30759. Good value with shared bath
in dorms, breakfast US$4, internet, kitchen.
Recommended.

Camping
Camping Municipal, Real de San Carlos,
T+598 (0)52-24444. US$5 per person.
Mini-*cabañas* (**C**), electric hook-ups, 100 m
from beach, hot showers, open all year, safe.
Recommended.

🍴 Eating

Tigre *p116*

🍴🍴-🍴 **Gato Blanco**, Río Capitán 80, T011-4728 0390, www.gatoblanco.com. 40-min trip by regular ferry from Tigre. Good international menu, as well as more traditional Argentine staples such as steak, pasta and pizza. Also has a bar and tea room. In elegant surroundings on terraces on the banks of the river. One of the delta's best.

🍴🍴-🍴 **Beixa Flor**, Arroyo Abra Viejo 148, T011-4728 2397, www.beixaflor.com.ar. Lovely setting with a private beach and great music. The food is all home-made.

Colonia del Sacramento *p119, map p118*

🍴🍴🍴 **Blanco y Negro**, Gen Flores 248, T+598 (0)52-22236, www.bynrestojazz.com.uy. Closed Tue and Wed. Set in historic brick building, smart, great range of meat dishes, live jazz every night. Cellar of local wines.

🍴🍴🍴 **Del Carmen**, Washington Barbot 283. T+598 (0)52-30460. Open from breakfast to dinner, fantastic views, great for evening drink. Recommended.

🍴🍴🍴 **Lo de Renata**, Flores 227, T+598 (0)52-31061. Open daily. Popular for its lunchtime buffet of meats and salads.

🍴🍴🍴 **Mesón de la Plaza**, Vasconcellos 153, T+598 (0)52-24807. 140-year-old house with a leafy courtyard, elegant dining, good traditional food.

🍴🍴🍴 **Viejo Barrio (VB)**, Vasconcellos 169, T+598 (0)52-25399. Closed Wed. Very good for home-made pastas and fish, renowned live shows.

🍴🍴🍴 **Yacht Club (Puerto de Yates)**, T+598 (0)52-31354. Ideal at sunset with wonderful view of the bay. Good fish.

🍴🍴🍴 **Arcoiris**, Av Gral Flores at Plaza 25 de Agosto. Very good ice cream.

🍴🍴 **Club Colonia**, Gen Flores 382, T+598 (0) 52-22189. Good value, frequented by locals.

🍴🍴 **El Drugstore**, Portugal 174, T+598 (0)52-25241. Hip, fusion food: Latin American, European, Japanese, creative varied menu, good salads and fresh vegetables. Music and show.

🍴🍴 **El Torreón**, end of Av Gen Flores. T+598 (0)52-31524. One of the best places to enjoy a sunset meal with views of the river. Also a café serving toasties and cakes.

🍴🍴 **La Amistad**, 18 de Julio 448. Good local grill.

🍴🍴 **La Bodeguita**, Del Comercio 167, T+598 (0)52-25329. Tue-Sun evenings and Sat-Sun lunch. Its terrace on the river is the main attraction of this lively pizza place that also serves good *chivitos* and pasta.

🍴🍴 **Lobo**, Del Comercio y De la Playa, T+598 (0) 52-29245. Modern interior, good range of salads, pastas and meat. Live music at weekends.

🍴🍴 **Mercosur**, Flores and Ituzaingó, T+598 (0)52-24200. Popular, varied dishes. Also café serving home-made cakes.

🍴🍴 **Parrillada El Portón**, Gral Flores 333. T+598 (0)52-25318. Best *parillada* in town. Small, relatively smart restaurant, good atmosphere. House speciality is offal.

🍴🍴 **Pulpería de los Faroles**, Misiones de los Tapes 101, T+598 (0)52-30271. Very inviting tables (candlelit at night) on the cobbled streets for a varied menu that includes tasty salads, seafood and local wines.

🍴🍴-🍴 **El Asador**, Ituzaingó 168. Good *parrillada* and pasta, nice atmosphere, value for money.

🛍 Shopping

Colonia del Sacramento *p119, map p118*
There's a large artist community, Uruguayan and International, with good galleries across town. There are leather shops on C Santa Rita, next to Yacht Club.

Afro, 18 de Julio 246. Candombe culture items from local black community, and percussion lessons.

Colonia Shopping, Av Roosevelt 458. Shopping mall on main road out of town (east) selling international fashion brands.

Eduardo Acosta, Paseo del Sol, Del Comercio 158. Decorative pottery by local artist.

El Almacén, Real 150. Creative gifts.

Oveja Negra, De la Playa 114. Recommended for woollen and leather clothes.

▲ Activities and tours

Tigre *p116*
Boat trips
See also Transport in Buenos Aires, page 108.
Catamarán Libertad, Puerto de Olivos.
At the weekends, longer trips (4½ hrs)
to the open Río de la Plata estuary.
Interisleña, Río Tigre, T011-4731 0261 and
Río Tur, Puerto de Frutos, T011-4731 0280.
Tourist catamarans, 5 services daily, 1- to
2-hr trips, US$3.50.

Colonia del Sacramento *p119, map p118*
City tours available with **Destino Viajes**,
General Flores 341, T+598 (0)52-25343,
destinoviajes@adinet.com.uy, or guided tours
with **Sacramento Tour**, Av Flores and Rivera,
T+598 (0)52 23148, sacratur@adinet.com.uy.
Asociación Guías de Colonia, T+598 (0)52-
22309/22796, asociacionguiascolonia@gmail.
com. Organizes walking tours (1 hr, US$5) in
the Barrio Histórico, starting daily 1100 and
1500, from tourist office next to Old Gate.

⊖ Transport

San Isidro *p114*
Taxi
Turismo York, T011-4743 0561, turismo
york@aol.com. Friendly and reliable taxi
company, cheaper than getting a Buenos
Aires company to come out to San Isidro.

Colonia del Sacramento *p119, map p118*
Book in advance for all sailings and flights
in summer, especially at weekends.

Air
For airport information, see page 119.
Flights to Aeroparque, **Buenos Aires**,
most days, generally quicker than hydrofoil.
Taxi to centre US$10.

Bus
To **Montevideo**, ½ hourly service, 2½ hrs,
US$9, COT and Tauril; to **Carmelo**, Mon-Sat,
4 per day, 1½ hrs (Tauriño), US$4
Chadre/Agencia Central.
  Bus company offices COT, Flores
432, T+598 (0)52-23121; Tauril, Flores and
Suárez; **Tauriño**, Flores 436.

Car hire
In bus terminal: **Avis**, T+598 (0)52-29842,
US$100 per day, **Hertz**, T+598 (0)52-29851,
US$90 per day. Thrifty by port, also at Flores
172, T+598 (0)52-22939, where there are
bicycles too (US$3 per hr), scooters (US$7
per hr) and golf buggies (US$15 per hr)
for hire, recommended as traffic is slow
and easy to navigate.

Ferry
For information on ferry transport, see
Buenos Aires, page 108.

Motorcycle and bicycle hire
Thrifty, Flores 172, T+598 (0)52-22939.
Rent bicycles, scooters, quadbikes and
golf buggies. Prices range from US$1.50
per hr (bicycle) to US$15 per hr (golf buggy).
Recommended. Traffic is slow and easy
to navigate.

⊙ Directory

Colonia del Sacramento *p119, map p118*
Currency exchange Cambio Dromer, Flores
350 and Suárez, T+598(0)52-22070, Mon-Fri
0900-2000, Sat 0900-1800, Sun 1000-1300 (also
outside the ferry dock, with car hire); **Cambio
Colonia** and **Banco de la República Oriental
del Uruguay** at the ferry port (dollars and
South American currencies); **HSBC**, Portugal
183, Mon-Fri 1300-1700, changes money,
and is located in a pretty colonial homestead.

Contents

Footprint features

Buenos Aires province

At a glance

○ **Getting around** Local bus and some short-distance trains. Hiring a car is recommended for visiting *estancias* and exploring the coast.

◉ **Time required** A long weekend is enough to visit one area.

☀ **Weather** The coastal areas can be pleasantly warm from Dec-Mar, but windy and cold the rest of the year. Inland, May-Aug is cold and can be unpleasant.

✖ **When not to go** The coast is popular with locals during Dec-Jan; you'll be lucky to find accommodation. May-Aug can be windy and cold but less crowded.

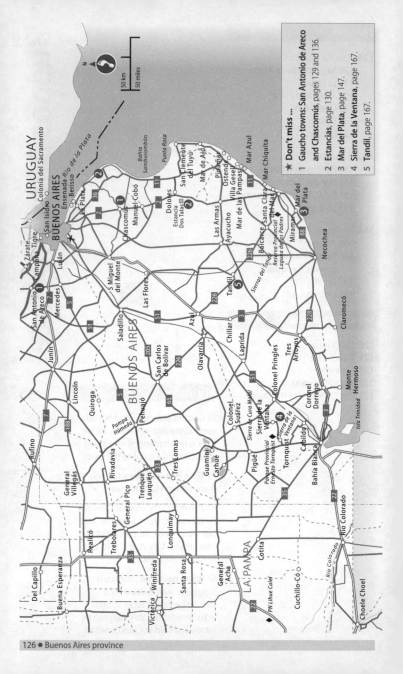

URUGUAY

Colonia del Sacramento

Don't miss ...

★ **Gaucho towns:** San Antonio de Areco and Chascomús, pages 129 and 136.

1 **Estancias**, page 130.

2 **Mar del Plata**, page 147.

3 **Sierra de la Ventana**, page 167.

4 **Tandil**, page 167.

BUENOS AIRES

LA PAMPA

The Pampas are the perfect antidote to the frenzied pace of Buenos Aires. These peaceful flatlands, stretching out in all directions towards dramatic mountains in the south and the unspoiled Atlantic coast to the east, are wonderful places for escape and relaxation within a few hours' drive of the capital.

Argentina's *estancias* (loosely translated as ranches) produce the superb beef that once made this country the breadbasket of the world, and staying in one is a quintessential part of Argentine life, complete with gauchos (cowboys) and *asados* (much more than a barbecue). Whether you choose a grand colonial mansion, or a simple working farm, you'll be welcomed as part of the family, and will gain a real insight into the culture, while enjoying the pleasure of life on the land. Ride your horse across the plains, and then tuck into a meal of succulent home-grown beef cooked on an open fire under the stars: an unforgettable experience. Gauchos are still very much part of Argentine rural life and you can enjoy their music and fine horsemanship in quaint Pampas towns such as San Antonio de Areco and Chascomús, virtually unchanged since the early 1900s.

The Atlantic beaches are a great way to cool down in the summer. Avoid the tawdry casinos of famous Mar del Plata and head instead for the chic resorts of Mar de los Pampas and Cariló, or escape to Pinamar where in summer you can party with the young *Porteños* of Buenos Aires. Two of the oldest mountain ranges in the world pop up from the flat pampas at Tandil and Sierra de la Ventana, attracting climbers, hikers and anyone looking for a relaxing weekend in beautiful countryside. For information on the region, see www.turismo.gba.gov.ar (in English).

The Pampas

The Pampas are home to one of the most enduring images of Argentina: the gaucho on horseback, roaming the plains. All over the Pampas there are quiet, unspoiled towns where gaucho culture is still very much alive. Two impeccably preserved gaucho towns very much worth visiting are San Antonio de Areco and Chascomús. The former is home to expert craftsmen, working silver and leather in the traditional gaucho way. Near here there are many of the finest and most historical estancias: two are recommended, El Ombú and La Bamba. Further southeast, Chascomús is similarly charming, a traditional cowboy town come to life, with pristine examples of 1870s architecture, a good museum of the Pampas and gauchos, and a lake for watersports in summer. There are fine estancias here too: friendly, relaxed La Fé, and best of all, Dos Talas, with its extraordinary history and beautiful grounds. Further inland, there are three more excellent estancias, La Concepción, Santa Rita, and the Loire chateau-style La Candelaria. Whether you stay the night or just visit for an afternoon to eat lunch and ride, you'll get an unforgettable taste of life on the land. The Pampas are also rich in wildlife, and on lakes and lagunas you're likely to spot Chilean flamingos and herons, maguari storks, white-faced ibis and black-necked swans. Ostrich-like greater rheas can also be seen in many parts. For more information, see www.turismolapampa.gov.ar (in Spanish). ▶▶ *For listings, see pages 137-141.*

Ins and outs

Getting around It's easy to get around the province with a network of buses to and from Buenos Aires, and between towns. Train lines operate to Mar del Plata, and to Chascomús and Tandil, stopping at many coastal towns on the way. You'll need to hire a car to reach the more remote *estancias*, and there are good, fast toll roads radiating out from the capital to Mar del Plata, via Chascomús, San Antonio de Areco and Lobos. Check out www.chascomus.com.ar, www.lobos.gov.ar, www.sanantoniodeareco.com/turismo, and www.turismo.gba.gov.ar; www.turismo.gov.ar also has links to all these small towns. ▶▶ *For further details, see Transport, page 141.*

Background

Travelling through these calm lands you wouldn't think they'd had such a violent past; but these are the rich fertile plains that justified conquering the indigenous people in the bloody 19th-century Campaign of the Desert (see box, page 135). Once the Spanish newcomers had gained control, their produce made Argentina the 'breadbasket of the world', and the sixth richest nation on Earth, exporting beef, lamb, wheat and wool when a growing Europe demanded cheap food and clothing. When you see these huge, perfect wheat fields, and superbly healthy Aberdeen Angus cattle roaming vast plains, you might wonder how a country with such riches can possibly have suffered an economic crisis. It's one of the great enigmas of Argentina. To get an idea of Argentina's former wealth, visit an *estancia* with history, like Dos Talas, and ask their owners what went wrong. Some blame Perón, and now the Kirchners, for taxing the farmers too harshly, or Menem for resorting to desperate measures to keep up with the US dollar by selling the nationalized industries. Farmers complain the government imposes impossible taxes for those who produce from the land. The fields of Buenos Aires province provide more than half of Argentina's cereal production, and over a third of her livestock, but many *estancia* owners have had to turn to tourism in order to maintain the homes built by their ancestors in more affluent times. Still, staying in an *estancia* is a rare privilege, to be wholeheartedly enjoyed.

Gaucho life

The gaucho is the cowboy of Argentina, found all over the country, and one of Argentina's most important cultural icons. Gauchos emerged as a distinct social group in the early 18th century. Brought over by the Spanish to tend cattle, they combined their Moorish roots with Argentine Criollo stock, adopting aspects of the indigenous peoples' lifestyle, but creating their own particular style and dress. The gaucho lived on horseback, dressing in a poncho, *bombachas* (baggy trousers) held up by a *tirador* (broad leather belt) and home-made boots with leather spurs. He was armed with a *facón* or large knife, and *boleadoras*, a lasso made from three stones tied with leather thongs, which when expertly thrown would wrap around the legs of animals to bring them swiftly to the ground. Gauchos roamed the Pampas, hunting the seemingly inexhaustible herds of wild cattle and horses in the long period before fencing protected private property. The gaucho's wild reputation derived from his resistance to government officials who tried to exert their control by the use of anti-vagrancy laws and military conscription. Much of the urban population of the time regarded the gaucho as a savage, on a par with the 'indians'.

The gaucho's lifestyle was doomed in the advent of railways, fencing and the redistribution of land that followed the massacre of indigenous peoples. Increasingly the term gaucho came to mean an *estancia* worker who made a living on horseback tending cattle. As the real gaucho disappeared from the Pampas, he became a major subject of Argentine folklore and literature, most famously in José Hernández' epic poem of 1872, *Martín Fierro*, and in Güiraldes' later novel *Don Segundo Sombra*. But you can still see gauchos in their traditional dress at work today in any *estancia*. Visit Mataderos, Chascomús, or San Antonio de Areco for displays of traditional gaucho horsemanship, music, silversmithing and leatherwork.

San Antonio de Areco → *For listings, see pages 137-141. Colour map 4, B5.*
Phone code 02326. Population 18,000.

San Antonio de Areco, 113 km northwest of Buenos Aires, is *the* original gaucho town and makes a perfect escape from the capital. Built in the late 19th century, much of its charm lies in the authenticity of its crumbling buildings surrounding an atmospheric plaza filled with palms and plane trees, and the streets lined with orange trees. The attractive *costanera* along the riverbank is a great place to swim and picnic. There are several *estancias* nearby, and the town itself has several historical *boliches* (combined bar and provisions stores), where you can lap up the atmosphere, listen to live music and meet locals. Gaucho traditions are on display in the many weekend activities, and the town's craftsmen produce wonderful silverwork, textiles and traditional worked leather handicrafts of the highest quality. Annual events include the *pato* games in January, a poncho parade in February and the **Fiesta Criolla** in March. Most important of all, however, is the **Day of Tradition**, in the second week of November (book accommodation in advance). For more information, see Festivals and events, page 140. The **tourist information centre** ① *Parque San Martín, Zerboni and Arellano, T02326-453165, www.sanantoniodeareco.com*, has friendly, helpful, English-speaking staff who can advise

Estancias

Argentina's *estancias* vary enormously from ostentatious mansions to simple colonial-style ranches that still work as cattle farms. Many now open their doors to tourists as paying guests, enabling you to experience traditional Argentine rural life. There are two main types of *estancia*: those that function as rural hotels, and those where you're welcomed as a guest of the family. The latter are particularly recommended as a great way to meet Argentine people. You dine with the owners and they'll often tell you about their family's history and talk about life on the farm, turning a tourist experience into a meeting of friends. Some *estancias* offer splendid rooms filled with family antiques. Others are simple affairs where you'll stay in an old farmhouse, and the focus is on peace and quiet. They can be the perfect place to retreat and unwind for a few days or to try an activity such as horse riding or birdwatching. Whichever kind you choose, a good *estancia* will give you an unparalleled taste of traditional hospitality: welcoming strangers is one of the things Argentines do best.

Activities These depend on the *estancia*, but almost all provide horse riding, which is highly recommended even if you've no experience. Galloping across the plains on a *criollo* horse has to be one of the biggest thrills of visiting the country. If you're a beginner, let your hosts know beforehand so that they can arrange for you to ride an especially docile creature. The horse-shy might be offered a ride in a *sulky*, the traditional open horse-drawn carriage, more relaxing but just as much fun. Cattle mustering, meanwhile, may sound daunting but is the best way to get

into life on the *campo*. You'll help your hosts move cattle while sitting astride your trusty steed. Gauchos will be on hand to guide you and by the end of the day you'll be whooping and hollering with the best of them.

Prices Usually around US$180/250 per person per night for the most luxurious, to US$65 for the simpler places, but bear in mind that all meals, and often drinks, as well as activities such as horse riding are also included. If this is outside your budget, consider coming for a day visit (*día de campo*), which usually costs around US$60 per person.

Access As *estancias* are inevitably located in the country you'll need to hire a car, although many will pick you up from the nearest town if you don't have one. If you're visiting for a few days ask your hosts to arrange a *remise* taxi; some *estancias* will arrange transfers on request. There are many *estancias* within easy access of Ezeiza International Airport in Buenos Aires, so it can be an ideal way to relax after a long flight at the start of your trip, or to spend your last couple of nights, allowing you to return home feeling refreshed and with vivid memories of Argentine hospitality.

Recommended *estancias* include, **Dos Talas** (pages 137 and 139), **Santa Rita** (page 138), **Juan Gerónimo** (page 138), **Casa de Campo La China** (page 138), **Palantelén** (page 154), **Ave María** (page 169) and **Siempre Verde** (page 170). A few useful websites are: www.estanciasargentinas.com; www.caminodelgaucho.com.ar and www.raturestancias.com.ar.

on gaucho activities in the town, as well as accommodation and transport. Other useful websites include www.pagosdeareco.com.ar and www.areco.mun.gba.gov.ar.

The **Museo Gauchesco Ricardo Güiraldes** ① *Camino Güiraldes, Wed-Mon 1100-1700, US$1, guided visits Sat, Sun 1230 and 1530,* is a replica of a typical *estancia* of the late 19th century, and houses impressive gaucho artefacts and displays on the life of the writer, who was a sophisticated member of Parisian literary circles and an Argentine nationalist who romanticized gaucho life. Güiraldes spent much of his early life on **Estancia La Porteña**, 8 km from San Antonio, and settled there to write his best-known book, *Don Segundo Sombra* (1926), which was set in San Antonio. The *estancia* and sights in the town, such as the old bridge and the Pulpería La Blanqueada (at the entrance to the museum), became famous through its pages.

Superb gaucho silverwork is for sale at the workshop and **Centro Cultural y Museo Taller Draghi** ① *Lavalle 387, T02326-454219, daily 1000-1230, 1530-1900, US$1.70 for a guided visit.* You can get a further idea of the life of the gauchos at the **Mueso Las Lilas** ① *Moreno 279, T02326 456425, www.museolaslilas.org, Thu-Sun 1000-2000 (1800 in winter) US$5,* which houses a collection of paintings by famous Argentine artist Florencio Molina Campos, who dedicated his life to the display of the gaucho way of life. Excellent chocolates are made at **La Olla de Cobre** ① *Matheu 433, T02326-453105, www.laollade cobre.com.ar* , with a charming little café for drinking chocolate and trying the most amazing home-made *alfajores.* There is a large park, **Parque San Martín**, spanning the river to the north of the town near the tourist information centre. While you're here, you should visit one of the old traditional bars, or *pulperías,* many of which have been lovingly restored to recreate the 1900s ambience, and are brought to life by a genuine local clientele every night. Try **La Vieja Sodería**, on General Paz and Bolívar, or **El Almacén de Ramos Generales Parrilla**, at Zapiola 143. Also at Alsina 66 is the city museum, **Centro Cultural y Museo Usina Vieja** ① *Tue-Sun 1100-1700, US$50.* There are ATMs on the plaza, and at the country club you can play golf or watch a polo match in restful surroundings; ask at the tourist office for directions.

Some of the province's finest *estancias* are within easy reach of San Antonio for day visits, offering an *asado* lunch, horse riding and other activities. One such place is **La Cinacina** ① *T02326-452045, www.lacinacina.com.ar,* which charges US$65 per person for a day visit. For a list of those offering accommodation, see Sleeping, page 137.

La Plata → *For listings, see pages 137-141. Colour map 4, B6.*

The capital of Buenos Aires province is La Plata, a modern university city with a lively student population, and consequently good nightlife, with lots of restaurants and bars. There's no particular reason to visit as a tourist, but if you're passing through or on a day trip from Buenos Aires (only 60 minutes by bus), you'll appreciate the broad avenues, leafy plazas and elaborate public buildings. It's a young and vibrant place, where football and rugby are major passions. At the east of the city there's a beautiful park, **Paseo del Bosque**, popular at weekends with families for *asados,* with its famous science museum, the magnificent but slightly run-down **Museo de Ciencias Naturales**.

Ins and outs → *Phone code 0221. Population 642,000.*

Getting there La Plata is 56 km southeast of Buenos Aires, 45 minutes by car. There are frequent trains, taking one hour 10 minutes. Buses from Buenos Aires leave every 30 minutes and take about 1½ hours. They leave the Retiro bus terminal day and night,

Argentine steak

So how did Argentina come to be synonymous with great beef? Cattle certainly aren't indigenous to the Pampas. But after Juan de Garay's expedition in 1580 brought cattle from Paraguay, the animals roamed wild on the fertile plains, reproducing so quickly that by the time the Spanish returned in 1780, there were 40 million of them. But by then, local indigenous groups were making a roaring trade, driving herds of cattle through the Andean passes to sell in southern Chile. Gauchos, meanwhile, were hunting cattle with the use of *boleadoras* (a lasso with three stone balls), and slaughtering them by the thousand for their hides alone, sometimes leaving the meat to rot. When salting plants – *saladeros* – arrived in 1810, the hides were transported to Europe, together with tallow for candles. The meat was turned into *charqui*, cut into strips, dried and salted, and sold to feed slaves in Brazil and Cuba. It was only with the invention of refrigerated ships that Argentina's produce was exported to meet the growing demand for beef in an expanding Europe. Cattle farmers introduced new breeds to replace the scrawny Pampas cattle, and sowed alfalfa as richer fodder than pampas grasses. Today Herefords and Aberdeen Angus are still bred for meat.

And why is Argentine beef so good? Because these cows are healthy! With such vast expanses of land to roam, the cattle burn off any fat, are well-toned and lean: the meat is even high in Omega 3. So head straight for the best *parrilla* in town, and, unless you're vegetarian, try a few different cuts. Better still, stay at an *estancia* to try home-reared beef cooked on the *asado*, the traditional way over an open wood fire. Delicious. A word of warning: learn some of the names for the parts of a cow so you don't end up eating hoof, intestines or glands. See the menu reader, page 707.

and from Plaza Constitución (less recommended), daytime only. If you arrive on an overnight bus at 0600, the *confitería* opposite the **bus terminal** (T0221-427 3186) is safe and will be open. Long-distance buses arrive here from all major cities. The terminal is at Calle 4 and Diagonal 74, and a taxi into the central area costs US$5.

Getting around The city is easy to get around, but note that the streets have numbers, rather than names, and diagonal streets cross the entire city, which can be very confusing. When you approach one of these crossroads with six choices, make sure you remember the number of the street you're on. There's an efficient network of buses all over the city, and taxis are safe, cheap and plentiful.

Tourist information The main tourist office is **Dirección de Turismo** ⓘ *Palacio Campodónico, Diag 79 between 5 and 56, Mon-Fri 1000-1800, T0221-422 9764, www.cultura.laplata.gov.ar, www.laplata.gov.ar*. There are also small **tourist booths** at Pasaje Dardo Rocha ⓘ *on 50 between 6 and 7, T0221-427 1535, daily 1000-1700*, and in the **bus terminal** ⓘ *on 42 between 3 and 4, Mon-Fri 0930-1330*. The provincial tourism website is www.turismo.gba.gov.ar (in English). A helpful office for exploring *estancias*, stables and for visiting craftsmen in the Pampas is **Camino del Gaucho** ⓘ *57 No 393, T0221-425 7482, www.caminodelgaucho.com.ar*. The English-speaking staff are extremely informative and will help you arrange your own itinerary.

Sights

The major public buildings are centred around two parallel north-south streets, 51 and 53, which run north from the Plaza Moreno to the Plaza San Martín, and from there to the Paseo del Bosque at the north of the city centre. On the west side of Plaza Moreno is the

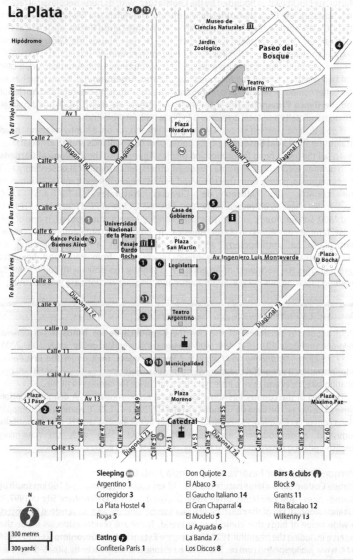

La Plata

To 9 12

Museo de
Ciencias Naturales

Hipódromo

Jardin
Zoológico

Paseo del
Bosque

4

Teatro
Martin Fierro

Av 1

Calle 2

Diagonal 80

Diagonal 77

Plaza
Rivadavia   5

Calle 3

8

Pol

Diagonal 78

Diagonal 79

Calle 4

Calle 5

Casa de
Gobierno

5

Calle 6

Universidad
Nacional
de la Plata

3

i

To El Viejo Almacén

To Bus Terminal

To Buenos Aires

Banco Pcia de
Buenos Aires

Pasaje
Dardo
Rocha

Plaza
San Martin

Plaza
D Bocha

Av 7

1

6

Legislatura

Av Ingeniero Luis Monteverde

7

Calle 8

Diagonal 77

Calle 9

11

Calle 10

3

Teatro
Argentino

Diagonal 73

Calle 11

Calle 12

14 13

Municipalidad

Plaza
3 J Paso

Av 13

Calle 49

Plaza
Moreno

Plaza
Maximo Paz

Calle 14

2

Calle 45

Calle 46

Calle 47

Calle 48

Diagonal 73

Calle 50

Av 51

Diagonal 74

Catedral

Av 53

Calle 54

Diagonal 74

Calle 55

Calle 56

Calle 57

Calle 58

Calle 59

Av 60

Calle 15

N

300 metres

300 yards

Sleeping
Argentino 1
Corregidor 3
La Plata Hostel 4
Roga 5

Eating
Confitería París 1

Don Quijote 2
El Abaco 3
El Gaucho Italiano 14
El Gran Chaparral 4
El Modelo 5
La Aguada 6
La Banda 7
Los Discos 8

Bars & clubs
Block 9
Grants 11
Rita Bacalao 12
Wilkenny 13

enormous brick neo-Gothic **cathedral** ① *daily 0900-1300, 1500-1800*, built between 1885 and 1936, and inspired by Cologne and Amiens. It has a beautiful and inspiring inside, and is definitely worth a visit. Opposite is the large, white building of the **Muncipalidad**, in German Renaissance style, with a striking clock tower. Plaza San Martín, six blocks east, is bounded by the **Legislature**, with its huge neoclassical façade and, opposite, the **Casa de Gobierno** is a mixture of French and Flemish Renaissance styles. On the north side of the plaza is the lovely **Pasaje Dardo Rocha**, designed as the main railway station in Italian Renaissance style. It now houses the **Centro Cultural** ① *Calle No 50 between 6 and 7, T0221-427 1843, gallery Mon-Fri 1000-1300, 1500-1800, Sat and Sun 1500-1800, free*, with a gallery of contemporary Latin American art, a café and two theatres. East of the Municipalidad, **Teatro Argentino** has its own orchestra and ballet company. Nearby on streets 6 and 7 are the imposing **Universidad Nacional** and the **Banco Provincial**. The main shopping streets are 8 and 12. A good market selling handicrafts and local *artesania* is in Plaza Italia at weekends.

If you do find yourself in La Plata at the weekend, or on a sunny evening, head straight for **Paseo del Bosque**, a pretty public park of woodlands and an artificial lake, where all the locals head for *asados* and picnics. There's also the **Zoological Gardens** with giraffes, elephants and pumas amongst others, an astronomical observatory and the Hipodromo, dating from the 1930s and one of the most important racecourses in the country. The **Museo de Ciencias Naturales** ① *T011-425 7744, www.fcnym.unlp.edu.ar/ museo, daily 1000-1800, US$2, free guided tours, Mon-Fri 1400 and 1600, Sat-Sun hourly, in Spanish and in English (phone first to request)*, is one of the most famous museums in Latin America. It houses an outstanding collection, particularly on anthropology and archaeology, with a huge collection of pre-Columbian artefacts including pre-Incan ceramics from Peru, and beautiful ceramics from the northwest of Argentina. It is slightly run-down with some exhibits needing replacing but the preserved animal and dinosaur sections are worth visiting.

Around La Plata → *For listings, see pages 137-141.*

Eight kilometres northwest of the city, the **República de los Niños** ① *Col General Belgrano and Calle 501, T011-484 1409, www.republica.laplata.gov.ar, daily 1000-2200, US$1, children free, parking US$1.30*, is Eva Perón's legacy, built under the first Perón administration, a delightful children's village, with scaled-down castles, oriental palaces, boating lake, cafés and even a little train. It's a fun place for families to picnic.

This area of the country has some lovely rural accommodation. A delightful option close to La Plata is the **Casa de Campo La China** ① *T0221-421 2931, www.casadecampola china.com.ar*, a charming 1930s adobe house set in eucalyptus woods, with beautifully furnished accommodation and far-reaching views. Stay with the charming English-speaking family, or visit for the day, ride horses and enjoy carriage rides.

Parque Costero Sur Reserve and Estancia Juan Gerónimo
Parque Costero Sur is a large nature reserve 110 km south of La Plata, and 160 km south of Buenos Aires – just two hours' drive away. Declared a UNESCO Biosphere Site in 1997, it extends along 70 km of the coastline of Bahía Samborombón, and was created to protect a wide range of birds that come here to breed. There are several *estancias* inside the reserve including the beautiful 1920s Tudor-style **Estancia Juan Gerónimo** ① *T0221-481 414, www.juangeronimo.com.ar*. The 4000-ha *estancia* is magnificently situated right on

The Conquest of the Desert

Until the 1870s, the Pampas, and indeed most of Argentina, was inhabited by indigenous tribes. After independence, President Rosas (see Background, page 671) launched the first attempt to claim territory in Buenos Aires province in his 1833 Campaign of the Desert. But in the 1870s, pressure grew for a campaign to defeat the indigenous people, since the withdrawal of Argentine troops to fight in the War of Triple Alliance had led to a series of increasingly audacious raids by *malones*, the indigenous armies. War minister Alsina planned a series of forts and ramparts to contain the indigenous peoples, and defend the territory won from them. But his successor General Julio Roca found these plans too defensive, and called for a war of extermination, aiming to make the whole of Patagonia available for settlement. Roca's Conquest of the Desert was launched in 1879, with 8000 troops in five divisions, one of them led by Roca himself. Five important indigenous chiefs were captured, along with 1300 warriors. A further 2300 were killed or wounded. Roca's view was that 'it is a law of human nature that the Indian succumb to the impact of civilized man'. He destroyed villages and forced the inhabitants to choose between exile in Chile, or life in a reservation. After the campaign,

mountain passes to Chile were closed, and any remaining indigenous groups were cruelly forced onto reservations.

Although Roca claimed victory in the Conquest of the Desert as a personal triumph, he was aided by technological advances: the telegraph gave commanders intelligence reports to offset the indigenous peoples' knowledge of the terrain and enabled them to co-ordinate their efforts. Railways moved troops swiftly, and Remington repeating rifles enabled any one soldier to take on five indigenous people and murder them all.

Roca was hailed as a hero, elected president in 1880, and dominated Argentine politics until his death in 1904. The land he conquered was handed out mainly to Roca's friends, since the campaign had been funded by mortgaging plots in advance, with bonds worth 25,000 acres being bought by only 500 people. Argentina has yet to come to terms with this shameful part of its history. But you can see that most statues of Roca throughout the country have been defaced with red paint symbolizing the blood he spilt. There is no attempt made by the authorities to stop this. In Buenos Aires the statue of Roca is on the corner of Perú and Roca, and it is covered in graffiti which is neither removed nor cleaned, unlike other public monuments.

the coast, and from here you can enjoy walking or horse riding in total peace and quiet – you can ride for three days here without ever repeating a route. The *estancia* is more of a village than a house, with a collection of Tudor-style buildings in the lovely grounds, including a tea house, a little cabin, stables and a rural school. The main house has a wonderful old library with an extensive collection of books on pre-Columbian culture, as well as literature in French, English and German. Its 11 guest bedrooms are beautifully decorated but best of all is the warm welcome you'll receive from the relaxed owner, Florencia Molinuevo. As well as horse riding along the coast, dunes and pampas, there's superb birdwatching and opportunities for swimming.

Chascomús → *For listings, see pages 137-141. Colour map 4, B6.*

This quaint historical town, 126 km south of Buenos Aires, is worth visiting to enjoy the vibrant combination of gaucho culture and fine 19th-century architecture, creating an atmosphere of colonial refinement with a Wild West feel. Chascomús was founded in 1779, when a fort was built as protection against the indigenous tribes. In 1839, it was the site of the Battle of the Libres del Sur (the Free of the South), and its streets are full of well-preserved buildings dating from the mid-1800s, and lined with mature trees. Despite the strong historical significance, the town has a lively feel and its position along the eastern edge of the huge Laguna Chascomús gives it an attractive *costanera*, which comes to life in summer. The **tourist office** ① *Av Costanera España y Espigón de Pesca, T02241-430405, www.chascomus.com.ar, and www.chascomus.net, daily 0900-1900*, is four blocks from the main avenue, Las Astras. You can take a boat out on the *laguna*, or head to a couple of fine *estancias* nearby.

Sights → *Phone code 02241. Population 40,000.*

Around the quiet Plaza Independencia are the fudge-coloured colonial-style **Palacio Municipal** and **Iglesia Catedral**. Southeast of the plaza is the extraordinary **Capilla de los Negros** (1862) ① *daily 1000-1200, 1700-1900*, a small brick chapel with earth floor, built as a place of worship for African slaves who were bought by wealthy families in the early 1800s; it's an atmospheric place that still holds the slaves' offerings. A highly recommended museum for an insight into gaucho culture is the **Museo Pampeano** ① *Av Lastra and Muñiz, T02241-425110, www.chascomus.com.ar/museo_pampeano2.php, daily 0900-1500, US$0.50*, which has lots of information on gaucho traditions, fabulous maps of the Spanish conquest, furniture and all the evident wealth of the early pioneers.

To the south of the town lies the **Laguna Chascomús**, one of a chain of seven connected lakes; the *costanera* is a pleasant place to stroll, you can sail and windsurf in the summer, and there are frequent regattas. It's also an important breeding site for *pejerrey* fish, with amateur fishing competitions held from November to March. The delightful *estancia* **La Fe** ① *www.estancialafe.com*, is nearby.

Dolores → *For listings, see pages 137-141. Colour map 4, C6. Phone code 02245. Population 30,000.*

Dolores is a pretty, sleepy little town, 204 km south of Buenos Aires. Founded in 1818, it was the first town in independent Argentina, and its attractive old buildings would be perfect as a film set for a 19th-century drama. There's an interesting little museum, **Museo Libres del Sur** ① *Parque Libres del Sur, daily 1000-1700*, with good displays on local history, in particular about the Campaign of the Desert and the subsequent revolt against Rosas. It also contains lots of gaucho silver, plaited leather *tableros*, branding irons and a huge cart from 1868. There's a charming plaza at the heart of the town, with a central obelisk and impressive classical-style church, the **Iglesia Nuestra Señora de Dolores**. In mid- to late February, the **Fiesta de la Guitarra** is held, with performances from internationally famous musicians, dancing and processions. This is a good time to visit, but book ahead. For further information, contact the **tourist office** ① *T02245-442432, www.dolores.gov.ar*. The railway station is 15 minutes' walk from the centre.

Estancia Dos Talas

The main reason to visit Dolores is its proximity to one of the oldest and most beautiful *estancias* in the Pampas, **Dos Talas** ① *10 km south of Dolores, 2 hrs' drive from Buenos Aires, T02245-443020, www.dostalas.com.ar.* The fabulously elegant house is set in grand parkland designed by Charles Thays, with a lovely chapel copied from Notre Dame de Passy and a fascinating history. Come for the day or, even better, stay. You'll be warmly welcomed by the owners, who are descendants of the *estancia*'s original owner, Pedro Luro. This beautifully decorated home is one of Argentina's really special places to stay.

◉ The Pampas listings

For Sleeping and Eating price codes and other relevant information, see Essentials pages 30-36.

◉ Sleeping

San Antonio de Areco *p129*
AL Patio de Moreno, Moreno 251, T02326-455197, www.patiodemoreno.com. Stunning modern rooms, in the middle of town, set in a wonderfully old building. Small pool, personal service and a cosy living room.
A Antigua Casona, Segunda Sombra 495, T02326-456600, www.antiguacasona.com. Charmingly restored 1897 house with 5 rooms opening onto a delightful patio and exuberant garden, very relaxing.
A Paradores Draghi, Lavalle 385. T02326-455 583, www.paradoresdraghi.com.ar. Beautifully renovated old colonial building, with traditional-style rooms, very comfortable, with kitchen and bathroom. Recommended.
B San Carlos, Zerboni and Zapiola, T02326-453106, www.hotel-sancarlos.com.ar. Simple and friendly hotel near the river with a small pool and only a short walk to the main plaza.
B-C Hostal de Areco, Zapiola 25, T02326-456 118, www.hostaldeareco.com.ar. Popular, with a warm welcome, very good value.
C Los Abuelos, Zerboni and Zapiola, T02326-456390. Neat hotel with well-equipped rooms and a small pool. Simple, modern-ish but comfortable.
C Posada del Ceibo, Irigoyen and Smith, T02326-454614, www.laposadadel ceibo.com.ar. Old-fashioned family place that looks like a bit like a 1950s motel. Basic rooms and a pool in the garden.

Estancias
Some of the province's finest *estancias* are within easy reach of San Antonio for day visits but it's best to stay overnight to appreciate the peace and beauty of these historical places. The following are recommended:
LL El Ombú, T02326-492080 (T011-4710 2795, office in Buenos Aires), Mon-Fri, www.estanciaelombu.com. A fine Italian neoclassical house with magnificent terrace, dating from 1890, with comfortable old-fashioned bedrooms, furnished with antiques. Offers horse riding and a warm welcome from English-speaking owners, the Boelcke family. The price includes meals, drinks and activities, but not transfer. *Día de Campo* (day on the ranch), US$70 per person. Taxi from Ezeiza US$115, from Buenos Aires centre or internal airport Aeroparque, US$90.
LL-L Estancia La Porteña, Ruta 8, Km 110, T011-155626 7347, www.laporteniadeareco. com. One of Argentina's most famous *estancias* which was once host to writers Ricardo Güiraldes and Antoine de Saint Exupéry. Stunning traditional building built in 1822, original features, large grounds with 150-year-old trees and working horses. There are 3 lovely houses where you can stay, including huge banquets of food (lots of meat), or you can spend a day here, enjoying the grounds.
LL-L La Bamba, T02326-456293 (T011-47321 269, office in Buenos Aires), www.la-bamba.com.ar. A plum-coloured, colonial-style building dating from 1830 with a fascinating history. It was originally a post-house on the Camino Royal (royal

road) connecting Buenos Aires with the north of the country. It was the first *estancia* to open to guests in the 1930s, and has attracted many famous visitors since then. It's set in beautiful parkland, with charming rooms and welcoming English-speaking owners, the Aldao family, who have lived here for generations. It's very relaxing, with only 5 rooms and highly recommended. Serves superb meals.

L El Rosario de Areco, T02326-451000, www.rosariodeareco.com.ar. A 19th-century house in lovely parkland, this is a traditional *estancia* for breeding polo ponies, and the children of the owners are keen polo players. Not surprisingly, there's excellent horse riding here, as well as a high standard of accommodation in attractive rooms, and superb food. Also 2 swimming pools.

A Santa Rita, near Lobos, 120 km west of Buenos Aires, T02227-495026, www.santa-rita.com.ar. Spectacular building in gorgeous lakeside setting where the Nüdemberg family make you welcome in their eccentric, late 18th-century home. Great fun, US$47 per person for a day visit. Highly recommended.

Camping
Auto-camping La Porteña, 12 km from town on the **Güiraldes Estancia**, good earth access roads. A beautiful spot with many *parrilladas* at picnic spots along the bank of the Río Areco.

Club River Plate, Av del Valle and Alvear, T02326-452744. The best of 3 sites in the park by the river. It's an attractive sports club offering shady sites with all facilities, a pool and sports of all kinds, US$6 per tent.

La Plata *p131, map p133*
Most hotels here are business-orientated.
A Hotel Argentino, Calle 46, No 536, between 5 and 6, T0221-423 4111, www.hotelargentino.com. Comfortable and very central, with bright rooms, all with bath and floral sheets. Also has apartments to rent.
A Hotel Corregidor, Calle 6, No1026, between 53 and 54, T0221-425 6800,

www.hotelcorregidor.com.ar. An upmarket, modern business hotel, with well-furnished rooms with bath, pleasant public rooms. Good value.
C Hotel Roga, Calle 54, No334, between 1 and 2, T0221-421 9553, www.hotelroga.com.ar. Basic, clean rooms, on a quiet street a short walk from the main plazas.

Hostels
F pp La Plata Hostel, Calle 50 No1066, T0221-457 1424, www.laplata-hostel.com.ar. Only 2 blocks from the cathedral, this hostel is well organized and set in a lovely turn-of-the-century house. High ceilings, original doors and a small garden to relax in. Simple but comfortable dorms.

Around La Plata *p134*
Estancias
L Estancia Juan Gerónimo, T0221-481414, www.juangeronimo.com.ar. 170 km south of Buenos Aires, 2 hrs' drive. The perfect place to relax in really elegant accommodation, this is a beautiful Tudor-style house right on the shore of the Río de la Plata, set in its own nature reserve, with 3238 ha of beach, dunes, forest and pampas to explore. You'll be personally welcomed by the charming owner Florencia and her family, who will take you riding or birdwatching, and share with you the *estancia*'s interesting history. Wonderful riding and food. Full board, all meals and activities included. English and French spoken. Day visit US$65. See also page 134.
AL-A Casa de Campo La China, 60 km from La Plata on R11, T0221-421 2931, www.casadecampolachina.com.ar. Beautifully decorated, spacious rooms off an open gallery, with great views. Day rates available. Charming hosts speak perfect English. Delicious food. Highly recommended.

Chascomús *p136*
There are a few very reasonably priced places to stay in town with more upmarket

accommodation to be found in the apart hotels and *cabañas* near the lake shore. See www.chascomus.com.ar for a complete list.
A Mi EspacioSur, Ayacucho 640, T02241-431786, www.miespaciosur.com.ar. Modern hotel, with clean doubles and triples. Large pool, and each room leads out onto a deck. Much cheaper during the week (**B**).
A Noble Blanco, Mazzini 130, T02241 436 3235, www.robleblanco.com.ar. By far the best place to stay in town. Modern comfortable rooms, a large heated pool with attractive deck and welcoming common areas, all in a refurbished 100-year-old house. Also a spa offering massages, sauna and treatments. Recommended.
B Chascomus, Lastra 367, T02241-422968, www.chascomus.com.ar. Stylish, turn-of-the-century public rooms and lovely terrace, this is an atmospheric and welcoming place. Breakfast is included and the staff are friendly.
C El Mirador, Belgrano 485, T02241-422273. An attractively renovated old building, with simple rooms but lovely original details in the public rooms. Spotlessly clean and simple.

Estancias

LL Estancia La Fe, R2, Km 116, T02241-155 42095, www.estancialafe.com.ar. A charming and typical place to come for a few days to get a feel for life on the land. Activities include horse riding, riding in carriages and walking in the grounds. Simple, comfortable rooms, wide views from the grounds, great *asado*.
LL Haras La Viviana, 45 km from Chascomús, T011-4702 9633, www.laviviana.com.ar. Perfect for horse riding as fine polo ponies are bred here. Tiny cabins in gardens by a huge *laguna* where you can kayak or fish. Very peaceful, wonderful welcome from the lady novelist owner who speaks fluent English. Can arrange collection from Chascomús.
AL La Horqueta, 3 km from Chascomús on R20, T011-4777 0150, www.lahorqueta.com. An 1898 Tudor-style mansion, lovely grounds with a *laguna* for fishing, horse riding, bikes to borrow. It's a good place for children, with

safe gardens to explore. 9 comfortable, lovely rooms, food is nothing special.

Camping

There are 7 sites all with good facilities: **Monte Corti** is closest, 2.2 km away, T0221-430767, but there are 5 on the far side of the *laguna*, including **La Alameda**, 12.6 km away, T0221-1568 4076; **Mutual 6 de Septiembre**, 8 km away, T011-155 182 3836, has a pool.

Dolores p136

LL-L Estancia Dos Talas, 10 km from Dolores, T02245-443020, www.dostalas.com.ar. One of the oldest *estancias*, you are truly the owners' guests here. The rooms and the service are impeccable, the food exquisite; stay for days, and completely relax. Pool, riding, English spoken. See also page 137.
C Hotel Plaza, Castelli 75, T02245-442362. Comfortable and welcoming old place on the plaza, all rooms with bath and TV, breakfast extra, good *confitería* downstairs. There's another good café next door.

Camping

Camping del Náutico, Lago Parque Náutico.

🍴 Eating

San Antonio de Areco p129

🍴 **Almacén de Ramos Generales**, Zapiola 143, T02326-456176, www.ramosgenerales areco.com.ar. Historical and very atmospheric old bar, or *pulpería*, dating from 1850; the perfect place to have a superb *asado*, or try regional dishes such as *locro*.
🍴 **El Almacén**, Bolívar 66. Popular with locals, serving good food in an original 1900s store.
🍴 **La Costa**, Zerboni and Belgrano, on the *costanera* near the park. Delicious *parrilla*.
🍴 **La Filomena**, Vieytes 395. An elegant, modern restaurant serving delicious food, with live music at weekends. Recommended.
🍴 **La Vuelta de Gato**, opposite the park. Good pizzas, local salami and *putero* wine.

La Plata *p131, map p133*

¶¶ **El Gaucho Italiano**, Diagonal 74 corner of Calle 50, T0221-421 5500. Large restaurant with friendly staff and a great menu of pizzas, pastas and sandwiches. They have another nicer restaurant on Calle 50, No 724 between Calles 9 and 10, T0221-483 2817.

¶¶ **El Modelo**, Calle 54 and 5. A traditional *cervecería*, with a good range on its menu, and great beer in German-style surroundings.

¶¶ **Los Discos**, Calle 48, No 441, T0221-424 9160. The best *parrilla* in town, superb steaks.

¶ **Don Quijote**, Plaza Paso 146. A very good restaurant, delicious food in welcoming surroundings. Well known and loved.

¶ **El Gran Chaparral**, Calles 60 and 117 (Paseo del Bosque). More basic *parrillada* situated in the lovely park.

¶ **La Aguada**, Calle 50, between Calles 7 and 8. The oldest restaurant in town is more for *minutas* (light meals) than big dinners, but famous for its *papas fritas* (chips); the chip soufflé is amazing.

2 fashionable places serving superb food: **El Abaco**, Calle 49 between 9 and 10, and **La Banda**, Calle 8 and 54, T0221-425 9521.

Cafés

Confitería París, corner of Calle 7 and Calle 49. The best croissants, and a great place for coffee.

Chascomús *p136*

¶¶ **El Viejo Lobo**, Mitre and Dolores. Good fish.

¶ **El Colonial**, Lastra and Belgrano. Great food, and very cheap, traditional old *parrilla*.

Dolores *p136*

¶¶ **Restaurant La Farola**, Buenos Aires 140. Welcoming, serves good pasta dishes.

¶ **Parrilla Don Pedro**, Av del Valle and Crámer. Ignore the unimaginative decor, order steak.

¶ **Pizzería Cristal**, Buenos Aires 226. Pizzas.

🍸 Bars and clubs

San Antonio de Areco *p129*

Pulpería La Ganas, Vieytes and Pellegrini. An authentic, traditional old bar, full of ancient bottles. Live music at weekends, from 2200.

La Plata *p131, map p133*

The following bars are popular and lively: **Block**, corner of Calles 122 and 50, and **Rita Bacalao**, in Gonnet, a pleasant residential area to the north of the city.

The Grants, Calle 49 corner of 9. Lively bar with cheap *tenedor libre* food.

Wilkenny, Calle 50 corner of 11. Hugely popular, Irish-style pub.

🎭 Entertainment

La Plata *p131, map p133*

El Viejo Almacén, Diagonal 74 and 2. Tango and tropical music.

Teatro Martín Fierro, Paseo del Bosque. Free concerts during the summer.

🎉 Festivals and events

San Antonio de Areco *p129*

Nov Day of Tradition, www.visiteareco.com/es/tradicion.php. Traditional parades, gaucho games, events on horseback, music and dance.

🚶 Activities and tours

San Antonio de Areco *p129*

Country Club, R8, Km 11, T02326-453073. Play golf (US$9) or watch a polo match in restful surroundings. Good food is also served. Ask tourist office for directions.

⊖ Transport

San Antonio de Areco p129
Bus
To **Buenos Aires**, every hr, 2 hrs, US$7, Chevallier or Pullman General Belgrano.

La Plata p131, map p133
Bus
To **Buenos Aires**, every 30 mins, 1½ hrs, US$3.

Train
To **Buenos Aires** (Constitución), run by TMR, frequent, 1 hr 10 mins, US$1. The ticket office is at Constitución, hidden behind shops opposite platform 6.

Chascomús p136
Bus
Frequent services, several per day, to **Buenos Aires**, US$9; **La Plata**; **Mar del Plata**; and daily to **Bahía Blanca**; **Tandil**; and **Villa Gesell**, with El Cóndor and El Rápido. To **Río de la Plata** with La Estrella.

Train
To **Buenos Aires** (Constitución), 2 daily, US$5, 1st class. Also 1 a week to **Tandil** and daily to **Mar del Plata**.

Dolores p136
Bus
To **Buenos Aires**, 3 hrs, US$14, and to **La Plata**, US$8, El Rápido T02245-441109.

Taxi
There is a stand at Belgrano and Rico, 1 block from plaza, T02245-443507.

Train
Daily service to **Buenos Aires**, US$7 .

Atlantic Coast

There are 500 km of beautiful beaches and some splendid resorts spread out along the great sweeping curve of coastline between La Plata and Bahía Blanca. Closest to Buenos Aires, there's a string of sleepy seaside towns known collectively as the Partido de la Costa, popular with older retired Argentines and better for sea-fishing than beachcombing. For more beautiful beaches, head further southwest to party town Pinamar, the jewel of the whole coast with its excellent hotels and fine restaurants. Its neighbour, smarter still, is chic Cariló, where the balnearios (swimming beaches) are exclusive and the cabañas luxurious. Nearby Villa Gesell is more of an ugly working town and best avoided. Nearby is a quieter resort becoming known for its natural beauty and complete peace: Mar de las Pampas, where you can find cabañas set in idyllic woodland right by to the sea.

Argentina's most famous resort, Mar del Plata was the very height of chic in the 1920s, but it's now a busy seaside city, with packed beaches and casinos – not the best place to relax but still interesting. To the west, two old-fashioned resorts are rather more appealing: Miramar is quiet and low-key, good for young families; and larger Necochea has an appealing woodland park along its coastline, with a vast area of unspoilt dunes, perfect for exploring on horseback. The southern stretch of beaches ends in the major port of Bahía Blanca, a useful transport hub if you're heading south, with an attractive town inland from the sea. ►► For listings, see pages 153-165.

Ins and outs

Getting there All resorts on the coast are linked to each other and to Buenos Aires by frequent bus services. Trains also leave to Mar del Plata, stopping at many coastal towns. If you're combining beaches and *estancias*, it's best to hire a car. The main artery south is the fast privatized toll road Route Provincial 2 (with US$2-3 tolls every 100 km), from Buenos Aires to Mar del Plata, via Chascomús and Dolores, with another fast road branching off to Pinamar from Dolores: take Route 63 and then 56. Alternatively, head along the coast from La Plata on Route Provincial 11, also fast and with tolls, to San Clemente del Tuyú and then parallel to the coast to Mar del Plata. Route Provincial 88 links Mar del Plata and Necochea, further southwest. Mar del Plata also has a domestic airport with flights from Buenos Aires. Remember to have small change for the tolls as they will not give change for large bills, and do not take credit cards. ►► *For further information see Transport, page 163.*

Best time to visit Avoid January if you can, when the whole coast is packed out with hordes of tourists from Buenos Aires. December and late February are ideal for hot weather and fewer crowds. Many resorts are very pleasant in spring and autumn, but out of season (and the season is from December to March) most resorts apart from the busy Mar del Plata are ghost towns. The winter wind can be harsh but if you want a quiet weekend away to read books and relax, then it can be a good time to travel. Some good deals can be had at resorts.

Tourist information There are well-organized tourist information offices in all resorts with complete lists of places to stay. There's plenty of accommodation along the coast, so only a small selection is listed. There's a useful provincial website, www.gba.gov.a (in Spanish). Each town has its own website: **Partido de la Costa** www.lacosta.gov.ar, www.lacostaturismo.com.ar; **Pinamar** www.pinamar.gov.ar and www.pinamarturismo.com.ar; **Mar de las Pampas** and **Mar Azul** www.mardelaspampas.com.ar; **Mar del Plata** www.mardelplata.gov.ar; **Miramar** www.miramarense.com.ar; **Necochea** www.necochea.gov.ar, www.necocheanet.com.ar; and **Bahía Blanca** www.bahia blanca.gov.ar.

Partido de la Costa → *For listings, see pages 153-165.*

Heading south from Buenos Aires, San Clemente del Tuyú is the first of a string of 14 small seaside towns, known as Partido de la Costa, stretching down to Mar de Ajó. First built in the 1930s, they lost popularity when the more glamorous resorts were built further south. It's not the best part of the coast and can't be recommended as most of the resorts are slightly run-down with peeling 1950s seafront hotels and tacky attractions, though they're also rather cheaper than the more upmarket resorts. The beaches are crowded in January but absolutely deserted at other times and particularly forlorn in winter. However, there is an interesting nature reserve and excellent sea fishing. The Río de la Plata has gained international recognition as the widest freshwater river in the world, and here at its mouth you can fish for shark, *pejerrey* and brotola from piers or from boats. Fish can often be bought on the beach from local fishermen. See www.lacosta.gov.ar for information on all the towns on this stretch of coastline.

San Clemente del Tuyú → *Colour map 4, C6. Phone code 02252. Population 11,400.*
Some 320 km south of Buenos Aires, San Clemente's main attraction is **Mundo Marino** ① *Av Décima No 157, signposted from the main road into town, T02252-430300, www.mundomarino.com.ar, daily Jan-Feb 1000-2000, Mar, Jul, Dec 1000-1800, off season Sat-Sun only, US$12.50, children US$8.* This is the biggest sea life centre in South America, where you can watch performing seals, dolphins, whales and penguins go through their completely unnatural routines; it's fun for children. There's also a smaller, far less spectacular theme park, **Termas Marinas** ① *take the road to Faro San Antonio at the far south of Bahía Samborombón, T02252-423000, www.termasmarinas.com.ar, daily 0900-1900 in summer, closing earlier in winter, US$9, children US$6.50,* where children can swim in thermal pools, identify birds and, for a small extra fee, ascend to the top of a historical lighthouse, which has impressive views.

Even more appealing is the unspoilt wildness of **Reserva Natural Punta Rasa** ① *2 km from San Clemente, take the road to Faro San Antonio and follow signs, free, managed by the Fundación Vida Silvestre, www.vidasilvestre.org.ar, www.puntarasa.com.ar.* This is a private reserve protecting a special area at the southernmost point of the Bahía de Samborombón, where a long tongue of dense sand stretches into the bay where the Río de la Plata meets the sea. Vast numbers of migrating birds and a resident population of crabs and shellfish make this an interesting place to spend an afternoon. It's a great place for a walk, with a short, self-guided trail and a lighthouse to visit. It's also a world-famous sea fishing site; the water around the peninsula can be up to 20 m deep, attracting large specimens of *corvina negra* (black sea bass) weighing over 20 kg. It's possible to drive along the 5-km peninsula but watch out for the tides. Information is available from *guardaparques* at the entrance and at the tip of the peninsula.

San Clemente has a busy fishing port, with yolk-yellow boats characteristic of the area, and the **Club Náutico**, at Tapera de López, offering all kinds of water sports. South of the centre, there's an attractive area of woodland, **Vivero Cosme Argerich** ① *T02252-421103, daily 0800-1900, free, guided visits offered,* a 37-ha park with woodlands, a plant nursery and sports centre. For further information on activities in the area, visit the **tourist office** ① *Calle 2 Sur and 63 Sur, San Clemente, T02252-430718, also at the bus terminal, T02252-422525, www.lacostaturismo.com.ar.*

Santa Teresita → *Phone code 02246. Population 13,000.*
From San Clemente, drive through Las Toninas and Costa Chica to reach Santa Teresita, where the biggest attraction is fishing, though there's also a good golf course, tennis and horse riding on offer. The **pier** ① *US$1*, is one of the largest on the coast, and is lit for night fishing. ›› *For further information, see Activities and tours, page 162.*

There's a **motor museum** Museo del Automóvil Santa Teresita ① *Av 32, No 1550, between 15 and 16, T02246-525786, www.museosantateresita.com.ar, daily 0930-2000 in summer, US$2, children US$1*, which has some stylish 1920s models and is fun for enthusiasts. The **tourist office** ① *Calle 3 and 42, T02246-420542, www.santateresita.com.ar*, can advise on accommodation.

Mar del Tuyú → *Phone code 02246. Population 6900.*
Approximately 20 km south of San Clemente del Tuyú, Mar del Tuyú is the administrative centre of Partido de las Costa. It's a tranquil place to visit in February, with a little more life than the other resorts nearby in winter. Boat trips are organized along the coast in summer, all the way to **Faro San Antonio**, where you can see whales basking at close proximity in August and September. Fishing is also a big attraction, see Activities and tours, page 162. The **tourist office** ① *town hall, Av 79 and Calle 13*, is helpful.

Mar de Ajó and around → *Colour map 4, C6. Phone code 02257. Population 13,800.*
Another quiet, old-fashioned resort, 40 km south of San Clemente del Tuyú, Mar de Ajó has a couple of natural attractions as well as motor racing, a shipwreck and a casino. The **Autódromo Regional** ① *follow signs from the access roundabout for Mar de Ajó, T02257-423342*, holds important motor-racing championships every summer. You can dive or snorkel at the *Naufragio Margarita*, a large German ship, wrecked off the coast here in 1880, and one of the oldest in the region. Mar de Ajó has one of the largest fleets of small fishing boats on the coast, as well as the largest pier. Boat trips to fish for *corvina*, *pescadilla*, and *cazón* sharks are offered by the best guide in the area, **Lopecito** ① *Av Costanera No 870, T02257-1563 8093*. A half-day trip including all equipment costs US$30 per person.

The most spectacular part of this area of coastline is **Altos Médanos**, a long stretch of high sand dunes that are, apparently, constantly changing shape. It's one of the wildest and most unspoilt areas of the coast, bordered along the shore by a wide flat beach, perfect for walking, horse riding or 4WD.

The best way to enjoy this area is by visiting one of the few *estancias* near the coast. **Estancia Palantelén** ① *15 km south of Mar de Ajó, T011-155 342 4120 or T02257-420983, www.palantelen.com.ar*, is owned by descendants of a pioneering Pampas family, whose atmospheric old house has views of the sea and is beautifully furnished and lined with mahogany panels salvaged from a shipwreck. Walk onto the sands, birdwatch or gallop across the miles of beaches, either on horseback or in a *sulky* (open horse-drawn carriage). Spend a few days here and absorb the complete peace; you could even have private tango lessons on the terrace under the stars. All highly recommended.

Pinamar → *Colour map 4, C6. Phone code 02254. Population 20,600.*
The two most desirable resorts on the coast are right next to each other, with the quieter old-fashioned **Ostende** in between (see below). Both party-town Pinamar and forested Cariló are upmarket places to stay, attracting wealthy Argentines, and have far smarter hotels here than elsewhere on the coast, not to mention sophisticated bars, fine restaurants and, in Pinamar, plenty of trendy beach bars and nightclubs. Pinamar is perfect

for young people and families, with live bands playing at its beach clubs in the evenings in high season (these are also quiet and elegant places to dine with superb seafood).

Access to the beach is mostly by day membership to a *balneario* (beach club). You pay a fee of US$20-40 per family or group of friends per day, and then you can make use of all the *balneario's* facilities. You can rent a *carpa* – little wooden beach huts, built in tightly packed rows perpendicular to the sea, and furnished with tables and chairs to use when you retreat from the hot sun. Alternatively, you can rent a big beach umbrella and stake a claim on an area closer to the sea. Renting either will allow you to use the *balneario's* showers, toilets, restaurants and even beach games. Pinamar's *balnearios* range from exclusive, quiet places with superb restaurants, to party spots with loud music, beach parties and live bands at night. There is free public access to the beach between the *balnearios*, but it's worth visiting one for a day to enjoy beach life. Their restaurants are open to those not renting *carpas* too.

The town also has golf courses and tennis courts, and there are lots of hotels and smart restaurants along the main street, Avenida Bunge, running perpendicular to the sea. Explore the dunes at **Reserva Dunícola**, 13 km north, by horse or 4WD. The **tourist office** ① *Av Bunge 654, T02254-491680, www.pinamar.gov.ar, www.pinamarturismo.com.ar, English spoken*, is helpful and can arrange accommodation. During the peak month of January, Pinamar is packed with Argentines, accommodation is extremely hard to get and very expensive. Best to visit in December or February/March. During the rest of the year, especially in June/July, the town virtually shuts down, and few hotels and restaurants are open. The **bus terminal** ① *Av Bunge and Intermédanos, T02254-403500*, is near the access road into town, a 20-minute walk to the beach, and the railway station is a few kilometres from town, but there are free bus transfers.

Cariló

Cariló is the most exclusive, and expensive, beach resort in Argentina, and you'll soon see why. It's a lovely huge area of mature woodland right on the beach, where luxury apart hotels and very chic *cabañas* are all tastefully concealed, so that its visitors have complete privacy – something that inevitably appeals to the many celebrities, sports stars and politicians who visit. The *balnearios* are neat and exclusive – **Hemingway** (T02254-470578) is *the* place to be seen for wealthy *Porteños*. Around the tiny centre, on Cerezo and Carpintero, there are good restaurants and chi-chi arcades with upmarket clothing shops where you can browse for top Argentine fashion labels among the usual international designers. You might find Cariló less friendly than Pinamar if you're in search of nightlife, since the emphasis is on exclusivity, but it's a good place for couples or for a quiet solo retreat. There is a **tourist office** ① *Boyero and Castaño, T02254-570773, www.carilo.com and www.parquecarilo.com (both in Spanish)*.

In between Pinamar and Cariló is **Ostende**, a small town founded by Belgian entrepreneurs in 1908. Little remains of the original resort, as it was abandoned when the settlers returned to Belgium on the outbreak of the First World War. The only building surviving from that period is the **Viejo Hotel Ostende**, formerly the **Hotel Termas**, which was a favourite of French writer Antoine de Saint-Exupéry. This is a wilder part of the coast and there are plenty of campsites. On the beach is the much-photographed old stone and wooden walkway, the *rambla*. For information on Ostende and surrounds, see www.pinamarweb.com (in Spanish).

Around Pinamar and Cariló

General Madariaga is a quaint 1900s town, 28 km inland, definitely worth visiting for the **Fiesta Nacional del Gaucho**, on the second weekend in December, when there are processions, singing and dancing. From General Madariaga, fishing enthusiasts could visit the **Laguna Salada Grande**, the largest lake in the province with a nature reserve and excellent *pejerrey* fishing. The **tourist office** ① *Guerrero 2039, T02267-421058, www.ruta0.com/general-madariaga.htm*, can advise on where to stay.

Villa Gesell → *Colour map 4, C6. Phone code 02255. Population 24,000.*

In complete contrast to overdeveloped Mar del Plata, and upmarket Pinamar, Villa Gesell, 22 km north, was planned by German inventor, Carlos Gesell, as an eco resort. He came to live here in 1931 with the aim of growing trees for wood on the barren sand dunes. His project then evolved into an ecological holiday retreat and the first guests were invited in the 1940s. He planned and built the town along environmentally friendly lines, and in harmony with nature, planting thousands of shady trees that would draw water to the surface, and constructing roads around the sand dunes. Today, however, it bears no resemblance to his idea. It is crammed full of decaying 1970s holiday homes and apartment blocks, broken cars, and tacky shops. Gesell would be aghast at the commercial feel of the main street, Avenida 3, filled with games arcades, fast-food shops and noisy cafés. It is best to avoid staying, although it can be much cheaper than in Pinamar only 10 minutes away. The main **tourist office** ① *Av de los Pioneros 1921, T02255-458596, daily 0800-2200 in summer, 0900-1900 in winter*, is on the right-hand side of the road as you enter the town. There's a good website with lots of accommodation and other information, www.gesell.gov.ar. The **bus terminal** ① *Av 3 and Paseo 140, information T02255-477253*, is at the southern end of town.

The **Reserva Forestal and Parque Cultural Pinar del Norte**, at the eastern end of Avenida 3, is where Carlos Gesell built his first house in the woods. It's now a museum, **Museo Casa Histórica** ① *T02255-468624, daily 1400-2100 in summer, Tue-Fri 1000-1600, Sat-Sun 1100-1700 in winter*, with inspiring biographical information (in English) and an interesting daily tour. Gesell's second house, **Chalet Don Carlos Gesell**, is now a cultural centre for exhibitions and concerts.

Mar de las Pampas and Mar Azul

Just 5 km south of Villa Gessell, two quiet resorts are developing: the pine forests and dirt-roads of **Mar de las Pampas** and the more commercial and less pretty **Mar Azul** are wilder and quieter places than anywhere on the coast, but have some appealing accommodation in more natural surroundings. There are lots of *cabañas* for rent and an increasing number of hotels but most people rent a house for the weekend; this is especially good if you are in a group. The beach here is broad and uncrowded, so although there is less to do than in Pinamar or Mar del Plata and no nightlife to speak of, you can completely relax and enjoy the sea in peace. It's a perfect retreat for writing or reflecting, or a cosy hideaway for couples, although in January you'll find traffic jams and queues at restaurants. Mar de las Pampas has a **tourist office** ① *Av 3 and Paseo 173, T02255-470324*. See also www.mardelaspampas.com.ar, for more information.

The oldest and most famous Argentine resort – built in 1874 – has lost much of its charm since its heyday in the 1930s but it is still an interesting place to stay. It's now a big city with plenty of entertainment, but unless you're a lover of crowds or casinos, there are better beaches elsewhere. There are some good new bars and cafés along Güemes and Alem, near the cemetery, and superb fish restaurants by the port and on the pier. There are hundreds of hotels, all busy and overpriced even in low season (although prices double in January and February), as this is a popular conference city. Winter is the best time to visit if you want to see the town itself and the sea lion colony, although the wind is relentless.

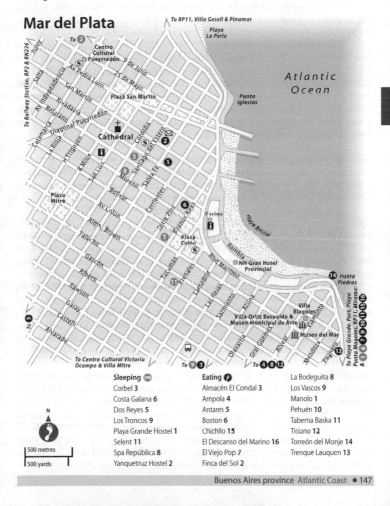

Mar del Plata

N

500 metres
500 yards

Sleeping	Eating	La Bodeguita **8**
Corbel **3**	Almacén El Condal **3**	Los Vascos **9**
Costa Galana **6**	Ampola **4**	Manolo **1**
Dos Reyes **5**	Antares **5**	Pehuén **10**
Los Troncos **9**	Boston **6**	Taberna Baska **11**
Playa Grande Hostel **1**	Chichilo **15**	Tisiano **12**
Selent **11**	El Descanso del Marino **16**	Torreón del Monje **14**
Spa República **8**	El Viejo Pop **7**	Trenque Lauquen **13**
Yanquetruz Hostel **2**	Finca del Sol **2**	

Ins and outs → *Phone code 0223. Population 542,000.*

Getting there There are daily flights from Buenos Aires (several in summer) to **Camet Airport**, 10 km north of town. In summer there are also flights to towns in Patagonia. Regular buses (bus No 542, US$1) run from the airport into town, or it's US$8 in a taxi.

The **bus terminal** ① *Alberti 1602, T0223-451 5406*, is in a former railway station, and is very central but squalid and short on facilities; avoid going there alone at night. Trains from Buenos Aires and Miramar arrive at **Estación Norte** ① *Luro 4599, T0223-475 3311*, about 13 blocks northwest of the centre. Buses Nos 511, 512, 512B and 541 run to the centre. Buses Nos 511 and 221 will take you into the centre, to the lighthouse, out to the beaches further to the south and to the port. The routes are fairly regular (every 10 minutes or so, until it gets late) and run all night (although the late-night service is less frequent). Single trips cost US$0.45-0.50, depending on how far you travel. **Note** Some buses, including No 511, can only be used with a top-up card available from any kiosk (a similar system to the Monedero in Buenos Aires capital). In general, buses are quick and comfortable.

Tourist information The city's **tourist office** ① *Belgrano 2740, T0223-494 4140 (ext 130 or 131) or, more conveniently, next to Casino Central, on Blvd Marítimo 2270, T0223-495 1777, daily 0800-2200 in summer, Mon-Sat 0800-2000, Sun 1000-1700 in winter, www.mardelplata. gov.ar, English spoken*, is very helpful and can provide good leaflets on events, information on bus routes and lists of hotels and apartment/chalet letting agents, including family homes (when everywhere else is full). There's another tourist office at the airport. For what's on, see www.todomardelplata.com.

Best time to visit There are several festivals throughout the summer, with live music shows, parades and the coronation of all kinds of carnival queens. For more details, see Festivals and events, page 162. If you're coming for the beaches, January is best avoided because of overcrowding; December or late February are much more pleasant and it's still warm.

Sights

The city centre is around **Playa Bristol**, where a broad promenade, the Rambla, runs past the fine casino (upper floor open to the public) and the new luxury refurbished **Gran Hotel Provincial**, both of which were designed by famous Argentine architect Bustillo, and date from the late 1930s. Six blocks north along San Martín is the Plaza San Martín, a good place for shopping, flanked by an attractive **cathedral**. Ten blocks southwest, at the end of Avenida Colón there are some impressive and attractive mansions dating from Mar del Plata's heyday, from mock-Tudor **Villa Blaquier** to Villa Ortiz Basualdo (1909), inspired by a Loire chateaux, now the **Museo Municipal de Arte** ① *Av Colón 1189, T0223-486 1636, daily 1700-2200 in summer, Wed-Mon 1200-1700 in winter, US$1, including tour*, with rooms furnished in period style. Nearby is the splendid **Museo del Mar** ① *Av Colón 1114, T0223-451 3553, www.museodelmar.com, daily 1000-2300 in summer, 1000-2000 in winter, US$2.70*, an imaginatively designed place on several levels, with a vast collection of 30,000 sea shells, a small aquarium, café and roof terrace. The **Centro Cultural Victoria Ocampo** ① *Matheu 1851, T0223-492 0569, daily in summer, Tue and mornings closed in winter; ring to check current opening times, US$1*, is in a beautiful 1900s wooden house in lovely gardens, where the famous author entertained illustrious literary figures. In summer, concerts are held in the grounds. Nearby is the **Villa Mitre** ① *Lamadrid 3870, www.loslobos.com.ar/villa_mitre.htm, Mon-Fri 0900-2000, Sat and Sun 1600-2000 in summer, closes at 1700 in winter, US$1*, owned by a son of Bartolomé Mitre, with an eclectic collection of artefacts including old photos of the city. There's no shortage of entertainment in the city, with lots of theatres and cinemas, live music and the casino. See Entertainment, page 162.

Beaches and port area

There are several beaches along this stretch of coast, each with a different feel. Fashionable **Playa Grande** has the best hotels and shops, as well as the famous golf course, with private *balnearios* attracting wealthy *Porteños*, and a small area open to the public. **Playa La Perla** is packed in summer and far from relaxing, while **Playa Punta Mogotes**, further west, is by far the most appealing beach. However, further towards the south (a short bus ride on No 511 or 221) will take you to some other quieter beaches, including La Morocha and La Arena, where it is also possible to park the car on the beach close to the sea for a small fee. The **port area**, south of Playa Grande, is interesting when the old orange fishing boats come in, and this is the place to head for at night, as there are many seafood restaurants gathered in one place; be selective as some are very touristy. A sea lion colony basks on rusting wrecks by the **Escollera Sur**, the southern breakwater that stretches out into the sea. Fishing for *pejerrey*, *corvina* and *pescadilla* is good all along the coast. Beyond the port are the **Punta Mogotes lighthouse**, built in 1891, and the **Bosque Peralta Ramos**, a 400-ha forest of eucalyptus and conifers, which is an excellent place to take a stroll. There's a tasty local restaurant, **El Descanso del Marino**, to dine in too (see Eating, page 160). If you want sea and sand, rather than bars and entertainment, the best beaches are further southwest of the city, along the road to Miramar. Here you'll find several fine broad beaches interrupted by high cliffs, and all easily reached by regular buses from the terminal.

Around Mar del Plata

Santa Clara del Mar is a low-key family resort 18 km north of Mar del Plata, and has *balnearios* and a relaxed feel. Though it's far from chic, it's a welcoming place. For further information, contact the **tourist office** ① *T0223-460 2433, www.marchiquitadigital.com.ar*. Beyond, some 34 km northeast of Mar del Plata, is the **Mar Chiquita**, a lagoon joined to the sea by a narrow channel, with huge dunes in between, offering good beaches, sailing, fishing and boating, and rich bird life. For excursions to the Laguna de los Padres and to Balcarce, see page 162.

Balcarce, 68 km northwest and inland from Mar del Plata, is an attractive small town, with some splendid art deco buildings and a leafy central plaza. The main reason for visiting, though, is to see the famous **Museo Juan Manuel Fangio** ① *Dardo Rocha 639, T02266-425540, www.museofangio.com, daily 0900-1900 US$6.50, children US$2*. Argentina's most beloved racing driver was born here, and the *municipalidad* on the plaza has been turned into a great museum, housing all his trophies and many of the racing cars he drove. Recommended for car enthusiasts. For further information, contact the **tourist office** ① *Calle 17 No 671, T02266-425758, www.sierrasdebalcarce.com.ar*.

The **Laguna La Brava**, 38 km away, at the foot of the Balcarce hills, offers *pejerrey* fishing, and plentiful birdlife in lovely wooded surroundings. Visit **Estancia Laguna La Brava** ① *R226, Km 37.5, T0223-4608062, www.lagunabrava.com/antcasco.htm*, for horse riding, trekking, mountain biking and water sports on the lake with fine views of Sierra Brava. ►► *For further information on fishing, see Activities and tours, page 162.*

Miramar → *Colour map 4, C6. Phone code 02291. Population 24,500.*

A delightful, low-key alternative to Mar del Plata, Miramar, lies 47 km southwest along the coast road, and is an old-fashioned little resort, known as the 'city of bicycles', and orientated towards families. It has a big leafy plaza at its centre, a good stretch of beach with soft sand, and a pleasant atmosphere providing a quieter, low-key alternative to Mar del Plata. The most attractive area of the town is away from the high-rise buildings on the seafront, at the **Vivero Dunícola Florentino Ameghino**, a 502-ha forest park on the beach, with lots of walks, restaurants and picnic places for *asado* among the mature trees. There's also a small **Museo Municipal**, with displays of animal fossils and indigenous Querandí artefacts. Further east is the dense wood of the **Bosque Energético**, possessed of an allegedly magical magnetic energy, which attracts large twigs to hang from tree trunks and groups of meditators to sit in hopeful silence. Golfers will enjoy the fine Scottish links-style course at **Golf Club Miramar** ① *4.5 km away from the centre on R91, T02291-420833,* known for its rough terrain, with no notable landmarks. There are plenty of banks with ATMs around the plaza. The **tourist office** ① *northern corner of the plaza, Calle 28 No 1086, T02291-420190, www.miramar-digital.com, Mon-Fri 0700-2100, Sat-Sun 0900-2100 in summer,* has helpful accommodation lists and maps. The **bus terminal** ① *T02291-423359,* is at Calle 34 and Avenida 23 and the **railway station** ① *T02291- 420657,* is at Avenida 40 and Calle 15.

From here, you can easily visit **Mar del Sur**, 14 km south, a peaceful resort with good fishing in a lagoon and bathing on the beach among dunes and black rocks.

Necochea → *Colour map 4, C5. Phone code 02262. Population 65,000.*

One of the most surprising resorts on the whole Atlantic coast, Necochea, 100 km west of Miramar, is a well-established town, famous for its enormously long (74 km) beach. While the central area is built up and busy in summer months, further west is a spectacular expanse of sand with high dunes, perfect for exploring on foot, horseback or 4WD. There's also a huge forest park, a golf club and rafting on the river Quequén.

Ins and outs There are several buses daily from Mar del Plata, Buenos Aires and Bahía Blanca to Necochea's **bus terminal** ① *Av 47 and Av 58, T02262-422470,* rather inconveniently northeast of the centre (3 km from the beach). Take local bus No 513 to the beach area, or a taxi for US$2.50. There's a good bus network all over the city. There is also a **train station** at the corner of streets 580 and 563 in Quequén, east of Necochea across the bridge. The town lies on the west bank of the Río Quequén, and is in two parts, with its administrative centre 2 km inland from the seafront area. On the opposite bank of the river, Quequén (population 15,000), is mostly a residential area, with one of the most important grain-exporting ports in the country. The two towns are linked by three bridges, one of them, Puente Colgante, a 270-m suspension bridge built in Cherbourg and opened here in 1929. There are a number of banks with ATMs and *locutorios* along the pedestrianized shopping street, Calle 83.

Tourist information There is a **tourist information office** ① *opposite main Av 79, which runs down to the sea, T02262-438333, www.necochea.gov.ar, www.necocheanet.com.ar, only open from Dec-Mar, Mon-Sat 0830-2100, Sun 0900-1900,* on the seafront, which is useful for accommodation and entertainment.

Sights The **Parque Miguel Lillo** (named after the Argentine botanist) is a wonderful dense forest of over 500 ha with more than a million trees, open to the public for all kinds of activities. It starts three blocks west of Plaza San Martín, and stretches along the seafront. There are lovely walks, many campsites and picnic spots, a swan lake with paddle boats, an amphitheatre, lots of restaurants, a couple of tiny museums and places to practise various sports.

West of Necochea, there's a natural arch of rock at the **Cueva del Tigre**, and beyond it stretches vast empty beach, separated from the land by sand dunes up to 100 m high, the **Médano Blanco**. This is an exhilarating area for walking or horse riding, and the dunes are popular for 4WD, riding and sand boarding. Vehicles and buses stop where the road ends at **Parador Médano Blanco** ① *T02262-1556 8931*, a good place for lunch where you can rent 4WDs (US$50, jeep for four). If you fancy exploring the distant sand dunes and far-flung beaches in 4WDs, head for **Expediciones del Este** ① *central balneario Palmeras del Este on Av 2 and Calle 83, T02262-526900, www.expedicionesdeleste.com.ar*.

East of Quequén harbour there are equally tranquil beaches, particularly **Balneario La Virazón**, and a lighthouse built in 1921, with a good 18-hole golf course.

Around Necochea

You can go rafting on the **Río Quequén**, and visit the **Cascadas de Quequén**, small waterfalls 13 km north. Nearby is the forested **Parque Cura-Meucó**, 70 km north, on the river, with the splendid **Balneario Puente Blanco**. There's also diving off the coast to a submerged diving park at **Parque Subacuático Kabryl**, just 1500 m from the coast. More information on diving is available at www.buceoprofundo.com.ar (in Spanish).

Bahía Blanca and around → *For listings, see pages 153-165. Colour map 4, C4.*

The province's most important port and a big naval base, Bahía Blanca is a busy city, and yet it's a relaxed and attractive place with some fine early 20th-century architecture around its large plaza. There's not much to attract tourists, but it's a useful stopping point on the route south, or a base for exploring the beautiful mountains 100 km north at Sierra de la Ventana. It's a city with the feel of a small town, where people are friendly and everyone knows everyone else.

Ins and outs → *Phone code 0291. Population 275,000.*

Getting there There are several flights daily from Buenos Aires to the airport, **Airport Comandante Espora** ① *information 10291-486 1456, 11 km north of town, US$6.50 in a taxi*, and weekly flights with **LADE** to many places in Patagonia. There are buses from all over the country to the **bus terminal** ① *Estados Unidos and Brown 1700, T0291-481 9615, 2 km east of the centre (connected by buses 512 and 514, or US$3 in a taxi, there are no hotels nearby)*. There are trains from Buenos Aires; the **railway station** ① *Av General Cerri 750, T0291-452 9196*, is six blocks east of the plaza.

Getting around The city is pleasant to walk around, with a small centre, and most things you'll need on streets Alsina or San Martín north/east of the plaza. There's a good network of local buses, taking *tarjebus* cards rather than cash (available from shops and kiosks), which you'll need to catch if you want to get to the shopping mall 20 blocks north. Taxis are cheap, plentiful and safe.

Tourist information The **tourist office** ① *main plaza, Alsina 65, through a small door on the outside of the building to the right, T0291-459 4007, www.bahiablanca.gov.ar, Mon-Fri 0730-1900, Sat 1000-1300*, is very helpful.

Background

Bahía Blanca was founded in 1828 as a fort, the Fortaleza Protectora Argentina, both to control cattle rustling by the indigenous population and to protect the coast from Brazil whose navy had landed in the area in 1827. Though the indigenous people of the area were defeated in the campaigns of Rosas, the fortress was attacked several times, notably by 3000 Calfucurá warriors in 1859. An important centre of European immigration, it became a major port with the building of railways connecting it with grain-producing areas of the Pampas. The biggest industry now is a huge petrochemicals plant 8 km from town at the port.

Sights

Bahía Blanca is pleasant to walk around, with well-preserved architecture from the early 20th century. At the city's heart is the large **Plaza Rivadavia**, a broad, well-kept leafy space, with a striking sculpture. On the west side is the Italianate **Municipalidad** (1904), and to the south the impressive French-style **Banco de la Nación** (1927); it's worth popping in to see its perfectly preserved interior. Three blocks north there's the classical **Teatro Municipalidad** (1922) ① *T0291-456 3973*, which hosts regular theatre, live music and dance. At the side of the theatre, the **Museo Histórico** ① *Dorrego 116, T0291-456 3117, mhistorico.bahiablanca.gov.ar, Tue-Sun 1700-2100*, has interesting displays on the city's history.

To the northwest of the centre, along the attractive Avenida Além, the **Parque de Mayo** is filled with eucalyptus trees, children's play areas and bars. Nearby there's a golf course, sports centre and a long area for walking by the river through a sculpture park.

Not to be missed is the **Museo del Puerto** ① *Torres and Carrega, 7 km away at the port area Ingeniero White, Mon-Fri 0830-1230, Sat-Sun 1530-1930, free, bus No 500A or 504 from the plaza, hourly Sat-Sun, or a taxi; US$5*. Set in a former customs building, this has entertaining and imaginative displays on immigrant life in the early 20th century, with witty photographs, evocative music and sound. And there's a great café in one of the exhibition spaces on Sundays. Highly recommended. The port also has a couple of fine fish restaurants in its red-light district: take a taxi.

Around Bahía Blanca

Bahía Blanca has both mountains and beach within an hour's drive. At **Pehuén-Có**, 84 km east, there's a long stretch of sandy beaches and dunes, all relatively empty and unspoilt (beware of jellyfish when the wind is in the south), signposted from the main road 24 km from Bahía Blanca. It has a wild and un-touristy feel, with a single hotel, several campsites well shaded by pine trees, and a couple of places to eat.

There's a more established resort at **Monte Hermoso**, 106 km east, with good hotels and better organized campsites, but still a quiet, family feel, and wonderful beaches for bathing. Its claim to fame is that it's one of the few places where the sun rises and sets over the sea (here too, don't swim when the wind is in the south because of jellyfish – ask a local if in doubt). To get there, **Combis Ariber** ① *T0291-456 5523, US$4*, runs a door-to-door minibus service; they will collect you from anywhere in town.

Santa Rosa de la Pampa → *Colour map 4, C2. Phone code 02954. Population 102,000.*

Santa Rosa is the capital of La Pampa province, founded in 1892, an important administrative centre 663 km from Buenos Aires. It's not a wildly exciting destination but it's a friendly place. There aren't really any tourist sights, though the **Teatro Español**, Lagos 44, dates from 1908, and 10 blocks west of the Plaza San Martín is **Laguna Don Tomás** and a park with sports facilities. There's a **tourist office** ① *San Martín and Luro, www.santarosa.gov.ar*, opposite the bus terminal, which is seven blocks east of Plaza San Martín.

The main reason to stop here is to visit the Parque Nacional Lihue Calel (see below). Closer however, is the **Parque Luro** ① *T02954-499000, www.parqueluro.gov.ar, 2 buses a day from Santa Rosa*, 32 km south of Santa Rosa, which covers over 6500 ha. This provincial park occupies the former estate of Pedro Luro, who created his own hunting grounds for aristocratic friends visiting from Europe, introducing red deer and wild boar, running wild in the park, with many species of birds. Luro's mansion, a French-style chateau, has been turned into a museum, and opposite is a **Centro de Interpretación Ecológico**, with displays on the flora and fauna of the Pampas.

Parque Nacional Lihue Calel

① *T02952-436595, lihuecalel@apn.gov.ar. For information see www.lihuecalel.com.ar and www.parquesnacionales.gov.ar. There's a camping area and toilets at the administration centre.*

The Lihue Calel National Park is situated 240 km southwest of Santa Rosa and 120 km from General Acha, and is reached by paved Route 152. The name derives from the Mapuche for 'place of life', and you can understand why when you see its low vegetated hills rising out of rather arid desert. Its microclimate allows it to support a wide variety of plant species, including a number of unique species of cactus in its rocky terrain. Wildlife includes pumas, but you're more likely to spot *maras* (Patagonian hare), vizcachas, guanacos and rheas as well as a wide variety of birds. The area was home to various groups of indigenous people 2000 years ago; there are geometric cave paintings in the **Valle de las Pinturas** and the **Valle de Namuncurá**, seen on one of two self-guided trails through the park. The other trail, **El Huitru**, climbs the highest hill in the park and explores some of its amazing flora. The park is best visited in spring.

⊕ Atlantic Coast listings

For Sleeping and Eating price codes and other relevant information, see Essentials pages 30-36.

⊖ Sleeping

San Clemente del Tuyú *p143*
See www.portaldesanclemente.com for a complete list.
B Altair Hotel, Calle 3, No2283, T02252-421 429, www.altairhotel.com.ar. A 3-star hotel with decent, simple rooms, some with balconies with sea views, in a modern block.
B Fontainebleau, Calle 3, No 2294, T02252-421187, www.fontainebleau.com.ar. Dated but comfortable 4-star hotel on the coast, good value, with an elegant entrance and light airy rooms. There is a pool and a restaurant.

B-C Sun Shine, Av Talas del Tuyú No 3025, T02252-430316, www.sunshinehotel.com.ar. The most recommendable of the cheaper places to stay.
C Morales, Calle 1, No 1856, T02252-430 357. A welcoming option that also has a large pool and a restaurant. Rooms are plain but comfortable.
D Sur, C 3 No 2194, T02252-521137, www.hotelsur.com.ar. A central location with simple accommodation.

Campsites
ACA, Av II No 96, T02252-421124, and Cetan, Av IX and Calle 45, T02252-421487.
Los Tres Pinos, T02252-430151, www.los3 pinos.com.ar. Nice, well-organized campsites (US$6 per person) as well as basic wooden

cabins (US$25 for up to 4 people). Good options for budget travellers.

Santa Teresita p144
See www.santateresita.com.ar for a complete list.

B San Remo Resort, Calle 35 No 344, T02246-420215, www.sanremohoteles. com.ar. The best of the 3-stars, this is a huge holiday hotel catering largely for families with a pool and jacuzzi. Includes breakfast.

B-C Sorrento, Calle 37 No 235, between Calles 2 and 3, T02246-420 0298, www.santateresita.com.ar/sorrento. Dated 3-star hotel with pleasant rooms, though somewhat on the kitsch side.

C Hostería Santa Teresita, Av Costanera No 747, between Calles 34 and 35, T02246-420202, www.go.to/hosteria. A nicely maintained, simple, family chalet-type hotel by the sea.

D Turista, Av 32 No 464, T02246-430334, www.santateresita.com.ar/turista.htm. Rather basic, with simple rooms around a central courtyard, but clean and friendly.

Campsites
Estancia El Carmen, Calle 23 and Playa, T02246-420220, www.estanciaelcarmen. com.ar. A really excellent site on the beach, but with grassy shaded areas, and all facilities, camping US$15 per tent for 2, including *cabañas* (**D**) for rent. Recommended.

Mar del Tuyú p144
There's little on offer in Mar del Tuyú itself, but Costa del Este next door has a couple of places, both comfortable; see www.mardeltuyu.com for a complete list.

B Seaside Forest Inn, Av Costanera No 355, T02246-434173.

B Terrazas al Mar, Av Costanera between 1 and 2, T02246-4375 3344, www.club52.com.ar.

Campsites
El Refugio, Calle 94 between 2 and 3, T02246-435195, gen@sinectis.com.ar.

Mar de Ajó and around p144
This town has a couple of good places to stay, but there is better accommodation offered at the next resort along, San Bernardo, see www.sanbernardo.com.ar for a complete list.

B Gran Playa Hotel, Costanera 190, Mar de Ajó, T02257-420001, www.hotelgran playa.com.ar. The best choice in town and also the oldest, still in the family of the original owners. A comfortable beach-front place. All rooms have bathrooms and sea views, some have jacuzzis too. Good buffet breakfast.

B Hostería Mar de Ajó, Av Costanera Norte 205, Mar de Ajó, T02257-421030, www.hosteriamardeajo.com.ar. A modest but comfortable beachfront *hostería*.

B Neptuno Plaza, Hernández 313, San Bernardo, T02257-461789, www.neptunoplaza.com.ar. A well-equipped 4-star place with good service.

Estancias
L Estancia Palantelén, 15 km south of Mar de Ajó, T011-155 342 4120 or T02257-420 983, www.palantelen.com.ar. The best place to stay for miles around. A delightful house close to the beach, where you can go horse riding, and even learn tango. Highly recommended. See also page 144.

Camping
ACA, Javier de Rosas y Melón Gil, San Bernardo, T02257-420230.

Pinamar p144
There are over 150 hotels of a high standard in Pinamar, all 4-stars have a pool. Book well ahead in Jan and Feb. See www.pinamar turismo.com.ar, for a complete list.

AL Del Bosque, Av Bunge 1550 and Júpiter, T02254-482480, www.hotel-delbosque.com. Smart, large, 4-star hotel in the woods with very attractive, minimalist and comfortable rooms. Although it's quite a way from the beach, it does have a pool, tennis courts, a good restaurant and a casino.

AL Reviens, Burriquetas 79, T02254-497 010, www.hotelreviens.com. Right on the beach, this is a modern, international-style hotel with luxurious rooms. Recommended.
AL Terrazas al Mar, Av del Mar and de las Gaviotas, T02254-480900, www.terrazas almar.com. A large luxurious chain hotel with very comfortable apartments with sea views in a prime position on Pinamar's most central beach. A spa, 2 pools and a restaurant.
A La Posada, del Tuyú and del Odiseo, T02254-482267, www.laposadapinamar. com.ar. Very comfortable and spacious hotel with renovated rooms on the 1st floor, and a quiet location next to the sea with a pretty garden for breakfast by a small pool. Excellent and a very attractive place wth lower rates (**B**) outside high season. Recommended.
A-B Las Araucarias, Av Bunge 1411, T02254 480812, hotel_araucarias@hotmail.com. Attractive, rather cottage-like rooms in this smaller hotel with pretty gardens.
A-B Playas, Av Bunge 250 and de la Sirena, T02254-482236, www.playashotel.com.ar. A lovely setting for this old-fashioned, large hotel with spacious, stylishly decorated rooms. Comfortable lounge, a small pool and really good service. Recommended.
A-B Soleado, Sarmiento and Nuestras Malvinas, T02254-490304, www.pinamar soleado.com. A lovely, bright, welcoming beachfront hotel with elegant entrance and cosy spacious rooms. Recommended.
C Trinidad, Del Cangrejo 1370, 102254 488 983, hoteltrinidad@telpin.com.ar. Open all year round. A lively, welcoming little hotel with simple rooms.

Estancias
AL Rincón de Cobo, access on R91, 30 km north of Pinamar, T02257-1563 8903, www.rincondecobo.com.ar. Just 3 secluded houses by the sea, separated from each other, and offering rustic comfort. The kind of service you'd expect in a hotel, with all the usual calm of the Pampas. It has its own airstrip in case you're tempted to fly here yourself.

A-B Viejo Hotel Ostende, Biarritz y El Cairo, Ostende, T02254-486081, www.hotel ostende.com.ar. Open summer only. This attractive, smallish hotel has been open since 1913, and writer Antoine de Saint-Exupéry was among its many renowned guests. Although it's now been renovated, the place retains some old-fashioned flavour, and it's comfortable in a simple way. There's a pool, the service is excellent, and the hotel has its own *balneario*.

Camping
There are several well-equipped sites (US$15 per day for 4 people in 2 tents) near the beach at Ostende.

Cariló *p145*
Most of the accommodation is in apart hotels and timeshares, see www.carilo.com for more options.
AL Cariló Village, Carpintero and Divisadero, T02254-470244, www.carilovillage.com.ar. Well-designed, cottage-style, attractive but not luxurious rooms and apartments; there is a very good restaurant, and a spa with 2 pools.
AL Marcin, Laurel and the oceanfront, T02254-570888, www.hotelmarcin. com.ar. Modern and large, very swish complex, right on the beach, with a spa and a restaurant.

Villa Gesell *p146*
There are many hotels scattered over the town, many between Av 3 and the beach. The tourist office has a complete list and a map showing where they are. See www.gesell.gov.ar for more listings.
AL Hotel Terrazas Club, Av 2, between 104 and 105, T02255-462181, www.terrazasclub hotel.com.ar. Closed off season. The most luxurious option in town is a modern tower right by the beach. It's not particularly attractive from the outside, but has very well-equipped apartments, great service, huge breakfasts, a restaurant and a nice pool, and access to the marvellous **Azulmarina Spa**, T02255-461245, www.spaazulmarina.com.ar.

A Delfín Azul, Paseos 104 No 459, T02255-462521, www.hoteldelfinazul.com.ar. Closed off season. Very cosy with attractive rooms and a pool in a large garden.

A-B De la Plaza, Av 2, between 103 and 104, T02255-468793, www.delaplazahotel.com. A small, spotless, very welcoming hotel with excellent service, open all year round. Rooms are plain but very comfortable. Excellent value. Across the garden there are also fully equipped apartments for 2-4, and a small pool.

C Hostería Gran Chalet, Paseo 105, No 447 and Av 4-5, T02255-462913, www.gesell.com.ar/granchalet. Closed off season. Spacious comfortable but dated rooms, a good breakfast and the owner Mariana knows all about the area. Good value.

Mar de las Pampas and Mar Azul *p146*
See www.mardelaspampas.com.ar for a complete list of accommodation.

LL-L La Mansión del Bosque, Juez Repetto and R Peñaloza, T02255-479555, www.lamansiondelbosque.com.ar. Open all year round. Just 150 m away from the sea, this attractive large house is beautifully decorated in minimalist style and has extremely comfortable rooms. It's one of the area's more pricey options, but there's a great spa that attracts affluent, stressed young *Porteños* from Buenos Aires.

AL Posada La Casona, Hudson between Roca and JV González, T02255-479693, www.posadalacasona.com.ar. A really stylish, comfortable place with a great restaurant. Excellent value.

AL-A Posada Piñen, Juan de Garay and R Payró, T02255-479974, www.posada pinen.com. A very comfortable *hostería*, with a wonderfully rustic atmosphere. Breakfasts are gorgeous and include delicious home-made pies.

Apart hotels
There are many apart hotels in the woods, the following is recommended: .

Village de las Pampas, Corvina and Roca, T02255-454244, www.villagedelaspampas. com.ar. Several apartments of different sizes, all very comfortable and attractively designed, and only a few metres from the sea.

Cabañas
There are many attractive, well-equipped *cabañas*, including **Arco Iris**, Victoria Ocampo between Los Alamos and Ombú, T02255-479 535, www.mardelaspampas.com.ar/arcoiris.

Mar del Plata *p147, map p147*
Busy traffic makes it impossible to drive along the coast in summer from beach to beach, so choose a hotel (there are over 700) near the beach you want. During the summer months it is essential to book in advance. Many hotels open in season only. See www.mardelplata. gov.ar for more listings.

LL-L NH Gran Hotel Provincial, Av Peralta Ramos 2502, T0223-499 5900, www.nh-hotels.com. Newly renovated, NH hotels have managed to recreate the grandeur of this beachside palace. Huge impressive foyer and lobby and the pleasingly modern rooms have flatscreen TVs, large bathrooms and great views of the town or the beach. Highly recommended.

LL-L Costa Galana, Blvd Marítimo 5725, T0223-486 0000, www.hotelcostagalana.com. A 5-star tower at Playa Grande with everything you'd expect from a modern luxurious hotel.

AL Dos Reyes, Av Colón 2129, T0223-491 0383, www.dosreyes.com.ar. Long-established but modernized town centre hotel with smart, well-equipped rooms. Guests have automatic access to a *balneario*, and the hotel offers a big breakfast, good service and is very good value off season.

AL Hotel Spa República, Córdoba 1968, T0223-492 1142, www.hotelsparepublica. com.ar. Friendly, modern hotel with attentive service and slightly overpriced rooms (all with their own kitchen and flatscreen TV), a swimming pool and spa, and a good restaurant.

A-B Corbel, Córdoba 1870, T0223-493 4424, www.hotellasrocas.com.ar/hotelcorbel. Closed off season. A modernized 1960s building with very pleasant rooms, good service and useful central location. Recommended.

B-C Los Troncos, Rodríguez Peña 1561, T0223-451 8882, www.hotellostroncos. com.ar. A small, chalet-style place with a homely atmosphere and a neat garden. In a nice, quiet, residential area, handy for the restaurants and bars along Güemes.

C Selent, Arenales 2347, T0223-494 0878, www.hotelselent.com.ar. Open all year round. This small and central, family-owned hotel is great value, with warm and welcoming staff and owners on hand. Quiet, very neat rooms, with good bathrooms. Highly recommended.

Hostels

F pp Playa Grande Hostel, Quintana 168, T0223-451 7307, www.hostelplayagrande. com.ar. 4 blocks from the beach. Set in an old house, this hostel is party-central surrounded by 40 bars and restaurants. Small dorms, and bigger doubles (**D**) available. They also run 2 other high-quality hostels, Hostel Playa Grand Suites and Hostel Playa del Sur (near the beach).

F pp Yanquetruz Hostel, 9 de Julio 3634, T0223-473 8098, www.yanquetruz.com.ar. A lovely old house in one of the oldest suburbs, recently refurbished. 20 mins' walk to the beach. Doubles (**D**) available.

Apartment rental

Prices vary a lot, with higher rates in Jan, slightly lower in Feb and even lower in Dec and Mar. Prices rise again at Easter and the long weekends through the summer months; cheap deals off season. The tourist office has a list of agents, and a helpful section in English on their website, www.mardelplata.gov.ar. Try **Gonnet**, Corrientes 1987 (and Moreno), T0223-495 2171, www.gonnet.com.ar.

Camping

Many on the road south of the city, but far better sites at Villa Gesell.

Around Mar del Plata p149
Camping

Campsites are plentiful, and include:
Club de Pesca Balcarce, at Laguna La Brava, R226, Km 39.4, T0223-460 8019. Well-organized site, with all facilities and good fishing.

Municipal, R55, Km 63.5, south of centre in Parque Cerro El Triunfo. Pools and good facilities, all kinds of sports too.

Parque Idoyaga Molina, at San Agustín, 25 km south of Balcarce, T0223-491075. A lovely park with mature trees and a pond, with the calm atmosphere of an old village in the hills: the perfect site for camping.

Miramar p150

There are dozens of hotels and apartments between Av 26 and the sea, see www.miramar-digital.com.ar for listings.

A América, Diag Rosende Mitre 1114, T02291-420847, www.hotelamericamiramar. com.ar. Open all year round. One of the most attractive places to stay. Located in a Spanish colonial-style building, surrounded by trees, with lots of games for children, bikes for hire, and lovely gardens. Recommended.

A-B Gran Rex, Av Mitre (Calle 23) No 805, T02291-420783, www.hotelgranrex.com.ar. Summer only. A rather austere block, old-fashioned but with comfortable rooms and good bathrooms.

C Brisas del Mar, Calle 29 No 557, T02291-420334, brisasdelmar@miramarnet.com.ar. Summer only. Family-run hotel on the sea-front with plain, very neat rooms and a cheery restaurant. Welcoming and good value.

Hostels

F pp **Aventureiro Hostels**, Calle 16,
T02291-430981, www.aventureiro.com.ar.
Fun and friendly hostel only 2 blocks from
the beach. Simple and rustic rooms, pool
table, small pool.

Camping

There are lots of campsites, including:
F pp **El Durazno**, R91, T02291-431984, 2 km
from town. Good facilities, shops, restaurant
and *cabañas*. Take bus 501 marked 'Playas'.

Necochea *p150*

Many hotels close off-season, when it's worth
bargaining with those remaining open. Most
hotels are in the seafront area just north of
Av 2 with at least 100 within 700 m of the
beach. There are many apartments for rent;
ask the tourist office for a list. For more
listings, see www.necochea.gov.ar/turismo.
A España, Calle 89 No 215, T02262-422896,
www.hotel-espana.com.ar (ACA affiliated).
Less luxurious than Ñikén, but a more modern
option open all year round. Well suited to
families, with warm and attentive staff.
A Ñikén, Calle 87 No 335, T02262-432323,
www.hotelniken.com.ar. The best hotel in
the seafront area. Just 2 blocks from the sea,
a very comfortable 4-star with a small pool,
good facilities, a good restaurant and
excellent service.
A Presidente, Calle 4 No 4040, T02262-423
800, www.presinec.com.ar. Only open in high
season. Another 4-star hotel, recommended
for its excellent service, comfortable rooms
and pool.
A-B Hostería del Bosque, Calle 89 No 350,
T/F02262-420002, www.hosteria-del-
bosque.com.ar. 5 blocks from the beach,
a quiet, comfortable place with a lovely
atmosphere. The attractive house, now
renovated, was formerly the residence of
a Russian princess in exile. Now it has rustic
rooms, individually designed and with old
furniture. Great restaurant.
B-C Marino, Av 79 No 253, T02262-520330,
www.laperlahotelmarino.com.ar. Open

summer only, this is a historic place, one
of the first hotels in town built in the 1920s.
It has a wonderful staircase and patios,
and although it's faded grandeur and a
bit run down, it's full of character.

Camping

The following are recommended:
Camping UATRE, Av 10 and 197, T02262-
438278. The best site, a few kilometres west
of town towards Médano Blanco, with great
facilities, and beautifully situated *cabañas*
too; US$3 per person per day.
Río Quequén, Calle 22 and Ribera Río
Quequén, T02262-428068, www.cabanias
rioquequen.com.ar. Lovely area, cabins (**B**)
available. Sports facilities, pool, bar and cycle
hire. Well-maintained in attractive setting on
the river. US$6 for 2 people per day.

Bahía Blanca *p151*

For more listings, see www.bahiablanca.gov.ar.
A Argos, España 149, T0291-455 0404,
www.hotelargos.com. 3 blocks from the
plaza, the city's finest is a smart 4-star
business hotel with comfortable rooms
and a good breakfast. Also has a restaurant.
A Austral, Colón 159, T0291-456 1700,
www.hoteles-austral.com.ar. A friendlier
4-star with plain, spacious rooms, nice
bathrooms and good views over the city.
Very attentive service and very decent
restaurant. Good position just a couple
of blocks from the plaza.
B Bahía Hotel, Chiclana 251, T0291-455
0601, www.bahia-hotel.com.ar. A new
modern business hotel, this is good value
for well-equipped rooms, though they're
comfortable rather than luxurious. Bright,
airy bar and *confitería* on street level.
Recommended.
C Italia, Brown 181, T0291-456 2700,
hitalia@rcc.com.ar. Set in a lovely 1920s
Italianate building, this is one of the town's
oldest, full of character, but the rooms are
badly in need of a facelift. There's a good
confitería, and it's very central.

Hostels

F pp **Hostel Bahía Blanca**, Soler 701, www.hostelbahiablanca.com. Light, spacious dorms and doubles (**D**) in this old colonial building. Close to town, offers lots of travel advice.

Camping

Best to head for Pehuen Có or Monte Hermoso – both lovely beach places 1 hr away by bus, with plentiful campsites.

Around Bahía Blanca *p152*

See www.monteweb.com.ar, for a complete list.

C-D Petit Hotel, Av Argentina 244, Monte Hermoso, T0291-491818, www.petitfrentealmar.com.ar. Simple rooms with bath, modernized 1950s style in this friendly, family-run place right on the beach. Has a relaxed atmosphere, and the cheap restaurant, **El Faro**, on the beach (breakfast extra) is recommended.

Camping

There are many sites around Monte Hermoso with good facilities.

Camping Americano, T0291-481149, www.campingamericano.com.ar, signposted from main road 5 km before town (bus or taxi from town). A lovely, sprawling, shady site by a quiet stretch of beach, with excellent facilities, hot showers, pool, electricity, restaurant, fireplaces, food shop and *locutorio*. US$10 for 2 per day. Recommended

Santa Rosa de la Pampa *p152*

See www.santarosa.gov.ar for a complete list.

A Club de Campiña, R5, Km 604, T02954-456800, www.lacampina.com. A rather more appealing option than below if you have transport. Wonderful old building, cosy rooms with high ceilings, attractive gardens, pool, gym and spa.

B Calfucura, San Martín 695, T02954-433 303, www.hotelcalfucura.com. A 4-star, business-oriented place with comfortable rooms. Pool, restaurants and a few apartments to rent.

Camping

There is a municipal site near the Laguna Don Tomás.

Parque Nacional Lihue Calel *p153*

See www.lihuecalel.com.ar for more details of the area.

ACA Hostería, R152, Km 152, T/F02952-436 101. There are 8 decent rooms with TV, and a restaurant. In an attractive setting in open landscape, 2 km south of park entrance.

Camping

There is a campsite near the park entrance with good facilities.

❼ Eating

Mar de Ajó *p144*

If self-catering, buy fresh fish on the beach when the fishermen come back at 1000.
El Quincho (♥), Francisco de las Carreras No 800, and **Parrilla San Rafael** (♥), Av Libertador 817, are both recommended.

Pinamar *p144*

The restaurants listed here are the best options in town.

♥♥ **Tante**, De las Artes 35, T02254-482735. A small, elegant place – and one of the most expensive – serving a good variety of dishes. Often recommended. Fantastic hot chocolate.
♥ **Tulumei**, Av Bunge 64. A nautical theme in the decor goes with the excellent fish served in this small and popular place.
♥ **Viejo Lobo**, Av del Mar and Av Bunge, T02254-483218. On the beach. Good seafood and international menu.

Cariló *p145*

♥♥ **Diviadero del Mar**, Benteveo and the beach, T02254-572010. Wonderful location overlooking the beach. Try the Caribbean salad, and the grilled salmon.
♥♥ **El Totem**, Av Divisadero and Cerezo, T02254-571936. Local favourite for pizzas and quick meals.

Mar de las Pampas and Mar Azul *p146*

†† Marechiare, Julio Roca and Corvina, T02255-453061. Next to the sea, with an excellent range of fish and seafood dishes.

†† Viejos Tiempos, Leoncio Paiva between Cruz del Sur y Peñaloza, T02255-479524. This is owned by local pioneers, who also serve some Mexican and German specialities together with more refined meals. Homely surroundings. This is *the* place to come for tea – worth a detour for the gorgeous cakes.

Mar del Plata *p147, map p147*

Besides the city centre, there are lots of seafood restaurants concentrated next to the fishing port, and in the **Centro Comercial del Puerto**. There are cheap pasta and *parrilla* restaurants along **Rivadavia**. But for more modern and chic places to eat and drink, head for 2 more areas that have become popular for attractive smaller shops, trendy bars, pubs and restaurants: Calle Güemes and the western end of Alem, next to cemetery, which is popular with young crowds late in the evening:

†† Pehuén, Bernardo de Irigoyen 3666. Eclectic and attractive decor in this very good and popular *parrilla*.

†† Tisiano, San Lorenzo 1332. Good pasta in this attractive place with a leafy patio.

† Almacén El Condal, Alsina and Garay. A charming old corner bar, popular with a young crowd for *picadas* and drinks.

† Ampola, Güemes 3064. Tiny chocolate shop and slightly larger tea room upstairs serving delicious biscuits, cakes and pastries.

† La Bodeguita, Castelli 1252. A Cuban bar with food and live music. An excellent place for a drink, great atmosphere.

Centre of town

†† Trenque Lauquen, Av Colón y Paunero. A traditional *parrilla*.

† Antares, Córdoba 3025. About 15 blocks west of the centre, this very popular brewery and restaurant attracts an eclectic crowd for its excellent beers and imaginative, good value food. Live shows every Mon.

† Boston, Buenos Aires 1927 and Blvd Marítimo 3887. A slightly old-fashioned *confitería* with very good set menus and a great range of excellent sandwiches and pastries.

† Finca del Sol, San Martín 2459. Cheap *tenedor libre* with vegetarian choices.

† Manolo, Rivadavia 2371, and on the coast at Blvd Marítimo 4961. Famous for *churros* (the sausage-shaped doughnuts) with hot chocolate for party-goers in the early hrs. Lively atmosphere, packed in high summer, tasty pizzas, sea view.

† Torreón del Monje, Paseo Galíndez. A picturesque stone building on a rocky point at the southern end of Bristol Beach, this is an unbeatable spot for its attractive terraces on the beach, serving decent food all day long. Recommended for breakfast.

Port area and Centro Comercial del Puerto

Good for seafood restaurants, although many are brightly lit and not very atmospheric.

†† El Viejo Pop, Av Martínez de Hoz 599, Candlelit and designed like a ship, this is the best option, and serves superb paella.

†† Los Vascos, Av Martínez de Hoz 643. A long-established atmospheric place for fish and seafood.

†† Taberna Baska, 12 de Octubre 3301. Another recommended option for good seafood next to the port.

††-† Chichilo, Centro Comercial del Puerto – Loc. 17, www.chichilo.com. Cheaper than the rest but by no means cuts back on portions or taste. A huge serving of *brotola* (a type of fish) can be bought for US$7, as well as a hefty portion of seafood paella.

El Bosque de Peralta Ramos

†† El Descanso del Marino, Yanquetruz and Diagonal M Gertrudis, www.eldescansodel marino.com.ar. Specializing in different types of fish and seafood. The owner, Adriana, will give you a personal talk about how the family came to work on the sea and how the restaurant was born. There are lots of history books, family photos and documents, to ponder over as you dine here. A treasure trove in the middle of nowhere that even has free Wi-Fi connection

Miramar *p150*
Lots of restaurants along Calle 21, and at the *balnearios*, on the seafront.
Ÿ **Cantina Italiana**, 9 de Julio and Calle 32. As its name suggests, this is a recommended place for good pasta, and seafood too; also offers a delivery service.
Ÿ **El Pescador Romano**, Calle 22, No 1022. Excellent fish in this popular family restaurant.
Ÿ **Mickey**, Calle 21 No 686. A lively long-established *confitería* serving cheap meals.

Necochea *p150*
ŸŸ **Cantina Venezia**, Av 59, No 259, T02262-424014. This is the most famous of the excellent seafood restaurants near the port, not to be missed.
ŸŸ **La Casona de Rocco**, Calle 8 and 81. A large house, popular with families. Home-made pastas and seafood, both recommended.
Ÿ **Chimichurri**, Calle 83, No 345. A popular place, recommended for *parrilla*.
Ÿ **Parrilla del Loco**, Calle 56, No 3202, T02262-437094. Classic *parrilla*, deservedly popular for superb steaks.
Ÿ **Pizzería Tempo**, Calle 83, No 310, T02262-425100. A lively, traditional place serving good pizzas.

Bahía Blanca *p151*
ŸŸ **Lola Mora**, Av Alem and Sarmiento. The city's most sophisticated restaurant serves delicious Mediterranean-style food, in an elegant colonial-style house. Excellent.
Ÿ **El Mundo de la Pizza**, Dorrego 53. Fabulous pizzas, made with thin bases and loaded with toppings. Big atmospheric place, the city's favourite. Unbeatable.

Ÿ **Micho**, Guillermo Torres 3875, Ingeniero White, T0291-457 0346. There are several good fish restaurants in the port area, but this elegant restaurant is the best. Take a taxi at night as it's in an insalubrious area.
Ÿ **Santino**, Dorrego 38. Italian-influenced menu, with a relaxed but sophisticated atmosphere, and a welcoming glass of sparkling wine. Very good value, recommended.

Cafés and ice-cream parlours
La Piazza, on the corner of the plaza at O'Higgins and Chiclana. Great coffee in a buzzing atmosphere, good salads and cakes.
Lepomm, Alsina 390. The best place for ice cream, especially their chocolate *amargo* and *flan de dulce de leche* – delicious.
Muñoz, O'Higgins and Drago. Sophisticated café for reading the papers.

Around Bahía Blanca *p152*
Ÿ **Marfil**, Valle Encantado 91, Monte Hermoso. The smartest option in town, serving delicious fish and pastas.
Ÿ **Pizza Jet**, Valle Encantado and Int Majluf, Monte Hermoso. Hugely popular for all kinds of food, arrive before 2130 to get a table.

◑ Bars and clubs

Mar del Plata *p147, map p147*
Many bars and nightclubs are on Alem or its surroundings and start at around 0200: **Bikein**, Formosa 254; and **Mr Jones**, Alem 3738, are both for trendy under-25 crowds. **La Llorona**, on Olavarría, near Blvd Marítimo and the Torreón del Monje, is the place if you're not 25 anymore.

Bahía Blanca *p151*
Lots of discos on Fuerte Argentino (along the stream leading to the park) mainly catering for under 25s: **Chocolate**, **Bonito** and **Toovaks**. The best place for the over 25s is **La Barraca**.

⊛ Entertainment

Mar del Plata *p147, map p147*
On Wed there is a 50% discount at all cinemas. Lots more listed in the free leaflet *Guía de Actividades* from the city tourist office. Reduced price theatre tickets are often available for theatre performances etc from **Cartelera Baires**, Santa Fe 1844, local 33, or from **Galería de los Teatros**, Santa Fe 1751, and some others on Santa Fe. Many shows, comedy especially, in summer. See *Guía de Actividades*.
Casino central, Dec-Apr 1600-0500; May-Nov, Sun-Thu 1500-0230, Fri-Sat 1500-0330, free. There are 3 other casinos that operate nearby in summer.
Centro Cultural Pueyrredón, 25 de Mayo 3102, T0223-499 7893. Every day screenings, music shows, plays or conferences, mostly free or for a small fee.

⊛ Festivals and events

Mar del Plata *p147, map p147*
Jan National Fishing Festival.
Dec Fiesta del Mar. One of the biggest festivals, it takes place mid-month.
Mar International Film Festival. This famous festival is in the 1st half of the month. Showcases new Argentine films and attracts some good premières from all over the world.

O Shopping

Bahía Blanca *p151*
There's a smart, modern shopping mall **Bahía Blanca Plaza Shopping**, 2 km north of town on Sarmiento, with a cheap food hall, cinema (T0291-453 5844) and supermarket. There's also the supermarket, **Cooperativa**, on Donado and plenty of clothes and shoe shops on Alsina and San Martín within a couple of blocks of the plaza.

▲▲ Activities and tours

Santa Teresita *p144*
Fishing
There are plenty of boats offering fishing trips off the coast, costing around US$30 per person for 3-4 hrs; book ahead. **Christian Maurs**, Calle 8, No 1043, T02246-430461, elcapitan pesca@telpin.com.ar; and **Choco**, Calle 38, No 1642, T02246-421730, are recommended.

Mar del Tuyú *p144*
Fishing
Excellent fishing either from the pier or on a boat trip.
El Pescador II, Calle 2, between 67 and 68, T02246-434728. Organizes day trips to Laguna La Salada, as well as the usual sea excursions.
Tiburon II, Av 1 BIS No 7503 and Calle 75, T02246-434698, eltiburon@infovia.com.ar. 3-hr boat trips, leaving daily at 0700.

Villa Gesell *p146*
Horse riding
Tante Puppi, Blvd and Paseo 102, T02255-455533. Every day on summer afternoons, offers horse rides in the dunes and also moonlit rides on the beach.

Mar del Plata *p147, map p147*
There are lots of tour operators at the port and in the town centre along the promenade where you can find information about city tours or tours to the surrounding areas.

Cycling
Bicicletería Madrid, Hipólito Yrigoyen 2249, on Plaza Mitre, T0223-494 1932 (take buses 573, 551 or 553). US$8 per day, also hires bikes for 2, US$14 per day.

Fishing
There is good fishing all year along the coast from the shore, and off shore in hired boats:

pejerrey and corvina abound; you can charter a private launch for shark fishing. Offshore fishing is best in Nov and Dec, when pescadilla are plentiful: winter is ideal for pejerrey. Deep-sea fishing yields high salmon and sea bass. Contact the tourist office for advice, T0223-495 1777, www.mardelplata.gov.ar.

Fishing licences are available from **Dirección de Fiscalización Pesquera**, Mitre 2853, T0223-493 2528, and fishing gear shops.

Golf
Mar del Plata Golf Club, Aristóbulo del Valle 3940 (near Playa Grande), T0223-486 2221. This is a great course, and deservedly famous, in a wonderful elevated position by the beach.

Horse riding
El Cobijo, Camino JM Bordeu, Km 2 (Sierra de los Padres), T0223-463 0309. Horse riding in the picturesque hilly setting of Sierra and Laguna de los Padres.

Tour operators
City tours leave from Plaza España and Plaza Colón. Tours also to Miramar and the sierras. 1-hr boat trips along the city coast on the *Anamora*, several times daily in summer, Sat-Sun only in winter, from Dársena B, Muelle de Guardacostas in the port, US$9, T0223-489 0310.

Around Mar del Plata *p149*
Fishing
Club de Pesca Balcarce, Villa Laguna Brava, T0223-460 8019, www.irapescar.com (in Spanish).

Necochea *p150*
Cycling
There are several options for bike hire in the park, Av Pinolandia between 2 and 10.

Fishing
There's splendid *pejerrey* fishing on beautiful *lagunas* at **Estancia La Pandorga**, T02262-1550 4419, near Energía (70 km west of Necochea), and at Laguna Loma Danesa, near La Dulce (60 km northwest of Necochea), T02262-1550 6504.

For boats, contact **Melluso Brothers**, Calle 26, No 4044, T02262-426065, for 1-hr tours or full-day fishing trips.

Fishing shop: **Gómez Pesca**, Av 59, No 1168, T02262-427494.

Golf
Golf club, Armada Argentina and 575, Quequén, T02262-450684.

Horse riding
Caballo's, Villa Marítima Zabala and Av 10, T02262-423138.

Bahía Blanca *p151*
Tour operators
ASATEJ, Zelarrayán 267, T0291-456 0666, ww.asatej.com.ar.

● Transport

San Clemente del Tuyú *p143*
Bus
To **Mar del Plata** (and to resorts in between) services are frequent, US$10, 5 hrs, **El Rápido**, El Rápido Argentino. To **Buenos Aires**, US$18, several companies.

Pinamar *p144*
Bus
For bus terminal information, see page 145. Buses to **Buenos Aires**, 4-5 hrs, US$21. To **Mar del Plata**, US$6, 2½ hrs, Rápido Argentino.

Train
For information about the railway station, see page 145. To **Buenos Aires** (Constitución), US$13 Pullman, US$10, the cheapest class.

Villa Gesell *p146*
Bus
For bus terminal information, see page 146.

To **Buenos Aires**, with Plusmar, Plaza, El Rápido Argentino 5-6 hrs, US$21. To **Pinamar**, US$1.50, 25 mins, Rápido Argentino. To **Mar del Plata**, with El Rápido and El Rápido Argentino, 1½ hrs, US$3.

Mar del Plata *p147, map p147*
Air
For airport information, see page 148.

Daily flights to **Buenos Aires**, Aerolíneas Argentinas/Austral, T0223-4960101. LADE flies in summer to towns in **Patagonia** once a week.

Airline offices Aerolíneas Argentinas, Austral, Moreno 2442, T0223-496 0101; LADE, Rambla Casino Loc 5, T0223-493 8211.

Bus
For bus terminal information, see page 148.

Local El Rápido del Sud line 212 from Terminal goes south along the coast via **Miramar** up to **Mar del Sud**; line 221 goes north from the southern beaches and **Punta Mogotes** up to **Mar Chiquita**. From the bus terminal, line 511 and 221 will take you into the centre, to the lighthouse, out to the beaches further to the south and to the port. The routes are fairly regular (every 10 mins) and run all night (although the late-night service is less frequent). **Note** Some buses, including the 511, can only be used with a top-up card, available from any kiosk (a similar system to the Monedero in Buenos Aires capital).

Long distance To **Buenos Aires**, 5-6 hrs, US$23. To **San Clemente del Tuyú**, frequent, 5 hrs, US$10, El Rápido. To **Pinamar**, 2 hrs, US$6 and to **Villa Gesell**, 1½ hrs, US$3 with El Rápido and El Rápido Argentino. The former company also goes southwest to **Miramar**, hourly, 45 mins, US$2.50; to **Necochea**, 2 hrs, US$6; and to **Bahía Blanca**, 6 daily, 7 hrs, US$21. To **Bariloche**, 20 hrs, US$83, Vía Bariloche. To all Patagonian towns along R3, ending

at **Río Gallegos**, 36 hrs, US$98, with Transportadora Patagónica. To **Mendoza**, daily, 19-22 hrs, US$73, Andesmar. To Posadas, 20 hrs, US$76, **Tigre Iguazú**.

Car hire
Avis, at airport, T0223-470 2100; Budget, Córdoba 2270, T0223-495 2935; Hertz, Córdoba 2149, T0223-496 2772.

Train
For information on the railway station, see page 148.

To **Buenos Aires** (Constitución) daily, 5½ hrs, US$17 Pullman, US$14 the cheapest class. Also services to **Miramar**.

Around Mar del Plata *p149*
Bus
Frequent services to Balcarce from **Mar del Plata**, El Rápido, T0223-451 0600 (in Mar del Plata).

Miramar *p150*
Bus
To **Buenos Aires**, 6 hrs, US$32, several companies. To **Mar del Plata**, 45 mins, US$2.50, El Rápido del Sud.

Train
To **Buenos Aires** (Constitución), via **Mar del Plata**, daily in summer, once a week off season, US$12.

Necochea *p150*
Bus
For bus terminal information, see page 151.

To **Buenos Aires**, 8 hrs, US$31, La Estrella/El Cóndor, Parque Plus-Mar; to **Mar del Plata**, US$6, El Rápido; to **Bahía Blanca**, US$12, El Rápido .

Bahía Blanca and around *p151*
Air
For airport information, see page 151.

Daily flights to **Buenos Aires** with AR/ Austral, T0291-456 0561/T0810-2228 6527; LADE, T0291-452 1063. LADE has weekly flights to **Bariloche**, **Mar del Plata**, **Neuquén**, **Puerto Madryn**, **San Antonio Oeste**, **San Martín de los Andes** (may involve changes). Book ahead in summer.

Airline offices Aerolíneas Argentinas, San Martín 198, T0291-426934. LADE, Darregueira 21, T0291-437697.

Bus

For bus terminal information, see page 151. **Local** You need to buy *tarjetas* (Tarjebus cards) from kiosks for 1, 2, 4 or 10 journeys.

Long distance To **Buenos Aires** frequent, 8½ hrs, US$39, shop around, several companies. Most comfortable by far is **Plusmar** suite bus, T0291-456 0616, with completely flat beds, US$27. To **Mar del Plata**, 7 hrs, US$21, El Rápido; to **Córdoba**, 12 hrs, US$38; to **Neuquén**, 6 a day, 8 hrs, US$19; to **Necochea**, 5 hrs, US$12, El Rápido; to **Viedma** 4 hrs, US$13, Ceferino, Plusmar and Río Paraná (to **Carmen de Patagones**); to **Trelew**, 10½ hrs, US$40, Don Otto and others; to **Río Gallegos**, US$86, Don Otto; to **Sierra de la Ventana** (town), US$6.50, Expreso Cabildo and La Estrella/El Cóndor. Also *combi* (minibus) with Geotur, T0291-450 1190, terminal at San Martín 455.

Bus companies Andesmar, T0291-481 5462, Ceferino, T0291-481 9566, Don Otto, T0291-481 8585, Rápido del Sur, T0291-481 3118.

Taxi

Taxi Universitario, T0291-452 0000, T0291-453 0000.

Train

For information on the railway station, see page 151.
To **Buenos Aires** 3 weekly, 12½ hrs, Pullman US$16, own compartment.

Santa Rosa de la Pampa *p152*
Bus

To **Buenos Aires**, 8 hrs, US$25; to **Neuquén**, 8 hrs, US$21, Andesmar, T02954-432841, El Valle (Via **Bariloche**) T02954-423554.

ⓞ Directory

Mar del Plata *p147, map p147*
Banks Many ATMs all around the central area, along Peatonal San Martín, at Santa Fe and Rivadavia, and 2 close together around the casino. **Currency exchange** Casas de Cambio Jonestur, San Martín 2574, and Av Luro 3181, gives the best rates for cash exchange. **Internet** Broadband internet is available in most places. **Post office** Av Luro 2460, also international parcels office (open till 1200). **Telephone** There are many *locutorios* around the town.

Bahía Blanca *p151*
Banks Many ATMs on plaza (all major cards). Lloyds TSB Bank, Chiclana 299, T0291-455 3263; Citibank, Chiclana 232; Pullman, San Martín 171. **Embassies and consulates** Chile, Güemes 102, T0291-455 0110; Italy, Colón 446, T0291-454 5140; Spain, Drago 70, T0291-422549. **Internet** Try places along Estomba and Zelarray and near plaza. **Laundry** Laverap, Av Colón 197; Las Heras, Las Heras 86. **Post office** Moreno 34. **Telephone** Big *locutorio* at Alsina 108, also internet. **Visas and immigration** Migraciones, Brown 963.

Southern Sierras

The south of Buenos Aires province has two ranges of ancient mountains rising suddenly from the flat Pampas; both are easily accessible and offer great opportunities for a weekend escape. The Sierra de Tandil range, due south from Buenos Aires, is 340 km long and 2000 million years old – among the oldest in the world. The beautiful, curved hills of granite and basalt offer wonderful walking and riding, with the pleasant airy town of Tandil as a base. There are plenty of small hotels, though nearby estancias offer the best way to explore the hills.

Further west, the magnificent Sierra de la Ventana is the highest range of hills in the Pampas, and so called because craggy Cerro de la Ventana has a natural hole near its summit. Next to the Parque Provincial Ernesto Tornquist, it is within easy reach of Bahía Blanca for a day or weekend visit, and the attractive villages of Villa Ventana and Sierra de la Ventana nearby are appealing places to stay, with plenty of accommodation options. These mountains are not quite as old as those in Tandil, but offer more demanding hikes in wilder terrain, with stunning views from their summits. There are daily buses and combis from Bahía Blanca, but you could break the journey at the quaint sleepy town of Tornquist. ▸▸ For listings, see pages 169-172.

Tornquist → For listings, see pages 169-172. Colour map 4, C4. Phone code 0291. Population 6066.

Tornquist, 70 km north of Bahía Blanca, is a pretty, sleepy, rural town that you will pass through if travelling to Sierra de la Ventana via Route 33. It has an attractive church on the large central plaza (which is more like a tidy park), a strangely green artificial lake, and a big children's play area. It's not a touristy place, but that's precisely its appeal, and it's a good starting point for excursions into the sierras. About 11 km east of town is the Tornquist family mansion (not open to tourism), built in a mixture of French styles. The town is named after Ernesto Tornquist (1842-1908) the son of a Buenos Aires merchant of Swedish origin. Under his leadership the family established an important industrial investment bank and Tornquist helped to establish the country's first sugar refinery, meat-packing plant and several chemical plants. There's a **tourist office** ① *Plaza Ernesto Tornquist, 9 de Julio and Alem, T0291-494 0081, www.tornquist.gov.ar*, for information.

Parque Provincial Ernesto Tornquist → For listings, see pages 169-172. Phone code 0291.

The sierras are accessed from the Parque Provincial Ernesto Tornquist which is 25 km east of Tornquist on Route 76. There are two main access points, one at the foot of Cerro Ventana and the other one, further east, at the foot of Cerro Bahía Blanca. It's US$2 to enter the park. Other than the Campamento Base (see below), the nearest places for accommodation are the two towns of Sierra de la Ventana and Villa Ventana. ▸▸ For transport to the park, see page 172.

Cerro Ventana
① To enter this section of the park, turn left after the massive ornate gates from the Tornquist family home. There are showers and a food kiosk.
There is an **information point** ① *Dec-Easter daily 0800-1700*, and *guardaparques* who you can ask for advice and register with for the longer walks. Nearby is the hospitable **Campamento Base** ① *T0291-156 495 304, www.haciafuera.com.ar/campamentobase.htm*, with hot showers, dormitory accommodation and an attractive campsite. From this

entrance, it's a three-hour walk, clearly marked, but with no shade, up **Cerro de la Ventana** (1136 m), which has fantastic views from the 'window' in the summit ridge. Register with *guardaparques* and set off no later than midday. Alternative hikes are a gentle stroll to **Garganta Olvidada** (one hour each way), where you can set off up to 1700, to the **Piletones**, small pools (two hours each way), and **Garganta del Diablo** (six hours return) a wonderful narrow gorge with waterfalls. Guides are available for the walk to Garganta Olvidada, for a minimum of 10 people.

Cerro Bahía Blanca

The entrance to this section of the park is 4 km further east along Route 76. There's a car park and **interpretation centre** ① *T0291-491 0039, Dec-Easter 0800-1800*, with *guardaparques* who can advise on walks. From here you can go on a guided visit to **Cueva del Toro** (only with your own vehicle, four to five hours), natural caves, and the **Cueva de las Pinturas Rupestres** which contains petroglyphs. There are also good walks, including up **Cerro Bahía Blanca** (two hours return), a gentle climb rewarded with panoramic views, highly recommended. There's lots of wildlife to spot, but you're most likely to see grey foxes, guanacos, wild horses and red deer.

Villa Ventana

Some 10 km further from the park's second entrance (Cerro Bahía Blanca section) is an attractive laid-back wooded settlement with weekend homes, *cabañas* for rent and a municipal campsite by the river with all facilities. There's an excellent tea shop, **Casa de Heidi**, and good food served in rustic surroundings at **Las Golondrinas**. The pretty village is the base for climbing **Cerro Tres Picos** (1239 m), to the south of the park, which is the highest peak in the province. The ruins of the **Hotel Club Casino** (1911) can still be seen; once the most luxurious hotel in Argentina, it burned down in 1983. There's a helpful **tourist office** ① *T0291-491 0001*, at the entrance to the village.

Sierra de la Ventana → *Colour map 4, C4. Phone code 0291. Population 1800.*

Continuing east, the town of Sierra de la Ventana is a good base for exploring the hills, with a greater choice of hotels than Villa Ventana, and wonderful open landscapes all around. There is an 18-hole golf course and good trout fishing in the Río Sauce Grande. There's also a wonderful tea shop, **La Angelita**, in the leafy lanes of Villa Arcadia (across the river), and several places on the river to bathe. The helpful **tourist information** ① *Av Roca 15, just before railway track, T0291-491 5303, www.sierradelaventana.org.ar*, has a complete list of all hotels, *cabañas* and campsites with availability and prices.

Tandil → *For listings, see pages 169-172. Colour map 4, C5. Phone code 02293. Population 101,000.*

Tandil is an attractive town, with a light breezy feel, and a centre for outdoor activities, making it a good base for exploring the nearby sierras. There are a couple of marvellous *estancias* in the area and a clutch of restaurants, cafés and bars within the town. On the south side of the main Plaza Independencia are the neoclassical **Municipalidad** (1923), the former **Banco Hipotecario Nacional** (1924) and the **Iglesia del Santísimo Sacramento** (1878), inspired (apparently) by the Sacre Coeur in Paris. Six blocks south of the plaza, up on a hill, is the **Parque Independencia**, with a granite entrance in Italianate style, built by the local Italian community to celebrate the town's centenary. Inside the park, the road winds up to a vantage point, where there's a Moorish-style **castle**, built by the Spanish community to mark the same event, with marvellous views over the surrounding sierras. At the base of the hill is an amphitheatre, where a famous community theatre event takes place during Easter week (book accommodation ahead). South of the park is the **Lago del Fuerte**, a popular place for water sports; bathing is possible at the Balneario del Sol in a complex of several swimming pools. For more information on the city, see www.tandil.com (in Spanish).

West of the plaza on the outskirts of town is **Cerro Calvario**, an easy walk leading to the **Capilla Santa Gemma** at the top. Further away, 5 km from town, **Cerro El Centinela** has a large, attractive, family-oriented tourist complex that includes a 1200-m cable car ride, a good restaurant (book your table in advaance) and swimming pools.

It's easy to get out of the city to explore the hilly countryside on foot or by bike. Heading south past the lake, follow Avenida Don Bosco or one of the nearby tree-lined roads into the beautiful surroundings. Note that you should not enter any private land without permission. Instead, contact local tour operators who have arranged exclusive

Tandil

Sleeping
Ave Maria **6**
Bed & Breakfast **1**
Cabañas Brisas Serranas **2**
Casa Chango **10**
Chacra Bliss **11**
El Solar de las Magnolias **12**
Hermitage **3**
Hostal de la Sierra del Tandil **5**

Jazmines en la Sierra **7**
Las Acacias **9**
Plaza de las Carretas **4**
Siempre Verde **8**
Tanta Pacha Hostel **13**

Eating
1905 **11**
El Molino **2**
El Viejo Sauce **9**

Epoca de Quesos **3**
Parador del Sol **7**
Taberna Pizuela **10**

Bars & clubs
Antares **12**
Liverpool **6**
O'Hara **13**

200 metres
200 yards

access with the land owners. The main **tourist information office** ① *at the access to town (next to R226), Av Cte Espora 1120, T02293-432 225, Mon-Sat 0800-2000, Sun 0900-1300*, is very well organized and has good brochures and urban maps. There are other offices in the **main plaza** ① *near the corner of General Rodríguez NS Pinto, Mon-Fri 0600-1300, 1800-2000, www.tandil.gov.ar*, and at the **bus terminal** ① *Av Buzón 650, T02293-432092, Mon-Sat 0800-1800, Sun 0700-1900*, 12 blocks northeast of the centre. The **railway station** ① *Av Machado and Colón, T02293- 423002*, is 15 blocks north of the plaza.

Six kilometres south is the 140-ha **Reserva Natural Sierra del Tigre**, with good views over Tandil from **Cerro Venado**. Wild foxes and guanacos can be seen occasionally, as well as llamas.

⦿ Southern Sierras listings

For Sleeping and Eating price codes and other relevant information, see Essentials pages 30-36.

⦿ Sleeping

Tornquist *p166*
C-D San José, Güemes 138, T0291-494 0152, www.sanjose-hotel.com.ar. A small, central hotel with faded, simple rooms.

Villa Ventana *p167*
See www.villaventana.com for a complete list.
B-C El Mirador, R76, Km 226, before reaching Villa Ventana, T0291-494 1338, www.complejoelmirador.com.ar. Great location at the foot of Cerro Ventana with basic rooms and a good restaurant.
C San Hipólito, R76, Km 230, T0291-156 428 281. A few fully furnished, small, comfortable houses in a large ranch with welcoming owners, Polito and his wife. Ideal for families with kids. Enjoyable horse rides in the hills.

Sierra de la Ventana *p167*
See www.sierradelaventana.org.ar.
B Cabañas La Caledonia, Los Robles and Ombúes, on leafy Villa Arcadia, T0291-491 5268, www.lacaledonia.com.ar. Well-equipped and comfortable *cabañas* in large gardens.
B Las Vertientes, R76, Km 221, T0291-491 0064, www.com-tur.com.ar/lasvertientes. A long-established ranch with charming hosts and an attractive main house.

A beautiful location for outdoor activities or just for relaxing in peaceful surroundings.
C Alihuen, Calle M Frontini and E Torquist, T0291-491 5074, www.com-tur.com.ar/alihuen. A delightful old place near the river.
C Provincial, Drago 130, T0291-491 5024, hotelprovincial@laredsur.com.ar. An old 1940s state-owned hotel, more quaint than comfy, but with good views, restaurant and a pool. Very good value.

Tandil *p167, map p168*
See www.tandil.com for a complete list.
LL-L Ave María, Paraje la Portena, T02993-422843, www.avemariatandil.com.ar. One of the most exquisite small hotels in the whole province, this may call itself a *hostería*, but the splendid Norman-style building set in beautiful gardens overlooking the rocky summits of the sierras is much more like an *estancia*. Charming owner Asunti encourages you to feel completely at home and ramble around the place as you please. There are only 8 rooms, all impeccably designed with everything you could possibly need, some with doors opening directly onto the gardens. The discreet staff speak perfect English. A great place to relax and swim in the pool or walk in the grounds, hills and woodland. Prices are half-board and discounts apply Mon-Thu. Highly recommended, not to be missed.
AL Las Acacias, Av Brasil 642, T02293-423373, www.posadalasacacias.com.ar.

Hostería in a restored 1890s dairy farm in the Golf Club area, with very comfortable rooms looking out on to large gardens with a splendid pool. Friendly owners who speak English and Italian, and excellent staff help to create a welcoming and homely atmosphere for a delightful stay. Recommended.

AL-A El Solar de las Magnolias, Ituzaingo 941, T02293-428618, www.solarmagnolias. com.ar. New apartment complex of lovely roomy traditional single-storey buildings, with a mix of antique and modern furniture. Parking and breakfast included.

A Cabañas Brisas Serranas, Scavini y Los Corales, T02293-406110, www.brisas serranas.com.ar. Very comfortable and well-furnished *cabañas*, pool, lovely views and welcoming owners.

B Chacra Bliss, Paraje La Porteña, T02293-1562 0202, www.cybertandil.com.ar/ chacrabliss. Charmingly decorated rooms with simple but comfortable furniture, a welcoming pool and a long veranda that catches the afternoon sun. Very relaxing.

B Bed and Breakfast, Belgrano 39, T02293-426989/1560 7076 (text preferred), hutton@ speedy.com.ar. The most welcoming place in town, charming and helpful English owners. There are 2 comfortable, secluded rooms for couples or families, 1 modern double and the large apartment, La Torre, for up to 6, in an idyllic walled garden with small pool. Breakfasts are gorgeous. Host Judy is a delight. Recommended.

B Hostal de la Sierra del Tandil, Av Avellaneda 931/41, T02293-422330, www.hostaldeltandil.com.ar. Spanish-style building, with boldly designed rooms with bath, appealing areas to sit, a good restaurant for residents only, and a pool.

B Jazmines en la Sierra, Libertad 316, T02293-422873,www.jazminesenlasierra. com.ar. 6 attractive rooms with a colour theme, a lovely cottage garden and slightly less appealing common areas with fireplace.

B Plaza de las Carretas, Av Santamarina 728, T02293-447850, www.plazadelascarretas. com.ar. An early 20th-century family house, now a homely and quiet place to stay, with good rooms with eclectic decor and a nice garden at the back.

C Hermitage, Av Avellaneda and Rondeau, T02293-423987, www.hermitagetandil.com. ar. Good value in this quiet, old-fashioned hotel next to the park. There are some smart modernized rooms, though these aren't very different to the standard ones, all very simple, but the service is welcoming.

Hostels

F pp Casa Chango, 25 de Mayo 451, www.casa-chango.com.ar. Bright, colourful hostel set in an old house with lovely communal areas. Central and friendly. Also room for camping.

F pp Tanta Pacha Hostel, Dabidos 1263, T02293-1554 5967, www.tantapacha.com. Lovely, spacious hostel set in an old country house in attractive grounds. Rustic wooden furniture, dorms only.

Estancias

The real experience of Tandil lies in the beauty of its surroundings, best explored by staying in an *estancia*.

L Siempre Verde, 45 km southwest of Tandil (next to Barker), T02292-498555, www.estanciasiempreverde.com. With the most magnificent setting amongst the sierras, this typical 1900s house has a long history. The traditional-style rooms with wonderful old-fashioned bathrooms and lots of antiques have good views over the grounds. The owners, descendants of one of Argentina's most important families, are very hospitable and helpful. Staying here provides a real insight into traditional *estancia* life. Extensive horse riding and walking among the magical sierras in the estate, fishing and *asados* on the hill side. Also offers camping. Highly recommended.

🍴 Eating

Tandil *p167, map p168*
Local produce here traditionally includes cheese and sausages, both excellent and served as part of the *picadas* (nibbles with drinks) offered in local bars and restaurants, or available to take away in several good delis in town, such as **Syquet**, General Rodríguez and Mitre, or **Epoca de Quesos**.
🍴 1905, Av Santamarina and San Martín. A minimalist setting in a charming old house that serves excellent, finely elaborate meals.
🍴 El Molino, Juncal 936. A small, simple place with a little windmill, which specializes in different cuts of meat cooked traditionally *al disco* – in an open pan on the fire.
🍴 El Viejo Sauce, Av Don Bosco and Suiza. Next to the Reserva Sierra del Tigre, in attractive natural surroundings, this is an ideal stopover at tea time for its cakes and home-made jams.
🍴 Epoca de Quesos, San Martín and 14 de Julio, T02293-448750. An atmospheric 1860s house serving delicious local produce, wines, home-brewed beers and memorable *picadas* to share, which include a great range of cheeses, salami, sausages and traditional pampas bread. Recommended.
🍴 Parador del Sol, Zarini s/n, T02293-435 697. Located in the attractive *balneario* by Lago del Fuerte, serving great pastas and salads in a smart beach-style trattoria.
🍴 Taberna Pizuela, Paz and Pinto. Attractive old place serving a broad range of very good simple dishes, including pizzas, their speciality.

🍸 Bars and clubs

Tandil *p167, map p168*
Antares, 9 de Julio 758. A popular brewpub, lively in the late evening with excellent beers, good meals and live music every Mon.
Liverpool, 9 de Julio and San Martín. Pictures of the Beatles in this relaxed and friendly bar.

O'Hara, Alem 665. An unbeatable selection of whiskies attracts a mixed crowd. Wines, *tapas* and live music too in this Irish pub.

⛰ Activities and tours

Sierra de la Ventana *p167*
Geotur, San Martín 193, Sierra de la Ventana, T0291-491 5355, www.com-tur.com.ar/geotur. Trekking, mountain-biking and horse-riding excursions. Also operate a minibus which leaves a few times a day along R76 from Sierra de la Ventana to Tornquist, dropping you off at the entrance to the park.

Tandil *p167, map p168*
Golf
Tandil Golf Club, Av Fleming s/n, T02293-406976, www.tandilgolfclub.com.

Horse riding
Gabriel Barletta, Avellaneda 673, T02293-427725. Recommended rides with Gabriel, expert on native flora, who might end your tour with an informal acoustic guitar session.

Trekking
To find an approved guide who will take you to otherwise inaccessible land for trekking, see www.guiasdetandil.com.ar.
Eco de las Sierras, Maipú 714, T02293-442 741, www.ecodelasierras.com. Run by Lucrecia Ballesteros, a highly recommended guide who is young, friendly and knowledgeable. Day trips (paragliding, lunch and swimming) from US$46.
Kumbre, Av Alvear 124, T02293-434313, www.kumbre.com. Trekking, mountain biking and some climbing guided by experienced Carlos Centineo.
Valle del Picapedrero, T02293-430463, www.valledelpicapedrero.com.ar. Guided walks along a beautiful nearby valley with Ana Maineri, a geology expert.

☺ Transport

Parque Provincial Ernesto Tornquist *p166*
Bus
La Estrella/El Cóndor has daily services connecting Tornquist and Sierra de la Ventana with Buenos Aires and **Bahía Blanca**. To **Bahía Blanca** also Expreso Cabildo and a few minibus companies.

Tandil *p167, map p168*
Bus
To **Buenos Aires**, 5-6 hrs, US$24, with La Estrella/El Cóndor, Parque and Río Paraná. Río Paraná goes daily also to **Bahía Blanca**, 6 hrs, US$21, and to **Mar del Plata**, 4 hrs, US$10. El Rápido goes to **Mar del Plata**, 3 hrs, US$11.

Taxi
Alas, on the main plaza, T02293-422222. A *remise* taxi company.

Train
To **Buenos Aires**, 1 service a week, US$8.

Contents

Footprint features

At a glance

⊖ **Getting around** Short-distance minibuses are frequent and comfortable. A hire car is helpful if you want to see more in less time.

◉ **Time required** Between 3 and 5 days allows you to visit some small towns and see Córdoba city.

☀ **Weather** The mountain air stops the summers from being too humid and the winters from being too windy.

✖ **When not to go** Jan is busy with family holidays, as is Easter, and during Oktoberfest it can be hard to find accommodation.

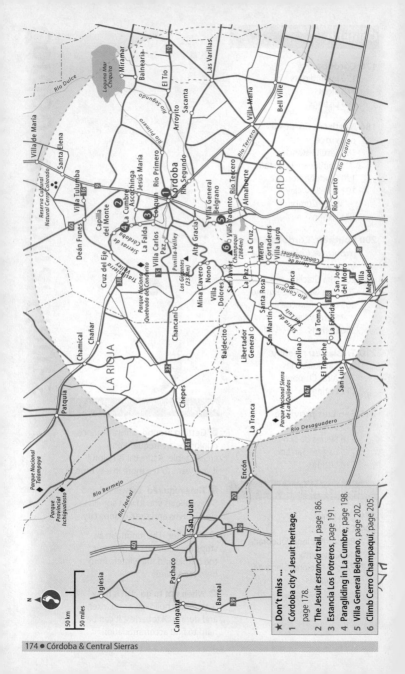

★ **Don't miss ...**

1 Córdoba city's Jesuit heritage, page 178.
2 The Jesuit *estancia* trail, page 186.
3 Estancia Los Potreros, page 191.
4 Paragliding in La Cumbre, page 198.
5 Villa General Belgrano, page 202.
6 Climb Cerro Champaquí, page 205.

Córdoba, Argentina's second biggest city, has an entirely different character from Buenos Aires. The sparky Cordobeses are known for their quick wit and warm welcome, and are understandably proud of their city's history. The Jesuits established the country's oldest university here in the 17th century, with a centre of learning funded by *estancias* all over the province. These magnificent *estancias*, tucked away in the Sierras Chicas, are the main tourist attraction, while the mountains themselves are best explored on horseback. Here, at hilltop Estancia Los Potreros, you can live the real gaucho life in comfort, or steep yourself in presidential luxury at grand Estancia La Paz, before heading north to the remote reaches of Cerro Colorado, where there are amazing displays of rock art in a bizarre rocky landscape.

South of the city in Alta Gracia is Che Guevara's childhood home, but don't miss the best Jesuit museum inside the spectacular *estancia* in the centre of town. Nearby Villa General Belgrano remains a German stronghold, with chalet-style architecture and endless microbreweries and *apfelstrudel*. Escape from the crowds to Córdoba's most stunning scenery, high along the Camino de las Altas Cumbres into the Traslasierra Valley. Hike into the mountains and gaze at condors in flight at the Parque Nacional Quebrada del Condorito, where majestic birds wheel above the dramatic peaks, and teach their young to fly.

Further west, the sleepy provincial capital of San Luis lies at the foot of its own magnificent sierra which intrepid travellers can explore in Parque Nacional Sierra de las Quijadas, with its dramatic red sandstone canyon. At sleepy villages El Trapiche and Carolina, you can even mine for gold.

Córdoba city

→ Colour map 4, A2. Phone code 0351. Population 1,370,000.
At the centre of an area of great natural beauty lies a modern city with a fascinating past. Córdoba is the capital of one of the country's most densely populated and wealthy provinces, with a lively student population and buzzing atmosphere. It lies on the Río Suquía, extending over a wide valley, with the sierras visible in the west. The city has been an important trade centre since the area was colonized in the 16th century, and it retains an unusually fine set of colonial buildings at its heart, the astonishing Manzana de los Jesuitas, complete with its temple still intact. Cordobeses are renowned throughout the country for their sharp sense of humour, defiant attitude and a lilting accent that other regions delight in imitating. However, along with their strong sense of civic pride, their warm welcome makes Córdoba one of the most hospitable areas in the country. For more information, see www.turismocordoba.com.ar and www.disfrutacordoba.com, or www.cordobaturismoafull.com.ar (in Spanish). ▸▸ For listings, see pages 180-185.

Ins and outs

Getting there
There are frequent flights from Buenos Aires (two hours), Santiago de Chile and major northern Argentine cities to Córdoba's airport, **Pajas Blancas** ① T0351-434 1692, 12 km northwest of centre. The **airport** is best reached by taxi (US$8), as the bus service is unreliable. Long-distance buses connect the city with almost everywhere in the country and arrive at the central **bus terminal** ① Blvd Perón 380, T0351-434 1694, eight blocks east of the main plaza. The terminal has restaurants, internet facilities, a supermarket, left-luggage lockers for US$1 per day (coins only), a *remise* taxi desk, an ATM and a tourist office on the lower level, where the ticket offices are. To leave the terminal go upstairs and cross the bridges towards the city centre. A taxi to Plaza San Martín costs US$2.50. Minibuses that travel to nearby towns stop at the main terminal and then stop at the **minibus terminal** ① Blvd Illia 155, T0351-425 2854. ▸▸ For further information, see Transport, page 184.

Getting around
Most of the city's sights can easily be visited on foot within a day or so. There's a leafy pedestrian shopping area to the north of the Plaza San Martín, and the historical Manzana de los Jesuitas is two blocks southwest of here. Buses share the main roads with trolleybuses. Both charge a fixed fee of US$0.45, and don't accept cash; buy tokens (*cospeles*) or cards from kiosks. Ordinary yellow taxis are usually more convenient for short distances than green *remise* taxis, which are better value for longer journeys. Tourists are allowed to park free in the centre, but must display a sticker, free from hotels and tourist offices, valid for a week and easily renewable.

Best time to visit
Avoid the hot and stormy summer months from December to February, when daytime temperatures are around 30°C. The dry season is April to September, with clear skies, cooler temperatures, but still pleasantly warm.

Córdoba

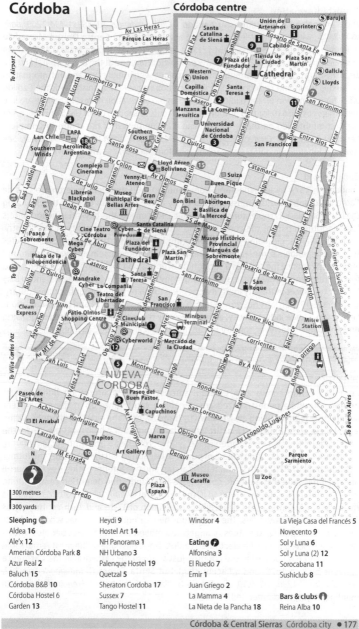

Córdoba centre

Sleeping 🛏

Aldea **16**
Ale'x **12**
Amerian Córdoba Park **8**
Azur Real **2**
Baluch **15**
Córdoba B&B **10**
Córdoba Hostel **6**
Garden **13**
Heydi **9**
Hostel Art **14**
NH Panorama **1**
NH Urbano **3**
Palenque Hostel **19**
Quetzal **5**
Sheraton Cordoba **17**
Sussex **7**
Tango Hostel **11**
Windsor **4**

Eating 🍴

Alfonsina **3**
El Ruedo **7**
Emir **1**
Juan Griego **2**
La Mamma **4**
La Nieta de la Pancha **18**
La Vieja Casa del Francés **5**
Novecento **9**
Sol y Luna **6**
Sol y Luna (2) **12**
Sorocabana **11**
Sushiclub **8**

Bars & clubs 🍸

Reina Alba **10**

Tourist information

There are helpful tourist offices at **Cabildo** ⓘ *Independencia 30, T0351-434 1200, daily 0800-2200* , with a small gallery, restaurant and bookshop; at **Centro Obispo Mercadillo** ⓘ *Rosario de Santa Fe 39, T0351-434 1215*; at **Patio Olmos Shopping Mall** ⓘ *Av San Juan and Vélez Sarsfield, T0351-420 4100, www.patioolmos.com,* and at the **bus terminal** and the **airport**. All are open early morning until late at night, with useful city maps and information on guided walks and cycle tours. See www.cordoba.gov.ar (in Spanish). Visit the Cabildo office for information on the daily tours they run (no reservation necessary); some are free and others cost US$10 for two or more people. Tours in Spanish or for US$5 in English. For the best information on the province, head 8 km northwest of the centre to **Complejo Ferial** ⓘ *Av Cárcano, Chateau Carreras, T0351-434 8260, dacyt.turismo@cba.gov.ar.* See www.cordobaturismo.gov.ar (in Spanish), for information on the whole province.

Background

Founded in 1573 by an expedition from Santiago del Estero led by Jerónimo Luis de Cabrera, Córdoba was the most important city in the country in colonial times. During the late 16th and 17th centuries, the Jesuit Order made the city their headquarters for the southern part of the continent and founded the first university in the country, giving the city its nickname 'La Doctora' (the Learned). In 1810, when Buenos Aires backed independence, the leading figures of Córdoba voted to remain loyal to Spain, and after independence the city was a stronghold of opposition to Buenos Aires. It's remained fiercely independent ever since, supporting many Radical party governments, and in May 1969 disturbances in the city ignited opposition to military rule throughout the country. Since the 1940s Córdoba has grown from a cultural, administrative and communications centre into a large industrial city, though recently the recession has resulted in growing unemployment. However, the city has an upbeat feel and a fabulous nightlife.

Sights

Old City

Córdoba's centre comes as a pleasant surprise. Its most interesting buildings are grouped around a pedestrianized area, enabling you to gaze up at the magnificent architecture without being mown down by traffic. Most of the older buildings lie within a few blocks of the **Plaza San Martín**, which dates from 1577 when it was the site for the odd bullfight. Now it's a wide open space, with lots of cafés, a fine statue of San Martín, and jacaranda trees creating a mass of purple in late spring. On the west side, the former **Cabildo**, built in 1610, with characteristic arches and two interior patios, has a colourful history. It has served as a prison, courthouse and clandestine detention centre during the last military dictatorship. Next to it, the **cathedral** ⓘ *daily 0800-1200, 1630-2000,* is the oldest in Argentina, an extraordinary confection of 17th- and 18th-century styles from successive renovations. The marvellous neo-baroque interior has wooden doors from a Jesuit temple and statues of angels resembling the indigenous peoples, with a silver tabernacle and lavishly decorated ceiling. Don't miss one of the most remarkable collections of religious art in the country, just south of the cathedral in the **Carmelite convent** built in 1628, and adjacent chapel of **Santa Teresa** ⓘ *Independencia 122, Wed-Sat 0930-1230, US$0.50, guided visits also in English and French*. A beautiful building; highly recommended.

On the west side of the pleasant Plaza del Fundador, one block west, the convent and church of **Santa Catalina de Siena**, founded in 1613 but rebuilt in the late 19th century, contains a splendid collection of paintings from Peru as well as colonial Spanish tapestries and carpets. For more contemporary art, the **Museo Municipal de Bellas Artes** ① *Av General Paz 33, T0351-433 1512, Tue-Sat 1000-2000,* has a permanent collection by celebrated Argentine artists in an early 20th-century French-style mansion.

The **Manzana Jesuítica**, contained within the streets Avenida Vélez Sarsfield, Caseros, Duarte Quirós and Obispo Trejo, has been declared a World Heritage Site by UNESCO. The **Iglesia de la Compañía**, at the corner of Obispo Trejo and Caseros, was originally built between 1640 and 1676, and its curious vaulted ceiling is a ship's hull, created by a Jesuit trained in the Dutch shipyards. Behind the church, on Caseros, is the smaller, most beautiful **Capilla Doméstica**, a private 17th-century Jesuit chapel, accessible only with a guided tour, but worth seeing for the indigenous painting on the altar. The main building of the **Universidad Nacional de Córdoba** ① *T0351-433 2075, Tue-Sun 0900-1300, 1600-2000, US$5, guided visits (in English) to the church, chapel, university (called Museo Histórico) and school leave from Obispo Trejo 242, Tue-Sun 1000, 1100, 1700 and 1800,* originally the Jesuit Colegio Máximo, now houses one of the most valuable libraries in the country, as well as the Colegio Nacional de Montserrat, the most traditional high school of the province. Guided visits are obligatory, see details above.

Other fine examples of religious architecture are the **Iglesia de San Francisco**, Buenos Aires and Entre Ríos, on a leafy plaza, and the **Iglesia de San Roque**, Obispo Salguero 84. One block east of plaza San Martín is the **Museo Histórico Provincial Marqués de Sobremonte** ① *Rosario de Santa Fe 218, T0351-433 1661, Tue-Fri 0900-1300,1500-1900, Sat 0900-1300, Sun 1000-1300, US$1,* with texts in English and German, the only surviving colonial family residence in the city, dating from 1760, and a labyrinth of patios and simply decorated rooms. The **Basílica de La Merced**, at 25 de Mayo 83, has a fine gilded wooden pulpit dating from the colonial period and beautifully carved wooden doors, with fine ceramic murals revealing Córdoba's history on the outside by the local artist Armando Sica.

Nueva Córdoba

Over the past few years Nueva Córdoba (south of the Plaza San Martín) has become the hippest part of town, due in part to the numbers of students that frequent the area (the university is a short walk from here). There are cute shops, cafés and lots of hostels and, at night, the area is taken over by bars and clubs; head to Rondeau and Cañada, or Blvd San Juan and Larrañaga, to be part of the action. There is an eclectic mix of building styles along Avenida Hipólito Yrigoyen. The new **Paso del Buen Pastor** ① *Av Hipólito Yrigoyen 325, T0351-432272,* has a cultural centre at its heart with an art gallery ① *Tue-Sun 1000-2000, free,* a book shop, a wonderful café ① *T0351-422 0768, daily 0900-0030,* and a beautifully presented chapel. Next door the neo-Gothic **Iglesia de los Capuchinos** ① *T0351-433 3412, Tue-Sun 1100-1900,* displays the night skies for every month of the year. Stop off at Colores Santos, a fantastic café with comfy chairs and view of the church, for morning tea. Further up towards the park are two worthwhile art galleries. Set in an amazing turn-of-the-century palace, the **Museo Superior de Bellas Artes Evita-Palacio Ferreyra** ① *Av Hipólito Yrigoyen 511, T0351-434 3636, Tue-Sun 1000-2000, US$1,* has 12 salons spread out over three floors and shows a range of Argentine and international artists. Opposite, in front of Plaza España, is the modern **Museo de Bellas Artes Emilio Caraffa** ① *Av Hipólito Yrigoyen 651, T0351-433 3412, www.museocaraffa.org.ar, Tue-Fri 1000-2000, Sat-Sun 1030-1900, free,* which is dedicated to presenting the best of

Cordobese visual arts. **Parque Sarmiento** is the largest green area of the city, laid out by French architect Charles Thays in 1889 with small lakes, a neat rose garden and a **zoo** ① *T0351-421 7643, daily 0900-1900, US$1.50*, set among steep hills.

Other sights

The magnificent **Mitre railway station**, near the bus terminal, has a beautiful tiled *confitería*, still in use for Sunday evening tango shows (see Entertainment, page 182). The lively, crowded market, **Mercado de la Ciudad**, provides a taste of local urban culture.

⊙ Córdoba city listings

For Sleeping and Eating price codes and other relevant information, see Essentials pages 30-36.

⊜ Sleeping

Córdoba city *p176, map p177*
There are several small places next to the bus terminal, but they're unreliable. For more listings, see www.cordobaturismo.gov.ar or www.disfrutacordoba.com.
AL Azur Real Hotel Boutique, San Jerónimo 243, T0351-424 7133, www.azurrealhotel.com. The best place to stay in Córdoba. Spread over 2 levels this listed 1915 building has 14 immaculately modern rooms (each with a choice of 6 pillows!) centred around a courtyard, as well as a wonderful deck and plunge pool. Located next to the historical centre this hotel is perfect. They also have a restaurant which is open to the public. Recommended.
AL Sheraton Córdoba, Duarte Quirós 1300, T0351-526 9000, www.sheratoncordoba. com. All the services you would expect from a 5-star hotel, plus great views over the city and a stunning triangle-shaped swimming pool on the roof.
AL Windsor, Buenos Aires 214, T0351-422 4012, www.windsortower.com. A small and smart 4-star, with a warm atmosphere, large breakfast, and use of sauna, gym and pool.
A Amerian Córdoba Park, Blvd San Juan 165, T0351-420 7000, www.amerian.com. Swish, modern hotel with marbled foyer and professional service. Rooms are hardly inspired in their decor, but they are very comfortable, the breakfasts are superb and

this is a convenient and reliable place to stay. Also has a spa and pool.
A NH Panorama, Marcelo T de Alvear 251, T0351-410 3900, www.nh-hoteles.com. Situated on La Cañada stream, this 4-star has comfortable business-style rooms and excellent views of the sierras from its upper floors. Small pool, gym and a restaurant. The **NH Urbano**, a block further south on Marcelo T de Alvear(La Cañada) 363, T0351-410 3960, is more central, if a little more business-like.
B Córdoba B&B, Tucumán 440, T0351-423 0973, www.cordoba-byb.com.ar. Sparsely decorated but clean doubles and triples, close to the centre. Buffet breakfast, Wi-Fi and parking all included. Budget option in this price bracket.
B Garden Hotel, 25 de Mayo 35, T0351-421 4729, www.garden-hotel.com.ar. A friendly and attractive budget hotel under new management. Great location.
B Heydi, Blvd Illia 615, T0351-423 3544, www.hotelheydi.com.ar. This spotless, quiet 3-star has pleasant rooms with TV and homely decor, breakfast included.
B Sussex, San Jerónimo 125, T0351-422 9070, www.hotelsussexcba.com.ar. The 110 rooms are basic with flouncy bedspreads, but it's clean and extremely central. Ask for a room with a view of Plaza San Martín. Pool, breakfast is included.
C-B Alex, Blvd Illia 742, T0351-421 4350, www.alexhotel.com.ar. A good-value hotel, modern and cosy inside the slightly off-putting exterior. All rooms have bath and include breakfast and a *mate* kit. Staff are

very friendly, there is a small pool and it's very close to the bus station. Recommended.
C Quetzal, San Jerónimo 579, T/F0351-422 9106. Refurbished with dubious taste, this is good value as the rooms are spotless with bath. Breakfast extra.

Hostels

F pp Tango Hostel, Fructuoso Rivera 70, T0351-425 6023, www.latitudsurtrek.com.ar. Good hostel accommodation in the Nueva Córdoba district, right in the heart of student heaven, with nightclubs and bars all around. Breakfast is included any time of day, rooms sleep 2-5 and there's a kitchen and library. Dinner also offered, as are lots of trips in and around Córdoba city with the good company, **Latitud Sur**.
F pp Córdoba Hostel, Ituzaingo 1070, Nueva Córdoba, T0351-468 7359, www.cordobahostel.com.ar. The biggest hostel in Córdoba. Great location, helpful staff, an on-site bar and basic dorms and doubles. There is a nice courtyard for BBQs and the reception can book extreme and not-so-extreme adventure sports .
F pp Aldea, Santa Rosa 447, T0351-426 1312, www.aldeahostel.com. Only about 8 blocks from the centre of town, this hostel is nicely designed and decorated. Welcoming outdoor terrace and clean bathrooms. Ping-pong, cable TV and a pool table to keep you entertained. Dorm prices vary depending on the number of people you share with.
F pp Baluch, San Martín 338, T0351-422 3977, www.baluchbackpackers.com. Lively, friendly and popular, this hostel has a great rooftop bar, clean and inviting dorms, and small but pleasant doubles (**D**). Located on a busy, slightly ugly market pedestrian street, 6 mins' walk from the main plaza. Recommended.
F pp Palenque Hostel, Av General Paz 371, T0351-423 7588, www.palenquehostel. com.ar. Lovely hostel set in a 100-year-old terrace building with spacious common areas, a well-equipped kitchen and small but friendly dorms and doubles (with TV).

F pp Hostel Art, Corro 112, T0351-423 0071, www.hostelart.com.ar. New hostel, a bit out of the centre, that sells art works, and is connected to a tattoo parlour. Fantastic 1950s style throughout the common areas, and colourful clean dorms. Friendly staff.

🍴 Eating

Córdoba city *p176, map p177*
♦♦♦ Sibaris, Buenos Aires 214, T0351-425 4477. Not for those on a budget, the newly renovated restaurant at the **Hotel Windsor** is a culinary delight. Large wine menu, and delectable mains.
♦♦♦-♦♦ Juan Griego, Obispo Trejo 104, T0351-1557 39760. Located on the 7th floor of the Colegio de Escribanos with a view of the Jesuit Manzana, this modern Argentine restaurant is unmissable. Only open at lunch.
♦♦ Cebiche, Jerónimo Luis de Cabrera 1041, T0351-422 3470. Peruvian food, full of colour, flavor and innovation.
♦♦♦ Novecento, Dean Funes 33, at the Cabildo, T0351-423 0660, www.bistronovecento.com. A smart, lively place with a lovely light patio and appealing decor with dark wooden tables and immaculate tablecloths. Superb, fresh Mediterranean-style cooking, lots of fish and pasta, and excellent service. Lunch only, bar open 0800-2000. Recommended.
♦♦ Sushiclub, 11 Irigoyen 419, T0351-482 1753. Part of the Sushiclub chain, this is a great place to eat something other than meat. Well made and nicely presented sashimi.
♦♦-♦ La Nieta de la Pancha, Jujuy 278, T0351-468 1920. Local home-cooked goodies including pastas, roast meat (beef, rabbit and goat's meat).
♦ Sol y Luna, Gral Paz 278, T0351-451189, www.solylunaonline.com.ar. A life-saver for vegetarians and those in need of some vegetable goodness. Try the *humitas*, or the breaded aubergine slices.
♦ Alfonsina, Duarte Quirós 66, T0351-427 2847. Young urban crowds flock to this inviting old house for, great simple meals,

pizza, *empanadas árabes*, *milanesas* or breakfasts with home-made bread. Warm atmosphere.

Ψ **Emir**, Bv Illia 33. Recommended Middle Eastern food.

Ψ **La Mamma**, Santa Rosa and F Alcorta. Good-quality affordable pizzas and pastas.

Cafés

Cafeto, Caseros 88. Just next to the Manaza in one of Córdoba's prettiest streets, this café, with its charming patio, is a good place to stop for lunch. Good salads.

El Ruedo Bar, Obispo Trejo and 27 de Abril. Lively *confitería*, also serving light meals.

Mandarina, Obispo Trejo 171. Central, very welcoming place with lovely decor. Lots of great breakfasts, and good for lunch and dinner too. Friendly staff. Highly recommended.

Sorocabana, Buenos Aires and San Jerónimo. Good cheap breakfasts for US$2.50, popular place on plaza San Martín.

🍸 Bars and clubs

Córdoba city *p176, map p177*
Córdoba has a rich and varied nightlife, with young crowds gathering in different areas of the city mainly on Fri and Sat, but on weekdays too during the holidays.

In **Nuevo Córdoba** head to Rondeau, Larrañaga or Cañada streets. **Alfonsina**, Duarte Quirós 66, if you need to express yourself with a piano or guitar. **Johnny B Good**, Av Hipólito Yrigoyen 320. **Boca del Lobo**, Buenos Aires 883. Relatively chilled bar, with a good atmosphere.

El Abasto district, on the river (about 8 blocks north of plaza San Martín) has several good, cheap places: **Casa Babylon**, Blvd Las Heras 48, has a disco night on Fri and rock music on Sat; and in **Dorian Gray**, Las Heras and Rs Peña, you can enjoy good music and a lively scene. Best Thu-Sat.

Another popular nightlife area lies further northwest in **Chateau Carreras**: Carreras,

Av Ramón J Cárcano, is the most popular club, frequented by trendy crowds in their 20s.

Zen, Julio A Roca 730, and **Beep**, Sucre and Colón, are 2 popular gay clubs with good beats and a good atmosphere.

🎭 Entertainment

Córdoba city *p176, map p177*
See free listings magazines *La Cova* and *Ocio en Córdoba*, local newspaper *La Voz del Interior*, and www.cordoba.net, for events.

Cinema

Mainstream films at **Complejo Cinerama**, Av Colón 345; and **Gran Rex**, Av General Paz 174. Independent, old and foreign language films at **Cineclub Municipal**, Blvd San Juan 49; and at **Cine Teatro Córdoba**, 27 de Abril 275.

Cuarteto

Very definitively a Cordobés invention, this music has given fame to 'La Mona' Jiménez, and many impersonators, whose gigs are attended by enthusiastic crowds.

The most popular venues are **Asociación Deportiva Atenas**, Aguado 775; **Estadio del Centro**, Santa Fe 480; and **La Vieja Usina**, Av Costanera and Coronel Olmedo.

Tango

This Buenos Aires tradition also has a home in Córdoba, every Sun from 2000 at **Confitería Mitre**, Blvd Perón 101 (in the railway station), tango class before *milonga* begins, US$3.

El Arrabal, Belgrano and Fructuoso Rivera, www.elarrabal.com.ar, is a popular restaurant with a tango show after 2400, Fri and Sat, US$2 extra.

For classes contact **Prof Hugo Arriagada**, T0351-156 744 119, huguitotanguerito@hotmail.com, or **Eugenia Goytea**, T0351-155 450 994, goytea.eugenia@gmail.com, to arrange personalized lessons – or ask at El Arrabal.

Theatre

The **Teatro del Libertador**, Av Vélez Sarsfield 367, T0351-433 2312, is traditional and sumptuous, with a rich history. On Plaza San Martín is **Real**, San Jerónimo 66, T0351-433 1669. Smaller places next to Puente Alvear include **Espacio Cirulaxia**, Pasaje Agustín Pérez 12; and **Quinto Deva**, Pasaje Agustín Pérez 10.

✿ Festivals and events

Córdoba city *p176, map p177*
Oct The Festival of Latin American Theatre.

○ Shopping

Córdoba city *p176, map p177*
The main shopping area is along the pedestrian streets north of the plaza. On Belgrano, 700 and 800 blocks, there are several antique shops.

Bookshops

Librería Blackpool, Deán Funes 395. Imported English-language books.
Tienda de la Ciudad, on a patio at the Cabildo. Specializes in books of local and regional interest.
Yenny-El Ateneo, Av General Paz 180. English-language titles.

Handicrafts

Mundo Aborigen, Rivadavia 155; **Unión de Artesanos**, San Martín 42 (Galería San Martín, local 22).
Paseo de las Artes, Achával Rodríguez and Belgrano, Sat and Sun 1700-2200, free. Market selling ceramics, leather, woodcrafts and metalware.

Outdoor equipment

Buen Pique, Rivadavia 255; **Suiza**, Rivadavia and Lima.

Shopping malls

Córdoba Shopping, José de Goyechea 2851 (at Villa Cabrera), T0351-420 5001.
Dinosaurio Mall, Rodríguez del Busto 4086, T0351-526 1500.
Nuevocentro, Av Duarte Quirós 1400, T0351-482 8193.
Patio Olmos, Av Vélez Sarsfield and Blvd San Juan, T0351-420 4100. The best shopping mall, located in a wonderful old palace with a stylish food area.

▲ Activities and tours

Córdoba city *p176, map p177*
Tour operators

On average, operators charge around US$25 per person for ½-day excursions and US$45 per person for a full-day trip. The main destinations are in the Punilla, Calamuchita and Traslasierra valleys and all Jesuit-related places. The city tourist office offers city tours on foot or bike, as well as cheap guided visits to the Jesuit *estancias* in Jesús María and Alta Gracia. The tourist office at the Cabildo, T0351-468 0019, guiasdecordoba@qmail.com, runs daily city tours, including **Córdoba Underground**, the **Historical Centre** and the **Manzana**, the **Church Circuit** and more. Some are free and others cost US$10 for 2 or more people. Tours in Spanish or for US$5 in English.
Córdoba City Tour, T0351-424 6605, www.cordobacitytour.com.ar. Big red bus leaving every day except Wed from outside the cathedral at 1630. See the website for additional times.
Córdoba Renta Bike, San Martín 5, T0351-421 8012, cordobarentabike@gmail.com. Full-day (US$20) and ½-day (US$9) hire with either mountain bikes or street bikes.
Explorando, T03543-437901, www.explorandosierras.com.ar. Alternative tours including birdwatching, mountain biking, horse riding and local excursions.

Itatí, 27 de Abril 220, T0351-422 5020. Good local company with tours in the province.
Nativo, 27 de Abril 11, T0351-424 5341, www.cordobanativoviajes.com.ar. Huge range of tours, very professional and reliable.
Southern Cross, Av General Paz 389, T0351-424 1614, www.terraargentea.com. Off the beaten track.

⊖ Transport

Córdoba city *p176, map p177*
Air
For airport information, see page 176.

There are several daily flights to **Buenos Aires**, about 2 hrs, with Aerolíneas Argentinas. Aerolíneas Argentinas also fly daily to **Mendoza**, **Tucumán** and **Ezeiza airport**, and 3 times weekly to **Jujuy** and **Salta**. Lan Chile has daily flights to **Santiago de Chile**, 1½ hrs. Lloyd Aéreo Boliviano flies weekly to **Santa Cruz de la Sierra**, via Salta. Sol flies daily to **Rosario**. Gol has weekly flights to Brazil and Uruguay.

Airline offices Aerolíneas Argentinas/Austral, Av Colón 520, T0351-410 7600, Tue-Fri 0900-1900, Sat 0900-1300; Lan Chile, Figueroa Alcorta 206, T0351-422 3058; Lloyd Aéreo Boliviano, Av Colón 119, 3rd floor office 6, T0351-421 6458; Southern Winds, Figueroa Alcorta 192, T0810-777 7979; Gol, T0810-266 3232, www.vogol. com; Sol, T0810-444 4765 www.sol.com.ar.

Bus
For bus terminal information, see page 176.

Buses and trolleybuses charge US$0.50, only payable in tokens (*cospeles*) or cards from kiosks. Minibuses, *diferenciales*, depart from a nearby platform; tickets can be bought on the bus or from offices in the terminal, 1st floor. Minibuses that travel to nearby towns stop at the main terminal and then stop at the minibus terminal, Blvd Illia 155, T0351-425 2854, which may be more convenient for accommodation.

Local To **Alta Gracia**, Sarmiento; SATAG; and **Sierras de Calamuchita** (stops on the highway, 30-min walk from centre or US$2 taxi), 1 hr, US$5. To **Cerro Colorado**, 3 weekly, 4½ hrs, US$7, **Ciudad de Córdoba**. To **Jesús María**, 1 hr, US$3, Ciudad de Córdoba, Colonia Tirolesa.
To **Laguna Mar Chiquita**, Expreso Ciudad de San Francisco goes to Miramar, 3½ hrs, US$7. Transportes Morteros goes to **Balnearia**, 3 hrs, US$6. To **Punilla valley**, Ciudad de Córdoba, TAC (La Falda, US$4; La Cumbre, US$5), and El Serra, La Calera, Lumasa, Transierras. To **Río Ceballos**, 1 hr, US$4, La Quebrada; Ciudad de Córdoba goes also to **Río Ceballos** and continues north to **Ascochinga** and then, **Jesús María**. To **Río Cuarto**, 3-3½ hrs, US$10, TUS. To **Traslasierra valley**, Ciudad de Córdoba, TAC (**Mina Clavero**, 3 hrs, US$7), and Sierra Bus and Panaholma minibus services. To **Villa Carlos Paz**, Ciudad de Córdoba, also Car-Cor and El Serra minibus services, 45 mins, US$3. To **Villa General Belgrano**, TUS, Sierras de Calamuchita (also runs minibus services, like Lep, La Villa and Pájaro Blanco), 1½-2 hrs, US$4.

Long distance To **Buenos Aires**, 9-11 hrs, US$43 (*coche cama*), Chevallier; General Urquiza; TAC. To **Catamarca**, 5-7 hrs, US$20, General Urquiza; TAC. To **Jujuy**, 12 hrs, US$47, Balut; TAC. To **La Rioja**, 6-7 hrs, US$18, Chevallier, General Urquiza, Socasa. To **Mendoza**, 10-12 hrs, US$34, Andesmar; Autotransportes San Juan-Mar del Plata; CATA; Expreso Uspallata; TAC. To **Puerto Iguazú**, 20 hrs, US$75, Crucero del Norte and Expreso Singer. To **Rosario**, 5-6 hrs, US$25, General Urquiza, TAC. To **Salta**, 12 hrs, US$35, Chevallier, La Veloz del Norte. To **San Luis**, 7 hrs, US$21, Andesmar, Autotransportes San Juan-Mar del Plata, TAC. Andesmar and TAC have connecting services to several destinations in Patagonia.

To Bolivia Take Balut or Andesmar
services to the border at **La Quiaca**, 19 hrs,
US$60, or **Pocitos**, 17 hrs, US$66.

To Chile To **Santiago**, 17-19 hrs, US$25,
CATA; TAC.

To Peru To **Tacna**, US$75, with change
at Mendoza and Santiago de Chile.

Car hire
Avis Blvd San Juan 137, T0351-426 1110;
Rentauto, San Jerónimo 131, T0351-421
1240; **Travel Rent a Car**, Humberto Primo
244, T0810-333 2763.

Remise taxis
Alta Córdoba Remis, T0351-471 0441;
Auto Remis, T0351-472 7777.

Train
There are weekly trains from the Mitre station,
Blvd Perón 371 (next to bus terminal) to **Villa
María** and Buenos Aires, T0351-426 3565.

❶ Directory

Córdoba city *p176, map p177*
Banks Open in the morning only. Banco
de Galicia; Boston Bank; Banco de la Nación;
Lloyds Bank, all on Plaza San Martín, all have
ATMs. **Currency exchange** Exchange and
TCs at **Barujel**, Rivadavia and 25 de Mayo;

Exprinter, Rivadavia 47; Western Union
branch, in the post office. **Embassies and
consulates** Bolivia, San Jerónimo 167,
6th floor, T0351-424 5650; Chile, Crisol 280,
T0351-469 0432. **Internet** Many places
charge US$0.50 per hr including: **Cyber
Freedom**, 27 de Abril 261; **Cyber world**,
Obispo Trejo 443; **Mandrake Cyber**, Marcelo
T de Alvear 255; **Mega Cyber**, Marcelo T de
Alvear 229, open until 0500. **Language
schools** Caseros Spanish School, Caseros
873, T0351-424 7877, www.cordoba-spanish.
com.ar. Located just 2 blocks from the
Manzana this friendly school with small
classes can organize excursions. Espanex,
Av General Paz 55, 18th floor, www.espanex.
org, large organization with schools in
Bariloche and Buenos Aires too, can arrange
accommodation; Set Idiomas, Corrientes 23,
T0351-421 1719, www.set-idiomas.com.ar,
centrally located school offering all levels of
classes in grammar, conversation and local
culture. **Medical services** Hospital Córdoba,
Av Patria 656, T0351-434 9000; Hospital
de Clínicas, Santa Rosa 1564, T0351-433
7010; Nuevo Hospital de Niños Santísima
Trinidad, Bajada Pucará 1900, T0351-434
8800, children's hospital. **Post office**
Av Colón 210, parcel service on the ground
floor beside the customs office. **Visas
and immigration** Dirección Nacional de
Migraciones, Caseros 676, T0351-422 2740.

Northern Córdoba province

Stretching north from Córdoba city are two parallel chains of mountains known as the Sierras Chicas, with wonderfully wild landscapes to explore. There are two main routes north offering quite different pleasures. Head up Route 9, named by the tourist board as the Camino de la Historia, to visit Jesús María and the Jesuit estancias, the cultural highlights of Córdoba province. Hiring a car is the best way to really enjoy them, as you can stop off at the more attractive villages in the hills and stay at rural estancias too, such as luxurious La Paz in Ascochinga; if you don't, the local minibuses are clean and efficient, and taxis are cheap. North of here, Route 9 leads to the Reserva Natural Cerro Colorado, where there are extraordinary prehistoric paintings in red rocky landscapes, or further northwest, the old Camino Real, now Route 60, leads you to quaint unspoiled villages where you can hide away in remote estancia San Pedro Viejo. The alternative route north along the Punilla Valley (Route 38) takes you through depressing built-up tourist towns, so keep going until you reach the pretty little mountain town of La Cumbre, which offers spectacular paragliding, golf and the laid-back, friendly villages of Capilla del Monte and San Marcos Sierras nearby are great bases to explore the mountains.

The region's most interesting rural landscapes lie between these two valleys, where there are beautiful rolling mountains, best explored on horseback from the traditional rural estancia, Los Potreros, just an hour from Río Ceballos in the valley. You could easily spend a week here and not exhaust the places to explore. Birdwatchers would be entertained here too, though keen twitchers should head east to Laguna Mar Chiquita, a lake the size of a small sea, which is a paradise for migratory birds. See www.lacumbrecita.gov.ar, and www.cordoba turismo.gov.ar (both with English option), for help with planning.
▸▸ *For listings, see pages 194-199.*

Jesuit estancias: Camino de la Historia → *For listings, see pages 194-199.*

The real jewel in the crown of Córdoba province is the collection of fine 17th-century Jesuit *estancias* in the hilly, rural areas to the north of the provincial capital. Three of the oldest *estancias* lie close to what used to be the **Camino Real** (the 'royal road'), used by the Spanish to link Córdoba with Lima and the Alto Perú mines. The Jesuit missionaries established huge, enterprising *estancias* in the country that were used to finance their educational and artistic work in the city. The elegant residences and beautiful chapels built for the priests still remain, complete with some wonderful art and walled gardens. These can be explored at **Jesús María**, 40 km north of Córdoba, **Estancia Caroya** nearby, and **Santa Catalina**, 20 km further northwest. You could visit all three Jesuit *estancias* in a day's drive from Córdoba, but part of the charm of exploring the sierras is to enjoy a night or two in the area's marvellous *estancias* – the kind where you're offered fine wine with dinner and horse riding, rather than religious instruction. For more information, visit www.sierraschicas.net and www.cordobaciudad.com/estancias jesuiticas.

Jesús María → *Colour map 4, A3. Phone code 03525. Population 27,000.*

The sleepy town of Jesús María, with its avenues lined with trees, is a good base for exploring two of Córdoba's oldest Jesuit *estancias*. It's typical of towns that grew through a wave of immigration from Friuli in the north of Italy, starting with 60 families in 1878. There's a distinctly Italian influence to the food, with some superb salamis to be found in the cafés and shops. Jesús María itself has little to offer tourists, but during the first half of January it hosts the **Festival de Doma y Folclore**, a popular *folclore* music and gaucho event whose profits benefit local schools.

There are two **tourist offices** ① *bus station, Belgrano 580, T03525-426113; and on the way into town on R9, T03525-426773, www.jesusmaria.gov.ar*, which provide useful information. Ask for the leaflet *Caminos de las Estancias Jesuíticas*, which includes a handy map of the *estancias* in relation to Córdoba, a map and some information on each *estancia* (in Spanish). From the main road into town, Estancia de Jesús María and Estancia Caroya are clearly signposted.

Estancia Jesús María

① *1 km northeast of the centre of Jesús María, T03525-420126. Mon-Fri 0800-1900, Sat and Sun 1000-1200, 1500-1900, US$1.50, Mon free. Guided tours 0900, 1000, 1100, 1430, 1530, 1730 (in Spanish).*

This is a well-conserved example of a Jesuit-built *estancia*, whose produce supported the schools in Córdoba. Argentina's first vineyards were created here and wine from Jesús María was reputed to have been the first American wine served to the Spanish royal family. The residence and church, built mainly in 1618, form three sides of a square enclosing a neat garden with pleasing cloisters on two sides. The imposing façade of the church is in good condition, with tall, plaster-covered pillars contrasting with the stonework of the main building, but it's a sober affair compared with the opulent interior of the church, with its finely decorated cupola. In the adjoining **Museo Jesuítico**, beautiful Cuzco-style paintings, religious objects and a curious collection of plates are on display, together with early winemaking artefacts. There are no longer remains of the housing for slaves and indigenous workers, or the cultivation areas, but, with its lovely pond underneath mature trees and a small graveyard to the left of the church, the whole place is very attractive and peaceful. Highly recommended for a few hours' visit.

You can get there by taxi ($2, 'Pancho' from Rapi-taxi, T0351-1552 7213 is recommended), or it's an easy 15-minute walk from the Jesús María bus station: take Avenida Juan B Justo, north, turn left at Avenida Cleto Peña, cross the bridge over the river and follow a dirt road right about 300 m.

Estancia de Caroya

① *In the southern suburbs of Jesús María, T03525-426300. Mon-Fri 0900-1800, Sat-Sun 0900-1500. US$1.*

Estancia de Caroya, dating from 1616, was the first of the Jesuit establishments to be built in the area and has an interesting history. It was acquired in 1661 by the Jesuit founder of the Colegio Convictorio de Montserrat (in Córdoba city). While its agricultural activities funded the college, it was also used as a holiday home for the students. Between 1814 and 1816, it was used as a weapons factory for the Army of the North fighting in the Wars of Independence, and then in 1878 the first Italian immigrants stayed here. A simpler construction than Jesús María, Santa Catalina consists of single-storey cloisters around a central patio, with access to kitchens, dining rooms, and a simple stone chapel. The fascinating history is well presented in the displays here, including a room with artefacts from the Italian immigration (although the tour is informative your guide may not speak English). Ruins of a dam and a mill can be seen in the surrounding gardens.

You can go by taxi ($2) or it's a 20-minute walk from the bus station: take Avenida Juan B Justo, south, and turn right at Avenida 28 de Julio. After 500 m, the gates of the *estancia* are on the left side of the road. Ask the staff at the *estancia* to call you a taxi to get back into town, they are very helpful.

Around Jesús María

Next to Jesús María, **Colonia Caroya** was the heart of the Italian immigration, and you can taste delicious salami at any of the local restaurants. The long access road is beautifully lined by an uninterrupted avenue of mature sycamore trees, where you'll find **Bodegas La Caroyense** ① *Av San Martín 2281, T03525-466270, www.lacaroyense-sa.com. ar, Mon-Fri 0800-1200, 1500-1900, Sat-Sun 1000-1800, free*, a winery offering guided visits.

Set picturesquely among hills, 22 km west of Route 9, the attractive village of **Villa Tulumba** has hardly changed since colonial times. It's worth visiting for the beautiful 17th-century baroque tabernacle in its church, crafted in the Jesuit missions.

Estancia Santa Catalina

① *T03525-421600, www.santacatalina.info. Tue-Fri 1000-1300, 1500-1930, Sun 1000-1800 in summer, Tue-Fri 1000-1300, 1400-1800 in winter. Only open Sat-Sun during Jan, Feb, Jul, Easter and bank holidays, US$2.*

This is the largest of the *estancias*, beautifully located in rolling fertile countryside northwest of Jesús María, and not to be missed. It is also the best preserved of all the *estancias* and the only one that remains in private hands, having the added advantage of being close to Ascochinga (see below), which has some good accommodation.

The house is still in use by the extended Díaz family as their weekend and summer home, but the church and all the outbuildings are open to the public. The guided tour (Spanish only) is included in the entrance price and provides lots of information on the way of life here, as well as allowing you to visit the seminary buildings and the second and third patios (not during January, February, July and Easter), which are rich in architectural detail. Access is by a 14-km dirt road branching off Route E66 to Ascochinga, 6 km west of Jesús María (signposted, 20 km in total). From Jesús María bus station, *remise* taxis charge US$31 return including two hours' waiting time at the *estancia*. Good lunches are available at **La Ranchería de Santa Catalina** ① *T03525-424467*, a simple rustic restaurant on the right as you approach the *estancia*. It also has two small guest rooms (**B-C**) with shared bathroom.

Built in 1622, the church has the most wonderful baroque façade, with swooping curves and scrolls in white plaster, and twin bell towers. The beautifully maintained interior has a fabulous gold pulpit and retable, brought from Alto Perú, with religious figures made by indigenous craftsmen betraying certain anatomical details of their makers, such as their big knees and robust workmen's thighs. There are superb Cuzco-school paintings representing the Passion and, opposite the retable, an intriguing articulated sculpture of Jesus on the cross. This was used by the Jesuit priests as a teaching device to evangelize the indigenous peoples, and unlike most such figures, this Jesus has his eyes open: his arms could be lowered to enact scenes from his life, pre-crucifixion, and then raised, as he was mounted on the cross. A moving and fascinating figure.

The house has a beautiful central patio, where just three priests lived in spacious splendour, organizing a staff of 600 and a workforce of thousands of African slaves and local indigenous peoples. Santa Catalina was the most important of the *estancias* economically, with its 25,000 head of cattle and extensive agriculture. To the right of the church is a huge vegetable garden and, further out, a little brick building with six tiny rooms where novice priests were trained. The slaves' quarters were even more miserable and can be found on the road leading to the *estancia*, now converted into a restaurant.

The servants for the main house were housed in the second patio, and in the third patio were wood and metal workshops. In the lovely surrounding parkland, you can see the *tajamar* – a reservoir used for the sophisticated watering system for crops.

Ascochinga and Estancia La Paz

The upmarket little village of **Ascochinga**, 13 km west of Santa Catalina, is full of second homes for rich *Córdobes* and has a couple of shops, a part time *locutorio*, an ACA petrol station and plenty of accommodation options. A fabulously opulent place to stay is the historical **Estancia La Paz** ① *Ashcochinga, www.estancialapaz.com*, which was owned by President Roca from 1872 until his death in 1914, and remains almost untouched. Just try not to think about him planning the massacre of the indigenous peoples in the Conquest of the Desert when he stayed here. Roca added the neoclassical Italianate touches to the building, and commissioned a splendid 100-ha park from Argentina's most famous landscape architect Charles Thays, whose work includes the parks at Palermo, Tucumán and Mendoza. There are grand bedrooms, with enormously high ceilings, coming directly off a long terrace with wonderful views across the huge ornamental lake where you can go rowing if the mood takes you. There are immense groves of exotic trees and blissful, private places to sit on the 1930s garden furniture and order tea from the impeccable staff. Old-fashioned opulence is combined with more modern luxuries such as an Olympic-sized pool, tennis courts, a spa with expert masseuse and a superb restaurant, making this a real treat. They also offer day-rates, if you don't have the time or the money to stay the night.

Asochinga to La Cumbre

From Asochinga a spectacular route heads over the mountains to La Cumbre (see page 193). The road courses through wonderful landscapes of rounded mountain ridges and deep valleys and is much loved by rally drivers and cyclists in training. This winding dirt road, full of hairpin bends, is probably best not attempted in the dark or in bad weather. Keep your speed below 40 kph, watch out for hares and perdis crossing the road, and allow at least two hours for the journey. The vegetation varies from lush subtropical woodlands to lush scrub on the summits, and there are consistently great views on a fine day.

Northeast of Córdoba → *Colour map 4, A3. Phone code 03563.*

From Route 9 north of Ascochinga you can head east to Argentina's largest inland sea, the **Laguna Mar Chiquita** ('Lagoon of the Small Sea'), set on the borders of the Pampas and the Chaco, 192 km northeast of Córdoba. The lake is very shallow (maximum depth 12 m) and has no outlet into any rivers, so its size varies (from 65 km by 80 km, to 30 km by 40 km) according to rainfall patterns. At times, the water is apparently so salty you can float in it.

A reserve, called the **Reserva Natural Bañados del Río Dulce y Laguna Mar Chiquita** ① *www.promarmarchiquita.com.ar*, has been created to protect the huge numbers of migratory birds that flock here in summer from the northern hemisphere. So far, over 300 species of bird have been spotted here, returning to different parts of the lagoon each year. There are also large resident populations of flamingos representing all three species extant in South America. It's the site of greatest biodiversity in the province, and is also popular for fishing *pejerrey* all year round. During the summer, human visitors flock here too, since the salty waters are used in the treatment of rheumatic ailments and skin diseases. It's a singular and spectacular landscape and, although you may feel it's not worth a big detour, if you're spending some time in the area, it would make a good relaxing day out. Park administration is in Miramar on the southern shore, the only settlement nearby, where there are a few hotels and campsites. There's a **tourist office** ⓘ *Libertad 351, T03563-493003.*

Córdoba Norteña → *For listings, see pages 194-199.*

If you're enjoying getting off the beaten track and want to see where the Camino Real leads, keep going northwest from Jesús María along Route 60 into the northernmost extreme of the province. In **Deán Funes** (118 km from Córdoba), you'll find a couple of decent hotels, plenty of places to eat and a **tourist information office** ⓘ *Sáenz Peña 466, T03521-421444, www.deanfunes.gov.ar.*

From Deán Funes head east on provincial road 16 to find **San Piedro Viejo** ⓘ *www.sanpedroviejo.com.ar.* This tiny hamlet has a beautiful little church, built in adobe with a squat square bell tower, and an *estancia*, where you can stay for a few nights to completely unwind and explore the rolling land on foot or horseback. This place has a history: it was an important staging post on the royal road between the Río de la Plata and Perú, and such illustrious figures as General San Martín and President Belgrano stayed in the building which is now a chic and rustic boutique hotel.

Reserva Cultural y Natural Cerro Colorado
ⓘ *Daily 0700-1300, 1400-2000 in summer, daily 0800-1900 in winter. US$2, www.cordobaturismo.gov.ar/CerroColorado.aspx (in Spanish and English).*
Some 104 km north of Jesús María, reached by an unpaved road (12 km) that branches off Route 9 at Santa Elena (see Transport, page 199), is this provincial park covering 3000 ha of rocky hills and woodlands protecting some 35,000 rock paintings in around 200 sites, some of them underground. It's thought that they were painted by the indigenous Comechingones people sometime between the 10th century and the arrival of the Spanish roughly 600 years later. The strikingly bold paintings, in red, black and white, portray animals and plants, hunting scenes, magic rituals and dancing; even battles against the Spanish, mounted on horseback. There are lots of more enigmatic paintings with geometric patterns, open to wildly imaginative interpretations. There are two small museums: **Museo Arqueológico** ⓘ *daily 0700-1300, 1400-2000, guided visits at 0830, 1030, 1600 and 1800,* at the foot of Cerro Intihuasi, has information on the site itself; **Museo Atahualpa and Yupanqui** ⓘ *T0351-155 198715, daily 0900-1300, 1600-2000,* at the end of the winding road to Agua Escondida, also offers guided tours. The vegetation is interesting with lots of ancient algarrobo trees, molles and a rare *mato* forest in the park, where you can also spot small armadillos.

The park can only be visited as part of a guided tour which lasts 1½ hours and is included in the entry fee. For tours, ask in the administration building, or for private guides contact **Justo Bustamante**, T0351-156 820 866; **Luis Martínez**, T0351-156 522 480; or **Ramón Bustos**, T03522-1551 5069. There's a hotel and a few *cabaña* complexes nearby in the sprawling villages at the foot of the Cerro, and plenty of handicrafts for sale. Useful websites include www.cerrocolorado.infoturis.com.ar (in Spanish) and www.cordobaciudad. com/cerrocolorado (in English and Spanish). A helpful leaflet, *El Chasqui de Cerro Colorado,* is available from tourist offices in Córdoba city.

Sierras Chicas and Estancia Los Potreros
To really get into the wild, remote country that is the Sierras Chicas, you need to spend a few nights away from civilization, and the best way to do this is to stay at an *estancia* such

as **Estancia Los Potreros** ⓘ *T011-6091 2692, T/F03548-452121 (office), T011-4313 1410 (Córdoba),www.estancialospotreros.com*. One of Argentina's finest riding *estancias*, this is situated in the middle of its own range of peaks, yet it's easily accessible: just an hour from the airport. It's run by a British family, Robin and Kevin Begg, who were brought up on this land and who breed fine horses and offer a wonderful mixture of real gaucho Argentine ranch culture and British hospitality. If you're not a rider, you can walk, birdwatch, swim or simply relax, and enjoy the peace and immense vistas. If you'd like to learn to ride, the Beggs are the most patient teachers and the horses very tame and sure-footed. It's best to stay for at least three nights to get the feel of the place, for those with more time, a riding tour of the sierras taking several days can be arranged. As well as enjoying spectacular scenery, a longer tour allows you to explore remote mountain villages with their tiny churches and schools, and stay at other mountain *estancias* in the region, gaining invaluable insights into the local culture and communities that you could never otherwise access. This is an unmissable experience of the Sierras de Córdoba.

Punilla Valley to La Cumbre → *For listings, see pages 194-199.*

The Punilla Valley, situated between the Sierra Chica to the east and the Sierra Grande to the west, was the first area of the sierras to become populated by weekend and summer visitors from the cities of Córdoba and Buenos Aires back in the 1920s. Sadly, these once-idyllic weekend retreats have now developed into one long string of built-up urban areas alongside Route 38: **Villa Carlos Paz**, **Cosquín**, **Valle Hermoso** and **La Falda**. There's no real reason to stop, unless you're keen to visit Cosquín's famous *folclore* music festival, which is held every year in January and attracts the country's best musicians and budding talent. The whole valley is unbearably busy during the Argentine holiday periods of January, February and Easter, when it is best avoided. Any time of the year, it is preferable to head straight for **La Cumbre** further north (see page 193), where there's a more civilized pace of life and plenty of appealing places to stay in this pretty hill-side town. A brief description of the main Punilla Valley towns is followed by a more complete description of La Cumbre. For further information, see www.lacumbre.gov.ar and www.alacumbre.com (both in Spanish).

Villa Carlos Paz and around → *Colour map 4, A2. Phone code 03541. Population 56,000.*

Ghastly Villa Carlos Paz, 35 km west of Córdoba, is a large and overpopulated resort, crammed with hotels and brimming with Argentine tourists in summer. There are lots of

ESTANCIA LOS POTREROS

The Riders Estancia
bookings@ride-americas.com
www.estancialospotreros.com

activities on offer and a chairlift runs from the Complejo Aerosilla to the summit of the Cerro de la Cruz, but your only reason to come here would be if everywhere else is full, or to use it as a base for the area's superb trekking. There are plenty of hotels, and some quieter places to bathe and hang out, such as the *balnearios* along Río San Antonio, and **Villa Las Jarillas**, 15 km south of town. See www.villacarlospaz.com and www.villa carlospaz.gov.ar (both in Spanish) for more information on the area.

Villa Carlos Paz is on the road to Traslasierra further west (see page 210). If you're not going that far, and are into hiking or climbing, it's certainly worth heading for **Cerro Los Gigantes** (2374 m), 39 km west of Villa Carlos Paz, with its spectacular views and challenging walks. To get there, take the unpaved Route 28 via **Tanti** over the Pampa de San Luis towards **Salsacate**. Los Gigantes is signposted at Km 30, where you turn off left; here you'll find the nearest base for climbing the granite massif. By public transport, you'll need to get a local bus from Villa Carlos Paz to Tanti, and from there to Los Gigantes. Daily buses with **TAC** to Salsacate stop at Los Gigantes. *Remise* taxi charges about US$20. There is **tourist information** ① *T03541-498250, tanti@cba.gov.ar, www.tanti.gov.ar*, at Tanti.

Cosquín and around → *Colour map 4, A2. Phone code 03541. Population 19,800.*

Cosquín, 20 km north of Carlos Paz, is not an attractive town, but its setting on the banks of the wide Río Cosquín gives it several *balnearios* (swimming areas), of which **Pan de Azúcar** is the quietest option. Cosquín is also known as the national *folclore* capital, and Argentina's most important *folclore* festival is held here in the last two weeks of January. The country's most famous bands and singers play every night on **Plaza Próspero Molina**, and there are plentiful food and handicrafts stalls. An increasingly popular rock festival (www.cosquinrock.com) is held here in early February, so accommodation is almost impossible to find between 10 January and 10 February. There is a **tourist office** ① *Av San Martín 560, Plaza Próspero Molina, T03541-450397, www.visitecosquin.com.ar*, and a bus terminal at Perón and Salta.

La Falda and around → *Colour map 4, A2. Phone code 03548. Population 16,000.*

La Falda, 20 km north of Cosquín, is another seething and tawdry tourist town, once the destination of Argentina's wealthy and influential who all stayed at the magnificent **Hotel Edén**. The hotel is now sadly in ruins but the bar gives you a flavour of its former grandeur, with an exhibition of old photographs. The town is known for its nightlife, bars and casinos abound, but it's really a place to avoid unless you want to use it as a base for hiking in the surrounding hills and pampas. The **tourist office** ① *Av España 50, T03548-423007, www.lafalda.gov.ar*, is at the former railway station and the **bus terminal** ① *Av Buenos Aires (R38)*, is a five-minute walk north of Avenida Edén.

The sierras to the east of La Falda are a good place for hiking. **Cerro La Banderita** (1350 m), which is also popular with paragliders, is a 1½-hour walk from the town centre and provides panoramic views of the valley: leave from the left side of Hotel Edén and take the street called Austria. Ask at tourist office for a map and directions. From La Falda you could also head out west to the Pampas: an 80-km rough, winding road goes to La Higuera, on the west side of the Cumbres de Gaspar. It crosses the vast **Pampa de Olaén**, a grass-covered plateau at 1100 m, where you'll find the tiny Capilla de Santa Bárbara (1750), 20 km from La Falda, and waterfalls Cascadas de Olaén, 2 km south of the chapel. There are more beautiful rivers and waterfalls at **Río Pintos** (26 km from La Falda) and **Characato** (36 km from La Falda). Jesuit **Estancia La Candelaria** lies further along this road, 53 km west of La Falda. This is a great area for cycling, but take water.

La Cumbre and around → *Colour map 4, A2. Phone code 03548. Population 7200.*

By far the most attractive town in this whole area, La Cumbre sits at the highest point of the Punilla Valley at 1141 m. It's only 1½-hour's drive from Córdoba, if you head straight here without stopping on the way. It was founded by the British engineers and workers who built the railway here in 1900 and who have given the place its distinctive flavour, with trees lining the avenues in the attractive residential area to the east of town, where you'll find the best hotels. **Golf Club La Cumbre** ① *T03548-452283, www.lacumbregolf. com.ar, US$15 for a round,* to the southeast of town, was built 90 years ago and is beautifully landscaped, with mature trees and a quaint Tudor-style clubhouse. Further east you'll find lots of craftsmen selling their wares. Unlike the rest of the valley, this friendly little town still feels authentic and the town centre bustles busily just before midday. There are some classy shops, as well as lots of places to eat and a couple of tea rooms selling superb cakes. For the more adventurous, there's excellent paragliding nearby in **Cuchi Corral** southwest of the town (see Activities and tours, page 198). There are also plenty of places to walk in the mountains, with access from residential areas **Cruz Chica** and **Cruz Grande**, on the road to **Los Cocos**.

The **tourist office** ① *Av Caraffa 300, T03548-452966, daily from early morning until late in the evening,* is in the old train station, and many of the friendly staff speak English. They'll give you a very helpful map listing all the hotels and restaurants. See also www.ala cumbre.com.ar and www.turismolacumbre.com.ar (both in Spanish). The **bus terminal** ① *Juan José Valle and Ruznak, T03548-452442,* is around the corner from the tourist office.

As a visitor to Argentina, you might not have noticed the national obsession with *alfajores,* the soft cakey biscuits made of a double layer of cornflour sponge, and sandwiched with *dulce de leche.* The chocolate-covered ones from **Havanna** *alfajores* shops in any town centre are particularly recommended. While you're in La Cumbre, you could visit the famous *alfajores* factory, **Estancia El Rosario** ① *R66, 5 km east of town, T03548-451257, www.estanciaelrosario.com.ar, daily 0800-1900,* to see them being made and try a fine specimen or three. The factory has been operating since 1924 and was, for many years, a major tourist attraction. These days there are still free guided visits to the small factory where fruit preserves and other sweet delicacies are also made.

Head east from the golf course along Route 66 for the spectacular mountain crossing that leads to Ascochinga (for a route description, see page 189). North of La Cumbre, there are more hotels in the lovely leafy residential areas of Cruz Chica, Cruz Grande and Los Cocos. Further along this picturesque road are two popular places for families: **El Descanso**, with its well designed garden and maze, and **Complejo Aerosilla** (www.aerosilla.com), with a chairlift to the nearby hills (US$3), an aquarium and toboggans.

Capilla del Monte and around → *Colour map 4, A2. Phone code 03548. Population 8940.*

Capilla del Monte is a quiet town which offers a base for good trekking and paragliding, and for exploring nearby rock formations, Agua de los Palos. The landscape is hilly and scrubby, with places rather reminiscent of the lunar landscapes in Ischigualasto – Valle de la Luna in San Juan (see box, page 266). The **tourist office** ① *T03548-481903, www. capilladelmonte.gov.ar, www.capilladelmonte.com.ar (in Spanish),* is at the end of the diagonal Buenos Aires. The town is overlooked by dramatic **Cerro Uritorco** (1979 m), which you can climb: head 3 km east of town and it's another 5 km to the summit, though be warned that this is a four-hour climb each way with no shade (US$2.50 entry).

UFO-spotters flock to the amazing landscape of **Quebrada de la Luna**, **Los Terrones** and **Parque Natural Ongamira**, where there are curious rock formations. Ask in the tourist office for more information and for a *remise* to take you there.

For Sleeping and Eating price codes and other relevant information, see Essentials pages 30-36.

⦿ Sleeping

Jesús María *p186*
A-B Hotel Jesús María, Calle Almafuerte 177, T03252-445888, www.hoteljesusmaria. com.ar. New hotel with rooftop pool, small gym and modern, spacious rooms.
B La Cabaña del Tío Juan, R9, Km 755, T03525-420563, www.lacabanadeltiojuan. com.ar. *Estancia*-style building with basic but appealing doubles, a small, slightly old-fashioned restaurant and a lovely pool in the gardens.
B-C Napoleón, España 675, T03525-423 020, hotelnapoleon@coop5.com.bar. Only 2 blocks from bus station, with a/c and a pool.
C La Gringa, Tucumán 658, T03525-425249, 1 block across the railway lines from the bus station. A/c, breakfast included.

Estancia Santa Catalina *p188*
A Posada Camino Real, 10 km from Santa Catalina, T0351-422 3422, T0351-155 525 215, www.posadacaminoreal.com.ar. Descendants of the original owners of this *estancia*, the Díaz family, have made this a welcoming and comfortable place to stay with 8 elegant stylish rooms and a pool complex, offering all the usual *estancia* pursuits: walking, riding, picnics, plus the less common *asado* of local kid and llama. Massages also on offer.
C La Ranchería de Santa Catalina, 10 m before the entrance to **Estancia Santa Catalina**, on the right-hand side, T03525-424467. Basic, but convenient for visiting the Jesuit *estancia*. 2 small rooms in the former slaves' quarters. Separate bathroom.

Ascochinga and Estancia La Paz *p189*
LL Estancia La Paz, Route E66, Km 14, a few kilometres from Ascochinga, signposted, but ring for directions, T03525-492073, www.estancialapaz.com. Opulence and splendour, presidential style, but this is a warmly welcoming luxury *estancia* with impeccable service and beautiful parkland. Offers golf, horse riding and a spa. Bilingual reception staff. Recommended.
B Hotel Parque, right in the middle of Ascochinga village and next to the golf course, T03525-492020, www.hotel-parque. com.ar. One of the many hotels built by Perón in the 1940s to allow workers' unions to go on holiday economically, this has been converted into a comfortable place to stay, but remains slightly institutional in its neatness.

Córdoba Norteña *p190*
AL Estancia San Pedro Viejo, R96, San Pedro Norte, San Pedro Viejo, T0351-155 293 682, www.sanpedroviejo.com.ar. A quaint, historical post house converted into a chic boutique hotel with 1-m-thick walls, old fireplaces, and ancient trees near a charming lake. 6 bedrooms decorated with antiques, some with jacuzzi. Great food and wines, relaxing walks and horse riding in the nearby hills. A lovely retreat.
C San Jorge, España and Buenos Aires, Deán Funes, T03521-421873, hotelsanjorge@ solutionsystem.com.ar. Drab, modern exterior, but reasonably comfortable rooms with a/c, TV and a snack bar on the ground floor.

Reserva Cultural y Natural Cerro Colorado *p190*
There are several places to stay in the hamlets around the foot of the *cerro*, and you can also stay with local families if the hotel is full. The tourist office produces a helpful free leaflet, *El Chasqui de Cerro Colorado*, available in Córdoba city before you set off. A few to try (all **C**) are **Cerro Colorado**, T03522-1564 8990; **Complejo Argañaraz** , T0351-156 466 778; and **La Italiana**, T0351-424 6598/156 870 445.

Sierras Chicas and Estancia Los Potreros *p190*

L Estancia Los Potreros, Sierras Chicas, either take a bus to the nearest town, Río Ceballos, or the owners will arrange a taxi from Córdoba city or the airport, 1 hr, T011-6091 2692, T/F03548-452121 (office), www.estancialos potreros.com. Warm hospitality from this exceptional English-Argentine family who grew up on these lands and now offer extremely comfortable rooms in their beautifully restored 1900s house. In a remote hilltop location in the middle of the sierras, offer superb horse riding on their impeccably trained and calm polo horses. Learn to play polo, relax by the pool, go birdwatching, enjoy delicious food and wines – all included in the price. 3 nights minimum stay. Highly recommended.

Cosquín and around *p192*

B La Puerta del Sol, Perón 820, T03541-452 045, www.lapuertadelsolhotel.com.ar. This hotel quite undeservedly has the best reputation in town. Still, it's a decent choice if you want to use the pool or take advantage of the half-board deals or car hire.
C Siempreverde, Santa Fe 525 (behind Plaza Molina), T03541-450093, www.hosteria siempreverde.com. Spotless place. Some rooms are small but still comfortable and there's a gorgeous garden. Breakfast included.

Camping

Several campsites, but **San Buenaventura**, 8 km west on Río Yuspe, is in the nicest location with shady trees and places for a good swim, US$35 per group (*remise* charge US$10 for an open return trip from Cosquín).

La Falda and around *p192*

About 80 hotels, all full in holiday season. For more listings, see www.visitelafalda.com.ar.
A L'Hirondelle, Av Edén 861, in the same block as **La Asuriana**, T03548-422825, www.lhirondellehostal.com. Lovely building, some rooms retain their original parquet floor and there's a large garden with a pool, and a restaurant. Welcoming owners.

B La Colonial, Avda. España 710, T03548-422406, www.hotellacolonia.com.ar. Though lacking comfort, there's well-preserved early 1950s decor in the reception and dining room. Includes the use of a large pool at the back.
B-C La Asturiana, Av Edén 835, T03548-422 923. Simple and comfortable rooms, a pool in a fabulously old colonial-style building, and a superb breakfast including rice pudding. Welcoming owners.
B-C Cabaña Tronco Piedra, Argentina 336, T03548-424419, www.troncopiedra.com.ar. A wood and stone cabin complex with 2 cabins sleeping 2-4 people. Cable TV, Wi-Fi, lovely rustic furniture and a small pool.

Camping

Balneario 7 Cascadas, next to the dam and the 7 falls (west of town), T03548-425 808. Nicely located site with hot showers, electricity and a food shop, US$4 a day per person. *Remise* taxi charges US$3.

La Cumbre and around *p193*

There are plenty of hotels but you're likely to want to stay in *cabañas* here, as these are particularly high quality and in attractive settings, ideal for larger groups who want the flexibility of self-catering. Cruz Chica is a lovely place to stay, but you'll need a car or taxi to get there. See www.alacumbre.com.ar for a complete list of accommodation.
LL-L El Castillo de Mandl, San Josemaría Escrivá 73, T03548-452727, www.elcastillo demandl.com. A huge luxury hotel in a charming 1930s mansion with a simply stunning location, surrounding by some of the best views in the area. Large beds, sumptuous linens and stylish furniture. A lovely pool and lots of attention to detail.
L-A Cruz Chica, Cruz Chica, Bartolomé Jaime, 3 km north of town, T03548-452780, www.hostalcruzchica.com.ar. A charming old stone building dating from 1886, in pleasant gardens. Has a spa (extra cost) and attractive rooms.
AL Angelus, Belgrano 560, T03548-451228, www.anguluslacumbre.com. With only 6

stylishly designed suites, this boutique hotel is small, and intimate, with a lovely garden surrounding the house, a pool and central heating.

AL Cabañas Villa Benitz, Av Benitz 102, T03548-451597, www.villabenitz.com. Stylish high-quality villas, all individually designed, make this upmarket place to stay and very good value for 4 or more people. They have everything you need: TV, grills for barbecues, and breakfast is delivered to your door in the mornings. Also has a pool and restaurant for guests. Recommended.

A-B Hostal Toledo, Bartolomé Jaime 1090, T03548-452898, www.toledohostal.com.ar. 1 of a pair of hotels owned by the same people on opposite sides of the road leading to Cruz Chica. In an attractive area, this is a Spanish-style stone building, with traditionally decorated interiors. Very comfortable and rooms are of a high standard.

A-B Gran Hotel La Cumbre, Posadas 680, T03548-451550, www.granhotellacumbre.com.ar. Alpine style on top of a hill and rather impressive, this hotel has wonderful views from its comfortable rooms. Larger rooms with balcony are 20% extra. Pool, restaurant and good breakfast is included.

A-B Posada los Cedros, Av Argentina 837, T03548-451028, www.posadaloscedros.com. A lovely old house set in the leafy residential area, close to the golf club. Attractive gardens and good service. An appealing option.

A-B Posada San Andrés, Av Benitz and Monteagudo, T03548-452547, www.posadasanandres.com. Popular with couples and families, this is a attractive old 1930s stone house, set back from the road in lovely gardens with a pool and mountains behind, great for walks. The owners are on hand to welcome guests, and good dinners are served in the restaurant.

B Cabañas Del Golf, JL Cabrera and J Hernández, T03548-452008, www.cabanasdelgolf.com. Attractive, well-equipped *cabañas* arranged in nice parkland with lush vegetation and lovely views.

B Posada Lambare, Bartolomé Jaime 880, on the right-hand side, high up on the road to Cruz Chica, T03548-451054, www.lambareposada.com.ar. Gardens with huge cedars and pines, a grand staircase leads up to the elegant main house with rustic rooms, and good views. Pool, no restaurant, very relaxing.

B-C Hotel La Viña, Caraffa 48, T03548-451388, www.hotellavina.com.ar. Nice budget option, with cosy flowery rooms, a large pool and pleasant gardens. Parking, cable TV and private bathrooms.

Hostels

F pp **Estancia Puesto Viejo**, T03548-482696, www.estanciapuestoviejo.com. Located on a huge (and I mean HUGE) property which takes around 1½ hrs to get to from La Cumbre, offering simple, clean dorms and doubles (**D**). Fantastic opportunity to experience country farm life. Own transport essential.

F pp **Hostel La Cumbre**, Av San Martín 282, T03548-451368, www.hostellacumbre.com. Large, friendly hostel set in an old homestead. Very basic single-sex dorms, simple doubles (**D**), a great pool with a view, and it is only 3 blocks from the bus station. HI discount.

Camping

Carpa Verde, Paraje Balata, 4 km from the centre of La Cumbre, T03548-1556 6847, www.carpaverde.com.ar. US$4 per person per day, or US$7 in the *refugio*. You can also rent tents here and there are excursions offered directly from the campsite. Hot water but no electricity.

Capilla del Monte and around *p193*
See www.capilladelmonte.gov.ar for more listings.

A-B Montecassino, La Pampa 107, T03548-482572, www.hotelmontecassino.com. Beautiful building from 1901, with lovely rooms, cable TV, jacuzzi and pool with stunning views.

C La Casona, Pueyrredón 774, T03548-482 679, www.cordobaserrana.com.ar/capilla/lacasona.htm. This 19th-century villa has a distinctly haunted-house look. At the top of a hill, surrounded by palm trees, there is a pool and the best views of the sierras. The interior retains examples of former opulence and the welcoming owners offer home-made meals. English spoken, recommended.

C Petit Sierras, Pueyrredón and Salta, T03548-481667, www.cordobaserrana.com.ar/capilla/petitsierras.htm. A renovated hotel with clean and comfortable rooms. The owners run the restaurant **A Fuego Lento**, on the edge of town, which serves good local trout. Discounts and free transport for guests.

Camping
G pp **Calabalumba**, 600 m north of the centre, T03548-481903. Municipal shady site with pool, hot water, *cabañas* for 4-6.

❶ Eating

Jesús María *p186*
♥ **Fertilia**, signposted from Av San Martín 5200, Colonia Caroya, T03525-467031, buses stop on the main road, from here it's a 15 min-walk along a dirt road to the farm. An unmissable treat. Welcoming farmers serve excellent quality salamis and ham accompanied by delicious local red wine.
♥ **Viejo Comedor**, Tucumán 360, T03525-421601. Popular for cheap meals.

Reserva Cultural y Natural Cerro Colorado *p190*
♥ **El Arco de Noe**, in Las Galerías, T03522-1545 6517. Bar and restaurant.
♥ **Inti Huasi**, in the visitor centre for **Córdoba Ambiente** agency. More of a café with food.
♥ **Purinqui Huasi**, opposite the archaeological museum, T03522-1564 8705. A *parrilla* with barbecued kid as the house speciality, also serves good pastas and salads.

Cosquín and around *p192*
♥♥♥ **La Encrucijada del Supaj-Ñuñú**, on the way to the Cerro Pan de Azúcar, T3541-1553 2267. Pleasant restaurant, tea house and

brewery, serving meals, fondue, cakes or sandwiches at moderate prices.
♥♥♥ **Wissen**, Av Juan B Justo and R38 (100 m north of bridge), T03541 454097. Open for lunch and dinner, this former German family residence with sumptuous decor and a pleasant terrace offers an unpretentious menu, with excellent home-made pastas, and several meat-based dishes. Moderate prices and a wide selection of wines.

La Falda and around *p192*
♥♥♥ **L'Hirondelle**, see Sleeping, above. Has a moderately priced restaurant open to non-residents, offering good set menus.
♥ **El Cristal**, San Lorenzo 39. Very good cooking, where the locals eat.
♥ **Pachamama**, Av Edén 127. If you're tired of eating beef, there is a health food shop with a few neat tables at the back where you can have cheap organic vegetable pies, or wholemeal pizzas and *empanadas*.

La Cumbre and around *p193*
♥♥♥ **El Enkuentro**, 25 de Mayo 283, T03548-452 053. Fabulous family restaurant and useful meeting place, central and well run. The home-made pastas are superb, and there are lots of excellent meat dishes on the menu too, including game. Highly recommended.
♥♥♥ **La Casona del Toboso**, Belgrano 349, T03548-451439. Also highly recommended for excellent food across a wide menu, including *parrilla*.
♥ **Dany Cheff**, opposite the tourist office, Av Caraffa and Belgrano, T03548-451379. The best place for afternoon tea, serves delicious pastries and cakes, and there's a lively buzz mid-morning when locals flock there.

❂ Festivals and events

Jesús María *p186*
Jan Festival de Doma y Folclore, www.festival.org.ar, entry US$3. Popular *folclore* music and gaucho event.The profits benefit local schools.

Cosquín and around *p192*
Jan Festival Nacional del Folclore, www.
visitecosquin.com.ar (in Spanish). Cosquín's
famous music festival attracts the country's
best musicians and budding talent. In the
last 2 weeks of Jan, the country's most
famous bands and singers play every
night on Plaza Próspero Molina.
Feb Cosquín Rock, www.festival.org.ar.
Showcases national rock singers and
groups, as well as international rock
bands from Spanish-speaking countries.

▲ Activities and tours

Cosquín and around *p192*
Cycling
Centro, Perón 937, T03541-1562 2983.
Mountain bike hire.

La Falda and around *p192*
Cycling
Club Edén 201, Av Edén 201. US$9 per day
for bike hire.

Tour operators
Turismo Talampaya, T03548-470412,
turismotalampaya@yahoo.com.ar. Run by
Teresa Pagni who guides 4WD full-day trips
to the Pampa de Olaen and Jesuit *estancia*
La Candelaria.
VH, T03548-424831, T03548-1556 2740,
vhcabal gatas@hotmail.com. 1-hr horse
rides to nearby hills from US$10 per person.

La Cumbre and around *p193*
Golf
Golf Club La Cumbre, Posadas, T03548-
452284, www.lacumbregolf.com.ar.
Follow Belgrano from the town centre,
opposite the tourist office, to reach the
corner of the golf course, then turn left
onto Posadas. Very attractive 18-hole golf
course, with caddies and coaching. Also
putting green and Olympic-sized pool.

Horse riding
Chachito Silva, T03548-451703, T03548-
1563 5673. Hires horses and offers ½-day,
1- and 2-day guided horse riding trips to
the sierras and Candonga.
La Chacra, Pasaje Beíro s/n, T03548-451703,
T03548-1557 0847. US$8 per hr, also ½-day
rides or rides for several days with guides.
La Granja de los Gringos, R38, T03548-1557
4317, lagranjadelgringo@yahoo.com.ar.
US$8 per hr, guides accompany your rides,
longer rides also offered.

Paragliding
See www.sierrascordobesas.com.ar. The
world-renowned paragliding site of **Cuchi
Corral** is just 9 km west of La Cumbre on
an unpaved road. From a natural balcony
overlooking the Río Pintos, a few hundred
metres below, northwest winds generate
thermal currents, that collide with the
mountains and make a superb place to
practise paragliding, or to try it for the first
time. Several local companies offer flights,
which start at US$70 for your 1st flight, the
Vuelo Bautismo, 20 mins, accompanied by a
trained paragliding instructor in tandem.
A 1-hr flight with instructor is US$100.

Trekking
Escuela de Montaña y Escalada, T03548-
451393, georgmallo@yahoo.com. Run by
Jorge González, for parapenting, but also
climbing and mountain trekking courses
and excursions, eg to the Cascada de los
70 Pies in Cruz Grande. Equipment hire.

Tour operators
4x4 Turismo Aventura, T03548-1556 6664;
Cerro Uritorco, Corrientes 96, T03548-451
470; **Gonzalo Gili**, T03548-492201. All these
operators go to Cuchi Corral and Río Pintos.
Aventura Family Club, T03548-423809,
www.estanciapuestoviejo.com. Covers
the area as part of a day trip to a remote
estancia, northwest of La Cumbre.

Capilla del Monte and around *p193*
Cycling
Claudio, Deán Funes 567. Mountain bike hire.

⊖ Transport

Jesús María *p186*
Bus
Direct to **Córdoba**, 1 hr, US$3, Ciudad de Córdoba; Colonia Tirolesa; or minibus Fono Bus, US$3.50. To **Córdoba** via Ascochinga, 2½ hrs, US$3.50, Ciudad de Córdoba. To **Colonia Caroya**, US$1, Ciudad de Córdoba; Colonia Tirolesa.

Northeast of Córdoba *p189*
Bus
Laguna Mar Chiquita to **Córdoba**, Expreso Ciudad de San Francisco (from **Miramar**), 3½ hrs, US$4.30; and Transportes Morteros (from **Balnearia**), 3 hrs, US$5.

Reserva Cultural y Natural Cerro Colorado *p190*
Bus
Buses Ciudad de Córdoba, T0351-424 0048 go to **Córdoba** 3 times weekly, but check for current days, 4½ hrs, US$7. There are also combis to **Santa Elena** with El Tatú, T0351-423 6335, and Río Seco, T0351-424 5610.

Remise taxis
Rapi-Taxi, T03525-15527213, ask for Pancho. Reliable and cheap radio taxis.

Cosquín and around *p192*
Bus
Ciudad de Córdoba, La Calera, and TAC run frequent buses along the **Punilla Valley** and to **Córdoba**; to **La Falda**, US$2.50; to **La Cumbre** US$2; to **Capilla del Monte** US$3. Several minibuses do same route, to **Córdoba**, 1-1½ hrs, US$4.

Remise taxis
El Cerro, Av San Martín 1036, T03541-450444.

La Falda and around *p192*
Bus
Chevallier, General Urquiza and Sierras de Córdoba go daily to **Buenos Aires** and to several other domestic destinations. Ciudad de Córdoba and La Calera run frequent buses along the **Punilla Valley** and to **Córdoba**; to **Cosquín**, US$2; to **La Cumbre**, US$2.20; to **Capilla del Monte**, US$3. Several minibuses also travel the same route, to **Córdoba**, US$4.

Remise taxis
Casa Blanca, 9 de Julio 541, T03548-426323.

La Cumbre and around *p193*
Bus
Daily buses to **Buenos Aires** with El Práctico, T03548-452442, General Urquiza /Sierras de Córdoba, T03548-452400, 11 hrs, US$43. To **Córdoba** Ciudad de Córdoba, T03548-452442, La Calera, T03548-452300.

Car hire
Reynas, 25 de Mayo 448, T03548-452107, gustavobecker2003@hotmail.com. US$43 per day. Ask for a discount if you hire for several days. Bring credit card and passport.

Taxis
Auto Remis, López and Planes 321, T03548-451000, T0800 444 7040; Taxi Victoria 25 de Mayo 260, T03548-452150.

Capilla del Monte and around *p193*
Bus
Daily buses to **Buenos Aires**, 12 hrs, US$40 and to **Córdoba**, US$5. Ciudad de Córdoba and La Calera and minibuses El Serra run services along the **Punilla valley**. Twice a day, **Ciudad de Córdoba** goes to **Traslasierra Valley** via Cruz del Eje.

Remise taxis
El Cerro, Pueyrredón 426, T03548-482300.

Southern Córdoba province: Calamuchita Valley

South of Córdoba, there's another fascinating and well-preserved Jesuit estancia in the unprepossessing town of Alta Gracia, which is the gateway to a picturesque hilly area between the high peaks of the Sierra Grande and Sierra de Comechingones. Fans of that great 20th-century icon Ernesto 'Che' Guevara will also want to visit his childhood home. Further south still, there's superb walking in the wooded countryside near the quaint Germanic town of Villa General Belgrano and, prettier still, the mountain town, La Cumbrecita. It's well worth spending two or three days combining the Jesuit heritage with some walking or relaxing in the hills, to gain the essence of Córdoba's history and landscapes. For more information on the area, see www.calamuchita.com.
▶▶ *For listings, see pages 206-209.*

Alta Gracia → *For listings, see pages 206-209. Colour map 4, A2.*

Alta Gracia's great attraction is the wonderful 17th-century **Estancia Jesuítica Alta Gracia** (see below), whose church, residential buildings and small lake make a splendid hilltop centre to the town, around the scrappy Plaza Solares. The rather tawdry main commercial area spills down Belgrano, with everything you need, but no charm whatsoever. Head instead to the pretty residential area west of centre **El Alto**, where the most appealing restaurants are to be found. El Alto was built when the British came here to build the housing which the locals describe as typically 'British': two stories with corrugated-iron roofs. The rather grand **Hotel Sierras** ⓘ *www.hojoar.com*, stylishly built in 1907 as Argentina's first casino, was made popular by the rich upper classes who flocked to the area for the summer in the 1920s when Alta Gracia was in its heyday. It has been restored and now is a four-star hotel and casino (now run by international hotel chain Howard Johnson). There's also an attractive golf course in this area, whose club has one of the town's most recommendable restaurants, open to non-members (see Eating, page 207). All this aristocratic pleasure might sound an unlikely environment for the early years of Ernesto 'Che' Guevara, but his family house can now be visited, see the **Museo Casa de Ernesto Che Guevara**, opposite.

Ins and outs → *Phone code 03547. Population 42,600.*
The **bus terminal** ⓘ *T03547-427000*, is 10 blocks from the centre on the river at Butori and Perón 1977. The **tourist information** ⓘ *corner of Molino and Padre Viera, at the top of Av Belgrano, T03547-428128, www.altagracia.gov.ar*, is at the base of the clock tower on the corner of the Jesuit reservoir, the Tajamar. Staff don't speak much English but are helpful and will give you a map and a useful *Guía Turística*.

Estancia Jesuítica Alta Gracia and Museo Casa de Virrey Liniers
ⓘ *Plaza Solares, Av Padre Viera 41, T03547-421303, www.museoliniers.org.ar, Tue-Fri 0900-2000, Sat-Sun 0930-2000, in summer; Tue-Fri 0900-1300, 1500-1700, Sat-Sun 0930-1230, 1530-1830, in winter. US$2.50, free on Wed.*
Part of the same development of Jesuit establishments at Jesús María and Santa Catalina, which were declared a World Heritage Site by UNESCO in 2000, Alta Gracia is a fascinating testimony to the Jesuits' culture, and the entire *estancia* is now an excellent museum. If you

visit only one Jesuit *estancia* in Córdoba, make it this one. There's added interest in the life of Viceroy Liniers, who owned the house from 1810. An excellent guided tour is included in the entry ticket, but ask in advance for an English, French or German speaking guide. There are also informative laminated cards in several languages in each room.

Alta Gracia dates from 1643, when Córdoba was the capital of the Jesuit province of Paraguay, and this *estancia* – one of their most prosperous rural establishments – was built to fund the religious education of their young men in the Colegio Maximo in Córdoba city. The centre comprised a **Residence** (now a museum), the **Obraje** (industrial workshops), the **Ranchería** (where the slaves lived), the **Tajamar** (built by the Jesuits as a water reservoir), the **watermill** and the **church** ① *daily 0900-1200, 1300-2000, you can attend Mass*. This latter was started in 1659 and completed only in 1723. It has a splendid baroque façade and a grand cupola, which is the only part that has been renovated. The rest is all now sadly a little dilapidated, but it's the only Jesuit church that still functions today as the parish church.

The Jesuits built their ambitious project in two stages: first they lived in an adobe building while the main house was constructed of brick. This first building then became the *herrería* (smithy), where iron was smelted with the aid of bellows, and workers made all the tools they needed for construction. There are impressive locks, keys and nails on display, testimony to their fine metalworking skills. Just three Jesuit priests lived in the Residence, which was built on two floors around an enclosed patio; the lower floor was used only for storage. All the workers lived outside the *estancia*, but 310 African slaves lived on the premises in the Ranchería. They were of great importance to the Jesuits, as they were used as overseers in the ranches, and did carpentry, brickwork, and blacksmithing. In the Obraje, African women and girls learned to spin and knit. The Jesuits built canals to bring water here to the Tajamar, a large reservoir outside the *estancia*, which supplied them with the power to run a flour mill (*molino*), which was built in the wall of the reservoir; it's now ruined, but there is a good model upstairs in the Residence. There are also on display here some original clay tiles moulded on the thighs of the slaves.

Part of the Jesuits' evangelizing technique included using music, and their exquisite little organ can be seen here, made in the Guaraní missions further northeast. There are some fine paintings and sculptures on display, made by the local population under supervision by the Jesuit priests – beautiful in their simplicity. Even the toilets are impressive, complete with running water to wash the waste away, half of it channelled to be used in the kitchen garden. All the wooden doors and windows are original, and the overall impression is of sophisticated organization and pleasing aesthetics. A couple of rooms are filled with 18th- and 19th-century original furniture from Liniers' family, less interesting, but evocative of the life of a Spanish Viceroy of the Río de la Plata from 1807 to 1809.

Museo Casa de Ernesto 'Che' Guevara

① *Avellaneda 501, T03547-428579. Daily 0900-2000 in summer; Mon 1400-1900, Tue-Sun 0900-1900 in winter. US$1.50, Wed free. From the Sierras Hotel, go north along Vélez Sarsfield, which becomes Quintana, and turn left on to Avellaneda.*

Guevara's parents moved to Alta Gracia when the young revolutionary was four years old, hoping that the dry climate here would help the boy's asthma. For 12 years they lived in this pleasant middle class neighbourhood, where he grew up, got into scrapes with his friends and learned to play golf. Some details of these early years are related in the utterly disappointing museum inside this old house, which retains few relics of Guevara's upbringing. The biographical information is scant, the photographs are all photocopies and there is no intelligent thesis behind the displays. It's best to bring a biography with you, since the books on sale are in Spanish only. Cheap quality T-shirts are also on sale. For more information on 'Che', see box, page 410.

You will learn that his mother educated him at home in his early years, and that asthma should have prevented him from being too athletic, but he played rugby and golf, was a keen cyclist, and had a wide group of friends, among whom he was known as being fair-minded and kind to the poor. His motorcycle trips around Argentina in 1951-1952 and 1953-1956 are well-documented in his own book *The Motorcycle Diaries*, which is recommended reading. There are two videos shown here, a 10-minute extract of a longer documentary, which is almost unintelligible, in Spanish with English subtitles, and a short introductory documentary, with interviews of some friends and teachers from his childhood and the family's former maid. The best photos are in the video room, unfortunately, so you'll have to scoot around them fast between screenings of the videos.

Other sights

If you've time and energy for more museums, you might be interested in **Museo Manuel de Falla** ① *Carlos Pellegrini 1001, T03547-429292, museofallaaltagracia@yahoo.com, daily 0900-1900, free*, the charming home of the famous Spanish composer in the last four years of his life from 1942 to 1946. It's an attractive Spanish-style house with great views from its beautiful garden. There are concerts from April to November, and the **Festival de Falla** in November attracts some fine musicians.

There's an easy 5-km walk to **Los Paredones**, with the remains of a Jesuit mill in a rocky section of the river. To get there, follow Avenida Sarmiento to the west and cross the river, passing the bus station on your left. On the way is the **Gruta de Lourdes**, where, every 11 February, hundreds of pilgrims arrive on foot from Córdoba city. Nearby lies the **Laguna Azul**, a small lake surrounded by impressive cliffs. From Alta Gracia take Avenida Sarmiento, turn right at Vélez Sarsfield and left at Carlos Pellegrini until the end of the road, where you turn right and follow the road, passing Parque García Lorca on your left.

Some 21 km northwest of Alta Gracia is the **Observatorio Bosque Alegre** ① *Tue-Sun 1000-1300 in summer, Fri-Sun 1000-1300, 1500-1800 in winter, remise US$6 plus waiting time*, built in 1942 for astrophysics research. At 1250 m, it offers good views over Alta Gracia, Córdoba and the Sierra Grande. Visits are guided by astronomers.

Villa General Belgrano → *For listings, see pages 206-209. Colour map 4, A2.*
Phone code 03546. Population 6500.

Imagine a German theme park, Disneyland-style, with *bierkellers* and chocolate shops, carved wooden signposts everywhere and cute Alpine architecture, and you get an idea of what the centre of Villa General Belgrano is like. It's a pretty mountain town, with wooded avenues and wonderful views of the sierras beyond. It's a lovely place to spend a few days.

The town was founded in 1932 when two German immigrants bought land and sold it off through advertisements in the German newspapers, with the intention of starting a German colony. Its German character was boosted by the arrival of 155 sailors from the *Graf Spee* in 1939 (see box, page 204), many of whom later settled here. Plagues of locusts and heavy rainfall meant that the colony grew slowly at first, and so children from German schools in Buenos Aires were encouraged to come here for holidays, bringing the very first influx of tourists to the town. German is still spoken by older inhabitants, and the architecture along the main street, Avenida Julio Roca, is dominated by Swiss chalet-style buildings and German beer-houses. You can find genuine German smoked sausages and a wide variety of German breads, delicious Viennese cakes and locally brewed beer. You can even celebrate **Oktoberfest** ⓘ www.elsitiodelavilla.com/oktoberfest, when the town is packed with 12,000 tourists. This is not the best time of year to appreciate the town, but the **Viennese Pastry Festival** in Easter week and the **Alpine Chocolate Festival** during the July holidays are certainly worth a visit. Book accommodation in advance at these times.

The town makes a great centre for hikes in the nearby hills, with plenty of places to stay and good restaurants. The souvenir shops along the main street are crammed with Tirolean hats, beer mugs and *Graf Spee* memorabilia, however there are also fine chocolates for sale and a handicrafts market near the small oval plaza on Sundays and during the holidays. Note that the street of Julio Roca changes its name to San Martín at the oval plaza, halfway along. For help with planning your visit, see www.elsitiodelavilla.com (in Spanish and German).

Ins and outs
To reach Villa General Belgrano from Alta Gracia, take the new faster route via Portrero de Garay. The **tourist office** ⓘ *Av Roca 168, T03546-461215, or call T125 free from inside the town, www.vgb.org.ar, daily 0830-2030*, has friendly English- and German-speaking staff, who'll give you a great map, accommodation list and a free booklet with loads of tourist information. You can go to the top of the tower above the tourist office for amazing fews of the surrounding hills. There is also a good internet café next door, downstairs, open 1600-1900 every day.

Walks around Villa General Belgrano
There are plenty of walks in and around the town itself; a map is available from the tourist office, ask for directions before setting off. Two rivers run through the town, **La Toma** and **El Sauce**, and a lovely shaded area for walking has been created along their banks. You could also hike up the **Cerro de la Virgen** (one hour), the hill to the east of town. Start at Ojo de Agua, 200 m east of Avenida Julio Roca. Walk along Ojo del Agua, turn right onto the main road, Route 5, then left where signposted. It's a steep walk, but there are rewarding views. Alternatively, a lower and easier hike is up to **Cerro Mirador**, northeast of town. To get here, walk along Avenida las Magnolias, turn left on the main road and then right along Pozo Verde (one hour). From the top there are great views of the valley and the town.

La Cumbrecita and Sierra villages → *For listings, see pages 206-209. Phone code 03546.*

To get right into the mountain scenery, head west from Villa General Belgrano via the tiny hamlet of **Los Reartes** with its old chapel to **La Cumbrecita**, a charming, Alpine-style village hidden away in the forested hills, where there are no cars permitted. Although crowded in summer, life here is very tranquil indeed and if you visit during spring or autumn to walk in the surrounding mountains, you'll probably have them all to yourself. It's an excellent centre for trekking or horse riding, with walks from half a day to three days, including to **Cerro Champaqui**, though this peak is better accessed from Villa Alpina (see below). There are short walks to a 14-m-high waterfall **La Cascada**, and to a small lake of crystalline water, **La Olla**, a natural pool with sandy beaches that is good for swimming. Longer walks or horse rides follow footpaths or 4WD vehicle tracks to the **Cerro Cristal**, the pools along **Río del**

Graf Spee

The famous *Graf Spee* was a German 'pocket' battleship, successful because she was of cruiser size and speed, but with the fire power of a battleship. Early in the Second World War, in 1939, the *Graf Spee* sank nine merchant ships in the Atlantic before being cornered outside Uruguay on 13 December by three Allied cruisers sent to find and destroy her. After the 14-hour Battle of the River Plate, in which one British ship was badly damaged, the *Graf Spee's* commander Captain Hans Langsdorff retreated into the neutral port of Montevideo, where he landed most of his crew, and the 36 dead German crewmen were buried. Langsdorff was granted just two days to repair his ship by the Uruguayan government which operated the neutral harbour, under British pressure, and on 17 December the *Graf Spee* sailed out to sea. Crowds lined the shore expecting to see another battle, but watched the vessel sink within minutes. All the remaining crew and 50 captured British seamen on board were rescued. Langsdorff had been trapped into believing that a superior British force was waiting for him over the horizon and Hitler had given him the order to scuttle the vessel rather than allow it to be captured. Two days later in Buenos Aires, Langsdorff wrapped himself in the flag of the Imperial German Navy and committed suicide.

Most of the crew were interned in Argentina and warmly welcomed by the German community of Buenos Aires, but British pressure forced the Argentine government to disperse them. In Mendoza, they were stoned by the locals and beaten up by the police.

In Córdoba they were welcomed by the governor, while the German embassy tried to enforce military discipline and prevent the men from getting too friendly with local women.

In 1944, the US and British governments demanded the repatriation of all the men to Germany. Nearly 200 managed to avoid this by marrying Argentine women, and another 75 escaped: after six years in Argentina, many had no wish to return to a country shattered by defeat. German communities created a distinctive culture in many areas, no more so than Villa General Belgrano in Córdoba, with its German architecture, beer festival and superb chocolate and pastries, where many members of the *Graf Spee* crew made their homes. Meanwhile the carcass of the *Graf Spee*, once visible above the sea line, has been lying on the sea floor for some six decades. In 2003 permission was granted to the Graf Spee Project, www.lummifilm.com/grafspee, by the Uruguayan government to raise – piece by piece – what is left of the pocket battleship. However, the German government has caused some delays with the project, which is far from being complete. Efforts to raise the ship will continue slowly, and there are plans for a museum in Montevideo. In the meantime, the Montevideo Naval base cemetery and museum are holding information and relics from the ship and its crew. More recently Langsdorff's log book was made public, giving historians the chance to consider the captain's problems and decisions looking at the facts. For more information, see www.grafspee.com.

Medio, or for spectacular panoramic views, hike up **Cerro Wank** (1715 m), two hours return. A footpath leads south to another quaint village, Villa Alpina, but it's a six-hour walk (return) and you should take a guide. You can also go horse riding, try rappelling, or explore the area with 4WDs. Many visitors in summer just come for the day, but there are plenty of places to stay and eat including *cabañas* for hire, and tasty food in chalet-style restaurants with lovely settings and great views. For general information, see www.calamuchita.com and www.lacumbrecita.gov.ar (both in Spanish).

There's a **tourist office** ⓘ *T03546-481088*, where staff can advise on walking guides and where to get information on riding and other activities. A useful website with information in English and German is www.lacumbrecita.info.

Villa Alpina and Cerro Champaquí

South of La Cumbrecita is another quaint mountain village, **Villa Alpina**, a small remote resort set in the forested upper valley of **Río de los Reartes**. On the map it looks close to La Cumbrecita, but there's no road connecting the two so the only direct way to get there is to walk, which takes three hours. By vehicle, you'll need to head back to pretty wooded Villa Berna, and from there it's 38 km west, along a poor gravel road. See www.turismocordoba.com.ar/losreartes (in Spanish).

Villa Alpina is the best base for the three-day trek to **Cerro Champaquí** (2790 m), 19 km from the village. It's possible to take a 4WD almost to the summit, but the longer walk is much more rewarding for the superb mountainous scenery and the chance to meet local inhabitants as you stop at the *puestos* on the way. You'll need an all-season sleeping bag to stay in the *puestos*, and be aware that it can snow even in summer. Take a local guide to avoid getting lost. Information is available from Villa General Belgrano tourist office (see page 203), or in La Cumbrecita (see above).

There are more picturesque hilly landscapes with streams and falls close to **Yacanto de Calamuchita**, a village in the mountains, reached via Santa Rosa de Calamuchita, the largest town in this part of the valley, and a very popular, but drab resort. From Yacanto de Calamuchita you can drive almost to the summit of Cerro Champaquí, thanks to a dirt road climbing up to Cerro de los Linderos, leaving you with only a 40-minute walk. Regular minibuses go to Los Reartes, Villa Berna, La Cumbrecita, Villa Alpina, Santa Rosa and Yacanto de Calamuchita. See www.villayacanto.gov.ar for planning information (in Spanish).

For Sleeping and Eating price codes and other relevant information, see Essentials pages 30-36.

⊜ Sleeping

Alta Gracia *p200*

AL El Potrerillo de Larreta, on the road to Los Paredones, 3 km from Alta Gracia, T03547-423804, www.potrerillodelarreta. com. Fabulous old-fashioned 1918 resort and country club in gorgeous gardens with wonderful views. Tennis courts, 18-hole golf course, swimming pool and grand grounds. Great service.

AL-A Hotel & Casino Sierras, Av Vélez Sarfield 198, T011-4701 6900 (in Buenos Aires), www.hojoar.com. A Howard Johnson chain hotel, but tastefully done. Refurbished 1901 hotel, set in parklands. Casino attached, indoor and outdoor pools.

B 279 Boutique Bed + Breakfast, Giorello 279, T03547-15459493, www.279altagracia. com. This small bed and breakfast is the best place to stay in town. It is immaculately clean, just a short stroll to the centre of town and on a quiet residential street. Host Silvia is friendly and helpful. Recommended.

B Fincas del Virrey, Las Rosas 970, near the golf course, T03547-423913, www.fincasdel virrey.com.ar. Extremely smart self-catering houses, a bit sparse, but well-equipped, with lovely pool and TV, games for kids and private gardens.

B Hispania, Vélez Sarsfield 57, T03547-426 555. Run by a Spanish family, this old residence offers very comfortable and spotless rooms with breakfast. Indulge yourself by sitting on the veranda enjoying a fine panoramic view of the sierras while trying some excellent tapas.

B Solares del Alto, Blvd Pellegrini 797, T03547-429042, www.solaresdelalto.com. Modern and comfortable, this smart little hotel on the edge of the lovely residential district is recommended for its friendly bilingual staff, pool and spa (extra cost).

Neat rooms with good bathrooms. **Leyendas** sports bar and café is part of the hotel, and serves good lunches and snacks.

D Asturias, Vélez Sarsfield 127, T03547-423 668. Welcoming owners have clean but cramped rooms in a small building at the back of the old house; breakfast extra.

Hostels

F pp Alta Gracia Hostel, Paraguay 218, T03547-428810, www.altagraciahostel.com. ar. Extremely friendly, family-run hostel, with dorm beds. Nice clean bathrooms and kitchen. Only 3 blocks from the main street. Highly recommended.

Camping

Los Sauces, Parque Federico García Lorca, northwest corner of town, T03547-420349. The site goes down to a river. Lots of facilities including hot showers, food shop, restaurant, volleyball, pool and bike park.

Villa General Belgrano *p202*

Endless *cabaña* complexes here, but book ahead in Jan, Feb, Jul and Easter, when all hotels raise their prices into the next bracket. See www.elsitiodelavilla.com for a full list.

AL-A Posada Chamonix, 2 km out of town on the quiet road to Los Reartes, T03546-464 230, www.chamonixposada.com.ar. This is a beautiful, chic, chalet-style building with splendid views across the valley. Attractive rooms, luxurious accommodation, indoor and outdoor pools, tennis courts and spa. Prices include a buffest breakfast and use of all hotel facilities.

A Bremen, Cero Negro 173, T03546-461133, www.hotelbremen.com. Huge, chalet-style hotel with lots of amenities and attractive gardens with pool, tennis and pretty rooms.

B Berna, Vélez Sarsfield 86, T03546-461097, www.bernahotel.com.ar. Next to the bus station, this vast agency hotel is Swiss-owned, with good service, tidy rooms, ample breakfast and a large garden with a pool.

B Edelweiss, Ojo de Agua 295, T03546-461 317, www.edelweissresort.com. Huge chalet-style place with pool, volley ball and tennis, dated decor but everything you need.

B-C Aitue, Veléz Sárfield 36, T03546-463439, www.aitueposada.com. Only 5 mins' walk from the main street and the bus terminal. Large, basic rooms with a nice pool and garden, Wi-Fi and breakfast included.

C La Posada de Akasha, Los Manantiales 60, T03546-462440, www.laposadadeakasha. com. Extremely comfortable, spotless chalet-style house with small pool and welcoming owners.

D Posada Novalis, Julio A. Roca 36, T03546-462323, www.posadanovalis.com. Right on the main street, small and friendly hotel with only 5 rooms. 2 rooms have a small balcony onto the street and all rooms have cable TV. A bit noisy, but great budget option, especially for lone travellers. Recommended.

Hostels

F pp El Rincón, Fleming 347, T03546-461 323, www.hostelelrincon.com.ar. The only hostel in town is beautifully set in hills with dense forests and green spaces. Welcoming owners offer dormitories, very good double or single rooms with bath for US$12, and camping (US$6 per person). US$1 extra for bedlinen or superb breakfasts. 20% ISIC and HI discounts available, ½-price for children under 16. A 10-min walk from the bus terminal, look for the sign across the road. Recommended.

La Cumbrecita and Sierra villages *p203*

Lots of *cabañas*, ask in the tourist office or see www.lacumbrecita.gov.ar, for a list.

A Suites de la Colina, T0351-155 904 662, http://suitesdelacolina.com. 5-star luxury in a chalet-style lodge with unmissable views. Each of the 7 huge suites has a bath/spa with a view, a large bed, LCD TV and a *hidromasaje* for 2 included in the price. Highly recommended.

A-B La Cumbrecita, T03546-481026, www.hotelcumbrecita.com.ar. Charming

chalet-style building with plain rooms in a lovely setting. Horse riding and fishing. Full or half board can be included if requested.

B Solares Cumbrecita, 2 blocks from the main street, contact the **Solares del Alto** in Alta Gracia (see opposite), T03547-429 042, www.solaresdelalto.com. A lovely old sierras hotel with pool and great views. Modernized, also 4 apartments. Restaurant, spa, massage centre, horse riding and hiking arranged.

B-C Cabañas de la Compañía, T03564-481102, www.delacompania.com.ar. By far the nicest *cabañas* in town with great views of the river. These are beautifully designed, chic and spacious, with wood stoves and TVs. Good low season prices.

B-C Las Verbenas, T03546-481008, www.las verbenashotel.com.ar. A traditional chalet hotel with a nice pool and welcoming service from its owners.

C Cabañas Amancay, De Graciela, by the car park at the town entrance, T03547-481 158, www.lacumbrecita.gov.ar/amancay.htm. A cute chalet-style building where *alfajores* are made, also *cabañas*.

C El Ceibo, T03546-481060, elceibo@lacum brecita.info. Neat, clean rooms for 2-4, near the entrance to the town. Bathrooms, TV, great views and access to the river.

Hostels

F pp El Viaje Hostel, T0351-155 735 085, www.elviajelacumbrecita.com. Clean and friendly hostel in a pretty location. Cheapest in town. Double (**D**) available.

🍴 Eating

Alta Gracia *p200*

🍴 **Alta Gracia Golf Club**, Av Carlos Pellegrini 1000, T03547-422922. Superb food in elegant surroundings in this charming neighbour-hood golf club, with the added advantage that you can watch the machinations of small town upper echelons social life unfold around you. Recommended.

Morena, Av Sarmiento 413, T03547-426365. Excellent menu of imaginative contemporary Argentine cuisine in the welcoming atmosphere of an old house. Also delivers. Recommended.

Betos, Av del Libertador 917, T03547-430996. Great value *parrilla*, plus pizzas, *empanadas* and snacks, as-much-as-you-can-eat deals including drinks and dessert.

Hispania, Urquiza 90. Excellent restaurant serving fish and seafood, including paella and *fidebua*, with sangría and occasionally gazpacho. Desserts such as *crema catalana* are fabulous.

Leyendas, Blvd Pellegrini 797, T03547-429 042. This American-style, sport-inspired bar has cosy nooks to sit in, and really good hamburgers and snacks. A buzzing atmosphere and friendly, welcoming staff. Recommended.

Villa General Belgrano *p202*

Bierkeller, Av Las Magnolias and R5, T03546-461425. Look for the giant beer bottle outside. A chalet-style building with a welcoming family feel. Goulash and *spatzle* recommended, trout too. Slow service but the staff wear jolly Tyrolean outfits. Recommended.

Blumenhaus, Roca and Bolivia, where Roca divides, T03546-462568. Touristy but with nice gardens. Pretty place to sit outside.

El Clervo Rojo, Av Julio Roca 210, T03546-461345. This unmissable Alpine-style building on the main street is the most typical German beer house in town, with a Tyrolean band playing on Sat and dancing. Lots of typical German food.

El Viejo Munich, Av San Martín 362, T03546-463122, www.cervezaartesanal.com. The first brewery in the town, serving superb beer. There are 9 different kinds of the stuff on draft (ask for 'Chopp') and legendary cold cuts of meat (*fiambres*), superb smoked meats, hams and trout, in a charming rustic Bavarian-style interior. Recommended.

La Casa de Dina, Los Incas 463, T03546-461104. Superb cakes and fondues in this cheery and welcoming place.

La Posta del Arroyo, Ojo de Agua 174, T03546-461767. Smart *parrilla* that also serves such delicacies as kid and frogs. Good pastas, welcoming atmosphere.

Ottilia, Av San Martín y Strauss. A traditional cosy Austrian tea room. Delicious *apfelstrudel* and *kirschtorte*.

⊛ Festivals and events

Alta Gracia *p200*
Nov Festival de Falla.

Villa General Belgrano *p202*
Easter week Viennese Pastry Festival.
Jul Alpine Chocolate Festival.
Oct Oktoberfest, www.elsitiodelavilla.com/oktoberfest.

▲ Activities and tours

Alta Gracia *p200*
Golf
Alta Gracia Golf Club, T03547-422922, www.aggc.com.ar. Beautifully landscaped 9-hole golf course, with a fine restaurant (see Eating, above).

Paragliding
Fly Experience, T0351-156 315 016, flyexperience@argentina.com. Daily flights in tandem over the valley, US$25 for 2 people.

Sky diving
Paracenter, Aero Club de Alta Gracia, Route C45, T0351-155 413 816, www.paracenter.com.ar. Sky diving in tandem and courses

Villa General Belgrano *p202*
Cycling
Fly Machine, Av Roca 50, T03546-462425. Bike hire.

Tour operators
Aero Club, Av Jorge Newbery, T03546-462 502. Short flights over the valley, US$35 for 2 people.
DAPA, Av Roca /6, T03546-463417, dapa turismo@calamuchitanet.com.ar. Day trips to La Cumbrecita and guided walks in the surroundings for US$9 per person; Cerro Champaquí in 4WD and a 40-min walk to the summit for US$20 per person; to El Durazno or San Miguel de los Ríos for US$13 per person.
Alto Rumbo, www.champaqui.com.ar. Often recommended tour company that specializes in alternative tours. They run trips for beginners and also experienced climbers.
Diego Caliari, T03546-461510, T03546-1547 5576, mlturismo@yahoo.com.ar. An excellent, trained, friendly young guide who has worked extensively in Traslasierra, and who can take you hiking up Champaquí or on other walks, or arrange horse-riding trips in the area.
Friedrich, Av Roca 224, T03546-461372, friedrich@calamuchitanet.com.ar. Reliable company offering adventure tourism, 4WD hire and day trips to La Cumbrecita or Yacanto de Calamuchita. Also a 10-hr walk across Sierras Chicas along Camino de los Chilenos.
Peperinatur, Julio Roca 235, T03546-461800, peperinatur@vgb.org.ar. Great company organizing trekking to Champaquí, Traslasierra and trips in 4WD.

⊖ Transport

Alta Gracia *p200*
Bus
For **Villa General Belgrano** and other towns in Calamuchita valley, buses stop at the bus

terminal and at the El Crucero roundabout, a 30-min walk from centre. To **Córdoba**, buses leave every 15 mins, 1 hr, US$3, **Empresa La Serranita** T03547-420369; Sarmiento T03547-426001; Sierras de Calamuchita T0351-422 6080 (from El Crucero). To **Villa Carlos Paz**, 1 hr, US$5, Sarmiento. To **Villa General Belgrano**, 1 hr, US$4, Sierras de Calamuchita. To **Buenos Aires**, 10-11 hrs, US$35, Chevallier, T03547-425585; Sierras Cordobesas; TUS, T03547-429370; Valle de Calamuchita.

Car hire
Rodar Rent a Car, T03547-1557 9927, www.autosrodar.com.ar.

Villa General Belgrano *p202*
Bus
To **Córdoba**, 1½-2hrs, US$3, La Villa; Lep; Pájaro Blanco; Sierras de Calamuchita. To **Buenos Aires**, 10-11 hrs, US$30, Chevallier, Sierras Cordobesas, TUS, Valle de Calamuchita; to **La Cumbrecita**, every 2-4 hrs, 1½ hrs, US$4 return, Pájaro Blanco. Pájaro Blanco, Av San Martín 105, T03546-461709, also goes to the nearby villages of **Los Reartes**, **Villa Berna**, **Villa Alpina** and **Yacanto de Calamuchita**.

Remise taxi
Central de Remises, Av Roca 95, T03546-462000.

La Cumbrecita and Sierra villages *p203*
Bus
Reliable daily bus service to **Córdoba city**, 2½ hrs, US$5; from **Villa General Belgano**, 1½ hrs, US$4).

Traslasierra Valley

Situated west of the Sierra Grande, Traslasierra (literally, 'across the mountains') is far less developed for tourism than neighbouring valleys, but ideal for those looking for an adventure. With its drier climate and generally slower pace of life, it's also a perfect place to relax for a few days. It can either be accessed from Córdoba city by the camino de las Altas Cumbres from the north, via the long but not uninteresting Route 15 across the Pampa de Pocho, or from the south, via Villa Dolores into San Luis province. See www.valledetraslasierra.com.ar and www.turismotraslasierra.com.ar (in Spanish). ➤➤ *For listings, see pages 212-214.*

Camino de las Altas Cumbres → *For listings, see pages 212-214. Phone code 03544.*

The first town you reach, Mina Clavero, is probably too busy if you've come to escape the crowds, but it is really picturesque, and further south lie Nono and Los Hornillos which are less busy and just as pretty. They and San Javier, even further south, both make a great base for hiking. The main road to the Traslasierra Valley from Córdoba is the most spectacular route in the sierras. Running southwest from Villa Carlos Paz, the road passes Villa Icho Cruz before climbing into the Sierra Grande and crossing the Pampa de Achala, a huge granite plateau at 2000 m, and descending into the Traslasierra valley near Mina Clavero.

Mina Clavero → *Colour map 4, A2. Phone code 03544. Population 6800.*

Mina Clavero (915 m) has the best nightlife and most raucous atmosphere in the entire valley (during school holidays), with nightclubs, theatres, a casino and dozens of hotels, restaurants and small shops. It's a good base for trips into the surrounding natural beauty. It lies at the foot of the **Camino de las Altas Cumbres** and at the confluence of the Río Panaholma and Río Mina Clavero, which form many small falls among impressive rocks right in the town centre, and there are attractive views along the riverside. The large **tourist office** ① *next to the intersection of Av San Martín and Av Mitre, T03544-470171, www.minaclavero.gov.ar, www.minaclavero.com, daily 0900 until very late,* has an ATM. The bus terminal can be found in the centre at Avenida Mitre 1191.

On the other side of the rivers is the quieter **Villa Cura Brochero**, named after Father Brochero who built schools, roads and aqueducts here at the end of the 19th century. Every March, around the 20th, he is remembered with the *Cabalgatas brocherianas*, a gaucho procession on horses and mules that follows a section of the former road he helped to build across the mountains.

Around Mina Clavero

Nearby rivers offer several attractive places for swimming among huge rocks and waterfalls, all busy in high season. About 5 km north of Villa Cura Brochero, a dirt road passing San Lorenzo branches east to the **Cascada de Toro Muerto**, where icy water falls into a 7-m-deep pool. The *balneario* (bathing area) serves very good meals.

Las Maravillas, a *balneario* set in a deep ravine, is 4 km north of San Lorenzo, and it's another 7 km to the hamlet of Panaholma with its old chapel. The **Camino de los Artesanos** is an 18-km stretch of road from Mina Clavero to Villa Benegas along which a dozen families offer hand-woven handicrafts and distinctive black ceramics.

North of Villa Cura Brochero, Route 15 crosses the vast **Pampa de Pocho**, a strange landscape covered by palm trees, with small inactive volcanoes in the background.

At Taninga, Route 28 branches off east across the Sierra Grande and the northern edge of Reserva Hídrica Pampa de Achala to Villa Carlos Paz.

Nono and around → *Colour map 4, A2. Phone code 03544. Altitude 900 m*

Nono, 8 km south of Mina Clavero, is an attractive little town. On the plaza there is a handicraft market in summer and a lovely little church. Among other well-conserved houses is the historic **Casa Uez**, which serves as a shop, café and basic hotel, and has been the lively meeting point for locals since 1931. **Traslasierra Tur** runs an excellent **tourist office** ① *T03544-498310, www.traslasierra.info, daily 0900-1500, 1600-2200*, at a wood cabin next to the petrol station, with internet facilities. The most visited sight is the extraordinary **Museo Rocsen** ① *5 km east, following Av Los Porteños, T03544-498218, www.museorocsen.org, daily 0900 till sunset, US$2, US$3.50 by taxi*. This eclectic selection of fabulously bizarre objects spanning archaeology, anthropology and human history is the personal vision of Frenchman Juan Santiago Bouchon. Not to be missed.

A network of minor roads east and southeast link the town with the foot of the mountains across a pretty landscape of rivers and hamlets, such as **Paso de las Tropas** and **El Huayco**. To the west, a dusty road leads from the church to the sandy beaches of **Río Los Sauces** and 11 km beyond to the village of **Piedras Blancas**. Cerro Champaquí is accessible from Nono (via San Javier) but you need to take a guide. See www.traslasierra.com/nono and www.nono-cordoba.com (in Spanish) for planning advice.

Los Hornillos and around → *Phone code 03544.*

South of Nono, Route 14 skirts the base of some imposing mountains amid lush vegetation and there are scattered villages offering some accommodation. At Los Hornillos (15 km from Nono) there are good walks 500 m east of the road (left of campsite), along Río Los Hornillos. From there, footpaths lead to the nearby summits, such as the five-hour trek to **La Ventana** (2300 m) passing a 50-m fall halfway. A 1½-hour walk upstream along the riverbed takes you to **Piedra Encajada**, a huge rock with waterfalls. At **Los Hornillos**, the Von Ledebur family has run the lovely hotel **Alta Montaña** ① *www.hosteriaalta montania.com*, since 1947. Ten kilometres northwest is **Dique La Viña** with a large reservoir and an impressive 106-m-high dam, not recommended for vertigo sufferers.

West of the sierras the main town is **Villa Dolores**, a useful transport hub, with a couple of banks and a few hotels, though there's no reason to stop here, unless you're keen to see the potato festival in January. There's an informative **tourist office** ① *T03544-423023*, at the bus station. For more, see www.villadolores.gov.ar.

San Javier and Yacanto → *Phone code 03544.*

These two neighbouring villages lie at the foot of the **Cerro Champaquí** (2790 m), the highest peak in the sierras. They are both very pleasant, peaceful places to stay, with old houses under mature trees, and even if not keen to climb the peak itself, you could relax by the streams or stroll around the picturesque area. The ascent up the Champaquí takes about seven hours from San Javier along the Quebrada del Tigre, but take a guide, as many people get lost. For more information, contact the **Municipalidad** ① *T03544-482041, www.sanjavieronline.com.ar*.

Further south there are more small resort towns where tourism is developing, such as **La Población**, **Luyaba**, **La Paz** and nearby **Loma Bola**, which lie along the road to Merlo, 42 km of San Javier. All these towns are linked by regular TAC buses services, which run between Villa Dolores and Merlo (via San Javier).

Parque Nacional Quebrada del Condorito

Covering 37,000 ha of the Pampa de Achala and the surrounding slopes at altitudes of between 1900 and 2300 m, the park was created in 1996 to protect the central section of Córdoba's sierras, including the spectacular Quebrada del Condorito. This 800-m-deep gorge is the easternmost habitat of the condor. Since you're at the same level as the top of the gorge, it's possible to see fledgling birds taking their first flying lessons. Though condors are elusive and sightings are not guaranteed, you may be lucky enough to see them take a bath under the waterfalls. It takes about three hours to get to the first vantage point (Balcón Norte) and two more hours to the Balcón Sur, by crossing the Río de los Condoritos. Tours are available from Villa Carlos Paz. There's great trekking on the *pastizal de altura* (high-altitude grassland) which is the furthest south that rare tabaquillo trees can be found. The only accessible section of the park is its northeast corner, reached by a short walk from La Pampilla (well signposted), on Route 34, 55 km southwest of Villa Carlos Paz. The landscapes are superb. The climate is warm sub-tropical but take a warm jacket.

Accommodation La Posta del Qenti (AL), 19 km west of La Pampilla, T03544-426450, www.qenti.com.ar. It's a pricey but comfortable resort at 2300 m offering rooms and dorms together with outdoor activities. Book in advance, and ask about their full-board promotional offers.

There are three camping areas with no facilities, along the path to Balcón Norte and Balcón Sur.

Transport Ciudad de Córdoba and TAC buses will both stop at La Pampilla on their way from Villa Carlos Paz to Mina Clavero, 1 hr, US$2.50. If you go with your own vehicle, park it at the NGO Fundación Cóndor (9 km before La Pampilla), beside the handicraft shop (1 km before La Pampilla) or at El Cóndor (7 km after La Pampilla).

Park information There's a national park administration office in Villa Carlos Paz at Resistencia 30 Sabattini 33, office 2, T3541-433371/486287, www.que bradadelcondorito@apn.gov.ar. For an excellent guide for trekking and horse riding, contact **Diego Caliari** T03546-461510/15475576, dfcaliari@yahoo.com.ar. For further information, see www.condoritoapn.com.ar www.que bradacondorito.com.ar (in Spanish).

◉ Traslasierra Valley listings

For Sleeping and Eating price codes and other relevant information, see Essentials pages 30-36.

● Sleeping

Mina Clavero *p210*

There are over 70 hotels, though many are closed in the low season. See www.mina clavero.com for a complete list.

B Hostería Santa María de las Casas Viejas, Camino de los Artesanos, R14, Km 128, T03544-1557 0995, www.santamariade lascasasviejas.com. Located just outside of town, this small stone-built hotel of only 10 rooms, is stylishly decorated. Fantastic restaurant, excursions can be arranged.

C Abuelo Juan, Los Pinos 1919 (take Bolívar to the west from Av Mitre), T03544-470562, www.hosteriaabuelojuan.de. In a residential area south of town, next to the amphitheatre. Run by artists, there is a large garden with a pool and 8 spotless, cosy rooms with a large breakfast. It is aimed at guests with no kids.

Hostels

F pp Hostel Andamundos, San Martín 554, T03544-470249, www.andamundos hostel.com.ar. Centrally located, this well-maintained hostel is brightly painted and has a great atmosphere. They can organize local excursions.

F pp Oh La La Hostel, Villanueva 1192, T03544-472634, www.ohlalahostel.com.ar. Only a short walk from the centre of town (800 m), this hostel has a lovely garden, pool and nice views. It is spacious, well designed and the simple dorms are clean and freshly painted. Recommended.

Camping

Several sites in Mina Clavero, but better to go to the less crowded Villa Cura Brochero.

Nono and around *p211*

Several family houses next to the plaza have signs offering rooms for rent by the day. See www.traslasierra-nono.com.ar for a full list.

AL Gran Hotel Nono, Vicente Castro 289, T03544-498022, www.granhotelnono.com.ar. On the riverside with views of the sierras and surrounded by a large and leafy park with a pool and tennis courts, this is a comfortable and welcoming place with rustic decor. It has a restaurant, and breakfast is included (lots of fruit). Rates are for half-board.

AL La Lejanía, T03544-498960, www.la lejania.com. Lovely little house surrounded by 1000 ha of wilderness. Great swimming pool, tennis courts and a fantastic breakfast.

B La Gloria, on the way to Museo Rocsen, 800 m from Calle Sarmiento, T03544-498231, www.hostal-lagloria.com.ar. On the rural outskirts set in 5 ha of park, this old house has comfortable though not luxurious rooms in a relaxed atmosphere. It has a pool and access to the river. Delicious breakfast included.

C-D Lo de Teresita López, Sarmiento 216 (no sign, just knock), T03544-498030. Welcoming former head teacher offers comfortable rooms and the kitchen in her home. The garden has a beautiful view of the sierras. Recommended.

Camping

A road to the left of the church goes west to the river where there are 3 sites, of which **Los Canadienses**, T03544-498259, is the best choice. A well-kept shady place with clean bathrooms and electricity supply; no pets or large groups allowed. Open high season only. From US$7 a day per tent.

Los Hornillos *p211*

A Alta Montaña, 300 m east of road to the mountains (signposted), T03544-499278, www.hosteria altamontania.com. Neat, comfortable rooms with splendid views from the grounds to the sierras. Pool, restaurant and 8 ha of virgin land by the river. Rates are for half-board; 50% discount for children under 7. Recommended.

San Javier and Yacanto *p211*

A San Javier, T03544-482006, www.san javier-cordoba.com.ar. Lovely gardens, a pool and good rooms with a large breakfast. Several excursions can be arranged.

B Yacanto, T03544-482002, www.hoteya canto.com.ar. A traditional 1920s hotel with comfortable rooms and a beautifully situated 9-hole golf course. In low season there is only half-board.

❶ Eating

Mina Clavero *p210*

♥♥ Rincón Suizo, down by the river, on Calle Recalde, 1 block off Av San Martín. This is an unmissable treat. It's basically a cosy tea room serving rich strudel or chocolate cakes.

Nono and around *p211*

♥♥ La Casona de Nono, Sarmiento 302. Not very attractive, but offers *pollo al disco* (grilled chicken) and *humita* as its specialities.

♥♥ La Pulpería de Gonzalo, on the plaza, opposite the church. Alfresco dining in the wonderful, romantically lit patio. *Parrilla* dishes are the speciality, but fish is also recommended.

▲ Activities and tours

Mina Clavero *p210*
Cycling
Mountain bikes can be hired from Urquiza
1318, for US$6 per day.

Tour operators
Short ½-day trips to the surrounding area
cost about US$9 per person and the longer
Camino de los Túneles costs US$9 per person.
Andar, T03544-471426, andar@arnet.com.ar;
Conocer, behind bus station, T03544-472539.

Nono and around *p211*
Camp Aventura, T0351-156 535 014. An old
lorry is used for weekend short trips to the
surroundings of Dique La Viña, leaving from
1 block east of plaza.
Traslahuella, Vicente Castro 210, T03544-498
084, traslahuella@yahoo.com.ar. Local guide
Martín Zalazar runs ½-day guided treks and
mountain-bike tours along the river and to
the nearby mountains for US$10 per person.
Also available is a day walk to the summit of
Cerro Champaquí for US$30 per person with
a meal included. Mountain bikes can be hired
for US$7 per day.

⊖ Transport

Mina Clavero *p210*
Bus
To **Córdoba**, Ciudad de Córdoba (via Altas
Cumbres), 3 hrs, US$5 (via Cruz del Eje),
6 hrs, US$8; and **TAC** (stopping at villages in
Pampa de Pocho), 6 hrs, US$6. To **Buenos
Aires**, 12 hrs, US$30, Chevallier, Expreso del

Oeste, TAC; to **Mendoza**, 9 hrs, US$18,
Andesmar; to **Merlo**, 2 hrs, US$5, Expreso
del Oeste, Monticas.
Minibuses **Expreso Mina Clavero** go to
Villa Cura Brochero and south to **Nono**
and **Villa Dolores**, calling at villages in
between. Panaholma and Sierra Bus go
direct to **Villa Dolores**, 45 mins, US$5;
and **Córdoba**, 3 hrs, US$6.

Remise taxis
Servicar, T03544-471738; Valle, T03544-472145.

Around Mina Clavero *p210*
Bus
TAC buses go to **Panaholma** and some
villages in the **Pampa de Pocho**. Other
nearby places are only accessible with own
vehicle or with a *remise* taxi (eg to **Toro
Muerto**, US$12; to **Villa Benegas**, US$10).
No buses go along the Camino de los
Túneles, only tour operators.

Nono and around *p211*
Bus
Expreso Mina Clavero going to **Villa
Dolores**, 50 mins, US$2; or up to **Villa Cura
Brochero**, 15 mins, US$2, runs the only bus
and minibus services that stops hourly at
Nono centre. Other companies stop on route.

Remise taxis
Tele Taxi, Sarmiento 94, T03544-498115.

Los Hornillos *p211*
Bus Expreso Mina Clavero stops at Los
Hornillos on its way between **Villa Dolores**
and **Villa Cura Brochero**.

San Luis province

The province of San Luis has always been considered Córdoba's poorer sister: it's further from Buenos Aires, lacking a grand city centre and is not popular with tourists, apart from the overvisited resort town of Merlo on the border. However, there's a spectacular national park, Sierra de las Quijadas, with a great red sandstone canyon and fossil-strewn lunar landscape and you can still find remote places where rural life is sleepy and traditional. ▸▸ *For listings, see pages 218-222.*

San Luis city → *For listings, see pages 218-222. Colour map 4, B2.*

The city of San Luis was founded in 1594, but it wasn't until the late 19th century that it really started to grow, with a flood of European immigration. There was further development in the 1980s when tax incentives encouraged industry to the area. The result is a modern city with a few colonial buildings, but little to attract visitors. However, it is a friendly place with decent accommodation and food, and is a good starting point for exploring the Sierras de San Luis and the Parque Nacional Sierra de las Quijadas. See www.sanluisturismo.com.ar and www.lasquijadas.com for more information.

Ins and outs → *Phone code 02652. Population 162,000.*

The **airport** ① *T02652-422427*, is 3 km northwest from town. Access the airport via Colón, Avenida Justo Daract and Sargento Baigorria. Ordinary and *remise* taxis charge about US$2.50 to the centre. The **bus terminal** ① *Av España 990, T02652-424021*, is a triangular shaped building with offices and bus stops on all sides. To reach the city centre, take Rivadavia. There is left luggage at Kiosko Portos (facing the University), which is open 24 hours, US$1.50 per item for a half-day.

Sights

The centre of the city is the attractive, leafy **Plaza Pringles**, filled with beautiful jacarandas and palm trees and thronging with young crowds after sunset. It's worth popping into the **cathedral** ① *daily 1000-1300, 1830-2000, US$1*, with its slender towers and sumptuous interior, to see replicas of famous Murillo paintings and an extraordinary *pesebre electrónico* – a personal vision of the birth of Christ, with moving figures to the accompaniment of Beethoven's *Ninth Symphony* and Scottish pipes; kitsch and marvellous. Northwest of the plaza, there's a magnificent, decaying former railway station. At the corner of Avenida Illia and Junín, the large **tourist office** ① *T02652-423479, www.sanluisturistico.com.ar*, has little information.

For hotels and bars, stroll along Avenida Illia, which becomes very lively at night. There's a tiny **Museo de Historia Natural** ① *university campus, Italia y Ejército de los Andes, T02652-423917 (ext 43), museo.unsl.edu.ar; Tue-Sun 0900-1300, Thu-Fri 1330-1730; US$0.50*, which traces the evolution of San Luis, including the fossil of an alarming giant spider and a dinosaur footprint. The main commercial heart of the city is on Rivadavia, and three blocks away there's the quieter Plaza Independencia, with its extraordinary Moorish Dominican temple, with a Moorish façade. You can see rugs being woven at the **Centro Artesanal San Martín de Porres** ① *25 de Mayo 955, T02652-424222, Mon-Fri 0800-1300*.

Sierras de San Luis → *For listings, see pages 218-222.*

Northeast of the city of San Luis, there's a beautiful range of hills which remains little known to travellers, and where there are just two frequently visited resorts, the small town of El Trapiche and the reservoir in La Florida. The rest of this vast hilly region is sparsely inhabited, with quiet villages which maintain old rural traditions and a simple way of life. The eastern edge of the sierras and the upper valleys and high pampas around Carolina can be visited by taking Route 9 north from San Luis. Regular buses go up to Carolina and Intihuasi.

El Trapiche → *Phone code 02651.*
At Km 40, El Trapiche is an attractive village set on the Río Trapiche in wooded hills. There are summer homes, hotels and picnic sites, and some good easy walks to **Los Siete Cajones**, on the sparkling waters of Río Grande, and 6 km west, to the pleasant surroundings of the rivers **Virorco** and **De las Aguilas**.

Carolina → *Colour map 4, A2. Phone code 02651. Population 200.*
Carolina is a former gold-mining town founded in 1792 at the foot of Cerro Tomolasta (2018 m) which offers great views from its summit. It's a picturesque village with stone houses and a gold mine, which can be visited through San Luis tour operators (see page 220). The local **Huellas agency** ① *16 de Julio and El Minero, T02651-490224, huellashuellas@hotmail.com*, dresses you up as a miner and guides you along a 300-m tunnel for about 1½ hours (English spoken), and provides tools in case you suddenly feel the desire to dig. From Carolina a rough track leads north over the Cuesta Larga to San Francisco del Monte de Oro, on Route 146. Two other roads in better condition cross attractive scenery of undulating pampas and volcanic peaks to Libertador General San Martín or to La Toma. **Tourist information** is available in the **Municipalidad** ① *16 de Julio s/n, T02651-490214, www.slcarolina.com.ar.*

Eastern San Luis → *For listings, see pages 218-222.*

Villa Mercedes → *Colour map 4, B2. Phone code 02657. Population 90,000.*
Founded in 1856 as a fortress, Villa Mercedes is an important route centre and an alternative transport hub, though of little interest to the tourist. It lies on Route 7, 100 km southeast of San Luis. Accommodation is mainly found along Avenida Mitre (six blocks east of the bus terminal). The **bus terminal** ① *T02657-428035*, and **tourist office** are both at Avenida 25 de Mayo 1500. Villa Mercedes is also the gateway to the southern plains with dozens of small lakes, attractive for anglers. *Pejerrey* is the main catch and the fishing season runs from November to August. Accommodation is available at local *estancias* (ask at the tourist office). For more, see www.villamercedes.gov.ar (in Spanish).

Conlara Valley → *Phone code 02656. Population 90,000.*
Lying east of the Sierra de San Luis and west of the Sierra de Comechingones, this broad valley runs into the Traslasierra Valley to the north, with a number of attractive places to visit and stay. **San José del Morro** has an 18th-century chapel in its blissful traditional village. Nearby, the **Sierra del Morro** (1639 m) is the remains of a collapsed volcano; inside its crater are small volcanic cones, and lots of rose quartz can be found here (access through Estancia La Morena). On 3 May, at tiny **Renca**, one of the most popular religious

Parque Nacional Sierra de Las Quijadas → Phone code: 02652

Situated 125 km northwest of San Luis in the northwestern corner of the province, the park covers 150,000 ha of wonderful scenery, in one of the hottest and most arid areas of Argentina. Its only accessible area, **Potrero de la Aguada**, is an immense natural amphitheatre of nearly 4000 ha surrounded by steep red sandstone walls, eroded into strange shapes. There's a small archaeological site next to the access road, and the fossil-rich field of Loma del Pterodaustro shows intriguing evidence of dinosaurs and pterosaurs (winged reptiles). The vegetation is largely scrub, and *jarillas* are very common though there are trees such as the *quebracho blanco*. Wildlife includes guanaco, collared peccaries, pumas, tortoises, crowned eagles, peregrine falcons and condors.

Near the park warden's office is **Mirador de Elda**, the first of the two vantage points on the Potrero. From here two optional footpaths go to **Mirador Superior** (an easy 45-minute return) or down to the *huella* (a more demanding two-hour return walk to a dinosaur footprint). This path also leads to the impressive cliffs of **Farallones**, reached by a five-hour return walk and only advisable well after midday.

Tours and access Open from dawn till dusk. Visit early in the morning or late afternoon for the best views and to avoid the heat. To get there, take the 6-km unpaved road that turns off from Route 147 (San Luis to San Juan) at Hualtarán. There are a few companies with daily services that link San Luis and San Juan, the two main ones are **Autotransportes San Juan** (US$16) and **Del Sur y Media Agua** (US$14), both stop at Hualtarán.

Tour operators in San Luis and Merlo run half- or full-day tours to the park. Entry costs US$10.

Accommodation Luxury cottages of Complejo La Aguada, T02652-1565 0245, www.laaguada.com. Price (LL-L) includes all meals and activities. The only site for camping (free) is 100 m from the park warden's office next to a basic canteen.

Further information T02652-490182, www.parques nacionales.gov.ar, and www.lasquijadas.com (in Spanish).

festivities in the region, **El Señor de Renca**, is celebrated. **Santa Rosa del Conlara** is a pleasant small town by a river, a good alternative for accommodation when Merlo is packed (reached by bus or *combi* from San Luis). A more scenic journey is via Provincial Route 1, which runs parallel to the east of Route 148 along the base of the Sierra de Comechingones through a string of pretty villages: **Papagayos**, surrounded by natural palm tree groves of *Trithrinax campestris*; **Villa Larca**, where the waterfall **Chorro de San Ignacio** and upper natural pools offer lovely walks; **Cortaderas**; **Carpintería** and up to the well-promoted Merlo.

Merlo → *Colour map 4, A2. Phone code 02656. Population 11,000.*

The **airport** ① *T02656-492840*, is on Route 148, 23 km west of Merlo and the bus terminal is on Route 1, next to the roundabout and a 10-minute walk to the plaza. Situated almost at the San Luis-Córdoba border, Merlo is a popular holiday centre on the steep western slopes of the Sierra de Comechingones. It has lost much of its charm in recent years, due to mass tourism which has made it busy and overpriced. It claims to have a special microclimate, and sunny days can certainly be enjoyed throughout the year. The town was founded in 1797, but the **church** on the plaza, said to be of Jesuit origin, dates from the early 18th century, and is soon to be replaced by the huge new red-brick church behind. There's a modern **airport** and **bus terminal** and two **tourist offices**: ① *at the roundabout on R5 and R1; and next to the plaza at Coronel Mercau 605, daily 0900-1900, T02656-476079, www.lavillademerlo.com.ar, www.turismo-merlo.com.ar.*

Merlo's surroundings are still pleasant for walking at the foot of the mountains or to their summits (the **Circuito de Damiana Vega** takes three to four hours). The slopes are covered with woods and scrub and there are numerous refreshing streams with falls. Higher up there are some excellent sites for paragliding; an experienced pilot recently reached heights of 5000 m. A paved road (15 km long) leads to the top of the sierras at **Mirador del Sol**, where there are wonderful panoramic views, best at sunrise or sunset. The mirador is accessible by bus and is the starting point for a rough track leading across 82 km of pampas and Sierras de Córdoba to Embalse del Río Tercero.

Quieter places to stay are spread in the neighbouring small settlements of **Piedra Blanca** (4 km north) or **Rincón del Este** (4 km east), but book ahead in high season.

◉ San Luis province listings

For Sleeping and Eating price codes and other relevant information, see Essentials pages 30-36.

● Sleeping

San Luis city *p215*

For more listings, see www.sanluisturistico.com.ar.

AL Vista Suites & Spa, Av Pte Illia 526, T02652-425794, www.vistasuites.com.ar. Stunning hotel with a lovely view from the rooftop pool. Stylish, modern rooms. Great bar and restaurant.

A Aiello, Av Illia 431, T02652-425609, www.hotelaiello.com.ar. Pricey but good rooms with a/c, welcoming staff, breakfast included, good pool and internet access.

A Hotel Quitana, Av Pte Illia 546, T2654-438400, www.hotelquintana.com.ar. 6 floors and 84 rooms make this hotel one of San Luis' biggest. The rooms are a little dated but the staff are friendly and the location is great.

C Belgrano, Belgrano 1440, T02652-435923. This is probably the best budget option, with welcoming staff, renovated rooms with fan and bath, and breakfast included.

Hostel

F pp San Luis Hostel, Falucho 646, T02652-424188, www.sanluishostel.com.ar. Large, welcoming gardens, basic dorms and slightly old-fashioned furniture. Central, but take a taxi from the bus station (US$4).

Around San Luis

A Hotel Potrero de los Funes, R18, Km 16, T02652-440038, T02652-423898, www.hotelpotrero.sanluis.gov.ar. Set in a mountainous area, this impressive lakeside resort offers affordable rooms, some with splendid views (slightly pricier). A pool and sport facilities are included (also ATM), as well as a large breakfast.

A Los Tamarindos, Balde, T02652-442220, www.jardinesdetamarindos.com. Rates at this attractive spa resort include breakfast and rooms with a/c in small flats for up to 6; there are both indoor and outdoor pools accessible to non-guests for US$4 per person. Also cabins with a/c where you can rest after the baths for US$5 per hr.

B-C Campo La Sierra, 19 km east of San Luis (access via R20), T02652-494171, www.campo lasierra.com.ar. A warm welcome at this Swiss-owned, 70-ha farm with native flora (cacti experts visit annually). German-style cooking, breakfast, pool and archery.

El Trapiche *p216*

B Hostería El Trapiche, Route 9, Km 39, T02652-493226, www.hosteriaeltrapiche.com. Charming bed and breakfast with personalized

service, cane armchairs and large garden to explore – all with stunning views.
C Villa Alinor, T02652-493038, villalinor. webege.com. Price is per house. A group of small houses at a most attractive location on a natural rocky balcony next to the river. Each house sleeps 4-6 with kitchen, fridge and phone; bedlinen and towels extra.
F pp Hostería El Parque, Av Costanera, T02651-493176. A family-orientated hotel with full- or half-board accommodation; children under 5 free.

Camping
At the north end of town, to the right side of the bridge. Nearby is the La Florida reservoir which offers good fishing, accessible via a paved road encircling the lake. On its northern shore there is a small natural reserve, intended to preserve the original flora and wildlife.

Carolina p216
B-C Hostería Las Verbenas, 10 km south of Carolina, T02652-430918, www.lasverbenas. com.ar. Situated in the beautiful Pancanta Valley, this is an ideal base for walking and horse riding or for enjoying a relaxing stay. Price is for full board.
B-C La Posta del Caminante, R9, Km 0.83, T02651-490223, www.lapostadelcaminante. com.ar. Housed in a former residence for mining engineers. Offers comfortable rooms with bath and breakfast (cheaper with shared bath), pool in natural setting, and has a small restaurant next door. Walks to the mines and horse-riding excursions are also arranged.

Conlara Valley p216
B-C Hotel Río Conlara, Rivadavia and San José, T02656-492012, www.hotelrioconlara. com.ar. Next to a nicely maintained *balneario*, where the river was dammed, this place has clean, comfortable rooms. Breakfast included.

Merlo p217
Book in advance for high season: Jan and Feb, Easter, Jul and Aug. See www.turismo-merlo. com.ar and www.lavillademerlo.com.ar for more listings.
AL La Quinta Resorts, Román Gonzáles s/n, Piedra Blanca, T02656-479598, www.laquinta resort.net. Huge complex with a jacuzzi, pool and tennis courts just outside of town. Lovely cabins, stylishly recorated.
A-B Villa de Merlo, Pedernera and Av del Sol, T02656-475335, www.hotelvillademerlo. com.ar. Comfortable rooms with splendid views of the sierras and a large garden with pool. There are sport facilities, though the quiet atmosphere of this rather exclusive 3-star hotel is more appealing for a relaxing holiday. Moderately priced restaurant.
B Altos del Sol, Andrada and Borges, T02656-478399, www.altosdelsol.com. Charming *cabañas* set above town with endless views. For 2-7 people, nice rooms and a pool.
B Rincón de los Troncos, Av José Percau 164, T02656-476768, www.rincondelos troncos.com.ar. Huge rustic but comfortable cabins for 2-6 people. Wonderful alpine wood and stone building within tranquil grounds and 2 large pools, only a short distance to the centre of town. Often recommended.
C Colonial, Av Dos Venados y P Tisera, T02656-475388, www.hchosteriacolonial.com.ar. Probably the best value, in a quiet residential area not far from the centre. This attractive, neo colonial building has simple rooms on a patio with an incredibly small pool. Breakfast is included, internet access available for a fee.

Camping
Las Violetas, Chumamaya and Av Dos Venados, T02656-475730, lasvioletas@merlo-sl.com.ar. The closest site to the centre has a small shady area for tents, a pool, canteen, grocery shop and clean but not spotless bathrooms. US$6 per campsite plus US$0.50 per day.

● Eating

San Luis city *p215*

Chivito (kid) is the main local dish. Its usual accompaniment is *chanfaina* (a stew whose main ingredients are the goat's entrails).

¶¶ La Porteña, Junín y General Paz, T02652-431722. Simple meals such as the *plato del día*. Prepare for enormous portions in the enjoyable atmosphere of this popular place.

¶ Crocantes, San Martín 630. A bakery where cheap and superb sandwiches are prepared at your request and with your chosen bread.

¶ Grand Palace, Rivadavia 657. At the hotel of the same name, the experienced chef Pedro Pardo offers a selection of very good dishes based on grilled meats, fish or pork, with scrumptious home-made desserts.

¶ La Pulpería del Arriero, 9 de Julio 753, T02652-432446. With tasty regional specialities and live folk music in the evenings, this is the place for trying *empanadas* or *asado* during a lively night out. The set menus are good value.

¶ Los Robles, Colón 684, T02652-436767. Formal atmosphere and very good food, you can eat at moderate prices at this smart *parrilla*. There is a wide choice of dishes (*bife de chorizo* is great), including *chivito* and trout. Recommended.

Cafés and bars

There's a cluster spread along Av Illia and Rivadavia between 0800 and 1000. During the day, 2 enjoyable cafés on the plaza are **Aranjuez** and **Ocean**. Try also **Liberato**, Av Illia 378, popular with young crowds at night; and **Macedonio**, San Martín 848, a laid-back café-bookshop.

Conlara Valley *p216*

¶ Manía, San Martín 199. Very good pizza, and simple and cheap meals.

Merlo *p217*

¶¶ El Ciprés, Av del Ciprés 114. Popular with the locals. Good, filling meals are guaranteed though the menu is pretty standard.

¶¶ El Establo, Av del Sol 450. Handsome *parrilla*, where the grill or *asador* is strangely trapped in a glass enclosure. Try *chivito* here.

¶¶ La Vieja Posada, Av del Sol 2. A simple place with more than 30 different pizzas with a folk music show on Sat evenings.

¶ La Estrella de Merlo, Becerra y Av del Sol. Locals come here for tasty home-made pastas.

✸ Festivals and events

San Luis province *p215*

3 May Cristo de la Quebrada. This popular religious festival takes place at Villa de la Quebrada.

25 Aug King Saint Louis. A religious procession that commemorates King Saint Louis. A national holiday across the province.

▲▲ Activities and tours

San Luis city *p215*

All agencies offer similar tours at standard rates (rates in leaflets usually do not include fees to national parks). A ½-day tour to Sierra de las Quijadas is the most popular (US$25 per person, plus entry) and includes a walk to Los Miradores (1-1½ hrs) and to La Huella (2-2½ hrs). Weather permitting (usually not in summer), a more demanding walk to Los Farallones (4-5 hrs) is organized (US$26 per person, plus entry). The Circuito Serrano Chico (US$11 per person) is a short walk around El Volcán, Potrero de los Funes and the town itself, while the Circuito Serrano Grande (US$13 per person) adds El Trapiche and La Florida. Circuito de Oro (US$19 per person) goes up to Carolina and Intihuasi and may include the Circuitos Serranos. There are also tours to religious sites in Suyuque and Villa de la Quebrada, and to the hot springs of Balde and the salt flats in Salinas del Bebedero. A day trip to Merlo via La Toma is also available (US$24 per person).

Bruno Aliberti, T02652-426021, T02652-1550 2971, guide only, for those with their own vehicle; **Dasso**, Rivadavia 540, T02652-421017, T02652-1564 5410; **Gimatur**, Av Illia y Caseros, T02652-435751, gimatursl@hotmail.com, English spoken; **Luciano Franchi**, Chile 1430, T02652-420345, T02652-1565 7441; **Remises Sur**, T02652-455000, good-value trips for 3 or 4 of you.

Merlo *p217*
Cycling
Sis, Coronel Mercau and Los Huarpes (2 blocks north of plaza). Bike hire.

Tour operators
Excursions to local sights and provincial attractions, including full-day tours to Sierra de las Quijadas (US$25 per person, plus entry fee). Closer destinations include ½-day trips to Mina Los Cóndores (US$10 per person, plus entry fee) and to Bajo de Véliz, an over-promoted palaeontological site, where giant spiders used to live millions of years ago (US$10 per person). Surrounding villages may also be explored for a few hours (US$8 per person). These more conventional tours are organized by **La Plaza**, Becerra y Av del Ciprés, T02656-476853; and **Sol**, Av del Sol 171, T02656-475346.

More demanding activities like climbing hills, visiting a remote ghost mining town, sleeping in caves or crossing rivers are also on offer, run by **Cimarrón Incursiones**, Av del Sol 300, T02656-478934, T02652-1566 4251; **Juan Carlos Sciamarella**, T02652-1554 8536; or **Los Tabaquillos**, Av de los Césares 2100, T02656-474010.

● Transport

San Luis city *p215*
Air
For airport information, see page 215. Flights to **Buenos Aires**, 1¼ hrs, CATA (from Merlo), Av España 950, T02652-439156.

Bus
For bus terminal information, see page 215. Check at office where your bus leaves from.

To **Buenos Aires**, 10-11 hrs, US$43-71, several companies. To **La Rioja**, 7½ hrs, US$15, Socasa; to **Mendoza**, 3-4 hrs, US$9, several companies. To **Córdoba**, 6 7 hrs, US$10, several companies. To **San Juan**, 4 hrs, US$9, Andesmar; Autotransportes San Juan; Autotransportes San Juan-Mar del Plata; Del Sur y Media Agua; TAC. To **Santa Rosa** (La Pampa), 10 hrs, US$9.50, Dumas; also to destinations in southern San Luis. To **Merlo**, 3 hrs, US$5, Automotores Merlo (packed minibuses); Expreso Uspallata; SENA; TAC. To **Balde** and **Salinas del Bebedero**, 2 daily Mon-Fri, 45 mins, US$0.50; and 1 hr, US$, Dasso. To **El Trapiche**, US$1, María del Rosario, San José; same services go to La Florida and Río Grande. To **Carolina** and **Intihuasi**, Polos, 3 daily (unreliable timetable), US$2 and US$2.50.

To Peru To **Lima**, 2½ days, US$110, El Rápido Internacional (direct).

To Chile To **Santiago**, 9-10 hrs, US$20, Cata; Tas Choapa; Tur Bus.

Car hire
Budget, Belgrano 1440, T02652-440288; **Travel**, Chacabuco 649, T02652-438500, www.travelrentacar.com.ar.

Remise taxis
Cosmos, Chacabuco 1151, T02652-440000; **Zoo**, Bolívar y Falucho, T02652-421000.

Merlo *p217*
Air
For airport information, see page 217.

To **Buenos Aires**, 1 hr 50 mins, CATA (stops at San Luis), desk at tourist office (at Merlo roundabout), T02656-478460.

Bus
Frequent services to **San Luis**, 3 hrs, US$5, Automotores Merlo; Expreso Uspallata; SENA; TAC. To **Buenos Aires**, US$43-70, 10-12 hrs, Autotransportes San Juan-Mar del Plata; Chevallier; Expreso del Oeste; Sierras Cordobesas; TAC. To **Córdoba**, 5 hrs, US$9, Andesmar; Expreso Uspallata; Monticas; TAC. To **Mina Clavero**, 2 hrs, US$5, Expreso del Oeste; Monticas. To **Villa Dolores**, 2 hrs, US$2 (via San Javier), TAC; or 1 hr, US$3 (via R148), Sierras Cordobesas and TAC. La Costa goes daily along R1 to Cortaderas, Villa Larca and Papagayos. STU

runs frequent services to **Mirador del Sol**, stopping there for 10 mins, US$2.50 return.

Remise taxis
Avenida, Becerra 575, T02656-476031; **Unión**, Videla 114, T02656-478444.

❶ Directory

San Luis city *p215*
Banks Banex, Rivadavia and Pringles, T02652-440004. **Currency exchange** Banco de Galicia, Colón and Pringles; Montemar, Belgrano 980. **Internet** Cyberclub Buskar, Pedernera 1305, US$0.50 per hr (US$0.35 per hr after 2400); Ego!, Av Illia 320, US$0.90 per hr (US$0.45 per hr after 2200); Telecentro, Av Illia 127, US$0.90 per hr. **Post office** San Martín y Av Illia, offers Western Union services. **Telephone** *Telecentros* on C San Martín and on Av Illia.

Contents

Footprint features

Border crossings

Argentina–Chile, *see pages 251
   and 258.*

Mendoza & the West

At a glance

◎ **Getting around** The local buses
are the best way to get around, but
a bicycle can be a great way to see
the wineries.

◉ **Time required** At least 4-5 days
to explore the city and wineries.

☀ **Weather** Mild summers
(Dec-Mar), but winters (May-Aug)
can be cold and windy.

✖ **When not to go** From May-Aug
it can be particularly cold, with
harsh winds coming down off
the Andes. Some hotels and tour
operators close during this time.

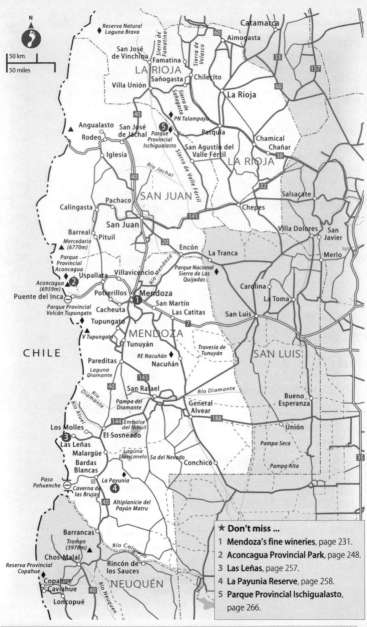

★ **Don't miss ...**
1 **Mendoza's fine wineries**, page 231.
2 **Aconcagua Provincial Park**, page 248.
3 **Las Leñas**, page 257.
4 **La Payunia Reserve**, page 258.
5 **Parque Provincial Ischigualasto**, page 266.

Argentina's west is wild and largely unvisited, despite having one of the country's most stylish and vibrant cities at its heart. Mendoza is the centre of the biggest wine-producing region in Argentina, and with its setting at the foothills of the Andes, and fine restaurants, it's a great base for exploring the surrounding vineyards for a few days. The secret to Argentina's successful wine industry is the climate: hot days and cool nights, and a consistent supply of pure snow-melt from the Andes. You could happily spend a week visiting bodegas, before heading west to climb Mount Aconcagua, South America's highest mountain. If this is too daunting, there are many other dramatic peaks to hike up in summer, or ski down in winter, with the country's most famous ski and snowboarding resort, Las Leñas, in the south of the province.

South of Mendoza, find sparkling wine producers in San Rafael, or set off for adventures in the wild landscapes beyond. Go rafting in the eerie ravine of Cañón del Atuel; find yourself seduced by the quieter charms of Llancanelo where thousands of flamingos rise from the Prussian-blue waters; or ride a horse through the starkly beautiful volcanic landscape of La Payunia, where *guanacos* roam unhindered. A spirit of adventure is definitely needed to explore the quieter provinces of San Juan and La Rioja, but the intrepid will be rewarded with forgotten valleys offering perfect peace and natural beauty. But the undoubted stars of the region are two national parks; each likely to make you feel dwarfed by both time and space. The 'Valley of the Moon' at Ischigualasto is indeed an other-worldly landscape: a 200-million-year-old lake-bed, strewn with fossils from first life forms to dinosaurs. And Talampaya's vast canyons of terracotta rock, eroded by wind into gigantic sculptures, are magnificent at sunset when they turn a vivid red.

Mendoza city

→ *Colour map 3, A2. Phone code 0261. Population of Greater Mendoza: 110,000.*

Mendoza is undoubtedly the tourism centre of the west of Argentina, and a good place to spend a few days, with its pretty plazas, wide boulevards and sophisticated nightlife. Its flourishing economy is based entirely around wine, as it is the centre of Argentina's rapidly growing wine industry. Any trip to the city should include a tour of some of the vineyards at Maipú and Luján de Cuyo, to the south of the city. There are large flashy commercial bodegas and smaller family wineries, and after seeing the process of winemaking, you'll be treated to a generous tasting to appreciate why Argentina's wine is receiving such worldwide acclaim. Wine is a part of the city's culture too, in the profusion of wonderful vinotecas where you can taste fine wines, and in the spectacular festival held to celebrate the wine harvest every March in Mendoza's splendid Parque San Martín. The city has some small interesting museums, and a lively nightlife, with sophisticated restaurants serving all kinds of fine food. It's a good place to plan a trip into the mountains to the west; the snow-capped peaks form a dramatic backdrop to the city. You can hire ski gear, get expertise on climbing Aconcagua or find specialist adventure tour operators for climbing or rafting elsewhere in the West. The city is well set up for tourism, with a huge range of comfortable hotels, and plentiful bilingual tour operators. For more information, see www.welcometomendoza.com.ar (in English) and www.viajeamendoza.com (in Spanish).▸▸ *For listings, see pages 236-245.*

Ins and outs

Getting there

Mendoza is 1060 km west of Buenos Aires. **El Plumerillo Airport** ① *T0261-520 6000*, 8 km north of the city, has a bank, tourist information, a few shops, restaurant, *locutorio* and left luggage. Bus No 60 heads to the centre from the airport (Alem and Salta streets) every 35 minutes (make sure it says 'Aeropuerto' on the front; 40 minutes, US$0.90. A taxi costs US$7. Daily flights connect Mendoza with Buenos Aires, Córdoba and Santiago de Chile. Long-distance buses arrive at Mendoza from almost everywhere in the country, with several services daily to Buenos Aires, Salta and Bariloche, as well as the nearby cities of San Rafael and San Juan. Mendoza is a good stopping point for routes in and out of Chile with frequent services to Santiago, and at least one bus a day stopping at Uspallata and the mountainous region on the way to the Chilean border for those wanting to trek or ski. Beware of thieves at all times in the bus station and note that there are generally long waits for taxis. ▸▸ *For further information, see Transport, page 243.*

Getting around

Mendoza's city centre is easy to find your way around on foot, with the large leafy Plaza Independencia occupying four blocks at its centre. Pedestrianized Sarmiento runs between the plaza and the main shopping street, San Martín, which runs north to south. The bodegas (wineries) in the nearby towns of Luján de Cuyo and Maipú, just to the south, can be reached by bus, but if you're keen to see more than one, it's better to hire a car. Each bus has two numbers – a big number painted onto the bus at the top front corner (the bus company or *grupo*), and a smaller number (*subnúmero*) on a card propped in the window, which is the actual route (*recorrido* or *línea*). For example, if you're going to the bodega La Rural in Maipú (US$0.75), you'll need bus No 10, *subnúmero* 173; don't be tempted to get on all the other 10s that go past.

San Martín El Libertador

If you learn about only one Argentine hero on your trip, make it San Martín, one of the greatest independence heroes of South America. Celebrated by statues in every town in the country, José Francisco de San Martín hoped to unite Spanish America after independence, and though he failed to achieve this aim, his military genius played a major role in securing independence. He possessed a tremendous organizational ability, even when leading troops scattered over large distances and mountainous terrain, and his epic crossing of the Andes in 1817 was a turning point in the Wars of Independence, and the bloody campaigns that followed in Chile and Peru ended Spanish rule in South America.

Born in Yapeyú, Corrientes, in 1778 and educated in Spain, San Martín served in the Spanish army in North Africa, Spain and France from the age of 15. In 1811 he resigned from the army and made contact with Francisco de Miranda and other supporters of South American independence, returning to Buenos Aires in 1812 to train the new cavalry regiment. The following year, he replaced Belgrano as commander of the northern armies and, once appointed governor of Cuyo province, spent the next two years preparing to capture Peru from his base in Mendoza by means of a giant flanking movement through Chile and up through the coast to Lima. His 'Army of the Andes' was drawn from regular troops sent by Buenos Aires, but San Martín personally reconnoitred the mountain passes to plan the crossing to Chile himself. He also planned a brilliant deception, calling a meeting of Pehuenche chiefs to ask their permission to cross their territory to invade Chile via mountain passes south of Mendoza. As he'd expected, spies carried this news across the Andes, leaving San Martín free to use a more northerly route, with the main force crossing by Los Patos and Uspallata passes. Some 3778 men set out on 19 January 1817, with equipment and 10,791 horses and mules, and they crossed the Andes in 21 days, arriving on time at their intended destinations. Within days, the army defeated the Spanish at Chacabuco and entered Santiago, Chile, in triumph, though the conclusive victory was at the Battle of Maipú in April 1818.

With Chilean independence secure, San Martín led his forces by sea to Peru in 1820. Avoiding battle against the larger Spanish forces, he negotiated a truce. Finally entering Lima in triumph in July 1821, he assumed political and military command of the new republic of Peru. Afterwards, San Martín resigned his post and returned to his small farm in Mendoza, before travelling to Europe in 1824 to settle in Brussels and then Grand Bourg, France. He died in Boulogne-sur-Mer in 1850, and his remains now lie in the Buenos Aires cathedral. Symbolizing to many Argentines the virtues of sacrifice, bravery and the lack of personal gain, he's remembered by street names in even the smallest towns.

Within the city, buses are US$0.60 per trip, payable with change on the bus, or you can buy the magnetic card, which you can top up like a phonecard. If you are only visiting for a short time, it's not worth the hassle. There are eight trolleybus routes, a streetcar that runs only in the centre and a tourist trolleybus that has just two daily departures. You're unlikely to need transport in the centre, but if you do, taxis are plentiful and safe.

Best time to visit

The biggest festival of the year, **Fiesta de la Vendimia**, is held from mid-February to mid-March to celebrate the start of the wine harvest. The festival includes a carnival queen, a procession of floats and outdoor extravaganzas in the park – but little wine tasting. A parallel event is the less-promoted but equally entertaining **Gay Vendimia Festival** with parties, shows and the crowning of the Festival Queen. Bodegas can be visited all year round and at harvest time (March and April) you'll see the machinery in action. If you're heading beyond Mendoza to explore the landscape, trekking in the mountains is only possible from November to April, when the snow has melted. The most pleasant time for trekking is December to February, which is the only feasible season for trekking at higher altitudes. Skiing at Los Penitentes (on the road to Chile) is from July to October, though Las Leñas further south is open from mid-June.

Tourist information

Mendoza has a well developed tourism infrastructure, with tourist offices all over the city. The city's **main office** ① *San Martín 1143, opposite Sarmiento, T0810-666 6363, or T0261-420 2800, daily 0900-2100*, provides information on the whole province. There's also a useful booth on the street outside, for city information only (T0261-420 1333). Both offices have English-speaking staff who can provide city maps, information on bodegas and explain the buses. Smaller offices are open Monday to Friday, 0800-1300, and can be found in the **civic centre** ① *9 de Julio 500, T0261-449 5185*, and at ① *Las Heras 670 y Mitre*,

Mendoza

Sleeping 🛏
Argentino 1 *A4*
Confluencia 13 *A4*
Damajuana 5 *B2*
Deptosmendoza 2 *B5*
El Portal Suites 14 *A3*
Gran Mendoza 9 *A4*
Hostel Suites Mendoza 11 *A4*
Huentala 3 *B5*
Independencia 15 *A4*
Kapac 10 *A3*
Mendoza Inn 4 *B1*
NH Cordillera 19 *A4*
Nutibara 16 *B4*
Park Hyatt 18 *B4*
Park Suites 20 *B4*
Petit 8 *A3*
Provincial 21 *A3*
Sosahaus 6 *A3*
Villaggio 7 *B3*

Eating 🍴
Anna Bistro 3 *A2*
Azafrán 1 *B3*
Comida de Campo 7 *B5*
Comida Poblana 2 *B2*
Facundo 6 *B3*

T0261-425 7805. There are two small but very helpful kiosks at the airport and at the bus terminal, and another extremely helpful office at the entrance to **Parque San Martín** ① *daily 0800-1800*. For online information visit www.turismo.mendoza.gov.ar (in English), or www. mendoza.com.ar. For city information, try www.ciudaddemendoza. gov.ar (in Spanish). Another very useful site, designed by English expats, is www.welcometomendoza.com.ar (in English).

Background

Mendoza was founded by Pedro del Castillo in 1561, when he was sent from the Spanish colony in Chile by Captain General García Hurtado de Mendoza to cross the 4000-m pass over the Andes, and start a new city. Mediterranean fruits were introduced to the region soon afterwards, and thrived in its sunny climate, aided by pre-Hispanic irrigation channels that are still used today to water the dry lands with abundant snow-melt from the Andes. The city's wealth grew, although it remained largely isolated throughout the colonial period, being governed from Chile and having little contact with modern-day Argentina. The city's greatest blow came on Easter Saturday in 1861 when it was completely destroyed in a devastating earthquake which killed some 4000 of its 12,000 inhabitants. Very quickly, a new centre was built by the French architect Ballofet, several blocks to the southwest of the original. This modern city was designed with low, quake-proof buildings and broad avenues with many plazas to aid evacuation in case of further tremors. Plane trees were planted on all the streets, watered by a network of irrigation channels which still gush with water every spring. Nowadays, Mendoza's main industry is wine, though a busy university and, increasingly, tourism help to sustain its wealth and lively character.

Sights

The large **Plaza Independencia** is a popular meeting place for *mendocinos* with its shady acacia and plane trees and pretty fountains. In the middle is the small **Museo de Arte Moderno** ① *Mon Sat 0900 2100, Sun 1600-2100, US$1*, originally designed to be an emergency bunker for victims of earthquakes, it now houses temporary exhibitions. On the western side is the new and luxurious **Park Hyatt Hotel** ① *www.mendoza.park.hyatt.com*, was once a splendid 1920s palace where Juan Perón and Evita stayed. The eastern side of the park is filled with a handicrafts market at weekends, where Sarmiento runs to San Martín. Around the four corners of this central plaza, just a block further out, are four smaller plazas. The most attractive is the **Plaza España**, to the southeast. Its floor and benches are beautifully tiled and

Ferruccio Soppelsa **17** *A4*
Il Dolce **19** *B5*
La Marchigiana **10** *A4*
La Sal **20** *B3*
Las Tinajas **4** *A5*
Mi Tierra **21** *B4*
Montecatini **12** *A4*
Por Acá **14** *B1*

Sr Cheff **15** *B5*
Terrazas del Lago **23** *A1*
Vía Civit **16** *B2*

➡ **Mendoza maps**
1 Mendoza, page 228
2 Mendoza wineries, page 232

it's a lovely place to sit under the trees and gaze at the rather sentimental mural displaying historical episodes as well as scenes from *Don Quijote* and the famous gaucho poem, *Martín Fierro*. Four blocks west along Montevideo, with its pretty Italianate and colonial-style buildings, is **Plaza Italia**, with wonderful mature tipa trees. Nearby it's worth visiting the small **Museo del Pasado Cuyano** ① *Montevideo 544, T0261-423 6031, Mon-Fri 0900-1230, US$0.50*, housed in a beautiful 1873 mansion owned by the Civit family. There's lots of San Martín memorabilia, and an exquisite Spanish 15th-century carved altarpiece. The director will give you an excellent tour and insights into the city's history.

The original city centre, destroyed by the earthquake in 1861, was located 12 blocks to the northeast of today's Plaza Independencia, and is now known as the **Area Fundacional**. Here there is a broad tranquil plaza and a beautifully designed **museum** ① *Beltrán and Videla Castillo, T0261-425 6927, Tue-Sat 0800-2000, Sun 1500-2000, US$1 (underground chamber, extra US$0.50), kids under 6 free*, whose glass floor reveals continuing excavations of foundations from the old Cabildo and the buildings that followed, with an array of objects salvaged from the rubble. The informative free tour is highly recommended to give you a picture of Mendoza's history. To get there, take buses 1 (line 13) and 3 (line 112). Under the plaza you can see the first fountain to bring running water to the city, and nearby, at the corner of Ituzaingó and Beltrán, are the ruins of the Jesuit **Iglesia de San Francisco**. **Plaza Pellegrini** is another attractive little plaza, at Avenida Alem and Avenida San Juan, where wedding photos are taken on Friday and Saturday nights, and there's a small antiques market on Friday at lunchtime.

Ten blocks west of Plaza Independencia, wrought-iron gates mark the entrance to the great **Parque General San Martín**, 350 ha of lavishly planted parkland designed by famous Argentine landscape architect Charles Thays, with sports facilities, a big lake where regattas are held, a sports stadium and an amphitheatre. On a hill in the park is the **Cerro de la Gloria**, popular with paragliders, giving splendid views of the Andes to the west. There's also a monument to San Martín, showing various episodes of his leading his army across the Andes to liberate Argentina and Chile from the Spanish. From the east end of the park, on Avenida Libertador, an hourly bus ('Oro Negro') runs to the top of the Cerro de la Gloria – otherwise it's a 45-minute walk. On the side of the Cerro is the **Jardín Zoológico** ① *T0261-427 1559, www.zoo.mendoza.gov.ar, Tue-Sun 0900-1800, US$2*, one of the country's best zoos. There's a helpful **tourist information office** next to the main gates. The lakeside restaurant **Terrazas del Lago** is open from breakfast to the early hours of the morning. At the south end of the lake is the **Museo de Ciencias Naturales y Antropológicas** ①*T0261-428 7666, Mon-Fri 0800-1300, 1400-1900, Sat-Sun 0800-1300,1500-1900, US$1*, with an ancient female mummy amongst its fossils and stuffed animals. Not far from the Area Fundacional, at the southern end of Parque O'Higgins, kids might enjoy the small aquarium **Acuario Municipal** ① *Ituzaingó and Buenos Aires, daily 0900-1230, 1500-2030, US$1*. Across the street is a small **Serpentario** ① *daily 0930-1300, 1500-1930, US$1*, with plenty of snakes and lizards.

The city's best art gallery is in the nearby suburb of **Luján de Cuyo**, where there's a small, charming collection of Argentine paintings in the house where Fernando Fader painted his beautiful murals, at the **Museo Provincial de Bellas Artes** ① *Casa de Fader, Carril San Martín 3651, Mayor Drummond, T0261-496 0224, Tue-Fri 0800-1800, Sat-Sun 1400-1900, US$0.50*. There are also sculptures in the lovely gardens. To get there, take bus 1 (line 19) Empresa Trapiche, 40 minutes. For the **Museo Nacional del Vino**, see Maipú page 235.

Around Mendoza

The sight of distant purple mountains is bound to draw you from the city sooner or later up into the dramatic Andes to the west, on the road to Chile. This area, known as Alta Montaña, is the undoubted highlight of the region, with Mount Aconcagua at its heart, and plenty of other places for walking in Parque Provincial Aconcagua. These are described in the next section, but if you're thinking of taking a day trip from Mendoza city, bear in mind that you'll get very little chance to walk around, and that you'd be better off hiring a car and spending a few days exploring. You'll pass through the pretty town of Uspallata reached by two possible routes west: either Portrerillos or Vallecitos. These routes and the town are described in more detail in the next section, but just to whet your appetite: there are thermal springs and a good place for lunch at the pretty village of Cacheuta, 40 km west of Mendoza city, which also has a good hotel. At **Potrerillos**, 68 km west of Mendoza on Route 7, you could do a day's rafting, walking or horse riding, but if you're driving, note there's no road between the two since the river was dammed, even though they're only 10 km away from each other.

The alternative route to Uspallata takes you up to **Villavicencio**, 47 km north, where there are gentle walks and a charming rustic restaurant in spectacular mountain scenery, though the famous hotel you see on all the bottles of Villavicencio water is undergoing renovation (due to open in 2012). Further west, the road climbs up to Paramillos at 3200 m, a spectacular and much more adventurous route to reach Uspallata valley and the Alta Montaña circuit. This is offered in some tours, but is more fun in your own transport (see Transport, page 245, for more details). For water sports, **Embalse El Carrizal**, an artificial lake 60 km south of Mendoza, has yachting and fishing, campsites and picnic areas. For skiing in the winter, you can do two resorts in day trips. **Los Penitentes** (www.penitentes.com), 183 km away, is by far the better of the two, but since there's plenty of accommodation there, it's better to go for a couple of days. **Vallecitos** is closer, at 95 km, but it's a very basic little ski resort and the *ripio* roads can be tricky.

Wine region → *For listings, see pages 236-245.*

No trip to Mendoza is complete without a tour of the local wineries. Wine is at the heart of Mendoza's landscape and industry, and the bodegas are beautiful places to visit. Surrounded by semi-arid lands with little vegetation, the rich green vineyards seem miraculous, stretching out in perfectly ordered rows towards the dramatic backdrop of snow-dusted mauve mountains beyond. Most establishments are delighted to show you around, with a tour to teach you about the winemaking process, and to invite you to taste their excellent produce. Some of the more interesting bodegas have good restaurants too, and many have opened smart and comfortable boutique hotels. These tend to be on the expensive side, but they are beautiful places to stay, since you're in the middle of vineyards, with the added advantage that you can enjoy superb wine with your meal and not have to worry about driving. **Tapiz** ① *www.tapiz.com*, is one of the best and is gaining a reputation for excellence. **Cavas Wine Lodge** ① *www.cavaswinelodge.com*, is also frequently recommended. ▶▶ *For further information on visiting bodegas, see box, page 244.*

There are three main wine-producing areas in Mendoza province. The **High zone of Río Mendoza**, the oldest wine-producing area, is immediately to the south of Mendoza city with bodegas sprinkled among two towns, Maipú and Luján de Cuyo. Wineries in this region are described in more detail below. The second region is the **Uco Valley**, to the south of the small town of Tupungato which lies southwest of Mendoza in the foothills of the Andes. And the third region is around **San Rafael** (286 km south of Mendoza city). Only the first region is described here, since both Tupungato and San Rafael are described in Southern Mendoza (see page 254).

Mendoza wineries

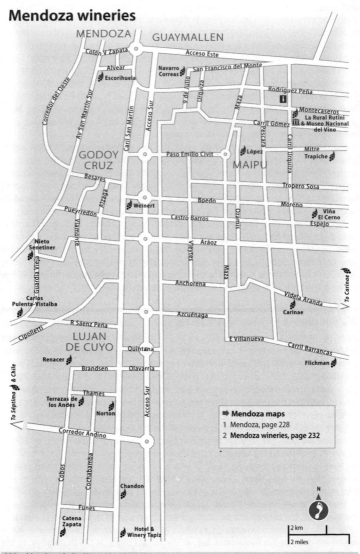

➡ **Mendoza maps**
1 Mendoza, page 228
2 **Mendoza wineries, page 232**

2 km

2 miles

N

Argentina's wine industry has grown considerably in recent years (see box, page 234). Now it's being shaken up by the arrival of foreign investors who have bought extensive vineyards in the region: and as well as British, French, Dutch, Spanish, American and Australian wine growers, there are other enthusiasts who have settled down here and started up more related businesses, running bodega tours, wine clubs, wine magazines and opening restaurants. This area of tourism is bound to change dramatically in the next few years, so check for new information if you're serious about your wine. For more information on the wine-growing region in general, see the following websites: www.bestofmendoza.com.ar; www.turismo.mendoza.gov.ar (has maps and information on the Camino del Vino); www.mendoza.com.ar (in Spanish and English with lots of information); www.vendimia.mendoza.gov.ar (covers the annual wine harvest festival in Mendoza); www.welcometomendoza.com.ar (another very useful site, designed in English by expats with a good general overview).

While you're on your way around Argentina, perhaps anticipating a trip to Mendoza, it's a good idea to try some of the famous brands in restaurants so that you know what you like when you're choosing vineyards to visit. This is a list of the best known and longest established names whose wineries you can visit in Mendoza province: López, Valentín Bianchi, Escorihuela, J&F Lurton, Trapiche, Flichman, La Rural, Norton, Félix Lavaque, Navarro Correas, Nieto Senetiner, Chandon and Weinert. ▶ *See the map of Mendoza wineries opposite, to find these bodegas in Maipú and Luján de Cuyo.*

Zona Alta del Río Mendoza → *For listings, see pages 236-245.*

The area immediately to the south of Mendoza city, around the sprawling centres of Maipú and Luján de Cuyo, contains the oldest and some of the most famous vineyards in the province, producing wines with a high concentration of fruit. Malbec, particularly, thrives here, in altitudes between 650 and 1050 m, and it's said that although the grape was brought from France, it is in Argentina that it's found its real home, and in Zona Alta del Río Mendoza that it's at its best. Winegrowing styles are eclectic in the various vineyards here, but this area produces premium wines, thanks to the unique combination of soil and climate. Other grape varieties grown here are Cabernet Sauvignon, Merlot, Chardonnay, Syrah and Tempranillo. This is the closest region to the city of Mendoza, and easily visited in a few hours. But since the wineries are spread out along pretty country roads, with few signs to guide you, it's worth taking a map, and contacting the bodegas ahead of your visit.

Escorihuela
ⓘ *Belgrano 1188, Godoy Cruz, T0261-424 2282, www.escorihuela.com.ar.*
Before you reach Maipú or Luján de Cuyo, it's worth stopping to visit one of the most famous bodegas in the country, in the suburb of Godoy Cruz. The closest winery to the city is the historical Escorihuela. Founded in 1884 by Spanish immigrants, it retains its traditional atmosphere in the original buildings. They export wine to the UK under the Gascón label and still produce Pont L'Eveque, which was Perón's favourite brand. The winery is only about 20 blocks south of the centre, five minutes away by taxi, or easily reached by all buses going south along Avenida San Martín. Belgrano runs parallel to Avenida San Martín, one block east. Escorihuela also has an excellent and expensive restaurant, **1884 Francis Mallman** (see Eating, page 240) with a superb menu – the perfect complement to the bodegas' fine wines, and run by the famous

Argentine wine

Wine is grown in Argentina along the length of the Andean foothills, from Cafayate in Salta to the Río Negro valley in Neuquén, with the oldest and most famous wine-producing areas in Mendoza and San Juan provinces, where the climate is ideal: warm, almost consistently sunny days, and cold nights, with a 'thermal amplitude' of 15°C which gives grapes such a rich flavour. Water is the other magical ingredient: wine was made in Argentina long before the Jesuits planted their first vines here in the 1550s, and irrigation canals made by pre-Incan cultures still carry pure, mineral-rich snow-melt from the Andes today, compensating for the low rainfall, less than 200 mm a year.

When Argentina was flooded with Spanish and Italian immigrants in the late 19th century, wine-growing became an imperative, and modern grapes were introduced, so that today the main grapes grown are Cabernet Sauvignon, Merlot, Malbec and Syrrah; Chardonnay, Chenin and Sauvignon Blanc. 'High-altitude wine' is a tiny, but fast-growing industry in Salta's Calchaquí Valley, with superb boutique wineries Colomé and El Estecco producing wines of extraordinary intensity. Cafayate is the only place on earth where the white Torrontés grape thrives, producing a deliciously dry, fruity wine with an aromatic bouquet.

Argentina was among the five biggest wine producers of the world in the early 20th century, but exported very little, since home consumption used up all that was produced. However, in the 1970s, after the local market became glutted with cheap wine – much of it of inferior quality – wine drinking slumped, Argentines preferring beer and soft drinks with their steaks. In the 1990s, Chile's vigorous marketing campaign secured their wines a place on every European supermarket shelf, but Argentina failed to compete, despite the fact that their wines, particularly their reds, are generally superior. But in the last five years the Argentine wine industry has been revolutionized, producing far more sophisticated premium wines, and resulting in a renaissance of wine drinking within the country, and a boom in exporting wine. Try a bottle or two at home before you visit the bodegas of Mendoza or Salta, and look out for the famous names in Argentine restaurants: Valentín Bianchi, Trapiche, Flichman, Navarro Correas, Senetiner and Norton. In Argentine supermarkets, wines can be bought for US$1.50-10 a bottle, but better by far to go to a *Vinoteca* (specialist wine shop) where US$15 will buy you a superb bottle, you'll get expert advice, and can try smaller labels.

Fur further information go to: www.argentinewines.com/ing/; www.vinosdeargentina.com; www.turismo.mendoza.gov.ar; www.welcome argentina.com/vino; and magazine *El Conocedor*, www.elconocedor.com.ar, as well as the wonderful free English-language magazine *Wine Republic* distributed in cafés and shops. Learn about Argentine wines and improve your Spanish at AEAV Spanish & Wine School, http://cable modem.fibertel.com.ar/aeav, or email aeav@fibertel.com.ar.

chef Francis Mallman. The stunning centrepiece of your tour is in the cellars, where there's an ornately carved barrel from Nancy, France. If your Spanish isn't strong, you might like to visit this bodega before the others for its helpful brochure explaining the whole process in pictures.

Maipú

ⓘ *From Mendoza take bus No 10 (173), at Rioja y Garibaldi.*

The satellite town of Maipú sprawls immediately southeast of Mendoza. You may find it useful to collect information from the local **tourist office** ⓘ *Urquiza and Montecaseros, Plazoleta Rutini, 10261-497 7437*, where bus No 10 (173) stops. There are many famous brands in this area, and some more intimate bodegas described here.

If you've only time for one bodega, make it **La Rural** ⓘ *Montecaseros 2625, Coquimbito, T0261-497 2013, www.bodegalarural.com.ar*. Bus No 10 (173) stops not far from the bodega. This is a large traditional bodega founded in 1885 by Felipe Rutini, which has been modernized recently with the latest technology allowing it to bottle 6000 units per hour. This bodega is renowned not only for its excellent wines but also for the marvellous **Museo Nacional del Vino** ⓘ *T0261-497 5255, Mon-Sat 0900-1700, Sun 1000-1400*, where you can see the history of winemaking through an amazing display of implements dating back to the pre-Colombian skin of an entire cow, where grapes were trodden in the belly so that juice flowed out of its neck. Felipe Rutini and Trumpeter labels are exported worldwide: look out for the San Felipe bottles in the UK.

Quite a long way east of Maipú town centre, and 35 km east of Mendoza, is the large and highly developed **Familia Zuccardi winery** ⓘ *R33, Las Margaritas, Km 7.5, San Roque, T0261-441 0000, www.familiazuccardi.com, Mon-Sat 0900-1730, Sun 1000-1630*. This is an exceptionally welcoming winery with a good restaurant, extensive wine tasting, a tea room, and occasional music concerts on offer. Anyone wanting to pick grapes during the harvest is always welcome, and cookery lessons are available with the restaurant's chef. Their wines are easily found abroad, where they're known as Q and Santa Julia (which you can find easily in the UK and Australia).

There are also several wineries in Coquimbito district, immediately east of Maipú. Two smaller family-owned wineries, both delightful for a visit, lie very close to each other. **Tempus Alba** ⓘ *Perito Moreno 572, Coquimbito, T0261-481 3501, www.tempusalba.com*, is a modern bodega where the Biondolillo family takes great pride in their attention to detail and are happy to share it with you. **Viña El Cerno** ⓘ *Perito Moreno 631, Coquimbito, T0261-481 1567, www.elcerno.com.ar*, has a lovely country house, a restaurant and olive groves. Founded in 1887, the historic bodega of **Inti Huaco** ⓘ *Carril Gómez 3602, Coquimbito, T0261-155 652 630, bodegaintihuac@infovia.com.ar* , has elegant mid-range rooms coming off a central courtyard in beautiful surroundings.

Another charming, small and welcoming winery is the French-owned **Carinae** ⓘ *Videla Aranda 2899, Cruz de Piedra, south of Maipú town centre, T0261-499 0470, www.carinaevinos. com, daily 1000-1800*. As the name might suggest, wines aren't the only passion of Philippe and Brigitte, but astronomy too. They have an interesting collection of telescopes, which you can use. They produce Malbec, Syrah and Cabernet Sauvignon under the Carinae name (for export), and Octans and El Galgo labels (within Argentina).

Luján de Cuyo

Southwest of Maipú, **Luján de Cuyo** is another wine-producing area in whose leafy suburb, Chacras de Coria, you'll also find restaurants and small hotels. For information, contact the local **tourist office** ⓘ *Roque Sáenz Peña 1000, T0261-498 1912, www.lujandecuyo.gov.ar*.

The large and impressively modern Mayan-pyramid-like bodega, **Catena Zapata** ⓘ *Cobos, Agrelo (see map), T0261-490 0214, www.catenawines.com*, is in one of the most beautiful settings in the region. It's owned by a traditional family who produce outstanding wines that are exported under the names Catena Alta, Alamos, Nicolás

Catena Zapata and Catena. There is a restaurant too. Another large, modern bodega with fantastic mountain views is **Séptima** ① *R7, Km 6.5, Agrelo (see map, page 232), T0261-498 5164, www.bodega septima.com.ar, Mon-Fri 1000-1700, Tue and Thu also open for amazing sunset tasting sessions.*

There are now several wineries that offer accommodation, but the most famous and deservedly popular is the exquisite **Tapiz** ① *Pedro Molina, Russell, T0261-496 3433, www.tapiz.com*, a small winery that owns a *finca* in Luján de Cuyo. There's a restored 1890s main house, beautifully decorated with impeccable taste, which is the region's most exclusive hotel and has one of the finest restaurants in Mendoza. See also Sleeping, page 238.

A smaller winery, but also highly developed, **Carlos Pulenta-Vistalba** ① *Roque Sáenz Peña 3135, Vistalba (west of Luján de Cuyo town centre), T0261-498 9400, www.carlospulenta wines.com*, is renowned for its marvellous Vistalba wines and for having on its ultra-modern premises, **La Bourgogne**, one of the best restaurants east of the Andes.

The Malbec grape flourishes wonderfully at **Renacer** ① *Brandsen 1863, Perdriel (south of Luján de Cuyo town centre), T0261-488 1247, www.bodegarenacer.com.ar*, which produces Punto Final Reserva, one of the top Argentine Malbec wines. Quite close to here, you'll find **Achával Ferrer** ① *Cobos by the Mendoza river, Perdriel (southwest of Luján de Cuyo town centre), T0261-498 4874, www.achaval-ferrer.com*, a young, modern and repeatedly prize-winning boutique bodega which produces the finest quality red wines, including the great Finca Altamira. **El Lagar de Carmelo Patti** ① *Av San Martín 2614, Mayor Drummond (north of Luján de Cuyo town centre), T0261-498 1379*, is highly recommended for its welcoming owner, who personally leads the tours, and takes pride in serving his excellent Cabernet Sauvignon or his Gran Assemblage for tasting, even straight from the barrel. Spanish only.

◉ Mendoza city listings

For Sleeping and Eating price codes and other relevant information, see Essentials pages 30-36.

◉ Sleeping

Mendoza city *p226, map p228*
Like all tourist areas in Argentina, hotels fill up quickly in the holiday periods of Jan, Jul and Easter, and during the Vendimia festival from mid-Feb to mid-Mar. For more listings, see www.mendoza.com or www.viajeamendoza.com (both in Spanish).
LL-L Park Hyatt, Chile 1124, on main plaza, T0261-441 1234, www.mendoza.park.hyatt. com. Extremely swish and very comfortable with an excellent and affordable restaurant, pool, spa and casino.
L-AL El Portal Suites, Necochea 661, T0261-438 2038, www.elportalsuites.com.ar.

Stylish, spacious and very comfortable rooms in this small apart hotel on Plaza Chile. Excellent value.
AL Huentala, Primitivo de la Reta 1001, T0261-420 0766, www.huentala.com.
A 1970s building tastefully refurbished into an exclusive hotel. Enormous wine cellar and tasting room. Standard doubles are comfortable and there is a small pool.
AL NH Cordillera, España 1324, on Plaza San Martín, T0261-441 6464, www.nh-hotels. com. A modern business hotel with smart, comfortable, well-equipped minimalist rooms, a small heated pool and a restaurant. Superior rooms have their own stylish terraces (some looking onto the plaza).
AL-A Park Suites, Av Mitre 753, T0261-413 1000, www.parksuites.com.ar. Very comfortable apartments in this excellent modern 15-storey tower block business hotel,

with a restaurant, pool, conference rooms, gym and sauna. All rooms are warmly decorated and have a small kitchen, and great views from the top floors. A fantastic new hotel in the same chain (same website) called the **Diplomatic (L-AL)** has opened on Belgrano 1041, same website. Good location.
A Gran Hotel Mendoza, España 1210 y Espejo, T0261-425 2000, www.hotelmendoza.com. Spacious rooms and stylish decor make this an appealing though slightly pricey option. However, it's very central and there are larger rooms for families. Splendid views from its small restaurant El Mirador on the 10th floor.
A Hotel Argentino, Espejo 455, T0261-405 6300, www.argentino-hotel.com. Fabulous hotel, right on Plaza Independencia, with smartly furbished rooms, a pool and a fantastic restaurant. Recommended.
A Villaggio, T0261-524 5200, Av 25 de Mayo 1010, www.hotelvillaggio.com.ar. Central boutique hotel will 28 luxury rooms and a small stylish spa on the 5th floor for the exclusive use of guests.
A-D Deptosmendoza, Alem 41, T0261-4299222, www.deptosmendoza.com.ar. Attractive short-term apartments for 2-6 people with full kitchen and wonderful bathrooms. Prices start at (**C**) for 2 people per night.
A Nutibara, Av Mitre 867, T/F0261-429 5428, www.nutibara.com.ar. Welcoming, slightly old fashioned place, with eclectic decor but a lovely pool, a leafy patio, comfortable rooms, and a quiet but central location.

A-B Provincial, Belgrano 1259, T0261-425 8284, www.hotelprovincialmza.com. Welcoming, spotless, small hotel, though a bit pricey. The best feature is the great view of the Andes Cordillera at breakfast.
C Petit, Perú 1459, T0261-423 2099, www.petit-hoteles.com.ar. Small hotel with good value but slightly old-fashioned budget rooms a short walk from the centre. Across the street is their other hotel **Kapac**, T0261-425 0682, which is slightly more upmarket.

Hostels

C Confluencia, España 1512, T0261-429 0430, www.hostalconfluencia.com.ar. This central *hostería* is not really a hostel, with its small hotel atmosphere and immaculate, simple rooms. Rooms are for 2-4 and have own bath but it is separate. Breakfast included, free internet access and cooking facilities. An excellent budget choice.
E pp **Damajuana**, A. Villanueva 282, T0261-425 5858, www.damajuanahostel.com.ar. One of the best hostels in town. Intimate dorms and lovely doubles (**C**) decked out with colonial-style dark wood beds and attractive linen. Amazingly large chill-out area downstairs, with a huge garden, large pool and a games room. A little expensive but worth it. Highly receommended.
E-F pp **Mendoza Inn**, Aristides Villanueva 470, T0261-420 2486, www.campobase. com.ar. One of 3 hostels run by Campo Base. Well-organized dorms, ask for the quieter rooms upstairs. Great bar and garden area,

as well as a fair-sized pool. A little deserted in low season.

F Hostel Suites Mendoza, Patricias Mendocinas 1532, T0261-423 7018, www.hostelsuites.com. Central, free Wi-Fi and on-site travel agent.

F pp Independencia, Mitre 1237, T0261-423 1806, www.hostelindependencia.com.ar. A lovely Tudor-style house in an attractive central location. Wooden floors add warmth to the spartan dorms and double rooms (**D**), all with own bath and breakfast included. Huge kitchen and organic wines for sale. A travel agency, **Aconcagua**, www.aconcagua-xperience.com.ar, organizes excursions.

F pp Sosahaus, Av Juan B Justo 56, T0261-425 4586, www.sosahaus.com. Small, friendly hostel 10 mins' walk from the centre. Good size, clean dorms, large kitchen and a nice terrace. Option of (**C**) doubles with Wi-Fi, pristine private bathrooms as well as heating or a/c. Cheaper than others. Best budget option.

Camping

Camping Suizo, Av Champagnat, El Challao, 6 km from city, T0261-444 1991, www.alojar.com.ar/campingsuizo. Modern with pool, barbecues, hot showers and nice leafy surroundings. Friendly and recommended.

Churrasqueras del Parque, T0261-452 6016, T0261-155 123 124. Right in the centre of the beautiful Parque General San Martín (next to the football stadium), at Bajada del Cerro de la Gloria.

Saucelandia, Tirasso 5165, 9 km east at El Sauce, Guaymallén, T0261-451 1409. Large pool and a restaurant. Take insect repellent.

Zona Alta del Río Mendoza *p233*
LL Cavas Wine Lodge, Costaflores, Alto Agrelo, Luján de Cuyo, T0261-410 6927, www.cavaswinelodge.com. A pricey but heavenly experience, ideal for a romantic and wonderfully relaxing stay. 14 incredibly spacious rooms in a rural mansion now beautifully restored to a very high standard with creativity and impeccable taste. Each

room has a fireplace and its own little terrace, with a pool for a cool dip, in addition to the main swimming pool, with the most wonderful views of the Andes. A restaurant and a spa complete this unique place. Highly recommended.

AL Casa Glebinias, Medrano 2272, Chacras de Coria, Luján de Cuyo, T0261-496 2116, www.casaglebinias.com. 2 detached houses set in large landscaped gardens are delightful places to stay. Decoration is simple, but there's a homely feel, a tempting swimming pool, and beautiful trees and flowers in the grounds. An art historian and a scientist are the very welcoming owners of this charming rural hotel.

AL Club Tapiz, C Pedro Molina, Russell, Maipú, T0261-496 3433, www.tapiz.com. Surrounded by vineyards, Tapiz is a small, beautifully restored neo-Renaissance Italian-style villa, where the minimalist style helps you unwind in the comfort of the 7 guest rooms. A spa and superb cuisine in the **Terruño** restaurant make this unquestionably one of the top hotels in Mendoza. A member of the impressive chain of quality NA Town and Country Hotels, www.newage-hotels.com. See also page 236.

AL Parador del Angel, 100 m from main plaza, Chacras de Coria, Luján de Cuyo, T0261-496 2201, www.paradordelangel.com.ar. This 100-year-old adobe house has been restored with traditional materials and decorated in tasteful rustic style, making it a thoroughly relaxing place to stay. Surrounded by gardens and with a pool.

❻ Eating

Mendoza city *p226, map p228*
There are 2 main areas to eat in the centre of the city: around the main Plaza Independencia with restaurants along Sarmiento and around Las Heras; or along C A Villanueva, just a 10-min walk southwest of the main plaza where Mendoza's hipper crowd hang out in lively bars and chic restaurants. If you have your own transport,

there are also excellent restaurants throughout the wine region. It's essential to book a
table for the top restaurants.

City centre

Azafrán, Sarmiento 765, T0261-429 4200.
A fine-wine lover's heaven, with an extensive
range from all the best bodegas, expert advice
on wines and a fabulous delicatessen where you
can enjoy superb *picadas*. Its menu changes
with the season: basically Argentine style with
some international touches. Recommended.

Bistro M, Park Hyatt Hotel, Chile 1124,
T0261-441 1200. Recommended for its
impeccably stylish setting, imaginative
menu, and offering cheaper choices too.
Great views over the plaza.

Anna Bistro, Av Juan B Justo 161,
T0261-425 1818. One of the most attractive
restaurants in town, this is an informal
French-owned place, cleverly designed
and very welcoming, with good food and
drink at all times. The short menu combines
French and Italian flavours, open for lunch
and dinner. Excellent value, and open till
late for laid-back drinking. Recommended.

Comida de Campo, Sarmiento 55. Resist
the 1st café along Peatonal Sarmiento and
head here instead for good set menu lunches
and a vast range from pastas *caseras* to great
traditional *Mendocino* steaks. Recommended.
Groups are welcome.

Facundo, Sarmiento 641, T0261-420 2866.
A welcoming and friendly *parrilla* with lots
of other choices and a good salad bar.

La Marchigiana, Patricias Mendocinas
1550, T0261 423 0751. One of Mendoza's
best restaurants and great value. Wonderful
Italian food served in spacious surroundings
with charming old-fashioned service.

La Sal, Belgrano 1069, T0261-420 4322. Stylish
and lively atmosphere with a creative menu
which changes with the seasons. The wine list is
extensive and there's good live music here too.

Mi Tierra, Mitre and San Lorenzo.
Recommended for wine tasting with expert
advice, this is an elegantly restored 1890s
house with 4 rooms, each devoted to a

different *bodega*: Norton, Catena Zapata,
Chandon and Terrazas de los Andes. A
limited menu with traditionally cooked
meat-based dishes.

Montecatini, General Paz 370, T0261-425
2111. Good Italian food is the speciality here,
and also *parrilla* and seafood. The decor has
been smartened, but this is slightly lacking in
atmosphere. Popular with families.

Por Acá, Aristides Villanueva 557. The most
original place in the area, a cosy and stylish
place serving pizzas and drinks till late, and
often noisier with crowds of people partying.

Sr Cheff, Primitivo de la Reta 1071. One
of the city's longest-established restaurants
with a good reputation for *parrilla* and fish.

Terrazas del Lago, Av Las Palmeras s/n,
T0261-428 3438. The main reason to come
here is for the really splendid setting by the
lake in Parque San Martín. The food is good.

Las Tinajas, Lavalle (between San Martín
and San Juan). Great buffet-style restaurant.
Pizzas, pastas, stir fries, and roast meat.
Affordable wine list.

Ferruccio Soppelsa, Espejo and Patricias
Mendocinas, Plaza Independencia, and other
branches. For the best ice cream with a great
range, including wine flavours.

Il Dolce, Sarmiento 81. A friendly place
for inexpensive set lunches and dinners,
and good vegetarian options.

Via Civit, Emilio Civit 277. Wandering back
to town from the park, try the wonderful
sandwiches, tasty tarts and exquisite pastries
in the relaxed but refined atmosphere of
an elegant traditional bakery. Open from
breakfast time onwards.

Market food

Try the atmospheric indoor market on
Las Heras at night for cheap and delicious
pizza, *parrilla* and pasta. Also heaps of cured
meats, dried fruits, pastries, wines, herbs
and a cheap snack bar.

Comida Poblana, Av Villanueva 217.
Turkish food, in a friendly environment.
Order the water pipe and smoke it outside
with a *shawerma*.

Zona Alta del Río Mendoza *p233*

TTTT 1884 Francis Mallman, Bodega Escorihuela, Belgrano 1188, Godoy Cruz, T0261-424 2698. This is the place to go for a really special dinner. Mallman is one of the country's great chefs and here he's created an exotic and imaginative menu. Open for lunch and dinner, but reservations are advisable. Highly recommended. See also page 233.

TTT La Bourgogne, Bodega Carlos Pulenta, Roque Sáenz Peña 3531, Vistalba, Luján de Cuyo, T0261-498 9421. Top French cuisine using the best local ingredients, served in the stylish, new, ultra-modern premises of the Pulenta winery. See also page 236.

TTT Terruño, Bodega Tapiz, Calle Pedro Molina, Russell, Maipú, T0261-496 3433. Refined minimalist decor in beautifully restored rooms of an Italian-style residence. Exquisite dishes such as Mediterranean flavours with a dash of Asian style, and high-quality local produce. Recommended. See also page 236.

TT Almacén del Sur, Zanichelli 709, Maipú, T0261-410 6597. A restored farmhouse surrounded by delightful gardens with leafy patios makes an attractive setting for this delightful restaurant, where your vegetables are grown close to where you eat them. A good range of delicious and imaginative dishes, beautifully served. Lunches are particularly recommended: 4-courses.

TT Karma, Italia 6076, Chacras de Coria, Luján de Cuyo, T0261-496 1731. A truly exotic little gem. Owned by one of the Tibetan actors from *Seven Years in Tibet*, which was filmed in Uspallata. Tasty Asian food.

🎶 Bars and clubs

Mendoza city *p226, map p228*

Av Villanueva is the area for an evening stroll and the more exciting bars and restaurants, popular with a younger crowd, and just 10 mins' walk southwest of the main plaza. (Note that this street changes its name to Colón at Belgrano). You'll find it quiet if you're heading out for an early dinner, but it livens up after 2400 when the bars are full. See www.mendozanoduerme.com.ar (in Spanish):

Antares, Av Villanueva 153. Popular place to hang out Fri nights, try the microbrewery beer.

Iskra, Av San Martín Sur 905. Late night club, with live music.

The Liverpool Pub, San Martín, y Rivadavia. Beatles memorabilia. Try the Liverpool burger.

⚙ Festivals and events

Mendoza city *p226, maps p228 and p232*

Feb-Mar Fiesta de la Vendimia, www. vendimia.mendoza.gov.ar. The biggest festival of the year, held to celebrate the start of the wine harvest.

Feb-Mar Gay Vendimia Festival. At the same time as the Fiesta de la Vendimia, less promoted but equally entertaining.

O Shopping

Mendoza city *p226, maps p228 and p232*

Shops usually close for siesta 1300-1600, when the city centre is completely dead. The best area for clothes shopping is Av San Martín and Av Las Heras, where there are good souvenir, leather and handicraft shops, and a vast sports emporia. Further north on San Martín are cheap fabric shops and old department stores such as **C&A**. Las Heras has an attractive indoor market with good food, next to the corner of Patricias Mendocinas.

Books

Centro Internacional del Libro, Lavalle 14. Small selection of classics and paperbacks in English and *Buenos Aires Herald* usually available from kiosks on San Martín.

SBS, Gutiérrez 54. For more books in English.

Camping equipment

Casa Orviz, Juan B Justo 532/36, CP5500, T/F0261-425 1281, www.orviz.com. Sales and rental of camping and climbing equipment; also provides climbing information.

Handicrafts

There are handicraft markets on the eastern side of Plaza Independencia at weekends, and on Plaza España, Thu-Sun.

El Turista, Av Las Heras 351. Sells most of the traditional local souvenirs, piled high and pretty cheap.

Las Viñas, Av Las Heras 399. Good range of T-shirts, *ponchos* and ornate *mates*.

Mercado Artesanal, Av San Martín 1133. Traditional leather, baskets and weaving.

Raíces, España 1092, just off Peatonal Sarmiento. High quality goods.

Shopping centres

Centro Comercial Mendoza Plaza, about 5 km east in Guaymallén, T0261-449 0100, daily 1000-1200. Known as **Mendoza Plaza Shopping**, this is the best indoor shopping mall with supermarkets, shops, fast food and cinemas, and a play area for kids. Free transfers from town; call to arrange.

Palmares, 7 km south in Godoy Cruz. Much smaller than the **Mendoza Plaza**, but includes a supermarket, shops, cinema and restaurants. Arrange a free transfer from the centre or your hotel by calling Palmares shopping centre office, T0261 4319 9052.

Wine stores/vinotecas

All the bodegas sell their produce 10% cheaper than in shops, and stock many wines you can't find elsewhere. But there are an increasing number of *vinotecas* in town: specialist wine stores that stock bottles from many bodegas

together, and offer expert advice on what to buy. The following are recommended:

Central, Mitre and Espejo, T0261-459 0658. English spoken, tastings are arranged in advance.

Marcelino, Tiburcio Benegas and Martín Zapata, T0261-429 3648, Mon-Fri only. Also offers courses on wine tasting.

Puracepa, Av Sarmiento 644, T0261-423 8282. English spoken; offers delivery service worldwide. Stocks an incredible range of wine from US$5-230.

The Vines, Espejo 567, T0261-438 1031, www.vinesofmendoza.com. Daily 1100-2200, booking advisable. Unique in its type and highly recommended. A lovely restored house with a peaceful atmosphere and patio, where you can try a selection of premium wines, and wines from the top boutique bodegas in chic minimalist wine-tasting rooms. Bottles are not sold on the premises, but they can be shipped to North America and Europe. An office next door takes reservations for visiting bodegas. Not to be missed.

▲ Activities and tours

Mendoza city *p226, map p228*
Cycling
Bikes can be hired from the following places: **Cycles El Túnel**, at the exit of the subway passage coming from bus terminal, hires, buys and sells cycles, also does repairs, friendly; **Indiana Aventuras**, Espejo 65, T026-429 0002,

info@indianaventuras.com.ar; **Adventure World**, Sarmiento 231, T0261-429 0206.

Mountain climbing

Aconcagua Spirit, Av España 1185, T0261-454 9721, www.aconcaguaspirit.com.ar. Trekking and mountain expeditions, with guides and lots of local knowledge.

Club Andinista, F L Beltrán 357, Guaymallén, T0261-431 9870, www.clubandinista.com.ar. See also page 248 for more information on climbing Aconcagua.

Inka Expediciones, Juan B Justo 345, T0261-425 0871, www.inka.com.ar. Bespoke climbing expeditions, including treks to Aconcagua base camps and alternative routes to the summit. Highly professional. Fixed departure dates. Mules for hire.

Skiing

There are 3 resorts within reach of Mendoza. Equipment can be hired from **Piré**, Av Las Heras 615, T0261-425 7699, and other agencies. For useful information, see www.mendozaski.com.

Los Penitentes, T02624-420110 (or Mendoza T0261-424 5648), www.penitentes.com, 183 km west on the road to Chile. A quiet family resort with a range of pistes, plus hotels, restaurants and affordable equipment hire. It's too far for a day trip from Mendoza but there is good accommodation.

Vallecitos, 95 km from Mendoza, on the winding road from Potrerillos, T02622-423 6569, www.skivallecitos.com. A tiny ski centre and very basic place with simple accommodation but it can be reached on a long day trip from Mendoza.

Swimming pools

Gimnasia y Esgrima, Gutiérrez 261, T0261-425 0315. Indoor swimming pool, Turkish baths and sauna.

Marina Natación, San Lorenzo 765, T0261-423 6065. Indoor swimming pool.

Tour operators

There are lots of operators, especially on Peatonal Sarmiento. Most go to the same

places but shop around for the best deals. As a rough guide: Mendoza city tour US$9, ½-day wine tour US$12, Alta Montaña US$24. There are also longer excursions including a long trip to the Valle de la Luna, US$54 (more comfortable from San Juan) and to Cañón del Atuel, US$34 (easier from San Rafael). The following companies are recommended:

Areauca, T0261-496 5439, www.areauca.com. Flying School offering hand-gliding, thermal flying, cross-country flying and courses.

Aymara Turismo, 9 de Julio 1023, T0261-420 5304, www.aymara.com.ar. Excellent, professional company offering a huge range of activities such as adventure tourism, rafting, climbing Aconcagua and the spectacular 10-day Andes horseback crossing to Chile every summer, as well as more conventional excursions to bodegas and Alta Montaña.

Bikes and Wines, Plazoleta Rutini, Maipú, T0261-410 6686, www.bikesandwines.com. Open 1000-1800. Cycle tours to Maipú wineries including lunch; also bike rental.

Campo Base, Peatonal Sarmiento 229, T0261-425 5511, www.campobaseadv enture.com. The same company that owns a chain of hostels offers wine tours aimed at younger travellers, as well as much more demanding 3- and 6 day-long summer treks to Aconcagua base camps.

El Cristo, Espejo 228, T/F0261-429 1911, www.turismo-elcristo.com.ar. A good range of tours, including Valle de la Luna and some cheap deals for the usual tours.

Huentata, Las Heras 699, T0261-425 3108, www.huentata.com.ar. The usual short tours plus full-day excursions to Villavicencio and up to Cruz de Paramillo, and then down to Uspallata, and another tour to Cañón del Atuel.

Kahuak, San Martín 1134, T0261-424 3380, www.kahuak.com.ar. Great local company that offers horse riding, winery tours, rafting, canopy, trekking, paragliding, rappelling and lots more. Recommended.

Malbec Travel, Av España 1185, T0261-425 9721, www.malbectravel.com.ar. Also run trips to Puente del Inca, rafting, trekking and horse riding.

Mancagua, España 967, T0261-429 7398, www.mancaguaviajes.com.ar. Recommended for its friendly staff and many wine tour options, combining different bodegas with lunches, wine included.
Mendoza Viajes, Peatonal Sarmiento 129, T0261-461 0210, www.mdzviajes.com.ar. Imaginative tours in comfortable coaches, including to the valleys of Uspallata and Calingasta. Professional service, cheap deals.
Trout and Wine, Sarmiento 133 (in the arcade), T0261-425 5613, www.troutand wine.com. Luxury wine tours including a gourmet 5-course lunch. Also organize fly-fishing tours.

Whitewater rafting

The most popular place for rafting is on the challenging Río Mendoza at Potrerillos (see page 231, but there's also quieter rafting for beginners among the colourful green rocks of Río Atuel, to the south near San Rafael. Further south still, there are more remote sites for rafting along the upper Ríos Atuel, Diamante, Grande and Andinos in southern Mendoza.
Argentina Rafting, P de la Reta 992, www. argentinarafting.com. Popular adventure sports agency which also offers kayaking, canopying, mountain bikes and trekking.
Ríos Andinos, Sarmiento 717, T0261-429 5030, www.riosandinos.com. The most experienced operator for rafting on Mendoza river. Also run horseback rides and do some rock climbing.

Wine tours

Most of the companies above offer wine tours. The following specializes in them.
The Grapevine, Peatonal Sarmiento 133, Galería San Marcos local 12, T0261-429 7522, www.thegrapevine-winetours.com. British and Irish owned, the company organizes personalized tours in the wine region, including flights, combined with bodega visits and lunch. They also organize their own wine club meetings and publish a very informative free magazine, which is available everywhere.

⊙ Transport

Mendoza city *p226, map p228*
Air
For airport information, see page 226. To reach the airport take bus No 60 from Alem and Salta, every hour at 35 mins past the hour, and make sure there is an 'Independencia-Aeropuerto' sign on the driver's window.
Daily flights to **Buenos Aires**, 1 hr 50 mins; **Córdoba**, Aerolíneas Argentinas/Austral; **Santiago** (Chile) and **Buenos Aires**, Lan.
Airline offices Aerolíneas Argentinas/ Austral, Sarmiento 82, T0261-420 4100. Lan, España 1012 and Rivadavia, T0261-425 7900.

Bus
Long distance The big terminal is on the east side of the major road Av Videla or Costanera, 15 mins' walk from centre, via an underpass which leads from the corner between platforms 38 and 39 to Alem. A taxi to the centre costs US$2-2.50. Call the helpful information centre for all companies and times, T0261-431 5000. There is an ATM, a *locutorio*, *confiterías*, lockers (US$2 in 2 US$1 coins), left luggage US$1.50 (next to platform 52) and a travel agency opposite the information desk. Ticket offices for domestic and some provincial services are along a corridor behind the information desk; for the closer provincial destinations, including **Expreso Uspallata** services for Alta Montaña, go to the left (facing the information desk) and for Chile, Perú and Uruguay, go to the right. **Andesmar**, España and Espejo, T0261-429 3894, and at the bus terminal, T0261-432 4800.
Provincial services To **San Rafael**, many daily, 3½ hrs, US$6, Expreso Uspallata; TAC. To **Malargüe**, 6 hrs, US$12, Expreso Uspallata, also combi service, Transporte Viento Sur, 3 a day (Mon-Fri), 2 on Sat, 1 on Sun, 4½ hrs, US$12. To **Cacheuta**, 5-7 daily, 1 hr, US$1.30, Expreso Uspallata. To **Alta Montaña** destinations, only with Expreso Uspallata, T0261-432 5055; to **Potrerillos**,

Visiting bodegas

Transport

There are plenty of tours on offer from agencies in Mendoza city, allowing you to visit a couple of bodegas in an afternoon. These are fine if you haven't got a car, but it's much more interesting to go independently, so that you can choose where you'd like to visit, and take your time over the visits. Touring wineries by bus really isn't an option, since almost all the bodegas are some way out of any town, it's easy to get lost in labyrinthine rural roads with little signposting, and you might waste a lot of time waiting for buses. Cycle tours are an appealing alternative to exploring one limited area, such as Mapiú, with a couple of specialized agencies based in the wine regions, and reasonable distances to cover: you could put together a tour of bodegas that are a five- to 20-minute ride from each other.

Reserve in advance

If you choose to visit the bodegas, remember always to ring and book your tour first, and if you don't speak Spanish, ask if they have an English-speaking guide. You'll be able to get a vague idea of the process but it will be far more interesting if you understand the detail.

Map

Get hold of a map of the wine region: there are lots of maps available in free tourist brochures, but the best is the *Winemap Turístico*, www.winemap turistico.com, sold in some restaurants and wine stores: very good and informative. There is also a good free wine magazine in English called *Wine Republic,* pick one up if you can.

Variety

Limit yourself to four or five bodegas in a day, especially if you're driving. It's worth trying to see both a big modern winery and smaller and more intimate places, since their processes are quite different, and often a smaller winery will take even more time and trouble to share their produce with you.

Try it at home

One of the great things about visiting these bodegas is that often you'll be trying wines that are available in your own country, so that even if you can't carry a crate home with you, you can buy the same wine from your home wine supplier, and share it with friends as you show them the photos of where the wine was grown.

---

6 daily, 1½ hrs, US$2; to **Uspallata**, 6 a day, 2-2½ hrs, US$4.50. To **Los Penitentes** or **Puente del Inca**, 3 a day, 3 hrs, US$7. To **Las Cuevas**, 2 a day, 4 hrs, US$5, fewer services in winter. To **Tunuyán**, several a day, 1-1½ hrs, US$3, ECLA. To **Tupungato**, several a day, 1½-2 hrs, US$4, Empresa Mitre 380.

National services To **Buenos Aires**, 13-17 hrs, US$52, Andesmar; Central Argentino; Chevallier; El Rápido; Sendas; TAC; Tramat. To **Bariloche**, 1 daily, 19 hrs, US$68, Andesmar, book ahead (or an alternative is TAC to Neuquén, and change). To **Córdoba**, 9-12 hrs, US$35, Chevallier; Mercobus Plus Ultra; San Juan Mar del

Plata; TAC; Tramat. To **San Luis**, TAC frequent, other companies including San Juan Mar del Plata, 3-3½ hrs, US$11. To **San Juan**, TAC, frequent, Andesmar; San Juan Mar del Plata and others, 2-2½ hrs, US$8. To **Tucumán**, 12-15 hrs, US$49, Andesmar; Flecha Bus; TAC; Tramat, all via **San Juan; La Rioja**, 6-7 hrs, US$30; and **Catamarca**, 8-9 hrs, US$37. To **Salta**, Andesmar; Flecha Bus; Tramat (via San Juan, La Rioja and Catamarca), 17-19 hrs, US$69. To **Mar del Plata**, San Juan Mar del Plata; TAC, daily, 17-19 hrs, US$64. To **Neuquén**, Andesmar; Del Sur y Media Agua; TAC, 5 daily, 11-12 hrs, US$45.

To **Comodoro Rivadavia**, 3 a day, 30-31 hrs, US$106, Andesmar. To **Río Gallegos**, 1 daily, 40 hrs, US$150, Andesmar. To **Santa Fe**, 13 hrs, US$64, TAC. To **Rosario**, 12 hrs, US$44, TAC.

To Chile To **Santiago**, several daily, 6-7 hrs depending on border crossing, US$24, Ahumada; CATA; Chile Bus; El Rápido; Tas Choapa; Tur Bus. There are also minibus services on similar rates, run by **Chiar**, **Nevada** and **Radio Móvil**. Passport required when booking, tourist cards given on bus. Children under 8 pay 60% of adult fare, but no seat: Book at least 1 day in advance, shop around.

The journey over the Andes is spectacular (see page 250 for a description). If you want to return, buy an undated return ticket Santiago–Mendoza; it is cheaper. Almost all the same companies also go to **Viña del Mar** 5½ hrs, US$23. Tas Choapa goes to Valparaíso, 1 daily. CATA and Chile Bus go to **La Serena**, 3 a week, 12-16 hrs, US$30. CATA goes weekly to **Arica**, 1½ days, US$60.

To Uruguay To **Montevideo**, Tue, 20-21 hrs, El Rápido, US$59; EGA.

Car hire

Shop around and barter for cheap car hire since international tourists are charged double the Argentines' rate. Sometimes you'll find several companies on Primitivo de la Reta, next to Plaza Pellegrini.

Avis, Primitivo de la Reta 914, T0261-429 6403, www.avis.com.ar, or at airport, T0261-447 0150, reliable and efficient; **Dollar**, Gutiérrez 567, T0261-425 0430, www.dollar.com.ar; **Hertz**, Espejo 415 and at the airport, T0261-423 0225, www.hertzargentina.com.ar.

Motorcycle

Motos Parra, Av Zapata 344, T0261-429 0340, motosparra@yahoo.com.ar. For motorcycle repairs.

❶ Directory

Mendoza city *p226, map p228*
Banks Most have branches with ATMs on plaza San Martín or on nearby streets. **Currency exchange** Many *casas de cambio* on San Martín, corner with Espejo/Catamarca. **Embassies and consulates** Chile, Belgrano 1080, T0261-425 4844; Spain, Agustín Alvarez 445, T0261-425 3947; Italy, Necochea 712, T0261-423 1640; France, Av Houssay 790, T0261-423 1542; Germany, Montevideo 127, 2nd floor, D1, T0261-429 6539; Israel, Lamadrid 738, T0261-428 2140; UK, Bodega Domaine Vistalba, T0261-498 3504. **Emergencies** Medical, T0261-428 0000. **Internet** Find the largest places along Av Las Heras or Av San Martín. **Language schools** Academia Buenos Aires, Hispámerica, www.hispamerica.com.ar, small school, specializing in small groups; Intercultural-Mendoza, Rep de Siria 241, T0261-429 0269, www.spanishcourses.com.ar, established school which offers the traditional 1-on-1 or group classes, but also offers classes tours such as 'Español y Vino'. **Medical services** Central Hospital near bus terminal, Alem and Salta, T0261-420 0600, T0261-449 0500; Hospital Pediátrico Humberto Notti, Bandera de los Andes 2603, Guaymallén, T0261-445 0045; Lagomaggiore, public general hospital at Timoteo Gordillo s/n, T0261-425 9700. **24-hr pharmacies** Del Aguila, Av San Martín and Buenos Aires; Del Puente, Av Las Heras 201, T0261-423 8800; Mitre 2, San Martín 701. **Post office** San Martín and Colón, T0261-429 0848. Mon-Fri 0800-2000, Sat 1000-1300. United Parcel Service, 9 de Julio 803, T0261-423 7861. **Telephone** There are many *locutorios* around the centre: a huge one on Av San Martín and Garibaldi, also at Av San Martín y Lavalle.

Alta Montaña

The high Andes to the west of Mendoza city are the world's highest mountains outside the Himalayas, and offer some of the country's most amazing scenery. The spectacular setting offers hiking, mountain climbing and adventures of all kinds, and is easily accessible from Route Nacional 7 to Chile, and simply driving west along Route 7 is an unforgettable experience. Alta Montaña is an essential part of any trip to the province, even if you're not crossing the border, or planning to climb Aconcagua. From the pretty oasis town of Uspallata, the road to Chile climbs up between the jagged snow-capped mountains, with staggering views of Volcán Tupungato in the distance to the south and Aconcagua closer at hand to the north. In winter, you'll quickly reach the snowline, the charming small ski resort of Los Penitentes and, beyond it, the natural wonder of the bridge at Puente del Inca, near the base for climbing Aconcagua. The road climbs finally to the border crossing at Túnel Cristo Redentor, and if you continue to Chile, the steep descent on the other side offers yet more superb views. In winter, this road is sometimes blocked by snow, so check conditions from Mendoza or Uspallata before setting off. Snow can lie as late as September and October, so bring appropriate clothing, even if you're just going for a day trip. For more information, see www.viajeamendoza.com (in Spanish). ▶▶ *For listings, see pages 252-253.*

Mendoza to Upsallata → *For listings, see pages 252-253.*

There are two ways to reach Uspallata from Mendoza, both offering great views. Most dramatic is the climb north via many hairpin bends past the (abandoned) spa resort of Villavicencio (104 km, of which 52 km is on unpaved roads), or alternatively, you can head south from Mendoza to pleasant Potrerillos (102 km, all paved roads) and take a short detour to the thermal springs at Cacheuta.

Villavicencio → *Colour map 3, A2. Phone code 0261.*

Famous to all Argentines from the image of its Alpine-style 1940s hotel seen on bottles of the ubiquitous mineral water, Villavicencio (1800 m, Km 47) is reached by a wonderful drive. From Mendoza, head north along Route 52, across flat plains growing nothing but scrubby *jarilla* bushes, and following the *pre-cordillera* mountains on your left. The road rises steeply to climb through thickly forested mountains to the beautiful old spa resort, closed for many years but under renovation (open 2012), and now the centre of its own little nature reserve – a good place for a picnic and a stroll. The reserve protects the sources of mineral water and the whole area is owned by the French company **Danone**, who run a smart information centre on the local wildlife and employ *guardaparques* who can direct you to nearby walks. You can also stroll around the splendid grounds of the hotel, visit its chapel and eat at the **Hostería Villavicencio** ① *T0261-424 6482*, run by a friendly local family who offer good value lunches and teas with fine local produce such as *jamón crudo* (prosciutto) and *chivo* (goat), which you can enjoy at tables outside.

Beyond Villavicencio the *ripio* road climbs up over the spectacular **Cruz de Paramillo**, via Caracoles de Villavicencio, the many (allegedly 365) hairpin bends that give the road its name *La Ruta del Año* (Route of the Year). At an altitude of 3050 m there are breathtaking views all around, and this is a marvellous introduction to the vast peaks of Aconcagua, Tupungato and Mercedario. Descending to the fertile valley of Uspallata, there are rocks popping up like jagged teeth through the earth, in extraordinary colours from aubergine through to oxidized copper green, orange and creamy white. There are no bus services, but many tour operators include this trip. With your own transport, this makes for a great route to Uspallata. Cyclists should carry plenty of water and be warned of the dangers of altitude and lack of shade. Take your time.

Cacheuta

An alternative route to Uspallata and into the Andes is via the pretty villages of Cacheuta and Portrerillos, offering thermal spa and watersports respectively. If you're driving, note that since the river has been dammed there is no direct road between Cacheuta (1245 m) and Potrerillos, so you need to take a detour to get to Cacheuta. From Mendoza, head south out of the city by Avenida J Vicente Zapata, access Route 7, leading to Ruta 40. Follow signs to Cacheuta, passing the area's biggest petrochemical plant, before you climb up into the hills. Cacheuta's pretty setting in a narrow valley merits the extra journey to reach it. There's a huge complex of several thermal pools where you can spend a day, and next to this, a fine hotel in attractive gardens with a good restaurant. It's better to stay at least a night to really enjoy the mountain scenery.
➤ *For further information, see Sleeping, page 252.*

Potrerillos → *Colour map 3, B1. Phone code 02624.*

Potrerillos (1354 m, Km 68), just 10 km further on from Cacheuta, is a charming, laid-back village sprawling among the foothills of the Cordón del Plata mountains. In the summer it's a popular retreat among *Mendocinos*, but it's excellent for a weekend's walking or horse riding at any time of year, though particularly lovely in spring, or in autumn, when the avenues of *álamo* (poplar) trees are a rich yellow against the mauve haze of mountains beyond. From December to February, you can go rafting and kayaking on Río Mendoza, which runs through the valley below the village. The water level depends on the time of year and the amount of snow melt swelling the river, so that the high season varies from year to year. In summer you can hike from Potrerillos to Vallecitos over two days. There's also a lovely walk to Cascada del Salto, but the path isn't marked, so take a guide (see Activities and tours, page 253).

From Potrerillos' centre – where there's little more than a hotel, campsite and YPF station on a crossroads – you could take the road south up to Vallecitos via the little hamlets of El Salto, Las Vegas and San Jorge, with its small *cervecería* (microbrewery). There are *parrilla* restaurants, tea rooms and lots of *cabañas* for hire around these areas, and the views are wonderful.

Vallecitos → *Phone code 02622.*

This tiny hamlet (2900 m) is 27 km west of Potrerillos along a madly winding *ripio* road, certainly not to be attempted in poor weather conditions. There's little here apart from a couple of *refugios* with hostel accommodation and a rather basic family ski resort, but it's popular as a day trip from Mendoza. The **ski centre** ① *Valles del Plata Centro de Esqui, T0261-496 5577, www.skivallecitos.com, lift pass US$26 per person per day, equipment hire from US$15*, has 4.7 km of pistes, mostly intermediate standard, seven ski lifts and a ski school. Vallecitos is used as a base camp by climbers for training in the nearby peaks, before attempting Aconcagua. Contact **Expediciones El Plata**, ① *T0261-488810, www.expedicioneselplata.com.ar*, to take part in a climbing expedition to the beautiful summits of the Cordón del Plata range. They're less well known than Aconcagua, but also spectacular.

Parque Provincial Aconcagua

The Aconcagua Provincial Park is 190 km west of Mendoza city, and apart from Aconcagua itself – the highest peak in the world outside the Himalayas, at 6959 m – it includes 30 other peaks over 4000 m, nine of them over 5000 m, making it a great centre for hiking and climbing. Mount Aconcagua gets its name from the Quechua for 'stone sentry', and it is indeed a majestic peak with five great glaciers hanging from its slopes. It's a demanding climb even for the experienced, and it's absolutely essential to take at least eight to 10 days just to adapt to the altitude before you ascend. Pulmonary and cerebral oedema are serious risks and the dangers should not be underestimated: climbers die on the mountain every year. If you're planning to climb Aconcagua, it's essential to seek expert advice and plan your trip carefully. See the official website, www.aconcagua.mendoza.gov.ar, for more details (in English, Spanish, German and French).

Access

Valle de los Horcones (2950 m), 2 km west of Puente del Inca and another 2 km off R7: *guardaparque* (ranger station) and free camping, open in the climbing season. This is the last accessible point for vehicles. No permits are required, but there is an entrance fee of US$1.50 for the short walk to the mirador or Laguna Horcones, where you have excellent views of Aconcagua's southern face.

Advice

Climbers are advised to make use of the medical services where they're available (some base camps) to check for early symptoms of altitude sickness and oedema. For more advice and online discussion, see www.aconcagua.org.ar and www.aconcagua.com.ar. Tents must be able to withstand 160-kph winds. Clothing and sleeping gear for temperatures below -40°C. Always carry plenty of water, as there are very few sources. Take all your rubbish out with you: no litter is to be thrown away in the park, and bags are handed out at the park entrance to be collected when you leave. Bring a stove and sufficient fuel; no wood is to be used for lighting fires. For emergencies only, use the *guardaparques* radio frequency 142.8 Mhz.

Permits

It's essential to obtain a permit for trekking or climbing at any time of year: pay a fee (much cheaper for Argentine nationals) and fill in a form. You'll need to submit certain other documents for some specific activities. The rules vary according to time of year and activity. For climbing in the high season (15 December-31 January) you must obtain a permit in person in Mendoza, at the Subsecretaría de Turismo, Avenida San Martín 1143. In the winter season (1 April-14 November) permits to climb Aconcagua are sold at Dirección de Recursos Naturales Renovables, next to the gates of Parque General San Martín in Mendoza. Permits vary in price, depending on the season and the activity. An ascent permit lasts for 20 consecutive days from the moment it is stamped at the park entrance, and prices vary from US$384 (US$520 via Plaza Guanacos) in high season to US$512 (for any route) in winter. Fees are much lower in mid season (1-14 December and 1-20 February), low season (15-30 November and 21 February-31 March), and in the special winter season (April). Be warned that places selling the permits, and fees, may change, so it's vital to check the official website (www.aconcagua.mendoza.gov.ar). Trekking permits are needed for all walks up to any of the base camps (excluding

Plaza Guanacos camp, at the end of the only ascent trek) and are sold near the park itself at Horcones ranger station. These cost: US$153 for seven consecutive days; US$66 for three consecutive days in high season; US$46 the rest of the year. Day permits are also available for US$20.

Trekking and climbing routes

There are two access routes to Aconcagua's summit, Río Horcones and Río de las Vacas, which lead to the two main base camps, Plaza de Mulas and Plaza Argentina respectively. For climbing Aconcagua, allow two weeks for the complete trip. Getting to the summit is not technically difficult: the problem is in taking sufficient time for your body to adjust to the high altitude. Most people fail simply because they take it too fast. All climbers should allow at least one week for acclimatization at lower altitudes before attempting the summit. Allow another few days for the weather. The best time is from the end of December to end of February.

Day permits allow you to walk from Horcones four hours up to Confluencia Base Camp (3390 m), where the upper Horcones meets the lower Horcones river, and then two hours back, all along the Quebrada del río Horcones. The walk presents no difficulties, except for the high altitude – so be prepared to take your time, and don't be surprised that some people in your group will be affected more than others. Altitude sickness affects everyone differently.

Confluencia Base Camp can get horribly crowded in summer, but has an interesting international atmosphere with dozens of climbers and many more mules. There is a ranger station, public showers and medical services (in high season). From here you can either take the North Face route, used by 80% of climbers, to Plaza de Mulas (4365 m), in eight hours, or the South Face route to Plaza Francia (4250 m), in five hours. It's a tiring, rather monotonous walk up to Plaza de Mulas, another busy camp, with a ranger station, medical services and the highest hotel in the world another 20-minute walk away.

South Face route leads from Confluencia to Plaza Francia base camp (five hours), with a mirador after about four hours looking over the lower Horcones glacier, with an outstanding view of the 3000-m high rock and ice walls of Aconcagua's south face. Plaza Francia Camp is less crowded, but has no services at all.

Route via the Polish Glacier: This little-used route starts at Punta de Vacas (2400 m), 16 km east of Puente del Inca (also used to reach the Falso de los Polacos route that connects with the normal route). Plaza Argentina (4200 m) is the base camp with intermediate camps at Pampa de Leñas (2900 m), with ranger station, reached after four hours of easy walking from Punta de Vacas, and Casa de Piedra (3240 m), reached after a further moderate six-hour walk along the same Quebrada del río de las Vacas, also with ranger station. From here, it's a steep seven-hour walk to Plaza Argentina (ranger station and medical services).

Facilities and services

Mules are available from Puente del Inca: about US$140 for 60 kg of gear one way to Plaza de Mulas or US$260 for 60 kg one way to Plaza Argentina; arrange return before setting out for a reduced two-way price. Organized trekking expeditions and tours can be booked in Mendoza, whether several days' trekking or climbing to the summit, with all equipment and accommodation/camping included (see Tour operators, Mendoza, page 242, and the official website).

Uspallata → *Colour map 3, A2. Phone code 02624. Population 3400.*

The picturesque village of Uspallata (1751 m, 120 km from Mendoza and 52 km from Potrerillos) lies in its own side valley, very close to the high Andes, and so it's become a popular stopping point on the road to Chile. All routes pass through it, and yet it has retained a rather charming unspoilt atmosphere – out of peak season at least. With distant mountains glimpsed through a frame of *álamo* (poplar) trees, it is reminiscent of the Himalayas and was the setting for *Seven Years in Tibet*. Stay for a day at least to explore the mysterious white egg-shaped domes of **Las Bóvedas** ① *2 km on R39 north, US$0.50*, built by the indigenous Huarpes people, under instruction by the Jesuits, to melt silver. There is a small, interesting museum.

From Uspallata, the Route Provincial 39 leads north to **Calingasta** and **Barreal** (see pages 266 and 267), unpaved for its first part and tricky when the snow-melt floods it in summer. Here you'll find the remains of the Inca road, one of the most important archaeological sites in the region, with foundations of an Inca Tambo (post house) too; look for signs on the left-hand side of the road. Uspallata has a few hotels, a hostel, food shops, bakeries, a post office and a YPF station with restaurant, shop and *locutorio*, open 0900-2200.

Route to Chile via Parque Provincial Aconcagua → *For listings, see pages 252-253.*

This dramatic road, which runs past the foothills of Aconcagua, is one of Mendoza's most memorable sights and not to be missed. From Uspallata, a good paved road to Chile crosses a broad plain, with maroon and chalk-white rocks sticking up from the rolling land. The road winds alongside a ravine with a thread of turquoise water below, before climbing up into a mountain pass with amazing terracotta rock formations and a heart- stopping glimpse of Volcán Tupungato – one of the giants of the Andes, rising to 6600 m. The first tiny village you come to, **Punta de Vacas**, has a large *gendarmería* (police station) but little accommodation. The road continues, climbing quickly beyond the snowline in winter, to the charming small ski resort of **Los Penitentes** (2580 m) ① *Km 183, T0261- 428 3601, www.penitentes.com, May-Sep, daily ski hire US$19, lift pass US$35.* Named after the majestic mass of pinnacled rocks on its mountainside, which you might think looks vaguely like a group of cowled monks climbing upwards, this is a low-key family ski resort right by the road, though it's surprisingly quiet. There is good skiing on the 28 pistes (total length of 25 km, with 10 lifts); most of them are graded difficult but there are a couple of long descents of medium difficulty and three beginners' slopes. It's good value and uncrowded.

Another low-key ski resort in the area is **Los Puquios** ① *www.lospuquios.com.ar*, 5 km west. It's small, ideal for beginners and cheap – a day pass costs US$20. It's also used as a base camp for climbers for acclimatization to the high altitudes, and as a departure point for mule caravans to higher base camps closer to Aconcagua. On the southern side of Route 7, opposite, you'll find a cemetery for climbers who have died on Aconcagua's slopes; a reminder that this summit is not to be undertaken lightly.

Puente del Inca → *Colour map 3, B1. Phone code 02624.*

Puente del Inca (2718 m, Km 190), 7 km further on, is set among breathtaking mountains and is a great base for exploring the peaks on foot or on horseback, with access to the Parque Provincial Aconcagua. The naturally formed bridge, after which the village is named, is said to be one of the Great Wonders of South America. Crossing Río Mendoza at a height of 19 m, the natural bridge is 21 m long and 27 m wide and seems to have been

Border essentials: Argentina–Chile

Las Cuevas

The paved road to the border goes through the 3.2-km **Cristo Redentor tunnel**, 0930-2030 in winter and 24 hours in summer, US$4 for cars (no cyclists), into Chile. The last settlement before the tunnel is tiny forlorn Las Cuevas, 16 km from Puente del Inca, offering only a *kiosko*, café and hostel accommodation. In summer you can take the old road over La Cumbre pass to **El Cristo Redentor** (Christ the Redeemer), an 8-m-high statue erected jointly by Chile and Argentina in 1904 to celebrate the settlement of their boundary dispute. If you want to see this, take an all-day excursion from Mendoza, or drive up in a 4WD, after the snow has melted, or walk from Las Cuevas (4½ hours up, two hours down – only to be attempted by the fit, in good weather). Expreso Uspallata runs buses to here from Mendoza.

Accommodation Arco de las Cuevas (F pp, doubles C), T0261-426 5273, www.arcodelas cuevas.com.ar. Set right above the old road to Cristo Redentor on a picturesque old Alpine-like stone and wooden arch, this has very spartan though comfortable dorms, a restaurant and a bar that mostly attracts climbers, some skiers and mountain guides. They can organize adventure trips into Chile.Transfer for access to Aconcagua Provincial Park for an extra US$4.

Precautions There are many dangerous bends on this route so drive slowly, and at Km 1097 the 13-m bridge over Río Blanco is only 4.70 m wide, so there is only one car allowed past at any one time. Due to fog, snow, mud or falling rocks, this route is sometimes closed. For up-to-date information **Escuadrón 27 Punta de Vacas**, T0261-4205 275, esc27p_vacas@fullzero.com.ar. For information on the curves and look outs see, www.gendarmería.gov.ar/pasos/ficheris.htm (in Spanish).

Chilean customs The Chilean border is beyond Las Cuevas, but customs is back near Los Horcones, 2 km west of Puente del Inca.

Note No fresh food can be taken into Chile. Hire cars need special papers, and the number plate engraved in the window: tell your hire company if you plan to take the car into Chile.

formed by sulphur-bearing hot springs below which have stained the whole ravine an incredible ochre yellow, and left the bridge an eerie orange colour. Underneath the bridge are the ruins of a 1940s spa hotel, destroyed by a snow avalanche and now mostly washed away by the river, but a torrent of hot sulphurous water still gushes from its walls. (Watch your footing on the steps as they are extremely slippery.) The old baths, to the side of the river, between the bridge and the small church, have basic facilities, but are still good for a soak amidst magnificent scenery.

West of the village there is a fine view of Aconcagua, sharply silhouetted against the sky. **Los Horcones**, the Argentine customs post, is 1 km west. To visit the Laguna Horcones in the Parque Provincial Aconcagua, see page 248.

For Sleeping and Eating price codes and other relevant information, see Essentials pages 30-36.

● Sleeping

Cacheuta *p247*
AL Hotel & Spa Termas Cacheuta, R82, Km 38, T02624-490152, www.termas cacheuta.com. A warm and inviting place with comfortable rustic-style rooms and thermal water piped into the private bathrooms. There's a large swimming pool, a good restaurant and access to the lovely spa included. Prices are full board and are cheaper Sun-Thu. Entry into the **Thermal Spa Park** US$41 for a full day spa. Recommended.

Potrerillos *p247*
B Cabañas Andinas, Av Los Cóndores y El Plata, El Salto, T0261-438 0505, www.cabanas andinas.com. Very comfortable with fabulous views and beautiful gardens. Recommended.
B-C Gran Hotel Potrerillos, R7, Km 50, T02624- 482130. A large, faded 1940s resort hotel in a lovely hilltop location with simple rooms and a pool. Rates are for half-board.

Camping
ACA campsite, R7, Km 53, T02624-482013. Excellent, nicely maintained, well-shaded site, with pool and hot water after 1800. US$5.50 per tent and car. Public phone on the road outside.

Vallecitos *p247*
B Refugio San Antonio, T0261-423 7423, www.cordondelplata.com. Down the hill from the ski centre this cosy *refugio* has been converted into an attractive hostel with a few warm, simple rooms with their own baths. Half board included. They also run excursions through their own travel agency **Cordón del Plata**. There's no public transport to the resort. Rooms with private bathroom cost more (**A**).

Parque Provincial Aconcagua *p248*
AL Hotel Plaza de Mulas, book through www.aconcaguaspirit.com.ar/pmulas.htm or see www.refugioplazademulas.com.ar. Full-board or **B** without meals. Good food, information, medical treatment, also camping area, open high season only. Recommended.

Uspallata *p250*
A Hotel Uspallata, R7, Km 1149, towards Chile, T02624-420066, www.atahoteleria. com.ar/uspallata. One of several hotels built in Perón's post-war era, now modernized and spacious, in a lovely location with big gardens and a pool, all a couple of kilometres from the centre. Cheap restaurant.
A Valle Andino, R7, T02624-420095, www.hotelvalleandino.com. The town's best. A modern, airy place with good functional rooms, a heated pool and a restaurant.
C Los Cóndores, T02624-420002. Great value, bright neat rooms, good restaurant with tasty pasta and cheap set menu. Highly recommended.

Hostels
F pp **Hostel Uspallata**, R7, Km 1141.5 (south of centre), T0261-429 3220, www.hostel uspallata.com.ar. A large house with mature trees in quiet, attractive surroundings. Rooms are basic and clean, sleeping 4-8, some with bathroom and doubles (**D-C**) available. Lively bar and restaurant. Tours arranged. Discounts to HI members.

Route to Chile via Parque Provincial Aconcagua *p250*
Los Penitentes
Hotels on the same side of the road as the ski resort offer a 20% reduction on ski passes.
AL Hostería Penitentes, T02624-420110, www.penitentes.com. A cheery place near the slopes offering cheap deals for several nights. Good café, the friendly owner speaks perfect English. Recommended.

A Apart Hotel Las Lomas Blancas. Modern, functional units, clearly visible from the road, handy for the ski lifts, and there's lively laid-on nightlife. Prices are for an apartment for 4

E pp **Campo Base Penitentes**, T0261-425 5511, www.penitentes.com.ar. One of the cheapest options in the Andes for staying at a ski resort. Lively atmosphere. Slightly cramped dorms with shared bath, bar and restaurant, and all the usual hostel facilities. Minibus transfers to Mendoza. Ski programmes in season, though the hostel is open all year.

Puente del Inca *p250*
B Hostería Puente del Inca, R7, Km 175, T02624-420 5304. Next to the small ski centre at Los Puquios, has doubles and rooms for 4-8, huge cosy dining room, helpful advice on Aconcagua, good atmosphere. Warmly recommended. Full board optional.

Camping
At Los Puquios and at Laguna Horcones inside the park.

⊙ Eating

Potrerillos *p247*
¶ **El Futre**, opposite the ACA campsite. Open all day, summer only. Typical Cuyo food, vegetarian dishes and home-made pizzas.
¶ **Los Pinos**, Av Los Cóndores, on the left as you go up the hill. Recommended for trout.
¶ **Tomillo**, Av Los Cóndores, El Salto. Open all day. Excellent home-made cooking in this welcoming and simple place.

Uspallata *p250*
There are several reliable *parrillas* in town; the cheapest is **La Estancia de Elías**, opposite the YPF station. Right on the crossroads, **Pub Tibet** is a welcoming bar with photos from the filming here of *Seven years in Tibet*, and a warm atmosphere.

▲ Activities and tours

Potrerillos *p247*
Argentina Rafting, Route Perilago, T02624-482037, www.argentinarafting.com. Reliable company. Guide Rodolfo Navio can organize all kinds of activities including mountain biking, climbing and a 2-day hike from Potrerillos to Vallecitos in summer. Full day rafting and zip-line costs around US$70, with all equipment and transport included.

Uspallata *p250*
Desnivel Turismo Aventura, Ejército de los Andes, T02624-420275, www.desnivel aventura.com. Rafting, mountain biking, trekking, riding, climbing and skiing.

⊖ Transport

Mendoza to Upsallata *p246*
Bus
Expreso Uspallata, T0261-432 5055, has daily services to and from **Mendoza** with stops at all towns along R7. Fewer services in winter, when roads can be blocked by snow, west of **Uspallata**. Between Uspallata and **Mendoza**, there are 6 services a day; between **Puente del Inca** and **Mendoza**, 3 a day, and between **Las Cuevas** and **Mendoza**, 2 a day. From **Potrerillos** to **Mendoza**, 1½ hr, US$2.50; from **Uspallata**, 2-2½ hrs, US$4.50; from **Puente del Inca**, 3 hrs, US$5.50; from **Las Cuevas**, 4 hrs, US$5.50. Buses going to Chile do not pick up passengers on their way.

Cacheuta *p247*
Bus
Daily Expreso Uspallata service to **Mendoza**'s bus terminal.

Southern Mendoza province

The southern half of the province is wilder and less visited by tourists than the area around Mendoza city, and it's well worth taking a few days to explore. There are two main centres, the closest of which, and most appealing, is the charming town of San Rafael, the centre of its own wine-growing region, with tree-lined streets and excellent bodegas. Near here, there's rafting heaven in the extraordinary Cañón del Atuel, a canyon of weird rock formations with a wonderful fast-flowing river running through it. The other centre, much further south, is the fledgling tourist town of Malargüe, which you could use as a base for skiing at Las Leñas, or for visiting remote areas of natural beauty at La Payunia and Llancanelo. There are two possible routes to the south of the province: you can take the fast Ruta 40 directly to San Rafael or the picturesque route from Potrerillos along the Cordón del Plata to Tupungato, a sleepy place with superb wineries and the starting point for long excursions into Tupungato Provincial Park. An appealing detour here is to scenic Manzano Histórico, right in the foothills of the Andes. ▸▸ *For listings, see pages 259-263.*

Tupungato → *For listings, see pages 259-263. Colour map 3, B2. Phone code 02622. Population 11,700.*

To reach the quiet little town of Tupungato (1050 m), take the picturesque road from Potrerillos (Route 89), descending along the Cordón del Plata mountain range, with splendid views of the mountains, and through the fertile fruit- and vine-growing Uco Valley. Otherwise, take Route 86 from Route Nacional 40, south of Mendoza. Nearby are the stunningly wild mountain landscapes of Tupungato Provincial Park, named after the imposing peak of its volcano, 6600 m, and inaccessible to the public unless you go with an approved guide, see page 262. There are also superb wild landscapes on the upper Río de Las Tunas, to the west of town; contact the tourist office at Tupungato to stay overnight at the nearby Refugio Santa Clara (they'll direct you to the army for the key). The best way to get to the park is to go on a trip with Rómulo Nieto's company (see Tour operators, page 262). **Tourist information** on Tupungato and the surrounding area is available from the foyer of **Hotel Turismo** ① *Belgrano 348, T02622-488007, www.tupungato.gov.ar* . Ask them about nearby bodegas and *estancia* visits for horse riding.

There are many vineyards around Tupungato; one of the most famous is **Bodega Salentein** ① *Los Arboles, 15 km south, T02622-429090, www.bodegasalentein.com, tours of the bodega daily 1000-1600,* whose fine wines you may have noticed in many restaurants. With a beautiful setting against the foothills of the Andes, the bodega produces some of the country's finest wine (the Malbec is exquisite) and you can stay in **Posada Salentein (L)** which has comfortable rooms, extremely welcoming hosts, and there's perfect peace in which to walk, ride and relax. Recommended.

A much newer winery also worth visiting is the Spanish-owned **O Fournier** ① *Los Indios, La Consulta, west of San Carlos, T02622-451088, www.ofournier.com*. Its output is dedicated mainly to Tempranillo grapes, and here you can admire both the vines and the avant-garde architecture of the winery building, which is strictly functional and state of the art.

Continue south from Salentein to **Manzano Histórico**, a tiny hamlet in fabulous scenery, where a statue of San Martín marks his victorious return via this route from Chile. A *hostería* and campsite make this a good base for trekking, and there's a little shop and bar for provisions.

San Rafael (688 m, 236 km south of Mendoza) is a charming, quiet, airy town in the heart of fertile land which produces wine, fruit and olives in abundance. It's a relaxed place, smaller and less sophisticated than Mendoza but with a good range of accommodation. It makes an ideal base for exploring the vineyards and for trying adventure sports at nearby Cañón del Atuel or more challenging activities further west. There are lovely, leafy boulevards of French-influenced buildings, thanks to the arrival of a significant French community here in the early 1900s, and it's a trim and well-maintained place, where everyone cycles around – there are more bicycles than cars on the streets. The main street is Avenida Hipólito Yrigoyen, changing names at the central north/south Avenida San Martín (called Avenida El Libertador south of Avenida H Yrigoyen).

The airport is at Las Paredes, a few kilometres west of town; there is access from Route 143. The central bus terminal is at Coronel Suárez and Avellaneda. There are ATMs and *locutorios* all along Yrigoyen, and a friendly and helpful **tourist office** ⓘ *7 blocks west of San Martín at Av H Yrigoyen and Balloffet, T02627-437860, www.sanrafael.gov.ar (in Spanish), www.sanrafael.com.ar (in English), and www.sanrafael-tour.com (in Spanish).*

Sights → *Phone code 02627. Population 158,000.*

Río Diamante runs just south of the town, with a lovely park, **Parque Mariano Moreno**, 2 km from the centre, on an island, the Isla del Río Diamante. Among its attractions are a zoo and a small museum, the **Museo Municipal de Historia Natural** ⓘ *Tue-Sun 0800-2100, free, take Iselin bus along Av JA Balloffet.* San Rafael is at the heart of an important wine-producing region, whose wines are at least as excellent as those around Mendoza. One of the country's most important *bodegas* is **Bianchi** ⓘ *T02627-422046, www.valentinbianchi.com* , which can be visited on a commercialized tour.

The **Bianchi** champagne house ⓘ *R143, 5 km west of town*, is also worth seeing for the fascinating process and rather over-the-top pseudo-classical building (take a taxi, US$3.50, as buses are infrequent). Their more traditional bodega is in town, at the corner of Comandante Torres and Ortiz de Rosas, and also gives an excellent and detailed tour, and sells the top wines at reduced prices after a generous tasting. Look for their exported wines abroad under the names Elsa, Elsa's vineyard or Valentín Bianchi Premium. There's a smaller, more intimate bodega **Jean Rivier** ⓘ *H Yrigoyen 2385, T02627-432675, www.jeanrivier.com* , which also produces excellent wine, and can be visited Monday to Saturday.

Around San Rafael

San Rafael is a great centre for all kinds of activities, including rafting, horse riding, trekking, climbing and fishing. The most spectacular place for adventure is the nearby **Cañón del Atuel**, 35 km southwest. It's an atmospheric drive along the *ripio* road through this 20-km-long ravine of extraordinary rock formations, of cream and pink, and metallic sulphurous greens next to vivid terracotta. There are constantly changing views and an eerie feel in places, in the darker recesses of the canyon, where birds of prey wheel overhead. The gorge lies between two lakes 46 km apart, **El Nihuil** (9600 ha) and **Valle Grande** (508 ha). From San Rafael three buses (Iselin, T02627-435998) a day go to the Valle Grande at the near end of the gorge (35 km, US$2); there is no public transport through the gorge to the El Nihuil dam. The best place for rafting is near Valle Grande, 2 km down the river from the Valle Grande Dam (about 40 km from San Rafael). On the south side of the river, near the bridge, you'll see plenty of adventure tour operators (see page 262 for the most reliable ones). Many offer river rafting (Grade II for beginners) and horse riding, and several offer excursions to places further afield for more challenging rafting, such as the upper Atuel or Diamante river (up to Grade V, experience required). There are plenty of hotels and campsites lining the pretty riverbanks on the north side of the river, in a 13-km stretch from this bridge back in the direction of San Rafael.

Lago Los Reyunos is another popular excursion, 35 km west of San Rafael, a lake set in a barren rocky landscape, which can only be reached on a tour, as there are no buses. But far more spectacular is the **Laguna Diamante**, 200 km northwest of San Rafael, an ultramarine blue expanse of water, whipped by perpetual winds, set against the craggy backdrop of the Andes and the perfectly conical Volcán Maipo. Only 4WD vehicles will make it over the last 60 km or so of track, and it's best to go on an excursion from San Rafael with **Taiel Viajes** (see page 262). There is some superb horse riding in the region into the Andes. You could take an excursion from El Sosneado (see below) or Tupungato to the place where the Uruguayan plane crashed into the mountains, subject of the book and film *Alive!*. This is less gruesome than you might think, since the landscapes are amazing: stark and very beautiful. **Laguna del Atuel**, 200 km west of San Rafael, has incredible turquoise water lapping against ochre mountains, and makes for another fabulous five-day horse-riding trip.

El Sosneado and around → *For listings, see pages 259-263.*

If you're heading south to ski or hike in Las Leñas (www.laslenas.com), or explore the area around Malargüe, you might like to stop off at El Sosneado. A good paved road (Ruta 144 and then Ruta 40) leads west from San Rafael across the vast plain of the Río Atuel, passing saltflats and marshland as you head towards stark snow-dusted mountains rising steeply out of the ochre-coloured land. **El Sosneado**, at Km 138, is the only settlement, with a service station, *hostería* and a small shop for fine home-cured hams and olives, where you can also take away delicious sandwiches. The YPF station sells snacks and hot drinks. El Sosneado is also the starting point for good rafting and treks into the mountains, but there is little infrastructure in the village itself, and most visitors prefer to arrange their trips before coming here, in San Rafael or Malargüe. However, if you're feeling spontaneous, tours can be arranged at **Hostería El Sosneado** (see Sleeping, page 260).

Nearby there's a good lake for trout fishing, **Laguna El Sosneado**, 42 km away, reached by a *ripio* side road following the valley of the Río Atuel northwest. Some 13 km or so further on from the lake, there are natural thermal pools, the **Termas el Sosneado**, where you can bathe in the sulphurous waters for free, since there's no organization here, and the **Hotel Termas El Sosneado** is in ruins. Ahead, you'll see the Overo volcano (4619 m).

Los Molles → *Colour map 3, B1. Phone code 02627.*

The greatest attraction in the area is the superb ski resort of Las Leñas, reached by a road 21 km southwest of El Sosneado and 156 km southwest of San Rafael following the Río Salado west into the Andes. After 30 km, the road passes through the tiny hamlet of Los Molles, a small, faded old thermal resort, now little more than a cluster of hotels, the oldest of which has access to thermal springs. None of these establishments is luxurious but they offer an alternative to expensive Las Leñas hotels, plus some adventure tourism trips in the summer that mainly include horse riding to nearby sites. Opposite Los Molles a *ripio* road leads to the *refugio* of the **Club Andino Pehuenche** and, 8 km further on, to the **Laguna de la Niña Encantada**, a beautiful little lake and shrine to the Virgin. Continuing towards Las Leñas, there are the strange **Pozo de las Animas** (Well of the Spirits), two natural circular pits filled with water (the larger is 80 m deep), where wind blowing across the holes makes a ghostly wail, hence the name. They're a curious sight if you happen to be passing, but don't quite merit a special excursion.

Las Leñas → *Colour map 3, B1. Phone code 02627.*

ⓘ *T02627-471100, www.laslenas.com, lift pass in high season US$64 per day, equipment hire from US$30 daily, 13 ski lifts.*

Las Leñas (2250 m), 49 km off the San Rafael–Malargüe road, is internationally renowned for its excellent skiing and snowboarding. As a result, it's one of the most expensive resorts in the country, full of beautiful people in trendy bars and wealthy Argentine families. Set at the end of a spectacular valley, in the middle of five snow-capped peaks, it has powder snow throughout the season on 27 pistes with a total length of 64 km, and despite the frequent bad weather and lack of tree cover, its steep slopes, with a vertical drop of some 1230 m, and the fact that you can walk straight out of your hotel onto the pistes, make it the best resort in South America. A constantly circulating free bus service picks up guests from further-flung hotels in the resort. The season runs from mid-June to early October but the busiest and most expensive time is July and August, when prices are at least 50% higher. The resort also has a ski school, a special snowboard park, many cafés, bars and restaurants (several right on the pistes), a useful information point where there are lockers, banks, doctors and tourist information. There are also many ski patrol units all over the pistes, so you are in safe hands here. In summer, Las Leñas operates as a resort for adventure sports, such as trekking and climbing. Beyond Las Leñas the road continues into **Valle Hermoso**, a beautiful valley accessible only from December to March.

Malargüe → *For listings, see pages 259-263. Colour map 3, B2. Phone code 02627. Population 23,100.*

Situated 186 km southwest of San Rafael in reach of really spectacular unspoilt landscapes, Malargüe (1426 m) is slowly developing as a centre for hiking and horse riding. It promotes itself rather grandly as the national centre for adventure tourism with a few good hostels. However, it's certainly a cheap alternative to Las Leñas in the ski season when there are frequent minibus services between the two and a 50% reduction on your ski pass if you stay in a hotel in Malargüe. However the best time to come is from spring to autumn, when you can make the most of the landscape for walking and riding. The **Fiesta Nacional del Chivo** (locally produced kid, a local delicacy) is held in the first fortnight of January, with live music and partying, attracting national *folclore* stars, as well as Chilean performers and public from across the Andes.

The **bus terminal** is at Aldao and Beltrán. The **airport** ⓘ *T02627-471600*, is on the southern edge of town. Malargüe has a broad main street, San Martín, with an assortment of small shops, *locutorios*, cafés and the odd run-down hotel, but the best accommodation is in the outskirts, north of the centre. On the way into town from the north, there's an impressive modern conference centre on the right, built for conventions of the nearby Philip Auger Observatory of Cosmic Rays, but mostly used for showing films. It has a smart bar. Next to it is the helpful **tourist office** ⓘ *T02627-471659, daily 0800-2130, www.malargue. gov.ar*, which can arrange visits to the nearby provincial parks.

Border essentials: Argentina–Chile

Paso Pehuenche

Paso Pehuenche (2553 m) is reached by a *ripio* road that branches off Ruta 40, 66 km south of Malargüe. On the Chilean side the road continues down the valley of the Río Maule to Talca.

Opening hours The border is open from 0800-1700. See http://www.gendarmeria. gov.ar/pasos/fichpehuenche.htm for detailed information (in Spanish).

Around Malargüe

The wild untouched landscape around Malargüe is surprising and extraordinarily beautiful. There are three main places to visit, all pretty remote and with little to no public transport, so unless you have your own vehicle, they can only be visited on a tour. Even if you do have your own transport, you must be accompanied by an authorized guide, which must be arranged in advance and requires a certain amount of planning.

La Payunia Reserve, 208 km south, is the most remarkable of the three, and dominated by the majestic peaks of several snow-capped volcanoes. The vast expanse of seductive altiplano grasslands is ridden with volcanic peaks, and deep red and black crags of extraordinary sculpted lava. The appearance of hundreds of guanaco running wild across your path adds to the magic. The entrance is 100 km south of Malargüe on sandy *ripio* roads. You can bring your own vehicle here and the *guardaparques* will show you around in their 4WD. Ask at the tourist office in Malargüe for directions; they will also radio the *guardaparques* and tell them to expect you. The best way to enjoy the reserve is on horseback, on a three-day expedition, or you can take a tour from Malargüe with **Karen Travel** ① *www.karentravel.com.ar*.

The **Laguna Llancanelo** (pronounced *shancannello*), 65 km southeast, is filled with hugely varied birdlife in spring, when 150 species come to nest on its lakes. At any time of year you'll see Chilean flamingos, rising in a pink cloud from pale turquoise waters where volcanic peaks are perfectly reflected. You may also see tern, curlews, grebes, teal and black-necked swans, among others. To get there, contact the Llancanelo *guardaparques* via the tourist office, or go on a trip from Malargüe.

At **Caverna de las Brujas** ① *2- to 3-hr guided tours, lights and helmets provided, children over 7 welcome*, there are 5 km of underground caves to explore, taking you through different eras of the earth's development, from the Jurassic period onwards, and a fantastic variety of elaborate stalactites and stalagmites. There is no independent access to the caves, and all visits must be arranged with one of the authorized tour operators in Malargüe. The tourist office in Malargüe will show you pictures of the caves, and recommend a tour operator (see Activities and tours, page 262).

For Sleeping and Eating price codes and other relevant information, see Essentials pages 30-36.

● Sleeping

Tupungato *p254*

L-AL Chateau d'Ancon, R89, San José, Tupungato, T02622-488245, www.estancian con.com. Open mid-Oct to Apr. At the foot of the mighty Tupungato volcano, a 1933 French-style rural mansion is at the heart of a traditional *estancia* owned by the Bombal family, who were originally French, but have been living in Mendoza since 1760. The magnificent park was designed by famous Argentine landscape architect Charles Thays and all the fruit and vegetables used for meals here are grown in nearby orchards and kitchen gardens. A wonderfully comfortable place to stay, with elegant decor inside the house, and excellent service.

C Hostería Don Romulo, Almirante Brown 1200, T02622-489020, www.donromulo. com.ar. This *hostería* is owned by Rómulo Nieto, who runs his own tour company (see Tour operators, page 262). There are simple rooms with TV and bath for 2-4 with a cosy lounge to relax in and decent, very inexpensive food from the restaurant.

C Hotel Turismo, Belgrano 1060, T02622-488007. A slightly modernized 1940s place, basic but comfortable rooms with wonderful kingfisher-blue tiles in the bathrooms, some family rooms, a pool and a good restaurant.

Camping

Camping San Antonio, R94, Km 27.5, T0261-429 4099, www.campingsanantonio. com.ar. There are various attractive spots in the Manzano Histórico, but this one is particularly recommended for its good, well-kept facilities, including a large pool. They also rent out small *cabañas*.

Patios de Correa, Calle La Costa, El Peral, 4.3 km northwest of Tupungato, T02622-1567 3299. A good site in woods of willow and walnut trees, on the riverbank, also a good picnic spot.

San Rafael *p255*

AL-A Tower, Av Yrigoyen 774, T02627-427190, www.towersanrafael.com. International-style hotel easily spotted on the main street, an 8-storey peachy yellow building. It's slightly soulless, but has luxurious rooms, great bathrooms, very professional service, a small pool and a spa.

A Red Wine Club, Salta 424, T02627-447 474, www.redwinehotel.com. Smart bed and breakfast hotel which has smallish rooms with colour schemes that match different types of wines. Swimming pool and spa.

A-B Nuevo Mundo, Av Balloffet 725, T02627-445666, www.hnmsanrafael.com.ar. This small, modern business-hotel has minimalist decor in its rooms, good service, and is great value. There is a restaurant and a spa, and it's close to the town centre.

A-B San Rafael, C Day 30, T/F02627-428251, www.hotelsanrafael.com.ar. A decent option with plain comfortable rooms, welcoming bar area and very reasonable prices.

C Rex, H Yrigoyen 56, T02672-422177, www.rexhotel.com.ar. Good budget option, small but clean rooms set around a large courtyard in a 1940s building. All rooms have private bathrooms ,TV and heating.

D Tonin, Pellegrini 330, T02627-422499, www.sanrafael-tour.com/tonin. A lovely, quiet, family-run place, with modern spacious rooms, TV and bath. Good location next to the plaza.

Hostels

F pp Tierrasoles, Alsina 245, T02627-433449, www.tierrasoles.com.ar. Close to the bus station, this is a lively, welcoming, well-kept house with all the usual hostel facilities. Basic dorms and doubles, all with shared bath. Lots of excursions and activities on offer, including bikes for hire.

F pp **Trotamundos Hostel**, Barcala 300, T02627-432795, www.trotamundoshostel. com.ar. Close to town, this social hostel is fitted out in rustic style with lots of wood. BBQs every Fri night, small dorms but a great patio for drinking beer in the afternoon. Excursions and tours organized.

Camping
El Parador, at the park on Isla Río Diamante, 5 km southeast, T02627-420492, www.com plejoelparador.alojar.com.ar.

There are also many sites at Valle Grande in the Cañón del Atuel.

Around San Rafael p255
B Valle Grande Hotel & Resort, T02627-1558 0660, www.hotelvallegrande.com. Well situated on the banks of the river in the Cañón del Atuel, with a big terrace and good views from its restaurant, this has smart rooms, a pool and friendly service. There are lots of activities laid on for guests. Also *cabañas* for hire (**A**), popular with families and very lively in summer.
B Finca El Maitén, Mercado 1405, T02762-1551 6690, www.fincaelmaiten.com.ar. Charming B&B, 10 km from town in the wine-growing region. Spacious, rustic-style double, and a lovely garden to relax in.

El Sosneado and around p256
C-B pp **Hostería El Sosneado**, T02627-1567 0283. Simple clean rooms and 5 *cabañas* sleeping 4-6, with breakfast included. Welcoming owners, who also organize horse-riding excursions to the 'Avión de los Uruguayos', or to Laguna del Atuel, rafting and 4WD trips.

Los Molles p256
Accommodation here is much cheaper than at Las Leñas, but it's all very basic.
A-B Cabañas en los Molles, road to Laguna Niña Encantada, T02762-1551 6690, www.cabanasenlosmolles.com.ar. Cosy cabins for up to 8 people, 15 mins' drive from the ski resort.

B-C Lahuen-Co, on left-hand side of road, T02627-499700, http:///hotellahuenco.com. This hotel, built in 1938, is pretty kitsch. Its special feature is the sulphurous thermal baths, in private cabins in a decaying extension at the back.

Las Leñas p257
Budget travellers should consider staying in Malargüe or Los Molles. Most of the accommodation here is expensive, although some cheaper apart hotels and dorms houses are available. For further information, T02627-471100, www.la[.]enas. com. The following options (**L-A**), can be found on the Las Leñas website and have restaurants:
Acuario right in the thick of the action; **Aries**, 4-star, with a sauna, gym and pool; **Escorpio**, great views; **Geminis**, an apart hotel, also with pool and sauna; **Piscis**, 5-star with exceptional facilities and pools, including an outdoor heated pool, fine restaurants, casino and shows.

Malargüe p257
Guests staying for more than 2 nights are issued with a voucher for 50% discount on a Las Leñas ski pass. For more options, see www.malargue.gov.ar.
A Maggio, Ing Alvarez y M Ruibal, T02627-472496, www.maggiohotel.com.ar. A good-value place with very stylish modern rooms, large beds and good showers. Good option.
A Microtel Inn & Suites, R40 Norte (north of centre), T02627-472300. Comfortable rooms and also well-equipped *cabañas*, all very functional and simply decorated. Heated pool, sauna and a large restaurant.
B Rincón Sur, R40 Norte (north of centre), T02627-1551 4816, www.posadarinconsur. com. In an attractive setting near the river, this is a small complex of simple though reasonably comfortable *cabañas*.
C SeuSek, Colonia Pehuenche I, Prolongación Constitución Nacional, T02627-1558 7890, www.seusek.com.ar. Rustic 'rural' *cabaña*, with nicely decorated doubles, huge break-fast included. A little out of town, 5 km from the centre. Call for directions.

D La Posta, Av San Martín 646, T02627-472 079, laposta_malargue@yahoo.com.ar. A welcoming cheap place with wood-panelled entrance hall and rooms. Also has a *parrilla*, a few blocks away, serving good kid and trout.

Hostels
F pp Campo Base, Telles Meneses 897, T02627-471534, www.backpackers malargue.com.ar. A lively hostel with basic comfort in its dorms and doubles, all with shared bath. Excursions arranged.
F pp Eco Internacional, Prolongación Constitución Nacional (Finca No 65), 2 blocks from R40 Norte, south of town, T02627-470391 or T02627-1540 2439, www. hostelmalargue.com. An appealing eco-hostel in rural surroundings. It has its own farm with dairy production and organic fruit and vegetables for delicious meals. Basic, comfortable accommodation in dorms and doubles (**D**). Run their own travel agency.
F pp Hostel International Malargue, Rutino Ortega 158, T02627-1540 2439/470391, www.hostelmalargue.com. Fun and friendly but basic hostel in the centre of town with dorms and doubles (**C**) available. They can organize tours and ski passes.

Camping
Castillos de Pincheiras, 27 km west of town, office in town at Rufino Ortega 423, T02627-471283, www.pincheira.com.ar. In wonderful wild surroundings by the river and at the foot of strange rock formations, this is a complex with campsite, a restaurant serving regional specialities and a tea room. A base for lots of excursions, including a fabulous horse-riding trip to a remote mountain hut.
Camping Municipal Malargüe (Alfonso Capdevila s/n, T02627/470691, US$3 per tent for up to 5 persons, at the north end of town.

Around Malargüe *p258*
B-C Puesto La Agüita, R186, 140 km south-east of Malargüe, T02627-1558 8635 (T011-4524 2993 in Buenos Aires), www.kinie.com.ar. At the edge of La Payunia reserve, this country house is set in a remote and unbeatably beautiful location, where the welcoming Sagal family offer all kinds of excursions into Payunia's volcanic world. Decorated in rustic style, offering comfortable accommodation. Guide **Ariel Sagal** organizes guided walks, 4WD excursions or horse riding into the park. Call in advance. Price is for full board.

🍴 Eating

Tupungato *p254*
Apart from the hotels' restaurants, there are a few pizzerias and cafés to choose from on the main street, Belgrano.
♥♥ La Posada del Jamón, R92, Km 14, Vista Flores, Tunuyán, T02622-492053. Pork rules on the menu here, in this charmingly rustic and very popular roadside restaurant. There are other tasty dishes on offer though, and excellent local wines.

San Rafael *p255*
San Rafael is lacking in exciting places to eat but most are clustered along the western end of Av H Yrigoyen, and you won't have to walk far for a steak. All are mid-range to cheap.
♥♥ El Restauro, Comandante Salas y Day, T02627-445482. An outstanding restaurant, and an exception in this town. The 1 elegant place to eat, where chef Ana Paula makes the most of regional ingredients, served in the minimalist rooms of a lovely restored house.
♥♥ La Fusta, Av H Yrigoyen 538. A smart, traditional restaurant with really delicious Italian-style food, superb *parrilla* and good home-made pastas. Warmly recommended.
♥♥ Tienda del Sol, Av H Yrigoyen 1663. The town's busiest place serves everything in a cheery family atmosphere. Recommended for pizzas and pastas.
♥ Pagoda, Av Mitre 216. Chinese *tenedor libre*, with a huge variety. Very cheap.

Cafés
There are lots of cafés but most appealing for a drink or coffee is **Nina**, Chile and San

Martín, with tables outside and a cosy wooden interior. Fantastic *lomitos*, too.

Malargüe *p257*
⍩ El Nido del Jabalí, R40, Cañada Colorada, T02627-471589. One of the most famous *parrillas* in town, welcoming owners.
⍩ El Bodegón de María, Rufino Ortega and Villegas. A cosy, simple place for home-cooked food, pizzas and pastas, lunch and dinner. Very welcoming. Recommended.
⍩ Puli Huen, Av San Martín 224, at the otherwise not recommendable **Hotel de Turismo**. Unpretentious traditional place serving good food.

▲ Activities and tours

Tupungato *p254*
Tour operators
A highly recommended guide is **Rómulo Nieto**, www.donromulo.com.ar. He organizes trekking and horse-riding excursions into the provincial park, where he also runs the base camp **Refugio El Cóndor**. In summer, Rómulo offers trekking to the summit and horse riding along the old path to Chile from Manzano Histórico to Portezuelo de los Piuquenes.
Tupungato Expedición, Liniers 1139, T02622-489791, www.tupungatoexpedicion.com.ar. Run by 2 professional guides, 1- and 2-day treks or 18-day adventures.

San Rafael *p255*
Travel agencies run all-day excursions to Cañón del Atuel and there are several rafting companies at Valle Grande, all of whom charge around US$13 for 20 mins' rafting.

Rafting
Portal de Atuel, Valle Grande, T02627-1558 6662, www.portaldelatuel.com. Rafting and catamaran trips across Lago Grande and 4WD excursions to nearby sand dunes.
Raffeish, Valle Grande, T02627-436996, www.raffeish.com.ar. Recommended for being very professional, offering a range of

rafting from very secure family trips to more adventurous expeditions for the experienced. Also rock climbing and rappel, and a great trekking excursion too, returning by boat.
Sport Star, Valle Grande, T02627-1558 1068, www.sportstar.com.ar. Another good company, which also offers whitewater rafting excursions on the upper Atuel and Diamante rivers, among other adventures.

Tour operators
Cañón del Atuel, Day 45, T02627-424871, www.rumbosanrafael.netfirms.com. Conventional tours to local bodegas, to Los Reyunos lake, and through the canyon itself.
Taiel Viajes, Av H Yrigoyen 707, T02627-427840, www.taiel.com.ar. Both conventional and adventure tours of all kinds. Wonderful 7-day horse-riding trips to Laguna del Atuel, 4WD trips to sand dunes and to Laguna el Diamante and Volcan Maipo, and rafting of all grades. Very helpful and professional.
Risco Viajes, Av HYrigoyen 284, T02627-436 439, www.riscoviajes.com. Well-organized, run local excursions in their own minivan.

Malargüe *p257*
Horse riding
Valles Aventuras, T02627-1566 6190, www.vallesaventura.com.ar. Horse-riding trips which include the famous Cruz de los Andes where you ride along the ridges.

Tour operators
Choique, Av San Martín and Rodríguez, T02627-470391, www.choique.net. A great range of excursions to all nearby sites and provincial parks. Daily transfers to Las Leñas ski resort.
Karen Travel, San Martín 54, T02627-470342, www.karentravelcom.ar. Highly recommended for excursions to all the nature reserves above and also horse-riding trips, such as the 4-day excursion to the crashed Uruguayan plane site known as *Viven* (*Alive!*). Their amazing photos of the spectacular landscapes will convince you it has to be done.

Around Malargüe *p258*
Horse riding
Kiñe tourism, www.kinie.com.ar. Horse riding in La Payunia reserve, and accommodation at the *hostería*, **Puesto La Agüita**.

⊖ Transport

Tupungato *p254*
Bus
To **Mendoza** and Las Heras and D Chaca, Empresa Mitre 380, daily, 1½-2 hrs, US$3.50.

San Rafael *p255*
Air
To **Buenos Aires**, 6 flights a week, 1 stop at San Luis, 2½ hrs, with Aerolíneas Argentinas, T02627-435156 (office in town, Av H Yrigoyen 395, T02627-438808).

Bus
To **Mendoza**, frequent, 3-3½ hrs, US$6, Expreso Uspallata and TAC; to **Neuquén**, 8-9 hrs, US$33, Andesmar; to **Buenos Aires**, US$56, 12-13 hrs, Andesmar; Chevallier; La Unión; TAC, to **Malargüe**, daily, 2½ hrs, US$4.50, Expreso Uspallata.

El Sosneado and around *p256*
Bus
Buses that pass daily to **Malargüe** from **San Rafael** stop at El Sosneado, and you can pick up buses from either places passing through to **Los Molles** and **Las Leñas**.

Las Leñas *p257*
Bus
Bus to **San Rafael**, 2 companies Isolin and Butini, daily in winter only, both US$6. Service varies from year to year, so check first. To **Malargüe**, Autotransportes Malargüe, runs a daily service, winter only, US$5.50 return. No regular bus service to Las Leñas off season, other than minibuses run by tour operators. To **Buenos Aires**, 15 hrs, ski season only.

Malargüe *p257*
Air
Charter flights to **Buenos Aires** (ski season).

Bus
Daily to **Mendoza** with Expreso Uspallata, 6 hrs, minibuses with Transporte Viento Sur, 4½ hrs, both US$11.

San Juan province

The province of San Juan extends north and west from the capital, San Juan city, which lies in the broad valley of the Río San Juan, and is the centre of a wine-producing area as big as Mendoza's but not of the same quality. The city itself is sleepy and not wildly interesting for visitors, but there are two areas in the province that might lure you here. San Juan's jewel is the little-visited west of the province, where the foothills of the Andes rise in ranges separated by beautiful, lush valleys such as the lovely Calingasta. There is great climbing and trekking here, with several Andean peaks to explore, including the mighty Mercedario (6770 m) and incredibly peaceful ancient hamlets provide charming places to completely unwind. The northeast of the province near the border with La Rioja offers two more famous attractions: Ischigualasto Provincial Park, often known as the Valle de la Luna (Valley of the Moon), where millions of years of the planet's history, and dinosaur fossils are on display in dried-out lagoons; and Talampaya National Park, just over the border in La Rioja, with fabulous dramatic canyons and eroded rocks. This northern region is inhospitably hot and dry almost all year round, but the landscapes are impressive: empty and starkly beautiful. For more information, see www.ischigualasto.com. ▸▸ *For listings, see pages 269-271.*

San Juan city → *For listings, see pages 269-271. Colour map 3, A2.*

The provincial city, 177 km north of Mendoza, is much less inviting than the marvellous landscape all around and you're most likely to arrive here on the way to the Calingasta Valley or the parks further north. However, it's a good base for organizing those trips as there are several good places to stay and eat, and some good bodegas for wine tasting. There's also one sight of fascinating cultural interest in the shrine to pagan saint La Difunta Correa. Although the city was founded on its present site in 1593, little of the original settlement remains since the most powerful earthquake in Argentine history struck in 1944, killing over 10,000 inhabitants. Though it's been rebuilt in modern style, San Juan has not yet recovered, unlike Mendoza. It was at a fundraising event at Luna Park in Buenos Aires for the victims of the tragedy that Juan Perón met Eva Duarte, the radio actress who became his second wife.

Ins and outs → *Phone code 0264. Population of Greater San Juan 422,000.*

There are no regular buses from **Chacritas Airport**, 11 km southeast of the city on Route 20, but a *remise* taxi to the centre costs US$4. The **bus terminal** ① *Estados Unidos and Santa Fe, terminal information T0264-422 1604*, is nine blocks east of the city centre and buses No 33 and 35 will get you there for US$0.50. Alternatively, take a taxi for US$3.

Sights

This is an important wine-producing area and there are lots of bodegas to visit, if you haven't seen those in Mendoza. Those offering tours include: **Santiago Graffigna** ① *Colón 1342 N, Desamparados, northwest of centre, T0264-421 4227, www.graffigna wines.com, Tue-Fri, Sun mornings only, Sat all day*, the oldest in San Juan, with an interesting museum displaying winemaking machinery and old photos, and a wine bar. **Fabril Alto Verde** ① *R40, between Calle 13 and 14, Pocito, south of centre, T0264-492 1905, www.fabril-altoverde. com.ar. Mon-Sat*, is an organic winery with a smart showroom and small bar. **Antigua Bodega** ① *Salta 782 N, near the ring road, northwest of centre, T0264-421 4327, www.antiguabodega.com, Tue-Sun*, has a museum, below where the sparkling wine is made. **Viñas de Segisa** ① *Aberastain and Calle 15, La Rinconada, Pocito, south of centre, T0264-492 2000, www.saxsegisa.com.ar,* is a small boutique bodega with attractively renovated buildings. Not far from here is the charming, small, family-run bodega **Las Marianas** ① *Nueva, La Rinconada, Pocito, south of centre, T0264-423 1191.* **Cavas de Zonda** ① *R12 Km 15, Rivadavia, west of centre, T0264-494 5144, http://cavasdezonda.com/,* has an interesting setting right inside a mountain and a champagne house at the end of a tunnel carved into the rocky hills, where wines are made following traditional Spanish and French methods. The **Mercado Artesanal Tradicional** ① *España and San Luis, T0264-421 8530,* sells the woven handicrafts, such as blankets and saddlebags, for which the province is famous. If you haven't time for a bodega tour, there are a few wine stores where you can buy the local produce, such as **La Bodega** ① *25 de Mayo 957 Este,* or **La Reja** ① *Jujuy 424 Sur.*

San Juan's museums are mostly rather dry, but if you're interested in Argentine history, pop into **Museo Casa Natal de Sarmiento** ① *Sarmiento 21 Sur, www.casanatalsarmiento. gov.ar, daily 0900-1300, also Tue-Fri and Sun 1700-2000 in summer; Tue-Fri and Sun 0900-1900, Mon and Sat 0900-1400 in winter, US$0.80, free on Sun,* dedicated to the important Argentine President and educator, Domingo Sarmiento. The **Museo de Ciencias Naturales** ① *Predio Ferial, España and Maipú, T0264-421 6774, daily 0930-1330, US$1.70,* has some of the fossils from Ischigualasto Provincial Park, which you won't see at the site itself. There is a basic **tourist office** ① *Sarmiento Sur 24 and San Martín, T0264-421 0004, www. turismo.sanjuan.gov.ar or www.ischigualasto.com (both in Spanish), daily 0800-2000, also at the bus terminal.* Note that the main street, Avenida San Martín, is often called Libertador.

Around San Juan → *See page 266 for Parque Provincial Ischigualasto.*
There's a wonderful collection of pre-Hispanic indigenous artefacts including several well-preserved mummies at the **Museo Arqueológico** ① *University of San Juan, Acceso Sur entre Calle 5 and Progreso, Rawson, a few kilometres south of centre, T0264-424 1424, Mon-Fri 0800-2000, Sat-Sun 1000-1800, US$1.* To get there, take buses 15, 49, 50 from the centre. The museum offers fascinating insights into the culture of the indigenous Huarpe peoples and into the Incan mountain-top sacrifice practices.

At **Vallecito**, 64 km east of San Juan city, the famous shrine to Argentina's most beloved pagan saint, **La Difunta Correa** has to be seen to be believed, and will give you far more insight into the Argentine character than any cathedral. By now, you'll have noticed piles of bottles at roadside shrines all over Argentina. The legend goes that the beautiful young Correa was making the long walk to reclaim the body of her young husband, killed in the wars of independence, when she fell by the roadside and died of thirst. No one would help her. But by some miracle, the baby she was carrying suckled at her breast and survived, and thus La Difunta Correa became the pagan patron saint of all travellers. People leave bottles of water by her shrine to quench her thirst, and to thank her for her protection on their journey. During Holy Week, 100,000 pilgrims visit this extraordinary series of shrines at Vallecito, to make offerings to splendidly florid effigies of Difunta and her child. Testimony to their faith is a remarkable collection of personal items left in tribute, filling several buildings, including cars, number plates from all over the world, photographs, stuffed animals, tea sets, hair (in plaits), plastic flowers, trophies, tennis rackets and guitars – and vast numbers of bottles of water (which are used for the plants, and the plastic recycled). There are cafés, toilets, a hotel and souvenir stalls. Bizarre and fascinating. Buses from San Juan to La Rioja stop here for five minutes, or Vallecitos runs a couple of services a day. See www.visitedifuntacorrea.com.ar for more information.

Parque Provincial Ischigualasto → *Colour map 3, A2.*

Popularly known as the Valle de la Luna (Valley of the Moon), this protected area covers 62,000 ha of spectacular desert landforms, and is the site of important palaeontological discoveries. Named after a Huarpe chief, the site occupies an immense basin, which was once filled by a lake, lying, at an average altitude of 1200 m, between the scarlet red Barrancas Coloradas to the east and the green, black and grey rocks of Los Rastros to the west. The vegetation is arid scrub and bushes; you may be lucky enough to see guanacos, vizcachas, Patagonian hares or red foxes and rheas. For many visitors, the attraction lies in the bizarre shapes of massive hunks of rock eroded into fantastical shapes, dotted throughout the park's other-worldly terrain. With the Argentines' charming penchant for naming all natural structures after things that they resemble, these are signposted accordingly: 'The Submarine', 'The Kiosk', '*Gusanos*' (Worms), and '*La Cancha de Bochas*' (the Bowling Green) – extraordinary spheres of fine compacted sand. Sadly, '*El Hongo*' (the Mushroom) has fallen over. However, the park's real fascination lies in the 250 million years of strata that you can see in the eroded cliffs of the rocks where fossils from all the geological periods have been found, among them fossils of the oldest dinosaurs known, including *Eoraptor*, 225 million years old and discovered in 1993. Your tour guide will show you the extraordinary strata, but you'll be disappointed to discover that there's no evidence of the dinosaur fossils here: you'll have to go to the Museo de Ciencias Naturales in San Juan (see page 265). The views throughout the park are impressive though, and the span of time you can witness here is mind-blowing. Highly recommended.

Tours and access

Entrance costs US$17, including a tour. The tour route is about 40 km long, lasting three hours, visiting only a part of the park but encompassing the most interesting sites. If you're in your own vehicle, you'll be accompanied by one of the rangers, whose knowledge and interest vary greatly: with luck you'll get a knowledgeable one. There's no fee but

Calingasta Valley → *For listings, see pages 269-271.*

The most beautiful part of the province, this long fertile valley lies 100 km west of San Juan between the jagged peaks of the snow-capped Andes *cordillera* and the stark crinkled range of the Sierra del Tontal, west of San Juan city. Inhabited since at least 10,000 BC, the Calingasta Valley was once the route of the Camino del Inca and though little of this history remains today, it still carries a compelling attraction. Its few oasis villages are charming places to stay to explore the hills, utterly tranquil and unspoilt.

The valley is reached from San Juan by the scenic paved Route Provincial 12. About halfway between Calingasta and Barreal, this passes, to the east, the Cerros Pintados, a range of red, white and grey stratified hills, striped like toothpaste. There are beautiful views of the whole valley here with its meandering river, a ribbon of green running through the dusty plain between the *cordillera* and Sierra del Tigre.

Calingasta → *Phone code 02648. Population 2100.*

The road from Pachaco to Calingasta follows the winding course of the Río San Juan through a steep sided gorge of astonishingly coloured and stratified rock. After Pachaco, a tip is appreciated. It can be crowded at holiday times, January, Easter and July. There are no regular buses that reach the park, so your only alternative is to take an excursion, either from San Juan, La Rioja or San Agustín. From San Juan, tours cost around US$70 (including breakfast and lunch) and take 14 hours. In San Agustín, there are a couple of small agencies (**Paula Tour**, T02646-420096; you'll see them at bus terminal) charging US$30, and giving you less time in the bus (ask at tourist office); they also offer a useful day trip combining Ischigualasto with Talampaya Park. Talampaya Park (in La Rioja province) lies only 94 km away from Ischigualasto, and some agencies organize a combined visit to both parks in one intense day: explore this option before you set off, and plan accordingly. For around five days every full moon, the park runs Full Moon tours, US$20 plus entrance fee.

A taxi to the park costs US$38 from San Agustín (recommended if there are four or five people), more expensive out of season. If you are travelling in your own transport, plan to overnight at San Agustín or the less lovely Villa Unión, as the drive is long, hot and tiring. From San Juan, both Ischigualasto and Talampaya can be reached by taking Route 20 east through Caucete and joining Route 141, via Difunta Correa to Marayes, then turning north onto Route 510 for 174 km northwest up to Los Baldecitos, from where it's 17 km to the entrance to Ischigualasto. If you're driving, beware of the donkeys and goats wandering across the roads.

Accommodation
You can camp opposite the ranger station in the park (US$2.50), which has a small museum, but bring all food and water as there's only an expensive *confitería* here, and nothing else for miles.

Further information
Visit www.ischigualasto.org, excellent website full of interesting research and articles about the park, well worth a look before you come; www.ischigualasto.com for tourism in San Juan (both in Spanish).

the landscape opens out, and Calingasta village lies at the confluence of the Ríos de los Patos and Calingasta, a vivid green splash on the otherwise arid landscape. This idyllic, secluded little village (1430 m, 135 km west of San Juan) is a delightful place to rest for a few days or plan a trek into the mountains. The Jesuit chapel, **Capilla de Nuestra Señora del Carmen**, is worth seeing, a simple adobe building dating from the 1600s, with the ancient original bells. There is a **tourist information office** ① *Av Argentina s/n, T02648-421066, or at the Municipalidad in Tamberías, Lavalle and Sarmiento, T02648-492005.*

Barreal → *Colour map 3, A2. Phone code 02648. Population 2400.*
Another peaceful oasis, Barreal (1650 m) offers more accommodation and services than Calingasta, and is the best base if you plan to trek into the Andes. However, it's still small and quiet enough to feel like a village, and offers spectacular views of the peaks all around. From here you can explore the mountains of **Sierra del Tontal**, which rise to 4000 m and give superb views over San Juan, Mercedario and Aconcagua, or climb the mighty **Cerro Mercedario** (6770 m) itself, one of the Andes' greatest peaks. For information, contact the **tourist office** ① *Calle Las Heras s/n, T02648-441066,* in Barreal.

Barreal is famous for *carrovelismo* (wind-car racing), thanks to its vast expanse of flat land known as Barreal del Leoncito, parallel to the main road, south of town. A more tranquil attraction are the two observatories at nearby **El Leoncito** (2348 m) ① *T02648-441088, www.casleo.gov.ar, daily 1000-1200, 1400-1800*. The observatories were built here because the climate is so sunny, with 320 clear nights a year, making it a perfect place for observing the stars and planets. The observatories are set within an immense nature reserve, covering 76,000 ha of the western slopes of the Sierra del Tontal and rising to over 4000 m. To the west there are fine views of Mercedario and other peaks in the *cordillera* with the flat plain and lush valley between. But hiking in the reserve is limited to one short walk to a small waterfall, near the entrance. Fauna includes suris (rheas), guanacos, red and grey foxes and peregrine falcons. There's no public transport except *remise* taxis from Barreal; take the partly paved road (17 km) that turns off the Route 412, 22 km south of Barreal. The **administrative office** ① *Calle Belgrano, T02648-441240, elleoncito@apn.gov.ar*, is in Barreal. There's also a ranger post at the observatory entrance; but no facilities, so if you if you want to camp, take all supplies.

Cerro Mercedario

Known in Chile as El Ligua and rising to 6770 m, the mighty peak of Mercedario, south-west of Calingasta, is considered by many mountaineers to be a more interesting climb than Aconcagua. It was first climbed in 1934 by a Polish expedition which went on to climb the nearby peaks of Pico Polaco (6050 m), La Mesa (6200 m), Alma Negra (6120 m) and Ramada (6410 m). This is a serious climb, and requires the same time to adjust to the altitude and the careful preparation as Aconcagua. You must not consider this expedition without hiring an experienced mountain guide (*baqueano*), who can provide mules if necessary, as there are no facilities and no rescue service. The best time to climb is from mid-December to the end of February. No authorization is required to climb but it is advisable to inform the *Gendarmería Nacional* at Barreal. Note that the mountain passes to Chile here are not officially open, making the crossing illegal.

San Agustín del Valle Fértil → *Phone code 02646. Population 3900.*

San Agustín is a charming little town, 250 km northeast of San Juan, and is definitely the best base for exploring the Ischigualasto park, with several good places to stay and eat. You could also fish in the Dique San Agustín, and buy ponchos and blankets from the local weavers here. There's a very helpful **tourist information office** ① *municipalidad, on the plaza, General Acha 52, T02646-420104, daily 0700-2200*, who can give you a map and advise on accommodation.

◉ San Juan province listings

For Sleeping and Eating price codes and other relevant information, see Essentials pages 30-36.

◉ Sleeping

San Juan city *p264*

Hotels in the **A-C** range all include breakfast and parking.

A Alkázar, Laprida 82 Este, T0264-421 4965, www.alkazarhotel.com.ar. A well-run, central 4-star hotel with very comfortable rooms, pool and gym. Excellent restaurant, where you can eat well for US$12 including wine.

C Alkristal, Av de Circunvalación 1055 Sur, T0264-425 4145, www.alkazarhotel.com.ar. One of the city's best bargains can only really be enjoyed if you have your own transport. Very comfortable, well-equipped rooms in a new high-rise international-style hotel with a pool. Poor breakfast but otherwise recommended, good value.

B-C Gran Hotel Provincial, Ignacio de la Roza 132 Este, T0264/4227501, www.granhotel provincial.com. Under new management this hotel is stylish and smart. A lovely pool, good service and modern rooms.

C América, 9 de Julio 1052 Este, T0264-427 2702, www.hotel-america.com.ar. A smart, modern hotel, nicely designed and very comfortable with good service. Tours arranged. Recommended.

C Selby, Rioja 183 Sur, T0264-422 4766, www.hotelselby.com.ar. Old-fashioned building, but this is a welcoming place with comfy rooms, good service and a restaurant.

Hostels

F pp **Triásico**, Pedro Echagüe 538 Este, T0264-421 9528, www.triasicohostel.com.ar. There's a homely feel in this house with simple dorms and doubles (**D**), some with own bath. Large patio with a pool in summer. Free transfer from bus station. They run their own travel agency (see Activities and tours).

F pp **Zonda**, Caseros 486 Sur, T0264-420 1009, www.zondahostel.com.ar. This is a central, slightly unfriendly hostel with a neat backyard. Rooms are simple and light, if not a little run-down, for 2-6, all with shared bath, and breakfast at any time is included.

Calingasta Valley *p266*

C-D Hotel de Campo Calingasta, take the left fork from the *gendarmería*, cross the river and continue 2 km, hotel is up a hill on your right, T0264-421220. A restored colonial-style building with airy rooms coming off a colonnaded patio, with open views to the mountains, and a pool in the garden. Very tranquil. Meals also available. Recommended.

Barreal *p267*

A La Querencia, C Florida, T0264-15436 4699, www.laquerenciaposada.com.ar. The upmarket choice is a small, homely place in rural surroundings with 6 comfortable rooms, all with a fireplace and beautiful views. Huge pool with a clear view to the Andes.

B Posada San Eduardo, Av San Martín s/n and Los Enamorados, T0264- 441046 . Charming, colonial-style house, where rooms open onto a courtyard. Very pleasant and relaxing. Also has a good restaurant. Recommended.

B-C Cabañas Doña Pipa, Mariano Moreno s/n, T0264-441004, www.cdpbarreal. com.ar. Attractive *cabañas* sleeping 6-8, well equipped, breakfast included, with a swimming pool, and great views to the mountains, open all year. Owned by the charming mountain guide Ramón Luis Ossa who opened an amazing Spa, Posada Don Ramón, which also has accommodation (www.posadadon ramon.com.ar). Highly recommended.

Hostels

F pp **Hostel Don Lisandro**, San Martín s/n, T0264-154 680 346, www.ansiltaturismo. com.ar. Small hostel set in lovely gardens. Rooms for 4 available at a cheaper price. US$1.50 extra for breakfast.

Camping

There is a municipal site in Barreal, C Belgrano, T0264-441241, which is well maintained with shady sites, *cabañas* and a pool. Open all year.

San Agustín del Valle Fértil *p268*

At Easter all accommodation is fully booked. There are a couple of good hotels, and lots of *cabañas*, but these are recommended:
B Finca La Media Luna, La Majadita, T0264-420 1950, www.fincalamedialuna.com.ar. Only 12 km from the centre of Barreal, each room in this hotel has a private outdoor area, with views over the trees to the mountains. A lovely well-sized pool adds to the attraction. Cabins for up to 4 (**A**) available.
B Hostería Valle Fértil, Rivadavia s/n, T02646-420015, www.alkazarhotel.com.ar. Smart, comfortable hotel with fine views from its elevated position above town (though it's an ugly building), also has *cabañas* and a good restaurant open to non-residents.
C Cabañas Valle Pintado, Tucumán y Mitre, T0264-434 5737, www.vallepintado.com.ar. Incredibly good-value option with cabins for up to 6 people (**B**) also available. Basic, clean rooms, with a large swimming pool surrounded by trees.

Hostels

F pp **Campo Base**, Tucumán between San Luis and Libertador, T02646-420063, www.hostelvalledelaluna.com.ar. Lively, cheerful hostel with basic dorms, shared bath and small kitchen. Discounts to HI members. Tours arranged to Ischigualasto.
F pp **Los Olivos**, Santa Fe and Tucumán, T02646-420115, posada_losolivos@hotmail. com. Welcoming and simple, with hostel accommodation and a good restaurant.

Camping

There are several campsites, of which the most highly recommended is **La Majadita** in a lovely spot on the river 8 km to the west of town with hot showers and great views. There's a municipal campsite in the town, on Calle Rivadavia, 5 blocks from the plaza, T02646-420104 (municipal office for information on both sites).

● Eating

San Juan city *p264*
ÝÝ Las Leñas, San Martín 1674 Oeste, T0264-423 5040. For superb steak, head straight to this popular and atmospheric *parrilla* in *quincho* (ranch) style with wooden interior. Arrive at 2100 to avoid queues later in the evening. Next door **Las Leñas** has another vegetarian restaurant at Rincón Verde.
ÝÝ Palito-Club Sirio Libanés, Entre Ríos 33 Sur, T0264-422 3841. A large, long-established place with pleasant decor, and good tasty food that includes Middle Eastern dishes.
ÝÝ Remolacha, Sarmiento Sur and Rivadavia, T0264-422 7070. Stylish, warm and welcoming place with superb Italian-inspired menu, delicious steaks and pastas. Recommended.
Ý Soychú, Av Ingnacio de la Roza 223 Oeste, T0264-422 1939. Excellent vegetarian food. Highly recommended, very good value.

San Agustín del Valle Fértil *p268*
Ý El Astiqueño, Tucumán next to the Dique. Good regional specialities.
Ý Noche Azul, General Acha s/n, off the plaza. *Parrilla* offering local *chivito* (kid).

▲ Activities and tours

San Juan city *p264*
Tour operators
Nerja Tours, Entre Ríos 178 Sur, T0264-421 5214, www.nerja-tours.com.ar. Conventional tours, local trips and combined visits to Valle de la Luna (Ischigualasto) and Talampaya.
Triásico, Pedro Echagüe 520 Este, T0264-4219528, www.triasico.com.ar. Day tours to Valle de la Luna (Ischigualasto), Calingasta and Las Quijadas Park in San Luis.

Valley Moon, Rivadavia 414 Oeste, T0264-421 4868, www.valleymoon.com. Excellent alternatives to conventional tours, and offering activities such as rafting and wind surfing at Rodeo, horse rides in remote valleys, climbing expeditions into the Andes peaks, including a 14-day ascent to Mercedario and tours to Calingasta and Valle de la Luna, with highly experienced guides. Recommended.

Barreal p267
Tour operators
Fortuna, C Mariano Moreno, T0264-404 0913, www.fortunaviajes.com.ar. Ramón Ossa is an expert guide for 1- to 15-day treks, horse-riding expeditions, and 4WD excursions into the Andes including up Mercedario and into the Cordón del Plata. Highly recommended.

☉ Transport

San Juan city p264
Air
For airport information, see page 264.

To **Buenos Aires**, Aerolíneas Argentinas/Austral, Av Libertador San Martín 215, T0264-422 0205, daily, 1½ hr.

Bus
For bus terminal information, see page 264.

Hourly departures to **Mendoza** with TAC and Media Agua and others, 2-2½ hrs, US$7-10. To **La Rioja**, 5-6 hrs, US$20-28, 6 companies including Andesmar and Flechabus; to **Catamarca**, 7-8 hrs, US$27-30, 6 companies. To **Tucumán**, 10-12 hrs, US$38-43, 6 companies;

to **Córdoba**, 8-9 hrs, US$20-28, 20 de Junio; Cata; Chevallier; San Juan-Mar del Plata; Socasa. To **Buenos Aires**, 20 de Junio; Auto-transporte San Juan; San Juan-Mar del Plata; TAC, 14-16 hrs, US$55-65.

Local To **San Agustín** with Vallecito, 3 daily, 4 hrs, US$10. Daily services in the afternoon (morning bus on Mon, Fri, Sat) to **Barreal**, 5 hrs, US$11, and **Calingasta**, 4 hrs with El Triunfo, T0264-421 4532.

Car hire
Avis, Laprida 82, T0264-425 4017; Classic, Av San Martín 163, T0264-422 4622.

Barreal p267
Bus
There is at least 1 bus daily to **San Juan**, 5 hrs, US$11, El Triunfo. Also minibus run by José Luis Sosa, T02648-441095.

San Agustín del Valle Fértil p268
Bus
Empresa Vallecito runs few services a day to **San Juan**, 4 hrs, US$10, and also 3 buses a week to **La Rioja**, 3 hrs, US$7.

☉ Directory

San Juan p264
Banks Open 0800-1300. Banelco and Link ATMs accept international credit cards. **Currency exchange** Cambio Santiago, General Acha 52 Sur, T0264-421 2232, Mon-Fri until 2100, Sat until 1300. **Internet** Several *locutorios* have internet, those at Rivadavia and Acha, on the plaza, and Mendoza 139 Sur are open on Sun.

La Rioja province

La Rioja is usually visited for the wonderful Parque Nacional Talampaya, a vast canyon of rock sculpted by wind and water into fantastic shapes, declared a World Heritage Site by UNESCO. However, there's also stunning scenery beyond the national park and places where you can find perfect tranquility, since the area is sparsely populated and little visited. Between the mountain ranges of the west are the extended Famatina and Vinchina valleys with verdant oasis villages at the foot of colourful eroded hills. In the arid southeast are the plains known as Llanos de los Caudillos, with the beautiful Sierra de los Llanos and extraordinary salt flats nearby. The city of La Rioja itself has two fine museums of indigenous art. For more information, see www.lariojaturismo.com (in English). ▶▶ *For listings, see pages 277-280.*

La Rioja city → *For listings, see pages 277-280. Colour map 1, C2.*

Though not obviously touristy, the capital of the province does offer decent accommodation and is a good starting point for a trip to more remote parts of the province. Founded in 1591 at the edge of the plains, with views of Sierra de Velasco, La Rioja has a few interesting museums, some neo-colonial houses and the oldest building in the country. Sleepy, and oppressively hot from November to March, the town becomes very lively every day after siesta time and during the celebrations of the local carnivals such as 'chaya' and the 'Tinkunaco'.

Ins and outs → *Phone code 03822. Population 170,000. Altitude 498 m.*

Airport VA Almonacid ① *T03822-439211*, is 5 km northeast of La Rioja city and taxis charge US$4 to the centre. The **bus terminal** ① *information T03822-425453*, is a few kilometres out of town at Avenida Circunvalación and Ortiz de Ocampo, T03822-468467. It offers left luggage from 0600 to 2100 (US$1.50 a day). To get into town take bus No 2, US$0.50, 15 minutes, or you could walk, 45 minutes to one hour.

Sights

The centre of the city is **Plaza 25 de Mayo** with its shady tipas, sycamores, araucarias and pine trees. Here, in 1637, the head of the native leader of an insurrection was exhibited as a trophy by the Spaniards. On the plaza is the early 20th-century **cathedral** with the image of San Nicolás de Bari and a room full of silver offerings.

Other interesting sights on the plaza are the neo-colonial government buildings, **Casa de Gobierno** and **Poder Judicial**, together with the pink building of the **Club Social**. The oldest surviving church in Argentina is one block northeast, the **Church of Santo Domingo** ① *Pelagio B Luna y Lamadrid*. It's a quaint stone temple, sparsely decorated inside but with magnificent carved wooden doors, dating from 1623 and renovated in later centuries. There is a lovely patio in the adjacent convent.

By far the most interesting sight in the town is the **Museo Arqueológico Inca Huasi** ① *JB Alberdi 650, Tue-Fri 0900-1300, 1700-2100, Sat 0900-1300, Sun and Mon closed, US$0.50*, which houses one of the most important collections of pre-Hispanic ceramics in Argentina. These beautiful pieces were made by the ancient cultures that originally inhabited the region, and include a remarkable funerary urn from the Aguada culture 1500 years ago.

The **tourist offices** ① *Av Perón 728, Mon-Fri 0800-1200, 1600-2000, or the provincial Luna 345, daily 0800-2100, T03822-426384, www.larioja.gov.ar*, are friendly, helpful and hand out a map of the city. Ask here about accommodation, including rooms with families (*casas de familia*).

Around La Rioja city

The **Quebrada del Río Los Sauces** is the fastest escape from the heat of the city, 10 km west via Route 75. There's a shaded river with campsites and a reservoir amidst lovely mountain scenery. From there, a 13-km dirt track (no shade) leads to the summit of the **Cerro de la Cruz** (1648 m) with great panoramic views, popular with hang gliders. Seven kilometres west of La Rioja is **Las Padercitas**, where there is a large, stone temple protecting the adobe remains of what is supposed to have been a Spanish fortress in the 16th century. Route 75 continues north and passes Las Padercitas, before following the Quebrada for 4 km to the reservoir of Dique Los Sauces. Regular minibuses or *diferenciales*, as they're called here, with **Transal** ① *T03822-421577*, to Villa Sanagasta from Rivadavia 519, take you to Quebrada and **Dique Los Sauces**, US$1.50. *Remise* taxis charge US$7.50. Some tour operators also run excursions.

Northeastern La Rioja (La Costa) → *For listings, see pages 277-280.*

If you have time and want a tranquil place to hang out or retreat to for a few days, with no distractions, head for the long narrow strip of land known as La Costa, lying at the edge of the plains at the foot of the Sierra de Velasco mountains. There are delightful small villages dotted about, green oases with old chapels, surrounded by vineyards, orchards and olive groves. Two roads head north from La Rioja. Route 75 to Aimogasta is the more interesting of the two, passing through Villa Sanagasta, Aminga and Anillaco and all the small towns of La Costa. Alternatively, Route 38 runs northeast to Catamarca and you could take a detour to visit thermal baths at **Termas Santa Teresita** ① *Km 33 take R9 (later 10) to Villa Mazán, Km 99.* The *termas* are some 7 km north and there's a budget **Hostería Termas Santa Teresita** ① *T03827-420445*, which has an open-air thermal pool, thermal baths in all rooms and breakfast included.

The first town you'll come across on the way to La Costa is **Villa Sanagasta**, nicely set among orchards and where, on the last Friday in September, there is a big religious procession to La Rioja. A few kilometres further, at **Agua Blanca**, there is a lovely Alpine-style cabin, **El Alpino** where good meals are served.

There are a few curious sights near Anillaco: a house that looks like something from a fairy tale or horror story (depending on your mood), called **Castillo de Dionisio**, at Santa Vera Cruz, built on a rock and surrounded by cacti; the massive **Señor de la Peña**, a naturally shaped rock and very popular religious sanctuary during Holy Week, lying in a desert plain 30 km east of Anillaco; and the 18th-century **chapel of Udpinango**. The largest town in the area, at the heart of the olive production, is **Aimogasta**, which serves as a good transport hub with links to several towns in the province of Catamarca.

Famatina Valley → *For listings, see pages 277-280.*

One of the richest areas of the province and only a few hours west of the capital, this immense valley is attractively flanked to the west by the magnificent Famatina Mountains, 6000 m high, and to the east by the Sierra de Velasco, rising to 4000 m. Once an important mining area, it's now famous for its tasty wines, olives and walnuts. You can combine the most challenging treks in the region with a relaxing stay in a calm, rural *finca*.

Parque Nacional Talampaya → *Phone code: 03825*

Extending over 215,000 ha at an altitude of 1200 m, Talampaya is remarkable for its impressive rock formations, of which the main feature is the 4-km canyon surrounding the River Talampaya. A stroll through this vast chasm gives you the unforgettable experience of being entirely dwarfed by the landscape. Though some sections of the park are only accessible by vehicle, guided walks and cycle rides are possible.

The park and circuits

The park itself occupies a basin between the Sierra Morada to the west and the Sierras de Sañogasta to the east. This is the site of an ancient lake, where piled-up sediments have since been eroded by water and wind for the last 200 million years, forming a dramatic landscape of pale red hills named **Sierra de los Tarjados**. Numerous fossils have been found, and some 600-year-old petro-glyphs can be seen not far from the access to the gorge. As in Ischigualasto, along the canyon there are extraordinarily shaped structures which have been given names such as 'the balconies', 'the lift', 'the crib' or 'the owl'. At one point, the gorge narrows to 80 m wide and rises to 143 m deep. A refreshing leafy spot in the centre of the gorge has been named 'the botanical garden' due to the amazing diversity of plants and tree specimens living here. The end of the canyon is marked by the imposing cliffs of 'the Cathedral' and the curious 'King on a camel'. 'The chessboard' and 'the monk', 53 m high, lie not far beyond the gorge, marking the end of the so-called **El Monje circuit**. Only accessible with 4WD vehicles, another circuit, **Circuito Los Cajones**, continues in the same direction up to '*los pizarrones*', an enormous wall of rock covered with petroglyphs, and then to '*los cajones*', a narrow pass between rock walls. Two additional circuits in other areas within the park are organized from an entrance on Route 76, Km 134. **Ciudad Perdida**, southeast of the gorge, accessible only with 4WD vehicles, leads to an area of high cliffs and a large number of breathtaking rock formations, and the **Arco Iris circuit** leads to a multi-coloured canyon.

Access and information

The park is reached by Route 76: turn off at Km 134 (217 km from La Rioja), 61 km north of the police checkpoint at Los Baldecitos and 55 km south of Villa Unión, onto a paved road, 14 km long. Independent access is possible, since buses or *combis* (minibuses) linking

---

Chilecito → *Colour map 1, C2. Phone code 03825. Population 30,000. Altitude 1074 m.*

The second biggest town in the province and certainly the most attractive, Chilecito lies at the foot of the snow-capped Famatina Mountains in an area of vineyards and olive groves, and is the best base for exploring the hills and nearby villages. Founded in 1715, its name derives from the influx of Chilean miners in the 19th century. The town centre, with lots of cafés and a modern church, is centred around Plaza de los Caudillos, beautifully shaded with mature pine and red gum trees, and two pergolas covered with grapevines. Each February the plaza is the focus of the *chaya* celebrations (see Festivals and events, page 278) and the anniversary of the town's foundation. The bus station can be found on Avenida Perón (on the south access to town).

There is good local wine to sample at the **Cooperativa La Riojana** ① *La Plata 646, T03825-423150, www.lariojana.com.ar, free 45-min guided visits and a smart wine shop open in the morning*, where you can watch local grapes being processed to make a wide

La Rioja and Villa Unión stop at the park entrance, but note that it's a long (14 km), lonely and unshaded walk to the administration building. No private vehicles are allowed beyond the administration building, where you have to park, and arrange alternative transport around the park: either a park vehicle, walking or bicycle.

Accommodation

The only option inside the park is a basic campsite, next to the administration office (US$1.50 per person). The closest base for visiting the park is the small town of La Unión, 67 km north, see under Western La Rioja, page 276, see www.turismovillaunion.gov.ar.

Tour operators

Tour operators in La Rioja and Chilecito organize tours into the park, sometimes combining a visit with Ischigualasto, which is otherwise difficult to access. Check when you book that both the entrance fee and guides' fees are included in the cost of your tour.

Tours of the park along the **El Monje**, and **Circuito Los Cajones** circuits can be arranged at the administration office, but not for the **Ciudad Perdida** and **Arco Iris** circuits. These both take 4½ hours and cost US$22 per person each; tours start from Route 76, Km 133.5. For more information, call T03822-1568 1114.

Guided walks, cycle rides and tours

Guides speak English.

Guided walks to Quebrada Don Eduardo, a secondary gorge, next to the canyon (about three hours, US$17 per person).

Guided bike rides (three hours, US$17 per person, cycle and helmet provided) follow the whole length of the *cañón* up to *'la catedral'*. A shorter journey is also on offer up to 'the botanical garden'.

Guided visits in a park vehicle for El Monje circuit (two hours, US$22 per person), Circuito Los Cajones circuit (four hours, US$24 per person).

Best time to visit

The best time to visit is in the morning, when the natural light is best, avoiding the strong winds in the afternoon.

Entry cost

US$6.50, September to April 0800-1800, May to August 0830-1730.

Further information

Call the park administration T0351-570 9909, or see www.talampaya.com (in English) or www.talampaya.gov.ar (in Spanish), for more information on excursions and for advance bookings.

---

variety of red and white wines, including organic products, many of which are exported to Europe under the labels Inti, 7 Days, Pircas Negras or Santa Florentina. For an easy five-minute walk from the plaza, head along El Maestro, past the pleasant Parque Municipal and up to the **Mirador El Portezuelo** where there are splendid panoramic views of the town and the Velasco and Famatina mountains. Another delightful nearby attraction is the botanical garden at **Chirau Mita** ① *Av Primera Junta, Km 0.25, take Arturo Marasso northwards, turning right at Primera Junta, and it's on the way to La Puntilla, T03825-424531, www.chiraumita.com.ar*. The beautiful private garden has rich collection of over 1500 cacti and succulent plants (native and non-native species) growing on terraces on the rocky slopes, and using the same techniques ancient Andes people used for cultivation. Not to be missed. For further information contact the **tourist office** ① *Castro and Bazán 52, T03825-422688*. A useful website is www.chilecitotour.com.

One of the pleasures of Northwestern Argentina is a visit to a *finca*, or farm. **Finca Samay Huasi** ⓘ *San Miguel, 3 km southeast of town, T03825-422629, Mon-Fri 0800-1300, 1330-1930, Sat-Sun 0800-1200, 1500-1900 (till 1800 in winter), closed 22 Dec-6 Jan, US$1*, is an attractive place to come and relax for a day, or stay overnight. The estate was once the summer residence of Joaquín V González, founder of La Plata University, who designed the gardens using native trees and strange stone monoliths expressing his love of ancient cultures. There's also a small natural-history museum.

Around Chilecito

While the Famatina Mountains are best explored on a guided tour, you can amble to the villages around Chilecito quite easily, with their old adobe houses and historical chapels. In **Famatina**, Good Friday and Christmas Day are celebrated with fabulous processions, and there's also a good site for paragliding. At **Santa Florentina** (8 km northwest of Chilecito), the impressive remains of a huge early-20th-century foundry can be reached from Chilecito and La Mejicana mine by cable car. A few kilometres west of Sañogasta, Ruta 40 leads to the eroded red sandstone rocks of **Cuesta de Miranda**, one of the most spectacular routes in the province. Winding its way between Sierra de Famatina and Sierra de Sañogasta, it rises to 2020 m and drops again, passing through 320 bends in 11,500 m.

Western La Rioja → *For listings, see pages 277-280.*

Western La Rioja is remote and undiscovered, but you might want to base yourself in the town of La Unión for Talampaya Park, or to visit the strange otherworldly landscapes of the Reserva Natural Laguna Brava. The westernmost inhabited valley in La Rioja (also known as Valle del Bermejo) follows the **Río Vinchina** which flows along the western side of the Sierra de Famatina. The valley can be reached from La Rioja city along Route 26 via the Parque Nacional Talampaya, or from Chilecito by Ruta 40, via the spectacular **Cuesta de Miranda**.

Villa Unión and around → *Colour map 1, C1. Phone code 03825. Population 4700.*

Some 92 km west of Nonogasta, Villa Unión (1240 m) is the largest settlement in the valley and is another base for visits to the Parque Nacional Talampaya, 67 km south. North of Villa Unión, paved Route 76 heads along the arid valley to **Villa Castelli** and **Vinchina** (70 km north of Villa Unión) offering the last comfortable accommodation option before the high mountains (**C-D**), **Corona del Inca** ⓘ *T03825-1567 5945, www.coronadelinca.com.ar*.

On the west side of Route 76, on the northern outskirts of town, there is an extraordinary testament to ancient cultures, the **Estrella de Vinchina**, the only surviving star-shaped stone mosaic made by ancient settlers centuries ago. Immediately north of Vinchina, Route 76 enters the spectacular **Quebrada de la Troya** and 36 km northwest of Vinchina, it reaches **Jagüe** (1900 m), with food and basic facilities, and where you will be approached by park wardens of the nearby Reserva Natural Laguna Brava (see below). This is the starting point for a 154-km-long road to Chile through the Andean mountain pass of **Pircas Negras** (4165 m). About every 20 to 30 km you'll see stone huts, built in the 19th century to shelter cattle wranglers on their way across the Andes. The road also gives access to a vast, empty territory of the Reserva Natural Laguna Brava.

Reserva Natural Laguna Brava → *Colour map 1, C1.*

ⓘ *Entry US$2 per person.*

This reserve protects Laguna Brava, a salt lake, 4271 m, 16 km long, 3 km wide, and some 405,000 ha of mountains and a high plateau, rising from 3800 m to 4360 m. The lake lies further northwest beyond the Portezuelo del Peñón, with superb views over the lake, and some of the mightiest volcanoes on earth in the background. From the left, these are: the perfect cone **Veladero** (6436 m), **Reclus** (6335 m), **Los Gemelos** (6130 m), **Pissis** (6882 m) the highest volcano in the world, though inactive, and **Bonete** (6759 m) which is also visible from Villa Unión and Talampaya. The park is home to thousands of flamingos and *vicuñas*, the more elegant cousins of the llama. There are many organized 4WD tours on offer here, which take you to the high plateau, the Laguna Brava itself and, occasionally, the small lagoon Corona del Inca lying at the crater of a volcano at 5300 m (see Activities and tours, page 279). The nearest settlement is Jagüe, at the western end of Route 76, and from here, 4WD or mountain bike are essential to enter the park. The nearest accommodation is at Villa Unión. Access is limited by summer rainfall and winter snow, so the best times for a visit are April and early May.

⦿ La Rioja province listings

For Sleeping and Eating price codes and other relevant information, see Essentials pages 30-36.

⦿ Sleeping

La Rioja city *p272*
A fan or a/c are essential for the hot summer nights. High season is Jul and winter holidays.
AL Naindo Park Hotel, San Nicolás de Bari 475, T03822-470700, www.naindoparkhotel. com. Central 5-star hotel with huge slightly dated doubles, access to the heated swimming pool and a gym.
AL-A Plaza, San Nicolás de Bari y 9 de Julio (on Plaza 25 de Mayo), T03822-425215, www.plazahotel-larioja.com. Attractive 4-star place with a great pool on the top floor and breakfast included; all rooms with a/c. Some have good plaza views but can be noisy.
A King's, Av F Quiroga 1070, T03822-422122. A pricey 4-star hotel with buffet breakfast included, a/c, gym, pool and fine rooms. Car rental available.
B Vincent Apart Hotel, Santiago del Estero 10 y San Nicolás de Bari, T03822-432326. Spotless new flats for up to 4 people with a/c. Dining room, small kitchen with fridge, and breakfast is included. Excellent value for a group of 3-4. Recommended.

C Savoy, San Nicolás de Bari y Roque A Luna, T03822-426894, hotelsavoy@infovia.com.ar. Located in a quiet residential area, this is a neat, comfortable hotel with breakfast and a/c included, though it has some strangely shaped rooms. It's worth paying the extra 30% for more spacious rooms with renovated bathrooms on the 2nd floor.

Camping
There are several sites along Av Ramírez de Velasco, in the northwest suburbs on the way to Las Padercitas and Dique Los Sauces, but the most appealing with pool, hot water and electricity is the one belonging to Sociedad Sirio-Libanesa at Quebrada de los Sauces, 13 km west of town.

Northeastern La Rioja (La Costa) *p273*
E Hostería Anillaco (ACA), T03827-494064. The best place to stay in the area. Breakfast included, a pool and also a decent restaurant.

Chilecito *p274*
C Chilecito (ACA) T. Gordillo and A G Ocampo, T03825-422201. A/c, comfortable with breakfast, safe parking, pool and cheap set menus.

C Finca del Paimán, Mariano Moreno 6 and Santa Rosa (at San Miguel, 3 km southeast of town), T/F03825-425102. Accommodation rates include breakfast and transport to or from Chilecito. The *finca* is a delightful 4.5-ha farm where you can just chill out or plan an excursion to the mountains. Warmly recommended, book in advance.
C Mary Pérez, Florencio Dávila 280, T03825-423156, hostal_mp@hotmail.com. Best value in town for its comfortable rooms. Good breakfast. Recommended (though check if the nearby sports club is holding a party).

Hostels
F pp Hostel del Paimán, El Maestro 188, T03825-425102, www.fincadelpaiman.com.ar. This is the best budget choice, with the same owners as **Finca del Paimén**, above. An old house in the town centre, friendly and welcoming, with dorms, singles, doubles and rooms for 3-4, with or without own bath. All basic and open onto a lovely, peaceful garden. Discounts to HI members.

Camping
There are 3 sites at Santa Florentina and Las Talas, 8 km northwest of Chilecito (*remise* taxis charge US$4).

Villa Unión and around *p276*
B Pircas Negras, R76, T03825-470611, www.hotelpircasnegras.com. Easy to spot as it stands out a mile: the only large building at the side of the road amongst the other more humble dwellings, this modern place is the most comfortable in town, with good rooms, a restaurant, a pool and lots of excursions on offer.
C Noryanepat, Joaquín V González 150, T03825-470133. A small, modern, family-run hotel; good value, although rooms are a bit cramped, but they do have a/c and breakfast is included.

❶ Eating

La Rioja city *p272*
❝❝ El Corral, Av Quiroga and Rivadavia. Try the traditional rustic *comidas de campo*, a rich *locro* (traditional stew) or a *puchero*, *asado* or *pollo al disco* (chicken cooked in an open pan on the fire); there are good local wines too.
❝❝ La Vieja Casona, Rivadavia 427, T03825-425996. A popular smart *parrilla*. The *lechón a la parrilla* (pork) with apple sauce is superb.
❝ La Aldea de la Virgen de Luján, Rivadavia 756, T03825-460305. Fill up cheaply in a small and popular place and try also the Middle Eastern dishes.

Chilecito *p274*
❝❝ El Rancho de Ferrito, Pelagio B Luna 647, T03825-422481. A very popular *parrilla*, where grilled meats and regional dishes such as *locro* can be enjoyed with local wines.
❝ Capri, 25 de Mayo and Joaquín V González. Traditional *confitería* on the plaza serving snacks and some basic meals.
❝ Club Arabe, 25 de Mayo, entre Zelada y Dávila and Famatina. Despite its name, Middle Eastern food only available on request, but you can eat the usual dishes on tables outside under thick grapevines.

❸ Festivals and events

La Rioja city *p272*
It's worth planning your visit to coincide with one of La Rioja's 2 lively festivals.
Feb Chaya. At this very popular festival, flour and basil are thrown, and percussion music is played for 4 nights at the Estadio del Centro.
Jan Tinkunaco. Beginning on New Year's Eve and lasting 4 days, this festival is a vestige of the peacemaking efforts of San Francisco Solano. A colourful procession accompanies the meeting of the images of San Nicolás de Bari and the Niño Alcalde in front of the cathedral.

▲ Activities and tours

La Rioja city *p272*
The most common destination, Talampaya, is usually offered together with Valle de la Luna (Ischigualasto Provincial Park) in 1 long day tour, plus occasionally Cuesta de Miranda in 1 or 2 days. Check if park entry, IVA (VAT) and meals are included in the price. Trips to the high mountains and plateaux in the west are restricted to good weather conditions, Sep-Apr.

Aguada, D Vélez Sarsfield 742, T03822-433 695. Highly professional services for full-day excursions to Talampaya, combined either with Valle de la Luna or Chilecito, or consider an amazing 4-day trip including Talampaya, Valle de la Luna, Laguna Brava and Chilecito. Some English and French spoken.

Corona del Inca, Pelagio B Luna 914, T03822-450054, www.coronadelinca.com.ar. A wide range of excursions including Talampaya and Valle de la Luna, and also including outstanding 4WD expeditions to the Corona del Inca lake at 5300 m. English spoken, email or call first.

Extreme, T03822-437690 or T03822-1566 1189, www.expedition-extreme.com.ar. Several excursions to the parks and the provincial valleys, and climbing expeditions in the Andes plus a trip to the Sierra de los Llanos to spot condors in a deep ravine.

Néstor Pantaleo, Ecuador 813, T03822-422 103. Pantaleo is an experienced photographer and runs 4WD trips to La Costa, Talampaya, Valle de la Luna and the mountainous west. Several languages spoken.

Chilecito *p274*
Chilecito is an excellent base not only for amazing treks in the Famatina Mountains, but also for day trips to Talampaya and Valle de la Luna.

Alejo Piehl, T/F03825-425102, www.fincadel paiman.com.ar. Experienced guide Alejo offers all-inclusive 1-day tours to Talampaya and Valle de la Luna for US$65 per person and a variety of unforgettable 2- to 3-day

treks (US$45-140 per person) to the colourful slopes of nearby Famatina, visiting abandoned cable-car stations on the way to the summit. Also 1-day 4WD trips to El Oro or La Mejicana (at 4400 m). Recommended. **Inka Ñan**, T03825-423641. Organizes excursions to the main attractions in the province.

⊖ Transport

La Rioja city *p272*
Air
For airport information, see page 272.

To **Buenos Aires**, Aerolíneas Argentinas, flights usually stop at **Catamarca**.

Airline offices Aerolíneas Argentinas, Belgrano 63, T03822-426307.

Bus
Note there is a new bus terminal a few kilometres out of town at Av Circunvalación y Ortiz de Ocampo, T03822-468467. It offers left luggage 0600-2100 (US$1.50 a day). To get into town take bus No 2, US$0.50, 15 mins, or you could walk, 45 mins-1 hr.

To **Buenos Aires**, 15-17 hrs, US$72, Chevallier, General Urquiza; to **Catamarca**, 2 hrs, US$8, many companies; to **Córdoba**, 6½ hrs, US$23, **Chevallier**, General Urquiza, Socasa. To **Mendoza**, 6-7 hrs, US$22, many companies, to **San Juan**, same companies, 5-6 hrs, US$21. To **Tucumán**, 5-6 hrs, US$20.50, several companies. To **San Agustín del Valle Fértil**, 3 hrs, US$13, Vallecito. Facundo and Nuevo Cuyo go daily to several destinations, mainly **Chilecito**, 3 hrs, US$6; **Villa Unión**, 4 hrs, US$9; **Vinchina**, 5 hrs, US$11.

Minibus (diferenciales or combis)
Popular alternative to buses, booked in advance, and costing a few extra pesos, but usually faster and more frequent (though fewer on Sun) than ordinary buses. All arrivals and departures are from their offices: **El Zonda**, Dorrego 79, T03822-421930;

to **Pagancillo**, **Villa Unión** and **Vinchina**. Transal, Rivadavia 519, T03822-421577; to **Villa Sanagasta** (via **Quebrada** and **Dique Los Sauces**), US$1.50; and **Las Padercitas**. La Riojana and Family Bus, El Maestro 61, T03822-435279 or T03822-420222; to **Chilecito** and **Aimogasta** (via **La Costa**). Maxi Bus, Rivadavia y Dávila (Esso petrol station), T03822-435979; to **San Blas de los Sauces**.

Car hire
King's, Av F Quiroga 1070, T03822-422122; Winner Rent a Car, Santa Fe 642, T03822-431318.

Remise taxi
Libertad, T03822-432000.

Chilecito *p274*
Bus
To **Buenos Aires**, T03822-423279, 17 hrs, US$63, **General Urquiza**; via **Córdoba**, 7 hrs, US$26. To **La Rioja**, 3 hrs, US$6, **Facundo** and **Nuevo Cuyo**.

Remise taxis
San Cayetano, T03822-424848; San Roque, T03822-425002.

Around Chilecito *p276*
Minibus
Daily service with several minibuses (*combis*) from **Chilecito** to many villages in the valley.

⊕ Directory

La Rioja city *p272*
Currency exchange US$ cash changed at **Banco de Galicia**, Buenos Aires and San Nicolás de Bari. More ATMs along San Nicolás de Bari. **Internet** A handful of good broadband centres on the plaza 25 de Mayo and surroundings. **Post office** Av Perón 258, Western Union branch.

Chilecito *p274*
Currency exchange US$ cash can be changed at **Banco Macro**, Castro Barros 50 (on plaza). **Internet** *Telecentro* with internet on the plaza. **Post office** Joaquín V. González and Pelagio B Luna, Western Union branch.

Contents

Footprint features

Border crossings

Argentina–Chile, *see pages 299
  and 329*
Argentina–Bolivia, *see page 327*

At a glance

◉ **Getting around** The cheap local buses, although slow and hardly modern, connect even the smallest towns in the region.

◉ **Time required** A minimum of 5-7 days will allow you to see both Jujuy and Salta, with a stop in Cafayate and the Quebrada de Humahuaca.

☼ **Weather** Mostly warm days and cool nights year round with temperatures rising to 47°C in summer.

✖ **When not to go** Jan-Feb can be extremely hot and Easter can be very busy – accommodation books up and tour companies sell out.

The Northwest

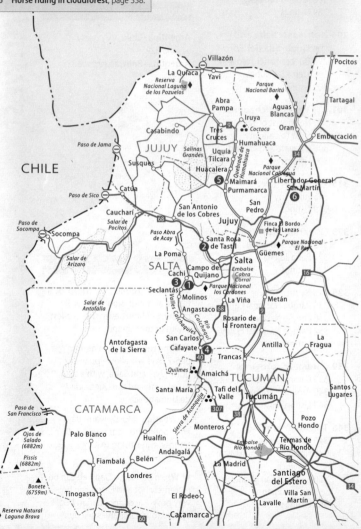

N

50 km
50 miles

BOLIVIA

CHILE

Villazón
La Quiaca
Yavi
Pocitos
Reserva
Nacional Laguna
de los Pozuelos
Parque
Nacional Baritú
Tartagal
Abra
Pampa
Iruya
Aguas
Blancas
Casabindo
Tres
Cruces
Coctaca
Oran
Embarcación
Paso de Jama
JUJUY
Salinas
Grandes
Humahuaca
Uquía
34
Susques
Tilcara
Huacalera
Quebrada de Humahuaca
Parque
Nacional Calilegua
Catúa
5
Maimará
Libertador General
San Martín
Paso de Sico
Cauchari
Salar de
Pocitos
San Antonio
de los Cobres
Purmamarca
San
Pedro
6
Paso de
Socompa
Socompa
Salar de
Arizaro
Jujuy
Finca El Bordo
de las Lanzas
68
Paso Abra
de Acay
Santa Rosa
de Tastil
Parque Nacional
El Rey
Salar de
Antofalla
La Poma
2
Güemes
Salta
SALTA
Campo de
Quijano
Embalse
Cabra
Corral
Cachi
3
1
16
Seclantás
Parque Nacional
los Cardones
Antofagasta
de la Sierra
Molinos
La Viña
Metán
Angastaco
68
Rosario de
la Frontera
9
San Carlos
Cafayate
4
Antilla
La
Fragua
Quilmes
40
Trancas
Amaichá
TUCUMAN
Santa María
Tafí del
Valle
Santos
Lugares
Paso de
San Francisco
CATAMARCA
Sierra de Aconquija
307
Tucumán
Pozo
Hondo
38
Ojos de
Salado
(6882m)
Palo Blanco
Hualfín
Monteros
Termas de
Río Hondo
34
Pissis
(6882m)
Embalse
Río Hondo
Bonete
(6759m)
Fiambalá
Belén
Andalgalá
La Madrid
Santiago
del Estero
Reserva Natural
Laguna Brava
Tinogasta
Londres
La Madrid
Villa San
Martín
60
El Rodeo
Lavalle
Catamarca

The northwest of the country is a different Argentina. The Andes here are wilder and less travelled, and ancient civilizations have left ruined cities sprawling over rugged mountainsides in the vast canyons at Quilmes, Purmamarca and Santa Rosa de Tastil. Traditional Andean culture is thriving, with lively celebrations of the ancient *Pachamama* (Mother Earth) festivities throughout the indigenous communities. The poorer province of Jujuy has even more spectacular riches in the stunning Quebrada de Humahuaca, a vast gorge of stratified rock where tiny white churches are filled with treasures, and Easter draws thousands of musicians in a moving procession.

Landscapes of the northwest are among Argentina's most breathtaking: winding roads snake up the Quebrada del Toro, steep gorges clad with cloudforest, through terracotta canyons dotted with giant cacti and then streak across the endless expanse of the high-altitude *puna*, with its shimmering salt flats and vast skies. Set off up the dramatic Cuesta del Obispo to the magical Valles Calchaquíes, to find giant cacti set against snow-capped mountains, and tranquil villages at Cachi and Molinos, or sophisticated wineries at Colomé and the charming village of Cafayate – a wine-growing region to rival Mendoza.

Salta is the splendid colonial city at the heart of the region, with fine hotels in its plazas of crumbling buildings and waving palm trees, vibrant *peñas* where passionate *folclore* music is sung live, luxurious *fincas* all around for great hospitality and unforgettable horse riding up into the cloudforest. For more information on the area, see www.norteargentino.gov.ar (in Spanish) or www.turismoensalta.com (in English).

Salta city and around

→ *Colour map 1, B3. Phone code 0387. Population 490,000. Altitude 1190 m.*

Salta is one of Argentina's most charismatic and historical cities; its colourful past is tangible in palm-filled plazas lined with crumbling 17th-century buildings, such as the plum-coloured Iglesia San Francisco and the handsome colonial Cabildo. Its fine museums chart the city's fascinating past, including the amazing finds from an Inca burial site on remote Mount Llullaillaco. Salta's tourist infrastructure is well established, and agencies offer trips south to the beautiful Calchaquí Valley, where oasis villages are timeless retreats, and there are splendid wineries around Cafayate. You could take the 'train to the clouds' into the dramatic Quebrada del Toro, or take your time to explore the ancient archaeological site of Santa Rosa de Tastil. Head further west into the shimmering salt flats, and discover the ancient way of life of the puna (high-altitude desert).

Salta city is worth at least a couple of days of your trip. It buzzes with life in the mornings, comes to a complete halt at lunchtime and comes alive again at night. Balmy evenings are perfect for wandering the streets to find live music played with passion in the local peñas of calle Balcarce. Or sample the superb food such as the locro, tamales and humitas for which Salta is famous, as you quaff a glass or two of fine 'high-altitude' wine grown in the Calchaquí Valley. This region is rich in indigenous culture, and you can buy the characteristic blood-red Güemes ponchos, as well as other handicrafts, in smart shops around the main plaza, or in the Mercado Artesenal. Sit in the atmospheric plaza cafés at midday to get a flavour of Salteño society: from elegant aristocrats to businessmen having their shoes shined, farmers from the outlying campos chewing coca and crowds of indigenous teenagers. The city is particularly lively in the second week of September, when the Fiesta del Milagro is celebrated with a huge procession uniting the population in an ancient communal act of superstition: parading the Christian figures that keep Salta safe from earthquakes.
➤➤ *For listings, see pages 289-295.*

Ins and outs

Getting there
There are daily flights from Buenos Aires to Salta's **airport** ① *T0387-4243115*, 12 km south of the city. The airport has a café, *locutorio* with internet, ATM and car rental companies. There's also a **Movitrack** stand, useful for information on tours as you wait for your luggage. **Tourist information** is in the main hall, next to **Avis**, but isn't always open. **Transfer del Pino** buses meet all flights, US$3.50 to the centre; or take a *remise* taxi, US$8, 15 minutes. The **bus terminal** ① *T0387-421 4716, information T0387-401 1143*, is eight blocks east of the main plaza; walk along Avenida Yrigoyen and then Caseros, or take a taxi to the centre for US$2.50. There is a *confitería*, toilets, *locutorio*, café, *panadería*, kiosks, ATM and left luggage (U$1.50 for 6 hours), but no internet. The **train station** ① *20 de Febrero and Ameghino*, is nine blocks north of Plaza 9 de Julio, a taxi costs US$2, and receives only the tourist *Tren a las Nubes* (Train to the Clouds), and cargo trains from Chile along the Quebrada del Toro. ➤➤ *For further details, see Transport page 294.*

Getting around
The best way to get around Salta is on foot, allowing you to soak up the atmosphere and see the main examples of its splendid architecture, all within four blocks of the main plaza, 9 de Julio. The main area for nightlife (Thursday to Saturday), and site of a weekend handicraft market is Calle Balcarce, 10 blocks north and west of the main plaza. This is five minutes in a

taxi (US$1.50), but it's a pleasant stroll, past attractive Plaza Güemes. There is also a hop-on, hop-off bus called the BTS (Bus Turístico Salta) which does a circuit of the town, www.busturisitcosalta.com.ar. To get a grand overview of the whole city, take the cable car from central Parque San Martín to the top of Cerro San Bernardo (or it's a 45-minute walk if you have the energy). At the top there are impeccably manicured gardens, waterfalls and a café with an amazing view. The countryside is on your doorstep, with lush jungle to explore on horseback in nearby San Lorenzo – also a good place for a relaxing evening. Salta city is certainly worth a day or two of your trip to enjoy the nightlife and museums, before you head off to explore the spectacular landscape all around.

Tourist information

The **provincial tourist office** ⓘ *Buenos Aires 93 (1 block from main plaza), T0387-4310950, www.turismosalta.gov.ar, Mon-Fri 0800-2100, Sat and Sun 0900-2000*, is helpful and provides free maps, both of the city and the province, as well as offering advice on accommodation and tours. Staff speak English. The **municipal tourist office** ⓘ *Caseros 711, T0800 -77 0300, Mon-Fri 0800-2100, Sat and Sun 0900-2100*, is for Salta city only and is small but helpful. There is also a **national parks office** ⓘ *España 366, 3rd floor, T0387-431 2683, Mon-Fri 0800-1500, elrey@apn.gov.ar*. Useful websites include www.saltaciudad.com.ar, www.saltargentina.com.ar, and www.redsalta.com.

Background → *See also History, page 668.*

The first Spanish expedition, led by Diego de Almagro from Cuzco (Peru), entered Argentina in 1536 and soon a busy trade route was established through the Quebrada de Humahuaca (now Jujuy). Along this route the Spanish founded a group of towns: Santiago del Estero, Tucumán, Salta and Jujuy. Throughout the colonial period these were the centres of white settlement and *encomiendas* were established to subdue the indigenous population. Jesuit and Franciscan missions were also attempted, but resistance was fierce, especially in the Calchaquí and Humahuaca valleys and, as a result, this is one of the few areas in Argentina that retains a rich indigenous culture.

The city of Salta was founded in 1582 and became one of the viceroyalty's most important administrative centres, governing a wide area, and gaining considerable wealth from the fertile outlying areas. The city also had an important role in the Wars of Independence between 1810 and 1821, when General Güemes led gaucho anti-Royalist forces to victory, utilizing their detailed knowledge of the terrain and inventing the now-famous red poncho which his men wore. Through the 19th century, Salta suffered a decline, since trade went directly to the country's new capital, Buenos Aires. Relatively little immigration and expansion allowed the city's colonial buildings to survive, boosted by neo-colonial architecture in the 1930s when there was a large influx of newcomers. Today, Salta retains its old aristocratic upper-class population but has a more affluent middle class than its neighbour, Jujuy. Tourism has taken off since devaluation in 2002, and is now the province's main source of income.

Sights

Plaza 9 de Julio and around

In just a few hours you can get a feel for the city. At its heart is the pleasant Plaza 9 de Julio, richly planted with wonderful tall palm trees, orange trees and surrounded by colonial-style buildings. The whole area has been spruced up and three sides of it are now pedestrianized with cafés where you can sit and watch teenagers hanging out on the plaza and smart businessmen having their shoes shined. There's an impressive **Cabildo** built in 1783, one of the few to be found intact in the whole country, and behind its

Salta

N

100 metres
100 yards

pleasingly uneven arches is an impressive museum, the **Museo Histórico del Norte** ① *Tue-Fri 0900-1800, Sat and Sun 0900-1330, closed Mon, US$1.50 (free on Wed)*. In a series of rooms around two open courtyards, the collection charts the region's history from pre-Hispanic times, with particularly good displays on the Wars of Independence and on Güemes leading the gauchos to victory. Upstairs, among some lovely religious art, is a fine golden 18th-century pulpit and some Cuzco school paintings, while outside are carriages and an ancient wine press. Fascinating and informative.

Opposite the museum, on the north side of the plaza, is the lovely **cathedral**, built 1858-1878, now strangely painted pastel pink, and open mornings and evenings so that you can admire a huge baroque altar (1807) and the images of the Cristo del Milagro and of the Virgin Mary. These are central to Salta's beliefs and psyche, and the focus of Salta's biggest mass ritual. In 1692 Jesuit priests were amazed to discover that two statues, of Christ and the Virgin of Rosario, had survived a severe earthquake intact. During a series of tremors they paraded them through the streets in procession, and the following day, 14 September, the tremors stopped. The **Milagro** (miracle) is now the biggest event of Salta's year, when thousands of pilgrims walk to the city from hundreds of kilometres away.

Ironically these images are now just a stone's throw from the precious beings involved in the Incas' attempts to avert earthquakes and volcanic eruptions. The *Niños de Llullaillaco*, a sacred burial unearthed by a National Geographic expedition in 1999, are now housed in the **Museo de Arqueología de Alta Montaña** (MAAM) ① *Plaza 9 de Julio at Mitre 77, next to the cathedral, T0387-437 0499, www.maam.org.ar, Tue-Sun 0900-1930, US$8, shop and café*. Controversially, MAAM now has on show the famous mummified remains of sacrificial children. You can also see many of the other fabulous objects found in the burial, well displayed in this museum, with texts in English and a guided tour included in the entry price. The guides are trained by resident archaeologist Christian Vitry, and there's a fine library too. Opposite MAAM on the other side of the plaza is the interesting **Museo de Arte Contemporáneo** ① *Zuviria 90, T0387-421 3635, Tue-Sat 0900-2000, Sun 1600-2000*, which is also worth a look.

Near the plaza, there are also a couple of historical houses worth visiting for a glimpse of wealthy domestic life, of which the best is **Casa de los Uriburu** ① *Caseros 417, Tue-Fri 0930-1330, 1530-2030, Sat 1600-2000, Sun 0930-1300, US$1*, situated in the former mansion of the Uriburu family, the most distinguished of *Salteño* families, containing furniture, clothes and paintings.

A block west of the Cabildo, on one of the main pedestrian streets, are a couple of interesting museums housed in colonial mansions. The **Casa Leguizamón**, Caseros and Florida, has interesting architecture and the **Casa Arias Rengel**, next door, now houses the **Museo de Bellas Artes** ① *Florida 20, T0387-421 4714, Mon-Fri 0900-1930, Sat 1000-1300, 700-2000, US$1*, which has the city's finest collection of paintings, including superb Cuzqueño school works and small exhibitions of Salteño painters and sculptors.

Across the street is the **Museo de la Ciudad 'Casa de Hernández'** ① *Florida 97 and Alvarado, T0387-437 3352, www.museociudadsalta.gov.ar, Mon-Fri 0900-1300, 1600-2030, Sat 1700-2030, free*, in a fine 18th-century mansion with a collection of old furniture, musical instruments and dull portraits, but a marvellous painting of writer Güemes.

East of Plaza 9 de Julio

Walk east from the plaza, along Caseros, an appealing street of slightly crumbling buildings. After a block, you'll come to the **Iglesia San Francisco** (1796) ① *Caseros and Córdoba, daily 0730-1200, 1700-2100*, one of the city's landmarks, with its magnificent plum-coloured façade ornately decorated with white and golden stucco scrolls, and its elegant tower (1882) rising above the low city skyline. The interior is relatively plain, but there are some remarkable statues to admire, such as the rather too realistic San Sebastián. Two blocks further east is the **Convento de San Bernardo** ① *Caseros and Santa Fe*, built in colonial style in 1846, with an exquisitely carved wooden door dating from 1762. You can't enter the convent as it's still the home to nuns, but they'll open up the little shop for you, with its little collection of quaint handicrafts.

Continuing along Caseros for two blocks and turning right at Avenida Yrigoyen, you come to the wide open green space of **Parque San Martín**, where you'll find the **Museo de Ciencias Naturales** ① *Mendoza 2, T0387-431 8086, Tue-Sun 1530-1930, US$0.50*, with various stuffed animals. It's not a particularly elaborate park, but there's a boating lake, and from here you can take the *teleférico* (cable car) up to **Cerro San Bernardo** (1458 m) ① *daily 1000-1900, US$5.50 return, children US$3*, whose forested ridge looms over the east of the city centre. The top of the hill can be climbed in 45 minutes by a steep path (which starts beside the Museo Antropológico, see below). At the top there are lovely gardens and a great café with deck chairs and fabulous views. Recommended.

At the base of the hill is an impressive **statue** of General Güemes by Victor Gariño. His gaucho troops repelled seven powerful Spanish invasions from Bolivia between 1814 and 1821. The nearby **Museo Antropológico Juan M Leguizamón** ① *follow Paseo Güemes behind the statue, and up Av Ejército del Norte, Mon-Fri 0830-1900, Sat 0900-1300, 1500-1900, closed Sun, US$1.50, www.antropologico.gov.ar*, makes a good introduction to the pre-Hispanic cultures of the region. It has a superb collection of anthropomorphic ceramics and beautifully painted funerary urns. There's also an exhibition on high-altitude burial grounds, complete with mummies, objects found at the ancient ruins of Tastil (see page 298) and, most mysteriously, skulls flattened during the owner's life by wearing boards to squash the head (thought to confer higher intelligence). It's all very accessible and well laid out.

Around Salta city → *For listings, see pages 289-295.*

There are many lovely places close to Salta where *Salteños* go to relax: the smart leafy suburbs of **San Lorenzo**, 11 km to the west, or the **Dique Cabra Corral** for fishing and water sports, or jungly **Campo Quijano** on the way to Quebrado del Toro (see page 296).

Dique Cabra Corral

Salta makes a big deal of its only big lagoon – one of the largest artificial lakes in Argentina, the Dique Cabra Corral. It's popular with locals for fishing *pejerrey*, the tasty local delicacy, and for enjoying a bit of beach life, with water-skiing, fishing, camping and restaurants also on offer. The best place to stay is the **Hotel del Dique**, on the banks of the lake; the **Finca Santa Anita** is nearby and also gives you ready access to the water. The nearest town is the quaint gaucho town of **Coronel Moldes**, which while not perhaps worth a special trip, has a quiet charm all of its own. There's a strong sense of community with wonderful local processions of gauchos on the celebration days of the Patron saints, **Fiesta Patronal** (1 August).

Fincas around Salta

One of the great experiences of staying in this beautiful region is the access to the landscape and its people offered by a stay at its *estancias*, or *fincas* as they're known in this part of the country. The great thing about staying in an *estancia* is that you get to know real Argentines, and spend time with them in their homes as if you were a friend. Most owners speak English, are naturally extremely hospitable, and delighted to have guests from abroad to talk to. Stay for at least a couple of days to make the most of the facilities, which will usually include horse riding, a pool and lovely places to walk. There are many *fincas* throughout the region, but the following are some of the most distinctive within easy access of the city. Some are owned by Salta's aristocratic families and now welcome tourists, like **El Bordo de las Lanzas** ⓘ *www.estanciaelbordo.com*, with its immense tobacco plantation where you can ride for hours, dine with the owners and stay in splendid accommodation. Others are more modest affairs, offering less formality, but the kind of welcome that makes you feel like staying for days. **Los Los** ⓘ *www.redsalta. com/loslos*, near Chicoana, is a historical family house with superb views and fabulous riding in the jungle. **Santa Anita** ⓘ *www.santaanita.com.ar*, near Dique Cabra Corral, has twice won 'Slow Food' prizes for its superb goat's cheese, and has good horse riding. Not strictly speaking an *estancia*, but a luxurious place to stay, **La Casa de los Jazmines** ⓘ *www.houseofjasmines.com*, near La Silleta, offers utter luxury and a spa in an exquisitely modernized old house. Nearby, **El Manantial del Milagro** ⓘ *www.hotel manantial.com.ar*, is a peaceful retreat with lovely views. ▶▶ *For further details on* estancias, *see Sleeping, page 291.*

◉ Salta city and around listings

For Sleeping and Eating price codes and other relevant information, see Essentials pages 30-36.

● Sleeping

Salta city *p284, map p286*
Hotels fill up during Jul and around 10-16 Sep during El del Milagro. But it's best to book ahead all year round. Salta has excellent hotels, plenty of hostels and luxurious *estancias* within an hour's drive. For more helpful advice, see www.turismosalta.gov.ar.
L Legado Mítico, Mitre 647, T0387-422 8786, www.legadomitico.com. With only 11 rooms, this small, welcoming hotel is absolutely lovely. Each luxurious room has its own personality, and the personalized pre-ordered breakfasts are a fantastic way to start the day. Very highly recommended.
L Hotel Solar de la Plaza, Juan M Leguizamon 669, T0387-431 5111, www.solardelaplaza. com.ar. A great hotel, in the traditional house of an old *Salteño* family. A calm oasis on the lovely palm-filled Plaza Güemes. Faultless service, a great restaurant and a pool. Ask for

the spacious rooms in the old building, since newer rooms are noisier.
AL-A Ayres de Salta Hotel, General Güemes 650, T0387-422 1616, www.ayresdesalta. com.ar. Spacious 4-star hotel near the calm Plaza Belgrano that has everything you would expect in this price range. Spacious rooms, heated pool, great views from a roof terrace and walking distance from the centre.
A Del Virrey, 20 de Febrero 420, T0387-422 8000, www.hoteldelvirrey.com.ar. Luxurious bedrooms and bathrooms in this classy, colonial-style hotel. Well situated for the nightlife of Balcarce.
A Bloomers Bed & Brunch, Vincente López 129, T0387-422 7449, www.bloomers-salta.com.ar. Closed mid-May to mid-Jun. The best place to stay in this budget. Set in a refurbished colonial house, there are 5 spacious rooms (and a new self-contained apartment) each with their own colour scheme, 2 patios to relax in, a kitchen to use and a great library. The brunch menu, which is different each day, is their speciality. Very highly recommended.

B Hotel del Antiguo Convento, Caseros 113, T0387-422 7267, www.hoteldelconvento. com.ar. A small and very welcoming hotel. Lovely old-fashioned rooms around a neat patio at the front of this 100-year-old house. An unbeatable central location between San Francisco and San Bernardo churches make this a great choice in town.

B Hotel Boutique, Urquiza 427, T0387-421 5786, www.hotelbonarda.com. New modern hotel with attractive fixtures, clean nicely decorated rooms and good breakfast. Staff are friendly but the hotel lacks a welcoming atmosphere.

B Posada de las Nubes, Balcarce 639, T0387-432 1776, www.posadadelasnubes.com.ar. A charming new small hotel, offering simply decorated rooms around a central patio. Great location for the Balcarce nightlife.

C Las Rejas B&B, General Güemes 569, T0387-421 5971, www.lasrejashostel.com.ar. A lovely family house with just a few comfortable rooms. Central, peaceful and recommended.

C Munay, San Martín 656, T0387-422 4936, www.munayhotel.jujuy.com. This hotel is a great budget hotel. Nicely decorated with dark but smart bathrooms, welcoming staff and breakfast included. The same owners also have a hotel by the same name and standard in Jujuy and Cafayate.

D-C Sallka Hostal, Buenos Aires 753, T0387-4260785, www.hostalsallka.com.ar. A little out of the centre, this hotel is relaxed, clean and offers secure parking, Wi-Fi and breakfast.

Hostels

E Backpackers, Buenos Aires 930, San Juan 413 (**Backpackers Soul**) and Alvarado 751 (**Backpacker's City**), T/F0387-431 6476, www.backpackerssalta.com. The 3 official HI youth hostels are all owned by the same people and they share 1 website. Backpackers is 9 blocks from the centre, Backpacker's Soul is 6, and Backpacker's City is really central. They are all well run, offer dorm beds and doubles (**D-E**), a laundry, kitchen and budget travel information. Noisy, crowded and popular. Wi-Fi.

F pp Correcaminos Hostel, Vicente López 353, T0387-422 0731, www.hostelsalta.com. A lively hostel, 4 blocks from the plaza. Basic 8- and 4-bed dorms and 2 small double rooms, all with shared bathrooms, laundry, kitchen, free internet and a pleasant garden. Wi-Fi.

F pp Terra Oculta, Córdoba 361, T0387-421 8769, www.terraoculta.com. Set in a labyrinthine building, there is more of a party atmosphere with basic small dorms of 8 and 4, doubles (**E**). If you prefer something a little quieter, ask for a room in their *casona*, a renovated traditional building with a charming garden.

Around Salta city *p288*

It's worth considering staying outside Salta if you're in search of more tranquillity: at San Lorenzo (11 km); at the Dique Cabra Corral; at Campo Quijano; or at one of the many *fincas* within an hour of the city. See www.turismo salta.gov.ar for more information.

A El Castillo, Juan Carlos Davalos 1985, T0387-492 1052, www.hotelelcastillo.com.ar. Stunning building in an amazing location with lots of places to hike to. High ceilings, antique furniture, a lovely pool and a nice garden to enjoy. There is a good restaurant (**†↑**) which is open to non-guests.

A Hostería Punta Callejas, in Campo Quijano, R51, 30 km west at the entrance to the Quebrada del Toro, T0387-490 4086, www.puntacallejas.com.ar. Very clean and comfortable, with a/c, pool, tennis, horse riding, excursions and meals. Breakfast included.

A Hotel del Dique, Dique Cabra Corral, R47, Km 12, T0387-490 5112, www.hoteldel dique.com. Extremely comfortable, great lakeside position, with a pool and good food.

B Hostería de Chicoana, on the way to Cachi, on the plaza in Chicoana at Espana 45, 47 km south, T0387-490 7009, www.new sendas.com. A pretty colonial building, now slightly faded, but with the added advantage of expert guide Martín Pekarek, who runs wonderful adventure trips.

C Selva Montana, Alfonsina Storni 2315, T0387-492 1184, www.hostal-selva montana.com.ar.

Nestling high up in the lush leafy hills of San Lorenzo, just 15 mins by car from Salta. Complete comfort, and peace and quiet in stylish rooms, with a pool, horses and walking on offer. Take a taxi or bus **El Indio interurbano** from terminal.

Estancias/fincas

See also page 288.

L pp **Finca El Bordo de las Lanzas**, 45 km east of Salta, Rivadavia 298, El Bordo, T0387-490 3070, www.turismoelbordo.com.ar. Formal and luxurious, a taste of aristocratic life, with horse riding and charming hosts. Highly recommended.

L La Casa de los Jazmines, R51, 11 km south towards La Sileta, T0387-497 2005, www.houseofjasmines.com. Not exactly an *estancia*, but a beautiful place to unwind: old *finca* building redesigned to the height of luxury and good taste, perfumed with roses and jasmine, with a pool and superb spa offering a great range of treatments. Recommended.

AL Los Los, Chicoana, 40 km from Salta at the entrance to the Valles Calchaquíes, T0387-683 3121, www.redsalta.com/loslos. Open Mar-Dec. Most welcoming and highly recommended, beautifully situated on a hilltop with fabulous views from the colonial-style galleried veranda. Spacious rooms, decorated with old furniture, and beautiful gardens with a pool. Includes unforgettable horse riding into the forested mountains of the huge *finca*, where you will be cooked lunch in a remote rustic lodge. Reserve in advance.

A Finca Santa Anita, Route 68 Km 134 El Saladillo, 60 km from Salta, on the way to Cafayate T/F0387-490 5050, www.santa anita.com.ar. The whole family makes you welcome on this prize-winning organic farm with superb goat's cheese: great organic food and all activities included in the price. A traditional, colonial-style *finca*, beautiful views, swimming, guided walks to prehistoric rock paintings and horse riding in wonderful landscapes.

A-B pp **Finca El Manantial del Milagro**, La Silleta, 25 km from Salta, T/F0387-439 5506, www.hotelmanantial.com.ar. Beautiful views from the superbly decorated rooms in this historical *estancia*, offering swimming, walking and riding on the estate. Gorgeous.

Camping

There are several campsites including a municipal site at the entrance to Quebrada del Toro gorge, with hot showers, bungalows, and plenty of room for pitching tents.

● Eating

Salta city *p284, map p286*

There are lots of great *peñas* for live music, serving good regional food at night along the north end of C Balcarce.

¶¶¶ El Solar del Convento, Caseros 444, T0387-421 5124. One of Salta's finest restaurants and yet reasonably priced. You're greeted with a glass of sparkling wine, the surroundings are elegant and there's delicious *parrilla* and a fine wine list. Service is excellent. Recommended.

¶¶ Doña Salta, Córdoba 46 (opposite Iglesia San Francisco, with gaudy sign), T0387-432 1921, www.donasalta.com.ar. In an 1820s house, serving delicious *carbonada, locro* delicious *empanadas*, and other regional delicacies in attractive rustic surroundings. Recommended and cheap.

¶¶ Gauchos de Güemes, Uruguay 750, T0387-421 7007, www.gauchosdesalta. com.ar. Excellent regional specialities at this *peña* set in a fantastic historical building.

¶¶ La Casa de Güemes, España 730. Atmospheric house where Güemes lived, serving *empanadas, tamales, humitas*, and *asado*, cooked in the traditional way.

¶¶ La Casona del Molino, Caseros 2500. Another *peña* in a crumbling old colonial house with good food and drink. Popular with *folclore* stars who often burst into song.

¶¶ Entre Indyas, Buenos Aires 44. A little hard to find as it's down an arcade, this fantastic vegetarian restaurant mixes Peruvian and Indian food and is highly recommended.

Goblin, Caseros 445. With over 40 artisanal beers and great pub food like shepherd's pie and chicken burgers, this bar is popular with travellers and locals alike. Close to the main plaza.

El Charrúa, Caseros 221, T0387-432 1859, www.parillaelcharrua.com.ar. A good, brightly lit family place with a reasonably priced and simple menu where *parrilla* is particularly recommended.

El Corredor de las Empanadas, Zuviria and Necochea, T0387-431 3816. Justifiably renowned, serves fabulous *empanadas* and delicious local dishes.

La Criollita, Zuviría 306. Small and unpretentious, this is a traditional place for juicy and tasty *empanadas*.

La Posta, España 456. A large, touristy place with a patio, but it's reliable, great for *parrilla* and pasta, with a good atmosphere and friendly service. An excellent value fixed-price menu.

Mama Paca, Gral Güemes 118. Recommended by locals, this traditional restaurant is great for seafood from Chile and home-made pastas.

Cafés

There are lots of cafés on Plaza 9 de Julio, a great place to sit now that it's largely pedestrianized. The 2 cafés outside MAAM, Havana and El Palacio, are very touristy.

Don Blas, Balcarce 401. A lovely old corner of Balcarce serving good coffee.

Fili, corner of Güemes and Sarmiento 297. The best ice cream in Salta, try the *dulce de leche* with almonds or cinnamon. Heaven.

MAAM, inside the museum, Plaza 9 de Julio. Lovely airy café for meals and drinks.

New Time, Plaza 9 de Julio, corner with Alberdi. Avoid the tourist cafés and go where the *Salteños* go. Great juice, salads, and light meals.

Plaza Café, next to **Hotel Salta**. This elegant café is popular with *Salteños* late morning, when the centre is buzzing. A nice spot for breakfast.

Around Salta city *p288*
See www.sanlorenzosalta.org.ar for more information.

Castillo de San Lorenzo, on the road up to the Quebrada, Juan Carlos Daválos 1985, just before the car park at the top, T0387-492 1052, www.hotelelcastillo.com.ar. Fabulous interior in this castellated building, delicious meals, stylish setting. Recommended.

Lo de Andrés, Juan Carlos Dávalos 960 and Gorritti (at San Lorenzo), T0387-492 1757. Fabulous restaurant. Great steaks and pasta.

⦿ Entertainment

Salta city *p284, map p286*
No trip to the northwest is complete without sampling its stirring *folclore* music. You can eat *empanadas* while watching great musicians playing live in Salta's *peñas* or listening to spontaneous performers in the crowd. Most are concentrated in the north end of C Balcarce, where you will find many *peñas* within 3 blocks. This area also has a number of popular rock and jazz bars, such as **Macondo** or **Café del Tiempo**, as well as intimate restaurants and nightclubs. The result is an entertaining and noisy mix, though there are quieter bars here too. This area is most alive Thu, Fri and Sat nights from 1900.

La Casa de Güemes, España 730. Close to Plaza 9 de Julio. Recommended for shows, and frequented by *Salteños*.

La Casona del Molino, Caseros 2500, T0387- 434 2835, daily and at lunchtime. West of the centre (reached by taxi), this is the most authentic place for spontaneous *peña*, where guests help themselves to guitars on the walls and play.

La Vieja Estación, Balcarce 885, T0387-421 7727. Particularly recommended *peña* for a great atmosphere; shows and sometimes spontaneous performances from the crowds.

⊛ Festivals and events

Salta city and around *p284, map p286*
Feb/Mar Carnival. Salta celebrates with
processions on the 4 weekends before Ash
Wed at 2200 along C Ibazeta; also on **Mardi
Gras** (Shrove Tue) there is a procession of
decorated floats and dancers with intricate
masks of feathers and mirrors. It is the custom
to squirt water at passers-by and *bombas de
agua* (small balloons to be filled with water)
are on sale for dropping from balconies.
16-17 Jun Commemoration of the death
of Martín Güemes. There's folk music in
the afternoon and a gaucho parade in the
morning around his statue.
Aug Fiesta de la Pachamama. On 1 Aug and
throughout the month. A wonderful tradition
of the indigenous peoples of the north and
entire Andean region, giving thanks to the
mother earth, *La Pachamama*, with offerings
of drinks and food, in a fascinating ceremony
that binds the whole community. Go to
San Antonio de los Cobres, Tolar Grande,
and other villages in the *puna*.
6-15 Sep Cristo del Milagro. Salta's biggest
event, where thousands of pilgrims add to
the city's population in a grand procession
around the town, with the Virgen and Señor
del Milagro, an amazing act performed since
the 17th century to prevent earthquakes. All
accommodation is heavily booked ahead, so
reserve at least a month in advance.

○ Shopping

Salta city *p284, map p286*
The best places for shopping are the parallel
pedestrianized streets of Alberdi, off Plaza 9
de Julio, and Florida, a block to the west.
There are pricey but high-quality local goods
on C Buenos Aires near the plaza, and in the
shopping centre next to MAAM on the plaza.
Librería Rayuela, Alvarado 570. Excellent
bookshop with foreign-language media.
Mercado Artesanal, C Balcarce. Weekends
and Fri evenings, an informal market of local

handicraft makers, some interesting jewellery,
wood and *mates*.
Mercado Municipal, San Martín and Florida.
Closed 1400-1700 and after 2100. Wonderful
place for cheap food; great fruit and
vegetables and some handicrafts.
Vea, Florida, between Caseros and Alvarado,
and Mitre corner with Santiago del Estero.
Big supermarket.

Around Salta city *p288*
Mercado Artesanal, San Martín 2550,
on the western outskirts of the city in the
Casa El Alto Molino, T0387-434 2808, daily
0900-2100. Take bus No. 5a from Av San
Martín in centre and get off as bus crosses
the railway line or ask the bus driver. If you're
short of time, head straight for this lovely
18th-century mansion, selling beautiful
handicrafts made by craftsmen in the
surrounding areas. Perhaps a little more
expensive than if you buy them from a tiny
village, but superb quality, and all under
one roof. Look out for soft and warm llama
wool socks, wonderful hand-woven ponchos,
delicately carved wood and weavings.

▲ Activities and tours

Salta city and around *p284, map p286*
Unless you hire a car, you can take a tour
to visit the Valles Calchaquíes and the *puna*
or you can take the long but efficient local
buses. Bear in mind that distances are huge
here, so as you're going to end up spending
many hours in a minibus, it's much better
to take 3 days, go by bus and spend time
in a place than just visit for an hour or 2.
There is lots of adventure tourism on offer,
including horse riding, rafting and trekking.
All agencies charge similar prices for tours:
Salta City, US$16; Quebrada del Toro and
San Antonio de los Cobres, US$48; Cachi,
US$39; Quebrada de Humahuaca, US$49;
2-day tour to Cafayate, Angastaco, Molinos,
Cachi, US$90.

Adventure tourism

BiciNorte, T0387-156 838 067, www.bicinorte.com.ar. Bike trips around the city and to the Valles Calchaquíes and the *puna*. You can book at **Clark Expediciones**, Caseros 121, T0387-421 5930.

Clark Expediciones, Mariano Moreno 1950, T0387-497 1024, www.clarkexpediciones.com. Specialist tours for birdwatchers, natural history and cultural tailored tours; they also offer a ½-day tour to Reserva El Huaico (in San Lorenzo), the closest cloudforest reserve to Salta. English spoken.

Norte Rafting, Cabañas and Camping Guanaquitos, R47, Km 48, Dique Cabra Corral, T0387-424 8474, www.norterafting.com. Fun and professional rafting trips along the Río Juramento to see dinosaur footprints.

Norte Trekking, Av del Libertador 1151B, T0387-436 1844, www.nortetrekking.com. Enormously experienced Federico Norte offers great trips to experience the Valles Calchaquíes, *puna* into Chile or Bolivia, mountains and *selva* in depth. He's one of the few authorized guides into El Rey cloudforest park, and his trips can combine trekking with 4WD, horse riding and rafting, personally tailored to the group's needs, and not expensive. .

Puna Expediciones, Agustín Usandivaras 230, T0387-434 1875, www.punaexpeditions.com.ar. Well-qualified and experienced guide Luis H Aguilar organizes treks in remote areas, US$35 a day, including transport to trekking region, food and porters. Recommended.

Salta Rafting, Buenos Aires 88, shop 13, T0387-401 0301, www.saltarafting.com. Wide range of rafting and kayaking excursions in the Río Juramento, canopying and rappel, professionally run. Also accommodation.

Socompa, Balcarce 998, 1st floor, T0387-422 8471, www.socompa.com. Excellent company specializing in trips to the *puna*, 1- to 3-day trips to giant salt flats and mighty volcanoes based at the beautiful and remote hamlet of Tolar Grande. English and Italian spoken by the knowledgeable guides, who will inform you all about the culture and

history of the places you'll visit. Unmissable. Highly recommended.

Bus Turístico Salta, 20 de Febrero 796, T387-422 7798, www.busturisticosalta.com.ar. With 14 stops around the city, this hop-on, hop-off bus pass allows you 12 hrs' unlimited travel around the city on a circuit. US$10 per person.

Tour operators

There are plenty of conventional agencies on C Buenos Aires, 1st couple of blocks from the main plaza, get a list in the tourist office.

MoviTrack, Caseros 468 (and desk at airport), T0387-431 6749, www.movitrack.com.ar. A dynamic and well-organized company offering imaginative trips in special 4WD vehicles. Highly recommended is their alternative to the Safari a las Nubes, US$125, which follows the same route as the train, either in an open bus or with the ultra-modern Oxy Bus (altitude-sickness-proof with pressurized and dust-free cabin) for a fantastic range of landscapes from *selva* to *puna* all in 1 day. Friendly, informative bilingual guides. Great 1- to 4-day trips, some getting off the beaten track.

TEA, Buenos Aires 82, T0387-421 3333, www.teaturismo.com. Offers well-organized tours to the usual places. Recommended.

⊖ Transport

Salta city and around *p284, map p286*
Air

For airport information, see page 284.

LAB to **Santa Cruz** (Bolivia) twice a week, once via Tarija. **Aerolíneas Argentinas** flies to **Buenos Aires**, 2¼ hrs.

Airline offices Austral, Caseros 475, T0387-431 0862; Lloyd Aéreo Boliviano, Caseros 529, T0387-431 1389.

Bus

For bus terminal information, see page 284.
Local Buses to local destinations, such as **Coronel Moldes**, and Cabra Corral can

be caught next to the cable car office, the *teleférico* on the corner of San Martín and Yrigoyen. To **Campo Quijano** via **Silleta**, hourly. To **Cafayate**, 6 times daily, 3 hrs, US$11, to **Santa María**, daily, 5½ hrs, US$11; to **Angastaco**, Mon-Fri, 5½ hrs, US$13; to **Belén**, Wed, 13 hrs, US$22. To **Cachi**, 2 daily, 4½ hrs, US$11, **Marcus Rueda**, spectacular journey which usually continues to **Molinos**, every 2 days, 6½ hrs, US$14; and to **La Poma**, 4 weekly, 6½ hrs, US$12, Marcos Rueda, T0387-421 4447. To **Rosario de la Frontera**, 2½-3 hrs, US$9. To **San Antonio de Los Cobres**, Mon-Sat 1500, Sun 1910, 5 hrs, US$10, El Quebradeño.

Long distance To **Buenos Aires**, several daily, 17-20 hrs, US$60-80, Brown; Chevallier; Flecha Bus; La Veloz del Norte; and other companies. Choose *coche cama* for maximum comfort and reclining seats. To **Córdoba**, several daily, 12-13 hrs, US$35-45, Flecha Bus; La Veloz del Norte; Tramat. To **Santiago del Estero**, 6-7 hrs, US$20. To **Tucumán**, 4hrs, US$15, several companies, including Andesmar; Flecha Bus; La Veloz del Norte. To **Mendoza** via Tucumán, daily, 16-18 hrs, US$63, several companies. To **Jujuy**, hourly 0600-2200, 'directo', 2 hrs, US$8, Andesmar; Balut Hnos; Flecha Bus; La Veloz del Norte; and others. To **La Rioja**, 10-11 hrs, US$28. To **Resistencia**, 13-16 hrs, US$40. To **Puerto Iguazú**, daily, 24-25 hrs, US$70.

To Bolivia **Santa Cruz de la Sierra** (connection at General Güemes), La Veloz del Norte; to **La Quiaca** (Bolivian border), several daily, 7 hrs, US$18, Andesmar; Balut; Flecha Bus. To **Pocitos** or **Aguas Blancas** (Bolivian border), daily, several companies.

To Chile To **San Pedro de Atacama**, Tue, Thu and Sun, 9 hrs, US$50, Géminis and Pullman Bus. To **Arica**, 12hrs, US$65.

Car hire

Avis, at the airport, R51, T0387-424 2289, and at Buenos Aires 88, T0387-431 7104 salta@avis.com.ar, efficient and very helpful, recommended; Hertz, Caseros 374, T0387-

421 6785, foarentacar@arnet.com.ar; NOA, Buenos Aires 1, T0387-431 7080, www.noarentacar.com, in Hotel Salta, helpful.

Train

For information on the railway station, see page 284. The only train running is the *Tren a las Nubes* (Train to the Clouds), which usually runs between Salta and La Polvorilla viaduct once a week from Apr-Nov, weather permitting, and on additional days in the high season (Jan-Feb and Jul-Aug). It departs promptly at 0705, returning to Salta 2300, US$120-140 per person (high season). Be warned: it's a very touristy experience but worth it. For more information, see box, page 297. Alternatively, consider the bus or tour options.

ⓘ Directory

Salta city *p284, map p286*
Banks Banks are open 0900-1400, all have ATMs (many on España). Banco de la Nación, Mitre and Belgrano. **Currency exchange** Banco de Salta, España 550 on main plaza, cashes TCs. **Embassies and consulates** Bolivia, Mariano Boedo 34, T0387-421 1040. Mon-Fri 0900-1400, unhelpful, better to go to Jujuy; Chile, Santiago del Estero 965, T0387-431 1857. **Cultural centres** Alliance Française, Santa Fe 20, T0387-431 2403. **Emergencies** T911. **Internet** There are many fast and cheap Internet places and *locutorios* in the centre: Cibercom, next to the tourist office on Buenos Aires, is one of the best and sells drinks. **Immigration office** Maipú 35, T0387-422 0438, daily 0730-1230. **Language schools** Bien Argentino, T0387-154 750 679, www.bien-argentino. com.ar, is the sister school to the one in Buenos Aires and organizes packages including excursions, accommodation and classes, it's recommended; Mercedes' School of Languages, 20 de Febrero 197, 5B, www.mercedesschool.com.ar, a small but welcoming school which also offers acting classes. **Medical services** Hospital San Bernardo, Tobías 69.

Northwest Salta and the Quebrada del Toro

The landscapes of northwestern Salta province are utterly spectacular. In one simple, unforgettable journey up the Quebrada del Toro from Salta city to the town of San Antonio de los Cobres, you'll travel through an extraordinary spectrum from dense forest, gorges of brightly coloured rock strewn with cactus, to the silent expanses of high-altitude desert in the puna. This is the route of Argentina's famous narrow-gauge railway, Tren a las Nubes (Train to the Clouds), but it's a long, frustrating and very touristy experience. Far better to take a minibus tour or hire a car, and take time to pause and explore on the way. You might stay a night in the forested weekend resort of Campo Quijano, and don't miss the superb ruined city of Santa Rosa de Tastil, one of Argentina's archaeological gems. Set in stunning rocky landscapes there's fascinating evidence of ancient pre-Inca and Inca civilizations here, and a local guide will bring it all alive. At the top of the gorge, the quiet mining town San Antonio de los Cobres is at its best for the Fiesta de la Pachamama in August, and a good stopping point before setting off into the puna. To offset altitude sickness, stop off for coca tea with typical puna family Sandro Yampa at el Mojón, and then be dazzled by the shimmering white expanse of the Salinas Grandes salt flats. From here you could drop to Purmamarca in the Quebrada de Humahuaca down the thrilling Cuesta de Lipán road. Or head west, further into the puna to discover tranquil isolation at Tolar Grande. ▸▸ For listings, see page 300.

Ins and outs

This part of Salta has traditionally been the sole preserve of the Tren a las Nubes, but in the last few years another tour operator, **Movitrack** ① www.movitrack.com.ar, has run very successful tours along the same route which actually allow you to see far more of the impressive engineering of the train track, and certainly absorb more of the landscape. Inevitably, other tour operators followed, and along Salta's Calle Buenos Aires, you'll find plenty of tours on offer, though Movitrack is the only company to have pressurized oxygen pumped vehicles to counter the inevitable effects of altitude. It's well worth hiring a car to explore the Quebrada del Toro, and to make time to see Santa Rosa de Tastil, which few agencies include in any detail. Ask the tourist office for latest information on local guides at the site, since there is a new project to put trained locals in place. There is comfortable accommodation at San Antonio de los Cobres, but very little on the way. If cycling, note that much of the road is *ripio*, that there is no shade, and it's extremely cold at night. However you travel, the effects of altitude are not to be underestimated, since you'll be climbing to nearly 4000 m. You must take time for your body to adjust if you're going to exert yourself beyond a gentle stroll. Drink plenty of water, avoid alcohol and don't overeat. Take it easy and you should feel fine.

Quebrada del Toro and Tren a las Nubes → For listings, see page 300.

The route for the Train to the Clouds is the same as the road through the Quebrada del Toro. The only difference is that travelling by road gives you the chance to get out and walk around – and to examine the spectacular feat of engineering of the train track – which of course you can't see from the train itself. You'll leave Salta's subtropical valleys via the jungle weekend retreat of **Campo Quijano**, at Km 30, which lies in a beautiful, thickly vegetated valley at the entrance to the gorge is an attractive place for a stop. The road and track then climb along the floor of the Quebrada del Toro, fording the river repeatedly amidst densely growing pampas grass and *ceibo*, Argentina's national flower,

Train to the Clouds

The famous narrow-gauge Tren a las Nubes is an extraordinary feat of engineering, and a good way to experience the dramatic landscape up to the *puna*.

Built to enable commerce over the Andes to Chile, the track, which runs 570 km from Salta to Socompa on the Chilean border, was the outstanding achievement of Richard Maury, an engineer from Pennsylvania. Work started in 1921 and took 20 years. The track starts in Salta at 1200 m above sea level, rising to 4200 m, up through the impossibly rocky terrain of the steep gorge Quebrada del Toro, with several switchbacks ('zig-zags') and 360° loops to allow diesel engines to gain height over a short distance with a gentler gradient. One thousand men worked with only the most basic tools through inhospitable conditions, detonating rock and carving away at steep mountainsides through howling winds and snow. Many died in the attempt. The destination of the tourist train (passengers no longer being allowed on the weekly cargo trains) is La Polvorilla viaduct, near San Antonio de los Cobres, a delicate bridge across a mighty gorge, spanning 224 m and 63 m high; it feels like you're travelling on air, both scary and exhilarating.

The tourist train is a comfortable ride, though a long day out. Leaving Salta at 0700 (cold and dark in winter) to the cheerful accompaniment of *folclore* singers on the platform, the train edges to the entrance of Quebrada de Toro, steep forested mountains tinged with pink as the sun rises, and a light breakfast is served. The landscape changes as you climb through the gorge, dotted with farms and adobe houses, to arid red rock where giant cacti perch, past sculptural mountains, coloured terracotta to chocolate, ochre and pink, to the staggeringly beautiful *puna*. The seven hours of the ascent are kept lively by chats from bilingual guides (English spoken, but French and Portuguese too on request). Altitude sickness hits many people, and oxygen is on hand. At La Polvorilla viaduct, you can get out briefly to admire the construction, and buy locally made llama wool goods from the people of San Antonio. Don't bother haggling: these shawls and hats are beautifully made, and these people's only source of income. At San Antonio, the Argentine flag is raised to commemorate those who worked on the railway, and the national anthem is sung, in a rather surreal ceremony. The descent, however, is slightly tedious, despite the constant stream of entertainment from *folclore* singers and Andean bands. Consider returning by road instead to see the ruins at Santa Rosa de Tastil. For more information, see www.trenalasnubes.com.ar.

with its striking fringed red blossoms. At **Chorrillos**, you'll see one of several identical wooden 1920s train stations along the route, with outside ovens built to heat steel fixings during the building of the track. From here the train track zigzags as it climbs past tiny farmsteads lined with *álamo* trees, and up into the dramatic **Quebrada Colorada** – so called because of its bright red, pink and green stratified rock – to Ingeniero Maury (2350 m, Km 65), where there is a police control point. From Km 96, now paved, the road climbs the **Quebrada de Tastil**, parting company from the railway which continues through the **Quebrada del Toro**. The road passes through the tiny hamlet of Santa Rosa de Tastil, where there are marvellous pre-Inca ruins, and the only accommodation before San Antonio de los Cobres.

Santa Rosa de Tastil

Spread out over 12 ha and looming 60 m over the Valle de Lerma in Salta's dry centre are the ruins of a complex pre-Inca civilization founded around 1336 AD. The site is one of the most complete archaeological sites in the country and the intricate houses (not built to any recognizable grid) sprawl haphazardly on the slope. As it hardly ever rains in this area, walls are still standing, pottery and arrow tips can still be found on the ground and erosion to the structures has been kept to a minimum (although some walls have been rebuilt). Abandoned around 1439 AD and rediscovered in 1903 by anthropologist Eric Boman, the site was once home to over 2000 people who traded with the neighbouring Andean towns and farmed at the foot of the mountains. They were excellent weavers, bred llamas and guanacos, and made stone and rustic pottery. No one is quite sure why the highly developed site was abandoned, but we can learn about their religion and beliefs from the rock paintings they left behind. If you are in the area, consider a trip to these remote and well-preserved ruins. They are a great example of the civilizations that lived peacefully up and down the Andes, until the Incas arrived.

Santa Rosa de Tastil → *Colour map 1, A2. Phone code 0387.*

This picturesque little hamlet (3080 m, Km 103) lies near the site of one of Argentina's most important pre-Hispanic settlements that once contained well over 400 houses and over 2000 people, believed to have been inhabited from AD 1336 to 1439. There is a small **museum** ① *at the side of the road, daily 1000-1800, US$.035*, which is recommended. It has some of the finds from this intriguing culture, among them a well-preserved mummy, delicate jewellery and a xylophone of sonorous rocks. The remains of this ancient city are extraordinarily beautiful; a vast expanse of regular walls and roads, stretching out on an exposed hillside with views along the entire gorge. The ruins themselves are well worth visiting, but be sure to ask for a local guide, since the site is extensive and you'll get more out of it with a little interpretation. Guides will show you around, but are unpaid so appreciate a tip.

San Antonio de los Cobres → *Colour map 1, B2. Phone code 0387.*
① *3774 m, 168 km northwest of Salta.*

Beyond Tastil the road climbs through green hanging valleys where cattle roam, and then up over the **Abra Blanca Pass** (4050 m) where the landscape changes dramatically, suddenly becoming vast, open and eerily empty. At the top of the pass, the road drops and runs across the *puna*, offering views of Mount Chañi (5896 m) to the right, Acay (5716 m) to the left, and Quewar (6102 m) in the far distance.

  San Antonio de los Cobres is a simple remote mining town of low adobe houses situated in a shallow hollow. There's nothing much to do here but it's a good introduction to the reclusive life of the *puna*, and it does have its subtle charms. It's also one of the few places here that retains authentic indigenous culture, and where the **Pachamama festival** is celebrated in style every August. Tourists are welcome at this great event, which is not to be missed. People are friendly and the handicrafts on offer are of high quality, and incredibly cheap. However, altitude sickness can strike heavily here, so avoid eating too much or drinking alcohol until acclimatized.

Border essentials: Argentina–Chile

Paso de Sico

The border is open daily 24 hours. Note that no fresh food may be taken into Chile (there is a search 20 km west of Paso de Sico).

Argentine immigration The offices are at the pass itself and in San Antonio de los Cobres at the other end of town from the *aduana* (customs house). There is a police checkpoint at Catúa, 26 km east of Paso de Sico and in Toconao.

Chilean customs and immigration San Pedro de Atacama.

Note This is a very high-altitude pass, with the road reaching up to 4080 m above sea level. From Salta the road is tarmac for the first 110 km of the Ruta Nacional 51, after that it is sealed road. For more detailed information, see www.gendarmeria.gov.ar/pasos/fichsico.htm.

Paso de Socompa

The border is open 24 hours. From Paso de Socompa a poor road runs to Pan de Azúcar, with roads west to the Pan-American Highway, or north via the Salar de Atacama to San Pedro de Atacama. No fuel is available until San Pedro or Calama.

Note This is a very high-altitude pass as well, with the road reaching up to 4080 m above sea level. Snow in this area is common from May to August and it can reach as high as 2 m. In winter temperatures can drop to -15°C. This route is rocky, with lots of bends and uneven roads, and as such it is not recommended. For more detailed information, see www.gendarmeria.gov.ar/pasos/fichsocom.htm.

From here you could head back south along Ruta 40 to La Poma and Cachi over the mighty Paso Abra del Acay (4900 m), see page 302. This road should only be attempted in a 4WD as it is very rough in places. Or you could head north to the fabulous salt flats at Salinas Grandes, and on to Purmamarca in the Quebrada de Humahuaca – a spectacular journey, see below. About 14 km west of San Antonio de los Cobres, there is a road that runs below the famous **La Polvorilla** railway viaduct, giving you the chance to photograph it.

San Antonio to Chile

From San Antonio there are two possible crossings to Chile. The best, closest, and most used, is the **Paso de Sico** (see box, above), due west on Route Nacional 51. Alternatively, at Caucharí, take Route Provincial 27 southwest across the giant Salar de Arizaro to the Chilean border at the **Paso de Socompa**. The road runs through very beautiful scenery including salt flats and desert, but be warned that it is extremely isolated, and there are no services whatsoever. Make sure you stock up on drinking water and fuel before setting out from San Antonio. Only for the very intrepid.

San Antonio to Purmamarca

Another road, the Ruta 40, leads north from San Antonio to Abra Pampa, or curves around to join a good route to Purmamarca in the Quebrada de Humahuaca (see page 325) which is recommended for a taste of the extraordinary landscapes. The road continues dead flat across the scrubby yellow *puna* – its horizons edged with pinkish mauve or bronze mountains, with the occasional flock of llamas or cows grazing. It's either wonderfully meditative or unbearably monotonous, depending on your point of view, but the salt flats, **Salinas Grandes**, which you'll reach in two hours from San Antonio, are certainly worth seeing. The huge expanses of dazzling white salt, crazy paved with crusted lines, are silent and other-worldly. There are crossroads some 20 north of the salt flats, where you could head west to Susques (in Jujuy, see page 328), up to Abra Pampa or follow the spectacular road to Purmamarca down the broad slalom bends of **Cuesta de Lipán** with breathtaking views of the valley below.

◉ Northwest Salta and the Quebrada del Toro listings

For Sleeping and Eating price codes and other relevant information, see Essentials pages 30-36.

⊜ Sleeping

Santa Rosa de Tastil *p298*
Basic accommodation in shared dorms is available in the village for US$3 per person – ask at the museum.

San Antonio de los Cobres *p298*
A-B Hostería de las Nubes, on the eastern outskirts, T0387-490 9059, www.hosteriade lasnubes.com.ar. A smart, well-maintained place with lovely comfortable rooms, including breakfast, and a good restaurant. Staff are friendly and can advise on routes nearby. Recommended.
D Hosteria El Palenque, Belgrano s/n, T0387-490 9019. Also a café, family-run.

⊘ Eating

Santa Rosa de Tastil *p298*
♛-♛ **Posta de los Cardones**, R51, T0387-499 1093. Tasty food by chefs Erick and Paula.

San Antonio de los Cobres *p298*
♛ **El Mojón**, 35 km from San Antonio on R40 to Salinas Grandes. Sandro Llampa and his family serve coca tea or lunch and will show you around their farm.

⊖ Transport

San Antonio de los Cobres *p298*
Bus
There are 2 departures daily with Ale Hnos bus to San Antonio de los Cobres via Santa Rosa de Tastil, 0730 and 1500. The journey takes 5 hrs and costs US$7.

Los Valles Calchaquíes

Dramatic, constantly changing and stunningly beautiful, the Valles Calchaquíes are perhaps the most captivating part of Salta province. The river Calchaquí springs 5000 m up on the slopes of the Nevado de Acay, just south of San Antonio de los Cobres, and flows– via a series of timeless oasis villages through a spectacularly long and broad valley– to Cafayate and beyond. The first village is La Poma, set in wide open red rocky land, but you're more likely to start exploring at the pretty town of Cachi, reached from Salta by a breathtaking drive up the Cuesta del Obispo and through the giant cactus park, Parque Nacional los Cardones. Cachi is set against the massive range of the Nevado de Cachi mountains with a hidden valley, Cachi Adentro, irrigated since pre-Inca times to produce the bright red peppers you'll see drying in the sun in April. Head south from Cachi, and there are unspoilt villages dotted along the valley: Seclantás, with its poncho weavers, Molinos, with its lovely church and Bodega Colomé to the west, Angastaco and San Carlos, all reached by the rough ripio Ruta 40. There are extraordinary rock formations at Quebrada de las Flechas, just north of the more established wine-growing centre of Cafayate. South of here, the valley and Ruta 40 continues to heavenly Santa María (Catamarca) and Amaichá del Valle (see page 349). The sun shines here all year and there is minimal rainfall, making it perfect to visit in the winter. ▶▶ For listings, see pages 309-314.

Ins and outs

It's possible to travel in the valleys using public transport from Salta to both Cachi and Cafayate. There are two different routes. To reach Cafayate quickly, there are several buses daily along the fast, paved Ruta Nacional 68. South of Cafayate, there are buses to Santa María (Catamarca) and Amaichá del Valle. If you're short of time, there are one or two day tours from Salta to the Cafayate and Calchaquíes valleys, but they are frustratingly brief, with many hours spent cooped up in a minibus.

Alternatively the more scenic route through the valley is the iconic Ruta 40. Only a few buses each day go from Salta to Cachi and Molinos along the nail-biting Cuesta del Obispo, Route Nacional 33, and the beautiful Ruta 40, quite an experience in itself. It's worth taking the extra time to explore the villages and stay the night in Cachi or Molinos. However, from Molinos there's only one bus a week along the Calchaquí Valley to Angastaco, leaving you stranded for days. The best way to see this region is to hire a car in Salta – note there is a rough stretch between Cachi and Cafayate and a 4WD is essential in summer, when rains swell the rivers.

Background

The whole vast Calchaquí Valley was densely populated in pre-Hispanic times by sophisticated people who built stone dwellings in large organized 'cities', the impressive remains of which you can see still at Las Pailas, near Cachi, and at Quilmes, further south. Much archaeological work has yet to be done to establish more detail about their daily lives and there are currently digs at Las Pailas and La Borgata, near Cachi Adentro. Often referred to as 'Diaguitan', the Diaguita was just one of several tribes in the valley. They left a rich legacy of ceramics, which you can see today in all the small museums throughout the region. From beautifully painted urns made to contain the bodies of their dead, to simple cooking pots and glazed black polished vessels, these artefacts speak of a population with a high degree of social organization.

After the defeat of the indigenous population in the Calchaquí Wars, the Spanish established missions and *haciendas* in the valley, which were run along feudal principles –

some until as recently as the 1980s. During the colonial period the valley prospered, providing pasturage for mules and herds of cattle en route to the mountain passes into Chile and Alto Perú (Bolivia). After independence, lower parts of the valley became the primary wheat-growing and wine-producing area for Salta city, but the local economy declined in the late 19th century when the railway brought cheap wheat from the Pampas and wine from Mendoza. Salta's endemic racism and the feudal legacy have meant that the indigenous people in the valley are only recently coming to value their own cultural inheritance. Rather than taking a commercial group tour from Salta, seek out local guides who will tell you about their fascinating history.

Northwest of Salta → *For listings, see pages 309-314.*

La Poma to San Antonio de los Cobres

La Poma (3015 m), with its modern adobe houses and a population of 600, lies beneath the massive Cumbre del Libertador General San Martín (6380 m). It's the first village in the valley but not the original one. The old village was destroyed by an earthquake in 1930, its ruins lie 2 km north at La Poma Vieja. North of La Poma, Ruta 40 continues over the **Paso Abra del Acay** (4900 m, Km 282), the highest pass in South America negotiable by car. Road conditions vary depending on the weather and whether the roads have been recently cleared; a 4WD vehicle is advised. The critical part of the route is south of the pass at **Mal Paso** (Km 257), where summer rains can wash the road away. Buses do not travel on this road and anyone tempted to try it on a bicycle should think twice. There is no shade, night temperatures are several degrees below freezing and you need to be well adapted to the altitude. Take plenty of water and an arctic sleeping bag. North of the pass, the road runs across the *puna* to San Antonio de los Cobres.

To explore La Poma on a day trip from Cachi, contact local guide, **Santiago Casimiro**, T03868-1563 8545, santiagocasimiro@hotmail.com, who can bring you here in your car or taxi, via the fascinating Inca grain storage caves at **Los Graneros**, and visiting the ex-feudal village of Palermo, with lots of interesting history and culture thrown in.

Salta to Cafayate → *For listings, see pages 309-314.*

Chicoana and the journey from Salta to Cachi

Cachi is 170 km west of Salta, along one of the most unforgettable routes in Argentina. Head south from Salta on Ruta Nacional 68, and turn right at El Carril to the quaint little colonial town of **Chicoana**, where you could stay the night in the splendid **Finca Los Los** ① *www.redsalta.com/loslos*. There's not much to do in Chicoana, but it's an interesting example of a colonial-style town, sitting amidst some of the finest tobacco-producing land in the world, and with lots of buildings dating from the 1900s. Religious festivals are celebrated with much enthusiasm, and the **Carnaval** (February) and the **Fiesta Patronal** (16 July) are particularly recommended for a fun day out. Easter celebrations are impressive too, with the Passion re-enacted throughout the town. The weekend afterwards (around 23 July) is the town's famous **Fiesta de Tamales** when regional delicacies such as meat and corn tied up in corn-husk bundles are traditionally made on a massive scale, famous *folclore* musicians come to sing, and gauchos compete in Doma contests – roughly equivalent to rodeo and very impressive.

From Chicoana, the road enters the fertile **Quebrada de Escoipe**, and a good wide road hugs the mountains as it snakes up the breathtaking **Cuesta del Obispo**. The road here is mostly still *ripio*. There are two places to stop for tea roughly halfway to Cachi. At **El Maray** (70 km from Salta), there's a nice *confitería* in a yellow building on the right and, opposite, delicious jams and walnuts are sold. Further on, **Café Margarita** serves coffee and layered *tortillas* for bus passengers. Throughout the journey, you'll pass tiny hamlets of adobe houses shrouded in low cloud. As the cloud clears, you'll glimpse dramatic views of the vast bronze, green-velvety mountains, and there's a fantastic panorama as you round the head of the valley. From here you might like to take the turning off down to the **Valle Encantado**, an eerie, fascinating place for a picnic amongst bizarre wind-sculpted terracotta rocks. Take great care if you drive the Cuesta del Obispo in fog, which often hangs in the valley in the early mornings, or in rain. It is not advisable at night.

Beyond the arid **Piedra del Molino Pass** (3347m), where you'll want to stop for photos, the road runs west along a dead-straight stretch known as **La Recta del Tin-Tin**, passing through the **Parque Nacional Los Cardones**, at altitudes between 2700 m and 5000 m, an astonishing landscape of huge candelabra cacti. Walking amongst these giant sentinels, their arms thrust up to the cloudless sky, with a backdrop of stratified bright pink rock, is an extraordinary experience. There are occasionally *guardaparques* at Recta del Tin-Tin, but no services. Camping is officially not allowed. About 11 km before reaching Cachi is the small village of **Payogasta**, where you can find the national park administrative office ① *T03868-491066, loscardones@apn.gov.ar*, and the **Hostería de Payogasta** ① *T03868-496034*.

Cachi → *Colour map 1, B2. Phone code 03868. Population 7000. Altitude 1228m.*

Cachi is a beautiful, tranquil town (180 km from Salta) in a wide green valley at the foot of the majestic Nevado del Cachi, whose nine peaks are snow-covered for much of the year and whose highest summit is **San Martín** (6380 m). Founded in 1694, it had been a Diaguita settlement long before the Incas arrived in 1450, and the extensive irrigation channels they built to channel the Nevado's snow-melt are still used today to make the valley green and to grow huge fields of peppers. These are an amazing sight when harvested in April and laid out to dry in huge scarlet squares, which stand out against the arid mountains beyond. The tourist office ① *on the plaza, opposite side to the church, Av Gral, Güemes s/n, T03868-491902, www.cachi.todowebsalta.com.ar, daily 0900-1200, 1500-2000*, can provide a basic leaflet and map. No one speaks English, but they are well meaning and will give advice if you're patient. A private tourist office has opened, **Casa de Turismo de Cachi** ① *by the entrance to the town on the left*. Local guides can be found here, and they sell crafts.

Cachi has a pleasingly simple church, the **Iglesia de San José**, whose roof and lecterns are made of cactus wood. Next door, there's a fascinating survey of pre-colonial Calchaquí culture in the **Museo Arqueológico** ① *T03868-491080, Mon-Fri 0900-1800, Sat-Sun 1000-1300, US$0.80*, with impressive painted funerary urns and an intriguing cat/man petroglyph. With its sunny climate, Cachi is the perfect place for a few days' rest, but there are satisfying walks into the mountains to see extraordinary pre-Inca ruins, and panoramic views from its spectacularly sited hilltop cemetery, just 20 minutes' walk from the plaza.

The town feels more like a small village and has a lively community life with fiestas throughout the year, where you can hear traditional *folclore* music as well as the *bagualas*, and *coplas* coming from the indigenous traditions. The **Fiesta de la Tradición Calchaquí**, held in the third week in January, and the **Carnaval** in February, are particularly worth experiencing. **Pachamama** is celebrated in August. Cachi has the special advantage of being one of the few original towns in the region with trained local guides. Don't miss **Las Pailas** archaeological site, and **Cerro de la Virgen** makes a satisfying day's hike. Serious climbers should plan to spend a week or so to climb the spectacular Nevado de Cachi. ▶▶ *For further information, see Activities and tours, page 313.*

Cachi has a great tradition in weaving, and you can buy beautiful handmade ponchos, shawls, rugs and wall hangings at the government-run **handicrafts shop** in the same room as the tourist office on the plaza. But these are more expensive than if bought directly from weavers, and they receive hardly any of the profit. Instead, go up the street, and find the workshop of **Oscar Cardozo** ① *Juan Calchaquí, opposite the monument, T03868-491037*. Oscar teaches weaving and can direct you to other weavers in his association. There's an ATM, restaurants and cafés on the plaza at Güemes and Ruiz de los Lanos.

Around Cachi

There are walks to **La Aguada**, 6 km southwest along the lush valley fringed with *álamo* trees and dotted with adobe farmhouses. Leave town by Calle Benjamín Zorrilla at the southwest of the plaza, and walk along the *ripio* track. There's wonderful accommodation here at the *finca* **El Molino** (see Sleeping, page 309), with its tiny *bodega* and charming hospitality.

But you shouldn't miss the ancient ruins at **Las Pailas**, 16 km northwest of Cachi (via Cachi Adentro), with intriguingly complex circular dwellings, long irrigation channels and worked stone cultivation terraces. The views are breathtaking, with huge cacti set against the snow-topped Nevado de Cachi behind. To get there take a bus to Las Arcas from where it's a two-hour walk. The bus leaves Cachi early in the morning (check the current timetable with the tourist office) and returns in the afternoon. However, it's better to go with one of the local guides (see page 313).

Cerro de la Virgen is another rewarding day hike near Cachi, up through a pretty hanging valley and slopes strewn with giant boulders to a peak with wonderful views over the Calchaquí Valley beyond. The hamlet **Cachi Adentro**, on the opposite side of the valley from La Aguada, has more fine views, a school, church and dairy farm, **El Tambo**. To climb any of the peaks in the **Nevado de Cachi**, you must take a mountain guide who is trained and familiar with the route. Do not attempt these peaks alone. See page 313 for details of recommended guides, or ask in the tourist office.

Seclantás and Molinos → *Colour map 1, B2. Phone code 03868. Population 900.*

The road continues from Cachi on the west side of the river, via the hostería **Casa de Campo La Paya** (see Sleeping, page 310), 9 km from Cachi, where there are interesting archaeological ruins of an important pre-Inca town and administrative centre. For a pretty detour via the hamlet of **Seclantás**, cross the river and follow signs. This is a quaint tranquil village with simple colonial-style houses and an interesting church dating from 1835. Seclantás' weavers are among the finest in the country, and they sell ponchos directly from their workshops on the side of the road; look for the looms strung up between the pillars on a porch. The quality is higher and prices are much lower than in the Cachi tourist office shop, and you have the satisfaction of knowing that the profits go directly to the weavers. Wander down the main street and ask around for *telares* (weavers), as there are few signs. There's currently nowhere great to stay in Seclantás, but a couple of places sell food and snacks and there is a camping ground.

Some 52 km from Cachi, you come to the village of **Molinos** (2220 m), hidden away 1 km off Ruta 40 at Km 118. Set in a bowl of craggy mountains with a wide plaza and neat adobe houses, it's a peaceful place and an idyllic retreat for relaxing and doing very little.

Founded in 1659, it has a fine church dating from 1692, with a simple gold *retablo*, containing the mummified body of the last Royalist governor of Salta, Don Nicolás Severo Isasmendi. The house he built, opposite the church, is now the **Hostal Provincial de Molinos**. There are a couple of satisfying two-hour walks: either across the river bed (usually dry) and then up the hill opposite; or up to the Cross above the town. Both offer fine views of Molinos and the surrounding country.

Accommodation is limited in Molinos, but the nuns opposite the church have pristine little rooms to rent, and there are several families that rent rooms in the village. There are a few simple places to eat near where the bus to Cachi stops – ask around, or at the basic **tourist office** ① *municipalidad, on the plaza at 9 de Julio s/n, daily 0800-2200, low season daily 0900-1300, 1600-2100*. No one speaks English here but they are kind and want to help. Molinos celebrates **La Virgen de la Candelaria** in February, with processions, music and handicrafts.

Just 20 km from Molinos along a road running west into the mountains, is the extraordinary and fabulous winery, **Colomé** ① *4 hrs from Salta, 2½ hrs from Cafayate via a short cut, Km 20, T03868-494044, www.estanciacolome.com/*. Owned by charming art collector Donald Hess and his wife Ursula, this remote retreat is more than just a swish place to stay. As well as having a stunningly lovely setting, the bodega produces the highest-altitude wines in the world, at 2300 m. In an arid valley of red and grey rock, surrounded by mountains, there are hundreds of hectares of rare pre-Phylloxera vines, producing Malbec-heavy wines of exquisite intensity – and all grown on organic and biodynamic principles. A Spanish-style house with nine rooms provides ultra-luxurious accommodation, delicious meals, and there is great walking and riding in the extensive *finca*. It's impressive in terms of social responsibility too, since the Hesses have built a church, clinic and community centre for the 400 families living on their land, and take great care of their well-being.

Angastaco → *Colour map 1, B2. Population 881.*

From Molinos, Ruta 40 weaves its way through some of the most exquisite scenery in the region. But the road is rough *ripio*, and only manageable in a hire car as long as it hasn't rained. Consider hiring a 4WD for safety. The landscape is beautiful: tiny settlements with green fields and orchards, against the constant backdrop of the rugged Andes. Angastaco (1900 m) is a modern village, 2 km off Ruta 40, at Km 77, less picturesque than Cachi, but it does have an **archaeological museum** in the Centro Cívico. The church is modern, so it's worth the trek to the much older one, the **Iglesia del Carmen de Angastaco** (1800) about 8 km further north on the **Finca El Carmen**. Stop in Angastaco to try the *vino patero*, for which the town is famous. This sweet red or white wine is traditionally made by treading the grapes in the traditional manner – hence the name (*pata* is the informal word for leg). The **Fiesta Patronal Virgen del Valle** is held on the second weekend of December, with processions, music, dancing, gauchos and rodeos. Information is available from the **tourist office** ① *in the municipalidad on the plaza, Mon-Fri 0900-1400*.

San Carlos and the Quebrada de las Flechas → *Colour map 1, B2.*

The highlight of your trip on this fabulous route will probably be the next stretch of road through the **Quebrada de las Flechas** (the gorge of arrows) to San Carlos. You'll find yourself surrounded by massive rocks, eroded into complex forms and massive sharp peaks towering above you, jutting like giant vertical valleys into the blue sky. All very photogenic. **San Carlos** (1710 m, Km 24) is a pleasant place and was the most important village in the valley until the growth of Cafayate. The main buildings are on the pretty plaza, including the church, the largest in the valley, which was built between 1801 and 1860. Nearby, there's a small **archaeological museum** ⓘ *daily 1000-1400*, which contains superb archaeological finds from the region, including fine funerary urns. Also on the plaza are artisans' shops and workshops, and a craft market.

Cafayate and around → *For listings, see pages 309-314.*

Cafayate (1660 m) is beautifully situated in a broad stretch of the valley at the confluence of the Santa María and Calchaquí rivers. There are mountains on all sides, and the valley is filled with vineyards, which have long produced wine to rival Mendoza in quality, if not in quantity. There's lots of accommodation and one exquisite place to stay, **Patios de Cafayate** ⓘ *www.patiosdecafayate.com*, making this a good base for exploring the dramatic scenery all around or just relaxing for a couple of days. Cafayate has long been a popular excursion destination for visits to the bodegas which open their doors to tourists with free tours and wine tastings. There are superb red grapes grown at high altitude here, and it's worth asking specifically to try the white Torrontés grape, which is grown in few places other than Argentina and flourishes in the annual 350 days of sunshine, and the cool nights.

Ins and outs → *Colour map 1, B2. Phone code 03868. Population 11,785.*
Getting there and around There are several buses daily from Salta along the fast Ruta Nacional 68, and it's an easy drive in a hire car, though the road is winding for the last 30 km as you enter the amazing rock formations of the Quebrada de las Conchas. Alternatively, and even more scenic, is the Ruta 40 via Cachi and the Valles Calchaquíes (see above) but the road is rough *ripio* and there are very few buses between Molinos and Angastaco. There are many excursions on offer from Salta to Cafayate (US$32, including lunch and visit to a *bodega*), with brief stops to see the strange rock formations in the Quebrada de las Conchas. But these make for a long day, and you'll miss the chance to walk around the region. Cafayate is easy to get around on foot, with restaurants and shops located around the main plaza, but you'll need transport to reach many of the bodegas further out. Take a taxi or hire a bike, available from shops on the plaza.

Tourist information There's a tiny but informative **tourist centre** ⓘ *20 de febrero, T03868-422442, culturcafayate@yahoo.com.ar, daily 0800-2200*, in a hut on the northeast corner of the plaza. They have a basic map with the bodegas marked, and an accommodation list. Tour operators can be found along Calle General Güemes (this street changes names from Norte to Sur across the plaza, and, confusingly, identical numbers can be found on both sides).

Sights
Conventional sights aren't Cafayate's strong point; it's much more interesting to explore the landscape and the bodegas. The **Museo de la Vid y El Vino** ⓘ *Güemes Sur, 2 blocks south of the plaza, Daily 0800-2000, US$1.50*, contains old winemaking equipment and a display on the history of wine. The **Museo Arqueológico Rodolfo I Bravo** ⓘ *Colon 191, daily 1100-2000, US$1.50*, is tiny but has some beautiful funerary urns, black ceramics from the fifth century, and Inca pieces too – well worth seeing if you haven't come across them elsewhere.

Bodegas

Cafayate's wines are sophisticated and generally of very high quality, with intense high-altitude reds (Malbec and Cabernet Sauvignon predominate), and the famous white Torrontés. This superbly fruity dry wine with delicious floral aromas is grown only in the Valles Calchaquíes, and makes an excellent aperitif. There are several bodegas that can be visited and all are shown on the tourist office's map; the best are described below. Tours usually take around 45 minutes, most are free, and are followed by a free tasting. Ask if the guides speak English.

The most highly recommended bodega, with an informative tour, is **El Esteco** ① *at the junction of R68 and R40, T03868-421201, www.elesteco.com.ar, 8 daily Mon-Fri (1st at 1000, last at 1830), Sat-Sun 1000, 1100, 1200.* Visitors can learn more about the process of winemaking and tasting in one of the courses on offer. There are various tours available. Next door is Cafayate's best accommodation: the sumptuous **Patios de Cafayate** (see Sleeping, page 311), formerly part of the bodega and now with luxury spa. It's also a great place for lunch.

Another excellent bodega is **Etchart** ① *2 km south on R40, Km 1047, T03868-421310, www.bodegasetchart.com, tours daily on demand, open Jan, Feb, Jul, closed for lunch, book in advance,* which produces high-quality wines, some of which are exported to Europe.

The diminutive **San Pedro de Yacochuya** ① *7 km behind Cafayate, T03868-1540 0890, www.sanpedrodeyacochuya.com.ar, phone to arrange a tour, Mon-Fri 1000-1700, Sat-Sun 1000-1300,* is a boutique bodega, beautifully situated high up into the hills, making exquisite wines. To get there, take Ruta 40 in the direction of Cachí, after 2 km turn left on Ruta 2, then follow this for 6 km until you reach the bodega.

Once you've visited the best three, you could go to **Finca de las Nubes** ① *3 km above Cafayate, on the Camino al Divisadero,*

Cafayate

To Cachi & Molinos (RN40)

beyond Hotel Viñas de Cafayate, T03868-422129, www.bodegamounier.com, guided visits are available Mon-Sat 0930-1700, Sun 1000-1500, dramatically set against the mountains. This is a small family bodega, which produces fine wines and offers simple meals so you can sit and enjoy a bottle of wine on the terrace. If you buy the wine, the visit is free (otherwise it's US$4).

Then there are two interesting mass-production bodegas that can also be visited: **Domingo Hermanos** ① *3 blocks south of the plaza on 25 de Mayo, T03868-421225, www.domingohermanos.com,* and **Vasija Secreta** ① *outskirts of Cafayete, next to ACA hostería, T03868-421850.*

If you only have an hour spare and don't want to wander far from the centre of town, head to **Nanni** ① *Chavarría 151, T03868-421527, www.bodegananni.com, US$1.25,* also recommended. It's only one block from the plaza, but once you're inside, you feel you're in the outskirts of town with only vineyards and the mountains in sight. The bodega is very traditional, family-owned for over 100 years. They grow Malbec, Torrontés, Tannat and Cabernet Sauvignon grapes, and produce organic wines.

Around Cafayate

There are lots of good walks around Cafayate. To see the amazing rock formations of Quebrada de las Conchas, go along Ruta Nacional 68 towards Salta (see below for a description), or the **Quebrada de las Flechas** on Ruta 40 towards San Carlos, see page 305. There are also lots of places to walk, cycle or drive to from the town itself. **Cerro San Isidro**, 5 km west, has cave paintings and views across the Aconquija mountains in the south and to the Nevado de Cachi in the north. Behind it, the waterfalls of **Río Colorado** are a pretty place for bathing in summer. For a stroll and a good view, take Vía Toscano west out of the centre up to **Cerro Santa Teresita**, 2 km each way.

Quebrada de las Conchas

Heading north from Cafayate towards Salta, the Ruta Nacional 68 enters the Quebrada de las Conchas (Gorge of Shells), though no one seems to know why it has this name. It's a truly magnificent stretch of road, with huge ochre, burgundy and terracotta rocks carved into extraordinary forms by wind and rain. These formations have been helpfully labelled, in true Argentine style, with the names of things they most resemble: *El Anfiteatro* (the amphitheatre) Km 48; the *Garganta del Diablo* (devil's throat), Km 49; *El Sapo* (the toad), Km 35; and *El Fraile* (looks vaguely like a praying friar), Km 29. Take a few minutes to walk inside the Garganta del Diablo, particularly, and to stop to photograph *Los Castillos* (the castles), Km 20. The best light for photography is in the early morning or late afternoon. The valley floor beside the Río de las Conchas is richly green with tipa and algarrobo trees, contrasting beautifully with the chocolate-coloured mountains and raspberry ripple strata. There's lots of birdlife to be spotted, including *ñandúes* (ostrich-like rheas). If you haven't got a car but want to experience the Quebrada, take a bus from Cafayate towards Salta and get off at Los Loros, Km 32, or at the Garganta del Diablo, walk back, and catch a return bus from Salta. Or, hire a bike, take it on the 0500 El Indio bus and cycle back.

Vegetation becomes increasingly dense as you approach Salta, with a river winding by your side. There's one decent place to stop: the **Posada de las Cabras** ① *T03868-499 1093,* and look out for the strange town of **Alemania**, once a busy trading place on the train line but deserted since the train stopped passing through.

For Sleeping and Eating price codes and other relevant information, see Essentials pages 30-36.

⏺ Sleeping

Northwest of Salta *p302*
La Poma
D Hostería La Poma, Sarmiento and Belgrano 40, T03868-491003. Welcoming place, breakfast included, also serves meals.

Salta to Cafayate *p302*
Chicoana
A Los Los, Chicoana, 40 km from Salta at the entrance to the Valles Calchaquíes, T387-683 3121, www.redsalta.com/loslos. Open Mar-Dec. Most welcoming and highly recommended, beautifully situated on a hilltop with fabulous views from the colonial-style galleried veranda, where you can completely relax. Spacious rooms are decorated with old furniture and there are beautiful gardens with a pool. Includes horse riding into the forested mountains of the huge *finca*, where you will be cooked lunch in a remote rustic lodge.
A Sayta, 2 km from Chicoana, T0387-156 836 565, www.saltacabalgatas.com.ar. Very welcoming *estancia* that has rustic accommodation. The real draw card is owner Enrique and his staff who run horse treks through the tobacco fields and the Sierras de Chicoana. The food is plentiful and home cooked. Often recommended.
B-C Hostería de Chicoana, on the right-hand side of the plaza in Chicoana, at España 45, T0387-490 7009, www.new sendas.com. A pretty colonial building, now slightly faded, but with the added advantage of expert guide Martín Pekarek on hand, and horses for hire.

Cachi and around *p303*
L-AL El Molino de Cachi Adentro, 9 km out of Cachi on the road to La Aguada, T/F03868-491094, www.bodegaelmolino.com.ar.

A great luxurious choice, this is a beautiful place to stay. 6 exquisitely tasteful rooms around a restored 300-year-old mill. Lovely views down the valley from the garden and pool, and superb food. Nuny and Alberto Durand are charming (and bilingual) hosts, and make sure every detail is perfect. They'll happily collect you from Salta airport, arrange personally designed tours on horseback or 4WD. Their miniature bodega produces wonderful wines, and there are lovely places to walk and sit all around. Reservations essential.
L-AL La Merced del Alto, Fuerte Alto 2 km from Cachi, T03868-490030, www.lamerced delalto.com. Stunning hotel set in a historical house amongst endless vineyards. 14 smart, modern and clean rooms, some with breathtaking views of the surrounding hills. Recommended.
AL Finca Santana, take the road to Cachi Adentro , on right at top, T0387-432 1141, adrianab@texilesandinos.net. Just 2 lovely rooms in this beautifully situated boutique B&B right in the heart of the valley, with spectacular views, and a complete sense of privacy and silence. Friendly young owner Adriana makes you feel at home in this stylish house, with spacious living room, terrace and garden. Twin or double both with private bath and gourmet breakfast, trekking can be arranged.
AL-A El Cortijo, just opposite the ACA, on Av Automóvil Club s/n, T03868-491034, www.hostalelcortijo.com.ar. Small, family-owned boutique hotel, with delightful rooms decorated simply in great style, with lovely paintings and religious icons from Peru and local areas. Recommended.
A ACA Hostería Cachi, at the top of Juan Manuel Castilla, up a steep slope behind the monument from Av Automóvil Club Argentina, T03868-491105, www.soldel valle.com.ar. Very comfortable, modern rooms with wheelchair access, great views from its hilltop position, and a pool. The

restaurant serves excellent food – the best in Cachi by far – with friendly staff and a warm welcome. Recommended.

A-B Casa de Campo La Paya, 12 km south of Cachi at La Paya, clearly signposted from the road, T03868-491139, www.casadecampo lapaya.com.ar. A restored 18th-century house with a pool, all elegant rooms with bathroom, also serves excellent dinners. Friendly welcome from the owners. Recommended.

B-C Cabañas Inti Killa, opposite the municipal campsite, T0387- 491345, T0387-154 154 325, www.cabanasintikilla.com.ar. *Cabañas* for 2-6, with heating and TV, and views of the Nevado de Cachi.

B-C Hostería Llaqta Mawk'a, Colonel Ruiz de los Llanos s/n (20 m from the plaza), T03868-491016, www.hotellllaqtamawka. todowebsalta.com.ar. An old building, nicely renovated, with comfortable rooms, pool and good breakfasts. The helpful local owners can give tourist information, organize trekking, horse riding, and arrange collection from Salta.

C-D Samay Huasi, on the road to La Aguada, just 1 km further on from El Molino, T03868-425 0625, reservas@samayhuasi.com. Great views but the rooms are run down and very basic. A laid-back place.

E Hospedaje Don Arturo, C Bustamente s/n, T03868-491087, hospedajedonarturo. blogspot.com. Homely and welcoming, with small but very clean rooms on a quiet old street, signposted from the plaza, and with very sweet owners who don't speak English but make you feel at home.

E-F Hospedaje El Nevado de Cachi, Ruiz de los Llanos and Federico Suárez, T03868-491912. The cheapest option, right next to the bus stop. Characterful with impeccable small rooms, all with bathrooms, arranged around a central courtyard.

Camping

Municipal campsite, at the end of the Av Automóvil Club Argentina s/n, T03868-491053. With pool and sports complex, also has basic *cabañas* and a hostel.

Seclantás *p304*
B-C Hostería El Capricho, Abrahan Cornejo s/n, T0383-421 6322, www.elcaprichosalta. com.ar. With 4 nicely decorated double rooms set around a well-kept courtyard, this *hostería* is the best choice in town. Includes breakfast.

E-F Hostería La Rueda, Abrahan Cornejo and Pedro Ferreyra, T03868-498041. The small, basic rooms in this clean *hostería* are the cheapest option. Welcoming staff make up for the lack of luxuries.

Molinos *p304*
LL-L Colomé, 20 km west of Molinos, T03868-494044, www.bodegacolome.com. Leave town via the *vicuña* farm and follow signs, or phone for directions from Cafayate. The most luxurious place to stay in the Valles Calchaquíes, this winery is beautifully set in the mountains, and has wonderful accommodation in 9 gorgeous rooms with spectacular views, great horse riding and walks, *bodega* tours and wine tastings that attract world-class connoisseurs. The entire *finca* is biodynamic, all the food is organic and the power is hydroelectric. One of Argentina's best places to stay. Highly recommended.

A Hacienda de Molinos, Abrahan Cornejo (by the river), T03868-494094, www.hacienda demolinos.com.ar. Open all year round. Stunning 18th-century *hacienda*, with rooms around a courtyard. Great attention to detail, the rooms are an oasis of calm. Swimming pool with a view of the Cachi mountains.

E Cardones de Molinos, Sarmiento and San Martín, T03868-494061, cardonesmolinos@ salnet.com.ar. Real family experience in this haphazard but welcoming home run by the charming young owner, Miriam. Don't expect luxury, but this is the real thing.

F pp Hospedaje San Agustín, Sarmiento and Abraham Cornejo, T03868-494015. The nuns here have small but impeccably clean, neat rooms for rent, some with private bathroom. They don't like them to be advertised, though, so just ask around in a gentle way for *'las monjas'* in the street behind the church, and someone will come and give you a key.

Camping
Municipal campsite, in the sports complex, Alvarado and Mitre, T03868-495110. Hot showers, electricity, US$1.50 per tent, cabins US$7.

Angastaco *p305*
D Hostería de Angastaco, Av Libertador s/n, T03868-491123. Breakfast included, and prices negotiable in low season. Rooms are basic but comfortable, and this place is especially recommended for its warm welcome from reception staff who are very helpful and can provide information on the region. Pool, and meals on request.

San Carlos and the Quebrada de las Flechas *p305*
C La Casa de Los Vientos, Las Alfareras s/n, San Carlos, T03868-495075, www.casadelos vientos.com.ar. Comfortable accommodation in a colonial-style house built almost entirely of adobe, recreating a traditional Calchaquí residence. Just 8 rooms, and it's rustic but very welcoming with the friendly Swiss owner on hand to make your stay enjoyable. Excellent value, with breakfast included.

Camping
Municipal campsite, Rivadavia and San Martín, T03868-495110. Well tended with plenty of shade.

Cafayate and around *p306, map p307*
There's lots of accommodation here but Cafayate is popular, so book ahead during holiday periods (Jan, Easter and late Jul), and it's all much cheaper off season. To see other options, visit www.turismosalta.gov.ar (in English).
LL Patios de Cafayate, Routes 68 and 40, T0387-432 3030, www.luxurycollection.com/ cafayate. A stunning hotel, in the converted building of the old winery (now **El Estecco**, see

page 307 for visits to the *bodega*), with beautifully designed rooms, sumptuous lounges, and set in gorgeous gardens with a lovely pool. There are interesting wine-oriented treatments in their spa and the restaurant serves fine food, has a lovely terrace and excellent wines. Highly recommended.
AL Viñas de Cafayate, R21, Camino al Divisadero, T03868-422272, www.cafayate wineresort.com. High up on a hillside above Cafayate, this hotel is built in colonial style, with large, airy public rooms, and pretty, spacious bedrooms, some with stunning views. The restaurant looks simple, but the chef (ex-Marriott) is excellent, and there are superb local delicacies on the menu, open to non-residents too, with reservation. Full buffet breakfast. Recommended.
AL-A Killa, Colón 47, T03868-422254, www.killacafayate.com.ar. A delightfully restored colonial house with a rustic decor in all the well-equipped rooms. Pleasing views, tranquillity and comfort. Martha, the lovely owner, makes you feel absolutely at ease and keeps a fascinating collection of plants growing in the garden. Breakfasts are just great.
A La Casa de la Bodega, R68, 18 km from Cafayate, T03868-421888, www.lacasadela bodega.com.ar. A large brick *estancia* set amongst vineyards, with a suburb view. Prices include a fantastic breakfast, Wi-Fi, and a private wine tasting.
A Villa Vicuña, Belgrano 76, T03868-422145, www.villavicuna.com.ar. Located only ½ a block from the main plaza, and containing 2 colourful patios lined with tiles, the rooms are bright and large, making this a nice, calming place to stay. Afternoon tea with home-made pastries is served on demand. Recommended.
A Portal del Santo, Silvero Chavarria 250, T03868 422-400, www.portaldelsanto.com.ar. A new family-run hotel with lovely large clean rooms overlooking a beautiful pool and garden. Recommended.
C Hostal del Valle, San Martín 243, T03868-421039, www.nortevirtual.com (search under

Cafayate). Highly recommended for comfort and great value, this homely place has beautifully maintained spacious rooms, all with bath, around a lovely plant-filled patio. A new living room at the top offers splendid views of the valley. For extra few pesos, the upper rooms have really nice views. Breakfasts of home-made delicacies.

D-C Lo de Peñalba, Nuestra Señora del Rosario 79, T03868 422-213, www.lode penalba.com.ar. You can't get more central than this small 5-room hotel directly off the main plaza. With high ceilings and rustic furnishings, rooms face an internal courtyard. Recommended.

Hostels

E Rusty K Hostal, Rivadavia 281, T03868-422 031, www.rustykhostal.com.ar. Slightly ugly building from the outside, but inside there are neat, basic rooms and a great garden with BBQ. 2 blocks from the main square.

E Hostel Ruta 40, Güemes Sur 178, T03868-421689, www.hostel-ruta40.com. The cheapest and most sociable accommodation option. Clean and friendly, R40 is recommended. Discount for HI members.

F El Balcón, Pasaje 20 de Febrero, T03868 421-739. The cheapest option. The rooms are basic, but the location is very central and the views from the roof are wonderful.

Camping

Camping Luz y Fuerza, T03868-421568, also on R40, south of the town. More appealing than the municipal site and quieter.

Camping El Jardín, Córdoba 250, T03868-421234. Only 4 blocks from the centre, and offering hot showers for US$2 a tent.

● Eating

Cachi *p303*

▼▼▼-▼▼ La Merced del Alto, Fuerte Alto, T03868-490020. Set in luscious surroundings, this is a treat to your taste buds and your eyes. Make sure you try a local wine.

▼▼ ACA Sol de Valle, Av AC Argentino, at the top of town, T03868-491105. A surprisingly extensive menu, with lovely views.

▼ Confitería del Sol, on the plaza, next to Oliver. Good, cheap, regional food, big groups at lunchtimes in high season.

▼ El Aujero, General Güermes, on the corner by the bus station. Interestingly decorated with old farm tools, the food is average but it's a good place to hang out and meet people. Regional specialities or European classics.

▼ Oliver Café, on the plaza. Sandwiches, juices and ice creams in a friendly tiny café. Good for breakfast or tea and pizzas.

Molinos *p304*

▼▼▼-▼▼ Bodega Colomé, 157 km from Cachi, T03868-494044. Good local specialities. After eating world-class delicacies on the terrace, stay around and try out the inviting spa. Pure luxury.

Cafayate and around *p306, map p307*

Cafayate has lots of lovely choices around the plaza, most of them huge and prepared for coach parties. In summer many provide live music. The following are recommended:

▼▼▼ Viñas de Cafayate, R21, Camino al Divisadero, T03868-422272. Elegant food, simple surroundings, but lovely views from this hotel. Book ahead.

▼▼ Restaurante Colorado, Belgrano 28, T0868-421280. Charming new restaurant with a great selection of local food and wine. Recommended.

▼▼ Criollo, Güemes Norte 254. A small *parrilla*, recommended.

▼▼ El Rancho, Toscano 4, T03868-421256. A traditional restaurant on the plaza serving *parrilla* and good regional dishes (try the *tamales*).

▼▼ La Carreta de Don Olegario, Güemes Sur 20 and Quintana de Niño, T03868-421004. Huge, but does good set menus for the usual meat dishes and pastas. Good wine menu.

▼▼-▼ Baco, Güemes Norte and Rivadavia. An attractive corner and a lively place serving basic sandwiches, *empanadas*, pizzas and trout-based dishes, with a great range of local wines and beers. Becomes lively at night with live music. Recommended.

Ice cream parlours
Helados Miranda, Güemes Norte 170. Cafayate's unmissable treat is this fabulous home-made ice cream. The creative owner makes wine-flavoured ice cream as well as many other delicious flavours.

O Shopping

Cachi *p303*
Artesanía Juan Calchaquí, near the monument at the bottom of the hill from the service station, T03868-491037. Oscar Alfredo Cardozo is the leading weaver and teacher in Cachi, and promotes local weavers through this shop, which sells their work at far lower prices than the government shop in the tourist office.
Artesanía Kuyaymasi, opposite the ACA Hostería, T03868-1563 9615, oscartesano@yahoo.com. Oscar Valenzuela works with alpaca and makes fine jewellery but also sells a good selection of local weavings, leather and woodwork. He's also a good tourist guide and leads conventional trips to Las Pailas, La Paya and La Poma.

Cafayate and around *p306, map p307*
Lots of fairly trashy souvenir shops have opened on the plaza, but there are some fine handicrafts shops to be found if you dig around. There's the **Calchaquí tapestry exhibition** of Miguel Nanni on the main plaza (Güemes 65), silver work at **Jorge Barraco**, Colón 157. Oil paintings, wood-carving, metalwork and ceramics by **Calixto Mamani** can be seen in his gallery, Rivadavia 452, or contact him at home (Rivadavia 254). Ceramics are also made by **Manuel Cruz**, Güemes Sur 288 (the building itself is worth seeing). Local

pottery is sold in the **Mercado Municipal de Artesanía** on the plaza.

▲ Activities and tours

Salta to Cafayate *p302*
Sayta, 2 km from Chicoana, T0387-156 836 565, www.saltacabalgatas.com.ar. Very welcoming *estancia* runs tours in the area. The real draw card is owner Enrique and his staff who run horse treks through the tobacco fields and the sierras de Chicoana.

Cachi *p303*
Horse riding
Hostería Llaqta Mawk'a , T03868-491016, www.hotelllaqtamawka.todowebsalta. com.ar, see Sleeping, above. Ask for Ariel Villar.

Tour operators
Fernando Gamarra, corner of Benjamín Zorrilla and Güemes, T0387-431 7305, fg_serviciosturisticos@yahoo.com.ar. More conventional trips around Cachi with genial Fernando, who is good company, to Las Pailas, La Poma and Seclantás, including the beautiful Laguna de Brealito. Knowledgeable, reasonably priced, especially if divided amongst a group.
Santiago Casimiro, T03868-1563 8545, santiagocasimiro@hotmail.com. Particularly recommended for all mountain hikes; he's a nurse trained in mountain rescue, and has lived in the valley all his life. He'll take you to La Poma, Cerro de la Virgen, and up the Nevado peaks, all very reasonable. Highly recommended.
Susana Guantay, T0387-154 134 135. Charming local Susana will take you on informed walks around the town, to La Poma and Las Pailas. Also informed guide on the archaeological museum.
Tourism Urkupiña, Benjamin Zorrilla s/n, T03868-491317, uk_cachi@hotmail.com. Local agency that can book tours and bus tickets.

Cafayate and around *p306, map p307*
Cycling
There are many places to hire a bike situated around the main plaza. Compare rates before renting.

Tour operators
Turismo Cordillerano, C Quintana de Niño 59, T03868-422137, www.turismocordillerano.com.ar.
Wichay Turismo Aventura, 9 de Julio 64, T03868-421333. Guided trips on mountain bikes, or high-mountain trekking and mountaineering.

⊖ Transport

Cachi *p303*
Bus
To **Salta**, daily 0700 and Tue and Sat 1330, Thu 1530, Sun 1730, 4 ½ hrs, US$11, **Marcos Rueda**, T03868-491063. To **Molinos**, daily at 1200.

Remise taxis
Los Calchaquies, T03868-491071; San José, T03868-491907.

Molinos *p304*
Bus
To **Salta** (via Cachi), Mon, Tue, Thu, Sat 0645, Sun 1245, 2 hrs to **Cachi**, US$7, 7 hrs to **Salta** US$13, **Marcos Rueda** (in Salta T0387-421 1327). From Salta to **Molinos**, Sun, Mon, Wed, Fri, 0700, arriving Molinos 1330, US$13.

Angastago *p305*
Bus
To **Salta**, Mon-Fri, US$11. To **Cafayate** via San Carlos, Mon-Fri, **El Indio**, US$8, T03868-421002 (in Cafayate).

Remise taxi
Alto Valle Remis, 12 de Octubre 233, Cachi, T03871-5502 0981. Taxi to **Molinos**, US$26.

San Carlos and the Quebrada de las Flechas *p305*
Bus
5 services a day to **Cafayate**, 30 mins, US$5, **El Indio**.

Cafayate and around *p306, map p307*
Bus
There are 2 separate bus terminals: for **Salta**, go to **El Indio** bus terminal on Belgrano, ½ a block from the plaza, T03868-421002; and for **Tucumán**, to the Aconquija terminal at Güemes Norte and Alvarado, T03868-421052. To **Salta** (via the Quebrada de Las Conchas), 3 a day, 3 hrs, US$11, **El Indio**, travel in daylight to see the rock formations. To **Angastaco**, 1 daily Mon-Fri, 1½-2 hrs, US$5, **El Indio**, but note this bus does not go further north along the R40 to Molinos and Cachi. To **Santa María** (for **Quilmes**) 4 daily, Aconquija; El Indio. To **Tucumán**, 3 daily (more services added from Santa María), 5½-6 hrs (6½-8½ hrs via Santa María), US$16 and **Tafí del Valle**, 3 daily (more connecting at Santa María), 4 hrs (5½ hrs via Santa María), US$10, with **Aconquija**, daily 0215, 0600, 1400, 1800. From Tafí de Valle there are 6-8 daily departures to Tucuman, 2½ hrs, US$5.

❶ Directory

Cafayate and around *p306, map p307*
Banks Banco de la Nación, Toscano and NS del Rosario. ATM; **Banco Salta**, Mitre and San Martín, ATM, open all year, good service. **Medical services** Pharmacy, F Pastor, Rivadavia 35. **Post office** Güemes 197. **Internet** Güemes Sur 155.

Jujuy province

→ Colour map 1, A3. Phone code 0388. Population 611,888.

The beautiful province of Jujuy lives slightly under wealthier Salta's shadow, but it has some of the richest culture of the whole country thanks to its large population of indigenous people, who most Argentines refer to as 'los indios'. Absorb the lively street life in Jujuy City, take part in a Pachamama (Mother Earth) ceremony, or witness the vibrant festival in remotest Casabindo, and you'll feel the palpable energy of the authentic Andean culture which has survived over 300 years of colonial rule. So while Jujuy is less developed in tourist infrastructure, it's definitely worth making the effort to explore, and as tourism brings more income to the region, bus services and hotels are opening up fast in response.

Jujuy's great attraction is the Quebrada de Humahuaca, made a World Heritage Site by UNESCO in 2003 for its spectacular beauty. Easter and Carnival are celebrated here in exuberant style, which combines Christian traditions with pre-existing Andean religious beliefs. Dotted along the Quebrada there are pleasant towns to hang out for a few days for walking and exploring. Purmamarca and Humahuaca are most appealing: famous for the Cerro de Siete Colores, there are now some fine hotels, walks to the stratified rocks of seven colours and a dramatic drive up to the salt flats. Tilcara is probably the best base for exploring the area, with lots of good accommodation, a lively market, a museum and the Pucará, the ruined hilltop town. From here the adventurous could trek west into the subtropical cloudforest park of Calilegua, or into the stunning Garganta del Diablo.

The Quebrada villages all have characteristic squat white adobe churches, but Uquía's is the most impressive, with an extraordinary collection of Cuzqueño school paintings. Further north, Humahuaca is popular and friendly, and you can take the bus from here to the exquisite remote hamlet of Iruya, just over the border into Salta. At the northernmost end of the Quebrada, off the road to Bolivia, the church in the village of Yavi is the country's most exquisite colonial treasure, its gold decoration seen in the lemony light from onyx windows. And east from here, there's the stunningly located village of Nazareno (Salta).

East and west of the province are two contrasting landscapes: in Jujuy's expanse of puna in the west, you'll find the fascinating small villages of Susques and Casabindo, famous for its bullfight in August. There are old Jesuit gold mines and Laguna de los Pozuelos with its wealth of birdlife. To the east, find cloudforest in Calilegua National Park, accessible from Libertador General San Martín. Or stay at eco-finca Portal de Piedra (www.ecoportaldepiedra.com.ar) for incredible horse riding into the same landscapes with greater comfort. For more information on travelling in and around Jujuy, see www.norteargentino.gov.ar (in English). → For listings, see pages 319-322.

Jujuy city → For listings, see pages 319-322.

Often overlooked by tourists, the city of Jujuy (pronounced whoo-whooey) may be Salta's poorer sister but it has plenty of life and culture to make it a good starting point for the Quebrada de Humahuaca which stretches northwest from here. Properly referred to by locals by its full name, San Salvador de Jujuy, it's the capital of Jujuy province and sits at 1260 m in a bowl of lushly wooded mountains, 100 km north of Salta. Jujuy was founded in 1593, between two rivers, the Río Grande and Chico, or Xibi Xibi, but it has sprawled south supporting a growing population on dwindling industry. Wars and earthquakes have left the city with few colonial buildings, but there's some fine architecture around its plaza and from the bridge over the Río Xibi

Xibi, with its brightly coloured market stalls, you have wonderful views of the dramatic purple mountains, contrasting with the thick green vegetation that fills the river bed. Although more chaotic than Salta, Jujuy has some lively bars where you can hear the region's wonderful *folclore* music, and its history is worth exploring, with two fine churches, a packed archaeological museum and a fabulous market. All this makes a good introduction to the province's rich indigenous culture and a handy base for exploring a variety of landscapes within easy reach. The region's most accessible cloudforest park, Calilegua, is just 125 km east of here. A great local website with lots of information is www.huhuhuy.com.ar (in Spanish).

Jujuy

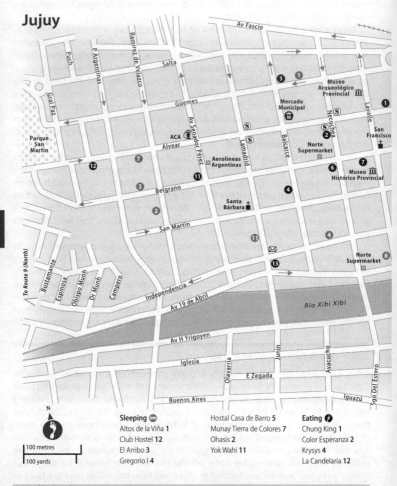

Sleeping 🛌
Altos de la Viña **1**
Club Hostel **12**
El Arribo **3**
Gregorio I **4**

Hostal Casa de Barro **5**
Munay Tierra de Colores **7**
Ohasis **2**
Yok Wahi **11**

Eating 🍴
Chung King **1**
Color Esperanza **2**
Krysys **4**
La Candelaria **12**

Ins and outs → *Colour map 1, A3. Phone code 0388. Population 238,000.*

Getting there Jujuy's airport, **El Cadillal** ① *T0388-491109*, is 32 km southeast of the capital. Minibuses (US$4.50) run between the airport (25 mins) and the **Aerolíneas Argentinas** office in town; a taxi costs US$10. The **bus terminal** ① *information T0388-422 1373*, is six blocks south of the main street, Belgrano, over the river on Dorrego and Iguazú. The terminal serves the whole province including all destinations north of the city and border towns with Bolivia, as well as south to Salta (four hours) and from there to most major destinations. There are direct overnight buses to Buenos Aires taking at least 19 hours. ▸▸ *For further details, see Transport, page 321.*

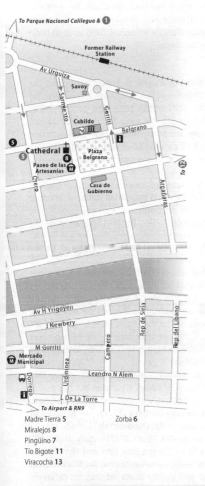

To Parque Nacional Calilegua & ❶

Former Railway Station

Av Urquiza

Savoy

Sarmiento

Gorriti

Cabildo ⑪

Belgrano

❺

Cathedral

❺

Plaza Belgrano

❽

Paseo de las Artesanías Ⓜ

Otero

Casa de Gobierno

Argañaraz

To ⑫

Av H Yrigoyen

J Newbery

Rep de Siria

Rep del Líbano

M Gorriti

Ⓜ Mercado Municipal

Canero

Urdininea

Leandro N Alem

Dorrego

L De La Torre

To Airport & RN9

Madre Tierra 5
Miralejos 8
Pingüino 7
Tío Bigote 11
Viracocha 13

Zorba 6

Getting around The city is pleasant to walk around and is particularly interesting around the plaza, the market opposite the bus terminal, and on the bridges. The most interesting sites are within six blocks and could comfortably be visited in a day.

Tourist information The **city tourist office** ① *on the plaza at Gorriti 295 and Belgrano, T0388-422 1326, Mon-Fri 0700-2200, Sat-Sun 0900-2100*, turismo@jujuy.gov.ar, has a helpful accommodation leaflet and a map, but little information about the rest of the province or transport. There is another smaller and limited office at the **bus terminal** ① *T0388-422 1343, www.turismo.jujuy.gov.ar (also in English), daily 0700-2100*, offering helpful advice on accommodation, though few staff speak English.

Background

Jujuy has an extraordinary history. The Spanish wanted to found a city to link the chain of settlements connecting Alto Perú with Córdoba but met extreme resistance from the indigenous people, who destroyed their first two attempts in 1561 and 1575. The city was finally established in 1593 and prospered until the 18th century, but the province of Jujuy bore the brunt of fighting during the Wars of Independence when the Spanish launched 11 invasions down the Quebrada de Humahuaca from Bolivia between 1810 and 1822. Then, in August 1812, General Belgrano, who was commander of the Republican troops, demanded an incredible sacrifice of

Jujuy's people when he ordered the city to be evacuated and destroyed before the advancing Royalist army. They left the city which was razed to the ground, but the people of Jujuy survived and remain proud of their sacrifice. This event is marked on 22-23 August by festivities known as **El Exodo Jujeño** with gaucho processions and military parades. As a tribute to the city for obeying his orders, Belgrano donated the flag which is displayed in the lavish Casa de Gobierno in Plaza Belgrano.

Jujuy has experienced growing poverty in recent years since its industries – traditionally sugar and tobacco – suffered in the economic crisis, with resulting widespread unemployment. It's one of the few Argentine cities where the population is largely indigenous, boosted in the last 20 years by considerable immigration from Bolivia. You may well find bus journeys in the region delayed en route by peaceful demonstrations of *piqueteros* blocking the road, protesting about job and benefit cuts. Tourism is the main growth industry in the area as the city is slowly waking up to its huge natural asset, the extraordinary beauty on its doorstep.

Sights

If you arrive in the city by bus, you will be greeted by a perfectly typical example of the usual mayhem of *boleterías* (ticket offices) for 20 different bus companies, crowds waiting with huge packages to be carried to remote parts of the *puna*, and people selling balloon-like plastic bags of pink popped corn. To get into town from the bus station, walk along Dorrego/Lavalle, crossing the bridge across the thickly vegetated river bed where the city teems cheerfully with life, and you'll pass the fabulous fruit and vegetable market with delicious *empanadas* and stalls selling razors and peaches, tights and herbal cures, pan pipes and plimsols.

In the eastern part of the city is the tranquil **Plaza Belgrano**, a wide square planted with tall palms and lined with orange trees, with a striking equestrian statue of Belgrano at its centre. On the south side stands the **Casa de Gobierno**, a cream French-style neoclassical building built in 1927. Inside, you can see the very flag that Belgrano gave the city in recognition of their great sacrifice in a sumptuously decorated long hall with pleasing art nouveau statues representing Justice, Liberty, Peace and Progress, by the Argentine sculptor, Lola Mora.

On the west side of the plaza is the **cathedral**, whose neoclassical façade – built in the late 19th century to replace the original, which was built in the early 1600s and destroyed by an earthquake – contains an exquisite jewel: a gold-plated wooden pulpit, carved by indigenous tribes in the Jesuit missions. Its elegant biblical illustrations are very moving and the delicate modelling of the dove overhead and on the angels' faces is stunning. It's one of Argentina's finest colonial treasures. There are also several fine 18th-century paintings. On the north side of the plaza is the **Cabildo**, built in 1867 and now occupied by the police, with a rather dull police museum inside.

The **Iglesia de San Francisco** ① *Belgrano and Lavalle, 2 blocks west of the plaza, daily 0730-1200, 1730-2100 (Thu till 2200), has well informed guides*, is modern but has a calm interior and contains another fine gilded colonial pulpit, with ceramic angels around it, like that at Yavi (see page 326). The **Iglesia de San Bárbara** (1777), San Martín and Lamadrid, is similar in style to the colonial churches in the Quebrada de Humahuaca.

The **Museo Arqueológico Provincial** ① *Lavalle 434, T0388-422315, daily 0900-1200, 1500-2100, US$1*, has some superb ceramics from the pre-Inca Yavi and Humahuaca cultures, and beautifully painted funerary urns, sadly, some containing the tiny bones of children. The museum may be underfunded and poorly displayed, but it's definitely worth visiting – particularly for a fabulous 2500-year-old sculpture of a goddess giving birth and the rather gruesomely displayed mummified infant.

If you like military portraits, you could visit the **Museo Histórico Provincial Juan Galo Lavalle** ① *Lavalle 256, T0388-421355, Mon-Fri 0800-1330, 1500-2000, Sat-Sun 0900-1300, 1600-2000, US$0.40,* though it's pretty dry and a whole room is dedicated to the death of General Lavalle which occurred in this house, a turning point in the civil war between Federalists and Unitarists. There are also a couple of fine Cuzco-school paintings dating from 1650.

Around Jujuy city

There's plenty of accommodation in Jujuy itself or you could head out to the **Termas de Reyes** ① *www.termasdereyes.com,* for the thermal baths. They have been closed recently due to a mudslide but should be opening up again at some point. Call beforehand. Tour operators offer full-day excursions from Jujuy into the *puna* and the Quebrada de Humahuaca, but if you have the time it's far better to take at least a couple of days to explore both areas properly. Jujuy is also the starting point for the cloudforest park of **Calilegua**, by bus via Libertador General San Martín.

◉ Jujuy province listings

For Sleeping and Eating price codes and other relevant information, see Essentials pages 30-36.

◉ Sleeping

Jujuy city *p315, map p316*
All hotels will be fully booked for the festival of **El Exodo Jujeño**, 22-23 Aug: book ahead. For a complete listing with prices, see www.turismo.jujuy.gov.ar.
A Altos de la Viña, Av Pasquini López 50, T0388-426 2626, www.hotelaltosdelavina. com.ar. Located just out of the city this 4 star hotel is set in 5 ha of parklands, with tennis, volleyball and football facilities, all with fantastic views over the city. The day spa offers day passes to non-guests (US$11).
A Ohasis, Ramírez de Velasco 244, T0388-424 1017, www.ohasishoteljujuy.com. Rooms are tastefully decorated, large spa offering treat- ments, a great restaurant and a rooftop pool.
B El Arribo, Belgrano 1263, T0388-422 2539, www.posadaelarribo.com.ar. Attractive, well located, newly opened boutique *posada* set in a restored colonial house with 12 modern, a/c rooms. Swimming pool, great breakfasts and smiling staff. Highly recommended.

B Gregorio I, Independencia 829, T0388-424 4747, www.gregoriohotel.com. Wonderful, small boutique hotel with only 20 rooms. Smart, modern style, with local art scattered throughout. Big buffet breakfast. Recommended in this price range.
C Munay Tierra de Colores, Alvear 1230, T0388-422 8435, www.munayhotel. jujuy.com. A small, clean, modern, quiet place with dark but comfortable rooms, all with private bath. Welcoming staff.

Hostels

F pp Hostal Casa de Barro, Otero 294, T0388-422 9578, www.casadebarro.com.ar. Lovely double, triple and quadruple rooms, whitewashed with simple decorations, shared bathrooms and a fantastic area for eating and relaxing. The wonderful staff provide dinner (US$4) on demand. Highly recommended.
F pp Club Hostel, San Martín 155, T0388-423 7565, www.hihostels.com. A fun hostel with a very small pool and lovely wooden furniture, next to the plaza with its own travel agency; **Noroeste** (see Activities and tours, below).
F pp Yok Wahi, La Madrid 168, T0388-4229608, www.yokwahi.com. An affordable,

centrally located hostel with clean and tidy dorms and 1 double with bath. Open 24 hrs, this is a lively and noisy hostel with great breakfasts included. Discounts to HI members.

Around Jujuy city *p319*
AL Hotel Termas de Reyes, Termas de Reyes, 19 km northwest of Jujuy, T0388-392 2522, www.termasdereyes.com. 6 buses a day from Jujuy bus terminal 0630-1945, returning 0700-2040, 1 hr, US$1.50. This sumptuous thermal spa resort with a grand neoclassical hotel is set among magnificent mountains at an altitude of 1800 m. Rates include the use of the thermal pools. No children allowed. Recommended for a day trip. The hotel recently closed due to mudslides but is expected to re-open. Call beforehand.
C-B La Escondida, Ejército del Norte s/n, T0388-156 822 141, laescondidadeyala. com.ar. This homestead is actually in the village of Yala, which is a great alternative (if you have car) to the bustle of Jujuy as it is only 14 km away. Minimum 2 night stay, lovely doubles, and also main homestead for rent (**AL** for up to 8), and a bungalow (**A** for up to 5). Impressive swimming pool set in luscious gardens.

Hostels
F pp **Aldea Luna**, Tilquiza, T0388-1550 94602, www.aldealuna.com.ar. A new concept in hostelling. Set in 900 ha of lush rainforest, native trees, rivers and mountains in a natural reserve, this hostel is 20 km from Jujuy. The dorm-style accommodation is in 4-share, solar-powered stone cottages with bathrooms (yes, there's hot water!). Prices include all meals and if you have the energy you can volunteer to work in the reserve or the garden and you'll get your accommodation free. Call to arrange a pick up from Jujuy US$15 for up to 4 people, or from Salta US$51 for up to 4. In summer, the 4WD can't make it all the way to the hostel, so you will have to walk the remaining 1 km. All the food served is vegetarian.

Cabañas
El Caserío, Finca Cerro Chico, Bárcena, 32 km north of Jujuy on R9, T0388-156 825 257, www.caseriojujuy.com. Beautiful *cabañas* (**B-A**) and a house available for rent in lovely wild parkland, with wide-open views (**L** for up to 8 people).

Camping
If you keep going north from Jujuy, up in the Quebrada de Humahuaca, there's a campsite in every town.
G pp **El Refugio**, R9, Yala T/F0388-490 9344, www.elrefugiodeyala.com.ar. This is the nearest campsite to the city and is actually at Yala, over the bridge in a pretty spot on the banks of the river, 14 km north of Jujuy city on R9. There's also a hostel with dorms (**F**) and doubles (**D**), pool, restaurant, and trekking and horse-riding excursions are on offer. Highly recommended, a great place to relax.

❼ Eating

Jujuy city *p315, map p316*
There are lots of great places to eat in Jujuy. For more information see www.jujuy.travel. Following Lavalle across the bridge to the bus terminal (where it changes names to Dorrego) there are lots of cheap places selling *empanadas*.
🍴🍴🍴 **Krysys**, Balcarce 272, T0388-423 1126. A popular bistro-style *parrilla* restaurant with excellent steaks.
🍴🍴 **Chung King**, Alvear 631, T0388-422 2982. This is an atmospheric and good-value place for regional food; note that their *peña* across the street has closed. The restaurant has been operating for over 60 years and is a local institution.
🍴🍴 **La Candelaria**, Alvear 1346, T0388-154 219 781. Closed Tue. A welcoming choice for *parrilla*, with good service. Highly recommended.
🍴🍴 **Miralejos**, Sarmiento 268. On the plaza, great restaurant serving local dishes

such as *humitas*, and local beers.
Highly recommended.
ŤŤ-Ť Zorba, Belgrano 802 (corner of
Necochea), Large, 2-level Greek-influenced
restaurant in the centre. Recommended
Ť Tío Bigote, Av Senador Pérez and Belgrano.
A hugely popular pizzeria.
Ť Viracocha, Independencia and Lamadrid.
Recommended for regional and spicy delicacies.

Cafés
There are several good cafés on the same
busy block of Belgrano between Lavalle
and Necochea, including **Pingüino**, the
best *heladería* in the town.
ŤŤ-Ť Madre Tierra, Belgrano 619. A great
place for vegetarians (or if you want a break
from all the meat). Behind the wonderful
wholemeal bakery of same name, a cool oasis
serves delicious food (only open for lunch).
Ť Color Esperanza, Necochea 376.
A small café also serving cheap *lomitos*
and hamburgers.

⊕ Entertainment

Jujuy city *p315, map p316*
Head for a *peña* to hear the region's
passionate *folclore* music played live here.
La Casa de Jeremías, Horacio Guzmán 306,
T0388-424 3531; **La Yapa**, Mejías 426; and
Savoy, Alvear and Urquiza, all have live music
and dancing at weekends, and during the
week in busy holiday periods. **Salamanka**,
San Martín 889. Has resident and guest DJs,
and good cocktails.

O Shopping

Jujuy city *p315, map p316*
Camping and fishing equipment
Can be hired at **Tierrita**, Necochea 508.

Food
You can't beat the colourful **Municipal market**,
Dorrego and Alem, near the bus terminal.

Outside it, women sell home baked
empanadas and *tamales*, and delicious goat's
cheese, as well as all kinds of herbal cures.
There is a **Norte** supermarket, Belgrano 825,
and a bigger branch at 19 de Abril y Necochea.

Handicrafts
Handicrafts are sold from stalls on Plaza
Belgrano near the cathedral. There's a better
range in the old train station north of the
plaza on Urquiza, and from the rather limited
Paseo de las Artesanías on the west side of
the plaza. Try also **Regionales Lavalle**, Lavalle
268; and **Mercado Municipal**, Balcarce 427.

▲ Activities and tours

Jujuy city *p315, map p316*
Tour operators
For visiting Calilegua under your own steam,
see Transport, below.
Noroeste, San Martín 155, T0388-423 7565,
www.noroestevirtual.com.ar. Excursions to
Quebrada de Humahuaca, salt flats, *the*
puna. Also offer adventure tourism. Located at Club
Hostel (see Sleeping, above). Recommended.
Siete Colores, Gorriti 291, T0388-422 6998/
155 106 064, www.sietecolores-jujuy.com.ar.
Organizes trips to the Yungas and the
Quebrada including Iruya.

⊖ Transport

Jujuy city *p315, map p316*
Air
For airport information, see page 317.
Flights to **Buenos Aires** and **Córdoba**
with Aerolíneas Argentinas.
Airline offices Aerolíneas Argentinas,
Belgrano 1053, T0388-422 7198.

Bus
For bus terminal information, see page 317.
Long distance Buses go almost hourly
up the Quebrada de Humahuaca – several
companies. Vía Tucumán to **Córdoba**,

daily, Panamericano and La Veloz del Norte; to **Tucumán**, 8 hrs, US$16, and **Córdoba**, 15-16 hrs, US$25.

To **Salta** hourly, 2 hrs, US$8. To the Bolivian border **La Quiaca**, 6½ hrs, US$12, Balut; El Quiaqueño; Panamericano. Several rigorous luggage checks en route for drugs, including coca leaves. To **Humahuaca**, several daily, 2½-3 hrs, US$6, Evelia and others; via **Tilcara**, 1½-2 hrs, US$4.

To **Buenos Aires**, several daily, 19-23 hrs, US$60-75, Flecha Bus; La Veloz del Norte; Panamericano. To **Orán** and **Aguas Blancas** (border with Bolivia, via San Pedro and Ledesma), daily, **Balut; Brown; Flecha Bus**. To **Purmamarca**, several daily US$5, 2 hrs **Cotta Norte, El Vallisto, Evelia, Panamericano** (check they call at Purmamarca village, off the main road). To **Susques**, Tue-Sun, 4-6½ hrs, US$8, Andes Bus. To **Calilegua**, almost every hr, various companies to Libertador General San Martín (also called Ledesma), eg **Balut**, from there take Empresa 23 de Agosto or Empresa 24 de Septiembre buses, leaving 0830 to Valle Grande, across Parque Nacional Calilegua. All **Pocitos** or Orán buses pass through **Libertador San Martín**.

Car hire
At the airport: Earth Rent a Car, T0388-491 2734, www.earthargentina.com.ar; Hertz, T0388-422 9582, www.hertzargentina.com.ar
In town: **Sudamerics**, Belgrano 601, T0388-422 9034/154 365 502, www.sudamerics.com.

❶ Directory

Jujuy city *p315, map p316*
Banks There are ATMs at Banco Francés, Alvear and Lamadrid; Banco Galicia, Alvear and Necochea; Banco Río, Alvear and Necochea. **Currency exchange** Banco Macro, Alvear and Lamadrid, changes dollars. **Embassies and consulates** Bolivia, Av Senador Pérez and Independencia, open 0900-1300. **Internet** Belgrano 969 in arcade. **Medical services** Pharmacy, Del Pueblo, Alvear 927, T0388-422 2339. **Post office** Independencia and Lamadrid. **Telephone** There are many *locutorios* in the centre.

Quebrada de Humahuaca

Since it was declared a World Heritage Site by UNESCO in 2003, the Quebrada de Humahuaca has attracted a deluge of visitors, and while a couple of its main towns are becoming transformed beyond recognition by tourism, much of the area retains its ancient authentic life. Starting at the city of Jujuy, the main route heading north to the Bolivian border is one of the most dramatic areas of natural beauty in the country, passing through a long gorge of intensely coloured rock, arid mountains of terracotta, yellow, orange, pink, cream and malachite green strata, speckled with giant cacti. In the fertile valley floor of the Quebrada are several small historic towns, some with their neat adobe houses now mingled with modern new developments, but all centred around the characteristic simple squat white 18th-century churches of the region. The pretty village of Purmamarca, with its backdrop of the Cerro de Siete Colores, Tilcara with its handicraft market and restored hill fort, Maimará with its hillside cemetery and La Paleta del Pintor, and the busy village of Humahuaca, all make good places to stay, to walk and to absorb the ancient history of the area. The indigenous culture is particularly rich here: there are pre-Incan ruins at Tilcara, and throughout the Quebrada there are weeks of riotous pre-Lent carnivals. Tilcara's Easter celebrations are justifiably famous: a traditional procession on Holy Thursday night is joined by thousands of pan pipe musicians making a huge procession from the mountain into the town: an overwhelming experience. For more tourist information, see www.turismo.jujuy.gov.ar and www.norteargentino.gov.ar (both in English). ➤➤ *For listings, see pages 329-334.*

Ins and outs

Getting around Public transport is easy to use and a number of bus companies go up and down the Quebrada from Jujuy to Humahuaca, stopping at Purmamarca, Tilcara, Maimará and Uquía. **El Quiaqueño**, **Panamericano** and **Balut** go all the way to La Quiaca on the Bolivian border. If driving, fuel is available at Volcán, Tilcara, Humahuaca and Abra Pampa, so you might need to take a spare can if you're heading far into rural areas. It's a good area for cycling, preferably away from the Ruta Nacional 9 where there can be a lot of traffic through the valley and there's not much shade.

Route 9 to Bolivia → *For listings, see pages 329-334.*

Purmamarca → *Colour map 1, A3. Phone code 0388. Population 2100. Altitude 2200 m.*

The first village you come to in the Quebrada, just off Ruta Nacional 9 at Km 61, Purmamarca is a perfect place to rest and acclimatize to the altitude. It's a tiny, peaceful, slightly expensive village with a choice of comfortable places to stay (no hostels) and a stunning setting at the foot of the Cerro de los Siete Colores – a mountain striped with at least seven colours, from creamy pink to burgundy and copper to green, best seen in the morning or afternoon light. Once the steady trickle of tour buses has left, Purmamarca retains its own quiet rhythm of life. There's a good market on the plaza, selling a mixture of locally made llama wool goods, but lots of alpaca spoons and weavings are imported from Bolivia. At the top of the plaza, there's a beautiful church, **Iglesia de Santa Rosa** (1648, rebuilt in 1778), typical of those you'll see elsewhere in the Quebrada, with its squat tower, whitewashed adobe walls and simple, well-balanced construction. Inside there's a splendid time-darkened cactus roof and pulpit, and a series of exquisite paintings depicting the life of Santa Rosa. Next to the church is an algarrobo tree thought to be 500 years old. There's a tiny, helpful **tourist office** on the plaza, which can provide maps, information on accommodation and bus tickets.

Maimará → *Phone code 0388. Population 2200. Altitude 2383 m.*

About 12 km from Purmamarca at Km 75, Maimará is a lovely, tranquil oasis village. Its green fields of onion and garlic are set in contrast with the backdrop of richly coloured marbled rock, known as La Paleta Del Pintor, to the east of the village. For an enjoyable walk in the low evening light, when the colours of the rock are at their warmest, walk along the old road to the east of Maimará, and take your camera: it's a beautiful sight. Just off the road, 3 km south, is **La Posta de Hornillos**, one of the chain of colonial posting houses that used to extend from Buenos Aires to Lima, also the scene of several battles and where Belgrano stayed. Now restored, the building houses a historical **museum** with a collection of 18th- and 19th-century furniture, as well as weapons and historical documents. North of Maimará there's a huge cemetery on the hillside, brightly decorated with paper flowers at Easter.

Tilcara → *Colour map 1, A3. Phone code 0388. Population 5600. Altitude 2461 m.*

Tilcara lies 22 km north of Purmamarca at Km 84. It's the liveliest Quebrada village and the best base for exploring the area, with plenty of places to stay and to eat. There's an excellent handicrafts market around its pleasant plaza, though be discerning as lots of the goods are mass produced in Bolivia. For fine local weavings, visit the women's weaving co-operative, **La Flor del Cardón**, next to the **tourist office** ① *Belgrano, next to Hotel de Turismo, T0388-495 5720, Mon-Fri 0800-1300, 1400-2130, Sat 0900-1300, 1400-2100, Sun 0900-1300*, which has very helpful staff. Useful websites include www.tilcara.com.ar (in English) and www.tilcarajujuy.com.ar (in Spanish).

Tilcara is the site of an important pre-Hispanic settlement, and you can visit the **Pucará** ① *Daily 0900-1800, US$1*, a restored hilltop fortress above the town with panoramic views of the gorge from its complex web of low-walled dwellings, made more splendid by mighty cacti. To get there, turn right off Belgrano where signposted; head up the hill and across the metal bridge over the Río Huasamayo. At the entrance to the Pucará, there's also a small handicrafts shop where you can get helpful information, and a small botanical garden with many species of cactus. On the plaza is a superb **Museo Arqueológico** ① *Belgrano 445, daily 0900-12.30, 1400-1800, US$1 including entry to Pucará, and vice versa*, with a fine collection of pre-Columbian ceramics, masks and mummies. There are four art museums in town, of which **Museo Regional de Pintura** ① *Rivadavia 459, Tue-Sat 0900-1800, Sun and public holidays 0900-1200, 1400-1800, US$0.50*, is worth a look, with paintings on the customs and traditions of Tilcara. There are fiestas throughout an extended Carnival period. At Easter, there's a famous gathering of thousands of pan pipe musicians, who play as they follow the procession of the Virgin de Copacabana down the mountain. It's an extraordinary, noisy and moving sight. Book accommodation well in advance.

Huacalera and Uquía

Huacalera lies 2 km north of the Tropic of Capricorn; a sundial 20 m west of the road marks the exact location. The church, several times restored, has a roof made of cactus wood and a small museum. **Uquía** is one of the smaller villages along the Quebrada, and is totally un-touristy with a tranquil atmosphere and a narrow main street of adobe houses. Close to the road, there's one of the valley's finest churches, its beautifully proportioned white tower very striking against the deep red rock of the mountain behind. Built in 1691, **Iglesia San Francisco de Paula** contains an extraordinary collection of Cuzqueño-style paintings of angels in 17th-century battle dress, the *ángeles arcabuceros*. Painted by local indigenous artists under the tuition of Jesuits, the combination of tenderness and swagger in these winged figures, brandishing their weapons, is astonishing.

Humahuaca and around → *Colour map 1, A3. Phone code 03887. Population 11,300.*

Although Humahuaca (2940 m) was founded in 1591 on the site of a pre-Hispanic settlement, it was almost entirely rebuilt in the mid-19th century. It is a labyrinth of narrow streets, with low adobe houses around a small central plaza. Despite being the most popular tourist destination for Argentines along the Quebrada, it retains its own culture. Accommodation here is more limited than at Tilcara, but once the coach trips have left, it's quiet, and is a useful stopping point for travelling north up to the *puna*, or to Iruya. **La Candelaria** festival is celebrated on 2 February, and the beginning of carnival here is famously lively with **Jueves de Comadres**, and **Festival de las Coplas y de la Chicha**, when everyone throws flour and water at each other and gets very drunk. Book accommodation ahead.

On the tiny plaza is the church, **La Candelaria**, originally constructed in 1631, rebuilt 1873-1880, containing wonderfully gaudy gold *retablos* and 12 fine Cuzqueño-school paintings. Every day at 1200, tourists gather outside **El Cabildo**, the neo-colonial town hall on the plaza, to watch a large mechanical figure of San Francisco Solano emerge to bless the town from his alcove high in the wall. You may find this kitsch rather than spiritually uplifting, but it's quite a sight. Overlooking the town and surrounded by fantastically large cacti is the **Monumento a la Independencia Argentina**, commemorating the scene of the heaviest fighting in the country during the Wars of Independence. There is a good **Feria Artesanal** on Avenida San Martín (on the far side of the railway line) and a fruit market at Tucumán and Belgrano. Several new restaurants have opened recently, with decent choices to eat. The small but helpful **tourist office** ① *Tucumán and Jujuy, daily 0900-1600*, can be found on the plaza in the lovely white Cabildo building. Ask for a map of the area; as they are underfunded and have no resources they ask you to make a small donation, but it is worth it as the map can be very helpful.

About 10 km northeast of Humahuaca, near **Coctaca**, there's an impressive and extensive (40 ha) series of pre-colonial agricultural terraces – the largest archaeological site in Jujuy, though you'll have to go with a guide to find them. Contact **Ser Andino** ① *Jujuy 21, Humahuaca, T03887-421659, www.serandino.com.ar*, who offers two- to three-hour tours to Coctaca from Humahuaca, US$10 per person. Highly recommended is a night or two at least in the peaceful hamlet of **Iruya** (see below), reached by a breathtaking (or hair-raising) three-hour bus ride. Ask the tourist office about trips over the mountains to enter **Parque Nacional Calilegua**, via the beautifully situated little hamlet of Abra Zenta.

Iruya → *Colour map 1, A3. Population 5500.*

To reach Iruya, a rough *ripio* road 25 km north of Humauaca runs northeast from the Ruta Nacional 9, 8 km to Iturbe (also called Hipólito Irigoyen). The bus stops here for five minutes, giving you a chance to glimpse captivating rural life and perhaps buy a woven hat from women waiting by the bus stop. There are no facilities. The road then crosses the broad river (manageable in an ordinary car only if it hasn't rained heavily) and climbs up over the 4000-m pass, Abra del Cóndor, where you have panoramic views, before dropping steeply, around an amazing slalom of many hairpin bends, into the Quebrada de Iruya.

Iruya is an idyllic small town tucked into a steep hillside, remote and hidden away, but full of warm and friendly inhabitants. In recent years, its character has started to change due to the influx of wealthier tourists staying at the *hostería* at the top of the town.

The town still retains its festivals, with a colourful **Rosario** festival on the first Sunday in October, and lively Easter festivities, when accommodation is booked up in advance. It's worth spending a few days here to lap up the tranquil atmosphere, and to go horse riding or walking in the beautiful valleys nearby. The hike to the even more remote hamlet of

San Isidro (seven hours return) is unforgettable. At **Titiconte**, 4 km away, there are some unrestored pre-Inca ruins, though you'll need to take a guide to find them. Iruya has a tourist office on Calle San Martín but the hours are irregular; there is also a *locutorio* and food shops. Wander up the tiny narrow main street to find a post office, a shop selling wonderful herbal teas of all kinds and dried peaches from a local co-operative, and another selling superb woven and knitted goods. Not to be missed. For more information see www.iruyaonline.com (in Spanish).

La Quiaca and into Bolivia → *Colour map 1, A2. Phone code 03885. Population 14,000.*

La Quiaca (3442 m) lies on the border with Bolivia, linked by a concrete bridge to **Villazón** on the Bolivian side. Neither town is appealing, but if you have to stay the night, La Quiaca is definitely preferable: there are a few decent places to stay, and if you're around here on the third weekend in October, you can see the three-day **Fiesta de la Olla** when villagers from the far reaches of the remote *puna* arrive on donkeys and in pickups to sell their ceramic pots, sheepskins and vegetables during a colourful festival that involves a lot of dancing and drinking *chicha*. ⏭ *For more information, see box, opposite.*

Yavi and around

ⓘ *Yavi is 16 km from La Quiaca but no buses go there. However, you take a remise taxi for US$10 from La Quiaca bus terminal (this includes up to 4 passengers).*

By far the best place to stay around here is actually in Yavi, 16 km east, which has a couple of good *hosterías*. Yavi is an intriguing *puna* village with a beguiling, hidden quality. Consisting of little more than a few streets of uniformly brown adobe dwellings, most often deserted, it was founded in 1667 and was the crossing point to Bolivia until rail and road connections were built through La Quiaca. The surrounding landscape is wide open with the distinctive swooping stratified hills of the Siete Hermanos to the east. These have long been an important landmark and their stark beauty immediately calls your attention, even before you stumble across the prehistoric petroglyphs on the rocks at the foot of the hills. Ask at **Hostal de Yavi** for a tour, see page 332.

Yavi also has perhaps the finest church in the northwest, well worth the detour from La Quiaca. The **Iglesia de Nuestra Señora del Rosario y San Francisco** ⓘ *Mon 1500-1800, Tue-Fri 0900-1200, 1500-1800, Sat-Sun 0900-1200*, was built in 1676-1690, a sturdy, white construction with buttresses and a single tower. Inside are the most magnificent gold *retablo* and pulpit, made by artisans who were brought, like the gold, from Peru. The *retablo* is adorned with a gold sculpture of an angel in 18th-century battle dress (like a three dimensional version of the paintings of Uquía) and the tabernacle is lined with mirrors to make candlelight within glow like the sun. Above the exquisite pulpit, decorated with ceramic cherubs, flies a golden dove. All this splendour is seen in the yellowy light from windows made of transparent onyx, giving the beautiful Cuzqueño paintings even more power. It's an impressive and moving sight.

Opposite the church is the 18th-century **Casa del Marqués Campero y Tojo** ⓘ *Mon-Fri 0900-1300, 1400-1800, Sat-Sun 0900-1800*, the austere former mansion of the family that was were granted large parts of the *puna* by Philip V of Spain. It's an imposing building with empty courtyards, whose one-room museum houses a strange and eclectic collection of 18th-century bedsprings, arrowheads and candelabras. There's a small but excellent selection of handicrafts for sale inside, and some nicely carved local slate with petroglyphs on a stall outside. There is a colourful evening procession during Easter week.

Border essentials: Argentina–Bolivia

La Quiaca

The border bridge is 10 blocks from La Quiaca bus terminal, 15 minutes' walk, taxi US$2.

Argentine customs and immigration Office open 0700-2400; but on Saturday, Sunday and holidays there is an extra fee of US$1.50 which may or may not be charged. If leaving Argentina for a short stroll into Villazón (not really advised), show your passport, but do not let it be stamped by Migración, otherwise you will have to wait 24 hours before being allowed back into Argentina. Formalities on entering Argentina are usually very brief at the border but thorough customs searches are made 100 km south at Tres Cruces. Leaving Argentina is very straight-forward, but travellers who need a visa to enter Bolivia (check with your embassy) are advised to get it before arriving in La Quiaca.

Transport There are at least nine buses a day from Jujuy to La Quiaca (stopping at most bigger villages in the Quebrada de Humahuaca), four to seven hours, US$9, and three hours, US$5.50 from Tilcara. The bus terminal in La Quiaca at España and Belgrano and there is luggage storage available. A taxi to the border from La Quiaca costs US$1.50.

Villazón

A grim place, little more than the centre of commercial activity in an otherwise remote and uninhabited area. The road from the border bridge, Avenida República de Argentina, is lined with shops and stalls selling sandals, toys, sunglasses, paper flowers, sacks of pink puffed corn and armfuls of coca leaves. Women in traditional Bolivian dress, with their enormous skirts (*cholitas*), spin wool and weave vividly coloured textiles on the pavement, and there's plenty of fresh orange juice and cheap ice cream for sale. However, there's nowhere decent to stay and no tourist information. The bus station has toilets, but they aren't pretty.

Note Argentine time is one hour behind Bolivian time depending on the time of year. Remember not to photograph the border area. For more detailed information, see www.gengarmeria.gov.ar/pasos/flchqulaca.htm (In Spanish)

For a really marvellous experience of the wild beauty and isolation of this region, make time to visit the remote town of **Nazareno**, a four-hour drive east of La Quiaca. The road crosses astonishingly bold rolling hills, before climbing up to the dramatic Abra del Cóndor, and then dropping thousands of metres to find Nazareno nestled in a crown of vermillion mountains. There are some wonderful walks along old Inca roads to Cuesta Azul and to Milagro. Accommodation is with local families; the hospitality is warm and the landscapes are unforgettable. If you speak Spanish and can chat to the people living here, you'll be able to get a real taste of fascinating Andean culture.

Puna Jujeña → *For listings, see pages 329-334.*

The Puna Jujeña (3700 m, Km 213) covers all the area to the west of the Quebrada de Humahuaca. It's a spectacularly remote and bleak place with few settlements, but extraordinary salt flats, lakes full of birdlife and plenty of history to be explored. If you have time it's definitely worth spending a few days in the area. The *puna* is high altitude (between 3000 and 4000 m) and it's an inhospitable area to travel alone, so although you could hire a 4WD vehicle and be independent, consider trips with adventure travel company **Socompa** ⓘ *www.socompa.com*, which enable you to explore the *puna* in the company of expert guides without having to worry about the many practicalities.

There are two main areas to explore. **Salinas Grandes** and **Susques** can be reached either from San Antonio de los Cobres in Salta, or from Purmamarca in the Quebrada de Humahuaca. The second area, in the far north, is the **Monumento Natural Laguna de los Pozuelos**, reached by turning west from Abra Pampa. You could do one round trip (now offered by **Movitrack** and other tour companies), setting off from Salta, climbing the Quebrada del Toro to San Antonio de los Cobres, and reaching the Salinas Grandes (Ruta 40), before descending via the spectacular **Cuesta de Lipán** (Route 52) to Purmamarca in the Quebrada de Humahuaca. ⏵⏵ *For further information, see Salta's activities and tours, page 293.*

Susques and Salinas Grandes → *Colour map 1, A2. Phone code 03887.*
The main crossing to Chile is via Route 52 which links Purmamarca and the Salinas with the little village of **Susques**, and on to the **Paso de Jama** (see box, opposite) over the awesome Abra Potrerillos pass (4170 m). Susques is the only settlement between Purmamarca and the border, lying in a hollow at the meeting of the Río Susques and Río Pastos Chicos. It has a stunning little church, dating from 1598 – one of the outstanding examples of colonial architecture in the region, with a roof of cactus-wood and thatch. Inside is an old bellows-organ. There are regular buses from Jujuy, with Andes Bus and Purmamarca (four hours), but it's best to hire a car or join a tour. There are a few basic places to stay and eat in Susques, see listings page 332.

The salt flats of Salinas Grandes are astonishing – a seemingly endless, perfectly flat expanse of white, patterned with eruptions of salt around regular shapes, like some kind of crazy paving. Against the perfectly blue sky, the light is dazzling. It's safe to walk or drive onto the surface, and you'll find men mining salt, creating neat oblong pools of turquoise water where salt has been cut away, and stacking up piles of white and brown salt blocks, ready for refining.

Casabindo → *Colour map 1, A3.*
Heading north from Susques on Route 11, you'll reach the tiny hamlet of **Casabindo** (3500 m), founded in 1602. It can also be approached by travelling 63 km southwest from Abra Pampa – quite a trip over the *puna*. There's a magnificent church, one of the finest in the whole region, with twin towers dating from 1772. It's beautifully proportioned and contains a superb series of 16th-century paintings of *angeles arcabuceros* (archangels in military uniforms) like those at Uquía. It's worth trying to visit on 15 August, when there's a lively celebration of **La Ascensión de la Virgen**, accompanied by the last remaining *corrida de toros* (running with bulls) in Argentina. **El Toreo de la Vincha** takes place in front of the church, where a bull defies onlookers to take the ribbon and medal it carries: a symbolic offering to the virgin rather than a gory spectacle. The only place to stay is at the village school, which offers basic dorm accommodation (T03887-491129). However, most visitors come on a day trip from Tilcara and return there to sleep at night.

Border essentials: Argentina–Chile

Paso de Jama

The border (4200 m) is open 0800-0000 and is 360 km west of Jujuy, reached by a 60-km road that branches off Route 70. This is one of the borders where long-distance buses cross and so the facilities are better than at most borders. There is a car park, toilets and phone services. **Note** Even in summer it can drop to -5°C at night. For more detailed information, see www.gendarmeria.gov.ar/pasos/fichjam.htm.

Argentine customs and immigration At Susques, where there is accommodation and fuel. On the Chilean side the road continues (unpaved) to San Pedro de Atacama (Km 514), where fuel and accommodation are available, and Calama.

Chilean immigration At San Pedro de Atacama.

Monumento Natural Laguna de los Pozuelos → *Colour map 1, A3. Phone 03887.*
ⓘ *Park office in Abra Pampa, T03887-491048, www.parquesnacionales.gov.ar.*
Monumento Natural Laguna de los Pozuelos (3650 m) is a nature reserve 50 km northwest of Abra Pampa and centred around the lake. Laguna de los Pozuelos hosts 44 species of birds, and is visited by huge colonies of up to 25,000 flamingos. It's a stunning landscape, well worth exploring if you have a few days. Be warned though that this is high-altitude *puna*, and temperatures can drop to -25°C at night in winter; don't attempt camping unless you have high-mountain gear and all the food, warm clothing and drinking water you're likely to need, plus spare supplies. There is a ranger station at the southern end of the Laguna with a campsite nearby. At **Lagunillas**, further west, there is a smaller lagoon, which also has flamingos. There are no visitor services and no public transport. Unless you have your own car, the only real option is to go with a guide. Try **Socompa** (see opposite).

If you're keen to explore the wild *puna* further, you could head for the tiny village of **Santa Catalina**, 67 km west of La Quiaca, along *ripio* Route 5. There's a *centro artesanal*, La Negra, and a 19th-century church with a dazzling gold and red interior, and a small museum of artefacts from local history housed in the oldest building in the village.

ⓔ Quebrada de Humahuaca listings

For Sleeping and Eating price codes and other relevant information, see Essentials pages 30-36.

ⓢ Sleeping

See also www.turismo.jujuy.gov.ar and www.welcomeargentina.com.

Purmamarca *p323*
See also www.gopurmamarca.com.ar.
L-AL El Manantial del Silencio, R52, Km 3.5, T0388-490 8081, www.hotelmanantial. com.ar. Signposted from the road into Purmamarca. One of the most luxurious options in the Quebrada, this is an elegant traditional *estancia* building, with beautifully designed comfortable minimalist rooms, grand spacious sitting areas, a huge fire, pool and wonderful views all around. Good service from the professional staff. The restaurant (residents only) serves superb food and wine, and the breakfasts are sumptuous. Recommended.

AL La Comarca, R52 Km 3.8, T0388-490 8001, www.lacomarcahotel.com.ar. A small complex of very comfortable rooms plus a few *cabañas*, all built with local materials in rustic style in this bright pink building. The location is unbeatable, amidst colourful mountains on the outskirts of Purmamarca. Rooms are comfortable, service is excellent, there's a heated pool, a mini spa, and a restaurant serving regional cuisine.

A Hostería del Amauta, C Salta, T0388-490 8043, www.hosteriadelamauta.com.ar. Not quite as sophisticated as **La Comarca** or **El Manantial**, but this central option offers spacious and nicely appointed rooms with attractive rustic decor, and also has a restaurant. Perfectly comfortable.

A-B La Posta de Purmamarca, C Santa Rosa de Lima, T0388-490 8029, www.postade purmamarca.com.ar. Highly recommended, with a beautiful elevated setting against the mountain, just 4 blocks up from the plaza. All of its standard rooms are spacious and comfortable, with modern bathrooms. Beautiful cacti plants for sale.

B Terrazas de la Posta, beside La Posta, above, T0388-490 8053, www.terrazasde laposta.com.ar. Very good rooms that open onto a veranda, with wonderful views over the little town.

B-C Casa de Piedra, Pantaleon Cruz 6, T0388-490 8092, www.postadelsol.com. Well-situated new hotel made of stone and adobe with very comfortable rooms.

C El Viejo Algarrobo, just behind the church, T0388-490 8286, elviejoalgarrobo@hotmail. com. Modest but recommended, with small but pleasant rooms, cheaper with shared bath.

Maimará *p324*

B La Casa de Té, Belgrano s/n, T0388-425 0230, www.lacasadeltata.com.ar. Nicely decorated and welcoming *hostería* serving great breakfasts which include home-baked pastries. Rooms have cable TV and newly fitted bathrooms. They also serve a fantastic afternoon tea with 7 varieties of cakes.

C Posta del Sol, Martín Rodríguez y San Martín, T0388-499 7156, www.postadelsol.com. Comfortable *hostería* with a good restaurant. The owner, a tourist guide, can take you on a tour of the area and has helpful information.

Tilcara *p324*

A Posada con los Angeles, Gorriti 156 (signposted from access to town), T0388-495 5153, www.posadaconlosangeles.com.ar. A much-recommended favourite with charming rooms, each in a different colour, all with fireplace and door to the garden with beautiful mountain views. Warmly recommended.

B Alas de Alma, Dr Padilla 437, T03881-5682 9926, www.alasdelalma.com. The newest and most central hotel. Relaxed atmosphere, spacious doubles, and *cabañas* for up to 4 people. 2 mins from the main street. Breakfast included.

B Posada de Luz, Ambrosetti and Alverro, T0388-495 5017, www.posadadeluz.com. ar. Gorgeous views of the Quebrada from the private terraces behind each room in this small, comfortable and rustic hotel surrounded by large gardens. Recommended.

B Quinta La Paceña, Padilla and Ambrosetti, T0388-495 5098, www.quintalapacena.com.ar. This architect-designed traditional adobe house is a peaceful haven and the nicest place to stay in Tilcara. The garden is gorgeous and wonderfully kept. Recommended.

B Uwa Wasi, Lavalle 564, T0388-495 5368, www.uwawasi.com.ar. Small and intimate, this adobe house not only has history, but its rooms have a welcoming, rustic-style. Peaceful garden to relax in.

Hostels

E pp **Malka**, San Martín s/n, 5 blocks from plaza up steep hill, T0388-495 5197, www.malkahostel.com.ar. The most welcoming place to stay in Tilcara. A superb youth hostel, one of the country's best. It has beautifully situated rustic *cabañas* (**A** up to 8), dorms for 4 people and doubles with bath (**B**). Catch a taxi from town or walk for 20 mins. Highly recommended.

F Casa los Molles, Belgrano 155, T0388-495 5410, www.casalosmolles.com.ar. Not really a hostel, this affordable *casa de campo* offers simple dorms in a friendly atmosphere, as well as a charming double (**D**) and 2 comfortable

cabañas (**B-C** for up to 4 people). Small and central, book in advance. Wi-Fi available.
F Tilcara Hostel, Bolívar 166, T0388-495 5105, www.tilcarahostel.com. Located on a quiet street, this hostel is welcoming, clean and easy to find. Also offer comfortable doubles (**D**). Highly recommended.

Camping
Camping El Jardín, access on Belgrano 700, T0388-495 5128, www.eljardintilcara.com.ar. Camping US$2 per person, with hot showers (only in the afternoon). Also basic but clean rooms available with bath (**E**).

Huacalera and the Uquía *p324*
B Solar del Trópico, T0388-154 785 021, www.solardeltropico.com. A short distance (2 km) from Huacalera, this small B&B is run by a lovely Argentine/French couple who will cook some fusion food for you on request. 3.25 ha of lovely organic gardens surround the house, where the rustic and spacious bedrooms are inviting. There is an artist's studio and workshops are run regularly. Tours offered. Call to arrange a pickup beforehand.
C Hostal de Uquía, Güermes and Padre Lozano, next door to the Iglesia San Francisco de Paula, T0388-490508, www.hostaldeuquia.com.ar. Simple rooms around a courtyard and very good food.
C Hostal La Granja, Huacalera, R9, 99 km, T0388-426 1766, www.hostal-lagranja.com. A welcoming, rustic place with pool, outstanding food and service. A good base for exploring the region.

Humahuaca and around *p325*
A El Mollar de Calete, Camino a Calete, 6 km from Humahuaca, T0388-154 179 693, www.elmollardecalete.com.ar. Attractive single-storey adobe house, just outside of town with rustic bedrooms and a fantastic view.
B Camino del Inca, Calle Ejército del Norte s/n, signposted on the other side of the river, T03887-421136. A modern hotel in traditional style with large rooms off colonnaded galleries, all rather overpriced. Good restaurant.

C Hostal Azul, over the bridge and 500 m further, Barrio Medalla Milagrosa, T03887-421598, www.hostalazulhumahuaca.com.ar. This small house is a good choice, offering simple rooms with bath around a central patio, and with an agreeable dining room. It lies in a quiet semi-rural area on the outskirts of the town, and the owners are young and friendly.
C Kuntur Wasi, Santa Fe 420, T03887-421 337, kunturwasi@argentina.com. Also a great resto-bar at night, each double room is smartly decorated and has a view over the town and across to the hills. Friendly staff. Recommended.
C-D El Portillo, Tucumán and Corrientes, T03887-421288, www.elportillohumahuaca.com.ar. If you don't stay here, at least try the restaurant. Basic but comfortable rooms with private bathrooms, breakfast included.

Hostels
F Hostal Humahuaca, Buenos Aires 447, T03887-421064, www.humahuacahostal.com.ar. The small rooms set around a patio are slightly dark and a bit cramped, but the friendly owner and its location (½ block from the main plaza) make this a good option. Double (**C**) available.
F pp Posada el Sol, over the bridge and 500 m further, signposted, Barrio Medalla Milagrosa, T03887-421466, www.posadael sol.com.ar. The surroundings are lovely and peaceful, on the semi-rural outskirts of town, and there are some doubles (**D**) as well as small dorms with shared bath, plus a well-equipped apartment for 6 with bath and breakfast. Discounts to HI members.

Iruya *p325*
AL-A Hostería de Iruya, T03887-154 070 909, www.hosteriadeiruya.com.ar. Extremely comfortable hotel with 15 beautifully simple rooms, smart bathrooms and excellent food. Has great views from the top of the village and offers tours. Highly recommended.
A-B Mirador de Iruya, La Banda s/n, T03887-421318, www.elmiradordeiruya.

com.ar. Cross the river and climb a little to reach this new hostal. Doubles, triples and quads available. Spot condors from the terrace with fantastic views.

Hostels
D Hostal Tacacho, Plaza La Tablada s/n, T0387-154 045 522, www.iruyaonline.com/iruya-tacacho.html. Charming but basic hotel with doubles and triples. Centrally located. Breakfast included.
F Hospedaje Asunta, Belgrano s/n (up the hill), T0387-154 045 113, www.hospedaje asuntadeiruya.blogspot.com. New friendly hostel with 28 beds. Fantastic views. Recommended.

La Quiaca and into Bolivia *p326*
B Hostería Munay, Belgrano 51/61, T03885-423924, www.munayhotel.com.ar. A very pleasant place with comfortable and spotless rooms. Very good value. Recommended.
B-C Hotel de Turismo, Siria and San Martín, T03885- 422243. The smartest place to stay, this has comfortable rooms with TV, a heated pool and a good restaurant.
C-D Cristal, Sarmiento 539, T03885-422255. Basic functional rooms with bath, in this old-fashioned place, not far from the bridge.

Hostels
D Hostel Copacabana, Pellegrini 141, T0388-423875, www.hostelcopacabana.com.ar. Friendly new hostel, only a few blocks from the bus terminal and the plaza. Clean dorms and comfortable living areas.

Camping
Camping Municipal, R5, on the route to Yavi, T03885-422645. Very basic facilities and quite a way out of town. US$2 per person.

Yavi and around *p326*
C Hostal de Yavi, Güemes 222, T03887-421659, www.hostaldeyavi.blog spot.com. Simple bedrooms with bath, and some hostel space. Cosy sitting room, good food cooked by the hospitable Javier

and Gino. Tours also arranged: to see cave paintings; moonlight walks; trekking; and trips to the Laguna de los Pozuelos. Recommended.
D-E Posada La Casona, Senador Pérez and San Martín, T03885-422316, mccailsaya@laquiaca.com.ar. Homely and welcoming.

Susques and Salinas Grandes *p328*
C El Unquillar, R52, Km 219 (2 km west of Susques), T03887-490201. An attractive *hostería* decorated with local weavings, with 6 rooms. Also has restaurant open to non-residents. Phone for pickup.
C Pastos Chicos, R52, Km 220 (at Casas Quemadas, 3 km west of Susques), T0388-423 5387/154 874 709, www.pastoschicos.com.ar. A rustic building providing comfortable accommodation. Good value. Its restaurant serves delicious regional specialities and is open to non-residents. Wi-Fi available. Phone for pickup.
D-E Residencial Las Vicuñitas, San Martín 121, T03887-490207, opposite church, atamabel@imagine.com.ar. This very basic budget accommodation is the only place to stay in Susques itself.

Casabindo *p328*
The only accommodation here is in the local school, T03887-491129. Basic, hostel-type beds, with shared bath. US$10 per person.

🍴 Eating

Purmamarca *p323*
🍴🍴🍴 **El Manantial del Silencio**, R52, Km 3.5, T0388-490 8080. Gourmet regional food in a wonderful setting. Highly recommended.
🍴🍴 **El Rincón de Claudia Vilte**, Libertad s/n, T0388-490 8088. *Folclore* music and regional dishes served at this pretty restaurant 1 block from the main plaza.
🍴🍴 **Los Morteros**, C Salta (behind the church), T0388-490 8063. A smart restaurant, combining chic and traditional style with a high standard of regional cuisine. Open lunch and dinner. Often recommended.

La Posta, Rivadavia s/n, on the plaza. Excellent local dishes – *humitas* and *tamales* especially recommended. Touristy, but the service and the food are good. A small handicrafts shop next door sells high-quality goods.

Cafés

Arte y Té, C Sarmiento. Ideal for tea, or for regional *picadas* with a drink, in the informal atmosphere of an artist's home.

Tilcara *p324*

Posada con los Angeles, Gorriti 156, T0388-495 5153. Few choices but superb food with well-balanced flavours, based on the best local ingredients (quinoa, llama meat, Andean potatoes, lamb, goat's cheese and herbs), excellently prepared and served by chef José María. Book ahead.

El Patio, Lavalle 352. This is a popular place, with rustic tables and chairs in a few small rooms. Tasty Andean meals are served. Great atmosphere, recommended.

Pucará, C Padilla, at the top of the hill on the right on the road to the *pucará*, T0388-495 5721. Really imaginative twists on traditional dishes, such as llama quinoa and risotto, all served in a rustic intimate atmosphere and really delicious. Open for dinner all year round and open for lunch in high season. Highly recommended.

Esperanza (Bar del Centro), Belgrano 547, T0388-495 5462. A small restaurant and café serving delicious local dishes in a small elegant patio. It's a lovely place to eat. Both the restaurant and crafts shop next door sustain an NGO that organizes free art and music workshops for local children.

Humahuaca and around *p325*

El Portillo, Tucumán 69, T0387-424 9000. A simply decorated room, serves slightly more elaborate regional meals than the usual, such as llama with a fine plum sauce.

La Cacharpaya, Jujuy 295, T0387-421 442. This brightly lit, large place lacks sophistication, but it's central and the food is good. Attracts an interesting mix of clientele.

Iruya *p325*

All hotels have their own restaurant, see Sleeping, above. They all serve regional meals (*locro, empanadas, humita, tamales*). **Hostal Federico Tercero** (on the plaza at the bottom of the hill) is the most welcoming place to hang out, but the most sophisticated and elegant place to eat is the pricey **Hostería de Iruya** (at the top of the town).

Comedor Margarita, near the plaza, T0388-1549 0926. Good home-made food, a menu that changes daily. The *menú del día* is always good.

Comedor Iruya, Lavalle and San Martín. Basic but tasty menu serving local cuisine.

La Quiaca and into Bolivia *p326*

Frontera, Belgrano and Siria, T03885-422269. An atmospheric place, where the generous set menu will cost you around US$4.

Ruta 9, R9, on the way out of town to the south. The best place to eat.

Bars and clubs

Tilcara *p324*

El Cafecito, Rivadavia s/n, on the plaza. Serves good coffee and wonderful locally grown herbal teas during the day, and has superb live *folclore* and jazz music at weekends from celebrated local musicians.

La peña de Carlitos, Lavalle 397, on the plaza, www.lapeniadecarlitos.com.ar. Regional music from the charismatic and delightful Carlitos, also cheap meal-of-the-day, *empanadas* and drinks. A selection of all the typical music of the area, with bits of history and culture thrown in, in a great show by the inimitable Carlitos. Recommended

Activities and tours

Tilcara *p324*
Cycling
Malka Hostel, T0388-495 5197. Rents bikes but it's a hike to get there if you're not a guest.

Tour operators

Caravana de Llamas, Alverro and Ambrosetti, T0388-495 5326, www.caravanadellamas.com.ar. Hiking into the mountains while llamas carry your belongings, reviving the ancient tradition. Explore magnificent mountain landscapes, ½- to 3-day excursions every day. **Cerro Morado**, T0388-495 5117, T03881-5682 3007, www.cerromorado.com.ar. Oscar Branchesi will take you to meet locals, giving you great insight into indigenous culture. Recommended.

Humahuaca and around *p325*
Tour operators

El Cardón, La Banda, T03887-421625, www.cabanaselcardon.com.ar. Guided horse treks in the area and also camping. **Ser Andino**, Jujuy 21, T03887-421659, www.serandino.com.ar. Really nice people offering an attractive range of trips along the Quebrada plus Iruya and to the *puna*, including to Laguna de los Pozuelos. They also go to Coctaca in 2- to 3-hr tours from Humahuaca. From US$14 per person.

Iruya *p325*
Tour operators

For local guides (walking and mules) in the surrounding area, ask at the tourist office in Iruya, T03887-482001. If you're short of time, it's probably a good idea to contract a guide in Humahuaca or Salta.
Norte Trekking, T0387-436 1844, www. nortetrekking.com. The region's most experienced guide, Federico Norte, runs small tours to Iruya, including other adventurous options, according to the groups needs. Highly recommended.

☉ Transport

Purmamarca *p323*
Bus

To **Jujuy** and up to **Humahuaca**, several buses daily, 1 hr, US$6, **Cotta Norte**;

El Vallisto; **Evelia**; **Panamericano**. To **Susques**, Tue-Sun, US$5.

Tilcara *p324*
Bus

There are frequent services to all towns on the **Quebrada** and to **Jujuy**, 1½-2 hrs, US$4.

Humahuaca and around *p325*
Bus

There are various buses to **Tilcara** and **Purmamarca** leaving every 10 mins. To **Iruya**, daily 0830 and 1030, Sun-Fri 1800, 3-3½ hrs, US$4, **Empresa Mendoza**.

Iruya *p325*
Bus

Tickets are available from the bus station, and from the food shop round the corner from the church. Buses stop outside Hostal de Gloria in Iruya.

To **Humahuaca**, Mon-Sat 0600, daily 1400, 1515, 1600, 3-3 ½ hrs, US$4, **Empresa Mendoza**, T03887-421442. Enquire with **Panamericano de Jujuy** buses about seasonal direct buses to **Jujuy** and **La Quiaca**.

La Quiaca and into Bolivia *p326*
Bus

There are several buses a day to **Salta**, 6-6½ hrs, US$18, **Andesmar**; **Balut**; **La Veloz del Norte**. To **Humahuaca**, several daily, 3-4 hrs, US$8; and to **Jujuy**, 5-6½ hrs, US$8. Take your own food, as there are sometimes long delays. Buses may be stopped for routine border police controls and searched for coca leaves. To **Buenos Aires** (via Jujuy), 26-28 hrs, US$70, including meals. **Andes Norte** links several villages west of R9, including **Santa Catalina**, Mon-Fri, US$4.

Remise taxis

Remises La Quiaca, Belgrano 169 (round the corner from terminal), T03887-423344. You can take a *remise* taxi to Yavi for US$11.

Las Yungas

In complete contrast to the puna and the Quebradas, the Yungas (pronounced shungas) are areas of cloudforest jungle lying along the eastern edges of the Salta and Jujuy provinces. Receiving heavy rainfall, these forests support an incredible wealth of wildlife and vegetation, together with fragile indigenous communities. Hence three national parks were created to protect them: Baritú and El Rey in Salta, and Calilegua in Jujuy. All three are very much worth visiting, but you'll need to be determined. Access is limited, and planning is required as infrastructure is still limited. If you don't have a 4WD vehicle, contact one of the few adventure tourism agencies who are allowed to operate in the parks. For more information, see www.redyaguarete.org.ar/yungas and www.welcome argentina.com/parques (both in English). ▸▸ *For listings, see page 338.*

Best time to visit

All three parks are difficult to access during the rainy season, January to March, when the roads are mostly impassable. There are lots of mosquitoes all year round so take plenty of repellent. The prevalence of malaria varies from year to year so check with your doctor about medication, especially in mid-summer.

Accommodation

There is no accommodation inside the parks themselves, except for very basic campsites with few facilities. However, there are some highly recommended places to stay nearby that can also arrange trips into the parks. ▸▸ *For further information, see Sleeping, page 338.*

Parque Nacional Calilegua → *For listings, see page 338.*

The park protects an area of peaks, sub-tropical valleys and cloudforest on the eastern slopes of the Serranía de Calilegua. There are some surprisingly high peaks including **Cerro Amarillo** (3720 m), which you can climb in a three-day trek round trip, starting from the entrance, and **Cerro Hermoso** (3200 m), which lies closer to the road, but is attempted by few visitors as you must go with a guide. Several rivers flow southeast across the park into the Río Ledesma. The wildlife is wonderful with at least 300 species of bird including the red-faced guan and the condor, and over 60 species of mammal. You're likely to see tapirs, otters, taruca (Andean deer) and perhaps even pumas. The unpaved Route 83 runs through the park climbing from southeast to northwest and affording splendid views, before reaching Valle Grande beyond the park's borders. From Valle Grande there is a basic road leading via Aparzo to the Quebrada de Humahuaca. Or you could hike west from the park to Humahuaca and Tilcara (allow at least four days); you'll need to take a guide.

Ins and outs

Parque Nacional Calilegua is 125 km northeast of Jujuy and the most accessible of the three cloudforest parks in the region. The park entrance is at Aguas Negras, 12 km northwest of Libertador General San Martín, reached by Route 83, which runs off Route 34 just north of town. There are frequent buses, including **Balut** ⓘ *T03886-422 2134*, from Jujuy's terminal to Libertador General San Martín (also called Ledesma). From there, buses run to the park, where you'll be met by the *guardaparque* guides. Hitching is also possible. The **park headquarters** ⓘ *San Lorenzo 4514, Calilegua, T03886-422046,* *calilegua@apn.gov.ar*, is 4 km northeast of Libertador. There is another *guardaparque* at Mesada de las Colmenas, 13 km further northwest along Route 83. The climate is subtropical with average temperatures ranging from 17°C in winter to 28°C in summer. Mean annual rainfall is 2000 mm, falling mainly in summer (November to March).

Walks
Within the park, there are 22 km of trails for trekking, most of which are close to the Aguas Negras ranger station. There are also some roads crossing the park for cars and bikes, and horse riding is allowed. A good tourist circuit is to **Calilegua** and then on to **Aguas Calientes**, a very rural place, where there are *hosterías* and a covered pool. You can do this in a day, if it hasn't rained, and it is accessible in an ordinary vehicle.

Cerro Amarillo ① *3720 m*. A three-day trek starting from the entrance. Ask the *guardaparques* for advice on directions.

Alto Calilegua Near the base of Cerro Amarillo. You could walk to an interesting shepherds' hamlet, at 2700 m. It's actually outside Calilegua park, but close to its northern border and only accessible on foot (eight to 10 hours, one way) or on horseback (three hours, one way). Mules can be hired from San Francisco (contact Luis Cruz). There are some small pre-Hispanic ruins near the hamlet, but the main point of visiting is to witness a culture that has remained isolated for centuries, in a picturesque mountainous setting. Locals will tell you they're tired of transporting everything by mules, and long for a road to be built. Visit now, before the road comes.

Parque Nacional Baritú → *For listings, see page 338.*

Baritú is Argentina's only tropical park, lying north of the Tropic of Capricorn. It protects several species close to extinction, such as the yaguareté which lives only in a few eco-regions of this kind, and whose only rival carnivore is the puma. There is rich birdlife, and there are also rare plant and tree species here, making the park a great destination for serious nature lovers. Although the park lies entirely within Salta province, to reach it you'll have to go into Bolivia first (check if you need a visa), on Route 50 via Aguas Blancas (see below). The climate here is wet and hot, with summer rains bringing between 900 and 1300 mm, making roads completely impassable in January and February. This makes Baritú one of the most inaccessible parks in the country, and you'll have to be determined to make a visit. But it's spectacularly beautiful, covering 72,439 ha of the eastern slopes of the Andean foothills and with peaks rising to around 2000 m, mostly covered by cloudforest. You'll see many of the same birds and animals as in Calilegua. Fauna is also abundant and varied. There are no facilities apart from ranger posts, campsites at the entrances and rustic *cabañas*. It's the hottest of the three parks, with average temperatures of 21°C in winter and 30°C in summer.

Ins and outs
Access is only now possible through Bolivia. Start in Orán (full name San Ramón de la Nueva Orán) and travel up Route 50 to Aguas Blancas region. Then drive 110 km through Bolivian territory – a beautiful winding road through hills – to reach the international bridge El Condado–La Mamora. Take Route 19 south (now back in Argentina). After 14 km you'll reach the region known as Los Toldos; keep heading south for a further 26 km until

you reach the northern boundary of the park. Remember to bring your passport (with a Bolivian visa if necessary) and, if hiring a car in Argentina, warn the hire company that you plan to take it into Bolivia. Fill up with fuel in Orán or Aguas Blancas. Check the state of the roads before setting off at Salta's **tourist office** ① *T03487-431 2683*, or call the park directly (T03487-431 2683). Information in English is also available on the website www.parquesnacionales.gov.ar; follow links to the 'Protected areas'.

Walks
There are many walks in the northeast area of the park, allowing you could close contact with the many species of birds in the park. A recommended walk is to **Termas de Cayotal**, two hours' walk from the *guardaparque's* office in El Lipeo. Another is to the settlement of **Campo Grande**, where you can meet local indigenous peoples living in the park, and get a glimpse of their rich culture. From here, you could also walk the seven hours to **Angosto del Río Lipeo**.

Parque Nacional El Rey

Parque Nacional El Rey is the closest of the three cloudforest parks to Salta city (196 km), though still not easily accessible unless you go with a specially arranged expedition. Covering 44,000 ha, it was once a privately owned estate, 'El Rey' (the king), on the eastern border of the Spanish territory. It belonged at one time to Coronel Fernández Cornejo, who carried out the expulsion of the Jesuits, and the remains of his 18th-century house can still be found in the park. With a warm climate and relatively high average rainfall, the park's vegetation is extremely varied as the landscape stretches from arid steppe in the east, at 750 m above sea level, to mountainous regions at over 2000 m. So in the east, you can find Chaqueño-serrano forest, then transition jungle in the middle and high mountain forest at the most western extreme. The natural amphitheatre formation of the park's landscape is created by the horseshoe-shaped ridge of the Sierra de la Cresta del Gallo, northwest of the park, reaching heights of around 1700 m, and from it there are rivers descending through lush jungle to the Río Popayán flowing below. There's abundant wildlife, much of it easily spotted – visitors to the park are few and far between, and there's little vehicular access. Toucans abound and other birdlife too, though these are rather more shy, but you might be lucky enough to spot wild cats and tapirs.

Ins and outs
Getting there The park entrance is 46 km off Route 5, but no public transport reaches the park so it's best to take a tour from Salta city with one of the three operators licensed to take groups into the park. **Federico Norte** ① *www.nortetrekking.com*; **Movitrack** ① *www.movitrack.com.ar*; and **Clark Expediciones** ① *www.clarkexpediciones.com*. These are highly recommended, with expert guides to the interesting flora and fauna in the park, offering one- and two-day trips in 4WD vehicles with walks in the park, and camping. No other accommodation is possible in the park.

Park information The best time to visit is May to November, avoiding the very rainy season of January to March. There is a rangers' office near the entrance with a clearing where you can camp. This is a simple campsite with drinking water and bathrooms. There is a **park office** ① *España 366, 3rd floor (4400), T03487-431 2683, pnaciorey@ish.com.ar*, in Salta. More information is available on the Parques Nacionales website, www.parquesnacionales.gov.ar.

Walks

There are several good paths you can take to explore the park's varied landscape and accompanying wildlife. **Los Patitos** is a small lake, 1.5 km from the *guardaparques* centre and a great one-hour walk for spotting aquatic birds and mammals. **Popayán River** is 10 km (a two-hour walk) from the *guardaparques* centre. **Pozo Verde** path is 12 km from the *guardaparques* centre and challenging for the first 3 km. Part of the way there is a footpath with interpretation information called 'Los Ocultos'. **Santa Elena Field and Los Lobitos waterfall** is a challenging hike but good for seeing transition jungle; 4 km from the *guardaparques*, two hours each way; you'll need a guide. **Chorro de los Loros** is a pedestrian path of medium-high difficulty. It is 10 km long and crosses the transition jungle. It starts in the *guardaparques* centre.

◉ Las Yungas listings

For Sleeping and Eating price codes and other relevant information, see Essentials pages 30-36.

◉ Sleeping

Parque Nacional Calilegua *p335*
AL-A Posada del Sol, Los Ceibos and Pucará, Barrio La Loma, Libertador General San Martín, T03886-424900, www.posadadel soljujuy.com.ar. Comfortable and welcoming hotel with good rooms, gardens and a pool. The best place to stay close to Calilegua National Park. Trip advice and excursions to the Yungas.

A Finca Portal de Piedra, Villamonte, Santa Bárbara, 12 km south of Palma Sola, via paved roads either by leaving R34, 10 km south of San Pedro, or 17 km north of Libertador General San Martín, T0388-156 820 564, portaldepiedra@yahoo.com. Convenient for Parque Nacional El Rey and Parque Nacional Calilegua. This fabulous *finca* is located inside its own nature reserve, Reserva Provincial Las Lancitas. Bilingual guides Carlos and Silvia run a guesthouse, and also a self-contained eco-cabin in the hills, and offer superb horse riding and excursions into the cloudforest, trekking in Calilegua, and birdwatching tours. Portal de Piedra can be reached by bus from Jujuy via San Pedro and Palma Sola. Highly recommended.

B Termas de Caimancito, Aguas Calientes, on R9, T03886-1565 0699,

www.termasdecaimancito.com.ar. A beautiful and tranquil place in tropical surroundings, owned by a welcoming, English-speaking family. Simple rooms with bath, a campsite, thermal pools and a small restaurant. Ask about excursions and trekking into the park, just a 30-min drive from here.

Camping

There is a campsite at Aguas Negras, near the 1st rangers' station and you'll find it when entering Calilegua from R34. There is drinking water from the river nearby, and some cooking facilities and tables. To camp at Mesada de las Colmenas ask permission at Aguas Negras.

▲ Activities and tours

Parque Nacional Calilegua *p335*
Tony Strelkov, T03886-1565 0699, www.termasdecaimancito.com.ar. Runs bilingual excursions, and runs the Termas de Caimancito in Aguas Calientes (see Sleeping, above).

Parque Nacional Baritú *p336*
Only **Movitrack** and **Clark Expediciones**, both in Salta are authorized to take visitors into the park. Both are recommended for specializing in natural history, with 1- to 2-day trips in 4WD vehicles, camping and walking inside the park.

Catamarca province

→ *Colour map 1, B2. Phone code 03833. Population 340,000.*

Most of the population of this large province lives in the capital, leaving the stunning countryside to the north and west virtually empty of people. Catamarca city is hot and quiet, livening up each July for the hugely popular Poncho festival, an excuse for a big forlclore music festival, food and dancing. There is a great tradition of weaving – wool, alpaca and llama – throughout the province of Catamarca, and while you can find poachers in the handicrafts centre in the city, you might want to explore the wild remote villages to the west, where you'll find many local weavers.

The small towns of Belén and Andagalá are animated oases on the way to the puna, where the tiny hamlets of Fiambalá and Tinogasta are fascinatingly remote last outposts and possible bases for climbing Mount Pissis in the highlands to the far west. The province has one really impressive archaeological find: the ruined Inca town of El Shincal, close to Londres, but accessible on a tour from Belén. With evidence of extensive Inca conquest and a sophisticated infrastructure, this is well worth visiting. From Belén, a lonely road leads north across the puna to remotest Antofagasta de la Sierra, surrounded by a vast expanse of salt flats. Catamarca's most appealing place to stay is the charming hilltop town of El Rodeo; a popular weekend retreat for Catamarqueños, with its refreshing microclimate and good walks. Further north, on the border with Tucumán, is the delightful village of Santa María, a lovely place to rest on the way to Salta, near the spectacular ruins at Quilmes.

The province is not the northwest's most accessible and the infrastructure can be frustratingly basic, but you'll be warmly welcomed in the remotest reaches; and you'll want to stuff olives, walnuts and superb woven textiles in your bag to bring home. For more information, see www.catamarcaguia.com.ar (in Spanish). ▶▶ *For listings, see pages 343-345.*

Catamarca city → *For listings, see pages 343-345.*

The provincial capital's real attraction is the rather lengthy San Fernando del Valle de Catamarca, and it is sleepy and traditional. Unless you're here for the Poncho festival in mid-July, there's little to draw you to the city. There are some attractive 19th-century buildings grouped around a large central plaza, and a wonderful museum, but the accommodation is basic, and the summers are unbearably hot with temperatures up to 45°C. El Rodeo, an hour away by regular minibus, makes a far more appealing alternative if you're on the way to the *puna* or Chile.

Ins and outs → *Colour map 1, C3. Phone code 03833. Population 172,000.*

Getting there Catamarca's airport, **Aeropuerto Felipe Varela** ⓘ *20 km south, T03833-430080*, has a daily flight from Buenos Aires. Alternatively, there are several daily buses from Buenos Aires, taking at least 14 hours. The **bus terminal** ⓘ *Av Güemes 881 and Tucumán T03833-437578*, is seven blocks southeast of the main plaza. It has shops, a café, an ATM and a *locutorio*. The entrance is through a car park. A taxi to Plaza 25 de Mayo costs US$3.

Getting around The city is small enough to walk around, with most hotels situated on Sarmiento, northwest of the plaza. Shops and banks are mostly on the pedestrianized street Rivadavia, which runs down the eastern side of the plaza and continues to the south. Buses link the city to outlying areas of the province, and there are many minibuses a day to Villa El Rodeo. ▶▶ *For further information, see Transport, page 345.*

Tourist information The tourist office ① *Saramiento 1040, T03833-437423, www.turismocatamarca.gov.ar, Mon-Fri 0700-1300, 1500-2000*, is helpful. There's also a **provincial tourist office** ① *Roca and Virgen del Valle, T03833-455308*, and an information point at the airport.

Best time to visit The best time to visit is during the **Poncho festival** in mid-July; book accommodation in advance. It's best to avoid the summer, when temperatures exceed 40°C. Very sensibly, the siesta is strictly observed here and everything closes down from 1230-1700.

Sights

The central, leafy **Plaza 25 de Mayo** was designed by the illustrious architect Charles Thays and contains tall trees of unusual species, providing much-needed shade from the scorching summer heat, and a rather striking equestrian sculpture of San Martín. There's the white stuccoed **Casa de Gobierno** (1891), designed by Caravati, and, to the west, the faded red bulk of his neoclassical **cathedral** (1878), looking rather forlorn but sporting a pair of fine mosaic- tiled cupolas on its towers. The interior is a rather un-celestial, peeling *eau de nil*, but the scenes from the life of Christ painted on the ceiling are lovely. In a chapel high above and behind the altar, you can visit the much-worshipped Virgen del Valle all dressed up, on a mighty gilded pedestal. Access is up a double staircase system to the *Camarín*, where the walls of the chapel are lined with plaques of offerings and cases crammed with thousands of silver arms, legs, hands and eyes offered by her followers over the years. One block north of the plaza, the **Iglesia de San Francisco** (1882) has an impressive colonial-style façade. Five blocks west of the plaza, the **Paseo General Navarro** is a rather scrappy park surrounded by huge trees, with good views over the town but not recommended for a quiet picnic.

For weavings and other handicrafts, try the **Mercado Artesanal** ① *Av Virgen del Valle 945, Mon-Fri, 0800-1200, 1500-2030*, in the 'Manzana de Turismo' (a 'block' for tourists, with no other obvious attractions), which is also a carpet factory.

The must-see of the city is the incredible **Museo Arqueológico 'Adán Quiroga'** ① *Sarmiento 450, T03833-437413, Mon-Fri 0700-1300, 1430-2030, Sat-Sun 0830-1230, 1530-1830, free*, containing an enormous collection of artefacts from the sophisticated pre-Hispanic cultures who inhabited the area from around 1000 BC. There are carved stone vessels with animal figures leaping off their sides, beautifully painted funerary urns, deliberately flattened skulls (compressed by the owners by wearing wooden boards), and quite a shocking mummified baby, naturally conserved above 5000 m. Allow at least an hour to discover the many fascinating finds. Highly recommended.

Around Catamarca city → *For listings, see pages 343-345.*

Heading north, towards El Rodeo, you'll pass through the **Valle de Catamarca**, with a series of attractive churches, built mostly in the 19th century. Look out for the ones at **San Isidro**, 5 km east, **Villa Dolores**, 1 km further north, and at **San José**, a further 4 km north, whose colonial church dates from 1780. Oldest of all is **La Señora del Rosario**, 2 km east of the city, a simple white building dating from 1715.

Some 25 km north of Catamarca, the **Dique Las Pirquitas** lake has good fishing and water sports, as well as trekking and mountain biking. To get to the lake, take bus No 1A from the bus terminal (every 30 minutes) to the **Hostería de Turismo** at Villa Pirquitas, from where it is about 45-minute walk.

However, the best place to head to escape from the city is the pretty weekend retreat of **El Rodeo**, some 37 km north of Catamarca in a lovely mountain setting with a cool microclimate and lots of good walks and horse riding. There's a great two-day hike to Cerro el Manchao 4550 m, and trout fishing in the Río Ambato. Ask for advice at the friendly **tourist information** ① *T03833-490043*. It's easy to get here by bus or hire car, and there are plenty of delightful *hosterías*, which make this a pleasant alternative to staying in the city. **El Rodeo Bus** runs several *combis* (minibuses) a day from the car park Estacionamiento San Martín, half a block east of the plaza on San Martín. US$8 each way, return buses the same day. If you plan to stay overnight, make sure you book beforehand as El Rodeo is popular with locals from Catamarca city, especially at weekends.

Las Juntas, a further 20 km away on the same road, is another rural retreat from the city, also in attractive mountainous countryside. **Los Hermanos Vergara** ① *T03833-427005*, run buses from Catamarca terminal Monday to Saturday at 1200 and 2000 (returning 0630 and 1500).

Northeast of Catamarca, there are fine panoramic views over the Valle de Catamarca at the **Cuesta del Portezuelo**, along the road snaking up the Sierra de Ancasti, 20 km northeast of the town. The Cuesta rises through 13 hairpin bends to 1680 m and, from the summit, with a vista over the city and valley below, the road continues via El Alto (950 m). There's a reservoir nearby, **Dique Ipizca**, good for *pejerrey* fishing.

Belén and around → *Colour map 1, B2. Phone code 03835. Population 8224.*

From whichever direction you approach Belén (1240 m) – whether from Andagalá on Route 46, or along the equally poor Ruta 40 – you'll be very relieved to arrive. Ruta 40 takes you across vast open plains fringed with chocolate-coloured flaking mountains and through the desolate little village of **Hualfín**, with thermal baths in summer at **Pozo Verde**, to the north. This is a better road than the Route 46, but still should not be attempted in the rainy season (February to March) when the rivers crossing the roads are high. Both roads are easier and safer in a 4WD.

There are good views from the **Cerro de Nuestra Señora de Belén**, a hill above the town, where a relatively new Virgen (the last one was struck by lightning) watches over the place. Information is available from the small **Dirección de Turismo** ① *at the bus terminal a block from the plaza on Rivadavia and Lavalle, T03835-461304, daily 0900-1300, 1600-2000*. For excursions by 4WD, go to the friendly and extremely helpful **Ampujaco** ① *General Roca 190, T03835-461189*, or ask at **Hotel Belén** ① *Belgrano and Cubas, T03835-461501, www.belencat.com.ar*, in town. This young agency organizes interesting tours to El Shinkal with tour guides and possibly an archaeologist, though you should specifically request this in advance.

Londres → *Population 2100.*

South of Belén, Ruta 40 is paved to Chilecito via **Londres** (1300 m), a pretty and quiet village with a remote feel. Founded in 1558, it is the second oldest town in Argentina, though its site was moved several times. It was named in honour of the marriage of Mary Tudor and Philip II. The municipalidad displays a glass coat-of-arms of the city of London and a copy of the marriage proposal. There are important Inca ruins at **El Shincal**, see below; they are signposted from the second plaza you come to after entering the village from Belén. Londres celebrates its walnut festival in January. There are no hotels here, but several *hospedajes*, an *estancia* (**Estancia La Casona**) and a campsite (T03835-491019) on the route to Shincal. Food can be bought from the few shops around the plaza.

El Shincal

ⓘ *7 km from Londres, daily 0700-1900. Cóndor buses linking Belén and Londres run three times daily (see Transport, page 345) and stop 100 m from the ruins, US$1.50. The site is quite small and you will only need around 2 hrs there. Tours are run by the helpful Ampujaco Tur in Belén, T03835-461189, General Roca 190, or at Hotel Belén, Belgrano and Cubas, T003835-461501. A tour for 4 with guide costs US$18 per person. In Spanish only. Taxis from Belén and Londres will take you there and wait for you. Prices vary but start at around US$25.*

This ruined town is one of the most astonishing remains of the Inca occupation of Argentina from the 1470s to their demise in 1532. The setting is superb, in a flat area between a crown of mountains and the river – a place the Incas clearly recognized as having sacred significance. Their religious beliefs were deeply entwined with their worship of mountains and their modification of natural forms – the most extreme example of which is Machu Picchu in Peru. Cuzco, too, follows strict conventions, sitting the town to line up auspiciously with sacred hills, water sources and the home of the ancestors. According to expert Ian Farrington, El Shincal is a 'little Cuzco', following precisely the same rules of orientation to mountains and water sources. There are large *kallankas* (thought to be either grain stores or military barracks), sleeping areas and a central plaza, lined up between two artificially shaped hills and perfectly aligned with the rising and setting sun at the solstice. In the middle of the plaza is a sacred platform with a specially designed trough for sacrifices. It's best to visit El Shincal with a guide, but you'll be lucky to find one in Londres so take a tour from Belén. It's a remarkable site, well worth visiting.

North of Belén

There are two routes north to Salta. The most direct is via Ruta 40 which runs northeast via Santa María (176 km, see page 349) and Cafayate (page 306). The alternative is via Ruta 43, which branches west off Ruta 40 at a point 52 km north of Belén and runs across the high *puna* to Antofagasta de la Sierra and San Antonio de los Cobres (see page 298). This route is challenging at the best of times, and impassable for ordinary cars after heavy rains. The stretch just after the junction with Ruta 40 is very difficult, with 37 km of fords. At Km 87 is Cerro Compo (3125 m), from which the descent is magnificent. At Km 99 the road turns right to Laguna Blanca, where there is a museum and a small vicuña farm (don't go straight ahead at the junction). There are thermal springs along this road at **Villavil**, 13 km further north, open from January to April. Drivers should note that you'll need enough fuel for 600 km on unmaintained roads, with fuel consumption being double at high altitudes. Fill up at Hualfín and San Antonio de los Cobres, and possibly carry extra.

Antofagasta de la Sierra → *Colour map 1, B2. Population 1000. Altitude 3365 m.*

ⓘ *Buses from Belén and Catamarca arrive Wed and Fri evening. Or hire a car.*

Antofagasta de la Sierra is the main settlement in the sparsely populated northwest corner of Catamarca province, situated on the Río Punilla, 260 km north of Belén and 557 km northwest of the provincial capital. With its low pinkish adobe buildings, surrounded by vast empty lunar landscapes and massive volcanoes, it's a wonderfully remote place. To the west are the salt flats of the **Salar de Antofalla**, though these are pretty much inaccessible. The **Salar del Hombre Muerto** on Ruta 43 can be visited, but it's best to hire a guide. It's a wonderful journey. There's nothing at all to do here and that's just the point. There are few places on earth that remain so wild and untouched, and these other-worldly landscapes are a paradise for photographers. If you're attracted to wild immense open spaces and long roads leading apparently to nowhere, you'll love it.

Within reach of Antofagasta de la Sierra are several interesting archaeological sites including the ruins at **Campo Alumbreras**, in the shadow of the volcano of the same name. There's a pre-Columbian *pucará* (fort) and some nearby petroglyphs. Guides can be found at the small but wonderful museum **Museo del Hombre** ① *Fiambalá Abaucán s/n, T03837-426250, Mon-Fri 0900-1200, 1500-1900*, which contains incredibly well preserved pre-Hispanic textiles and a 2000-year-old mummified baby. There's no petrol station, but fuel can be bought from the *intendencia*.

◉ Catamarca province listings

For Sleeping and Eating price codes and other relevant information, see Essentials pages 30-36.

◉ Sleeping

Catamarca city *p339*
See also www.turismocatamarca.gov.ar.
AL Amerian Park, República 347, T03833-425 444, www.amerian.com. A modern but expensive business hotel, with spacious, attractively decorated and very comfortable rooms. Large restaurant and pool.
AL Hostel Casino Catamarca, Esquiú 151, corner Ayachuco, T03833-432928, www.hotelcasinocatamarca.com. Large and surprisingly inviting hotel with comfortable beds, a nice swimming pool and a day spa.
A Ancasti, Sarmiento 520, T03833-435951, www.hotelancasti.com.ar. Aspiring to be a business hotel. The modernized rooms are comfortable but the bathrooms are tiny. There are sometimes cheaper deals that include dinner in the pleasant airy restaurant.
A La Aguada, 16 km from the city along Ruta 38, T03833-1536 5722, www.la-aguada.com. This wonderful boutique hotel has 5 beautifully decorated rooms. The friendly owners also offer trekking, horse riding and abseiling, as well as breakfast, local phone calls, laundry and bicycle hire included in the price.
A-B Arenales, Sarmiento 542, T03833-431329/330, www.hotel-arenales.com.ar. Welcoming, but slightly institutional in feel. Plain rooms with well-equipped bathrooms, minimalist though not exactly stylish. The most comfy in this price range.
B Grand Hotel, Camilo Melet 41, T03833-426715, www.grandhotelcatamarca.com.ar.

You'll get the friendliest welcome here and they have spacious and comfortable rooms, all with bath, TV and a/c.

Hostels
E pp Hostel San Pedro, Sarmiento 341, T03833-454708, www.hostelsanpedro. com.ar. Cheapest option in town, this new hostel offers brightly coloured dorms, a large garden, small pool and lively bar.

Around Catamarca city *p340*
B Hostería El Rodeo, R4, El Rodeo, T03833-490296. Lovely spacious rooms, pool, good restaurant and great views. Climbing, 4WD trips and excursions for children. Highly recommended.
C La Casa de Chicha, Los Gladiolos s/n, T03833-490082, www.lacasadechicha.com.ar. With fewer facilities than El Rodeo, but with a more idyllic setting right in the mountains, and rooms with antique furniture. Try the excellent restaurant for lunch and dinner, or have tea in the beautiful garden filled with pear trees.
E pp Hostel El Rodeo, Las Maravillas and Las Aljabas, T03833-490380. Although the dorms are basic and the double is small, this hostel has a nice, relaxed atmosphere. Bicycles for hire.

Belén and around *p341*
B Belén, Belgrano and Cubas, T03835-461 501, www.belencat.com.ar. The most comfortable place to stay. Refurbished with stylish plain rooms in a modern block in a little leafy garden, also a tour operator.

C Samay, Urquiza 349, T03835-461320, samaihotel@cotelbe.com.ar. Old fashioned but very welcoming, and its homely little rooms have bathrooms and fans.

Londres *p341*
A-B Estancia La Casona, Ruta 38, T03835-491995, lacasonadelondres@hotmail.com. With a capacity of 10 people, this *estancia* has basic rooms and can organize an excursion to El Shincal. In your free time you can help harvesting nuts and herbs.

Antofagasta de la Sierra *p342*
Several family houses have cheap, basic but very welcoming accommodation, some rooms including private bath and breakfast. Ask the tourist office for details, T03833-422300.
D Hostería Municipal de Antofagasta, T03835-471001, hosteriaantofagasta@yahoo.com.ar. This is the only really comfortable accommodation, and though its 23 rooms are simple, they're perfectly decent, and the owners also have a restaurant and offer travel advice.

❶ Eating

Catamarca city *p339*
There are few good restaurants, many cheap ones around the Plaza 25 de Agosto, and also at the bus terminal but this area is not safe at night.
¶¶¶-¶¶ La Tinaja, Sarmiento 533. T03833-435 853. The best eating choice by far, this delicious *parrilla* does excellent pasta. Slightly pricey, but worth it. Deservedly popular.
¶¶ Salsa Criolla, República 546, on the plaza, T03833- 433584. Traditional and popular *parrilla*. Sloppy service, but the beef is recommended. The same owner runs Italian-style **Trattoria Montecarlo** next door, where the speciality is pasta.
¶¶ Sociedad Española, Av Virgen del Valle 725, T03833-431897. Recommended for its quality and variety, serving paella, seafood and other Spanish specialities, with friendly

service. Worth the 5-block walk from the main plaza.

Belén and around *p341*
¶¶ 1900, Belgrano 391. Laid-back restaurant with affordable food. Popular with locals.
¶¶ El Unico, corner of General Roca and Sarmiento. Great *parrilla* for a drink and a light meal.

✿ Festivals and events

Catamarca city *p339*
Mar-Apr Virgen del Valle pilgrimage. In the week following Easter, there are pilgrimages to the Virgen del Valle. Hotel rooms are hard to find.
Jul Festival Nacional del Poncho. The city's major festival is the held in the 3rd week in Jul. It includes a huge *feria artesanal* with the best of the province's handicrafts, as well as those from other parts of the country, and 10 nights of excellent *folclore* music.
29 Nov-8 Dec Virgen del Valle pilgrimage. A crowded pilgrimage in which thousands of people show their devotion to the Virgin. Hotel rooms are hard to find.

Belén and around *p341*
20 Dec-6 Jan Fiesta de Nuestra Señora de Belén. The town's most important fiesta.
Feb Carnival. Celebrated in style.
Mar/Apr Easter. There are processions for the Virgin.

◯ Shopping

Catamarca city *p339*
Catamarca specialities are available from **Cuesta del Portezuelo**, Sarmiento 571, T03833-452675; and **Fábrica Valdez**, Sarmiento 578, T03833-425175. There's a range of handicrafts and you can see carpets being woven at the **Mercado Artesanal**, Av Virgen del Valle 945. The carpet factory is open Mon-Fri 0800-1200, 1500-2030.

▲ Activities and tours

Catamarca city p339
Tour operators and guides
Tours are offered to El Rodeo and there are various opportunities for adventure sports.
Alta Catamarca, Sarmiento 569, T03833-430333, www.altacatamarca.com. Local company that runs adventure-style trips into the mountains and visits to local villages and spa packages.
Aníbal Vázquez, T03835-471001, anibal.vazquez@hotmail.com. Walking expeditions in Antofagasta de la Sierra.
Catamarca Viajes y Turismo, Sarmiento 589, T03833-429450, www.catamarcaviajesytur.com.ar. Conventional tours to main sights in the eastern valleys of Catamarca.
La Lunita, T011-4776 7821, www.lalunita com.ar. Great trekking company that runs tours throughout the region.

○ Transport

Catamarca city p339
Air
Aerolíneas Argentinas flies to **Buenos Aires** and **La Rioja**.
  Airline offices Aerolíneas Argentinas, Sarmiento 589, T03833-424450/60.

Bus
Tucumán, 4 hrs, US$9, several companies. To **Buenos Aires**, daily, 16-18 hrs, US$55-60, 4 companies. To **Córdoba**, daily, 5 hrs, US$16, 6 companies. To **Santiago del Estero**, only 1 bus a day operates, 3½ hrs, US$8. To **Mendoza**, daily, 10 hrs, US$25-38, several companies. To **La Rioja**, daily, 2 hrs, US$9, several companies. To **Tinogasta**, 5 hrs, US$8, Gutiérrez; Robledo. To **Belén** via Aimogasta

and Londres, 4-6 hrs, US$7, 3 companies. To **Andagalá**, 4½-6 hrs, US$9, 4 companies including **Marín** (via Aconquija).

Belén and around p341
Bus
To **Santa María**, **San Cayetano** and **Parra** (connection there with other companies to Cafayate and Salta), daily, 5 hrs, US$8. To **Tinogasta**, 4 weekly, 2-3 hrs, US$5, Robledo. To **Antofagasta de la Sierra**, 2 weekly, 11 hrs, US$16, El Antofagasteño. For more frequent services to **Catamarca** or **La Rioja**, take bus to **Aimogasta**, 1 hr, US$3. Buses to **Catamarca** leave at 1200 and late at night, US$7, 4-6 hrs. Check with Gutiérrez, El Antofagasteño, and Robledo bus companies. To **Córdoba** US$20, 11-12 hrs.

El Shincal p342
Buses leave from **Belén** at 1000, 1200 and 1730, and return at 12.30, 1700 and 1900, with various companies, 30 mins, US$1.50.

Antofagasta de la Sierra p342
Bus
Buses to **Belén** and **Catamarca**, Mon and Fri 0800, with El Antofagasteño.

○ Directory

Catamarca city p339
Banks Many ATMs for all major cards, along Rivadavia and at bus terminal, and Banco de la Nación, San Martín 632. **Currency exchange** TCs can only be cashed at BBVA Banco Francés, Rivadavia 520. **Internet and telephone** Several *locutorios* with broadband access in the centre. **Post office** San Martín 753, slow, daily 0800-1300, 1600-2000.

Tucumán province

→ *Colour map1, B3. Phone code 0381. Population 1,242300.*

One of the country's largest cities lies in one of its smallest provinces. Its subtropical climate is ideal for growing sugar, tobacco and lemons. Outside the modern provincial capital, in the surrounding mountains to the north and west, is the popular weekend retreat of Tafí del Valle, with its cool microclimate. Further northwest, on the route to Cafayate in Salta, are the delightful small towns of Amaichá del Valle and Santa María, over the border in Catamarca, both good bases for exploring Quilmes – one of Argentina's most important archaeological sites. Here you can wander around the extensive remains of a city of 5000 Calchaquíes, built into the side of a mountain amidst breathtaking scenery. Combine Tucumán with Salta via the spectacular drive from Tafí del Valle and Amaichá, stopping at Quilmes, and then up the Valle Calchaquí along Ruta 40. It's an unforgettably beautiful experience. For more information, see www.tucumanturismo.gov.ar
►► *For listings, see pages 352-357.*

Tucumán city → *For listings, see pages 352-357.*

The city of San Miguel de Tucumán, known simply as Tucumán, lies almost equidistant between Catamarca and Salta on a broad plain, just east of the massive Sierra de Aconquija. It's the largest and most important city in the north of the province, though it has suffered economically during the recession. Visually, the city lacks Salta's style or architectural splendour despite being one of the first cities to be founded by the Spanish, and few of its colonial buildings remain. There are few attractions for visitors, and it's overwhelmingly hot in summer – the siesta is strictly observed from 1230 to 1630 – but it does have a couple of good museums and lively nightlife. It's a busy city with plenty of restaurants and a huge park designed by architect Charles Thays.

Ins and outs → *Colour map 1, B3. Phone code 0381. Population 472,000.*

Getting there **Aeropuerto Benjamín Matienzo**, 10 km east of town, is linked to the city by **Transfer Express** ① *office at the airport, T0381-426 7945*, which meets all flights and charges US\$1.50 from the airport to Plaza Independencia, or US\$5 to hotels in town. There are also buses (US\$2) or taxis (US\$7). There are daily flights from Buenos Aires (via Córdoba). This is one of the few places reached by long-distance train from Buenos Aires. There's a huge **bus terminal**, www.terminaltuc.com, seven blocks east of Plaza Independencia on Avenida Brígido Terán, where long-distance buses arrive from all parts of the country, as well as Chile and Peru. The bus terminal has a shopping complex, left luggage lockers (US\$1.50), fantastic **tourist information office** ① *Mon-Fri, 0800-2200, Sat-Sun 0900-2100* (by *boletería* 1), *locutorios*, toilets and an ATM. Bus No 4 goes to the centre from outside the terminal (on Avenida Benjamín Aráoz), to Córdoba and 25 de Mayo. A taxi to the centre costs US\$2.50.

Getting around The plaza is the city's heart along with the busy pedestrianized shopping streets to the north and west. It's an easy place to get around on foot, but taxis are cheap and reliable. There are several good accommodation options, but if this is a strategic stopover for you, it would be better to retreat to the cooler mountains of Tafí del Valle, as the *Tucumanos* do at weekends.

Best time to visit The city's big festivals are the **Day of Independence**, 9 July, when Tucumán is capital of the country for the day. On 24 September, the city celebrates the day Belgrano won the Battle of Tucumán with a huge procession. September also sees the **Tucumán Empanada Festival**. Summer is best avoided because of the heat, especially January and February.

Tourist information There's a very helpful **tourist office** ① *on the plaza, 24 de Septiembre 484, T0800-555 8828, www.tucumanturismo.gov.ar, Mon-Fri 0800-2200, Sat-Sun 0900-2100*. There are also offices in the bus terminal and airport – the bus station office is particularly helpful with finding accommodation. For more, see www.turismo entucuman.com (in Spanish).

Background

Tucumán was an important city in Spanish colonial times. Founded in 1565 and transferred to its present site in 1685, it was a strategic stop for mule trains on the routes from Bolivia to Buenos Aires and Mendoza. With a colonial economy based on sugar, citrus fruit and tobacco, it developed an aristocracy distinct from those of Buenos Aires and Córdoba. The city was the site of an important battle during the Wars of Independence. Belgrano's victory here in 1812 over a royalist army ended the Spanish threat to restore colonial rule over the River Plate area. Tucumán's wealth was derived from sugar and it remains the biggest industry, though lemons have also become vital exports in recent decades.

Sights

Plaza Independencia in the city's commercial centre, with its many tall palms and mature trees, gives welcome shade in the sweltering heat. At night it's full of *Tucumanos* eating ice cream from one of the many *heladerías*. Among its attractive buildings are the ornate **Casa de Gobierno** (1910), with tall palms outside and art-nouveau balconies. Next door is a typical *casa chorizo* (sausage house), **Casa Padilla** ① *25 de Mayo 36, daily 1000-2000, US$0.50*, a series of skinny rooms off open patios, whose collection of china and paintings belonging to a wealthy Tucumán family gives you a flavour of 19th-century life. Across the road, the **Iglesia San Francisco** (1891) has a rather gloomy interior, but a picturesque façade and tiled cupola. On the south side of the plaza, the neoclassical **cathedral** (1852) has a distinctive cupola, but a disappointingly bland modern interior, the ceiling painted with rainbows and whales.

South of the plaza, on Calle Congreso 151, is the **Casa Histórica** ① *Mon-Fri 0900-1300,1500-1900, Sat-Sun 1000-1300, 1600-1900, US$1.50, Fri-Wed son et lumière show (except in Jul) at 2030, US$1.50, children US$0.70*. Rooms are set around two attractive patios, filled with old furniture, historical documents and some fine Cuzqueño-school paintings. The highlight is the actual room where the Declaration of Independence was drafted, with portraits of the Congressmen lining the walls. Next to it is a room full of interesting religious artefacts. The **Museo Folklórico General Manuel Belgrano** ① *24 de Septiembre 565, Mon-Fri 0900-1300,1600-2100, Sat-Sun 0900-1300*, has an impressive collection of silverwork from Peru and musical instruments in an old colonial house. To see local art and sculpture, try the **Museo de Bellas Artes Timoteo Navarro** ① *9 de Julio 36, T0381-422730*. Set in a wonderfully restored building there are over 680 works of art.

Tucumán's enormous park, **Parque Nueve de Julio**, east of the centre, is a much-used green space designed by French landscape architect Charles Thays, who also designed the Parque Tres de Febrero in Buenos Aires. With many subtropical trees, it was once the property of Bishop Colombres who played an important role in the development of the local sugar industry, and whose handsome house is now the **Museo de la Industria Azucarera** ① *Mon-Fri 0800-1300, 1400-1900, Sat-Sun 0900-1900, free*, with a display on sugar-making. The park also has a lake and lots of sports facilities.

Northwest Tucumán province → *For listings, see pages 352-357.*

Tucumán has stunning mountain scenery to the west and north of the province, along the Nevados de Aconquija, where there are several attractive small towns to visit on the way to Salta. Of the two possible routes, Route 9, via Rosario de la Frontera and Güemes, is far quicker, but one of the most spectacular routes in the whole area is the Ruta 40 to Cafayate and up into the Valles Calchaquíes. The road rises up though verdant Tafí del Valle, over the massive Infiermillo pass and then there is spectacular landscape all the way to the archaeological site of Quilmes, with the added charms of small towns of Santa María and Amaichá del Valle on the way.

Tafí del Valle → *Colour map 1, B3. Phone code 03867. Population 11,483.*
The journey from Tucumán to Tafí is very satisfying. Route 307 leads northwest towards Cafayate, climbing through sugar and citrus fruit plantations, and then jungle subtropical forest, before entering the wide Valle de Tafí, surrounded by mountains densely covered in velvety vegetation. At Km 69 there is a statue to 'El Indio', with good views from the picnic area.

Tafí (2000 m) is a popular weekend retreat from the heat of the city for *Tucumanos*, since it has a cool microclimate, and makes a good base for walking, with several peaks of the Sierra de Aconquija providing challenging day-hikes. Within the sprawling town itself, you can walk by the Ríos El Churqui and Blanquito and to the Parque de los Menhires, where a collection of 129 engraved granite monoliths stand to the south of an attractive reservoir, the **Embalse Angostura**, in the valley below. For hikes into the mountains, it's best to go with a guide, available from **La Cumbre Hostel**, see Activities and tours, page 356. There's some excellent accommodation, especially at the upper end of the market, making this an appealing alternative to staying in Tucumán. There are also a couple of very fine *estancias*, including **Las Carreras** ① *www.estancialascarreras.com*. There is a small but welcoming bus station two blocks from the centre on Avenida Gobernador Critto, with a café, *locutorio*, toilets but no luggage storage. Most shops are on the main streets, Avenida Gobernador Critto (becoming Los Faroles to the west near the plaza) and Avenida Perón. At the junction you can buy good locally made cheese and delicious bread, while there's a basic **tourist office** ① *daily 0800-2200, from the bus station turn left onto Av Gobernador Critto and follow the road for 3 blocks up the hill*, opposite the park. They have a good map of the town and the surrounding areas, and listings of accommodation options. For more, see www.tafidelvalle.com (in Spanish).

Sights
Tafí's most historic building is the attractive **Capilla Jesuítica y Museo de La Banda** ① *Mon-Sat 0900-1900, Sun 0900-1600 (closing early off season), US$1 including guided tour.* This 18th-century chapel and 19th-century *estancia* has a small museum with interesting finds from the valley and 18th-century religious art. Cross the bridge over Río Tafí southwest of town, and the museum is on your left after 500 m. **Parque de los**

Menhires lies in an attractive spot at the south of the Dique la Angostura, 10 km south of the centre of Tafí del Valle. The *menhires* are 129 granite stones, engraved with designs of unknown significance, said by some to symbolize fertility. They are undeniably intriguing, however, it's not quite the mystical sight the tourist brochures claim it is, since the stones were unearthed in various places in the valley and put here in 1977. There's a decent campsite nearby and windsurfing and sailing are available on the reservoir in summer.

Five kilometres further west, **El Mollar** is another weekend village with campsites and *cabañas*, and is popular with teenage and student crowds.

Northwest of Tafí del Valle

One of Argentina's most memorable journeys is along Route 307 northwest from Tafí, climbing out of the valley up to the mountain pass **Abra del Infiernillo** (3042 m) at Km 130, on the way to Amaichá del Valle and Cafayate. There are panoramic views south over the **Cumbres de Mala Mala**, the steeply sided deep green valley below, then breathtaking vistas as you emerge over the pass, looking north over the **Cumbres Calchaquíes**, purple veiled in the distance, and finally over the dramatic Valles Calchaquíes. The road descends along hairy zig-zags to the beautiful rocky landscape of the valley of the **Río de Amaichá**.

Amaichá del Valle → *Colour map 1, B2. Phone code 03892. Population 1100.*

Claiming rather grandly to have the best climate in the world, Amaichá (1997 m) is a lovely tranquil little place that does indeed always seem to be sunny. There's a splendid museum, the **Complejo Museo Pachamama** ① *T03892-421004, daily 0830-1230, 1400-1830 (Sun closed in low season), US$2.50, explanations in English, guided tour in Spanish*, also known also as Casa de Piedra. The museum was designed by the well-known Argentine sculptor Héctor Cruz, who uses the iconography of the region's pre-Columbian art with bold flair in his own ceramics and weavings. It's part gallery, part archaeological museum, and a great place to relax for a couple of hours, with wonderful views from the mosaic cactus gardens. The shop sells an extensive range of handicrafts, and bold rugs and hangings, designed by Cruz and made by local weavers.

The road forks at Amaichá for Quilmes and Cafayate. Take Route 357 north for 14 km to the junction with Ruta 40, then follow it north. For Santa María and western Catamarca, take Route 307 south to join Ruta 40 heading south.

Santa María → *Colour map 1, B2. Phone code 03838. Population 10,800.*

With its lively village feel, still untainted by tourism, Santa María (1880 m) makes a very attractive place for a stopover on the road to either Tucumán or western Catamarca. There's a lovely plaza full of mature trees, several friendly places to stay and to eat, and a wonderful small museum. The **Museo Arqueológico Eric Boman** ① *Centro Cultural Yokavil, on the plaza, daily 0830-1300, 1630-2100, free*, houses a fine collection of sophisticated ceramics tracing the development of the various indigenous cultures who lived in the Calchaquí valleys. Ask the well-informed staff to show you around. In the same building is a handicrafts gallery selling weavings, wooden objects and the delicious local *patero* wine. There is a helpful but small **tourist office** ① *on the plaza, Belgrano and Sarmiento, T03838-421083*, which can provide a map and a list of places to stay.

In January the town has handicrafts fairs and a live music festival, with the crowning of *La Reina de Yokavil* (the old indigenous name for Santa María). For the **Fiesta de San Roque** on 16 August, thousands of pilgrims descend on the town, and accommodation fills up fast. There's a *locutorio* on the plaza, the only ATM for miles around on Mitre and

Sarmiento, taking Visa and MasterCard, a post office and several service stations. Buses arrive at Avenida 9 de Julio and Maestro Argentino, eight blocks south of the plaza.

Quilmes → *Colour map 1, B2.*

ⓘ *32 km north of Santa María, 5 km along a dirt road off R40 (no shade, tiring walk up hill), daily 0800-1830, US$2 including guided tour and museum. There is a hotel with restaurant, see Sleeping, page 354, and a good café, open until 1830.*

Quilmes is one of the most important archaeological sites in Argentina, sadly little known by most Argentines, who are more likely to associate the name with the country's most popular lager, see box, opposite. Located on the slopes of the Sierra de Quilmes, at an altitude of 1850 m, it has commanding views over the entire valley. The city was home to 5000 Diaguitan people, who lived here peacefully for hundreds of years until the Incas and then the Spanish arrived. What remains today is an extensive network of thousands of roofless rooms bordered with low walls, mostly heavily reconstructed, but walk up to the top of the mountain and you'll see a beautiful and elaborate lacework that continues right up from the valley to the higher slopes. It's a spectacular site, especially early or late in the day, when the silvery walls are picked out against the pale green of the enormous cacti.

For a day trip take the 0600 Aconquija bus from Cafayate to Santa María, and after an hour get off at the stop which is 5 km from the site. Alternatively, take the 0700 El Indio bus from Santa María, which runs Friday to Wednesday. Take the 1130 bus back to Cafayate for US$3. You can also take a tour from Cafayate, see Activities and tours, page 314.

South of San Miguel de Tucumán → *For listings, see pages 352-357.*

Once you travel past the city of Tucumán, on the highway you will enter the province of Santiago de Estero. For more information see www.turismosantiago.gov.ar and www.santiagodelestero.net (both in Spanish).

Santiago del Estero → *Colour map 1, B3. Phone code 0385. Population 328,000.*

This quiet, provincial town makes a handy stopping point if you're heading from the flat landscape of the Chaco to explore the northwest corner of Argentina but little of the architectural heritage of Argentina's oldest city remains. There are, however, some comfortable places to stay, a couple of museums worth seeing, and the people are among Argentina's most friendly and welcoming.

Santiago was founded in 1553 and was an important base for establishing other major cities in the northwest. As the other cities grew, Santiago was left behind and the town is now a rather impoverished older neighbour. It's a bit run down, with its plaza in a shambolic state of affairs, but it has a warm, laid-back atmosphere and the siesta here is legendary. The **bus terminal** ⓘ *Pedro Leon Gallo 480, T0385-421 3746*, has toilets, a *locutorio*, basic café and *kioskos*, as well as stalls selling food. A taxi into town from the bus terminal costs US$2, and this will save you a 12-block walk. However, if you find a taxi a little further from the terminal you'll avoid being surcharged by some taxi drivers. **Mal Paso airport** is on the northwestern outskirts of town.

On the Plaza Libertad stand the **Municipalidad** and **Jefatura de Policía**, built in 1868 in the style of a colonial *cabildo*. On the west side is the **cathedral**, the fifth on the site, dating from 1877. Two blocks southeast of the plaza is the **Convento de Santo Domingo** ⓘ *Urquiza and 25 de Mayo*, containing one of two copies of the 'Turin Shroud', but otherwise unremarkable. Six blocks east of the plaza is the welcome greenery of

Quilmes: not just a lager

Of all the indigenous peoples of Argentina, perhaps the most tragic was the fate that awaited the inhabitants of Quilmes. This ancient city, now an intricate lacework of terraces climbing high up the mountain-side, housed around 5000 people from 5000 years ago until AD 117, with a well developed social structure, and its own language, *kakán*, now extinct. The Quilmes people lived on the plains, but built the site as a defensive stronghold to retreat to in times of attack, since the whole Calchaquí valley was the site of frequent warfare between rival clans. Added to this excellent strategic position, they were hard to dominate thanks to their sophisticated weaponry: with *boleadoras* made from stones tied with llama hide thongs, and slings of plaited lamb's wool, they hurled egg-shaped stones with great accuracy over long distances. Their houses consisted of adjacent dwellings buried some way into the earth, and lined with stone walls, which also served as walkways between houses. Posts of sturdy algarrobo wood were used to support pitched roofs (now vanished), and they lived in clans or family groups. The higher social orders and those who held shamanic or religious positions in the community occupied dwellings highest up the mountainside, closest to the gods.

They cultivated fruit in the valley, beans, potato, pumpkins and maize, using irrigation canals to redirect snow-melt from the mountain tops. Chicha was the popular, mildly alcoholic drink made from ground and fermented algarrobo seeds, and their shamen cured people using local herbs and plants, as they do today.

The Incas were the first to dominate the Quilmes clan, in the late 15th century, but the Quilmes adapted and survived. It was the arrival of the Spanish in the 17th century that proved fatal. After resisting Spanish attacks for many years, the Spanish finally besieged them and cut off all their supplies. Their hillside position proved to be their downfall. In 1668, the Quilmes surrendered, the community was broken up, and the largest group was made to walk for weeks to an area now known as Quilmes, near Buenos Aires. In 1812, the last descendent died, and Argentina's most popular lager brewery was later built in the town. Few Argentines are aware that its namesake was this sophisticated civilization. The next time you have a sip of Quilmes, take a moment to think of its namesake people.

the **Parque Francisco de Aguirre** which stretches to the river, and includes the town's campsite. There's also a **tourist office** ① *Plaza Libertad 417, T0385-421 3253*.

The best museum is the **Museo de Ciencias, Antropológicas y Naturales** ① *Avellaneda 355, T0385-421 1380, www.wagnermuseo.gov.ar, Tue-Sun 0800-2000, free*, with the wonderfully eclectic collection of pre-Hispanic artefacts by brothers Emilio and Duncan Wagner, now sadly haphazardly presented and badly conserved. Amongst the stuffed armadillos, bone flutes, delicate spindles and board-flattened skulls is a breathtaking quantity of beautifully decorated funerary urns, some rare bronze ceremonial *hachas*, and anthropomorphic pieces.

Termas de Río Hondo → *Colour map 1, B3. Phone code 03858. Population 28,000. Altitude 265 m.*
Argentina's most popular spa town, 65 km northwest of Santiago del Estero, is also its most dreary. It was very popular in the 1950s but much of it remains unmodernized from

that era, and the only real reason to visit is if you want to take advantage of the warm mineral-laden waters, which are piped into every hotel in the city. Older Argentines hold it in fond regard and it's a mecca for visitors with arthritic or skin conditions in July and August, when you'll need to book in advance. Out of season, it's a depressing place. The **bus terminal** ① *Las Heras and España*, is eight blocks north of centre near Route 9, but buses will drop you at the plaza, on Alberdi, opposite the casino. With the casino dominating the scruffy triangular plaza, the resort consists of 160 hotels interspersed with *alfajores* shops (the much-loved chocolate and flour biscuit), mostly in run-down and flaking buildings. Even in high season, there's little to make you feel better here, and another biscuit isn't likely to help.

◉ Tucumán province listings

For Sleeping and Eating price codes and other relevant information, see Essentials pages 30-36.

● Sleeping

Tucumán city *p346*

For more listings, see www.tucuman turismo.gov.ar.

L Catalinas Park, Av Soldati 380, T0381-450 2250, www.catalinaspark.com. The most comfortable place to stay is this luxurious hotel, overlooking Parque 9 de Julio, with comfortable minimalist decor in the bedrooms, outstanding food and service, and pool (open to non-residents), sauna and gym. Good value and highly recommended.

AL Suites Garden Park, Av Soldati 330, T0381-431 0700, www.gardenparkhotel. com.ar. The competition next door is this smart and welcoming 4-star, with views over Parque 9 de Julio. Pool, gym, sauna and restaurant. Also apartments.

A-B Carlos V (Cinco), 25 de mayo 330, T0381-411 3666, www.hotelcarlosv.com.ar. Although the rooms aren't as smartly decorated as the swish lobby and restaurant, they are still spacious and welcoming. DVD players, cable TV and Wi-Fi.

B Premier, Crisóstomo Alvarez 510, T/F0381-431 0381, www.hotelpremier.com.ar. The rooms are spacious and comfortable, and those next to the street are noisy, but the bathrooms are modern and the staff helpful.

B-C Plaza Alberdi, Santiago 1054, T0381-430 3463, www.hotelplazaalberdi.com.ar. Good value for its price range, the simple doubles are on the small side but are clean, and newly constructed. Sauna and massages on offer.

Hostels

E pp Backpacker's Tucumán, Laprida 456, T0381-430 2716, www.backpackerstucuman. com. Under new management. Basic but welcoming dorms in this central 1900s restored house, with a quiet atmosphere and lovely patios. Free internet, a small travel agency and double rooms with own bath (**C**) add to the usual hostel services. Discounts for HI members. Prices include breakfast and dinner.

F pp Hostel Oh!, Santa Fe 930, T0381-430 8849, www.hosteloh.com.ar. Bright, cheerful hostel with a tiny pool and a ping-pong table. Doubles (**D**) available. A bit of a hike from the centre of town.

F pp Tucumán Hostel, Buenos Aires 669, T0381-420 1584, www.tucumanhostel.com. Friendly hostel located in a refurbished building, close to the centre. The cheapest option in town. Large, high-ceiling dorms, freshly painted. Slightly unkempt but chilled garden. Doubles (**E-D**). Recommended.

Private homes

The tourist office arranges homestays with families in the area who are willing to open their homes to foreign visitors. Rates vary.

Tafí del Valle p348

There's lots of comfortable accommodation in Tafí, tending towards the more expensive, with a good range of mid price hotels, most of them with great views. There's a good value *estancia*, though, right in the centre of town, and a welcoming small hostel. For more information, see www.tafidelvalle.com.

A Las Tacanas, Pte Perón 372, T03867-421821, www.estancialastacanas.com. Only a short walk to the centre, this *estancia* was built by Jesuits in the 17th century. With only 7 rooms, the whitewashed farmhouse by the river offers tranquillity and a piece of history. They accept cash only.

A Lunahuana, Av Gdor Critto 540, T03867-421330, www.lunahuana.com.ar. This is the most comfortable and best value hotel in Tafí centre with splendid views from its stylish rooms. There are spacious 2-floor 'duplex' rooms for 4, and a restaurant.

A Mirador del Tafí, on the R307 just east of the town, T03867-421219, www.mirador deltafi.com.ar. This is the best option in the valley, it's comfortable and spacious with spectacular views, a fine restaurant and wonderful service. Recommended.

A-B Posada la Soñada, Ruta 307 Km 64, T03867-421744, www.posadalasoniada. com.ar. New boutique hotel with only 3 rooms, all with wonderful views over the valley. Up on the hill a short distance from the centre, you can enjoy an uninterrupted vista while you eat breakfast. Rooms have comfortable wooden furniture and the bathrooms are well designed and clean.

B Estancia Los Cuartos, on Av Miguel Critto, 150 m from the bus station, T0381-155 874 230, www.estancialoscuartos.com. Very good value and full of character, this 200-year-old *estancia* is right in the middle of town. There are 3 original rooms, hardly restored, with an eclectic collection of antiques. New rooms fit in well with the old style, but benefit from touches of modern comfort. They also offer a day at the *estancia*, with lunch, excursion and horse riding and a great *té criollo*, with farm cheese. Prices are higher in Jan, Feb and Jul.

B Hostería Tafí del Valle, Av San Martín and Gobernador Campero, T03867-421027, www.soldelvalle.com.ar. Right at the top of the town, with splendid views, a pool and an airy restaurant. Its standard rooms are comfortable though rather small; worth paying extra for the larger special ones. Lovely pool and good Wi-Fi connections.

B Hotel Tafí, Av Belgrano 177, T03867-421007, www.hoteltafiweb.com.ar. Simple, welcoming and comfortable rooms in a central location make this a very good choice among mid-range hotels. Buffet breakfast included.

Hostels

F pp La Cumbre, Perón 120, T03867-421768, www.lacumbretafidelvalle.com. The most central hostel, only a 5-min walk from the bus station. The basic rooms are made up for by friendly staff and its location. You can also book hiking, trekking and horse rides with the hostel's own travel agency. Doubles (**D**) available.

F pp Nomade Hostel, Av Los Palenques and Calamico, T03867 420179, www.hostels. org.ar (search for Tafi de Valle). Affordable hostel, in a nicely decorated building only 6 blocks from the bus station. Ask the lovely staff about activities in the area. Doubles (**D**) available.

Amaichá del Valle p349

A Altos de Amaicha Posada, Ruta 307 at Km 117, just outside of town, T03892-421430, www.hotelesdelnorte.com.ar (search for Amaichá del Valle). Wonderful boutique hotel with 7 well-decorated rooms, an amazing pool and a notable restaurant. Ask for a room with a view of the mountains. Recommended.

F pp El Portal de Amaichá, on the main road, next to the petrol station, T03892-421140, www.elportaldeamaicha.8m.com. Quiet and comfortable accommodation with great views either in simple rooms, dorms or in *cabañas*.

F pp La Rocca Camping, Ruta 337 La Puntilla, T011-1562 491964, www.larocca camping.com.ar. Fantastic new camping facility from the team behind the popular La Rocca hostels. They offer rented tents, mountain bikes and also can organize trekking trips. The facilities are new and comfortable.

Santa María p349
C **Hotel de Turismo Cielos del Oeste**, San Martín 450, corner 1 de Mayo, T03892-420240, cielosdeloeste@yahoo.com.ar. Occupying a block of its own 2 blocks east of the plaza, this large institutional place is the best option, with several newer and very comfortable rooms. Free internet, a restaurant and a pool surrounded by a large garden.
D **Inti-Huaico**, Belgrano 146, T03892-422060, pirka@cosama.com.ar. A bargain with nice clean rooms with bath, friendly owners and lovely gardens.
D **Plaza**, San Martín 258, on the plaza, T03892-420309. Small, simple and rather dark but comfy rooms all with bath and TV, breakfast included. Triples (**D**) available.

Camping
Municipal campsite, at end of Sarmiento, about 6 blocks east of the plaza, T03892-425064, with *albergue* (**G**) and restaurant.

Quilmes p350
B **Parador Ruinas de Quilmes**, T03892-421075. Make the most of the site by staying in this peaceful, very comfortable hotel. Its spacious, stylish interior is filled with weavings and ceramics, there's a good restaurant, a nice pool and free camping. Best of all, there are great views of Quilmes: get up early and have them to yourself. Restaurant open to residents only. Recommended.

Santiago del Estero p350
See also www.santiagodelestero.net.
A **Carlos V**, Independencia 110, T0385-424 0303, www.carlosvhotel.com. On the corner of the plaza. The most expensive and luxurious hotel is still good value for a really comfortable international-style hotel with an indoor pool, a good restaurant, and elegant rooms. Go for the spacious superior rooms if you can afford it. Includes parking and breakfast.

B **Hotel Centro**, 9 de Julio 131, T0385-421 9502, www.hotelcentro.com.ar. Light, simply decorated rooms, all with good bathrooms and minibar. Airy 1st floor restaurant.
B **Hotel Libertador**, Catamarca 47, T0385-421 9252, www.hotellibertadorsrl.com.ar. This slightly dated place has a spacious, light lounge and plain, well-equipped rooms. There's an attractive leafy patio with pool (summer only) and a elegant restaurant, also open to non residents. A peaceful place to stay 5 blocks south of the plaza in the better-off part of town.
B **Savoy**, Tucumán 39, T0385-421 1234, www.savoysantiago.com.ar. Most characterful is the faded grandeur of this central, art-nouveau building with swirling stairwell. Rooms are plain but large, and are an excellent budget option.
C **Nuevo Hotel Santiago**, Buenos Aires 60, T0385-421 4397, nuevohotelsantiago@arnet. com.ar. Modernized and comfortable, this is the best of the remaining decent budget choices. The rooms are small but well equipped and it's quiet for such a central location, a block from the plaza.

Camping
Las Casuarinas, Parque Aguirre, T0385-421 1390. Insect repellent essential.

Termas de Río Hondo p351
Ask the helpful tourist office for accommodation advice, at Caseros 268, T03858-421969, or at Av Alberdi 245, T03858-421571, or www.lastermasderiohondo.net.
L **El Hostal del Abuelo**, Francisco Solano 168, T03858-421489, www.elhostaldelabuelo. com.ar. Most central in town, this spa hotel has a huge range of facilities, comfortable rooms but is a bit pricey.
L-AL **Hotel de los Pinos**, Maipú 201, T03858-421043, www.lospinoshotel.com.ar. The best option in an attractive Spanish-style building a little removed from the centre in a huge park, with fantastic pools and rooms with private thermal baths. Rates are for minimum 3-night all-inclusive stays.

🍽 Eating

Tucumán city *p346*
There are plenty of places to eat along
25 de Mayo, which stretches north from
the west side of the plaza.

†††-†† La Leñita, 25 de Mayo 377, T0381-422
9241. Highly recommended for excellent
parrilla and superb salads, one of the best
on the street, also offering live *folclore*
music at weekends.

†† Il Postino, 25 de Mayo and Córdoba, T0381-
421 0440. A hugely popular pizza place and
café, stylishly designed, with lots of brick and
wood and a buzzing atmosphere. Generous
pizzas, tapas and tortillas. Recommended.

†† Los Negros, Laprida 623, T0381-430 4624.
Good for *parrilla* and *tenedor libre* for US$11.

† Cosas del Campo, Lavalle 857, T0381-420
1758. South of centre, next to Plaza San
Martín, this small place is becoming an
unmissable point in town for its delicious
empanadas. Also offers takeaways.

† El Portal, 24 de Septiembre 351 (at the
back of a craft market), T0381-422 6024.
Unpretentious and popular, this large place
and its attractive patio make an ideal settom
for gorgeous *empanadas, locros, humitas*
and *tamales*.

† Mercado del Norte, Maipú between
Mendoza and Córdoba, Mon-Sat 0900-1400,
1630-2100. Indoor market and bazaar
featuring cheap and yummy regional
foods, meat and local produce.

Cafés
Café de París, Santiago del Estero 502 (25 de
Mayo corner). Tapas bar and stylish restaurant.
Filipo, Mendoza y 25 de Mayo. A very
popular smart café, with a nice atmosphere.
Good place for a coffee or a drink.
Panadería Villecco, Corrientes 751. Superb
bread, pastries, and *pan integral* (wholemeal).

Tafí del Valle *p348*
†† Mirador del Tafí, see Sleeping, above.
Excellent food at this hotel, good value.

††† Parrilla Don Pepito, Av Perón 193.
Very good food, excellent *empanadas*.

† El Portal de los Valles, Perón 221. Pleasant
café with a large menu. Good for breakfast
or lunch.

† Parador Tafinisto, at the bottom of
Av Perón. Frequently recommended for
parrilla with plenty of regional dishes, and
live *folclore* music at the weekends.

Santa María *p349*
There are some good and lively places
on the plaza, including:
† El Colonial del Valle. Serves *empanadas* and
other meals, and it is also a nice *confitería*.
† Jandar. Serves excellent and cheap
empanadas, pizzas and salads.

Santiago del Estero *p350*
The better restaurants are at **Libertador**
and **Carlos V** hotels.
† Mia Mamma, on the plaza, 24 de
Septiembre 15, T0385-429 9715. Often
recommended, this is a cheery place for
parrilla and tasty pasta, with good salad
libre starters and friendly service.
† Periko's, on the plaza. Lively, for *lomitos*
and pizzas, popular with a younger crowd.

Cafés, bakeries and heladerías
Cerecetto, a couple of blocks from the plaza,
Córdoba and Libertad. Best ice cream in town.

Termas de Río Hondo *p351*
San Cayetano (††) or homely **Renacimiento**
(††), both on the main drag Sarmiento, are
reasonably priced for *parrilla*. **El Chorizo
Loco** (†), Alberdi and Sarmiento, is a very
cheap and lively pizzeria.

🍸 Bars and clubs

Tucumán city *p346*
Plaza de Almas, Santa Fe and Maipú, north
of centre. This bar attracts young crowds
in the late evenings.

Costumbres Argentinas, San Juan 666.
Good atmosphere in this intimate bar for
late drinks.

Santiago del Estero *p350*
Chester Bar, Roca 525, corner Pellegrini,
T0385-421 4477, www.chesterbar.com.
Lively bar with a friendly atmosphere.

▲ Activities and tours

Tucumán city *p346*
Tour operators
Duport Turismo, Congreso 160, T0381-422
0000, duporttur@tucbbs.com.ar. Same tours
as Turismo del Tucumán, plus a circuit of the
local valleys, 6 hrs, US$20; Parque Alpa Puyo,
½-day US$17; El Cadillal, ½-day US$17.
Montañas Tucumanas, Laprida 196, 1st
floor, T0381-467 1860, www.montanas
tucumanas.com. Great company that
organizes trekking, rappelling, horse riding,
canyoning and paragliding, to name but a few.
Turismo del Tucumán, Crisóstomo Alvarez
422, T0381-422 7636, www.turismodel
tucuman.com. Informative tours to local
places, Quilmes, full-day, US$38; Tafí del
Valle, full-day US$26.

Tafí del Valle *p348*
Tour operators
Aucache Expeditions, Los Palenques, at
Hostel Nomade (see above), T03867-421378,
www.aucachexpediciones.com.ar. Friendly
agency, that can organize rappelling,
trekking, and day trips to Quilmes ruins
and areas around the valley.
La Cumbre, Av Presidente Perón 120,
T03867-421768, www.lacumbretafidel
valle.com. An energetic and friendly company
who offer 4WD excursions and full-day walks
to all the nearby peaks, to waterfalls Cascada
lo Alisos, and to the ruins at Valle de la
Ciénaga. Also a recommended trek to Cerro
Muñoz (4437 m), with an *asado* at the summit.

◷ Transport

Tucumán city *p346*
Air
For airport information, see page 346.
To **Buenos Aires** via **Córdoba**, AR/
Austral, 9 de Julio 110, T0831-431 1030.

Bus
For bus terminal information, see page 346.
Local bus services operate on *cospeles*,
US$0.40, which you buy in advance at
kiosks. For long-distance services, the
modern terminal has 70 ticket offices.
There is a helpful bus information kiosk
opposite **Disco**, T0381-422 2221.
To **Buenos Aires**, 14-16 hrs, US$40-65.
To **Tafí del Valle**, 2½ hrs, US$7, **Aconquija**.
To **Salta** direct (not via Cafayate), 5 hrs,
US$15. To **Cafayate**, 5½ hrs (6½ hrs if
via Santa María), US$14, **Aconquija**.
To **Posadas**, 16 hrs, US$30, **Vosa**. To
Mendoza, 14 hrs, US$36, vía **Catamarca**,
La Rioja, and **San Juan**. To **Catamarca**,
4 hrs, US$10, **Aconquija** and others.
To **Andalgalá**, 1 daily, US$9, **Gutiérrez**.
To **Córdoba**, 8 hrs, US$19. To **Santiago
del Estero**, 2 hrs, US$6. To **La Quiaca**,
10-11 hrs, US$19, **Andesmar** and **Balut**.
To Chile To **Santiago** via **Mendoza**,
daily, 22-24 hrs, US$55, **Andesmar**
and **El Rápido Internacional**.
To Peru To **Lima**, 3 a week, 3½ days via
Mendoza, US$160, **El Rápido Internacional**.

Car hire
Budget Rent a Car, 25 de Mayo 230, T0381-
497 6036, www.budget.com; **Movil Renta**,
San Lorenzo 370, T0381-431 0550,
www.movilrenta.com.ar, and at the airport.

Train
To **Buenos Aires** via **Rosario**, Ferrocentral,
T0381-430 9220, for more information see
Buenos Aires Mitre line, page 109.

Tafí del Valle *p348*
Bus
Smart **Aconquija** terminal on Av Critto, which you might mistake for another hotel, with café, public phones and toilets. There are no luggage lockers, T0381-421025. To **Tucumán**, 8 daily, 2½ hrs, US$7, **Aconquija**. To **Cafayate**, 3 a day, 2½ hrs, US$8 (4 hrs via **Santa María**). To **El Mollar** several daily, US$2. Buses to **Tucumán** stop at El Mollar on request.

Amaichá del Valle *p349*
Bus
To **Tucumán**, 6 daily, 5 hrs, US$5, sit on the right for best views. To **Santa María**, 15 mins, US$1, **Gutiérrez**.

Santa María *p349*
Bus
To **Tucumán**, 5 daily, 4½-5 hrs, US$6, **Aconquija**. To **Cafayate**, daily, 2 hrs, US$4, **Aconquija** and **El Indio**. To **Salta**, daily, 5-6 hrs, US$12, **El Indio**. To **Belén**, 4 hrs, US$8, check with tourist office for current times, **Cayetano** and **Parra**. To **Amaichá del Valle**, 15 mins, US$2, **Gutiérrez**. To **Catamarca**, Sun-Fri, US$12, **Gutiérrez**.

Santiago del Estero *p350*
Air
To **Buenos Aires** and **Tucumán**, Aerolíneas Argentinas/Austral.
   Airport offices Aerolíneas Argentinas, 24 de Septiembre 547, T0385-422 4335.

Bus
Córdoba, 6 hrs, US$12; to **Jujuy**, 8 hrs, US$14; to **Salta**, 6-6½ hrs, US$12; to **Tucumán**, 2 hrs, US$7; to **Catamarca** go via Tucumán.

Termas de Río Hondo *p351*
Bus
For bus terminal information, see page 352.
   To **Santiago del Estero**, 1 hr, US$3, and to **Tucumán**, 2 hrs, US$5; several to **Buenos Aires**, 13-14 hrs, US$45.

❶ Directory

Tucumán city *p346*
Banks Most along San Martín, especially the 700 block between Junín and Maipú. **Currency exchange** Maguitur, San Martín 765, T0381-431 0127, accepts TCs; Maxicambio, San Martín 779, T0381-431 0020. **Post office** Córdoba and 25 de Mayo, Mon-Fri 0800-1400, 1700-2000, Sat 0900-1300. **Telephone** There are lots of *locutorios* all over the centre.

Tafí del Valle *p348*
Banks Banco de Tucumán, Miguel Critto 311, T03867-421033. ATM for all major cards.

Santiago del Estero *p350*
Banks Banco Francés, 9 de Julio and 24 de Septiembre.

Contents

Footprint features

Border crossings

The Northeast

At a glance

Getting around Local buses and minibuses are the best option.

Time required With 5 days you can visit both sides of the falls, and the mission ruins of San Ignacio. Add at least 3-4 more if you intend to visit the Esteros del Iberá.

Weather Dec-Feb is hot and humid. Temperatures average 25°C in summer, 15°C in winter.

When not to go Jan-Feb can be hot and humid, and Easter is very busy. There is more rain in Mar and Jun.

★ Don't miss ...
1 Boat ride under Iguazú Falls, page 363.
2 The ruins of San Ignacio, page 382.
3 Colonia Carlos Pellegrini and the Esteros del Iberá, page 394.
4 Carnival in Gualeguaychú, pages 400 and 406.
5 El Monumento de la Bandera, Rosario, page 409.

Of all Argentina's many natural wonders, there is nothing quite as spectacular as Iguazú Falls. With a magical setting in subtropical rainforest, alive with birdsong and the constant dancing of butterflies, the colossal Garganta del Diablo waterfall at their centre is an unforgettable sight. Take a boat underneath and get drenched in the spray, or stroll along nature trails at first light. Along red earth roads through emerald green vegetation, Misiones province holds other delights: Jesuit missions unearthed from the jungle at San Ignacio, and the extraordinary Saltos de Moconá, 3000 m of falls more horizontal than vertical.

El Litoral's wealth of wildlife is astounding. In the vast wetlands of Esteros del Iberá, giant storks and caiman nestle between floating islands and water lilies. In Mburucuyá tall palms wave in grasslands and passion flowers thrive in abundance. In the Chaco, watch out for pumas and monkeys, while the palm forests of Entre Rios are centuries old. Stop on the lazy Paraná river for relaxed, pretty Colón with its port and sandy beaches and the faded splendour of Paraná. For more stimulation, historical Corrientes is a riot at Carnival time, and lively Rosario's hotbed of culture produces the country's finest musicians.

The northeast's rich culture stems from its indigenous peoples, the Guaraní and Wichí, who produce beautiful art. The gently meandering rivers set the pace, giving the land its lush vegetation and generating in its people a charming laid-back warmth. *Yerba mate* is grown for the nation's favourite drink, and everywhere you'll encounter friends gathered on riverbanks on balmy afternoons sipping from their *mate* gourd. For more details on the *mate* ritual, see the box on page 36.

Iguazú Falls

Any trip to Argentina should include the Iguazú Falls. They're the biggest falls in South America – half as high again as Niagara – and a spectacular experience. You can get right up close to the water as it gushes down, along paths that enable you to enjoy the natural splendour of their subtropical setting, filled with birdsong and vividly coloured butterflies. In all, there are 275 falls stretching over 2.7 km but the main attraction is the Garganta del Diablo (devil's throat), where walkways take you right above the falls to see the smooth river transformed in an instant into a seething torrent as the water crashes 74 m over a horseshoe-shaped precipice onto basalt rocks below, filling the air with bright spray and a deafening roar. The whole chasm is filled constantly with billowing clouds of mist in which great dusky swifts miraculously wheel and dart, and an occasional rainbow hovers. Then you can walk close to the bottom of the immensely wide Saltos Bossetti and Dos Hermanos, or take a boat trip, which speeds you beneath the falling water to get a total drenching. Viewed from below, the rush of water is unforgettably beautiful, falling through jungle filled with begonias, orchids, ferns, palms and toucans, flocks of parrots, cacique birds and myriad butterflies. There are some longer trails enabling you to enjoy the diverse flora and fauna in this national park, and several excellent guides on hand whose expertise will considerably add to your enjoyment. The whole experience is uplifting, the park itself is clean and well organized, and the area is easily worth at least a couple of days of your itinerary.

Argentina shares the falls with Brazil and you can visit them from either side for two quite different experiences. The Brazilian side has a smaller, more restricted park and offers a panoramic view from its limited trails but you're kept at a distance from the falls themselves. If you have to choose just one, go for the Argentine side, where you can get closer to the falls, walk in the jungle and explore the rainforest. Allow at least two days to see both sides, or to return to the park a second time in Argentina (half price if you keep your ticket). The most pleasant place to stay is undoubtedly the laid-back Argentine town of Puerto Iguazú, where hotels are cheaper and the streets are far safer than in the Brazilian city of Foz do Iguaçu, where accommodation is plentiful but there is a serious crime problem. On either side, most establishments will accept Brazilian reais, Argentine pesos or dollars.

In this chapter the Argentine side of the falls is described first, with the national park, then Puerto Iguazú, and all the listings information. The Brazilian side follows, with Foz do Iguaçu and its listings. For more information, see www.iguazuargentina.com and www.fozdoiguacu.pr.gov.br (both in English). ▸▸ For listings, see pages 370-374.

Ins and outs

Getting there and around The falls on both sides are contained within national parks, both of which charge entry fees and have well-organized free transport to take you to the waterfalls. **In Argentina**, park entry costs US$21, and you should allow at least a day (it takes six hours to see the main attractions if you do it quickly), starting early (the park opens at 0800). If you find a brisk pace exhausting in the heat of summer, you can revisit the park the next day at half the price – make sure you keep your ticket. Just opposite the entrance, a free mini-train takes you from the visitor centre to Estación Garganta, where a 1-km-long walkway leads to the Garganta del Diablo falls and then to Estación Cataratas, where two trails, taking at least an hour each, offer great views of the falls and a free boat crossing to Isla San Martín for even closer views. **On the Brazilian side**, park entry costs US$10 (payable in reais only), and a visit takes around two hours, with free buses taking you to the start of a walkway with steps down to the falls, and some basic restaurants with fantastic views. The park opens at 0900; see also www.cataratasdoiguacu.com.br.

Dos and don'ts

- Get to the park as early as you can to spot wildlife and avoid queues.
- Wear a hat, good sunscreen and sunglasses: the sun is fierce here.
- In the rainy season, when water levels are high, wear waterproof coats or swimming costumes for some of the lower catwalks and for boat trips.
- Bring insect repellent, bottled water and some snacks.

- Wear shoes with good soles, as the walkways can be very slippery.
- Protect cameras and binoculars from the spray with a plastic bag.
- Take all rubbish out of the park with you, or use the bins.
- Don't feed animals or birds, don't damage the flora, and walk quietly so as not to disturb wildlife.
- Get your ticket stamped on entry; your next day visit will be half price.

On both sides there are optional extra boat trips right up to the falls themselves: **Jungle Explorer** ⓘ *www.iguazujunglexplorer.com*, on the Argentine side is best, with a great trip that takes you rushing right underneath the falls. You will get wet. Both parks have visitor centres, though the Argentine centre is far superior. There are also cafés and restaurants.

When to visit The falls can be visited all year round. There's officially no rainy season, though it tends to rain more in March and June and there can be heavy downfalls in summer. The average temperatures are 25°C in summer and 15°C in winter. The busiest times are the Argentine holiday periods – January, Easter week and July – when you must book accommodation in advance, and on Sundays when helicopter tours over the falls from the Brazilian side are particularly popular (and noisy). Remember that between October and March Argentina is one hour behind Brazil (daylight saving dates change each year) and, from December to March, one hour behind Paraguay.

Background The first recorded European visitor to the falls was the Spaniard Alvar Núñez Cabeza de Vaca in 1542, on his search for a connection between the Brazilian coast and the Río de la Plata: he named them the *Saltos de Santa María*. Though the falls were well known to the Jesuit missionaries, they were unexplored until the area was covered by a Brazilian expedition sent out by the Paraguayan president, Solano López, in 1863.

Parque Nacional Iguazú (Argentina) → *For listings, see pages 370-374.*

Created in 1934, the park extends over an area of 67,000 ha of dense subtropical rainforest. There is excellent access to the falls themselves from various angles and along two further trails that wind through the forest to give you an experience of the wildlife.

Ins and outs

Getting there The park lies 20 km east of the town of Puerto Iguazú along Route 12. **El Práctico** buses ⓘ *T03757-420377*, run from the Hito Tres Fronteras junction in Puerto Iguazú, 0700-1930 on the hour and 30 minutes past, stopping at the main bus terminal 10 minutes later, and arriving at the visitor centre after 45 minutes, US$2.50. Buses return from the park 0750-2020. You can get on or off the bus at any point in the journey.

For transport between the Argentine and Brazilian sides see Foz do Iguaçu, page 376, and the border box, page 367. ▶▶ *For further information, see Transport, page 374.*

Park information The park is open every day of the year: 16 September to 15 March from 0800-1800, and 15 March to 15 September from 0800-1700. Entry is US$21 for all foreign visitors. Get your ticket stamped as you leave for half-price entry for the next three days.

There's an excellent **visitor centre (Centro de Interpretación)** on the right after you enter, with information and photographs of the flora and fauna, and the history of the area from the earliest settlers. Opposite, you'll find plenty of places to eat in the **Patio de Comidas**, including a pizzeria, *parrilla* and snack bar. As you walk towards the barriers where you pay the entry fee, there are excellent souvenir shops selling both commercial souvenirs and local Guaraní handicrafts (note that these are cheaper when bought from the Guaraní people themselves, just inside the entrance). These shops will also download digital photos to CD. Opposite are clean toilets, *locutorio* (a public phone centre) and

Around the Iguazú Falls

Sleeping 🛏
Complejo Americano **5**
Das Cataratas **1**
Del Parque Ibirá Retá **4**
Hostel Inn Iguazú **5**
Loi Suites Iguazú **3**
Paudimar Campestre **11**
Riotropic **6**
Sheraton Internacional
Iguazú Resort **2**

ATMs. Further along the 'Sendero Verde' towards the start of the 'Circuitos Inferior' and 'Superior' there's a great open-air café (the fresh orange juice and fruit salad is recommended), *locutorio* and *parrilla* (US$9 for *parrilla tenedor libre*). At the **Estación Garganta** there's another little café and shop selling postcards and water.

The **guardería** (ranger station) is next to the Estación Cataratas, on the way to the Circuitos Inferior and Superior. The *guardaparques* are hugely knowledgeable about the park and will give you detailed information on wildlife and where to spot it, and will even accompany you if they're not too busy. They also hand out a helpful leaflet with a clear map of the park, and another in English, *Birds of Iguazú*.

Recommended books *The Laws of the Jungle* by Santiago G de la Vega, and *Iguazu Life and Colour*, both around US$6, available in English from visitor centres throughout Puerto Iguazú. Also, *Birds of Southern South America and Antarctica*, by De la Peña and Rumboll, published by Harper Collins, 1998.

➡ **Iguazú Falls maps**
1 Around the Iguazú Falls, page 364
2 Puerto Iguazú, page 368

Wildlife

You'll see amazingly rich wildlife whatever time you visit the park: there are more than 430 species of birds, 70 species of mammals and over a hundred species of butterflies. But you'll need to come in the early morning or late afternoon to stand a good chance of seeing the more elusive species: pumas and tapirs. Look out for restless and curious brown capuchin monkeys, seen in groups of around 20, howler monkeys and friendly coati with their striped tails. Toucans are ubiquitous, with their huge orange cartoon beaks, and also the curious plush crested jays, black with pale yellow breasts, which can be seen perched inquisitively around the park's restaurants. You'll also see two kinds of vultures wheeling above the falls themselves, both with fringed wing tips: the red-headed turkey vulture, and the black vulture whose wing tips are white. You should spot blue-winged parakeets, the red-rumped cacique which builds hanging nests on *pindo* palms, and fruit-eaters like the magpie tanager and the colourful purple-throated euphonia. The butterflies are stunning: look out for electric blue *morpho* butterflies, as big as your hand, the poisonous red and black *heliconius*, and species of *Papilionidae* and *Pieridae*, with striking black and white designs.

Trails

Garganta del Diablo From the visitor centre a mini-train (free), the *Tren de la Selva*, whisks visitors on a fantastic 25-minute trip (2.3 km) through the jungle to Estacíon Garganta, from where it's a 1-km easy walk along boardwalks (fine for wheelchairs) across the wide River Iguazú to the park's centrepiece, the Garganta del Diablo falls. Trains leave Estación Central, just beyond the visitor centre, on the hour and 30 minutes past the hour, and leave Estación Cataratas at 15 and 45 minutes past the hour (either direction). Allow at least two hours for the whole trip: train, walking, watching the falls and photos.

Circuito Inferior and Circuito Superior There are excellent views of the wider range of falls, from Salto San Martín to Salto Dos Hermanos, from the two well-organized trails along sturdy walkways: the **Circuito Superior** (650 m) and **Circuito Inferior** (1400 m), both taking around 1½ to two hours to complete. To reach them, get off the train at the Estación Cataratas (after a 10-minute journey) and follow signs a short distance to where the trails begin. Alternatively, you can walk from the visitor centre along the Sendero Verde to the Estación Cataratas, which takes 10-15 minutes and avoids the crowds waiting for the next train.

Start with the **Circuito Superior**, a level path that takes you along the westernmost line of falls – Saltos Dos Hermanos, Bossetti, Bernabé Mendez, Mbigua (Guaraní for cormorant) and San Martín – allowing you to see these falls from above. This path is safe for those with walking difficulties, wheelchairs and pushchairs, but you should wear supportive, non-slippery shoes.

The **Circuito Inferior** takes you down to the water's edge via a series of steep stairs and walkways with superb views of both San Martín falls and the Garganta del Diablo from a distance, and then up close to Salto Bossetti. Wheelchair users, pram pushers, and those who aren't good with steps should go down by the exit route for a smooth and easy descent. There's a café on the way down and plenty of shade. You could then return to the **Estación Cataratas** to take the train to Estación Garganta, at 10 minutes and 40 minutes past the hour, and see the falls close up from above.

Isla San Martín An optional extra hour-long circuit is to take the free two-minute ferry ride (leaves every 10 minutes, or on demand) at the very bottom of the Circuito Inferior, which crosses to the small hilly island of Isla San Martín where two trails lead to miradores (viewpoints): take the right-hand path for good close views of the San Martín Falls and straight ahead to Salto Rivadavia, or left for a longer walk to the same place. Bathing on the beach here is strictly speaking not allowed, but there are usually a few Argentines sunning themselves. Note that the paths down to the ferry and up to the miradores on the island are very steep and uneven. Take water to drink, as there are no services. The ferry ride can be suspended by high waters at times. Ask at the entrance.

Alternative trails The park offers two more trails through the forest which allow you to get closer to the wildlife: the **Macuco Nature Trail** allows you to see particularly superb birdlife, 7 km return (allow six hours), starts from the path leading from the visitor centre to the Sheraton Hotel, and is a magnificent walk down to the river via a natural pool (El Pozón) fed by a slender, ice-cold, 20-m-high waterfall **Salto Arrechea**. This is a good place for bathing (and the only permitted place in the park), and the walk is highly recommended. See the helpful leaflet in English produced by the Iguazú National Park: *Macuco Nature Trail*. The first 3 km are easy but the next 150 m are more challenging, as the path descends steeply, before the final easy 200 m; the elderly and children may find this route tough. The path is

Border essentials: Argentina–Brazil

Puente Tancredo Neves

This crossing is straightforward. If crossing on a day visit, no immigration formalities are required, so you should state clearly if you need your passport stamped on re-entry for another three months in the country.

Argentine immigration At the Brazilian end of the bridge, and if entering Argentina, buses stop at immigration and wait for the officials. Before setting off, check to see if you need a visa for Brazil.

Brazilian consulate In Puerto Iguazú: Av Guaraní 70, T03757-421348, consular@conbrasilcordoba.org.ar.

Transport Buses leave Puerto Iguazú terminal for Foz do Iguaçu every 20 minutes, US$2. At the border the driver waits while everyone gets their passports stamped. Keep your ticket as you will need it to exit Brazil, you can get a new one for a fee if you loose it though. Taxis between the border and Puerto Iguazú cost US$20.

open April to August 0800-1730 and September to March 0800-1830, but leaving in the early morning is recommended. There are no services, so bring water and lunch and contact tour agencies for guides. The **Sendero Yacaratiá** trail starts from nearer the visitor centre and reaches the river by a different route, ending at **Puerto Macuco**, where you can take the *Jungle Explorer* boat to see the falls themselves. This trail is really for vehicles and less pleasant for walkers, so it's best visited on a 'Safari in the Jungle' with **Explorador Expediciones.** ▸▸ *For further information, see Activities and tours, page 373.*

Puerto Iguazú → *For listings, see pages 370-374. Colour map 2, A3.*

Puerto Iguazú (210 m) is a friendly, atmospheric place, its low white buildings splashed with the red dust from roads, and bright green vegetation growing abundantly everywhere. Its houses are neat, decorated with flowers, and although the centre is slightly chaotic, the town has an appealing authentic life of its own, despite the massive daily influx of tourists on whom the economy depends. It's a pleasant place to walk around, and with several comfortable and economical places to stay, it's a much more appealing base than Foz on the Brazilian side.

 Iguazú means 'big water' in the local Guaraní language (i = water, guazú = big)

Ins and outs → *Phone code 03757. Population 31,000.*

The **airport** ① *T03757-420595,* is some 20 km southeast of Puerto Iguazú near the falls. A bus service runs between the airport and the bus terminal to connect with plane arrivals and departures, US$5, and will drop you at or collect you from your hotel. Taxis charge US$12 to the Hotel Sheraton, and around US$19 to Puerto Iguazú; US$23 to Foz do Iguaçu; and US$30 to the Brazilian airport. The **bus terminal** ① *Av Córdoba and Av Misiones, T03757-421916,* has a *locutorio*, restaurant, various tour company desks and bus company offices, who might look after your luggage if you ask nicely.

Tourist information

The **tourist information office** ① *Av Victoria Aguirre 396, T03757-420800,* is useful only for the very patient and those who speak good Spanish. They are not always friendly but they do have a basic map with useful phone numbers and bus timetables. Also try www.misiones.gov.ar and www.iguazuturismo.gov.ar.

Sights

The town's main street is Avenida Victoria Aguirre where, at No 66, you will find the Iguazú National Park information office, **Parque Nacional Iguazú** ① *T03757-420722, daily 0900-2200, www.iguazuargentina.com, in park T03757-420180.* This avenue runs northwest from the entrance to the town to the little plaza at its hub, and changes names to Avenida Tres Fronteras as it turns east and heads to the spectacular viewpoint high above the meeting of rivers Paraná and Iguazú, known as the **Hito Tres Fronteras** (three borders landmark). You can also reach this point via an attractive *costanera*, running above the Río Iguazú, past the small port where boats leave for cruises along the Paraná and to Paraguay. At the Hito, there's a string of touristy souvenir stands, where children will press you to buy orchid plants, and little rolls of the local *chipita* bread, made from mandioc root (very tasty). The views over the rivers and neighbouring Paraguay and Brazil are impressive.

Puerto Iguazú

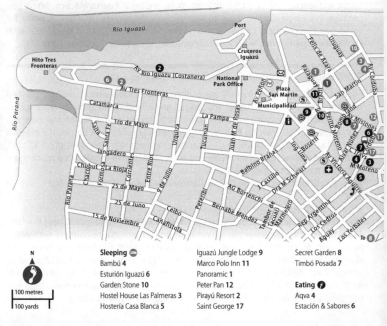

Sleeping	Iguazú Jungle Lodge 9	Secret Garden 8
Bambú 4	Marco Polo Inn 11	Timbó Posada 7
Esturión Iguazú 6	Panoramic 1	
Garden Stone 10	Peter Pan 12	**Eating**
Hostel House Las Palmeras 3	Pirayú Resort 2	Aqva 4
Hostería Casa Blanca 5	Saint George 17	Estación & Sabores 6

N

100 metres
100 yards

Border essentials: Argentina–Paraguay

Puente de la Amistad

The ferry service from the port in Puerto Iguazú to Tres Fronteras is for locals only (no immigration facilities). Crossing to Paraguay is via Puente de la Amistad to Ciudad del Este. There is a US$4 tax to enter Paraguay, but it is rarely charged. Most buses won't even stop.

Transport Direct buses leave Puerto Iguazú terminal every 30 minutes, US$2, 45 minutes, liable to delays especially when crossing the bridge to Ciudad del Este.

There are a couple of interesting projects worth visiting. **La Aripuca** ① *T03757-423488, www.aripuca.com.ar, US$3, turn off Ruta 12 at Km 4.5 just after Hotel Cataratas; or get off the bus here and walk 250 m,* is a charming centre for appreciation of the native trees of the forest – a good option for families if it's raining. An Aripuca is a traditional Guaraní trap for birds, and a giant version of the pyramidic structure that they use has been made from the fallen logs of 30 ancient trees of different species. A 30-minute guided tour (English, Spanish or German) explains all about the tree life, and then you can clamber up their trunks, or enjoy the sculpture from enormous chairs made from tree roots. Sponsor a living tree in the forest to protect it. Recommended. Nearby, **Güira Oga** (Casa de los Pájaros) ① *guiraoga.fundacionazara. org.ar, T03757-423980, daily 0830-1800, US$2,* is a sanctuary for birds that have been injured, or rescued from traffickers. Here, they are treated and reintroduced to the wild; there are exquisite parrots and magnificent birds of prey. To get there, turn off Ruta 12 at Hotel Orquídeas Palace, and the entrance is 800 m further along the road from Aripuca. A 1-km-long trail from the road winds through the forest, and through the large aviaries, with families of monkeys in trees overhead. Endangered species are bred here, and eagles and hawks are taught to hunt. It is an entirely self-funded family enterprise. A guided visit in English or Spanish takes 40 minutes, after which you can wander around at your leisure, and enjoy the peace. It is inspiring and informative.

➡ **Iguazú Falls maps**
1 Around the Iguazú Falls, page 364
2 **Puerto Iguazú, page 368**

Fatto in Casa **9**
La Esquina **3**
La Rueda **5**
La Tribu **10**
Parilla El Quincho de
Tío Querido **8**

Pizza Color **7**
Pizzería La Costa **2**
Tango Bar Iguazú **11**

Bars & clubs 🎵
Cuba Libre **1**

For Sleeping and Eating price codes and other relevant information, see Essentials pages 30-36.

🛏 Sleeping

Parque Nacional Iguazú *p363, map p364*
LL-L Sheraton Internacional Iguazú Resort, Iguazú National Park, T03757-491800, www.sheraton.com/iguazu. The only hotel within the park itself, with unsurpassable views of the falls from half of the stylish rooms, the others have attractive forest views. There is open access to all the trails directly from the gardens, so that you can even visit the park and its wildlife before breakfast. It's the standard international style, but waking up to see the falls is priceless. There's a pool, tennis courts, putting green, sauna and bikes for hire. Taxi to airport US$13.

Puerto Iguazú *p367, map p368*
The Brazilian side is favoured by tour operators because of the profusion of large hotels, but the city can be a little dangerous at night, so it's much better to stay on the Argentine side. For more listings, see www.welcome argentina.com/puertoiguazu/.
LL Posada Puerto Bemberg, Fundadores Bemberg s/n, T03757-496500 (In Buenos Aires), www.puertobemberg.com. Wonderful luxury accommodation in a 1940s bungalow surrounded by lush gardens. Huge living

areas, beautifully decorated rooms and helpful staff. Highly recommended.
LL Esturión Iguazú, Av Tres Fronteras 650, T03757-420100. On the road to Hito Tres Fronteras, above the river, with panoramic views from its lovely pool. A beautiful luxury hotel with smartly designed rooms and *cabañas*. Nightly entertainment, pool, tennis courts, volleyball and football.
LL-L Loi Suites Iguazu, Selva Iryapú s/n, T03757-498300, www.loisuites.com.ar. A little out of the city on the way to the falls, this fantastic hotel has 4 pools, an attractive outside deck, large modern rooms and a spa. Recommended.
L Panoramic, Paraguay 372, T03757-498133, www.panoramic-hoteliguazu.com. Located on a hill overlooking the meeting point of Argentina, Brazil and Paraguay, this hotel is simply stunning. Serene outdoor pool with great views, large well-designed rooms and all 5-star inclusions.
AL-A Iguazú Jungle Lodge, Hipólito Irigoyen and San Lorenzo, T03757-420600, www.iguazujunglelodge.com. The most luxurious place in the town itself, a beautifully designed complex of *cabañas* and loft apartments, just 7 blocks from the centre, by a river and with a lovely pool. Each self-contained apartment is incredibly comfortable and stylish, equipped with everything you need, including a/c, Wi-Fi

POSADA PUERTO BEMBERG
Hotel de Selva · Iguazú Argentina

Info & Reservas
(+54) 3757 496500
info@puertobemberg.com
www.puertobemberg.com

and DVDs to borrow. Some sleep 7, so they're good value if you fill them up.

AL-A Saint George, Córdoba 148, T/F03757-420633, www.hotelsaintgeorge.com. Comfortable modern-ish rooms (ask for the most luxurious ones) around a leafy pool area, with attentive service and a friendly atmosphere. Good restaurant **La Esquina** (see Eating, below). Good location next to the bus station. Tours arranged. If you can't afford the upgraded rooms, don't stay here as the cheaper rooms are small, musty and not recommended.

A Secret Garden, Los Lapachos 623, T03757-423099, www.secretgardeniguazu.com. Small B&B with attentive owners, and a precious fern garden surrounding the house. Spacious rooms and a relaxing atmosphere.

B Pirayú Resort, Av Tres Fronteras 550, on the way to the Hito, T03757-420393, www.pirayu.com.ar. Comfortable and well-equipped *cabañas*, with lovely river views, and sports of all kinds, lots of games for children, attractive pool and entertainment.

B Hotel Riotropic, C Montecarlo and Av los Inmigrantes, T03757-1540 5574, www.riotropic.com.ar. 10 simple but comfortable rooms set around a pool, with a friendly host and lovely garden. US$5 taxi ride or 20-min walk to town.

C Del Parque Ibirá Retá, R12, Km 4, T03757-420072, www.ibirareta.com.ar. Snuggled in the middle of Parque Botánico Ibirá Retá, the lodge is small, intimate and decorated in simple modern colours, with TV, cable and a/c. Breakfast included and there is the option of including dinners as well.

C Hostería Casa Blanca, Guaraní 121, 2 blocks from bus station, T03757-421320, www.casablancaiguazu.com.ar. Good value, with breakfast included. Conveniently central, family-run place with impeccably clean, pleasant and spacious rooms. Simple but beautifully maintained.

D Timbó Posada, Misiones 147, T03757-422698, www.timboiguazu.com.ar. Only 100 m from the bus station. Doubles have

a/c and Wi-Fi. There is a kitchen and they serve good breakfasts. Options for triples and quads make it affordable for groups.

Hostels

F pp Hostel Inn Iguazú, R12, Km 5, T03757-421823, T03757-420156, www.hostel-inn.com. 20% discount to HI members and 10% discount on long-distance buses. Large, well-organized and clean hostel which used to be a casino. Huge pool and free internet, pool tables, ping-pong and a range of free DVDs to watch. They also organize package tours to the falls, which include accommodation. Recommended.

E pp Marco Polo Inn, Av Córdoba 158, T03757-425559, www.hostel-inn.com. The biggest and most central hostel in town, right in front of the bus station. It's newly built, has Wi-Fi throughout, a nice pool and clean rooms. There is a fun bar at night (open to non-residents). It gets busy so reserve in advance. Recommended.

F pp Bambú, Av San Martín 4, T03757-425 864, www.hostelbambu.com. Small hostel, with cramped but friendly dorms, a great bar outside and a good-sized kitchen. A short walk to the bus station.

F pp Garden Stone, Av Córdoba 441, www.gardenstonehostel.com. Lovely new hostel with a homely feel set in nice gardens, with a large outdoor eating area. They have plans for a pool but in the meantime the garden is the perfect place to relax in. Recommended for a tranquil stay.

F pp Peter Pan, Av Córdoba 267, T03757-423 616, www.peterpanhostel.com. Just down the hill from the bus station, this hostel is impeccably clean, has a central pool and large open kitchen. The doubles (**B-C**) are lovely. Helpful staff.

G pp Hostel House Las Palmeras, Av Córdoba 341, T03757-425 604, info@ laspalmerashostel.com.ar. The cheapest place in town. The rooms are basic, small common area with a pint-sized pool. Good atmosphere. For those on a real budget.

Estancias

LL Yacutinga Lodge, 30 km from town, will collect visitors in their jeep, www.yacutinga.com. A wonderful experience, staying in this beautifully designed lodge in the middle of the rainforest, with activities filling your 2-day stay. Accommodation is in rustic adobe houses in lovely tropical gardens. Superb food and drinks are included, as are boat trips and walks to spot wildlife and plant trees. Highly recommended as the perfect complement to seeing Iguazú Falls.

Camping

Complejo Americano, R12, Km 5, T03757-420190, www.complejoamericano.com.ar. The town's best site with 3 pools in pleasant, nicely tended wooded gardens, 5 km from town, and also *cabañas* (**B**). Camping is US$6 per person, and there's a food shop, electricity, games area, pool and barbecue facilities. Recommended.

❶ Eating

Puerto Iguazú *p367, map p368*
Take a break from steak and try the delicious local fish which is the speciality here: *surubí*, *pacú* and *dorado*. All the 5-star hotels listed above have high-quality restaurants that can be visited by non-guests.

₸₸₸ Iguazú Grand Hotel Resort and Casino, R12, Km 1640, T03757-498000. This swanky hotel's swish restaurant is open to non-residents who book in advance. Posh food and international cuisine for an elegant night out.

₸₸ Aqva, Av Córdoba and Corlos Thays, T03757-422064. Just down from the bus station, this lovely restaurant serves dishes made with ingredients from the area. Try the stuffed *pacú* or the *surubí*.

₸₸ La Esquina, corner of Av Córdoba 148, T03757-425778. Very good restaurant next to Hotel Saint George. Good beef, salads and local fish. Warm and friendly service.

₸₸ La Rueda, Córdoba 28, T03757-422531. A family-run restaurant with a warm and lively atmosphere inside a cosily decorated rustic cabin, often with mellow live music. There's a superb menu with delicious food, including well-prepared locally caught *surubí* and *pacú* fish, steaks and pastas.

₸₸ Tango Bar Iguazú, Av Brasil 1, T03757-422008. New bar which serves pizzas and pastas. It turns into a milonga with tango classes and dancing at night.

₸₸-₸ Fatto in Casa, Av Brasil 126. Reasonable Italian food in a lively part of town. Often recommended by locals.

₸ Estación & Sabores, Terminal de Omnibus. Located at the bus station, this restaurant is actually quite good, serving regional specialities; in the evenings they open up their deck area.

₸ Parrilla El Quincho de Tío Querido, Bompland 110, T03757-420151. The best *parrilla* in town, and much loved by locals. Great value. Live music in high season.

₸ Pizza Color, Córdoba 135, T03757-420206. Great for pizzas and *parrilla*. Reasonably priced, very central.

₸ Pizzería La Costa, Av Río Iguazú on the Costanera. Popular with locals, this is an informal pizzeria high above the river on the coast road. Looks basic, but the pizzas are really superb.

Cafés

At the end of Av Misiones, near the meeting point of Brasil and P Moreno, is a nice inter-section known as 7 Bocas, where there are a lot of cafés and resto-bars for a cheap meal, or an evening drink. Try Puerto Bambú or Nae.

❶ Bars and clubs

Puerto Iguazú *p367, map p368*
Cuba Libre, Av Brasil and Paraguay, T03757-422531. Just a block from the newly popular area of town for eating out, this is a fun place for a drink, or if you fancy dancing salsa. Owned by a Cuban, the music is great and the atmosphere lively at weekends.

La Tribu, Av Brasil 149. A pub/club which has cheap, good and live shows.

▲ Activities and tours

Parque Nacional Iguazú *p363, map p364*
A day trip from Puerto Iguazú to the
Argentine side of the falls, including transfer
from your hotel and guide (request English
speakers) costs US$23, and to the Brazilian
side is US$22, but neither includes park
entrance fee (US$21). The tour to the Brazilian
side of the falls will inevitably stop at the
Duty Free Shop, a large, flash indoor mall
between the 2 customs points. Perfumes
and cosmetics, electrical goods, spirits and
cigarettes at reduced prices. If you want to
visit the Jesuit ruins at **San Ignacio Mini**,
250 km (4 hrs) away, a trip to an open mine
for semi-precious stones at **Wanda**, 60 km
away, is likely to be included. Full-day
US$42, plus park entrance to the Jesuit ruins
(US$10). For tour operators in Puerto Iguazú,
see page 374. It is recommended that you
visit San Ignacio's ruins overnight as there
are some wonderful places to stay and
there are some great excursions you can
do with Misiones Excursions, see page 390.

There are also **Full Moon Walks**:
night-time walking tours to the falls when
the moon is full. The 1½-hr guided bilingual
walks may or may not include dinner before
or afterwards at the Restaurante La Selva.
Bookings must be done in person at the
park, see the *guardaparques*, T03757-
491409 or www.iguazuargentina.com.
US$30 with dinner, US$20 without.

Boat trips

Jungle Explorer, T03757-421696, www.
Iguazujunglexplorer.com. Run a series of
fabulous boat trips, all highly recommended:
Aventura Náutica is a fast and exhilarating
journey by launch along the lower Río Iguazú,
from opposite Isla San Martín right up to the
San Martín falls and then into the Garganta
del Diablo, completely drenching passengers
in the mighty spray. Great fun; not for the
faint-hearted, 12 mins, US$26.
Gran Aventura combines the Aventura
Nautica with a longer boat trip along rapids

in the lower Río Iguazú to Puerto Macuco,
followed by a jeep trip along the Yacaratiá
trail, 1 hr, US$51. Other combinations at
reduced prices and tailor-made tours.
Tickets available at all embarkation points.
Paseo Ecológico takes you floating silently
3 km down the river from Estación Garganta
to appreciate the wildlife on its banks:
basking tortoises, caiman, monkeys and
birdlife. A wonderful and gentle introduction
to the river, 30 mins, US$15.

Mountain biking
The **Sheraton**, T03757-491800, hires
mountain bikes (US$6 for 2 hrs).

Tour operators
Argecam Turismo, T03757-423085,
www.argecamturismo.com. Can arrange
tours to the mines and San Ignacio from
Puerto Iguazú.
Ecomundo Turismo, Av República Argentina
and Guatambú, T03757-424142,
www.ecomundo.tur.ar. As well as offering
excursions to the ruins and the mine, this
local company also runs adventure travel.
Iguazú Forest, T03757-421140, www.iguazu
forest.com. Runs a ½- or full-day's adventure
in the jungle offering the chance to try
canopying, climbing waterfalls, repelling and
mountain biking. Great for kids and teenagers.

Wildlife safaris
Explorador Expediciones, T/F03757-421632,
www.rainforestevt.com.ar. Offers 2 good
tours in small groups:
Safari a la Cascada takes you by jeep to the
waterfall Arrechea, stopping along the way
to look at plants, bird and animal life,
identifying tracks, and involving a short
walk to the falls, 2 hrs US$20.
Safari in the Jungle is a more in-depth
interpretation of the natural life all around,
in open jeeps along the longer version of
the Yacatariá trail, 2 hrs, US$28. Daily at 1030
and 1600, though you can request special
departures. Expert guides will bring the
natural world alive and both trips will provide

fantastic insights into the jungle. Astonishing and highly recommended.

Puerto Iguazú *p367, map p368*
Tour operators
Aguas Grandes, Entre Ríos 66, T03757-425500, www.aguasgrandes.com. Runs conventional tours to both sides of the falls and Iguazú Forest. Adventure activities in the forest, including ½-day, US$28, good fun.
Cabalgatas por la Selva, R12, just after the Rotonda for the road to the international bridge, T03757-1554 2180 (mob). Highly recommended for 3-hr horse-riding trips in the forest, US$23.
Cabalgatas Ecológicas, T03757-1543 9763, www.cabalgatasecologicas.com. Good personalized horse-riding tours around Iguazu. 1 hr US$17, 2 hrs US$21.
Hostel Inn and Marco Polo Inn, for details see Sleeping, above. These hostels run friendly and efficient travel agencies where you can arrange trips to the falls and surrounding area.

⊖ Transport

Puerto Iguazú *p367, map p368*
Air
For airport information, see page 367.
Aerolíneas Argentinas flies direct to **Buenos Aires**, 1 hr 40 mins, flights fill up fast in Jan, Feb, Easter and in Jul.
Airline offices Aerolíneas Argentinas, Brasil and Aguirre 295, T03757-420168.

Bus
For bus terminal information, see page 367.
To **Buenos Aires**, 18 hrs, US$57-84 (for the nearly horizontal comfortable seats in Suite Bus), with Crucero del Norte; Tigre Iguazú and Via Bariloche, daily, US$57 *semi cama*. To **Posadas**, hourly, 5 hrs, US$12, **Corrientes**, 10 hrs, US$17 *servicio común*, and **Santa Fe**, 14 hrs, US$40 *servicio común*; all with **Empresa Horianski** T03757-454559.

To **San Ignacio**, US$11 *servicio común*.
Agencia de Pasajes Noelia, local 3, T03757-422722, can book tickets beyond Posadas for other destinations in Argentina, very helpful, ISIC discounts available. To Salta, US$61-80 (for executive class), 23 hrs, with **Flecha Bus**. To Santa Fe, US$57, 14 hrs, 5 departures daily, various companies.

Car hire
Alamo, Aguirre 271, T03757-423780, cars may be taken to the Brazilian side for an extra US$12; **Avis** at airport and M Moreno 85, T03757-424125.

Taxi
El Sol is a very reliable company, T03757-421 532 (ask for Ruben); or Taxi Transtam, T0299-155 813 409.
To the **airport** US$18; to **Argentine falls** US$12; to **Brazilian falls** US$23; to **centre of Foz** US$25; to **Ciudad del Este** US$28; to **Itaipu** US$50 return.

⊙ Directory

Puerto Iguazú *p367, map p368*
Banks Banks are generally open 0800-1300. Many ATMs in town, including at **Banco de la Nación** and **Macro Misiones** (which is just down from the bus station). There can be queues at the ATM so leave yourself time.
Currency exchange Cambios Links, Av Victoria Aguirre 226, T03757-423332; **Libres Cambios** in the Hito Tres Fronteras, T03757-421566, open 0800-2200. **Embassies and consulates** Brazil, Av Córdoba 264, T03757-421348. Paraguay, T03757-424230.
Internet There are several places at the town's hub, Aguirre and Brasil, opposite tourist office. **Medical services** Hospital SAMIC, T03757-420288. **Telephone** Plenty of *locutorios*, but Telecom, Victoria Aguirre and Los Cedros, is central, open all afternoon, and has internet too.

Parque Nacional Foz do Iguaçu (Brazil)

The Brazilian National Park was founded In 1939 and declared a World Heritage Site in 1986. The park covers 170,086 ha, extending along the north bank of the Rio Iguaçu, sweeping northwards to Santa Tereza do Oeste on the BR-277. The experience is less impressive than on the Argentine side since you are not immersed in the jungle but it's fascinating to see the whole panorama from a distance and because there are less crowds, it is more tranquil. You will see more wildlife. For more information on the park, see www.cataratasdo iguacu.com.br (in English). ▸▸ *For listings, see pages 377-379.*

Ins and outs

Getting there
It is 17 km from the city of Foz do Iguaçu to the park entrance. Buses leave Foz do Iguaçu, from the Terminal Urbana on Avenida Juscelino Kubitschek and República Argentina every 40 minutes starting at 0730-1800, and are clearly marked number 400, 'Parque Nacional'. You can get on or off at any point on the route past the airport and **Hotel das Cataratas**, 40 minutes US$1.50 one way, payable only in reais or pesos. The driver will either wait at the park entrance while passengers purchase entry tickets (see below) or you will change buses to a complimentary transfer. Tickets are checked by a park guard on the bus. A taxi costs US$11, US$45 return. ▸▸ *For further information, see Ins and outs, page 376.*

Getting around
From the entrance, shuttle buses leave every 10-15 minutes for the 8-km journey to the falls, stopping first at the start of the Macuco Safari. From there it's another 10-minute drive to the **Hotel Tropical das Cataratas**, and a short walk to the falls.

Park information
Entry is US$10, payable in reais only, and the park is open daily, apart from Monday mornings, 0800-1700 in winter, 0800-1800 in summer. At the entrance to the park there's a smart modern visitor centre, with toilets, an ATM, a small café and a large souvenir shop, but little information on the park or wildlife. There's also a **Banco do Brasil** *câmbio*, open from 0800 1900. If possible, visit on a weekday when the walks are less crowded.

Wildlife
Most frequently encountered are the little and red brocket deer, South American coati, white-eared opossum and brown capuchin monkey Much harder to see are the jaguar, ocelot, puma, white-lipped peccary, bush dog and southern river otter. The endangered tegu lizard can also been seen. Over 100 species of butterfly have been identified, among them the electric blue *morpho* and the poisonous red and black *heliconius*, and the birdlife is especially rewarding for the birdwatcher. Five members of the toucan family can be seen including toco and red-breasted toucans.

Trails
The 1200-m paved walk from **Hotel Tropical das Cataratas** to the falls is an easy walk, taking you high above the Río Iguazú, giving splendid views of all the falls on the Argentine side from a series of galleries. At the end of the path, you can walk down to a viewing point almost right under the powerful **Floriano Falls**, a dramatic view, since you're in the middle

Border essentials: Brazil–Paraguay

Ponte de Amizade/Puente de Amistad (Friendship Bridge)

The Ponte de Amizade/Puente de Amistad (Friendship Bridge) over the Río Paraná, 12 km north of Foz, leads straight into the heart of Ciudad del Este. Crossing is very informal but keep an eye on your luggage and make sure that you get necessary stamps – so great is the volume of traffic that it can be difficult to stop, especially with the traffic police moving you on. It is particularly busy on Wednesday and Saturday, with long queues of vehicles. Pedestrians from Brazil cross on the north side of the bridge allowing easier passage on the other side for those returning with bulky packages.

Immigration Paraguayan and Brazilian immigration formalities are dealt with at opposite ends of the bridge. There is a US$3 charge to enter Paraguay, but it is hardly ever charged. Remember to adjust your watch to local time.

Transport Buses (marked Cidade-Ponte) leave from the Terminal Urbana, Avenida Juscelino Kubitschek, for the Ponte de Amizade (Friendship Bridge), US$3. If you want to cross by private vehicle, this presents no problem if you're only visiting the national parks.

of the river. A catwalk at the foot of the Floriano Falls goes almost to the middle of the river to give a good view of the **Garganta del Diablo**. From here, there are 150 steps up to the **Porto Canoas complex**, a quick and easy walk, but for those who find stairs difficult, you can return the way you came, and walk a little further along the road. The Porto Canoas complex consists of a big souvenir shop, toilets, a café, a fastfood place (cheeseburger, US$3) and smart restaurant (full three-course lunch, US$15), open Tuesday-Sunday 1130-1600. All are recommended and are good value with a fantastic view of the river above the falls. Return to the visitor centre and entrance either by the free shuttle bus, or walk back along the forest path as far as **Hotel Tropical das Cataratas** (where you can also eat a slightly more expensive but good lunch with a view of the falls), and take the bus from there. The visit will take you around two hours, allow extra time for lunch.

Foz do Iguaçu (Brazil) → *For listings, see pages 377-379. Colour map 2, A3.*

A small modern city, Foz lies 28 km from the falls, with a wide range of accommodation and good communications by air and road with the main cities of southern Brazil and Asunción in Paraguay. It's not a particularly attractive town, and Argentina's Puerto Iguazú makes a better base, with cheaper hotels and better access to the falls. Street crime has increased in Foz in recent years, but the inhabitants are friendly and welcoming, and there are some good places to eat.

Ins and outs → *Phone code +55-(0)45. Population 232,000.*

Getting there Iguaçu international Airport ① *T+55-(0)45-3521 4200*, is 19.5 km south of town near the falls. In arrivals there is a Banco do Brasil and Caribe Tours e Câmbio, car rental offices, a tourist office and an official taxi stand. Taxis charge US$17 for a trip into town. All buses marked Parque Nacional, No 400, pass the airport in each direction, and cost US$1.50, daily 0525-0040, to anywhere around town, they allow backpacks but not lots of luggage. Many hotels run minibus services for a small charge.

The **bus terminal** ① *Av Costa e Silva, T+55-(0)45-3522 2590*, is 4 km from the centre on the road to Curitiba. To get to the centre, take any bus that says 'Rodoviária', US$1.50, or a taxi for US$8. There's a tourist office open 0630-1800, **Cetreme** desk for tourists who have lost their documents, *guarda municipal* (police), ATM and luggage store.

Tourist information The **main tourist office** ① *T+55(0)45-0800 451516 (freephone 0700-2300)*, is at Praça Getúlio Vargas 69, a small plaza at the corner of Avenida JK and Schimmelpfeng. The staff are extremely helpful and well organized, and speak English. There's also a tourist office at the **bus terminal** at the end of Avenida José María de Brito, and at the **airport** open for all arriving flights, with map and bus information. If you arrive without a place to stay there are plenty of agencies to help you find a hotel and transfer you there. A newspaper, *Triplice Fronteira*, carries street maps and other tourist information. Tourists are warned not to stray from the main roads in town, not to wear jewellery, and to leave their passport in the hotel. Take taxis or tours wherever possible. Avenida Kubitschek and the streets south of it, towards the river, have a reputation for being unsafe at night as there is a *favela* or shanty town, nearby. Having said that there are some nice places to stay here with restaurant options, so you shouldn't need be in town too often.

Sights

Apart from the Parque Nacional do Iguaçu there are a couple of other attractions. The world's largest hydroelectric dam at **Lago Itaipu** ① *15 km away, T+55-(0)45-5206 999, www.complexoitaipu.tur.br, buses run from Terminal Urbano, Av JK and República Argentina, to a village 200 m away from the visitor centre, US$1.50, marked 'Usina Itaipu'*, is quite a feat of human achievement, an interesting contrast to the natural wonder of the falls. There are eight free guided tours daily. Wear long trousers and sensible shoes. Check times with the tourist office and take your passport. There are also attractive artificial **beaches** on Lake Itaipu, **Bairro de Três Lagoas**, at Km 723 on BR-277, and in the municipality of **Santa Terezinha do Itaipu**, 34 km from Foz, good places for relaxing in the summer. The **Parque das Aves** ① *www.parquedasaves.com.br (in English), 0830-1730 (1800 in summer), US$12, next to the visitor centre at Rodovia das Cataratas Km 18, just before the falls*, contains some local and Brazilian species, but most of its beautiful caged birds are from Africa and Asia. It's a picturesque setting, particularly the butterfly house, with hummingbirds whirring about, but It's far more satisfying to spot birds in the wild, or at Guira Oga on the Argentine side of the falls.

◉ Parque Nacional Foz do Iguaçu (Brazil) listings

For Sleeping and Eating price codes and other relevant information, see Essentials pages 30-36.

◉ Sleeping

Parque Nacional Foz do Iguaçu *p375*
Good selection of hotels and many also offer excursions to the falls. The excellent tourist office has a full list. Note that Av Juscelino Kubitschek and the streets south of it, towards the river, are unsafe at night.

Taxis only good value for short distances when you have your luggage.

LL Hotel das Cataratas, directly overlooking the falls, 28 km from Foz, T+55-(0)45-521 7000, www.hoteldascataratas.com. Elegant, pale pink colonial-style building with a pool in luxuriant gardens, where you might spot wildlife at night and early morning. The rooms are disappointingly plain and sombre, but there's a small terrace with views of the falls at the front of the hotel. The restaurant is open to non-residents; lunch and dinner buffet, US$20; à la carte dishes and dinner with show.

Foz do Iguaçu *p376*
AL Rafain Centro, Mel Deodoro 984, T+55-(0)45-3521 3500, www.rafaincentro.com.br. Smart and comfortable hotel, attractive pool area, good restaurant. Wi-Fi.
A Aguas do Iguaçu, Av Brasil, 84, T+55-(0)45-3521 6000, www.aguasdoiguacuhotel.com.br. Large, clean rooms, attractive pool.
B Luz, Av Costa and Silva, Km 5, near Rodoviaria, T+55-(0)45-3523 1619, www.luz hotel. com.br. Standard rooms with a/c, TV, and small pool. Friendly and comfortable.
C Tarobá, Rua Tarobá, 1048 T+55-(0)45-3523 9722, www.hoteltaroba.com.br. Highly recommended as a good-value central place, with a/c, a small indoor pool and good breakfast. They offer singles (**D**) and triples (**A** for the room).
D Pousada Evelina Navarrete, Rua Irlan Kalichewski 171, Vila Yolanda, T+55-(0)45-3574 3817, www.pousadaevelina.com.br. Lots of tourist information and English, French, Italian, Polish and Spanish spoken. Helpful, good breakfast and location, near Chemin Supermarket, near Av Cataratas on the way to the falls. Recommended.

Hostels
E pp **Paudimar Campestre**, Rodovia das Cataratas Km 12.5, Al Cailbí, 201, T+55-(0)45-3529 6061, www.paudimar.com.br. Huge, fun HI-affiliated hostel. One of the cheapest and best budget options in Foz. Swimming pool, bar, football field and room for camping. The rooms are a little small, and it is a fair way out of town, but there are transfer services from the airport and the bus station. Doubles (**D**) are available.
E pp **Paudimar Falls**, Rua Antonio Raposo 820, T+55-(0)45-3574 5503, www.hihostels.com. Sister hotel of the Paudimar Campestre. Situated closer to town, with a small pool and basic rooms. Friendly staff, and transfers from airport and bus station. Doubles (**D**) available.

❷ Eating

Foz do Iguaçu *p376*
Many restaurants stay open till midnight and accept a variety of currencies. There are lots of restaurants along Av JK.
♥♥♥ Bufalo Branco, Rebouças 530. Sophisticated, with attentive service. Superb all-you-can-eat *churrasco*, including filet mignon, bull's testicles, and a good salad bar.
♥♥♥ Rafain, Av das Cataratas, Km 6.5. Touristy but entertaining affair, an extravaganza with live *folclore* music from all over South America, dancing and a buffet.
♥♥ Bier Garten, Av Jorge Schimmelpfeng 228. Pizzeria; beer garden in name only but there are some trees.

❶ Bars and clubs

Foz do Iguaçu *p376*
There are lots of bars concentrated along the 2 blocks of Av Jorge Schimmelpfeng from Av Brasil to R Mal Floriano Peixoto. Wed and Sun are the best nights.
Amazém, R Edmundo de Barros 446. Intimate and sophisticated, it attracts discerning locals. Good atmosphere, mellow live music, US$1 cover. Recommended.
Oba! Oba!, Av das Cataratas 370 (Antigo Castelinho). Live samba Mon-Sat 2315-0015, very popular, US$14 for show and a drink. Also known as **Coopershow**.
Pizza Park, opposite Bier Garten on Av Jorge Schimmelpfeng, open from 2000. Good pizzas in a lively atmosphere, popular with tourists and residents.

▲ Activities and tours

Parque Nacional Foz do Iguaçu *p375*
Tour operators
Macuco Safari, T+55-(0)45-3574 4244, www.macucosafari.com.br. Run the Macuco Safari Tour, 1 hr 40 mins, US$45, which leaves from the 1st stop on the free shuttle bus

service. Ride down a 3-km-long path through the forest in open electric jeeps, and then a motor boat takes you close to the falls themselves, similar to **Jungle Explorer** on the Argentine side, but it's more expensive, and the guides aren't as good. Portuguese, English and Spanish spoken.

Helisul, Rodovia das Cataratas, Km 16.5, T+55-(0)45-3529 7474, www.helisul.com. Offer helicopter tours over the falls, leave from near the entrance and Parque das Aves, US$30 per person, 8 mins. The altitude has had to be increased to avoid disturbing birdlife and visitors, making the flight less attractive.

Lots of companies organize conventional tours to the falls – convenient as they collect you from your hotel, ½-day, US$13, plus park entrance. **Conveniotur**, Rua Rui Barbosa 820, T+55-(0)45-3523 3500, www.conveniotur. com.br; and **Central Tours**, Hotel das Cataratas, BR469, Km 28, T+55-(0)45-3521 4258, www.centraltours.com.br.

Cânion Iguaçu, T+55-(0)45-4529 6040, www.campodedesafios.com.br. Local adventure company that can organize abseiling, rafting and rock climbing in the area.

Foz do Iguaçu *p376*
Tour operators
Caribe Tur, at the international airport, and Hotel das Cataratas, and Hotel Bourbon, T+55-(0)45-3523 1612, www.grupocaribe. com.br. Run tours from the airport to the Argentine side, and **Hotel das Cataratas**.
STTC Turismo, Hotel Bourbon, Rodovia das Cataratas, T+55-(0)45-3529 8580. Cruises on the Río Paraná, with dinner and show, T03757-421111 (Argentina), ventas@crucerosiguazu.com.

⊖ Transport

Foz do Iguaçu *p376*
Air
For airport information, see page 376.
Ther are daily flights to **Rio de Janeiro**, **São Paulo**, **Curitiba** and other Brazilian cities.

Airline offices Rio Sul, and Varig, J Sanways 779, T+55-(0)45-3529 6601; TAM, T+55-(0)45-3523 6246 (free transport to Ciudad del Este for its flights, all border documentation dealt with); **Varig**, Kubitschek 463, T+55-(0)45-3523 2111; **Vasp**, Brasil 845, T+55-(0)45-3523 2212.

Bus
For bus terminal information, see page 377. For transport to the falls, see page 375.

To Brazil To **Curitiba**, 9-11 hrs, paved road, US$50, **Pluma**, Sulamericana. To **Guaíra** via Cascavel only, 5 hrs, US$20. To **Florianópolis**, 16 hrs, US$64, **Catarinense** and Reunidas; to **Porto Alegre**, US$58-67, Reunidas. To **São Paulo**, 16 hrs, new buses Kaiowa, and Pluma US$50, *executivo* 6 a day, plus 1 *leito*. To **Rio de Janeiro**, 22 hrs, several daily, US$104.

To Paraguay To **Asunción**, direct at 1430, US$26, **Pluma**, RYSA.

Car hire
Localiza at the airport, T+55-(0)45-3523 4800; Av Juscelino Kubitschek 2878, T+55-(0)45- 3522 1608.

⊕ Directory

Foz do Iguaçu *p376*
Banks There are plenty of banks on Av Brasil. Banco 24 Horas, Oklahoma petrol station; Banco do Brasil, Brasil 1377, has ATM, charges high commission for TCs; Bradesco, Brasil 1202; HSBC, Av Brasil 1151, MasterCard ATM; Itaú, ATM at Kubitschek e Bocaiúva and the airport. Currency exchange Corimeira, Av Brasil 248; Vento Sul, Av Brasil 1162. **Embassies and consulates** Argentine, Travessa Eduardo Bianchi 26, T+55-(0)45-3574 2969, open Mon-Fri 1000-1500. **Internet** L@n Zone, Av Sílvio Américo Sasdelli 2431, fast but noisy; Net pub@, Av JK and Rua Rui Barbosa 549; Zipfoz.com, R Barão do Rio Branco 412 and Av JK, smart, a/c, US$2.50 per hr. **Post office** Praça Getúlio Vargas 72. **Telephone** Posto 1, Edmundo de Barros 281, Calçadão and Brasil.

Misiones province and the Jesuit missions

There are wonderfully evocative remains of several Jesuit missions in the south of picturesque Misiones province. Testimony to their great organization and extensive expansion in the early 17th century, they make a worthwhile stop on your way south from Iguazú Falls. And if you're interested in seeing more, there are the ruins of San Ignacio Miní, Santa Ana, and Loreto, all are within reach of the small pleasant town of San Ignacio, or on a long day trip from Iguazú (not recommended). Misiones' lush landscapes of red earth roads cutting through fecund green jungle and forest plantations are matched by a rich culture, generated by the mix of indigenous Guaraní and European immigrants, particularly from Eastern Europe, together with a constant flow of Paraguayans and Brazilians from over the borders. The fertile land produces pine forests for wood, huge plantations of tea, and most important of all, the yerba for mate, the Argentine drink without which the country would grind to a halt (see box, page 36). It's a fairly wet region: the annual rainfall exceeds 2000 mm, generating hundreds of rivers and waterfalls, the most magnificent of which are the overwhelming Iguazú Falls, at the province's northernmost tip. But there are more falls, the Saltos de Moconá, almost as spectacular and staggeringly wide, on the southeasternmost edge of the province and accessible for those adventurous enough to make the trip. With time to spare, you could head inland to Oberá, whose 35 churches represent immigrants from an amazing 15 countries, but beyond the laid-back way of life, there's little to hold you in the province for long. The climate might be uncomfortably hot for much walking in summer, but it's pleasantly warm in winter, while flowers and birdlife are most abundant in spring. For more information, see www.turismo.misiones.gov.ar (in Spanish), or www.misionesvive.com.ar (in Spanish and English). ▸▸ For listings, see pages 388-392.

Ins and outs

Getting there and around The Jesuit missions at San Ignacio are near the southwestern end of the province, and while you could visit these on a long day trip from Puerto Iguazú, you'll see more of the region's lush landscapes if you stop off at the small town of San Ignacio itself – also a stop if you're combining a trip to Iguazú with the Esteros del Iberá further south. From the region's capital, the unattractive business-hub of Posadas an hour south of San Ignacio, two parallel roads run northeast to the Iguazú Falls, but only Route 12, the northernmost one is tarmacked and negotiable in an ordinary vehicle. The Jesuit ruins at San Ignacio are 60 km north of Posadas and the road continues, via a series of small towns such as Eldorado, to Wanda, famous for its open mines of semi-precious stones, to Puerto Iguazú, the best base for visiting the falls. The other road, Route 14, runs parallel and south along the interior of the province, via Oberá to Bernardo de Irigoyen. It's paved but there are no buses. To visit the Saltos de Moconá, you'll need to take a rough road further south, Route 2, which is unpaved from Alba Posse onwards (about halfway), so you'll need a 4WD vehicle. ▸▸ For further information, see Transport, page 391.

Best time to visit Summers are incredibly hot here, with temperatures reaching 40°C from November to March, but winters are warm and sunny.

Posadas and around → For listings, see pages 388-392. Colour map 2, B2.

Posadas is the lively but unattractive capital of Misiones, set on a bend on the southern bank of the Río Paraná, with views over the river from its *costanera* (riverbanks). It was founded in 1814, and developed after the War of Triple Alliance as a useful strategic post.

It's a modern city, and there aren't any particularly remarkable sights. If you are looking for a place to stop on your way from the Esteros del Iberá to Iguazú head up to the small town of San Ignacio instead.

Ins and outs → *Phone code 03752. Population 280,500.*

General San Martín Airport ① *T03752-457413*, is on Route 12, 12 km west. A *remise* taxi to the airport takes about 25 minutes and costs US$9. The **bus terminal** ① *Av Santa Catalina and Av Luis Quaranta, T03752-456106*, is 3 km south of the centre on the road to Corrientes – take a taxi (US$4). At the terminal use the taxi company **Nivel Líneas Rotavías** whose rank is underneath the terminal's stairs. They are the safest company. Offers left luggage facilities, Monday to Friday 0730-2100, and Saturday 0730-2000 (US$0.50). You can also catch a bus into town, cross over the street from the terminal and look for buses 15, 21 or 8 to the centre, US$1.50.

Tourist information The **tourist office** ① *2 blocks south of the Plaza 9 de Julio at Colón 1987, T03752-447540, www.posadas.gov.ar (in Spanish), daily 0800-2000*, can provide a basic map but not much else. There is a small tourist office in the bus station but it isn't often open. For information on the whole province, visit www.turismo.misiones.gov.ar (in Spanish).

Sights

The centre of the city is the Plaza 9 de Julio, with its French-style cathedral and government building, and several hotels. Banks and ATMs can be found one block west on San Martín, or one block south on Félix de Azara. Two blocks southeast, there's a peaceful spot at Paseo Bosetti, a quiet plaza with mural paintings. There are a couple of rather old-fashioned museums near the Plaza, the **Museo de Ciencias Naturales e Historia 'Andrés Guaçurarí'** and the **Museo Regional de Posadas** with the obligatory collection of stuffed animals. There's also a cultural centre and arts exhibition hall at **Museo de Arte Juan Yaparí** ① *Sarmiento 319, daily 0800-1200, 1400-1800, free*, a block north of the plaza, and next door is **Mercado de Artesanías**, where Guaraní handicrafts are for sale, and the **Museo Arqueológico** ① *General Paz 1865, daily 0800-1200, 1600-2000, free*.

Posadas' main feature is the long Costanera, extending northeast of the centre alongside the broad river Paraná and a good place for a stroll. In the afternoon you'll see residents sitting on folding chairs sipping *mate* as the sun goes down. **Avenida Andrés Guaçurarí** (referred to also as Avenida Roque Pérez) is a pretty boulevard which becomes livelier by night with several popular bars. A few blocks northwest is the small **Parque Paraguayo** and the **Museo Regional Aníbal Cambas** ① *Alberdi 600, Mon-Fri 0700-1200, 1600-1900, free*. This is Posadas' most interesting museum with a permanent exhibition of Guaraní artefacts and pieces collected from the nearby Jesuit missions, including the façade of the temple at San Ignacio Mini.

Around Posadas

There is a marvellous traditional *estancia* nearby, **Estancia Santa Inés** ① *R105, Km 8.5, 20 km south of Posadas, T03752-436194, www.estancia-santaines.com.ar*, a traditional *estancia* of 2000 ha, growing *yerba mate*. Activities include walking, horse riding and, between February and October, helping with *mate* cultivation. Half-day activities, US$22; taxi from Posadas, US$20. However, if you're here in July, you might like to visit the **Fiesta Nacional de la Yerba Mate** (*mate* festival) in **Apóstoles**, a prosperous town 65 km south of Posadas, founded in 1897 by Ukrainian and Polish immigrants on the site of a Jesuit mission dating from 1633. The festival attracts *folclore* singers to this town set in the heart of *yerba mate* plantations in a picturesque hilly region – reached by regular buses.

The **Museo Histórico Juan Szychowski** ① *13 km further at La Cachuera, follow the 6-km dirt road, branching off R1, 7 km south of Apóstoles*, is worth a trip if you have a car. It displays tools and machinery invented by a young Polish immigrant, mills for processing rice, corn and *yerba mate*, and his hydraulic works, which can be seen in the grounds, still amaze engineers. He was the founder of a *yerba mate* processing plant, **La Cachuera** ① *T03758-422443, www.yerbamanda.com.ar*, still operating, now under the brand name of *Amanda*.

For Esteros del Iberá, see page 393; you could also cross the border to Encarnación in Paraguay to visit more Jesuit missions at Trinidad and Jesús.

San Ignacio and the Mini Jesuit Mission → *For listings, see pages 388-392.*
Colour map 2, B2.

The pleasant town of San Ignacio is the site of the most impressive Jesuit mission in Misiones province, 63 km northeast of Posadas. The site, together with the nearby Jesuit missions of Loreto and Santa Ana, was declared a World Heritage Site by UNESCO in 1984. It's a very sleepy place, but is a lovely place to recharge for a few days if you have just been in busy Puerto Iguazú. There is only a few paved streets, the rest have red dirt. It's rural and welcoming.

Ins and outs → *Phone code 03752. Population 6300.*
Getting there Buses from Posadas and further south stop in San Ignacio on their way to the falls. Most come into town but a few stop on the highway, leaving a 15-minute walk into town. They are currently building a new bus terminal on the highway, which will mean that there are more options into town, but luckily at the moment the centre of town is being used. San Ignacio Mini Jesuit Mission is located six blocks from Avenida Sarmiento on the northwest side of town, entrance at Calle Alberdi, exit to Calle Rivadavia. Walk straight ahead of you down Sarmiento, and you'll see signposts 'To the Ruins'. Keep walking and you'll find the ruins on your right. Note that the entrance is 200 m further on than the exit, round the corner of the block to your right. There are plenty of restaurants and cafés along this road near the ruins.

Tourist information There is an extremely helpful **tourist office** ① *Sarmiento and Rivadavia, T03752-470707, 0900-2200*, who also run day tours in the area, including trips to the Jesuit ruins of Santa Ana and Loreto. See Activities and tours page 390. There is free Wi-Fi in the office, they rent bikes (the best way to get around) and you can leave your bags there for a few hours free of charge.

At the ruins there is a **tourist information office** ① *daily except Christmas Day 0700-1900, T03752-470186*. Entrance fees are US$8. A free leaflet gives basic information in English and Spanish. You can reliably leave your luggage in a room behind the ticket office. Tips are appreciated. Basic toilet facilities, though there are plenty of cafés across the road. Keep hold of your ticket, as it gives you entrance to the other Jesuit ruins at Santa Ana, Santa María La Mayor and Loreto, within a 15-day period. Every night there is an impressive sound and light show at 1930; you need to pay the US$8 entrance again for this, but it's worth it. The effects are eerie and they give you an idea of what the working mission would have looked like.

The Jesuit mission

Jesuits were the religious force that accompanied the Spanish conquest of much of northern Argentina, and though their impact on indigenous culture was far more positive, their rule remains controversial. Were they pioneers of a primitive socialism or merely exploiting the local Guaraní in the name of religious enlightenment?

Between 1609, when they built their first *redacción* or mission, in present-day Brazil, and 1767 when they were expelled by the Spanish King, the Jesuits founded about 50 missions around the upper reaches of the rivers Paraná, Paraguay and Uruguay. In 1627, they were forced to flee southwards, when their northern missions were attacked by slave-hunting *bandeirantes*. The priests led some 1000 converts down the Parapanema river into the Paraná on 700 rafts, only to find their route blocked by the Guaíra Falls. They pushed on for eight long days through dense virgin forest, built new boats below the falls and continued their journey. Some 725 km from their old homes, they re-established their missions, and trained militias to protect them from further attacks.

The missions prospered on agricultural produce, which raised profits to fund religious teaching. The Guaraní grew traditional crops such as manioc (the local root vegetable), sweet potatoes and maize, plants imported from Europe, such as wheat and oranges, and they also kept horses and herds of cattle and sheep. The missions became major producers of *yerba mate* (see page 36), favoured by the Jesuits as an alternative to alcohol. Apart from common lands the Guaraní also farmed their own individual plots.

Due to their growing wealth, they became a powerful force in the Americas and in time they were considered a threat to Spanish rule in the area.

The decision by Carlos III to expel the Jesuits from South America in 1767 was made under the conditions of highest secrecy: sealed orders were sent out to the colonies with strict instructions that they should not be opened in advance. On the appointed date, over 2000 members of the order were removed by force and put on ships for Italy. Jesuit property was auctioned, schools and colleges were taken over by the Franciscans and Dominicans, and many missions fell into disuse, or were destroyed.

The Jesuits had attracted many enemies since their wealth and economic power angered landowners and traders, and their control over the Guaraní irritated farmers short of labour. Rumours circulated that the missions contained mines and hoards of precious metals, which gold diggers still look for today. In fact, when building the new bridge just outside of San Ignacio government workers found 60 kg of Jesuit gold! The Jesuits may have exploited their manpower of the Guaraní, but they certainly defended the Guaraní from enslavement by the Spanish and Portuguese, and many feel their societies were a vanished arcadia.

Only four of the missions retain their former splendour: San Ignacio Miní in Argentina, Jesús and Trinidad in Paraguay, and São Miguel in Brazil. The first three can be visited with ease from San Ignacio, along with several others, including Santa Ana and Loreto, which are a short bus ride away.

Background

San Ignacio Mini ('small' in comparison with San Ignacio Guazu – 'large' – on the Paraguayan side of the Río Paraná) was originally founded in 1610 near the river Paranapanema in the present Brazilian state of Paraná, but frequent attacks from the *bandeirantes* (hunting for slaves as workers) forced the Jesuits to lead a massive exodus south together with the neighbouring Loreto mission. Taking their massive Guaraní population down the river by a series of rafts, they established San Ignacio on the river Yabebiry, not far from its present site, which was settled by 1696.

At the height of its prosperity in 1731, the mission housed 4356 people. Only two priests ran the mission; a feat of astounding organization. Latin, Spanish and Guaraní were taught in the school, and nearly 40,000 head of cattle grazed in the surrounding land, where *yerba mate* and cotton, maize and tobacco were also cultivated. The mission itself once covered around 14 ha: today you can see remains on only 6 ha – still an impressive sight with the immense central plaza lined with buildings in dramatic red sandstone. For almost a hundred years, the Jesuit *reducciones* operated successfully, growing in size from a population of 28,000 in 1647 to 141,000 in 1732. But after the expulsion of the Jesuits in 1767 by the Spanish king, the mission rapidly declined. By 1784 there were only 176 Guaraní, and by 1810 none remained. In 1817, by order of the Paraguayan dictator, Rodriguez de Francia, San Ignacio was set on fire. The ruins, like those of nearby Santa Ana and Loreto, were lost in the jungle until the late 19th century when attempts at colonization forced the founding of new towns, and San Ignacio was founded near the site of the former mission. It wasn't until the 1980s that there was some attempt to give official protection to the ruins, which were declared a national monument at last in 1943.

The mission

Like other Jesuit missions, San Ignacio Mini was constructed around a central plaza: to the north, east and west were about 30 parallel one-storey buildings, each with a wide veranda in front and each divided into four to 10 small, one-room dwellings for slaves. Guaraní communities lived in the surrounding areas. The roofs of these buildings have gone, but the massive 1-m-thick walls are still standing except where they have been destroyed by the *ibapoi* trees. The public buildings, some still 10 m high, are on the south side of the plaza. In the centre are the ruins of the church, 74 m by 24 m, finished in about 1724. To the right is the cemetery, which was divided for men and women, priests and children, to the left are the cloisters, the priests' quarters, guest rooms, and the workshops for wood and metal work, gold and silver. Sculpture was of particular significance in San Ignacio, and some of the most pleasing details are to be found in the red sandstone masonry. While the architecture is the traditional colonial baroque style found in all Jesuit public buildings, the influence of the Guaraní culture can be seen in the many natural details in bas-relief on walls and lintels: elegantly entwined grapes, fruit and flowers, together with naïve human forms and angels, so that even the buildings reveal a harmony between the Jesuit priests and their Guaraní workers. The chapel was designed by two Italian *sacerdotes*, and it took 36 years to build. Along the same stretch of terrace, you will see the remains of the music conservatory, library and kitchen. Many of the porticos and windows are elaborately carved, testimony to the highly trained workforce and high standards of aesthetics. The whole area is excellently maintained and is a most impressive sight.

Just 40 m inside the entrance to the ruins is the **Centro de Interpretación Jesuítico-Guaraní**, with a fine model of the mission in its heyday, and an exhibition which

Border essentials: Argentina–Paraguay

Puente San Roque

A bridge, the Puente San Roque, links Posadas with Encarnación. Pedestrians and cyclists are not allowed to cross the bridge; cyclists must ask officials for assistance. Argentine pesos are accepted in Encarnación, so there is no need to change them. Paraguay is one hour behind Argentina, except during Paraguayan summer time.

Immigration and customs The border is open 24 hours. Formalities are conducted at respective ends of the bridge. The Argentine side has different offices for locals and foreigners, T03758-435329; Paraguay has one for both. Formalities for boat crossing are carried out at both ports.

Argentine consulate At Mallorquín 788, T03758-3446.

includes representations of the lives of the Guaraní before the arrival of the Spanish, displays on the work of the Jesuits and the consequences of their expulsion.

Other sights

Follow Avenida Sarmiento to its very end and turn right for a picturesque view of a row of wooden houses on a reddish road amidst lush vegetation. Next to the Jesuit missions site entrance is **Galería Bellas Artes** ① *La Casa de Inés y Juan, San Martín 1291*, where painter Juan Catalano exhibits and sells his works which feature geometrical motifs, or typical local scenes, mounted on wooden boards. Another interesting collection is at the **Museo Provincial Miguel Nadasdy** ① *Sarmiento 557, T03752-470130, only Sat 0700-1900, Sun 0900-1200, 1500-1800*, which contains a collection of artefacts from the Guaraní and Jesuits of the missions, some beautiful examples of stone carving, and a bas-relief of San Ignacio de Loyola, founder of the Jesuit order.

On the opposite side of the town, there's a really delightful stroll to the house of celebrated Uruguayan writer Quiroga, a 20-minute walk (with little shade) along San Martín, in the opposite direction to the ruins. Walk to the end of the street, past the *Gendarmería* and two attractive wooden and stone houses. After 200 m the road turns left and 300 m later, a signposted narrow road branches off leading to the **Casa de Horacio Quiroga** ① *T03752-470124, daily 0800-1900, US$0.50 including a 40-min guided tour; ask for an English guide*. Quiroga (1878-1937) lived here for part of his tragic life as a farmer and carpenter between 1910-1916, and again in the 1930s. Many of his fantastical short stories were inspired by this subtropical region and its inhabitants. The scenery is beautiful, with river views, a garden with palms and an amazing bamboo forest planted by him. There's a replica of his first house, made for a movie set in the 1990s, while his second house is still standing, and contains an exhibition of a few of his belongings. Return to the main road, follow it down the slope amongst thick vegetation for a gorgeous riverside (25-minute) walk.

Other missions: Loreto and Santa Ana

If you have time, it's interesting to complement your visit to San Ignacio with a trip to see the ruins of two other Jesuit missions nearby. The mission of **Loreto** ① *daily 0700-1830, US$4, or free with your ticket from San Ignacio within 15 days*, has far fewer visitors than San

Ignacio, and under thick shady trees, the silence of the still air and the refreshing darkness add an attractive touch of mystery. The mission was moved to its present site in 1631, after the exodus from the former Jesuit province of Guayrá, and more than 6000 people were living here by 1733. It's thought that this was the site of the first printing press in the Americas, and of an extensive library, as well as being impressively productive: cattle and *yerba mate* were grown here, and ceramics were made. Little remains of this once-large establishment other than a few walls, though excavations are in progress. Note the number of old trees growing entwined with stone buttresses. Access is via a 3-km dirt road (signposted) off Route 12, 10 km south of San Ignacio; no public transport enters Loreto, but take a tour from San Ignacio with Misiones Excursions or catch one of the minibuses which leave every 15 minutes from outside the church on the square. Ask the driver to drop you outside the mission. You can ask for help at the tourist office if your Spanish isn't up to it.

Some 16 km south of San Ignacio at **Santa Ana** ① *daily 0730-1930 (1830 in winter), US$3, or free with your ticket to San Ignacio within 15 days, regular buses stop on R12*, are the ruins of another Jesuit mission, not as extensive as San Ignacio, but revealing interesting architectural adaptation to the terrain, and founded much earlier, in 1633. Moved to its present site in 1663, Santa Ana housed the Jesuit iron foundry. In 1744 the mission was inhabited by 4331 people and covered an area of 37 ha, of which only 10 remain. The impressively high walls are still standing and there are beautiful steps leading from the church to the wide-open plaza. The ruins are 700 m along a path from Route 12 (signposted).

You could also explore the ruins of **Santa María la Mayor**, 76 km southwest, on paved Route 2 linking San Javier and Concepción de la Sierra, 9 km west of Itacaruare. They date from 1637 and were never restored. Remains of the church and a jail are still standing, and a printing press operated there in the early 18th century.

Oberá → *For listings, see pages 388-392. Colour map 2, B3. Phone code 03755. Population 51,400.*

Oberá is the second largest town in Misiones, located amongst tea and *yerba mate* plantations, with factories open for visits. It's one of the province's biggest centres of 20th-century European immigration, and there are around 15 different nationalities here, including Japanese, Brazilian, Paraguayan and Middle Eastern communities, represented every September in the annual Fiesta Nacional del Inmigrante, held in the Parque de las Naciones. The town has over 35 churches and temples, but there's little reason to make a special trip. Oberá's **tourist office** ① *Plazoleta Güemes, Av Libertad 90, T03755-21808, Mon-Fri 0700-1900, Sat-Sun 0800-1200, 1500-1900, www.obera.gov.ar*, has information on local *estancias* open to visitors. There is a **zoo** ① *Italia y Venezuela*, with the **Jardín de los Pájaros** ① *T03755-427023, daily 0700-1900 (1800 in winter), US$1*, which houses native birds.

Monte Aventura ① *T03755-422430, Tue-Sun 1000-1800, US$1, access from Av José Ingenieros*, is a park with forest trails and entertainment for kids. If you're more interested in tea, you could head for **Campo Viera**, 21 km north of Oberá on Route 14. The 'national capital of tea', it has about 8000 ha of tea fields and 25 processing plants. The **Fiesta Nacional del Té** is held here every September with the Queen of Tea coronation (for more information, go to the **Casita del Té**).

There's a dazzling array of **orchids** some 28 km southwest of Oberá on Route 14 at Leandro N Alem (regular public transport from Oberá), where **Blumen Haus** ① *T03755-497090*, is a nursery and an arboretum of 36 ha with native trees.

San Ignacio to Puerto Iguazú

From San Ignacio Route 12 continues northeast, running parallel to Río Alto Paraná, towards Puerto Iguazú, through appealing landscapes of bright red soil and green vegetation: plantations of *yerba mate*, manioc and citrus fruits can be seen as well as timber yards, and *yerba mate* factories. The road passes through several small, modern, uninteresting towns including Jardín America, Puerto Rico, Montecarlo and Eldorado. If you're driving and feel like an extra stop you could consider the **Salto Capioví**. Just 100 m from Route 12 in Capioví, 60 km from San Ignacio, this 7-m waterfall is immersed in a patch of jungle, with a campsite. Nearby, there's the **Parque Natural Las Camelias**.

At 100 km south of Puerto Iguazú is **Eldorado** ① *www.eldorado.gov.ar*, a quaint, friendly and typical little Misiones town with an interesting archaeological collection at the **Museo Municipal** ① *T03751-430788, Thu-Sun 1500-1800, free*. The bus stops here between Puerto Iguazú and San Ignacio, and it's the closest town for **Estancia Las Mercedes** ① *www.estancialasmercedes.com*. The best way to explore this lovely landscape is on horseback from Las Mercedes. For information visit the **tourist office** ① *Av San Martín 2060, 2nd floor, T03751-421152*.

If you're interested in seeing how amethyst and quartz are mined, you might like to stop off at **Wanda**, 50 km north, a famous opencast mine, which also sells precious gems. There are daily guided tours to two mines, Tierra Colorada and Compañía Minera Wanda, from 0700-1900. Consult tour operators in Eldorado or Puerto Iguazú.

Saltos del Moconá → *For listings, see pages 388-392.*

While the main tourist route through Misiones runs along Route 12, if you have time, a 4WD and a spirit of adventure, you might well want to get off the beaten track and explore Misiones' hilly interior. Beautiful waterfalls are hidden away in the dense subtropical forests, and, at the furthest end of the track, you'll find the remote Saltos de Moconá. Tourist services are less well developed here, but you can stay next to the falls or in San Pedro or El Soberbio.

For a staggering 3 km, on the Argentine side of the Río Uruguay, water falls over a vast shelf of rock from 18 m up to 120 m, creating one of the most magnificent sights in the region. The rocky edge is quite easily reached on foot from the bank of the river, in an area surrounded by dense woodland, and protected by the Parque Estadual do Turvo (Brazil) and the Parque Provincial Moconá, the Reserva Provincial Esmeralda and the Reserva de la Biósfera Yabotí (Argentina). The **Parque Provincial Moconá** covers 1000 ha with vehicle roads and footpaths, and accommodation nearby where all activities are arranged, including excursions to the falls. In all three natural reserves the hilly forested landscape offers tremendous trekking, kayaking, birdwatching and exploring in 4WD vehicles. Alternative bases for exploring the remains are the small towns of **El Soberbio** (70 km southwest) or **San Pedro** (92 km northwest). Roads from both towns to Moconá are impassable for ordinary vehicles after heavy rains. There are regular bus services from Posadas to El Soberbio and San Pedro and from Puerto Iguazú to San Pedro, but no public transport reaches the falls.

For Sleeping and Eating price codes and other relevant information, see Essentials pages 30-36.

🛏 Sleeping

Posadas *p380*

The standard of accommodation in Posadas is pretty low compared to other provincial capitals. It attracts mainly business travellers and so there are few good budget options and the prices are high. If you just need somewhere to stay near the missions, try the pleasant hotels in San Ignacio instead. They are cheaper and the little town is a nice alternative to the busy capital city.

A Julio César, Entre Ríos 1951, T03752-427 930, www.juliocesarhotel.com.ar. Large 4-star with pool, gym and spacious rooms. Breakfast included. Rooftop pool

B Continental, Bolívar 1879 (on plaza 9 de Julio), T03752-433707, www.hoteleramisiones.com.ar. Comfortable standard rooms but more spacious VIP rooms (**A**) available, some with river views. Restaurant on 1st floor.

B Hotel Canciller, Junín 1710 and San Martín, T03752-440 599, www.hotelcanciller.com.ar. A dated 4-star hotel, with a gloomy reception but the rooms are slightly better. Good central location.

B Posadas, Bolívar 1949, T03752-440888, www.hotelposadas.com.ar. Busy business-oriented hotel with good standard rooms and bigger, more special rooms. Restaurant, gym and free internet access. Good location.

C City, Colón 1764, T03752-433901, citysa@arnet.com.ar. Right out of the 1970s, but good a/c rooms, some overlooking the plaza. Breakfast included, restaurant on 1st floor.

C Le Petit, Santiago del Estero 1630, T03752-436031, lepetithotel@ciudad.com.ar. Very good value small hotel a short walk from the centre on a quiet and shady street. Spotless rooms have a/c, and breakfast is included.

C Residencial Colón, Colón 2169, T03752-42085, www.residencialcolon.blogspot.com. Small but affordable rooms with a/c and TV,

and parking. Also apartments for up to 6 people. Lots of floral bedspreads.

E pp Residencial Misiones, Félix de Azara 1960, T03752-430133. Welcoming owners offer very basic rooms with fan and bath in a centrally located old house with a patio (sounds nicer than it is). No breakfast is served, but cooking and laundry facilities are available. Popular with Europeans.

Hostels

E pp Hostel Vuelo el Pez, 25 de mayo 1216, www.vuelaelpez.com.ar. Posadas' first hostel. Small hostel with basic but comfortable facilities, brightly coloured walls and lots of friendly advice. Doubles (**D**) also available.

San Ignacio *p382*

Easier and cheaper than staying in Posadas.

C pp Club de Río, 3 km from San Ignacio (ring for directions), T03755-1557 0843, www.clubderio.com.ar. Outside of town. Attractive *cabañas* in 32 ha of rural setting in this tourist complex which has a huge pool and a beach onto the lake.

C El Descanso, Pellegrini 270, T03755-470 207. Small detached house, a short walk (5 blocks) from the main square. Comfortable rooms with camping.

C La Toscana, H Irigoyen and Uruguay, T03752-470777, www.hotellatoscana.com.ar. By far the best place to stay in town is this family-run 12-bedroom hotel with their rustic welcoming rooms and a wonderful pool. There is cable TV, a terrace overlooking the pool and friendly Italian owners. It's an easy 10-min walk from the tourist office and main square. Highly recommended.

C Portal del Sol, Rivadavia 1295, T03752-470096, www.lacarpaazul.com, across from the mission ruins. A/c, a large pool and a restaurant. Not very friendly staff, slightly run down.

C San Ignacio, San Martín 823, T03755-470422, hotelsanignacio@arnet.com.ar. Good if not dated rooms with a/c and self-catering apartments for 4-5 people. Breakfast US$2.50. Phone booths and an interesting view of town from the reception.

Hostels

F pp **Adventure Hostel**, Independencia 469, T03752-470955, www.sihostel.com.ar. Large hostel with a fantastic pool, rooms for camping and a games area. The common areas are spacious and double rooms are comfortable (**D**). Camping available (US$5). Short walk to centre of town.

F pp **Hostel El Jesuita**, San Martín 1291, T03727-470542, www.hosteleljesuita.com. Lovely welcoming owners, Darío and Graciela, run this small and friendly hostel. Fully equipped kitchen, spacious double rooms (**D**) with their own exit to the lush garden, and a small but comfortable dorm. Only 1½ blocks from the ruins. Call when you arrive and they will come and get you. Lots of travel advice. 3 camping spots available (US$3.80 with breakfast). Recommended.

Camping

Sites on the river are splendidly situated and very well kept. On a small sandy bay among rocky promontories, they are reached by a 45-min walk from town at the end of the road leading to Quiroga's house: **Club de Pesca y Deportes Náuticos**, on hilly ground with lush vegetation at Puerto Nuevo, 3 km from San Ignacio, www.pesca sanignacio.netfirms.com. US$2 per person per day, plus US$1.50 per tent. **Playa del Sol**, T03752-470207. On the beach side. US$2 per person per day, plus US$1.50 per tent.

Oberá p386

Ask the tourist office for details of farms run by host families of different nationalities. **A Cabañas del Parque**, Ucrania y Tronador, T03755-426000, www.hotelcabanas.com.ar. Situated next to the Parque de las Naciones, this is a tourist complex of several houses or rooms for 2 to 8 people. Kitchen, a/c

and breakfast included. Also has a large swimming pool and a restaurant.
B-C Premier, 9 de Julio 1114, T03755-406 171, hpremier@hotmail.com. A good central option, with a/c but no breakfast.
D Cuatro Pinos, Sarmiento 853, T03755-1558 3278. A well-located hotel.

San Ignacio to Puerto Iguazú p387
Eldorado

AL-A Estancia Las Mercedes, just south of Eldorado, 120 km from Iguazú, T03751-431 511, www.estancialasmercedes.com.ar. A great place for a couple of nights. Traditional Argentine *estancia* founded by British pioneers, it has a quaint historical old house, gorgeous grounds with pool, horse riding through virgin rainforest, and rafting on the river. Owner Edie Lowe makes you extremely welcome. Price is for full board, all activities included (half-board an option). Recommended. **Delmonte** travel agency in Eldorado (see page 391) can arrange transfer from the falls.

Saltos del Moconá p387

AL pp **El Refugio Moconá**, 3 km from access to the reserve, 8 km from the falls (or contact at Bolívar 1495, in Posadas), T03752-421829, www.refugiomocona.com. Price for 3-day package. Rustic rooms for 4-5 with shared bath, campsite for US$6 a day per tent, tents for rent at US$9 a day, meals for US$5. Many activities, such as 30-min boat trips to the falls (US$80 per group of up to 5), 1-hr walk to the falls (US$30 per group), and several other excursions on foot and by 4WD. There is also a kayak journey down the river Yabotí (US$33 per person). Transfer with sightseeing to and from San Pedro, 2 hrs, US$90 for up to 8.
B-C Hostería Puesta del Sol, C Suipacha s/n, El Soberbio, T03755-495161 (T011-4300 1377 in Buenos Aires). A splendid vantage point overlooking town, with a swimming pool and a restaurant. The rooms are comfortable with breakfast and a/c. For full board add US$7 per person.

🍴 Eating

Posadas *p380*

Most places offer the *espeto corrido* system, as much *parrilla* as you can eat for a fixed price: pork, beef, sausages, entrails or chicken, grilled and brought to the table speared on a long brochette or *al galeto*. Instead of the usual potato or bread with meat, in Misiones it's common to eat *mandioca*, a potato-like root. The typical dessert is *mamón en almíbar* (papaya in syrup). If you haven't already tried *chipá*, small bread rolls made with manioc flour, there are lots to try in Posadas. Delicious.

₮₮ De La Costa, Av Costanera. Hugely popular with locals, this place on the riverbank has 2 floors, with great views from the upper floor and a cheerful buzz on Sat.

₮₮ El Mensú, Fleming and Coronel Reguera (in the Bajada Vieja district). A very attractive house in the picturesque old port area with a varied menu of fish and pasta, with a large selection of wines. Closed Mon.

₮₮ La Querencia, Bolívar 1849 (on plaza 9 de Julio). A large traditional restaurant offering *parrilla* served *al galeto*, *surubí* and pastas.

₮₮ Plaza Café, Bolívar 1979 just outside the shopping centre. Great salads and large mains, including 'wok' vegetables. Busy during the day and busier at night. Highly recommended.

₮ Bar Español, Bolívar 2085. Open since 1958, this restaurant has tasty Spanish-influenced food. Have an ice cream for dessert next door at Duomo.

₮ La Nouvelle Vitrage, Colón and Bolívar. Good pizzas, sandwiches and coffee. Friendly staff, a good view of the plaza and free Wi-Fi.

San Ignacio *p382*

There are several restaurants catering for tourists on the streets by the Jesuit ruins.

₮₮ La Carpa Azul, Rivadavia 1295. Large restaurant near the ruins serving quality meals but you will be surrounded by tour buses.

₮ Hotel San Ignacio, San Martín 823, see Sleeping, above. Closed Mon. Restaurant at the hotel offers simple meals.

₮ La Misionera, Rivadavia 1105. Offers a tourist meal. Nicely decorated.

₮ Pizzería La Aldea, Rivadavia and Lanusse, opposite the entrance to the ruins. Friendly place serving good cheap pizzas, *empanadas* and other simple meals. Will make sandwiches to take away. Recommended.

Oberá *p386*

₮₮₮ Del Monte, Costa Rica 334. Great modern fare.

₮₮₮ Engüete, Cabeza de Vaca 340. Good food and a varied menu is available.

🎉 Festivals and events

Oberá *p386*

Sep Fiesta Nacional del Inmigrante Vibrant festival that lasts a week around Sep 4 (Immigrants' Day). In the Parque de las Naciones, houses built in various national styles are the attractive setting for folk dances, parades, tasting national dishes and the election of a queen. Very popular.

🔺 Activities and tours

Posadas *p380*

Abra, Colón 1975, T03752-422221, www. abratours.com.ar. Runs tours to San Ignacio, including Santa Ana Jesuit ruins; to Jesuit ruins in Paraguay, and in Brazil; to Jesuit ruins in Misiones and waterfalls; to Saltos del Moconá, a 2-day trip.

Guayrá, San Lorenzo 2208, T03752-433415, www.guayra.com.ar. Tours to Iberá, US$65 per person (if 4 people); to Saltos del Moconá, US$85 per person (if 4 people); both sites in a 5-day excursion for US$240 per person (if 4 people). Also car rental and transfer to Colonia Carlos Pellegrini (for Esteros del Iberá).

San Ignacio *p382*

Misiones Excursions, Rivadavia and Sarmiento, T03752-470707, www.misionesexcursions.

blogspot.com. Excellent, small company with its office in the Tourist Information Centre. They run personalized tours around San Ignacio, including visits to the other ruins of Santa Ana and Loreto, local Guaraní villages, and a *yerba estancia*. All cost US$21 per person. They also organize kayaking trips, cycling excursions and can organize a full day trip into Paraguay to see the famous mission ruins of Trinidad (US$65). If you contact then in advance they can organize 2-night excursions to the Esteros de Iberá, including luxury accommodation, breakfast, a boat trip on the wetlands and personal 4WD transfers, for US$83pp. Recommended.

Oberá p386
Transit 21, Ucrania and Tronador, 1st floor, T03755-402121, www.transit21.com.ar. Ask here for a transfer to the Saltos de Moconá.

San Ignacio to Puerto Iguazú p387
Eldorado
Delmonte, Av San Martín 1734, Km 9, T03751-422113, cebrera@ceel.com.ar. Transfers from Iguazú to San Ignacio, and to *estancias* like Las Mercedes.

Saltos del Moconá p387
Hostería Puesta del Sol, see Sleeping, above. Boat excursions arranged to the falls, 7-8 hrs, landing and meal included, US$2520 per person (minimum 4 people). The journey to the falls is by a boat crossing to Brazil, then by vehicle to Parque do Turvo, 7 hrs, meal included, US$30 per person. Otherwise, a 4WD journey on the Argentine side with more chances for trekking takes 7 hrs, with a meal included, US$35 per person.

⊖ Transport

Posadas p380
Air
For airport information, see page 381. The airport can be reached by Bus No 8 or 28 with stops along C Junín in centre, 40 mins,

US$0.50, or take a *remise* taxi. Flights to **Buenos Aires**, twice daily with Aerolíneas Argentinas, 1 hr 25 mins (direct), some flights call at **Corrientes** or **Formosa**, 1 hr 50 mins.
   Airline offices Aerolíneas Argentinas, Ayacucho 1728, T03752-433340.

Boat
At Río Paraná, port access from Av Costanera and Av Andrés Guaçurarí, T03752-425044 (**Prefectura**). Boat crossing to Encarnación (Paraguay), 6-8 mins, almost every hour Mon-Fri 0800-1800, US$2. Ticket office at main building.

Bus
For bus terminal information, see page 381. The terminal is quite a way from the centre of town. It can be reached by Bus No 4, 8, 15, 21, with stops along C Junín in centre, 20 mins, US$0.50. Platforms at both levels, so check. It is easier to take a taxi, but only use the company downstairs underneath the platforms called Nivel Líneas Rotavias, T03752-428500, as they are the most reliable. There is a tourist office in the terminal but as it's hardly ever open it's best to visit the one in the centre.
   Buses to **Buenos Aires**, 12-13 hrs, US$44, Crucero del Norte, T03752-482223; Expreso Singer, T03572-455800; Expreso Tigre Iguazú, T03752-455200; Río Uruguay, T03752-455833; **Vía Bariloche**, T03572-45300. Choose *coche cama* for real comfort.
   To **Mendoza**, 30 hrs, US$51, Autotransportes Mendoza, T03752-454833. To **Tucumán**, 16-18 hrs, US$55, Autotransportes Mendoza; La Nueva Estrella, T03752-455455. To **Salta**, 18 hrs, US$52 (*coche cama*), La Nueva Estrella (change at Resistencia). To **Puerto Iguazú**, hourly, 5-6 hrs, US$12, Aguila Dorada Bis; Expreso Singer; Horiansky; Kruse. Several companies run frequent services to almost all main provincial destinations, including San Ignacio, 1 hr, US$2; Oberá, 1½ hrs, US$2.50; El Soberbio, 3½-4½ hrs, US$6.
   If going to **Esteros del Iberá**, there are more frequent services from **Mercedes**,

which is the nearest town. You may have to take a transfer from Posadas – your *estancia* in Iberá can arrange this. The only way to get from Posadas to Colonia Carlos Pellegrini is via a private 4WD for around US$154 one way. Speak to the tour agencies. Apart from travelling to Mercedes, the best way may be to organize a package from Posadas or San Ignacio, see Activities and tours, above. Or contact Iberá Expediciones, www.ibera expediciones.com, who can organize it for you.

To Paraguay To **Encarnación**, Servicio Internacional, 50 mins, US$2, leaving at least every 30 mins from platforms 11 and 12 (lower level), tickets on bus.

Car rental
Alamo, Junín 1696, T03752-4322454; Avis, at airport T03752-596660, or San Martín, T03752-1556 1430.

Remise taxi
JC, Entre Ríos 1945, T03752-431185; Nivel, Córdoba 194, T03752-428500.

San Ignacio *p382*
Bus
Stop in front of church, leaving every hour to **Posadas**, US$2, or to **Puerto Iguazú**, US$11, and all towns along R12. Don't rely on the terminal at end of Av Sarmiento, as only a few buses actually stop here. More buses stop on R12 at the access road (Av Sarmiento).

Remise taxis
Stop at Av Sarmiento and San Martín.

Oberá *p386*
Bus
To **Posadas**, 1½ hrs, US$2.50, **Capital del Monte**; Don Tito; Expreso Singer; Horiansky. Capital del Monte also goes to **Campo Viera**, **Aristóbulo del Valle** and **Leandro N Alem**. Don Tito goes to **El Soberbio**.

❻ Directory

Posadas *p380*
Banks Banco de La Nación, Bolívar 1799; Banco Río, Félix de Azara; Citibank, San Martín and Colón; HSBC, Félix de Azara. **Currency exchange** Mazza, Bolívar 1932. **Embassies and consulates** Paraguay, San Lorenzo 179, T03752-423858, Mon-Fri 0730-1400. **Immigration** Dirección Nacional de Migraciones, Buenos Aires 1633, T03752-427414. **Internet** Anyway, Féliz de Azara 2067, cheaper evenings and weekends; Cyber Nick, San Luis 1847; Mateando, on Félix de Azara, next to San Martín, US$0.75 per hr; Misiol@n, San Lorenzo 1681, open 24 hrs, US$0.75 per hr. **Medical services** Hospital Dr Ramón Madariaga, Av L Torres 1177, T03752-447000. **Post office** Bolívar and Ayacucho, Western Union branch.

Esteros del Iberá

Still one of Argentina's secret natural wonders, the Esteros del Iberá is a vast nature reserve of lagoons and marshes, home to an astonishing array of bird and animal life. The area has been loved by ornithologists for some time, and they still come here in great groups to tick off rare species, which can't be seen elsewhere, and certainly not at such close quarters. But you don't have to be an expert to appreciate this natural paradise. Among the 370 species of birds, herons and egrets soar elegantly from bush to bush, swifts and kingfishers swoop low on the water, giant storks nest on the many floating islands, rich with plant life, and there are tiny bright red-headed federal birds, long-tailed flycatchers, families of southern screamers – chajá – with their fluffy heads and rasping cry, amongst many species.

These immense and beautiful wetlands are among the largest expanse of virgin lagoons in South America, bettered only by the far more famous Pantanal in Brazil. Fed by an expanse of freshwater the size of Belgium, the Esteros (marshes) del Iberá host an incredible diversity of bird and animal life in one of Argentina's most exquisite landscapes. Great stretches of water are interrupted by embalsados, huge floating islands where marsh deer can be glimpsed among lush foliage, and on whose banks alligators wait, half submerged, for something to eat. The great appeal of a stay here is that you don't have to be an expert birdwatcher to find the varied birdlife fascinating. Stay in one of the estancias at Colonia Carlos Pellegrini, or further south at Rincón del Socorro, and your accommodation includes at least one boat trip on the lagoons, with a guide who can tell you all about the flora and fauna. In this country of so many natural wonders, it's one of the most unforgettable experiences. Come here soon before everyone else does. For more information, see www.esterosdelibera.com (in Spanish).

On the western side of the region, in an area of lowlands and higher woodlands, is the Parque Nacional Mburucuyá, where natural conditions are ideal for a close view of the local wildlife.
▸▸ *For listings, see pages 397-399.*

Ins and outs

Getting there and around Part of the magic of the Esteros del Iberá is that they are isolated. Transport can be organized by the *estancias*. The quickest way is to fly from Buenos Aires to Posadas (twice daily, 1½ hours) but the flight leaves Buenos Aires at 0600. A better option may be to take the overnight bus (*coche cama*, 10 hours) from Buenos Aires to **Mercedes**, and ask your *estancia* or hotel to arrange a 4WD *remise* transfer from there. There's a bus from Merdedes to Colonia Carlos Pelegrini but it takes forever and leaves at inconvenient times (see Transport, below). From **Posadas**, the 200 km journey takes four to five hours as the roads are earth and gravel after the first 60 km, and negotiable only in a 4WD vehicle, impassable after heavy rain. It's best not to hire a car. The hotels are all near the Iberá Lagoon, the easiest lagoon to access in the Esteros, reached by boat from one of several small hotels and *estancias* with their own stretch of waterfront in the sleepy little village of **Colonia Carlos Pellegrini**. **Estancia Rincón del Socorro** ⓘ *www.rincondelsocorro.com*, 30 km south of Pellegrini, is one of the most beautiful *estancias*, and slightly closer to Mercedes. They will arrange transfers. ▸▸ *For further information, see Transport, page 399.*

Best time to visit Autumn, winter or spring are the best times to visit to avoid the intense heat of midsummer. There is less chance of rain and thunderstorms during these months.

Background

This beautiful area at the heart of Corrientes province has only just opened to tourism as until recently it was a rich territory for hunters and grazing land for cattle ranchers. Since the creation of a nature reserve here in 1983, several local *estancias* have opened to guests, keen to enjoy the perfect tranquillity here as much as the birdlife. The Esteros have yet to gain national park status, however, which would ensure their greater protection. North American conservationist Douglas Tompkins is campaigning for this, and has been buying up huge sections of the land from private owners, in order to rescue it from cattle farming and rice growing which pollute the pristine waters. Though he's a controversial figure, his aims are sincere: he plans to give all the land to Argentina if it can be guaranteed national park status.

Mercedes → *For listings, see pages 397-399. Colour map 2, B1. Phone code 03773. Population 30,900.*

Mercedes is the most convenient access point for Colonia Carlos Pellegrini and the Esteros del Iberá, with regular overnight buses from Buenos Aires. It is 120 km from Pellegrini (but note that this takes two hours on the gravel roads) and 250 km southeast of Corrientes. A chirpy little town, with some quaint 1900s buildings, there are a couple of decent places to stay overnight, and a few restaurants, internet facilities and ATMs around the plaza, where there is also a small **tourist office**. Both Calle Pujol and Calle San Martín lead from the bus station to the plaza, and you're likely to see *gauchos* hanging around here in the distinctive outfits of Corrientes province, their red berets. A few kilometres west of town, on the road to Corrientes, is a shrine to **pagan saint Gauchito Gil** at the place where it's said he was killed. Shrines to Gil can be seen all over the country, with their distinctive red flags.

Colonia Carlos Pellegrini → *For listings, see pages 397-399. Colour map 2, B2.*
Phone code 03773. Population 900.

With a remote setting on the beautiful Laguna Iberá 120 km northeast of Mercedes, the sprawling village of Pellergini is the only base for visiting the Esteros del Iberá. A quiet, very laid-back place with only 900 inhabitants, there are just a few blocks of earth roads, and all the hotels are just a few hundred metres away from each other. There are not many restaurants or shops and no ATMs, so bring everything you may need. Most shops don't accept credit cards so bring extra money.There are, however, several hotels and *estancias*, most very comfortable, and these all offer full board, or a picnic if you're out during the day. They also offer boat trips on the lake as part of your accommodation, and some *estancias* offer walking and horse riding too. A two-night stay allows you to do at least one two-hour boat trip, but you may want to plan to stay for three or four nights to really unwind and lap up the tranquil atmosphere. Most accommodation will include or charge extra for a walk to see the howler monkeys in a patch of lovely jungle near the visitor centre, but you can actually do that yourself. It is clearly marked, each new species of tree is labelled and it takes about 20 minutes to complete. There are few streetlights in the village so carry a torch at night. Bring a hat, mosquito repellent, plenty of sunblock, and binoculars too if you're keen to spot the more distant birds as well as those right by your boat. The **Visitor Centre 'Aguas Brillantes'** ① *Mbigua and Yacare, daily 0730-1200, 1400-1800*, is just by the bridge as you come into town on the right. See www.coloniapellegrini.gov.ar for more information.

Reserva Natural del Iberá

This reserve protects nearly 13,000 sq km of wetlands known as the Esteros del Iberá, a vast flat flooded plain which is one of the most important natural areas in all Argentina for its superb wildlife. The area is really only accessible to visitors from the little village of Colonia

Carlos Pellegrini, from where excursions depart. There's a **Park Rangers office and visitor centre** ① *by the bridge at the access to Colonia Carlos Pellegrini, daily 0730-1200, 1400-1800*, where you can chat to the *guardaparques*, study a map of the natural reserve, and get more information on the flora and fauna. They also sell an excellent guide to all the plants, birds and animals you'll find here – *Iberá, Vida y Colour*, in Spanish and English with the Latin names noted as well – which is indispensable if your guide on the boat trip doesn't speak English. Opposite the visitor centre is a stretch of jungle where howler monkeys hang out – a *guardaparque* may accompany you if your trip doesn't include this.

The Esteros del Iberá – 'shining water' in the Guaraní language – are fed exclusively by fresh water from rain: no rivers flow into it. The marshes extend 250 km northeast to Ituzaingó on the Alto Paraná, and are some 70 km wide at their broadest. Clear waters cover 20-30% of the protected area, and there are over 60 *lagunas*, or small lakes, astonishingly no more than a few metres deep, the largest being the **Laguna Iberá** and **Laguna de la Luna**. The area is rich in aquatic plants, including the beautiful purple *camelote*, tiny cream-coloured star-shaped flowers, *irupé* (*Victoriana cruziana*) which forms a kind of floating plate supporting animal and birdlife, and when it stretches along the shoreline, it's hard to differentiate the land from the lake. The area owes its rich animal life to the profusion of *embalsados*, which sit like islands in the *lagunas*, but are just floating vegetation, dense enough to support large animals, such as the marsh deer, and sizeable trees and bushes. *Carpinchos* (capybaras) make their homes along the edges, and alligators can be seen basking on any protruding clump of mud. Watch out for the ghastly but ingenious colonial spiders, weaving enormous horizontal nets for unsuspecting insects in the late afternoon. Prolific birdlife is all around. The boat trip is at its most exciting when you travel down narrow creeks between these *embalsados*, and when you're invited to walk on them – they are amazingly stable, but yield subtly to your

Colonia Carlos Pellegrini

To Cementario
To Galarze
To Mercedes
Bridge
Ruta 40
To Mercedes
Laguna Iberá
Municipalidad

N
Not to scale

Sleeping 🛏
Aguapé **1**
Don Justino Hostel **2**
Irupe Lodge **3**
Nandé Retá **4**
Pa Sapukay **5**

Posada de la Laguna **6**
Rancho Iberá **7**
Rancho Inambú **8**
Rincón del Socorro **9**

Eating 🍴
Don Marcos **1**
El Esquinazo **2**
La Caserita **3**
Santa Rita **4**
Yacanú Purá **5**

feet with a pleasing springiness. In case you don't understand your guide's instructions in Spanish: if you suddenly start sinking, you're advised to spread out your arms before the *embalsado* closes in over you. But don't worry – this is very unlikely to happen.

Boat trips

Your hotel or *estancia* will offer at least one boat trip included in your accommodation into Laguna Iberá to visit areas where there are lots of birds, alligators and capybaras. Depending on the time of day, these usually take two to three hours, and in summer it's best to go out in the early morning or later evening, to avoid the intense heat and to stand a better chance of seeing more birds. Do ask your hotel or *estancia* at the time of booking if there are guides who speak your language: many of the local guides are excellent and know the lagunas like the back of their hands, complete with all the resident wildlife, but speak little English. You can be guaranteed English-speaking guides at **Posada de la Laguna**, Irupé Lodge and **Rincón del Socorro**. If you're lucky, your trip will be timed to return as the sun sinks on the water – sunsets here are really spectacular, when the whole world of water and sky is tinted vivid vermillion, an unforgettably moving sight. Some *estancias* also offer walks to the jungle to see and hear howler monkeys, swinging off the trees, and roaring, especially when rain is approaching. Night safaris are fun too: mammals, vizcachas, owls and lots of capybaras running around by the light of your guide's lamp.

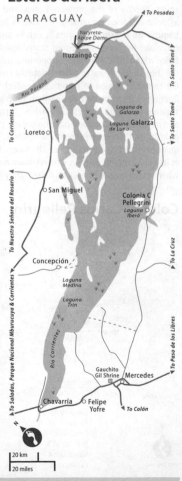

Esteros del Iberá

Parque Nacional Mburucuyá

If you can't make it over to the Esteros del Iberá and are in Corrientes city, you might like to visit this park, which stretches north from the marshlands of the Río Santa Lucía. It's 180 km southeast of Corrientes, 12 km east of the small town of Mburucuyá (where there are two places to stay overnight), accessible by a 47-km-long road branching off at Saladas. Unpaved Route 86 (later Route 13) links Mburucuyá with the park and this sandy road leads northeast to Itá Ibaté, on Route 12, 160 km east of the provincial capital. Buses go from

San Antonio Corrientes daily to Mburucuyá, the journey takes 2½ hours and costs US$4. A *remise* taxi from there to the park is US$12.

The land was donated by Danish botanist Troels Pedersen, whose long research had identified 1300 different plants, including some newly discovered species. There's a variety of natural environments, ranging from savanna with *yatay* palms and 'islands' of wet Chaco forest, with *lapacho* trees (with purple blossom in late winter) and *timbó* trees to the aquatic vegetation of the *esteros*. You'll also see *mburucuyá* (passion flower) that gives its name to the park. Lots of interesting wildlife too: capybaras, the rare *aguará guazu* (maned wolf) and the *aguará pope*, similar to the North American raccoon – though these are both nocturnal animals – deer such as *corzuela parda* (*Mazama gouazoubira*) and *ciervo de los pantanos*, foxes *aguará-í*, monkeys and many bird species, such as the lovely *yetapá de collar* (*Alectrurus risora*) or strange-tailed tyrant, with its beautiful double tail.

Provincial Route 86 (unpaved) crosses the park for 18 km, to the **information centre** and free **campsite** (hot water and electricity) at the centre of the park. From there, two footpaths branch off the access road. The **Sendero Yatay** goes south to a vantage point on Estero Santa Lucía, winding 2.5 km through gallery forests and grassland with mature palms. The Sendero Aguará Popé goes north 1.2 km, through thick vegetation and wet Chaco forests and near the western access to the park, the road crosses the *arroyo Portillo*, where 2-m-long *yacarés negros* alligators are often spotted. See www.parquesnacionales.gov.ar for more information or call the National Park Office T03782-498907.

◉ Esteros del Iberá listings

For Sleeping and Eating price codes and other relevant information, see Essentials pages 30-36.

● Sleeping

Mercedes *p394*

C Hotel Sol, San Martín 519 (between Batalla de Salta and B Mitre), T03773-420283, www.mimercedes.com.ar/hotelsol. Comfortable rooms around a wonderful patio with black and white tiles, and lots of plants. Lovely.

C La Casa de China, Mitre y Fray Luis Beltrán, call for directions, T03773-1562 7269. Welcoming old house with clean rooms and a lovely patio, breakfast included. Recommended.

Hostel

F pp Delicias del Iberá Hostel, Dr Rivas 688, T03773-423167, www.deliciasdelibera.com. Located 9 blocks from the city and 2 from the main plaza, this hostel is set in a wonderful old building with a huge inviting veranda. Nicely decorated rooms and friendly staff. They offer a free taxi from the bus station. Call to arrange.

Colonia Carlos Pellegrini *p394, map p395*
See also www.coloniapellegrini.gov.ar.

LL pp Rincón del Socorro, T03782-497161, www.rincondelsocorro.com, offer transfers from Mercedes. Incredibly luxurious, this *estancia* is part of an impressive conservation project by North American millionaire Douglas Tompkins. Beautifully set in its own 12,000 ha, 35 km south of Carlos Pellegrini. Furnished with impeccable taste throughout: 6 spacious bedrooms, each with bathroom and little sitting room. 3 *cabañas*, elegant sitting rooms and dining rooms. Delicious organic food is grown in the kitchen garden, and you'll receive a charming welcome from Leslie and Valeria, who speak perfect English, and organize excellent trips on the *lagunas* with expert, bilingual guides, *asados* at lunchtime, night safaris and wonderful horse riding. Gorgeous gardens, pool with superb views all around. Highly recommended.

L pp Posada de la Laguna, T/F03782-499413, www.posadadelalaguna.com. The loveliest place to stay in Pellegrini, this little *estancia* was built by the current owner, Elsa Güiraldes, granddaughter of one of

Argentina's great writers. She's created a stylish and welcoming home here, where guests share the spacious sitting and dining rooms, but have their guesthouse with elegant bedrooms coming off a terrace with open views onto the *laguna*. There is direct access to the water from the lovely gardens, and a pool. Price includes all boat trips, use of the canoes and all the delicious meals. Elsa speaks fluent English and some French, and makes you feel entirely at home. She also guides the boat trips, and will arrange transfers. A beautiful place. Highly recommended.

L-AL pp **Posada Aguapé**, T03773-499412 (T011-4742 3015 in Buenos Aires), www.ibera esteros.com.ar. Named after the pale yellow water lilies that abound nearby, this *estancia* combines relaxed living with extremely good food and a very high standard of activities. Run by a welcoming couple, Rafael and Elena, accommodation is in high-ceilinged traditional galleried rooms, with big windows directly onto the simple gardens going down to the lagoon. Rafael speaks good English and is an excellent guide to the local wildlife, but note that other guides speak little English. Recommended.

AL Hostería Ñandé Retá, T/F03773-499411, www.nandereta.com. The first house to receive guests at the Esteros, this big old wooden house is set under shady trees and offers friendly and relaxed accommodation in 9 rooms, full board with excursions included, as well as a playroom on the upper floor.

A pp **Irupé Lodge**, T03773-1540 2193, www.ibera-argentina.com. Built right on the *laguna*, with great views from the dining room, this is a rustic place with lovely rooms, offering some less conventional trips such as camping on remote islands, *asado* with local musicians playing *chamamé*, and diving and fishing for piranha. Several languages spoken, including English. Fantastic hosts and a fabulous new pool add to the package. Highly recommended.

C pp **Posada Ypa Sapukai**, T03773-420155, www.ypasapukai.com.ar. This cosy house is run by friendly Pedro Noailles, who has lived here for 10 years and is an expert guide to the lagoon's wildlife. His wife Claudia speaks

English, and they offer excellent excursions to the laguna. Shared, single rates available (**E** pp). Rates are for full board and include 2 3-hr boat trips, or a walk or horse riding.

C Rancho Iberá, Caraguatá and Aguará, T03783-153 18 5 940, www.posadarancho ibera.com.ar. Designed like an old Argentine country house, there is a *posada* with double and triple beds and a well-maintained garden.

C Rancho Inambú, T03773-1543 8485, Yeruti, between Aguapé and Pehuajó www.rancho inambu.com.ar. Having recently moved to the *posada* category the owners have added extra services such as tours, 24-hr water, a lovely common area and a great bar (open to non-guests). Nice rustic rooms set in lush gardens.

Hostels

F pp **Don Justino Hostel**, Curupi and Yaguareté, T03773-499 415, book through www.hosteltraveler.com. Small and friendly hostel 3 blocks from the lake, 2 from the plaza. Organizes tours and boat trips.

Estancias

B pp **San Juan Poriahú**, at Loreto, T03781-4794 8964, gesino@fibertel.com.ar. Closed in Jan, Feb and Jul holidays. An old *estancia* with an attractive house run by Marcos García Rams, situated at the northwestern edge of the Esteros del Iberá, next to the village of Loreto, and accessible by a paved road from nearby R12. Rates include full board accommodation (½ rate for under 12s), and activities such as horse riding and boat trips to appreciate the rich wildlife in an area where there has been no hunting at all.

B pp **San Lorenzo**, at Galarza, T03756-481 292, www.estanciasanlorenzo.com. Closed in Jan and Feb. Set next to 2 of the biggest lakes of the Iberá (at the northeast edge of the region), this *estancia* is in a splendid place for wildlife watching, especially rare deer *venado de las pampas*. Welcoming, full board, activities (riding, walking, boat trips to Lagunas de Luna and Galarza) are included in the rates. Boat excursions by night, charged separately. Transfers can be arranged from Gobernador Virasoro or Posadas for an extra charge.

① Eating

Mercedes *p394*

¶¶ **El Quincho**, Av San Martín and Alvear. Upmarket, but still very inexpensive and serves delicious food.

¶ **Pizza Libre**, Sarmiento and San Martín, opposite the main church, serves great pizzas as well as *parrilla* and *lomitos*. A simple place but excellent value for a filling meal.

Colonia Carlos Pellegrini *p394, map p395*

There aren't many restaurants here since all hotels and *estancias* offer full board. There are a couple of *kioskos* selling cold drinks and snacks on the road leading to the bridge, these have unreliable opening times. The following are all within walking distance of the main plaza:

¶ **Don Marcos**, RP 40 and Guasuvirá, T03773-1540 4159. Offering a variety of *empanadas* and *milanesas*, but also regional dishes such as *chastaca*, *bai pui*, *carbonada* and *locro*.

¶ **La Caserita**, Timbó s/c, house 16, T03773-1543 3228. Take away store with home-made bread and *empanadas*. Vegetarians catered for.

¶ **Santa Rita**, Curupí and Tuyuyú, T03773-1541 1053. Pizza, pastries and delicious home-made desserts.

¶ **Yacarú Porá Restaurant**, Yaguarte and Cara Huata, T03773-1541 3750. Tasty BBQ, pasta, pizzas and *empanadas*. Vegetarians catered for.

▲ Activities and tours

Colonia Carlos Pellegrini *p394, map p395*

As part of your stay at most lodges you will have at least a few activities included but local enterprises also offer several tours, such as boat trips, horse riding and kayaking. Expect to pay around US$21 per person. Ask at the visitor centre for details.

Iberá Expediciones, Yaguarete and Pindo, T03773-1544 3602, www.iberaexpediciones. com. Small but professional tour agency run by the informative José Martín, who can organize boat trips, birdwatching tours, horse riding and treks. He can also help you find

accommodation and is happy to help with information on the area. Recommended.

⊖ Transport

Mercedes *p394*

Bus

To **Colonia Carlos Pellegrini**, Itatí II *combi* provides a service Mon-Sat 1230 (but check as times change), from Pujol 1166, T03773-420184, T03773-1562 9598, 4-5 hrs, US$8. Note that it spends 1 hr picking up passengers from the whole of Mercedes after leaving the office. Returns from Pellegrini the next day at 0430 (doesn't run on Sun). Ask in the bus terminal. 3 times a week (Wed, Fri and Sun) there is a 4WD that carries passengers between the 2 towns (US$24 one way if full). Ask at the tourist office for details as they change regularly.

To **Buenos Aires**, 9-10 hrs, US$35, **Aguila Dorada Bis**; **Flecha Bus**; **Itatí**; **Nuevo Rápido Tata**; **San Cristóbal**. To **Corrientes**, 3 hrs, US$9, several companies. To **Posadas** 6 hrs, US$12 with **Crucero del Norte**. To **Puerto Iguazú**: there are 2 options: via Corrientes or via Posadas. Expect to pay around US$22 for the whole journey (via Posadas). To **San Ignacio**, catch a bus to Posadas and change (Posadas to San Ignacio, 1 hr, US$9).

Colonia Carlos Pellegrini *p394, map p395*

Bus

To **Mercedes**, Itatí II *combi*, daily at 0400, 3-5 hrs, US$7. Booking is required before 2200 the night before, at the office in a local grocery (ask for directions). To **Posadas**, either catch the bus back to Mercedes and up to Posadas or organize a transfer through your hotel or *estancia*, 4-5 hrs (impassable after heavy rain). Your hosts will be happy to sort this out by email before you arrive. Or try **Fermín Cruz**, ferbenitez cruz@hotmail.com. Transfer prices are per vehicle, so cheaper if there are a few of you. **Mercedes** to **Colonia Carlos Pellegrini**, US$100; **Pellegrini** to **Corrientes** US$250. From Posadas, see Tour operators, page 390.

Along the Río Uruguay

The mighty Río Uruguay is over 1600 km long, and a staggering 10 km wide in places. It forms Argentina's eastern boundary with Uruguay and Brazil, and along the Argentine side are dotted a few interesting towns and cities. With time to spare you could return from the northeast to Buenos Aires via the river. Gualeguaychú is so keen to party, it celebrates its carnival every weekend for two months, but you can calm down in Concepción del Uruguay, with its attractive old buildings, or Colón, with its historic port area and sandy beaches. There's a national park protecting splendid palm forests, though the reserve La Aurora del Palmar is more accessible. You can stay on colonial estancias, jungle islands, and with small communities at Irazusta and Arroyo Barú. The section that follows takes you from south to north along the Río Uruguay. ▸▸ For listings, see pages 404-407.

Gualeguaychú → *For listings, see pages 404-407. Colour map 4, A5.*

Ins and outs → *Phone code 03446. Population 74,700.*
The **bus terminal** ① *Blvd Artigas and Blvd Jurado, T03446-440688*, is a 30-minute walk from the centre; a *remise* taxi charges US$2 for the trip. The terminal has tourist information, a post office, phones, a small restaurant and 24-hour left luggage (US$1 per day).

Sights
The first town of any size on the route north, Gualeguaychú is famous for its extended carnival. It's lively throughout the summer, with an attractive *costanera* on the Río Gualeguaychú, where there are several *balnearios* and restaurants, a pleasant place for a stroll with views of the picturesque port. Carnival is celebrated at the local *corsódromo* (arena), a hugely popular event lasting well beyond the usual fortnight to fill every weekend for a couple of months. The port and *balneario municipal* (town bathing spot) are the departure points for short boat excursions and city tours, T03446-423248 (only in high season). About 200 m south of the port in Plazoleta de los Artesanos, local handicrafts are sold at weekends in summer. A thatched hut houses the local **tourist office** ① *T03446-423668, www.gualeguaychuturismo.com, daily 0800-2000 (closing 2200 in summer)*.

On the *costanera* at Gervasio Méndez is **El Patio del Mate** ① *T03446-424371, www.elpatiodelmate.com.ar, daily 0800-2100*, a workshop where dedicated craftsmen make the cups from which *mate* is drunk, varying widely from simple dyed gourds to ornate silver goblets.

Around Gualeguaychú
Villa Paranacito is a village set in the delta islands, 100 km south of Gualeguaychú, where houses are built on tall stilts and boats are the essential means of transport. It's popular with anglers in the waters of the nearby Río Uruguay (half an hour further by boat), and anyone looking for a quiet place to stay, immersed in the islander culture. There are campsites, a hostel and *cabañas* offering boat excursions. There's delicious local fish at **Villa Paranacito Annemarie**. Villa Paranacito is accessible only via a 22-km dirt road, branching off Route 12, 10 km south of Ceibas. There are daily buses with Nuevo Expreso from Gualeguaychú, Zárate and Buenos Aires.

Estancia La Azotea ① *10 km north of Villarancito, on Route 12 in Ceibas, T03446-4794 8964, gesino@fibertel.com.ar*, is a 19th-century house popular for day visits, with cattle ranching, horse riding, an *asado* lunch and the use of a pool in summer. Very good value.

Border essentials: Argentina–Uruguay

Libertador General San Martín Bridge

Situated 33 km southeast of Gualeguaychú, the Libertador General San Martín Bridge (5.4 km long) provides the most southerly route across the Río Uruguay, to Fray Bentos (see below). Open 24 hours.

Customs and immigration These are at opposite ends of the bridge and it's an uncomplicated crossing; formalities take about 10 minutes. Passport details are noted when booking bus tickets and passed to officials at the border, and passports are inspected on the bus. **Note** Pedestrians and cyclists can only cross in motor vehicles, though officials may arrange lifts. Vehicle toll is US$6. Don't carry any dairy products, meat, fruit and vegetables, flowers, plants and seeds, or animals.

Argentine consulate At 18 de Julio 1225, T+598-(0)562 3225, Fray Bentos.

Transport From Gualeguaychú to Fray Bentos, there are two daily buses (one on Sunday) with **Ciudad de Gualeguay**, T03446-440555, 1¼ hours, US$3.50. Arrive 30 minutes before departure to do the border paperwork.

Note Due to ongoing demonstrations regarding the building of various paper mills in the area, the bridge and border are sometimes closed. For updates, email: e6curuguay@gendarmeria.gov.ar.

Into Uruguay: Fray Bentos → *Colour map 4, A6. Phone code +598-(0)562. Population 22,000.*
Fray Bentos is the main port on the east bank of Río Uruguay, a friendly little town with an attractive *costanera*. The main reason to visit is to see the meat-packing factory. The name Fray Bentos was synonymous with corned beef in Britain throughout the 20th century, and the factory (*frigorífico*) known as El Anglo, which produced Oxo for many years, has been beautifully restored as the **Museo de La Revolución Industrial** ① *T+598 (0)562-3690, www.maquinascnc.com.ar daily 0900-1800, US$5 (or US$8 with a guided tour), tour 2 hrs in Spanish, may provide leaflet in English,* and business park, with a restaurant, *Wolves*. The office block in the factory has been preserved and some of the old machinery can be seen. See also the Bovril *estancia*, **Vizcacheras** ① *www.vizcacheras.com.ar,* page 417. The **tourist office** ① *T+598(0)562-2369,* is at Puente General San Martín.

Concepción del Uruguay and around → *For listings, see pages 404-407. Colour map 2, C1.*

Ins and outs → *Phone code 03442. Population 64,500.*
The **bus terminal** ① *Rocamora and Los Constituyentes, T03442-422352,* is 11 blocks from Plaza Ramírez. A *remise* to the centre costs US$1. Luggage can be left free of charge at the information desk.

Sights
Concepción del Uruguay lies on the western shore of the Río Uruguay 74 km north of Gualeguaychú, with views of islands in the river opposite. Founded in 1783, it was capital of Entre Ríos province between 1813-1821 and 1860-1883, and retains some fine architecture in its public buildings. It has a distinctively lively character, thanks to a young student population. The **tourist office** ① *9 de Julio 844, T03442-425820, Mon-Fri 0700-1300, 1400-2000, and Sat-Sun 0700-2200 in high season,* is two blocks from the plaza.

There is another **information point** ① *T03442-440812, daily 0800-2000,* on the access road at Galarza and Elías with the same hours.

The old town is centred on beautiful **Plaza Ramírez**, with the Italian neoclassical-style **Basílica de la Inmaculada Concepción**, containing the remains of General Urquiza on its western side. Next to it is the **Colegio Superior Justo José de Urquiza**, the first secular school in the country, although its 19th-century buildings were largely replaced in 1935. One block northeast of the plaza is **Museo Casa de Delio Panizza** ① *Galarza and Supremo Entrerriano 58, daily 0900-1200, 1600-1900, US$0.50,* in a mansion dating from 1793 and containing 19th-century furnishings and artefacts.

Around Concepción del Uruguay

① *Buses going to Paraná or Rosario del Tala will stop at El Cruce or Caseros, and from here, the palacios are 4 km and 8 km away, respectively (take a remise taxi from Caseros). Remise taxis charge about US$10 (with a 1½-hr wait included). Tour operators run combis (minibuses) only in high season for about US$9 including entrance (check companies at tourist office, since they change every year). A train service arrives on Sat from Villa Elisa. Basavilbaso has regular buses which link Concepción del Uruguay and Paraná or Rosario del Tala.*

Palacio San José ① *32 km west of the town, www.palaciosanjose.com.ar, Mon-Fri 0800-1900, Sat-Sun 0900-1800, US$3.50, information in Spanish, French and English, free guided visits at 1000, 1100, 1500, 1600, plus 1200 and 1400 on weekends,* is the former mansion of General Urquiza, which dates from 1848, built in Italian style with 38 rooms and a chapel. It was once the country's most luxurious residence. Now a museum with artefacts from Urquiza's life, the palace stands in a beautiful park with an artificial lake. It can be reached by taking Route 39 west and turning right after Caseros train station. There is also a second palacio, **Palacio Santa Candida** ① *www.santacandida.com,* which is another wonderfully old *estancia* that can be visited and stayed in.

Basavilbaso, 68 km west, is a historical small town which in the early 20th century was an urban centre for Lucienville, inhabited by Jewish immigrants from Russia. There's a **tourist office** ① *Lagocen and Hipólito Yrigoyen, T03445-481015, www.turismoentrerios.com/basavilbaso* , and information is available at **Asociación Israelita** ① *T03445-481908*. There are three well-preserved synagogues, of which the **Tefila L Moises** has a beautifully painted wooden ceiling. It's also worth visiting the **Navibuco synagogue**, 2.5 km out of town, dating from 1895, and two Jewish cemeteries nearby. Basavilbaso was a busy transport hub and though the last passenger train left in 1992, the station now houses a museum where the rich history of the local railway can be explored.

Colón → *For listings, see pages 404-407. Colour map 2, C1.*

One of the prettiest towns on the river, Colón was founded in 1863 as a port for the Swiss colony of San José, 9 km west, and it's an excellent base for several very interesting places nearby, including the **Parque Nacional El Palmar** ① *www.colonentrerios.com.ar/elpalmar/*. It is also linked by a bridge to the Uruguayan city of Paysandú, with its interesting old buildings (see below). Colón itself has many well-preserved early 19th-century houses, and a beautiful riverbank with long sandy beaches and shady streets. The **bus terminal** ① *Paysandú and Sourigues, T03447-421716,* is 10 blocks away from the main plaza. Not all long-distance buses enter Colón: buses going north from Colón will stop at Ubajay. At the bus terminal there is a 24-hour bar where luggage is kept for US$0.50 a day; and the owner provides information on bus timetables.

Sights → *Phone code 03447. Population 19,200.*

The most attractive part of town is the port district, next to the Plaza San Martín, with fine old houses on the plaza and nearby streets leading down to the riverside. The former passenger boat terminal now houses the **tourist office** ① *Av Costanera Quirós and Gouchón, T03447-421233, www.colonentrerios.com.ar, Mon-Fri 0630-2100, Sat-Sun 0800-2100.*

At the corner of Avenida 12 de Abril and Paso is **La Casona** (1868), where there's a handicrafts exhibition and shop. North of the port, Calle Alejo Peyret gives access to the *balnearios* and their sandy beaches on the river and Calle Belgrano leads to the **Complejo Termal** ① *T03447-424717, daily 0900-2100, US$2*, where there are 10 thermal pools (ranging from 34-40°C) in an attractive setting, very popular for treating a variety of ailments. Most shops and banks can be found on Avenida 12 de Abril, with the old **Teatro Centenario**, opened in 1925.

Excursions

Some 40 km north of Villa Elisa is **Arroyo Barú**, a rural village whose inhabitants have opened their houses to visitors who want to enjoy the tranquillity of its small community. This place, together with Irazusta (west of Gualeguaychú), are both study cases for NGO research. Contact Señora Marta, T03447-496048, turismoenbaru@hotmail.com. The village is reached via a 35-km-long dirt road, branching off Route 130, 5 km west of Villa Elisa, where *remise* taxis (T03447-496010) and *combis* (T03447-496013), will take passengers in good weather.

Parque Nacional El Palmar → *Colour map 2, C1.*

① *T03447-493049, US$7. There is a bus from Colón, 1 hr, US$2. Coming from the north you will be dropped at the entrance, from where you can walk or hitch the last 12 km to the park administration. Remise taxis from Colón or from Ubajay offer tours (eg from Colón, US$20 for a 4-hr round trip, including a tour or waiting time in the park). Enquire in Ubajay at bus stop Parador Gastiazoro or at petrol station for park wardens who might be going to the park.*

On the west bank of the Río Uruguay 51 km north of Colón and 53 km south of Concordia, this park covers 8500 ha of gently undulating grassland and mature palm forest, including *Yatay* palms hundreds of years old. These graceful trees were once found all over the Pampas, until the introduction of cattle, who found the young seedlings irresistible. Growing in *palmares*, or groves, mature trees may reach 12 m in height, with fronds some 2 m in length. Along the Río Uruguay, and the *arroyos* streams that flow into it, there are gallery forests of subtropical trees and shrubs. You'll find indigenous tombs hidden away on the edge of the Río Uruguay where there are **beaches** and the remains of an 18th-century quarry and port. Look out for capybaras, foxes, lizards and vizcachas as well as rheas, monk parakeets and several species of woodpecker.

The entrance gates to the park are on Route 14, where you are given a map and information on walks, and a *ripio* road leads to the administration centre, in the east of the park, near the Río Uruguay, with access to several viewpoints: **Mirador de La Glorieta**, **Mirador del Arroyo El Palmar**, **Mirador del Arroyo Los Loros** and to the coast of the Río Uruguay. There are walks between 300 m and 1000 m and you are free to walk around the main roads, though there's little shade. The administration centre is the departure point for guided walks and cycle tours run by *Capybara Aventura* (English spoken). Nearby there's camping (US$5 per person, plus US$2 per tent in high season) with electricity, hot water, a restaurant opposite and a small shop. Visit at any time of year, but note that the park is very popular at weekends in summer and during Easter week. In summer there are more chances of thunderstorms and very hot weather.

Border essentials: Argentina–Uruguay

General José Artigas Bridge

Open 24 hours. 7 km southeast of Colón, the General José Artigas Bridge gives access to the Uruguayan city of Paysandú. Toll US$3.50.

Argentine consulate At Gómez 1034, T03447-22253, Mon-Fri 0800-1300.

Immigration Argentine and Uruguayan formalities are both dealt with at the Uruguayan end of the bridge. *Migraciones* officials board the bus, but non-Argentines or Uruguayans should get off bus to have their passports stamped. When driving you don't need to get out of your car, just present your passport and car registration details when asked.

Note It's better to fill your tank up on the cheaper Argentine side.

Transport From Colón to Paysandú, take a **Copay** bus, 45 minutes, US$3.

Refugio de Vida Silvestre La Aurora del Palmar

① *Buses from Colón or from the north will drop you at the entrance. Remember to tell the driver you're going to La Aurora del Palmar, to avoid confusion with the national park. Remise taxis from Ubajay charge US$3.*

More accessible than the National Park, the wildlife reserve of La Aurora del Palmar was created to protect a similar environment. Situated 3 km south of Ubajay, on Route 14, Km 202, it covers 1150 ha, of which 200 are covered with a mature palm forest. There are also gallery forests along the streams and patches of *espinal*, or scrub. There's lots of birdlife, but capybaras can also be spotted along the streams. The administration centre is only 500 m from Route 14, and it offers far more organized services for visitors. Since entry is free, you could reach the vantage point of the *quincho panorámico* for a drink (try the *yatay* spirit), while enjoying the view of the palm forest. Guided excursions include horse riding into the palm forest and the Arroyo de los Pájaros (two hours, US$6.50 per person, minimum two people); canoe journeys along Arroyo El Palmar (US$8 per person, minimum two people); and walks to the Mirador del Cerro de Piedra (US$4.50 per person, minimum three people, only at weekends). All recommended.

◉ Along the Río Uruguay listings

For Sleeping and Eating price codes and other relevant information, see Essentials pages 30-36.

◉ Sleeping

Gualeguaychú *p400*
Accommodation is scarce during the carnival. Prices double Dec-Mar, Easter and long weekends.

B Puerto Sol, San Lorenzo 477, T03446-434017, www.hotelpuertosol.com.ar. Appealing place to stay with good basic rooms with a/c, next to the port. The hotel runs a small resort on a nearby island (transfer and access included in room rates) where you can spend the day relaxing.

B Tykuá, Luis N Palma 150, T03446-422625, www.tykuahotel.com.ar. Red-brick hotel with breakfast included, 3 blocks from the bridge. Triples are rather small for 3 people (**D** in low season).

Hostels

F pp **Top Maló**, T03446-495255, topmalo@ infovia.com.ar. HI-affiliated (discounts for members), this place has basic houses (**E**), built on stilts 3 m above ground for 2 and 4 people with cooking facilities and shared rooms for up to 5 people. Kitchen and bed-linen included, and there's a campsite with hot showers and electricity for US$5 a day plus US$0.50 per person payable only for the 1st day. Attractive rustic style and a warm atmosphere.

Camping

There are several sites along the riverbank, next to the bridge and north of it.

Costa Azul, 200 m northeast of bridge, T03446-423984. A shady willow grove, and a good location on the riverside. Camping (US$5 a day for a 2-man tent), new wooden cabins and small flats with cooking facilities. **El Ñandubaysal**, 15 km southeast, T03446-423298, www.nandubaysal.com. The smartest campsite and the only one to have a beach on the beautiful Río Uruguay. Very good facilities (US$9 per tent plus access fee) and a 'VIP' sector (US$11 per tent plus access fee).

Concepción del Uruguay and around p401

A Antigua Posta del Torreón, Almafuerte 799, T03442-432 618, www.postadeltorreon.com.ar. A lovely hotel set in a 19th-century mansion. Comfortable rooms, inviting courtyard and a small plunge pool. Recommended

C-B Grand Hotel, Eva Perón 114, T03442-422851, www.grandpalaciotexier.com.ar. Originally a French-style mansion with an adjacent theatre built in 1931 for the Texier family, it retains some of its former splendour, especially in the hall and casino. Superior rooms (25% more expensive) have a/c and TV but are otherwise similar. Both include a large breakfast.

D Nuevo Residencial Centro, Moreno 130, T03442-427429, www.nuevorescentro.com.ar. One of the cheapest options in town. Basic but clean rooms in a traditional 19th-century building with a lovely patio. Only 1½ blocks from the plaza.

Estancias

Founded by Urquiza, these offer excellent accommodation and all meals are included:
AL pp Estancia Santa Cándida, T03442-4343 2366, www.santacandida.com. Offers half-board and is situated in a gorgeous old manor.

A pp Estancia San Pedro, Near Villa Mantero, 39.5 km west of Concepción del Uruguay. T03442-4794 8964 www.estanciasanpedro. com. Owned by descendants of Urquiza, this has old rooms full of antiques, very good accommodation. It is popular with hunters who come for the hundreds of red deer on the property (best to stay away if this upsets you).

Colón p402

A Hotel and Spa Costarenas, Av Quirós and 12 de Abril, T03447-425050, www.costarenas. com.ar. Well-designed modern rooms, some with a wonderful view. Clean and inviting spa, sauna and a high-quality restaurant (open to non-guests). Best upmarket option in town.

A Quirinale, Av Costanera Quirós and Noailles 3280, T03447-421133, www.hquirinale.com.ar. A large, rather overpriced 5-star overlooking the river. Panoramic views from some of the rooms, spa treatments charged separately. Restaurant, casino, and open-air and indoor pools, the latter with thermal waters.

B Hostería Restaurant del Puerto, Alejo Peyret 158, T03447-422698, www.hosteriadecolon.com.ar. By far the best-value place to stay. This old building has been redecorated offering comfort but retaining the period-style atmosphere. Rooms for 4 at the front on 1st floor have balconies overlooking the river, but off-season are also offered as doubles. Breakfast is included.

C La Posada de David, Alejo Peyret 97, T03447-423930. A pleasant family house with a garden. Welcoming owners offer very good double rooms with breakfast and one with cooking facilities.

Hostels

F pp Sophie Hostel, Laprida 128, T03447-422 385 (formerly Casamate Hostel), www.hostels club.com. HI-affiliated (discounts for members), this is a renovated old house with a nice backyard and a pleasant sitting room with a fireplace. The very welcoming young owners provide excellent information on local sights and on bus connections. Good rooms with shared baths (bedlinen provided), as well as doubles (**C**) with own bath. Free use of cycles are also available.

Camping

Consult the tourist office for their extensive list as there are many campsites along the riverside, getting quieter the further you go from the centre, as well as some on nearby rivers. They all charge about US$5 a day per tent for up to 2 people.
Camping Municipal Playa Norte, T03447-422074. A few blocks north of the port.
Piedras Coloradas, T03447-421451. On the river south of Av 12 de Abril.

Refugio de Vida Silvestre La Aurora del Palmar *p404*
F pp **Pernoctar en La Aurora**, T03447-421549, www.auroradelpalmar.com.ar/alojamiento.htm. Offers one of the most extraordinary places to stay, converted train carriages (**C-D**) for doubles with bath and breakfast provided, also available for 3 to 6 people. Book in advance or check availability for the excursions.

Camping

There is a campsite in the park, US$4 per person a day plus US$2 per tent.

⓸ Eating

Gualeguaychú *p400*
Ⓣⓣ Campo Alto, San Lorenzo and Concordia, T03446-429593. A large *quincho* (rustic place to eat) at the end of the *costanera*, lots of local fish such as *surubí*, *boga*, *dorado* and *patí* on the menu.
Ⓣ Dacal, Av Costanera and Andrade, T03446-427602. A traditional restaurant, serving good food; the *surubí* is recommended.

Concepción del Uruguay *p401*
Ⓣⓣ El Remanso, Rocamora and Eva Perón, T03442-428069. Good food, popular and with moderately priced *parrilla*.

Colón *p402*
Ⓣⓣ La Cosquilla de Angel, Alejo Peyret 180, T03447-423711. The smartest place in town with attractive decor, live piano music in the evenings and tables outside at lunchtime. Varied and moderately priced meals, including fish of the day and also a reasonable set menu.
Ⓣⓣ Viejo Almacén, Urquiza and Paso, T03447-422216. A cosy place offering very good cooking and excellent service. The *surubí* is tasty *al limón* or with a delicate sauce. In the basement there's a great place for trying wines and *picadas* (cheese and ham nibbles).

⊛ Festivals and events

Gualeguaychú *p400*
Jan/Feb Carnival, www.carnavaldelpais.com.ar (in Spanish). Local teams or *comparsas* compete in colourful parades, to the powerful drumbeats of the *batucada*, with the spectacularly decorated *carrozas* and dancers dressed in brightly coloured costumes and feathers. Carnival is celebrated every weekend throughout Jan and Feb at the *corsódromo*, a purpose-built carnival parade ground with grandstand, at the back of the former railway station, Piccini y Maipú. It's US$15 for a seat, and while the spectacle is quite amazing, it lacks the spontaneity of a street festival.

Colón *p402*
Feb Fiesta Nacional de la Artesanía. Held over 9 evenings in Parque Quirós, where craftspeople display a wide variety of handicrafts. There are also *folcore* and pop music concerts.

▲ Activities and tours

Gualeguaychú *p400*
Ahoniken, 25 de Mayo 581, T03446-430706. Local trips and travel advice.

Colón *p402*
Ita i Cora, San Martín 97, T03442-423360, www.itaicora.com. Very welcoming and

informative people run boat trips on the Río Uruguay, where you can lie on the beaches or take long walks in shallow waters, stopping off at islands to give you a taste of trekking through jungle, 45 mins, 2½ hrs, US$10-25 per person. Also short 4WD trips, including a visit to Pueblo Liebig, 1½-2½ hrs, US$9-18. Boat departures from Av Costanera Quirós and Noailles, ½-price for children under 10.

Parque Nacional El Palmar *p403*
Capybara Aventura T03442-1544 5170, pnpalmar@ciudad.com.ar (at park administration), T03447-493053, capybaraaventura@ciudad.com.ar. Guided walks, 1-3 hrs, US$7 per person; cycle tours with mountain bikes and helmets, 1½-3 hrs, US$5 per person. Call first in low season.

● Transport

Gualeguaychú *p400*
Bus
For bus terminal information, see page 400.

To **Buenos Aires**, 3-3½ hrs, US$13, Flecha Bus; Nuevo Expreso; Nuevo Rápido Tata. To **Paraná**, 4½-5 hrs, US$9, Ciudad de Gualeguay; Jovi Bus; Nuevo Expreso. To **Concepción del Uruguay**, 1 hr, US$3.50, Flecha Bus; Jovi Bus; Nuevo Expreso. To **Colón**, 1½-2 hrs, US$4.80, Flecha Bus; Jovi Bus; Nuevo Expreso. To **Villa Paranacito**, daily, 2 hrs, US$5, Nuevo Expreso. To **El Ñandubaysal**, several daily in high season, US$4 open return includes entry fee, Expreso Ñandubaysal.

Remise taxi
San José, San José and Rivadavia (on plaza), T03446-431333.

Around Gualeguaychú *p400*
Bus
Buses to **Zárate** or **Buenos Aires** stop at **Ceibas**, not far from Estancia La Azotea, and there are regular buses from **Gualeguaychú** to **Larroque** and **Urdinarrain**, where *remise* taxis will take you to **Irazusta** and **Aldea San Antonio**.

Concepción del Uruguay *p401*
Bus
For bus terminal information, see page 401.

To **Buenos Aires**, 4 hrs, US$15, Flecha Bus; Nuevo Rápido Tata. To **Paraná**, 5 hrs, US$11, Flecha Bus; Itapé; Nuevo Rápido Tata. To **Colón**, 45 mins, US$5, several companies. To **Palacio San José**, 30 mins, US$2, Itapé; Paccot; San José (stopping at El Cruce or at Caseros). To **Gualeguaychú**, 1 hr, US$3.50, several companies.

Colón *p402*
Bus
For bus terminal information, see page 402.

Not all long-distance buses enter Colón. Buses going north from Colón will stop at **Ubajay**. At Ubajay, **Parador Gastiazoro**, T0345-490 5026, is a busy bus stop where you can take daily **Expreso Singer** to **Puerto Iguazú**, US$30.

To **Buenos Aires**, 5-6 hrs, US$17, Flecha Bus; Nuevo Expreso; Nuevo Rápido Tata. To **Mercedes** (for getting to Iberá), 6-7 hrs, US$14, Flecha Bus; Nuevo Rápido Tata. To **Paraná**, 4-5 hrs, US$11, Flecha Bus; Paccot. To **Concepción del Uruguay**, 45 mins, US$2, several companies. To **Gualeguaychú**, 1½-2 hrs, US$3, several companies. To **San José**, 20 mins, US$1, Paccot. To **Pueblo Liebig**, 45 mins, US$1.50, Paccot. Access to **Parque Nacional El Palmar**, 1 hr, US$3, Flecha Bus; Itapé; Jovi Bus. To **Villa Elisa**, 1 hr, US$2, Itapé; Mitre Bus; Transporte Ogara.

Remise taxi
Palmar, Laprida 37, T03447-421278.

● Directory

Gualeguaychú *p400*
Banks Banco de la Nación, 25 de Mayo and Alberdi; Credicoop, Rivadavia and Perón. **Embassies and consulates**, Uruguay, Rivadavia 810, T03446 426168, Mon-Fri 0800-1400.

Río Paraná

Running parallel to the Río Uruguay, the Río Paraná weaves its lazy course right across the northeast of Argentina, from Misiones to Buenos Aires where it forms a vast delta. If you have time for a road trip from Buenos Aires to Corrientes, you will pass through the major cities of Rosario and Santa Fe. There are two main routes north: an interesting journey is along the eastern banks of the river, through Paraná via small towns with wildlife spotting and fishing and onwards to Goya and Corrientes; or the more major route north along the western banks, through the cities of Rosario and Santa Fe to Reconquista and Resistencia. This chapter explores the western route first, as far as Santa Fe, and then crosses to the eastern bank to the city of Paraná, and areas north and south.
▶▶ *For listings, see pages 415-423.*

Rosario → *For listings, see pages 415-423. Colour map 4, A5.*

Rosario is Argentina's third largest city, renowned for its rich cultural life, since it is home to many famous artists and pop musicians. Although little visited by travellers, it has some fine buildings in its attractive centre, and a well-kept *costanera* alongside the Paraná river. The nightlife is lively, with plenty of cafés, restaurants and nightclubs, and there are daily theatre and live music shows at venues all around the city. To recover from all that entertainment, visit the nearby islands in the river, just minutes away from the centre, where you can relax on sandy beaches. It is a fantastic place to spend the weekend.

Ins and outs → *Phone code 0341. Population 1,159,000.*

Fisherton airport ① *T0341-451 3220*, is located 15 km from the centre. *Remise* taxis charge US$6 for the journey to town. Transfers are also arranged by airline companies. The **bus terminal** ① *Santa Fe and Cafferata, T0341-437 3030*, is about 30 blocks from the Monumento de la Bandera. The terminal has an information point, post office, shops, restaurants and left luggage (open 24 hours, US$1.50 a day per piece). For local buses a magnetic card must be bought at kiosks in the centre or near bus stops (US$0.50 per trip). A *remise* taxi from the bus terminal to the centre will cost US$3, alternatively there are several bus to the centre with stops on Córdoba (eg 101, 103, 115). There is also the **Rosario Norte railway station** ① *Av del Valle and Av Ovidio Lagos*.

Background

Unlike most Spanish American cities, Rosario was never officially founded. Though a fort was established in 1689 by Luis Romero de Pineda, it was just a place to export mules and tobacco throughout the 18th century. However, it grew rapidly in the late 19th century, with the opening of a railway line to Córdoba in 1870 and the increase of shipping along the Paraná: its port became a major exporter of grain and beef, while new industries were established, including breweries, grain mills and leather industries. In the late 20th century, Rosario attracted thousands of immigrants from the northern provinces of Argentina who settled on the outskirts, later forming one of the largest deprived communities in the country. The main **tourist office** ① *Av Belgrano and Buenos Aires, on the riverside park down from the Monumento a la Bandera, T0341-480 2230, www.rosarioturismo.com (in English)*, has very efficient staff and a free tourist card is given for discounts at several hotels, restaurants and other services around the city. See also www.visitarosario.com (in Spanish).

Sights

The old city centre is on the Plaza 25 de Mayo, just a block south of the Parque a la Bandera which lies along the riverside. Around it are the cathedral, in somewhat eclectic style and containing the *Virgen del Rosario*, and the Palacio Municipal. On the north side is the **Museo de Arte Decorativo** ① *Santa Fe 748, T0341-480 2547, Thu-Sun 1600-2000, free,* a sumptuous former family residence housing a valuable private collection of paintings, furniture, tapestries, sculptures, and silver, brought mainly from Europe. To the left of the cathedral, the **Pasaje Juramento** is the pedestrian access to the imposing **Monumento a la Bandera** ① *T/F0341-480 2238, Mon 1400-1800, Tue-Sun 0900-1800 (in summer till 1900), US$1 (tower), free (Salón de las Banderas),* an impressively large monument built on the site where General Belgrano raised the Argentine flag for the first time in 1812. The tower has a vantage point 70 m high with excellent panoramic views over the city and the river.

Rosario

Sleeping
Anamundana
  Guest House 2
Boulevard 8
Esplendor Savoy 3
Garden 11
Hostel Passers 6
Hostelpoint 15
Libertador 1
Merit Majestic 7
Plaza Real 9

Presidente 14
Punto Clave Hostel 10
República 4
Riviera 5
Ros Tower 13

Eating
Albaca 13
Amarra 1
Bruno 2
Café de la Opera 10

Cuernavaca 6
Don Ferro 4
Kaffa 11
La Estancia 5
La Sede 12
Rich 7
Rock&Feller's 14
Sr Ming 8
Verde Que Te Quiero
  Verde 9

¡Che!

Ernesto 'Che' Guevara is one of the most recognized faces in the word, and his image can be seen on T-shirts, posters, mugs and key rings virtually everywhere you go. His is an enduring image of youthful revolutionary zeal, something he would have never predicted when he set off on his now legendary travels around South America with a friend and a beaten-up motocycle called *el poderoso*, the powerful one.

The future revolutionary was born into a middle-class family in Rosario in 1928, but his parents soon moved with their asthmatic son to the healthier climate of the Sierras of Córdoba. You can visit the house where they lived in Alta Gracia (see page 200). After growing up in a small town, his eyes were soon opened to the plight of South America's poor during his famous journey around the continent documented in his book *The Motorcycle Diaries*, which is a recommended and entertaining read. Rather than pursue a career in medicine, he decided mid-trip to dedicate the rest of his life to the fight for the 'liberation of the American continent'.

In 1956 he met Fidel Castro in Mexico and together they planned to create the ideal Socialist model in Cuba, as well as establish links with other sympathetic nations. His overriding ambition had always been to spread the revolutionary word, and take the armed struggle to other parts. So he began his fight in Bolivia. After spending a little time in La Paz, he then travelled to a guerrilla base at Nanchuazú. However, the constant movements of the group aroused the suspicion of neighbours and the army were alerted. The group fled and spent several months wandering the steep valleys of eastern Bolivia. In August 1967, the small group was ambushed by Bolivian troops and Ernesto Guevara was executed, photographed and buried in an unmarked grave, aged just 39. In 1997 his body was exhumed and taken to Cuba. The name 'Che' was given to him as a form of reverence. Che in Argentina roughly translates as 'mate' or 'buddy', and is used by friends and family.

From Plaza 25 de Mayo, Calle Córdoba leads west towards Plaza San Martín and the **Paseo del Siglo**, the largest concentration of late 19th- and early 20th-century buildings in the city. The palm-lined **Boulevard Oroño** leads north to the riverside parks, the Rosario Norte railway station and south to the **Pichincha district**, popular for nightlife, and to **Parque Independencia** at the south end. This beautiful 126-ha park was designed by the famous landscape architect Charles Thays. It has a large lake and a **tourist information** ① *Mon-Fri 1500-2100, Sat-Sun 1300-1930*. There are gardens with fountains and fine statues, shady avenues, the Newell's Old Boys football club stadium and three museums in the area.

Just outside the park, the **Museo de Bellas Artes J B Castagnino** ① *J B Castagnino, Av Pellegrini 2202, T0341-480 2542, Wed-Mon 1400-2000, US$1*, is considered one of the best fine arts museums in the country, with a large collection of European paintings, particularly French Impressionist, Italian Baroque and Flemish works, and one of the best collections of paintings and sculpture by renowned Argentine artists.

Next to the stadium is the **Museo Histórico Provincial** ① *Av Pellegrini and Oroño, T0341-480 2542, Tue-Fri 0900-1700, Sat 1500-1800, Sun 1000-1300 (Thu-Sun 1000-1300 in summer), free*, which has a very well displayed collection of Latin American aboriginal artefacts and valuable pieces of religious art including Cuzco-school paintings and a magnificent altar covered with silver plaques, which was used by Pope John Paul II in 1987.

The riverside is lined with several parks, making it a very attractive place to walk. Eight blocks south of the Monumento a la Bandera is an open-air theatre, **Parque Urquiza** ① *T0341-480 2533, shows on Sun 2000, US$01, museum open Sat-Sun 1830-2100, US$1*, and the **Complejo Astronómico Municipal** with an observatory, a planetarium and a small science museum.

Further north is the **Estación Fluvial** where boats leave for excursions around the islands and where you'll find the **Museo del Paraná y las Islas** ① *T0341-440 0751, Wed-Sun 1600-1930, US$0.65*, which gives an insight into islander culture through local art and artefacts. At the foot of the monument is the **Parque a la Bandera**, one of the most appealing parks, and the tourist office, beyond which is the **Parque de España**, a modern red-brick development which incorporates the old railway arches as an exhibition centre and offers fine views over the Río Paraná. Further up the river is the fantastic **Museo de Arte Contemporáneo** (MACRO) ① *Blvd Ortoño on the river shore, T0341-480 4981, www.macromuseo.org.ar, Thu-Wed 1400-2000, US$0.50*. Located inside a massive old silo, this remarkable museum is 10 levels high with one small gallery on each level, and at the top is a viewing deck. Highly recommended.

On Sunday afternoons (from 1500 onwards) there is a great craft market and many antique and vintage-clothing stalls along the river starting at Boulevard Ortoño. Great fun and less crowded than Buenos Aires' markets.

The most popular destination for locals as well as visitors are the dozens of riverside resorts on the islands and sandy banks opposite Rosario. These have restaurants and bars, and most have comfortable facilities for an enjoyable day's stay, with woods, beaches and lagoons. There are campsites and *cabañas* for rent on some of them. Boats depart daily in summer from *La Fluvial* or from *Costa Alta* to the island resorts, each with its own transfer service. Weekend services run throughout the rest of the year.

Santa Fe → *For listings, see pages 415-473. Colour map 4, A5.*

Santa Fe is capital of its province, one of the oldest cities of the country, though there's little architectural evidence and this is not really a tourist destination. It lies near the confluence of the Santa Fe and Salado rivers in a low-lying area with lagoons and islands just west of the Río Paraná and was severely flooded in May 2003, one of Argentina's most shocking disasters. It is connected to the smaller city of Paraná, on the east bank of the river, by road bridges and a tunnel. For more information, see www.turismosantafe.com.ar.

Ins and outs → *Phone code 0342. Population 451,600.*
The airport, **Sauce Viejo** ① *T0342-499 5064* , is located 17 km from the centre. The **bus terminal** ① *Belgrano 2910, T0342-457 4124*, is near to the centre and taxis normally charge US$2. There are luggage lockers available for US$1.50.

Sights
The city's **commercial centre** lies a few blocks southwest of the bus terminal, along the partially pedestrianized San Martín. This street leads southwards to the historic centre, with the oldest buildings and a few museums. On the plaza itself is the cathedral, dating from 1751 but remodelled in 1834, its twin towers capped by blue-tiled cupolas.

Southeast of the plaza is the **Museo Histórico Provincial** ① *3 de Febrero 2553, T0342-457 3529, Tue-Fri 0830-1200, 1500-1900, Sat-Sun 1600-1900, free*, in a former family house dating from 1690 (one of the oldest surviving civil buildings in the country), worth visiting for the house itself rather than the exhibition of two 17th-century Cuzco-school paintings. About 100 m south is the **Iglesia y Convento de San Francisco** built between 1673 and 1695. The church has walls nearly 2 m thick and fine wooden ceilings, built from timber floated down the river from Paraguay, carved by indigenous craftsmen and fitted without the use of nails. The pulpit and altar are 17th-century baroque.

On the opposite side of the park is the superb **Museo Etnográfico y Colonial** ① *Tue-Fri 0830-1200, 1530-1900, Sat-Sun 1530-1830, US$0.50*, with a chronologically ordered exhibition of artefacts from aboriginal inhabitants from 2000 BC to the first Spanish settlers who lived in Santa Fe la Vieja, the town's original site. The most remarkable objects are delicate zoomorphic ceramic pots, Spanish amulets and board games, and a model of both Santa Fe towns, showing that the distribution of the main buildings remained unchanged after the moving.

The city has three very good **tourist information** points: at the **bus terminal** ① *T0342-457 4123, daily 0700-1300, 1500-2100*; at **Paseo del Restaurador** ① *Bulevar Pellegrini and Vittori, T0342-457 1881, daily 0700-1900*; and at **Boca del Tigre** ① *JJ Paso and Dr Zavalía, daily 0700-1900, www.santafeciudad.gov.ar*.

Paraná → *For listings, see pages 415-423. Colour map 4, A5.*

Capital of Entre Ríos province, Paraná stands on the eastern bank of a bend in the Río Paraná, opposite Santa Fe. Its centre lies on a hill offering fine views over the river, and if you're travelling up the Paraná river, it is a good place to stop on a journey north. It was founded in 1649, when Santa Fe was moved from its original spot and settlers crossed the river in search of higher ground for cultivation, and a suitable port. In the mid-19th century it gained importance as capital of the Argentine Confederation and a subsequent period of growth left some sumptuous public buildings. The city's faded splendour creates a quiet, rather melancholic atmosphere but there is an appealingly calm pace of life here. For more information, see www.turismoparana.com.ar.

Ins and outs → *Phone code 0343. Population 247,600.*
Getting there and around The **bus terminal** ① *Av Ramírez 2598, T0343-422 1282*, is 10 blocks from Plaza Primero de Mayo. Leave the small plaza on your right and take Avenida Echagüe right to the centre, or buses No 1, 6, US$0.40. A *remise* taxi will cost US$3. Left-luggage facilities are available Monday to Saturday 0700-2300, and Sunday 0800-1200, 1730-2300, US$2 a day per piece.

The city can easily be visited on foot, since the most interesting sights lie around the two main plazas, Plaza 1 de Mayo and, three blocks north, Plaza Alvear.

Tourist information Paraná has four city **tourist offices** (all open daily 0800-2000): in the centre at ① *Buenos Aires 132, T0343-423 0183*; at the **bus terminal** ① *T0343-420 1862*; at **Parque Urquiza** ① *Av Laurencena and Juan de San Martín, on the east side, T0343-420 1837*; and at the **Hernandarias tunnel**.

Sights

From Plaza Alvear, Avenida Rivadavia leads to the beautiful **Parque Urquiza** and the riverside. Though nothing remains from the colonial period, the city retains many fine 19th- and 20th-century public buildings, centred around Plaza Primero de Mayo. On the east side is the impressive **cathedral**, built in 1883 in Italianate neoclassical style, with a fine dome and colonnaded portico, though the interior is plain. Also on the plaza are the **Municipalidad** (1890), with its distinctive tower, and the **Club Social** (1906), for years the elite social centre of the city. Take pedestrianized San Martín half a block west of the corner with 25 de Junio to see the fine **Teatro 3 de Febrero** (1908). Two blocks north is the **Plaza Alvear**, and opposite one of its corners, the provincial **tourist office** ⓘ *Laprida 5, T0343-422 2100, www.turismo.entrerios.gov.ar, Mon-Fri 0800-2000, Sat 0800-1400*. On the same block is the mildly engaging **Museo Histórico Martiniano Leguizamón** ⓘ *Laprida and Buenos Aires, T0343-431 2735, Tue-Fri 0800-1200, 1530-1930, Sat 0900-1200, 1600-1900, Sun 0900-1200, US$0.75*.

On the west side of the plaza is the **Museo de Bellas Artes** ⓘ *Buenos Aires 355, T0343-420 7868, Tue-Fri 0700-1300, 1500-1900, Sat 1000-1400, 1700-2000, Sun 1000-1300, US$0.75*, housing a vast collection of Argentine artists, with many works by painter Cesáreo Bernaldo de Quirós. On the north side of the plaza is the **Museo de Ciencias Naturales y Antropológicas** ⓘ *Carlos Gardel 62, T0343-420 8894, Tue-Sat 0800-1230, 1400-1800, Sun 0900-1200, US$0.90*, particularly appealing for kids, with an insect collection (see the 25-cm-wide moth), and lots of stuffed animals. Among fascinating artefacts by Guaraní people are a rare ornate urn, with red geometrical paintings, and small utensils made by groups of indigenous peoples to the north, and a rather alarming display of jars containing human foetuses, from five weeks to six months old.

From the northwestern corner of the plaza, it's a pleasant stroll along tree-lined Avenida Rivadavia, with the monumental **Escuela del Centenario** (1910) ⓘ *Av Rivadavia 168*, to reach the city's pride and joy, the **Parque Urquiza**. Extended along the low cliffs of the Paraná river, with wonderful views and many fine statues, the park is well planted with *lapachos, palos borrachos* and pines. There's an open-air theatre, and steps to the Avenida Costanera. The cobbled street **Bajada de los Vascos**, which in the 19th century gave access to the port area, is now known as Puerto Viejo and retains some original buildings. The Avenida Costanera is lively, with restaurants, sports clubs and sandy beaches on the river. The **Paraná Rowing Club** ⓘ *T0343-431 2048, charges US$4 per day* for beach access, including the use of its pool.

North of Paraná → *For listings, see pages 415-423.*

Heading north from Paraná along the Río Paraná, you can take monotonous Route 11 to Resistencia on the western bank, or Route 12 north to Corrientes, which closely follows the eastern banks of the river through varied landscapes giving access to two attractive small towns on the coast with good fishing: Santa Elena and La Paz, and a marvellous traditional *estancia*, **Vizcacheras** ⓘ *www.vizcacheras.com.ar*.

Santa Elena → *Phone code 03437. Population 18,000.*

Santa Elena lies on the Río Paraná about 150 km north of the capital. It is a small port whose fishing attracts many anglers and its history has been associated with that of its meat-packing factory run by British firms from the late 19th century, before it closed down in 1993. The red-brick buildings of the *frigorífico* can still be seen in town. At the end of the *costanera* is the Paseo La Olla, with beautiful views over the river. There is a **tourist office** ① *Eva Perón y 9 de Julio, T03437-481223*.

La Paz → *Colour map 4, A5. Phone code 03437. Population 22,700.*

La Paz, 68 km north of Paraná, is a small port in an area popular for fishing, where the fishing festivals **Fiesta Provincial del Surubí** and **Fiesta Provincial del Dorado** are held respectively every April and September. The undulating terrain and the cliffs above the river make a picturesque setting for the old houses still standing in the town. The **tourist office** ① *Vieytes and España, T03437-422389*, can provide information on accommodation at a few nearby *estancias*.

There is a **Museo Regional**, a small history museum at the Parque Berón de Astrada, from where there are fine views, while another park, the **Parque de la Aventura**, has trails along the riverside for walking or cycling. Access is on the way to La Armonía, reached by Bulevar 25 de Mayo and then Yrigoyen.

Corrientes → *For listings, see pages 415-423. Colour map 1, B6.*

Capital of Corrientes province, some 30 km southwest of the meeting of the rivers Paraná and Paraguay, the city is mainly a service centre for its agricultural hinterland which produces beef, cotton, tobacco, rice and *yerba mate*. Although Corrientes is a less important transport hub than Resistencia, it is a pleasant place for a stopover. The city centre, with its peaceful traditional streets and squares, is well preserved and its *costanera* is one of the most attractive in the country. The national capital of Carnival, the city is also famous as the location of Graham Greene's novel *The Honorary Consul*. In summer the air can be oppressively hot and humid, but in winter the climate is pleasant.

Ins and outs → *Phone code 03783. Population 316,500.*
Camba Punta airport ① *T0343-458684*, is 10 km from the city and is reached by Route 12. *Remise* charge US$4. The **bus terminal** ① *Av Maipú 2600, T0343-446666*, is 5 km from the centre. From the terminal to the centre, take bus No 103 which stops next to the parking area, on Avenida Maipú. A left-luggage facility is available at Crucero del Norte office for US$1 a day, open 0530-0100.

There is a **city tourist office** ① *on the central Plaza Cabral, T03783-428845*, with an information point at Pellegrini 542 ① *T03783-423779, daily 0700-2100*, where you can ask for a good map. The **provincial tourist office** ① *25 de Mayo 1330, T03783-427200, www.corrientes.gov.ar/, Mon-Fri 0700-1300, 1500-2100*, also provides information on the city, as well as other destinations in Corrientes province.

Background

Founded in 1588 on the Paraná river, next to seven relatively high *puntas*, or promontories, by an expedition from Asunción, led by Juan Torres de Vera y Aragón, Corrientes became important as a port on the route between Buenos Aires and Asunción. Numerous shipyards led to the development of a naval industry that endured for centuries. The Guaraní population that inhabited the region were mainly absorbed into the Jesuit missions or became workers for the *estancias*. They progressively mixed with the Spanish newcomers giving the local society a distinctive character, still evident today in the faces of the inhabitants, and also in the daily use of Guaraní words and a particular accent in the spoken Spanish.

Sights

The main Plaza 25 de Mayo, one block inland from the *costanera*, is a beautiful shady space. You could take a pleasant stroll from here around the surrounding blocks, with their fine old houses and river views, and to the Avenida Costanera. On the north side of the plaza is the **Jefatura de Policía**, built in 19th-century French style. The **Museo de Artesanías** ① *Quintana 905, Mon-Fri 0800-1200, 1600-2000, free,* is a large old house with an exhibition of handicrafts made from the most diverse materials imaginable, by indigenous groups, as well as by contemporary urban and rural artisans. Tiny skeleton-shaped images represent San La Muerte, a popular devotion that ensures the bearer a painless death. A large room at the front is a workshop where you can watch the patient work of the local craftspeople. On the east side of the plaza are the Italianate **Casa de Gobierno** (1881-1886) and the **Ministerio de Gobierno**. On the south side is the church **La Merced**, where there are confessionals carved by the indigenous inhabitants of Misiones in the mid-18th century, and a colonial-style altar. The **Casa Lagraña**, a huge building with three interior patios, built in 1860 for the governor, lies one block south. At 9 de Julio 1044 is the **Museo Histórico** ① *Tue-Fri 0800-1200, 1600-2000, free,* displaying among other pieces a collection of religious objects dating from the 18th and 19th centuries. Only two blocks north is the **Teatro Juan de Vera** ① *San Juan 637, T03783-427743,* a lively cultural centre and a beautiful building itself (1913). Across the road is the **Museo de Bellas Artes** ① *San Juan 634, Tue-Fri 0800-1200, 1630-2030, free,* a small arts museum with temporary exhibitions and a permanent collection including valuable works by the painters Petorutti, Fader and Quinquela Martín. The quite impressive **Iglesia y Convento de San Francisco** ① *Mendoza 450,* was rebuilt in 1861 on the site of the original which dated from 1608. Six blocks south of the Plaza 25 de Mayo is the leafy Plaza de la Cruz and opposite, the church of **La Cruz de los Milagros** that houses the Santo Madero, a miraculous cross placed by the founder of the city, the miracle occurring, allegedly, when the indigenous residents who tried to burn it were killed by lightning from a cloudless sky. Near the plaza, the **Museo de Ciencias Naturales 'Amadeo Bonpland'** ① *San Martín 850, Mon-Sat 0900-1200, 1600-2000,* has a large archaeology collection and plants with a remarkable display of 5800 insects including a huge wasp nest.

The attractive Avenida Costanera, lined with *lapachos* and *palos borrachos*, leads along the Río Paraná from its southwestern end, next to the bridge, to **Parque Mitre**, from where there are good views of sunsets over the river. On the intersection with Junín, there is a small **zoo** ① *Tue-Sun 0900-1830,* by the river, with animals from the region.

◉ Río Paraná listings

For Sleeping and Eating price codes and other relevant information, see Essentials pages 30-36.

● Sleeping

Rosario *p408, map p409*
For more listings, see www.rosarioturismo.com (in English).
AL Plaza Real, Santa Fe 1632, T0 341-440 8800, www.plazarealhotel.com. This 139-room hotel does everything a luxury 5-star hotel should. Modern, spacious rooms, good service and a nice pool.
AL Ros Tower, Mitre 299, T0341-529900, www.rostower.com.ar. Stunning 5-star hotel with wonderfully big beds, great views and a luxurious spa complex. Check special deals.
AL-A Esplendor Savoy, San Lorenzo 1022, T0341-429 6007, www.esplendorsavoy rosario.com. The recently remodelled hotel is the best in Rosario. Originally opened in 1910, this grand hotel fell into disrepair;

however, now it is back with uber-stylish modern rooms, a chic pool, a spa and sauna, roof garden and the wonderful **Restaurant Savoy Grand Café**.

A Garden, Callao 39, T0341-437 0025, www.hotelgardensa.com.ar. This is a good, though pricey, option a little way from the centre in the Pichincha district (next to Blvd Oroño) with comfortable superior rooms (**A**) and a great pool. Also restaurant and children's play area.

A Riviera, San Lorenzo 1460, T0341-424 2058, www.solans.com. A 4-star hotel whose superior rooms (**A**) are very good while the cheaper standard rooms are smaller but still comfortable, with a warmer decor. Both include a large breakfast, and there is a sauna, a gym and a restaurant. The same chain owns 3 more hotels: **Libertador**, Av Corrientes 752, T0341-424 1158; **Presidente**, Av Corrientes 919, T0341-424 2789; and the slightly cheaper **República**, San Lorenzo 955, T/0341-424 3395.

B Merit Majestic Hotel, San Lorenzo 980, T0341-440 5872, www.amerian.com. Newly opened and reburbished, this 3-star hotel is modern and inviting. The 51 rooms are well designed and the ornate turn-of-the-century building adds a stylish atmosphere.

C Hotel Boulevard, San Lorenzo 2194, T0341-447 5795, www.hotelboulevard. com.ar. This small 1920s house has been tastefully renovated, and now is a charming bed and breakfast with doubles and triples. Recommended.

Hostels

F pp **Hostel Point**, Catamarca 1837, T0341-440 9337, www.hostelpoint.com.ar. Central and wonderfully designed, this hostel is a gem. Brightly coloured dorms and a lovely double (**D**) make this a great place to stay. Recommended.

F pp **Anamundana Guest House**, Montevideo 1248, T0341-424 3077, www.anamundanahostel.com. Located in an old terraced house that has been sparsely but stylishly decorated, this hostel has dorms and doubles with high celings and original windows and doors. It can be noisy at times.

F pp **Punto Clave Hostel**, Ituzaingo 246, T0341-481569, www.puntoclavehostel. com.ar. A fun, brightly coloured hostel with spacious dorms, a comfortable common area with big bean bags and helpful owners. Recommended.

F pp **Passers Hostel**, 1 Mayo 1117, T0341-155896242, www.passershostel.com.ar. Funky wallpaper and furniture make this hostel stand out from the rest. The dorms aren't as nicely decorated but they are clean and spacious. Located only a few metres from the Monumento a la Bandera.

Sante Fe *p411*

All listed hotels lie within 10 blocks of the bus terminal. For more listings, see www.santafe-turistica.com.ar.

A Conquistador, 25 de Mayo 2676, T0342-400 1195, www.oha.com.ar/santafe/hotel conquistador. Worth the price only if you use the pool, the sauna and the gym, all included in the rate.

A Riogrande, San Gerónimo 2580, T0342-450 0700, www.hotel-riogrande.com.ar. Santa Fe's best hotel has very good rooms, with slightly smaller standard ones. A large breakfast is included.

B Castelar, 25 de Mayo 2349 y Peatonal Falucho, T/F0342-4560999, www.castelar santafe.com.ar. On a small plaza, this old-style hotel built in the 1930s is a good-value option, offering comfortable accommodation in a formal atmosphere. Breakfast is included. It has a smart but welcoming restaurant on the ground floor.

B Hostal Santa Fe de la Veracruz, San Martín 2954, T0342-455 1740, www.hostalsf.com. Traditionally one of the top hotels in town, with 2 types of room categories, both good value. Price includes a large breakfast, checkout is at 1800. Has a restaurant, use of the sauna is extra.

Hostels

F pp **Santa Fe Hostel**, Blvd Galvez 2175, T0342-455 4000, www.santafe-hostel.com. Very basic hostel, 11 blocks from the centre.

Paraná *p412*
AL Marán Suites & Towers, Av Rivadavia y Mitre, T0343-423 5444, www.maran.com.ar. An impressive modern tower on Parque Urquiza with very comfortable, light, functional and simply decorated rooms. The splendid views over the park and the river are the main reasons for choosing this pricey hotel.
B Gran Hotel Paraná, Urquiza 976, T0343-422 3900, www.hotelesparana.com.ar. Overlooking Plaza Primero de Mayo, this large hotel offers 3 types of room (all with breakfast included), pricey standard rooms, but very comfortable and spacious superior rooms. It has a gym and the smart restaurant, La Fourchette.
C San Jorge, Belgrano 368, T/F0343-422 1685, www.sanjorgehotel.com.ar. With palm trees growing on the street outside, this is an attractive renovated house, made welcoming by friendly staff and owners. There are cheaper old-style rooms (avoid noisy rooms closer to reception) or modern ones at the back with renovated bathrooms and TV. A light breakfast is included, and there are cooking facilities.

Hostels
F Paraná Hostel, Andrés Pazos 159, T0343-455 0847, www.paranahostel.com.ar. A small, central hostel with a nice living room, with cable TV and comfy sofas. Smart dorms and private rooms available. Best budget option in the area.

Santa Elena *p413*
A pp Estancia Vizcacheras, R12, Km 554.5, T011-4719 5613 (in Buenos Aires), www.vizcacheras.com.ar. South of Santa Elena, the Bovril *estancia* was built in the early 1900s in British colonial-style with Argentine touches. The owners are extremely hospitable, making guests feel at home in luxuriously furnished bedrooms, all with their own bathroom (some with old fashioned baths) and private verandas. Have drinks on the terrace with splendid views of the gardens and the grasslands beyond, and delicious dinner served under the stars. You'll be invited to see the daily routines of the working cattle ranch, with walking and horse riding, fishing and birdwatching also arranged. Highly recommended.

La Paz *p414*
C Milton, Italia 1029, T03437-422232, www.miltonhotel.com.ar. Central, with comfortable enough rooms. A/c and breakfast extra.
C Posta Surubí, España 224, T03437-421128, www.postasurubipesca.com.ar. Nicely located by the river with good rooms and fine views. Has a restaurant. Breakfast included.

Corrientes *p414*
For more listings search for Corrientes in www.welcomeargentina.com (in English).
L La Alondra, 2 de abril 827, T03783-430555, www.laalondra.com.ar. The best place to stay in town. 7 beautiful rooms, a dining table to die for, and a wonderful communal area. Antique furniture throughout, exquisite styling and a wonderful homely feel. Lovely patio and 12-m pool. Simply unmissable.
AL-A Corrientes Plaza, Junín 1549, T/F03783-466500, www.hotel-corrientes. com.ar. A large, business-oriented hotel with plain, comfortable rooms, gym and small pool.
A Gran Hotel Guaraní, Mendoza 970, T03783-433800, www.hguarani.com.ar. A 4-star business-oriented hotel with restaurant, pool and gym. 4 types of room, slightly differing in comfort, all functional, well equipped but with plain decor. Large breakfast included.
B-C Costanera Hotel, Plácido Martínez 1098, T/F03783-436100. Standard rooms are nothing special, but the superior ones (**B**) are certainly more comfortable. There's a small pool on the roof and a restaurant, and breakfast is included.

Hostels
F pp Bienvenida Golondrina, La Rioja 455, T03783-435316, http://bvngolondrina. blogspot.com/. The first and only hostel in the city. Just ½ a block from the port, this century-old building has been renovated and carefully remodelled. Bright, freshly

painted dorms, an ultra-modern kitchen, a roof-top terrace and lots of internal patios to relax in. Recommended.

🅞 Eating

Rosario *p408, map p409*

See www.rosarioalacarta.com.ar, for a comprehensive list of dining options. A lot of restaurants can be found along Av Pellegrini from Blvd Oroño to Buenos Aires, and the whole area is packed at weekends.

♔♔-♔♔ Sr Ming, La Fluvial, T0341-411 8000, walk along the coast from the monument to the flag until you see this restaurant. Fantastic view over the river in a wonderful Japanese-style garden. Upmarket sushi joint. Recommended.

♔♔ Amarra, Av Belgrano 720 and Buenos Aires, T0341-447550. Good food, including fish and seafood, served in a formal atmosphere. Cheap set menus Mon-Fri lunchtimes.

♔♔ Bruno, Montevideo and Av Ovidio Lagos. For home-made pastas and a good wine list.

♔♔ Don Ferro, España (next to the river), T0341-421 1927. Very stylish café overlooking the river. Good seafood and pizzas.

♔♔ Escauriza, Bajada Escauriza and Paseo Ribereño, north of centre at La Florida. The most traditional fish restaurant in Rosario serving tasty *dorado*, *surubí*, *pacú* or *boga*.

♔♔ La Estancia, Av Pellegrini 1510 and Paraguay. Typical good *parrilla* popular with locals a few blocks east of Parque Independencia.

♔♔ Rich, San Juan 1031, T0341-411 5151. This is a classic in Rosario. The food is superb. There's a widely varied menu and good set meals including delicious pastas, excellent meats and many different salads. Rarities such as *milanesa de yacaré* (alligator *milanesas*) are occasionally served. Recommended.

♔ Cuernavaca, Blvd Oroño and Wheelwright, T0341-455 0968. Great western-themed *parrilla* restaurant opposite the riverside Sun markets. Good option for lunch.

Cafés

Café de la Opera, Mendoza and Laprida 1235 (next to the access to the Teatro El Círculo), T0341-421 9402. Open afternoons and evenings. Regular performances of jazz, tango, Russian folk music, poetry and storytelling in this pretty, antique café.

Kaffa, Córdoba 1473. Good coffee served inside the large bookshop El Ateneo.

La Sede, San Lorenzo and Entre Ríos. An extremely popular café, crowded at lunchtimes with office workers.

Rock&Feller's, Córdoba 2019. Open every day from 0800, this is a great place for eating outside on their patio, inside in the wooden, antique bar or whilst watching a game of football. International fare including great Tex-Mex options. Popular at night too. Highly recommended.

Verde que te quiero Verde, Córdoba 1358, www.verdequetequiero.com. Great vegetarian café open everyday, serving a fantastic brunch and lots of good veggie options. Recommended.

Victoria, Jujuy and Blvd Oroño. One of the oldest cafés in town and most traditional, turns into a bar at night.

Sante Fe *p411*

♔♔ El Quincho de Chiquito, Av Almirante Brown 1700 and Obispo Príncipe, next to boxer Carlos Monzón's statue (on Costanera Oeste). A classic fish restaurant, excellent food and good value, with huge helpings.

♔♔ España, San Martín 2644. An elegant place, serving good food.

♔ Club Sirio Libanés, 25 de Mayo 2740. Very good Middle Eastern dishes, reasonably priced. It is popular with families at Sun lunchtime.

♔ El Brigadier, San Martín 1670. This colonial-style place next to the Plaza 25 de Mayo serves superb *surubí al paquete* (stuffed fish) and many *parrilla* dishes.

♔ Rivadavia, Rivadavia 3299. Traditional *parrilla* serving excellent grills and good pastas.

Paraná p412

Giovani, Urquiza 1047. A popular place in the centre, good for pasta.

La Fourchette, Urquiza 976 (at Gran Hotel Paraná). The finest restaurant in town is a small, stylish place. Choose from a small menu of really fine dishes. Perfect for a sophisticated, intimate dinner.

Club de Pescadores, access from Av Estrada at Puerto Viejo. Another good traditional fish restaurant in the old and picturesque section of the port.

Coscoino, Corrientes 373. A relaxed family establishment serving good and very filling home made pastas, *tenedor libre*, except Sat evenings and Sun lunchtime.

El Viejo Marino, Av Laurencena 341, the opposite end of Av Costanera. Well-prepared fish dishes.

Nos sobran los motivos, Colón and San Juan, for very good tapas in a cheerful atmosphere that includes live shows on Thu and Sun.

Playa, Av Costanera (at Club Atlético Estudiantes). Nicely situated on a sandy beach with fine views of the river. A good place for fish such as *surubí*, *boga* or *pejerrey* (caught upstream in Corrientes or Misiones).

Cafés

Viejo Paraná, Buenos Aires and Av Rivadavia (on Plaza Alvear). Appealing café.

Corrientes p414

Most options are in the centre and on the *costanera*.

El Mirador, Av Costanera and Edison. A large place, good for *parrilla*, and local fish.

El Solar, San Lorenzo 830. With an informal atmosphere, and busy at lunchtime, this self-service restaurant serves decent and cheap salads, pastas and *milanesas*.

Las Brasas, Av Costanera and San Martín (near beach). Another large place good for *parrilla*, and local fish.

Cafés

Martha de Bianchetti, 9 de Julio and Mendoza. A smart café and bakery.

Panambí, on pedestrianized Junín, near Córdoba. A traditional central *confitería*, ideal for delicious pastries and the regional bread-like speciality, *chipá*.

Bars and clubs

Rosario p408, map p409
Bars

Rock & Feller's, Córdoba 2019. American-style bar, with a mix of pop icons and the sumptuous art-deco design of an old house.

Roots Reggae Bar, Pte Roca 1051. This lively place is owned by the people who run the HI hostel in town. Good music, always busy.

Piluso, Catamarca and Alvear. A lively meeting point at night, also open during the day.

Victoria, Jujuy and Blvd Oroño. One of the oldest cafés in town and the most traditional.

Sante Fe p411

Santa Fe has a long tradition of brewing, and is one of the few places where local lagers can compete with the big national monopoly, Quilmes. Beer is usually sold in a *liso* (not a very large glass). There are lively areas of bars and nightclubs, popular with young crowds, all along the Costanera Este, beyond the bridge on Laguna Setúbal, in the Recoleta district, north of centre, around plaza Los Constituyentes, and next to Blvd Pellegrini and to Blvd Gálvez.

Don Ernesto, San Martín and General López. A traditional café in the civic centre.

Las Delicias, Hipólito Yrigoyen and San Martín. A well-preserved, early 20th-century café and bakery, with beautiful decor, serving a wide variety of coffees and sweet pastries. Try their speciality, the *alfajorsantafesino*.

Tokio, Rivadavia y Crespo (on Plaza España). Another café with a rich history in Santa Fe.

☻ Entertainment

Rosario *p408, map p409*
A good listings guide can be found in a section of the daily paper *Pagina 12*: *Rosario 12*, as well as www.viarosario.com.

Cinema
In the centre there is **Del Siglo**, Córdoba and Presidente Roca (at the Shopping Mall Del Siglo); **El Cairo**, Santa Fe 1120; and **El Patio**, Sarmiento 778. In the mall, **Alto Rosario**, Caning and Junín.

Cultural centres
Centro Cultural Bernardino Rivadavia, San Martín 1080, T0341-480 2401, www.ccbr. gov.ar. A large centre holding all year round art exhibitions, video screenings, plays, music shows, seminars and puppet shows.
Centro Cultural Parque de España, on Parque de España, T0341-426 0941, www.ccpe.org.ar. Shows temporary art exhibitions, photography and plays at the **Teatro Príncipe de Asturias**.
Centro de Expresiones Contemporáneas, Sargento Cabral and el Río (on the riverside, opposite Ex Aduana building), T0341-480 2245, www.cecrosario.org.ar. A large warehouse with almost daily music, theatre and cinema events.

Theatre
De la Comedia, Cortada Ricardone y Mitre, T0341-480 2597; **El Círculo**, Laprida 1235, T0341-424 5349; **Lavarden**, Mendoza and Sarmiento, T0341-472 1462.

☻ Festivals and events

Rosario *p408, map p409*
20 Jun Flag Day. It is worth going to the Monumento a la Bandera for the swearing-in ceremony made by hundreds of school pupils to the country's flag.
Nov Fiesta de las Colectividades. Every year during the first part of Nov at the Parque

a la Bandera (opposite the monument) the town celebrates the diverse origins of the inhabitants, offering food, folk music and dancing from 1800 onwards. The main show is on 11 Nov, the **Day of Tradition**.

Corrientes *p414*
Feb Carnival, www.carnaval-corrientes. com.ar. Has been one of the most popular celebrations for decades in Argentina and is celebrated on Fri and Sat evenings throughout Feb at the Corsódromo. This stadium lies a little distance from the centre reached by bus No 105 along 9 de Julio. The colourful parade opens the competition among the different *comparsas*, passionately supported by the audience as football teams. Tickets are not sold in the stadium, but in many shops in the centre.
Dec/Jan Chamamé Festival. The regional music *chamamé* has its own festival in Corrientes at Anfiteatro Tránsito Cocomarola, Barrio 1000 Viviendas, 10 blocks south of Av 3 de Abril. This cheerful music is danced in couples with the upper body close, legs far apart. Join in!

☉ Shopping

Rosario *p408, map p409*
The main shopping street is the pedestrianized Córdoba.

Books
Balcarce, San Lorenzo 1576, a massive place for second-hand books and vinyl records; **El Ateneo**, Córdoba 1473; **Stratford**, Santa Fe 1340, sells English books.

Markets
Feria del Boulevard, Blvd Oroño and Rivadavia. A weekend handicraft market.
Mercado de Pulgas, next to the tourist office on the riverside. Flea market at weekends,
Mercado Retro La Huella, Av del Valle and Callao (next to Rosario Norte railway station at Pichincha district). Every Sun and bank holiday there is a large flea market.

Outdoor gear
Central de Pesca, San Juan 1089;
El Combatiente, San Martín 816.

Shopping malls
Alto Rosario, Caning and Junín, an impressive
mall; Del Siglo, Córdoba and Presidente Roca;
Palace Garden, Córdoba 1358.

▲▲ Activities and tours

Rosario *p408, map p409*
Swimming
On Laguna Setúbal, from El Espigón; the
Club de Regatas, next to the bridge; or
from Piedras Blancas on Costanera Este.

Tour operators
For city tours check agencies at Asociación
Rosarina de Agencias de Viaje, T0341-421
3554, www.arav.org.ar.
Barco Ciudad de Rosario, T0341-449 8688,
www.barcocr1.com. A large passenger
boat leaves from the pier next to Estación
Fluvial for 2-hr excursions on the river on
weekend afternoons.
Catamarán Victoria Austral, leaving on
weekend afternoons from Estación Fluvial.
Transporte Fluvial del Litoral, T0341-
454 4684. This operator used to run the
regular boat service to Victoria (check if
it's still running, recommended) from
Estación Fluvial; also has boats for hire
at US$25 per hr for up to 10 people.

Paraná *p412*
Tour operators
Costanera 241, Buenos Aires 212, T0343-
423 4385, www.costanera241.com. City tours
and boat excursions on the Paraná river.
Equilibrio, General López 3697, T0343-
459 9663. Offer day trips and city tours.

⊖ Transport

Rosario *p408, map p409*
Air
For airport information, see page 408.
    Daily flights to Buenos Aires with
Aerolíneas Argentinas and Aerovip, 45 mins.
    Airline offices Aerolíneas Argentinas,
Santa Fe 1412, T0341-424 9333; Aerovip,
Mitre 830 local 32, T0341-449 6800.

Boat
Modern terminal called Estación Fluvial
(known as La Fluvial), Av de los Inmigrantes
410, opposite Monumento a la Bandera,
T0341-447 3838. The main departure point
for boat transfer to the island resorts.
    At Costa Alta, situated between La
Florida and the suspension bridge, is a pier
also used for passenger boats going to the
island resorts. Tickets US$5 return, boat
services every 30 mins in the summer to
some resorts, with a few weekend services
during the rest of the year.

Bus
For bus terminal information, see page 408.
    From the centre, take buses on Plaza
25 de Mayo, via C Santa Fe to the bus
terminal. Taxi US$3. Several companies go
to the main destinations. To Buenos Aires,
5 hrs, US$16; to Córdoba, 6 hrs, US$22;
to Santa Fe, 2 hrs 20 mins, US$6. To Puerto
Iguazú, 18 hrs, US$65.

Car hire
Avis, San Nicolás 620, T0341-435 2297;
Hertz at the airport, T0341-451 3220;
Olé, Gorriti 151, T0341-438 6593.

Taxi
Radio Taxis (painted in black and yellow),
T0341-482 2222. For a *remise* taxi, contact
Nuevo Estilo, T0341-454 3000; Primera
Clase, T0341-454 5454.

Train

The **Buenos Aires–Tucumán** service operated by TBA, T0800-333 3822, stops weekly in Rosario, though at inconvenient times in the day and tickets are only sold just before departures, at the station. To **Tucumán**, US$20; to **Buenos Aires**, US$10.

Sante Fe *p411*
Air

For airport information, see page 411. Taxis charge US$5 from the bus terminal and a bus with a yellow 'L', signed Aeropuerto, stops on C San Luis (1 block from bus terminal), 20 mins, US$1.

Daily flights to **Buenos Aires** with Aerolíneas Argentinas and Aerovip.

Airline offices Aerolíneas Argentinas, 25 de Mayo 2287, T0342-452 5959; Aerovip, Lisandro de la Torre 2570, T0342-452 2491.

Bus

For bus terminal information, see page 411.

To **Buenos Aires**, 6 hrs, US$23, several companies. To **Córdoba**, 5 hrs, US$21, several companies. To **Paraná**, 50 mins, US$3, ETACER, Fluviales. To **Rosario**, 2 hrs 20 mins, US$2, several companies. To **Cayastá** (marked Helvecia), 1 hr 40 mins, US$2, Paraná Medio.

Car hire

Hertz, 25 de Mayo 1925, T0342-458 2583.

Taxis (radio and remise)

Santa Fe, Moreno 2512, T0342-459 5906.

Paraná *p412*
Bus

For bus terminal information, see page 412.

To **Buenos Aires**, 6-7 hrs, US$25, Basa; Flecha Bus; San José. To **Santa Fe**, every 20 mins, 50 mins, US$2, ETACER; Fluviales. To **Corrientes**, 8-9 hrs, US$23, Flecha Bus. To **Puerto Iguazú**, 15 hrs, US$58, Expreso Singer. To **Colón**, 4-5 hrs, US$7, Flecha Bus; Paccot. To **Diamante**, 1 hr, US$2, several

companies. To **La Paz**, 3 hrs, US$5, ETA. To **Victoria**, 2-3 hrs, US$4, several companies.

Car hire

Travel Rent a Car, Malvinas 102, T0343-423 1707.

Remise taxis

Ciudad Paisaje, T0343-423 2100; Tele-Radio, T0343-424 6565.

Corrientes *p414*
Air

For airport information, see page 414. Minibus pick-ups from hotels to the airport, T0343-450072, US$3 (US$3.50 to Resistencia airport).

Flights to **Buenos Aires** with Aerolíneas Argentinas, 1 hr 20 mins.

Airline offices Aerolíneas Argentinas, Junín 1301, T0343-428678.

Bus

For bus terminal information, see page 414. To reach the terminal take bus No 103 (check with the driver, as same line has many different routes) from Carlos Pellegrini and Córdoba (or any stop along Carlos Pellegrini and Salta), 20 mins, US$0.70. Bus tickets can be bought at same prices at many offices other than the company's own.

From the town centre, several buses or *combis* go to nearby towns from the centre, with stops around Plaza Cabral or along central streets. To **Santa Ana**, bus No 11 (Santa Ana), from 9 de Julio y Catamarca, 30 mins, US$1.50. To **Paso de la Patria**, Mir, office in Paso de la Patria at La Rioja and 12 de Octubre, T0343-494654, or Silvitur, 8 de Diciembre 234 (in Paso de la Patria), T0343-494260; both charge US$2. To **Empedrado**, Empedrado minibus, Mendoza 837, T0343-1568 7431, US$3. These destinations also have regular buses from terminal. The port area around Av Costanera and La Rioja is another transport hub with buses Chaco-Corrientes leaving regularly to **Resistencia**, 40 mins, US$2 return.

To **Empedrado**, US$2.50, López;
Nuevo Expreso; San Justo. To **Mburucuyá**,
2½ hrs, US$5, San Antonio. To **Mercedes**,
3 hrs, US$12. To **Paso de la Patria**, 5 daily,
US$2.50 (tickets on bus), **Paso de la Patria**.

To **Santa Ana**, bus No 11 (Santa Ana),
US$2 (tickets on bus), every 2 to 3 hrs.
To **Posadas**, 3½-4 hrs, US$14, several
companies. To **Puerto Iguazú**, 8-9½ hrs,
US$29, **Aguila Dorada Bis** (change at
Posadas); Autotransportes Mendoza;
Crucero del Norte; Expreso Singer. To
Resistencia bus terminal, 30 mins, US$2
(for going to city centre, get off at traffic
lights immediately after supermarket
Libertad and take bus No 9, US$0.50,
stopping there; not recommended at
night), Puerto Tirol.

To **Buenos Aires**, 11-12 hrs, US$41,
several companies. To **Salta**, 13-14 hrs,
US$40, **Norte Bis** or La Nueva Estrella
(change at Resistencia). To **Tucumán**,
12-15 hrs, US$39, **La Nueva Estrella**;
Nuevo Rápido Tata; Vosa.

Remise taxi
Interprovincial, Av Costanera and La Rioja.

◑ Directory

Rosario p408, map p409
Banks Many banks along Córdoba, east
of plaza San Martín. **Currency exchange**
Banex, Mitre and Santa Fe; Transatlántica,
Mitre and Rioja; **Western Union**, Laprida y
San Juan. **Emergencies** Medical
emergencies T107, T0341-435 1111; Police
T101, T0341-448 6666. **Internet** Several
places in centre charging US$0.50 per hr.
Language schools Global Idiomas, San
Martín 876, 2nd floor, T0341-424 4407,
www.globalidiomas.com.ar, small central
school that can book travel within Argentina

as well as accommodation in Rosario;
Punto Spanish, Italia 1209, T0341-447 7212,
www.puntospanish.com, Spanish school
that can also organize accommodation
and, in the future, volunteering in the area.
Medical services Hospital de Emergencias
Clemente Alvarez, T0341-4808111; Hospital
de Niños Víctor Vilela (Children's Hospital),
T0341-480 8133. **Post office** Córdoba and
Buenos Aires.

Sante Fe p411
Banks Banking district around San Martín
and Tucumán. **Currency exchange**
Columbia, San Martín 2275; Tourfe, San
Martín 2500. **Internet** El Shuk, San Martín
and Corrientes, US$0.50 per hr; Xiver, 9 de
Julio 2344, US$0.40 per hr. **Post office**
C San Martín between Tucumán and
La Rioja, Western Union branch.

Paraná p412
Banks Banco de la Nación, San Martín 1000;
Banco Francés, San Martín 763; Banco Río,
Pellegrini 29. **Internet** Several broadband
places in the centre and along Av Rivadavia.
Medical services Hospital San Martín,
Perón 450, T0343-431 2222. **Police** T0343-
420 9038. **Post office** 25 de Mayo and
Monte Caseros, Western Union branch.

Corrientes p414
Banks Bank Boston, San Juan and Carlos
Pellegrini; Banco de la Nación, 9 de Julio and
Córdoba. **Currency exchange** El Dorado,
9 de Julio 1343, Western Union branch.
Emergencies Medical emergencies: T107;
Police T101. **Internet** Brujas, Mendoza 787,
US$0.70 per hr. **Post office** San Juan and
San Martín. **Medical services** Hospital
Escuela General San Martín, Rivadavia 1250,
T03783-420695; Sanatorio del Norte, Carlos
Pellegrini 1358, T03783-421600.
Telephone Several *locutorios* in centre.

The Argentine Chaco

Little visited by travellers, the Argentine Chaco is just part of an immense sprawling lowland some 900 km wide, covering half of Paraguay and huge areas of Bolivia and Brazil. Rising gently from east to west, it's crossed by meandering rivers, and filled in central parts with cattle and cotton fields, soya and sunflowers. Though much of the Chaco is inaccessible, with little public transport, and rough roads that become almost impassable after heavy rains, two national parks can easily be reached all year round, both hosting a rich diversity of wildlife largely uninterrupted by human activity: Parque Nacional Chaco reached from Resistencia, and Parque Nacional Río Pilcomayo reached from Formosa. These are the region's two main cities, both close to Río Paraguay, and the only other settlement is uninspiring Presidencia Roque Sáenz Peña, 170 km northwest of Resistencia, though its thermal waters are among the country's finest.

The most fascinating aspect of the Chaco is its pure and extensive indigenous population. Two of the largest groups are the Toba, mainly settled in towns next to the Paraná river, and the semi-nomadic Wichí in the west, who maintain their traditions of fine weaving, woodwork and ancient fishing techniques. For more information, see www.chacoturismo.com. ▸▸ For listings, see pages 428-430.

Ins and outs

Getting there From Resistencia and Formosa, parallel Routes 16 and 81 head dead straight northwest across the plains until they encounter the first hills of eastern Salta, which mark the border of this vast territory. Buses to Salta take Route 16, while Route 81 has long unpaved sections west of the small town of Las Lomitas, making the journey tough going after heavy rains.

Background

The Chaco falls into two distinct zones along a line south of the boundary between Chaco and Formosa provinces: the Wet Chaco and the Dry Chaco. The **Wet Chaco** spreads south from the Río Pilcomayo (the border with Paraguay) and west of the Río Paraguay, fertile wetlands supporting rich farming and abundant vegetation, marshlands with savanna and groves of *Caranday* palms, hosting many species of birds. Further west, as rainfall diminishes, the **Dry Chaco** is arid and wild, with little plant life, or indeed human life. The scrub vegetation, dotted with the algarrobo trees, white quebracho, the spiny bloated trunks of palo borracho and various types of cacti. This is one of the hottest places in South America – the western part of the Chaco has been known as 'El Impenetrable'.

Resistencia → *For listings, see pages 428-430. Colour map 1, B6.*

The hot and energetic capital of the Province of Chaco, Resistencia is the commercial centre for the Chaco region together with the port of Barranqueras, just to the south on the Río Paraná. It's a modern city, not architecturally rich, but boasting an impressive number of sculptures by renowned artists, earning it the title of 'city of statues'. There's also a splendid central plaza, a nature reserve and the lovely **Isla del Cerrito** within easy reach, making it an appealing alternative stopover to neighbouring Corrientes on the journey between Iguazú and Salta.

Ins and outs → *Phone code 03722. Population 274,500.*

The **airport** ① *T03722-424425*, is 8 km west of town. There is no bus and taxis charge US$4. The **bus terminal** ① *Av Malvinas Argentinas and Av MacLean, T03722-461098*, is on the western outskirts, taxis charge US$2. Left luggage on the platform, open 24 hours, US$0.50 a day.

Sights

The large Plaza 25 de Mayo occupies four blocks in the centre of the city, with a variety of indigenous plants and palms turning it into a mini botanical garden. Here, you'll find the city **tourist office** ① *Mon-Fri 0800-2000, T03722-458289*. If they can't give you a map try the **provincial tourist office** ① *Santa Fe 178, T03722-423547, Mon-Fri 0630-2000, Sat 0800-1200*, where you can also get information on other destinations.

Five blocks from here, there's an informal cultural centre, **Fogón de los Arrieros** (literally, 'the hearth of the muleteers') ① *Brown 350 (between López and Planes and French), T03722-426418, open to non-members Mon-Sat 0900-1200, Mon-Fri 2100-2300, US$2*. This rather wonderful institution was formed in the late 1960s by artists who decided to make the city an open-air gallery, with public spaces filled with sculpture and murals. The centre itself still operates as a meeting place and exhibition space. Inspiring, and highly recommended. In the surrounding streets, you'll find more than 175 pieces of art by the country's finest artists.

Take López and Planes (later Sáenz Peña) and turn right at Juan B Justo to reach the **Museo del Hombre Chaqueño** ① *Juan B Justo 280, Mon-Fri 0800-1200, 1600-2000, free*. This small anthropological museum covers the story of colonization in the region, with a fine exhibition of handicrafts by native Wichi, Toba and Mocoví peoples, together with a fascinating mythology section in which small statues represent the Guaraní peoples' beliefs. Many of the rituals detailed are still practised in rural areas today, and are characterized by creatures of the marsh and woodland.

The **Isla del Cerrito**, a beautiful island northeast of Resistencia at the confluence of the Paraná and Paraguay rivers, has a provincial nature reserve of 12,000 ha, covered mainly with grassland and palm trees. At the eastern end of the island (51 km from Resistencia), on the Río Paraná, in Cerrito, there's an attractive tourist complex with white sand beaches, a history museum, accommodation and restaurants, all very busy during the **Fiesta Nacional del Dorado** on the opposite shores in Paso de la Patria. Follow Route 16 east and turn north 3 km before the bridge to Corrientes: from here a road, the last 20 km of which are dirt (difficult after heavy rain), leads to a bridge, from where it is 17 km further to Cerrito. **Combi Arco Iris** ① *3 daily at 0600, 1100 and 1900, 1 hr's journey, stopping 30 mins there, US$1.75*, has daily services to Cerrito, leaving from bus stop at Juan B Justo and Avenida Alberdi (off Banco Hipotecario).

Parque Nacional Chaco → *Colour map 1, B6.*
① *Access to the park is free, open 24 hrs, T03725-496166.*

The Chaco National Park, 115 km northwest of Resistencia, extends over 15,000 ha and protects one of the last remaining untouched areas of the Wet Chaco with its exceptional *quebracho colorado* trees, *Caranday* palms and dense riverine forests, with orchids growing along the banks of the Río Negro. It is a very good place for birdwatching, with 340 species having been sighted in the park, including the parrot *loro hablador*. You're certain to be woken in the morning by the loud screams of *Carayá* monkeys, though other mammals living in the park may be less obtrusive, like the collared *peccary*, the *corzuela parda*, the puma and the *yaguarundí cat* (*Felis jaguamindi*).

At 300 m from the park's entrance there's a visitor centre and a free campsite with hot showers and electricity. There you can hire bicycles or horses for US$4 an hour, and move freely along the park's inner roads. Two short footpaths, *sendero del puente colgante* and *sendero del abuelo*, respectively lead to the banks of the Río Negro, and to an 800-year-old specimen of the *quebracho* tree. A vehicle road goes north 6 km up to two high *mangrullos* or viewpoints, overlooking the two lakes, Laguna Carpincho and Laguna Yacaré, where, with a bit of patience, you'll see *yacarés* (alligators). Another track, suitable only for 4WD vehicles, goes south, through a forest of *quebracho* trees, and after 9 km reaches the peaceful Laguna Panza de Cabra. There is a campsite by the lake, without facilities, and where you'll often hear the rare maned wolf *(aguará guazú)* at night. Tour operators run day-long excursions to the park from Resistencia.

Paved Route 16 goes northwest from Resistencia and after about 60 km Route 9 branches off it, leading north to Colonia Elisa and beyond to Capitán Solari, which lies 5 km east of the park entrance via a dirt road. If there's a group of you, call the park in advance to be picked up at Capitán Solari. Regular buses La Estrella daily link Resistencia and Capitán Solari, where *remise* taxis should not charge more than US$2 for the short journey to the park, which can also be made on foot.

North of Resistencia → *For listings, see pages 428-430.*

Route 11 runs north to Formosa and then onwards to the Paraguayan border near **Clorinda**, with the city of Asunción just over the border. Crossing low-lying pastures with streams and *Caranday* palms, this route offers views of the diverse birdlife of the Wet Chaco, and is beautiful in the evening.

Formosa → *Colour map 2, A1. Phone code 03717. Population 198,100.*

Formosa is the capital of its province and the only Argentine port of any note on the Río Paraguay. Oppressively hot from November to March, the city is the base for boat trips along the rivers in the eastern part of the province during the winter, when the weather is mild. It's also a possible stopover on the way to the **Parque Nacional Río Pilcomayo** or the **Bañado La Estrella**, and it's close to the Paraguayan capital, Asunción. From the town's small port, boats cross the river to Alberdi (only if you have a multiple entry visa).

Tourism is not well developed here yet, but increasingly activities are offered: guided excursions and accommodation at *estancias*; ask at the **tourist office** ⓘ *José M Uriburu 820 (on Plaza San Martín), T03717-420442, www.formosa.gov.ar/turismo.html, Mon-Fri 0700-1300.* **El Pucu Airport** ⓘ *T03717-452490, is 5 km southwest, and remise taxis charge US$2 to the centre. The* **bus terminal** ⓘ *Av Gutnisky and Av Antártida Argentina T03717-451766, is 15 blocks west of plaza San Martín and remise taxis to centre cost US$2.*

Parque Nacional Río Pilcomayo → *Best visited in winter*

ⓘ *Access to the park is free and open 24 hrs, administration centre at town of Laguna Blanca, Av Pueyrredón and R86, T03718-470045, Mon-Fri 0700-1430. From Formosa, take R11 to Clorinda, and from there take R86 going west. After 47 km, a 5-km dirt road leads north to the entrance to the Laguna Blanca area. Follow R86 for a few kilometres further for the 5-km access dirt road to the entrance to the Estero Poí section. Buses Godoy run from Formosa or Resistencia to the small towns of Laguna Naick-Neck, 5 km from the park (for going to Laguna Blanca) and from Laguna Blanca, 8 km from the park (for going to Estero Poí). Remise taxis from both towns should charge no more than US$3 for these short journeys.*

Border essentials: Argentina–Paraguay

Puente Loyola

The easiest crossing into Paraguay is by road via the Puente Loyola, 4 km north of Clorinda. From Puerto Falcón, at the Paraguayan end of the bridge, the road runs 40 km northeast, crossing the Río Paraguay to reach Asunción.

Immigration The border is open 24 hours. Formalities for entering Argentina are dealt with at the Argentine end, at Puerto Pilcomayo, closed at weekends for tourists, and for those leaving Argentina at the Paraguayan end at Itá Enramada, easy crossing, open 24 hours.

Transport Crucero del Norte and El Pulqui run buses at 0030, and 0730 from Corrientes to Asunción, 5-7 hours, US$13. Alternatively Empresa Falcón, US$1, every hour from the border, last bus to the centre of Asunción 1830. The other route is by cargo and passenger ferry from Puerto Pilcomayo, close to Clorinda, to Itá Enramada (Paraguay), US$2, five minutes, every 30 minutes. Then take bus No 9 to Asunción.

This park, 162 km north of Formosa, covers 48,000 ha of Wet Chaco environment bordering Paraguay on the southern bank of the Río Pilcomayo. The lower parts may be flooded during the rainy season and the resulting lakes and *esteros*, or marshlands, create the park's most beguiling landscapes. The rest is grassland with *Caranday* palm forests, where rheas can be seen, with some Chaco forest in the upper lands, habitat of three monkey species and several types of woodpecker. Due to its significance as a natural wetland, the park is a Ramsar site with diverse birdlife, including herons and three different species of stork. Anteaters, capybaras, coatis, two species of yacarés and aguará guazu are on the list of animals protected within the park.

The park has two entrances leading to different areas. The most visited and easier to reach if you are on foot is Laguna Blanca, where there's an information point and a free campsite with electricity and cold water. From there, a footpath leads to the **Laguna Blanca**, the biggest lake in the park where you'll spot alligators among the rich aquatic plant life. The lake is not recommended for swimming, since the resident piranhas have a penchant for human toes. The second of the entrances leads to **Estero Poí**, another information point and a campsite without facilities. Here take the 1200-m footpath, which has informative signs on the botany of the upper areas of the park. A vehicle road goes into the park up the Río Pilcomayo and the international border, but can only be used with special permission.

◉ The Argentine Chaco listings

For Sleeping and Eating price codes and other relevant information, see Essentials pages 30-36.

◉ Sleeping

Resistencia *p424*
B Niyat Urban Hotel, Hipólito Yrigoyen 83, T03722-448451, www.niyaturban.com.ar. The newest and best hotel in town. Modern building, with spacious and stylish rooms overlooking the greenery of the park. Buffet breakfast, cable TV and efficient staff.
B Amerian Hotel Casino Gala, Juan Domingo Perón 330, T03722-452400, www.hotelcasino gala.com.ar. Smart 5-star hotel in the centre of town. Attractive pool and spa.
B Covadonga, Güemes 200, T03722-444444, www.hotelcovadonga.com.ar. Comfortable rooms with a/c. Pool, flatscreen TVs, sauna and gym, breakfast included. Good but no 'wow' factor.
C-D Bariloche, Obligado 239, T03722-421 412, jag@cpsarg.com. Definitely the best budget place in town, with a welcoming owner and decent rooms with bath and a/c. Unfortunately no breakfast here, but there's a nearby café at **Gran Hotel Royal**.

Formosa *p426*
A-B Turismo, San Martín 769, T03717-431 122, hoteldeturismoformosa@arnet.com.ar. A large, strangely shaped building by the river offering good views. Though the rooms are pricey, all have a/c and breakfast is included.
B Casa Grande Apart-Hotel, Av González Lelong 185, T03717-431573, www.casa grandeapart.com.ar. Situated 8 blocks north of Av 25 de Mayo and next to the river, these are good 1- and 2-room apartments, with kitchen, a/c, breakfast, a gym and pool.
C Colón, Belgrano 1068, T03717-426547, www.hotelcolonformosa.com. Comfortable rooms, a/c, breakfast included.

◉ Eating

Resistencia *p424*
There is a lack of choice when it comes to good-value restaurants but these are recommended:
♥♥ **Kebon**, Don Bosco and Güemes, T03722- 422385.
♥ **San José**, Roca and Av Alberdi, Plaza 25 de Mayo. A popular café and *confitería* with excellent pastries (try the *medialunas*) and ice creams.

Formosa *p426*
♥♥ **Asador Criollo**, Av Gutnisky. A popular *parrilla* where *chivito* (kid) is on the menu.
♥♥ **El Fortín**, Mitre 602. A traditional place, good varied local fish dishes.
♥ **El Tano Marino**, Av 25 de Mayo 55. An Italian restaurant, fine home-made pasta.
♥ **Yayita**, Belgrano 926. Regional dishes such as *soyo*, or *sopa paraguaya* are offered in this central restaurant.

◉ Festivals and events

Resistencia *p424*
10-12 Oct Fiesta Nacional de Pescado de los Grandes. Celebrated every Oct in the Río Antequeros, 14 km away from Resistencia.

Formosa *p426*
Mar/Apr The world's longest *Via Crucis* pilgrimage with 14 stops all the way along R81 (already registered in the *Guinness Book of Records*) takes place every **Easter** week, starting in Formosa and ending at the border with the province of Salta, 501 km northwest.
31 Jul Festival de la Caña Con Ruda. On the night of the last day of Jul, when a drink

of the Paraguayan *caña* flavoured by the ruda plant is taken as a protection for the mid-winter blues. The celebration is very popular and organized annually by the local authorities (ask at tourist office about the venue). It's also a good chance to try regional dishes.
Nov Festival Provincial de Folclore. Held at Pirané (115 km northwest), the major music festival in the northeast, attracting national stars of stirring *folclore* music.

O Shopping

Resistencia *p424*
Fundación Chaco Artesanal, Carlos Pellegrini 272. A charity selling fine handicrafts made by Toba, Wichi and Mocoví native groups in varied materials, whose profits return to those communities.

▲ Activities and tours

Resistencia *p424*
Sudamericana, San Buenaventura del Monte Alto 866, T/F03722-435954, sudevt@ciudad.com.ar. 1-day tours to nearby sights all for a minimum of 5 people. Isla del Cerrito, lunch included; Parque Nacional Chaco, US$13 per person.

Formosa *p426*
Domínguez Excursiones, San Martín 1577, T03717-421264, dominguez_excursiones@yahoo.com.ar. Excursions to all sights in the province, including the National Parks and Bañado La Estrella.
La Corvina, Mitre 164, T03717-423702, corvinaderio@hotmail.com. Reinaldo Saporiti is a fishing guide running excursions to Herradura on Paraguay river.
Pedro Iznardo, Paraguay 520, T03717-420 780, iznardo@uol.com.ar. Freddy is a knowledgeable guide specializing in canoeing, who runs very interesting excursions down the nearby rivers lasting

several days, such as the Riacho Monte Lindo Grande, north of Formosa. Good for birdwatching. He also runs excursions to Bañado La Estrella.

⊖ Transport

Resistencia *p424*
Air
For airport information, see page 425.
Flights to **Buenos Aires** only with Aerolíneas Argentinas, 1 hr 15 mins.
Airline offices Aerolíneas Argentinas, Juan B Justo 184, T03722-445550.

Bus
For bus terminal information, see page 425. Buses No 3 and 10 from Oro and Perón, 1 block west of plaza, go to the bus terminal, 20 mins, US$1. Bus tickets can be bought for the same prices at several offices.
To **Corrientes**, Chaco–Corrientes buses stop opposite Norte supermarket on Av Alberdi e Illia, 45 mins, US$5 return. To **Capitán Solari** (for going to Parque Nacional Chaco), La Estrella, 3¼ hrs, US$3. To **Corrientes** bus terminal, Puerto Tirol, 30 mins, US$5 50 (drops you off at a small plaza at Av 3 de Abril and Av España; Corrientes centre lies 6 blocks north on Av España).
To **Buenos Aires**, several companies, 12-13 hrs, US$46. To **Puerto Iguazú**, 8-10½ hrs, US$33, Aguila Dorada Bis (change at Posadas); Autotransportes Mendoza; Expreso Singer, Río Uruguay.
To **Salta**, Flecha Bus, La Nueva Estrella, 12½ hrs, US$35. To **Tucumán**, Almirante Brown, Vosa, 12 hrs, US$35. To **Formosa**, 2-2½ hrs, US$6.50, several companies. To **Laguna Blanca** or **Laguna Naick-Neck** (for Parque Nacional Río Pilcomayo), 8 hrs, US$8.50, Godoy.
To Paraguay To **Asunción**, Brújula; Crucero del Norte; El Pulqui, Godoy, 5-5½ hrs, US$11.

Taxi
Radio Taxi, T03722-438535.

Formosa *p426*
Air
Aerolíneas Argentinas to **Buenos Aires**, direct 1 hr 30 mins (2 hrs 20 mins when calling at Corrientes or Resistencia).

Airline offices Aerolíneas Argentinas, Av 25 de Mayo 601, T03717-429314.

Bus
For bus terminal information, see page 426.

To **Asunción**, 3 hrs, US$7, **Brújula**; El Pulqui; Godoy. To **Resistencia**, 2½ hrs, US$6.50, several companies. To **Buenos Aires**, 15-17 hrs, US$55, El Pulqui; Flecha Bus; Godoy; Puerto Tirol. To **Laguna Blanca** or **Laguna Naick-Neck** (for **Parque Nacional Río Pilcomayo**), 3 hrs, US$5, **Godoy**. To **Las Lomitas** (for Bañado La Estrella), 4 hrs, US$9, **Giroldi Travel**.

Remise taxi
Libertad, José M Uriburu 750, T03717-420700.

❶ Directory

Resistencia *p424*
Banks Banco de Galicia, Mitre 153; Banco de la Nación, Güemes and Av 9 de Julio. **Currency exchange** El Dorado, J M Paz 50, Western Union branch. **Emergencies** Police T101, T03722-432002. **Internet** Klap, Illia 12, US$1 per hr, open 24 hrs. **Medical services** Hospital Pediátrico (Children's Hospital), Juan B Justo 1136, T03722-441477; Hospital Perrando, Av 9 de Julio 1101, T03722-425050. **Post office** Av Sarmiento and Hipólito Yrigoyen on Plaza 25 de Mayo.

Formosa *p426*
Banks Banco de Galicia, Av 25 de Mayo 160; Banco de la Nación, Av 25 de Mayo 602. **Emergencies** Medical emergencies T110; Police T101, T03717-429000. **Medical services** Hospital Central, Fotheringham 550, T03717-426194; Hospital de la Madre y el Niño (for children), Ayacucho 1150, T03717-426097.

Contents

Footprint features

Border crossings

Argentina–Chile, *see pages 449, 463,
475, 478, 492 and 526*

Lake District

At a glance

◉ **Getting around** Minibuses
connect even the smallest towns
and some campsites. A car or
bicycle gives more freedom.

◉ **Time required** At least 4-7 days
for Bariloche, 1-2 for towns and hikes
or skiing.

☼ **Weather** Rainy and cold from
May-Aug, and high temperatures
from Nov-Mar.

✖ **When not to go** May-Jul, unless
skiing. In Aug Bariloche can be busy
with students.

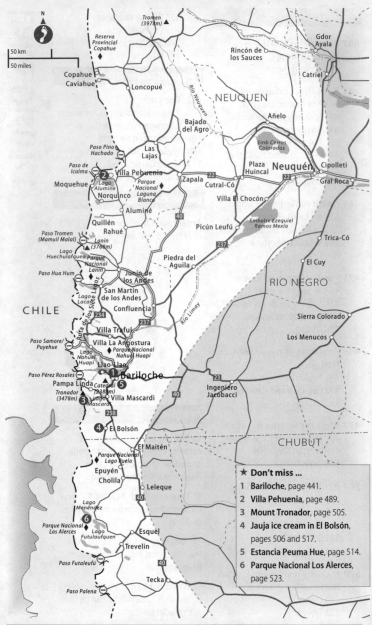

★ Don't miss ...
1 Bariloche, page 441.
2 Villa Pehuenia, page 489.
3 Mount Tronador, page 505.
4 Jauja ice cream in El Bolsón, pages 506 and 517.
5 Estancia Peuma Hue, page 514.
6 Parque Nacional Los Alerces, page 523.

Trek amongst craggy snow-capped peaks flanked by glaciers and crystalline rivers running through virgin Valdivian rainforest to lakes of peppermint green and Prussian blue. Ski down long pistes with panoramic views of lagoons below or hike for days through a mountain-top nirvana without seeing any signs of civilization. Take a slow boat across fjords or a hair-raising whitewater rafting trip. Or simply step onto the terrace of your lakeside hotel and sip a Malbec as the sun sinks over the mountains. Whatever you choose to do, Argentina's Lake District is spectacular and unforgettable.

Bariloche is the best starting point, a friendly but large town in alpine style with chocolate shops, lakeside hotels and chalet-style restaurants selling wild boar and smoked trout. Towering above is a range of peaks where you can hike, ski or cycle. Or take a cable car and admire the incredible views. Bariloche could easily entertain you for a week. A magical road winds through seven lakes and three national parks to the pretty tourist towns of Villa La Angostura and San Martín de los Andes. Retreat to Lago Huechulafquen, where perfectly conical Volcán Lanín is reflected in cobalt blue waters. North of here, it's wilder and less visited. Pehuenia is a quiet haven with its forests of prehistoric monkey puzzle trees, broad lagoons and the rich culture of the native Mapuche people. At the southern end of the lakes, El Bolsón and Esquel are wonderfully relaxed places for a few days' hiking, where the mountains are magnificent, and the local *cerveza* is excellent. Take the *Old Patagonian Express*, try a Welsh tea in quaint Trevelin, and then explore the region's most unspoilt national park, Los Alerces. A jade-green river flows between the cinnamon trunks of *arrayán* trees and 1000-year-old *alerce* trees tower above you.

Ins and outs

Getting there

Air There are several flights daily from Buenos Aires to Bariloche, Esquel (for the southern lakes) and San Martín de los Andes (for the northern lakes), as well as flights from Santiago in Chile to Bariloche. In addition, the army airline **LADE** runs weekly flights connecting Bariloche with other Patagonian towns. If you're short on time, flying is preferable to long bus journeys, and it's relatively inexpensive. Consider buying two singles (same price as a return), flying to San Martín de los Andes in the north and leaving from Esquel in the south, allowing you to see the whole area by hired car or bus. Book well in advance from December to March.

Bus Long-distance buses connect busy Neuquén and Bariloche with Buenos Aires and all major cities in Argentina, as well as over the Chilean border. But distances are huge and these long journeys will probably take a day or more out of your holiday – Bariloche to Buenos Aires is 22 hours; to Mendoza, 19 hours; and to Puerto Madryn, 14 hours. Unless your budget is really tight, it's better to fly.

Train One of the country's few long-distance trains runs to Bariloche from Viedma on the east coast, a comfortable overnight service that will also carry your car. This isn't convenient unless you're already in Viedma. Check out www.interpatagonia.com/trenpatagonico/.

Getting around

Bicycle The area is fabulous for cycling with unparalleled views, lots of hills, but generally good roads, even where they are *ripio* (gravel). The Seven Lakes Drive is gradually being paved but is full of potholes for 50 km in the middle. Avoid cycling in January and early February when there is lots of car traffic around the lakes. During the rest of the year there are few cars and you'll have some superb rides. There are good bike shops in Bariloche and San Martín that carry a wide range of spares and can also do repairs. You can also rent bikes, although they're not of the highest standard. Carry plenty of food and water, as services are few and far between, though there are plenty of campsites. There is almost no shade on the stretch from Bariloche to Esquel.

Boat There are lots of boat trips around Lago Nahuel Huapi which can be used as a means of transport, as well as a day out. The Three Lakes Crossing to Chile from Bariloche is a good way of getting to Puerto Montt in Chile, but the bus is cheaper. ▶▶ *For more information on the Three Lakes Crossing, see border box, page 449.*

Bus and car Hiring a car is the most appealing option as it allows you to stop where you like and explore places off the beaten track. However, if you're travelling alone, you might find the distances tedious. There are excellent bus services around Bariloche, on the road to Llao Llao, and to Pampa Linda, making it possible to do long hikes in these more remote areas. There are also regular bus services running north/south between Junín de los Andes, San Martín de los Andes, Bariloche and El Bolsón, and on to Esquel, with less frequent services via Cholila, Lagos Puelo and Epuyen. Many big buses will take bicycles, but always arrange this beforehand. The national parks are less easy to access by bus, although there is a daily bus into and out of Los Alerces from Esquel. Reaching Pehuenia and the dinosaur region near Neuquén are both almost impossible by bus. These places largely cater for Argentine tourists, who mostly bring their own cars. Unless you have a lot of spare time to wait for buses, hiring a car or arranging a tour is the best way to get the most out of the northern lakes.

Bariloche is the best starting point for visiting the lakes, and there are excellent transportation and accommodation options.

Car hire is easiest in Bariloche, but is also possible in San Martín de los Andes, El Bolsón, and Esquel. Costs tend to be around US$50 a day; and for an extra charge of around US$40 the better companies will allow you to drop the car off at a different town from where you hired it (arrange this at the time of hire). If you plan to take a hire car over the border into Chile, let the car-hire company know ahead of time as by law the vehicle must have its registration number etched on the windows.

Walking There are plenty of *refugios* in the mountains behind Bariloche making it possible to plan four- or five-day hikes. They vary in quality but most will provide hot meals and advice on routes. There are more *refugios* near Pampa Linda, in the hills around El Bolsón, and a couple in both Los Alerces and Lanín national parks. Get advice from park offices or **Club Andino Bariloche** (see page 442). Bus services around Bariloche are well set up to help hikers get about; again, ask in Club Andino for an updated schedule.

Best time to visit
Summer (December to February) is the obvious time to come, but be aware that January is impossibly busy throughout the region as this is when Argentines take their holidays en masse and accommodation is hard to find. Come in March and early April instead, when days are still likely to be clear and there are far fewer visitors, making it much easier to get flights and be spontaneous with accommodation. Late spring and early summer (October to November) can be lovely, though cool, and also busy. Autumn is the most beautiful time of year to visit, with brilliant displays of autumn leaves in late April to early May. The skiing season runs from late June to September and is busiest in July, when prices rise and Bariloche is inundated. Outside the peak season, transport services are fewer, requiring more flexible schedules, but well worth it to enjoy greater tranquillity. Hotels are all more expensive in peak periods, with the highest in January and July.

Tourist information
The best centre is in Bariloche. It is well set up for tourism with good tour operators and well-organized boat and cable-car services to make the most of the stunning mountain landscape nearby. Tourist offices can be found in each town, but to plan your trip and for more information before you come, check out these sites: www.neuquentur.gov.ar (in English); www.barilochepatagonia.info (a great site in English, French, Portuguese and German); www.visitchile.org; www.interpatagonia.com (excellent site for general information on the area in English); www.clubandino.org (for walks and mountain climbing); www.active patagonia.com.ar (hiking and trekking expeditions); and www.revistapatagonia.com.ar (a useful magazine).

National parks
There are five national parks covering enormous swathes of the Lake District, and these areas are generally where you'll find the best hiking, rafting and horse riding, in the most unspoilt forests and mountain landscapes you can imagine. The area's main centre, **Bariloche**, is inside **Parque Nacional Nahuel Huapi**, and has a well-developed

infrastructure for activities in the park, see page 441. Inside this park is another tiny park, **Parque Nacional Los Arrayanes**, accessed from **Villa La Angostura**. Immediately to the north of Nahuel Huapi is **Parque Nacional Lanín**, which contains the town of **San Martín de los Andes**, and has also superb hiking, especially around **Volcán Lanín** (see page 474). South of Bariloche there is the tiny but beautiful **Parque Nacional Lago Puelo**, just south of **El Bolsón**. Finally, **Los Alerces** is the most pristine of all the parks, with just one road running through it, and most areas accessible only on foot. The nearest towns are **Esquel** and **Trevelin**, see pages 520 and 522. Each park has a ranger's station, where *guardaparques* will give you a map and advise on walks in the park, as well as on accommodation and state of the paths.

Parque Nacional Nahuel Huapi

Nahuel Huapi is the national park you're most likely to visit since Bariloche is right at its heart. It stretches along the Andes for over 130 km, from south of Lago Mascardi to north of Villa Traful, and so there are no official entry points like most of the other national parks. It was Argentina's first ever national park, created in 1934 from a donation made to the country by naturalist Francisco 'Perito' Moreno of 7500 ha of land around Puerto Blest. Extending across some of Argentina's most dramatic mountains, the park contains lakes, rivers, glaciers, waterfalls, torrents, rapids, valleys, forest, bare mountains and snow-clad peaks. Among those you can climb are Tronador (3478 m), Catedral Sur (2388 m), Falkner (2350 m), Cuyín Manzano (2220 m), López (2076 m), Otto (1405 m) and Campanario (1052 m). The outstanding feature is the splendour of the lakes and the pristine nature of the virgin forests. For more information, see www.nahuelhuapi.gov.ar. ▸▸ *For listings, see pages 450-460.*

Ins and outs

There are many centres within the park, at Villa la Angostura and at Villa Traful, for example. But Bariloche is the usual first port of call for park activities, and here you can equip yourself with information on transport, walks and maps. The **Nahuel Huapi National Park intendencia** ① *San Martín 24, T02944-423111, www.nahuelhuapi.gov.ar, daily 0900-1400*, is fairly unhelpful, with little hard information. Much better information on walks, *refugios* and buses, and great maps, are available from the trained guides and mountaineers at **Club Andino Bariloche** (CAB) ① *20 de Febrero No 30, T02944-422266, www.clubandino.org, Mon-Fri 0900-1300 (1600-2100 in high season).*

You can also contact the **Association of Guides**, all of whom are trained, and know the geography, flora and fauna. Ask for English speakers. They sell excellent maps showing walks, with average walking times, and *refugios*, and can advise on which have room. Ask for the *Sendas y Bosques* (walks and forests) series, which are 1:200,000, laminated and easy to read, with good books containing English summaries of the walks, www.guiasendasybosques.com.ar, the *Active Patagonia* map, with fabulous detail, and the *Carta de Refugios, Senderos y Picadas* for Bariloche. They can also tell you about transport: services vary from year to year and between high and low season, so it's best to check.

Flora and fauna

Vegetation varies with altitude and climate, but you're most likely to see large expanses of southern beech forest – the magnificent *coihue* trees (small-leaved evergreen beeches) – many over 450 years old, and near the Chilean border where rainfall is highest, there are areas of magnificent virgin rainforest. Here you will see an *alerce* tree over 1500 years old, with the ancient species of bamboo cane *caña colihue* growing everywhere. Eastern parts of the park are more steppe-like with arid land, supporting only low shrubs and bushes. Wildlife includes the small pudú deer, the endangered huemul and river otter, as well as foxes, cougars and guanacos. Among the birds, scarlet-headed Magellan woodpeckers and green austral parakeets are easily spotted as well as large flocks of swans, geese and ducks.

Parque Nacional Nahuel Huapi

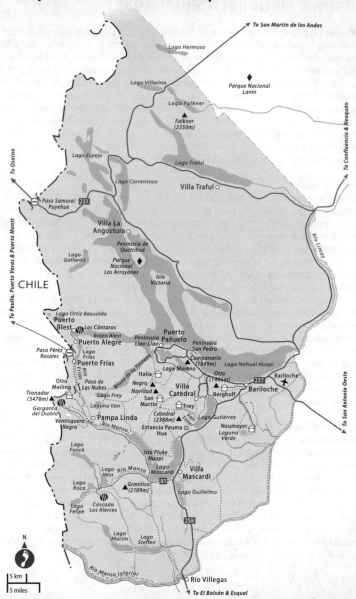

Around the park

Lago Nahuel Huapi

The centrepiece of the park is its largest lake, Lago Nahuel Huapi, a huge 531 sq km and 460 m deep in places, particularly magnificent to explore by boat since the lake is very irregular in shape and long fjord-like arms of water, or *brazos*, stretch far into the west towards Chile, where there is superb virgin Valdivian rainforest, and north towards the Parque Nacional Los Arrayanes (a park inside a park), which contains a rare woodland of exquisite *arrayán* trees with their bright cinnamon-coloured flaky bark. There are many islands: the largest is Isla Victoria with a luxurious hotel (www.islavictoria.com). The tourist town of Bariloche is the best base for exploring this area, with plentiful accommodation all along the southern shore of Lago Nahuel Huapi and hiking, rafting, tours and boat trips on offer.

North of Bariloche

North of the small, upmarket village of Villa La Angostura (see page 462), a winding road takes you through spectacular and largely unspoiled landscapes on the famous Seven Lakes Drive (see page 461) to San Martín de los Andes (see page 476). The northernmost stretch of this drive and three of its lakes are in Parque Nacional Lanín (see page 471), which borders Nahuel Huapi National Park. Lagos Correntoso and Espejo both offer stunning scenery, and tranquil places to stay and walk. Another tiny centre, Villa Traful (see page 464), lies on the shore of navy blue Lago Traful, the perfect place to escape to, with fishing, camping and walking.

South and west of Bariloche

West of Bariloche, there are glaciers and waterfalls near Pampa Linda, the base for climbing Mount Tronador and starting point for the trek through Paso de las Nubes to Lago Frías. South of Lago Nahuel Huapi, Lagos Mascardi, Guillelmo and Gutiérrez have even grander scenery, offering horse riding, trekking and rafting along the Río Manso. An excellent base for exploring this area is **Estancia Peuma Hue** ⓘ www.peuma-hue.com, on the southern shore of Lago Gutiérrez, with great walking, riding and rafting arranged by the *estancia*. See page 514, for hotels along their shores.

Activities

Trekking This is obviously the main attraction here, with many well-marked routes in the peaks south of Bariloche, Mount Tronador and others. There are plenty of *refugios* offering accommodation, all of which are very busy in January. See Walks around Bariloche, page 447.

Skiing Cerro Catedral ⓘ www.catedralaltapatagonia.com, is a world-class ski resort and is very popular throughout the season, from June to September. All hotels fill up in July and August. For more information, see page 446.

Boat trips There are day trips across Lago Nahuel Huapi from Puerto Pañuelo to Bosque de Arrayanes (which can also be reached by boat or on foot from Villa La Angostura), and to Isla Victoria (see page 447). Boats also cross to the extreme west of Lago Nahuel Huapi for the Three Lakes Crossing to Chile, see page 449. Sailing is not available to tourists on the lake as winds are so unpredictable, but there are plans to offer trips on sailing boats as

Parque Nacional Los Arrayanes

This park covers the Quetrihué Peninsula, which dips south from Villa La Angostura into the Lago Nahuel Huapi, and lies within the Parque Nacional Nahuel Huapi. It was created to protect a rare forest of *arrayán* trees, since it's one of the few places in the world where the *arrayán* grows to full size, and some of the specimens are 300 years old. This myrtle-like tree grows near water in groves, and likes to have its roots wet, since it really has no bark. The trunks are extraordinary: a smooth powdery or peeling surface, bright cinnamon in colour and cold to the touch. They have no outer bark to protect them, but the surface layer is rich in tannins that keep the tree free from disease. They have creamy white flowers in January and February, and produce blue-black fruit in March. The sight of so many of these trees together, with their twisting trunks, creates a magical light, and is really fairy-tale wonderful. The most rewarding way to see the wood is to take the boat trip across the deep-blue lake, fringed with spectacular peaks, to the tip of the peninsula, and then take a leisurely walk along the wheelchair-friendly wooden walkways through the trees, waiting until the guided tour has left. Halfway along you'll see a small wooden café which serves tea and coffee and has great views of the forest. Stroll back to the port through the mixed forest, passing two pretty and secluded lakes, Laguna Patagua, and Laguna Hua Huan.

Ins and outs

The entrance to the park lies a walkable 2 km south of the port area of Villa la Angostura, known as La Villa. Bus company **15 de Mayo** runs buses from El Cruce to La Villa every two hours (15 minutes). Entrance costs US$6, and a taxi to Villa costs US$3.50. The **park office** is found at Inacayal 13, 2nd floor, T02944-494004, www.bosquelos arrayanes.com.ar.

Walking and cycling

There's a clear path all the way from the tip of the Quetrihué Peninsula where the boat arrives, through the prettiest part of the *arrayán* forest, and then running the length of the peninsula back to La Villa. You can walk or cycle the whole length: three hours one-way walking; two hours cycling (for cycle hire, see page 469).

Boat trips

Two companies run catamarans from the pier in La Villa to the end of the peninsula, and take passengers on a short guided tour through the forest. **Catamarán Patagonia Argentina**, T02944-494463, www.catamaran patagonia.com.ar. **Greenleaf Turismo**, T02944-494004, www.bosquelos arrayanes.com.ar; tickets from **Hotel Angostura**, US$20 one-way, US$38 return. Boats also run from Bariloche, via Isla Victoria, with **Turisur**, T02944-426109, www.barilche.com/turisur.

a passenger. Rafting is excellent along the Río Manso, in the southwestern area of the park, with trips organized from Bariloche; see Activities and tours, page 457.

Swimming In the larger lakes such as Nahuel Huapi swimming is not recommended, as the water is extremely cold all year round, but smaller lakes can be very pleasant in summer.

Bariloche and around

→ *Colour map 5, B2. Phone code 02944. Population 100,000.*

Beautifully situated on the steep and wooded southern shore of Lago Nahuel Huapi, surrounded by high peaks, San Carlos de Bariloche (it's official name) is an ideal base for exploring the Lake District. It's right in the middle of Nahuel Huapi National Park and there's so much on offer from the town itself that you'd be quite content to spend a week or so around here. There's hiking and adventure sports of all kinds in the mountains behind the town, fantastic restaurants and some wonderful boutique hotels on the lakeshore heading west.

The town was founded in 1902 but really took off in the 1930s when the national park was created. The chalet-style architecture was established at this time by early German and Swiss settlers. The famous hotel Llao Llao (www.llaollao.com) and the Civic Centre were designed by major Argentine architect Bustillo, who set the trend for 'Bariloche Alpine style', with local stone, brightly varnished wood and carved gable ends, now ubiquitous throughout the region.

Bariloche is well set up for tourism with the main street, Mitre, bustling with tour operators, outdoor clothing shops and chocolate makers. There are also many restaurants serving fondue, as well as delicious local trout and wild boar, some of them bordering on kitsch, but appealing nevertheless. There are plenty of hotels and restaurants in the town centre, but the best places are sprinkled along the shore of lake Nahuel Huapi, towards Llao Llao, where Argentina's most famous hotel enjoys a spectacularly beautiful setting. To the immediate south of Bariloche there are fabulous walks in the mountains, and up giant Mount Tronador, reached from Pampa Linda further south. On the way are two gorgeous lakes: Gutiérrez, with Estancia Peuma Hue on its shores for excellent horse riding and relaxing; and Mascardi, with access to rafting on the Río Manso. In summer there are good bus and boat services to reach these mountains and lakes, as well as cable cars up two of the peaks behind Bariloche. Ski resort Cerro Catedral is arguably the best in South America, and makes a great base for trekking in summer. →→ *For listings, see pages 450-460.*

Ins and outs

Getting there

The **airport** ① *T02944-405016*, is 15 km east of town, taxis charge US$10.50. A shuttle bus service meets each arriving flight (US$5). Bus and train stations are both 3 km east of town; a taxi costs US$2.50, or there are frequent buses (Nos 10, 20 and 21) to the centre, US$1. The **bus terminal** ① *T02944-432860*, has toilets, a small *confitería*, *kiosko* and *locutorio*. Left luggage costs US$2 per day. If you are staying in one of the many hotels on the road to Llao Llao, west of town, expect to pay a little more for transport to your hotel.

Getting around

Bariloche is an easy city to walk around and to orient yourself in, since the lake lies to the north and the mountains to the south. The main street is Mitre, running east to west, and unmistakable with its souvenir and chocolate shops. Here you'll find all the tour operators, *locutorios* and internet cafés, as well as banks and some food shops. The tourist information office (see below) is in the distinctive chalet-style Centro Cívico, with an open space giving good views onto the lake, and most hotels and restaurants are gathered within three or four blocks from here, with cheaper accommodation and hostels tending to be a few blocks further south on the upper slopes of town. More upmarket hotels and many restaurants are spread out along Avenida Bustillo, the road running beside the southern shore of Lago Nahuel Huapi for some 25 km, as far as the famous **Hotel Llao Llao**, and in an area known as Colonial Suiza. This is a viable place to stay even if you haven't got a car since frequent local buses, run by **3 de Mayo**, run along its length. Take No 20 to Llao Llao, for lakeside hotels and restaurants and Puerto Pañuelo; No 10 to Colonia Suiza and Bahía López for trekking; No 50 to Lago Gutiérrez, via the base for the cable car to Cerro Otto; and the bus labelled 'Catedral' for Cerro Cathedral.

Tourist information

The **tourist office** ① *Centro Cívico, T02944-429850, www.barilochepatagonia.info, daily 0900-2100*, has helpful staff who speak English, French and German, and have maps showing the town and whole area, with bus routes marked. They can also help with accommodation and campsites in the area. **Nahuel Huapi National Park intendencia** ① *San Martín 24, T02944-423111, www.nahuelhuapi.gov.ar, daily 0900-1400*, is pretty unhelpful; far better to go straight to **Club Andino Bariloche** (CAB) ① *just above the Centro Cívico, 20 de Febrero No 30, T02944-422266, www.clubandino.org, Mon-Fri 0900-1300 (1600-2100 in high season only)*, for information on walks, hikes, mountain climbs, *refugios*, and buses to reach all the local areas for walking. They sell excellent maps and books for walks: *Infotrekking* produced by trekking company Active Patagonia is detailed, has great maps and is highly recommended. For climbing, get hold of the booklet *Guía de Escalada [climbing] en Roca*, by Eduardo (Tato) López, with

1 Bariloche

Lake Nahuel Huapi

Puerto San Carlos

➡ **Bariloche maps**
1 Bariloche, page 442
2 Bariloche – the road to Llao Llao, page 444

N

200 metres
200 yards

Sleeping 🛏
1004 **3** *A1*
7 de Febrero **4** *B3*
Antiguo Solar **1** *B2*

Below 41 **2** *B1*
Familia Arko **5** *B1*
Hostel Inn **9** *A1*
Hostería Güemes **11** *B1*
La Bolsa **13** *B2*
La Pastorella **14** *B1*
New Andino **6** *A2*
Panamericano **7** *A1*
Periko's **18** *B1*
Premier **20** *A2*
Pudu **8** *A1*

Ruca Hueney **22** *B2*
Tres Reyes **23** *A2*

Eating 🍴
Chez Philippe **11** *B1*
Corvita **12** *A3*
Dias de Zapata **2** *B2*
El Boliche de Alberto **1** *B2*
Huang Ji **5** *A2*
Jauja **6** *B2*
Kandahar **7** *B1*

La Alpina **3** *A2*
Map Room **18** *A2*
Tarquino **8** *B1*
Vegetariano **13** *B1*

Bars & clubs 🍸
Cerebro **14** *A1*
Pilgrim **10** *A2*
Roxxy **17** *A1*
Wilkenny **16** *A1*

translations in English and explanations of all the areas to climb. Excellent advice and current information given. All staff know the mountains well and some of them speak English, French or German.

Best time to visit

Bariloche is busiest in the school holidays (January and July), but it's also the destination for all graduating secondary school students in August, September and January, though these groups are now confined to special hotels (not listed here), and rarely stray beyond the city's bars and nightclubs for their inevitable rites of passage. Accommodation is cheaper outside of the peak periods, but the weather becomes unpredictable at the end of April. For skiing, July and August are best, though hotels are packed with mass tourism from Chile and Brazil. Try June or September instead, and always book well ahead.

Sights

At the heart of the city is the **Centro Cívico**, designed in 'Bariloche Alpine style' on an attractive plaza above the lake, where there's also a small museum, **Museo de la Patagonia** ① *Tue-Fri 1000-1230, 1400-1900, Sat 1000-1700, entry by donation, www.bariloche.com.ar/museo*, with some indigenous artefacts and material from the lives of the first white settlers. Mitre is the main commercial area, and here all the chocolate shops are clustered – a sight in themselves, and not to be missed. **Abuela Goye** and **Mamushka** are most highly recommended. The **cathedral**, built in 1946, lies south of Mitre and opposite is a huge rock left in this spot by a glacier during the last glacial period. On the lakeshore is the **Museo Paleontológico** ① *12 de Octubre and Sarmiento, Mon-Sat 1600-2100, US$0.30*, which has displays of fossils mainly from Patagonia including an ichthyosaur and replicas of a giant spider and shark's jaws. Bariloche's real sights are the mountains themselves; don't miss a trip up to one of their peaks in cable cars to either **Cerro Otto** or **Cerro Campanario** to see lakes and mountains stretching out in front as far as the eye can see.

The road to Llao Llao → *For listings, see pages 450-460.*

To really appreciate the splendid setting of Bariloche, you need to get out of town and head west along **Avenida Bustillo** running parallel to the lakeshore to the area known as **Llao Llao**, where boats leave from Puerto Pañuelo. Frequent buses run along this road, so it's easy to explore even without your own transport. Parallel to Avenida Bustillo is **Avenida de los Pioneros**, with more hotels, but mostly residential areas. There's easy access to the mountains above these roads, by driving to, or getting off the bus at, the kilometre stop you want. The free tourist office map, *Circuito Chico* shows the stops clearly. For information on some of the excellent hiking in the area, see Trekking and climbing, page 458. Cyclists beware that this is a busy road, and drivers will show you no mercy, expecting you to pull over onto the gravel verges as they pass.

Llao Llao

Llao Llao, named after the hotel, is a charming area 25 km west of Bariloche, and a lovely place for walking with gorgeous views. It's at the end of Avenida Bustillo, which runs along Lago Nahuel Huapi to the port (Puerto Pañuelo), where boat trips leave. **Hotel Llao Llao** (see Sleeping, page 452), is one of Argentina's finest hotels, and worth the extortionate rates for the view, spa and restaurant. The hotel was designed by Bustillo, and opened in 1937, originally almost entirely a wooden construction. It burned down within a few months of opening and was rebuilt using local stone. Superbly situated on a hill with incredible views over the lake, it's a good place for tea on the terrace. Even if luxury hotels aren't your thing, it's still worth coming to the area as there are superb walks in beautiful virgin forest, rich in wildlife, at **Parque Municipal Llao Llao**, just off the road west of the hotel. This small peninsula juts into the lake, with a small hill and a little beach, **Villa Tacul**, both offering good views. Take bus No 20, a lovely 45-minute ride, US$1. Buses leave from the big bus stop on Moreno and Rolando (for information T02944-425648). Alternatively, take a half-day tour to 'Circuito Chico', but beware that you won't get much time for walking, see below, or take a full day to cycle.

Cerro Campanario

At Km 17.5, a **chairlift** ① *T02944-427274, daily 0900-1800, 7 mins, US$6.50 return, extended opening in summer*, goes up to Cerro Campanario (1049 m) with superb views of the lake, edged with mountains, as well as San Pedro Peninsula below and Lago Moreno. Take bus No 10, 20 or 22 to Km 17.5. There is a restaurant and bar at the top with fabulous views.

Circuito Chico

Circuito Chico is the classic old Argentine tour: you sit in the car and gaze at the view. These days, you're more likely to want to stop, hike, take photos and find somewhere to

② Bariloche – the road to Llao Llao

Sleeping
Aldebaran **19**
Apart Hotel Andes y Sol **1**
Departamentos Bellevue **2**
Design Suites **3**

El Yeti **4**
Goye **5**
Hostel Alaska **6**
Hostería Katy **10**
Hostería Santa Rita **8**

Hueney Ruca **5**
Isla Victoria Resort **9**
La Caleta **11**
La Cascada **12**
Llao Llao **20**

eat, so the tour as offered by tour operators is a frustrating experience. Drive or cycle instead. The circuit itself is a great introduction to the area. Start by travelling along Avenida Bustillo, and turn off at Km 18.3 to go around Lago Moreno Oeste, past Punto Panorámico (with really great panoramic views) and continue around **Bahía López**, through the Parque Municipal Llao Llao with lovely walks, and on to Hotel Llao Llao and Puerto Pañuelo. You could extend the circuit by returning via **Colonia Suiza** and ski resort **Cerro Catedral** (2388 m), both of which are possible starting points for longer treks. This is a satisfying all-day cycle ride, but beware of impatient drivers.

Southwest of Bariloche → For listings, see pages 450-460.

Cerro Otto
At Km 5 on Avenida de los Pioneros, a cable car (*teleférico*) goes up to Cerro Otto (1405 m) with its revolving restaurant and really wonderful views over the lakes and mountains all around. Alternatively, 20 minutes' walk away on the summit at **Refugio Berghof** is a *confitería* belonging to Club Andino Bariloche. Highly recommended. Take the free hourly bus service from Mitre and Villegas, running from 1030 to 1730, returning hourly 1115 to 1915. Cable cars run from 1000 to 1800. A combined ticket for both bus and cable car is US$15 return (T02944-441031, www.telefericobariloche.com.ar). By car, take Avenida de los Pioneros, then the signposted dirt track 1 km out of town. To climb Cerro Otto on foot

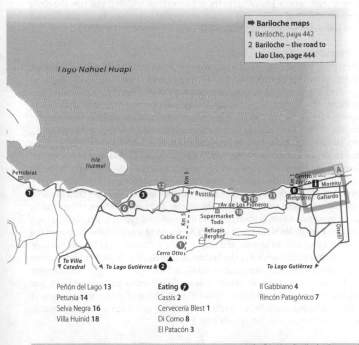

Peñón del Lago **13**
Petunia **14**
Selva Negra **16**
Villa Huinid **18**

Eating 🍴
Cassis **2**
Cervecería Blest **1**
Di Como **8**
El Patacón **3**

Il Gabbiano **4**
Rincón Patagónico **7**

(two to three hours): turn off Avenida de los Pioneros at Km 4.6, then follow the trail past **Refugio Berghof**, with splendid views. Not recommended alone, as paths can be confusing. ▸ *For more information on skiing on Cerros Otto, see page 457.*

Cerro Catedral

ⓘ *Slopes are open from mid-Jun to end of Sep and are busiest from 15 Jun-15 Aug (school holidays). Ski lifts are open 0900-1700, and adult passes cost around US$30 per day. Ski school, US$35 per hr for individuals.*

Cerro Catedral (2338 m), 21 km southwest of Bariloche, is one of the major ski resorts in Argentina; extremely well organized with a great range of slopes for all abilities. There are 70 km of slopes of all grades, allowing a total drop of 1010 m, starting at 2000 m, and 52 km of cross-country skiing routes, all with utterly spectacular views. There are also snowboarding areas and a well equipped base with hotels, restaurants, equipment hire, ski schools and nursery care for children. As a summer resort, there's a cable car to take you further into the hills, useful for starting walks to **Refugio Lynch** (from where you can walk on to Laguna Jakob) and **Refugio Frey**, or for cycling down to Lago Gutiérriez. To get to Cerro Catedral, the bus 'Catedral' from the bus terminal or the bus stop on Moreno and Palacios takes you to the ski station base (known as Villa Catedral). The bus leaves every 90 minutes, takes 35 minutes and costs US$1.50, taxis cost US$8. The **cable car** ⓘ *T02944-460090, www.catedralaltapatagonia.com*, from Villa Catedral is US$16 return. There is also superb cross-country skiing (called Nordic skiing here) around the wonderful Refugio Neumeyer, where you can also try out snowshoe walking, and stay the night or have dinner. Bilingual guides and equipment available for hire. Great fun. Contact Diversidad (see Activities and tours, page 457).

Mount Tronador and Pampa Linda

The highest peak around is the mighty mountain of Tronador ('The Thunderer', 3478 m), which overshadows the peaceful hamlet of **Pampa Linda** – the base for climbing the mountain itself or a number of other good walks. You can visit Pampa Linda on a day tour from Bariloche, which takes in the beautiful lakes Gutiérrez and Mascardi, and stops to appreciate the tranquillity of the place but offers little time for walking. However, it's better to take the bus from outside Club Andino and spend a few days at Pampa Linda, exploring. Usually included in the day tour, and fascinating, are the eerie, murky glacier **Ventisquero Negro** and the awesome falls at **Garganta del Diablo**, one of the natural amphitheatres on Tronador's slopes, where several waterfalls drop straight from the glacial shelf. It's well worth the trip to walk up through the *coihue* and *lenga* forests to the falls themselves. Also superb is the hike from Pampa Linda to **Refugio Otto Meiling**, where you can hire crampons and walk on the glacier. The lower sections of these paths are great for mountain biking in the forest, and there are more spectacular walks to Lago Blest along the **Paso de los Nubes**, and **Laguna Ilon**. A good way to make the most of the area is to take a tour with an agency, and then stay on at Pampa Linda to start trekking, returning with the minibus service run by **Transitando lo Natural** ⓘ *20 de Febrero number 28, T02944- 424531*. Buses to Pampa Linda run daily at 0900 in season, US$9. Alternatively, **Expreso Meiling** also run buses in season, leaving Club Andino Bariloche at 0830, and returning from Pampa Linda at 1700 (T02944-529875). There's a great simple *hostería* at Pampa Linda, offering lunch. ▸ *For further information on climbing Mount Tronador, see page 505. For Pampa Linda listings, see page 515.*

Boat trips on Lago Nahuel Huapi

Bosque de Arrayanes

A popular boat trip is across to Lago Nahuel Huapi to **Isla Victoria** and Bosque de Arrayanes, where these rare myrtle trees with their twisting cinnamon-coloured trunks create a magical fairy-tale atmosphere. The *bosque* (forest) can also be visited by boat or on foot from **Villa La Angostura** which allows you more time in the forest, and a good 13-km hike back. There are half-day excursions (1300-1830) from Puerto Pañuelo (bus No 10, 20 or 21 to get there) and on to Parque Nacional Los Arrayanes, on the Quetrihué Peninsula further north, in a full-day excursion (either 0900-1830, or 1300 till 2000 in season) costing US$20; take a picnic lunch.

Puerto Blest

The other great boat trip in the area is the all-day excursion to Puerto Blest, and **Cascada los Cantaros**, at the western end of Lago Nahuel Huapi, and **Lago Frías**, visiting native forest and Valdivian rainforest. Highly recommended. This is usually done as a nine-hour trip from Bariloche, leaving at 0900 from Puerto Pañuelo (Km 25.5), and sailing down to fjord-like Puerto Blest, where there's a good *hostería* and restaurant at the end of the lake. *Coihue*-clad mountains drop steeply into Prussian blue water, and it's usually raining, but very atmospheric. The tour then continues by short bus ride to **Puerto Alegre** on Lago Frías, and you cross the still, peppermint-green lake by launch. From Puerto Blest, the walk through beautiful forest to the **Cascada de los Cántaros** (one hour) is superb. Set off while the rest of the party stops for lunch, and you'll have time for your picnic by the splendid falls before the crowd arrives by boat. Or walk beyond them up to quiet **Lago de los Cántaros**, enclosed by vertical granite cliffs.

Boats fill up entirely in high season, and are much more pleasant in December and March. Boat trips cost US$20, plus extra US$7 for a bus transfer from Bariloche, or slightly cheaper if you take the 0730 bus (US$4) from the centre of town to Puerto Pañuelo where the boat excursion leaves for Puerto Blest at 0900. Tours are run by **Catedral** and **Turisur**. Boats are comfortable with a good (but expensive) *cafetería* on board. Stock up on picnic provisions from the shop next to the Shell garage just before you reach Puerto Pañuelo at Km 24.6. Set lunch at **Hostería Blest** is US$10; cheaper sandwiches are available from the snack bar next door. The **Hotel y Restaurant Puerto Blest** (C) is a small cosy hotel built in 1904, with homely rather than luxurious rooms. It's worth staying a night if you want to try any of the treks from here, or fish for trout, and the only other option is camping *libre* with no facilities. The *guardaparques* at Puerto Blest can advise on the many walks from here (and their state), but the seven-hour, 15-km trek to **Lago Ortiz Basualdo** is recommended (mid-December to March only).

Walks around Bariloche

There are many superb walks in this area, and there's not space here to do justice either to their descriptions or to detailed instructions. For all walks, contact **Club Andino Bariloche** (see page 442) who sell the excellent *Carta de Refugios, Senderos y Picadas* maps for Bariloche and the book *Infotrekking de la Patagonia*, which gives great detail on all the possible walks, times, distances and *refugios* where you can stay, with satellite-based maps to guide you. Ask the Club Andino Bariloche to check paths are open before you set off: crucial in spring when snow may not have cleared the upper slopes. You could also consider contacting a trekking company such as **Active Patagonia** ① *www.active patagonia.com.ar*, to take you on guided hikes rather than setting off alone. In summer *tábanos* (horseflies) are common on the lake shores and at lower altitudes; their bites are very annoying but not harmful, and the only solution is to climb higher.

Below is just a small selection of walks of various grades of difficulty, recommended for the surrounding natural beauty:

Around Llao Llao There are several easy and very satisfying walks from Llao Llao: a delightful easy circuit in virgin rainforest in the Parque Municipal Llao Llao (turn left off the road, just past the golf course, two hours), or the small hill Cerrito Llao Llao (900 m), for wonderful views (turn right off the road and follow signs – one to two hours), or a 3-km trail through to Brazo de la Tristeza (turn right off the road opposite the *guardebosque*), via tiny Lago Escondido, with magical views. Bus No 20 to Llao Llao, every 20 minutes.

Refugio López ① *2076 m, 5-7 hrs return*. This is a great hike with some of the most wonderful views of the whole area. Starting from the southeastern tip of Lago Moreno, go up alongside Arroyo López, and then along a ridge to the distinctive rose-coloured **Refugio López**, with its fabulous views. From Refugio López, you could do some climbing, or continue to make this a three- to four-day trek: head south to **Refugio Italia**, which is on the shores of the incredibly calm Laguna Negra at the foot of Cerro Negro. Then from here, you could hike on via Cerro Navidad to Laguna Jakob and **Refugio San Martín**. But note that this section is poorly signposted, and advisable only for very experienced walkers who are well equipped and can use a compass proficiently. Take a trekking guide if in any doubt, and always ask at CAB for the conditions of the paths. Bus No 10 to Colonia Suiza and Arroyo López (check return times), bus No 11 in summer only. Refugio López is the only *refugio* that is privately owned, and not part of CAB's chain. The owners may charge you to use the paths.

Refugio Frey ① *1700 m*. From the ski station at **Villa Catedral**, there are two ways up: 1) Walk up to Refugio Frey, or take the cable car to **Refugio Lynch** (check before you set off, as precise cable-car routes change each year) and from here walk along the ridge of Cerro Catedral to Refugio Frey which occupies a beautiful setting on a small lake (two to four hours one-way); or 2) from Villa Catedral, walk south and up alongside the Arroyo Van Titter to **Refugio Piedritas**, a very basic emergency shelter with no services, to reach Refugio Frey (three to six hours to climb one-way). The area around **Refugio Frey** is the best area for climbing in the whole region, with innumerable options in the granite walls around. From Refugio Frey there are several possibilities: walk on to Refugio Piedritas (four hours each way), and then down the Arroyo Van Titter to reach Lago Gutiérrez. Once you reach the lake, you could either walk around its southern head to join the Route 258, which runs from Bariloche to El Bolsón, or ask **Estancia Peuma Hue** (see page 514) to collect you at the start of a few night's stay there. (The same is also possible in reverse.)

Lago Gutiérrez You can reach this grand lake southwest of Bariloche by walking 2 km downhill from the ski base at Cerro Catedral, and along the northern lake shore, reaching the El Bolsón road (Route 258) where you can take a bus back to Bariloche (six hours). Or arrange with **Estancia Peuma Hue** (see Sleeping, page 514) to collect you by boat from the shore of Lake Gutiérrez, and stay a couple of nights at the *estancia* for more great walks.

Border essentials: Argentina–Chile

Three Lakes Crossing

The Three Lakes Crossing enters Chile via the Paso Pérez Rosales.

Argentine immigration and customs At Puerto Frías (open all year). For more information, see www.gendarmeria.gov.ar/pasos/fichperezro.htm.

Chilean immigration and customs At Peulla, open daily 0900-2000.

Transport The launches (and hence the connecting buses) on the lakes serving the direct route via Puerto Blest to Puerto Montt generally do not operate at weekends, but check (T02944-425216). No cars are carried on the ferries on this route.

Note There is a ban in Chile on importing any fresh food – meat, cheese, fruit – from Argentina. Chilean currency can be bought at Peulla customs at a reasonable rate.

Refugio Neumayer ① *has an office in town: Diversidad, 20 de Junio 728, T02944-428995, www.eco-family.com*. Some 12 km south of Bariloche, this makes a really charming centre for exploring the area, with eight paths to walk, information and guides on offer. Two are particularly recommended, to **Laguna Verde**, and to a mirador through Magellanic forest at **Valle de los Perdidos**. This is a cosy, friendly *refugio*, very well set up for walkers and families, and offering a wonderful range of activities.

Around Pampa Linda This blissful setting for a *hostería* and campsite is the starting point for a number of truly spectacular walks: firstly for climbing mighty Mount Tronador, or up to **Refugio Otto Meiling** (five hours each way), or to tranquil **Laguna Ilon** (5½ hours each way), or across Paso de las Nubes to **Puerto Frías**, where you can get the boat back to Bariloche (two days). For all of these, you must check with the excellent *guardaparques* in Pampa Linda on the state of paths (the Paso de las Nubes is often closed when boggy).

Into Chile → *For listings, see pages 450-460.*

Three Lakes Crossing to Chile

This popular route to Puerto Montt, with ferries across Lago Nahuel Huapi, Lago Frías and Lago Todos Los Santos, is outstandingly beautiful whatever the season, though the mountains are often obscured by rain and heavy cloud. It's a long and tiring journey, however, and is not recommended in really heavy rain. Book well ahead in high season (you can reserve online), and take your passport when booking with a tour operator. The journey can be done in one or two days: the one-day crossing (1 September to 28 February) arrives at Puerto Varas at around 2000 and does not allow a return to Bariloche next day, and you miss the walk to see the Cascada de los Cantaros. For the two-day crossing (operates all year round), there is an overnight stop in Peulla.

Tickets are sold by various operators, but all trips are run by **Turismo Catedral** ① *Palacios 263, T02944-425444, www.crucedelagos.com/tickets*. See also www.goargentina.net (there is a link on the right-hand side of the webpage), for a detailed description of the journey, prices and photos. Cost is US$230 (one day), plus cost of lunch at Peulla (US$25), and US$299 (two days with a hotel and breakfast included); credit cards are accepted and there are no student discounts. Book before 1900 the day before, and further in advance during the high season; and beware the hard sell. Take your own lunch, but eat it before you reach Chile, as no fresh food can be taken over the border.

Puerto Montt → *Phone code +56-(0)65. Population 175,000.*

Puerto Montt is a popular centre for excursions to the Chilean Lake District, and departure point for boats to Puerto Chacabuco and Puerto Natales. **El Tepual Airport** is 13 km northwest of town, and the **bus terminal** is on the seafront at Diego Portales and Lota. Facilities include telephones, restaurants, *casa de cambio* and left luggage (US$2.50 per item for 24 hours). A paved road runs 55 km southwest to Pargua, where there is a ferry service to the island of Chiloé. The little fishing port of **Angelmó**, 2 km west, has become a tourist centre with many seafood restaurants and handicraft shops (reached by Costanera bus along Portales and by *colectivo* Nos 2, 3 or 20 from the centre, US$1 per person). See Footprint's *South American Handbook* and *Chile* guide for further details. Accommodation is expensive in season, much cheaper off season. Details are available from **Sernatur** (Chilean tourist authority) in the **Intendencia Regional** ⓘ *Av Décima (X) Región 480, 3rd floor, T+56-(0)65-254580, Mon-Fri 0830-1300, 1330-1730*. There is also a kiosk on Plaza de Armas run by the municipality, open until 1800 on Saturday.

⊚ Bariloche and around listings

For Sleeping and Eating price codes and other relevant information, see Essentials pages 30-36.

⊜ Sleeping

Bariloche *p441, map p442*
Prices rise in 2 peak seasons: Jul and Aug for skiing, and mid-Dec to Feb for summer holidays. It's essential to book ahead in summer, but if you do arrive in the high season without a reservation, the tourist office can help. For more options, see www.barilochepatagonia.info (in English).
LL-L Panamericano, San Martín 536-570, T02944-425846, www.panamericanobari loche.com. Lovely views from these smartly decorated doubles on the lakefront. The building is a little dated but nicely renovated, and it includes a spa and casino. Central.
L Tres Reyes, 12 de Octubre 135, T02944-426121, www.hoteltresreyes.com. Traditional lakeside hotel with spacious rooms and lounge with splendid views, but it's all a bit dated. The friendly professional staff speak English. It's cheaper on the spot than if you reserve by email. It includes breakfast, security box, parking and Wi-Fi at the hotel

A Hotel 7 de Febrero, P Moreno 534, T02944-422244, www.hotel7defebrero. com.ar. Good central budget option with a slightly dated reception but nice, clean, simple doubles. Small breakfast included. Special prices for staying more than 5 nights.
A La Pastorella, Belgrano 127, T02944-424656, www.lapastorella.com.ar. A cosy, quaint little *hostería*, whose welcoming owners speak English.
A Premier, Rolando 263, T02944-426168, www.hotelpremier.com. Good economical choice in centre of town, with a light, spacious entrance and gallery, and neat, modern rooms with bath and TV. Wi-Fi, English spoken. Recommended.
B El Ñire, John O'Connor 94, T02944-423 041, www.elnire.com.ar. Comfortable rooms in this wooden alpine building close to the centre. Breakfasts are included, though they're nothing special.
B-C Antiguo Solar, Angel Gallardo 360, T02944-400337, www.antiguosolar.com. Only 2 blocks from the centre of town, this B&B has nice simple rooms on the upper level of an attractive traditional residential building. Includes breakfast, internet (Wi-Fi) and parking.

C Hostería Güemes, Güemes 715, T02944-424785. The charming hosts welcome you in this lovely, quiet B&B in a residential area, with lots of space in the living area and views of the lake. All the simple rooms have bath, and breakfast is included.

D Familia Arko, Güemes 691, T02944-423109, arko@eco-family.com. English and German spoken, cooking facilities, plentiful breakfast, helpful, good trekking information, beautiful garden. Often recommended.

Hostels

Bariloche has many good quality hostels, all charging around US$12-13 for a bed in a shared dorm. A lot of hostels are focused on and around Salta.

E pp Below 41, Juramento 94, T02944-436 433, www.hostel41below.com. Extremely cosy and welcoming hostel, with a great area to chill out filled with travel information. Small but ample kitchen and clean, attractive dorms. A lovely apartment (**B**) also available. Recommended.

E pp Hostel Inn Bariloche, Salta 308, T02944-426084, www.hostel-inn.com. Large, clean well-designed hostel with great views of the lake from the cosy communal areas and rooms. New comfortable beds and clean bathrooms, and a large well-equipped kitchen. Prices include free breakfast and dinner (at neighbouring Marco Polo Inn). The best feature is the great deck with a view in the garden. Only a short walk to the centre.

E pp La Bolsa, Palacios 405 (and Elflein), T02944-423529, www.labolsadeldeporte.com.ar. Recommended for its friendly, relaxed atmosphere, homely rustic rooms (some with lake views), and a great deck to sit out on. Doubles (**C**) available.

E pp Periko's, Morales 555, T02944-522 326, www.perikos.com. A warm and friendly atmosphere, with an *asado* every Fri, but otherwise a quiet, calm place. Also double (**B-C**) with own bath. Garden, free internet access, can organize horse riding and rent mountain bikes. Best to reserve by email: info@perikos.com.

E pp Pudu, Salta 459, T02944-429738, www.hostelpudu.com. An absolute gem in Bariloche. Run by a charming Irish couple, all dorms and doubles (**C**) have a spectacular view of the lake, and downstairs there is a small garden, an in-house bar and a huge kitchen. Long-term rates available. Recommended.

E pp Ruca Hueney, Elflein 396, T02944-433 986, www.rucahueney.com. A lovely calm place, with very comfortable beds and duvets. Spotless kitchen, quiet dining area, and very welcoming bilingual owners. Good double bedroom (**D**) with extra bunk beds, bathroom and great view. Free parking. Highly recommended.

F pp 1004, San Martín 127, 10th floor, T02944-432228, www.lamoradahostel.com/1004_english.html. Welcoming hostel at the top of a block of apartments with truly amazing views. Helpful staff, a big kitchen and cosy rooms. The big communal area is the great place to chill and watch the sunset. Their sister hotel La Morada (same website) is a wonderful place up on the hill behind Bariloche, the perfect retreat for a few days.

Estancias near Bariloche

LL Estancias Patagónicas, 20 km east of Bariloche in the steppe, R237, Km 1.6, www.estanciaspatagonicas.com. Offering riding, hunting and other *estancia* activities, this is more of a traditional *estancia* based in the historical Fort Chacabuco. The landscape is less dramatic, but it's interesting to see a working ranch.

The road to Llao Llao *p443, map p444*

There are lots of great places to stay along the shore of Lago Nahuel Huapi, many of them very close to the centre. All can be reached by buses which run every 20-30 mins.

LL Aldebaran, on Península San Pedro, reached from Av Bustillo, Km 20.4, T02944-465132, www.aldebaranpatagonia.com. At last a hotel that's not chalet style. Warm, stylish, minimalist rooms in a modern boutique hotel on the rocky lake shore, where your every need is catered for. There are superb views across the lake, chic food in the rustic-style restaurant and a wonderful sauna and spa with outdoor pool, so you can bask under the stars. The rates include transfer in/out and breakfast and they offer discounts at their restaurant and if renting for a week, they offer special prices.

LL La Cascada, Bustillo Km 6, T02944-441 088, www.lacascada.com. A traditional hotel with a stunning lakeside position and terrace going down to water. Good, reasonably priced restaurant. Not quite luxurious but comfortable.

LL Llao Llao, Bustillo, Km 25, T02944-448 530, www.llaollao.com. Deservedly famous, one of the world's most wonderful hotels in a superb location, with panoramic views from its perfect gardens, golf course, gorgeous spa suite, pools, water sports and superb restaurants. Excellent service, but some complaints about tiny rooms.

LL Peñón del Lago, Av Bustillo, Km 14, T02944-463000 (T011-4790 7979 in Buenos Aires), www.penondellago.com.ar. Hidden away in a forested park on the lake shore, this is stylish and bold design in chalet-style comfort, with a relaxed atmosphere, and a hip international feel. Rates include breakfast, transfers from the airport and to the ski centre in season.

LL Villa Huinid, Km 2.5, T02944-523523, www.villahuinid.com.ar. Luxurious *cabañas* for 2-8, and well-furnished rooms, though the service is variable.

L Design Suites, just 2.5 km from Bariloche centre, Av Bustillo, T02944-457000, www. designsuites.com. Refreshingly modern, with wonderful bold design in glass and wood in the stylish bar and restaurant area, this is a great place to stay. Huge spacious rooms with modern bathrooms, some with windowside jacuzzis, and all very comfortable. Rates include breakfast, pool, gym and return transfers. Recommended.

L Isla Victoria Resort, T011-439 499 605 (Buenos Aires), www.islavictoria.com. On Isla Victoria just off the coast, this is really

something special, and recommended if you want to escape from it all, amidst the spectacular island scenery. Pool, sauna, spacious and cosy places to sit and relax, riding and trekking organized, and good food. A fabulous and romantic treat.

AL Tunquelén, Bustillo Km 24.5, T02944-4444 8233, www.tunquelen.com. A real alternative to its close neighbour, Llao Llao, this is a comfortable 4-star hotel, on the lakeside with really splendid views and a secluded feel, wilder and closer to nature than its more famous cousin. Nicely decorated cottage-style rooms, attentive service and superb food. Much cheaper if you stay 4 days. Warmly recommended.

AL-A Hostería Santa Rita, Av Bustillo, Km 7.2, T/F02944-461028, www.santarita.com.ar. Bus 10, 20, 21 to Km 7.5. Close to the centre but with peaceful lakeside views, comfortable rooms, lovely terrace, and great service from the friendly family owners. Warmly recommended.

A Departamentos Bellevue, Av Bustillo, Km 24.6, T02944-448389, www.bellevue. com.ar. A dream come true: the famous tea room with the most beautiful view in Bariloche now offers accommodation. Access to beaches on the lake, incredible views, and gorgeous gardens and native forest. High-quality furnishings, extremely comfortable and well-equipped self-catering *cabañas*, delicious breakfast included.

A Hostería Katy, Av Bustillo, Km 24.3, T02944-448023 www.gringospatagonia.com. Delightful, peaceful place in a garden full of flowers, charming family welcome, breakfast included. Also offers adventure tourism and half-board.

A-B La Caleta, Av Bustillo, Km 1.9, T02944-1560 7727, www.bungalows-bariloche.com.ar. English-owned and very well-run, these *cabañas* sleep 4. Excellent value and have an open fire.

C Apart Hotel Andes y Sol, Av Bustillo Km 23.4, T 02944-448750, www.bariloche vacationrental.com. Open sky views of Lake Nahuel Huapi, the Andes and Chile make this cabin complex a recommended place to stay, as well as the attentive guest service. Rentals are private, yet are in close proximity to high-class dining, great hiking and the beach. Low-season rates start at US$40. Highly recommended.

Hostels

E pp **Hostel Alaska** (HI), Av Bustillo, Km 7.5, T02944-461564, www.alaska-hostel.com. To get there, take bus No 10, 20, 21, to Km 7.5. Well run, cosy chalet-style hostel open all year, doubles (**D**) and dorms. Kitchen facilities, internet access, rafting and riding.

Camping

A complete list of campsites is available from the tourist office, with prices and directions, www.bariloche.org. The following are recommended for their attractive locations and good facilities. Prices are around US$7 per person. To reach Av Bustillo, towards Llao Llao, take buses 10, 11, 20 or 21.
El Yeti, Km 5.8, T02944-442073, www.elyeti.alojar.com.ar. Pretty place, which also has *cabañas*.
Goye, Colonia Suiza, T02944-448627, www.campinggoye.com.ar, and **Hueney Ruca**, T02944 448622, omar@bariloche. com.ar, Colonia Suiza, buses 10 and 11 in season. These 2 sites both have *cabañas* and lots of facilities.
Petunia, Km 13.5, T02944-461969, www. campingpetunia.com. Well protected from winds by trees, a lovely shady lakeside site with beach. All facilities, a restaurant and a shop. Also *cabañas* (**D**) and dorms (**F**). Recommended.
Selva Negra, Km 2.95, T02944-441013, campingselvanegra@infovia.com.ar. Very attractive, well-equipped site. Highly recommended.

Southwest of Bariloche *p445*

For details of accommodation on Lago Gutiérrez, see page 514.
A Pire-Hue, Villa Catedral, T011-4807 8200 (Buenos Aires), www.pire-hue.com.ar.

Exclusive 5-star hotel with beautifully decorated rooms and all the facilities. Prices rise in Jul/Aug (**AL**) and fall in Jun/Sep (**B**).

Into Chile *p449*

AL O'Grimm Hotel, Gmo Gallardo 211, Puerto Montt, T+56 (0)65-252845, www.ogrimm.com. Lovely old building with clean and comfortable rooms but the decor is a little dated. Friendly staff.
A Tren del Sur Hostal, Santa Teresa 643, Puerto Montt, T+56 (0)65-343939, www.trendelsur.cl. Cosy eco-friendly boutique hotel with nicely decorated rooms, Wi-Fi and cable TV.
D pp **Res Palomita**, 50 m west of Hotel Puella, Puerto Montt. Half-board, family-run, simple, comfortable but not spacious, with separate shower. Book ahead in season. Lunches available.

Camping

There is a site opposite the Conaf office, US$7, and a good campsite 1 hr 45 mins walk east of Peulla, take food.

Eating

Bariloche *p441, map p442*
Bariloche is blessed with superb food: famous for locally smoked trout and salmon, and for wild boar, there are other delicacies to be sampled too, like the berries in season, and the fine chocolate. For details of more options, see www.guiasabores.com.ar.
¶¶¶ Chez Philippe, Primera Junta 1080, T02944-427291. Delicious local delicacies, really fine French-influenced cuisine, and delicious fondue, in this cosy place with a living-room feel. Book ahead. In high season open every day from 2000 to 2300; in low season they close on Tue.
¶¶¶ Kandahar, 20 de Febrero 698, T02944-424702, www.kandahar.com.ar. One of the nicer restaurants in town and highly recommended for its excellent food and intimate warm atmosphere. A romantic

and charming place. Tasty Argentine dishes and other imaginative cuisine served in style, in a cosy place run by ski champion Marta Peirono de Barber. Superb wines and the pisco sours are recommended. Dinner only. In high season they open every day from 2000, in low season they close on Sun.

†††-†† Jauja, Elflein 148, T02944-422952, www.restaurantjauja.com.ar. Specializing in local delicacies, this is a consistently pleasing place with a quiet, welcoming atmosphere, and great local trout and wild boar. Friendly and good value. Open every day for lunch and dinner, they accept credit cards, have a smoking room, and Wi-Fi.

†† Corvita, VA O'Connor, 511, T02944-421 708, www.covitacocinanatural.com.ar. New vegetarian restaurant (that serves fish too), set in front of the cathedral. Try the curries, masalas and pastas. They accept credit cards, open Mon-Sat for lunch and dinner from Thu-Sat.

†† Días de Zapata, Morales 362, T02944-423 128. Great on atmosphere, don't expect the Mexican food to be too authentic, but the staff are welcoming. Large menu, and the meals are tasty. Fun and friendly. Recommended. They open every day for lunch and dinner. They also have happy hours for margaritas and other drinks.

†† El Boliche de Alberto, Villegas 347, T02944-431433. Very good pasta and live *folclore* music. So popular that you'll have to queue in summer.

†† Tarquino, 24 de Septiembre and Saavedra, T02944-434774, www.restaurantetarquino.com.ar. Warm, welcoming design with trees growing through the boldly coloured room. This is great for steak and tasty pasta, with a good wine list and friendly service. They accept credit cards and are open every day for lunch and dinner.

†† Vegetariano, 20 de Febrero 730, T02944-421820, www.vegetarianpatagonia.com.ar. Basic vegetarian meals that are a little bland but beautifully served in a warm and friendly atmosphere. Dinner only except in high season. Recommended.

††-† Huang Ji, Rolando 268, T02944-428168. Good Chinese food, next door to the bowling alley.

Cafés

La Alpina, Moreno 98. Charming, old-fashioned Alpine-style place, as you'd expect, with delicious cakes, great for tea. They have the kitchen open all day, you can have sandwiches, fondue or other dishes at anytime. Wi-Fi available.

La Esquina, Moreno 10. Another traditional pub with good food and relaxed atmosphere. Wi-Fi.

The Map Room, Urquiza 248, T02944-456 856. Fantastic café/pub that serves large portions of interesting salads, burgers, and Bariloche's best brunch complete with hash browns and bacon. Recommended.

The road to Llao Llao *p443, map p444*

††† Cassis, opposite Arelauquen golf club, just off R82, call first for directions, T02944-476167, www.cassis.com.ar. This is without a doubt one of Bariloche's finest restaurants, with a stunning setting right on the waterfront of Lake Gutiérrez, in secluded gardens. Serves amazing food, local delicacies, exquisite dishes. Evenings only except in high season. Highly recommended.

††† Il Gabbiano, Av Bustillo, Km 24.3, T02944-448346. Closed Tue. Excellent Italian food in this intimate restaurant on the lakeside. Delicious trout, seafood and wild boar, and an extensive wine list. Booking essential. No credit cards. Highly recommended.

†††-†† Di Como, Av Bustillo. Km 0.8, T02944-522118. A 10-min walk from town. Good pizza and pasta place with a fantastic terrace and great views of the lake. Recommended.

†† El Patacón, Av Bustillo Km 7, T02944-442 898/800, www.elpatacon.com. The food here is good, but it's pricey. Romantic setting with beautiful interior woodwork and great example of old Patagonian luxury.

Rincón Patagónico, Av Bustillo, Km 14, T02944-463063, www.rinconpatagonico. com.ar. Traditional *parrilla* with tasty Patagonian lamb cooked *al palo* (speared over an open fire). Menu is huge. Service is marginal at times.

Cervecería Blest, Av Bustillo Km 11.6, T02944-461026, www.cervezablest.com.ar, open 1200-2400. One of Bariloche's many breweries, this is a great place to come at lunchtime or for an early dinner, with delicious beers – try their La Trochitastout – imaginative local and German dishes and, incredibly, steak and kidney pie. Warm rustic atmosphere. Come with friends and order the superb *picadas* with a selection of beers. Recommended.

Bars and clubs

Bariloche *p441, map p442*
Bars
Antares, Elflein 47, T02944-431454. Chilled modern bar with a good range of beer.
The Map Room (see Cafés, above). Quiet pub, with good food.
Pilgrim, Palacios 167, between O'Connor and Mitre. One of 2 Irish theme pubs in town, this serves a good range of beers in a lively pub atmosphere, also regional dishes. Reasonably priced.
Wilkenny, San Martín 435, T02944-424444. The other Irish pub, also lively. Expensive food but it really gets busy around 2400. Great place to watch televised sporting events.

Clubs
Cerebro, JM de Rosas 406, www.cerebro. com.ar. The party starts at 0130. Fri is best. Open Jun-Dec.
Roxvy, San Martín 240. Open for dinner and then moves into dancing from 0130. Very popular for locals and visitors. Open all year.

Shopping

Bariloche *p441, map p442*
The main commercial centre is on Mitre between the Centro Cívico and Beschtedt.

Bookshops
Cultura, Elflein 78, T02944-420193. A good range of books, some in English and German.
La Barca Libros, Quaglia 247, and another branch on Mitre 534, T02944-423170, www.patagonialibros.com. Mon-Fri 0930-2100, closed for lunch on Sat. For a wonderful range of books on Patagonia, and an excellent bookshop: the Mitre branch has a good selection of books in English.

Clothing and outdoor equipment
Arbol, Mitre in the 400 block. Sells good quality outdoor gear, lovely clothes and interesting gifts.
Cardón, San Martín 324, T02944-439997, www.cardon.com.ar. Reliable chain of shops all over Argentina selling quality leather and clothing.
Martín Pescador, Rolando 257, T02944-422 2275, also at Cerro Catedral in winter. Fly shop with fishing, camping and skiing equipment.
Patagonia Outdoors, Elflein 27, T02944-426768, www.patagonia-outdoors.com.ar. Maps and equipment, everything you might need, plus adventure tourism organized, trekking and rafting especially.
Scandinavian, Mitre 219, T02944-433170. Skiing and outdoor clothing, plus climbing gear – very reasonable prices.

Food and drink
The local chocolate is excellent, and there are many shops along Mitre selling it. It is an Argentine custom to bring home a box of Bariloche chocolates for friends and family – and is almost a sin if you don't!

Abuela Goye, Quaglia 221, www.abuela
goye.com. Daily 0800-2330. Delicious chocs.
A personal favourite. Also a cosy café, where
you can sit and plan which chocolates to
eat next.

Ahumadero Weiss, Mitre 131, T02944-
435874, www.ahumaderoweiss.com.
Just pop in to look around and you won't be
able to resist buying some smoked trout, local
wild boar, jam, beer, or fine wine. A great little
shop selling the home-smoked goods for
which the **Familia Weiss** restaurant is famed.

Fenoglio, Av Bustillo, Km 12, www.museo
delchocolate.com.ar. An actual museum
of chocolate and chocolate production.
Tastings and a great shop. Recommended.

Mamushka, corner of Mitre and Rolando.
Daily 0830-2230. 'The best'. No mistaking
the quality here in the handmade chocolate
bars. Try a piece for free as you're waiting to
be served: the filled chocolates are delicious,
US$17 a kilo. Nice little café here too.

Handicrafts

Burton Cerámica, Av Bustillo 41. Makes
and sells the renowned handmade
Patagonian pottery.

Feria Artesanal Municipal, Moreno and
Villegas, daily 0900-2100.

▲ Activities and tours

Bariloche *p441, map p442*
Rafting, horse riding, birdwatching, hiking,
climbing and skiing can all be arranged
through tour operators. There are many
along Mitre, but best to use one that's
recommended to you, or those below.

Tours include: San Martín de los Andes
(360 km) US$30, via the Seven Lakes Drive
and returning via Paso de Córdoba and
the Valle Encantado, 12-hr minibus
excursions. There are also tours around
the Circuito Chico (60 km), US$12, ½-day.
'Cerro Tronador' (they mean a view of
Tronador, not climbing it) and Cascada los
Alerces, full-day (255 km), U$25; El Bolsón

full-day (300 km, including Lago Puelo),
US$26. Whole-day excursions to Lagos
Gutiérrez, Mascardi, Hess, the Cascada
Los Alerces, Cerro Tronador and the
Ventisquero Negro, leaving at 0800, US$38,
lots of time spent on the bus. Useful as a
way to get to walks at Pampa Linda if the
bus from CAB isn't running.

Cycling
This is a great area for mountain biking, with
some fabulously challenging descents from
the peaks around Bariloche, also easily reached
by bus. Even the basic tourist information map
shows the main routes, but **Club Andino**
(see Trekking and climbing, page 458)
has more detailed maps and advice.

Cordillera Bike, Av Bustillo, Km 18.6, T02944-
4524828, arrayanes235@bariloche.com.ar.
Great, relatively new Zenith bikes for rent at
the start of Circuito Chico. Take bus No 20,
22 or 10 and save yourself the 60-km ride
from town. Recommended.

Dirty Bikes, VA O'Connor 681, T02944-425
616, www.dirtybikes.com.ar. Very helpful
for repairs – if pricey and also offer guided
excursions on bikes, with bikes for hire.
Recommended.

Diversidad, 20 de Junio 728, T02944-428995,
www.eco-family.com. Excellent mountain
biking around the beautiful **Refugio Neumeyer**.

Circuito Chico Mountain Bike, Av Bustillo,
Km 18, T02944-1536 1917, www.circuitochico
bikes.com. Rental of good quality 24-gear
bikes at the start of the Circuito Chico route.
Can provide advice and maps.

Fishing
Excellent trout fishing Nov-Apr; arrange boat
hire with tackle shops (permits required).
Check the itinerary before you book a tour.
For information, see www.interpatagonia.
com/pesca (in Spanish and English).

Baruzzi Deportes, Urquiza 250, T02944-
424 922, baruzzi@barilocher.com.ar. Fly
shop and offers guided fishing excursions
in the whole area (flycast, trolling, spinning)

for experts and newcomers; US$150-300 (Trout Unlimited membership discounts).

Fishing and Company, T02944-523103, www.fishingandcompany.com. Bilingual guides can take you to all the good rivers nearby for fly fishing.

Martín Pescador, Rolando 257, T02944-422 275, martinpescador@bariloche.com.ar. A great shop for fishing supplies (as well as camping and skiing) and experts there can organize all kinds of fishing expeditions.

Horse riding

Bastion del Manso, Mitre 415, 1st floor, T02944-437663, www.bastiondelmanso.com. Relaxed place with tuition and full-day's riding offered, including rafting and longer treks.

Diversidad, 20 de Junio 728, T02944-428 995, www.eco-family.com. Great 2-day ride to Pampa Linda, US$200 per person, everything included, or longer rides into the Steppe. Great all-round company.

Estancia Peuma Hue, Ruta 40, Km 2014, T02944 1550 1030, www.peuma-hue.com. The best riding in the region, starting at the beautiful *estancia* on the head of Lago Gutiérrez, with luxurious accommodation, and fine horses, with your own guide and horse whisperer. Day-long rides into the mountains all around, or longer rides to Pampa Linda and across the border into Chile.

Los Baqueanos, T02944-1555 4362. Based on the shore of Lago Gutiérrez, offering trips up to Refugio Frey.

Paragliding

Parapente Bariloche, T02944-1541 3715, fedemano@ciudad.com.ar. Gliding at Cerro Otto and Cerro Catedral in the winter.

Rafting

Río Manso, south of Bariloche, from the road that skirts Lago Mascardi, offers some of the best rafting in Argentina, with sections of river suitable for all levels. There are 2 main trips offered by the best companies, and they vary very little in what's on offer:

Aguas Blancas, Morales 564, T02944-432 799, www.aguasblancas.com.ar. Also offer full-day excursions, 'Duckies' (inflatable kayaks) for beginners, and the trip to Chile.

Extremo Sur, Morales 765, T02944-42/301, www.extremosur.com. Offering both trips for beginners and the more experienced, this is a very professional company with an excellent reputation. They also offer longer trips to Chile.

Skiing

There is skiing on Cerro Otto and Cerro Catedral, for more details see pages 445 and 446. Ski equipment can be rented by the day from **Cebron**, Mitre 171; **Martín Pescador** (see Fishing, above); or **Milenium**, Mitre 125.

Tour operators

Catedral Turismo, Palacios 263, T02944-425444, www.cruceandino.com. This company has the monopoly on the famous Three Lakes Crossing to Puerto Montt in Chile (see Transport, page 459), but you can buy it at any agency.

Cau Cau, Mitre 139, T02944-431372, www.isla victoriayarrayanes.com. Specializing in the trip to Isla Victoria and the Bosque de Arrayanes, these are fast modern boats with good catering facilities and professional guides.

Chaltén Travel, Moreno 126, loc 3, T02944-456005, www.chaltentravel.com. Well-organized and friendly tour company offering trekking, kayaking and specializing in the R40 from Bariloche.

Huala, San Martín 66, T02944-522438, www.huala.com.ar. Superb company offering all kinds of rafting, both Río Manso and also up to the Chilean border. Also cycling, trekking, horse riding, climbing and more challenging rafting offered for the more experienced. Bilingual guides, great value. Recommended.

Lagos del Sur, Quaglia 262, T02944-434188, www.lagosdelsurevt.com.ar. Recommended for affordable excursions around Bariloche including Circuito Chico, Isla Victoria, Trondador, as well as adventure tourism.

Turisur, Mitre 219, T02944-426109, www.bariloche.com/turisur. Boat trips to Bosque de Arrayanes, Isla Victoria and Puerto Blest, and conventional tours.

Trekking and climbing
There are fabulous peaks around Bariloche, allowing you to walk for an afternoon, or several days, staying at mountain *refugios* that provide beds and food, but cannot be booked. These are run by Club Andino Bariloche. The season runs from Dec-Apr; note that winter storms can begin as early as Apr at higher levels, making climbing dangerous. It's advisable to go with a guide. You should always check with *guardaparques* that paths are open where you're intending to walk. Horseflies (*tábanos*) frequent the lake shores and lower areas in summer: bring insect repellent.
Active Patagonia, 20 de Febrero 30, T02944-527966, www.activepatagonia.com.ar. Excellent company with very knowledgeable and well-trained guides. Ask for English speakers. Also produce good maps and walking books. Recommended.
Diversidad, 20 de Junio 728, T02944-428995, www.eco-family.com. Riding, walking, skiing, all kinds of great adventures offered by this friendly company with a great base in Refugio Neumeyer, 12 km south of Bariloche. Tremendous long treks can be tailor-made for you with bilingual guides adapted to your level. Highly recommended.
Extremo Sur, Morales 765, T02944-427301, www.extremosur.com. Professional company offering rafting and kayaking, all levels, full-day all-inclusive packages offered, and longer trips including accommodation. Check website for more details.
Huala, San Martín 66, T02944-522438, www.huala.com.ar. Excellent company with all kinds of adventure tourism on offer: rafting, riding, climbing, biking, and more. English speaking guides. Highly recommended.

⊖ Transport

Bariloche *p441, map p442*
Air
For airport information, see page 441.
Aerolíneas Argentinas runs several flights a day to **Buenos Aires**, and to **El Calafate** in summer. Chilean airline **LAN** also run flights to **Buenos Aires** and Chilean cities, excellent service. LADE flies weekly to many destinations in Patagonia, including **Bahía Blanca, Comodoro Rivadavia, Mar del Plata, Puerto Madryn**; book well in advance in peak seasons.
Airline offices Aerolíneas Argentinas, Mitre 185, T02944-423759, free phone from anywhere in Argentina, T0810-2228 6527, www.aerolineas.com, ask for English-speaking assistants; **LADE**, Villegas 480, T02944-423562, www.lade.com; **LAN**, Mitre 534, T02944-431043,T0810-999 9526, www.lan.com. Mon-Fri 0900-1300, 1600-2000, Sat-Sun 1000-1300 (only in Jan, Feb, Jul and Aug).

Bus
For bus terminal information, see page 441.
Most bus companies have offices at the bus station, some have an office in town as well: **3 de Mayo**, for local services, Moreno 480, T02944-425648; **Andesmar/ Albus**, T02944-430211; **Chevallier/La Estrella/ Koko**, also at Moreno 105, T02944-425914; **Cruz del Sur**, T02944-437 699; **Don Otto/ Río de La Plata**, T02944-437699; **Flechabus**, T02944-423090, www.flechabus.com; **TAC**, T02944-434727; **Vía Bariloche/El Valle**, also at Mitre 321, T02944-429012, bus station T02944-432 444, free-phone T0800-333 7575, www.viabariloche.com.ar.
Long distance To **Buenos Aires**, daily, 2-2½ hrs, US$63 *coche cama*, 6 companies including Andesmar. To **Bahía Blanca**, US$42, 3 companies. To **Mendoza**, 19 hrs, US$41, via Piedra de Aguila, Neuquén,

Cipolleti and San Rafael, Andesmar and TAC. To **Esquel**, via El Bolsón, 4 hrs, US$10, Andesmar; Don Otto; Mar y Valle; Vía Bariloche. To **Puerto Madryn**, 14 hrs, US$41, Don Otto and Mar y Vale. To **San Martín de los Andes**, 4 hrs, US$12, Koko. Direct bus to **Río Gallegos** with Transporte Patagonica; or you have to spend a night in **Comodoro Rivadavia** en route: daily, 14½ hrs, US$58, Don Otto. To **Calafate**, ask at hostel Alaska, or Periko's about Safari Route 40, a 4-day trip down R40 to **Calafate** via the Perito Moreno National Park, Cueva de Las Manos and Fitz Roy, staying at Estancia Melike and Río Mayo en route, US$136 plus accommodation at US$12 per day, www.visitbariloche.com/alaska, or see www.chaltentravel.com, who also organize this trip. For a budget trip which runs all year round, see Taqsa, T02944-423081, www.taqsa.com.ar, who run a no-frills services from Bariloche to El Calafate via the R40 once a week, long but interesting.

To Chile To **Osorno**, 4-6 hrs; to **Puerto Montt**, daily, 7-8 hrs US$32, Andesmar; Bus Norte; Cruz del Sur; Río de la Plata; TAS Choapa (sit on left side for best views). For **Santiago** or **Valdivia** change at Osorno.

Car hire

Let your hire company know if you're planning to drive over the border into Chile, as they'll need to rent you a vehicle that has its registration number engraved on the windows by law. Give 24 hrs' notice. Rates are around US$55 a day. You can arrange to drop the car at San Martín de los Andes, or Esquel for an extra charge, from US$35.

Budget, Mitre 106, 1st floor, T02944-422482, www.budget.com.ar; Rent a Car Bariloche, Rolando 258, T02944-426420, www.rentacarbariloche.com, reliable and good value; Travel Rent a Car, VA O'Connor 602, T02944-435374, www.travel rentacar.com.ar, reliable, English spoken.

Remise taxi

Melipal Remises, T02944-442300; Puerto Remises, T08009-990885 (freephone), T02944-435222; Radio Taxi Bariloche, T02944-422103; Remises Bariloche, T02944-430222; Remises del Bosque, T02944-429109.

Train

Booking office T02944-422450, closed Mon-Fri 1200-1500, Sat afternoon and Sun. Information available from the tourist office. Tourist service to **Viedma**, 16 hrs, US$12-50 .

The road to Llao Llao *p443, map p444*
Bus

Minibuses run to **Pampa Linda** and **Tronador**, Transitando lo Natural, 20 de Febrero 25, T02944-527926, transitando1@ hotmail.com. Buses to Pampa Linda daily at 0900 in season, US$10. Alternatively, **Expreso Meiling**, T02944-529 875, also run buses in season, leaving Club Andino at 0830, and returning from Pampa Linda at 1700.

Puerto Montt *p450*
Air

For airport information, see page 450.

An **ETM** bus runs from the bus terminal 1½ hrs before departure, US$3. To **Santiago** and **Punta Arenas** several daily flights by LanChile, Lan Express and Aero Continente. Flights fully booked in advance in summer: worth asking at the airport for cancellations.

Bus

There are services to all parts of the country from the bus terminal.

Sea

Shipping offices Cruce de Lagos, www.crucedelagos.com. Includes departures to **Puerto Vargas** and **Bariloche**.

❶ Directory

Bariloche *p441, map p442*
Banks Usually open from 0900-1300. ATMs at many banks along Mitre: **Banco Frances**, San Martín 332; **Banco Galicia**, Moreno and Quaglia; **Banco Nación Argentina** at Mitre 180; **Banco Patagonia**, Moreno 127. **Currency exchange** Sudamérica, Mitre 63, T02944-434555, exchange and TCs, best rates and service. **Customs** Bariloche centre T02944-425216; Rincón (Argentina) T02944-425734; Pajarito (Chile) T002944-236284. **Embassies and consulates** Austria, 24 de Septiembre 230, T02944-424873; **Chile**, Rosas 180, T02944-422842; **France**, T02944-441960; **Germany**, Ruiz Moreno 65, T02944-425695; **Italy**, Beschtedt 141, T02944-422247; **Switzerland**, Quaglia 342, T02944-426111. **Emergencies** Medical, T107; or San Carlos Emergencias, T02944-430000. **Immigration office** Libertad 191, T02944-423043, Mon-Fri 0900-1300.

Internet Many places along Mitre, and in the 1st block of Quaglia. **Language schools** La Montana, Elflein 251, 1st floor, T02944-524212, www.lamontana.com, friendly Spanish-language school with small classes, activities and accommodation organized, and a fantastic volunteering programme that supports the local community, highly recommended; **Steps**, Morales 764, T02944-422340, www.stepsonline.com.ar, established school that teaches Spanish, Portuguese and English; **Spanish in the Mountains**, C Isla Victoria, Villa Los Coihues, T02944-467597, www.spanishinthemountains.com, unique concept of teaching Spanish while exploring the area trekking, kayaking, climbing and skiing, can also organize accommodation. **Medical services** Hospital Zonal, Moreno 601, T02944-426100. **Post office** Moreno 175, Mon-Fri 0800-2000, Sat 0830-1300. **Telephone** Many *locutorios* along Mitre; Telecom at Mitre and Rolando is helpful.

North of Bariloche and Seven Lakes Drive

The journey north from Bariloche along the celebrated Seven Lakes Drive is a magical experience: a winding road through a wonderland of lakes embedded in forest-covered mountains. On the way to picturesque San Martín de los Andes, there are two good bases for further adventures. First, on the northern side of Lake Nahuel Huapi, is the pretty, upmarket town of Villa la Angostura. Much loved by wealthier Argentines, there's no shortage of smart places to stay and eat, such as famous and blissful boutique hotel, Las Balsas (www.lasbalsas.com). From Villa la Angostura you can visit the tiny national park, Los Arrayanes, created to protect a rare forest of arrayán trees with their cinnamon-coloured bark, and twisting trunks: a magical woodland where you can walk or take a boat. Further along the Seven Lakes Drive is another more remote village, Villa Traful. Tucked into a deep fold between dramatic, spired mountains, on the side of a navy blue sliver of lake, this is a peaceful place for a few days' rest, with a couple of good walks and some appealing places to stay.

Drive up through ever-changing combinations of lakes and mountains to find San Martín de los Andes sitting proudly at the head of Lake Lacar. With no shortage of chalet-style cabañas, this is a very comfortable base for exploring another fine national park, Lanín, whose conical volcano is visible for miles around, and which you can climb if you have a few days free. It's well worth hiring a car here to explore the park in detail, especially Lagos Huachulafquen and Paimun. Junín de los Andes makes an alternative base for lovers of fishing; it is the fishing capital of Argentina. Estancia Huechahue (www.huechahue.com) is nearby, with superb horse riding into the park and across the Andes to Chile. Heading further north still, you'll come eventually to Villa Pehuenia, a fledgling village in a spectacular setting on Lake Aluminé, with some superb accommodation and its own resident Mapuche community who will take you riding and skiing in season. Sleepier Lake Moquehue is a great place to hang out and do nothing. For more information, see www.interpatagonia.com/loslagos (in Spanish and English). ▸▸ For listings, see pages 465-470.

La Ruta de los Siete Lagos ➜ For listings, see pages 465-470.

The Seven Lakes Drive is the most famous tourist route in the Argentine Lake District. It follows Route 234 through the Lanín and Nahuel Huapi national parks, and passes seven magnificent lakes, all flanked by mixed natural forest and is particularly attractive in autumn (April to May) when the forested slopes turn red and yellow. The road is only partially paved, and mostly decent, apart from a very potholed stretch in the middle, not recommended after heavy rain or snowfall.

The seven lakes are (from south to north): Nahuel Huapi, Correntoso, Espejo, Villarino, Falkner, Machónico and Lácar. Leaving Villa la Angostura, you'll be treated to a superb view of Lago Correntoso, then turn off to reach gorgeous secluded Lago Espejo ('lake mirror'), which has lovely beaches on its shore, before passing the northwestern corner of Lago Traful at Km 58. At Km 77, Route 65 branches off to the east, running along the south shore of Lago Traful through Villa Traful to meet the main Neuquén–Bariloche highway (Route 237) at Confluencia. If you have a couple of days to spare, this is a lovely place to stop. At Pichi Traful, a beautiful spot by the wide green banks of the aquamarine blue river, there's a campsite and picnic ground amidst little beech trees by turquoise water with steeply rising mountains on all sides. Carry on though for the pretty, if exposed, free campsite (with no facilities) by the deep green Río Villarino. The road emerges to climb up overlooking the shores of Lago Villarino and you're suddenly shown a welcome open vista of the lake; from here the road is paved. Popular with fishermen, Lago Falkner opposite is wide and open with thickly forested fjord-like mountains descending steeply into it. There's a long narrow sandy beach on the roadside, a good place for a picnic stop, and wild camping, with no facilities, though **Camping Lago Falkner** nearby does have facilities.

You can see the route from the windows of a bus on a round trip excursion from either Bariloche or Villa la Angostura, which will take about five hours, but you may prefer your own transport, so you can stop and explore. Buses will stop at campsites on the route. It's a good route for cycling, you can really appreciate the beauty of the ever-changing landscape, though note that there's more traffic in January and February.

The direct route to San Martín de los Andes

There's a quicker route to San Martín and Neuquén if you're in a rush, or for the way back, when you've already seen the view. Further west, via **Confluencia**, it's also attractive. Take Route 237 from Bariloche to Confluencia running through the astounding **Valle Encantado**, where there are weird rock formations including El Dedo de Dios (The Finger of God) and El Centinela del Valle (The Sentinel of the Valley), and then north on Route 63, over the **Paso de Córdoba**, Km 77 (1300 m), and along the tranquil shore of Lago Meliquina. You could turn off to isolated Lago Filo-Hua-Hum at Km 54 (unpaved track).

Villa La Angostura and around → *For listings, see pages 465-470.*

This is a delightful little town which, apart from in January when it is packèd out, is an appealing place to stay, especially for those who like their nature seen from the comfort of a luxurious hotel. There are some superb restaurants here and some seriously chic hotels. *Cabaña* complexes and great hostels have mushroomed up everywhere, so there's no shortage of places to stay. And there are some good walks nearby, excellent fly fishing, and a golf course, as well as skiing in winter. The area is divided into several different *barrios*: around the sprawling town centre, **El Cruce**, around the lakeside area of **Puerto Manzano**, and around the picturesque port, known as **La Villa**, which is 3 km away at the neck of the Quetrihué Peninsula. For more information, see www.villalaangostura.com.ar.

Ins and outs → *Colour map 5, B2. Phone code 02944. Population 13,000.*

Getting there The small **bus terminal** ① *at the junction of Av 7 Lagos and Av Arrayanes*, is opposite the ACA service station. You can leave your baggage at the small café below for US$2.

Tourist information The **tourist office** ① *on the left-hand side of the road heading north, just opposite the bus terminal, Av Siete Lagos 93, T02944-494124, high season 0800-2100, low season 0800-2000*, is busy and helpful, with lots of information, and accommodation prices marked on a board inside. English spoken.

Sights

Villa La Angostura's great attraction is the **Parque Nacional Los Arrayanes** (see box, page 440), at the end of the Quetrihué Peninsula, which dips into the northern end of Lago Nahuel Huapi, and can be reached on foot or by boat from the port area of La Villa. Also from La Villa, a short walk leads to lovely **Laguna Verde**, an intense emerald-green lagoon surrounded by mixed *coihue* cypress and *arrayán* forests, where there's a 1-km

Border essentials: Argentina–Chile

Paso Samore

Officially known as Paso Samore, **Paso Puyehue** (1280 m) lies 125 km northwest of Bariloche on Route 231, which is unpaved from Villa La Angostura. It's a spectacular six-hour journey, with plenty of buses from Bariloche, making it a cheaper alternative to the expensive Three Lakes Crossing. The road is rough *ripio* here, with the occasional paved stretch.

Argentine customs and immigration Open daily 0900-2000, for more information, see www.gendarmeria.gov.ar/pasos/fichsamo.html.

Chilean immigration It's another 50 km to Chilean customs over a wonderful mountain pass. On the Chilean side the road is paved via Entre Lagos and Lago Puyehue to Osorno. Immigration is open mid-October to 1 May daily 0800-2100, 0900-2000 in winter. It's in the middle of a forest at Anticura, Km 146, 22 km west of the border.

Accommodation Termas Puyehue, Route 215, Km 76, T+56-(0)2-293 6000, www.puyehue.cl. Luxurious accommodation and excellent thermal baths at a huge complex set in beautiful open parkland, framed by mountains, with an impressive spa. Recommended.

Transport For bus services from Bariloche to Osorno, Puerto Montt and Valdivia, see page 458. For vehicles entering Chile, formalities take about 30 minutes, and include the spraying of tyres and wiping of shoes on a mat (US$3.50 fee). Have Chilean pesos ready. Argentine hire cars must have the necessary documentation, and the car's number plate etched on the windows. Tell your car hire company you plan to cross to Chile 24 hours in advance.

Note This route is liable to closure after snow.

---

self-guided trail, taking about an hour. A bus runs from El Cruce to La Villa every couple of hours, taking 15 minutes, but it's a pleasant walk.

There are no services in La Villa apart from a *kiosko*, a tea room in high season, and the restaurant at **Hotel Angostura**. About halfway between the two centres there is a chapel (1936), designed by Bustillo, the famous architect who gave this region's buildings their distinctive style, and nearby is **El Messidor** (1942), the summer resort of Argentine presidents, where you can visit the beautiful gardens with lake views.

In winter, there's good skiing at Villa La Angostura's popular ski resort **Cerro Bayo** ① *9 km north of town, T02944-494189, www.cerrobayoweb.com*, with 24 pistes, many of them fabulously long, and all with excellent views over the lakes below, 20 km in total, and a great area for snowboarding. This is one of Argentina's pricier resorts; a one day ski pass costs US$40 for adults for the day in high season. There's also a tiny museum, **Museo Regional** ① *Blvd Nahuel Huapi 2177, on the road to La Villa, Mon 0800-1400, Tue and Thu 0800-1630, Wed and Fri 0800-1630*, with interesting photos of the original indigenous inhabitants.

Walks around Villa La Angostura

Parque Nacional Los Arrayanes For an easy flat walk, take the boat to the head of the Quitrihué Peninsula and walk the 13 km back. See box, page 440.

Mirador Belvedere Offers fine views of Lagos Correntoso and Nahuel Huapi. It's a 3-km drive or walk up the old road, northwest of El Cruce; and from the mirador a path to your right goes to **Cascada Inacayal**, a waterfall 50 m high, situated in an area rich in native flora and forest.

Cascada Río Bonito A delightful walk leading to a beautiful waterfall, lying 8 km east of El Cruce off Route 66. The steep path gives tremendous views, and the falls themselves are impressive, falling 35 m from a chasm in basalt cliffs to an emerald-green pool. Further along the same path, you can reach the summit of Cerro Bayo (1782 m). Alternatively, 1 km further along the road, a ski lift takes you to the platform at 1500 m, where there's a restaurant with great views, and from here, it's a short trek to the summit. The ski lift runs all year; cyclists can take bikes up in the lift and cycle down.

Villa Traful → *Phone code 02944. Population 503.*
If you want to get off the beaten track, Villa Traful is ideal. It was created after the Nahuel Huapi National Park was set up, with the aim of giving visitors the greatest possible contact with nature. Approaching from the west, the winding road passes through forests of lenga and tall *coihue* trees, their elegant trunks creating a woody cathedral, with idyllic spots to camp all along the shore. The quiet pretty village sprawls alongside the narrow deep-blue sliver of Lago Traful, enclosed on both sides by stunning sharp-peaked mountains. There's not much to do here, but it's popular with fishermen, and there are a couple of wonderful walks and waterfalls to see, it's a pleasant place to unwind. The best time to visit is December or late February to March when the few restaurants aren't full of tourists. Traful is prone to mercurial winds, so check the forecast if you're coming for a few days as it's miserable being stuck here in bad weather and the buses are infrequent. At the heart of the village opposite the main pier is a pay phone, a kiosk selling basic supplies and bus tickets, and the best restaurant. There's a small but very helpful **tourist office** ① *on the lakeshore, just past Aiken* cabañas, *T02944-479099, see www.villatraful. com, www.interpatagonia.com/villatraful*, which has information on walks, riding and fishing. The national park *guardería* is opposite the pier, open only in high season, with advice on walks.

Walks around Villa Traful

A 1½-hour walk from the village centre there are the lovely **Cascadas dal Arroyo Coa Có y Blanco**, waterfalls thundering down through beech forest and *cañas colihues* bamboo. Walk up the hill from the Ñancu Lahuen restaurant and take the left-hand path to the mirador over Cascada Coa Có, and from here take the right-hand path through *coihue* forest to **Cascada Blanco**. A lovely ride by horse or mountain bike. Better still, there's a satisfying hike up to **Cerro Negro** (2000 m) five hours up, following uncertain yellow markers. Ask at the national park office to get the best advice on the route. It's a stiff climb to start with, through gorgeous *coihue* and *lenga* forest, and the views as you clear the tree line are unbelievable, with the dramatic spired peaks visible on the northern side of Lago Traful. There's a lot of scree near the summit, but the views of Lanín, Tronador and the others make it all worthwhile. Alternatively, cross the lake (15 minutes) by boat, leaving from the main pier, to reach a sand beach from where you can walk up a steep path to twin lagoons, and some superbly well conserved prehistoric cave paintings nearby. Ask in the tourist office to see which companies are currently running trips.

For Sleeping and Eating price codes and other relevant information, see Essentials pages 30-36.

◉ Sleeping

La Ruta de los Siete Lagos *p461*

A Hostería Lago Villarino, Lago Villarino, T02972-429483. A lovely setting, fantastic large rooms in an attractive 1940s-style lodge. Good food, also camping.
B Lago Espejo Resort, at tranquil Lago Espejo, set a little way off the road, T02944-494583, lago_espejo_resort@topmail.com.ar. A beautifully situated hotel, though not quite a resort as the name suggests, with simple camping area on the tranquil and secluded shore of the lake, surrounded by *coihue* trees. Lovely in good weather, and out of season.
D Hostería Lago Espejo, T02944-494584. Old fashioned and comfortable, with good food in the restaurant, open Jan-Mar only.

Camping

Lago Espejo Resort campsite (see above) is open all year. Facilities include toilets, drinking water and fireplaces, but no showers. US$5 per person.
Lago Espejo Camping, further along a dirt track. A magical spot on quiet shores of the lake and its incredibly blue-grey river. Open all year, mostly visited by fishermen from Nov-end Apr, US$5 per person, no showers, but toilets, drinking water and fireplaces. Also picnic spots. Busy in Jan, less so in Feb. Recommended.

The direct route to San Martín de los Andes *p462*

B Hostería ACA Confluencia, T02944-490800, at the ACA service station. *Confitería.*
B-C Hostería La Gruta de las Virgenes, Confluencia, T02944-426138, www.glvpatagonia.com.ar. On a hill with views over the 2 rivers, very hospitable.

Villa La Angostura and around *p462*

Accommodation is good here, but pricey. It's more pleasant, and cheaper, outside Jan and Jul peak seasons. See www.villa laangostura.com.ar, for more listings.
LL La Escondida, T02944-475313, www.hosterialaescondida.com.ar. Wonderful setting, right on the lake with only 14 rooms, heated pool and great midweek and week-end specials. They have special prices for staying more than 5 nights. Recommended.
LL Las Balsas, on Bahía Las Balsas (signposted from Av Arrayanes), T02944-494308 (T011-4700 1417 in Buenos Aires), www.lasbalsas.com. One of the best small hotels in Argentina, with fabulous cosy rooms, warm relaxed public areas, impeccable service, and a wonderfully intimate atmosphere in a great lakeside location with its own secluded beach. The chef, Pablo Campoy, creates really fine cuisine from top local produce. There's a beautiful lakeside pool (indoor and outdoor, both heated), and the best spa in the Lake District. Trips and excursions arranged, or transfers to the ski centre in season. This cannot be recommended highly enough.
LL-L Correntoso, discreetly hidden off the road, R231 and Río Correntoso, T02944-619728 (T011-4803 0030 in Buenos Aires), www.correntoso.com. Really fabulous setting for this intimate and stylish hotel with a superb restaurant. Very special. Recommended.
L La Posada, R231, Km 65, a few kilometres west of town on R231 towards Chile, T02944-494450/494368, www.hosterialaposada.com. In a splendid elevated position off the road with clear views over the lake, this is a welcoming, beautifully maintained hotel in lovely gardens, with pool and fine restaurant; a perfectly peaceful place to relax.

AL Casa del Bosque, Los Pinos 160, Puerto Manzana, T02944-475229, www.casadelbosque.com. Luxury and style in these wonderfully designed *cabañas*, with lots of glass, jacuzzis and all possible comforts, in secluded woodland. Price includes breakfast and spa services.

AL-A Hostal Las Nieves, Av 7 Lagos 980, T02944-494573, www.lasnieves.com. Chalet-style splendour, high standard of service and cuisine.

A Cabañas La Ruma Andina, Blvd Queitrhué 1692, La Villa, T02944-495188, www.rumaandina.com.ar. Top-quality rustic *cabañas* with lots of stone and wood, and cosily furnished, in a lovely setting with pool. Recommended.

A Casa Grande Resort, Blvd Quetrihué 338, T02944-494888, www.casagranderesort. com.ar. Spread over 4 ha are 3 lodges with 4 bedrooms each. Lovely designs, and spacious living inside and out. Price for entire lodge, up to 8 people.

A Hostería ACA al Sur, Av Arrayanes 8 (behind the petrol station), T02944-494168, www.acavillalaangostura.com.ar. New, modern and very attractive single-storey hotel with 20 well-designed rooms in the centre of town. Highly recommended.

A Hotel Angostura, T02944-494224, www.hotelangostura.com. Open all year, and beautifully situated on the lakeside at the port, La Villa. Handsome stone and wood chalet was designed by Bustillo in 1938, and retains a rather charming old-fashioned feel, with lovely gardens. Has an excellent restaurant and tea house open to non-residents in high season.

B-C Verena's Haus, Los Taiques 268, T02944-494467, www.verenashaus.com.ar. A quaint and welcoming wooden house, with cosy rooms, a pretty garden and delicious breakfasts. German and English spoken. No smokers or children allowed. Recommended.

C-D Hostería del Francés, Lolog 3057, located in a great position on the shore of Lago Correntoso, T02944-488055,

www.lodelfrances.com.ar. Excellent value. Lovely, chalet-style house with great views (although a little blocked by recent developments in the area) from all the rooms. Recommended.

Hostels

E pp Italian Hostel, Los Marquis 215, T02944-494376, www.italianhostel.com.ar. Closed from Apr-Oct each year, this small, central hostel offers dorms in a friendly and cosy oasis. The owners, artists who live next door, can help with local information. Recommended. Special for bike riders, they give assessments about routes, trips, and supplies needed. Cheapest hostel option in town. Maximum of days to stay here: 7.

E pp Bajo Cero Hostel, Av 7 Lagos, T02944-495454, www.bajocerohostel.com. Appealing lodge-style wood building with warm, cosy dorm rooms and a great games area, linen and breakfast included. Situated a little out of town, but an easy 5-min walk to a supermarket or 10-15 mins' walk to town. Doubles (**D-C**) available. Hire bikes at the hostel. Recommended.

E pp Hostel la Angostura, Barbagelata 157, T02944-494834, www.hostellaangostura. com.ar. 300 m up the well-signposted road behind the tourist office is this warm, luxurious and great value hostel, beautifully run and impeccably clean. All the small dorms have bathrooms, and the friendly young owners organize trips too. Pool, internet, bar, TV and bikes for hire. Doubles (**D-C**) available. Highly recommended.

Camping

Many sites, with good facilities along R231. **Osa Mayor**, signposted off main road, close to town, T02944-494304, www.camping osamayor.com.ar. Delightful leafy site on a hillside with good, shaded levelled camping spots, and all facilities. Clean bathrooms and run by a friendly family. US$8 per person. Also lovely rustic dorms (**E** pp) and *cabañas* (**C**) with heating and good views, for up to 4 people. Highly recommended.

Villa Traful p464

There are just a few places to stay clustered around the lake; most of them basic.

AL-A Marinas Puerto Traful, T02944-479117, www.marinaspuertotraful.com.ar. Gorgeous uninterrupted views of the lake. Comfortable. Good deals in low season.

A Ruca Lico, T02944-479004, www.inter patagonia.com/rucalico. Luxurious *cabañas*, in woodland above the lake, lavishly furnished in rustic chic style, with jacuzzi and balcony. Good value for 6, a fabulous treat for 2. Horse riding also organized. Highly recommended.

B Aiken, T02944-479048 (in Buenos Aires, T011-4568 2107), www.aiken.com.ar. Rustic and compact, well-decorated *cabañas* in spacious gardens with old trees and lovely open views of the lake below. All have *parrilladas* outside, so you can grill your own steaks, and still have a feeling of privacy. Cheap for 4 or 5. Also a restaurant. Recommended.

B-C Cabañas del Montañes, up behind the village, T02944-479035, www.interpatagonia. com/delmontanes. Accommodation in 4 charming *cabañas* offered by the company that makes *alfajores*. Lovely setting

B-C Hostería Villa Traful, T02944-479005, www.hosteriavillatraful.com. A delightful place to stay, this simple *hostería* is elevated above the lakeside in pretty gardens. Separate cabins, with comfortable furnishings and ample bathrooms. There are also *cabañas* for up to 6. Charming hospitality from the owner, whose son Andrés Quelin, T02944-479005, also organizes fishing and boat trips.

Hostels

E pp Vulcanche, Los Sorbus 67, T02944-479028, www.vulcanche.com. An attractive, huge chalet-style hostel and 2 cosy *cabañas* (**C**), very comfortable and set in lovely open gardens with good views. Also simple camping in a pleasant open site, US$7 per person with hot showers, phone and *parrilladas*. Breakfast US$3 extra.

Camping

There are many sites along the lake shore. **Camping Traful Lauquen**, on the shore, T02944-479030, www.traful-lauquen.com.ar. Open Nov-Mar. With 600 m of beach, this is among the loveliest of the many sites along the lake. Facilities include hot showers, light, fireplaces and restaurant. US$8 per person. A really calm and beautiful site, much favoured by families wanting a quiet time.

Costa Traful, T02944-479049, www.inter patagonia.com/costatraful. Open Dec-Apr. If you're young and you've got a guitar, or would like to meet somebody who has, camp at this lively place with 24-hr hot showers, restaurant, fireplaces and *provedería*. Popular with backpackers, US$7 per person. Also has shared bunk rooms and basic but rustic *cabañas* for hire (**B**). Fishing and horse-riding trips, as well as trips to see cave paintings on the other side of the lake (3-hr trek each way), US$20, full-day. Also offers a boat trip to see a submerged cypress forest, and diving for those with experience.

● Eating

Villa La Angostura and around p462

Plenty of places are to be found on the main Av Arrayanes, lots of them chalet-style, and open all day from breakfast onwards. Prices reflect the fact that this is a popular tourist town. Don't miss out on some of the really excellent places for fine cuisine here.

♦♦♦ Cocina Waldhaus, R231, Puerto Manzano, T02944-475323. Much recommended, this is 'auteur cuisine' with gorgeous local delicacies created by Chef Leo Morsella, served in a charming chalet-style building.

♦♦♦ Correntoso, Hotel Corentoso, Av 7 Lagos, T02944-619727. Another gourmet restaurant, this one specializing in Mediterranean cuisine, with Patagonian touches, like lamb and trout. Great wine list, gorgeous setting on the lake.

♦♦♦ Las Balsas, on the lake T02944-494308, www.las balsas.com. The chef, Pablo Campoy, creates really special food here.

The wines are superb too, and the whole atmosphere is a real treat. Non-residents are only admitted if the hotel is quiet, and you should book well in advance and dress up a bit. Highly recommended.

ᵀᵀ Gran Nevada, opposite **Nativa Café**. Good for cheap *parrilla* and *noquis* in a cheery, friendly atmosphere.

ᵀᵀ Los Pioneros, Av Arrayanes 267, T02944-495525. Famous for fine local dishes in a chalet-style building and great Argentine steaks, this is widely recommended. There is a great pizza place next door run by the same owners. Try the locally brewed beers.

ᵀᵀ Nativa Café, Av Arrayanes 198, T02944-495093. This is the most relaxed and welcoming on the main drag with a high-ceilinged chalet feel, good music playing, and a menu that manages to be international and individual. Excellent pizzas – try the smoked goat cheese – and a good place to hang out. Friendly, efficient staff and a mixed clientele: couples and families of all ages. Pizza for 2, US$9, huge salads. Recommended.

ᵀᵀ Tasca Placido, Av Siete Lagos 1726, T02944-495763. Owned by a Spaniard, this local hang-out serves great paella and lots of seafood.

ᵀᵀ-ᵀ El Esquiador, Las Retames 146 (behind the bus terminal), T02944-494331. Your best bet on a budget is this *parrilla*. Cheap, fixed-price 3-course menu.

ᵀ Hora Cero, Av Arrayanes 45. Hugely popular, heaving in summer, this serves a big range of excellent pizzas and *pizza libre* (as much as you can eat for US$5) on Wed and Sat, a great deal.

Cafés

ᵀ TemaTyCo, R231, Km 55, T02944-475211. Chic tea room serving amazing range of teas, *mate* and delicious cakes. Charming, welcoming and recommended.

Villa Traful p464

ᵀᵀ Costa Traful, R65, T02944-479049. The only restaurant set directly on the lake, also

has accommodation (see Sleeping, **Villa Traful**). Regional dishes and sandwiches.

ᵀᵀ Ñancu Lahuen, T02944-479017. The best restaurant for miles around, this is a delightful tea room and restaurant serving excellent trout and home-made pasta, all reasonably priced, and in a cosy setting. Great cakes and delicious home-made chocolates, a homely place to hang out if it's raining, with a big open fire.

ᵀ Parrilla La Terraza, T02944-479073. Recommended for delicious, locally produced lamb and kid on the *asado*. Panoramic lake views.

▲▲ Activities and tours

La Ruta de los Siete Lagos p461
Round-trip excursions along the Seven Lakes route, 5 hrs, are operated by several companies. Buses will stop at campsites on the route. It's a good area for cycling, though there is more traffic in Jan and Feb.

Villa La Angostura and around p462
Boat trips
There are 3 companies running catamarans: **Catamarán Patagonia Argentina**, T02944-494463, www.catamaranpatagonia.com.ar, runs trips on a 60-passenger catamaran; **Greenleaf Turismo**, www.bosquelos arrayanes.com.ar, runs *Catamarán Futuleufu*, T02944-494004, tickets from Av 7 Lagos 118, 1st floor, US$15 return; **Turisur**, T02944-426109, www.turisur.com.ar, runs boats from Bariloche, via Isla Victoria.

Velero Luz de Luna, T02944-494834, www.vela-aventura.com.ar, offers trips on sailing boats with a special meal on board, or a drink with *picadas* of smoked meat and fish.

Canopying
The new craze in the lakes is this terrifying (or exciting) business of hanging from a harness rolling along wires strung up high in the forest to get an adrenalin-filled aerial view.

Canopy Villa la Angostura, Curruhué and Melinquina, T02944-1557 9071, www.canopybariloche.com. Runs a great trail in the forest nearby, with over 1400 m of cable to zoom along.

Climbing
Club Andino Villa La Angostura, Cerro Bayo 295, T02944-494954. Excursions, maps and information.

Cycling
Expect to pay around US$10 per day for bike hire.
Free Bike's, Las Fucsias 45, T02944-1564 2985, www.freebikes.com.ar. Mountain bike hire and spares and repairs. Run guided and tailor-made tours.
Taquari Blcl Shop, Av Arrayanes 259. New bikes, knowledgeable staff.

Fishing
The season runs from mid-Nov to May. For permits and a list of fishing guides, ask at the tourist office.
Anglers Home Fly Shop, Belvedere 22, T02944-495222. Arranges fishing trips.
Banana Fly Shop, Av Arrayanes 282, T02944-494634. Fly shop.
PatagonFly, www.patagonfly.com. A fly shop and association of local fishing guides, also runs trips.

Horse riding
Rates are usually about US$15 per hr.
Cabalgatas Correntoso, Cacique Antrao 1850, T02944-1551 0559, www.cabalgata-correntoso.com.ar. Offers horseback excursions in the surrounding area and to Villa Traful.
Los Saucos, Av Arrayanes 1810, T02944-494853. Offers both short and long horse treks. Knowledgeable and friendly staff.

Kayaking
Angostura Adventura, T02944-1561 8680, www.angosturaaventura.com. Local guide Jose Rubén Ocampo offers guided kayaking tours as well as trekking.

Skiing
Cerro Bayo (www.cerrobayoweb.com), although smaller and more popular with families than the famous Cerro Catedral in Bariloche, is also very well worth visiting, with a 700-m drop, and more than 20 pistes of 4 levels of difficulty. There are spectacular views of the mountains and lakes all around.

Tour operators
Nómades de la Montaña, Ruca Choroy 38 y Cerro Inacayal 35, T02944-495562, www.nomades.tur.ar. Offering everything from trekking, mountain biking, rappel, diving and fly fishing.
Rucán Turismo, Av 7 Lagos 239, T02944-495075, info@rucanturismo.com. Offers skiing, riding, mountain biking and conventional tours.

Trekking
Alma Sur, T02944-1556 4724, www.alma-sur.com. Great trips in the local area and further afield, with bilingual, knowledgeable Anthony Hawes. A trained guide of Nahuel Huapi National Park, he creates really imaginative walks, which can include boats, climbing and hiking way off the beaten track. Recommended.

Villa Traful p464
Horse riding and boat trips are organized by Camping Costa Traful, see Sleeping.

Fishing
Andres Quelin, T02944-479005. A fishing guide who organizes boat trips to see a submerged cypress wood. Find him at **Hostería Villa Traful**, see Sleeping.
Osvaldo A Brandeman, Bahía Mansa, T02944-479048, pescaosvaldo@mail.com. Fishing expert and excellent guide. Find him on the lake shore 200 m from Arroyo Cataratas.

Mountain biking
Del Montanés, along the road running up the slope behind the centre of the village, T02944-479035. Rents mountain bikes.

☉ Transport

Villa La Angostura and around *p462*
Bus
For bus terminal information, see page 462.

For bus network information, **Albus**, T02944-1561 7578; **15 de Mayo**, T02944-495104; **Andesmar**, T02944-495247; Via Bariloche/El Valle, T02944-495415.

To **Bariloche**, several daily, 1¼ hrs, US$10, several companies. If going on to **Osorno** (Chile), you can arrange for the bus company to pick you up at **La Angostura**, US$10 to Osorno. Daily buses to **San Martín de los Andes**, 2 hrs, US$7, Albus and Koko. For other destinations, change at San Martín de los Andes and Bariloche.

Car hire
Angostura Rent a Car, Av Arrayanes 21, T02944-424621, www.angosturarentacar.com.ar. Reliable company, offering accessories such as baby seats and ski racks at no extra charge. Good value.
Giménez Vidal, Las Mutisias 146, T02944-494336.
Terpin Turismo, Los Notros 41, T02944-494 551, http://www.terpinrentacar.com.ar.

Taxi
Taxi Aldana, T02944-1560 3595, ask for the helpful Jorge Eduardo Betanzo; **Taxi de la Montaña**, T02944-1556 7744, good and reliable.

Villa Traful *p464*
Bus
In high summer, a daily bus between **Villa la Angostura** and **San Martín** stops here, but in low season, buses run only 3 times a week. Kiosko El Ciervo, by the YPF service station, sells tickets and has the timetable.

❶ Directory

Villa La Angostura and around *p462*
Banks Andina, Arrayanes 256, T02944-495197, for cash and TCs; **Banco de Patagonia**, Av Arrayanes 275, ATM; **Banco Provincia de Neuquén**, Av Arrayanes 172, ATM. **Internet** Punta Arrayanes, Av Arrayanes 90, T02944-495288. **Medical services** Hospital Rural Arraiz, Copello 311 (at *barrio* Pinar), T02944-494170. **Post office** Siete Lagos 26. **Telephone** Several *locutorios* along Av Arrayanes.

Parque Nacional Lanín

Some of the most beautiful sights in the Lake District are to be found in one of the country's largest national parks, Lanín, which stretches north from Nahuel Huapi National Park all the way to Lago Norquinco, to the west of Aluminé, and along the border with Chile for some 200 km. The park's centrepiece, and its most climbed peak, is the magnificent extinct snow-capped Volcán Lanín. The ascent takes two days, and starts from close to the border at Paso Tromen (also known as Paso Mamuil Malal). Lanín forms a dramatic backdrop to the beautiful landscapes all around the park, and is especially superb seen from two connected lakes, which make the most beautiful places in the park to visit: Lago Huechulafquen and Lago Paimún stretch west from Junín de los Andes, with great hiking, fishing and camping. Both lakes have shores of volcanic black sand, and there are comfortable hosterías, and basic campsites, as well as marked paths for several rewarding hikes. A fantastic boat trip allows you to see the spectacular heart of the park from the water, and access to Lago Epulafquen. These are the easiest parts of the park to visit, with a good road leading from Junín de los Andes. Southernmost parts of the park can be visited easily from San Martín de los Andes, which sits at the head of picturesque Lago Lacar (well set up for tourism), with boat trips and several beaches where you can bathe and rent canoes. Quiet Lago Lolog further north also offers good fishing, and it's worth the drive to find two more tranquil and very pretty lakes hidden away in mountains: Lago Curruhué Grande and Lago Chico. Further along the same road, there are thermal waters at Lahuen-Co, at the western end of Lago Epulafquen, which you could also reach in a spectacular two-day hike from Lago Paimún. Northernmost areas of the park are harder to access, and infrastructure here is building only slowly. But there are several Mapuche communities living in the park who organize campsites and horse riding, and sell home-made bread and other provisions, making this area interesting to visit. The whole park is definitely more rewarding if you visit in your own transport, as bus services are sporadic at best, and there is a great deal of unspoilt landscape to explore, varying from lowland hills in the east to steep craggy mountains in the west, all heavily clad in native beech trees, coihue, lenga and ñire. ➡ For listings, see pages 480-488.

Ins and outs

Getting there

Bus transport into the park is tricky, with services usually running to Lago Huechulafquen from San Martín de los Andes with KoKo Bus, but the timetable varies from year to year. There are boat trips along Lago Lacar from San Martín de los Andes, and rafting at its western end on the River Hua Hum: contact tour operators in San Martín for information (see page 487). There are *guardaparques* (rangers) offices at Huechulafquen and Tromen, who can advise on hikes. The park can be entered at two point. One is **San Martín de los Andes** which is the main tourist centre and gives easy access to Lago Lacar and the River Hua Hum on its western end, with plenty of tourist services, and further north, to remoter Lago Lolog. There are more good walks at the natural thermal pools at **Termas de Lahuen-Co** further west, accessed from Route 62, starting either south of Junín, or from Lago Lolog.

The other entrance is at **Lago Huechulafquen**, further north, which provides the easiest access to beautifully situated lakes, with some accommodation. Go to the more commercial town of Junín de los Andes, and take the good dirt road Route 61 west, past the fishing spot at the mouth of the Chimehuín river, 22 km further on. Stop off here for a moment, to appreciate one of Argentina's most celebrated fly-fishing spots, and the heavenly turquoise water, with black sandy shore. As soon as you cross the river, you'll be

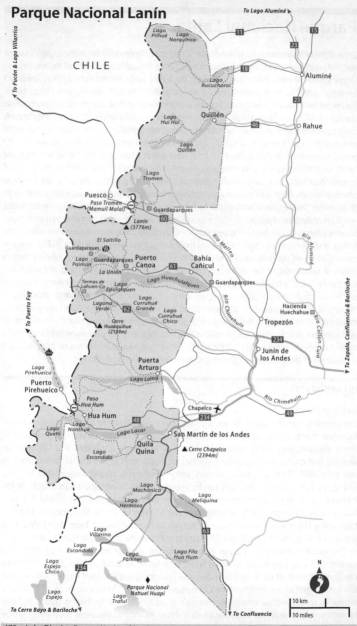

Parque Nacional Lanín

asked to stop at the *guardaparque* office, where you can get free maps and information on hikes. From Lago Huechulafquen there are fabulous walks up into the hills and along the shore, and along beautiful Lago Paimún further west. Three *hosterías* and great campsites offer accommodation, and there are simple food shops and places to eat. The very north of the park is hard to access, since the roads are poor, but It's possible to reach Quillén from Rahue by heading west along Route 46, which is signposted on Route 23. Roads are poor, and there's little infrastructure when you reach Quillén, but there are Mapuche communities to visit and some rural campsites.

Park information

Park entry is US$4.50 (paid at the entry point). You're supposed to register at the **park administration** ① *in San Martín de los Andes, the corner of Perito Moreno and Elordi, T02972-427233, www.lanin@apn.gov.ar, www.tresparques.com.ar/lanin/*, before setting out on any major treks at Huechulafquen. There is now a *guardaparque* office at the entrance to the park at the eastern end of Lago Huechulafquen, and they can advise on walks and should also always be notified before you set off for a hike. Ask them about your route, and if paths are open. They have two really good free leaflets: one on the park itself, and another on climbing Lanín, both with sections in English. Check out www.parque nacionallanin.gov.ar. Having a good map is essential: look out for the *Sendas y Bosques* (Walks and Forests) map for Parque Nacional Lanín, 1:200,000, laminated and easy to read (US$3), with a book containing English summaries of the walks, 'Lanín/Villarica' (US$5), www.guiasendasybosques.com.ar.

Around the park

There are some delightful walks here, with guides only needed for the longer treks where paths are not marked. (For these, ask in the Junín park office or at San Martín de los Andes, address above.) Yellow arrows indicate the paths; allow plenty of time to return before dark. Ask *guardaparques* for advice on routes before setting off. To cross to the other side of Lago Paimún at La Unión, there's a boat operated by the local Mapuche community; just ring the bell. Wherever you are in the park, fires are a serious hazard here: always put out with lots of water, not just earth. Obviously, take all rubbish away with you.

Trekking routes

El Saltillo Falls ① *2 hrs return, fabulous views.* Start from campsite **Piedra Mala** (where you can stock up on provisions) at Lago Paimún, and head west towards the Paimún *guardaparque* office. From here you can also walk on to Río Paimún, three to four hours one way, from Piedra Mala campsite.

Termas at Lahuen-Co It's well worth getting to beautiful Lago Curruhué and the rustic Termas. You could walk it from Lago Paimún: it is eight hours to reach the end of Lago Paimún, walking along the northern side, then four more to reach the Termas, best done over two days. You must consult the book of walks *Sendas y Bosques* for Parque Nacional Lanín, and notify *guardaparques*. It's a beautiful walk, and you'll be rewarded by a soak in these simple rustic pools. Start from beautiful **La Unión**, where Lago Huechulafquen meets Lago Paimún. If you can't face the two-day hike, go west along Route 62 south of Junín de los Andes on a good dirt road, passing the turning to Lago Lolog, Lago Curruhué Chico and Lago Grande, through ancient *pehuén* forests along the southern shores, and then past the impressive lava field at Laguna Escorial. It's worth

Climbing Volcán Lanín

One of the world's most beautiful mountains, Lanín (3776 m), is geologically one of the youngest volcanoes (though now extinct) of the Andes. It is a challenging three-day climb, with two *refugios* at 2400 m (both without charge), sleeping 14 to 20 people. The ascent starts from the Argentine customs post at the Tromen Pass, where you must register with *guardaparques*, and obtain a free permit. They will check that you are physically fit and experienced enough, and also check that you have the equipment listed below. If they judge that you are not experienced enough, they will insist that you hire the services of a trained and licensed guide to the park.

Access Possible only between November and May. Outside this period, climbing is subject to conditions; guides are not always available at this time. Set off between 0800 and 1400; to start climbing before 0800, obtain clearance the previous day before 2100. The number of climbers is limited to 60 per day; no bookings can be made.

Bring all rubbish down with you. You will be given numbered waste bags for this purpose. On your return, it is essential to check in with the *guardaparques*, so that they can log your safe return. Start hydrating 24 hours before setting off and continue doing so as you climb. Take at least two litres of water with you. Eat light and frequent snacks, including bananas, raisins, cereal bars and chocolate.

It's vital to get detailed descriptions of the ascent from the *guardaparques*, and take a detailed map. To climb the north face, follow the path through *lenga* forest to the base of the volcano, over Arroyo Turbio and up the Espina de Pescado (fish bone), following red and yellow marks. From here the path becomes steeper. Follow the signs to the Camino de Mulas (mule track), and then follow the red markers to reach the Nuevo Refugio Militar (new military shelter). From here keep right to the Viejo Refugio Militar (old military shelter) and the CAJA Refugio. From then on, the ascent is steep and requires ice-climbing techniques. The section to the *refugios* may be done in one day if you set out early and are mentally and physically prepared. See the excellent free leaflet produced by the Parque Nacional Lanín on the ascent, with all GPS references provided and English translation.

Because of its relative accessibility, the risks are often underestimated: crampons and ice-axe are essential. Other equipment you will be required to show includes: good walking boots, an all-season sleeping bag, stove and fuel, sunglasses, torch, first-aid kit, walking sticks, helmet and VHF radio (frequency is VHF 155675). An authorized guide (see below) is absolutely necessary for anyone other than the very experienced.

Mountain guides

Alquimia Viajes, Padre Milanesio 840, Junín de los Andes, T02972-491355, www.alquimiaturismo.com.ar, organize expeditions.
Víctor Gutiérrez, Las Mutisias 150, cabaña 5, Altos del Sol, San Martín de los Andes, T02972-421595, jano@smandes.neuquen.com.ar, is an experienced mountain guide, who also leads expeditions to Aconcagua.

checking in San Martín's tourist office before you set off. **Camping Agreste Lanín** is a lovely shaded spot with hot showers, toilets, *parrilladas* and places to wash, well run by friendly people; open December to April, US$6 per person.

Border essentials: Argentina–Chile

Paso Tromen (Mamuil Malal)

Paso Tromen, known in Chile as Paso Mamuil Malal, is 64 km northwest of Junín de los Andes and reached by *ripio* Route 60 which runs from Tropezón on Route 23, through Parque Nacional Lanín. Some 3 km east of the pass a turning leads north to Lago Tromen, and south of the pass is the graceful cone of the Lanín volcano. This is the normal departure point for climbing to the summit (see box, opposite). This crossing is less developed than the Hua Hum and Puyehue (now known as Paso Cerro Samore) routes further south; it is unsuitable for bicycles and definitely not usable during heavy rain or snow (June to mid-November), as parts are narrow and steep. Ring to check: T02972-491270, or customs, T02972-492163. This is a beautiful spot, with a good campsite, and some lovely walks: from the *guardaparque* centre, footpaths lead to a mirador (1½ hours round trip), or across a grassy prairie with magnificent clear views of Lanín and other jagged peaks, through *ñirre* woodland and some great araucaria trees to the point where Lago Tromen drains into Río Malleo (4 km).

Argentine immigration and customs Puesto Tromen, 3 km east of the pass, daily 0800-2000 open all year, co-ordinated with the Chilean side.

Chilean immigration and customs Puesco, 8 km west of the pass, December to March daily 0800-2100, April to November daily 0800-2000. On the Chilean side the road continues through glorious scenery, with views of the volcanoes of Villarrica and Quetrupillán to the south, to Pucón, 40 km west of the pass, on Lago Villarrica.

Transport Hire cars will need special documents (ask when you rent), and the car's number plate must be etched into all windows.

Note No fruit or vegetables are to be taken into Chile. For more detailed information, see www.gendarmeria.gov.ar/pasos/fichmamal.html.

Base of Volcán Lanín ① *8 hrs return*. A satisfying walk. Start from Puerto Canoa.

Cerro El Chivo ① *2064 m, 8-9 hrs return*. A more challenging walk through forest. Note that heavy snow can lie till January. Set off early, and register in campsite at Bahía Cañicul. Potentially dangerous without a guide. Consult *Sendas y Bosques* book for Parque Nacional Lanín, and notify *guardaparques*.

Horse riding

You can explore much of the area on horseback, including the trek to the base of Volcán Lanín. Five places along the lake hire horses: ask *guardaparques* for advice, or ask at the local Mapuche community where you see the signs, *cabalgatas* (horse rides). Also recommended for longer rides, and with really fine horses, is **Estancia Huechahue** ① *reached from north of Junín de los Andes, T02944-491303, www.huechahue.com*, see also page 484. Unbeatable riding and hospitality, and excellent rides into the park, enabling you to reach areas completely inaccessible otherwise.

Boat trips

A fantastic boat trip offers the chance to see Lanín and the beautiful surrounding mountains from the water, and to reach the relatively inaccessible Lago Epulafquen with its impressive

6-km lava deposit. Trips on the comfortable catamaran *José Julián* (T02972-429264, www.catamaranjosejulian.com.ar), start at Puerto Canoa, on the northern shore of Lago Huechulafquen, and there are some refreshments available on board.

San Martín de los Andes → *For listings, see pages 480-488.*

San Martín de los Andes is a charming upmarket tourist town in a beautiful setting on the edge of Lago Lacar, with attractive chalet-style architecture and lots of good accommodation. It's an excellent centre for exploring southern parts of the Parque Nacional Lanín and nearby lakes Lolog and Lacar, where there are beaches for relaxing and good opportunities for rafting, canoeing, mountain biking, trekking and even diving. There is also excellent skiing at Chapelco resort 10 km south, and Chapelco Airport, 12 km north, receives daily flights from Buenos Aires. Tourism information can be found at www.sanmartindelosandes.com (in English). ▶▶ *For further information, see Activities and tours, page 486.*

Ins and outs → *Colour map 5, A2. Phone code 02972. Population 25,000.*

Getting there The nearest **airport** is Chapelco, 20 km away on Route 234, see Junín de los Andes, page 488. The **bus terminal** ① *Villegas and Juez del Valle, information T02972-427044,* is reasonably central and has all the usual services, including luggage store, toilets and *locutorio*. There is a tiny tourist office open daily 1130-1730.

Getting around It's easy to orientate yourself here as the town nestles in a valley surrounded by steep mountains at the eastern end of Lago Lacar. Beware of confusing street names: Perito Moreno runs east-west, crossing Mariano Moreno, which runs north-south, and Rudecindo Roca which is two blocks north of General Roca.

Tourist information The large and helpful **tourist office** ① *San Martín y J M de Rosas 790, on the main plaza, T02972-427347, www.sanmartindelosandes.gov.ar/turismo, open all year 0800-2100*, hands out maps and has lists of accommodation, with prices up on a big board. Helpful staff speak English and French, but are very busy in summer, when it's advisable to go early in the day, before they get stressed. The **Parque Nacional Lanín office** is at ① *E Frey 749, T02972-427233, www.parquenacionallanin.gov.ar.* Also check out www.chapelco.com.ar, and www.sanmartindelosandes.gov.ar.

Sights

The main street, San Martín, runs perpendicular to the *costanera*, and here you'll find most shops and plenty of places to eat. Of the two plazas, the more interesting is Plaza San Martín, which has a sporadic crafts market. It's a pleasant 1½-hour walk north and west up the hill to **Mirador Bandurrias**, with great views and a great *quincho*-like restaurant, **Lola Mora**, run by the local Mapuche community. Start at the far northernmost end of the *costanera*, passing the fish trap (open winter 1100-1630, summer 1000-1300, 1600-1900) and walk along the shore before ascending the path, 40 minutes up. Even lovelier, set off from the costanera up to **Mirador Arrayán**, where there's a gorgeous tea room **La Casa de Té Arrayán**, and restaurant with spectacular views over the lake.

Around San Martín de los Andes

Surrounded by lakes and mountains you can explore, the most popular excursions are south along the **Seven Lakes Drive** to Lagos Traful, Meliquina, Filo Hua Hum, Hermoso,

Falkner and Villarino; north to the thermal baths at **Termas de Lahuen-Co** (which can also be reached on a long hike from Lago Huechulafquen). At the thermal baths there is a fantastic day spa and lodge (www.lahuenco.com), which organizes tours in the area. Other excursions go to Lagos Lolog and Lacar. **Lago Lacar** can be explored by car along much of its length, as there's a *ripio* road, Route 48, leading to the Chilean border at **Paso Hua Hum**, 41 km. **Río Hua Hum** has become a popular place for rafting, with some good stretches of rapids, as the river flows west towards the Pacific. You can float over the Chilean border: take a tour from an agency in town. You can cycle or walk all the way around the lake on rough track, and also to **Lago Escondido**, south of the lake. There are beaches at **Catrite**, and at the western end of the lake at **Hua Hum**. On the southern shore, 18 km away, there is a quieter beach at **Quila Quina**, where you can walk to a lovely waterfall, along a guided nature trail, or a two-hour walk that takes you to a tranquil Mapuche community in the hills above the lake. Both lakeshore villages can be reached by boat from the pier in San Martín, T02972-428427; to Quila Quina hourly, 30 minutes each way, US$9 return. To Hua Hum, US$22 return, three daily in season.

San Martín de los Andes

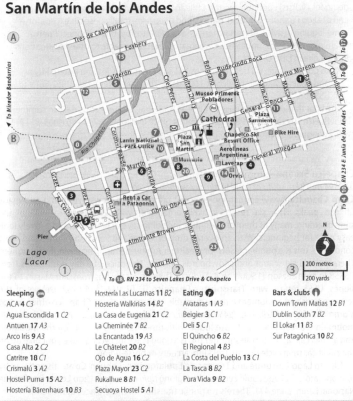

Sleeping 😴
ACA **4** C3
Agua Escondida **1** C2
Antuen **17** A3
Arco Iris **9** A3
Casa Alta **2** C2
Catritre **18** C1
Crismalú **3** A2
Hostel Puma **15** A2
Hostería Bärenhaus **10** B3

Hostería Las Lucarnas **11** B2
Hostería Walkirias **14** B2
La Casa de Eugenia **21** C2
La Cheminée **7** B2
La Encantada **19** A3
Le Châtelet **20** B2
Ojo de Agua **16** C2
Plaza Mayor **23** C2
Rukalhue **8** B1
Secuoya Hostel **5** A1

Eating 🍴
Avataras **1** A3
Beigier **3** C1
Deli **5** C1
El Quincho **6** B2
El Regional **4** B3
La Costa del Pueblo **13** C1
La Tasca **8** B2
Pura Vida **9** B2

Bars & clubs 🍸
Down Town Matias **12** B1
Dublin South **7** B2
El Lokar **11** B3
Sur Patagónica **10** B2

Border essentials: Argentina–Chile

Paso Hua Hum

Usually open all year round and is an alternative to the route via the Paso Tromen (Mamuil Malal), see page 475. Paso Hua Hum (659 m) lies 47 km west of San Martín de los Andes along Route 48 (*ripio*) which runs along the north shore of Lago Lacar and crosses the border to Puerto Pirehueico.

Accommodation Available in private houses in both Puerto Pirehueico and Puerto Fuy.

Immigration Argentine and Chilean immigration is open daily 0900-2000. For more information, see www.gendarmeria.gov.ar/pasos/fichhuahum.html.

Transport Buses leave early morning daily, two hours, US$4.50, check terminal for schedule (T02972-427044). They connect with boats across Lago Pirehueico and bikes can be taken. The ferries cross the lake between the two ports from January to February, three daily; from November to December and March to April, two daily; and from May to October they are daily except Sunday. The road (tough going for cyclists) continues on the Chilean side to Puerto Pirehueico at the southern end of Lago Pirehueico, a long, narrow and deep lake, totally unspoilt except for some logging activity. At its northern end lies Puerto Fuy. Buses connect Puerto Pirehueico with Panguipulli, from where transport is available to other destinations in the Chilean Lake District.

Koko goes to Chile, via boat crossings to Lago Pirehueico, leaving Puerto Fuy at 1230 and boat leaving Pirehueico at 1600 daily. The boat takes bikes (US$2.50) and cars (US$9).

The boat that crosses the pass to Chile at Hua Hum also takes cars daily in summer from Puerto Fuy to Puerto Pirehueico tourist office in Panguipulli, T+56 (0)63-311311, www.panguipulli.com.

Chapelco Ski and summer resort

ⓘ *2394 m, 19 km south of San Martín, www.chapelco.com.ar.*

Cerro Chapelco (www.cerrochapelco.com) offers superb views over Lanín and many Chilean peaks. The ski resort is well organized, with 29 pistes for skiing and snowboarding, many of them challenging, including several black runs and a lovely long easy piste for beginners. With an overall drop of 730 m and very good slopes and snow conditions, this is a popular resort for wealthier Argentines and, increasingly, foreigners. There's also a ski school and snowboards for hire. The price of a day pass varies from US$58 in high season (15 July to 4 August). There is a daily bus from San Martín to the slopes, US$5 return, with **Transportes Chapelco** ⓘ *T02944-1556 0247*. Details of the resort, passes and equipment hire are available in season from the **Chapelco office** ⓘ *San Martín and Elordi, T02972-427845, www.sanmartindelosandes.gov.ar*. At the foot of the mountain is a restaurant and base lodge, with three more restaurants on the mountain and a small café at the top. In summer this is a good place for cycling (take your bike up on the cable car then cycle down), trekking, archery or horse riding.

Trips to **Lago Curruhué** and **Termas de Epulafquen** or **Lahuen-Co** are also offered by tour operators, but you could cycle or drive along *ripio* roads from Lago Lolog. See Parque Nacional Lanín, page 471. There's no public transport to these places at present.

Situated on the Río Chimehuín, the quiet town of Junín de los Andes (773 m) is justifiably known as the trout-fishing capital of Argentina. It offers some of the best fly fishing in the country, and the fishing season runs from mid-November to May. Junín is also an excellent base for exploring the wonderful Parque Nacional Lanín and for climbing the extinct volcano, as well as rafting on Río Aluminé further north.

Founded in 1883, Junín is a real town; not as picturesque or tourist-orientated as its neighbour, San Martín – there are far fewer chalet-style buildings, and few chocolate shops here – but it's a quiet, neat place with genuinely friendly people. The hotels are not as upmarket as San Martín, but **Estancia Huechahue** nearby (see Sleeping, page 484) is superb, and there are some decent family-run hotels here, plus one excellent restaurant,

Junín de los Andes

To **5** & El Via Christi
To **1**

Gral Roca

Blvd Juan Manuel de Rosas

9 de Julio

YPF

Félix San Martín

O'Higgins

Casa de Cambio

San Martín

Plaza San Martín

P Milanesio

Santuario Nuestra Señora de las Nieves y Beata Laura Vicuña

Museo Salesiano

Don Bosco

Rim 26

Nogueira

25 de Mayo

Av Costanera

Río Chimehuín

E Serrano — J Iturra — Pedro Illera
Av Antártida Argentina — Olavarría — Chile — Patagonia — Leloig — Neuchea — Cam 6
Av Lonquimay — Villarino — Laura Vicuña — Gines Ponte — Cnel Suárez — Lamadrid

200 metres
200 yards
N

Sleeping
Hostería Chimehuín **3**
La Isla **9**
Mallín Laura Vicuña **8**
Milla Piuke **2**
Residencial Marisa **6**

Río Dorado Lodge
& Fly Shop **1**
San Jorge **5**
Tromen **7**

Eating
Centro de Turismo **2**
Ruca Hueney **3**

Bars & clubs
Rivendel **1**

making it worth an overnight stop to get a feeling of real life in a Patagonian town; you can try the celebrated local trout.

Chapelco Airport is 19 km southwest on the road to San Martín de los Andes, and can be reached by taking any bus to San Martín. A taxi to the centre will cost US$12. The bus terminal ① *Olavarría and Félix San Martín (do not confuse with General San Martín), information T02972-492038*, has a public phone but no other facilities. There is a fantastic tourist office ① *Domingo/Padre Milanesio and C Suárez, T02972-491160, www.juninde losandes.gov.ar, 0800-2200 in summer, 0800-2100 in winter*, on the main plaza, which has friendly staff who can advise on accommodation, and who hand out maps. The Parque Nacional Lanín office ① *T02972-491160*, is in the same building and is very helpful.

Sights
Most of what you need can be found within a couple of blocks of the central Plaza San Martín with its fine araucaria trees among mature *alerces* and cedars. The small Museo Salesiano ① *Ginés Ponte and Nogueira, Mon-Fri 0900-1230, 1430-1930, Sat 0900-1230*, has a fine collection of Mapuche weavings, instruments and arrowheads, and you can buy a whole range of excellent Mapuche handicrafts in the Feria Artesanal behind the tourist office. There's an impressive religious sculpture park, El Vía Christi ① *just west of the town, T02972-491684*. From the plaza walk up Avenida Ant Argentina across the main road, Route 234, to the end. Situated among pine forest on a hillside, the Stations of the Cross are illustrated with touching and beautifully executed sculptures of Mapuche figures, ingeniously depicting scenes from Jesus's life together with a history of the town and the Mapuche community. The sculptures are to be found along trails through the pine woods. A lovely place to walk, and highly recommended. The church, Santuario Nuestra Señora de las Nieves y Beata Laura Vicuña, also has fine Mapuche weavings, and is a pleasing calm space.

Some 7 km away, clearly signposted, at Km 7 on Route 61 towards Lago Huechuflafquen, is the Centro Ecológico Aplicado de Neuquén (CEAN) ① *Mon-Fri 0900-1300, US$1*, where trout are farmed, and ñandus and llamas can be seen; a good place for kids.

Fishing is undoubtedly one of the great attractions of Junín, and the best fishing is at the mouth of the Río Chimehuin on the road to Lago Huechualfquen, although there are many excellent spots around; see guides below. In the town itself, there are pleasant places to fish and picnic along the river, while there are several fishing lodges in the area, which cater for experts, with guides whose services you can hire.

◉ Parque Nacional Lanín listings

For Sleeping and Eating price codes and other relevant information, see Essentials pages 30-36.

● Sleeping

Parque Nacional Lanín *p471, map p472*
Lago Huechulafquen
LL Hostería San Huberto, R60, Km 33, T02972-491238, www.sanhubertolodge. com.ar. Luxury fishing lodge close to the river, also offers home-cooked meals.

LL-L Lahuen Co, T02972-424 709, www.lahuenco.com. Wonderful resort that has a professional spa (open to non-guests), stunning views, and a good-quality restaurant. The rooms are all very comfortable with fluffy towels, good heating and very modern appliances. They can organize adventure tours in the area. Recommended.
L Hostería Paimún, R61, Km 58, T02972-491201, www.hosteriapaimun.com. Open Nov-Mar. Best location, nicely decorated.

L Refugio del Pescador, R61, Km 57, leave messages at T02972-491319. The most basic and popular with fishermen. Full board offered, small golf course.

A Huechulafquen, R61, Km 55, T002972-427598, price for half-board. The most recommended and welcoming of the 3 options, with comfortable, small rooms lined with wood and well heated. Gardens going down to the lakeside, very peaceful. The owner is a fanatical fisherman, and there's an expert fishing guide on hand too (extra charge for this). In high season, lunches are served to non-residents here. Other choices for eating are limited, best to take a picnic.

Camping

There are lots of sites, all along the lake, run by local Mapuche communities, and often selling delicious *pan casero* (home-made bread), or offering horse riding. Easiest if you have your own transport and can keep going till you find one you like. They're all beautifully situated.

Bahía Cañicul, 48 km from Junín. All the facilities you'll need, including places to bring your boat ashore.

Camping Lafquenco, 53 km from Junín, just after the sign to Bahía Coihues. This campsite is highly recommended for its friendly welcome and facilities: hot showers, fireplaces and toilets. Wild camping is also possible in a beautiful spot nearby, but there are no facilities. Lafquenco is run by friendly and helpful Juan Andres, with a good open spot on the lakeside and lots of room, US$7 per person.

Piedra Mala, 65 km from Junín, on the shores of Lago Paimún. Hot showers, toilets, fireplaces, picnic tables, restaurant offering local dishes, good facilities and beautiful setting. Sites are spread under araucaria and beech trees by 2 beaches, with lovely walks along the water's edge to the end of the lake. US$7 per person. This is where the bus stops (when it's running).

There are 3 more campsites beyond Hostería Paimún, including **Mawizache**, just beyond the picturesque little chapel. Offers fishing trips with expert Raúl Hernández (US$15 per hr), and also picnic places in an amazing spot. Raúl and his wife Carmen have lived on the land all their lives, and know it well. Open all year.

San Martín de los Andes *p476, map p477*
Single room rates are expensive. There are 2 high seasons, when rates are much higher, and you must book ahead: Jan-Feb and Jul-Aug. For more accommodation options, see www.sanmartindelosandes.gov.ar.

LL Lois Suites, R234, Km 57.5, T02972-410 304, www.loisuites.com.ar. Wonderful 5-star golf resort set on 226 ha just outside of town. Lovely spa and restaurant.

LL Ten Rivers & Ten Lakes Lodge, Circuito Arrayanes Km 4.5, T02972-425571, www.tenriverstenlakes.com. Amazing views from this small lodge with only 4 rooms set on a hill overlooking the lakes. Includes a wonderful breakfast.

L La Casa de Eugenia, Coronel Díaz 1186, T02972-427206, www.lacasadeeugenia. com.ar. The most charming B&B in San Martín, this beautifully renovated 1900s house is more like an exclusive boutique hotel, but completely relaxing and unsnobby. Rooms are beautifully designed, incredibly cosy, and very welcoming. Breakfasts are luxurious. They have a lovely pool and also have a tea room open to the public. Highly recommended.

L La Cheminée, General Roca and Mariano Moreno, T02972-427617, www.hosteriala cheminee.com.ar. One of the most luxurious options, with pretty and cosy cottage-style rooms, spacious bathrooms and a small pool. Breakfast is included, but there is no restaurant. Overpriced in high season, reasonable otherwise.

L Le Châtelet, Villegas 650, T02972-428294, www.hotellechatelet.com.ar. Really chic and luxurious, everything in this beautiful chalet-style hotel has been thought of to make you feel utterly pampered. Cosy, wood-lined living room, and gorgeous bedrooms, video library, excellent service, spa and pool with massage and facial treatments. Also some suites.

L Tipiliuke Lodge, in the Chimehuin Valley, 35 km from San Martín de los Andes, T02972-429466 (or T011-4806 8877, ext 101 in Buenos Aires), www.tipiliuke.com. 10 mins from Chapelco airport. 9 rooms. Activities include fly fishing, golf, birding and trekking.

AL-A Plaza Mayor, Cl Pérez 1199, T02972-427302, www.hosteriaplazamayor.com.ar. A chic and homely *hostería* in a quiet residential area, with traditional touches in the simple elegant rooms, all decorated to a high standard. Pool, *quincho*, parking. Great home-made breakfast included.

AL Hostería Walkirias, Villegas 815, T02972-428307, www.laswalkirias.com. A lovely place, homely but smart, with very spacious and well furnished, tasteful rooms with big bathrooms. Breakfast and free transfer from the airport included. Sauna and pool room. Special prices available for staying a few nights and special discounts offered during the winter.Great value off season.

A Casa Alta, Obeid 659, T02972-427456. Deservedly popular, this is a welcoming B&B with charming multilingual owners, who will make you feel at home. Comfortable rooms, most with bathrooms, lovely gardens, and delicious breakfast. Closed in low season, book in advance.

B Crismalú, Rudecindo Roca 975, T02972-427283, www.interpatagonia.com/crismalu. Simple rooms in attractive chalet-style place, good value with breakfast included.

B Hostería Las Lucarnas, C Pérez 632, T02972-427085, www.patagoniasuperior. com.ar/hosterialaslucarnas. Really good value, a central and pretty place with simple comfortable rooms, and a friendly owner, who speaks English. They have special prices if you stay more than 5 nights. Open all year.

Hostels

D-E pp Hostería Bärenhaus, Los Alamos 156, Barrio Chapelco, 5 km outside town, free pick-up from bus terminal and airport. T/F02972-422775. The welcoming English- and German-speaking young owners have thought of everything to make you feel at home here: excellent breakfast, very comfortable rooms with bath and heating or great-value shared dorms. Open during ski season. Highly recommended.

E pp Hostel Puma, Fosbery 535 (take Rivadavia to the north, 2 blocks after crossing the bridge), T02972-422443, www.puma hostel.com.ar. HI discounts. A lovely hostel: warm, friendly and clean. Run by an enthusiastic mountain guide who organizes treks to Lanín, rooms for 4 with private bathroom, also twin and double rooms with bath (**C-D**), and kitchen facilities. Highly recommended.

E pp Rukalhue, Juez del Valle 682, T02972-427431, www.rukalhue.com.ar.

Large camp-style accommodation with one section full of dorm rooms and one section with doubles and triples (**C**). Great new apartments (**B**) with private bathrooms and kitchenette also an option.

E pp **Secuoya Hostel**, Rivadavia 411, T02972-42485, www.hostelsecuoya.com.ar. Charming hostel, 6 blocks from the bus terminal past the river. Small rooms are made up for by the welcoming common area. Doubles (**C-D**) also available. Closed in Jun.

Cabañas

Plentiful *cabañas* are available in 2 main areas: up Perito Moreno on the hill to the north of town, and down by the lakeside. Prices increase in high season, but are good value for families or groups.

Agua Escondida, Rohde 1162, T02972-422 113, www.aguaescondida.com.ar. Luxurious apart hotel, very comfortable, nicely designed, spacious apartments, great break-fasts, cosy, wood fires and internet access. The rooms are fully equipped, located downtown in close proximity to main street and supermarkets. In high season they rent the cabins for minimum of 1 week.

Antuen, Perito Moreno 1850, T02972-428340, www.antuen.com.ar. Modern, well-equipped, luxurious *cabañas* for 2-7, with jacuzzi, pool, games room and stunning views from its position above the valley.

Arco Iris, Los Cipreses 1850, T02972-429450, www.arcoirisar.com. Comfortable and perfectly equipped, spotless *cabañas* in a quiet area of town. Beautifully situated, with their own access to the river, so you can fish before breakfast or enjoy a drink at the water's edge in the evening. Each has 2 bathrooms, cosy living rooms with TV and spacious kitchen. Very good value for 4 in high season. Highly recommended.

La Encantada, Perito Moreno and Los Enebros, T/F02972-428364, www.laencantada.com. In a spectacular position above town in wooded surroundings, large, beautifully furnished cosy *cabañas* for 2 or more. A pool, game

room and fishing guides are offered. They have cabins for 4 people or more.

Ojo de Agua, Pérez 1198, T02972-427921, www.interpatagonia.com/ojodeagua. Well-equipped *cabañas* for 2-7, more like little urban chalet-style houses, crammed next to each other in quiet part of town near the lake. Great budget option.

Estancias

AL Estancia Lemu Cuyén, 60 km south via Lago Melinquina, T02972-428360, www.lemucuyen.com.ar. Chalet-style *cabañas* for rent, with adjoining restaurant serving great food made by the owner-chef. Great fishing, horse riding and lovely forests for walks. *Cabañas* for up to 5 or 8 people. Good value. Open in summer Oct-Mar.

Camping

Generally costing US$7-8 per person, and US$2 per car.

ACA, Koessler 2176 (on the access road), T02972-429430. Hot water, laundry facilities.

Catritre, R234, Km 4, T02972-411329. On the southern shore of the lake. Good facilities in a gorgeous position on the shore.

Quila Quina, T02972-426919. A pretty spot and a peaceful place (out of peak season) with beaches and lovely walks, 18 km from San Martín. Recommended.

Junín de los Andes *p479, map p479*
If there are several of you and you have your own transport, there are quite a few good *cabaña* complexes; ask at the tourist office.

L Río Dorado Lodge and Fly Shop, Pedro Illera 448, T02972-491548, www.riodorado.com.ar. The only 4-star in town. Luxury fishing lodge with comfortable, spacious rooms in log-cabin style, with huge beds and private bathrooms, lovely gardens and attentive service. Big 'American' breakfast included. Good fly shop.

A San Jorge, at the very end of Antártida Argentina, Chacra 54, T02972-491147, www.hotelsanjorge.com.ar. Open Nov-Apr. A big, modernized 1960s hotel, beautifully located with lovely views and large gardens, homely well-furnished rooms, all with bath and TV. Very good value, with good restaurant and internet access. English spoken. Recommended

C-B Hostería Chimehuín, tucked away at the end of the road by the river on Suárez y 25 de Mayo, T02972-491132, www.inter patagonia.com/hosteriachimehuin. Best value in town, a long-established classic fishing *hostería* with beautiful gardens and friendly owners, quaint cosy decor, and comfortable rooms all with bath and TV. Ask for the spacious newer rooms with balconies in the block next to the river. Good breakfasts. Recommended.

C Milla Piuke, set back from the road R234, at General Roca and Av los Pehuenes, T02972-492378, www.milla-piuke.com.ar. Delightful and welcoming *hostería*, with tastefully decorated and stylish rooms all with bath and TV, and apartments for families. Very warm hospitality from the owner Vilma. Breakfast included. Highly recommended.

C Residencial Marisa, JMI de Rosas 360, T02972-491175, residencialmarisa@ jdeandes.com.ar. A simple place with plain, clean rooms with TV and bathroom, and cheery family owners. *Confitería* downstairs, but breakfast is US$2 extra. It's on the main road, so a little noisy during the day, but handy for the bus terminal and cheap eating places.

Hostels

F pp Tromen, Lonquimay 195, T02972-491498. tromen@fronteradigital.net.ar. Small, friendly house which has dorms and rooms for up to 4 people. At night take a taxi from the bus station as the streets in the area have no signs, and there are no street lights.

Estancias

L Estancia Huechahue, north of town, off R234 (reached from the Junín–Bariloche bus), T02972-491303, www.huechahue.com. The best riding in the Lake District can be experienced at this marvellous self-sufficient,

traditional Patagonian *estancia*, where they breed horses and cattle, and welcome guests to stay in very comfortable wooden cabins. Superb horses, great *asados* in the open air, even a jacuzzi under the stars to rest tired muscles. Highly recommended.

Camping

Many sites in the area, 2 good ones in town: **La Isla**, T02972-492029. On the river. US$5 per person.

Mallin Laura Vicuña, Ginés Ponte 861, T02972-491149, campinglv@jandes.com.ar. On the river, with hot showers, electricity, small shop and discounts for stays over 2 days. Very good value *cabañas* for 4-7.

🍴 Eating

Parque Nacional Lanín *p471, map p472*
Lago Huechulafquen
There are lots of places to eat here, with *provedurías*, selling good *pan casero*, at Bahía and Piedra Mala.
Mawizache (see Camping, page 481) has a great restaurant serving fabulous local dishes very inexpensively, hot chocolate and cakes.

San Martín de los Andes *p476, map p477*
¶¶¶ Avataras, Teniente Ramayón 765, T02972-427104, Thu-Sat from 2030. One of the best in town, this pricey, inspired place is absolutely marvellous. The surroundings are elegant, the menu imaginative, with cuisine from all over the world, from fondue to satay, and superb wine, an excellent treat.
¶¶ El Quincho, Rivadavia and San Martín, T02972-422564. An excellent, much-recommended traditional *parrilla* for excellent steaks, also offering superb home-made pasta, with good old-fashioned service to match. Great atmosphere. Warmly recommended.
¶¶ El Regional, Villegas 953, T02972-425326. Hugely popular for regional specialities – smoked trout, pâtés and hams, and El Bolsón's home-made beer, all in cheerful German-style decor.

La Costa del Pueblo, on the *costanera* opposite pier, T02972-429289. This is one of the best-value places overlooking the lake. A big family-orientated place, where kids running around give the place a cheerful atmosphere, offering a huge range of pasta, chicken and trout dishes. Very cheap with good service. Recommended.

La Tasca, M Moreno 866, T02972-428663. A great atmospheric family restaurant with superb food, and a wonderful wine list of good Argentine wines, perfect with their tasty *picadas*. The food is traditional but with something extra, and the smoked boar and trout-filled pasta are both excellent. Recommended.

Pura Vida, Villegas 745, T02972-429302. The only vegetarian restaurant in town, small and welcoming, also serves fish and chicken dishes.

Deli, Villegas and Av Costanera, T02972-428631. Great affordable place with views of the bay and nice salads, pastas and pizzas. Wi-Fi and friendly service.

Tea rooms

Beigier, Av Costanera 814, T02972-427 037. Little hidden cottage with views of the bay serving a fantastic home-made afternoon tea with home-made goodies. Only a few tables. Friendly staff. Highly recommended.

Casa de Té Arrayán, head up to the Mirador Arrayán, and follow signs, T02972-425570, www.tenriverstenlakes.com. Fabulous views from this cosy and chic, rustic log cabin with delicious meals. Lunch and dinner (reservations essential) in the tea room. A real treat. Mon, Wed, Thu and Fri 1630-2030.

Junín de los Andes *p479, map p479*
Ruca Hueney, on the plaza at Col Suárez and Milanesio, T02972-491113, www.ruca-hueney.com.ar. The best place to eat in town, this popular place serves a wide menu, but try the 'famous' (enormous) *bife de chorizo Ruca Hueney*, the local wild boar, excellent *parrilla*, and the locally caught trout: all are

delicious. Also Middle Eastern dishes. Great atmosphere, and wonderful old-fashioned service. Highly recommended.

Centro de Turismo, Domingo Milanesio, on the plaza next to the **Tourist Information Centre**. Central café serving interesting regional specialities such as the Patagonic Sandwich with wild boar and venison.

La Posta de Junín, Rosas 160 (R234), T02972-492303. Good steaks, local trout, tasty home-made pasta and good wine list. Also offer takeaway.

🍸 Bars and clubs

San Martín de los Andes *p476, map p477*
Down Town Matias, Coronel Díaz y Calderón. Fantastic, welcoming building, good for a late night drink with snacks.
Dublin South Bar, Av San Martín 599. Huge pub (with no reference to Ireland at all) with comfy seats, great food – try the home-made pasta – and a great atmosphere.
El Lokar, General Roca and Sarmiento. Home-brewed beers and tapas.
Sur Patagónica, M Moreno 759. Not really a bar but a great selection of local and own brews. They have a deal for a taster of 3 beers and a bretzel for US$5.
The Switch, Av Koessler 2227. Popular music bar with live shows at weekends. Open Sat 2400.

Junín de los Andes *p479, map p479*
Rivendel, Bvd JM de Rosas and Ginés Ponte. Wine and beer bar with a beer garden, but also serving breakfast and café food.

🎉 Festivals and events

Junín de los Andes *p479, map p479*
Jan Agricultural show and exhibition of flowers and local crafts, at the end of the month.
Feb Fiesta Provincial de Puestero. Mid-Feb sees the election of the queen, handicrafts,

asados with local foods and fabulous gaucho riding. The most important country fiesta in the south of Argentina.

Mar Carnival.
Jul Festival of Aboriginal Arts, mid-month.
Nov Opening of the fishing season, 2nd Sat.
Dec Inauguration of the church of **Laura Vicuña**, with a special mass on the 8th and singing to celebrate the life of Laura Vicuña.

O Shopping

San Martín de los Andes *p476, map p477*
A great place for shopping, with chic little shops selling clothes and handmade jumpers, and a handicraft market in summer in Plaza San Martín. Lots of outdoor shops on San Martín sell clothes for walking and skiing.
Aquaterra, Villegas 795, T02972-429797. Outdoor equipment and clothing.
La Oveja Negra, San Martín 1025, T02972-428039. Wonderful handmade scarves and jumpers, esoteric crafts to a high standard, interesting souvenirs.
Mountain Ski Shop, San Martín 861.
Nomade, San Martín 881. Outdoor gear and camping equipment.

There are 2 recommended places for chocolates: **Abuela Goye**, No 807, T02972-429409, which serves excellent ice creams and a killer hot chocolate; **Mamusia**, No 601, T02972-427560, which also sells home-made jams.

Junín de los Andes *p479, map p479*
Craft stalls behind the tourist office sell good-quality local weavings and wood work.
Patagonia Rodeo, Padre Milanesio 562, 1st floor, T01972-492839. A traditional shop selling what real gauchos wear in the field, plus quality leather work: belts, wallets, saddlery. Look like the real thing before you turn up at the *estancias*.

▲ Activities and tours

Parque Nacional Lanín *p471, map p472*
Lahuen Co, T02972-424 709, www.lahuenco.com. This thermal spa resort can organize trekking, kayaking, biking and fishing excursions in the area, and afterwards you can relax in their thermal water pool.

San Martín de los Andes *p476, map p477*
Canopying
Canopy, T02944-1559 6215, www.canopyensmandes.com.ar. 8 km from the city, with 1400 m of course, spread over 10 different resting-stations with a height that varies from 8-20 m off the ground. Recommended.

Cycling
Many places rent mountain and normal bikes along San Martín, all charging more or less the same.
Enduro Kawa & Bikes, Elordi and Pto Moreno, T02972-427093. Good quality bikes.
HG Rodados, San Martín 1061, T02972-427 345, hgrodados@smandes.com.ar. Rents mountain bikes at US$10 per day, also sells spare parts and offers expertise.

Diving
Buceo de los Andes, Club Náutico SMA, Av Costanera and Obeid, T02944-1555 0006, info@buceodelosandes.com.ar. Diving courses and excursions throughout the year.

Fishing
The season runs from mid-Nov to May. For guides contact the tourist office or the park office. **Martín Castañeda**, T02972-422300, equis@smandes.com.ar, runs 1 or more day trips and the following outlets sell equipment and offer fishing excursions: **Fly Shop**, Pedro Illera 378, T02972-491548; **Jorge Cardillo Pesca Fly shop**, Villegas 1061, T02972-428 372; **Los Notros**, P Milanesio and Lamadrid,

T02972-492157; **Orvis Fly Shop**, General Villegas 835, T02972-425892; **Patagonian Anglers**, M Moreno 1193, T02972-427376, patagoniananglers@smandes.com.ar; **Rosario Aventura**, Av Koessler 1827, T02972-429233.

Flying
Aeroclub de los Andes, T02972-426254, www.aeroclubdelosandes.com.ar. For flights in light aircraft.

Skiing
Chapelco has very good slopes, and the snow conditions make this a popular resort with foreigners and wealthy Argentines. Details, passes and equipment hire available from the office at San Martín and Elordi, T02972-427845, www.chapelco.com.ar or www.sanmartindelosandes.gov.ar.

Tour operators
Many are advertised on a helpful board in the tourist office. These are the most professional (prices quoted are standard):
El Claro, Coronel Díaz 751, T02972-429363, www.interpatagonia.com/elclaro. Trips to the lakes, and also paragliding, horse riding and other adventure trips
El Refugio, Access from upstairs on C Pérez 830, just off San Martín, T02972-425140, www.elrefugioturismo.com.ar. Excellent company with friendly bilingual guides, offering conventional tours and boat trips: visiting Lagos Huechulafquen and Palmún, US$20; Villa la Angostura via Seven Lakes US$22; boat trip to Quila Quina US$15; mountain bike hire US$20 for the day; rafting at Hua Hum US$35 for the day; horse riding US$25; and trekking US$20. Lots more on offer. Recommended.
Lucero Viajes, San Martín 826, 2nd floor, office B, T02972-428453. Rafting at Hua Hum, horse riding, 4WD trips, and conventional tours to Hua Hum and Quila Quina, as well as selling ski passes in winter.

Net Sur, C Pérez 1124, T02972-427929, www.netsurpatagonia.com.ar. Offering rappelling, kayaking, mountain biking, rafting and horse trekking.

Junín de los Andes *p479, map p479*
Fishing
The season runs from 2nd Sat in Nov to May. For fly casting and trolling the best places are Lagos Huechulafquen, Paimún, Epulaufken, Tromen, Currehue, rivers Chuimehuin, Malleo, Alumine and Quilquihué. Ask the helpful tourist office and also see Tour operators below.
Jorge Trucco, based in fly shop **Patagonia Outfitters** in San Martín de los Andes, Pérez 662, T02972-427561, www.jorgetrucco.com. Expert and professional trips, good advice, and many years of experience.
Pesca Patagonia with Alejandro Olmedo, JM Rosas 60, T02972-491632, www.pescapatagonia.com.ar. Guides, tuition and equipment.
Río Dorado Lodge, Pedro Illera 448, T02972-491548, www.riodorado.com.ar. The luxury fishing lodge at the end of town has a good fly shop, and organizes trips, run by experts and passionate fishermen.

Tour operators
Alquimia Viajes and Turismo, Padre Milanesio 840, T02972-491355, www.alquimiaturismo.com.ar. Offers fishing excursions with expert local guides among a range of adventure tourism expeditions, including climbing Lanín, climbing in rock and ice, rafting, and transfers.
Picurú, C Suárez 371, www.picuruturismo.com.ar. Fun and friendly, offering horse riding, fishing, birdwatching, climbing and trekking.
Tromen, Lonquimay 195, T02972-491469. Trips up Volcano Lanín, horse riding, mountain biking, car rental and bicycle rental.

☉ Transport

San Martín de los Andes *p476, map p477*
Bus

For bus terminal information, see page 476.

Bikes can be carried on most routes, wheels removed, but ask first to be sure. To **Buenos Aires**, daily, 20 hrs, US$66 *coche cama*, 6 companies. To **Bariloche**, many daily, 3½ hrs (not via Seven Lakes Drive), US$12, T02972-425325, **Albus**, T02972-428100; minibus along the Seven Lakes Drive via Traful and La Angostura, 4 hrs, US$8; **Koko**, T02972-427422, daily, fast route via Confluencia. **Puerto Madryn** (changing Neuquén), US$34. To **Neuquén**, 2 daily, 6½ hrs, US$16, **Albus**.

To Chile Temuco Mon, Wed, Fri, Empresa San Martín, T02972-427294; Tue, Thu, Sat, 6-8 hrs, US$16, Igi-Llaima, T02972-427750 (heavily booked in summer), via Paso Hua Hum.

Car hire

Hansen Rent a Car, San Martín 532, T02972-427997, www.hansenrentacar.com.ar, reliable, friendly and very professional company with excellent rates, Mario Hansen is very helpful, recommended. **Hertz**, San Martín 831, 1st floor, T02972-420820; **Rent a Car La Patagonia**, Villegas 305, T02972-421807.

Taxi

Eco Taxi, also known as **Lacar**, T02972-428 817. Very helpful and efficient. If in town, find them on main street San Martín, or give Abuela Goye as useful meeting point.

Junín de los Andes *p479, map p479*
Air

For airport information, see page 480. Flights to **Buenos Aires**, Austral, LADE flights weekly from **Bahía Blanca**, **Esquel**, and **Bariloche**.

Bus

For bus terminal information, see page 480.

To **San Martín de los Andes**, several a day, 45 mins, US$5, **Airén**; **Centenario**; **Koko**. To **Neuquén**, 7 hrs, US$24, several companies. Ask about buses to **Huechulafquen**; every year a different company. To **Tromen**, Mon-Sat, 1½ hrs, US$6. To **Caviahue** and **Copahue**, change at Zapala, 3½ hrs, US$14. To **Bariloche**, 3 hrs, US$15, **Vía Bariloche**, Koko. To **Buenos Aires**, several companies, 21 hrs, US$60.

To Chile Service Temuco, daily, 5 hrs, US$15, via Paso Tromen/Mamuil Malal; 3 times a week, **Empresa San Martín**; 4 times a week, **Igi Llaima**.

☉ Directory

San Martín de los Andes *p476, map p477*
Banks Many ATMs along San Martín: Banelco, at the tourist office, San Martín 1093 and Rosas; Banco Nación, San Martín 687. **Currency exchange** Andina Internacional Cambio and Turismo, Cap Drury 876; Banco de la Nación, San Martín 687; Banco de la Provincia de Neuquén, Obeid and Belgrano, also has ATM, T02972-427243. **Internet** Punto.Com, inside Galería Azul, San Martín 866; Terminal, Vilegas 150. **Laundry** Laverap, Drury 880, daily 0800- 2200; Marva, Drury and Villegas, and Perito Moreno 980, fast, efficient and cheap. **Medical services** Hospital Ramón Carrillo, San Martín and Coronel Rodhe, T02972-427211. **Post office** General Roca and Pérez, Mon-Fri 0800-1300, 1700-2000, Sat 0900-1300. **Telephones** Cooperativa Telefónica, Drury 761; Terminal, Villegas 150.

Junín de los Andes *p479, map p479*
Currency exchange Banco Provincial Neuquén, San Martín and Lamadrid. TCs can be cashed at **Western Union**, Milanesio 570, 1000-1400, 1600-1930. **Internet** In the *galería* behind tourist office. **Post office** Suárez and Don Bosco. **Telephone** *Locutorio* near tourist office on plaza at Milanesio 540.

Pehuenia and northern Neuquén

At the northern end of the Lake District, Pehuenia is a wonderful expanse of unspoilt wilderness, which is only now opening up to visitors, around the picturesque villages of Villa Pehuenia and Moquehue. The area due west of Zapala, running along the border with Chile, is quite different from the southern lakes, thanks to its large forests of ancient pehuén *or araucaria – monkey puzzle trees. These magnificent silent forests exert a mysterious force and give a prehistoric feel to the landscape, while the sleepy backwater feel of the villages makes them appealing for a few days' rest or gentle walking. Further north there are two little-visited tourist centres, useful stopping points if you're heading to Mendoza. Caviahue is good for walking in rugged and unspoilt landscapes or skiing in winter, while bleaker Copahue is known for its high-quality thermal waters. See www.villa pehuenia.org and www.caviahue.com.* ▸▸ *For listings, see pages 493-496.*

Pehuenia → *For listings, see pages 493-496. Phone code 02942.*

The magical and unspoilt area of Pehuenia is named after the country's unique forests of *pehuén* trees, which grow here in vast numbers. Covering a marvellous open mountainous landscape, these ancient, silent trees create a mystical atmosphere, especially around the lakes of Aluminé and Moquehue, where a pair of small villages provides good accommodation. Villa Pehuenia is the best set up for tourism, with its picturesque setting on the lakeside, and a cluster of upmarket *cabañas* have opened here in recent years, with one exceptionally lovely boutique hotel, **La Escondida** ① *www.posadalaescondida.com.ar.* Moquehue is quite different in style: more sprawling and relaxed. There are more *cabañas*, excellent hiking up La Bella Durmiente, and good fly fishing. You'll need to hire a car to get the best out of the area. You can approach from Neuquén city, or, even closer, from Temuco over the border in Chile.

Villa Pehuenia

Getting there To reach Villa Pehuenia, take one of the daily buses from Neuquén city via Zapala, but these take a long time, and once you're here you may want to explore the area in your own transport so car rental may be the best option. Consider approaching from Temuco in Chile, which is just 1½ hours across the border, or hire a car in Neuquén (3½-hour drive) and drop it off in San Martín de los Andes or Bariloche afterwards. Route 13 continues to the Paso de Icalma crossing to Chile, just a few kilometres from Villa Pehuenia, with easy access to Temuco, 130 km further, on the other side.

Getting around The centre of the village is just off the main road, Route 13, where you'll find a service station, *locutorios*, food and handicrafts shops, and a pharmacy. There are two tour operators who can arrange trekking, boat trips on the lake and bike hire, and there is another area of restaurants and tea rooms by the lake side.

Tourist information There is a **tourist kiosk** ① *off the main road, by the turning for Villa Pehuenia, T02942-498044, www.villapehuenia.gov.ar,* which, along with most hotels, has the excellent free leaflet showing a detailed map of Villa Pehuenia with all the hotels and restaurants marked. In March, the harvest of the *piñones* is celebrated during the **Fiesta del Pehuén** with horse-riding displays and live music.

Monkey puzzle trees

The stunningly beautiful area of Pehuenia is remarkable for its forests of araucaria, or monkey puzzle trees (*Araucaria araucana*). Growing slowly to a mighty 40 m high, the trees exert a powerful presence when seen en masse, perhaps because their forests are silent, moving little in the breeze. A true conifer, the araucaria is a descendent of the petrified pines found in Argentina's *bosques petrificados*. For centuries the *pehuén* or *araucaria* have been revered by indigenous peoples, and the local Mapuche still eat its pine nuts, rich in vitamins and fats. The custom of collecting their nuts, around which a whole array of foods and a celebratory harvest festival are based, has been the source of a bitter territory dispute in parts of the northern Lake District. The Mapuche feel that they have a natural right to harvest the fruits of their trees, and local landowners, backed by local government, clearly don't agree.

There's a growing respect for the Mapuche in the area, and they are beginning to get involved in the provision of basic tourist services with great success. You'll see *pan casero* (home-made bread), *tortas fritas* (fried pastries) and handicrafts for sale on roadsides, as well as the winter sports centre near Villa Pehuenia, all run by the local Mapuche. These small enterprises enable them to survive financially, while retaining their traditions and customs, and with luck, access to the magnificent araucarias which they hold so sacred.

Sights This pretty village on sprawling Lago Aluminé's northern shore is picturesquely set amongst steep wooded hills, and makes a lovely base for a few days' relaxation or gentle walks in the hills and forests around. This is Mapuche land and was chosen for a settlement when the Mapuche were forcefully flushed out of Buenos Aires province in the late 19th century. It has special significance because seven volcanoes in a chain are visible from here, and because the area abounds with *pehuén* (monkey puzzle) trees, which are sacred to the Mapuche (see box, above). With the rapid building of *cabaña* complexes, tourism is slowly taking off here, and at the moment you have the best of both worlds: an unspoilt feel but enough tourist infrastructure to stay in comfort, with good restaurants. Walk onto the peninsula stretching out into the lake from the village for wonderful walks along the araucaria-fringed shore, and up to the **Mirador del Cipres** with fabulous views.

There is skiing and winter sports at the **Parque de Nieve Batea Mahuida** ① *www.inter patagonia.com/bateamahuida*, winter sports area (turn right just a few kilometres further along the main road, signposted). This reserve was created to protect an area of *pehuén* trees and the majestic volcano Mahuida (1900 m) which is regarded by the Mapuche peoples as sacred. This sports area is one of the few businesses in the area run by Mapuche people, and is a lovely place for walking in summer, with tremendous views of all seven volcanoes around, and good for limited skiing in winter, with snowmobile and snowshoe walking. Delicious home-cooked food is served. Contact the Mapuche Puel community at the entrance. It's a lovely walk up here (three hours), or one hour by bike.

Walks

For walks through the *araucaria* forests, drive west from Villa Pehuenia towards Chile and continue 4 km further along the road until you reach the end of the lake, where you turn left at the *gendarmería*, following a dirt road across the bridge over a narrow strip of water, La Angostura. Follow the arrow to a campsite 50 m further on, **El Puente** (a delightful place, recommended). Continue past it and, when you come to a little hut and a sign to Lago Redonda, take the right fork and follow the track. Park or leave your bike at the largest of the three small *lagunas*, and take the path due south when the track comes to an end at a farmstead by a large lagoon. Climb from here to a ridge with great views, and then take the path which drops and skirts around **Lago Moquehue** – the view is awe-inspiring. You could walk to Moquehue from here, but you need a map. Ask for the *Sendas y Bosques* map of Norte Neuquino, which shows the Pehuenia-Moquehue area, and some paths. This whole area is the heart of the Mapuche community: many houses offer *pan casero* (home-made bread), horse riding or walking guides. Alternatively, head further north to the weird other-worldly landscapes of **Paso de Arco**.

Lago Moquehue → *Phone code 0299. Population 600.*
Another 10 km on Route 13 brings you to the sprawling village of Moquehue. It's a wilder, more remote place than Villa Pehuenia, spreading out on the shores of its lake, with a lovely wide river. Famous for fishing, this is a beautiful and utterly peaceful place to relax and walk, and it has a less cultivated feel, inspiring adventurous treks. A short stroll through araucaria forests brings you to a lovely waterfall; a longer hike to the top of **Cerro Bandera** (four hours return) gives wonderful views over the area, and to Volcán Llaima. There are fine camping spots and a couple of comfortable places to stay. For more information, see www.villapehuenia.org (in English).

Aluminé → *Colour map 5, A2. Population 4000. Phone code 02942.*
In the splendid Aluminé Valley, on Route 23 between Pehuenia and Junín, lies the area's self-proclaimed rafting capital, the small town of Aluminé. There is indeed superb rafting (Grades II or IV to VI, depending on rainfall) nearby on Río Aluminé. There are places to stay, but despite the lovely setting, it's a drab place: far better to keep going to Villa Pehuenia unless you are here to go rafting. There's a very friendly **tourist office** ① *C Christian Joubert 321, T02942-496001, www.alumine.gov.ar, daily 0800-2100.* There's a service station too, the last before Villa Pehuenia. ►► *For further information, see Activities and tours, page 496.*

Rucachoroi
From Aluminé there is access to Lago Rucachoroi, 23 km west, the biggest Mapuche community inside the Lanín national park. In gentle farmland surrounded by ancient *pehuén* forests. Access is by a rough *ripio* road, best in a 4WD in winter, and spectacular in autumn when the deciduous trees are a splash of orange against the bottle-green araucarias. The only accommodation is in two campsites, both offering Mapuche food, and horse riding. Here too, there's a *quardería* where you can ask about a possible trek to Lago Quillén. The landscape is very beautiful and you will want to linger, but bring provisions and camping gear. Private transport is essential.

Lago Quillén
At the junction by the small town of Rahue, 16 km south of Aluminé, a road leads west to the valley of the Río Quillén and the exquisite Lago Quillén, from where there are fine views of Volcán Lanín peeping above the mountains. The lake itself is one of the region's most lovely, jade green in colour, with beaches along its low-lying northern coast. Further west, where annual rainfall is among the heaviest in the country, the slopes are thickly covered with superb Andean Patagonian forest. There's no transport, and the only accommodation (with food shop and hot showers) is at **Camping Pudu Pudu**

Border essentials: Argentina–Chile

Paso Pino Hachado

Paso Pino Hachado (1864 m) lies 115 km west of Zapala via Route 22, which is almost completely paved. On the Chilean side a *ripio* road runs northwest to Lonquimáy, 65 km west of the border. Temuco lies 145 km southwest of Lonquimáy.

Argentine immigration and customs 9 km east of the border, open daily 0900-2000. There are toilets and a kiosk. For more information, see www.gendarmeria.gov.ar/pasos/fichpihacha.htm.

Chilean immigration and customs Liucura, 22 km west of the border, December to March daily 0800-2100, April to November daily 0800-1900. Very thorough searches and two- to three-hour delays reported. Buses from Zapala and Neuquén to Temuco use this crossing.

Paso de Icalma

Paso de Icalma (1303 m) lies 132 km west of Zapala and is reached by Route 13 (*ripio*). It is used as an alternative border crossing when other crossings at higher altitude are closed due to snow. On the Chilean side this road continues to Melipeuco, 30 km west of the border, and then to Temuco. At the moment there are upgrades to the roads in process on the Argentine side, but it is still possible to travel through to Chile. For up-to-date information, see www.gendarmeria.gov.ar/pasos/fichicalma.html.

Argentine immigration and customs 9 km east of the border, daily 0800-2100 in summer, daily 0900-1900 approximately in winter. All paperwork is carried out at the customs office, clearly signposted.

Chilean immigration and customs Open December-March 0800-2100, April-November 0800-1900.

---

① *T02942-496001*, on the lake's northern shore, just west of the *guardería*. Here you can get advice about walks, and register with *guardaparques* if you plan to hike to Rucachoroi. There's another walk to the remote **Lago Hui Hui**, 6 km north from the second campsite (3½ hours return). For fishing, contact **Estancia Quillén** (see Sleeping, page 495).

Copahue and Caviahue → *For listings, see pages 493-496. Colour map 3, C1.*

The extraordinary landscape of **Reserva Provincial Copahue** at the heart of this region is formed by a giant volcanic crater, whose walls are the surrounding mountains. An arid, dramatic and other-worldly landscape, the park was created to protect the araucaria trees that grow on its slopes, and there are some wonderful walks that take you to unexpectedly stunning landscapes. About 150 km from Zapala, **Caviahue** is by far the most attractive of the two, with an appealing lakeside setting, and the best base for walking and horse riding; it converts into a skiing and winter sports centre from July to September and swells to a winter population of over 10,000. It has three ski lifts, excellent areas for cross-country skiing, snow-shoeing and snowmobiling, all with tremendous views, and it's one of cheaper resorts in the Lake District. **Copahue** (1980 m) is a thermal spa resort enclosed in a gigantic amphitheatre formed by mountain walls and boasting the best thermal waters in South America, though it's decidedly the bleaker of the two towns.

Ins and outs → *Phone code 02948. Population 700.*
Getting there Both towns are easily reached by public transport from Zapala, 150 km southeast, or by flying to Neuquén, 300 km southeast.

Tourist information In Caviahue, there is a **tourist office** ① *8 de Abril, bungalows 5 and 6, T02948-495036, www.caviahue-copahue.com.ar*. For information on the thermal waters, check out www.caviahuetours.com. To find out about the ski centre, contact **Caviahue Base**, www.caviahue.com. There's an ATM at the *municipalidad*, several restaurants and a tea room, as well as some decent accommodation. In Copahue, the **tourist office** is on the approach road into town, Route 26.

Around Caviahue

The Volcán Copahue last erupted, smokily, in 2000, destroying the bright blue lake in its crater, but it's still a popular destination for horse riding, and the views of the prehistoric landscape are astounding. Most highly recommended, though, is **El Salto del Agrio**, 15 km northeast along Route 27. This is the climax in a series of delightful falls, approached by a road passing between tall, ancient araucaria trees poised on basalt cliffs; a wonderful excursion by horse to see all seven falls. Other fantastic walks in the area are to the extraordinary **Las Máquinas**, 4 km south of Copahue, where sulphurous steam puffs through air holes and against a panoramic backdrop, making the weirdest noises. And at **El Anfiteatro**, there are thermal waters reaching 150°C, in a semicircle of rock edged with araucaria trees. Just above Copahue, there is a steep climb up to **Cascada Escondida**, a torrent of water falling 15 m over a shelf of basalt into a pool surrounded by a forest of araucaria trees; above it Lago Escondida is a magical spot.

ⓔ Pehuenia and northern Neuquén listings

For Sleeping and Eating price codes and other relevant information, see Essentials pages 30-36.

ⓢ Sleeping

Villa Pehuenia *p489*
You'll find 1 superb boutique hotel, and plenty of *cabañas*, many with good views over the lake and set in idyllic woodland. Email or ring first for directions, since there are no road names or numbers here. For more listings, see www.villapehuenia.org (in English).
L-AL La Escondida, western shore of the península, T02942-1569 1166, www.posada laescondida.com.ar. By far the best place to stay in the whole area, this is a really special boutique hotel with just 9 rooms in an imaginatively designed building on the rocky lakeside. Each room is spacious and beautifully considered, with smart bathrooms (all with jacuzzi), and private decks, all with

gorgeous views over the lake. The restaurant is superb and non-residents can dine here with a reservation. The whole place is relaxing and welcoming. Highly recommended.
AL Altos de Pehuén, T02942-1566 6849, www.altosdelpehuen.com.ar. Comfortable *cabañas* with lovely views, and a *hostería*.
A Complejo Patagonia, T02942-1557 9434 (T011-155 011 4470 in Buenos Aires), www.complejopatagonia.com.ar. Very comfortable indeed, these lovely *cabañas* are traditionally designed and the service is excellent. Recommended.
B Cabañas Bahía Radal, T02942-498057, www.bahiaradal.com.ar, on the peninsula (ask the tourist office for directions). Luxurious *cabañas*, with clear lake views from its elevated position.
B Las Terrazas, T02942-498036, www. lasterrazaspehuenia.com.ar. Recommended: the owner is an architect, who has retained

Mapuche style in his beautiful design of these comfortable *cabañas*, tasteful, warm and with perfect views over the lake. Also with bed and breakfast (**C**). He can direct you to magical places for walking, and to Mapuche communities to visit.

C Cabañas Caren, T02942-498057, www.cabanias.com/caren. Simple A-frame *cabañas*, but with open views and balconies, and made especially welcoming by the warm friendly owner Walter.

C La Serena, T011-154 794 0319, www.complejolaserena.com.ar. Beautifully equipped and designed *cabañas* for 2-6 people with lovely uninterrupted view, gardens going down to beach, sheltered from the wind and furnished with rustic-style, handmade cypress furniture, and wood stoves, all very attractive.

C Puerto Malén Club de Montaña, T02942-498007 (T011-4226 8190 in Buenos Aires), www.puertomalen.com. Well-built wooden *cabañas* with lake views from their balconies, and the highest-quality interiors. Also a luxurious *hostería* (**A**). Recommended.

Camping

Camping Agreste Quechulafquen, at the end of the steep road across La Angostura. Situated among lovely steep hills and dense vegetation, run by Mapuche Puels.

Camping El Puente, at La Angostura. US$3 per person, with hot showers. A simpler site, in beautiful surroundings.

Las Lagrimitas, just west of the village, T02942-498003. A lovely secluded lakeside site on the beach, with food shop. US$6 per person, hot showers and fireplaces.

Lago Moquehue p491

C Hostería Restaurante Moquehue, set high above the lake with panoramic views, T02942-1560 0301, www.hosteriamoquehue. netfirms.com. Cosy, stylish rooms, nicely furnished with good views and excellent food. Try the superb Moquehue trout and local *chivito*. Charming family hosts. Recommended.

D La Bella Durmiente, T0299-496172. In a rustic building with no heating, summer only,

the welcoming owner offers good food and also trekking, horse riding, diving in the lake and mountain biking. Call for directions.

Cabañas

A Cabañas Los Maitenes, T029942-421681, T02942-1566 5621, www.interpatagonia.com/cablosmaitenes. Right on the lake, well-equipped *cabañas*, with breakfast included and friendly owners. Recommended.

A La Busqueda, T02942-1566 0377, www.labusquedamoquehue.com.ar. Just north of the lake, before you reach the head of Lago Moquehue. Interesting design in these well-equipped *cabañas* with TV, including breakfast. Recommended

B Cabañas Melipal, T02948-495056, www.melipalcopahue.com.ar. Very attractive, rustic, stone-built *cabañas* in secluded sites on the lake. Lovely old-fashioned style, well equipped and warm, fabulous views from balcony, use of boats. Highly recommended.

C Cabañas Huerquen, T0299-440 1650, www.cabaniashuerquen.com.ar. Beyond Moquehue on the road to Norquinco, these lovely secluded stone *cabañas* are in beautifully tranquil surroundings.

Camping

Along R13, 11 km to Lago Ñorquinco, past mighty basalt cliffs with *pehuenes* all around, there's idyllic camping. Also idyllic, reached by R11, are the smaller campsites of **Lagos Pilhué** and **Ñorquinco Camping**.

Camping Trenel, www.trenel.alojar.com.ar. In a fabulous site elevated on the southern shore of Lago Moquehue, just beyond the **Hostería Moquehue**. Beautiful, well-kept sites in the thick of little *nirre* trees, with seats and *parrillas* overlooking the lake. Smart, hot showers, good restaurant, food shop, information and excursions. Recommended.

Ecocamping Ñorquinco, T02942-496155, www.ecocampingnorquinco.alojar.com.ar. There is 1 amazing rustic *cabaña* right on the lake, with a café by the roadside, US$8 per person per night, US$3 for under 12s, Dec or Mar, Apr to Easter. Great fishing, hot showers

and a *provenduría*. Lovely place to eat if it rains.
Los Caprichosos, on Lago Ñorquinco. Open
Nov-Apr only, with water and food shop.

Aluminé p491
AL Estancia Quillén, R46 near Rahue, near
the bridge crossing Río Aluminé, T02942-
496196, www.interpatagonia.com/quillen.
A comfortable, traditionally furnished house,
with spacious rooms and a restaurant, where
you'll be welcomed by the *estancia* owners.
Great for fishing and hunting. Open Dec-Apr.
AL Piedra Pintada, T02972-429510. Only
35 km from town, this is the best option. 12
rooms, stylishly fitted out, with a sauna, fantastic
views over the lake and impressive restaurant.
A-B Pehuenia, just off R23 at Crouzeilles 100,
T02942-496340, www.hotelpehuenia.com.ar.
A huge tin chalet-style building, not attractive
but with great views. The rooms are simple
and comfortable, the staff are friendly, and
it's good value. Horse riding, bike hire and
canoeing at the owner's campsite, **Bahía de
los Sueños**, 6 km from the red bridge north
of Aluminé.
C-D Aluminé, C Joubert 312, T02942-496
174, www.hosteriaaalumine.com.ar. In the
middle of town, opposite tourist information,
this is a drab 1960s place, with clean,
functional rooms. There's an excellent little
restaurant next door, **La Posta del Rey**.

Camping
There are campsites all over the area.
La Vieja Balsa, T02942-496001, just
outside Aluminé on R23 on the Río Aluminé.
Dec-Easter. A well-equipped site offering
rafting and fishing, US$8 per person per day
to camp. Hot showers, shop and fireplaces.

Rucachoroi p491
Camping
2 sites: **Rucachoroi 1** and **Rucachoroi 2**,
before and after the lake. Open all year, but
ideal only Dec-Feb. The 1st has more facilities,
with toilets, but no hot water, some food
supplies, including Mapuche home-made
bread and sausages, and horse riding.

Copahue p492
AL Aldea Termal, T0299-442 5605,
www.aldeatermal.com. Attractively decorated
chalet-style apartments. Recommended.
A Hotel Copahue, Olascoaga y Bercovich,
T0299-495117, www.copahuejunin.com.ar.
This lovely old place where you'll be warmly
welcomed by Pocho and Moriconi is the most
recommended place in Copahue. There are
well-built wood and stone *cabañas* (**A-C**).

Caviahue p492
A-B Lago Caviahue, Costanera Quimey-Co,
T02948-495110, www.hotellagocaviahue.
com. Better value than the Nevado;
comfortable but dated lakeside apartments
with kitchen, also a good restaurant and great
views. 2 km from the ski centre.
A-B Nevado Caviahue, 8 de Abril s/n, T02948-
495053, www.hotelnevado.com.ar. Plain,
modern rooms, and there's a restaurant and
cosy lounge with wood fire. Also 6 *cabañas*
(**A-B**), well-equipped but not luxurious.
B-C Farallón, Caviahue Base, T02948-
495085, www.hotelfarallon.com.ar.
Neat apartments, some with kitchens.
C La Cabaña de Tito, Puesta del Sol s/n,
T02948-495093. *Cabañas*, excellent meals.

Hostels
E pp **Hebe's House**, Mapuche y Puesta del
Sol, T02948-495237, www.hebeshouse.com.ar.
Lovely chalet-style building with great
communal areas and only 2 blocks from the
centre of town. Doubles (**D-C**) available.

Camping
Copahue, T02948-495111, Hueney Municipal.
Open summer only. Basic but well maintained.

🍴 Eating

Villa Pehuenia p489
🍴🍴🍴 **La Escondida**, on the western shore of the
peninsula, T02942-1569 1166, www.posadala
escondida.com.ar. By far the best in town.
Only open to non-residents with a reservation,

this is really special cuisine. All local ingredients, imaginatively prepared and served. Highly recommended.

₩₩ **Anhedonia**, on the lakeside, T02942-1566 9866. Fondue, beef and pasta.

₩₩ **Gnaien Chocolatería and tea room**, on the lakeside, T02942-498082. Good for tea, with lovely views of the lake, chocolate delicacies, *picadas* and range of wines.

₩₩ **La Cantina del Pescador**, on the lakeside, T02942-498086. Fresh trout.

₩ **Costa Azul**, on the lakeside, T02942-498 035. Tasty local dishes and pasta; *chivito* (kid) *al asado* is the speciality of the house.

Aluminé *p491*

₩ **La Posta del Rey**, next to the service station, opposite the plaza, Cristian Joubert, T02942-496248. The best place by far, with friendly service, great trout, local kid, delicious pastas and sandwiches. Recommended.

Copahue and Caviahue *p493*

₩ **Copahue Club Hotel**, Valle del Volcán. Serves good *chivito al asado* and local trout.

₩ **Hotel Lago Caviahue**. The most stylish place to eat with an inspired *chivo a la cerveza* (kid cooked in beer), along with more traditional favourites and local specialities.

⊛ Festivals and events

Villa Pehuenia *p489*

Mar Fiesta del Pehuén, www.villapehuenia. org (in Spanish). The harvest of the *piñones*, celebrated with riding displays and live music.

▲ Activities and tours

Villa Pehuenia *p489*

Los Pehuenes, T02942-498029, www. pehuenes.com.ar. Excellent company offering wide range of excursions and adventures, from trekking in the mountains; to rafting, US$35, for full day, Grade IV; horse riding, US$36 for full day with lunch; visits to the local Mapuche

communities, with kid *asado*, and local history and culture; and fishing and boat trips. Professional, helpful and friendly. Ask for Fernando. Can also arrange transfers to Pehuenia from San Martín and Neuquén.

Aluminé *p491*

Aluminé Rafting, Villegas 610, T02942-496 322, www.interpatagonia.com/aluminerafting. US$13-20, depending on difficulty, for 3 hrs rafting, Grades II-VI, all equipment included. Circuito Abra Ancha, 2½ hrs, Grade II, 6 km, very entertaining, suitable for everyone; Circuito Aluminé Superior, 12 or 15 km run, 5-6 hrs, Grade III-IV, very technical river leaving Lago Alumine, for those who like a thrill, passing little woods of araucarias and *ñirres*; family trips Grades I and II. Costs US$25 per person for Abra Ancha and US$65 per person for higher level. Trekking US$85 per day, trekking in Cordón de Chachil, US$122 per day, 2 days minimum, but can be up to a week, also kayaking and biking.

Caviahue *p492*

Caviahue Tours, San Martín 623, Buenos Aires, T02948-4314 1556. Good information.

⊖ Transport

Villa Pehuenia *p489*

There are 3 buses weekly to Villa Pehuenia and **Moquehue** from **Neuquén** (less predictable in winter, when the roads are covered in snow) and **Aluminé**, 5½ hrs.

Aluminé *p491*

Buses daily to **Zapala**, 3 hrs, US$7, Albus, T02942-496368; Aluminé Viajes, T02942-496 231. Twice a week to **Villa Pehuenia**, 1 hr, US$4. Twice a week to **San Martín de los Andes**, 4 hrs, US$9, Tilleria, T02942-496048.

Caviahue *p492*
Bus

To **Neuquén**, daily, 6 hrs, US$16, via Zapala (US$6), El Petroleo and El Centenario, T02948-495024.

Western Neuquén

The northern half of the Lake District falls into the province of Neuquén, encompassing an enormous region from just north of Bariloche to beyond Copahue and Caviahue, and ending at the border with Mendoza. The provincial capital is the pleasant modern city of Neuquén, centre of an important fruit-growing area, providing most of Argentina's apples, pears and grapes. You're likely to stop off only briefly here on the way to greater adventures in the mountains further west, but it's worth making time for a brief encounter with dinosaurs at several sites easily reached from Neuquén city. There are incredibly huge dinosaur footprints at Villa El Chocón, and you'll want to see the skeleton in the museum there as proof that the largest carnivores ever known actually stomped around these lands 100 million years ago. You could also try a spot of excavation yourself at Valle Cretacico, and not only dinosaur fans will be impressed by the skeleton of the largest herbivorous dinosaur on earth in Plaza Huincul. For more information, see www.neuquen.com. ▶▶ *For listings, see pages 501-503.*

Neuquén city and around → *For listings, see pages 501-503. Colour map 5, A3.*

The provincial capital is at the eastern tip of the province of Neuquén, an attractive industrial town, founded in 1904, just after the arrival of the railway. It's on the opposite side of the Río Neuquén from Cipolletti, a prosperous centre of the Río Negro fruit-growing region. While it has no major tourist attractions, it's a useful stopping point for the lakes and also a good base for exploring the dinosaur finds in the area to the immediate southwest. There's even a *bodega* you can visit, **Bodega del Fin del Mundo** ① *R8, Km 9, near San Patricio de Chañar, T0299-485 5004, www.bodegadelfindelmundo.com, Mon-Fri 1000-1600, weekends and bank holidays 1000-1700.* Free tours take an hour and include a tasting.

Ins and outs ➤ *Phone code 0299. Population 210,000.*
Getting there There are daily flights from Buenos Aires to the **airport** ① *T0299-444 0245*, 7 km west of town. Take a local bus into town (No 10 or 11) for US$0.50 (*tarjeta* bus card needed), or take a taxi for US$9. There are frequent long-distance buses to the **central bus terminal** ① *Mitre 147, T0299-445 2300*, from Buenos Aires and towns throughout the Lake District as well as north to Mendoza and west to Chile. The bus terminal is huge and modern, with lots of services and clean toilets. Left luggage costs US$2 a day per item.

Getting around The town can easily be explored on foot in a few hours, with most hotels and restaurants around the main street Avenida Argentina, which runs north from the disused railway track running east-west across the town, just south of General San Martín. Don't get confused with the street Félix San Martín, three blocks further south.

Tourist information The **tourist office** ① *Félix San Martín 182, T0299-442 4089, www.neuquentur.gov.ar, www.neuquen.com, Mon-Fri 0700-2200, Sat-Sun 0800-2000*, provides helpful lists of accommodation and a map.

Sights

At the northern end of Avenida Argentina at the Parque Centenario there is the **Mirador Balcón del Valle** with panoramic views over the city and the confluence of the rivers (be sure not to take the bus to Centenario industrial suburb). In the university buildings at the entrance of the park is the **Museo Paleontológico de Ciencias Naturales** ① *Argentina 1400*, which includes exhibitions of dinosaur fossils found in the region. The **former railway station**, at Olascoaga and Pasaje Obligado, has been converted into a cultural centre and exhibition centre. South of the centre there is also a pleasant walk along the Río Limay. Facing Neuquén and connected by bridge is **Cipolletti**. All the towns in the valley celebrate the **Fiesta Nacional de la Manzana** (apples are the main local crop) in the second half of March.

Routes to the lakes

From Neuquén, there are various ways to approach the lakes. An attractive route involves continuing due west to Zapala on Ruta 22, and then south to Junín de los Andes on Ruta 40. Or from Zapala, you could continue west to Villa Pehuenia, or north to Caviahue and Copahue. For the direct route to Bariloche, take Ruta 237, via **Piedra del Aguila** and the astounding scenery of the **Valle Encantado**, with mountains whipped into jaggy peaks. Río Limay appears, a mysterious milky turquoise as it flows into Embalse Alicura lake. The road continues to Lago Nahuel Huapi where there are fine views over Cerros Catedral and Tronador.

West of Neuquén → *For listings, see pages 501-503.*

To the southwest of Neuquén lies the huge lake **Embalse Ezequiel Ramos Mexía** in an area that has become famous in recent years for the wealth of dinosaur fossils found here from the Cretaceous period (100 million years ago). There are a number of places where you can see the finds, and even walk close to the footsteps of dinosaurs, and although the towns themselves are not appealing, they could make convenient stopping points along the road from Neuquén to the lakes, with a good museum at Villa El Chocón. You can even take part in dinosaur excavation at the **Centro Paleontológico at Lago Barreales** ① *www.proyectodino.com.ar.*

Villa El Chocón and around → *Colour map 5, A3. Phone code 0299.*

① *For information on reaching the footprints, and how they were formed, see www.interpatagonia.com/paseos/huellas (in English).*

Your only reason to visit Villa El Chocón at the northern end of Lago Ezequiel Ramos Mexía, 72 km from Neuquén, is to see the remains of dinosaurs. It's a neat, rather uninspiring town, a strictly functional place built for workers on the hydroelectric dam, but worth a stop for the amazing evidence of **dinosaurs**: take Route 237 towards Piedra del Aguila, and turn left at Barrio Llanquén, where indicated, to the lake shore. Red sedimentary rocks have preserved, in relatively good condition, bones and even footprints of the creatures that lived in this region during the Cretaceous period about 100 million years ago. Some of the fossils can be seen in the **Museo Paleontológico Ernesto Bachmann** ① *Civic centre, El Chocón, T0299-490 1223, www.interpatagonia.com/ paseos/ernestobachmann, daily 0900-1900 in winter, 0800-2100 in summer, US$0.50,* where guides give very good tours. Exhibits include fossils of the mighty 10-ton, 15-m long *Gigantosaurus carolinii*, a carnivorous dinosaur larger than the famous *Tyrannosaurus rex*. There's a well laid-out and informative display with information on these quite mind-boggling finds. Alejandro París of **Aventura Jurásica** ① *El Chocón, T0299-490 1243,* offers guided two- to three-hour visits to the museum and surroundings from US$3 per person not including transfers.

Excavation at Valle Cretacico

ⓘ *www.interpatagonia.com/paseos/valle_cretacico2, has information in English.*

The lunar landscape around Villa El Chocón is rather amazing and contains a surprising amount of dinosaur remains. So much so that an area has been named 'Cretaceous Valley'. The valley lies 18 km south of Villa El Chocón, near the Dique and has improbably shaped pedestals of eroded pink rock coming out of the blue water. There are two walks beside the lake to see the dinosaur footprints, which are amazingly well preserved.

If you're really into dinosaurs, you should consider visiting the **Centro Paleontológico at Lago Barreales** ⓘ *T0299-154 048 614, www.proyectodino.com.ar*, where you can even take part in dinosaur excavation. A team of palaeontologists is currently working on a large site, where some 30 fossils of dinosaur vertebrates have already been found, some of them belonging to a small dinosaur so far unnamed. Leave Neuquén on Route 7 and then take Route 51 towards Añelo. Before reaching this district, and after having passed Lake Mari Menuco, you'll find Lake Barreales. The entrance to the paleontological centre is located in the detour towards the lake.

Plaza Huincul → *Colour map 5, A2. Population 11,000.*

There are more dinosaur remains at a quite impressive little museum in the otherwise rather dull town of Plaza Huincul. The road to Zapala, Route 22, leaves Neuquén and passes through the fruit-growing region of the Río Limay and the much duller oil-producing zone. Situated 107 km west of Neuquén, Plaza Huincul was the site of the country's first oil find in 1918. The **Museo Municipal Carmen Funes** ⓘ *on the way into Plaza Huicul, at the crossing of R22 and R97, T0299-496 5486 for opening times*, includes the vertebrae of *Argentinossaurus huinclulensis*, believed to have weighed over 100 tons and to have been one of the largest herbivorous dinosaurs ever to have lived, as well as a nest of fossilized dinosaur eggs. It's mainly a centre for research, and you can see the results of the fieldwork in fossils, photographs and videos, as well as the skeletons themselves. For more information, see www.plazahuincul.com.ar and www.plazahuincul.gov.ar (In Spanish).

Zapala → *Colour map 5, A2. Phone code 02942. Population 35,000.*

Zapala (1012 m) lies in a vast dry plain with views of snow-capped mountains to the west. It's a modern and rather unappealing place, but you'll need to stop here if you want to take buses to Pehuenia, Copahue and Caviahue, or to cross the border into Chile at the Icalma Pass. There is a **tourist office** ⓘ *San Martín and Mayor Torres, T02942-421132, Mon-Fri 0700-1930, Sat-Sun 0800-1300, 1600-1900 in summer, closes earlier off season*. The **bus terminal** ⓘ *T02942-423191*, is at Etcheluz y Uriburu.

The **Museo Mineralógico Dr Juan Olsacher** ⓘ *Ejército Argentino and Etcheluz 52 (next to the bus terminal), Mon-Wed 0900-1400, free*, is one of the best fossil museums in South America; it contains over 2000 types of mineral and has the finest collection of fossils of marine reptiles and marine fauna in the country. On display is the largest turtle shell from the Jurassic period ever found and an ophthalmosaur, as well as photos of an extensive cave system being excavated nearby.

Parque Nacional Laguna Blanca → *Colour map 5, A2.*

Covering 11,250 ha at altitudes of between 1200 m and 1800 m, this park is one of only two reserves in the Americas created to protect swans and is 35 km southwest of Zapala. This is a rare example of high arid steppe, and its 1700-ha lagoon is one of the most important nesting areas of the black-necked swan in Argentina. Other birdlife includes

Walking with dinosaurs

Few countries are as important as Argentina for palaeontologists. The relative abundance of fossils near the surface has made the country one of the most important for the study of dinosaur evolution. The Ischigualasto and Talampaya parks (San Juan and La Rioja respectively) have yielded rich evidence of dinosaurs from the Triassic period (225-180 million years ago), among them, the small *Eoraptor lunensis*, 220 million years old. Ask your Ischigualasto tour guide to find some fossilized dinosaur bones for you to see.

Patagonia was home to Jurassic dinosaurs (180-135 million years old), with some outstanding examples found here: Cerro Cóndor in Chubut is the only site of Middle Jurassic period dinosaurs found in the Americas, and has given palaeontologists an important breakthrough in understanding the evolutionary stages of the period. Finding five examples of *patagosaurus* indicated that these dinosaurs were social creatures, perhaps uniting for mutual defence. In Santa Cruz, traces of dinosaurs from the Upper Jurassic period have been found in rocks which indicate that the climate was arid and desert-like at the time, surprising palaeontologists with the news that dinosaurs could live and breed in such adverse conditions.

Head for Neuquén and Chubut, where the most important discoveries of dinosaurs from the Cretaceous period (135-70 million years ago) have been made. Dating from the period of separation of the continents of South America and Africa, these provide evidence of the way dinosaurs began to evolve differently due to geographic isolation. The *Carnotaurus sastrie* has horns and small hands, for example, whereas the Patagonian dinosaurs are huge. The carnivorous *Gigantosaurus carolinii*, found near Neuquén city, was larger even than the better known *Tyranosaurus rex*, discovered in North America. You'll find dinosaur footprints, eerily well preserved, near Villa Chocón, southwest of Neuquén city, and more finds in the local museum. You can even take part in excavation at a site in Cretaceous Valley, and there are remains of the largest herbivorous dinosaur on earth at Plaza Huincul's famous museum. Trelew on the Atlantic coast has the country's finest dinosaur museum, and there's an excellent site with 40 million years of history near the Welsh village of Gaiman (see page 548). For more infor- mation, see www. welcomeargentina.com/paleontologiam.

several duck species, plovers, sandpipers, grebes and Chilean flamingos, with birds of prey such as the red-backed hawk and the peregrine falcon nesting on the steep slopes of the *laguna*. It's best visited in spring, when young can be watched at many sites around the *laguna*. The landscape is indeed very dry, and rather bleak, with fierce winds, encouraging only the lowest and most tenacious plant life. A rough track runs round the lake, suitable for 4WD vehicles only. Nearby the **Arroyo Ñireco** has eroded the volcanic rock to form a deep gorge, and it's worth seeking out a small cave, inhabited in prehistoric times, with cave paintings. Southwest of the park Route 46 continues through the spectacular Bajada de Rahue, dropping 800 m in under 20 km before reaching the town of Rahue, 120 km southwest of Zapala.

Park information The park entrance is 10 km from the junction of Route 46 (which runs across the park) with Ruta 40. The *laguna* itself lies 5 km beyond this. There's no public transport, so without your own vehicle the only option is a tour from Zapala. There's a *guardería* post near the southeast corner of the *laguna*, with a visitors centre and picnic area, entry is US$11. Take drinking water and a hat for the heat. There's a hiking trail which takes in 10 lagoons in all. There's free camping by the *guardaparque*, otherwise Zapala has the nearest accommodation, see www.parquesnacionales.gov.ar.

⊕ Western Neuquén listings

For Sleeping and Eating price codes and other relevant information, see Essentials pages 30-36.

◉ Sleeping

Neuquén city and around *p497*
LL Valle Perdido Wine Resort, RP7, Picada 6, San Patricio de Chañar, T011-6091 7777, www.valleperdido.com.ar. Located 50 km south of town on the way to Villa El Chocón this wonderful winery has top-notch 5-star accommodation. With only 16 huge boutique rooms and 2 even bigger suites all with spectacular views and a private deck, this is the best place around for miles.
AL Casino Magic Hotel, Teodoro Planas 4005, 10800-666 2442, www.casinomagic. com.ar/hotel.html. Surprisingly nice rooms with flatscreen TVs, and the use of the sauna, pool and gym is included.
AL Hotel del Comahue, Av Argentina 377, T0299-443 2040, www.hoteldelcomahue. com. This is an elegant 4-star, with spa and pool, an excellent restaurant, and very good service and facilities.
AL-A La Morada, Villegas 591, T0299-442 1379, www.lamoradaneuquen.com.ar. Small boutique hotel with attention to detail. Lovely sitting room with fireplace and Wi-Fi.
B Hostal de Caminante, R22 Km 1229, T0299-4440118, www.hostaldelcaminante. com.ar. Nicely presented, basic hotel which has tennis courts, a pool, parking and a mini-gym. Located south of the city.
B-C Royal Hotel, Av Argentina 143, T0299-448 8902, www.royalhotel.com.ar. Slightly dated, but clean hotel with en suites, parking and a/c.

Hostel
Fpp, **Hostel Punto Patagónico**, Julio Argentino Roca 1694, T0299-447 9940, www.puntopatagonico.com. A bit out of the centre, this clean and friendly hostel, with Wi-Fi, breakfast included and rustic furniture is recommended.

Camping
There's no camping in town.
Las Araucarios, 16 km from town, before Plottier on R22. Enjoy the activities of the *chacra* (farm) and pool, a great place for kids.

Villa El Chocón and around *p498*
See Valle Perdido Wine Resort, above.
B Cabanas los Acantilados, Costa del Lago, Barrio 1, T0299-490 1139 www.los-acantilados.com.ar. Three delightful cabins for 2-4 people with unbeatable views. Recommended.
B La Posada del Dinosaurio, on the lakeshore in Villa El Chocón, Costa del Lago, Barrio 1, T0299-490 1200, www.posada dinosaurio.com.ar. Convenient for dinosaur hunting, a place with plain but comfortable modern rooms, all with views over the lake, and a restaurant.
C Complejo Costa del Sol, Av 9 de Enero s/n, T0299-15408 2734. This small, quite depressing place is the only real budget accommodation. It is on the way to the dinosaur footprints.

Camping
Club Chocón Lauquen, R23, Barrio 2, T0299-156 318 719.
Las Flores, Barrio III, T0299-490 1155. Pretty location, close to the water. Basic facilities, clean.

Plaza Huincul *p499*
C Hotel Tortorici, Cutral-Co, 3 km west, Av Olascoaga and Di Paolo, T0299-496 3730, www.hoteltortorici.com.ar. The most comfortable option is this basic but slightly run-down hotel with neat rooms and a restaurant. Can arrange golf on a nearby course.

Zapala *p499*
A Hue Melén, Brown 929, T02942-422414, www.hotelhuemelen.com. Good value 3-star hotel, with decent rooms and a good restaurant serving the town's best food, including local specialities.
B Hostal del Caminante, 13 km south of Neuquén towards Zapala, T02942-444 0118, www.hostaldelcaminante.com.ar. Popular in summer, with pool and garden.
B Huincul, Av Roca 311, T02942-431422. A spacious place with a cheap restaurant, serving good, home-made, regional food.
C Coliqueo, Etcheluz 159, T02942-421308. Conveniently opposite the bus terminal, if the other options above are full (unlikely).
C Pehuén, Elena de Vega and Etcheluz, T02942-423135. Comfortable, 1 block from bus terminal. Interesting display of local maps.

Camping
Hostería Primeros Pinos, R93, T02942-422637, primerospinos@yahoo.com.ar. Municipal site.

● Eating

Neuquén city and around *p497*
♥♥♥ **1900 Cuatro**, at the Comahue Hotel, Av Argentina 377. Posh and a little pricey, but serves superb food.
♥ **El Reencuentro**, San Martín 29, T0299-443 1461. A popular *parrilla* recommended for delicious steaks in a warm atmosphere.
♥ **Buonapasta Trattoría**, Yrigoyen 36, T0299-448 3958. Fabulous filled pasta.
♥ **La Birra**, Santa Fe 19. Lots of choice and very welcoming, with chic modern surroundings.

♥ **Tutto al Dente**, Alberdi 49. Recommended for tasty home-made pasta.
♥ **Anónima**, corner of Av Olascoaga and Félix San Martín. This supermarket has a good *patio de comidas* (food hall), and games to amuse the kids.
♥ **Estación Quilmes Resto-bar**, Córdoba 194. Relaxed atmosphere with basic meals.

Cafés
There are lots of cheap cafés opposite the bus terminal on Mitre.

Bars
Mulligan's Irish Pub, Ministro González 47, What you would expect. Friendly staff and popular with locals.

Zapala *p499*
See Sleeping, above, for hotel restaurants.
♥♥♥ **Del Hotel Hue Melen**, Brown 929. Great value for money and has a varied menu.
♥ **Don Quijote**, Etcheluz 162. Rustic furniture but friendly staff serve home-cooked meals.
♥ **El Chancho Rengo**, Av San Martín and Etcheluz, T02942-422795. Where all the locals hang out.

▲ Activities and tours

Neuquén city and around *p497*
Arauquen, H. Yrigoyen 720, T0299-442 5101, www.arauquen.com. Great local agency that can organize day tours and trips further afield.

Plaza Huincul *p499*
Gondwana Tour, Córdoba 599 T0299-496 3355, geoda@copelnet.com.ar. Excursions to dinosaur sites nearby, and accommodation.

Zapala *p499*
Mali Viajes, Alte Brown 760, T02942-432251.
Monserrat Viajes y Turismo, Etcheluz 101, T02942-422497. Both offer traditional day tours to the surrounding area. Can help with bus and plane tickets.

⊖ Transport

Neuquén city and around *p497*
Air

For airport information, see page 497.

To **Buenos Aires**, daily with AR, Austral, and Aerolíneas Argentinas.

Airline offices Aerolíneas Argentinas/Austral, Santa Fe 52, T02942-442 2409; Lapa, Argentina 30, T02942-448 8335; Southern Winds, Argentina 237, T02942-442 0124.

Bus

For bus terminal information, see page 497.

About a dozen companies to **Buenos Aires**, daily, 12-16 hrs, US$40-50. To **Zapala** daily, 3 hrs, US$6. To **San Martín de los Andes**, 6 hrs, US$12. To **Bariloche**, 5-6 hrs, US$14, many companies. To **Mendoza**, daily, 12 hrs, US$20, Andesmar and 3 others. To **Junín de los Andes**, 5 hrs, US$10, many companies.

To **Aluminé**, 6 hrs, US$12, many companies. To **Plaza Huincul**, 1½ hrs, US$4, same companies. To **Caviahue** 6 hrs, US$12 and **Copahue**, 6½ hrs, US$13, Centenario.

To Chile Services to **Temuco** stop for a couple of hours at the border, 12-14 hrs, US$25. Some companies offer discount for return, departures Mon-Thu and Sat; 7 companies, some continuing to destinations en route to **Puerto Montt**.

Bus company offices Andesmar, T0299-442 2216; El Valle, T0299-443 3293, Vía Bariloche, T0299-442 7054.

Taxi

Confluencia, T0299-443 8880; Radio Taxi, T0299-442 2502.

Zapala *p499*
Bus

To **Neuquén**, several daily, 3 hrs, US$6, Albus, Centenario. To **San Martín de los Andes**, 3-4 hrs, US$11. To **Junín de los Andes**, several daily, 3 hrs, US$11, Albus, Centenario. To **Aluminé**, daily, 2½ hrs, US$6, several companies. To **Villa Pehuenia**, daily in summer, 4 a week in winter, 2½ hrs, US$8, most go on to **Moquehue**, but check first, 5-6 hrs, US$10. To **Caviahue**, 3 hrs, US$8; to **Copahue**, daily, 3½-4 hrs, US$9, Centenario. To **Bariloche**, Albus, TAC, Vía Bariloche change at San Martín. To **Buenos Aires**, 18 hrs, US$40-50, many companies.

To Chile Temuco Mon, Wed and Fri, US$17, Centenario (buy Chilean currency before leaving).

⊙ Directory

Neuquén city and around *p497*
Banks Lots of ATMs along Av Argentina. **Currency exchange** Exterior, San Martín 23; Pullman, Alcorta 144. **Embassies and consulates** Chile, La Rioja 241, T02942-442 2727. **Internet** Near the bus terminal at Mitre 43, T02942-443 6585, a block from bus station. **Post office** Rivadavia and Santa Fe. **Telephone** Many *locutorios* in the centre, often with internet access. Telecom, 25 de Mayo 20, daily till 0030, and Olascoaga 222, open till 2345, cheap.

Zapala *p499*
Banks Bansud, Etcheluz 108; Banco de la Nación Argentina, Etcheluz 465. **Internet** CPI, Chaneton and Garayta; Instituto Moreno, Moreno and López and Planes.

Bariloche to El Bolsón

Some of Argentina's most spectacular and unspoilt scenery lies south of Bariloche, where tourism has developed more recently and there is a wilder, more relaxed feel to the landscape. Route 258, the road south from Bariloche to El Bolsón, is breathtaking, passing the picturesque lakes of Gutiérrez and Mascardi, lying below a massive jagged range of mountains. There are some fabulous, peaceful places to stay here and wonderful hikes and horse riding. From Villa Mascardi, a road leads west along the Lago Mascardi's southern shore to glorious Pampa Linda, where there is enough excellent trekking to entertain you for several days, including access to climb Mount Tronador. Further south, Río Manso Medio has become famous for whitewater rafting, and at Lago Hess there is a hostería and the lovely Cascadas Los Alerces. El Bolsón is a pretty and relaxed town, sprawled out between two mountain ranges, with superb hikes nearby and beautiful rivers, waterfalls and mountains to explore. The town itself is a laid-back place which started as a hippy community in the 1970s. Now there are several microbreweries converting local hops into fine handmade beers, and craftsmen supplying the local market with wood and leather work, as well as delicious jams from the abundant soft fruits in summer. Further south, Lago Puelo is a tiny national park, offering great fishing, some good walks, and a boat trip to the Chilean border. As you head south, Cholila might attract Butch Cassidy fans, but the cabin where he and the Sundance Kid hid out has been brutally reconstructed. And though Cholila feels authentically like the Wild West, there's little appeal here now. ►► For listings, see pages 514-519.

Lago Gutiérrez → Phone code 02944.

Easily accessible by bus from Bariloche, Lago Gutiérrez feels like a fjord, with mountains dropping steeply into its western side and spectacular views all around. There are many ways to access the lake and it can be explored on foot or bike almost all the way round. There are several campsites, a hostel and fine hotels at its northern end, or a fabulous comfortable *estancia*, **Peuma Hue** ① www.peuma-hue.com, see page 514, on the southern lakeshore and the base of the mountain, with great trekking and horse riding.

For an adventurous approach, you could hike down from **Refugio Frey** or walk or cycle down the stony track from Cerro Catedral (which can be reached by bus). Or just get off any bus heading from Bariloche to El Bolsón to explore either end. Water sports can be practised on the lake in summer, and there's a golf course at Arelauken on the northern shore.

Lago Mascardi → Colour map 5, B2. Phone code 02944.

At the southern end of Lago Mascardi (Km 35), **Villa Mascardi** is a small village from where the *ripio* Route 81 runs towards Lago Hess and Cascada Los Alerces. This road operates a one-way system: going west 1000-1400, east 1600-1800, two-way 1900-0900; times may vary, check with the Bariloche **tourist office** ① T02944-423022. From this road, another *ripio* road runs along the lakeside to reach Pampa Linda, with access to climb Mount Tronador. Bariloche to El Bolsón buses can be taken to and from here, enabling you to visit the lake itself. Park entry costs US$5.

Along Lago Mascardi, there are several beautifully situated places to stay, all easily reached by car, or bus when the service is running in summer, including the luxurious **Mascardi Lodge** ① www.mascardilodge.com.ar, with biking, rafting and horse riding. Opposite the lovely straight beach of Playa Negro, handy for launching boats and fishing, is the peaceful **Camping La Querencia** (www.campinglaquerencia.com) at Km 10 on Route 258 to Tronador. Shortly afterwards, the road forks, with the left-hand branch following the crystalline Río Manso Medio to Lago Hess. This is a beautiful spot for a picnic, and there is also good camping at **Camping Los Rápidos** (www.losrapidos.com.ar). The **Río Manso** is popular for rafting (arranged through tour operators in Bariloche, see page 457). At **Lago Hess** is Hostería Lago Hess ① *T02944-462249, piccino@bariloche.com.ar*. The right fork follows a narrow arm of Lago Mascardi, with a viewpoint in lovely woodland to see Isla Piuke Huapi in the centre of the lake. A few kilometres further on is the lakeside paradise of Hotel Tronador before reaching Pampa Linda at the end of the road. ▶▶ *For further information, see Sleeping, page 514.*

Pampa Linda and Mount Tronador → *Phone code: 02944.*

① *Buses to Pampa Linda daily at 0900 in season, US$9. Alternatively, Expreso Meiling also run buses in season, leaving Club Andino at 0830 and returning at 1700, T02944-529875.*
Pampa Linda lies 40 km west of Villa Mascardi in the most blissfully isolated location, with spectacular views of Cerro Tronador towering above. There's a *guadería* (ranger station) with very helpful *guardaparques* who can advise on walks, and whom you must consult about the state of the paths and register your name with before setting out. From Pampa Linda, a lovely track (*ripio*) continues to **Ventisquero Negro** (Black Glacier), which hangs over a fantastically murky pool in which grey 'icebergs' float. The colour is due to sediment, and while not exactly attractive, the whole scene is very atmospheric. The road ends at the awesome **Garganta del Diablo**, one of the natural amphitheatres formed by the lower slopes of Mount Tronador. A beautiful walk (90 minutes' walk there and back) from the car park through beach forest takes you to a more pristine glacier, and up to the head of the gorge, where thin torrents of ice melt from the hanging glacier above and fall in columns like sifted sugar.

From Pampa Linda two other paths lead up **Cerro Tronador** (3478 m): the first is 15 km long and leads to **Refugio Otto Meiling** (2000 m), in itself a wonderful walk (five hours each way), situated on the edge of the eastern glacier. Another hour from the *refugio*, a path takes you to a view over Tronador and the lakes and mountains of **Parque Nacional Nahuel Huapi**. The other path leads to a *refugio* on the south side of the mountain. Otto Meiling is a good base camp for the ascent, with lots of facilities and activities, including trekking and ice climbing; always ask the *guardaparques* in Pampa Linda if there's space (capacity 60), US$8 per person per night, dinner US$6 (let them know in advance if you're vegetarian).

Paso de los Nubes

Pampa Linda is the starting point for a 22-km walk over Paso de los Nubes (1335 m) to **Laguna Frías** and **Puerto Frías** on the Chilean border. Allow at least two days; start the walk at Pampa Linda, rather than the other way around, as there's a gentler rise to the pass this way. There is camping at **Campamento Alerce** (after four hours) or **Campamento Glacier Frías** (after seven hours); from here it's another five hours to Puerto Frías. You'll see a spectacular glacial landscape, formed relatively recently (11,000 years ago), and the pass lies on the continental divide, with water flowing north to the Atlantic, and south to the Pacific. Views from the Río Frías valley are tremendous, and from Glacier Frías you enter Valdivian rainforest. Boats cross Lago Frías three times a day in summer at roughly 1115, 1315 and 1630, but check this before leaving Bariloche. You must register with *guardaparques* at Pampa Linda before setting out, and check with them about conditions. The route is not always well marked and should only be attempted if there is no snow on the pass (it's normally passable only between December and February) or if the path is not excessively boggy. Do not cross rivers on fallen bridges or trees. Get advice from the very helpful *guardaparques* here, and buy the map produced by Infotrekking for Mount Tronador/Paso de las Nubes before you leave Bariloche (available from **Club Andino Bariloche**, see page 442). See the excellent leaflet for *Paso de las Nubes* produced by Parque Nacional Nahuel Huapi. From Puerto Frías a 30-km road leads to Peulla on the shore of Chilean Lago Todos Los Santos. Or you can take a boat back to Bariloche; highly recommended. Another pleasant walk is to tranquil **Laguna Ilon** (5½ hours each way), with bathing on the shore in summer. Also to **Refugio Otto Meiling**. Check with *guardaparques* before setting out.

Río Manso Medio and Lago Hess
Some 9 km west of Villa Mascardi, a road runs 18 km through the beautiful valley of the Río Manso Medio to Lago Hess and on to the nearby **Cascada Los Alerces**. This is the starting point for trekking excursions in a more remote area of small lakes and forested mountains, including Lagos Fonck, Roca, Felipe, and Cerros Granito and Fortaleza. Check with *guardaparques* at Lago Hess about the conditions of the paths. There is also wonderful rafting here, but you have to take a trip starting in Bariloche. Contact a reputable company such as **Extremo Sur** ⓘ *www.extremosur.com*, or **Huala** ⓘ *www.huala.com.ar*. Note that there is also rafting on the **Río Manso Inferior**, further south, heading west from **Villegas**, on Route 258. This is the place for wilder rafting, and the trip to the Chilean border, run by the same rafting companies. ➤➤ *For further information, see Activities and tours, page 457.*

Lago Steffen and Lago Martín → *Phone code: 02944.*
About 20 km south of Villa Mascardi, another one-way dirt road leads to Lago Steffen, where a footpath runs along both northern and southern shores (of Lago Steffen) to Lago Martín. Both lakes are quite outstandingly lovely, fringed with beech and *álamo* trees, with far-off mountains in the distance, and pretty beaches where you can sit at the water's edge. There's also great fishing here. The *guardería* is at Lago Steffen, and further north, wild camping is possible on the lake shore. Further south, a road leads west along the Río Manso Inferior towards Chile. There is excellent rafting on the river, and several places where you can buy home-made produce.

El Bolsón → *For listings, see pages 514-519. Colour map 5, B2.*

El Bolsón is a very seductive little place. With its laid-back atmosphere, sprawled out in a broad fertile valley 130 km south of Bariloche, it is contained within huge mountain ranges on either side (hence it's name 'the big bag'), and it makes a great base for relaxing for a few days and for hiking in the tempting peaks around. The great serrated ridge of Cerro Piltriquitrón (2284 m) dominates the town, apparently emitting healthy positive ions, which might be why you feel so relaxed while you're here. Certainly it's a magical setting, and it's not surprising that it inspired thousands of hippies to create an ideological community here in the 1970s. What remains is a young, friendly place where the locals make lots of handicrafts, and with the sparkling Río Azul running close by, and a warm sunny microclimate, you're likely to want to stay for a few days to try the home-brewed beers and fruit for which the town is famous. A craft market is held in the semicircular plaza on Tuesday, Thursday and Saturday 1000-1600. Argentina's finest ice cream is made at **Jauja**, also the town's best restaurant, with organic milk and local berries: there are 11 flavours of chocolate alone.

El Bolsón

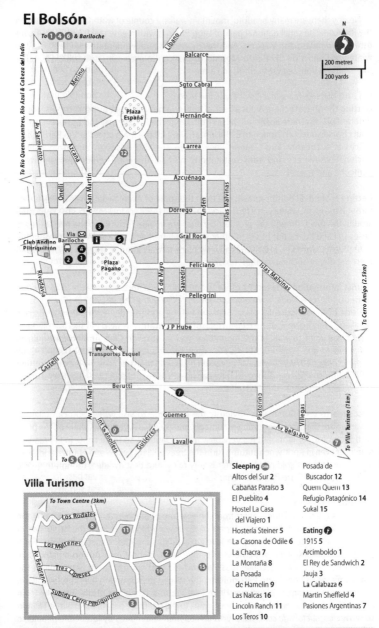

To ① ④ ⑥ & Bariloche

Balcarce

Sgto Cabral

J Hernández

Plaza España

Larrea

Azcuénaga

To Río Quemquemtreu, Río Azul & Cabeza del Indio

Av Sarmiento

Onelli

Azcona

Av San Martín

Dorrego

Anden

Islas Malvinas

Gral Roca

Via Bariloche ✉

Club Andino Piltriquitrón

③

⑤

❶

④

⑤

②

❶

Plaza Pagano

⑥

Feliciano

25 de Mayo

Saavedra

Pellegrini

Islas Malvinas

⑭

To Cerro Amigo (2.5km)

Rivadavia

Y J P Hube

French

ACA & Transportes Esquel 🚌

Castelli

Berutti

❼

Pastorina

Güemes

To Ville Turismo (1km)

Av San Martín

In˙s sarolera

Gütierrez

Lavalle

Av Belgrano

Villegas

⑨

To ⑤ ⑬

❼

200 metres
200 yards

N

Villa Turismo

To Town Centre (3km)

Los Rodales

⑧

⑪

Los Maitenes

②

Av Belgrano

Tres Cipreses

⑩

⑮

Subida Cerro Piltriquitrón

③

⑯

Nearby there are many beautiful mountain walks, a couple of waterfalls and rafting on the Río Azul. The small national park of Lago Puelo is within easy reach 18 km south, for fishing, swimming and walking. And there's a small family-orientated ski centre in the winter, at **Centro de Ski Perito Moreno** ⓘ *www.bolsonweb.com/aventura/ski.htm*. For more information, see www.elbolson.com.

Ins and outs → *Phone code 02944. Population 16,000.*

Getting there Note there is not a central bus terminal. Different bus companies stop at different places. There are hourly buses from Bariloche (two hours) and buses every two hours from Esquel (2½ hours) to El Bolsón, arriving off the main street at **Via Bariloche**'s offices at Sarmiento and General Roca. There are also buses to and from Parque Nacional Los Alerces, and from destinations in Chile. There are equidistant airports at Bariloche and Esquel.

Getting around El Bolsón sprawls out from the spine of Avenida San Martín which runs through the town, where you'll find places to eat, and there are lots of places to stay dotted around the town, though the prettiest *cabañas* are in Villa Turismo up the hill. There are buses to Lago Puelo, but buses to other sites are infrequent, and geared to locals rather than tourists. However, El Bolsón is a lovely place to walk around, you can hire bikes and there are plenty of cheap *remises* (taxis).

Tourist information The **tourist office** ⓘ *San Martín and Roca opposite the big post office (correo), T02944-492604, www.elbolson.gov.ar, daily 0900-2100, till 2400 in summer*, is on the side of the semicircular plaza. Staff are helpful and friendly (with plenty of English speakers). They'll give you an excellent map of the town and the area, and suggest places to stay. If you want to walk in the mountains, you must go to **Club Andino Piltriquitrón** ⓘ *Sarmiento and Roca, T02944-492600, www.capiltriquitron.com.ar, Mon-Fri 1800-2000 (summer only, till 31 Mar)*, who will advise on hikes, and registers all walkers before setting off. The tourist office can also give limited advice on hikes and sells two quite useful maps, but you will need more detailed advice.

Best time to visit Summer is obviously the best time to visit, when you can take full advantage of the blissful rivers and mountains, and there's a lively atmosphere on the plaza with live music at nights. But it´s very busy here in January, so try to come in February or March, or even in April, when autumn turns the trees brilliant yellow and orange, and there are sunny days but cold nights. Winter is very rainy, and best avoided, though there is a basic ski resort at Cerro Perito Moreno.

Around El Bolsón

El Bolsón's great attraction – apart from the pleasure of being in the town itself – are the superb hikes up to the mountains west of the town which start from the other side of turquoise Río Azul, where there are lovely places to sunbathe, camp and picnic. For a pleasant hour-long walk, with views over the town, climb **Cerro Amigo**. Follow Calle General Roca east until it becomes Islas Malvinas and continue up the hill. Better still are the panoramic views from **Cerro Piltriquitrón**, the jagged peak looming over the town, from where you can paraglide in summer. Drive, take a tour, or take a taxi 10 km east of the town up winding earth roads. Then it's an hour's walk to the sculpture park of the **Bosque Tallado** ⓘ *www.elbosquetallado.com*, sculptures carved from fallen trees by local craftspeople, to the mirador with fabulous views over the valley to the Andes beyond. It's a six- to seven-hour round trip walking all the way. Food and shelter are available at the *refugio* (1400 m), and from there it's three hours' walk to the summit. A useful map, *Sendas y Bosques El Bolsón and Los Alerces*, is available from the tourist office. You can also do paragliding from here. ►► *For further information, see Activities and tours, page 518.*

There are also good views from **Cabeza del Indio**, so called because the rock's profile resembles a face, a good 6-km drive or bike ride from the centre. Take Calle Azcuénaga west to cross the bridge over Río Quemquemtreu, follow signs to Cabeza del Indio. From here, there's a new walk marked leading to Cascada Escondida.

To the north of the town, in woods reached from winding gravel roads, there's an impressive sweep of waterfalls at **Cascada Escondida**, 10 km northwest, a good place for a picnic, with a botanical garden. This area is also worth visiting for a good rustic *parrilla* **El Quincho**, for local lamb and great meat (vegetarians: don't even think about it) signposted from the road. There are rather less exciting falls at **Cataratas Mallín Ahogado**, a little further north, but it's still a pleasant spot for a stop. **La Golondrina** runs three buses daily Monday to Friday from the plaza to the loop around Mallin Ahogado, but extra walking is required to reach both falls. See the tourist office map for details. There are many microbreweries dotted around town – **Cervecería El Bolsón** ⓘ *R258, Km 123.9, just north of town, www.cervezaselbolson.com*, is particularly worth a visit, with brief guided tour, restaurant and no fewer than 18 different beers on offer, including three for celiacs. You could also try **Otto Tipp** ⓘ *www.ottotippcervezaartesanal.blogspot.com*, Tue-Sun after 2000 (restobar), Mon 0900-1400, Tue-Sat 0900-1800.

The famous narrow gauge railway **La Trochita** ⓘ *www.latrochita.org.ar* (also known as the *Old Patagonian Express*) is a novel way of seeing the landscape and a catching a glimpse into Patagonia's past. As well as the better known route from Esquel, there's another journey from at El Maitén, near El Bolsón, where you can see the fascinating steam railway workshops too. ►► *For further information, see Activities and tours, page 518.*

El Bolsón benefits from a gentle microclimate which means it's warmer than most of the Lakes District, even in winter. However, there is a ski centre, **Centro de Ski Perito Moreno** (www.bolsonweb.com/aventura/ski.htm), on the upper slopes of Cerro Perito Moreno (2216 m). With good snow and no wind, its 720 skiable metres are good for families. It's a newish centre and the only place to stay at the moment is the **Refugio Perito Moreno** ⓘ *www.bolsonweb.com/aventura/peritomoreno.htm*, with 120 beds, but there are three ski lifts and ski instructors too. Ask the tourist office for more information. Leave town by Route 258, and take the left-hand turn to Río Azul. Follow signs to Refugio Perito Moreno.

Walks → *For Parque Nacional Lago Puelo, see below.*

There are wonderful treks to the mountains west of the town. For all walks, get the *Sendas y Bosques* (Walks and Forests) map and book for El Bolsón, Lago Puelo and Los Alerces. Maps are 1:200,000, laminated and easy to read, and the book is full of great walks, with English summaries. Register for all walks before setting off at the **Club Andino Piltriquitrón** (see Tourist information, above).

Cerro Lindo Due west of town, there's a great hike up Arroyo Lali to Cerro Lindo (2105 m), in one of the most beautiful mountain landscapes of the whole area, with **Refugio Cerro Lindo** halfway up, after a five-hour walk. From here, you can reach an ancient glacier and climb onwards to several viewpoints. You'll need a map, and check the route before setting off. The altitude difference is pretty extreme here, so you're advised to go slowly and steadily.

Cerro Hielo Azul This is a more serious and demanding hike up to Cerro Hielo Azul (2255 m), where you can stay at **Refugio Cerro Azul** (at 1300 m). It's steep and takes six hours one-way. From the comfortable *refugio*, you can also walk to the glacier on the slopes of Cerro Hielo Azul (three hours return), or on to Cerro Barda Negra. It's often suggested that you could walk from here via **Refugio Natación** to **Refugio Cajón de Azul**, but this is really not to be recommended without a local guide. The path can be confusing in places, the area remains marshy well into the summer months, and people have got lost, with dangerous consequences. Ask in the **Club Andino Piltriquitrón** (see page 508).

Cajón de Azul One of the loveliest and most accessible walks can be done in a day, although once you reach the delightful *refugio* (600 m) at Cajón de Azul, you're going to wish you could stay at least a night. It's a fabulous four-hour walk up the Río Azul which flows from a deep canyon. Set off early to allow for a leisurely lunch at the top, or spend the night in the *refugio*, with its lovely gardens, in the company of Atilio and friends, who make a fine dinner with produce from the garden. Take a *traffic* (minibus) to Wharton, leaving El Bolsón at 0900. There's a well-marked path. It's a bit hairy crossing the two wood-and-wire bridges (and only one at a time, so there are queues in January), but worth it for a dip in the sparkling turquoise water on the way down. You'll be collected by the *traffic* at 2000. Buses and information from **Nehuén**, at Belgrano and Perito Moreno, in the same office as Andesmar.

Refugio Los Laguitos A wonderful four-day walk that takes you right into the deepest part of the Andes Cordillera, almost to the border with Chile, and through outstanding *alerce* forests. Allow four hours to **Refujio Cajón de Azul**, another three hours to the Mallín de los Chanchos, and another four hours on from there to reach the basic **Refugio Los Laguitos**, in a beautiful spot on the shore of Lago Lahuán. A map and guidebook are absolutely essential; seek advice before setting out.

Parque Nacional Lago Puelo → *For listings, see pages 514-519.*

This lovely green and wooded national park is centred around the deep turquoise-coloured Lago Puelo, 15 km south of El Bolsón on the Chilean border, surrounded by southern beech forest and framed with the spiky peaks of snow-dusted far-off mountains. It's a blissful spot out of the busy holiday season. With relatively low altitude (200 m) and high rainfall, the forest is rich in tree species, particularly the cinnamon-bark *arrayán* and the *pitra*, *coihues* (evergreen beech) and cypresses. There's lots of wildlife, including the *huemul*, *pudu* and foxes, and the lake is known for its good fishing for trout and salmon. There are gentle walks on marked paths around the northern shore area, boat trips across the lake, and canoes for rent. *Guardaparques* at the park entrance can advise on these, and hand out a basic map.

Ins and outs
Getting there Entry fee US$5. The main entrance is along a pretty road south from El Bolsón, through *chacras* (small farms) growing walnuts, hops and fruit, to Villa Lago Puelo, 3 km north of the park, where there are shops, plenty of accommodation and fuel. From here the road is unpaved. Entry is also possible at **El Desemboque**, on the eastern side of the park: take the bus from El Bolsón to Esquel, alight at El Hoyo, then walk 14 km to El Desemboque. There are regular buses, US$4, from Avenida San Martín and Dorrego in El Bolsón to the lake via Villa Lago Puelo. It's best to come between November and

April, though the northern shore of the lake can get crowded in January and February. The lake is glorious in April, when the trees turn a vivid yellow.

Park information The **Intendencia** ① *500 m north of the lake, T02944-499232, lagopuelo@apn.gov.ar, www.lagopuelo.com, Mon-Fri 0800-1500, with a booth at the pier in summer,* can provide a helpful leaflet and advice on walks. You must register here before embarking on long hikes, and register your return. In the town of Lago Puelo there's a **tourist office** ① *Av 2 de Abril and Los Notros, T02944-499591, www.lagopuelo.gov.ar, 0900-2100 in summer, 0900-1900 in winter,* on the roundabout as you enter town. Staff are helpful, English-speaking and can advise on accommodation.

Walks
For all walks, get the *Sendas y Bosques* (Walks and Forests) map and book for El Bolsón, Lago Puelo and Los Alerces. Maps are 1:200,000, laminated and easy to read. The book is full of great walks, with English summaries, www.guiasendasybosques.com.ar.

Bosque de las Sombras (Forest of the Shadows). A delightful overgrown forest which you wander through on wooden walkways, on the way to the shingle beach at 'La Playita', with guided trails and signs telling you what trees you're passing. It's an easy 400-m walk.

Senda los Hitos A 14-km (five hours each way) walk through marvellous woods, to the rapids at Río Puelo, on the Chilean border (passport required), and there is some wild camping on the way at **Camping de Gendarmería**, after two hours.

Cerro Motoco There's a tremendous two-day hike up Cerro Motoco, with **Refugio Motoco** at the top of the path. Leave Lago Puelo heading north, and cross the hanging bridge to access Río Motoco. It's 25 km altogether, and could be done in seven hours, one way, but you'll want to stay at the top. Take the walks book with you.

Cerro Plataforma From the east of the lake, you can hike to **El Turbio** and Cerro Plataforma, crossing the lake first by boat to El Desemboque (or taking the bus and walking 14 km). At Cerro Plataforma, there's a tremendous amount of marine life in evidence, as this was a beach in the ice age. It's about seven hours to Río Turbio, where there's a *guardaparque*, and then 12 hours to Cerro Plataforma; allow three days for the whole trip. There's also a three-day trek through magnificent scenery to **Glaciar y Cerro Aguaja Sur**: get advice and directions from the *guardaparques*.

Other activities
There is wonderful **fly fishing** in the park, thanks to the fact that this is the lowest crossing in the whole of the Andes region (at only 190 m) so there is no snow, and with mild warm summers in the microclimate here, Pacific salmon come here in large numbers. Contact fishing guides through the park *guardería*. Also check out **Puelo Trout** for fishing trips. There are boat trips across Lago Puelo with **Juana de Arco**, as well as kayaking with **Kayak Lago Puelo**. ▸▸ *For further information, see El Bolsón Activities and tours, page 518.*

Epuyén → *Colour map 5, B2. Phone code 02944. Population 1500.*

Forty kilometres southeast of El Bolsón on Route 258, the little settlement of Epuyén (pronounced epooSHEN) is relatively undeveloped for tourists, and there's nothing much to do here except stroll around Lago Epuyén. There's a simple *hostería*, which also has rustic *cabañas* with meals on request. A fire destroyed trees all over one hillside a few years ago, making the area less attractive for walks, but there's a good trek around the lakeside, and good fishing in the lake.

Cholila → *Colour map 5, B2. Phone code 02945. Population 2000.*

Cholila is a real Patagonian settlement, which one day will make a great place to stay, with its lovely setting in broad open landscape with superb views of Lago Cholila, crowned by ranges of mountains all around. Cholila lies 76 km south of El Bolsón on Route 71, which branches off Route 258 at Km 179. There's excellent fishing, canoeing and kayaking on rivers nearby, but very little tourist infrastructure. The accommodation is extremely limited, and there's little information.

You might have heard that the reason to visit Cholila is to see the wooden cabins where **Butch Cassidy**, the **Sundance Kid** and **Etta Place** lived between 1901 and 1905 (see box, opposite). You can understand why they hid out here for so long: Cholila still feels remote and untouched, and the views from their land are breathtaking. The cabins themselves were rather evocative, falling to pieces, patched up with bits of wood and with a lichen-stained slatted roof, but in 2006, the owner of the land started to 'renovate' them, by replacing the tattered timbers with brand new bright orange beams, doors and window frames. As a result, it is unlikely to please visitors keen to see what remained of the authentic cabins where Butch and Sundance lived. Unless you're a true fan it might not be worth the considerable effort required to visit them. To get there make a detour from Route 258 heading south from El Bolsón, towards Los Alerces National Park's northern entrance; 13 km north of Cholila along Route 71, look out for a sign on the right, park by the little kiosk and walk 400 m to the cabins. Entry US$2.50, if anyone's around to charge you.

There is a good walk around **Lago Mosquito**: continue down the road from El Trébol past the lake then take a path to the left, following the river. Cross the river on the farm bridge and continue to the base of the hills to a second bridge. Follow the path to the lake and walk between the lake and the hills, crossing the river via a suspension bridge just past El Trébol – six hours.

Leleque → *Colour map 5, B2.*

Ruta 40 (paved) is a faster way to get from El Bolsón to Esquel than Route 71 via Cholila, and this is the route the bus takes. You could stop off at Leleque to see the **Museum of Patagonia** ① *off the R40, Km 1440, 90 km from Esquel and 80 km from El Bolsón, US$1.50, daily (except Wed) 1100-1700*, in the vast estate owned by **Benetton**, the Italian knitwear company. To their credit, they have created a remarkable museum here. There's a beautifully designed exhibition on the lives of indigenous peoples, with dwellings reconstructed of animal skins, using the original construction techniques, a huge collection of delicate arrowheads and the *boleadoras* for catching cattle. Other moving exhibits include one on the first pioneers in Patagonia, especially the Welsh. There's an attractive café in a reconstructed *boliche* (provisions shop and bar).

Butch Cassidy and the Sundance Kid

Near Cholila, south of El Bolsón, is a wooden cabin which was home to infamous US bank robbers Butch Cassidy (Robert LeRoy Parker) and the Sundance Kid (Harry Longabaugh) immortalized by Paul Newman and Robert Redford in the 1969 film. In America in the late 1890s, the two were part of a loosely organized gang, known variously as the Train Robbers' Syndicate, the Hole in the Wall Gang and the Wild Bunch, which carried out hold-ups on railway payrolls and banks in the borders of Utah, Colorado and Wyoming. In 1900, the gang celebrated the wedding of one of their colleagues by having their photo taken: a big mistake. The photo was recognized by a Wells Fargo detective, and with their faces decorating Wanted posters across the land, Cassidy, Sundance and his girl- friend Etta Place escaped to Argentina in February 1901.

Using the names Santiago Ryan and Harry Place, the outlaws settled on government land near Cholila and applied to buy it, but Pinkerton detectives hot on their trail soon tracked them down and informed the Argentine authorities. The three lay low in their idyllic rural retreat until 1905, when, needing money to start up elsewhere, the gang raided banks in Villa Mercedes and a particularly audacious job in Río Gallegos. Posing as ranching company agents, they opened a bank account with US$7000, spent two weeks at the best hotels and socialized with the city's high society, and then entered the bank to close their accounts and empty the safe before escaping to Chile. Then Etta returned to the United States, and disappeared from the history books.

Butch and Sundance moved to Bolivia, and worked at the Concordia tin mine, disappearing every now and then to carry out the occasional hold-up. Lack of capital to settle as respectable ranchers was, however, their undoing. In 1908, near Tupiza in southern Bolivia, they seized an Aramayo mining company payroll, but gained only a fraction of the loot they expected. With military patrols in pursuit and the Argentine and Chilean forces alerted, they rode into the village of San Vicente and were recognized. Besieged, they did not, as in the film, run into the awaiting gunfire. Their deaths were not widely reported in the United States until the 1930s, and rumours abounded: Butch was said to have become a businessman, a rancher, a trapper and a Hollywood movie extra, while Sundance had run guns in the Mexican Revolution, migrated to Europe, fought for the Arabs against the Turks in the First World War, sold mineral water, founded a religious cult, and still found time to marry Etta.

Their ramshackle wooden cabin was, until June 2006, an evocative place to visit. Now the owner has restored it with brand new bright orange wood, ruining the outlaw hideout feel. The location is still spectacular, however, and worth the trip for fans.

For Sleeping and Eating price codes and other relevant information, see Essentials pages 30-36.

◉ Sleeping

Lago Gutiérrez *p504*

LL-L Arelauquen Golf and Country Club, on the eastern shore of Lago Gutiérrez, T02944-467626 (T011-4311 1919 in Buenos Aires), www.arelauquen.com. Upmarket golf and country club, with tennis, squash and horse riding. Luxury accommodation in a beautiful chalet-style building. Smallish but luxurious rooms, excellent restaurant and golf bar, exclusive atmosphere.

AL Estancia Peuma Hue, on the southern shore of Lago Gutiérrez, 3 km off the road, T02944-501030, www.peuma-hue.com. One of the finest places to stay in the whole area, this *estancia* combines a gorgeous rural setting on 2 km of private shoreline on Lago Gutiérrez, right up against the foot of Cerro Catedral Sur, with luxurious accommodation in 2 beautifully designed country houses and a mountain cabin. Prices include meals and superb activities such as trekking into virgin forest on the mountain to find waterfalls and amazing wildlife; great horse riding with the resident horse whisperer; exploring the lake in kayaks; and rafting in Río Mansos. Also massage and yoga. Highly recommended.

AL-A El Retorno, Villa Los Coihues, on the northern shore, T02944-467333, www.hosteriaelretorno.com. With a stunning lakeside position, this is a traditional family-run hotel in tasteful hunting lodge style, with lovely gardens running down to the beach, tennis courts, and comfortable rooms, as well as 5 self-catering apartments. Also has a restaurant. Very relaxing.

Camping

Villa los Coihues, Lago Gutiérrez, T02944-467479, www.campingloscoihues.com.ar. Well equipped and beautifully situated. Camping from US$6 and dorm rooms from US$10.

Take bus No 50 or 51, or take the track down to Gutiérrez from Cerro Catedral (4WD advisable) or the road to El Bolsón (R258), and follow signs.

Lago Mascardi *p504*

AL-A pp Hotel Tronador, T02944-441062, www.hoteltronador.com. A lakeside paradise, mid-Nov to Easter, the lovely rooms have terrific lake views from their balconies, there are beautiful gardens, and they run tourist excursions. Rates include full board. Highly recommended.

B Mascardi Lodge, R258, Km 36.8, on the road to Pampa Linda and Tronador on Lago Mascardi, T2944-490518, www.mascardi lodge.com.ar. Just a few kilometres from the turning off R258 is this luxurious place with a delightful setting in lovely gardens on its own beach by Lake Mascardi. There's a restaurant and tea room, and horse riding, mountain biking, rafting and fly fishing in the Río Guillelmo can also be arranged.

Camping

Camping La Querencia, T02944-426225, www.campinglaquerencia.com, further on towards Pampa Linda, at Km 10. A pretty and peaceful spot on the side of the river and on banks of lake, opposite the lovely straight beach of Playa Negro. Camping from US$6 per person.

Camping Las Carpitas, also on Lago Mascardi, at Km 33, T02944-490527, www.campinglas carpitas.com.ar. Set in a great lakeside position, summer only, with *cabañas* and restaurant. Camping from US$6 and dorms from US$12.

Camping Los Rápidos, R258, Km 37, T/F02944-461861, www.losrapidos.com.ar. Attractive shaded site going down to the lake, with *confitería*, food store and all facilities, US$6 per person. Also bunk beds in a basic *albergue* US$10 per person (sleeping bag needed). Friendly owners organize trekking, kayaking, fishing and mountain biking.

Pampa Linda and Mount Tronador *p505*

A-B Hostería Pampa Linda, T02944-442 038, www.hosteriapampalinda.com.ar. This *hostería* is a luxurious base for climbing Tronador, or a comfortable retreat from which to start other treks. Simple, comfortable rooms, all with bath and stunning views. The owners are charming; Sebastián de la Cruz is one of the area's most experienced mountaineers. Horse riding can be organized, as well as trekking and climbing courses. Full board, and packed lunches for hiking available.

Camping

Pampa Linda, T02944-424531. Idyllic spacious lakeside site, *confitería* serving good meals and food shop. Excellent service, run by the Club Andino Bariloche.

Río Manso Medio and Lago Hess *p506*

LL Río Manso Lodge, T02944-490546, www.riomansolodge.com. Spectacularly set on the bank of the Río Manso in beautiful mountainous scenery, this is a top-class fishing lodge, with lovely rooms with great views from their large windows, fine food and great fishing. Loved by experts. Transfers organized.

El Bolsón *p506, map p507*

There are lots of *cabañas* and *hosterías* up on a hill in the Villa Turismo, 3 km southeast of the centre, a good hour's walk, or a cheap taxi ride. It's difficult to find accommodation in the high season: book ahead. For more information, see www.elbolson.com.

LL-L Las Nalcas, Villa Turismo, T02944-493 054, www.lasnalcas.com. Amazing set of 5 lovely fully equipped lodges for 4-6 people, surrounded by lush forest. Heated pool.

A La Posada de Hamelín, Int Granollers 2179, T02944-492030, www.posadade hamelin.com.ar. One of the most welcoming places in the whole region, lovely chalet-style house with quaint, comfortable rooms all with bathroom, very central. Highly recommended.

C La Casona de Odile, Barrio Luján, T02944-492753, www.interpatagonia.com/odile.

A really special place to stay, in rustic wooden cabins on this idyllic lavender farm by a stream, with delicious French cooking by the wonderful charismatic owner Odile. Ask the tourist office for directions. Recommended.

C Sukal, high on a hill in Villa Turismo, Subida Los Maitenes, T02944-492438, www.sukal arteyflores.com.ar. Gorgeous B&B, a haven of peace in a flower-filled garden, with glorious views. Welcoming owners.

Hostels

E pp El Pueblito, Barrio Luján, T02944-493560, www.elpueblitohostel.com.ar. Wonderfully friendly rustic wooden hostel, a US$3 taxi ride from the centre, set in woodland. Lots of free travel information and huge living room with log fire. Doubles (**C**) available. Recommended.

E pp Altos del Sur, Villa Turismo, T02944-498730, www.altosdelsur.bolsonweb.com. In a lovely setting in Villa Turismo, with beautiful views from the terrace, and nice welcoming sitting areas, this is a peaceful hostel with shared rooms and 1 double (**D**) with private bath. Dinner available and breakfast included, lovely welcoming owner Mariela will collect from bus station if you book in advance. Otherwise a US$4 taxi ride. Highly recommended.

E pp Refugio Patagónico, Islas Malvinas and Pastorino, T02944-483628, www.refugio patagonico.com. Basic hostel, with small dorms all with bathrooms, in a spacious house set in open fields, where you can also camp, with great views of Piltriquitrón, and just 5 blocks from the plaza.

E pp Hostel La Casa del Viajero, Liberdad and Las Flores, Barrio Usina, T02944-493092, www.lacasadelviajero.com.ar. Just a little out of the centre, this cosy hostel is surrounded by organic gardens. The rooms are simple and comfortable but the wonderful setting is why you come. Call them and they will pick you up from the centre of town.

E pp Posada de Buscador, Diagonal Líbano 3015, T02944-492263, posadadelbuscador. blogspot.com. Lovely house in the middle of town (but too many floral bedspreads), great common areas, friendly hosts.

Cabañas

There are many *cabañas* in picturesque settings with lovely views, in the Villa Turismo, costing around US$55 for up to 5 people per night, though prices vary widely between high and low seasons. Call each *cabaña* complex for directions. Buses to Villa Turismo run by **Comarca Andina**, opposite Vía Bariloche, T02944-455400, or take a *remise*, US$4. Recommended are:
Cabañas Paraíso, T02944-492766, www.cabaniasparaiso.com.ar. Lovely wooden cabins in a gorgeous setting amongst old trees. Pool, good service.
La Montaña, T02944-492776, www.montana. com.ar. Very well-equipped, smart *cabañas* spaced out in a big complex with pool, children's play area and lovely views of Piltriquitrón. The most appealing option.
Lincoln Ranch, T02944-492073, www.lincolnranch.com.ar. Big, modern, well-maintained *cabaña* complex with open views, and pool.
Los Teros, ask for the road leading up Vía Los Tres Cipreses, T02944-455 5569, www.cabanas losteros.com.ar. Lovely cabins, well spaced in parkland with good views of the mountains, a pool and complete peace. Recommended.

Camping

There are many good sites, fully equipped and lively particularly in Jan.
La Chacra, Belgrano 1128, T02944-492111. A 15-min walk from town, well-shaded, good facilities, lively atmosphere in season.
Quem Quem, on the banks of Río Quem-quemtreu, T02944-493550, quemquem @elbolson.com. Well-kept, lovely site with hot showers, good walks, free pick-up from town.
Refugio Patagónico, see hostels above. A great open site with hot showers and fireplaces, lovely views.

Parque Nacional Lago Puelo *p510*

There are lots of *cabañas*, shops and fuel. Apart from wild camping, there's no accommodation in the park itself, but plenty in Villa Lago Puelo, just outside, with *cabañas*, restaurants and campsites spread out along R16 through the little village.

Cabañas

A Lodge Casa Puelo, R16, T02944-499 539, www.casapuelo.com.ar. *Cabañas* for up to 6. Beautifully designed rooms and self-catering cabins right against forested mountains where you can walk, with good service from friendly English-speaking owner Miguel, who knows the local area intimately. Very comfortable, dinner offered. Free internet access. Recommended.
A-B La Yoica, just off R16, Km 5, T02944-499 200, www.layoica.com.ar. Charming Scottish owners make you feel at home in these traditional *cabañas* set in lovely countryside with great views. Price for up to 4 people.
B La Granja, 20 m from Río Azul, T02944-499 265, www.interpatagonia.com/lagranja. Traditional chalet-style *cabañas* with simple furnishings, nothing out of this world, but there's a pool, and these are good value.
B-C Frontera, isolated in woodland, off the main road heading for Esquel, T02944-473 092, www.frontera-patagonia.com.ar. *Cabañas* for 4 (**B**) and *hostería* (**C**), furnished to a very high standard, in a lovely building set in native forest, and offering delicious breakfasts and dinner if required.
B-C San Jorge, a block from the main street, on Plaza Ilia, Perito Moreno and Azcuénaga T02944-491313, www.elbolson.com/ sanjorge. Excellent value, neat but dated self-catering apartments in a pretty garden, with friendly, helpful owners.

Camping

There are 2 free sites in the park itself, on Lago Puelo, of which **Camping del Lago** is most highly recommended; it offers all facilities, and rafting, fishing and trekking.

Outside the park there are many good sites with all facilities, these are recommended: **Ailin Co**, Km 15, T02944-499078; **La Pasarela**, Km 10, T02944-499061; **Los Quinchos**, Km 13.

Epuyén *p512*

D El Refugio del Lago, T02945-499025, www.elrefugiodellago.com.ar. Buses between El Bolsón and Esquel stop (briefly) at Epuyén, though some don't enter the village itself. Transfers available on request. A relaxed place with rustic comfortable rooms in a lovely wooden house, a short walk from the shore, with breakfast included, also good meals. Also offers camping (US$3 pp) and *cabañas*. Recommended.

● Eating

El Bolsón *p506, map p507*

¶¶ Jauja, San Martín 2867, T02944-492448, www.heladosjauja.com. The best in town by a long way, Jauja is a great meeting place, with a friendly and welcoming atmosphere, good mellow music playing, and really tasty food. There's a broad menu, lots of local specialities, but the trout-filled pasta and apple strudel are particularly fabulous, and whatever you do, don't miss the country's best handmade ice creams, including Patagonian *calafate* berry flavour. All made from organic milk, and locally grown fruit, so that they're entirely natural, with exquisite flavours. There are 11 kinds of chocolate alone. Highly recommended.

¶¶¶ Pasiones Argentinas, Av Belgrano and Berutti, T02944-483616, www.pasionesresto bar.com.ar. Traditional Argentine food, in a wonderful cosy setting.

¶¶ Martin Sheffield, Av San Martín 2760, T02944-491920. Conveniently central and serving good food, Patagonian specialities, menu of the day, with or without a drink.

¶ 1915, San Martín and Roca 336. Wonderful café/restaurant with views over the park, lake and the markets. Good option for breakfast as it opens at 0800. Recommended.

¶ Arcimboldo, San Martín 2790, T02944-492137. Good-value *tenedor libre* that includes dessert and drinks, smoked fish and draught beer.

¶ El Rey de Sandwich, Roca 345, T02944-491076. The cheapest sandwiches in town at this *rotisería*, next to **Via Bariloche** bus terminal.

¶ La Calabaza, Av San Martín 2518, T02944-492910. Nice little place for a soup or a quiche. Good option for vegetarians.

Breweries and tea rooms

Cervecería El Bolsón, R258, Km 123.9, T02944-492595, www.cervezaselbolson. com. The best microbrewery in El Bolsón, and a great place to visit to see how the beer is made – and sample the 18 varieties. Try the delicious *picadas* served with your beer, sitting outside in the gardens, and take a few bottles away with you. Highly recommended.

El Mirador, R258, Km 137, Las Golondrinas, T02944-1541 4491, www.restaurantel mirador.com.ar. Open for breakfast and afternoon tea, with delicious home-made cakes, in pretty gardens.

Parque Nacional Lago Puelo *p510*

¶¶ Familia von Fürstenberg, R16 on the way to the national park, T02944-499392, www.vonfuerstenberg.com.ar. In a delightful perfectly decorated Swiss-style chalet, try the beautifully presented traditional waffles and home-made cakes. Sumptuous. Also *cabañas* (**A-B**) to rent.

¶¶ Sabores de Patagonia, R16 on the way to national park, T02944-499532, www.sabores delapatagonia.com. Good for lunch or tea, locally caught trout and smoked salmon. Slow service, but the food is worth waiting for.

Cholila *p512*

La Casa de Piedra, R71 outside village, T02945-498056. Welsh tea room, chocolate cake recommended.

⊛ Festivals and events

El Bolsón *p506, map p507*
Jan Fiesta de la Fruta Fina (Berry Festival) at the nearby El Hoyo.
Feb Fiesta del Lúpulo (Hop Festival), at the end of the month.
Oct Fiesta de la Cerveza Artesanal. The home-brewed beer festival, much more civilized than an Oktoberfest!
Dec Jazz festival. Attracts many famous musicians, lasts 10 days.

○ Shopping

El Bolsón *p506, map p507*
The handicraft and food market is on Tue, Thu and Sat in season 1000-1600 around the main plaza. Some fine leather and jewellery, carved wood and delicious organic produce.
Centro Artesanal, Av San Martín 1866, daily 1000-2000, T02944-491150. If the market's not open, a selection of the best crafts can be bought here: wood, leather, precious stones, ceramics and candles.
Granja Larix, R258, Km 118.5, T02944-498 018, alejandra@bariloche.com.ar. Fabulous smoked trout and home-made jams.
La Huella, Sarmiento and Dorrego, T02944-491210. For tent hire and outdoor equipment.
Laten K'Aike, T02944-491969. Also known as **Piedras Patagónicas**, for exquisite semi-precious stones.
Mercado Artesanal, Av San Martín 1920, Mon-Fri 0800-1300, 1400-2000, Sat 0900-1300. Wonderful Mapuche weavings can be bought here in this co-operative of local weavers, and you can watch women spin and weave beautiful rugs, scarves and bags, in the traditional way. Also knitted goods, all incredibly high quality and beautifully made. Recommended.
Talabartería Poyetun, Dorrego 443, T02944-498606. Excellent leather goods: belts, hats, boots and bags, locally made to traditional designs.

⚠ Activities and tours

Lago Gutiérrez *p504*
Horse riding
Estancia Peuma Hue, see Sleeping, above. From the *estancia* on the southern shore of Lago Gutiérrez, you can ride into the mountains, and over to Pampa Linda.
Los Baqueanos, signposted from R258, on the eastern shore of Lago Gutiérrez, T02944-1555 4362, baqueanos@bariloche.com.ar.

Lago Mascardi *p504*
Boat trips
Victoria II Lago Mascardi Paseos Lacustres, T02944-441062, lmascardi@bariloche.com.ar. Trips on Lago Mascardi are a wonderful way to see the mountains in summer.

Rafting
Rafting on the Río Manso is arranged through operators in Bariloche; see page 457.

El Bolsón *p506, map p507*
Ask at the tourist office for their *Agro-turismo* leaflet, with information on the *chacras* (fruit farms) you can visit in summer, for delicious, freshly picked soft fruits and berries, jams and other delights. Throughout El Bolsón and El Hoyo, further south.

Cycling
La Rueda, Sarmiento 2972, T/F02944-492465, daily 0830-1330, 1530-2130. US$12 per day for bike hire.

Tour operators
Grado 42, Av Belgrano 406, on the corner with Av San Martín, T02944-493124, www.grado42.com. Excellent company offering wide range of tours, including La Trochita's lesser-known trip from El Maitén, where there is a superb steam railway workshop and you can learn all about how the trains work. Also rafting on the Río Manso; horse riding in glorious countryside at Cajón de Azul; wonderful fishing in Lago Puelo; paragliding from Plitriquitron.

Huara, Dorrego 410, T02944-455000, www. huaraviajesyturismo.com.ar. Mon-Sat. Horse riding, rafting, trekking and mountain biking.
Juana de Arco, San Martín and Juez Fernández, T02944-493415, www.inter patagonia.com/juanadearco. Boat trips across Lago Pielo, US$24 for a 3-hr trip to the Chilean border, including walk through Valdivian rainforest. Also run fishing trips, email for details. Recommended.
Puelo Extremo, Callejón La Lydia s/n, T02944-499588, www.puelo extremo.com.ar. Trekking and canoeing in the park.
Puelo Trout, T02944-499430. Boat trips and all-inclusive fishing trips, equipment included.

Kayaking
Kayak Lago Puelo, T02944-499197, www.kayaklagopuelo.com.ar. Kayaking on the lake with guide and instructor Alberto Boyer.

⊖ Transport

Lago Mascardi *p504*
Bus Services from Bariloche to **El Bolsón** pass through **Villa Mascardi**. Buses to **Los Rápidos** run from the terminal in Bariloche at 0900, 1300, 1800 daily in summer. Check with **Vía Bariloche/El Valle**, or Bariloche Bus station for times (see below).

Pampa Linda and Mount Tronador *p505*
There is a bus that departs from the Club Andino (20 de Febrero and Juramento, www.clubandino.org) which leaves at 0830 daily in the summer, passing by Los Rápidos at 0930 and arriving at Pampa Linda. The bus then departs again at 1630, US$8 one way.

From Pampa Linda you can also often get a lift with an excursion trip returning to **Bariloche**, if there's room, US$10.

El Bolsón *p506, map p507*
Bus
Buses to **Lago Puelo**, every 2 hrs, 4 on Sun, 45 mins, US$3, **Vía Bariloche**. To Bariloche and Esquel, buses leave every hour, US$4, 2 hrs, various companies. To **Parque Nacional Los Alerces** (highly recommended route), once a day, 4-5 hrs, US$6, via Cholila and Epuyen, **Transportes Esquel** (from ACA service station). If you arrive early in the morning the best thing to do is wait at the ACA on Av San Martín. They have phones, and serve tea and coffee. You can order a taxi from there to take you to your accommodation.

Taxi (Radio and remise)
Pepe (*remise*), T02944-1566 1744, friendly Pepe works with El Pueblito hostel (see page 515), but not exclusively; **Piltri**, T02944-492272.

Parque Nacional Lago Puelo *p510*
Transportes Esquel run daily buses connecting Lago Puelo with **Cholila**, **PN Los Alerces** and **Esquel**.

⊕ Directory

El Bolsón *p506, map p507*
Banks Exchange cash at **Banco Patagonia**, San Martín and Roca, with ATM outside.
Internet Various places open and close, currently functioning: **Ciber Café La Nuez**, Av San Martín 2175, T02944-455182.
Post office San Martín 1940.

Esquel, Trevelin and Parque Nacional Los Alerces

This southernmost area of the lakes is the most Patagonian in feel, with pioneer towns Esquel and Trevelin caught between the wild open steppe to the east and the dramatic mountains of the Andes to the west. Esquel retains the quiet charm of an ordinary country town – with one very famous attraction. It's the starting point for the narrow-gauge railway known as 'La Trochita' (www.latrochita.org.ar), an atmospheric way to see the surrounding landscape, but the town also boasts a family ski resort and a few places to trek and mountain bike. Far more tranquil is the village of Trevelin, which still bears signs of its origins as a Welsh colony: Welsh is still spoken in the streets, you can try an enormous 'traditional' Welsh tea, and there's a fascinating old flour mill to visit in the pretty landscape towards the Chilean border. Both towns make good bases for exploring the most unspoilt national park in the Lake District: Los Alerces. With just one road running through it, the park has pristine forested mountains and several stunning lakes, and is best enjoyed on foot. There are wonderful hikes, boat trips to see ancient alerce trees, and some unforgettable views, like Río Arrayanes and Lago Verde. Since this area is less developed for tourism than the rest of the lakes, it's best to hire a car to see it independently if you don't want to do a full-day tour. ▸▸ *For listings, see pages 527-531.*

Esquel → *For listings, see pages 527-531. Colour map 5, B2.*

One of the most authentic towns in the Lake District, Esquel is a pleasant, breezy place that still feels like a pioneer outpost, set where the steppe meets the mountains. It's a typical Patagonian country town, with many buildings dating from the early 1900s, and battered pickups filling the streets in the late-morning bustle when local farmers come into town. There are few tourist sites, but it's all the more appealing for that. It is the starting point for the narrow-gauge railway, 'La Trochita' (www.latrochita.org.ar), made famous by Paul Theroux as the *Old Patagonian Express*, which chugs off into the steppe from a charming old-fashioned station just north of town. It's the best base for visiting the Parque Nacional Los Alerces, and for skiing at La Hoya (www.cerrolahoya.com) in winter. The tranquil village of Trevelin, where the Welsh heritage is more in evidence, is just 25 km away. For more information, see www.esquelonline.com (in Spanish).

Ins and outs → *Phone code 02945. Population 30,000.*

Getting there and around Esquel has its own **airport** ⓘ *T02945-451354, enquiries T02945-450588*, 20 km east of town, reached by bus (US\$3.50) or taxi (US\$10), and a smart modern **bus terminal** ⓘ *Av Alvear 1871, T02945-451584*, six blocks from the main commercial centre around Avenida Fontana. Buses arrive here from Comodoro Rivadavia on the Atlantic coast and Bariloche, with connections from those places to all other destinations in Patagonia and to the north. The terminal has toilets, *kiosko*, *locutorio*, and left luggage (US\$1.50 per item per day). Buses also run daily into Los Alerces National Park.

Tourist information The **tourist office** ⓘ *in a little hut on the corner of Av Alvear and Sarmiento, T02945-451927, www.esquel.gov.ar, daily 0900-2200, closed May-Jul*, is friendly enough, but doesn't seem to have much information. They do hand out a useful town map, however, and another leaflet it's worth asking for, with a yellow map of Los Alerces National Park showing all access and accommodation in the park, as well as crossing to Chile via Paso

Futulaeufú. You might have to press them patiently for bus timetables. For further information on Los Alerces and the whole area, see www.comarcadelosalerces.com.ar.

Sights

There aren't any sights, as such, and the whole point of visiting Esquel is to get to Los Alerces, or Trevelin, but it's a pleasant place to walk around. All the food shops and services you need are contained within a few blocks east of Avenida Alvear, between Mitre and the wide Avenida Fontana. The famous narrow-gauge railway, **La Trochita** (*Old Patagonian Express*) ① *station office Estación Viejo Expreso Patagonico, T02945- 451403, www.latrochita.org.ar, US$38, children under 6 free, Jan-Feb 3 departures a week, other times Sat and sometimes Tue only at 1000, tour operators in town sell tickets*, also known in Spanish as *El Viejo Expreso Patagónico*, leaves from a pretty old station six blocks north of the town centre at the corner of Brown and Roggero. While it's obviously a tourist experience, this is a thoroughly enjoyable trip, and as the steam train rumbles across the lovely valleys and mountains of the *precordillera* on tracks just 75 cm wide, you'll find yourself wanting to know how it works. There's Spanish and English commentary along the way, the quaint carriages each have little wood stoves, and there's a small tea room on board. But it's worth waiting for the home-made cakes (and handicrafts) for sale at the wild and remote Mapuche hamlet of **Nahuel Pan**, where the train stops, and where you'll hear an interesting explanation of how the engine works. Recommended. Sometimes there's an extra service from El Maitén at the northernmost end of the line on Saturday, taking six hours, US$12, with a dining car.

There's good skiing on high quality powder snow over a long season at the low-key family resort of **La Hoya**, 15 km north. It is popular with Argentines, since it's one of cheapest and friendliest. There are 22 km of pistes, many of them suitable for kids or beginners, with good challenging pistes too, and seven ski lifts. For information, try asking the tourist office, and see www.cerrolahoya.com. There are three daily buses to La Hoya from Esquel, US$12 return. A skipass costs US$24 per day in high season, with reductions for a week or longer, and equipment hire ranges from US$15 a day.

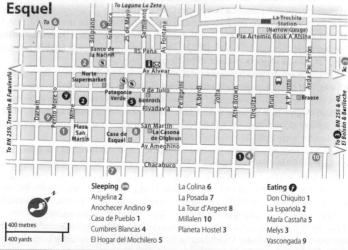

Esquel

400 metres
400 yards

Sleeping		La Colina 6	Eating	
Angelina 2		La Posada 7	Don Chiquito 1	
Anochecer Andino 9		La Tour d'Argent 8	La Española 2	
Casa de Pueblo 1		Millalen 10	María Castaña 5	
Cumbres Blancas 4		Planeta Hostel 3	Melys 3	
El Hogar del Mochilero 5			Vascongada 9	

There are also some challenging walks and mountain-bike trails in the surrounding mountains. See the map *Sendas y Bosques* (Walks and Forests) for El Bolsón, Lago Puelo and Los Alerces, which has the trails clearly marked. It's an easy climb along a clear path to **Laguna La Zeta**, 5 km from the centre of town, with good views and a lake with birdlife. From there, head further north up the Río Percey or towards Cañadón Huemul. The path is signposted from the end of Avenida La Fontana. Another good hike, with spectacular view, is to **Cerro La Cruz**, five hours return; walk from the centre of town signposted from the end of the street 25 de Mayo. There are longer hikes to **Cerro Veinte Uno** (five to eight hours return) and the pointy cone of Cerro Nahual Pan (eight hours return).

Trevelin → *For listings, see pages 527-531. Colour map 5, B2.*

The pretty village of Trevelin, 25 km southwest of Esquel, was once an offshoot of the Welsh colony Gaiman on the Atlantic coast (see box, page 547), when the Welsh travelled west to find further lands for growing corn. The name means Town (*tre*) of the Mill (*velin*) in Welsh, you can still hear Welsh spoken here, and there is plenty of evidence of Welsh heritage in several good little museums around the town. With a backdrop of snow-capped mountains, the village is an appealing place to rest for a few days, to go fishing and rafting on nearby Río Futuleufu, or see the beautiful waterfalls at the reserve of Nant-y-fall.

Sights → *Phone code 02945. Population 5000.*

Trevelin remains a quiet village with a strong sense of community, and its history is manifest in several sights. The Welsh chapel (1910), **La Capilla Bethel**, can be visited, with a guided tour to fill you in on a bit of history. The fine old flour mill (1918) houses the **Museo Histórico Regional** ① *Molino Viejo 488, T02945-480545, daily 1500-1800, US$2.50*, which has fascinating artefacts from the Welsh colony. The **Museo Cartref Taid** ① *El Malacara s/n, ask for directions in the tourist office, T02945-480108, daily 0900-2100*, is another great place for exploring the Welsh pioneer past. It's the house of John Evans, one of Trevelin's first settlers, and filled with his belongings. There's another extraordinary and touching relic of his life in **La Tumba del Caballo Malacara** ① *200 m from main plaza, guided tours are available, US$2.50*, a private garden containing the grave of his horse, Malacara, who once saved his life. The enthusiastic and helpful staff at the **tourist office** ① *central octagonal plaza, T02945-480120, www.trevelin.gob.ar*, speak English and can provide maps and advice on accommodation and fishing.

Eisteddfods are still held here every year in October, and you'll be relieved to hear that **Té Galés**, that other apparently traditional Welsh ritual, is alive and well in several tea rooms, offering a ridiculous excess of delicious cakes. Extensive research has established that **Nain Maggie** is, in fact, the town's best. There are good day walks in the region, in idyllic scenery around the town. Get directions on routes from the tourist office. It's also a good area for horse riding or mountain biking.

For a gentle outing with quite the best insight into the Welsh history in Patagonia, visit the rural flour mill **Molino Nant Fach** ① *T0268-4280836, entry US$2.50*, on Route 259, 22 km southwest towards the Chilean border. This beautiful flour mill was built by Merfyn Evans, descendant of the town's founder Thomas Dalar Evans, as an exact replica of the first mill built in the town in 1899. Merfyn's fascinating tour (in Spanish, but English booklet available to read) recounts a now familiar tale of the Argentine government's persistent mismanagement of natural resources and industry, through the suppression of the Welsh prize-winning wheat industry. It's a beautiful spot, and Merfyn tells the rather tragic story in a wonderfully entertaining way. Highly recommended. On the same road, but 5 km earlier (the **Nant-y-fall Falls**), 17 km southwest of Trevelin, on Route 259 heading to the Chilean border, before you reach Molino Nant Fach are a series of spectacular waterfalls reached by an easy 1½-hour walk along a trail through lovely forest. There's a charge of US$5 per person which includes a guide to take you to all seven falls.

Fishing is popular in many local rivers and lakes, most commonly in Río Futuleufú, and Corintos, and Lagos Rosario and Corcovado. The season runs from the end of November to mid-April, and the tourist office can advise on guides and where to go.

Parque Nacional Los Alerces → *For listings, see pages 527-531.*

One of the most magnificent and untouched expanses of the whole Andes region, this national park was established to protect the stately *alerce* trees (*Fitzroya cupressoides*). The *alerce* is among the longest-living-tree species in the world, and there are some specimens in the park over 4000 years old. They grow deep in the Valdivian rainforest that carpets these mountains a rich velvety green, beside vivid blue Lago Futalaufquen and emerald Lago Verde. There are several good hikes, rafting and fishing in the park, and idyllic lakeside campsites and *hosterías*, making this a great place to spend a few days.

The park, 60 km west of Esquel, is enormous, over 200,000 ha, and it remains the most virgin park in the whole Lake District, since much of it is only accessible on foot. There are four large lakes: navy-blue **Lago Futalaufquen**, with fine fishing; **Lago Menéndez**, which can be crossed by boat to visit the ancient *alerce* trees; the exquisite green **Lago Verde**; and the almost inaccessible **Lago Amutui Quimei**. In order to protect this fragile environment, access by car is possible only to the eastern side of the park, via *ripio* Route 71 which runs between Cholila and Trevelin alongside the eastern side of Lagos Futalaufquen, Verde and Rivadavia, with many good camping spots and small *hosterías* on their shores. The western side of the park, where rainfall is highest, has areas of Valdivian forest, and can only be accessed by boat or by hiking to Lago Krügger. Lago Futalaufquen has some of the best fishing in this part of Argentina (the season runs from end November to mid-April), and local guides offer fishing trips, and boat transport. Ask in the *Intendencia* (see Ins and outs, below), or **Hostería Cume Hue** (see Sleeping, page 528).

Ins and outs

There are two main entrances to the park, both off Route 71, at the northern end of Lago Rivadavia, and 12 km south of Lago Futulaufquen. At the southern tip of this lake is the park's administration centre, the *Intendencia* (park office) with a **visitor centre** ① *T02945-471064*, offering useful information on the park. Helpful *guardaparques* give out maps and advise on walks. Right by the *Intendencia*, and less than 2 km from Route 71, **Villa Futulaufquen** is a little hamlet which is very useful for services. There's a petrol station, *locutorio*, two food shops and a restaurant, **El Abuelo Monje**. Fishing licences can be obtained either from the food shops, the *kiosko* or **Hostería Cume Hue**. Park entrance costs US$8. A daily bus runs along Route 71 in each direction, picking up and dropping off passengers at campsites and *hosterías*, and also at the petrol station, opposite the *Intendencia*. Ask at the petrol station for bus times, or contact T02945-471020, www.parquesnacionales.gov.ar. ▸▸ *For further information, see Transport, page 531.*

Walks

① www.guiasendasybosques.com.ar.
For all walks, get the *Sendas y Bosques* (Walks and Forests) map and book for El Bolsón, Lago Puelo and Los Alerces. Maps are 1:200,000, laminated and easy to read, and the book is full of great walks, with English summaries and detailed directions in Spanish. The park office *Intendencia* also has leaflets listing the walks, but there is insufficient detail.

Cave paintings There are *pinturas rupestres* to be found just 40 minutes' stroll from the park *Intendencia* (Km 1). You'll also pass a waterfall and a mirador with panoramic views over Lago Futulaufquen.

Lago Verde The most beautiful walk in the whole park, and unmissable, no matter how little time you have, is across the suspension bridge over Río Arrayanes (Km 34.3) to heavenly Lago Verde. A self-guided trail leads around a peninsula and to Lago Menéndez, to the pier where boat trips begin, Puerto Chucao. Go in the early evening to see all kinds of birdlife from the beach by Lago Verde, swifts and swallows darting all around you. Signposted off Route 71, **Pasarella** (walkway) **Lago Verde**. While you're in the area, take a quick 20-minute stroll up to **Mirador Lago Verde** where you'll be rewarded with gorgeous views up and down the whole valley and can appreciate the string of lakes, running from Lago Futulaufquen in the south, Lago Verde, to Lago Rivadavia in the north.

Cerro Dedal For a great day hike, there is a longer trek up Cerro Dedal (1916 m), a circular walk, at least eight hours return, with a steep climb from the *Intendencia*, and wonderful views over the lake and mountains further west. Register with *guardaparques* and get detailed instructions. You're required to start before 1000. Carry plenty of water.

Lago Krügger There is also a long but rewarding two- to three-day (12- to 14-hour) hike though *coihue* forest to the southernmost tip of **Lago Krügger**, where there is a *refugio* (open only in January and February), and campsite, as well as a *guardaparque's* office. Here you can take a boat back to Puerto Limonao, but check when the boat is running before you set off, and always register with the park's *Intendencia*. From Lago Krügger, you could walk south along the course of Río Frey, though there is no *refugio* here. For information on the boat service and the *refugio* contact **Hostería Lago Krügger** ① *T02945-453718, www.lagokrugger.com*, a little rustic fishing lodge.

Cascada Arroyo A satisfying and easy four-hour walk where you can see waterfalls, passing various miradors.

Boat trips

All boat trips run frequently in high season (1 December to 31 March), and all can be booked through **Safari Lacustre** ① *T02945-15465941, www.brazosur.com.ar*, and **Patagonia Verde** ① *Esquel, T02945-454396, www.patagonia-verde.com.ar*, or when you get to the pier, though tickets tend to sell out in high season. Boat trips leave from Puerto Limonao at the southern end of Lago Futulaufquen: follow signs up the western side of the lake, just for a few kilometres; or from Puerto Chucao, which is reached from the suspension bridge crossing Lago Verde, halfway along Route 71. Trips start at Puerto Limonao, and then call in at Puerto Chucao, before setting off across Lago Futulaufquen and along the pea-green Río Arrayanes, lined with the extraordinary cinnamon-barked *arrayán* trees. Even more spectacular, from Puerto Chucao, across Lago Menéndez (1½ hours) where you land, and walk a short distance to see a majestic 2600 year old *alerce* tree, known as 'el abuelo'. From here you walk to the hidden and silent jade-green Lago Cisne, and then back past the rushing white waters of Río Cisne. An unforgettable experience. From Puerto Limonao, cost US$40, set off 1000, return 1900. From Puerto Chucao, cost US$30, set off 1200, return 1700. Boats also go from Puerto Limonao to Lago Krügger or you can trek there, and take the boat back, but check boat times before you set off. Boats sail in summer only.

Parque Nacional Los Alerces

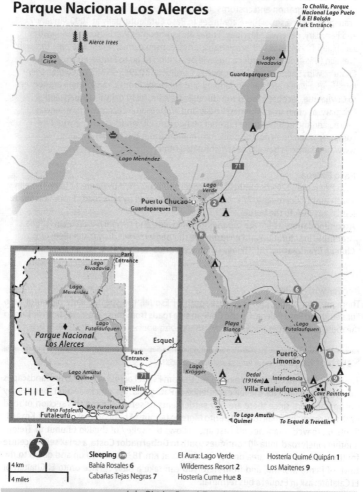

Sleeping
Bahía Rosales **6**
Cabañas Tejas Negras **7**

El Aura: Lago Verde
Wilderness Resort **2**
Hostería Cume Hue **8**

Hostería Quimé Quipán **1**
Los Maitenes **9**

Border essentials: Argentina–Chile

Paso Futaleufú
Paso Futaleufú is 70 km southwest of Esquel via Trevelin and is reached by Route 259 (*ripio* from Trevelin). The border is crossed by a bridge over the Río Futaleufú, and formalities should take no longer than an hour.
Argentine immigration and customs On the Argentine side of the bridge. Open 0800-2000 in summer and 0900-2100 in winter. Eat all your fresh food, as no fruit or vegetables may be taken into Chile.
Chilean immigration and customs In Futaleufú, 9 km west of the border.
Transport From Esquel there are buses to Paso Futaleufú, daily at 1000 January and February, otherwise Monday, Friday and sometimes Wednesday, US$4, with Jacobsen, T02945-453528, www.transportejacobsen.com.ar, these also pass through Trevelin (US$4). At the border a bus will be waiting to go to Futuleufú and on to Chaitén, with **Ebenezer** and **Transportes Cordillera**, T02945-258633, between them four times a week, and daily in January and February. From Chaitén there are services to Coyhaique. Jacobsen buses run through Trevelin, 0830 daily in January and February, at other tmes Monday, Friday and Wednesday. Cars must have special papers and the number-plate number etched into all windows: advise your hire company when booking. For more information about this border crossing, see www.gendarmeria.gov.ar/pasos/fichfutaleu.html.

Paso Palena
Paso Palena lies 120 km southeast of Esquel and is reached by Route 17 from Trevelin which runs to Corcovado, 75 km east of Tecka (reached by *ripio* road). From Corcovado it is 26 km west to the border.
Accommodation There are *cabañas* in Corcovado and several *pensiones* in Palena.
Argentine immigration and customs At the border, open daily 0900-1800.
Chilean immigration At Palena, 11 km west of border.

Border with Chile
There are two border crossings just south of Esquel, the spectacularly beautiful Paso Futaleufú and Paso Palena. On the Chilean side roads from these crossings both link up to the route to Chaitén. ▶ *For further details, see box, above.*

South of Esquel → *For listings, see pages 527-531.*

The iconic Ruta 40 continues (paved) south from Esquel across very deserted landscapes that give you a taste for the full experience of Patagonia. It's a tricky section for travel by public transport, since there are few settlements or services along this section of road until you reach the small town of Perito Moreno (about 14 hours' drive). At **Tecka**, Km 101, Route 62 (paved) branches off east and follows the valley of the Río Chubut to Trelew: another lonely road. Ruta 40 continues south to **Gobernador Costa**, a small service centre for the *estancias* in this area on the Río Genoa at Km 183. Buses go up and down to the town of Perito Moreno, and from here you can take a daily service on to El Chaltén or El Calafate: ask in Esquel's bus terminal.

Río Pico → *Colour map 5,C2. Phone code 02945. Population 1000.*

Río Pico lies in a wide green valley close to the Andes and has become quietly known among trout-fishing circles as a very desirable place to fish. It is the site of an early 20th-century German settlement and some old houses remain from that period. Nearby are several lakes, good for fishing and free camping, ask locals for hitching advice; the northern shore of Lago Tres, 23 km west of town, is a peaceful and remote place, with a rich birdlife and wild strawberries at the end of January. Some 30 km north of Río Pico lies the huge Lago Vintter, reached by Route 44. There are also smaller lakes good for trout fishing. Permits are available from the *municipalidad* in Gobernador Costa.

South of Gobernador Costa

At Km 221, Ruta 40 (poor *ripio*) forks southwest through the town of **Alto Río Senguer** from which visits can be made to the relatively unexplored Lago Fontana and Lago La Plata. Provincial Route 20 (paved) heads almost directly south for 81 km, before turning east towards Sarmiento and Comodoro Rivadavia. At La Puerta del Diablo, in the valley of the lower Río Senguer, Route 20 intersects provincial Route 22, which joins with Ruta 40 at the town of Río Mayo in Patagonia (see page 573). This latter route is completely paved and preferable to Ruta 40 for long-distance motorists.

⊙ Esquel, Trevelin and Los Alerces National Park listings

For Sleeping and Eating price codes and other relevant information, see Essentials pages 30-36.

⊙ Sleeping

Esquel *p520, map p521*
There are now many *cabañas* for rent in Esquel: ask at tourist office for the full list. For more hotel listings, see www.inter patagonia.com/esquel (in English).
AL Canela, Los Notros, Villa Ayelén, on the road to Trevelin, T02945-453890, www.canela-patagonia.com. Comfortable B&B and tea room. The English-speaking owners are knowledgeable about Patagonia.
A Cumbres Blancas, Ameghino 1683, T02945-455100, www.cumbresblancas. com.ar. A little out of the town centre, this lovely *hostería* has great views, comfortable traditional rooms and an airy restaurant serving good food. Recommended.
B Angelina, Alvear 758, T02945-452763, www.hosteriaangelina.com.ar. A warm welcoming place, open high season only, serving good food. Italian spoken.
B-C La Chacra, Km 5 on R259 towards Trevelin, T02945-452802,

www.lachacrapatagonia.com. Tranquil place with spacious rooms and huge breakfast, Welsh and English spoken.
B-C La Tour d'Argent, San Martín 1063, T02945-454612, www.latourdargent.com.ar. With breakfast, the bright, plain, modern rooms are very good value in this friendly family-run hotel with a lovely garden. Recommended.
C La Posada, Chacabuco 905 and Roca, T02945-454095, laposada@ar.inter.net. A real find, this welcoming, tasteful *hostería* is in a quiet part of town, with a lovely lounge to relax in, good spacious rooms and breakfast included. Excellent value. Recommended.

Hostels

E pp **Anochecer Andino**, Av Ameghino 482, T02945-450498, www.anocheceranndino. com.ar. Only 4 blocks from the commercial centre and 2 from the mountains, this basic but friendly hostel can organize ski passes and excursions. They also can provide home-made dinner and there is a bar on site.
E pp **Casa de Pueblo**, San Martín 661, T02945-450581, www.epaadventure.com.ar. A friendly, welcoming hostel with smallish

rooms, kitchen and laundry. Also run rafting, trekking, climbing and mountain biking.
E pp Planeta Hostel, Av Alvear 2833, T02945-456846, www.planetahostel.com. A 15-min walk from town, this small cosy hostel has dorm rooms for 4-6 people, and 1 double (**D**), and is limited to only 16 guests at any one time. Recommended.

Camping
E pp La Colina, Darwin 1400, T02945-455264, www.lacolinaesquel.com.ar. Complex a little out of the centre offering cramped dorms (**E** pp), nice doubles (**C**) and camping from US$6.
El Hogar del Mochilero, Roca 1028, T02945-452166. Camping in summer only (Jan-Mar), also has laundry facilities, 24-hr hot water, friendly owner, internet and free firewood.
La Rural, 1 km on road to Trevelin, T02945-1568 1429. Well-organized and shady site with facilities.
Millalén, Ameghino 2063, T02945-456164. Good services.

Trevelin p522
L Campo Cielo Grande, south of Trevelin on the banks of Lago Rosario, www.threes adventures.com. Exclusive luxury 5-star camping on raised decks, with heating, huge beds and million-dollar views. Friendly hosts Trey and Shelby can arrange activities in the area. Minimum 3-night stay.
L-AL Challhuaquen, Los Cipreses, T02945-501032, www.challhuaquen.com. Charming place set high up with beautiful views over the river. Good-quality accommodation and food, aimed at the fly-fishing market with expert resident fishing guide.
A La Patagonia Lodge, R71, Km 1, T02945-480752, www.lapatagonialodge.com. Has been recommended as a great fishing lodge.
A-B Casa de Piedra, Almirante Brown 244, T02945-480357, www.casadepiedratrevelin. com. Lovely stone and wood cottage in the suburbs of Trevelin. King-size beds, wonderful heating and a charming common area make this hotel popular.

C Pezzi, Sarmiento 353, T02945-480146, hpezzi@intramed.com.ar. Jan-Mar only. An attractive small hotel with a garden. English spoken.

Hostels
E pp Casa Verde Hostal, Los Alerces s/n, T/F02945-480091, www.casaverdehostel. com.ar. Run by the lovely Bibiana and Charley, who'll make you welcome in their cosy log cabin, with gardens and views over Trevelin. Comfortable dorms for 4-6 people all have bathrooms. Kitchen facilities, laundry, lounge, HI discount and meals available. They also run trekking and rafting excursions into Los Alerces National Park. There's a very comfortable *cabaña* (**B**) for hire. All highly recommended.

Camping
There are many sites, especially on the road to Futuleufú and Chile.
Aikén Leufú, on the road to Futaleufú dam, T02945-1568 1398. Full facilities and *cabañas* for 2.
Puerto Ciprés, on the banks of Río Futuleufú, T02945-450913. Peaceful place, right on the riverbank, simple facilities.

Parque Nacional Los Alerces p523, map p525
East side of Lago Futalaufquen
LL El Aura: Lago Verde Wilderness Resort, T011-4816 5348 (Buenos Aires), www.hosteria selaura.com. Exquisite 3 stone cabins and a guesthouse on the shore of Lago Verde. Luxury in every respect, attention to detail, ecologically friendly. Impressive place.
A Hostería Cume Hue, T02945-453639, http://cumehue.patagoniaexpress.com. A rather overpriced fishing lodge with spartan rooms and basic bathrooms, and enclosed in woodland, so that only some rooms have views, but great for anglers. You can fish directly from the shore here, or on boat trips organized by the owners. Prices are full board.

A Hostería Quimé Quipán, T02945-425423,
www.hosteriaquimequipan.com.ar.
Delightful, comfortable rooms, impeccably
clean and attractively decorated, with
uninterrupted lake views and dinner
included. Wonderfully peaceful. Paths lead
down to a small rocky beach and there are
gardens to sit in. Prices soar over Jan/Feb.
Recommended.

B Bahía Rosales, T02945-471044, www.
bahiarosales.alojar.com.ar. A welcoming,
family-run place with spacious *cabañas*
to rent, in an elevated position above the
lake, also *refugio*-style little *cabañas* to
share (**F** pp), and camping in open ground
with great views, fireplaces and tables,
and hot showers, restaurant and *quincho*.
All recommended.

D Cabañas Tejas Negras, T02945-471046.
Next door to **Pucón Pai**, these are really
comfortable *cabañas* and good facilities for
camping. Also recommended tea room.

Camping

There are several campsites on the eastern
side of the lake, at Lagos Rivadavia, Verde
and Río Arrayanes, ranging from free to US$5
depending on facilities. All have marvellous
views, lake access and fireplaces, and can be
busy in high season. If walking, register with
guardaparques before you set off, bear in
mind that it takes at least 10 hrs to reach
the *refugio* at Lago Krügger, and camping
is possible (1 night only) at Playa Blanca,
where fires are not permitted.

Krügger Lodge www.lagokrugger.com.ar.
Lago Krügger has a *refugio* (**A**) and campsite,
with hot showers, food shop, meals provided,
fishing guides and boat trips.

Lago Rivadavia, close to lake, T02945-
454 381. Basic facilities.

Los Maitenes, Villa Futalaufquen, T02945-
450354. Excellent, US$2.50 per person,
US$5 per tent.

Pucón Pai, close to lake, T02945 451425.
Basic facilities.

Eating

Esquel *p520, map p521*

♥♥ **Don Chiquito**, Av Ameghino 1641,
T02945-450035. The walls are lined with
number plates, and the owner will entertain
you with magic and mind-teasing games
while you wait for your pasta and pizzas.

♥♥ **La Española**, Rivadavia 740, T02945-451
509. Excellent beef, salad bar and tasty pasta.
Recommended.

♥♥ **Vascongada**, 9 de Julio and Mitre, T02945-
452229. Fabulous *parrilla*. Good trout and
local specialities.

♥ **La Tour D'Argent**, San Martín 1063,
T02945-454612. Delicious local specialities,
good-value set meals and a warm ambience
in this popular, traditional restaurant.

Cafés and tea rooms

Maria Castaña, Rivadavia and 25 de Mayo.
A popular place for excellent coffee, reading
the papers and watching street life.

Melys, Miguens 346 (off Ameghino 2000).
Welsh teas and also a good breakfast.

Trevelin *p522*

♥♥ **Patagonia Celta**, 25 de Mayo and Molino
Viejo, T02945-480722. This is the best place
to eat by a long way. Really delicious local
specialities, superbly cooked fresh trout,
steaks and vegetarian dishes in elegant
stylish surroundings. Very welcoming,
and reasonably priced.

♥ **Parrilla Mirador del Valle**, R259, Km 46,
T02945-1568 8951. Excellent *parrilla* and
other delicious dishes. Recommended.

♥ **Parrilla Oregon**, Av San Martín and Murray
Thomas, T02945-480408. Large meals
(particularly breakfast).

Cafés and tea rooms

Nain Maggie, P Moreno 179, T02945-
480 232, www.casadetenainmaggie.com.
The best tea room, offering a huge *té galés*
and excellent *torta negra*. Recommended.

O Shopping

Esquel *p520, map p521*
Benroth, 9 de Julio 1027. Sells chocolates.
Braese, 9 de Julio 1959. Home-made
chocolates with other regional specialities.
Casa de Esquel, 25 de Mayo 415. A range
of rare books on Patagonia, also souvenirs.
La Casona de Olgbrun, San Martín 1137.
A variety of handicrafts and souvenirs.
Librería Patagonica, 25 de Mayo 415,
T02945-452544. Rare books on Patagonia
and recent editions, with friendly service.
Norte, 9 de Julio and Roca. Huge supermarket.

▲ Activities and tours

Esquel *p520, map p521*
Fishing
Lots of guides and equipment for hire. See
Frontera Sur, under Tour operators, below.
Jorge Trucco and Patagonia Outfitters,
Pérez 662 (San Martín de los Andes) T2972-
427 561, www.jorgetrucco.com. Arrange
tours and accommodation in fishing lodges.

Skiing
Sol del Sur, 9 de Julio 1094 and Sarmiento,
T02945-452189, www.hotelsoldelsur.
guiapatagonia.net. Hires ski equipment.

Tour operators
Frontera Sur, Av Alvear and Sarmiento,
T02945-450505, www.fronterasur.net.
Good company offering adventure tourism
of all sorts, as well as more traditional
excursions, ski equipment and trekking.
Patagonia Verde, 9 de Julio 926, T/F02945-
454396, www.patagonia-verde.com.ar.
Excellent local tours to Los Alerces, including
the wonderful boat trip across Lagos
Menéndez and Cisnes, and La Trochita.
Also adventure excursions: horse riding,
US$13 ½-day; rafting, US$29 per day,
Grades II-IV; fishing, US$110 per day, all
inclusive; and fabulous 4WD trips to trek

in tunnels of ice, US$22 full day. Helpful,
professional and English spoken.
Quehumanque, Los Maitanes 890,
Villa Ayelen, T02945-451869,
www.quehumanque.com.ar. Good local
company that runs small-group excursions
in the area including snow-shoeing, kayaking,
canyoning and mountain biking.

Trevelin *p522*
Gales al Sur, Patagonia 186, in the same
building as the *locutorio*, T02945-480427,
www.galesalsur.com.ar. Tours to Chilean
border; Los Alerces National Park and
Futaleufú dam; La Trochita. Recommended
for their rafting, trekking, biking, 4WD
and horse-riding excursions. Friendly
and English spoken.

Parque Nacional Los Alerces *p523,
map p525*
Agencies in Esquel or Trevelin run tours
including the boat trip across Lago
Menéndez to the *alerce* trees. For short
guided excursions, ask at the *intendencia*
in Villa Futalaufquen.

O Transport

Esquel *p520, map p521*
Air
For airport information, see page 520.
Weekly to **Buenos Aires** with Aerolíneas
Argentinas (agent), Av Fontana 408,
T02945-453614; **LADE**, Av Alvear 1085,
T02945-452124, to **Bahía Blanca**, **Bariloche**,
Comodoro Rivadavia, **El Bolsón**, **Mar del
Plata**, **Neuquén**, **Puerto Madryn**.

Bus
For bus terminal information, see page 520.
To **Comodoro Rivadavia**, 4 times a week,
9 hrs, US$17, Don Otto, T02945-453012 (but
usually arrives from Bariloche full in season).
To **Bariloche**, 4-5 hrs, US$10, **Andesmar**,
Don Otto; Mar and Valle; T02945-453712;

Vía Bariloche, T02945-453528. To **El Bolsón**,
2 hrs, US$8, on bus to **Bariloche**, or via
Los Alerces National Park, see below.
To **Trelew**, daily, 9 hrs, US$17, **Don Otto**;
Emp Chubut; Mar y Valle. To **Trevelin**,
Mon-Fri, hourly 0700-2100, every 2 hrs at
weekends, US$2.50, **Jacobsen**, T02945-
453528. To **Los Alerces National Park**,
Jacobsen, T02945-453528, runs a daily bus
through the park from Esquel bus terminal
at 0930, arriving at **Futulaufquen** (the
entrance and *guardería*) 1100, and on to
Lago Verde 1215. You can get on or off
at any of the campsites or *hosterías* in park,
US$5 each way. Returns to Esquel from
Futulaufquen at 2000, arriving **Esquel**
2115. Ring to check times as they vary
from season to season.

Car hire
Avis, Av Fontana 331 and at the airport,
T02945-455062, www.avis.com; Travel
Rent a Car, Av Alvear 1069, T02945-455811.

Taxi
Gerardo Parsons, T02945-1568 7702,
gerardoturismo@yahoo.com.ar; **Unión**,
Roca 477, T0800-333 2806

Train
For information about La Trochita
(the *Old Patagonian Express*), in English
including schedules, T02945-495190
(El Maitén), T02945-451403 (in Esquel),
www.latrochita.org.ar.

Trevelin *p522*
Bus
To **Esquel**, Mon-Fri, hourly 0700-2100,
every 2 hrs weekends, US$2.50, with
Vía Trevelin, T02945-455222.

Parque Nacional Los Alerces *p523, map p525*
Bus
From Esquel there are 2 services running at
the time of writing: Jacobsen, as described
above, and Transportes Esquel, T02945-
453529, runs daily buses at 0800 from Esquel
(returning at 2115) along the east side of
Lago Futalaufquen, passing **Villa
Futalaufquen** 0915 (return 2000), **Lago
Verde** 1030 (return 1845), **Lago Rivadavia**
1120 (return 1830), and continuing on to
Cholila, **El Bolsón** and **Lago Puelo**
(return 1500). The driver will drop you at your
accommodation, and you can stop the bus
at any point on the road, US$5 each way.

South of Esquel *p526*
Bus
From Esquel to **Río Pico**, Mon, Wed and Sat,
4½ hrs, US$4, Jacobsen, T02945-453528.

South of Gobernador Costa *p527*
Bus
From Esquel to **Alto Río Senguer**, Mon and
Thu, **ETAP**.

⊕ Directory

Esquel *p520, map p521*
Banks Banco de la Nación, Alvear and
Roca, open 0730-1300. ATM accepts all cards;
Banco Patagonia, 25 de Mayo 739, ATM;
Bansud, 25 de Mayo 752, ATM. **Internet**
Best & Best, Av Fontana and Ameghino,
T02945-450632; Cyberplanet, San Martín
996, T02945-452228; lots more in the centre.
Post office Alvear 1192 and Fontana,
Mon-Fri 0830-1300 and 1600-1930, Sat
0900-1300. **Telephone** Many *locutorios*
in centre including Unitel, 25 de Mayo 528,
Central Sur Rivadavia 949, and bus terminal.

Contents

Footprint features

Border crossings

Argentina–Chile, *see page 575 and 593*

Patagonia

At a glance

◔ **Getting around** Long distances dictate many hours on buses. Car hire is preferred, as are local flights if your budget allows.

◍ **Time required** 7-9 days is enough to see El Calafate, do a short hike near El Chaltén and see the whales in Puerto Madryn.

◐ **Weather** May-Jul is extremely cold and the months either side can bring low temperatures. It warms up from Dec-Mar/Apr, but the winds never really stop.

◉ **When not to go** Accessible all year round, but from May-Oct the weather is cold and windy, some places close down and transport is less frequent.

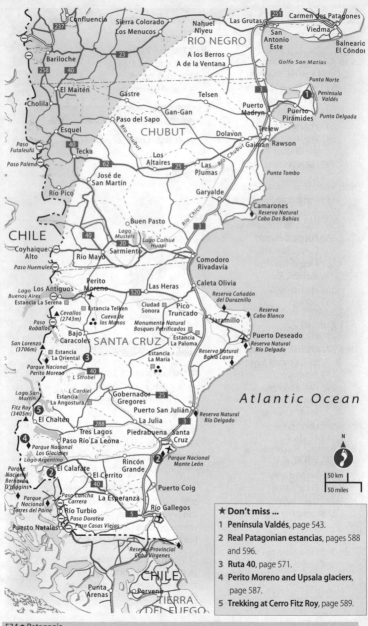

★ Don't miss ...
1 Península Valdés, page 543.
2 Real Patagonian estancias, pages 588 and 596.
3 Ruta 40, page 571.
4 Perito Moreno and Upsala glaciers, page 587.
5 Trekking at Cerro Fitz Roy, page 589.

Patagonia has become the stuff of legends, and for good reason. It's more immense than you can possibly imagine, more empty, more windswept and more beautiful. No wonder it has attracted pioneers and runaways from the modern world. From Welsh settlers to Butch and Sundance; from Bruce Chatwin to Ernesto 'Che' Guevara riding the Ruta 40, Patagonia invites adventure.

East of the Andes, Patagonia makes up the whole southernmost cone of the Americas: a vast expanse of treeless steppe, dotted with the occasional sheep *estancia*. But at its edges are extraordinary extremes: whales bask and thousands of sea lions cavort at Península Valdés, and descendants of the Welsh still hold Eisteddfods (Welsh Festival of Arts) at Gaiman. Thousands of handprints are testimony to Stone Age life at Cueva de las Manos, and there are two petrified forests of mighty fallen monkey puzzle trees.

Take the Ruta 40 south, and you'll travel hundreds of kilometres without seeing a soul, until the magnificent granite towers of Mount Fitz Roy rise up from the flat plains: this trekking heaven is far less crowded than Torres del Paine, and on the southern ice field there are no beaten tracks whatsoever. El Calafate is the base for boat trips to the Perito Moreno Glacier: put on your crampons and walk their sculpted turquoise curves, or escape to splendidly isolated Estancia Cristina. Once you've seen Upsala Glacier stretching out as far as the eye can see, silent and pristine, calving below you into a milky Prussian-blue lake, you'll be addicted. Allow plenty of time, bring walking boots and don't forget your camera.

Ins and outs

Patagonia is vast, and it's no surprise that getting around takes some organization. Strictly speaking, Patagonia is the whole southern cone of South America, combining all parts of Argentina and Chile, south of the Río Colorado, which runs from west to east, just north of Viedma. It includes the Andes, running north-south along the extreme west (marking the Chilean border) and therefore the Lake District, which has been given its own chapter in this book, see page 431. The Patagonia chapter includes all of Argentine Patagonia apart from the Lake District and Tierra del Fuego, the island at the very bottom, which also has its own chapter, see page 635.

For Puerto Madryn, whale watching at Península Valdés, and the Welsh village of Gaiman, see the Northern Atlantic Coast section, page 539. For marine wildlife reserves at Puerto Deseado and Puerto San Julián, and the petrified forest, see the Southern Atlantic Coast section, page 558. For the Cueva de las Manos, *estancias* and the Parque Nacional Perito Moreno, see Ruta 40, page 571. And finally, for both trekking around Mount Fitz Roy from El Chaltén, and for visiting the glaciers from El Calafate, see Parque Nacional Los Glaciares, page 582. The main centres, with good accommodation and services, are Puerto Madryn, El Calafate, Río Gallegos (which all have airports) and El Chaltén.

Getting there

Fortunately Patagonia is served by good public transport. There are daily flights from Buenos Aires to Viedma, Trelew, Comodoro Rivadavia, Río Gallegos, El Calafate's airport Lago Argentino and also to Ushuaia. However, it's vital that you book these flights in advance in the summer (December to March) and the winter ski season for Ushuaia (July and August). **Aerolíneas Argentinas** ① *freecall from within Argentina T0810-222 86527, www.aerolineas.com.ar*, and **LADE** ① *freecall from within Argentina T0810-810 5233, www.lade.com.ar*, fly these routes, and flights get booked up very quickly. At other times of the year, flights can be booked with just a few days' warning. The Chilean airline, **Lan Chile** ① *freephone from within Chile T0600-526 2000, freecall from within Argentina T0810-999 9526, www.lan.com*, now flies to Ushuaia from Argentine destinations as well as Punta Arenas, Puerto Montt and Santiago in Chile.

Getting around

Air Flying between these small main towns is complicated without flying all the way back to Buenos Aires, since there are only flights with the army airline **LADE** connecting all the towns. To get between Puerto Madryn and Ushuaia or El Calafate, for example, your best bet is an overnight bus. Long-distance buses cover the whole of Argentina, are very comfortable – if you choose *coche cama* (bed seat) – and reasonably cheap. There are several daily services between all the towns in Patagonia, though tourist routes book up quickly.

Road There are two main routes south: Ruta 3 along the Atlantic coast, and the Ruta 40 (made famous when Ernesto 'Che' Guevara travelled along it on his motorcycle) running along the Argentine side of the Andes. This road is fabulously bleak and empty, mostly unsurfaced, and there is very little traffic, but a number of bus companies run daily services in summer for tourists between the lovely oasis of Los Antiguos and stunning El Chaltén. From Los Antiguos you can reach Chile and the Lago General Carrera, and from El Chaltén there are frequent services to El Calafate. Some buses stop over at Cueva de las Manos, and if you have the time (14 hours) it's a great way to get a feel for Patagonia, with fine views of the Andes and plenty of wildlife to be spotted.

Hiring a car gives you great flexibility if you want to be independent, but isn't recommended if you're travelling alone – not that you're at risk from people, since Patagonia's rural inhabitants are among the world's most friendly and helpful – but the elements are harsh, distances are enormous and if you run out of petrol or get a stone through your windscreen, it's not a place to be stranded alone. However, hire companies will now let you rent a car in one place and drop it off in another for a rather large but worthwhile fee, so you could consider combining flying with driving.

Driving and cycling in Patagonia require care and patience. Most of the roads are *ripio* (gravel) limiting driving speeds to 60 kph, or slower where surfaces are poor, and it's worth driving your hire car very carefully, as there are huge fines for dents or turning them over. Carry spare fuel, as service stations may be as much as 300 km apart, carry warm clothing in case of breakdown at night, and make sure your car has anti-freeze. There are lots of cattle grids (watch out for signs saying *guardaganados*) to be crossed with care. Hitchhiking is difficult, even on Ruta 3 in the tourist season, and hitching along the Ruta 40 is only possible with a lot of luck and a little help from locals; it helps to speak good Spanish. The Ruta 40 has become a long-distance favourite among hardy cyclists, and it is an amazing experience. But do your research first: winds are fierce; there are few places to get food and water and a complete absence of shade. A tent is essential, with camping allowed pretty much everywhere, but very few *hosterías* or places to stay.

Train There's just one long-distance train across this expanse: a comfortable overnight service between Viedma and Bariloche in the lakes, also taking cars. Check out www.trenpatagonico-sa.com.ar for further information. It's cheap, but takes as long as the bus, and is only useful if you happen to be in Viedma in the first place, or you have a particular love of trains.

National parks

There are many national parks in the region, of which **Parque Nacional Los Glaciares** is the most famous. At the northern end the main centre is El Chaltén for trekking around **Mount Fitz Roy**, and at the southern end are the glaciers, reached from El Calafate. Both have *guardaparques* offices where staff speak English and other languages, hand out maps, and can advise on where to walk and camp. See www.parquesnacionales.gov.ar (in Spanish) for more information.

Parque Nacional Perito Moreno is also spectacular, and well worth the considerable effort involved in reaching its remote lakes and mountains. Access is via the Ruta 40, but there is almost no infrastructure whatsoever, little information for visitors and no services. The best way to see the park is to stay at an *estancia*, such as **La Maipú**, and ride horses into the park: an unforgettable experience.

Marine life abounds on the Atlantic Coast in Península Valdés, reached by organized tour or hire car from Puerto Madryn. This is a well-organized area for visits and there are also several *estancias* on the peninsula where you can stay in great comfort. Further south, **Parque Nacional Monte León** is reached by Ruta 3, you'll need your own transport, but there is a comfortable *hostería*. There are many other colonies of penguins and other sea life reserves along the Atlantic Coast, and two other tourist sites; at **Cueva de las Manos**, and a petrified forest. Unless you have your own transport it's best to take an organized tour to reach these, as services are few at the sites themselves.

Best time to visit

The summer months from December to mid-April are best for trekking. However, January should be avoided everywhere but the most remote places if possible, as this is when most Argentines go on holiday, and transport and accommodation are both heavily booked. From mid-April onwards most hotels close until mid-November and many bus services don't operate. This is because temperatures in the south plummet to -20°C, making it very inhospitable. For Península Valdés, the season for spotting whales is between September and November, when all services are open.

Tourist information

There are tourist offices in even the smallest towns that have any tourist potential, although the best ones are inevitably in El Calafate and El Chaltén, with excellent information centres in Puerto Madryn, Trelew and Río Gallegos. Many have good websites, worth a look before you set off, some with links to hotels for booking accommodation: **Puerto Madryn** and **Península Valdés**, www.madryn.gov.ar; **Chubut province** (northern half of Patagonia), www.chubutur.gov.ar; **Santa Cruz province** (southern half of Patagonia), www.santacruz.gov.ar; **El Chaltén**, www.elchalten.com; **El Calafate**, www.turismo.elcalafate.gov.ar. Also worth visiting is the national parks site, www.parquesnacionales.gov.ar. For information on towns and tourist services, try the site www.interpatagonia.com. For articles on specific places, see www.revistapatagonia.com.ar; for *estancias*, see www.lastfrontiers.com and www.estanciasdesantacruz.com; and for fly fishing, see www.pescaenlapatagonia.com.ar.

Background

Patagonia was inhabited by various groups of indigenous peoples from thousands of years ago until colonization by the Europeans. The region gets its name from early Spanish settlers' first impressions of these native people: big feet (*pata* being the informal word for leg). The first European visitor to the coast of Patagonia was the Portuguese explorer Fernão Magalhães in 1519, who gave his name to the Magellan straits, by which he discovered a safer route through the southern extreme of the continent, going north of the island of Tierra del Fuego, rather than the perilous route south around Cape Horn. The first to traverse Patagonia from south to north was the English sailor, Carder, who survived a shipwreck in 1578 in the Strait of Magellan, walked to the Río de la Plata and arrived in London nine years later.

For several centuries European attempts to settle along the coast were deterred by isolation, lack of food and water, and the harsh climate, as well as understandable resistance from the indigenous peoples. Sadly, the indigenous population was almost wiped out in the bloody war known as the Conquest of the Desert in 1879-1883 (see box, page 135). Before this there had been a European colony at Carmen de Patagones, which shipped salt to Buenos Aires, and the Welsh settlement in the Chubut Valley from 1865. After the Conquest of the Desert, colonization was rapid. Welsh, Scots and English farmers were among the biggest groups of immigrants including sheep farmers from Las Malvinas/Falkland Islands, as well as Chilean sheep farmers from Punta Arenas moving eastwards into Santa Cruz. The discovery of large oil reserves in many areas of southern Patagonia brought wealth to Chubut and Santa Cruz provinces in the 1900s. However, when President Menem privatized the national oil company YPF in the 1990s, much of that wealth immediately diminished. One of the few people to gain from it all was former president and the husband of Argentina's current president, Christina Kirchner, who had been governor of Santa Cruz province while it was rich and influential within the country.

Northern Atlantic Coast and Puerto Madryn

The sight of a mother and baby whale basking in quiet waters just a few metres from your boat is an unforgettably moving sight. Not, perhaps, what you expected to see after travelling for days in the wild unpopulated open plains of Patagonia. But the whole Atlantic coast hosts huge colonies of marine life, and there is no region quite as spectacular as Península Valdés. This wide splay of land stretching into the Atlantic from a narrow isthmus enclosing a gulf of protected water attracts an astonishing array of wildlife which comes to breed here each spring, most famously the southern right whales, who can be seen from September to November. The small breezy town of Puerto Madryn is the best base for exploring the peninsula, though there are estancias on Valdés itself. Just to the south, Trelew is worth a visit for its superb palaeontological museum, and to reach the old Welsh pioneer villages of Gaiman and Dolavon further west. If you're heading south by road, consider stopping off at historic Carmen de Patagones, a quaint Patagonian town. Patagonia's fine estancias start here, with riding and sheep mustering at La Luisa.➔ For listings, see pages 549-557.

Viedma and Carmen de Patagones ➔ *For listings, see pages 549-557. Colour map 5, A5.*

These two towns straddle the broad sweep of the Río Negro, about 250 km south of Bahía Blanca, and while neither has any real tourist attractions, you could stop off here on the way south and find warm hospitality and a couple of decent places to stay. The two towns face each other and share a river, but little else. Capital of Río Negro province, Viedma, on the south bank, was founded as Mercedes de Patagonia in 1779, but was destroyed almost immediately by floods, after which Carmen de Patagones was founded on higher ground on the north bank later that same year. The towers of a handsome church thrust above the town's roofs and the little town prospered for many years as it successfully shipped salt to Buenos Aires. However, in 1827, it was the site of an extraordinary battle and was destroyed. Poor old Viedma was rebuilt, but destroyed again by floods in 1899. Now, it's a rather dull place, employing most of its residents in the administrative centre for the province of Río Negro, and rather less attractive than Patagones. However, Viedma does have a perfect bathing place along the shaded south bank of the river, a delightful spot in summer. Patagones (as it's called by the locals) has more tangible history, with charming streets of 19th century adobe houses near the river, where the tiny ferry takes you across to Viedma, and there's a fabulous little museum. For information on Patagones, see www.patagones.gov.ar.

Viedma ➔ *Phone code 02920. Population 80,000.*

Viedma is quite different in character from Carmen de Patagones: it's the provincial administrative centre, rather than the home of farmers and landowners. The **bus terminal** ① *Av Pte Perón and Guido*, is 15 blocks from the plaza; take a taxi (US$1.50). An attractive *costanera* runs by the river, with large grassy banks shaded by willow trees, and the river water is pleasantly warm in summer and clean. On a calm summer's evening, when groups gather to sip *mate*, the scene resembles Seurat's painting of bathers. There are two plazas, with the cathedral, built by the Salesians (1912), on the west of Plaza Alsina. The former convent next door was the first chapel built by the Salesians (1887) in the area, and is now a cultural centre housing the **Museo del Agua y del Suelo** and the **Museo Cardenal Cagliero**, which has ecclesiastical artefacts. Two blocks east, on the Plaza San Martín, are the French-style **Casa de Gobierno** (1926) and, opposite, the **Museo Gobernador Tello** ① *San*

Martín 262, T2920-425900, daily 0900-1230, 1700-1930 in summer, with fossils, rocks and indigenous *boleadoras*. Most diverting, though, is the **Museo Gardeliano** ① *Colón 498 (1st floor), Mon, Wed, Fri 0930-1130*, a fabulous collection of biographical artefacts of tango singer Carlos Gardel. Along the attractive *costanera*, the **Centro Cultural**, opposite Calle 7 de Marzo, houses a small **Mercado Artesenal** selling beautifully made Mapuche weavings and woodwork. The rather impoverished **tourist office** ① *3 blocks east of Plaza Alsina, T02920-427171, www.viedma.gov.ar, daily 0900-2100*, is also on the *costanera*.

Carmen de Patagones → *Population 18,189.*
This is by far the more dynamic of the two places (which isn't saying much) and although you'll still find this is a very sleepy town, there's a feeling of positive bustle on the main street on weekday mornings. The town centre, just east of the river, lies around the Plaza 7 de Mayo, and just west is the **Iglesia del Carmen**, built by the Salesians in 1880. Take a stroll down the pretty streets winding down to the river to find many early pioneer buildings along the riverside: the **Torre del Fuerte**, tower of the stone fortress built in 1780 against indigenous attacks; the **Casa de la Tahona**, a disued 18th-century flour mill now housing the **Casa de la Cultura**; and another late-colonial building, **La Carlota**, one block east. Nearby there's the fascinating **Museo Histórico Regional 'Emma Nozzi'** ① *JJ Biedma 64, T02920-462729, Mon-Fri 1000-1200, 1700-1900, Sat 1700-1900 only*, giving a great insight into early pioneer life. There are Tehuelche arrowheads, stone *boleadoras*, silver gaucho stirrups and great early photos – one of a baptism by Salesians of a 100-year-old Tehuelche man in a field, next to delicate tea cups. There are great guided tours too. The **Museo de la Prefectura Naval** ① *Mitre 350, T02920-461742, www.prefecturanaval.edu.ar/museo/, Mon-Fri 0800-1300, 1500-1800, Sat-Sun 1000-1200, 1600-1900*, is also worth a look if you're into ships – it's housed in a building dating from 1886 and contains a marine history of the area.

Patagones is linked to Viedma by two bridges and a very small ferry which takes four minutes and leaves every 15 minutes, US$1. There's a helpful and dynamic **tourist office** ① *Bynon 186, T02920-462054*. The town is packed out for the **Fiesta de 7 de Marzo**, which celebrates the victory at the Battle of Patagones. It's great fun but make sure you book accommodation in advance. ►► *For more information, see Festivals and events, page 554.*

Around Viedma and Carmen de Patagones
At **El Cóndor**, 30 km south (also known as La Boca) there is a beautiful beach, with the oldest lighthouse in the country, dating from 1887. Facilities include a hotel, restaurants and shops (open January and February only). There's free camping on a beach 2 km south. There are three buses a day in summer.

This whole stretch of coast is great for shore fishing, with *pejerrey*, variada and even shark among the many other species. **Playa Bonita**, 12 km further south is known as a good fishing spot, and offers more good beaches. Equipment is available in Viedma (see Shopping, page 554). Ask the tourist office for their leaflet *Lobería Punta Bermeja*; 60 km south is a sea lion colony visited by some 2500 sea lions in summer, which you can see at close range (daily bus in summer; but hitching is easy). There's also an impressive visitor centre (with toilets). There's more lovely coastline and a well-established little fishing resort at **Bahía San Blas**, 100 km from Patagones, an area renowned for its shark fishing. There's lots of accommodation here, including **Resort Tiburón** ① *www.resort tiburon.com.ar*. For more information, see www.bahiasanblas.com.

The undoubted highlight of the whole Atlantic Coast in Patagonia is the splendid array of marine wildlife on Península Valdés, best visited from Puerto Madryn. This seaside town has a grand setting on the wide bay of Golfo Nuevo, and is the perfect base for setting off to Valdés, just 70 km east, as there are plenty of hotels and reliable tour operators running excursions to the peninsula, including boat trips to see the whales. During the breeding seasons (broadly speaking, September to December) you can see whales, penguins and seals at close range, or go diving to explore life underwater. It's possible to stay on the peninsula if you hire a car, with several *estancias* right in the middle of the wild nature, and conventional hotels at the small popular resort of **Puerto Pirámides**. Puerto Madryn is a good place to enjoy the sea for a couple of days, with lots of beachfront restaurants selling superb locally caught seafood.

Ins and outs → *Phone code 02965. Population 74,000.*

Getting there **Puerto Madryn Airport** ① *T02965-456774*, is 8 km west of the centre and can be reached by taxi, US$12. There are weekly flights with **LADE** from Buenos Aires to Puerto Madryn's airport, 10 km west. However, there are more frequent flights with **Aerolíneas Argentinas** from Buenos Aires, El Calafate and Ushuaia to Trelew's airport, some 60 km south, with buses to Puerto Madryn that meet all flights. **Transportes Eben Ezer** runs a bus service from the airport to Puerto Madryn's bus terminal for US$4.50; the journey takes one hour. **Mar y Valle** runs a bus every hour from Trelew's bus terminal to Puerto Madryn's bus terminal. The **bus terminal** ① *T02965-451789*, is at Yrigoyen y San Martín (behind the old railway station), and has a café, clean toilets, *locutorio* and a small but helpful tourist office. Walk three blocks down Roque Sáenz Peña to get into town.

Getting around The city centre is easy to get around on foot, with many restaurants and hotels lined up along the seafront at Avenida Roca, and most shops and excursion companies on the streets around 28 de Julio, which runs perpendicular to the sea and past the town's neat little plaza, all contained within four or five blocks.

Best time to visit Much of Península Valdés' wildlife can be enjoyed throughout the year, with sea lions, elephant seals, dolphins and many species of bird permanently resident. The bull elephant seals can be seen fighting for females from September to early November, and at this time too, killer whales can sometimes be sighted off the coast, staying until April. Penguins can be seen from September to March, and the stars of the show, the southern right whales, come to these waters to breed in spring (September to November).

Tourist information Efficient and friendly, the **tourist information centre** ① *Av Roca 223, just off 28 de Julio, T02965-453504, www.madryn.gov.ar, Mon-Fri 0700-2300, Sat-Sun 0800-2300*, is found on the seafront, next to the shopping complex. The staff are extremely well organized and speak English and French. They have leaflets on Península Valdés and accommodation, and can advise on tours.

Background

Puerto Madryn was the site of the first Welsh landing in 1865 and the town is named after the Welsh home of the colonist, Jones Parry. However, it wasn't officially founded until 1889, when the railway was built connecting the town with Trelew to enable the Welsh living in the Chubut Valley to export their produce. The town is a modern, relaxed and friendly place, and hasn't been ruined by its popularity as a tourist resort, with a large workforce occupied by its other main industry: a huge aluminium plant (which you can visit by arrangement through the tourist office). Accommodation is generally of a high standard, but can be pricey. This is one of several tourist centres in Argentina where higher rates apply for foreigners than Argentines for hotel rooms and some entrance fees. It's hopeless to argue.

Sights

You're most likely to be visiting the town to take an excursion to Península Valdés (see opposite), and it's certainly worth spending at least a day enjoying the wildlife there. During the right season, you can also spot whales directly from the coast at the long beach of **Playa El Doradillo**, 16 km northeast, along the *ripio* road closest to the coast.

In the town itself, the real pleasure is the sea, and it's a pleasant first day's stroll along the long stretch of beach to **El Indio**, a statue on the road at the eastern end of the bay, marking the gratitude of the Welsh to the native Tehuelche people whose shared expertise ensured their survival. As the road curves up the cliff here, there's the splendid **EcoCentro** ① *Julio Verne 3784, T02965-457470, www.ecocentro.org.ar, daily 1500-1800 (Tue usually closed in winter and is open longer in summer, but check with tourist office as times change), US$7*, an inspired interactive sea-life information centre that combines an art gallery, café, and fabulous reading room with comfy sofas at the top of a turret. The whole place has fantastic views of the bay. Take bus No 2 from 25 de Mayo and Belgrano, and walk the five minutes from the university.

Just a little closer to town, perched on the cliff, is the tiny **Centro de Exposición de Punta Cuevas** ① *daily www.puntacuevas. org.ar, 1700-2100, US$2.50*, of interest if

Puerto Madryn

To Playa El Doradillo & Puerto Pirámides

III Museo de Ciencias Naturales y Oceanográfico

La Anónima Supermarket

Norte Supermarket

Portal de Madryn

Plaza San Martín

Banco Nación

Argentina Visión

To ② ① ② ⑬, El Indio, EcoCentro, Centro de Exposición de Punta Cuevas & Punta Loma Reserve

200 metres
200 yards

Sleeping 🛏
ACA Camping 2
Australis Yene Hue 9
Bahía Nueva 1
Casa de Pueblo 15
El Gualicho 3
El Retorno 8
Gran Palace 14
Hostería Torremolinos 4
La Tosca 13
Marina 5
Muelle Viejo 6
Patagonia 12
Península Valdés 7
Tolosa 10

Eating 🍴
Caccaros 3
Centro de Difusión de la Pesca Artesanal 2
De Miga 4
La Casona del Golfo 5
Lizard Café 8
Los Colonos 7
Mitos 10
Nativo Sur 5
Plácido 11
Taska Beltza 12
Vernardino 13

Bars & clubs 🍸
La Frontera 6
Margarita 9
Mr Jones 14

you're tracing the history of the Welsh in Patagonia. It's little more than a couple of rooms of relics near the caves and basic huts on the cliffs where the settlers first lived, but enthusiastic guides make the visit worthwhile. A more conventional museum, with displays on local flora and fauna, is the **Museo de Ciencias Naturales y Oceanográfico** ① *Domecq García y J Menéndez, T02965-451139, Mon-Fri 0900-1200, 1500-1900, Sat 1430-1900, US$2*, informative and worth a visit.

Around Puerto Madryn

Península Valdés is the main attraction, with whale-spotting boat trips leaving from Puerto Pirámides, on the southern end of the peninsula. There's more marine life on the coastline – and both are included in one organized tour from Puerto Madryn. There are also sea lions at the **Punta Loma Reserve** ① *US$8, child US$3*, 15 km southeast of Puerto Madryn, open during daylight hours and best visited at low tide in December and January. Access is via the coastal road from town and, like the road to the north, makes a great bike ride; allow 1½ hours to get there. Puerto Madryn is also Patagonia's **diving** capital, with dives to see wildlife and many off-shore wrecked ships, together with all kinds of courses from beginners' dives to the week-long PADI course on offer from tour operators, such as **Puerto Madryn Buceo**. You can also hire mountain bikes and windsurfing boards here, from many places along the beachfront. ▸▸ *For more information, see Activities and tours, page 555.*

There are several *estancias* on the peninsula which allow you to really appreciate the space and natural beauty of the land, and give you much more access to some of the most beautiful places, with great wildlife to observe. Ask the tourist office for their leaflet and advice. Day trips can also be arranged, which might include wildlife trips with an *asado*, and perhaps horse riding. **Estancia Rincón Chico** ① *T02965-471733, www.rinconchico.com.ar*, and **Estancia La Elvira** ① *T02965-474248, www.laelvira.com*, are both particularly recommended.

Península Valdés → *For listings, see pages 549-557.*

Whatever time of year you visit Península Valdés you'll find a wonderful array of marine life, birds and a profusion of Patagonian wildlife such as guanacos, rheas, Patagonian hares and armadillos. But in spring (September-November), this treeless splay of land is host to a quite spectacular numbers of whales, penguins and seals, who come to breed in the sheltered waters of the gulf south of the narrow isthmus Ameghino, and on beaches at the foot of the peninsula's chalky cliffs. The land is almost flat, though greener than much of Patagonia, and at the heart of the peninsula are large salt flats, one of which, **Salina Grande**, is 42 m below sea level. The peninsula is privately owned – many of its *estancias* offering comfortable and wonderfully remote places to stay in the middle of the wild beauty – but it is also a nature reserve and was declared a World Heritage Site by UNESCO in 1999. The beach along the entire coast is out of bounds and this is strictly enforced. The main tourist centre for accommodation and whale trips is **Puerto Pirámides**, on the southern side of the isthmus.

Ins and outs

Getting there You need a 4WD to reach Península Valdés. You can get as far as Puerto Pirámides by local bus which leaves the bus station in Puerto Madryn three times a week (daily in November to March), and it costs US$3 each way.

Getting around Península Valdés can most easily be visited by taking one of the many well-organized full-day excursions (see Tour operators, page 555) but if you'd rather see the peninsula independently, you can hire a car relatively inexpensively for a group of four, and then take just the boat trip to see the whales (September to November) from Puerto Pirámides. Note that distances are long on the peninsula, and roads beyond Puerto Pirámides are *ripio*, so take your time – hire companies charge a heavy excess if you damage the car. A cheaper option is the daily bus to Puerto Pirámides with 28 de Julio, leaving the terminal daily at 0930, returning at 1900, 1½ hrs, US$3 each way. This would only allow you to see the whales though, since there is no public transport to other areas of the peninsula. The island is almost entirely undeveloped, and the only tourist centre is at Puerto Pirámides, where there's a few good hotels, a few hostels, places to camp and a handful of restaurants. Otherwise, the most comfortable accommodation is in one of several *estancias* on the island, recommended for a longer stay as it offers closer contact with nature and the incredible wildlife.

Tour operators in Puerto Madryn offer full-day trips that usually include a whale-watching boat trip, which departs from Puerto Pirámides (see below), together with a stop or two on the eastern coastline to see sea lions, penguins and other wildlife at close hand. Minibus travel, the boat trip and transfers to your hotel are included, but not lunch or entrance to the peninsula.

Tourist information About 45 km northeast of Puerto Madryn is the entrance to the reserve, where you buy the ticket for visiting all the sites within the peninsula. Entry costs for non-Argentines are US$12 (US$7 for children). Twenty kilometres beyond, on the isthmus, there's an interesting **interpretation centre** with stuffed examples of the local fauna, many fossils and a wonderful whale skeleton, which makes a great complement to seeing the real thing gracefully soaring through the water. Ask for the informative bilingual leaflet on southern right whales.

Wildlife → *The following are the main marine wildlife colonies.*
Isla de los Pájaros, is in the Golfo San José, 5 km from the interpretation centre. Its seabirds can only be viewed through fixed telescopes (at 400 m distance). Only recognized ornithologists can get permission to visit. Between September and April you can spot wading birds, herons, cormorants and terns. **Caleta Valdés**, 45 km south of Punta Norte in the middle of the eastern shore, has huge colonies of elephant seals which can be seen at close quarters. In the breeding season, from September to October, you'll see the rather unappealing blubbery masses of bull seals hauling themselves up the beach to make advances to one of the many females in their harem. During the first half of August the bull seals arrive to claim their territory, and can be seen at low tide engaging in bloody battles over the females. At **Punta Cantor**, just south of here, you'll find a good café and clean toilets. There are also three marked walks, ranging from 45 minutes to two hours. **Estancia La Elvira** is a short distance inland from here, and is clearly signposted.

Punta Delgada, at the southeastern end of the peninsula, 110 km from the entrance, is where elephant seals and sea lions can be seen from the high cliffs in such large numbers that they seem to stretch out like a velvety bronze tide line on the beautiful beach below. It's mesmerizing to watch as the young frolic in the shallow water, and the bulls lever themselves around the females. There's a hotel nearby, **Faro Punta Delgada** (see Sleeping, page 550), which is a good base for exploring this beautiful area further.

Punta Norte, at the northern end of the peninsula, 97 km from the entrance, is not often visited by the excursion companies, but it has colonies of elephant seals and sea lions. Killer whales (orca) have also been seen here, feeding on sea lion pups at low tide in March and April. **Estancia San Lorenzo** is nearby.

Puerto Pirámides → *Colour map 5, B5. Population 429.*

Puerto Pirámides, 107 km east of Puerto Madryn, is the centre for visits to the peninsula, and whale-watching boat trips leave from its broad sandy beach. Every year, between June and December, 400 to 500 southern right whales migrate to the Golfo Nuevo to mate and give birth. It is without doubt one of the best places in the world to watch these beautiful animals, and in many places these whales come within just a few metres of the coast. From Puerto Pirámides, boat trips take you gently close to basking whales, and if you're lucky, you may find yourself incredibly close to a mother and baby. Sailings are controlled by the Prefectura (Naval Police), according to weather and sea conditions (if you're very prone to sea sickness, think twice before setting off on a windy day). There's one four-star hotel, right by the beach where boat trips begin, and plenty of other places to stay strung out along the road from the beach in this touristy little place, plus a campsite, and a good range of places to eat. All are packed out in January and February. There is a small **tourist office** ① *T02965-495084, www.puertopiramides.gov.ar*, on the edge of Puerto Pirámides, offering useful information for hikes and driving tours.

Welsh colonies in the Chubut Valley → *For listings, see pages 549-557.*

The Río Chubut is one of the most important rivers in Patagonia, flowing a massive 820 km from the eastern foothills of the Andes into the Atlantic at Bahía Engaño. It's thanks to the Río Chubut that the Welsh pioneers came to this part of the world in 1865, and their irrigation of the arid land around it enabled them to survive and prosper. You can trace their history west along the valley from the pleasant airy town of Trelew to the quiet little village of Gaiman, with a wonderful museum, and *casas de té* (cafés serving traditional Welsh afternoon tea). Further west, past little brick chapels sitting amidst lush green fields, is the quieter settlement of Dolavon, with an old brick chapel. And if you're keen to investigate further into the past, there's a marvellous museum full of dinosaurs in Trelew, and some ancient fossils in the Parque Palaeontológico Bryn-Gwyn near Gaiman. From Trelew you could visit South America's largest single colony of Magellanic penguins on the coast at Punta Tombo.

Trelew → *Colour map 5, B5. Phone code 02965. Population 90,000*

Some 70 km south of Puerto Madryn, Trelew is the largest town in the Chubut Valley. Founded in 1884, it was named in honour of Lewis Jones, an early settler, and the Welsh colonization is still evident in a few remaining chapels in the town's modern centre. It's a cheerful place with a quietly busy street life, certainly more appealing than the industrial town of Rawson, 20 km east on the coast. Trelew boasts a splendid paleontological museum, a great tourist office and a couple of fabulous cafés.

Ins and outs There are flights from Buenos Aires, El Calafate and Ushuaia to Trelew's airport, 5 km north of centre. A taxi costs US$5, and local buses to Puerto Madryn will stop at the airport entrance if asked. The **bus terminal** ① *T02965-428021*, is northeast of the centre and taxis charge about US$3. Alternatively, it's a 10-minute walk from the main plaza, where you'll find the very helpful **tourist office** ① *Mitre 387, T02965-420139, www.trelew.gov.ar, Mon-Fri 0800-2000, Sat-Sun 0900-2100*. They'll give you an excellent map, directing you to the town's older buildings.

Sights There's the lovely shady **Plaza Independencia** in the town centre, packed with mature trees, and hosting a small handicraft market at weekends. Nearby is the **Capilla Tabernacle**, on Belgrano between San Martín and 25 de Mayo, a red-brick Welsh chapel dating from 1889. Heading east, rather more impressive is the **Salon San David**, a Welsh meeting hall first used for the Eisteddfod of 1913, and now sadly, used for bingo. On the road to Rawson, 3 km south, you'll find one of the oldest standing Welsh chapels, **Capilla Moriah**. Built in 1880, it has a simple interior and a cemetery with the graves of many original settlers, including the first white woman born in the Welsh colony.

Back in Trelew itself, not the oldest but quite the most wonderful building is the 1920s **Hotel Touring Club** ① *Fontana 240, www.touringpatagonia.com.ar*. This was the town's grandest hotel in its heyday. Politicians and travellers met in its glorious high-ceilinged mirrored bar, now full of old photographs and relics. You can eat lunch here and there's simple accommodation available; you should also ask the friendly owner if you can see the elegant 1920s meeting room at the back: almost perfectly preserved.

The town's best museum – and indeed one of the finest in Argentina – is the **Museo Paleontológico Egidio Feruglio** ① *Fontana 140, T02965-420012, www.mef.org.ar, daily 0900-2000 in spring and summer, Mon-Fri 1000-1800, Sat and Sun 0900-2000 in autumn and winter, US$8, full disabled access, guides for the blind*. Imaginatively designed and beautifully presented, the museum traces the origins of life through the geological ages, displaying dynamically poised dinosaur skeletons, with plentiful information in Spanish. Tours are free, and are available in English, German and Italian. There's also a reasonably cheap café and a shop. Highly recommended and great for kids. Also ask about the **Parque Paleontológico Bryn-Gwyn** ① *8 km from Gaiman T02965-420012, for visits consult www.mef.org.ar, Tue-Fri 1000-1700, US$3, taxi from Gaiman US$4.50*, with fossil remains from over the last 40 million years.

The **Museo Regional Pueblo de Luis** ① *Fontana and Lewis Jones 9100, T02965-424062, Mon-Fri 0800-2000, Sat-Sun 1700-2000, US$2*, is appropriately housed in the old railway station, built in 1889, since Lewis Jones founded the town and started the railways that exported Welsh produce so successfully. It has interesting displays on indigenous societies, on failed Spanish attempts at settlement, and on Welsh colonization. Next to the tourist office is the wonderful new **Museo Artes Visuales** ① *Mon-Fri 0800-2000, Sat-Sun 1400-2000, free*, the visual arts museum, located in an attractive wooden building. Recommended.

Around Trelew

The two most popular excursions are to see the penguin colony at **Punta Tombo**, 125 km south, and the Welsh valley towns of **Gaiman** and (less so) **Dolavon**. The **Embalse Florentino Ameghino**, 120 km west, however is not so interesting. There is a lovely rock and sand beach at **Playa Isla Escondida**, 70 km south, with secluded camping but no facilities.

Take a tour or drive, if you have a car, to the **Reserva Natural Punta Tombo** ① *park entrance US$10, US$5 for children*. Tours from Trelew and Puerto Madryn, US$50, allow 45 minutes at the site, where there's a café and toilets, and usually include a stop in the Welsh town of Gaiman. A paved access leaves Route Nacional 3, 60 km south of Trelew, and takes you to Route 1, a *ripio* road between Trelew and Camarones (closed late March to September). This reserve is the largest breeding ground for Magallenic penguins in Patagonia, and the largest single penguin colony on the South American continent. This nature reserve is best visited from September to March, when huge numbers of Magallenic penguins come here to breed. Chicks can be seen from mid-November, and

Welsh Patagonia

Among the tales of early pioneers to Argentina, the story of Welsh emigration, in search of religious freedom, is one of the most impressive. The first 165 settlers arrived in Patagonia in July 1865. Landing on the bay where Puerto Madryn now stands, they went south in search of drinking water to the valley of the Chubut river, where they found cultivatable land and settled.

The settlement was partly inspired by Michael D Jones, a non-conformist minister whose aim was to create a 'little Wales beyond Wales', far from the intruding influence of the English restrictions on Welsh religious beliefs. He provided much of the early finance and took particular care to recruit people with useful skills, such as farmers and craftsmen, recruiting settlers through the Welsh language press and through the chapels. Between 1865 and 1915, the colony was reinforced by another 3000 settlers from Wales. The early years brought persistent drought, and the Welsh only survived through creating a network of irrigation channels. Early settlers were allocated 100 ha of land,

and when, by 1885, all irrigable land had been allocated, the settlement expanded westwards along the valley to the town of Trevelin in the foothills of the Andes.

The Welsh colony was tremendously successful, partly due to the creation of their own cooperative society, which sold their excellent produce and bought necessities in Buenos Aires. Early settlers were organized into chapel-based communities of 200 to 300 people, which were largely self-governing, and organized social and cultural activities. The colony thrived after 1880, producing wheat from the arid Chubut Valley which won prizes all over the world. However, the depression of the 1930s drove wheat prices down, and poor management by the Argentine government resulted in the downfall of the Welsh wheat business. Many of the Welsh stayed, however, and most of the owners of Gaiman's extraordinary Welsh tea rooms are indeed descendants of the original settlers. The Welsh language is kept alive in both Gaiman and Trevelin, and Gaiman's festival of the arts – Eisteddfod – is held every October.

they waddle to the water in January or February. It's fascinating to see these creatures up close, but noisy colonies of tourists dominate the place in the morning; it's quieter in the afternoon. You'll see guanacos, hares and rheas on the way.

Gaiman → *Colour map 5, B4. Phone code 02965. Population 45,750.*

The quaint village of Gaiman is west of Trelew, in the floodplain of the Río Chubut, and was made beautifully green and fertile thanks to careful irrigation of these lands by Welsh settlers. After travelling for a few days (or even hours) on the arid Patagonian steppe, it will strike you as a lush green oasis, testimony to the tireless hard work of those hardy Welsh emigrants. Gaiman is the first village you come to on Route 25, which heads past Dolavon before continuing through attractive scenery to Esquel in the Andes, and the other Welsh colony of Trevelin. On the way, you'll find old Welsh chapels tucked away amongst the poplars in this green valley. Gaiman is a pretty little place with old brick houses, which retains the Welsh pioneer feel despite the constant influx of tourists, and it hosts the annual **Eisteddfod** (Welsh Festival of Arts) in October. Around its pretty plaza are several tea rooms, many of them run by descendants of the original pioneers, serving delicious and 'traditional' Welsh teas and cakes (expect to pay about US$11). Before you fill up on all that though, spare a thought for the spartan lives of those idealistic pioneers. There's the wonderful tiny **Museo Histórico Regional Galés** ① *Sarmiento and 28 de Julio, T02965-491007, Tue-Sun 1500-1900, US$1*, with an impressive collection of Welsh artefacts, objects and photographs, all evocative and moving testimony to extraordinary lives in harsh conditions. This is a great resource if you're looking for books on the subject or trying to trace your emigrant relatives.

Many older buildings remain, among them the low stone first house, **Primera Casa** (1874) ① *corner of main street, Av Tello y Evans, daily 1400-1900, US$1*; the **old railway station** (1909), which now houses the regional museum (see above); the old hotel (1899), at Tello and 9 de Julio; and the **Ty Nain tea room** (1890), on the Plaza at Yrigoyen 283 (see below). On the south side of the river there are two old chapels: cross the bridge, and then take the first right to find the pretty **Capilla Bethel** (1913) and the **Capilla Vieja**.

A far more recent monument to human energy and inspiration is the extraordinary creation **El Desafío** ① *Brown 52, 2 blocks west of plaza, daily until 1800, US$2*, an imaginative sculptural world, made entirely from rubbish by the eccentric Joaquín Alonso. Painted plastic bottles, cans and wire form pergolas and dinosaurs are sprinkled liberally with plaques bearing words of wisdom and witty comments. Beginning to fade now, but still good fun. The **tourist office** ① *Av Belgrano S/N, T02965-491571, www.gaiman.gov.ar, Mon-Sat 0900-2000, Sun 1100-1800*, is on the plaza.

Some 8 km south of town, there are fossil beds dating back 40 million years at the **Parque Paleontológico Bryn Gwyn** ① *T02965-420012, for visits consult www.mef.org.ar, Tue-Fri 1000-1700, US$3, taxi from Gaiman US$4*. This is a mind-boggling expanse of time brought to life by a good guided tour. It takes two hours to do the circuit, with fossils to see, as well as a visitor centre where you can try some fieldwork in palaeontology.

Dolavon → *Colour map 5, B4. Phone code 02965. Population 2700.*

Founded in 1919, Dolavon is the most westerly Welsh settlement in the valley, and not quite as inviting as Gaiman, though its quiet streets are rather atmospheric, and on a short stroll you can find a few buildings reminiscent of the Welsh past. The main street, Avenida Roca, runs parallel to the irrigation canal built by the settlers, where willow trees now trail into the swiftly flowing water, and there's a Welsh chapel, **Capilla Carmel**, at its quieter end. The old **flourmill** ① *to arrange a visit, call T02965-492290, Mon-Sun 1100-1900, US$3.50*, at Maipú and Roca dates from 1927 and can be visited. There's **Autoservicio Belgrano** at the far end of San Martín for food supplies, but there is only one tea room, **El Molienda** ① *Maipú 61, T0265-492290, US$10*, and nowhere really to stay, though there's a municipal campsite two blocks north of the river which is free and has good facilities.

Welsh chapels

If you're in your own transport, it's worth driving on from Dolavon back towards Gaiman via the neat squared fields in this beautiful irrigated valley, where you'll see more Welsh chapels tucked away among poplar trees and silver birches. Follow the main road that leads south through Dolavon, and then turn left and then the next right, signposted to Iglesia Anglicana. The **San David Chapel** (1917) is a beautifully preserved brick construction, with an elegant bell tower, and sturdy oak-studded door, in a quiet spot surrounded by birches. Further on you'll cross the raised irrigation canals the Welsh built, next to them small orchards of apple trees, with tidy fields bordered by *álamo* trees.

For Sleeping and Eating price codes and other relevant information, see Essentials pages 30-36.

● **Sleeping**

See www.estanciasdesantacruz.com for information on *estancias*.

Viedma and Carmen de Patagones *p539*

The best places to stay are all in Viedma.
A-B Austral, 25 de Mayo y Villarino, T02920-422615, www.hoteles-austral.com.ar. Along the *costanera*, this ugly hotel has well-equipped, but old-fashioned rooms. Wi-Fi available.
B Nijar, Mitre 490, T02920-422833, www.hotel nijar.com. Very comfortable, smart modern rooms, a quiet relaxed atmosphere, and good attentive service. The best of the 2 decent, modern mid-range hotels. Recommended.
C Peumayén, Buenos Aires 334, T02920-425222, www.hotelpeumayen.com.ar. An old-fashioned, friendly place on the plaza.

Camping

At the sea lion colony, **La Lobería**, T02920-428883, and **Trenitos**, T02920-497098, both have good facilities and charge US$4 per person.
Municipal Campsite near the river, T02920-421341. Good site, US$2 per person, offers all facilities including hot showers.

Puerto Madryn *p541, map p542*

For more hotels, see www.madryn.gove.ar/turismo. There is a huge range of hotels, but all are heavily booked ahead of time in summer.
LL-L Australis Yene Hue Hotel and Spa, Roca 33, T2965-471214, www.australiset.com.ar. New luxury hotel on the beachfront with a small spa, clean modern rooms, and nice buffet breakfast. Ask for a room with a view.
AL Península Valdés, Av Roca 155, T02965-471292, www.hotelpeninsula.com.ar. A good place on the seafront, great views from many of its spacious rooms. Spa, sauna and gym.

International prices here, plus 30% extra for bookings made from outside Argentina.
A Bahía Nueva, Av Roca 67, T02965-451677, www.bahianueva.com.ar. One of the best seafront hotels, with a welcoming reception area, and high standards in all details. Rooms are on the small side, but comfortable, breakfasts are generous, and staff are helpful and professional. Cheaper in low season, but be aware that this hotel has higher prices for non-Argentines. Recommended.
A-B Marina, Av Roca 7, T/F02965-454915, teokou@infovia.com.ar. Great little seafront place with well-equipped apartments for up to 5 people. Welcoming owners will also arrange excursions. Price quoted for 5. Worth booking ahead.
B Casa de Pueblo, Av Roca 475, T02965-472500, www.madryncasadepueblo.com.ar. Once apparently the first brothel in town, now a charmingly renovated seafront chalet with functional rooms and a homely atmosphere. Good value.
B Muelle Viejo, H Yrigoyen 38, T02965-471284, www.muelleviejo.com. Ask for the stylish, comfortable modernized rooms in this funny old place. Excellent value, large rooms sleep 4 and there are *parrilla* and kitchen facilities if you want to cook.
B Patagonia Hotel and Apart Hotel, Albarracin 45, T02965-452103, www.patagoniaaparthotel.com. Modern and spacious rooms and apartments are of a high standard and are a good option if you want an apartment.
B Tolosa, Roque Sáenz Peña 253, T02965-471850, www.hoteltolosa.com.ar. An extremely comfortable modern place with flawless personal service and great breakfasts. Note that the superior rooms are much more spacious and have full wheelchair access. Bookings made from outside Argentina will be international tourist prices. Free use of bicycles and internet. Highly recommended.
B-C Hostería Torremolinos, Marcos A Zar 64, T02965-453215. Nice modern place

with 7 simple, well decorated rooms with large beds, bathrooms and cable TV.
D Gran Palace Hotel, 28 de Julio 390, T02965-471009. Attractive entrance to this central and economical place, but rooms are a bit squashed and rather dark, thanks to the mahogany-effect wallpaper. But they're clean and have bathroom and TV, good value.

Hostels
E-F pp El Gualicho, Marcos A Zar 480, T02965-454163, www.elgualichohostel. com.ar. By far the best budget place in Puerto Madryn, this hostel is beautifully designed. It is run by a friendly and enthusiastic owner, and they offer free pick-up from the bus terminal. Breakfast is included and there's a garden, attractive double rooms and bikes for hire – book ahead. Wi-Fi and discounts for HI members. Highly recommended.
E-F El Retorno, Bartolomé Mitre 798, T02965-456044, www.elretornohostel.com.ar. Only 3 blocks to the beach, this hostel is clean and friendly. They have an endless supply of hot water, a cosy common area and they rent bikes. Double rooms (**C**) available.
E-F La Tosca, Sarmiento 437, T02965-456 133, www.latoscahostel.com. Great mattresses and friendly staff. Dorm rooms all have private bathrooms, and if you call them from the bus station, they'll pick you up for free. Centrally located. Doubles are small but cosy (**C**).

Camping
ACA, Blvd Brown, 4 km south of town centre (at Punta Cuevas), T02965-452952, open Sep-Apr. Hot showers, café, shop, no kitchen facilities but shady trees and it's close to the sea. Family-friendly.

Península Valdés *p543*
LL Las Restingas, Primera Bajada al mar, T02965-495101, www.lasrestingas.com. The top hotel in town has an exclusive location on the beach, and 8 of its 12 suites have their own balcony for splendid sea views. All very comfortable, with minimalist decoration, and there's a small restaurant

serving a sophisticated selection of regional food. The hotel is a member of the excellent NA Town & Country Hotels group, www.new age-hotels.com. Great deals in low season.
AL-A Cabañas en el Mar, Av de las Ballenas s/n, T02965-495049, www.piramides.net. 5 comfortable, well-equipped, 2- to 6-bed *cabañas*. Sea view.
AL-A The Paradise, at the far end of the main street, T02965-495030, www.hosteria paradise.com.ar. Huge, very comfortable, light rooms, smart bathrooms, and splendid suites with jacuzzis. Also a fine restaurant serving delicious squid, among other seafood.
AL-A del Nomade Eco Lodge, Av de las Ballenas s/n, T02965-495044, www.eco hosteria.com.ar. Wonderful eco-hotel that provides solar-heated water and heating in their 8 lovely rooms. There is a comfortable common area and the breakfasts are delicious. Recycled water in the toilets and in the garden. Charming hosts Lala and Laura.
B La Nube del Angel, Segunda Baja, T02965-495070, located on a quiet street, 5 mins' walk from the beach. Open all year. Small *cabañas* built for 2-6 people, lovely owners.
B Motel ACA, Av de las Ballenas 25, T02965-495004, aca@piramides.net. Slightly old fashioned, but still modern in feel, this has welcoming rooms and is handy for the beach. Also has a good seafood restaurant, and you might even spot whales from the terrace. Jan and Feb are reserved for ACA members only.

Estancias
For more *estancias* in Patagonia, see www.interpatagonia.com/estancias.
LL Estancia La Ernestina, near Punta Norte, T02965-458061, T02965-1566 3713, www.laernestina.com. The very welcoming Familia Copello offers comfortable accommodation in simple rooms, with all meals and excursions included. Open from mid-Sep to mid-Apr. No credit cards accepted.
LL-L Faro Punta Delgada, next to the Punta Delgada's lighthouse, T02965-458444, www.puntadelgada.com. Comfortable accommodation, offering ½ and full board,

excellent food, horse riding and guided walks. Some activities are included in the basic rate. Credit cards not accepted. Recommended.
L Rincón Chico, office in Puerto Madryn: Brown 1783, T02965-471733, www.rincon chico.com. A working sheep farm close to Punta Delgada, still owned by the original pioneer family who built it. Luxurious accommodation in 8 lovely rooms opening onto an attractive veranda. Beautifully situated, and with well-organized circuits for walking and bike riding. Half and full board also available. Recommended.
AL Estancia La Elvira, T02965-1569 8709, office in Puerto Madryn: Av Yrigoyen 257, T02965-474248, www.laelvira.com. Comfortable accommodation in an outstanding location on Caleta Valdés, near Punta Cantor. Traditional Patagonian dishes served.

Camping
Camping Municipal, near the beach, T02965-495084. Has a shop but hot showers in evening only. It's a bit scruffy and very busy, so get there early to secure a place; do not camp on the beach, as people have been swept away by the incoming tide.

Trelew p545
Trelew is not a touristy town, and so there's limited choice of accommodation, particularly for low budgets, though there is a good campsite. The great tourist office will be able to help.
A Galicia, 9 de Julio 214, T02965-433802, www.hotelgalicia.com.ar. The smallish rooms don't quite live up to the grand entrance, but are extremely comfortable and well decorated, and the staff are friendly. Excellent value (breakfast included) and recommended.
A Libertador, Rivadavia 31, T02965-420220, www.hotellibertadortw.com. Breakfast is included in this large modern place, which is highly recommended for its friendly service and comfortable rooms. The newer, more spacious rooms are slightly pricier but worth it. Reserve ahead.

A Rayentray, San Martín y Belgrano, T02965-434702, www.cadenarayentray.com.ar. Huge, modernized 1960s place with comfortable rooms and professional staff – the spacious 'superior' rooms are worth the extra, with sitting area and good bathrooms, and splendid 1970s leather panelling. Swimming pool on top floor is free for guests, but gym, sunbed and sauna cost extra.
C Rivadavia, Rivadavia 55, T02965-434472, hotelriv@infovia.com.ar. Simple, comfortable rooms with TV and bath, and some even cheaper, rather spartan rooms without. Good and well located. Breakfast extra.
C Touring Club, Fontana 240, T02965-433 997, www.touringpatagonia.com.ar. After the gorgeous faded style of the bar, the vast staircase and light corridors, the rooms here are on the plain side, but they're quiet and spacious with big bathrooms. Breakfast is extra, but this hotel is good value and the bar is marvellous.

Camping
Camping Patagonia, R7 and Rawson, 11 km from town, T02965-1540 6907, leave Trelew on R7 in the direction of Rawson, pass a roundabout, the road bends sharply to the right, take right fork, a *ripio* road, and the campsite is after 3 blocks on the right. Pretty site with *parrilla*, hot showers, football pitch and *proveduría* (food shop). US$5 per person.

Gaiman p547
B Posada Los Mimbres, Chacra 211, 6 km west of Gaiman, T02965-491299, www.posada losmimbres.com.ar. A farmstead in idyllic surroundings with just a few rooms in the charming old house or in a modern one. Gorgeous meals. Wonderful place to unwind.
C Casa de Té Ty Gwyn, 9 de Julio 147, T02965-491009, tygwyn@cpsarg.com. The next best option in town are these smart rooms above the tea house.
C Hostería Ty'r Haul, Sarmiento 121, T02965-491880, www.hosteriatyrhaul.com.ar. Centrally located in a listed historical building, rooms are comfortable and well lit. Recommended.

C Plas Y Coed, Irigoyen 320, T02965-491133, www.plasycoed.com.ar. A lovely place run by the charming Marta Rees, descended from a Welsh tea pioneer family. Double and twin rooms with bath and TV. Breakfast included.
C Unelem, Av Tello and 9 de Julio, T02965-491663, www.unelem.com. Most expensive in this price bracket, but very comfortable. This is a restored hotel from 1867, the restaurant serves Welsh cuisine.

Camping

Los Doce Nogales, south of the river at Chacra 202, close to **Ty Te Caerdydd** tea room, T02965-1551 8030. An attractive site, with showers.

❼ Eating

Viedma and Carmen de Patagones p539

❢❢❢ La Balsa, on the river at Colón and Villarino. By far the best restaurant, inexpensive with a pleasant atmosphere. Delicious seafood, and a bottle of superb Río Negro wine, Humberto Canale Merlot, are highly recommended.
❢❢ Parrilla Libre, Buenos Aires and Colón. Well-priced *tenedor libre* steaks in a cheerful atmosphere.
❢ Camilla's Café, Saavedra and Buenos Aires. A smart and relaxing place for coffee and to watch Viedma trundle by on its errands.

Puerto Madryn p541, map p542

One of the unmissable pleasures of Puerto Madryn is its great seafood. While you're here, try at least one plate of *arroz con mariscos* (rice with a whole selection of squid, prawns, mussels and clams). Most restaurants are mid-range and charge around the same price, but differ widely in quality. Without doubt, the best place to eat in town is the wonderful Taska Beltza (see below), though there's plenty of choice along the coast road.
❢❢❢ Caccaros, Av Roca 385, T02965-453767. Stylish, simple place on seafront with relaxing

atmosphere, good-value seafood menu and cheap lunch menu.
❢❢❢ Plácido, Av Roca 506, T02965-455991, www.placido.com.ar. For a special dinner or a romantic place to eat, overlooking the sea, and beautifully designed, with stylish tables and intimate lighting. Has excellent service and a good range of seafood, with cheaper pasta dishes and lots of options for vegetarians.
❢❢❢ Taska Beltza, 9 de Julio 345, T02965-1566 8085. Open Tue-Sun. Chef and owner 'El Negro' cooks superb seafood with great passion and a Basque influence. Even if you're on a budget, his *arroz con mariscos* is cheap and superb. Highly recommended. Book ahead.
❢❢ Centro de Difusión de la Pesca Artesanal, Brown, 7th roundabout, T02965-1553 8085. Grandly named, but with no sign outside, this is a basic *cantina* on the coast road east, opposite the municipal campsite, where the fishermen's families cook delicious meals with their catch. Hugely popular with locals, so come early. Far more authentic than **El Náutico**.
❢❢ Los Colonos, Av Roca y A Storni, T02965-458486. You can't miss this place as it's partly built into the wooden hull of a boat. A big place but with a cosy atmosphere, the speciality is *parrilla*, very reasonably priced, and there's seafood and pasta too. Great for families with a big soft-play area for kids.
❢❢ Nativo Sur, Blvd Brown 2000, T02965-457 403. Smarter than its more popular sister restaurant Yoaquina, Nativo Sur is a good place for a quiet dinner on the beachfront, with an imaginative menu of local Patagonian produce and seafood.
❢❢ Vernardino, Blvd Brown 860, T02965-474 289, www.vernardinoclubdemar.com.ar. One of the nicest restaurants on the beach, serving great seafood and pasta. Good choice for lunch.
❢ La Casona del Golfo, Av Roca 349, T02965-455027. Good value *tenedor libre* with lots of choices including good *parrilla* and seafood, and *helados libre* – as much ice cream as you can eat. Great for families, kids pay ½-price.

Cafés

De Miga, 9 de Julio 160, T02965-475620. Cosy local favourite with affordably priced sandwiches and pizzas.

Kebom, Av Roca 542, T02965-474094. Popular ice cream place with a big soft-play area for kids.

Lizard Café, Av Roca and Av Gales, T02965-455306. Lively, funky place with friendly people. Good for plentiful pizzas or for late-night drinks on the seafront.

Mitos, 28 de Julio 80, T02965-474980. Friendly and welcoming stylish café with good atmosphere, and pictures of tango stars and jazz musicians on the walls. Great for breakfast or lunch and open until the early hours. Recommended.

Península Valdés p543

There are many restaurants on the main street and reasonably priced ones at Punta Norte, Punta Cantor and the Faro in Punta Delgada. These recommendations are on the beach:

₸₸₸ **Las Restingas**, Primera Bajada on the beach, T02965-495101. Perfect for a romantic dinner, sea views and tranquillity. An imaginative menu combines quality local produce with a touch of sophistication.

₸₸ **The Paradise**, Av De los Bellenas y Segunda Bajada, T02965-495030. Just off the beach, good atmosphere and great seafood. Also offers lamb and a few vegetarian choices.

₸₸ **Quimey Quipan**, Primera Bajada opposite Las Restingas, T02965-1569 3100. By the beach and next to *Tito Bottazzi*, this family-run place specializes in delicious seafood with rice and has a cheap set menu. Always open for lunch, ring to reserve for dinner. Recommended.

₸ **Margarita Resto Bar**, Av de los Bellenas, T02965-1520 2659, Fri-Sat 2100-0500, Sun-Thu 2100-0230. Midway along the main street, small and intimate bar serving light meals.

Trelew p545

₸₸ **El Quijote**, 25 de May 90, T02965-434564. Traditional *parrilla*, popular with locals.

₸₸₸ **El Viejo Molino**, Gales 250, T02965-428 019, Tue-Sun 1130-0030. The best restaurant in town, and well worth a visit to see the first flour mill that was built here in 1886. Beautifully restored with a fine restaurant and café in relaxed and stylish surroundings. There's an imaginative menu with Patagonian lamb and home-made pasta, a good value set menu with wine included, and Welsh teas. Recommended.

₸₸₸ **La Bodeguita**, Belgrano 374, opposite the cinema, T02965-437777. Serves superb home-made pasta in a warm and lively atmosphere, with interesting local art on the walls. Recommended.

₸ **Café de mi Ciudad**, Belgrano 394, T02965-426748. A smart café serving great coffee; read the papers while watching street life.

₸ **Delikatesse**, Belgrano y San Martín, T02965-430716. Serves pizzas in a cheery atmosphere, good for families.

₸ **Hotel Touring Club**, Fontana 240, T02965-433997. Open from breakfast till the small hours for sandwiches and drinks, worth a visit to see the splendid 1920s bar.

Gaiman p547

There's a stylish small restaurant, **El Angel**, Rivadavia 241, serving delicious food in an old-fashioned intimate atmosphere; a high quality *panadería* **La Colonia** on the main street; and **Siop Bara**, Tello and 9 de Julio, sells cakes and ice creams.

Welsh teas

You're unlikely to be able to resist the Welsh teas for which Gaiman has become famous, though quite how the tradition sprung up remains a mystery. It's hard to imagine their abstemious ancestors tucking into vast plates filled with 7 kinds of cake and scones at one sitting. Inevitably, the teas are not cheap. Tea is served from 1500, all the tea rooms charge about the same – US$11 – and include the most well known of the Welsh cakes, *torta negra* – a delicious dense fruit cake. The first 3 are all near the Plaza:

Plas Y Coed, Irigoyen 320. The first house to start serving tea, now in renovated premises. Its owner Marta Rees is a wonderful raconteur and fabulous cook who can tell you all about her Welsh forebears; she was married in this very house. Highly recommended.

Ty Cymraeg, down by the river. Lovely spot with room for big groups. Sells good cakes.

Ty Gwyn, 9 de Julio 147. This large tea house serves a very generous tea in a more modern venue with traditional features; the owners are welcoming. Recommended.

Ty Nain, Irigoyen 283. The prettiest house and full of history. Owner Mirna Jones is charming; her grandmother was the first woman to be born in Gaiman.

Ty Te Caerdydd, Finca 202, 2 km from the centre, but well signposted. A staggering theme park of its own, with manicured lawns and dressed-up waitresses; its main claim to fame is that Princess Di took her tea here. The atmosphere is entirely manufactured.

🌓 Bars and clubs

Puerto Madryn p541, map p542
La Frontera, 9 de Julio 254. Popular with locals, this nightclub only really gets busy about 0300, and closes at 0500.

Margarita, RS Peña 15, T02965-470885, next to Ambigu on RS Peña and Av Roca. Late-night bar for drinks and live music, serves expensive but tasty food.

Mr Jones, 9 de Julio 116, T02695-475368. With over 45 Argentine and imported beers, this pub is a popular hang-out. The pub food is good value and there is a great atmosphere.

❋ Festivals and events

Viedma and Carmen de Patagones p539
Mar Fiesta de 7 de Marzo, www.maragato.com.ar. Celebrates victory at the Battle of Patagones with a week of music

and handicrafts, fine food, a huge procession, gaucho horse-riding displays and lots of meat on the *asados*.

🛍 Shopping

Viedma p539
Patagonia Out Doors Life, 25 de Mayo 340; **Tiburón**, Zatti 250, stock fishing equipment.

Puerto Madryn p541, map p542
You'll find clothes, T-shirts, high quality Patagonian handicrafts and leather goods, and artesanal *alfajores* and cakes in streets 28 de Julio and Av Roca.

For fishing tackle, guns and camping gear, try **Nayfer**, 25 de Mayo 366. For diving gear, there's **Acquablu**, Av Roca 329, www.acquablu.com.ar; and **Pino Sub**, Yrigoyen 200, www.pinosub.com.

Cardon, Shopping El Portal de Madryn, Av JA Roca and 28 de Julio. Recommended for regional goods and leather bags.

Portal de Madryn, 28 de Julio and Av Roca. The indoor shopping centre has all the smart clothes shops, a café on the ground floor, and a kids games area with a fast, but not cheap, food place **Mostaza** on the top floor.

Trelew p545
The main shopping area is around San Martín, and from the plaza to Belgrano. Though Trelew can't compare with Puerto Madryn for souvenirs, it has a good little handicrafts market on the plaza. There is a supermarket, **Norte**, Rivadavia y 9 de Julio.

▲ Activities and tours

Viedma and Carmen de Patagones p539
Tour operators
Mona Tour, San Martín 225, Viedma, T02920-422933. Sells flights as well as tickets for the train to Bariloche, www.trenpatagonico-sa.com.ar.

Puerto Madryn *p541, map p542*
Diving
Lobo Larsen, Roca 885, T02965-470277, www.lobolarsen.com. Friendly company that specializes in diving with the sea lion colony at Punta Lomas Provincial Widlife Reserve.
Ocean Divers, Blvd Brown (between 1st and 2nd roundabout), T02965-472569, www.oceandivers.com.a. Advanced courses (PADI) and courses on video, photography and underwater communication.
Puerto Madryn Buceo, Blvd Brown, 3rd roundabout in Balneario Nativo Sur, T02965-1551 3997, www.madrynbuceo.com. Offer courses of all kinds from beginners' dives to the week-long PADI course, around US$190, or US$60 for a day excursion.
Scuba Duba, Blvd Brown 893, T02965-452 699. Courses, excursions and night dives.

Fishing
Raul Díaz, T02965-450812; Juan Domínguez, T02965-1566 4772

Horse riding
Huellas y Costas, Blvd Brown 1900, T02965-1563 7826. Also hires kayaks and windsurf boards.

Mountain bike hire
El Gualicho, Marcos A Zar 480, T02965-454163, **Vernardino Club Mar**, on beach at Blvd Brown 860, T02965-455033.

Tour operators
Lots of agencies in Puerto Madryn run tours to Península Valdés, usually taking in the same places: the interpretation centre and viewing point for the Isla de los Pájaros, (both on the narrow isthmus at the entrance to the peninsula), and then Puerto Pirámides, where the boat trip to see the whales costs US$32 extra. They go on to Punta Delgada and Caleta Valdés, with time to look at wildlife. Trips take 12 hrs, so you should bring water and lunch, though there are places to eat in Puerto Pirámides. All charge US$55,

plus entrance to the peninsula – but shop around to find out how long you'll spend at each place, how big the group is, and if your guide speaks English.

Most tour companies (addresses below) stay 50-60 mins on location. Usually ½-price for children under 10, free for those under 6. Tours are also offered to see the penguins at Punta Tombo, or the Welsh village of Gaiman with Ameghino Dam thrown in, but these are both 400 km round trips and better from Trelew.
Alora Viaggio, Av Roca 27, T02965-455106, www.aloraviaggio.com. A helpful company which also has an office at the bus terminal (T02965-456563).
Argentina Visión, Av Roca 536, T02965-451 427, www.argentinavision.com. Offers 4WD adventure trips and can arrange *estancia* accommodation at Punta Delgada. Can also contact **Estancia San Lorenzo** to arrange great day excursions to a beautiful stretch of coast to see penguins close up in one of the peninsula colonies, as well as birdwatching and horse treks. English and French spoken.
Cuyun Co, Av Roca 165, T02965-451845, www.cuyunco.com.ar. Offers a friendly, personal service and a huge range of conventional and more imaginative tours: guided walks with biologists, 4WD expeditions, and can arrange *estancia* accommodation. Bilingual guides. Recommended.
El Gualicho, Marcos A Zar 480, T02965-454 163, www.elgualicho.com.ar. Located inside the hostel, the tours on offer cater more to the backpacker market. Open to non-guests. Great guides and helpful reception staff.
Flamenco Tour, Av Roca 331, T02965-453 275, www.flamencotour.com.ar. Slightly more sedate trips and charming staff.
Tito Botazzi, Blvd Brown and Martín Fierro, T02965-474110, www.titobottazzi.com, and at Puerto Pirámides (T02965-495050). Particularly recommended for small groups. Well informed, bilingual guides. Very popular for whale watching.

Puerto Pirámides *p545*

Hydrosport, near the ACA Primera Bajada al Mar, T02965-495065, hysport@infovia.com.ar. Rents scuba equipment and boats, and organizes land and sea wildlife tours to see whales and dolphins.

Punta Bellenas, Segunda Bajada al Mar, T02965-495012. Offers diving expeditions and provides equipment. Tours do not run after heavy rain in the low season.

Whales Argentina, Primera Bajada al Mar, T02965-495015. Recommended for whale watching.

Trelew *p545*

Tour operators

Agencies run tours to Punta Tombo, US$36; Chubut Valley (½-day), US$45; both together as a full day US$65. Tours to Península Valdés are best done from Puerto Madryn.

Nieve Mar, Italia 98, T02965-434114, www. nievemartours.com.ar. Punta Tombo and Península Valdés, bilingual guides (reserve ahead). Organized and efficient.

Patagonia Grandes Espacios, Belgrano 338, T02965-435161, infopge@speedy.com.ar. Good excursions to Punta Tombo and Gaiman; palaeontological trips, staying in *chacras*; whale watching. Recommended.

Transport

Viedma and Carmen de Patagones *p539*
Air

LADE fly to **Buenos Aires**, **Mar del Plata**, **Bahía Blanca**, **Neuquén**, **San Martín de Los Andes**, **Trelew** and **Comodoro Rivadavia** from Aeropuerto Gobernador Castelo.

Airline offices LADE, Saavedra 403, T/F02920-424420.

Bus

For bus terminal information, see page 539.

To **Buenos Aires**, 3 daily, 14 hrs, US$54, Don Otto; La Estrella; Cóndor. To **San Antonio Oeste**, several daily, 2½ hrs, US$9,

Don Otto. To **Bahía Blanca**, 4 daily, 4 hrs, US$12, Río Parana.

Train

A comfortable sleeper train, which also carries cars, goes from Viedma to **Bariloche** overnight once a week, Fri 1800, and arrives in the morning. On board there's a restaurant and a cinema car showing videos. All reasonably comfortable. US$60 for a bed, US$30 for a *semi-cama* seat (the cheapest is US$15 for a small non-reclining seat), T02944-431777, www.trenpatagonico-sa.com.ar. Book ahead.

Puerto Madryn *p541, map p542*
Air

For airport information, see page 541.

Only **LADE** operate from here. Flights once a week to **Buenos Aires**

Airline offices LADE, Roca 119, T02965-451256.

Bus

For bus terminal information, see page 541.

To **Buenos Aires**, 18-19 hrs, US$68-79, several companies of which **Andesmar**, T02965-473764, is recommended. To **Río Gallegos**, 18 hrs, US$64, Andesmar; El Pingüino (connecting to El Calafate, Punta Arenas, Puerto Natales), T02965-456 256; Transportadora Patagónica/Don Otto, T02965-451675. To **Trelew**, every hr, 1 hr, US$4.50 with **28 de Julio/Mar y Valle**, T02965- 472056. To **Puerto Pirámides**, daily, 1½ hrs, US$5, **28 de Julio**. To **Esquel**, daily, 11-12 hrs, US$41, Ejecutivo de Chubut. To **Comodoro Rivadavia**, 5½ hrs, US$21.

Car hire

More expensive than in other parts of Argentina, and note the large insurance excess for turning the car over. Drive slowly on unpaved *ripio* roads.

Avis-Andres Rent A Car, Roca 493, T02965-475 4222, www.andesrentacar. com.ar; Localiza, Roca 15, T02965-458 000, recommended for efficient and helpful service.

Taxi
Taxis can be found outside the bus terminal,
T02965-452966.

Trelew *p515*
Air
Aerolíneas Argentinas have flights to
Buenos Aires.
   Airline offices Aerolíneas Argentinas,
25 de Mayo 33, T02965-420170.

Bus
Long distance To **Buenos Aires**, daily,
19-20 hrs, US$80, several companies
including Andesmar, T02965-433535;
El Cóndor, T02965-433748; El Pingüino,
T02965-427400; Que Bus, T02965-422760;
Transportadora Patagónica/Don Otto,
T02965-432 4346. To **Comodoro Rivadavia**,
5 hrs, US$18, many companies; to **Reserva
Natural Cabo Dos Bahías**, Mon, Wed
and Fri 0800 (return 1600), 2½ hrs, US$8,
with El Nandu; to **Río Gallegos**, 17 hrs; US$50
(from here to **El Calafate**, **Puerto Natales**,
Punta Arenas), many companies. To **Esquel**,
9-10 hrs, US$45, Empresa Chubut; Mar y
Valle; Transportadora Patagónica/ Don Otto.
   Local Mar y Valle and 28 de Julio both
go frequently to **Rawson**, 30 mins, US$1;
to **Gaiman**, 30 mins, US$2.50; to **Dolavon**
1 hr, US$2.50; to **Puerto Madryn**, 1hr, US$3;
to **Puerto Pirámides**, daily, 2½ hrs, US$8,
Mar y Valle.

Car hire
Car-hire companies' desks at the airport are
staffed only at flight arrival times and cars
are taken quickly. All have offices in town.
   AVIS, Italia 98, T02965-436060; Hertz, at
the airport, T02965-424421, T02965-1540
5495; Localiza, Urquiza 310, T02965-435344.

Gaiman *p547*
Bus
Buses to **Trelew**, several a day, 30 mins,
US$2.50, with **28 de Julio**.

Dolavon *p548*
Bus
Buses to **Trelew**, several a day, 1 hr, US$2.50,
28 de Julio.

⊙ Directory

TCs are hard to change throughout Patagonia,
and it's easier, and safer, to use credit or debit
cards to withdraw cash. There are ATMs in
all the main towns in Patagonia (even in
El Chaltén which recently got its first).

**Viedma and Carmen de
Patagones** *p539*
Banks ATMs at Colón and San Martín
in Viedma; and Carmen de Patagones at
Bynon and Alsina or Bynon and Paraguay.

Puerto Madryn *p541, map p542*
Banks Banco del Chubut, 25 de Mayo 154;
Banco Nación, 9 de Julio 117; Río, 28 de
Julio 56, all have ATMs. **Internet** Internet
Centro Madryn, 25 de Mayo and Belgrano,
US$1.50 per hr; Re Creo, Roque Sáenz Peña
101. **Medical services** There are chemists
all along 28 de Julio, and a late night
pharmacy on Belgrano and 25 de Mayo.
Post office Maíz 293, daily 0900-1200,
1500-1900. **Telephone** There are many
locutorios in the centre.

Trelew *p545*
Banks Mon-Fri 0800-1300. Banco de la
Nación, 25 de Mayo and Fontana; Banco del
Sud, 9 de Julio 320, cash advance on Visa.
Currency exchange Patagonia Grandes
Espacios, Belgrano 338. **Internet** 25 de
Mayo 219. **Post office** 25 de Mayo and
Mitre. **Telephone** Telefónica, Roca and Pje
Tucumán, and several *locutorios* in the centre.

Southern Atlantic Coast

Quieter, and much less visited by tourists than Puerto Madryn and Península Valdés, the southern stretch of the Atlantic coastline from Camarones to Río Gallegos is extremely rich in marine life of all kinds. There are several wonderful reserves protecting a wide variety of species of birds and mammals, and a few good bases for exploring them at the coastal towns of Camarones, Puerto Deseado and Puerto San Julián, with good services and accommodation. If you have your own transport, you could head out to the only national park on the coast, Monte León, where you can walk the shore for miles and stay in a remote but comfortable hostería. And on the last spit of land before Tierra del Fuego, there's ancient history to explore near the coast at Cabo Vírgenes.

There are two cities in this huge region, of which the most appealing is the southernmost town on the Argentine mainland, Río Gallegos. It's a small pleasant place, with fair accommodation, and tours offered to penguin colonies, though there's little to draw you here unless you're changing buses. The other city, Comodoro Rivadavia, is probably best avoided if possible, unless you're keen to see the petroleum museum. Aside from coastal attractions, this region also boasts the country's finest petrified forest, the Monumento Natural Bosques Petrificados, difficult to reach on public transport, 250 km west of Puerto Deseado. ▶▶ For listings, see pages 565-570.

Comodoro Rivadavia and around → For listings, see pages 565-570. Colour map 5, C4.
Phone code 0297. Population 145,000.

The largest city in the province of Chubut was established primarily as a sheep-exporting port, and early settlers included Boer immigrants fleeing British rule in southern Africa. Its compact centre is at the foot of Cerro Chenque, 212 m high, a dusty bluff overlooking the town unattractively adorned with radar masts, with its own shanty town. The city began to flourish suddenly when oil was discovered here in 1907, bringing in many international companies. However, since the petrol industry was privatized by President Menem in the 1990s, there's been consequent unemployment and now the town has a slightly sad, rather unkempt feel. You're most likely to end up here if you need to change buses, and there's little to make you want to stay. Comodoro Rivadavia has a **tourist office** ⓘ *Rivadavia 430, T0297-446 2376, www.comodoro.gov.ar, Mon-Fri 0900-2100, Sat-Sun 1500-2100*, which is very helpful and English is spoken.

Situated at the end of the Bioceanic Corridor, a fast road to Chile, Comodoro is the hub for terrestrial transport and a bus nexus from all areas of Patagonia, though there are some smart hotels and a popular beach nearby. The **airport** is 9 km north and bus No 6 leaves hourly for the bus terminal, 45 minutes, US$0.75. A taxi from the airport costs US$6. The **bus terminal** ⓘ *Pellegrini 730, T0297-336 7305*, is conveniently located in the centre and has a luggage store, good *confitería* upstairs, toilets, excellent tourist information office (open from 0800 to 2100) and a few kiosks.

If you're really stuck for something to do, you could visit the **Museo Nacional del Petróleo** ⓘ *T0297-455 9558, Tue-Fri 0900-2000, Sat-Sun 1500-2000, taxi US$4, only 3 km north of the centre at San Lorenzo 250*, for a good history of local oil exploitation. Some 20 km north is **Museo Paleontológico de Astra** ⓘ *Sat-Sun 1500-1800*, which has fossils and reconstructions of dinosaurs. There's a good view of the city from **Cerro Chenque**, a dun-coloured hill whose cliffs give the town its drab backdrop. It's interesting to take a taxi up there, if you don't feel like the walk, to see the first pioneers' homes, now dilapidated, but with panoramic views of the bay.

There's a good beach at the resort of **Rada Tilly** 12 km south, where you can walk along the beach at low tide to see sea lions. **Expreso Rada Tilly** runs buses every 30 minutes; they're packed in summer. You could use Comodoro Ravadavia as a base for exploring a second petrified forest, the Bosque Petrificado Héctor Szlápelis (see page 573), but the little town of **Sarmiento**, some 140 km west, is far more pleasant. See www.coloniasarmiento.gov.ar, for more details (in English). ▸▸ *For further information on getting to Sarmiento, see Transport, page 568.*

Camarones → *Colour map 5, B5. Phone code 0297. Population 1100.*
Camarones is a quiet fishing port on Bahía Camarones, between Comodoro and Trelew, whose main industry is harvesting seaweed. This is prime sheep-rearing land, and Camarones wool is world-renowned for its quality. Aside from the salmon festival in early February, the only real attraction is a penguin colony, which you can walk to from the town.

There's another well-known penguin colony with lots more species of marine life, 35 km southeast at **Reserva Natural Cabo Dos Bahías** ① *there are buses to the reserve from Trelew, see page 557.* This is a small reserve at the southern end of the bay, reached by a dirt road. It protects a large penguin colony of some 12,000 couples, which you can see close up, but also sea lions and whales. The reserve is open all year, US$5 per person and US$1 per car, and you can see seals and sea lions any time, but there are whales from March to November, and killer whales might be spotted from October to April.

South to Río Gallegos → *For listings, see pages 565-570.*

Caleta Olivia → *Colour map 5, C4. Phone code 0297. Population 40,000.*
Caleta Olivia lies on the Bahía San Jorge, 74 km south of Comodoro Rivadavia. Founded in 1901, it became the centre for exporting wool from the *estancias* of Santa Cruz. It boomed with the discovery of oil in 1944, but has suffered since the petroleum industry was privatized in the 1990s, and is now a rather sad place with heavy unemployment. However, there's a lovely 70 km stretch of pebbly beach, popular with locals for bathing, and lots of fishing nearby. There's a **tourist information office** ① *San Martín 1059, T0297-485 0988, extension 476, daily 0700-2200 in high season, 0800-1700 in low season.*

At **Pico Truncado**, some 50 km southwest, there's the gas field that feeds the pipeline to Buenos Aires, and an enterprising art project, **Ciudad Sonora** ① *www.ciudadsonora.net,* in a spectacular open setting; the wind sings through structures made of metal and marble, producing strange and eerie sounds. There's a daily bus service from Caleta Oliva, and nearby Pico Troncado has a few simple hotels, a campsite, and **tourist information** ① *T0297-499 2202.*

Monumento Natural Bosques Petrificados
① *256 km west of Puerto Deseado. Access is via Route 49 shooting west from the main route south, the R3, at Km 2063, 86 km south of the small town of Fitz Roy. Daily 1000-2000, entry by donation. There is no public transport, and no accommodation in the park. Camping is not allowed, and you're advised to bring your own food and drink.*
Extending over 10,000 ha in a bizarre, wind-wracked lunar landscape surrounding the **Laguna Grande**, this park contains much older petrified trees than the forests further north around Sarmiento. The trunks, mainly of giant araucaria trees, are up to 35 m long and 150 cm in diameter. They were petrified in the Jurassic period 140 million years ago by intense volcanic activity in the Andes cordillera which blew ash over the entire area.

It was the silicates in this volcanic ash which petrified the trunks of fallen trees, and created these strange jasper-like hulks, which were only revealed when other organic matter around them was eroded. The place is more eerie than beautiful, but it does exert a strange fascination, especially when you consider that the fossils of marine animals that you see on the site are a mere 40 million years old, belonging to a sea which covered the land long after the trees had turned to stone. There is a small visitor centre and museum, and a well-documented 1-km trail that takes you past the most impressive specimens. You may be very tempted to take away your own personal souvenir: don't.

The only way to visit the park, unless you have your own transport, is with a tour from either Comodoro Rivadavia, or the more appealing Puerto Deseado. ⇥ *For further information, see Activities and tours, page 568.*

Puerto Deseado → *For listings, see pages 565-570. Colour map 6, A4. Phone code 0297. Population 10,200.*

Puerto Deseado is a pleasant fishing port on the estuary of the Río Deseado, which drains, curiously, into Lago Buenos Aires in the west. It's a stunning stretch of coastline, and the estuary has a wonderful nature reserve, Ría Deseado, with Magellanic penguins and several species of cormorants among its inhabitants; as well as being the breeding grounds of Commerson's dolphin. Within reach are more reserves, protecting sea lions and penguins. The **Museo Regional Mario Brozoski** ① *Belgrano (9050) and Colón, Mon-Fri 1000-2000, Sat-Sun 1500-1900,* has remains of an 18th-century ship that sank off the coast here in 1770, as well as some evocative photos. Outside the former railway station, a rather fine old building, in vaguely English medieval style, is the **Vagón Histórico** ① *San Martín 1525, T0297-487 0220,* an 1898 carriage now used as the tourist office.

The **Reserva Natural Ría Deseado**, the submerged estuary (*ría*) of the Río Deseado, 42 km long, is an important nature reserve, and a stunning area to visit. Among many varieties of seabird, there's a colony of Magellanic penguins, and the crumbling chalky cliffs, mauve and ochre, splattered with *guano* (droppings), are home to four species of cormorants including the unique red-legged cormorant, most appealing with their smart dinner-jacketed appearance. These birds nest from October to April on four islands off the shores. The reserve is also the breeding grounds of Commerson's dolphins, beautiful creatures, who frolic playfully around your boat. Excellent tours (see Tour operators, page 568), run from the town's pier, they last about two hours, and are best in early morning or late evening. There are several other nature reserves within easy reach if you have transport, and all offer good places to walk.

North of Puerto Deseado, some 90 km on the northern shore of the peninsula, is **Cabo Blanco**, the site of the largest fur seal colony in Patagonia. It's another magnificent area, a rocky peninsula bursting out from flat lands, with one of the oldest lighthouses on the coast perched on top, and thousands of seals perched on the rocks below. The breeding season is December to January. A little further west, you should also visit **Reserva Cañadón de Duraznillo** in the *estancia* of **La Madrugada**. Here you'll see lots of guanacos, *ñandues*, foxes and birds, as well as the largest seal colony in the province on spectacular unspoilt beaches. The *estancia* is a great place to visit or stay, see Sleeping, page 566.

South of Puerto Deseado are two more reserves: **Isla Pingüino**, an offshore island with a colony of Magellanic penguins, as well as cormorants and steamer ducks, and the **Reserva Natural Bahía Laura**, an uninhabited bay where black-necked cormorants, ducks and other seabirds can be found in abundance. Isla Pingüino can be reached by boat, and Bahía Laura by *ripio* and dirt roads. ►► *For further information, see Activities and tours, page 568.*

The **Gruta de Lourdes**, 24 km west, is a cave which attracts pilgrims to see the Virgen de Lourdes. Further south along the same road is the **Cañadón del Puerto**, a mirador offering fine views over the estuary.

Puerto San Julián → *For listings, see pages 565-570. Colour map 6, A4. Phone code 02962. Population 6200.*

The quiet port town of Puerto San Julián, lying on the Bahía San Julián 268 km south of Fitz Roy, is the best place for breaking the 834-km run from Comodoro Rivadavia to Río Gallegos. It has a fascinating history, although little of it is in evidence today. The first Mass in Argentina was held here in 1520 after the Portuguese explorer Magellan had executed a member of his mutinous crew. Then in 1578, Francis Drake also put in here to behead Thomas Doughty, after amiably dining with him. There's plenty of wildlife to be seen in the area, and a paradise of marine life in the coastal Reserva Natural San Julián, all very accessible from the town.

After the 16th-century visitors, there was an attempt to found a colony here in 1780 which failed due to scurvy. The current town was founded in 1901 on a peninsula overlooking a fine natural harbour, as a port to serve the sheep *estancias* of this part of Santa Cruz. There's a little regional museum, **Museo Regional at Rivadavia and Vieytes**, which houses the amazingly well preserved dinosaur footprint found in the town. There are also superb tours offered to see the wildlife in the reserve, which you can ask about at the **tourist office** ① *Av Costanera and 9 de Julio, or San Martín 1126, T02962-454396, centur@uvc.com.ar, www.sanjulian.gov.ar.*

The **Reserva Natural San Julian**, on the shores of Bahía San Julian, includes the islands **Banco Cormorán** and **Banco Justicia**, thought to be the site of the 16th-century executions, where there is a colony of Magellanic penguins and nesting areas for several species of cormorants and other birds. You're also very likely to spot Commerson's dolphins. It's a lovely location and the concentration of marine life is stunning. Highly recommended. There are excellent Zodiac boat trips, lasting 90 minutes, run by **Excursiones Pinocho** ① *Av Costanera between San Martín and Mitre, T02962-452056, www.pinochoexcursiones.com.ar,* The best time to visit is in December to see dolphins and cormorants, though there's plenty to see from December to April. **Cabo Curiosa**, 15 km north, has fine beaches: there are 30 km of spectacular coastline, and it's a popular bathing place for the whole of the region. You can also visit the ruins of **Florida Blanca**, 10 km west, the site of the failed colony founded in 1870 by Antonio Viedma. It's certainly worth visiting **Estancia La María**, 150 km west, with one of the main archaeological sites in Patagonia: a huge canyon with 87 caves of paintings including human hands and guanacos, 4000-12,000 years old. The *estancia* offers transport, accommodation in dorm beds, and is highly recommended; contact **Fernando Behm** ① *Saavedra 1168, T02962-452328.*

Piedrabuena → *Colour map 6, B3. Phone code 02962. Population 4900.*
Known officially as Comandante Luis Piedrabuena, this quiet town is named after the famous Argentine explorer and sailor, Piedra Buena, who built his home on Isla Pavón, an island in the river Santa Cruz, in 1859. On this small mound in the deep emerald green fast-flowing river you can visit the **Casa Histórica Luis Piedra Buena**, a reconstruction of

the original building where he carried on a peaceful trade with local indigenous groups. However, the island has become most popular as a weekend resort for those fishing steelhead trout. It's a world-renowned fishing spot, and there's a smart four-star *hostería* as well as an attractive campsite to cater for anglers and their families on weekend breaks (see Sleeping, page 566). In March there's a national trout festival. Piedrabuena is a good base for exploring the Parque Nacional Monte León, which protects 40 km of coastline and steppe, 30 km south (see below).

Parque Nacional Monte León → *For listings, see pages 565-570.*

Ins and outs → *www.parquesnacionales.gov.ar, www.vidasilvestre.org.ar.*
It's difficult to reach the park unless you have a 4WD; access is along 23 km of poor *ripio* road which branches off Route 3, 36 km south of Piedrabuena. Or fly from Buenos Aires to Río Gallegos, and from the airport take a taxi (two hours, US$130 for up to four passengers). The old house at the heart of the *estancia* has been converted to a *hostería*, and by far the best way to enjoy the park in comfort is to stay at the traditional but beautifully modernized Estancia Monte León (see Sleeping, page 566).

Sights
The only national park on Argentina's long Atlantic coastline, Monte León is a beautiful stretch of steppe and shore, south of Piedrabuena. It includes 40 km of coastline, where there are many species of seabirds, the world's fourth largest colony of penguins and colonies of sea lions in its many caves and little bays, as well as the tiny island Monte León, an important breeding area for cormorants and terns. It was acquired for the Argentine nation by North American millionaire Douglas Tompkins (who also owns Parque Pumalín in Chile, and **Rincón del Socorro** in Los Esteros del Iberá, see page 397), and looked after by the organization **Vida Silvestre**, before being made a national park in 2004. It's not easy to access the park, but your efforts to get here will be rewarded by wonderful walks along wide isolated beaches with their extraordinary rock formations, and cliffs dotted with vast caverns, fabulous at low tide. The park also protects an important habitat of sea-shore steppe, which is home to pumas and wolves as well as guanacos and choiques. Improved access is one part of the plan for the national park, which will also include turning the old shearing shed into a visitor centre.

Río Gallegos → *For listings, see pages 565-570. Colour map 6, B3.*

The capital of Santa Cruz province lies on the estuary of the Río Gallegos (pronounced rio ga-shay-gos), the river famous for its excellent brown trout fishing. It's a pleasant, airy town, founded in 1885 as a centre for the trade in wool and sheepskins, and is by far the most appealing of the main centres on Patagonia's southern Atlantic Coast (which isn't saying a great deal). It has always been a major transport hub, but receives fewer visitors since the airport opened at El Calafate. However, if you come here to change buses, you could visit the penguin reserve at **Cabo Vírgenes** some 130 km south, or Monte León National Park 210 km north. The town itself has a couple of museums, and boasts a few smart shops and restaurant.

Ins and outs → *Phone code 02966. Population 75,000.*

Getting there Flights arrive at the airport from Buenos Aires, Ushuaia and Río Grande, as well as **LADE** flights connecting all major Patagonian towns. The **airport** is 10 km from the centre; a *remise* taxi should cost US$6. The bus terminal is inconveniently 3 km from the centre, at the corner of Route 3 and Avenida Eva Perón. Bus Nos 1 and 12 will take you into town, or take a taxi for US$3.50. The **bus terminal** is crowded, there's no left luggage, but there is a *confitería*, toilets and some kiosks.

Tourist information The **tourist information office** ① *Av Roca 1587, T02966-436920, www.turismo.mrg.gov.ar, Mon-Fri 0700-2000, Sat and Sun 0700-1400, 1600-2000,* is excellent and well organized, with information for the whole province. The staff are extremely helpful, speak English and have a list of *estancias* in Santa Cruz. They'll also phone hotels for you. There's a tourist information office at the airport, and a small desk at the bus terminal, T02966-442159.

Sights

The tidy, leafy Plaza San Martín, two blocks south of the main street, Avenida Roca, has an interesting collection of trees, many planted by the early pioneers, and a diminutive corrugated iron **cathedral**, with a wood-panelled ceiling in the chancel and stained-glass

Río Gallegos

Sleeping
Apart Hotel Austral **1**
Comercio **2**
Covadonga **3**
Hostería Santa Cruz **4**
Nevada **5**
París **6**
Punta Arenas **9**
Sleepers Inn **8**

Eating
Bar Español El Horreo **4**
Chino **3**
El Club Británico **7**
Laguanacazul **1**
Puesto Molino **6**

windows. The best of the town's museums is the small **Museo de los Pioneros** ⓘ *Elcano and Alberdi, T02966-437763, daily 1000-1900, free.* Set in a house built in England and shipped here in 1890, there are interesting photographs and artefacts telling the story of the first Scottish settlers, who came here in 1884 from the Falklands/Malvinas Islands, by government grants of land. There's an interesting tour given by the English-speaking owner, a descendent of the Scottish pioneers, and great photos of those first sheep-farming settlers. There's work by local artists at **Museo de Arte Eduardo Minichelli** ⓘ *Maipú 13, Mon-Fri 0800-1900, Sat-Sun and holidays 1400-1800 (closed Jan-Feb).* There's **Museo Regional Provincial Padre Jesús Molina** ⓘ *Av San Martín y Ramón and Cajal 51, Mon-Fri 1000-1700, Sat and Sun 1200-1900,* in the Complejo Cultural Santa Cruz, with some dull rocks and fossils and a couple of dusty dinosaur skeletons.

Around Río Gallegos

Laguna Azul, 62 km south near the Monte Aymond border crossing, is nothing more than a perfect royal-blue lagoon in the crater of an extinct volcano. But it does have a certain atmosphere, set in an arid lunar landscape, and is a good place for a walk. Take a tour, or get off the bus along Route 3, which stops on the main road.

Reserva Provincial Cabo Vírgenes ⓘ *entry US$5,* 134 km south, is a nature reserve protecting the second largest colony of Magellanic penguins in Patagonia. There's an informative self-guided walk to see their nests amongst the *calafate* and fragrant *mata verde* bushes. It's good to visit from November to January, when chicks are born and there are nests under every bush. Fascinating for anyone, and wonderful for children. You can climb the **Cabo Vírgenes lighthouse** (owned by the Argentine Navy) for wonderful views. Both these are usually included in a tour organized from Río Gallegos. There's a *confitería* close by for snacks and souvenirs. Branch off Route 3 onto Route 1 (unpaved), 15 km south of Río Gallegos, and from here it's 119 km, 3½ hours. South of Cabo Vírgenes are the ruins of **Nombre de Jesús**, one of the two settlements founded by Pedro Sarmiento de Gamboa in 1584 and where, tragically, all its settlers died.

Estancia Monte Dinero ⓘ *T02966-428922, www.montedinero.com.ar,* 13 km north of Cabo Vírgenes, is a wonderful base for visiting the reserve. It is a working sheep farm, where the English-speaking Fenton family offers accommodation, food and excursions; all excellent.

For Sleeping and Eating price codes and other relevant information, see Essentials pages 30-36.

◉ Sleeping

Comodoro Rivadavia *p558*

Hotels are either luxurious or basic, with little in between.

AL-A Austral Hotel, Moreno 725, T0297-447 2200, www.australhotel.com.ar. Big new 5-star hotel near the water, large modern rooms, good service and great hot showers. Suites (**LL-L**) are also available.

AL Lucania Palazzo Hotel, Moreno 676, T0297-449 9300, www.lucania-palazzo.com. A stylish and luxurious business hotel, with a lovely airy spacious reception, and superb rooms, many with sea views. A huge American breakfast, and use of the sauna and gym are included. Good value and recommended.

B-C Hotel Azul, Sarmiento 724, T0297-446 7539, www.hotelazul.com.ar. Direct from the 70s, this is a quiet, old place, with bright rooms, friendly owners and great panoramic views from the *confitería*. Breakfast is extra.

C Hospedaje Cari Hue, Belgrano 563, T0297-447 2946, www.hospedajecarihue.com.ar. Sweet rooms, with separate bathrooms, coming off a central hallway, very nice owners who like backpackers. Breakfast is extra. The best budget choice.

C Rua Marina, Belgrano 738, T0297-446 8777. All rooms have TV and bath, and breakfast is included; the newer rooms are particularly comfortable. Recommended for the friendly welcome. This is the best budget choice.

Camping

Camping Municipal, Rada Tilly, reached by **Expreso Rada Tilly** bus from town. Hot showers.

San Carlos, 37 km north on R3, T0297-456 0425. Offers 20 ha, open all year.

Camarones *p559*

B Complejo Indalo Inn, Sarmiento and Roca, T0297-496 3004, www.indaloinn.com.ar. Simple but clean, doubles and singles with en suite. Good food and the owner runs trips to the penguin colony. Recommended.

There are 2 other hotels in town (**C**), the one by the power station is not recommended.

Caleta Olivia *p559*

B Patagonia Hotel, Av Eva Perón 1873, T0297-483 0517, www.patagoniahotelco.com.ar. Welcoming, slightly dated hotel with clean bright rooms and views of the ocean.

B-C pp Hotel Robert, San Martín 2152, T0297-485 1452, www.hotelrobert.com.ar. Comfortable option. All rooms have bathroom, and breakfast is included.

D Grand Hotel, Mosconi and Chubut, T0297-485 1393. Reasonably comfortable rooms.

Camping

Municipal campsite, T0297-485 0999, ext 476. Hot showers and near the beach. US$4.50 per person.

Monumento Natural Bosques Petrificados *p559*

There are no services, no water source anywhere close by, and no accommodation in the area, apart from camping at **Estancia la Paloma**, 25 km away, T0297-443503. Note that camping is not allowed near the park.

Puerto Deseado *p560*

B-C Isla Chaffers, San Martín y Mariano Moreno, T0297-487 2246, www.hotelislachaffers.com.ar. The town's best; modern and central.

C Los Acantilados, Pueyrredón and España 1611, T0297-487 2167. Beautifully located hotel, popular with anglers. Comfortable rooms with bathrooms, and a good breakfast.

Estancias
AL-A La Madrugada, situated on the Atlantic coast, 120 km from Puerto Deseado, reached from the R281 to Km 79, then R68, T0297-4794 8964, gesino@fibertel.com.ar. Splendid views and plenty of places to spot wildlife from the *estancia* itself. Good Patagonian home cooking, and comfortable accommodation. The owners also arrange excursions to the sea lion colony and cormorant nesting area. English spoken, recommended.

Camping
Camping Cañadón de Giménez, 4 km away on R281, T0297-487 2135; **Camping Municipal**, Av Lotufo, on the seafront, T0297-487 2728. Lovely locations but the sites are a bit run down.

Puerto San Julián *p561*
A Hotel Bahía, San Martín 1075, T02962-454028, www.hotelbahiasanjulian.com.ar. Modern and comfortable rooms, good value.
B Hotel Sada, San Martín 1112, T02962-452 013, www.hotelsada.com.ar. Simple rooms, on a busy road.

Estancias
C Estancia La María, 150 km west, contact Fernando Behm, Saavedra 1163, T02962-452233. Simple accommodation in a modern house, with amazing cave paintings nearby. The owners also organize trips to see marine and birdlife.

Camping
Municipal campsite, Magellanes 650 and M Moreno, T02962-452806. US$3.50 per site plus US$2.50 per person. Offers all facilities. Recommended.

Piedrabuena *p561*
A Hostería El Álamo, Lavalle 8, T02962-497249, www.hosteriaelalamo.com. Quiet, breakfast extra. Recommended.
A-B Hostería Municipal Isla Pavon, Isla Pavón, T02966-1563 8380, www.yaten. com.ar. Luxurious 4-star catering to fishermen of steelhead trout.

C Res Internacional, Ibáñez 99, T02962-497197. Recommended.

Camping
Sites south of town on R3; also on Isla Pavón.

Parque Nacional Monte León *p562*
LL-L Estancia Monte León, R3, www.monteleon-patagonia.com. Open Nov-Apr. 4 tasteful rooms, all decorated with Douglas Tompkins' considerable style. There's a good library, living room and even a small museum. Fishing is good here, too. It's a fantastic place to stay.

Río Gallegos *p562, map p563*
Most hotels are situated within a few blocks of the main street, Av Roca, running northwest to southeast. Do not confuse the street Comodoro Rivadavia with (nearby) Bernardino Rivadavia.
A Hostería Santa Cruz, Av Roca 701, T02966-420601, www.hotelsantacruzrgl. com.ar. Smart business hotel only a short walk to the commercial centre. The more expensive rooms have flatscreen TVs, cable and larger bathrooms.
B Apart Hotel Austral, Roca 1505, T02966-435588, www.apartaustral.com. A smart newly built apart hotel, with bright rooms and attractive sunny decor. Very good value, particularly the superior duplexes. The kitchen facilities are a bit basic, but certainly adequate for a couple of nights. Breakfast is US$1.70 extra.
B Comercio, Roca 1302, T02966-422458, www.hotelcomercio-rgl.com.ar. Good value, nicely designed, comfortable rooms with bathrooms, and breakfast included. There is an attractive cheap *confitería* on the street.
C Covadonga, Roca 1244, T02966-420190, hotelcovadongargl@hotmail.com. Attractive 1930s building. Basic rooms have bath and TV, and come off a long corridor to a courtyard. Breakfast is included, and though rooms are small, it's all clean and well maintained.

C Nevada, Zapiola 480, T02966-435790.
A good budget option, with clean, simple
spacious rooms, nice beds and good
bathrooms. Breakfast not included.
C Paris, Roca 1040, 102966-420111.
Fairly simple rooms with bath, set back
from the street. A good-value choice,
though breakfast is extra.
D Punta Arenas, F Suphur 55, T02966-
427743. Smart and new, rooms in new
wing cost more, as do rooms with private
bathrooms (**C**).

Hostels
E Sleepers Inn, F Sphur 78, T02966-444
037, sleepersinn@gmail.com. The 1st and
only hostel in town. Simple, clean rooms
with shared bath. Note it can be a little noisy.

Estancias
AL Monte Dinero, near Cabo Vírgines,
T02966-428922, www.montedinero.com.ar.
Comfortable accommodation on a working
sheep farm. The house is lined with wood
rescued from ships wrecked off the coast,
and the food is delicious and home-grown.
Highly recommended.
AL-A Hill Station, 63 km north of Río
Gallegos on R58, T02966-423897 (in Río
Gallegos). An estancia with 120 years of
history, run by descendants of the founder,
William Halliday. A sheep farm, also breeding
criollo horses, this offers wonderful horse
riding to see flora and fauna of the coast,
and also simple accommodation.

Camping
Camping ATSA, R3, en route to bus terminal,
T02966-420310.
Chacra Daniel, Paraje Río Chico, 3.5 km from
town, T02966-423970, ofaustral@ciudad.com.
US$5 per person per day, with *parrilla* and full
facilities. Recommended.
Club Pescazaike, Paraje Güer Aike, T02966-
423442, info@pescazaike.com.ar. Some 30 km
west of town on R3. Well equipped, and an
attractive place. Also *quincho* and restaurant.

ⓘ Eating

Comodoro Rivadavia *p558*
Ⓨ Cayo Coco, Rivadavia 102, T0297-447
3033. A welcoming little bistro, with very
cheery staff and excellent pizzas. Good
value and recommended.
Ⓨ Dionisius, 9 de Julio y Rivadavia 324,
T0297-446 3369. A smart and elegant *parrilla*,
popular with a more sedate clientele, serving
excellent set menus for US$8.
Ⓨ La Barca, Belgrano 935, T0297-447 3710.
Welcoming and cheap, *tenedor libre*.
Ⓨ La Tradición, Mitre 675, T0297-446 5800.
Another popular and recommended *parrilla*,
good *asado*.
Ⓨ Peperoni, Rivadavia 481, T0297-446 9683.
A cheerful modern place with good range of
home-made pastas, filled with exciting things
like king crab, as well as serving seafood and
parrilla. US$5-8, for a main dish.

Cafés
Ⓨ La Barra, San Martín 686, T0297-446
6551. A pleasant, bright café for breakfast,
very good coffee or a light lunch.

Puerto Deseado *p560*
Ⓨ El Pingüino, Piedrabuena 950, T0297-
487 2105. Established *parrilla* which serves
fabulous rice pudding.
Ⓨ Puerto Cristal, España 1698, T0297-487
0387. Panoramic views of the port, a great
place for Patagonian lamb and *parrilla*.

Puerto San Julián *p561*
Ⓨ Bar Sportsman, Mitre 301 and 25 de Mayo.
Excellent value.
Ⓨ El Muelle Viejo, Mitre 1 and 9 de Julio,
T02962-453009. Good seafood, the *pejerrey* is
recommended. Also has bars and tearooms.
Ⓨ La Rural, Ameghino 811 and Vieytes,
T02962-454066. Good, but not before 2100.

Río Gallegos *p562, map p563*
There are lots of good places to eat here, many serving excellent seafood, and some smart, new, inexpensive restaurants.

† Bar Español El Horreo, Roca 863. Next door to Puesto Molino. A more sophisticated option, rather like a bistro in feel, serving delicious lamb dishes and good salads. Recommended.

† El Club Británico, Roca 935, T02966-427 320. Doing its best to look like a London gentleman's club, though lacking in atmosphere, serves cheap set lunches.

† Laguanacazul, Sarmiento y Gob Lista, T02966-444114. Chic and not expensive. Near the river, with open views across the Plaza de la República, this has an imaginative menu, and is reasonably priced.

† Puesto Molino, Roca 862, opposite the tourist office. A relaxed, airy place, its design inspired by life on *estancias*, with bold paintings, wooden tables and excellent pizzas (US$5 for 2) and *parrilla* (US$10 for 2). Recommended.

† Chino, 9 de Julio 29. Cheap and varied *tenedor libre*.

▲ Activities and tours

Caleta Olivia *p559*
Zoyen Turismo, Güemes 2121, T0297-485 1632, www.zoyenturismo.com.ar. New tour operator who can also help with R40 connections, and *estancia* visits. They also have an office in Perito Moreno.

Puerto Deseado *p560*
Darwin Expediciones, España 2601, T156-247554, www.darwin-expeditions.com and **Los Vikingos**, Estrada 1275, T0297-487 0020, www.losvikingos.com.ar, both offer excursions by boat to Río Deseado reserve, and Reserva Provincial Isla Pingüino, as well as trips to see the Monumento Natural Bosques Petrificados.

Puerto San Julián *p561*
Tur Aike Turismo, Av San Martín 446, T02962-452086.

Río Gallegos *p562, map p563*
Fishing
The southern fishing zone includes rivers Gallegos, Grande, Fuego, Ewan, San Pablo and Lago Fagnano, near Ushuaia. It is famous for runs of sea trout. Ask the tourist office for fishing guides, and information on permits, or visit www.pescaenlapatagonia.com.ar (in Spanish).

Tour operators
Maca Tobiano Turismo, Roca 998, T02966-422466, macatobiano@macatobiano.com. Air tickets and tours to Pingüinero Cabo Vírgenes, all-day trip US$22 also to the mystical Laguna Azul, a ½-day trip to a beautiful lake in a volcanic crater, and to Estancia Monte León, as well as tickets to El Calafate and Ushuaia. Recommended.

⊖ Transport

Comodoro Rivadavia *p558*
Air
For airport information, see page 558.
To **Buenos Aires**, Aerolíneas Argentinas; Austral. LADE flies once a week to **Puerto Madryn**, **Esquel**, **Bariloche**, and **El Calafate**, among other towns in **Patagonia**.
Airline offices Aerolíneas Argentinas, 9 de Julio 870, T0297-444 0050; LADE, Rivadavia 360, T0297-447 0585.

Bus
For bus terminal information, see page 558.
Services to **Buenos Aires**, 2 daily, 28 hrs, US$99. To **Mendoza**, 28 hrs, US$107, Andesmar, T0297-420139. To **Bariloche**, 14 hrs, US$44, Don Otto, T0297-4470450. To **Esquel** (paved road), 8 hrs direct with ETAP and Don Otto, US$30, in summer

buses usually arrive full so book ahead.
To **Río Gallegos**, daily, 11 hrs, US$39,
Don Otto; Pingüino; and TAC, T0297-444
3376. To **Puerto Madryn**, US$24. To **Trelew**,
3 daily, 4 hrs US$8, several companies
including Don Otto. To **Caleta Olivia**,
hourly, US$4, La Unión. To **Sarmiento**,
3 daily, 2½ hrs, US$7, Etap, T0297-447 4841.
   To Chile To **Santiago** (Coyhaique),
35 hrs, US$185, Etap Angel Giobbi. To
Coyhaique, twice a week, 12 hrs,
US$28, Etap Angel Giobbi.

Car rental
Avis, 9 de Julio 687, T/F0297-496382;
Patagonia Sur Car, Rawson 1190,
T0297-446 6768.

Camarones *p559*
Bus
Bus to **Trelew**, Mon-Fri 1600, 2½ hrs,
Don Otto.

Caleta Olivia *p559*
Bus
To **Río Gallegos**, El Pingüino, T0297-485
2929, US$39, overnight. Many buses to
Comodoro Rivadavia, 1 hr, US$8 and
3 daily to **Puerto Deseado**, US$16. To
El Calafate, 5 hrs; to **Perito Moreno** and
Los Antiguos, daily, 5 hrs, US$25.

Puerto Deseado *p560*
To **Caleta Olivia**, daily, US$16, Sportman and
La Unión, at the bus terminal, T0155-928598.

Puerto San Julián *p561*
Air
Weekly services (Mon) with LADE, Martín
1552, T02962-452137, to **Santa Cruz**, **Río
Gallegos**, **El Calafate**, **Puerto Deseado**,
Gobernador Gregores, **Comodoro
Rivadavia**, and **Río Turbio**.

Bus
To **Buenos Aires**, Transportadora
Patagónica, T02962-452072; El Pingüino,
T02962-452425. To **Río Gallegos**, 6 hrs,

US$13, El Pingüino. To **Mendoza**, US$60,
Andesmar, T02962-454403.

Río Gallegos *p562, map p563*
Air
For airport information, see page 563.
   Regular flights to **Buenos Aires**, **Ushuaia**
and **Río Grande** with Aerolíneas
Argentinas. LADE to **Río Turbio** and **El
Calafate**, twice a week, to **Ushuaia** and
Comodoro Rivadavia once a week. LADE
flights should be booked as far in advance
as possible. The Ladeco service from **Punta
Arenas** to **Port Stanley** on the **Falkland
Islands/Islas Malvinas** stops once a month
in either direction.
   Airline offices Aerolíneas Argentinas,
San Martín 545, T02966-422020; LADE,
Fagnano 53, T02966-422326 (closed in
low season).

Bus
For bus terminal information, see page 563.
   To **El Calafate**, 4-5 hrs, US$16, Taqsa and
Interlagos. To **Los Antiguos**, daily at 2100,
US$41, Sportman. To **Comodoro Rivadavia**,
10 hrs, US$143, El Pingüino; Don Otto; and
TAC. To **Bariloche**, daily 2130,
Transportadora Patagónica, 24 hrs, US$87.
To **Buenos Aires**, several daily, 33 hrs,
US$124, El Pingüino; Don Otto; and TAC.
To **Río Grande** and **Ushuaia**, Tue, Thu, Sat
1000, 8-10 hrs, US$37-51, Tecni Austral.
   Both Pingüino and Interlagos can
arrange packages to **Calafate** including
accommodation and trip to Moreno
Glacier from their offices at the airport.
   To Chile To **Puerto Natales**, Sat, 7 hrs,
US$11, Pingüino; Tue and Thu 1700,
Bus-Sur. To **Punta Arenas**, daily, US$15,
El Pingüino and others.

Car
To Chile First make sure your car papers
are in order – go to the tourist office for
necessary documents, then to the customs
office at the port, at the end of San Martín.
It's very uncomplicated. Then let the hire

company know, and allow 24 hrs to get the appropriate papers. The car's windows should be etched with the licence plate number.

It is essential to book car rental in advance in high season. **Cristina Vehiculos**, Libertad 123, T02966-425709; **Localiza**, Sarmiento 245, T02966-436717.

Taxis
Hiring a taxi for group excursions may be the same price as a tour bus. Taxi ranks are plentiful, the rates controlled, and *remise* slightly cheaper. Also consider hiring a car with driver from **Todo Transfer Patagonia** www.interpatagonia.com/todotransfer/.

ⓘ Directory

Comodoro Rivadavia *p558*
Banks Banco de la Nación, San Martín 102; Banco del Chubut, San Martín 833, ATMs. **Currency exchange** ETAP, in the bus terminal; Thaler, Bartolomé Mitre 943, Mon-Fri 0900-1400. **Embassies and consulates** Chile, Sarmiento 936.

Internet Rivadavia 201, and along San Martín at Nos 131, 394, 808, 263 and 699. **Post office** San Martín and Moreno.

Puerto San Julián *p561*
Banks Banco de la Nación, Mitre and Belgrano; Banco de la Provincia de Santa Cruz, San Martín and Moreno. **Post office** Belgrano and San Martín.

Río Gallegos *p562, map p563*
Banks Change TCs here if going to El Calafate, where it is even more difficult. 24-hr ATMs for all major international credit and debit cards all over the centre. Banco Tierra del Fuego, Roca 831, changes TCs. **Currency exchange** Cambio El Pingüino, Zapiola 469; and Thaler, San Martín 484, will both change Chilean pesos as well as US$. **Embassies and consulates** Chile, Mariano Moreno 136, Mon-Fri, 0900-1300; tourist cards issued at border. **Internet** Neo, Roca 1085 (next to British Club on Roca); also various *locutorios* offer internet services, US$1.50 per hr. **Post office** Roca 893 and San Martín. **Telephone** *Locutorios* all over town.

Ruta 40

The Ruta 40 – known in Argentina, with affection and awe, simply as 'la cuarenta' – is one of the wildest and least-travelled roads on the planet. It runs the whole length of Argentina, from La Quiaca on the border with Bolivia in the north, all the way down to El Chaltén and Río Gallegos in the south. And almost the entire length of the Ruta 40 crosses extraordinarily beautiful countryside: at times dramatic, at times eerily remote. Ernesto 'Che' Guevara travelled along much of it in his famous motorcycle jaunts and his experience of the poverty and adversity he encountered helped form his revolutionary spirit. You can get a flavour of the toughest parts by travelling this southernmost stretch through Patagonia on bicycle, motorbike, or by bus, which might be quite enough adversity for some travellers. In the 14 hours it takes to go from Los Antiguos to El Chaltén, you're likely to see no more than a few cars, and this experience alone convinces you of the sheer emptiness of Patagonia. You'll also spot condors wheeling high above the Andes, the occasional Patagonian fox, and not much else apart from the clouds, whipped into amazing shapes by the ubiquitous winds.

Along the way you could veer off the battered track to hide out at a number of isolated estancias, visible from miles away where you see a fringe of tall poplars protecting a cluster of buildings from the relentless wind. Many estancias in this area welcome guests, and you can enjoy horse riding, walking and the warm hospitality of their owners, who will share their experience of a hardy life. There's a wonderful national park to explore, Perito Moreno (not to be confused with Glaciar Perito Moreno, which is in Parque Nacional Los Glaciares, further south). Estancia La Oriental is the best way to see the park's stark and beautiful landscapes, many of which are inaccessible by car. To the north of this stretch, the Ruta 40 has a couple of strange attractions. One that belies the incredible emptiness of Patagonia is the Cueva de las Manos. Near the small towns of Los Antiguos and Perito Moreno, in the beautiful canyon of the Río Pinturas, are caves containing thousands of human handprints, made more than 8000 years ago. Mind blowing, especially after travelling for 14 hours without seeing a soul. Just to the north, near Sarmiento, there's a petrified forest, with huge trunks of monkey puzzle trees turned to stone 140 million years ago.

And when at last you arrive at Mount Fitz Roy, whose great turrets of granite can be seen rising up from the flat steppe from 100 km away, you may well think you've imagined it. It's one of the most magnificent sights in the whole country, made all the more spectacular by hours or days of relentless flat lands, with only condors and the clouds for company. For travel information on the Ruta 40, see www.rutanacional40.com (in Spanish with great maps) ⟫ For listings, see pages 578-581.

Ins and outs

Getting around
Travelling along the Ruta 40 is quite an experience, and unless you're taking the bus, it's one that requires careful planning. Travelling south, the road is paved as far as Perito Moreno, and then good *ripio*, improving greatly after Las Horquetas. From Río Mayo to El Calafate, the wide stony *ripio* track of the Ruta 40 zigzags its way across windswept desolate land. Every few hundred kilometres or so, there will be a small, improbable signpost to an *estancia*, somewhere off the road unseen, but be warned that not all accept paying guests, and many are just ordinary sheep farms. There are only a few service stations for fuel along the whole stretch, and few places offering accommodation. The best time to go is between October and April. Outside of these months travel is still possible but accommodation and transport is harder to find, and the winter is deadly cold.

Bus The most efficient way to travel this stretch is by making use of the bus services offered by two companies, **Chaltén Travel** and **Itinerarios y Travesías**, who between them run one service daily in each direction between Los Antiguos and El Chaltén. Departure times and the itinerary can change throughout the year, but if you're keen to stop off at Cueva de las Manos, both companies run a service that visits the caves at dawn at least a couple of times each week. A new year-round no-frills service run by local bus company **Taqsa** departing daily in summer and twice a week the rest of the year between El Calafate and Bariloche via the Ruta 40 is making the route even more accessible. Cueva de las Manos can also be reached with a tour organized from quite Perito Moreno or the more attractive Los Antiguos (www.losantiguos.gov.ar).

Car/motorbike/bike Hiring a car in one town, and dropping it off in another is possible, and allows great flexibility. But it can be expensive and is only fun if you're not travelling alone. Make sure you know exactly where the next petrol station is, as they can easily be 300 km apart: carry spare fuel, and allow more time than you think before nightfall. It's not advisable to travel faster than 60 kph on *ripio* roads. Take warm clothes, liquids and a blanket, in case you become stranded at night. If cycling, note that food and water stops are scarce, the wind is fierce, and there is no shade whatsoever. Hitching along this road is virtually impossible, and isn't recommended, as you could be stranded for days.

Crossing the border from Chile You might be wondering how to start your journey along the Ruta 40. There are several options. Travelling from north to south, you could reach Río Mayo from Comodoro Rivadavia, with regular buses along the Route 26. There are also daily buses from Esquel, at the southernmost end of the Lake District. But you may well have crossed from Argentina into Chile at Futuleufú (near Trevelin) and come south along the Carretera Austral in Chile. In this case, take the ferry across Lago General Carrera/Lago Buenos Aires, from south of Coyhaique to Chile Chico, and cross the border back into Argentina at Los Antiguos. This is one starting point of the bus journey south along the Ruta 40.

Accommodation Be warned that there are few decent places to stay along this entire route. The best bases for accommodation after Esquel in the north are the pretty little town of Los Antiguos, near the border with Chile, and Perito Moreno – also in the north. After that, there are only remote rural *estancias*, and some very bleak one-horse towns until you reach the tourist haven of El Chaltén. Take a tent if you're on a bike. To get to the *estancias*, you'll need to have booked in advance, and you'll need your own transport to get to them. Various companies organize tours along the route, with *estancia* stays and travel included; for more information see www.guiatierrabuena.com.ar and www.lastfrontiers.com. There's a useful site for information on the *estancias* in the area, although this organization offers no real logistical help, www.estanciasdesantacruz.com.

Colonia Sarmiento and the petrified forests → *For listings, see pages 578-581.*
Colour map 5, C3. Phone code 0297. Population 9000.

The vital east–west road link between Chile and the Atlantic is Route 26, also known as the Bioceanic Corridor, which runs east from the Andes across the steppe amid oil wells, from the Chilean border and the Chilean towns of Coyhaique and Puerto Aisén to Comodoro Rivadavia. Mainly used by lorries, it gives access to two unusual sights – the petrified araucaria forests of José Ormachea and Héctor Szlapelis, both within easy reach of the small town Colonia Sarmiento.

Sarmiento lies 156 km west of Comodoro Rivadavia on the Río Senguer just south of two great lakes, **Lago Musters** and **Lago Colhué Huapi**, both of which offer good fishing in summer. Founded in 1897 and formally known as Colonia Sarmiento, its early settlers were Welsh, Lithuanians and Boers. It's a quiet and relaxed place, sitting in fertile, well irrigated land, and little visited by tourists, though it's the best base for visiting two areas of petrified forest nearby. Most accessible is the **Bosque Petrificado José Ormachea** ① *US$3.50*, 32 km south along a *ripio* road. Less easy to reach is the rather bleaker **Bosque Petrificado Héctor Szlápelis**, some 40 km further southwest along the same road (follow signposts, the road from Sarmiento is in good condition). These forests, 60 million years old, of fallen araucaria trees nearly 3 m in circumference and 15 to 20 m long, are a remarkable sight, best visited in summer as the winters are very cold. There are *guardaparques* (rangers) at both sites, who can give tours and information. The **tourist office** ① *Pietrobelli 388, T0297-489 8220*, is helpful and has a map of the town. A *combi* (minibus) service runs to Bosque Petrificado Héctor Szlápelis twice daily from December to March; contact the tourist office. A taxi from Sarmiento to the forests costs around US$20 (three passengers), including a one-hour wait. Contact **Señor Juan José Valero** ① *Uruguay 43, T097-489 8407*, the *guardaparque*, for guided tours. Ask him about camping.

Río Mayo → *For listings, see pages 578-581. Colour map 5, C2. Phone code 02903. Population 2900.*

Set in beautifully bleak landscape, by the meandering Río Mayo, there's little of tourist interest in this very rural little town, and you're most likely to find yourself here to change for buses or pick up fuel. But every November, it is the site for an extraordinary display of dexterity at the **Fiesta Nacional de la Esquila** (national sheep-shearing competition). Teams of five or six *esquiladores*, who travel around Patagonia from farm to farm in shearing season, compete to shear as many sheep as possible. A good shearer might get through 20 in an hour. The re'sa little **tourist office** ① *Av Ejército Argentino s/n, T02903-420400, riomayoturistico@yahoo.com.ar.* From Río Mayo, a road continues west 140 km to the Chilean border at Coyhaique Alto for Coyhaique in Chile. South of Río Mayo Ruta 40 is unpaved as far as Perito Moreno (124 km, high-clearance advised).

Perito Moreno → *For listings, see pages 578-581. Colour map 5, C2. Phone code 02963. Population 3000.*

Not to be confused with the famous glacier of the same name near El Calafate, nor with Parque Nacional Perito Moreno, this Perito Moreno is a spruce little town, 25 km west of Lago Buenos Aires, and the nearest but not the most attractive base for exploring the mysterious cave paintings at the **Cueva de las Manos**, to the south. The town has no sights as such, apart from the pleasure of watching a rural community go about its business. But southwest of the town is **Parque Laguna**, where you can see varied birdlife including flamingos and black-necked swans, and go fishing. You could also walk to the crater of **Volcán Cerro**, from a path 12 km outside Perito Moreno: ask at the tourist office for directions. The friendly **tourist office** ① *San Martín 1222, T02963-432222, low season 0800-2000, high season 0700-2300*, can advise on tours to the cave and *estancias*. You could also visit Santa Cruz's **tourist office** ① *Suipacha 1120, T011-4325 3102, www.epatagonia.gov.ar*, in Buenos Aires. The bus terminal is on the edge of town next to the EG3 service station. There are two ATMs in the main street, at

Banco de la Provincia de Santa Cruz and Banco de la Nación. Traveller's cheques can be cashed at Banco Santa Cruz SA, Avenida San Martín 1385, T02963-432028 where they also change US dollars, euros and Chilean pesos. The airport is 7 km east of town, and the only way to get there is by taxi, US$8.

Cueva de las Manos → Colour map 6, A2. Phone code 02962.

ⓘ US$13, under 12 free. Entrance only with rangers between 0900 and 1900.

Situated 47 km northeast of Bajo Caracoles, the canyon of the **Río Pinturas** contains outstanding examples of handprints and cave paintings, estimated to be between 9500 and 13,000. In the cave's four galleries, shelves in the rock in a stunning canyon, are over 800 paintings of human hands, all but 31 of which are of left hands, as well as images of guanacos and rheas, and various geometrical designs. Painted by the Toldense peoples in red, orange, black, white and green, the pigments were derived from earth and calafate berries, and fixed with a varnish of guanaco fat and urine. They are mysterious, and rather beautiful, albeit indecipherable. However, the canyon alone is worth seeing, 270 m deep and 480 m wide, with strata of vivid red and green rock, especially beautiful in the early morning or evening light. Access is via an unpaved road which branches east off Ruta 40, 3 km north of Bajo Caracoles. *Guardaparques* living at the site give helpful information and a tour. It is one of the major cultural and archaeological sites in South America, declared a World Heritage Site by UNESCO in 1999, and definitely one of the highlights of any trip to Patagonia. Worth the trip for the setting, especially. The best time to visit is early morning or evening. The road can be difficult after rain. The minibus **Itinerarios y Travesías** from El Chaltén to Los Antiguos stops here in the early morning for a couple of hours. ▶▶ *For further information, see Transport, page 581.*

Los Antiguos and border with Chile → Colour map 6, A2. Phone code: 02963. Population 3000.

Though there are two crossings to Chile west of Perito Moreno, the easiest and most commonly used is via the pretty little village of Los Antiguos, which lies just 2 km east of the border. The town lies on the southern shore of Lago Buenos Aires, the second largest lake in South America, extending into Chile as Lago General Carrera, where the landscape is very beautiful and unspoilt. The Río Baker, which flows from the lake, is world-renowned for excellent trout fishing. ▶▶ *For further information on crossing the border here, see box, opposite.*

Los Antiguos is a sleepy little place, but has a pleasant atmosphere, thanks largely to its warm microclimate, and it's certainly a nicer place to stay than Chile Chico or Perito Moreno. New hotels are being built and there are countless new services including restaurants, new bus terminal and internet. It is good place to stay for two days or longer and to stock up on basics before continuing the journey. It's a rich fruit-growing area with a popular **cherry festival** in early January (**Fiesta Nacional de la Cereza**), which attracts national *folclore* stars, and is a nice place to spend a day or two. While you're here, there are two local *chacras* (small farms) worth visiting. You can walk from the main street to **Chacra Don Neno**, where there are strawberries growing and jam for sale. You'd have to drive, or take a taxi, though, to the idyllic **Chacra el Paraíso**, where the charming owners make really exquisite jams and chutney. Recommended. The **parque municipal** at the east end of the town is a pleasant place to walk, along the bank of the river, with birdlife to look at, and two blocks down, there's a superb campsite. There is a small but willing **tourist office** ⓘ *Av 11 de Julio 446, T02963-491261, www.losantiguos.gov.ar, daily 0800-2200 in summer, mornings only at other times.*

Border essentials: Argentina–Chile

Paso Huemules and Coyhaique Alto

There are two roads crossing the border into Chile to take you to Coyhaique from here. The southernmost of the two, via Paso Huemules, has better roads. Paso Huemules is reached by a road that branches off Ruta 40 some 31 km south of Río Mayo and runs west 105 km via Lago Blanco (small petrol station), where there is an *estancia* community, 30 km from the border. There's no hotel but the police are friendly and may permit camping at the police post. This road continues from Balmaceda on the Chilean side of the border to Coyhaique. This is the crossing used by buses between Comodoro Rivadavia and Coyhaique. The border is open 0900-2000 in winter and 0800-2200 in summer. For more information about the border crossing, see www.gendarmeria.gov.ar/pasos/fichhuemul.html.

Coyhaique Alto is reached by a 133-km road (87 km *ripio*, then dirt) that branches off Ruta 40 about 7 km north of Río Mayo. On the Chilean side this road continues to Coyhaique, 50 km west of the border.
Chilean immigration Coyhaique Alto, 6 km west of the border, May to July daily 0800-2100, September to April daily 0700-2100.

Los Antiguos

The main reason to enter Chile here is either to explore the largely unvisited and lovely southern shore of Lago General Carrera, or to take the ferry over the lake north to Puerto Ibáñez with bus connections on to Coyhaique, the main town for visiting the Carretera Austral. You can also drive to Puerto Ibáñez, via the paved road that goes around the north side of Lago Buenos Aires.
Transport Transportes VH buses cross the border by the bridge to the drab village of Chile Chico, 8 km west, US$3.75, 45 minutes. If crossing from Chile at Los Antiguos, there are two buses daily in summer, which take one hour and cost US$4, run by La Union, T02963-432133.

Bajo Caracoles and south to Tres Lagos → *Colour map 6, A2. Phone code 0297. Population 100.*
After hours of spectacular emptiness, even tiny Bajo Caracoles is a relief. It's nothing more than a few houses with an expensive grocery store and very expensive fuel. West of Bajo Caracoles, 72 km along Route 39 are **Lago Posadas** and **Lago Pueyrredón**, two beautiful lakes with contrasting blue and turquoise waters separated by a narrow isthmus. Guanacos and rheas can be seen and there are sites of archaeological interest.

Border with Chile From Bajo Caracoles Route 41 (unpaved) goes 99 km northwest to the **Paso Roballos** border with Chile, and from there 201 km onwards to Cochrane. Route 41 runs past Lago Ghio and Lago Columna. On the Chilean side this road continues to Cochrane, Km 177. Though passable in summer, it is often flooded in spring (September to November). There's no public transport available here.

South to Tres Lagos South of Bajo Caracoles Ruta 40 crosses the Pampa del Asador and then, near Las Horquetas, Km 371, swings southeast to follow the Río Chico. Some 92 km south of Bajo Caracoles is the turn-off west to Lago Belgrano and Parque Nacional Perito

Moreno (see below). About 23 km east, along Route 521 is **Tamel Aike**, Km 393, where there is a police station and water but little else. ('Super' grade fuel is available in most places, but carry extra, since the nearest fuel before Tres Lagos involves a 72-km detour to Gobernador Gregores.) At Km 464, Route 25 branches off to **San Julián** via **Gobernador Gregores**, 72 km southeast, where there is fuel and a good mechanic, while the Ruta 40 continues southwest towards Tres Lagos. At Km 531, a road heads west to Lago Cardiel, a very saline lake with no outlet and good salmon fishing.

From the Parque Moreno junction to Tres Lagos, Ruta 40 improves considerably. From Tres Lagos, Ruta 40 deteriorates rapidly and remains very rugged until after the turn-off to the Fitz Roy sector of Parque Nacional Los Glaciares. Twenty-one kilometres beyond is the bridge over Río La Leona, with delightful **Hotel La Leona** whose café serves good cakes. **Tres Lagos**, at Km 645, is a solitary village with a supermarket and fuel at the junction with Route 288. A road also turns off northwest to Lago San Martín, which straddles the border (the Chilean part is Lago O'Higgins).

Parque Nacional Perito Moreno → For listings, see pages 578-581.

ⓘ *Accessible only by own transport. Open all year round. There is no public transport into the park. Free. For more information, see www.parquesnacionales.gov.ar.*

Situated southwest of Bajo Caracoles on the Chilean border, this is one of the wildest and most remote parks in Argentina. There is good trekking and abundant wildlife within this large, interconnected system of lakes, lying between glaciated peaks of astonishing beauty. However, since much of the park is dedicated to scientific study, it's largely inaccessible. **Lago Belgrano**, in the park's centre, is the biggest in the chain of lakes, a vivid turquoise, contrasting with surrounding mountains streaked with a mass of differing colours; on its shores, you might find ammonite fossils.

Ins and outs

The **park office** ⓘ *Av San Martín 409, T02962-491477*, is 220 km away in the nearest town, Gobernador Gregores, and you can get information here before reaching the park itself. Entrance to the park from Gobernador Gregores is via the paved Ruta 40, before you turn off west, 100 km south of Bajo Caracoles, onto 90 km of unpaved road. The *guardaparques* office is 10 km beyond the park entrance, and has maps, and leaflets on walks and wildlife. It's essential to get detailed maps here and to ask advice about hikes and paths. You should always inform *guardaparques* before setting out on a hike. The best time to visit is in summer (December to February). However, the access road may be blocked by snow from November to March. Bring an all-season sleeping bag and plenty of warm clothing: the climate here is mercurial. There is nowhere to buy fuel inside the park, unless you're staying at one of the *estancias*, and cyclists should bring water: there is no source along the 90 km branch road.

There are two *estancias* inside the park boundaries: **Estancia La Oriental** and **Estancia Menelik**. There are also several good sites for camping (free) – although much of the park is closed to visitors. The most accessible part is around Lago Belgrano, 12 km from the entrance. ⏵ *For more information, see Sleeping, page 579.*

Around the park

Just outside the park, but towering over it to the north, is **Cerro San Lorenzo** (3706 m), the highest peak in southern Patagonia. Between the lakes are other peaks, permanently

Exploring Argentina

Francisco 'Perito' Moreno was one of Argentina's most prolific explorers, he played a leading role in defending Argentine rights in Patagonia and was pivotal in creating Argentina's first national park. Born in Buenos Aires in 1852, he showed an interest in flora and fauna early on, and by the age of 14 he had created his first collection of specimens – a collection that would go on to form the basis of the famous La Plata History Museum. When he was 20 he embarked on a series of explorations for the Argentine Scientific Society, and it was through these expeditions that he became a household name throughout the fledgling nation. He began with a survey of the uncharted Río Negro territory, which had just opened up thanks to Roja's Conquest of the Desert campaign (see box, page 135), and by 1876 he had reached Lake Nahuel Huapi in the Lake District. On the same trip, he 'discovered' El Chaltén in the south and named Cerro Fitz Roy. His second expedition was, however, decidedly more dangerous as he was captured by an unfriendly Tehuelche tribe and taken prisoner. He managed to escape down a river, with an injured leg the day before his execution. After several more expeditions, namely to claim Patagonian land for Argentina, he was given the name 'Perito' (expert) in 1902. For his exploring efforts the government gave him land in the Lake District, which he subsequently donated in order to create the country's first national park, Parque Nacional Nahuel Huapi. Ironically, Perito Moreno never set eyes on the famed Perito Moreno Glacier; it was simply named after him as he extensively explored the surrounding lakes and mountains.

snow-covered, the highest of which is Cerro Herros (2770 m). The vivid hues of Sierra Colorada run across the northeast of the park: the erosion of these coloured rocks that has given the lakes their differing colours. At the foot of Cerro Casa de Piedra is a network of caves containing cave paintings, accessible only with a guide. Wildlife in the park includes guanacos, foxes and one of the most important surviving populations of the rare huemul deer. Birds include flamingos, ñandus, steamer ducks, grebes, black-necked swans, Patagonian woodpeckers, eagles and condors. The lakes and rivers are unusual for Argentina in that only native species of fish are found here, whereas in the rest of the country, trout and salmon have been introduced for fishing.

Hiking

Several good hikes are possible from here. There are also longer walks of up to five days. Ask the *guardaparques* for details, and see the website.

Lago Belgrano ① *1-2 hrs*. Follow the Senda Natural Península Belgrano to the peninsula of the lake, 8 km, where there are fine views of Cerro Herros, and an experience of transition landscape from steppe to forest.

Lago Burmeister ① *via Cerro Casa de Piedra, 16 km*. The trail follows the northern shore and offers nice views of the lake. There is free camping (no fires permitted). It is hard to find the official trail in parts but if in doubt, follow the shore.

Cerro León ① *4 hrs*. Start at **Estancia La Oriental**. This walk has fabulous panoramic views over the park, and offers the chance to see condors in flight.

For Sleeping and Eating price codes and other relevant information, see Essentials pages 30-36.

● Sleeping

Colonia Sarmiento and the petrified forests *p572*

B-C Chacra Labrador, 10 km from Sarmiento, T0297-489 3329, agna@coopsar. com.ar. This is an excellent place to stay on a small *estancia*, breakfast included, all other meals extra and available to non-residents. English and Dutch spoken, runs tours to petrified forests at good prices, will collect guests from Sarmiento (same price as taxi).

Camping
Camping Municipal near Río Senguer, 2 km north of centre on R243. Basic, no shower, US$5 for tent, US$2 per person.

Río Mayo *p573*
LL Estancia Don José, 2.5 km west of Río Mayo, T02963-420015 or 0297-156 249155, www.guenguel.com.ar. Excellent *estancia*, with superb food, rooms and cabins. The family business involves sustainable production of guanaco fibre.
C Covadonga, San Martín 575, T02903-420 014, www.hotelcovadonga.guiapatagonia. net. The oldest hotel in town, established for travelling salesmen in the 1940s, and now restored with comfortable rooms, and a decent restaurant.

Camping
There is a free campsite on the northern outskirts, near the river.

Perito Moreno *p573*
A Hostería Cueva de Las Manos, 20 km from the cave, also known as Los Toldos, see below.
C Americano, San Martín 1327, T02963-432 538. With breakfast, has a decent restaurant, new ownership.

C Belgrano, San Martín 1001, T02963-432019. This hotel is often booked by Ruta 40 long-distance bus companies, basic and not always clean, one key fits all rooms, helpful owner, breakfast included.
C El Austral, San Martín 1386, T02963-432 538. Bath, breakfast and a decent restaurant.
D Alojamiento Dona Maria, 9 de Julio 1544, T02963-432452. Clean and basic.
E pp Santa Cruz, Belgrano 1565. Simple rooms.

Estancias
L pp Telken, 28 km south on R40, T02963-432079, Buenos Aires T011-4797 7216, jarinauta@santacruz.com.ar. Open Oct-Apr. Formerly a sheep station, now aimed at tourism. Comfortable accommodation in the farmhouse; charming simple bedrooms. All meals shared with the warmly welcoming owners, Joan and Reynaldo Nauta, who also offer horse riding (Cueva de las Manos US$80). Highly recommended.
A Las Tóldos/Hostería Cueva de Las Manos, 60 km south on R40, 7 km off the road to Bajo Caracoles, T02963-432856 (Buenos Aires, T011-4901 0436), www.estanciasdesantacruz.com. Open Nov-Apr. The closest *estancia* for visiting the Cueva de las Manos. A modest building, but set in wonderful landscape, the owners Alicia and Martín Molina organize trips by horse and 4WD to see the cave paintings, as well as to the lakes and the Perito Moreno park. They also have an *albergue*.
D Estancia Turística Casa de Piedra, 75 km south of Perito Moreno on R40, in Perito Moreno ask for Sr Sabella, Av Perón 941, T02963- 432199. Price is for rooms (camping **G**), hot showers, home-made bread, use of kitchen, excursions to Cueva de las Manos and volcanoes by car or horse.

Camping
Camping Municipal, 2 km at Laguna de los Cisnes, T02963-432072. Basic facilities.

Los Antiguos p574

Los Antiguos is being forever transformed by the opening of 2 new hotels/hostels.
L-AL Mirador Hostería & Spa, will be located 2 km from town. Horses, jacuzzi on the rooftop, cosy elegant rooms, Wi-Fi, restaurant and small library. Rents bicycles. Recommended. Contact Nicolas van Schie from **Viva el Viento**, T0297-15-4216133, www.vivaelviento.com, for updates.
A Antigua Patagonia, on the lakeside, signposted from R43, T02963-491038, www.antiguapatagonia.com.ar. Luxurious rooms with beautiful views from this modern building on the shore of the lake, with wide open vistas and big skies reflected in its waters. There's also an excellent restaurant. The charming owner Alejandro arranges small tours to the Cueva de las Manos and nearby Monte Cevallos. Highly recommended.
A-D Mora, Av Costanera. Will accommodate up to 170 people in rooms ranging from dorms to 1st-class accommodation with private bathrooms.
C Argentino, 11 de Julio 850, T02963-491 132. Comfortable rooms, decent restaurant.

Hostels

D-F pp Albergue Padilla, San Martín 44 (just off main street) T02963-491140. The town's cheapest place to stay. Big shared rooms for 4-8 with bathrooms, cosy *quincho* and garden to sit in, where you can also camp. Very friendly. They sell the El Chaltén travel tickets and collect passengers off the bus from El Chaltén. Recommended.
F pp Albergue y Bungalows Sol de Mayo, Av 11 de Julio, Chacra 133 'A', T02963-491 232. Another budget option. Basic rooms with shared bathrooms, very central location.

Camping

Camping Municipal, T02963-491265. An outstanding campsite with hot showers and every other facility. In lovely grounds 2 km from centre, US$4 per person. Cabins (**F**) available for up to 4 people. Linen not provided.

Bajo Caracoles and south to Tres Lagos p575

LL Hostería Lagos del Furioso, Lago Posadas, on the peninsula between the lakes, reached along R39, T02963-490253 (Buenos Aires, T011-5237 4043), www.lagosdelfurioso.com. Open mid-Oct to Easter. Extremely comfortable accommodation in cabins in a really incredible setting by the lake. Offers superb Patagonian cooking with home-grown produce and good wines. Also offers horse riding, trekking and excursions in a 4WD. 2 nights minimum – you'll want to stay longer.
C Hotel Bajo Caracoles, T02963-490100. Old-fashioned 1920s building, with plain, spacious rooms, but a rather institutional feel, and not quite welcoming. There are meals, and given the wilderness all around you'll probably be glad of a bed.

Estancias

There are some superb *estancias* in this region: tricky to get to without your own transport, but offering an unforgettable experience of Patagonian life.
A pp La Angostura, 55 km from Gobernador Gregores, T02962-491501, www.estanciala angostura.com.ar. Offers horse riding, trekking and fishing. Recommended.

Camping

The campsite is in the middle of town. Rooms (**E** pp) are also available. A simple and welcoming place, also runs excursions to Cueva de las Manos, 10 km by vehicle then 1½-2 hrs' walk, and to nearby volcanoes by car or horse. Ask for **Señor Sabella**, Av Perón 941, Perito Moreno, T02963-432199.

Parque Nacional Perito Moreno p576

L Estancia Menelik, follow R40 until the turn-off for Las Horquetas along R37, T011-4311 5550, www.estanciasde santacruz.com/Menelik/menelik_e.htm. Homely and comfortable, 3 double rooms with 1 quadruple, plus a *refugio* where you can sleep with your sleeping bag.

A Estancia La Oriental, T02962-452196, elada@uvc.com.ar. Open Nov-April, full board. In a splendid setting, rooms are comfortable and there's superb horse riding. A taxi from Gobernador Gregores costs US$95.

Camping

Camping is possible and there are 4 free sites inside the park: **Alberto de Agostini**; **Cerro de Vasco**; **Lago Burmeister**; and **Mirador Lago Belgrano**. There are no facilities and no fires are permitted.

❶ Eating

Perito Moreno *p573*

There's good food at **Pipach**, next to Hotel Austral; and **Parador Bajo Caracoles**. Nono's, on 9 de Julio and Saavedra, serves pizzas.

Los Antiguos *p574*

2 great *parrilla* restaurants on the main street.
♔ **Agua Grande**, 11 de Julio 871, T02963-491217. Slightly more modern and busier than **El Negro 'B' Parrilla**.
♔ **El Negro 'B' Parrilla**, 11 de Julio 571, 3 blocks away from **Agua Grande**, T02963-491358. Welcoming staff, looks outdated.
♔ **Viva El Viento**, 11 de Julio 477, T02963-491109, www.vivaelviento.com. Dutch-owned, good atmosphere, very good tasty food and coffee, 0900-0100, also has Wi-Fi, lots of information, flights over the lake, and boat trips arranged. Recommended.
♔ **Confitería y Restaurante El Tío**, Av11 de Julio 508.
♔ **Pizza Uno**, 11 de Julio 895, T02963-491471. A great, affordable pizzeria. Delivery service.

▲ Activities and tours

Colonia Sarmiento and the petrified forests *p572*
Tour operators

The operators listed below all offer tours to the petrified forest:

Aonikenk Viajes, Rawson 1190, T0297-446 6768, www.aonikenk.com.ar; **Atlas**, Rivadavia 439, T0297-447 5204; **Monitur**, Brown 521, T0297-447 1062, monitur@amadeusmail.com.ar.

Perito Moreno *p573*
Tour operators

Guanacóndor Viajes Turismo, Perito Moreno 1089, T02963-432117, guana condor@argentina.com; and **Las Loicas**, Transporte Lago Posados, T02963-490272, www.losloicas.com, both offer an all-day tour with the option of collecting passengers from Bajo Caracoles, US$40-50. Both do the Circuito Grande Comarca Noroeste, one of the highlights of Santa Cruz, taking in some of the province's scenery.
Zoyen Turismo, San Martín near Saavedra, T02963-432207, www.zoyenturismo.com.ar. The friendly staff can help with R40 connections and *estancia* visits.

Los Antiguos *p574*
Fishing

Los Antiguos is a great place to catch rainbow trout, and there are 2 local fishing guides who will take you out on the beautiful lake: **Mario Rodrigo**, T02966-1551 4923, and **Osvaldo Zeme**, T0297-154 137 813.

Tour operators
Turismo Toscas Bayas, 11 de Julio 797, T02963-491016, toscasbayas@yahoo.com.ar. Can arrange trips to the Cueva de las Manos, Monte Zeballos, Lago Posadas and more. They also run city tours, 4 hrs, US$10. Friendly.

❸ Transport

Colonia Sarmiento and the petrified forests *p572*
Bus

Overnight services to **Esquel**, Sun-Fri, with **Etap**, T0297-454756; take food for the journey, as cafés are expensive. Frequent buses to **Comodoro Rivadavia**.

To Chile Via Río Mayo, Giobbi, 3 weekly, 0200, seats are scarce in Río Mayo.

Río Mayo p573
Bus
To Chile Giobbi buses from **Comodoro Rivadavia** to **Coyhaique** pass through Río Mayo 3 times a week.

Perito Moreno p573
Air
LADE flies to **Perito Moreno** from **Río Gallegos**, **Río Grande**, **Ushuaia**, **El Calafate** and **Gobernador Gregores**.

Airline offices LADE, Av San Martín 1059, T02963-432055.

Bus
For bus terminal information, see page 573.

To **Comodoro Rivadavia**, with La Unión, 0630, 1700 and Sportman, 1700, 6 hrs, US$18 (latter also to Río Gallegos, US$43). There are 3 main companies that run to **El Chaltén**, 1000 (on even days), **Chaltén Travel**; and 1800 (on odd days), US$70, Itinerarios y Travesías and Taqsa. It's a 14-hr, 582-km journey over bleak emptiness. Northbound buses with Itinerarios y Travesías stop at the **Cueva de las Manos** for a couple of hours at dawn, and while it's a shame to miss the ride in daylight, it's a great way to see the caves.

Car
Perito Moreno is a great place to service your car. There are several mechanics on both Rivadavia and San Martín streets.

Taxi
Parada de taxi El Turista, Av San Martín and Rivadavia, T02963-432592.

Los Antiguos p574
Bus
There is brand new bus terminal on Av Tehuelches. It has a large, moderately priced cafeteria/restaurant with free Wi-Fi. Most bus companies will agree to store the luggage. Vans from Chile now arrive at this terminal.

To **Comodoro Rivadavia** (via Perito Moreno and Caleta Olivia), daily, 7½ hrs, US$19, **Co-op Sportman**, T02963-491175, from near Hotel Argentino. To **El Chaltén** and **El Calafate** (via Perito Moreno), daily, US$70, **Chaltén Travel**, booked through Albergue Padilla, San Martín 44 Sur, T02962-491140, or through the Chaltén Travel agency on San Martín 44, T02693-491140, www.chaltentravel.com. Itinerarios y Travesías run buses along the route every odd day and tickets can be bought in their office in **El Chaltén**, Perito Moreno 152, T02962-493088, or at Albergue Patagonia, Av San Martín 493 (only open during high season), El Chaltén, T02962-493019, patagoniahostel@yahoo.com.ar. Taqsa have the same schedules as Itinerarios y Travsías but run a no-frills service once a week, all year round, US$60. Sportman and Taqsa (Av Tehuelches terminal, T0297-156 234 882), to **Río Gallegos**, daily, US$46, 15 hrs. To **Chile**, La Unión to Chile Chico, 8 km west, US$3.75, 45 mins, including border crossing.

Remise taxis
There are several companies that run *remise* taxi services, **Los Antiguos**, T0297-156 215 073, or T0297-491451, is recommended.

Parque Nacional Los Glaciares

Of all Argentina's impressive landscapes, the sight of these immense glaciers stretching out infinitely and silently before you may stay with you longest. This is the second-largest national park in Argentina, extending along the Chilean border for over 170 km, almost half of it covered by the Southern Ice Cap – at 370 km long. From it, 13 major glaciers descend into two great lakes: Lago Argentino in the southeast and Lago Viedma to the northeast. Two quite different areas of the park are centres for tourism. At the southern end, the spectacular glaciers themselves can be visited from El Calafate, with bus and boat trips to Glaciares Moreno, Upsala and Spegazzini. At the northern end, there is superb trekking around the dramatic Fitz Roy massif, and ice climbing on glaciers near its summit, reached from El Chaltén, 217 km northwest of El Calafate. The central section, between Lago Argentino and Lago Viedma, is composed of the ice cap on the western side, with a couple of estancias open to tourists. East of the ice fields, there's plentiful southern beech forest, but further east still, the land flattens to the typical wind-blasted Patagonian steppe, with sparse vegetation. Birdlife is surprisingly prolific, and you'll spot the scarlet-headed Magallenic woodpecker, black-necked swans, and perhaps even the torrent duck, diving for food in the streams and rivers. Guanacos, grey foxes, skunks and rheas can be seen on the steppe while the rare huemul inhabits the forest. The entire national park is a UNESCO World Heritage Site. For more information, see www.losglaciares.com. ▸▸ For listings, see pages 594-604.

Ins and outs

Getting there
Access to the park is very straightforward at both El Calafate and El Chaltén. There are regular bus services from El Calafate, as well as many tourist excursions, combining bus access with boat trips, walking and even ice trekking on Glaciar Perito Moreno. There are flights to El Calafate from Buenos Aires, Ushuaia, Río Gallegos, Esquel, Comodoro Rivadavia, Bariloche and Puerto Natales in Chile. All transport gets heavily booked in the summer months of January and February. From El Chaltén you can hike directly into the park, with a well established network of trails leading to summits, lakes and glaciers around Mount Fitz Roy, with many campsites. There are several buses daily to El Chaltén from El Calafate.

Best time to visit
Although this part of Patagonia is generally cold, there is a milder microclimate around Lago Viedma and Lago Argentino, which means that summers can be reasonably pleasant, with average summer temperatures between 5°C and 22°C, though strong winds blow constantly at the foot of the Cordillera. Rainfall on the Hielo Sur, up to 5000 mm annually, falls mainly as snow. In the forested area, rainfall is heavier, and falls mainly between March and late May. In winter, the whole area is inhospitably cold, and most tourist facilities are closed, although El Calafate and the Perito Moreno Glaciar are open all year round. The best time to visit is between November and April, avoiding January and early February, when Argentines take their holidays, campsites are crowded and accommodation is hard to find.

Park information
Entrance fee to the park is US$16, to be paid at the gates of the park, 50 km west of El Calafate. There is an **El Calafate park office** ① *Av del Libertador 1302, T02901-491005,*

Parque Nacional Los Glaciares

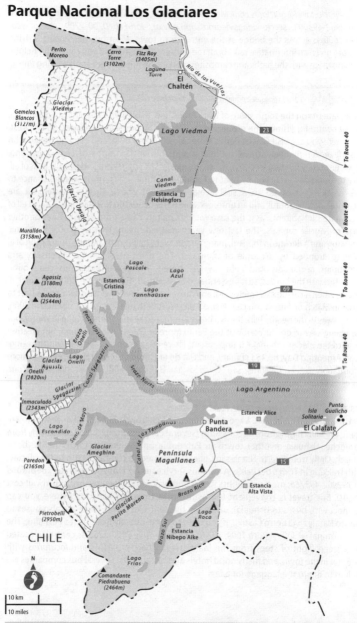

CHILE

10 km
10 miles

parquenacional@losglaciares.com, Mon-Fri 0800-1600, in town. The **El Chaltén park office**
ⓘ *T02962-493004, seccionallagoviedma@apn.gov.ar, Jan-Feb 0700-2200, rest of year 0900-1600,* is across the bridge at the entrance to town. Most bus passengers arriving here are given an informative talk about the park and its paths, and you can ask for helpful trekking maps with the paths and campsites marked, giving distances and walking times.

El Calafate → *For listings, see pages 594-604. Colour map 6, B2.*

El Calafate sits on the south shore of Lago Argentino, a town existing almost entirely as a tourist centre for visiting the glaciers in the Parque Nacional los Glaciares, 50 km west. From here you can visit Glaciar Perito Moreno by bus and boat, and even go trekking on its surface. Alternatively, travel by boat along the western arms of Lago Argentino, between stately floating icebergs, to see the glaciers of Spegazzini and Upsala. Best of all, take the long day excursion by boat to **Estancia Cristina**, which gives you the chance to trek or ride horses up to a spectacular viewpoint above Upsala Glacier. All are breathtakingly beautiful, and an unforgettable part of your trip to Patagonia. Almost all of El Calafate's inhabitants, as is the case with El Chaltén, came from Buenos Aires or other large provincial capitals. The last few years, marked meant that by global economic recession and a decline in tourism, many people went back north and the population of El Calafate dropped by a couple of thousand. The town itself can be expensive, and sometimes in January and February the hotels, hostels and *cabañas* can't quite accommodate the hordes, so it's essential to book ahead. The town is empty and quiet all winter, when it can be extremely cold, and most tourist services close down, so it's best to come in March or April if you can. A small ski resort with just four pistes opened in 2006, 11 km away in the nearby hills: this is a brave attempt to keep visitors coming in winter, but has a long way to go. You can visit the Perito Moreno Glacier all year round, but weather close to the glacier can make it unpleasant. There are a couple of festivals worth seeing: **Lago Argentino Day**, on 15 February, and **Día de la Tradición**, on 10 November. For more information on El Calafate, see www.losglaciares.com and www.todocalafate.com.
▶▶ *For more information, see Festivals and events, page 600.*

Ins and outs → *Phone code 02902. Population 8000.*
Getting there The airport, **Lago Argentino** ⓘ *T02902-491230*, is 23 km east of town. There are daily flights from Buenos Aires (several daily in summer). You can also fly from Bariloche, Ushuaia or other towns in Patagonia on the weekly **LADE** flights (book ahead). Or fly from Puerto Natales in Chile (in summer) to combine a trip to the glaciers with trekking in Torres del Paine. A minibus service run by **Transpatagonia Expeditions** ⓘ *T02902-493766*, meets all flights (US$4 one way, US$7 open return); a taxi will cost US$10. Bus travel is convenient too, with buses from Río Gallegos (where you can connect with buses to Ushuaia) arriving in the centre of town. There are also buses to Puerto Natales, via Cerro Castillo, if you want to come directly from Torres del Paine. The **bus terminal** ⓘ *Julio A Roca 1004, T02902-491090, daily 0800-2200*, is centrally located up a steep flight of steps from the main street. There are ATMs and *locutorios* with internet in the town, and many good hotels and restaurants. Several bus companies are willing to guard the luggage for a fee.

Getting around El Calafate's shops, restaurants and tour operators can mostly be found along its main street, Avenida del Libertador, running east to west, with hotels lying within two blocks north and south and smaller *hosterías* scattered through the residential areas sprawling up the hill, and north of centre, across the river. There are many *estancias* on the way to the national park, and also campsites. A small local public transport system carries people from one end of the city to the other, which is useful if you are staying at some of the hotels on the edge of town. Bus travel and tour trips to the Perito Moreno glaciers are well organized. The cheapest method is with a regular bus service, but tours can be informative and some include a boat trip.

Tourist information There is a small not particularly helpful **tourist office** ① *T02902-491 090, www.elcalafate.gov.ar, Oct-Apr daily 0800-2200, May-Sep 0800-2100,* at the bus terminal. They have folders of helpful information that you can browse.

El Calafate

Sleeping 🛏
América del Sur **1** *B3*
AMSA **9** *C3*
Ariel **13** *B1*
Blanca Patagonia **2** *C1*
Cabañas Nevis **3** *B1*
Casa de Grillos **12** *A2*
Design Suites **4** *A2*
Hostel del Glaciar 'Libertador' **7** *C3*
Hostel del Glaciar 'Pioneros' & Punto de Encuentro Restaurant **19** *C3*
Hostel de las Manos **6** *A2*
I Keu Ken Hostel **8** *C2*
Kau-Yatún **20** *C3*
Kosten Aike & Ariskaiken Restaurant **14** *B2*
Lago Azul B **5** *B2*
Los Alamos & La Posta Restaurant **15** *B2*

Los Sauces Casa Patagónica **10** *A1*
Michelangelo & Restaurant **17** *B2*
Patagonia Rebelde **16** *B3*
Santa Monica Aparts **21** *B3*
Sir Thomas **11** *A2*
Vientos del Sur **18** *C1*

Eating 🍽
Casablanca **1** *B2*
Casimiro Biguá **12** *B2*
El Puesto **2** *B2*
Heladería Aquarela **4** *B2*
La Cocina **7** *B2*
La Tablita **11** *B3*
Mi Viejo **6** *B2*
Pascasio **3** *B2*
Pura Vida **5** *C1*
Rick's Café **6** *B2*
Viva la Pepa **10** *B3*

Bars & clubs 🍸
Borges y Álvarez **14** *B2*
Elba'r **9** *B2*
Shackleton Lounge **8** *C1*

Sights

Though El Calafate was founded in 1927, it grew very slowly until the opening of the road to the Perito Moreno Glacier in the 1960s, and has since expanded rapidly as a tourist town. Following the economic collapse in 2001, many people flocked here from Buenos Aires to start hotel and restaurant businesses, and escape the economic stress of the city. Tourism here is very transient: most people stay here no longer than two or three nights.

Just west of the town centre is **Bahía Redonda**, a shallow part of Lago Argentino that freezes in winter, when ice-skating and skiing are possible. At the eastern edge of the bay, **Laguna Nímez**, there's a bird reserve where there are flamingos, black-necked swans and ducks; recommended for an hour's stroll either early morning or late afternoon. From the **Intendencia del Parque** ① *Av del Libertador 1302*, follow Calle Bustillo up the road to cross the bridge. Keep heading north across a pleasant new residential area: the *laguna* is signposted. Guides lead walks in the summer that last two hours, US$1, and take place Monday to Saturday. On the way back, you can stop by the **Centro de Interpretación Histórica** ① *Av Brown and Bonarelli, T02902-492799, US$3*, a small well-run centre housing a very educating exhibition created by an anthropologist and a historian with pictures and bilingual texts about the region. There's also a very relaxing café and library.

Around El Calafate

For the main excursions to the glaciers, see Glaciar Perito Moreno below. El Calafate has a number of other attractions, worth considering if you're here for a few days, and some good places for trekking, horse riding and exploring by 4WD. At **Punta Gualicho** (or Walichu) on the shores of Lago Argentino, 7 km east of town, there are cave paintings. Though they're rather badly deteriorated, the six-hour horse ride (US$40 per person) is worthwhile. Some tour operators run excursions to the top of nearby hills for views of the silhouette of the southern end of the Andes, **Bahía Redonda** and Isla Solitaria on Lago Argentino. An easy five-hour walk (or horse ride) is possible to the top of Cerro Calafate for panoramic views too. Ask for directions at the **Hostel del Glaciar Pioneros**.

Several *estancias* are within reach, offering a day on a working farm, a lunch of Patagonian lamb, cooked *asado al palo* (speared on a metal structure over an open fire), and activities such as trekking, birdwatching and horse riding. **Estancia Alice** ① *T02902-491793 (T011-4312 7206 in Buenos Aires), www.estanciaalice.com.ar*, also known as 'El Galpón del Glaciar', 21 km west, is a lovely house with views of Lago Argentino offering the 'El Galpón' tour, including tea with home-made cakes, walks through a bird sanctuary where 43 species of birds have been identified, displays of sheep shearing, *asado*, and music shows, all for US$60 per person (includes transfer to and from hotels); English spoken. Trekking, 4WD or horse-riding trips to the top of Cerro Frías (1030 m) for fantastic views of Mount Fitz Roy, Paine and Lago Argentino are organized by **Cerro Frías** ① *Libertador 1857, T02902-492808, www.cerrofrias.com*, for around US$45 per person, including lunch.

Lago Roca, 40 km southwest, is set in beautiful open landscape, with hills above offering panoramic views, perfect for lots of activities, such as trout and salmon fishing, climbing, walking, and there are *estancias*, such as the beautifully set **Estancia Nibepo Aike** ① *www.nibepoaike.com.ar*, or book through Lago San Martín agency, *www.lagosanmartin.com*, where you can watch typical farm activities, such as the branding of cattle in summer. There is good camping in a wooded area and a restaurant. At **Estancia Quien Sabe**, strawberries and walnuts are grown, and you can see beehives and sheep shearing, and eat an *asado* lunch; contact **Turismo Leutz**, *www.leutzturismo.com.ar*.

Lago Argentino

Glaciar Perito Moreno

The sight of this expanse of ice, like a frozen sea, its waves sculpted by wind and time into beautiful turquoise folds and crevices, is unforgettable. Immense and silent, you'll watch in awe, until suddenly a mighty roar announces the fall of another hunk of ice into the milky turquoise water below. Glaciar Moreno is one of the few accessible glaciers in the world which you can see visibly advancing. Some 30 km long, it reaches the water at a narrow point in one of the fjords, **Brazo Rico**, opposite Península Magallanes, and here, where it's 5 km across and 60 m high, it occasionally advances across Brazo Rico, blocking the fjord. As the water pressure builds up behind it, the ice breaks, reopening the channel and sending giant icebergs (*témpanos*) rushing down the appropriately named **Canal de los Témpanos**. This has only happened in recent decades, February 1988, March 2004, March 2006, and quite unusually in winter 2008, raising concern that global warming may be to blame for the marked change in the glacier's behaviour. Walking on the ice itself is a wonderful way to experience it, climbing up the steep curves of what appear from a distance to be vertical fish scales, and are in fact huge peaks, with mysterious chasms below, lit by refracted bluish light.

Access There are various ways to approach the glacier. All excursions not involving boat trips (and the regular bus service) will take you straight to the car park situated 77 km west of El Calafate (around 30 km further from the gates of the park) where you begin the descent along a series of extensive wooden walkways (*pasarelas*) to see the glacier slightly from above, and then, as you get lower, directly head-on. There are several wide viewing areas, where in summer crowds wait expectantly, cameras poised, for another hunk of ice to fall from the vertical blue walls at the glacier's front into the milky turquoise lake below with a mighty roar. There is a large and fairly inexpensive café at the site with clean bathrooms. You could also approach the glacier by boat from two different piers. To survey the glacier from the south (and for trekking on the glacier), boats leave from Bajo de las Sombras pier (7 km east of the glacier). To approach from the north, boats leave regularly from Perito Moreno pier (1 km north of the glacier, where there is a restaurant). This latter service is offered as an extra when you book your standard excursion to the glacier or it can also be booked directly at the pier. To get closer still, there are guided treks on the ice itself, known as Big Ice and Minitrekking, where you can walk along those crevices and frozen wave crests in crampons, which are provided. The latter is possible for anyone with a reasonable level of fitness, and not technically demanding. The glacier is approached by a lovely walk through lenga forest, and there's a place to eat your lunch outside, with wonderful views; but bring your own food and drink. Tour companies in El Calafate offer all of these, or some in combinations. ▶ *For further information, see Activities and tours, page 601.*

Glaciar Upsala

The fjords at the northwestern end of Lago Argentino are fed by four other glaciers. The largest is the Upsala Glacier, named after the Swedish university that commissioned the first survey of this area in 1908, a stunning expanse of untouched beauty. It's three times the area of the Perito Moreno Glacier, and the longest glacier flowing off the Southern Patagonian icefield. Unusually it ends in two separate frontages, each about 4 km wide and 60 m high, although only the western frontage can be seen from the lake excursion. It can be reached by motorboat from Punta Bandera on Lago Argentino, 50 km west of Calafate, on a trip that also goes to other, much smaller, glaciers. **Spegazzini**, further south, has a frontage 1.5 km wide and 130 m high. In between are **Agassiz** and **Onelli** glaciers, both of which feed into **Lago Onelli**, a quiet and very beautiful lake, full of icebergs of every size and sculpted shape, surrounded by beech forests on one side and ice-covered mountains on the other. However, unlike its cousin Perito Moreno, Upsala suffers tremendously from global warming. At the end of 2009 a huge part of it broke from the main mass of ice, blocking most of the lake and all tourist activities.

The best way to see Upsala Glacier is to visit the remote **Estancia Cristina** ⓘ *9 de Julio 69, El Calafate, T02902-491133 (T011-4814 3934 in Buenos Aires), www.estancia cristina.com*. Lying on a lonely lakeside spot, on the northern shores of the lake, not far from Upsala Glacier, it's beautiful, utterly wild, and yet an unbeatably comfortable base for exploring the region. Accommodation is available, or you can come on a full-day visit that includes lunch and the option to go hiking for five hours, horse riding or driving in sturdy 4WD vehicles to a vantage point high above the lake. You'll walk through incredible ancient landscapes, alongside massive rocks polished smooth by the path of glaciers, to see Upsala Glacier from above. This is an overwhelmingly beautiful sight, stretching apparently endlessly away from you, with the deep still Prussian-blue lake below, and all around, rocks the colour of fire. Boat trips to **Estancia Cristina** are run by Fernández Campbell (see Activites and tours, page 602).

Cerro Fitz Roy and around

The soaring granite towers of Mount Fitz Roy rise up from the smooth baize of the flat steppe, more like a ziggurat than a mountain, surrounded by a consort of jagged snow-clad spires, with a stack of spun-cotton cloud hanging constantly above them. **Cerro Fitz Roy** (3405 m) is one of the most magnificent mountains in the world, towering above the nearby peaks, its polished granite sides too steep for snow to settle. Its Tehuelche name was El Chaltén ('smoking mountain' or 'volcano'), perhaps because occasionally at sunrise the pink towers are briefly lit up bright red for a few seconds, the *amanecer de fuego* ('sunrise of fire'). Perito Moreno named the peak after the captain of the *Beagle* who saw it from afar in 1833, and it was first climbed by a French expedition in 1952. It stands in the northern end of Parque Nacional Los Glaciares, at the western end of Lago Viedma, 230 km north of El Calafate. Around it are **Cerros Torre** (3102 m), **Poincenot** (3002 m), and **Saint-Exupery** (2558 m), in an area of lakes and glaciers that makes marvellous trekking country, every bit as satisfying as Torres del Paine across the border.

Ins and outs

Getting around The base for walking and climbing around Fitz Roy is the tiny town of El Chaltén. Most paths are very clear and well worn, but a map is essential, even on short walks: the park information centre provides helpful maps of treks, but the best are published by *Zagier and Urruty*, www.patagoniashop.net, regularly updated, in varied scales (1:50,000; 1:250,000; 1:350,000), US$6-12, available in shops in El Calafate and El Chaltén. Do not stray from the paths. Always wear sunscreen (factor 30 at least), and be prepared for bad weather. In summer, **Restaurant Las Lengas** runs a regular minibus to Lago del Desierto, passing several starting points for treks and the wonderful **Hostería El Pilar**. There is a one-hour hike to Chorillo del Salto, a small but pristine

Trekking advice and information

- There are campsites at Poincenot, Capri, De Agostini and Laguna Toro. (**Note** Rio Blanco is only for climbers with prior permission arranged.) Campsites have no services, but all have toilets, apart from Laguna Toro.
- Access is free. There's no need to register before you leave on walks, and the paths are well marked. But stick to the centre of the path so as not to make it any bigger and walk in single file (at times that means you'll be walking in a rut).
- The park information centre will give you a good map which recommends lots of walks, times for walking and tells you where campsites are.

Times given on their sheet are for walking one way only.

- As you leave El Chaltén, don't let the dogs follow you, as they frighten the huemules (rare wild deer, an endangered species).
- Don't bathe in rivers and lakes, and take water away from source to wash.
- Don't go to the toilet near water sources, and take all rubbish down the mountain with you.
- A gas/alcohol stove is essential for camping as fires are prohibited everywhere in the park.
- Take plenty of warm clothes and a good sleeping bag. It is possible to rent equipment in El Chaltén; ask at the park office or Rancho Grande hostel.

waterfall. Follow the road to Lago del Desierto for about 30 minutes, then stay on marked path. No guide necessary.

Park information The national park office is across the bridge, right at the entrance to the town, T02962-493004, www.parquesnacionales.gov.ar, January-February 0700-2200, the rest of year 0900 1600. Visitors are met by the friendly *guardaparques* (some speak English), and you should ask for their helpful trekking maps with paths and campsites marked, giving distances and walking times.

Best time to visit Walking here is only really viable mid-October to April, with the best months usually March to early April when the weather is generally stable and not very cold, and the autumn colours of the beech forest are stunning. Midsummer (December and January), and spring (September to October) are generally very windy. In December and January the campsites can be full to bursting, with many walkers on the paths. Outside of these months most accommodation and many services close.

Trekking

Always ask at your accommodation or at the tourist office for up-to-date information on trails and weather conditions.

Laguna Torre For a dramatic approach to Cerro Torre, take the path to Laguna Torre (three hours each way). After 1½ hours you'll come to Mirador Laguna Torre with views of Cerro Torre and Fitz Roy, and after another 1¼ hours, to busy Camping De Agostini (formerly Bridwell), next to the lake, with fantastic views of the Cordón Torre.

Laguna de los Tres For closer views of Cerro Fitz Roy, take the path to Laguna de los Tres (four hours each way). Walk up to **Camping Capri** (just under two hours), with great views of Fitz Roy, then another hour to **Camping Poincenot**. Just beyond it is **Camping Río Blanco** (only for climbers, previous registration at park office required). From Río Blanco you can walk another hour, though it's very steep, to Laguna de los Tres where you'll get a

The Fitz Roy area

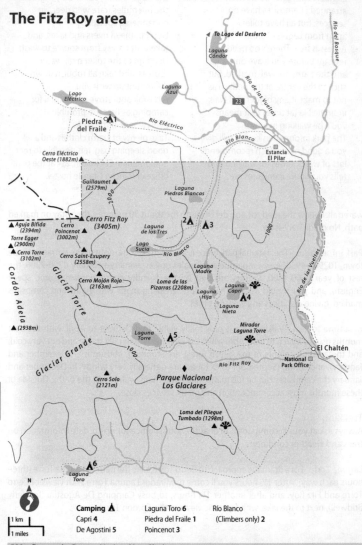

Camping ⛺

Capri **4**
De Agostini **5**

Laguna Toro **6**
Piedra del Fraile **1**
Poincenot **3**

Río Blanco
(Climbers only) **2**

spectacular view (not a good walk if it's cloudy). In bad weather, you're better off walking an hour to Piedras Blancas (four hours total from El Chaltén). You can connect the two paths (between Laguna Torre and Laguna de los Tres) by taking a transverse path (two hours) that links a point northwest of Laguna Capri and another one east of **Camping De Agostini**, passing two lakes, Laguna Madre and then Laguna Hija; but note that this alternative can take more than one day.

Loma del Pliegue Tumbado A recommended day walk is to the Loma del Pliegue Tumbado viewpoint (four hours each way) where you can see both *cordones* and Lago Viedma. There's a marked path from the *guardería* with excellent panoramic views, best in clear weather. The trek to **Laguna Toro**, a glacial lake on the route across the ice cap (seven hours each way) is for more experienced trekkers.

Piedra del Fraile The trek up Río Blanco to Piedra del Fraile (seven hours each way) is beautiful. It starts at Campamento Río Blanco running north along the Río Blanco and west along the Río Eléctrico via Piedra del Fraile (four hours) to Lago Eléctrico. Piedra del Fraile can be reached more easily from the road to Lago del Desierto in about two hours. At Piedra del Fraile, just outside the park, there are *cabañas* (E per person, hot showers) and a campsite, US$6 per person. From here a path leads south, up Cerro Eléctrico Oeste (1882 m) towards the north face of Fitz Roy (two hours); it's tough going but offers spectacular views. You should take a guide for this last bit. The best day walks are Laguna Capri and Mirador Laguna Torre, both of which have great views.

Climbing

Base camp for Fitz Roy (3405 m) is Campamento Río Blanco. Other peaks include Cerro Torre (3102 m), Torre Egger (2900 m), Cerro Solo (2121 m), Poincenot (3002 m), Guillaumet (2579 m), Saint-Exupery (2558 m), Aguja Bífida (2394 m) and Cordón Adela (2938 m): most of these are for very experienced climbers. The best time to climb is generally mid-February to end March; November to December is very windy; January is fair; winter (May to July) is extremely cold, but weather is unpredictable and it all depends on the specific route being climbed. Permits for climbing are available at the national park information office. Guides are available in El Chaltén, see Activities and tours, page 602. **Fitz Roy Expediciones** are recommended.

El Chaltén → *For listings, see pages 594-604. Colour map 6, B2.*

The small modern town of El Chaltén is set in a wonderful position at the foot of Cerro Fitz Roy and at the mouth of the valley of the Río de las Vueltas. The village was founded very recently, in 1985, in order to settle the area and pre-empt Chilean territorial claims. However, it has grown very rapidly, along with its popularity as a centre for trekking and climbing in summer, and for cross-country skiing in winter. It can be an expensive and not particularly attractive place, especially when the harsh wind blows. But its visitors create a cheerful atmosphere, there are some great bars and from its concrete and tin you can walk directly into breathtaking landscapes. Tourist infrastructure is still developing, and so far there is only one ATM (right next to the gas station at the entrance to town), so consider taking extra cash in case it isn't working. Luckily credit cards are accepted in all major hotels and most restaurants. Accommodation is available and ranges from camping and hostels to not-quite-luxurious *hosterías*, and some top hotels, all overpriced in high season. Food is expensive too, though there is increasingly plenty of choice.

Ins and outs → *Phone code 02962.*

The quickest way to reach the town is by flying to El Calafate's airport, 220 km away, and from there it's a four-hour bus journey. There are frequent bus connections from El Calafate, and regular bus services in summer from Ruta 40 in the north, useful if you've come from the Lake District in either Argentina or Chile. The **tourist information office** ① *Güemes 21, T02962-493270, www.elchalten.com, Mon-Fri 0900-2000, Sat-Sun 1300-2000 only in high season*, has an excellent website with accommodation listed. They hand out trekking maps of the area, with paths and campsites marked, distances and walking times.

Sights

There is a small chapel, the **Capilla Tomás Egger**, named after an Austrian climber killed on Fitz Roy and built entirely from materials brought from Austria. The main attraction here is clearly the trekking around Fitz Roy or Torre cordons. But there is also stunning virgin landscape to explore around the **Lago del Desierto**, 37 km north of El Chaltén. The long skinny lake is fjord-like, surrounded by forests, and a short walk to a mirador at the end of the road gives fine views. It's reached by unpaved Route 23, which leads along the Río de las Vueltas via **Laguna Cóndor**, where flamingos can be seen. A path runs along the east side of the lake to its northern tip, from where a trail leads west along the valley of the Río Diablo to Laguna Diablo. There is also the possibility of walking to Chile (border control at the Gendarmería, only open November to April) in two hours. To get to Villa O'Higgins (Chile), the southernmost town on the Carretera Austral, take the Las Lengas transfer to Lago del Desierto, then a 45-minute boat trip goes to the northern

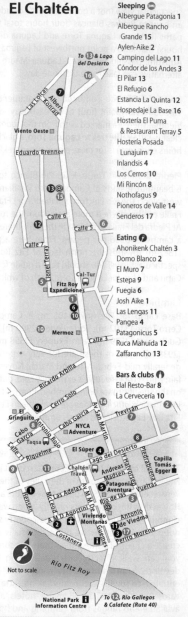

El Chaltén

To ⑬ & Lago del Desierto
16
Las Loicas
Albert Konrad
⑦
Viento Oeste ▢
Eduardo Brenner
⑬@
⑮
⑫
Calle 6
Calle 5
Calle 7
Lionel Terray
⑤
Fitz Roy Expediciones
Cal-Tur 🚌
①
⑥
⑩
⑩ Mermoz
Calle 3
Ricardo Arbilla
Cerro Solo
El Gringuito ⑨
Cabo García
Antonio Rojo
Trevisán
NYCA Adventure
Cerro García
Taqsa
Riquelme
El Súper
Lago del Desierto
Chaltén Travel
Andreas Madsen
⑨ ⑪
Patagonia Aventura ⑤
Capilla Tomás + Egger
McLead
Las Adelas
M.M De Güemes
Río de las Vueltas
Hansen
A M D Agostini
② Viviendo Montañas
Antonio de Viedma
⑪ ③⑰
Costanera
N
i ▢
Perito Moreno
Not to scale
Río Fitz Roy

National Park Information Centre 🏛

To ⑫, Río Gallegos & Calafate (Ruta 40)

Border essentials: Argentina–Chile

Paso Río Don Guillermo/Cancha Carrera

The Paso Río Don Guillermo or Cancha Carrera, 129 km west of La Esperanza and 48 km north of Río Turbio, open all year, is the most convenient crossing for Parque Nacional Torres del Paine. In Chile, the road continues 7 km to Cerro Castillo, where it meets the road from Puerto Natales, 65 km south, to Parque Nacional Torres del Paine. Open all year, daily 0900-2300. For more information, see www.gendarmeria.gov.ar/pasos/fichdguille.html (in Spanish).

Argentine customs and immigration Cancha Carrera, 2 km east of border, fast and friendly.

Chilean immigration On the Chilean side the road continues 14 km to the Chilean border post at Cerro Castillo, where it joins the road from Puerto Natales to Torres del Paine. Open daily 0830-1200, 1400-2000.

Paso Mina Uno/Dorotea

Paso Mina Uno/Dorotea is 5 km south of Río Turbio and is open all year, daily 0900-0100. On the Chilean side this runs south to join the main Puerto Natales–Punta Arenas road. This is the crossing used by buses from Río Turbio to Puerto Natales. For more information, see www.gendarmeria.gov.ar/pasos/fichdorotea.html.

Paso Casas Viejas

Paso Casas Viejas is 33 km south of Río Turbio via 28 de Noviembre. Open all year, daily 0900-0100. Runs west on the Chilean side to join the Puerto Natales–Punta Arenas road.

---

end (US$18), or walk up a path alongside the east shores 4½ hours to reach the northern end. From there you can trek or go on horseback (seven hours with guide, US$33) to Puerto Candelario Mancilla on Lago O'Higgins (lodging at *estancia*). Next day, take a boat from Candelario Mancilla to Bahía Bahamóndez (three hours, US$45), then a bus to Villa O'Higgins, 7 km, US$3.30. The border is closed from May to November (check at www.villaohiggins.com for tours and boat availability). The **Estancia El Pilar** is the best place to stay on the way to the lake; it's in a stunning position and has views of Fitz Roy. Visit for tea and use it as an excellent base for trekking up Río Blanco or Río Eléctrico, with a multi-activity adventure circuit. Highly recommended. Contact **Fitz Roy Expediciones** (see Activities and tours, page 602) for trekking circuits that connect Lago Viedma and Lago San Martín. Lago Viedma to the south of El Chaltén can also be explored by boat. The trips usually pass Glaciar Viedma, with the possibility of ice trekking too.

El Calafate to Chile → *For listings, see pages 594-604.*

If travelling from El Calafate to Torres del Paine by car or bike, you'll cross a bleak area of steppe; about 40 km before reaching the border there are small lagoons and salt flats with flamingos. From El Calafate you can take the paved combination of Route 11, Route 40 and Route 5 to **La Esperanza** (165 km), where there's fuel, a campsite and a large but expensive *confitería* (accommodation D with bath). From La Esperanza, paved Route 7 heads west along the valley of the Río Coyle. A shorter but rougher route (closed in winter), missing Esperanza, goes via El Cerrito and joins Route 7 at Estancia Tapi Aike. Route 7 continues to the border crossing at Cancha Carrera (see box, page 593) and then meets the good *ripio* road between Torres del Paine and Puerto Natales (63 km). For bus services along this route, see Transport, page 603.

Río Turbio → *Colour map 6, B2. Phone code 02902. Population 6600.*

A charmless place you're most likely to visit en route to or from Torres del Paine in Chile. The site of Argentina's largest coalfield hasn't recovered from the depression that hit the industry in the 1990s. It has a cargo railway connecting it with Punta Loyola, and visitors can see Mina 1, where the first mine was opened. There's a small ski centre nearby, **Valdelén**, which has six pistes and is ideal for beginners; there is also scope for cross-country skiing between early June and late September. There is **tourist information** on Plazoleta Agustín del Castillo, T02902-421950. For more information, see www.welcomeargentina.com/rioturbio.

◉ Parque Nacional Los Glaciares listings

For Sleeping and Eating price codes and other relevant information, see Essentials pages 30-36.

⬤ Sleeping

El Calafate *p584, maps p583 and p585*
Dec-Feb most hotels are booked up. Reserve ahead. Low season (May-Sep) is a great time to find a deal at one of the top hotels. For more hotels, see www.todocalafate.com.
LL Design Suites, C 94 No 190, T02902-494525 (T011-5199 7465 in Buenos Aires), www.designsuites.com. Large, stylish hotel with one of the best views of Lago Argentino. Heated pool, spa treatments and gym. A little out of town but worth the short drive. Low-season prices move this hotel down a category (**L**). Recommended.
LL Los Sauces Casa Patagónica, Los Gauchos 1352/1370, T02902-495854 (T011-4348 5189 in Buenos Aires), www.casalossauces.com. Incredibly stylish, and welcoming boutique hotel close to town. Attention to detail and great accommodation packages make this a hotel a must. Member of Small Luxury Hotels. Highly recommended.
L Kosten Aike, Gobernador Moyano 1243, T02902-492424, www.kostenaike.com.ar. A special place, relaxed and yet stylish

with large elegant rooms, king-sized beds throughout, jacuzzi and gym. The restaurant **Ariskaiken** is open to non-residents and has an excellent chef; there's a cosy bar with a wood fire and a garden. The staff are extremely attentive and speak English.
L Los Alamos, Gobernador Moyano y Bustillo, T02902-491144, www.posadalos alamos.com. Located in 2 separate chalet-style buildings, this is an extremely comfortable and large hotel, with charming rooms, beautifully decorated and equipped, good service, lovely gardens, golf course and without doubt the best restaurant in town, **La Posta**. Recommended.
AL Blanca Patagonia, Parque Nacional Los Glaciares No149, T02902-493370, www.blancapatagonia.com. With only 13 rooms, this small *hosteria* offers cabins for 2 and 4 people, as well as doubles. Fantastic views from the main building, as it is situated within the city heights. Recommended.
AL Cabañas Nevis, Av del Libertador 1696, T02902-493180, www.canasnevis.com.ar. Large complex of spacious, A-shaped *cabañas* for 5 and 8, some with lake views, west of the centre. Great value and quiet location.

AL Patagonia Rebelde, José Haro 442, T02902-494495, www.patagoniarebelde. com. Charming building in traditional Patagonian style, resembling an old inn with its corrugated zinc walls and rustic decor, all looking pretty basic though offering good comfort with well-heated bedrooms and comfy sitting rooms.

A Michelangelo, Espora y Gobernador Moyano 1020, T02902-491045, www.michelangelohotel.com.ar. A lovely, quiet and welcoming place, modern and stylish in design, with a really excellent restaurant. The menu is innovative and includes hare, steak, and ink squid ravioli. All rooms have TV, bath and minibar, breakfast is included. Excellent value. Recommended.

A Santa Mónica Aparts, Josefa Freile 42, T02902-491835, www.santamonicaaparts. com.ar. Located right in the middle of town, just off the main street, this little collection of wooden cabins is perfect for couples or groups of up to 4. Very convenient.

A Vientos del Sur, a little way up the hill at Río Santa Cruz 2317, T02902-493563, www.vientosdelsur.com. One of the most welcoming places in town, this tranquil retreat is worth the short taxi ride for the views over the lake, comfortable rooms with bath, TV in a large wooden cabin, and a great welcome. Recommended.

A-B Ariel, Av del Libertador 1693, T02902-493131, www.hotelariel.com.ar. A modern, functional place west of centre, very clean and well-maintained rooms with bath and TV. Breakfast included.

A-B Casa de Grillos, Los Cóndores 1215 corner of Las Bandurrias, T02902-491160, www.casadegrillos.com.ar. Marta and Alejandro are the welcoming hosts at this B&B situated next to Nímez nature reserve. It has all the comfort and charm of a family house.

B Sir Thomas, Comandante Espora 257, T02902-492220, www.sirthomas.com.ar. A relatively cheap option for El Calafate, this is a chalet-type house with sparse but spacious wood-lined rooms and private bathrooms.

E pp Lago Azul 'B', Perito Moreno 83, T2902-491419. Cheapest in the area, this pioneer house with a couple of simple and spotless rooms to share is the most welcoming budget choice, with charming Sra Echeverría and her husband offering traditional Patagonian hospitality. Recommended.

Hostels
E pp Hostel del Glaciar 'Libertador', Av del Libertador 587 (next to the bridge on the access to town), T02902-491792, www.glaciar.com. Clean, modern and open almost all year round (closed in Jun) with good, functional, well-heated rooms. Private doubles (**A**) or rooms to share for 4, all with own bath. Breakfast is only included in the high season rate for the private rooms; free transfer from bus station. Discounts to HI members. Recommended.

E pp América del Sur, Puerto Deseado 153, T02902-493525, www.americahostel.com.ar. A short walk from the centre of town on a hilltop, each room in this hostel has uninterrupted lake views. Friendly staff, and a no shoes policy makes this a great choice.

E pp Hostel del Glaciar 'Pioneros', Los Pioneros 251, T02902-491243, www.glaciar. com. Larger, older and a bit further from the centre, this is cheaper than its sister hostel **Libertador**. A long-established, lively and often recommended hostel, open only in high season (Oct-Mar), offering a great range of accommodation for all budgets: shared dorms for up to 4 people, standard private doubles (**C**, also for 3 and 4) with bath, and larger superior doubles with bath (**B**). They also run **Patagonia Backpackers agency** with the much loved Alternative Glaciar Tour (see below), organize a booking service for Navimag and hotels and transport throughout Patagonia, and run a free shuttle service from the bus terminal. Book well in advance.

E-F pp I Keu Ken Hostel, FM Pontoriero 171, T02902-495175, www.patagoniaikeuken. com.ar. Basic dorms, but well-equipped kitchen, and fantastic views. Also on offer are 2 cabins (**B**) which are nicely decorated and great for a couple or group.

F pp **Hostal de las Manos**, Egidio Feruglio 59, T02902-492996, wwwhosteldelasmanos. com.ar. Clean, comfortable private rooms (**F**) and basic dorms available at this welcoming hostel 6 blocks from the main street. Take a taxi from the bus station and they will reimburse you. Call first to arrange.

Estancias

LL Hostería Alta Vista, 35 km west of El Calafate (on the way to Lago Roca-R15), T02902-499902, www.hosteriaaltavista. com.ar. Set within the land of **Estancia Anita**, the largest *estancia* in the area (74,000 ha), Alta Vista is a famous *estancia* with all facilities you could possibly need, and only 15 guests. Favoured by celebrities and politicians, the lovely house was built in the 1930s and mostly retains its original style. Full-board is possible, with excellent cuisine and wines included. There are attractive walks and a great range of excursions all within the vast expanse of the ranch. Recommended.

LL Kau-Yatún, Estancia 25 de Mayo (10 blocks from town centre, east of Arroyo Calafate), T02902-491059 (T011-4783 2930 in Buenos Aires), www.kauyatun.com. This is the very comfortable renovated main house of an old *estancia*, on the outskirts of town, and surrounded by 4 ha of very well-kept gardens, where vegetables are grown for the meals served in its 2 excellent restaurants. The welcoming hosts successfully combine a homely feel with rustic decor, typical of a traditional Patagonian *estancia*. Either half-board or all-inclusive programmes with excursions in the park included.

LL Los Notros, in front of the glacier, www.losnotros.com (T011-4814 3934 in Buenos Aires). An exclusive retreat by the lake with luxurious accommodation in spacious, well designed rooms. The only option if you want to wake up to views of the Perito Moreno Glacier. You can walk, hike, trek and ride horses here. Expensive, but there are all-inclusive packages with free

transfers to the glacier *pasarelas* included. Triple rooms available.

AL Estancia Nibepo Aike, in the far south of the park on the shores of Brazo Sur of Lago Argentino (T02966-436010 in Río Gallegos), www.nibepoaike.com.ar, www.lagosanmartin.com. Open Oct-Apr. In a spectacular setting inside the national park, near the shores of the lake. The house has 15 simple rooms, decorated with lovely old furniture, and there's a cosy sitting room. Lots of activities are possible in the park, or the surrounding 12,800 ha. The premises are open for day visits too.

Camping

AMSA, Olavarría 65 (50 m off the main road, turning south at the fire station), T02902-492247. Only open in summer. US$6 per person, hot water, security.

There are 2 campsites in the park en route to Lago Roca: **El Huala**, 42 km from El Calafate, free with basic facilities and open all year round; and **Lago Roca**, 50 km from El Calafate, T02902-499500, beautiful setting, with hot water, public phone, restaurant and bike hire, US$6 per person.

El Chaltén *p591, maps p590 and p592*
The tourist office has a full list, see www.elchalten.com. Some hotels close from Apr-Sep, and from Dec-Mar, when finding accommodation can be challenging. Book ahead.

LL Hotel Los Cerros, San Martín s/n, T02962-493182 (T011-4814 3934 in Buenos Aires), www.loscerrosdelchalten.com. On a hilltop position above the town, this large hotel (44 rooms) is by far the most sophisticated choice in the area. Stylish yet informal, all rooms are very comfortable with impressive attention to detail. Half-board and all-inclusive packages with excursions run by **Fitz Roy Expediciones**, see page 602. Heated swimming pool.

L Hostería El Puma, Lionel Terray 212, T02962-493095, www.hosteriaelpuma. com.ar. The most desirable place in town, set a little apart, and with splendid views up the valley. Has a welcoming lounge with log fire and tasteful stylish furnishings, spacious comfortable rooms with lots of brick, and plush bathrooms. Transfers and a big American breakfast are included. They can also arrange tours through their excellent agency, Fitz Roy Expediciones.

AL El Pilar, on R23, Km 17, T02962-493002, www.hosteriaelpilar.com.ar. A special place to stay a little way out of town on the road to Lago del Desierto. This simple country house, in a spectacular setting on the confluence of Ríos Blanco and de las Vueltas, with views of Fitz Roy, offers the chance to sample the simple life with access to the less visited northern part of the national park and beyond. Spacious rooms, great food, recommended.

AL Hostería Posada Lunajuim, Trevisán 45, T02962-493047, www.elchalten.com/lunajuim. A stylish yet relaxed and welcoming place, with comfortable rooms (thick duvets on the beds), bathrooms, a lovely big lounge with wood fire, and art on the walls. Dinner is available to residents, and a full American breakfast is included. Friendly family, charming hosts. Recommended.

AL Senderos, near the bridge, T02962-493 336, www.senderoshosteria.com.ar. New and cosy wooden structure. Can arrange excursions. Excellent restaurant. Wi-Fi in public areas.

B Nothofagus, Hensen and Riquelme, T02962-493087, www.elchalten.com/nothofagus. One of the most appealing places to stay is this small cosy B&B, with simple double rooms with or without bath. A wonderful breakfast is included. Bright and welcoming.

C Hospedaje La Base, Lago del Desierto s/n, T02962-493031. Good rooms for 2, 3 and 4, all with bath, tiny kitchen, self-service breakfast included, great video lounge. Recommended.

C Inlandsis, Lago del Desierto 480, T02962-493276, www.elchalten.com/inlandsis. This small B&B only has 8 cosy rooms, some with magnificent views. Quiet, clean and affordable. Recommended.

C Mi Rincón, Cabo García 115, T02962-493 099, www.mirincon-elchalten.com.ar. Simple, clean and inviting doubles and triples with a view of Fitz Roy. Good value.

Hostels

E pp Albergue Patagonia, San Martín 493, T/F02962-493019, www.patagonia hostel.com.ar. Closed Jun-Sep. Most appealing of several hostels here is HI-affiliated, and a is a small, cosy, friendly place with rooms to share (4 to 6), with kitchen, and in a separate new section there are modern, clean doubles (**D**) with fantastic private bathrooms. Helpful information on Chaltén and also excursions to Lago del Desierto. Next door is their restaurant **Fuegia**, with Patagonian dishes, curries and vegetarian food.

E pp Albergue Rancho Grande, San Martín s/n, T02962-493005, www.hihostels.com. HI-affiliated, in a good position at the end of town with an attractive restaurant and lounge (open to non-guests), accommodates huge numbers of trekkers in rooms for 4, with shared bath, breakfast extra. Also (**C**) doubles, breakfast extra. Some reports of bed bugs.

E pp Aylen-Aike, Trevisán 125, T02962-493 142, www.elchalten.com/aylenaike/. Closed late-Apr to Oct. Large, modern yellow building on one of the quieter streets. Has friendly staff and the option of 4- or 10 bed dorms.

E pp Cóndor de los Andes, Av Río de las Vueltas y Halvorsen, T02962-493101, www.condordelosandes.com. Open Oct to mid-Apr. Friendly, small and modern, with nice little rooms for 4 to 6, and private doubles, all with bathrooms en suite, sheets included but breakfast extra. Washing service, library, kitchen. A calm place with a quiet atmosphere. Discounts to HI members. Recommended.

E pp Pioneros de Valle, San Martín 451, T02962-493079. Central, large hostel with basic, clean but slightly cramped dorms, and a modern kitchen.

Estancias

L Estancia La Quinta, on R23, 2 km south of El Chaltén, T02962-493012, www.estanciala quinta.com.ar. Open Oct-Apr. A spacious pioneer house with renovated rooms surrounded by beautiful gardens, very comfortable. A superb breakfast is included and the restaurant is also open for lunch and dinner. Transfer to and from El Chaltén bus terminals is included.

AL Estancia Lago del Desierto, at Punta Sur (southern tip of Lago del Desierto), R23, Km 37, T02962-493010 (contact **Hotel Lago del Desierto** in El Chaltén). Basic place, with hot showers for campers (US$6 per person) or for those staying in *cabañas* for 5 people.

A-B pp Estancia La Maipú, T02966-422613, Lago San Martín, www.estanciasdesantacruz. com/LaMaipu/lamaipu.htm. The Leyenda family offer accommodation at their working sheep farm, with meals, horse riding, trekking and boat excursions on the lake.

Camping

A gas or alcohol stove is essential as fires are prohibited in any campsites of the national park. Take plenty of warm clothes and a good sleeping bag. It is possible to rent equipment in El Chaltén; ask at park office or Rancho Grande.

Camping del Lago, Lago del Desierto 135, T02962-493010. Central, with hot showers.

Camping Piedra del Fraile, on Río Eléctrico beyond park boundary. Privately owned.

El Refugio, off San Martín just before Rancho Grande. Hot showers. Also a basic *refugio*.

Campsites in the national park: **Capri**; **De Agostini**; **Laguna Toro**; **Poincenot**; **Río Blanco** (only for climbers with prior permission arranged). None have services and fires are not allowed. All river water is drinkable. Take out all rubbish, do not wash or bury waste within 70 m of rivers.

Río Turbio *p594*

Hotels here are almost always full.

C De La Frontera, 4 km from Río Turbio, Paraje Mina 1, T02902-421979. The most

recommended option, has a hostel attached to the 3-star hotel.

D Hostería Capipe, Dufour, 9 km from town, T02902-482930, www.hosteriacapipe. com.ar. Simple rooms with bath. Friendly and has a restaurant.

Eating

El Calafate *p584, map p585*

For cheap meals (ᵀᵀ-ᵀ), there are 2 lively, packed places on the main street, Av del Libertador, with good atmosphere and cheapish food: **Rick's Café**, No 1091, T02902-492148, serving *parrilla tenedor libre* for US$15, and **Casablanca**, Av del Libertador and 25 de Mayo, T02902-491402. Welcoming place, serving omelettes, hamburgers and vegetarian food.

ᵀᵀᵀ **Casimiro Biguá**, Av del Libertador 963, T02902-492590. A popular, upmarket place with quality food, including the excellent stew *cazuela de cordero*.

ᵀᵀ **El Puesto**, Gobernador Moyano and 9 de Julio, T02902-491620. Tasty thin-crust pizzas served in this cosy old house. Also pricier regional meals and takeaway service. Recommended.

ᵀᵀ **La Cocina**, Av del Libertador 1245, T02902-491758. Pizzeria, a large variety of pancakes, pasta, salads, served in friendly atmosphere. Good wine list.

ᵀᵀ **La Tablita**, Coronel Rosales 28 (near the bridge), T02902-491065. The best place for a typical *parrilla* with generous portions and quality beef.

ᵀᵀ **Mi Viejo**, Av del Libertador 1111, T02902-491691. Popular *parrilla*, try the grilled lamb for US$6.

ᵀᵀ **Pascasio**, 25 de Mayo 52, T02902-492055. Cosy, exclusive and a very good spot for romantic dinners.

ᵀᵀ **Punto de Encuentro**, Los Pioneros 251 (at **Hostel del Glaciar 'Pioneros'**). Ideal for meeting fellow travellers over creative meals that include veggie options.

Pura Vida, Av del Libertador 1876. A relaxed place to eat well, with comfortable sofas, home-made Argentine food, lots of veggie options, and a lovely warm atmosphere with lake view. Recommended.

Viva la Pepa, Emilio Amado 833, T02902-491880. Closed Wed. A mainly vegetarian café with great sandwiches and crêpes filled with special toppings.

Ice cream parlours
Heladería Aquarela, Av del Libertador 1177. You'll be glad to hear that it does get hot enough for ice cream, and the best is served here – try the delicious (and beautifully coloured) *calafate* which is a local berry.

El Chaltén *p591, map p592*
Los Cerros, Hotel Los Cerros (see Sleeping), T02962-493182. Top cuisine in a sophisticated atmosphere, where regional meals such as *puchero patagónico* and *carbonada de liebre* sit well among other, more international standards. The wine list includes produce from the best bodegas.

Ahonikenk Chaltén, Güemes 23, T02962-493070. Large portions of pizza and pasta, and its central location, all sell this small café.

El Muro, San Martín 948, T02962-493248. Inviting indoor and outdoor restaurant/bar serving pastas, pizzas, and home-made beers. Strangely there is a climbing wall to practice on before you try the beer.

Estepa, Cerro Solo and Antonio Rojo. Tue-Sun from 1500. Small, intimate place with a varied menu that includes excellent lamb, selected wines and imaginative vegetarian options.

Fuegia, San Martín, T02962-493243. The usual international menu in a warm atmosphere, plus some Patagonian dishes and more imaginative options, such as curries and veggie food. Great breakfast menu, served until 1430 in high season.

Josh Aike, Lago del Desierto 105. Excellent *confitería* in a beautiful building. Delicious home-made food, recommended.

Pangea, Lago del Desierto and San Martín, T02962-493084. Open for lunch, dinner, drinks and coffee. Calm and comfortable, with good music and a varied menu; from pasta to steak, and trout to pizza. Recommended.

Patagonicus, Güemes and Madsen, T02962-493025. Daily 1200-2400. A lovely, warm, cosy, stylish place with salads, home-made pasta and the best pizzas. Great family photos of mountain climbers on the walls. Recommended.

Ruca Mahuida, Lionel Terray s/n. Widely regarded as the best restaurant with imaginative and well-prepared food.

Terray, Hostería El Puma, Lionel Terray 212, T02962-493095. Climbers, trekkers and other visitors chat about their expeditions, over excellent food in a homely atmosphere.

Zaffarancho, behind Rancho Grande. Bar-restaurant, good range and reasonably priced.

Domo Blanco, Costanera Sur 90. Makes superb home-made ice cream.

Las Lengas, Viedma 95, opposite tourist office. Plentiful meals, basic pastas and meat dishes. Cheaper than most, US$3 for meal of the day.

🍸 Bars and clubs

El Calafate *p584, map p585*
Borges y Alvarez, Av del Libertador 1015, 1st floor, Galería de los Gnomos, T02902-491 464. Cosy, wooden bar with huge windows looking out over the shopping street below. Affordable, with delicious lunch and dinner options, as well as live music and books for sale. A must.

Elba'r, 9 de Julio 57, T02902-493594. Just off the main street, this café/bar serves hard to find waffles and juices, as well as home-made beer and sandwiches.

Shackleton Lounge, Av del Libertador 3287, T02902-493516, on the outskirts of town (US$2.50 in taxi). A great place to relax, with lovely views of the lake, old photos of Shackleton, a great atmosphere and good music. Highly recommended for a late drink or some good regional dishes. Also serves afternoon tea.

El Chaltén *p591, map p592*
Elal Resto-bar, Lago del Desierto 410, T02962-493106, daily 0730-2400. Live shows attract large crowds in summer, and they follow up a good night by serving a great breakfast.
La Cervecería, San Martín 320. Packed-out café/bar serving home-brewed beers from their own microbrewery, as well as great vegetarian pizzas, sandwiches and soups. The wooden interior creates a homely feel.

⊕ Festivals and events

El Calafate *p584, map p585*
15 Feb Lago Argentino Day. Live music, dancing and *asados*.
10 Nov Día de la Tradición. Displays of horsemanship and *asados*.

○ Shopping

El Calafate *p584, map p585*
All along Libertador there are souvenir shops selling hats, fleeces and gloves, so that you can prepare yourself for those chilly boat rides to see the glacier. There are lots of fine quality handicrafts from all over Argentina and look out for Mapuche weavings and woollen items. There are also small handicraft stalls on Libertador at around 1200.
Abranpampa, Libertador 1341, T02902-491 697. Clothing and camping gear rentals, ranging from backpacks to tents to cookers.
Ferretería Chuar, a block away from the bus terminal. The only place selling white gas for camping and camping supplies.
La Anónima, Av del Libertador and Perito Moreno. A supermarket.

El Chaltén *p591, map p592*
Camping Center, San Martín, T02962-493 264. Buy or rent equipment for climbing, trekking and camping.
El Gringuito, Av San Martín. The best supermarket, though there are many others around. All are expensive and have little fresh food. Fuel is available.
El Súper, Lago del Desierto y Av Güemes, T02902-493039. Supermarket that also rents and sells camping and climbing equipment, maps, postcards, books and handicrafts.
Eolia rental & Outdoor shop, San Martín and Fonruge, T02962-493066. Enquire here about equipment hire, as well as advice on personalized APN-certified guides. These guys know their stuff when it comes to ice and rock climbing, and glacier trekking.
Viento Oeste, Av San Martín s/n, northern end of town, T02962-493021. Equipment hire; tents, sleeping bags, and everything else you'll need. Can arrange mountain guides. Also sell handicrafts.

▲ Activities and tours

El Calafate *p584, map p585*
Most agencies charge the same rates and run similar excursions. Note that in winter bad weather can limit boat trips or even cause them to be cancelled.

Ballooning
Hotel Kau Yatún (see Sleeping, above). Organizes balloon trips over El Calafate and Lago Argentino, weather permitting, US$160 per hr for a group of up to 7 people.

Boat trips
Boat trips to the Moreno and Upsala glaciers are organized by **Fernández Campbell** and **Hielo y Aventura**, see Tour operators, below. Alternatively, there's a marvellous 2-day

full-board programme for 14 passengers on the *Crucero Leal* ship, which includes a comfortable night on board, and the chance to enjoy the view of Moreno, Upsala and Spegazzini glaciers at leisure. US$350 pp, full board. See www.crucerosmarpatag.com, or call T02902-492118.

Fishing
Calafate Fishing, Calle Espora 33, T02902-496545, T02902-493311, www.calafate fishing.com. Offers regular ½- and full-day fishing excursions, plus longer expeditions, all for fly-casting.

Glacier trips
From Calafate there are regular buses by **Cal-Tur** and **Taqsa** to the car park above the walkways (US$20). Many agencies in El Calafate also run minibus tours in high season (park entry not included, US$16).

Hostels del Glaciar's alternative trips, highly entertaining and informative, go out by different route passing the Estancia Anita and are highly recommended, full-day US$43. Fantastic guides. Minitrekking (US$86) and Big Ice (US$116) are offered by **Hielo y Aventura**, wonderful walking trips on the glacier (crampons provided, bring lunch), 1-hr boat trip optional extra US$15.

Near the Perito Moreno pier (1 km away from walkways area) there is a basic restaurant and café. Out of season, trips to the glacier are more difficult to arrange, but there are still regular bus services or you can gather a party and hire a taxi. Taxis US$80 (300 pesos) for 4 passengers round trip including wait at the glacier for up to 3-4 hrs. Very good and friendly driver is Ruben, T02902-498707. There is a small but reliable taxi stand right outside the bus terminal.

Horse riding
Cabalgata en Patagonia, Av del Libertador 3600, T02902-493203, www.cabalgataen patagonia.com. For 2-hr rides (US$23 per person) along Bahía Redonda or 6-hr excursions (US$44 per person, lunch included) to Punta Bonita to see the Gualicho cave paintings by the lake.

Ice trekking
Walking excursions on the Perito Moreno Glacier (known as Minitrekking and Big Ice) are enormous fun (and not too physically challenging). Close-up experiences of the glacier are run by **Hielo y Aventura**, see Tour operators, below. Note that people under 18 and over 45 are not permitted to attempt ice trekking.

Mountain bikes
On Rent a Car, Av del Libertador 1831, T02902-493788, www.onrentacar.com.ar. US$20 per day.

Tour operators and trekking guides
Note that entry fee to the national park (US$16 per person), transfer to piers and food may not be included in tour prices. Most agencies charge the same rates for excursions: to the Perito Moreno Glacier, US$40; Minitrekking (on the glacier itself with crampons included, recommended), US$86; to Lago Roca, a full-day including lunch at Estancia Anita, US$40; horse riding to Gualicho caves, 6 hrs, US$45.
Always Glaciers, Gobernador Moyano 1226, T02902-492450, www.alwaysglaciers.com. Prolific agency that offers tours in the area. Their speciality is the packages they offer combining several tours in one. HI card-holders receive a discount.
Chaltén Travel, Av del Libertador 1174, T02902-492212, www.chaltentravel.com. The most helpful, with a huge range of tours: glaciers, *estancias*, trekking, and transfers and excursions to El Chaltén and a guided visit to Torres del Paine National Park in 1 long day for US$80. Also sells tickets along the Ruta 40 to Perito Moreno, Los Antiguos, US$70, and Bariloche, US$150, departures 0800 on odd-numbered days (0830 from El Chaltén) mid-Nov-Apr, overnight in Perito Moreno (cheaper to book your own accommodation), Offers advice, English spoken.

Fernández Campbell, Av del Libertador 867, T02902-491155, www.fernandezcampbell. com. This company runs most boat excursions on Lago Argentino, from 1-hr trips to the north side of Perito Moreno Glacier, US$15, to the much longer circuits for viewing Upsala, Onelli and Spegazzini glaciers, US$65. They also run the full-day excursion to Estancia Cristina, US$160 (see also www.estanciacristina.com). The Spirit of the Glaciers trip is a pricey though unmissable experience for those who can afford it (about US$350 per person).

Hielo y Aventura, Av del Libertador 935, T02902-492205, www.hieloyaventura.com. Run a handful of fantastic excursions: Safari Náutico, 1-hr boat trip for viewing Moreno Glacier from the south side, leaving regularly from Bajo de las Sombras pier, US$15 (tickets also sold at the pier; transfer not included); Brazo Sur boat trip, the same as Safari plus a landing to give you the chance to see more glaciers, US$35 (transfer included); Minitrekking, 90 mins walking on the glacier with crampons (supplied and fitted by them), after a walk through lovely lakeside *lenga* forests, US$86 (transfer included); and Big Ice, a much longer walk on ice in the same area as the Minitrekking, for young adults only, US$116 (transfer included). Recommended.

Lago San Martín, Av del Libertador 1215 p 1, T02902-492858, www.lagosanmartin.com. Specializes in *estancia* reservations in Santa Cruz province, very helpful.

Leutz Turismo, Av del Libertador 1440, T02902-492316, www.leutzturismo.com.ar. Daily excursion to Lago Roca 1000-1800, with optional lunch at Estancia Nibepo Aike, and an interesting tour of the sheep and fruit. Estancia Quien Sabe for a traditional *cordero asado* for dinner.

Mar Patag, www.crucerosmarpatag.com, T02902-492118 (T011-5031 0756 in Buenos Aires). They run the Spirit of the Glaciers luxurious boat trip, a recommendable 2-day exclusive experience for viewing Moreno, Upsala and Spegazzini glaciers (US$350 per person, full board).

Mil Outdoor Adventure, Av del Libertador 1029, T02902-491437, www.miloutdoor.com. Exciting alternative excursions in 4WD to see wild places with wonderful views, 3-6 hrs, US$50-100.

Overland Patagonia, www.overland patagonia.com. Visiting remote Parque Nacional Perito Moreno and Cueva de las Manos, with overnights at *estancias* or small hotels. Can be booked at **Patagonia Backpackers (Hostels del Glaciar)**.

Patagonia Backpackers, at Hostels del Glaciar: Los Pioneros 251 or Av del Libertador 587, T02902-491243, www.glaciar.com. This tour operator offers the best glacier trip, the Alternative Tour to Moreno Glacier. Entertaining and informative, it includes lots of information on the landscape and wildlife, and is followed by the boat trip (only included in high season), US$43. They also do a great 2-day trip to El Chaltén, 'Supertrekking en Chaltén', a 2-day hiking trip, featuring the best treks in the Fitz Roy massif, including camping and ice trekking US$162; and a 2-day visit to Torres del Paine National Park, including camping and trekking. Safari Route 40 is a 4-day excursion along R40 to Bariloche (see Bariloche Transport, page 458) which is run by Overland Patagonia, www.overlandpatagonia.com, but can be booked here. It visits the remote Parque Nacional Perito Moreno and Cueva de las Manos, with overnights at *estancias* or small hotels. Also sell tickets for the Navimag ferries in the Chilean fjords. Highly recommended.

El Chaltén *p591, map p592*
Tour operators and trekking guides
Chaltén Travel, Güemes 7, T02962-493092, www.chaltentravel.com. Diverse travel agent who can book local tekking, glacier visits, and R40 tours and transport.

Fitz Roy Expediciones, San Martín 56, T02293-436424, www.fitzroyexpediciones. com.ar.

Las Lengas, Viedma and Güemes, T02962-493023. Daily bus transfer to Lago del Desierto, Río Eléctrico, Hostería Pilar and Piedra Buena on the coast in summer.

NYCA Adventure, Cabo García 122, T02962-493185, www.nyca-adventure.com.ar. Ascents, trekking, ice-field expeditions and water sports.

Patagonia Aventura, San Martín 56, T02962-493110, www.patagonia-aventura.com.ar. Boat trips along Lago Viedma to see the Glaciar Viedma, including informative chat; transfers US$12 extra. Also a good full-day's trip along Lago Viedma, with ice trekking on Glaciar Viedma. They operate Lago del Desierto crossings, US$18 per person.

Viviendo Montañas, Av Güemes 68, T02962-493068, www.vivmont.com.ar. Young company, organizing climbing schools, and ice climbing expeditions (take sleeping bag and equipment), guides for trekking too.

⊖ Transport

El Calafate p584, map p585
Air
For airport information, see page 584. Note that there is an airport charge for departing air passengers, US$6.

Aerolíneas Argentinas, 9 de Julio 57, T02902-492814, flies daily to **Buenos Aires**, with many more flights in summer, when it also flies from Bariloche (check, as this varies from year to year). Also flights to Ushuaia all year round. **LADE**, T0810-810 5223, www.lade.com.ar, flies to **Río Gallegos**, **Comodoro Rivadavia**, **Esquel** and **Bariloche** but from May-Sep flights are not frequent. To **Puerto Natales**, daily (Nov-Mar only), **Aerovías Dap**, www.aerovlasdap.cl.

Bus
For bus terminal information, see page 584. Take your passport with you when booking bus ticket to Chile and just about anywhere.

To **Perito Moreno Glacier**, daily, 1½ hrs, US$20 return, **Cal-Tur**, T02902-491842; **Taqsa**, T02902-491843, goes only in summer. To **El Chaltén**, daily, 4-4½ hrs,

US$18, **Cal-Tur; Chaltén Travel**, US$14, T02902-491833; and **Taqsa**, US$18. To **Río Gallegos**, daily, 4 hrs, US$15, **Interlagos**, T02902-491179; **Sportman**, T02902-492680; and **Taqsa**. To **Ushuaia**, take a bus to Río Gallegos; **Taqsa** operates a 0300 service for the best connection (check first).

To **Perito Moreno**, **Los Antiguos**, US$70, **Chaltén Travel**, departures 0800 on odd-numbered days (0830 from El Chaltén) mid-Nov-Apr, overnight in Perito Moreno (chaper to book your own accommodation). To **Bariloche**, take a bus to **Río Gallegos** for connections or travel via the R40 with budget option **Taqsa** who runs a year-round service to Bariloche, 36 hrs, US$120. Alternatively, look into actual tours with **Chaltén Travel**, www.chaltentravel.com (only Nov-Mar on odd days), who run a 2-day bus service along R40 (US$150 for the full journey). These rates only include transport. Food and accommodation at the town of **Perito Moreno** cost extra.

Direct bus services to Chile (take passport when booking bus tickets to Chile). To **Puerto Natales**, daily in summer with **Cootra** (T02902-491444), via Río Turbio, 7 hrs, or with **Turismo Zaahj** (T2902-491 631), 5 hrs, Wed, Fri, Sun, or **Bus Sur**, 1 a week, US$20 (advance booking recommended, tedious customs check at border crossing). Note Argentine pesos cannot be exchanged in Torres del Paine.

Car hire
Average price under US$100 per day for small car with insurance but no unlimited mileage – usually only 200 km free. **Cristina**, Av del Libertador 1711, T02902-491674, crisrenta@rnet.com.ar. **Localiza**, Av del Libertador 687, T02902-491398, localiza calafate@hotmail.com. **ON Rent a Car**, Av del Libertador 1831, T02902-493788 or T02966-1562 9985, onrentacar@cotecal.com.ar. All vehicles have a permit for crossing to Chile included in the fee, but cars are poor. Bikes for hire, US$17 per day.

Taxi

El Cóndor, T02902-491655, T02902-492005;
Remise taxi, T02902-491745.

El Chaltén *p591, map p592*

Bus

In summer buses fill quickly so book ahead.
There are fewer services off season. Local
company **Las Lengas** (T02962-493023) runs
several services for trekkers: to Hostería El Pilar
(to start the Glaciar Pedras Blancas, Laguna
de los Tres, and Laguna Capri treks), 3 daily,
US$11; to Lago del Desierto (with a 2-hr stop),
2 daily, US$18, this service arrives in time for
the ferry to Villa O'Higgins in Chile. To **El
Calafate**, daily 4-4½ hrs, US$18 (1-way, most
stop on the way at El Calafate International
Airport), **Cal-Tur**, San Martín 451, T02962-
493079; **Chaltén Travel**, San Martín 635 (at
Albergue Rancho Grande), T02902-493005,
www. chaltentravel.com; and **Taqsa**, Av
Antonio Rojo 88, T02962-493294. To **Los
Antiguos** along the R40, **Itinerarios y
Travesías**, T002902-493088, overnight,
even dates (2nd, 4th, 6th, etc), includes trip
to Cueva de las Manos in the early morning.
Chaltén Travel runs a service Nov-Mar, leaving
on odd days to Bariloche, with a stopover at
the small town of Perito Moreno, US$130,
transport only. **Taqsa** also run a year-round
service from El Calafate, via El Chaltén (weather
permitting) to Bariloche stopping at Perito
Moreno, Los Antiguos, Esquel and El Bolsón.
It is long, and the bus is basic, but it is a great
way to see the famous R40, bring your own
food, 28 hrs, US$110. An alternative route to
Bariloche is via the coast, which is cheaper
and takes less time, offered by **Las Lengas**,
Viedma 95, T02962-493023, laslengasel
chalten@yahoo.com.ar. Unlike most
companies, instead of transiting through El
Calafate and then Río Gallegos on the way
to Bariloche, the bus travels directly through
Piedrabuena to the north (5 hrs, US$32) with
connections to Bariloche and Puerto Madryn.
0530, return 1300, daily.

Taxi

Very reliable **Servicio de Remis El Chaltén**,
Av San Martín 430, T02962-493042.

Río Turbio *p594*

Bus

To **Puerto Natales**, several daily, 1 hr,
US$5, **Bus Sur**, Baquedano 534, Pto Natales,
T+56(0)61-411859, www.turismozaahj.co.cl;
Cootra, Ttedel Castillo 01, T02902-421448
cootra@oyikil.com.ar; **Lagoper**, Av de Los
Mineros 262, T02902-411831. To **El Calafate**,
daily, 4½ hrs, US$14, **Cootra**; **Taqsa**. To
Río Gallegos, daily, 4 hrs, US$12, **Taqsa**,
www.taqsa.com.ar.

⑥ Directory

El Calafate *p584, map p585*
Banks ATMs at Banco de la Provincia de
Santa Cruz, Av del Libertador 1285; and
Banco de Tierra del Fuego, 25 de Mayo 34.
Currency exchange Best to take cash as
high commission is charged on exchange.
Thaler, 9 de Julio 57, www.cambio-
thaler.com. **Post office** Av del Libertador
1133. **Internet and telephone** Open
Calafate, Av del Libertador 996, a huge
locutorio for phones, also has 20 fast internet
computers, it's central but rather expensive;
Centro Integral de Comunicaciones, Av del
Libertador 1486, is more convenient, cheaper
and more comfortable.

El Chaltén *p591, map p592*
Banks There is one ATM, Av M M De
Güemes, right next to the gas station at the
entrance to town. **Internet and telephone**
Rancho Grande, San Martín 724, open late;
3 *locutorios* with phones and internet on
Av Güemes at the entrance to the town.
Wi-Fi is available at most hotels and cafés.

Contents

Footprint features

Border crossings

Chilean Patagonia

At a glance

⊖ **Getting around** Local buses are expensive and time-consuming but reliable. If you can afford it, a hire car is invaluable.

◉ **Time required** 3-5 days will allow you to hike in the Torres del Paine National Park and relax in Puerto Montt for a day afterwards.

☼ **Weather** Dec-Mar is usually warm and dry. The rest of the year can be cold and windy, or humid.

✖ **When not to go** May-Jun is cold and most places close down. Jan can be busy, with campsites over-crowded and hiking trails packed.

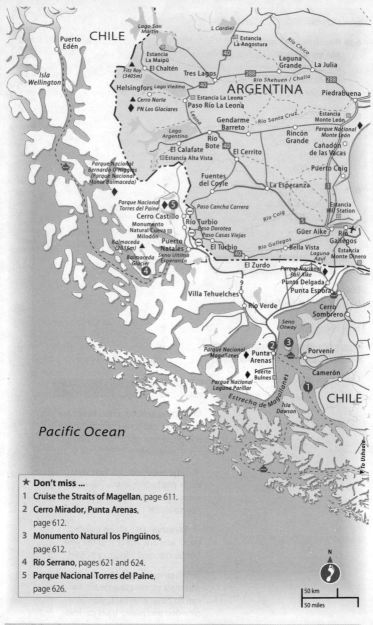

This remote land of silent fjords, hanging glaciers, pristine lakes and jagged mountains is the most visited part of Chile. Yet much of it remains a vast wilderness, with areas of staggering beauty. The Parque Nacional Torres del Paine offers both: trek around the mighty towers of granite, thrust up like fingers from a mass of basalt buttresses, passing minty-green and icy-blue glacial lakes in which icebergs float. In summer, you'll share the awe-inspiring landscape with a steady stream of walkers, but start out at dawn, and you'll find solitude and silence in some of the most dramatic landscape on earth.

The quaint port of Puerto Natales is the nearest town, with its tranquil views over the Ultima Esperanza Sound, fringed by lofty far-off peaks. Take a boat from here into Parque Nacional Bernardo O'Higgins where glaciers descend steeply into the water, and you can even trek on the ice.

Punta Arenas is Chile's southernmost city, a complete contrast to the endless windswept sheep farms all around. Here you'll find superb fish restaurants and classy hotels in grand 1900s stone buildings, relics from the city's heyday of sheep-farming millionaires. Sail from here through the Straits of Magellan to the Argentine city of Ushuaia, or head for adventure nearby in the Parque Nacional Pali Aike, to get a sense of how precarious civilization is in this wildest part of Patagonia. For general travel information on Chilean Patagonia, see www.interpatagonia.com.

Punta Arenas and around

→ Colour map 7, B1. Phone code 061. Population 150,000.

After hours of travelling through the barren steppe of Patagonia, Punta Arenas comes as a surprise. With a grand plaza surrounded by neoclassical mansions and several fine monuments, Chile's most southerly city has an affluent history. Its strategic position on the eastern shore of the Brunswick Peninsula made it a thriving port of call when trading ships sailed through the Strait of Magellan. Landowners Braun and Menéndez made their fortunes from sheep, building a sumptuous palace, filled with treasures: one of the city's two fascinating museums. The other recounts the more sombre history of the ousted indigenous peoples, and their own rich culture. While the cemetery, an oddly beautiful place, also deserves a visit.

Although no longer as wealthy on natural resources, Punta Arenas remains an upbeat breezy place, with traditional bright tin houses away from the handsome architecture of the centre. It's a good place to spend a couple of days, with plenty of decent accommodation, and some excellent fish restaurants. However, it's also the starting point for visiting the Magellanic penguins at Isla Magdalena, and the mysterious landscape of Pali Aike, as well as more challenging expeditions into the wilderness of Tierra del Fuego. For more information on Punta Arenas see www.welcomechile.com. ▶ *For listings, see pages 613-618.*

Ins and outs

Getting there
Punta Arenas is cut off from the rest of Chile. The only road connections are via Comodoro Rivadavia and Río Gallegos either to Coyhaique and the Carretera Austral (20 hours; one or two buses weekly in summer), or to Bariloche and on to Puerto Montt (36 hours, daily buses in summer); it is quicker, and often cheaper, to take one of the many daily flights to Puerto Montt or Santiago instead. Carlos Ibáñez del Campo Airport is 20 km north of town. **Buses Transfer** (Pedro Montt 966, T061-229613), and **Buses Pacheco** run services to Punta Arenas, scheduled to meet flights, for US$5. Buses from Punta Arenas to Puerto Natales will only stop at the airport if they are scheduled to pick up passengers there. There are also minibuses operated by Sandy Point costing US$5, which will drop you anywhere near the city centre. DAP have their own bus service to town, US$6. A taxi ordered at the airport costs US$14, but a Radio Taxi ordered in advance from the city is much cheaper. Transport to Tierra del Fuego is on the Melinka ferry to Porvenir (six weekly) or, further north, at Punta Delgada (many daily) to Cerro Sombrero. There are also direct flights to Porvenir, Puerto Williams and Ushuaia. Puerto Natales, 247 km north, is easily reached on a paved road (many buses daily). ▶ *For further details, see Transport, page 616.*

Getting around
Calle Pedro Montt runs east to west, while Jorge Montt runs north to south. Buses and *colectivos* in Punta Arenas tend to go either north along the 21 de Mayo–Magallanes–Bulnes axis, south down Chiloe, or east to west up Independencia. In either case, Punta Arenas is not a huge city and walking about is a pleasant way of getting to know it. Buses and *taxi-colectivos* (shared taxis) are plentiful and cheap (US$0.70 a ride): a taxi is only really necessary for out-of-town excursions.

Punta Arenas

To Instituto de la Patagonia, Free Port, Airport, Puerto Natales & Ferry to Porvenir

Carrera

Cemetery

Carrera

To 16

Sehoret

Av Bulnes

Jorge Montt

A

Angamos

Maipú

Sarmiento

Museo Regional Salesiano Mayorino Borgatello 🏛

Chiloé

Croacia

B

Mejicana

Bories

2

Magallanes

Mejicana

Croacia

Armando Sanhueza

Turismo Aonikenk 6

Lautaro Navarro

3

2

Abu-Gosch Supermarket

Carrera Pinto

Quillota

Fernández & Pingüino

Central de Pasajeros

Pacheco

11

Almte Señoret

7 21 3

Av Colón

O'Higgins

Teatro Cervantes

Bus Sur

Chocolatta 8

9

Aerovías DAP

J Menéndez

Payne Turismo & Rent a Car

Museo de Historia Regional 🏛

Ghisoni & Transfer

5

J Montt

14 13

Waldo Seguel

17

Turismo Comapa & Navimag

Pedro Montt

Ghisoni & Transfer 15

Mirador Cerro de la Cruz

Plaza Muñoz Gamero

Museo Naval y Marítimo 🏛

19 10

21

Cathedral ✝

1

Transtur to Ski Resort

6

Av Costanera

Viento Sur

Roca

Fagnano

Av España

J Nogueira

21 de Mayo

16

Turismo Tamana

12

1A

D

Errázuriz

Estrecho de Magallanes

Balmaceda

1

2

3

Ta V

To 7 & Parque María Behety

To Fuerte Bulnes & Puerto del Hambre

200 metres
200 yards

N

Sleeping
Backpackers Paradise **2** *B3*
Cabo de Hornos **1** *C2*
Finis Terrae **3** *C2*
Hostal Al Fin
  del Mundo **6** *C3*
Hostal del Sur **8** *B1*
Hostal El Conventillo **10** *C3*
Hostal Independencia
  23 *D2*
Hostal La Estancia **11** *B3*
Hostal Sonia
  Kuscevic **20** *A2*
José Nogueira (Palacio
  Sara Braun) **14** *C2*

Oro Fueguino **21** *C1*
Pink House **16** *A3*
Tierra del Fuego **22** *C2*

Eating 🍽
Café Montt **15** *C3*
Coffeenet **17** *C2*
Damiana Elena **3** *B3*
Dino's Pizza **2** *B2*
El Quijote **4** *C3*
Entre Fierros **16** *D3*
La Luna **19** *C3*
La Marmita **6** *B3*
La Tasca **1** *D2*
Lomit's **9** *C2*

O'Sole Mío **5** *C3*
Remezón **7** *D2*
Solitos **12** *D3*

Bars & clubs 🍸
La Taberna del Club
  de la Unión **13** *C2*
Olijoe **14** *D3*
Pub 1900 **21** *C2*
Santino **8** *C2*

Tourist information

Sernatur ⓘ *Navarro 999 and Pedro Montt, T061-225385, infomagallanes@sernatur.cl, www.patagonia-chile.com, Mon-Thu 0815-1800, Fri 0815-1700, closed Sat and Sun off season, English spoken*, is helpful and has lots of information. The **municipal tourist office** ⓘ *T061-200610, Mon-Thu 0800-1730, Fri 0800-1630, informacionturistica@punta arenas.cl*, on the plaza is also good. **CONAF** ⓘ *Bulnes 309, opposite the shepherd monument, between the racetrack and the cemetery, T061-238581, magallan@conaf.cl, Mon-Fri*, doesn't have much useful information.

Background

After its foundation in 1848, Punta Arenas became a penal colony modelled on Australia. In 1867, it was opened to foreign settlers and given free port status. From the 1880s, it prospered as a refuelling and provisioning centre for steam ships and whaling vessels. It also became a centre for the new sheep *estancias* in Tierra del Fuego since it afforded the best harbour facilities. The city's importance was reduced overnight by the opening of the Panama Canal in 1914. Most of those who came to work on the *estancias* were from Chiloé, and many people in the city have relatives in Chiloé and feel an affinity with the island (the *barrios* on either side of the upper reaches of Independencia are known as Chilote areas); the Chilotes who returned north took Patagonian customs with them, hence the number of *mate* drinkers on Chiloé.

Sights

Around the attractive **Plaza Muñoz Gamero** are a number of mansions that once belonged to the great sheep-ranching families of the late 19th century. A good example is the **Palacio Sara Braun** ⓘ *Tue-Sun 1000-1300, 1800-2030, US$2*, built between 1894 and 1905 with materials from Europe; the Palacio has several elegantly decorated rooms open to the public and also houses the **Hotel José Nogueira** ⓘ *www.hotelnogueira.com*. In the centre of the plaza is a statue of Magellan with a mermaid and two Fuegian Indians at his feet. According to local wisdom, those who rub or kiss the big toe of one of the Indians will return to Punta Arenas.

Just north of the plaza is the **Museo de Historia Regional Braun Menéndez** ⓘ *Magallanes 949, T061-244216, www.dibam.cl, Mon-Sat 1030-1700, Sun 1030-1400, US$2, children ½-price*, the opulent former mansion of Mauricio Braun, built in 1905. A visit is recommended. Part of the museum is set out as a room-by-room regional history; the rest of the house has been left with its original furniture. Guided tours are in Spanish only, but a somewhat confusing information sheet in English is also available. In the basement there is a café. One block further north is the **Teatro Cervantes**, now a cinema with an ornate interior.

Three blocks east of the plaza, the **Museo Naval y Maritimo** ⓘ *Pedro Montt 981, T061-205479, terzona@armarda.cl, Mon-Sat 0930-1230, 1400-1700, US$1.50*, houses an exhibition of local and national maritime history; sections on naval instruments, cartography, meteorology, as well as shipwrecks. There is a video in Spanish and an information sheet in English. West of the plaza Muñoz Gamero on Waldo Seguel are two reminders of British influence in the city: the **British School** and **St James's Anglican Church** next door. Nearby on Calle Fagnano is the **Mirador Cerro de La Cruz** offering a view over the city and the Straits of Magellan complete with its various shipwrecks. Three blocks further west is the **Museo Militar** ⓘ *Regimiento Pudeto, Zenteno and Balmaceda,*

A Cruise at the End of the World

From September to April, **Cruceros Australis** have two vessels running cruises between Punta Arenas and Ushuaia, the *Vía Australis* and the *Mare Australis*. The ships are almost identical, with 64 cabins apiece. In comfort, and treated to fine food and expert service, passengers sail through the Straits of Magellan and the channels and fjords between Tierra del Fuego and the islands that cling to its southern shore. These were the waters fished by the Yámana and Kawéskar people and surveyed by Robert Fitzroy and his crew.

From Punta Arenas the cruise takes four nights and from Ushuaia three. Each includes a visit to Cape Horn where, sea conditions permitting, you can land to see the monuments and to sign the visitor's book in the lighthouse, manned by a Chilean naval officer and his family. The landing obeys a rigorous procedure, everyone togged up in waterproofs and lifejackets, transferring from ship to Zodiac, disembarking with the aid of crew standing in the surf. 160 wooden steps lead up the cliff to wooden walkways. On a relatively benign day – sunny, with an icy breeze – it's hard to imagine the tragedies of so many mariners lost, of so many souls that, according to legend, have become albatrosses, and that this is the last piece of terra firma before Antarctica.

Other shore trips are followed by a whisky, mulled wine or hot chocolate. You need the sustenance, especially after a visit to Piloto and Nena glaciers in the Chico fjord. The blue ice of Piloto calves into the water, while Nena is scarred by rocky debris. All around water pours off the mountains; sleet and rain drive into your face as the Zodiac powers away.

En route from Ushuaia to Punta Arenas (the itinerary varies according to the route and the weather), there are two other landings. At Wulaia Bay on Isla Navarino two walks are available, up a hill or along the shore to look for birds and flora. A museum, in an old radio station, tells the history of the place. It was here that one of Fitzroy's Fuegians, Jemmy Button, who was briefly a celebrity in England in the 1830s, was reportedly present at the massacre of missionaries in 1859. The other visit is to Isla Magdalena, just off Punta Arenas. Here, between November and January, 60,000 pairs of Magellanic penguins breed in burrows.

At all times the ship is accompanied by giant petrels, black-browed albatross and king cormorants. Occasionally, dolphins ride the wake. If it is too cold on deck, you can go onto the bridge and be entertained by the navigator. The bar is open almost all the time; stewards and guides are on hand at any hour; and there are lectures and films, visits to the engine room and cookery lessons to fill the hours at sea. Everything runs like clockwork thanks to clear instructions for safety and fine-tuned organization: when the captain says you'll dock at 1100, dock at 1100 you will.

For more information on these cruises, see www.australis.com, and Activities and tours, page 615.

Ben Box

Tue-Sun 0900-1300, 1500-1700, free, with lots of knives, guns, flags and other military memorabilia plus many items brought from Fuerte Bulnes. Explanatory notes in excruciating English. Expect to be watched over by a young private.

North of the centre along Bulnes is the **Museo Regional Salesiano Mayorino Borgatello** ① *Colegio Salesiano, Av Bulnes 336, entrance next to church, T061-241096,*

Tue-Sun 1000-1230, 1500-1730, hours change frequently, US$4, an excellent introduction to Patagonia with a large collection of stuffed birds and animals from the region, exhibits on local history, geology, anthropology, aviation and industry. Easily the most complete and fascinating regional museum in Chile. Three blocks further on, the **cemetery** ① *Av Bulnes 929, daily 0800-1800*, is one of the most interesting places in the city, with cypress avenues, gravestones in many languages, which bear testimony to the cosmopolitan provenance of Patagonian pioneers, and many mausolea and memorials to pioneer families and victims of shipping disasters. Look out for the statue of Indicito, the little Indian, on the northwest side, which is now an object of reverence, bedecked with flowers. Further north still, the Instituto de la Patagonia houses the **Museo del Recuerdo** ① *Av Bulnes 1890, Km 4 north (opposite the zona franca), T061-207056, Mon-Fri 0830-1130, 1430-1830, Sat 0830-1300, US$2, children free*, an open-air museum with artefacts used by the early settlers, pioneer homes and botanical gardens.

Around Punta Arenas

Reserva Forestal Magallanes
① *7 km west of town, US$5, taxi US$8.*
Known locally as the Parque Japonés, Reserva Forestal Magallanes extends over 13,500 ha and rises to 600 m. **Viento Sur** (see Activities and tours, page 616) offers a scheduled transport service to the reserve, but it can also be reached on foot or by bike: follow Independencia up the hill and take a right turning for Río de las Minas, about 3 km from the edge of town; the entrance to the reserve is 2 km beyond. Here you will find a self-guided nature trail through lenga and coigue trees. The road continues through the woods for 14 km passing several picnic sites. From the top end of the road a short path leads to a lookout over the **Garganta del Diablo** (Devil's Throat), a gorge with views over Punta Arenas and Tierra del Fuego. From here a slippery path leads down to the Río de las Minas Valley and then back to Punta Arenas.

Cerro Mirador is 9 km west of town in the Reserva Nacional Magallanes. It is one of the few places in the world where you can ski with a sea view. The ski season is June to September, weather permitting. Transfer buses leave at 0900 and 1400 from in front of Hotel Cabo de Hornos, US$5 return (taxi US$12). A daily lift-pass is US$15 and equipment rental is US$10. There's a mid-way lodge with food, drink and equipment. Note that the ski centre is often closed due to lack of snow. There's also a good two-hour hike here in summer; the trail is clearly marked and flora are labelled. Skiing is also available at Tres Morros.

Isla Magdalena
A small island, 30 km northeast, Isla Magdalena is the location of the **Monumento Natural Los Pingüinos**, a colony of 150,000 penguins, administered by CONAF. Deserted apart from during the breeding season from November to early February, Magdalena is one of a group of three islands visited by Drake (the others are Marta and Isabel), whose men killed 3000 penguins for food. Boat trips to the island are run by **Comapa and Cruceros Australis** ① *Tue, Thu and Sat, 1600 (Dec-Feb), 2 hrs each way, 2 hrs on the island, US$40, subject to cancellation if windy; full refund given*. Beyond, Route 255 heads northeast via Punta Delgada to the Argentine frontier at Kimiri Aike and then along Argentine Route 3 to Río Gallegos, an unappealing city. For routes to Calafate in Argentina, see page 621.

Seno Otway

Seventy kilometres north of Punta Arenas, Seno Otway is the site of a colony of around 11,000 Magellanic penguins, which can be visited from October to mid-March, for US$5. There are beautiful views across the sound to the mountains to the north and rheas, skunks and foxes can also be seen. Several agencies offer trips to the colony lasting five hours (US$20 at peak season); if you wish to visit independently, a taxi from Punta Arenas will cost US$50 return. It is best to go early in the day. Try to avoid going at the same time as the large cruise ship tours – it is not much fun having to wait behind 200 people for your turn at the viewing stations.

◉ Punta Arenas and around listings

For Sleeping and Eating price codes and other relevant information, see Essentials pages 30-36.

● Sleeping

Punta Arenas *p608, map p609*
Hotel prices are substantially lower during winter (Apr/May-Sep), but winter visitors are on the increase, especially Mar-Apr. Most hotels include breakfast in the room price. Rooms are also available in private houses; ask at the tourist office. There are no campsites in or near the city.
LL Cabo de Hornos, Muñoz Gamero 1039, on the plaza, T061-715000, www.hoteles-australis.com. 4 star comfy, bright spacious rooms with good views from 4th floor up.
LL-L José Nogueira, Plaza de Armas, Bories 959, in former Palacio Sara Braun, T061-248840, www.hotelnogueira.com. Beautiful *loggia*. Slightly small rooms, but high ceilings. The rooms on the 2nd level are best. Good suites, lovely dining room, parking. Probably the nicest hotel in town. Recommended.
L Finis Terrae, Colón 766, T061-228200, www.hotelfinisterrae.com. Typical large hotel; some rooms are small, as are the bathrooms. Expensive suites. Views from the top 2 floors. The best thing about the hotel is the rooftop café/bar. English spoken, parking available.
L Tierra del Fuego, Colón 716, T061-226200, www.patagoniahotels.com. Spacious, tasteful, TV, 2nd floor rooms have kitchenette. Popular **Café 1900** downstairs, excellent restaurant open to non-residents. Recommended.

A Oro Fueguino, Fagnano 356, T061-249401, www.orofueguino.cl. Some rooms have no windows but all have TV and phone. Good breakfast. Often fills up with groups so book ahead. Cheaper in US$ than pesos. Recommended.
B Hostal del Sur, Mejicana 151, T061-227249, hostaldelsure@hotmail.com. Homely and impeccably kept late 19th-century house. The living room is top-of-the-range 1960s, but the rooms are modern. Excellent breakfast with cereal and cakes. Not central, but in a peaceful neighbourhood. Advance booking advised in summer. Highly recommended.
B Hostal Sonia Kuscevic, Pasaje Darwin 175, T061-248543, www.hostalsk.50megs.com. One of the city's oldest guesthouses, with breakfast, kitchen facilities, hot water, heating and parking. Better value for longer than short stays, good discount with HI card.
B-C pp Hostal La Estancia, O'Higgins 765, T061-249130, www.hostallaestancia.cl. Simple but comfy rooms, some with bath. Excellent breakfast, lots of information. Recommended.
B-C The Pink House, Caupolicán 99, T061-222436, pinkhous@ctinternet.cl. Impeccable rooms with or without bath, breakfast included. Pick-up from bus station. English spoken, internet access. Recommended.
C Hostal Al Fin del Mundo, O'Higgins 1026, T061-710185, www.alfindelmundo.cl. With breakfast. Bright cosy and friendly. Shared baths, central, helpful, laundry service, book exchange, internet, English spoken, helpful. Recommended.

Hostels

C-D Hostal El Conventillo, Pasaje Korner 1034, T061-242311, www.hostalelconven tillo.com. A new 'hip' hostel. Breakfast, rooms for 2-6 with shared bath, none with outside window. Cheerful, good value, free internet.
D Backpackers Paradise, Carrera Pinto 1022, T061-240104, backpackersparadise@ hotmail.com. Fun backpackers' with cooking facilities, limited bathroom facilities, basic dorms (**G** pp), lots of information, good meeting place, luggage store, internet access, laundry service, book exchange. Expensive bike rental. No privacy but recommended.
F Hostal Independencia, Independencia 374, T061-227572, www.chileaustral.com/ independencia. Friendly, small basic rooms, shared rooms (**G** pp), breakfast extra. Kitchen facilities, laundry service, internet, bike rental and cheap camping. Also *cabañas* away from the centre. Good value. Recommended.

● Eating

Punta Arenas *p608, map p609*
Note that many eating places in Punta Arenas are closed on Sun.

Visitors to Punta Arenas and the surrounding region should be especially wary of eating shellfish. In recent years, the nearby waters have been sporadically affected by a *marea roja* (red tide) of poisonous algae. While the *marea roja* only affects bivalve shellfish, infected molluscs can kill humans almost instantly. Do not pick and eat mussels from the shore of Punta Arenas; foreigners who have done this have died. However, all shellfish sold in restaurants have been inspected and so are theoretically safe.

♥♥♥ Remezón, 21 de Mayo 1469, T061-241 029, www.patagoniasalvaje.net. Regional specialities such as krill. Very good, and so it should be given the exorbitant prices.
♥♥♥-♥♥ La Tasca, Plaza Muñoz Gamero 771, above **Teatro Cervantes** in Casa Española.

Large helpings, limited selection, decent set lunch.
♥♥♥-♥♥ Solitos, O'Higgins 1138, T061-243565. Good service and excellent cuisine. Elegant and expensive. Recommended.
♥♥ Damiana Elena, O'Higgins 694, T061-222 818. Stylish restaurant serving Mediterranean food with a Patagonian touch. Popular with locals. Advance booking essential at weekends.
♥♥ La Marmita, Plaza Sampiao, T061-222056, daily 1230-1500, 1830-2330. Intimate, *mestizo* restaurant decorated in pastel shades. Regional dishes with an international twist, soups and vegetarian options, food nicely presented. Very good.
♥♥ Santino, Colón 657, T061-220511, Mon-Sat until 0300. Good pizzas, large bar, good service.
♥♥-♥ La Luna, O'Higgins 1017, T061-228555. Fish and shellfish including local specialities, huge pisco sours, lively atmosphere. Under same ownership is **O' Sole Mío**, O'Higgins 974, T061-242026, for cheap pasta dishes.
♥ Dino's Pizza, Bories 557. Good pizzas, huge sandwiches. For something different, try their rhubarb juice. Recommended.
♥ El Quijote, Lautaro Navarro 1087, T061-241225. Happy hour 1900-2100. Good burgers, sandwiches and fish dishes. Good-value set lunch. Recommended.
♥ Lomit's, Menéndez 722. A Punta Arenas fast-food institution serving cheap snacks and drinks, open when the others are closed, always busy. Recommended.

Cafés and snack bars

Café Montt, Pedro Montt 976, near Sernatur. Coffees, teas, cakes, pastries and snacks. Wi-Fi.
Coffeenet, Waldo Seguel 670, www.coffee net.cl. Big internet café opposite the police HQ, with broadband, good service and music, hot chocolate and coffee.
Entre Fierros, Roca 875, T061-223436. Open until 1900. Small diner that by all accounts has remained unchanged since the 1950s. It is famous for its banana milkshakes and tiny *choripan* (spicy sausage-meat sandwiches).

🅞 Bars and clubs

Punta Arenas *p608, map p609*
Note that anywhere that calls itself a
'nightclub' is in fact a brothel.
La Taberna del Club de la Unión, Plaza
Muñoz Gamero and Seguel, Mon-Sat
1830-late. For drinks, atmospheric pub in
the basement of the **Nogueira Hotel**.
Olijoe, Errazuriz 970. Reasonably plush
British-style pub with leather interior.
Recommended.
Pub 1900, Av Colón esquina Bories.
Friendly, relaxed atmosphere.
Santino, Colón 657, T061-220511. Pizzeria
that doubles as a bar at night. Popular.

🅦 Festivals and events

Punta Arenas *p608, map p609*
Late Jan/Feb Muestra custumbrista de
Chiloe. The Chilote community celebrates
its culture.
Jun Carnaval de invierno. The winter
solstice is marked by a carnival on the
weekend closest to 21 Jun.

🅞 Shopping

Punta Arenas *p608, map p609*
Punta Arenas is famous for the quality of
its chocolate. Delicious handmade chocolate
is for sale at several shops on Calle Bories.
Sports Nativa, Colón 614, camping
and skiing equipment; **The North Face**,
Bories 887, outdoor gear; **The Wool
House Patagonia**, Fagnano 675, by the
plaza, good quality, reasonably priced
woollen clothes.
Zona Franca, 3.5 km north of the centre,
on the right-hand side of the road to the
airport, take bus E or A from Plaza Muñoz
Gamero or a taxi (US$4). Open Mon-Sat
1000-1230, 1500-2000. Punta Arenas has
certain free-port facilities. Cheap perfume
and electrical goods are especially worth

seeking out, as is camping equipment.
The quality of most other goods is low
and the prices little better than elsewhere.

🅐 Activities and tours

Punta Arenas *p608, map p609*
Skiing
Club Andino, T061-241479,
www.clubandino.tierra.cl/. For information
on skiing facilities.

Tour operators
Most organize tours to Torres del Paine,
Fuerte Bulnes and *pingüineras* on Otway
Sound. Several also offer bespoke tours,
and adventure tourism on Chilean Tierra
del Fuego, which has very little tourist
infrastructure: shop around as prices vary.
Specify if you want a tour in English. There
are many more operators than listed here. For
more information ask at the **Sernatur** office or
email them at Infomagallanes@sernatur.cl.
Cruceros Australis, at Turismo Comapa,
Magallanes 990, T061-200200, www.australis.
com (in Santiago T02-442 3111, in Buenos
Aires 1011-4139 8400). Runs cruises on
the *Vía Australis* and *Mare Australis* between
Punta Arenas and Ushuaia, through the
Straits of Magellan and the 'avenue of
glaciers', with stops at Cape Horn, Isla
Navarino, glaciers and Isla Magdalena
(the itinerary varies according to route).
There are opportunities to disembark and
see wildlife. Very safe and comfortable,
1st-class service, fine dining, daily lectures,
an unforgettable experience. Advance
booking is essential; check-in is at **Comapa**.
Consistently highly recommended.
Pali Aike, Lautaro Navarro 1125,
T061-223301, www.turismopaliaike.com.
Wide range of tours including horse riding.
Solo Expediciones, J Nogueira 1255,
T061-710219, www.soloexpediciones.com.
Bespoke and off-the-beaten-track excursions
on and around the Straits of Magellan.

Turismo Aonikenk, Magallanes 619, T061-221982, www.aonikenk.com. Excellent company organizing informed tours to the usual places near Punta Arenas, as well as more imaginative options, such as Parque Nacional Pali Aike, and expeditions on Tierra del Fuego. Run by charming bilingual couple Sebastián and Marisol. Highly recommended.
Turismo Aventour, J Nogueira 1255, T061-241197, www.aventourpatagonia.com. English spoken, specialize in fishing trips, also organize tours to Tierra del Fuego.
Turismo Comapa, Magallanes 990, T061-200200, www.comapa.com. Tours to Torres del Paine (responsible, well-informed guides), Tierra del Fuego and to see the penguins at Isla Magdalena (3 times a week Dec-Mar, 5 hrs in all, US$40). Also sell tickets for sailings Puerto Montt to Puerto Natales.
Turismo Viento Sur, Fagnano 585, T061-710840, www.vientosur.com. For camping equipment, fishing excursions, horse riding, sea kayaking and cycle hire. English spoken, good tours.
Whale Sound, Lautaro Navarro1163, Whale-watching trips in the Straits of Magellan.

⊖ Transport

Punta Arenas *p608, map p609*
All transport is heavily booked from late Dec through to Mar; advance booking is advised.

Air
For airport information, see page 608.
  Domestic To **Balmaceda** (for Coyhaique), with **LanChile** (LanExpress), daily in summer, otherwise 1 a week or daily via Puerto Montt (more expensive). To **Puerto Montt**, with **LanChile** (LanExpress), **Aerolíneas del Sur** and **Sky Airline**, 10 daily, from US$120 return. Cheapest 1-way tickets with **Aerolíneas del Sur**. To **Santiago**, **LanChile** (LanExpress), **Aerolíneas del Sur** and **Sky Airline**, several daily, from around US$200 return, via Puerto Montt (sit on the right for views). To **Porvenir**, **Aerovías DAP**,

2 daily, Mon-Sat, US$35 (1-way), plus other irregular flights, with Twin-Otter and Cessna aircraft. To **Puerto Williams**, daily in summer, around US$95 (1-way), **Aerovías DAP**. Book a week in advance for Porvenir, 2 weeks in advance for Puerto Williams.
  International To **Ushuaia** (Argentina), 3 weekly in summer, 1 hr, around US$200 (1-way), **Lan Chile**; reserve well in advance from mid-Dec to Feb. To **Falkland Islands/Islas Malvinas**, Sat, US$600 return, LanChile. **International Tours & Travel**, T+500-22041, www.falklandstravel.com, serve as LanChile agents on the Falkland Islands.
  Airline offices Aerolíneas del Sur, Fagnano 817; **Aerovías DAP**, O'Higgins 891, T061-223340, www.dap.cl, daily 0900-1230, 1430-1930; **LanChile**, Bories 884, T600-526 2000, www.lan.cl; **Sky Airline**, Roca 933, www.skyairline.cl.

Boat
All tickets on ships must be booked in advance for Jan and Feb. Visits to the beautiful fjords and glaciers of **Tierra del Fuego** are highly recommended. Comapa runs a fortnightly 22-hr, 320-km round trip to the fjord d'Agostino, where many glaciers descend to the sea. The luxury cruiser *Terra Australis* sails from Punta Arenas on Sat via Ushuaia and Puerto Williams; details from Comapa; advance bookings (advisable) from **Cruceros Australis SA**, Miraflores 178, 12th floor, Santiago, T02-6963211, www.australis.com. For services to Porvenir, Tierra del Fuego, see pages 638 and 645.
  Government supply ships are only recommended for the young and hardy, but take a sleeping bag, extra food and travel pills. For transport on navy supply ships to **Puerto Williams** and **Cape Horn**, enquire at **Tercera Zona Naval**, Lautaro Navarro 1150, but be prepared for irregular sailings (about 1 every 3 months) and inaccurate information. You will almost certainly need a letter of recommendation. During the voyage across the Drake Passage, albatrosses, petrels, cormorants, penguins,

elephant seals, fur seals, whales and dolphins can be sighted.

Most cruise ships to **Antarctica** leave from Ushuaia (Argentina). However there are a few operators based in Punta Arenas. Try **Antarctic Dream Shipping** Ebro 2740 of 602, Las Condes, Santiago, T02-481 6910, www.antarctic.cl (in UK **Senderos**, T0117-946 7547, info@senderos.co.uk); or **Antarctic XXII**, Lautaro Navarro 987, Piso 2, T061-614100, www.antarcticaxxi.com. Otherwise, another possibility is with the Chilean Navy. The Navy itself does not encourage passengers, so you must approach the captain direct. Spanish is essential. 2 vessels, Galvarino and Lautaro, sail regularly (no schedule), isotop@mitierra.cl.

Shipping offices Comapa (Compañía Marítima de Punta Arenas), Magallanes 990, T061-200200, www.comapa.com; **Navimag**, Magallanes 990, T061-244400, www.navimag.com.

Bus

Services and frequencies change every year, so check on arrival at the helpful Sernatur office. Timetables are also printed daily in *El Austral*. The services detailed below are for high season only. Buses depart from the company offices, which are listed below.

Buses Pacheco, Buses Sur, Fernández, and Transfer (cheapest), all run services each day to **Puerto Natales**, 3½ hrs, last departure 2000, US$9 (1-way), US$16 return (although this means you have to return with the same company). Buses may pick up at the airport with advance notice. To **Coyhaique**, 1 per week via Argentina, 20 hrs, US$55, meals not included, **Buses Sur**. Cruz del Sur, Pacheco, and Queilen Bus have services through Argentina to **Osorno**, **Puerto Montt** and **Castro**, several weekly, 36 hrs to Castro, US$50-75.

To Argentina To **Río Gallegos**, Pingüino, departs 1245 daily, returns 1300; Ghisoni, 4 weekly, departs 1100; **Pacheco**, 5 weekly, departs 1130. All cost US$12 and take about 5 hrs depending on customs,

15 mins on Chilean side, up to 2 hrs on Argentine side. For services to **Buenos Aires** it is cheaper to go to Río Gallegos and buy an onward ticket from there. **Pacheco** and **Ghisoni** have buses most days to **Río Grande** via Punta Delgada, 8-10 hrs, US$33, heavily booked. To **Ushuaia** via Punta Delgada, 12-14 hrs, book any return at same time; **Tecni Austral**, Tue, Thu, Sat, Sun 0800 from **Ghisoni** office, US$50; **Pacheco**, Mon, Wed, Fri, 0715, US$50.

Bus companies Bus Sur, Menéndez 552 T061-614224, www.bus-sur.cl; Cruz del Sur, El Pingüino and Fernández, Sanhueza 745, T061-221 4429, www.buses fernandez. com; Gesell, Menéndez 556, T061-222896; Ghisoni, Lautaro Navarro 975, T061-613422, www.ghisoni.terra.cl; Los Carlos, Plaza Muñoz Gamero 1039, T061-241321; Pacheco, Colón 900, T061-242174, www.busespacheco.cl.

Car hire

Try looking in the local newspaper for special deals and bargain if you want to hire a car for several days.

Budget, O'Higgins 964, T061-241696; **Hertz**, O'Higgins 987, T061-248742, English spoken; also at airport, T061 210096, **International**, Sequel 443 and at airport, T061-228323, recommended; **Payne Rent a Car**, Menéndez 631, T061-240852, www.payne.cl, try bargaining, friendly

Taxis

Ordinary taxis have yellow roofs. *Colectivos* (all black) run on fixed routes within the city, US$0.60-70. Reliable service is available from **Radio Alce vip**, T061-710889; **Taxi Austral**, T061-247710/244409.

❶ Directory

Punta Arenas *p608, map p609*
Banks Several on or around Plaza Muñoz Gamero, many 24 hrs, all have ATMs. Mon-Fri 0830-1400. **Currency exchange** Mon-Fri 0900-1230, 1500-1900, Sat

0900-1230. Outside business hours try **Bus Sur** (see Transport, above), or the major hotels (lower rates). Argentine pesos can be bought at *casas de cambio*; good rates at **Cambio Gasic**, Roca 915, Of 8, T061-242396, German spoken; **La Hermandad**, Lautaro Navarro 1099, T061-243991, excellent rates, US$ cash for AmEx, TCs and credit cards; **Scott Cambios**, Colón y Magallanes, T061-227145; **Sur Cambios**, Lautaro Navarro 1001, T061-225656, accepts TCs. **Embassies and consulates** Argentina, 21 de Mayo 1878, T061-261912, Mon-Fri 1000-1530, visas take 24 hrs. UK, Cataratas de Niaguara 01325, T061-211535, helpful, with information on Falkland Islands. **Internet** Lots of places offer access, including at Magallanes and Menéndez, and below Hostal Calafate on Magallanes, ½ block north of Plaza. Prices are generally US$1 per hr. **Medical services** A list of English-speaking doctors is available from Sernatur. **Clínica Magallanes**, Bulnes 01448, T061-211527, private clinic, minimum charge US$45 per visit; **Hospital Regional Lautaro Navarro**, Angamos 180, T061-244 040, public hospital, for emergency room ask for '*la posta*'. **Post office** Bories 911 and Menéndez, Mon-Fri 0830-1930, Sat 0900-1400. **Telephone** There are several call centres in the city centre (shop around).

Puerto Natales and around

→ *Colour map 6, B3. Phone code 061. Population 17,000.*

Beautifully situated on the calm waters of Canal Señoret fjord, an arm of the Ultima Esperanza Sound, edged with spectacular mountains, Puerto Natales is a pretty, quiet town of brightly painted corrugated-tin houses. It's the base for exploring the magnificent Balmaceda and Torres del Paine national parks, and although inundated with visitors in the summer, it retains a quiet unhurried feel and is a recommended place to relax for a few days. ▶▶ *For listings, see pages 622-625.*

Ins and outs

Getting there
Puerto Natales is easily reached by many daily buses from Punta Arenas, as well as by daily buses from Río Turbio (Argentina) and El Calafate. There are also two buses weekly from Río Gallegos. The town is the terminus of the **Navimag** ship to Puerto Montt (for further details, see page 625). If driving between Punta Arenas and Puerto Natales make sure you have enough fuel.

Getting around
Puerto Natales is not a large place and taxis are only needed for journeys out of town.

Tourist information
There is a municipal **tourist office** ① *Bulnes 285, T061-411263, muninata@chilean patagonia.com,* and information is also available at **SERNATUR** ① *Pedro Montt 19, T061-412125,* on the waterfront. A great website for Puerto Natales and the rest of Chile is www.welcomechile.com.

Sights

The colourful old steam train in the main square was once used to take workers to the meatpacking factory at Puerto Bories, 5 km north of town, now converted into the **Museo Frigorífico Puerto Bories** ① *T061-414328, daily 1000-1900 in summer, www.museopuerto bories.cl, US\$6 with audioguide in several languages.* In its heyday the plant was the biggest of its kind in Chile with a capacity for 250,000 sheep. Bankrupted in the early 1990s, much of the plant was dismantled in 1993. Belatedly the plant was given National Monument status and is slowly being restored. Fascinating tours of the remaining buildings and machine rooms are given in English. It is a pleasant hour-long walk along the shore to Bories (US\$6 by taxi), with glimpses of the Balmaceda Glacier across the sound.

The slab-like **Cerro Dorotea** dominates the town, with superb views of the whole Seno Ultima Esperanza. It can be reached on foot or by any Río Turbio bus or taxi (recommended, as the hill is further off than it seems). The trail entrance is marked by a sign 'Mirador Cerro Dorotea'. Expect to be charged US\$6-8 in one of the local houses, where you will be given a broomstick handle, which makes a surprisingly good walking stick. It is a 1½-hour trek up to the 600-m lookout along a well-marked trail. In theory you can continue along the top of the hill to get better views to the north, but the incredibly strong winds often make this dangerous. Some 25 km to the north of Puerto Natales is the **Monumento Nacional Cueva Milodón**, a massive cave, 70 m wide, 220 m deep and 30 m high, formed by the lapping of glacial lakes in the ice age, which were then 300 m above the current lake. Remains have been found here of a prehistoric ground sloth, together with evidence of occupation by early Patagonian humans some 11,000 years ago. The ceiling of the cave is dimpled with mineral deposits, and inside the eerie depths it's as silent as a library with marvellous views through the letterbox slit of the cave's mouth. There's a small visitor centre with summaries in English, toilets and a restaurant. This was the end point of Bruce Chatwin's famous travelogue *In Patagonia*. Most tours to Torres del Paine stop at the cave but you can also get there by bus US$8, or taxi US$30 return.

Parque Nacional Bernardo O'Higgins

Often referred to as the Parque Nacional Monte Balmaceda, Bernardo O'Higgins covers much of the Campo de Hielo Sur, plus the fjords and offshore islands further west. A three-hour boat trip from Puerto Natales up the Seno de Ultima Esperanza takes you to the southernmost section, passing the Balmaceda Glacier, which drops from the eastern slopes of **Monte Balmaceda** (2035 m). The glacier is retreating; in 1986 its foot was at sea level. The boat docks further north at **Puerto Toro**, from where it is a 1-km walk to the

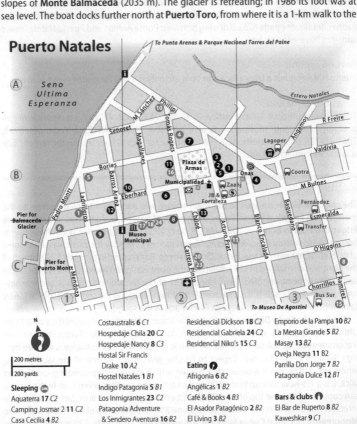

Puerto Natales

To Punta Arenas & Parque Nacional Torres del Paine

Seno Ultima Esperanza

Pier for Balmaceda Glacier

Pier for Puerto Montt

To Museo De Agostini

N

200 metres
200 yards

Sleeping
Aquaterra **17** C2
Camping Josmar 2 **11** C2
Casa Cecilia **4** B2
Costaustralis **6** C1
Hospedaje Chila **20** C2
Hospedaje Nancy **8** C3
Hostal Sir Francis
  Drake **10** A2
Hostel Natales **1** B1
Indigo Patagonia **5** B1
Los Inmigrantes **23** C2
Patagonia Adventure
  & Sendero Aventura **16** B2

Residencial Dickson **18** C2
Residencial Gabriela **24** C2
Residencial Niko's **15** C3

Eating
Afrigonia **6** B2
Angélicas **1** B2
Café & Books **4** B3
El Asador Patagónico **2** B2
El Living **3** B2

Emporio de la Pampa **10** B2
La Mesita Grande **5** B2
Masay **13** B2
Oveja Negra **11** B2
Parrilla Don Jorge **7** B2
Patagonia Dulce **12** B1

Bars & clubs
El Bar de Ruperto **8** B2
Kaweshkar **9** C1

Border essentials: Chile–Argentina

From Puerto Natales, the Argentine frontier can be crossed at three points, all of which meet Ruta 40, which runs north to El Calafate. These crossings are open, subject to weather conditions, 24 hours a day from September to May and daily 0700 to 2300 between June and August.

Paso Casas Viejas
This crossing, 16 km east of Puerto Natales, is reached by turning off Route 9 (the Punta Arenas road) at Km 14. On the Argentine side, the road (*ripio*) runs east to meet Ruta 40, en route to Río Gallegos (or north to El Calafate). This crossing is open all year.

Villa Dorotea
This crossing is reached by branching off Route 9, 9 km east of Puerto Natales and continuing north a further 11 km. On the Argentine side, the road (*ripio*) continues north to Ruta 40 via **Río Turbio**, see page 594.

Cerro Castillo
The most northerly of the three crossings, Cerro Castillo is reached by turning off the road north to Torres del Paine at Km 65.
Customs and immigration Chilean formalities are at Cerro Castillo; Argentine formalities are at Cancha Carrera, 2 km further east.
Transport On the Argentine side of the frontier, the road meets Route 40 in a very desolate spot – hitching may be possible, but this route is more feasible if you have your own transport.

base of the Serrano Glacier on the north slope of Monte Balmaceda. On the trip, dolphins, sea lions (in season), black-necked swans, flightless steamer ducks and cormorants can be seen. Take warm clothes, including a hat and gloves. There is a route from Puerto Toro along the **Río Serrano** for 35 km to the Torres del Paine administration centre (see page 627); guided tours are available. It is also possible to travel to the Paine administration centre by boat or Zodiac (four hours, US$65). Although the park is uninhabited, guest accommodation is available at **Hostería Monte Balmaceda (L)**, T061-220174. The cutter *21 de Mayo* sails every morning from Puerto Natales to the park in summer and on Sunday only in the winter, US$125 per person, minimum 10 passengers. Book through **Casa Cecilia** (see Sleeping, below), or directly through **Turismo 21 de Mayo** (see Activities and tours, page 625). Lunch is extra, so take your own food; snacks and drinks are available on board. The trip can be combined with a visit to Torres del Paine.

For Sleeping and Eating price codes and other relevant information, see Essentials pages 30-36.

⊜ Sleeping

Note that more information on where to stay, and tour companies, can be found at www.torresdelpaine.com (in English).

Puerto Natales *p619, map p620*
Most prices include breakfast. Hotels in the countryside are open only in the summer months; specific dates vary. In season, cheaper accommodation fills up quickly after the arrival of the **Navimag** ferry from Puerto Montt.

LL Altiplanico Sur, Huerto 282, T061-412525, www.altiplanico.cl. Lovely minimalist hotel with a unique design built into the hillside 1 km north of town and stunning views across the sound.

LL Costaustralis, Pedro Montt 262, T061-412000, www.hoteles-australis.com. The most expensive hotel in town but no better than the other big hotels. In effect you are paying for the view. The rooms facing inland are a waste.

LL Indigo Patagonia Hotel & Spa, Ladrilleros 105, T061-413609, www.indigo patagonia.com. Chilote-style house on the waterfront. Café and vegetarian restaurant downstairs. Internet access. Singles **C**. Would be overpriced except it has the best views of any hotel in town.

LL Remota, R9 Norte, Km 1.5, Huerto 279, T061-414040, www.remota.cl. Boutique hotel just outside town, unsual design with big windows. Lots of trips, activities and treks offered, spa, all-inclusive, good food.

L Weskar Patagonian Lodge, Km1, road to Bories, T061-414168, www.weskar.cl. Quiet lodge overlooking the bay, understated wooden interior. Most rooms with extensive views. Restaurant for guests and bike rental available. A good out-of-town place to relax.

AL Aquaterra, Bulnes 299, T061-412239, www.aquaterrapatagonia.com. Understated design. No frills but thought and effort have gone into it. Not cheap, but unlike many other places in the same price bracket you get the feeling that the staff are there to help and are able to answer any question you might have. Living room upstairs and a resto-bar downstairs. Alternative therapies also offered.

A Hostal Sir Francis Drake, Phillipi 383, T061-411553, www.hostalfrancisdrake.com. Simple, smallish but comfortable rooms with bath and cable TV. Pleasant living room on the upper floor with views. Recommended.

B-C Casa Cecilia, Tomás Rogers 60, T061-613560, www.casaceciliahostal.com. With good breakfast, some rooms with bath, some singles (**D-E**), clean, cooking facilities, English, French and German spoken, heating, luggage store, camping equipment rental, information on Torres del Paine, tours organized, bus tickets sold, credit cards accepted. Warmly recommended.

C Hospedaje Nancy, E Ramírez 540, T061-410022, www.natateslodge.cl. Cooking facilities, internet access, laundry service, tours and lots of information. Good budget option, singles (**F**). Helpful, recommended.

C-D Res Dickson, Bulnes 307, T061-411871, lodging@chileaustral.com. Good breakfast, clean, helpful, cooking and laundry facilities, internet, singles (**F**). Recommended.

C-D Residencial Niko's, E Ramírez 669, T061-412810, nikoresidencial@hotmail.com. With breakfast, basic rooms, some rooms with bath, singles (**F**), good meals, also dormitory accommodation. Recommended.

D Los Inmigrantes, Carrera Pinto 480, T061-413482, losinmigrantes@hotmail. com. Good breakfast, clean, kitchen facilities, equipment rental, luggage store, singles (**F**). Recommended.

D Residencial Gabriela, Bulnes 317, T061-411061. Clean, good breakfast, helpful, luggage store, heating, singles (**F**). Recommended.

E Hospedaje Chila, Carrera Pinto 442, T061-412328. Use of kitchen, laundry facilities and luggage store. Singles (**F**). Bakes bread, is welcoming and recommended.

Hostels See also the budget options above.

A-D Hostel Natales, Ladrilleros 209, T061-411081, www.hostelnatales.cl. All rooms with bath. Formerly a decent hotel converted into a luxury hostel. The place has been fully refurbished and is very comfortable, if overpriced.

C Patagonia Adventure, Tomás Rogers 179, T061-411028, www.apatagonia.com. Lovely old house, Bohemian feel, shared bath, dorms (**E** per person), good value. Home-made bread for breakfast, luggage store, equipment hire, bike and kayak tours and tour arrangements for Torres del Paine. No kitchen. Recommended.

Camping Camping Josmar 2, Esmeralda 517, in centre, T061-414417. Family-run, convenient, hot showers, parking, electricity, café, US$2.50 per site or **E** per person in double room.

Around Puerto Natales *p619*

Along the road from Punta Arenas are several decent hotels, including:

AL Hostal Río Penitente, Km 138, 1061-331 694. In an old *estancia*. Recommended.

AL Hostería y Refugio Monte Balmaceda, T061-220174, turismo@aventourpatagonia. com. Beautifully situated on Ultima Esperanza Sound, close to the Río Serrano. Comfortable rooms and *refugio* (**D**) with well-lit, giant tents, beds and bathrooms, restaurant. Also organize tours and rent equipment. Handy for boat trip up Río Serrano. Recommended.

AL-A Cisne de Cuello Negro, 6 km north of town, Km 275 near Puerto Bories, T061-244506, for bookings contact: Av Colón 782, Punta Arenas, T061-411498, www.pehoe.com. In a splendid lakeside setting, comfortable, excellent cooking.

A Posada Río Verde, Km 90, east off the highway on Seno Skyring, T061-311131. Private bath, heating. Recommended.

B Cabañas Kotenk Aike, 2 km north of town, T061-412581. Sleeps 4, modern, very comfortable, great location.

⓸ Eating

Puerto Natales *p619, map p620*

More suggestions for restaurants can be found at www.interpatagonia.com/puertonatales (in English).

₸₸₸ Afrigonia, Eberhard 343. A totally unexpected mixture, Patagonia meets East Africa in this Chilean/Kenyan-owned restaurant. One of the best in town.

₸₸₸-₸₸ Angélicas, Eberhard 532, T061-410 365, angelicas@rest.cl. A sign of how Puerto Natales has turned into a boutique town. Elegant Mediterranean-style restaurant originally from Santiago. Quality ingredients, well prepared. Pricey but more than reasonable for Natales, and customers invariably leave satisfied. Staff can be a little flustered when the restaurant is full. Recommended.

₸₸₸-₸₸ El Asador Patagónico, Prat 158 on Plaza. Specializes in spit-roast lamb. Recommended.

₸₸₸-₸₸ Parrilla Don Jorge, Bories 430 on Plaza. T061-410999. Another restaurant specializing in *Cordero al Palo*, but also serving fish, etc. The open plan leaves you feeling a little exposed when the restaurant is not full. Decent service.

₸₸ El Rincón de Don Chicho, Luis Cruz Martínez 206, T061-414339. One of the best *parrillas* in town. All-you-can-eat *parrillada*. Vegetarian options on request. 15 mins' walk from town centre. Recommended.

₸₸ La Mesita Grande, Prat 196 on Plaza, T061-411571, www.mesitagrande.cl. Fresh pizzas made in a wood-burning clay oven, as well as pasta and good desserts. Not much atmosphere, but has a fantastic antique till.

¶¶ **Oveja Negra**, Tomás Rogers 169, Plaza de Armas. Excellent local food and also has a book exchange.

¶ **Masay**, Bulnes 429. Cheap sandwiches.

Cafés

Café & Books, Blanco Encalada 224. Another cosy café with extensive 2-for-1 book exchange.

El Living, Prat 156, Plaza de Armas, www.el-living.com. Just what you need: comfy sofas, good tea, magazines in all languages, book exchange, good music, delicious vegetarian food. British-run, popular.

Emporio de la Pampa, Eberhard 226C, T061-510520. Small café/delicatessen selling wine and local gourmet products.

Patagonia Dulce, Barros Arana 233, T061-415285, www.patagoniadulce.cl. For the best hot chocolate in town.

🌓 Bars and clubs

Puerto Natales *p619, map p620*
El Bar de Ruperto, Bulnes 371, T061-414302, open 2100-0500. Good, English-run pub with a lively mix of locals and tourists. For a kick, try the chile vodka.

Kaweshkar, Bulnes 43, T415821. Laid-back bar, serving *empanadas*, hamburgers and vegetarian food. Try the parmesan mollusc tacos. Club at night with lounge music.

🔘 Shopping

Puerto Natales *p619, map p620*
Camping equipment
Balfer, Esmeralda and Baquedano. Camping gear and fishing tackle, but more expensive than the **Zona Franca** in Punta Arenas. Similar items at **Alfgal**, Barros Arana 299, T061-413622.

Outdoor clothing from **La Maddera**, Prat 297, T061-413318. Camping gas is available in hardware stores (eg Baquedano and O'Higgins). **Patagonia Adventure** and **Casa Cecilia** hire out good-quality gear (for both,

see Sleeping, above). Check all equipment and prices carefully. Average charges, per day: tent US$8, sleeping bag US$4-6, mat US$2, raincoat US$1, also cooking gear US$2. Note that deposits are required: tent US$200, sleeping bag US$100.

Food
Food prices are variable so shop around, although everything tends to be pricier than in Punta Arenas. There's a 24-hr supermarket on the Bulnes 300 block, and at Bulnes 1085. The town markets are also good.

🔺 Activities and tours

Puerto Natales *p619, map p620*
Reports of the reliability of agencies, especially for their trips to Torres del Paine National Park, are very mixed. It is better to book tours direct with operators in Puerto Natales than through agents in Punta Arenas, where huge commissions may be charged. Some agencies offer 1-day tours to the Perito Moreno Glacier in Argentina (see page 573), 14-hr trip, 2 hrs at the glacier, US$65 excluding food and park entry fee; take US$ cash or Argentine pesos as Chilean pesos are not accepted. However, if you have more time it is better to break the trip by staying in Calafate and organizing a tour from there.

Bigfoot Expediciones, Bories 206, T061-413247, www.bigfootpatagonia.com. Sea kayaking, trekking, mountaineering and ice-hiking trips on the Grey Glacier. Unforgettable if expensive. Recommended.

Estancia Travel, Casa 13B, Puerto Bories (5 km north of Puerto Natales), T061-412221, www.estanciatravel.com. English/Chilean operator offering a different way of experiencing Patagonia – on horseback. Bilingual guides and well-kept horses. Good ½-day trips to the Cueva del Milodón. Multi-day trips only for the well-off. Book direct or through agencies in Natales.

Onas, Blanco Encalada 211, T061-614300, www.onaspatagonia.com. Tours of Torres

del Paine and kayaking trips. Also trips to and from the park down the Río Serrano in Zodiac boats to the Serrano glacier in the Parque National Bernardo O'Higgins, and from there on the tour boats to Puerto Natales, US$95 per person all inclusive. Book in advance.
Sendero Aventura, at Hostal Patagonia Adventure, Tomás Rogers 179, T061-415 636, www.senderoaventura.com. Adventure Trekking in Torres del Paine, cycling and kayaking trips to the park, boats to Parque Nacional Balmaceda, camping equipment and bike hire. Recommended.
Skorpios, Prat 62, T061-412409, www.skorpios.cl. Catamaran trips up to the Fjordo de las montañas. Truly spectacular close-up vistas of glaciers and waterfalls given good weather. 2 sailings weekly.
Turismo 21 de Mayo, Eberhard 560, T061-4114/6, www.turismo21demayo.cl. Boat trips to Parque Nacional Bernado O'Higgins and on to Torres del Paine in Zodiac. This can be combined for a very long day with a trip to the park, returning by bus. Around US$125, including park entry and food.

⊖ Transport

Puerto Natales *p619, map p620*
Punta Arenas is served by Bus Fernández, E Ramírez 399, T061-411111; Bus Sur, Baquedano 668, T061-4614220; and Bus Transfer, Baquedano 414, T061-421616; several services daily, 3½ hrs, US$49, book in advance. Bus Sur runs to **Coyhaique**, Mon, US$50.

To Argentina Bus Sur has 2 weekly direct services to **Río Gallegos**, 4-5 hrs, US$18. Cootra runs services to **Río Turbio**, 2 hrs (depending on customs), US$5. To **Calafate**, Bus Sur and Bus Zaahj, daily

services, 4½ hrs, US$19; **Cootra** also runs a service via Río Turbio, 7 hrs, reserve at least 1 day in advance. Bus Sur also runs 3 buses a week to **Ushuaia**, Oct-Apr, 15 hrs, US$63.

Boat
The **Navimag** ferry *Eden* sails every Fri in summer to **Puerto Montt**, less frequently off season; confirmation of reservations is advised.

Shipping companies Navimag, Pedro Montt 262, Loc B, Terminal Marítimo, T061-411421.

❶ Directory

Puerto Natales *p619, map p620*
Banks Banks offer poor rates for TCs, which cannot be changed into US$ cash. **Banco de Chile**, Bulnes 544, MasterCard and Visa, ATM; **Banco Santander Santiago**, Bulnes y Blanco Encalada, MasterCard and Visa, ATM.
Currency exchange Shop around as some *casas* offer very poor rates (much better to change money in Punta Arenas). **Cambio Stop**, Baquedano 380; **Enio América**, Blanco Encalada 266, Argentine pesos can be changed here; there are 2 more at Bulnes 683 and 1087 (good rates, also change Argentine pesos), and others on Prat. **Internet** Concepto Indigo, Hospedaje María José (see Sleeping, above); El Rincón de Tata, Prat 236; Patagonianet, Blanco 330.
Laundry Lavandería Catch, Bories 218, friendly service; **Servilaundry**, Bulnes 513.
Post office Eberhard 417, Mon-Fri 0830-1230, 1430-1745, Sat 0900-1230.
Telephone CTC, Blanco Encalada 23 y Bulnes; **Entel**, Baquedano and Bulnes, phone and fax service; **Telefónica**, Blanco Encalada and Phillipi.

Parque Nacional Torres del Paine

→ *Colour map 6, B2.*

Parque Nacional Torres del Paine is spectacular. World-renowned for its challenging trekking, the park contains 15 peaks above 2000 m. At its centre is the glacier-topped granite massif Macizo Paine from which rise the vertical pink granite Torres (towers) de Paine and below them the strange Cuernos (horns) de Paine, swooping buttresses of lighter granite under caps of darker sedimentary rock. From the vast Campo de Hielo Sur ice cap on its western edge, four main glaciers (ventisqueros) – Grey, Dickson, Zapata and Tyndall – drop into vividly coloured lakes formed by their meltwater: turquoise, ultramarine and pistachio expanses, some filled with wind-sculpted royal blue icebergs. Wherever you explore, there are constantly changing views of dramatic peaks and ice fields. Allow five to seven days to see the park properly. The park is also one of the best places on the continent for viewing rheas and guanacos. Apart from the 3500 guanacos, 24 other species of mammals can be seen here, including hares, foxes, skunks, huemules and pumas (the last two only very rarely). For helpful·information on the park see www.torresdelpaine.com (in English). ►► *For listings, see pages 632-634.*

Ins and outs

Getting there

The most practical way to get to Torres del Paine is with one of the many bus or tour companies that leave Puerto Natales daily. From early November to mid-April daily bus services run from Puerto Natales to the park, leaving between 0630 and 0800, and again at around 1430 (2½ hours to Laguna Amarga, three hours to the administration centre), US$15 one-way, US$24 open return (return tickets are not always interchangeable between different companies). Return departures are usually around 1300 and 1800. Generally, buses will drop you at Laguna Amarga and pick you up at the administration centre for the return. The buses wait at Refugio Pudeto until the 1200 boat from Refugio Lago Pehoé arrives. Travel between two points within the park (eg Pudeto to Laguna Amarga) costs US$6. Services are provided by **Bus Gómez** ① *Prat 234, T061-411971*, **Trans Via Paine** ① *Bulnes 518, T061-413672*, and **JB** ① *Prat 258, T061-412824*. At other times, services by travel agencies are subject to demand; arrange your return date with the driver and try to coincide with other groups to keep costs down (Luis Díaz has been recommended, about US$17, minimum three persons).

If you want to drive, hiring a pickup from Punta Arenas or Puerto Natales is an economical proposition for a group (up to nine people), US$400 for four days. The new entrance to Torres del Paine (via a bridge over the Río Serrano) along the new paved route which cuts the distance from Puerto Natales to the park entrance by 100 km; it now takes about two hours to travel the 147 km from Puerto Natales to the administration. ►► *For further details, see Transport, page 633.*

Getting around

Allow a week or 10 days to see the park properly. Most visitors will find that they can get around on foot. However, there are minibuses running regularly between the CONAF administration and Guardería Laguna Amarga, as well as boats across Lago Pehoé. Roads inside the park are narrow and bendy with blind corners. Rangers keep a check on the whereabouts of all visitors: you are required to register and show your passport when entering the park or before setting off on any hike.

Tourist information

There are entrances at Laguna Amarga, Lago Sarmiento and Laguna Azul; foreigners pay US$25 (proceeds are shared between all Chilean national parks). The park is administered by CONAF, which has an **administration centre** ① *T061-691931, open daily 0830-2000 in summer, daily 0830-1230, 1400-1830 off season*, at the northern end of Lago del Toro. It puts on a good slide show at 2000 on Saturday and Sunday and there are also excellent exhibitions on the flora and fauna of the park in Spanish and English. There are six ranger stations (*guarderías*) in the park staffed by *guardaparques*, who give advice and store luggage (not at Laguna Amarga).

Best time to visit

The weather in the park can change in a few minutes. The warmest time is from December to March, although it can be wet and windy. The spring months of October and November are recommended for wild flowers. Rain and snowfall are heavier the further west you go and bad weather sweeps off the Campo de Hielo Sur without warning. Snow may prevent access in winter, but well-equipped hikers can do some good walking when conditions are stable. For information on weather conditions, in Spanish, phone the administration centre. The park is open all year round.

Trekking

There are about 250 km of well-marked trails. Visitors must keep to the trails: cross-country trekking is not permitted. It is vital not to underestimate the unpredictability of the weather, nor the arduousness of some of the long hikes. Some paths are confusingly marked and it is all too easy to end up on precipices with glaciers or churning rivers below; be particularly careful to follow the path at the Paso John Gadner on El Circuito (see below). The only means of rescue are on horseback or by boat; the nearest helicopter is in Punta Arenas and high winds usually prevent its operation in the park.

Equipment

It is essential to be properly equipped against cold, wind and rain. A strong, streamlined, waterproof tent is essential if doing El Circuito (although you can hire camping equipment for a single night at most *refugios*). Also essential are protective clothing, strong waterproof footwear, compass, good sleeping bag and sleeping mat. In summer also take shorts and sunscreen. You are strongly advised to bring all necessary equipment and your own food from Puerto Natales and not to rely on availability at the *refugios* within the park; the small shops at the *refugios* (see below) and at the **Posada Río Serrano** are expensive and have a limited selection. Note that rats and mice are a real problem around camping sites and the free *refugios*, so do not leave food in your pack (which may be chewed through); instead, the safest solution is to hang food in a bag on a wire. Note that you are not allowed to build fires in the park. A decent map is provided with your park entrance ticket; other maps (US$7-9) are obtainable in many places in Puerto Natales but most have one or two mistakes. The map produced by **Cartografía Digital** has been recommended as more accurate, as is the one produced by **Patagonia Interactiva**.

Treks

El Circuito ① *in theory, lone walkers are not allowed on this route.* The most popular trek is a circuit round the Torres and Cuernos del Paine. It is usually done anticlockwise starting from the *guardería* at **Laguna Amarga** and, although some people complete the route in less time, it normally takes five to six days. The circuit is often closed in winter because of snow; major rivers are crossed by footbridges, but these are occasionally washed away. From Laguna Amarga the route is north along the western side of the Río Paine to **Lago Paine**, before turning west to follow the lush pastures of the valley of the Río Paine to the southern end of **Lago Dickson** (it is possible to add a journey to the *campamento* by the Torres on day one of this route); the *refugio* at Lago Dickson lies in a breathtaking position in front of the icy white lake with mountains beyond. From Lago Dickson the path runs along the wooded valley of the **Río de los Perros**, past the Glaciar de los Perros, before climbing through bogs and up scree to **Paso John Gadner** (1241 m, the highest point on the route), then dropping steeply through forest to follow the Grey Glacier southeast to **Lago Grey**, continuing to **Lago Pehoé** and the administration centre. There are superb views en route, particularly from the top of Paso John Gadner.

The longest stretch is between Refugio Laguna Amarga and Refugio Dickson (30 km, 10 hours in good weather; two campsites on the way at Serón and Cairon), but the most difficult section is the very steep, slippery slope from Paso John Gadner down to the Campamento Paso; the path is not well signed at the top of the pass, and some people have got dangerously lost and ended up on the Grey Glacier itself. Camping gear must be carried, as some *campamentos* (including Campamento Paso and Campamento Torres) do not have *refugios*.

The 'W' The 'W' is a popular alternative to El Circuito. This three- to five-day route can be completed without camping equipment if preferred, as there is accommodation in *refugios* en route. It combines several of the hikes described separately below. From Refugio Laguna Amarga the first stage runs west via **Hostería Las Torres** and up the valley of the **Río Ascensio** via Refugio Chileno to the base of the **Torres del Paine** (see below). From here return to the Hostería Las Torres and then walk along the northern shore of **Lago Nordenskjold** via Refugio Los Cuernos to Campamento Italiano. Next climb the Valley of the **Río del Francés** (see below) before continuing to Refugio Pehoé. From here you can complete the third part of the 'W' by walking west along the northern shore of **Lago Grey** to Refugio Grey and the Grey Glacier before returning to Refugio Pehoé and the boat back across the lake to the Refugio Pudeto.

Valley of the Río del Francés From Refugio Pehoé this route leads north across undulating country along the western edge of **Lago Skottberg** to Campamento Italiano and then follows the valley of the Río del Francés, which climbs between Cerro Paine Grande and the Ventisquero del Francés (to the west) and the Cuernos del Paine (to the east) to Campamento Británico; the views from the mirador an hour's walk above Campamento Británico are superb. Allow 2½ hours from Refugio Pehoé to Campamento Italiano, 2½ hours further to Campamento Británico.

Treks from Guardería Grey Guardería Grey, 18 km west by road from the administration centre, is the starting point for a five-hour trek to Lago Pingo, recommended if you want to get away from the crowds, and one of the best routes in the park for birdwatching. From the *guardería* follow the **Río Pingo**, via Refugio Pingo and Refugio Zapata (four hours), with views south over Ventisquero Zapata (look out for plenty of wildlife and for icebergs in the lake) to reach the lake. **Ventisquero Pingo** can be seen 3 km away over the lake. Note there is a bridge over a river here, marked on many maps, which has been washed away. The river can be forded when it is low, however, allowing access to the glacier. Two short signposted walks from Guardería Grey have also been suggested: one is a steep climb up the hill behind the ranger post to **Mirador Ferrier**, from where there are fine views; the other is via a suspension bridge across the Río Pingo to the peninsula at the southern end of **Lago Grey**, from where there are good views of the icebergs on the lakes.

To the base of the Torres del Paine From Refugio Laguna Amarga, this six-hour route follows the road west to **Hostería Las Torres** (1½ hours), before climbing along the western side of the **Río Ascensio** via Refugio Chileno (two hours) and Campamento Chileno to Campamento Las Torres (two hours), close to the base of the **Torres del Paine** (be careful when crossing the suspension bridge over the Río Ascensio near Hostería Las Torres, as the path is poorly marked and you can end up on the wrong side of the ravine). The path alongside the Río Ascensio is well marked, and the Campamento Las Torres is in an attractive wood (no *refugio*). A further 30 minutes up the morraine takes you to a lake at the base of the towers themselves; they seem so close that you almost feel you could touch them. To see the Torres lit by sunrise (spectacular but you must have good weather), it's well worth carrying your camping gear up to Campamento Torres and spending the night. One hour beyond Campamento Torres is Campamento Japonés, another good campsite.

Laguna Verde From the administration centre follow the road north 2 km, before taking the path east over the **Sierra del Toro** and then along the southern side of **Laguna Verde** to the Guardería Laguna Verde. Allow four hours. This is one of the easiest walks in the park and may be a good first hike.

Parque Nacional Torres del Paine

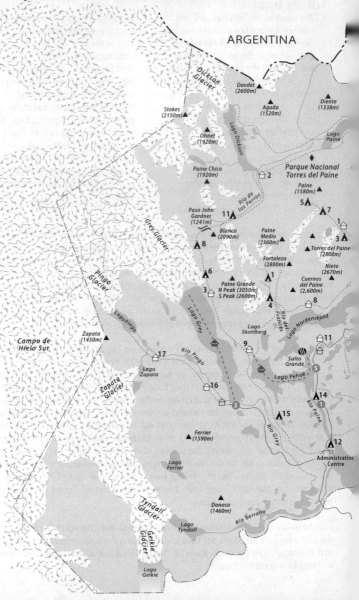

ARGENTINA

Dickson Glacier

Davdet
(2600m)

Aguda
(1520m)

Diente
(1338m)

Stokes
(2150m)

Lago Dickson

Lago
Paine

Ohnet
(1920m)

Paine Chico
(1920m)

2

Parque Nacional
Torres del Paine

Río de los Perros

Paine
(1580m)

5

7

Paso John
Gardner
(1241m)

11

1

Blanco
(2090m)

Paine
Medio
(2360m)

3

8

Grey Glacier

Fortaleza
(2800m)

Torres del Paine
(2800m)

6

Nieto
(2670m)

Pingo
Glacier

3

Paine Grande
N Peak (3050m)
S Peak (2600m)

1

Cuernos
del Paine
(2,600m)

4

8

Lago Grey

Lago
Skottberg

Río del Francés

Lago Nordenskjold

Zapata
(1450m)

Lago Pingo

Río Pingo

9

11

Campo de
Hielo Sur

17

Lago
Zapata

Salto
Grande

5

Zapata
Glacier

16

3

Lago Pehoé

14

15

Río Paine

Ferrier
(1590m)

Río Grey

12

Administration
Centre

Lago
Ferrier

Tyndall
Glacier

Donoso
(1460m)

Río Serrano

Geikie
Glacier

Lago
Tyndall

Lago
Geikie

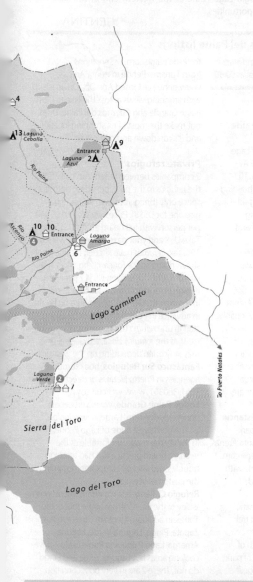

Sleeping
Explora **1**
Hostería Lago Grey **3**
Hostería Las Torres **4**
Hostería Mirador del Payne **2**
Hostería Pehoé **5**

Refugios
Chileno **1**
Grey **3**
Lago Dickson **2**
Lago Paine **4**
Laguna Amarga **6**
Laguna Verde **7**
Las Torres **10**
Lodge Paine Grande
  (formerly Lago Pehoé) **9**
Los Cuernos **8**
Pingo **16**
Pudeto **11**
Zapata **17**

Camping ▲
Campamento Británico **1**
Campamento Chileno **3**
Campamento Italiano **4**
Campamento Japonés **5**
Campamento Lago Paine **2**
Campamento Las Carretas **15**
Campamento Las Guardas **6**
Campamento Las Torres **7**
Campamento Paso **8**
Lago Pehoé **14**
Laguna Azul **9**
Las Torres **10**
Los Perros **11**
Serón **13**
Serrano **12**

Ranger stations (*guarderías*)

N

5 km
5 miles

To Laguna Azul and Lago Paine This route runs north from Laguna Amarga to the western tip of **Laguna Azul**, from where it continues across the sheltered **Río Paine** valley past Laguna Cebolla to the Refugio Lago Paine at the western end of the lake. Allow 8½ hours. Good birdwatching opportunities.

◉ Parque Nacional Torres del Paine listings

For Sleeping and Eating price codes and other relevant information, see Essentials pages 30-36.

◉ Sleeping

Parque Nacional Torres del Paine
p626, map p630

LL Explora, Salto Chico on edge of Lago Pehoé, T02-395 2533. Reservations: Av Américo Vespucci 80, p 7, Santiago, T02-206 6060, www.explora.com. Ugly building but the most luxurious and comfortable accommodation in the park, offering spectacular views, pool, gym, tours and transfer from Punta Arenas.

LL Hostería Lago Grey, T061-712100. Small rooms on edge of Lago Grey with views of Grey Glacier, decent restaurant.

LL Hostería Las Torres, Sarmiento 846 head office Magallanes 960, Punta Arenas, T061-360360, www.lastorres.com. Probably the best of the *hosterías* in the park. Nice rooms, although strangely none has a particularly good view, good restaurant, disabled access, English spoken, horse riding, transport from Laguna Amarga ranger station. Some cheaper rooms are also available.

LL Hostería Mirador del Payne (Estancia Lazo), on the eastern edge of the park, reservations from Fagnano 585, Punta Arenas, T061-226930, www.miradordelpayne.com. Beautifully situated on Laguna Verde with spectacular views, good fishing and restaurant. Recommended but an inconvenient base for visiting the park; own transport essential, or you can trek to it from within the park.

LL-AL Hostería Pehoé, 5 km south of Pehoé ranger station, 11 km north of park administration, T02-235 0252, pehoe@

torresdelpaine.com. Reservations from **Turismo Pehoé** in Punta Arenas, www.pehoe.cl. Closed Apr-Oct. On an island with stunning views across the lake to Cerro Paine Grande and Cuernos del Paine. Does not make the most of its stunning location and it's run down and overpriced.

Private refugios
2 companies between them run half of the *refugios* in the park, providing dormitory space only (bring your own sleeping bag or hire one for US$8). Prices are around US$40 per person with full board about US$35 extra. Take US$ and your passport as you will save 19% tax. *Refugios* have kitchen facilities, hot showers and space for camping. Most will hire out tents for around US$12 per night. In high season accommodation and meals in the non-CONAF *refugios* should be booked in advance in Puerto Natales, or by asking staff in one *refugio* to radio another. In winter most of the *refugios* close, although 1 or 2 may stay open depending on the weather.

Fantástico Sur Refugios, book through agencies in Puerto Natales or direct on T061-360361, www.wcircuit.com.

Lodge Paine Grande, www.verticepata gonia.cl/lodge.htm. Large, new *refugio* on the northwest edge of Lago Pehoe. In theory the most comfortable of the *refugios*, but in practice has had teething troubles and several complaints regarding the customer service.

Refugio Chileno, reservas@fantasticosur.com. Valley of the Río Ascensio at the foot of the Torres. In addition, there are 6 free *refugios*: Zapata, Pingo, Laguna Verde, Laguna Amarga, Lago Paine and Pudeto. Most have cooking areas but Laguna Verde and Pingo do not. These 2 are in very poor condition.

Refugio Grey, eastern shore of Lago Grey; Refugio Lago Dickson, on the northern part of the circuit; Refugio Las Torres, next to the Hostería Las Torres (see above); Refugio Los Cuernos, on the northern shore of Lago Nordenskjold; Vértice Refugios, book through agencies in Puerto Natales or www.verticepatagonia.cl.

Camping
The wind tends to increase in the evening so it is a good idea to pitch tents early (by 1600). In addition to sites at the private *refugios*, there are the following sites (see map, page 630, for locations): Lago Pehoé, run by Turismo Río Serrano, US$7pp, hot showers, beware of mice; Laguna Azul, hot showers; Las Torres, run by Estancia Cerro Paine, US$7pp, hot showers; Los Perros, run by Andescape, with shop and hot showers; Serón, run by Fantastico Sur, US$7pp, hot showers.

Free camping is permitted in 10 other locations in the park; these sites are known as *campamentos*. Fires may only be lit at organized campsites, not at *campamentos*. The *guardaparques* expect people to have a stove if camping. These restrictions should be observed, as forest fires are a serious hazard. *Guardaparques* also require campers to have a trowel to bury their waste. Equipment can be hired in Puerto Natales.

▲ Activities and tours

Parque Nacional Torres del Paine
p626, map p630
Before booking a tour check all the details carefully and get a copy in writing, as there have been increasingly mixed reports of the quality of some tours. Many companies who claim to visit the Grey Glacier, for example, only visit Lago Grey (you see the glacier in the distance). Note that after mid-Mar there is less public transport and trucks are irregular.

Several agencies in Puerto Natales offer 1-day tours by minibus, US$35 plus park entry; these give a good impression of the lower parts of the park, although you spend most of the day in the vehicle and many travellers would argue that you need to stay several days, or at least overnight, in the park to appreciate it fully. Cheaper tours are also available, but both guide and vehicle may not be as good as the established operators. There are many more operators based in Puerto Natales offering trekking, kayaking, ice-hiking, boat trips and other tours (see page 624).

Cascada Expediciones, Don Carlos 3219, Las Condes, Santiago, T02-232 9878, www.cascada.travel/. Small group tours to Torres del Paine.
Experience Chile, T02-5709436 (Santiago), www.experiencechile.org. Itineraries and accommodation in the region can be arranged by this UK-based operator.
Hostería Lago Grey, see Sleeping, above. Excursions by boat to the face of the Grey Glacier, 0900 and 1500, 3½ hrs, US$70 per person. Book direct.

✆ Transport

Parque Nacional Torres del Paine
p626, map p630
Bus
In season there are minibus connections from Laguna Amarga to the Hostería Las Torres, US$6, and from the administration centre to Hostería Lago Grey.

To go from Torres del Paine to **El Calafate** (Argentina), either return to Puerto Natales and catch a bus, or take a bus or hitch from the park to Villa Cerro Castillo and try to link with the Natales–Calafate bus schedule. In season, there is a direct bus from the park to El Calafate with **Chaltén Travel**, US$60.

Boat

A service runs across Lago Pehoé from near the Lodge Paine Grande to Refugio Pudeto, daily, 30 mins, US$19 (1-way), 1 piece of luggage free, tickets available on board, Departures from Paine Grande 1000, 1230, 1830; from Pudeto 0930, 1200, 1800. Reduced service off season, no service May-Sep. For more information, call T061-411380.

Contents

Footprint features

Border crossings

At a glance

⊖ **Getting around** Local buses will take you to the local attractions, but not much further afield. Some short-distance flights

◐ **Time required** 3-4 days will allow you to visit Ushuaia and the surrounding area.

☼ **Weather** Mar-Nov brings harsh winds and cold temperatures, with snow in Jun and Jul.

✕ **When not to go** The height of winter (May-Jul) can be unpleasantly cold, unless you want to ski.

Tierra del Fuego

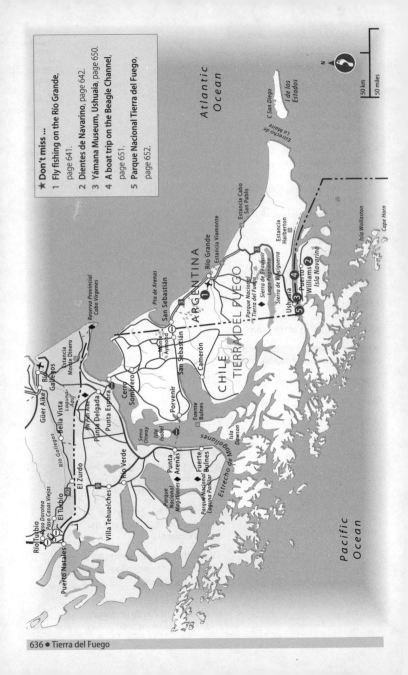

★ Don't miss ...
1 Fly fishing on the Río Grande, page 641.
2 Dientes de Navarino, page 642.
3 Yámana Museum, Ushuaia, page 650.
4 A boat trip on the Beagle Channel, page 651.
5 Parque Nacional Tierra del Fuego, page 652.

Atlantic Ocean

N

50 km
50 miles

I de los Estados

C San Diego

Estrecho de La Maire

Isla Wollaston

Cape Horn

Estancia Cabo San Pablo

Estancia Viamonte

Río Grande

Estancia Harberton

Parque Nacional Tierra del Fuego

Sierra de Beauvoir Lago Fagnano

Sierra de Valdivieso

Ushuaia

Puerto Williams
Isla Navarino

ARGENTINA

TIERRA DEL FUEGO

San Sebastián

Pta de Arenas

Monte Aymond

San Sebastián

Camerón

CHILE

Reserva Provincial Cabo Vírgenes

Estancia Monte Dinero

Güer Aike

Río Gallegos

Bella Vista

Laguna Azul

PN Pali Aike

Punta Delgada

Punta Espora

Cerro Sombrero

Porvenir

Fuente Bulnes

Isla Dawson

Seno Otway

Isla Isabel

Punta Arenas

Fuerte Bulnes

Parque Nacional Laguna Parrillar

Parque Nacional Magallanes

Estrecho de Magallanes

Villa Tehuelches

Río Verde

El Zurdo

Río Gallegos

El Tubbo

Paso Dorotea
Paso Casas Viejas

Río Turbio

Puerto Natales

Pacific Ocean

The island of Tierra del Fuego is the most mysterious and captivating part of all Patagonia. At the very foot of the South American continent and separated from the mainland by the intricate waterways of the Straits of Magellan, this is America's last remaining wilderness and an indispensable part of any trip to the south. The island is divided between Argentina and Chile by a north–south line that grants Argentina the Atlantic and southern coasts and gives Chile an expanse of wilderness to the west, where the tail of the Andes sweeps east in the form of the mighty Darwin range.

The Chilean side is largely inaccessible, apart from the small town of Porvenir, though expeditions can be organized from Punta Arenas to take you hiking and trout fishing. On the Argentine side, glaciers and jagged peaks give a dramatic backdrop to the city of Ushuaia, the island's main centre, set in a serene natural harbour on the Beagle Channel, with views of the Dientes de Navarino mountains on the Chilean island of Navarino opposite. Sail from Ushuaia along the channel to the pioneer home of Harberton; to Cape Horn; or even to Antarctica. Head into the small but picturesque Parque Nacional Tierra del Fuego for strolls around Bahía Lapataia and steep climbs with magnificent views out along the channel. The mountain slopes are covered in lenga forest, and if you visit in autumn you might think the name 'Land of Fire' derives from the blaze of scarlet and orange leaves. Elsewhere on the island, lakes and valleys can be explored on foot or on horseback, and in winter the valleys are perfect for cross-country skiing, while the slopes at Cerro Castor offer good powder snow, and skiing with spectacular views of the end of the world.

Ins and outs

Getting there

Air The **Argentine Tierra del Fuego** is easy to reach with several flights daily from Buenos Aires to Río Grande and Ushuaia, and less frequent flights from El Calafate, and some other towns in Patagonia. Flights are heavily booked in advance throughout the summer months (December to February). **Chilean Tierra del Fuego** is less easily accessed by air, but there are five flights a week from Punta Arenas to Porvenir in the summer, and four a week to Puerto Williams on Isla Navarino (summer only).

Ferry and bus There are no road or ferry crossings between the Argentine mainland and Argentine Tierra del Fuego. You have to go through Chilean territory. Note that accommodation is sparse, and planes and buses fill up quickly from November to March. It's essential to book ahead.

From Río Gallegos, Route 3 reaches the Chilean border at Monte Aymond, 67 km, passing Laguna Azul. Thirty kilometres into Chile is Kamiri Aike, with a dock 16 km east at Punta Delgada for the 20-minute Straits of Magellan ferry-crossing over the Primera Angostura (First Narrows) to Bahía Azul. At Punta Delgada is the Hostería El Faro where you can get food and drink. There are two boats working continuously, *Pionero* and *Fueguino*. On board is a café, lounge and toilets. Buses can wait up to 90 minutes to board and the boats run from 0700 to 0100 (0830 to 2345 from April to October), US$22 per vehicle, foot passengers US$2.50. See www.tabsa.cl for more information.

The road is paved to Cerro Sombrero, from where *ripio* roads run southeast to Chilean San Sebastián (130-140 km from ferry, depending on the route taken). It's 15 km east, across the border (24 hours), to Argentine San Sebastián. From here the road is paved to Río Grande (see below) and Ushuaia. For more information on crossing the border here, see box, opposite.

The second main ferry crossing is Punta Arenas to Porvenir. Route 255 from Kamiri Aike goes southwest 116 km to the intersection with the Punta Arenas–Puerto Natales road, from where it is 53 km to Punta Arenas. The ferry dock is 5 km north of Punta Arenas centre, at Tres Puentes. The ferry crosses to Bahía Chilota, 5 km west of Porvenir, Tuesday to Sunday (subject to tides) and takes two hours 20 minutes, US$54 per vehicle, bikes US$12, foot passengers US$8.65. **Transportadora Austral Broom** ⓘ *www.tabsa.cl*, publishes a timetable a month in advance. These are dependent on tides and subject to change so check in advance. Reservations are essential, especially in summer. From Porvenir a 234-km *ripio* road runs east to Río Grande (six hours, no public transport) via San Sebastián. Note that fruit and meat may not be taken onto the island, nor between Argentina and Chile.

There is also a weekly ferry service from Punta Arenas to Puerto Williams on Isla Navarino, 36 hours, no creature comforts, US$175 for a reclining seat, US$210 for a bunk, meals included.

Getting around

There are good bus links from Punta Arenas to Río Grande in Argentina, with an option of going via Porvenir, along the decent loop of road on the Chilean side. From Porvenir your options are limited to a *ripio* road around Bahía Inútil to near Lago Blanco, though there's no public transport here. Argentine Tierra del Fuego is much easier to get around, via Route 3 between Río Grande and Ushuaia with several buses a day. A fan of roads spreads

Monte Aymond

Monte Aymond is open 24 hours in summer and 0900 to 2300 from April to October.
Transport For bus passengers the border crossing is easy, although you have about a 30-minute wait at each border post as luggage is checked and documents are stamped (it's two more hours to Punta Arenas). Hire cars need a document for permission to cross the border.

Accommodation Chilean San Sebastián is just a few houses with Hostería La Frontera 500 m from the border. In Argentine San Sebastián there is a seven-room ACA hostería, T02964-425542, and a service station open from 0700 to 2300.

out south and west, from Río Grande to the *estancias* on the Argentine side, but these are unpaved and best attempted in a 4WD vehicle. A good *ripio* road leads from 40 km east of Ushuaia to Harberton and Estancia Moat on the south coast, and part of the way along the north coast to Estancia San Pablo; there is no public transport here either.

Background

Tierra del Fuego's narrated history began with the early 16th-century explorers, but the island had been inhabited by indigenous groups for some 10,000 years. The most populous of these groups, the Onas (also known as the Selk'nam), were hunter-gatherers in the north, living mainly on guanaco which they shot with bow and arrow. The south-eastern corner of the island was inhabited by the Haus or Hausch, also hunter-gatherers. The Yaganes or Yámana lived along the Beagle Channel and on the islands further south, and were seafaring people who survived mainly on seafood, fish and birds, physically smaller than the Onas but with a strongly developed upper body for rowing long distances. The fourth group, the Alacalufe, lived in the west of Tierra del Fuego as well as on the Chonos Archipelago, surviving by fishing and hunting seals.

The first Europeans to visit the island came with the Portuguese navigator Fernão Magalhães (Magellan), who, in 1520, sailed through the channel that now bears his name. It was Magellan who named the island Land of Fire when he saw the smoke from many fires lit along the shoreline by local inhabitants. As a result of numerous maritime disasters, including the failure of Sarmiento de Gamboa's attempt at colonizing the Straits in 1584, the indigenous population were left undisturbed for three centuries.

Fitzroy and Darwin's scientific visits in 1832 and 1833 recorded some fascinating interaction with the indigenous peoples, four of whom Fitzroy had earlier brought to London to see if they could be 'civilized', and of whom he now returned the surviving three. Fitzroy and Darwin's visits were a precursor to attempts to convert the indigenous groups to Christianity so that the island could be used by white settlers without fear of attack. Several disastrous missions followed, encountering stiff resistance from the inhabitants. In 1884, Reverend Thomas Bridges founded a mission at Ushuaia and was the first European to learn the Yámana language, and compiled his Yámana-English dictionary. He soon realized that his original task was a destructive one. The purpose of the missionary work had been to facilitate lucrative sheep farming on the island, however, the Ona were attracted to the 'white guanacos' on their land and hunting sheep proved far easier than the faste-footed guanaco. The colonists offered two sheep for each Ona that was killed (proof was provided by a pair of Ona ears), but Bridges realized that he would rather protect the Onas, as the indigenous groups were further ravaged by epidemics of European diseases. In a desperate attempt to save the Ona, Salesian missionaries founded three missions in the Straits of Magellan in the early 20th century, but, stripped of their land, the Ona lost the will to live; sadly the last Ona died in 1999. The Hausch also died out. The last of the Yámana, a woman called Cristina Calderón, presently survives near Puerto Williams. She is 82 years old.

Imprecision in the original colonial land division and the greed of the rush southwards led to border disputes between Argentina and Chile, which still rumble on today. The initial settlement of the dispute in 1883 was followed by a desire by both governments to populate the area by allocating large expanses of land for sheep farming. The main beneficiaries of this policy on Tierra del Fuego were the Menéndez and Braun families, already established in Punta Arenas.

For many years, the main economic activity of the northern part of the island was sheep farming, but Argentine government tax incentives to companies in the 1970s led to the establishment of new industries in Río Grande and Ushuaia and a rapid growth in the population of both cities; the subsequent withdrawal of incentives has produced increasing unemployment and migration. Tourism is increasingly important in Ushuaia.

For a detailed narrative account of Tierra del Fuego, the best book is the classic by Lucas Bridges, *Uttermost Part of the Earth*, out of print but easily obtained second-hand on www.abebooks.co.uk. Also fascinating is *Patagonia, Natural history, prehistory and ethnography at the uttermost part of the earth* (British Museum press). *Savage – The Life and Times of Jemmy Button* by Nick Hazelwood (Hodder & Stoughton) is also recommended.

Chilean Tierra del Fuego

The Chilean half of Tierra del Fuego is in two sections: the western half of Isla Grande (the main island) and the whole of Isla Navarino, to the south of the main island. Much less developed than the Argentine side of Tierra del Fuego, there are just two small towns where Chile's Fuegians are mostly concentrated: Porvenir on Isla Grande, easily reached by ferry from Punta Arenas, and Puerto Williams on Isla Navarino, which can only be reached by a flight from Punta Arenas. The northern part of Isla Grande is flat steppe, but the south is dominated by the Darwin range of mountains, which provide a dramatic visual backdrop, even if you can't easily get to them. Tourism on Chilean territory is very limited, but it's possible to organize trekking tours from Punta Arenas, and there are plenty of fishing lodges offering magnificent trout fishing, particularly on Río Grande.
▸▸ *For listings, see pages 643-645.*

Puerto Porvenir → *For listings, see pages 643-645.* *Colour map 6, C3. Phone code: +56 (0)61. Population 5500.*

Chilean Tierra del Fuego has a population of 7000, most of whom live in the small town of Porvenir – the only town on the Chilean half of the main island. Founded in 1894 during the gold boom, when many people came seeking fortunes from Croatia and Chiloe, Porvenir is a quiet place with a wide open pioneer feel, streets of neat brightly painted houses of corrugated zinc, and quaint tall domed trees lining the main avenue. There is a small museum, the **Museo Fernando Cordero Rusque** ① *Zavattaro 402, on the plaza, T061-580098, daily 0900-1800, US$1*, with archaeological and photographic displays on the Onas; and good displays on natural history and the early gold diggers and sheep farmers. There's little else to do here, but you could stroll around the plaza, with its **Iglesia San Francisco de Sales**, and down to the shoreside promenade, where there's a strange collection of 19th-century farm machinery, and a striking wooden monument to the Selknam.

There's a **tourist information office** ① *Zavattaro 424, T061-580094, www.patagonia-chile.com, www.porvenir-chile.cl*, but the tiny kiosk on the waterfront is more helpful and it also sells handicrafts.

Beyond Porvenir

Beyond Porvenir there is wonderfully wild virgin territory to explore. However, if you want an adventure, your best bet is to arrange a trip through tour operators in Punta Arenas, since there's still very little infrastructure on the Chilean side of the island. **Aonikenk** ① *www.aonikenk.com*, is recommended, offering several days' trekking into the remote mountains in the south of the island, horse riding and fly fishing. There are two tour operators in Porvenir itself, offering tours through the Cordon Baquedano to see the areas where gold was mined – recommended for great views of the Straits of Magellan and visits to traditional sheep-farming *estancias*. ▸▸ *For more information, see Activities and tours, page 644.*

The **fly fishing** in this area is becoming **fly fishing** world-renowned and it's now possible to stay in several comfortable lodges in Río Grande, Lago Escondido and Lago Blanco. This area is rich in brown trout, sea run brook trout and steelheads, weighing 2-14 kg, and you could expect to fish an average of eight trout a day in season. See specialist fly-fishing tour operators, or **Aonikenk** (see above). The season runs from 15 October to 14 April, with the best fishing from January to April.

Camerón

About 90 km east of Porvenir, roads head north to San Sebastián and south to Camerón. This large farm settlement is the only other community of any size on the Chilean part of the island and lies 149 km southeast of Porvenir on the opposite shore of Bahía Inútil. This wonderful windswept bay, with views of distant hills and the snow-capped Darwin range all along the horizon, was named 'useless' by British engineers making a hydrographic survey here in 1827 because it has no useful port. Nevertheless, as you near Camerón, the southern mountains loom ahead and the road passes secluded canyons and bays, interspersed with a few farms, and the whole feel is dramatic, isolated and somehow rather magical.

From Camerón a road runs southeast past an airfield and into the hills, through woods where guanacos hoot and run off into glades, and the banks are covered with red and purple moss. The north shores of **Lago Blanco** can be reached by cutting through the woods from Sección Río Grande, with superb views of the mountains surrounding the lake and the snows in the south, or from Estancia Vicuña. It's essential to organize any trip to this area through a reliable tour operator with solid infrastructure.

From Estancia Vicuña a trail leads southwest to the **Río Azopardo**, which also offers **trout fishing**. South of here trails run across the Darwin range to the **Estancia Yendegaia** near the Beagle Channel, a wonderful area for horse riding. For trips into this wild and undiscovered country, contact **Aonikenk** in Punta Arenas, www.aonikenk.com.

Isla Navarino → For listings, see pages 643-645.

Situated on the southern shore of the Beagle Channel, Isla Navarino is totally unspoilt and beautiful, offering great geographical diversity, thanks to the **Dientes de Navarino** range of mountains, with peaks over 1000 m, covered with southern beech forest up to 500 m, and south of that, great plains covered with peat bogs, with many lagoons abundant in flora. The island was the centre of the indigenous Yaganes culture, and there are 500 archaeological sites, the oldest dated as 3000 years old. Guanacos and condors can be seen inland, as well as large numbers of beavers, which were introduced to the island and have done considerable damage. The flight from Punta Arenas is beautiful, with superb views of Tierra del Fuego, the Cordillera Darwin, the Beagle Channel and the islands stretching south to Cape Horn.

Puerto Williams → Colour map 7, C2. Phone code 061. Population 2500.

The only settlement of any size on the island is Puerto Williams, a Chilean naval base situated about 50 km east of Ushuaia in Argentine seas across the Beagle Channel. Puerto Williams is the southernmost permanently inhabited town in the world; 50 km east- southeast is Puerto Toro, the southernmost permanently inhabited settlement on earth. Some maps mistakenly mark a road from Puerto Williams to Puerto Toro, but it doesn't exist; access is only by sea. Due to the long-running border dispute with Argentina here, Puerto Williams is controlled by the Chilean navy. Outside the naval headquarters, you can see the bow section of the *Yelcho*, the tug chartered by Shackleton to rescue men stranded on Elephant Island.

Your main purpose for visiting the island is likely to be the trekking on the Dientes de Navarino, but you should take time to explore the indigenous heritage here too. It's beautifully documented in the **Museo Martín Gusinde** ① *Mon-Thu 1000-1300, 1500-1800, Sat and Sun 1500-1800, US$1*, known as the Museo del Fin del Mundo (End of the World Museum), which is full of information about vanished indigenous tribes, local wildlife and the famous voyages by Charles Darwin and Fitzroy of the *Beagle*. A visit is highly recommended. A kilometre west of the town is the yacht club (one of

Puerto Williams' two nightspots), whose wharf is made from a sunken 1930s Chilean warship. The town has a **tourist information office** ① *Municipalidad de Cabos de Hornos, Presidente Ibáñez 130, T061-621011, closed in winter, www.imcabodehornos.cl*, where you can ask for maps and details on hiking, a bank, supermarkets and a hospital.

Exploring the island

For superb views, climb **Cerro Bandera**, which is reached by a path from the dam 4 km west of the town (it's a steep, three- to four-hour round trip, take warm clothes). There is excellent trekking around the Dientes de Navarino range, the southernmost trail in the world, through impressive mountain landscape, frozen lagoons and snowy peaks, giving superb views over the Beagle Channel. It's a challenging hike, over a distance of 53 km in five days, possible only from December to March, and a good level of fitness is needed. There is no equipment rental on the island. Ask for information in the tourist office at Puerto Williams, but it's best to go with an organized expedition from Punta Arenas.

Beyond Cerro Bandera, a road leads 56 km west of Puerto Williams to Puerto Navarino. There is little or no traffic on this route and it is very beautiful, with forests of lengas stretching right down to the water's edge. You can also visit Villa Ukika, 2 km east of town, the place where the last descendants of the Yaganes people live, relocated from their original homes at Caleta Mejilones, which was the last indigenous reservation in the province, inhabited by hundreds of Yagana descendants. At **Mejillones**, 32 km from Puerto Williams, is a graveyard and memorial to the Yámana people. Just before Estancia Santa Rosa (10 km further on), a path is said to cross the forest, lakes and beaver dams to Wulaia (four to six hours), where the Beagle anchored in 1833; however, even the farmer at Wulaia gets lost following this track.

Cape Horn

It is possible to catch a boat south from Isla Navarino to Cape Horn (the most southerly piece of land on earth apart from Antarctica). There is one pebbly beach on the north side of the island; boats anchor in the bay and passengers are taken ashore by motorized dinghy. A rotting stairway climbs the cliff above the beach, up to the building where three marines run the naval post. A path leads from here to the impressive monument of an albatross overlooking the wild, churning waters of the Drake Passage below.

◎ Chilean Tierra del Fuego listings

For Sleeping and Eating price codes and other relevant information, see Essentials pages 30-36.

◎ Sleeping

Puerto Porvenir *p641*
B-C España, Croacia 698, T061-580160. The largest hotel in town, decent standard, with spacious rooms (**C** singles) but slightly aloof service.
B-C Rosas, Phillippi 296, T061-580088. With bath, hot water, heating, a restaurant and bar, internet and laundry facilities. Recommended.

C Hostel Kawi, Pedro Silva 144, T061-581 638, hostalkawi@yahoo.com. A comfortable hostel, with rooms for 3, all with bath, and offering fly-fishing trips on the island.
E Residencial Dalmacia, Croacia 469, T061-580008, angelacardenas1945@hotmail.com. A basic *residencial* with a central location.

Beyond Porvenir *p641*
If you get stuck in the wilds, note that it is almost always possible to camp or bed down in a barn at an *estancia*.
B-E Hostería de la Frontera, San Sebastián, T061-696 004, escabini@tie.cl. Rooms with

bath, avoid the more basic accommodation in an annexe. Decent restaurant.

C-F Hostería Tunkelén, Cerro Sombrero, 46 km south of Primera Angostura, T061-345001, hosteria_tunkelen@hotmail.com. Rooms and dormitory accommodation. Recommended.

Puerto Williams *p642*
LL Hotel Lakutaia, out of the edge of Lauta bay, 2 km out of town, T061-621733, www.lakutaia.cl. The only upmarket place on the island. Simple attractive rooms. Lovely views from spacious common areas. A range of activities offered.
A Bella Vista Hostal, Tentiente Muñoz 118, T061-621010, www.victory-cruises.com/bella_vista_hostal.html. **B-C** singles. Some rooms with views and sailing trips offered. Also camping US$10.
B pp **Hostal Yagan**, Piloto Pardo 260, T061-621334, hostalyagan@hotmail.com. Singles and doubles. Good meals available. Clean and comfortable, friendly, tours offered.
B-C Hostal Akainij, Austral 22, T061-621173, www.turismoakainij.cl. Smallish but comfortable rooms with bath. Excellent meals served by lovely guests.Tours offered. Recommended.
C Hostal Pusaki, Piloto Pardo 222, T061-621116, pattypusaky@yahoo.es. Friendly. Good meals served.
C Hostería Camblor, T061-621033, hostalcamblor@hotmail.com. Price per person for full board. Gets very booked up. Good value.
E pp **Residencial Onashaga**, Uspashun 15, T061-621564, run by Señor Ortiz. Basic accommodation but a warm welcome. Good meals, helpful, full board available.

Eating

Puerto Porvenir *p641*
There are many lobster fishing camps nearby, where fishermen prepare lobster on the spot.

Club Croata, Senoret and Phillippi. On the waterfront, good food, lively.
El Chispa, Señoret 202. Seafood and other hearty home-cooked fare. Friendly service. Good value.

Puerto Williams *p642*
There are several grocery stores; prices are very high because of the remoteness. Most hotels and hostels will offer food. Away from **Club Náutico**, nightlife is at the **Dientes de Navarino**, a bar on the plaza.

▲ Activities and tours

Puerto Porvenir *p641*
For adventure tourism and trekking, it's best to go through tour operators in Punta Arenas.
Turismo Cordillera d Darwin, Señoreta 511, T061-580450, jebr_darwin@hotmail.com. Day tours of the area around Porvenir.

Puerto Williams *p642*
Sea, Ice and Mountains, Ricardo Maragaño 168, T061-621150, www.simltd.com. Sailing trips, trekking tours and many other adventurous activities.
Shila, O'Higgins 322 (the hut at the entrance to Centro Comercial), T061-621366, www.turismoshila.com. Trekking, fishing, equipment hire including bikes (US$10 per day), tents (US$4-8), sleeping bags, stoves and more. Trekking maps for US$1.60.

Sailing
Captain Ben Garrett, www.victory-cruises.com, offers recommended adventure sailing in his schooner *Victory* in Dec/Jan, including special trips to Ushuaia, voyages to Cape Horn, the glaciers, Puerto Montt and Antartica.
Crucero Australis, www.australis.com, calls at Wulaia Bay on the west side of Isla Navarino after visiting Cape Horn. You can disembark and take a short walk.

⊖ Transport

Puerto Porvenir *p641*
Air
Aerovías DAP, Señoret s/n, Porvenir, T061-580089, www.aeroviasdap.cl, flies from Punta Arenas (weather and bookings permitting), 2-3 times daily Mon-Sat, 15 mins, US$35 (1-way). Heavily booked so make sure you have your return reservation confirmed.

Bus
Buses from Punta Arenas to Ushuaia don't take on passengers in Chilean Tierra del Fuego.

Local buses run to **Camerón** from Manuel Señoret, in theory Tue and Fri 1600, 2 hrs, returning at 2030, US$3. There's also a service to **Cerro Sombrero**, leaving from opposite the Municipalidad, Mon, Wed, Fri 0800, 1¾ hrs, returning at 1700 or 1800, US$4.50.

Ferry
The *Melinka* sails from Tres Puentes (5 km north of Punta Arenas; catch bus A or E from Av Magallanes or *colectivo* 15, US$1; taxi US$3) to **Bahía Chilota**, 5 km west of Porvenir, Tue-Sun 0900 with an extra afternoon sailing Tue-Thu in season, 2½ hrs, pedestrians US$9, bikes US$12, cars US$54. The boat returns from Porvenir in the afternoon Tue-Sun.

Timetable dependent on tides and subject to change: check in advance. The crossing can be rough and cold; watch for dolphins. Reservations are essential especially in summer (at least 24 hrs in advance for cars); obtainable from **Transbordadora Austral Broom**, Bulnes 05075, Punta Arenas, T061-218100 (T061-580089 in Porvenir), www.tabsa.cl.

The ferry service from Punta Delgada on the mainland to **Punta Espora**, 80 km north of Porvenir, departs every 40 mins 0830-2300 (schedules vary with the tides) and takes 15 mins, pedestrians US$4, cars US$25. This is the main route for buses and trucks between Ushuaia and mainland Argentina. Before 1000 most space is taken up by trucks.

Puerto Williams *p642*
Air
Aerovías DAP, Centro Comercial s/n, T061-621051, www.aeroviasdap.cl, flies 20-seater Cessna aircraft from Punta Arenas, Mon-Sat, departure time varies, 1¼ hrs, US$96 (1-way). Book well in advance; there are long waiting lists. Luggage allowance 10 kg (US$2 per kg extra).

Ferry
There are no regular sailings to **Isla Navarino** from Ushuaia (Argentina). The following depart from Punta Arenas: **Austral Broom** ferry *Cruz Australis*, www. tabsa.cl, once a week, 36 hrs, US$175 for a reclining seat, US$210 for a bunk, meals included; **Navarino** (contact Carlos Aguilera, 21 de Mayo 1460, Punta Arenas, T061-228 066), 3rd week of month, 12 passengers, US$210 (1-way); *Beaulleu* cargo boat, once a month, US$360 return, 6 days. Some cruises to Ushuaia also stop at Puerto Williams.

Cape Horn *p643*
Crucero Australis cruises from Ushuaia stop at **Cape Horn**. In addition, the naval vessel *PSG Micalvi*, which sails once every 3 months from Punta Arenas via Puerto Williams, occasionally takes passengers to Cape Horn for US$300. Navy and port authorities in Puerto Williams may deny any knowledge, but everyone else knows when a boat is due; ask at the **Armada** in Punta Arenas. Otherwise ask at the yacht club about hitching a ride to Cape Horn.

⊕ Directory

Puerto Porvenir *p641*
Banks There is a bank on the plaza. The ATM accepts MasterCard but not Visa. Currency exchange available at Estrella del Sur, Santos Mardones, Santos Mardones and at Señoret 346.

Puerto Williams *p642*
Post office Av Pt Carlos Ibáñez, closes 1900. **Telephone** CTC, Av Pt Carlos Ibáñez, Mon-Sat 0930-2230, Sun 1000-1300, 1600-2200.

Argentine Tierra del Fuego

The Argentine half of Tierra del Fuego is much easier to visit than the Chilean half, and more rewarding. The northern half of the island is windswept steppe, and its only town, Río Grande, once rich in oil, is now very faded. But pause before you head straight for Ushuaia to visit two splendid estancias. Viamonte (www.estanciaviamonte.com) was built by Lucas Bridges to protect the indigenous Ona people, and is an evocative place to stay, while Estancia María Behety (see www.maribety.com.ar) is world famous for its brown trout fishing. The landscape turns to hills as you head south, and there's a lovely silent lake, Lago Fagnano, ideal for a picnic.

Ushuaia is the island's centre, beautifully set on the Beagle Channel, with a backdrop of steep mountains. With a picturesque national park on its doorstep, boat trips up the Beagle Channel to the Bridges' other superb estancia Harberton, and a ski centre at Cerro Castor, there's plenty to keep you here. Huskies will draw your sledge in winter, and in summer you can walk around Bahía Lapataia and contemplate the serenity of the end of the world. ▸▸ *For listings, see pages 654-664.*

Río Grande → For listings, see pages 654-664. Colour map 6, C4. Phone code: 02964. Population 53,000.

Río Grande is a sprawling modern coastal town, the centre for a rural sheep-farming community that grew rapidly in the 1970s, with government tax incentives. The new population was stranded when benefits were withdrawn, leading to unemployment and emigration, and leaving the rather sad, dusty town you find today. The people are friendly but there's little culture, and you're most likely to visit in order to change buses. There are a couple of good places to stay, however, and a small museum worth seeing. There is an **airport** ① *T02964-420600*, 4 km west of town; a taxi to the centre costs US$3.

Sights

The city's architecture is a chaotic mix of smart nouveau-riche houses and humble wooden and tin constructions. It seems to have defied municipal efforts at prettification, and the series of peeling and graffitied concrete 'sculptures' along some of the avenues do little to cheer it up. But if you do get stuck here, you could trace the city's history through sheep, missions, pioneers and oil in its interesting small museum, **Museo de la Ciudad** ① *Alberdi 555, T02964-430414, Tue-Fri 1000-1700.* The city was founded by Fagnano's Salesian mission in 1893, and you can visit the original building, **La Candelaria** ① *11 km north, T02964-421642, Mon-1000-1230, 1500-1900, US$2, afternoon tea US$3,* whose museum has displays of natural history and indigenous artefacts, with strawberry plantations, piglets and an aviary. A taxi ride there with wait costs US$7. The **tourist office** ① *Rosales 350, T02964-431324, www.tierradelfuego.org.ar, Mon-Fri 0900-1700,* in the blue-roofed hut on the plaza is small but helpful.

Around Río Grande

Estancia Viamonte, on the coast, 40 km to the south, is a working sheep farm with a fascinating history. Here, Lucas Bridges, son of Tierra del Fuego's first settler, built a home to protect the large tribe of indigenous Onas, who were fast dying out. The *estancia* is still inhabited by his descendants, who will take you riding and show you life on the farm. There is also a house to rent and superb accommodation, highly recommended. **Estancia María Behety**, built by the millionaire José Menéndez, is heaven for brown trout fishing.

Río Grande to Ushuaia → *For listings, see pages 654-664.*

From Río Grande, several roads fan out southwest to the heart of the island, though this area is little inhabited. The paved road south, Route 3, continues across wonderfully open land, more forested than the expanses of Patagonian steppe further north, and increasingly hilly as you near Ushuaia. After around 160 km, you could turn left along a track to the coast, and find **Estancia Cabo San Pablo**. It's a simple working *estancia* in a beautiful position (reserve in advance), open all year and with beautiful native woodland for walking and riding, birdwatching and fishing. There are also other trips to places of interest within reach. Route 3 then climbs up above Lago Fagnano and Tolhuin.

Tolhuin and around → *Phone code 02964.*

This is a friendly, small settlement close to the shore of Lago Fagnano, a large expanse of water, right at the heart of Tierra del Fuego. The village has a stretch of beach nearby and is a favourite Sunday afternoon destination for day-trippers from Ushuaia. There's a YPF service station just off the main road, but it's worth driving into the village itself for the famous bakery **La Unión**, where you can buy delicious bread, *empanadas* and fresh *facturas* (pastries). It's also a good source of information. There's a tiny, friendly **tourist office** ① *Av de los Shelknam 80, T02901-492125, daily 0900-1500,* with very helpful staff. Handicrafts are available at El Encuentro, including fine leather goods, half a block from the tourist information office. From the village a road leads down to the tranquil lake shore, where there are a couple of good places to stay. Further along Route 3, 50 km from Ushuaia, a road to the right swoops down to **Lago Escondido**, a fjord-like lake with steep, deep-green mountains descending into the water. After Lago Escondido, the road crosses the cordillera at Paso Garibaldi. It then descends to the Cerro Castor winter-sports complex and the Tierra Mayor Recreation area (see Activities and tours, page 662). There is a police control just as you enter the Ushuaia city limits; passports may be checked.

Ushuaia → *For listings, see pages 654-664. Colour map 6, C4. Phone code 02901. Population 45,000.*

The most southerly town in the world, Ushuaia's setting is spectacular. Its brightly coloured houses look like toys against the dramatic backdrop of vast jagged mountains. Opposite are the forbidding peaks of Isla de Navarino, and between them flows the serene green Beagle Channel. Sailing those waters you can just imagine how it was for Darwin, arriving here in 1832, and for those early settlers, the Bridges, in 1871. Though the town has expanded in recent years, sprawling untidily along the coast, Ushuaia still retains the feel of a pioneer town, isolated and expectant. There are lots of places to stay, which fill up entirely in January, a fine museum, and some great fish restaurants. There is spectacular landscape to be explored in all directions, with good treks in the accessible **Parque Nacional Tierra del Fuego** ① *www.tierra delfuego.org.ar,* just to the west of the city, and more adventurous expeditions offered into the wild heart of the island, trekking, climbing or riding. There's splendid cross-country skiing nearby in winter, as well as downhill skiing too, at **Cerro Castor** ① *www.cerrocastor.com.* And to the east, along a beautiful stretch of coastline is the historic *estancia* of Harberton, which you can reach by a boat trip along the Beagle Channel. Ushuaia is also the starting point for expeditions to Antarctica; for more information, see www.dna.gov.ar. For more about Ushuaia, see www.e-ushuaia.com.

Ins and outs

Getting there The airport, **Aeropuerto Internacional Malvinas Argentinas** ① *T02901-423970 for information*, is 4 km from town. A taxi to the centre costs US$4.60 (there is no bus). There are daily flights from Buenos Aires and Río Gallegos, and frequent flights from El Calafate and Punta Arenas, as well as weekly flights from other Patagonian towns to Ushuaia's airport, on a peninsula in the Beagle Channel, close to the centre. Buses and minibuses from Río Grande arrive at their respective offices around town. ▸▸ *For further information, see Transport, page 663.*

Getting around It's easy to walk around the town in a morning, since all its sights are close together, and you'll find banks, restaurants, hotels and shops along San Martín, which runs parallel to the shore, a block north of the coast road, Avenida Maipú. Boat trips leave from the Muelle Turístico (tourist pier) by a small plaza, 25 de Mayo on the seafront, Avenida Maipú between calles 25 de Mayo and Laserre. Ushuaia is very well organized for tourism, and there are good local buses to the national park and other sights, as well as many boat trips.

Best time to visit Ushuaia is at its most beautiful in autumn (March to May), when the dense forests all around are turned a rich red and yellow, and there are many bright clear days. Summer (December to February) is best for trekking, when maximum temperatures are around 15°C, but try to avoid January, when the city is swamped with tourists. Late February is much better. The ski season is mid-June to October, when temperatures are around zero, but the wind drops.

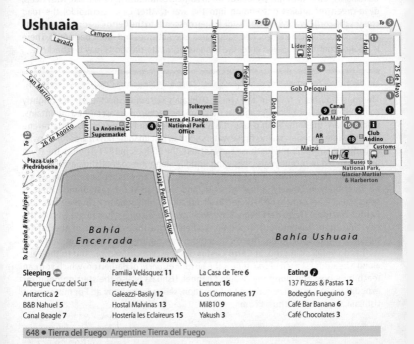

Sleeping 🛏
Albergue Cruz del Sur **1**
Antarctica **2**
B&B Nahuel **5**
Canal Beagle **7**

Familia Velásquez **11**
Freestyle **4**
Galeazzi-Basily **12**
Hostal Malvinas **13**
Hostería les Eclaireurs **15**

La Casa de Tere **6**
Lennox **16**
Los Cormoranes **17**
Mil810 **9**
Yakush **3**

Eating 🍴
137 Pizzas & Pastas **12**
Bodegón Fueguino **9**
Café Bar Banana **6**
Café Chocolates **3**

Tourist information The **tourist information office** ⓘ *San Martín 674, corner with Fadul, T02901-432000, www.tierradelfuego.org.ar, Mon-Fri 0800-2200, Sat-Sun and holidays 0900-2000, also an office at the pier (Muelle Turístico), T02901-437666, and a desk at the airport, T02901- 423970,* is one of the best in Argentina and the friendly and helpful staff speak several languages. They have a map and a series of leaflets about all the things to see and do, and can provide bus and boat times. Next door is the **Oficina Antártica** ⓘ *T02901-423340, antartida@tierradelfuego.org.ar, Mon-Fri 0900-1900.* **Tierra del Fuego National Park Office** ⓘ *San Martín 1395, T02901-421315,* has a basic map of the park.

Background

Founded in 1884 after missionary Thomas Bridges had established his mission in these inhospitable lands, Ushuaia attracted many pioneers in search of gold. Keen to populate its new territory, the government set up a penal colony on nearby Staten Island, which moved to the town in 1902, and the town developed rapidly. Immigration was largely Croatian and Spanish, together with those shipwrecked on the shores, but the town remained isolated until planes arrived in 1935. As the prison closed, a naval base opened and in the 1970s a further influx arrived, attracted by job opportunities in assemblage plants of electronic equipment that flourished thanks to reduced taxes. Now the city is capital of Argentina's most southerly province, and though fishing is still a traditional economic activity, Ushuaia has become an important tourist centre, particularly as the departure point for voyages to Antarctica.

Sights

There are several museums worth visiting If bad weather forces you indoors and the most fascinating is **Museo del Fin del Mundo** ⓘ *along the seafront at Maipú and Rivadavia, T02901-421863, www.tierradel fuego.org.ar/museo, Nov Apr daily 0900-1900, May-Oct Mon Sat 1200-1900, US$4,* in the 1912 bank building, which tells the history of the town through a small collection of carefully chosen exhibits on the indigenous groups, missionaries, pioneers and shipwrecks, together with nearly all the birds of Tierra del Fuego (stuffed), and you can get an 'end of the world museum' stamp in your passport. There are helpful and informed staff, and also an extensive reference library. Recommended. Further east, the old prison, Presidio, at the back of the naval base, houses the **Museo Marítimo** ⓘ *Yaganes and Gobernador Paz, www. museomaritimo.com, daily 0900-2000, US$12, ticket valid 48 hrs,* with models and artefacts from seafaring days, and, in the cells of most of the five wings of the huge building, the **Museo Penitenciario**, which

El Bambú **8**
El Turco **4**
Kaupé **5**
La Estancia **7**
Martinica **14**

Ramos Generales **18**
Sandwichería Kami **19**
Tía Elvira **13**
Volver **15**

details the history of the prison. Excellent guided visits (in Spanish only) also include a tour of the lighthouse (a life-size repliace of the original) that inspired Jules Verne's novel, *Around the World in Eighty Days*. Recommended. Much smaller is **Museo Yámana** ① *Rivadavia 56, T02901-422874, www.tierradelfuego.org.ar/mundoyamana, daily 1000-2000 high season, 1200-1900 in low season, US$3.50*, which has interesting scale models showing scenes of everyday life of Yámana people and the geological evolution of the island, also interesting and recommended.

Around Ushuaia → *For listings, see pages 654-664.*

Whatever you do, unless it's absolutely pouring with rain, take the chairlift up to **Cerro Martial** ① *daily 1000-1645 (last trip up), 1730 (last trip back down) in summer, daily 1030-1630 in winter, US$8.50,* 7 km from town, for exhilarating views along the Beagle Channel and to Isla Navarino opposite. To reach the chairlift, follow Magallanes out of town, allow 1½ hours. Several companies run minibus services from the corner of Maipú and Fadul, and there are frequent departures in summer, US$4. Taxis charge US$7 to the base, from where you can walk all the way back. There are several marked trails (a leaflet is given out at the lower platform), including to a viewpoint and to Glaciar Martial itself, from 600 m to 1 km. There is a splendid tea shop at the Cumbres de Martial *cabañas* at the base, and a basic *refugio* with no electricity up at the Cerro. Also by the lower platform is the **Canopy** ① *T02901-1551 0307, www.canopyushuaia.com.ar, US$30, US$18 for a shorter run,* a series of zip lines and bridges in the trees, eight stretches of about 500 m in total (to be extended). All visitors are accompanied by staff; it's safe and good fun. The café at the entrance, Refugio de Montaña, serves hot chocolate, coffee, cakes, pizzas and has a warm stove.

Parque Nacional Tierra del Fuego (see below), just outside Ushuaia, is easily accessible by bus and offers superb walks for all levels of fitness. The **Tren del Fin del Mundo** ① *www.trendelfindelmundo.com.ar, US$24 (tourist), US$46 (1st class) return, plus US$6 park entrance and transfer to the station,* is the world's southernmost steam train, running new locomotives and carriages on track first laid by prisoners to carry wood to Ushuaia. It's a totally touristy experience with relentless commentary in English and Spanish, but it might be fun for children, and is one way of getting into the national park to start a walk. There are three daily departures in summer and one in winter. Tickets can be bought at the station from **Tranex Turismo** ① *T02901-431600,* or from travel agencies in town. Sit on the left side on the outbound journey to get the views. Buses to the train station with **Kaupen** and **Pasarela** leave from the corner of Maipú and Roca at unreliable times; it's better to take a taxi for US$5.

The **Estancia Harberton** (see box, opposite), 85 km from Ushuaia, is the oldest *estancia* on the island, and is still run by descendants of the British missionary Thomas Bridges, whose family protected the indigenous peoples here. It's a beautiful place, with the attractive wood-framed house that Thomas built sitting in quiet contemplation on a tranquil bay. You'll get an excellent guided walk (bilingual guides) around the *estancia*, through protected forest, and delicious teas or lunches are served in the Manacatush tea room overlooking the water. Highly recommended. The impressive **Museo Akatushún** ① *T02901-422742, www.acatushun.org, 1000-1700, daily 15 Oct to 15 Apr, except Christmas, 1 Jan and Easter, tour of the estancia US$7, museum entrance US$3,* has skeletons of South American sea mammals, the result of 25 years' scientific investigation in Tierra del Fuego, with excellent tours in English. You can camp for free with permission from the owners, or stay in cottages (see Sleeping, page 658). Access is from a good

Estancia Harberton

In a land of extremes and superlatives, Harberton stands out as special. The oldest *estancia* in Tierra del Fuego, it was built in 1886 on a narrow peninsula overlooking the Beagle Channel. Its founder, the missionary Thomas Bridges (see box, page 653, for information on his life), was granted land by President Roca for his work amongst the indigenous people and for his help in rescuing victims of numerous shipwrecks in the channels. Harberton is named after the Devonshire village where his wife Mary was born, and the farmhouse was prefabricated by her carpenter father and assembled on a spot chosen by the Yámana people as the most sheltered. The English connection is evident in the neat lawns, shrubs and trees between the jetty and the farmhouse. Behind the buildings is a large vegetable garden, a real rarity on the island, and there's noticeably more wildlife here than in the Tierra del Fuego National Park, probably owing to its remoteness.

Still operating as a working farm, mainly with cattle and sheep, Harberton is run by Thomas Goodall, great-grandson of the founder, whose wife Natalie has created an impressive museum of the area's rich marine life with a thriving research centre. Visitors receive a guided tour of the museum, or of farm buildings and grounds with reconstructions of the Yámana dwellings. Tea or lunch (if you reserve ahead) are served in the tea room overlooking the bay, and you may well be tempted to rent one of the two simple cottages on the shore. There are wonderful walks along the coast, and nowhere in Argentina has quite the feeling of peace you'll find here. For more information, see www.estanciaharberton.com (in Spanish and English).

unpaved road (Route 33, ex 'J') that branches off Route 3 40 km east of Ushuaia and runs 25 km through forest before the open country around Harberton; marvellous views, about two hours (no petrol outside of Ushuaia and Tolhuin). **Boat trips** to Harberton run twice weekly in summer, and allow one to two hours on the *estancia*. Regular daily minibus service, with Ebenezer from Avenida Maipú and 25 de Mayo, US$33 return. Agency tours by land cost US$50 plus entrance. Excursions can be made to Lagos Fagnano and Escondido: agencies run seven-hour tours for US$35 per person without lunch (US$40 with lunch); or check the list of cheaper but rather unreliable minibuses that go there, which is available at the tourist office. Tour agencies offer many good packages, which include trekking, canoeing, birdwatching and horse riding in landscape accessible only by 4WDs. See boat trips and cruises, page 660, and the tourist office's list of excursions, indicating which companies go where.

Boat trips

All these trips are highly recommended, but note that the Beagle Channel can be very rough. Food and drink on all boats is pricey. Excursions can be booked through most agencies, or at the Muelle Turístico where boat companies have their ticket offices; boats leave from the Muelle Turístico, with a few excursions leaving from Muelle AFASYN (next to the old airport). If going to Harberton, check that your tour actually visits the *estancia* and not just the bay, as some do.

Most popular excursions visit the small islands southeast of Ushuaia in 2½-3 hours, all year round, passing next to the sea lion colony at Isla de los Lobos, Isla de los Pájaros and

Les Eclaireurs lighthouse. Alternatively, they add an hour or so for a landing on Bridges Island. Prices vary if trips are made on big catamarans (US$35), on more exclusive sailing boats (from US$45), or on the charming old boat *Barracuda*, with excellent commentary, US$30. A few pricier services include lunch onboard; otherwise a light snack or a coffee is served. Summer options add more services to the usual, with some that go further east past the Isla de los Lobos, Isla de los Pájaros, Les Eclaireurs lighthouse, Isla Martillo penguin colony, and then visit Estancia Harberton (note that this stop is not included in all trips). The round trip by catamaran takes six to nine hours, US$65, includes packed lunch and entrance; a few excursions go west to the national park in about 5½ hours. You can also set off from Ushuaia for expeditions to Antarctica, highly recommended, see Activities and tours, page 660, and Transport, page 663.

Parque Nacional Tierra del Fuego → *For listings, see pages 654-664.*

Covering 63,000 ha of mountains, lakes, rivers and deep valleys, this small but beautiful park stretches west to the Chilean border and north to **Lago Fagnano**, though large areas have been closed to tourists to protect the environment. Public access is at the park entrance 12 km west of Ushuaia, where you'll be given a basic map with marked walks. There's good camping in a picturesque spot at Lago Roca, with a *confitería*. All walks are best early morning or afternoon to avoid the tour buses. You'll see lots of geese, the beautiful torrent duck, Magellanic woodpeckers and austral parakeets.

Ins and outs
Access and information The park entrance is 12 km west of Ushuaia, on the main road west signposted from the town centre. The **park administration** ① *San Martín 1395,*

Parque Nacional Tierra del Fuego

Uttermost Part of the Earth

If you read one book about Patagonia, make it *Uttermost Part of the Earth*. The story of the first successful missionary to Tierra del Fuego, Thomas Bridges, and his son Lucas, is one of the most stirring in the whole history of pioneers in Argentina. An orphan from Bristol, Thomas Bridges was so called because he was found as a child under a bridge with a letter T on his clothing. Adopted by Rev Despard, he was taken as a young man to start a Christian mission in wild, uncharted Tierra del Fuego where no white man had survived. He brought his young wife and daughter after Despard had left following the massacre of the last lot of Christians by the indigenous inhabitants. Until his death in 1898, Bridges lived near the shores of the Beagle Channel, first creating the new settlement of Ushuaia and then at Harberton. He devoted his life to his work with the Yámanas (Yaghanes) and soon gave up converting them, in favour of compiling a dictionary of their language, and – ultimately – protecting them from persecution. His son Lucas (1874-1949), one of six children, spent his early life among the Yámanas and Onas, living and hunting as one of them, learning their languages, and even, almost fatally, becoming involved in their blood feuds and magic rituals. Lucas became both defender and protector of the indigenous people whose culture he loved and was fascinated by, creating a haven for them at Harberton and Estancia Viamonte when most sheep farmers were more interested in having them shot. Lucas's memoirs, *Uttermost Part of the Earth* (1947), trace the tragic fate of the native population with whom he grew up. A compelling account of 20th-century man colliding with an ancient culture (out of print, but easily obtained from www.abebooks.co.uk).

T02901-421315, *tierradelfuego@apn.gov.ar*, is in Ushuaia. Entry is US$6. In summer, buses and minibuses run an hourly service, US$7 return to Lago Roca, US$13.50 return to Bahía Lapataia, leaving from Ushuaia's tourist pier at the corner of Maipú and Roca or from Maipú and 25 de Mayo, and returning from either Bahía Lapataia or Lago Roca, hourly until last bus (2000 or 2100 in summer). Ask at the tourist office for bus details and a map of the park, with walks. There are no legal crossing points to Chile. Wear warm, waterproof clothing; in winter the temperature drops to as low as -12°C, and although in summer it can reach 25°C, evenings can be chilly. There's a helpful *guardaparque* (ranger) at Lago Roca.

For a really rich experience, go with guides who know the territory well and can tell you about the wildlife. Inexpensive trips for all levels are available with the highly recommended **Compañía de Guías de Patagonia** ① *www.companiadeguias.com.ar*.

Walks

The leaflets provided at the entrance show various walks, but these are recommended:
Senda Costera ① *6.5 km, 3 hrs each way* This lovely easy walk along the shore gives you the essence of the park, its rocky coastline, edged with a rich forest of beech trees and glorious views of the low islands with a backdrop of steep mountains. Start at Bahía Ensenada (where the boat trips start, and where the bus can drop you off). Walk along a well-marked path along the shoreline, and then rejoin the road briefly to cross Río Lapataia (ignoring signs to Lago Roca to your right). After crossing the broad green river and a second stretch of water (where there's a small camping spot and the *gendarmería*),

it's a pleasant stroll inland to the beautifully tranquil **Bahía Lapataia**, an idyllic spot, with views across the sound.

Senda Hito XXIV ① *Along Lago Roca, 4 km, 90 mins one way* Another easy walk, beside this peaceful lake, with lovely pebble beaches and through dense forest at times, with lots of birdlife. This is especially recommended in the evening, when most visitors have left. Get off the bus at the junction for Lago Roca, turn right along the road to the car park (passing the *guardaparque*'s house) and follow the lake side.

Cerro Guanaco ① *4 km, 4 hrs one way* A challenging hike up through the very steep forest to a mirador at the top of a hill (970 m) with splendid views over Lago Roca, the Beagle Channel and far-off mountains. The ground is slippery after rain: take care and don't rush. Allow plenty of time to return while it's light, especially in winter. The path branches off Senda Hito XXIV (see above) after crossing Arroyo Guanaco.

◉ Argentine Tierra del Fuego listings

For Sleeping and Eating price codes and other relevant information, see Essentials pages 30-36.

● Sleeping

Río Grande *p646*
Book ahead, as there are few decent choices. Several *estancias* offer full board and some, mainly on the northern rivers, have expensive fishing lodges, see www.tierradelfuego.org.ar.
A Posada de los Sauces, Elcano 839, T02964-432868, posadadelossauces@ speedy.com.ar. Nicely decorated and comfortable rooms, good restaurant and cosy bar. Breakfast included. Recommended.
B Hotel Isla del Mar, Güemes 963, T02964-422883. Right on the sea shore, a bit run down but cheap, with bathrooms and breakfast included. The staff are welcoming.
B Villa, Av San Martín 281, T02964-424998, hotelvillarg@hotmail.com. Central, modern, restaurant/*confitería*, with internet, TV and parking. A discount is given if you pay in cash.
C pp **Hotel Argentina**, San Martín 64, T02964-422546, hotelargentino@yahoo.com. The best cheap place to stay. A beautifully renovated 1920s building close to the sea. Kitchen and a bright sunny dining room, parking, Wi-Fi and a book exchange

Estancias
LL Estancia María Behety. Reservations at The Fly shop, www.maribety.com.ar. Established in 1897, 15 km from Río Grande, on a 40-km stretch of the river that has become legendary for brown trout fishing, with accommodation for 18 anglers, and good food. At US$5350 per week, this is one of the country's priciest fishing lodges, deservedly so. Guides, equipment and accommodation included.
L Estancia Viamonte, 40 km southeast on the coast, T02964-430861, T02964-156 1813, www.estanciaviamonte.com. For a really authentic experience, stay as a guest here. Built in 1902 by pioneer Lucas Bridges, writer of *Uttermost Part of the Earth*, to protect the indigenous Ona peoples, this working *estancia* is run by his descendants. You'll be warmly welcomed and will stay in traditional, beautifully furnished rooms, with comfortable bathrooms, and delicious meals (extra cost). Also a spacious cottage to let, US$320 for 7. Join in the farm activities, read the famous book, ride horses and completely relax. Recommended. Reserve a week in advance.
L Estancia Rivadavia, 100 km from Río Grande, on Route H, T02901-492186,

www.estanciarivadavia.com. A 10,000-ha sheep farm, owned by descendants of the original Croatian builder. Luxurious accommodation in a splendid house near the mountains and lakes at the heart of Tierra del Fuego, where you can enjoy a trip around the *estancia* to see wild horses and guanacos. Good food, and trekking to the trout lake of Chepelmut and Yehuin.

Camping

Club Naútico Ioshlelk-Oten, Montilla 1047, T02964-420536. Situated 2 km from town on the river. Clean, cooking facilities, camping, heated building in cold weather. YPF petrol station has hot showers.

Tolhuin and around *p647*

AL for 6 **Cabañas Khami**, T02964- 422296, www.cabaniaskhami.com.ar. Isolated in a lovely open spot at the head of the lake on low-lying land, very comfortable and well-equipped *cabañas* for 2-6 people, nicely decorated and with great views of the lake. Recommended.

A Hostería Petrel, at Lago Escondido, R3, Km 3186, T02901-433569, hosteria.petrel@ hotmail.com. In a secluded position amidst forest on a tranquil beach of the lake. Decent rooms with bath, and a good restaurant serving delicious lamb, open to non-residents. There are also tiny basic *cabañas* on the water.

C-D Parador Kawi Shiken, off the main road on the way to Ushuaia, 4 km south of Tolhuin on R3, Km 2940, T02964-424380. A rustic place with 3 rooms, shared bathrooms, *casa de té* and restaurant. Ring to arrange for local *cordero al asador* (barbecued lamb).

C-D Terrazas del Lago, R3, Km 2938, T02964-432300, terrazas@uol.com.ar. A little way from the shore, smart wooden *cabañas*, well decorated, and also a *confitería* and *parrilla*.

F pp Refugio Solar del Bosque, Lago Escondido, R3, Km 3020, 18 km from Ushuaia, T02901-421228, solardelbosque@tierradel fuego.org.ar. Basic hostel for walkers, with shared bathrooms, dorms for 4. Breakfast.

Camping

Camping Hain del Lago, T02964-425951, T02964-1560 3606, robertoberbel@hotmail. com. Lovely views, fireplaces, hot showers, and a *quincho* for when it rains.

Camping La Correntina, T02964-1560 5020, 17 km from Tolhuin. In woodland, with bathrooms, and horses for hire.

Ushuaia *p647, map p648*

The tourist office has accommodation lists and can help find you somewhere to stay, but in Jan you must reserve before you come. See www.e-ushuaia.com, for more listings.

L Canal Beagle, Maipú and 25 de Mayo, T02901-432303, www.hotelcanalbeagle. com.ar. ACA hotel (discounts for members), comfortable and well attended, with a small pool, gym, sauna and clear views over the channel from some rooms (others look out over the container dock), good restaurant.

L Lennox, San Martín 776, T02901-436430, www.lennoxhotel.com.ar. Boutique hotel on the main street, with breakfast. Services include internet, hydromassage, TV, frigobar, restaurant and *confitería* on 4th floor.

L Mil810, 25 de Mayo 245, T02901-437710, www.hotel1810.com. City hotel with 30 standard rooms, 1 with disabled access. No restaurant, but breakfast and *confitería*. All rooms with flatscreen TV, minibar and safe. Quite small but cosy, with calm colours, good views, a business centre and multiple use room where you can hang out while waiting for a flight.

AL Hotel El Viejo Lobo de Mar, Gobernador Godoy 98, T02901-424850/51, www.hotelel viejolobodemar.com. Located on the main street, these 2-, 3- and 4-bedroom apartments are good value for money with groups or if you want to cook. Clean and user-friendly.

A Cap Polonio, San Martín 746, T02901-422140, www.hotelcappolonio.com.ar. Smart, central modern city hotel with very comfortable minimalist rooms with bath, TV, phone and Wi-Fi. Some have views of the canal. Chic restaurant/café downstairs.

A Hostería les Eclaireurs, Staiyakin 2676, www.hosteriadelfaro.com. Only a couple of blocks from the centre, this hotel is clean, simple and nicely decorated. Comfortable common areas with a TV and couches. Plain but attractive rooms with small but modern bathrooms.

B Hostal Malvinas, Gobernador Deloqui 615, T02901-422626, www.hostalmalvinas.net. Central and well-run town-house hotel. Neat and comfortable, if rather small, rooms with excellent bathrooms and good views. A basic breakfast is included, as is all-day tea and coffee. Recommended.

B Hostería Posada Fin del Mundo, Gobernador Valdez 281, T02901-437345, www.posadafindelmundo.com.ar. A relaxed family atmosphere in a quiet area close to centre, homely, friendly staff. Good value.

C Galeazzi-Basily, Gobernador Valdez 323, T02901-423213, www.avesdelsur.com.ar. The best option by far is this cosy and stylish place, with welcoming owners Frances and Alejandro, who speak excellent English, in a pleasant residential area just 5 blocks from the centre. Delicious breakfast. There are also excellent value 4- and 5-bed *cabañas* (**A**) in the garden. Highly recommended.

C pp La Casa de Tere, Rivadavia 620, T02901-422312, www.lacasadetere.com.ar. Shared bath, with breakfast, home-made bread and cake, use of kitchen, some rooms get lots of sun, singles, doubles and triples, hot water, helpful owner.

D B&B Nahuel, 25 de Mayo 440, T02901-423068, www.welcomeargentina.com/bybnahuel. A family house with views over the channel, brightly painted and tasteful rooms. Expect a lovely welcome from the charming owner. Great value. Recommended.

Hostels

E pp Albergue Cruz del Sur, Deloqui 242, T02901-434099, www.xdelsur.com.ar. Very friendly atmosphere in this relaxed, small Italian-owned hostel, with cosy dorms, use of kitchen and a lovely quiet library room for reading.

E pp Antarctica, Antártida Argentina 270, T02901-435774, www.antarcticahostel.com. Welcoming and central hostel with a spacious chill-out room and an excellent bar open till the small hours. Dorms are rather basic and cramped, with larger private doubles (**C**). Cooking facilities, breakfast and the use of internet are included. Cycles for hire.

E pp Freestyle, Gobernador Paz 866, T02901-432874, www.ushuaiafreestyle.com. Very busy but good, central hostel with laundry (US$3), TV room, DVDs and pool table. Also has doubles with bath (**B-A**), at the **Alto Andino** hotel, which is built in front.

E pp Los Cormoranes, Kamshen 788 (corner Alem), T02901-423459, www.loscormoranes.com. Large hostel, with good views over the town. Cosy rooms, with lockers, OK bathrooms and a well-equipped kitchen. Doubles (**B**) available. They can also book tours for you in the local area. HI member discount.

E-F pp Yakush, Piedrabuena 118 y San Martín, T02901-435807, www.hostelyakush.com.ar. On a central corner, this is a well-run hostel with spacious rooms to share and a few private ones (**B-C**), a light kitchen and dining room, and a steep tiny garden with views. If a cheerful atmosphere prevails, there are also comfy and more secluded corners for oneself.

Private homes

C-D Familia Velásquez, Juana Fadul 361, T02901-421719, almayo@arnet.com.ar. Basic rooms with breakfast in cosy cheerful pioneer family home, where the kind owners look after you.

Around Ushuaia *p650*

LL Cabañas del Beagle, Las Aljabas 375, T432785/1551 1323, www.cabaniasdelbeagle.com. 3 rustic-style cabins ,1.3 km above the city, fully equipped with kitchen, hydromassage, fireplace, heating and phone. Self-service breakfast, very comfortable, with personal attention.

LL Cumbres del Martial, Luis F Martial 3560 (7 km from town), T02901-424779, www.cumbresdelmartial.com.ar. This charming cottage by a mountain stream on the forested slopes of Martial range has very comfortable rooms with balconies for viewing the Beagle Channel. A homely feel prevails in this small, relaxed and secluded place 7 km away from town. There are also 4 *cabañas*, in which rustic materials contrast with a cosy interior. All have a fireplace and big windows open onto the woods. Superb fondues are served in the restaurant and tea room.

LL Finisterris Lodge Relax, Monte Susana, Ladera Este, 7 km from city, T012901-1561 2121 (mob), Buenos Aires, T011-5917 8288, www.finisterris.com. In 17 ha of forest, 5-star luxury in individual cabins, with top-of-the-range fittings, hydromassage and private spa (massage arranged, extra). Rustic style but spacious, 'home-from-home' atmosphere, 24-hr attention from owner and you're given a mobile phone on arrival. Meals can be ordered in, or private chef and sommelier can be booked for you.

LL Las Hayas, Martial 1650 (road to Glaciar Martial), T02901-430710, www.lashayas. com.ar. A 5-star hotel, in a spectacular setting, high up on the mountainside with outstanding views over the Beagle Channel. Light, tasteful, impeccable rooms. Breakfast included and use of pool, sauna, gym, squash court, 9-hole golf course, shuttle from town (high season only), and transfer from airport. A lovely calm atmosphere, friendly staff. Recommended.

LL Los Cauquenes, at Bahía Cauquen, C Reinamora 3462, T02901-441300, www.los cauquenes.com. High-quality 5-star hotel overlooking the Beagle Channel, room price depends on room size and view. Spa, prize-winning restaurant with US$13 lunch menu, regional food on dinner menu.

LL Los Yámanas, Costa de los Yámanas 2850, western suburbs, T02901-445960, www.hotelyamanas.com.ar. In the same group as Canoero tour operator, all rooms with channel view, spacious, well-decorated with DirectTV, Wi-Fi, hydromassage, fitness centre, spa and conference centre outside in wooded grounds, shuttle to town. Very pleasant.

LL-L Patagonia Villa, Bahía Buen Suceso 563, T02901-435937, www.patagonia villa.com. This lodge in the middle of the bush is made with local rock and wood, and is filled with fantastic chunky wooden furniture and comfy couches. Rooms have big windows, soft beds and there is an endless silence. Very relaxing. The huge fire downstairs will keep you warm in the evenings. High-quality food.

L Tierra de Leyendas, Tierra de Vientos 2448, T02901-443565, www.tierrade leyendas.com.ar. In the western suburbs. 5 very comfortable rooms with views of the Beagle Channel or the mountains at the back, 1 room with jacuzzi, all others with shower. Excellent restaurant serving regional specialities, open only for guests for breakfast and dinner. Free internet, no cable TV, but DVDs, living room with games, library, deck overlooking Río Pipo's outflow. Only for non-smokers. Recommended. Part of the Rusticae chain.

Estancias

L Estancia Rolito, R21 (ex 'A'), Km 14, T02901-437351, www.tierradelfuego.org.ar/ rolito/. A magical place in the wooded heart of the island, with cosy accommodation in traditionally built houses, and friendly hosts, booked through Turismo de Campo, Fuegia Basket 414 (Ushuaia), T02901-432419, www.turismodecampo.com. Also day visits with recommended walks or horse rides in mature southern beech forest.

A-B pp Estancia Harberton, T02901-422742, harberton@tierradelfuego.org.ar. Open mid-Oct to mid-Apr, 90 km east of Ushuaia, along R3 and 33, a spectacular drive. 2 impeccably restored historical buildings on the tranquil lakeside, giving you space and privacy from the main house. Very simple accommodation, but wonderful views and beautiful walks on the *estancia's* coastline.

Camping

Camping del Solar del Bosque, R3, Km 19, T02901-435276. US$3 per person. At a small ski resort that in summer offers plenty of activities. Hot showers and also a large dorm with good facilities.

Camping Haruwen, in the Haruwen Winter Sports complex (Km 36), T02901-431099. US$4 per tent. Electricity, shop, bar and restaurant in a small winter-sports centre. Centre open in summer for outdoor activities.

La Pista del Andino, Leandro N Alem 2873, T02901-435890, www.lapistadelandino. com.ar. Set in the **Club Andino** ski premises in a woodland area, it has wonderful views over the channel. Electricity, hot showers, tea room and grocery store, US$11 per pitch. Very helpful.

Parque Nacional Tierra del Fuego *p652, map p652*
Camping

Camping Lago Roca, in Parque Nacional Tierra del Fuego, T02901-433313, 21 km from Ushuaia. By the forested shore of tranquil Lago Roc, this is a beautiful site with good facilities, reached by bus Jan-Feb, expensive small shop, *cafetería*, US$4 per person. Tents and sleeping bags for hire (with a US$100 deposit for a tent, US$40 for a sleeping bag).

🍴 Eating

Río Grande *p646*
🍴 **El Rincón de Julio**, next to Posada de los Sauces, Elcano 800 block. For excellent *parrilla*.

🍴 **La Nueva Colonial**, Av Belgrano and Lasserre, ½ a block from the plaza, next to **Casino Club**. Where the locals go for delicious pasta in a warm, family atmosphere.

🍴 **La Nueva Piamontesa**, Belgrano and Mackinlay, T02964-426332, to the side of the charming 24-hr grocery store. Cheap set menus and also delivers food.

🍴 **La Rueda**, Islas Malvinas 998, 1st floor. Excellent *parrilla* in a welcoming place. Has another branch on O'Higgins 200 block.

Cafés
El Roca (sic), Espora entre Av San Martín y Rosales, ½ block from Plaza. *Confitería* and bar in historic premises (the original cinema), good and popular.

Tío Willy, Alberdi entre Espora and 9 de Julio. Serves *cerveza artesanal* (microbrewery).

Tolhuin and around *p647*
On the same block as the famous **La Union** bakery, open 24 hrs, daily except Mon 2400-Tue 0600. There are pizzas at **Pizzería Amistad**, and more of a range at **La Posada de los Ramírez**, a cosy restaurant and *rotisería*, open weekends only, lunch and dinner.

Ushuaia *p647, map p648*
Lots of restaurants along San Martín and Maipú. Most open at lunchtime and again from 1900 at the earliest. Several cafés are open all the time. Ask around for currently available seafood, especially *centolla* (king crab) and *cholga* (giant mussels). Much cheaper if prepare your own meal; **Pesquera del Beagle**, Maipú 227, closed Sun 1600-1800, Mon 1300-1600, sells *centollón* (US$15 per kg ready to eat) and *centolla* (US$11 per kg; US$22.50 per kg ready to eat, just add lemon). Note *centolla* may not be fished Nov-Dec. Beer drinkers should try the hand-crafted brews of the Cape Horn brewery, Pilsen, Pale Ale and Stout.

🍴 **Bodegón Fueguino**, San Martín 859, T02901-431972. Tue-Sun 1200-1500, 2000-2400. In a stylishly renovated 1896 house in the main street, this stands out from the crowd by serving *picadas* with delicious and imaginative dips, good roast lamb, and unusual *cazuelas*, *picadas* and dips. A buzzy atmosphere and welcoming staff.

🍴 **Kaupé**, Roca 470 and Magallanes, T02901-437396. The best restaurant in town with exquisite food. King crab and meat dishes all beautifully served, in a lovely environment – a great treat.

🍴 **Tía Elvira**, Maipú 349, T02901-424725, open Mon-Sat. Has a reputation for excellent seafood, with a good choice of fresh fish and good views over the channel.

††† **Volver**, Maipú 37, T02901-423977. In an atmospheric, old 1898 house, with ancient newspaper all over the walls, so that you can read intriguing fragments while you eat. Cosy stoves and an intimate atmosphere. Delicious salmon and *arroz con mariscos*.

†††-†† **La Estancia**, San Martín 253, T02901-432700. Cheery and good-value *parrilla tenedor libre* for US$13.50 per person.

†††-†† **Moustacchio**, San Martín 272 and Gobernador Godoy, T02901-423308. Long established, good for seafood in a cosy atmosphere. Next door is a cheaper all-you-can-eat sister restaurant.

†††-†† **Parrilla La Rueda**, San Martín and Rivadavia, T02901-436540. A good *tenedor libre* for beef, lamb and a great range of salads. US$14 per person with dessert.

†† **137 Pizzas and Pastas**, San Martín 137. A brightly lit functional place with tasty and filling food. Also takeaway *empanadas* and pizzas.

††-† **Martinica**, San Martín between Antártida Argentina and Yaganes, daily 1130-1500, 2030-0000. Cheap, small and busy, sit at the bar facing the *parrilla* and point to your favourite beef cut. Takeaway (T02901-432 134) and good meals of the day, also pizzas and *empanadas*.

† **El Turco**, San Martín 1410. One of the few good and cheap places, very popular with locals, serving generous *milanesas*, pastas, steaks and pizzas.

Cafés

El Bambú, Piedrabuena 276. Purely vegetarian. Home-made food, delicious and good value. Takeaway only.

Café Bar Banana, San Martín 273, T02901-424021. Quite small, always busy, with a pool table at the back, offers good fast food, such as burgers, small pizzas, puddings, breakfasts and an all-day *menú* for US$7.50.

Café Chocolates, San Martín and 25 de Mayo. Hot chocolate heaven, home-made goodies.

Café de la Esquina, San Martín and 25 de Mayo. Lots of lunch choices, daily specials, sandwiches, *tortas, picadas, lomitos*, café and bar. Open for 15 years, used by locals and tourists.

Café Tante Sara, Fadul y San Martín, opposite tourist office. Smart and modern with an airy feel. Good coffee and tasty sandwiches.

Ramos Generales, Maipú 749, T02901-424317, www.ramosgeneralesushuaia.com. An old warehouse with wooden floors and shelves, and a collection of historic objects and dusty ledgers. Sells breads, pastries, wines and drinks, also cold cuts, sandwiches, salads, ice cream and coffee. Also has a dish of the day or soup for lunch, breakfasts till 1300, teas 1300-2000. Not cheap but atmospheric. Recommended.

Bars and clubs

Ushuaia *p647, map p648*
Dublin Bar Irlandés, 9 de Julio, and **Galway Irish Pub**, Lasserre 108, are both favourites with the locals and tourists.

Küar, Av Perito Moreno 2232, east of town, T02901-437396, daily from 1800. Great setting by the sea, restaurant, bar and brewery.

Lennon Pub, Maipú 263. Friendly atmosphere and live music.

Ushuaia Che, San Martín 452. A lively place with Mexican and Brazilian food.

Festivals and events

Río Grande *p646*
Jan Sheep Shearing Festival. Definitely worth seeing if you're in the area.
Feb Rural Exhibition. In 2nd week of Feb, exhibition with handicrafts.
Mar Shepherd's Day. An impressive sheep-dog display during the 1st week in Mar.
21-22 Jun Winter Solstice. The longest night. Fireworks and ice-skating contests; this is a very inhospitable time of year.

Ushuaia *p647, map p648*
Apr Classical Music Festival, www.festival
deushuaia.com.
21-22 Jun Winter solstice. The longest
night. Torch-lit procession and fireworks.
Aug Sled Dog Race. Held annually.
Aug Marcha Blanca. A ski trek from
Lago Escondido to Tierra Mayor valley.

O Shopping

Ushuaia *p647, map p648*
Ushuaia's tax free status doesn't produce as
many bargains as you might hope. Lots of
souvenir shops on San Martín and several
offering good quality leather and silverware.
In comparison, the Pasaje de Artesanías, by
the Muelle Turístico, sells local arts and crafts.
Atlántico Sur, San Martín 627. The duty-free
shop (not especially cheap).
Boutique del Libro, San Martín and
Piedrabuena and 25 de Mayo 62. A good
range of books on Patagonia and Antarctica,
also DVDs, English titles and guidebooks.
La Anónima, Gobernador Paz and Rivadavia
and San Martín y Onas. Large supermarket.
Norte, 12 de Octubre and Karukinka.
Supermarket, takeaway, fresh food and
fast-food diner.

▲ Activities and tours

Río Grande *p646*
Tour operators
Mariani Travel, Rosales 259, T02964-426010,
mariani@netcombbs.com.ar; **Tecni Austral**,
Moyano 516, T02964-432885. Bus tickets
to Ushuaia.

Tolhuin and around *p647*
Sendero del Indio, T02901-1561 5258,
http://senderoindio.com.ar. For horse riding.

Ushuaia *p647, map p648*
Boat trips and cruises
All short boat trips leave from the Muelle
Turístico. Take your time to choose the size
and style of boat you want. Representatives
from the offices are polite and helpful. All
have a morning and afternoon sailing and
include Isla de los Lobos, Isla de los Pájaros
and Les Eclaireurs lighthouse, with guides
and some form of refreshment. Note that
weather conditions may affect sailings, prices
can change and that port tax is not included.
Barracuda, T02901-437233, www.motonave
barracuda.com.ar. On a lovely old motor
yacht, the 1st tourist boat in Ushuaia,
US$32; their other boat, *Lanín*, includes
Isla Bridges, US$36; all trips include a
discount at the **Acuario** (see above).
Canoero, T02901-433893, www.catamaranes
canoero.com.ar. Catamarans for 60-100
passengers, 2½ hr trips to the 3 main sites
and Isla Bridges, US$36. They also have a 5-hr
trip almost daily to the Pingüinera on Isla
Martillo near Estancia Harberton (Oct-Mar
only), boats stay for 1 hr, but you cannot
land on Martillo. Passengers can return to
Ushuaia by bus: US$65 without stops on
bus ride, US$76 with stops.
Patagonia Adventure Explorer, T02901-
1546 5842, www.patagoniaadvent.com.ar.
Has a sailing boat and motorboats for the
standard trip, plus Isla Bridges: US$50 sailing,
US$40 motoring. Good guides.
Pira-Tour, T02901-1560 4646, www.piratour.
com.ar. Runs 2-3 buses a day to Harberton,
from where a boat goes to the Pingüinera
on Isla Martillo: 15 people allowed to land
(maximum 45 per day – the only company
licensed to do this). US$85 for a morning tour,
including lunch at Harberton and entry to
Acatushún Museum; US$70 for afternoon tour.
Tres Marías, T02901-421987, www.tres
mariasweb.com. The only company licensed
to visit Isla H, which has archaeological sites,

cormorants, other birds and plants. Also has sailing boat, no more than 10 passengers; specialist guide, café on board, US$40 on Tres Marías, US$50 on sailing boat.

Also **Rumbo Sur** and **Tolkeyen**; see Tour operators, below.

Ushuaia is the starting point, or the last stop, en route to Antarctica for several cruises from Oct-Mar that usually sail for 9-21 days along the western shores of the Antarctic peninsula and the South Shetland Islands. Other trips include stops at Falkland/Malvinas archipelago and at South Georgia. Go to **Oficina Antártica** for advice (see page 649). Agencies sell 'last-minute tickets', but the price is entirely dependent on demand (available 1 week before sailing). Coordinator for trips is **Turismo Ushuaia**, Gob Paz 865, T02901 436003, www.ushuaiaturismoevt.com.ar, which operates with IAATO members only. The website has a section for last-minute deals: expect to pay around $3,600-4,000 for 11-day cruises.

To reach Chile, **Cruceros Australis**, www.australis.com, operates 2 luxury cruise ships between Ushuaia and Punta Arenas, with a visit to Cabo de Hornos, frequently recommended. Full details are given under Punta Arenas tour operators. At **Muelle AFASYN**, near the old airport, T02901 435 805, ask about possible crossings with a club member to Puerto Williams, about 4 hrs, or if any foreign sailing boat is going to Cabo de Hornos or Antarctica. From Puerto Williams a ferry goes once a week to Punta Arenas. **Ushuaia Boating**, Deloqui 302 and Godoy, T02901 436193 (or at the **Muelle Turístico**), www.ushuaiaboating.com.ar. Operates a channel crossing all year round to Puerto Navarino (Isla Navarino), 20-90 mins depending on weather, and then bus to Puerto Williams, 1 hr, US$120 (1-way), not including US$8 taxes.

Fishing
The lakes and rivers of Tierra del Fuego offer great fishing for brown and rainbow trout, and stream trout in Lago Fagnano. Both flycasting and spinning are allowed, and permits must be bought. The trout season is 1 Nov-Apr (though this varies slightly every year), licences US$15 per day (an extra fee is charged for some rivers and lakes). Contact **Asociación de Caza y Pesca** at Maipú 822, T02901-423168, cazapescush@infovia.com.ar. Open Mon, Wed, Fri 1700-2100. They sell licences and are very helpful.

Hiking and climbing
Club Andino, Fadul 50, T02901-422335, www.clubandinoushuaia.com.ar. For advice, Mon-Fri 1000-1200, 1400-2030. Sells maps and trekking guidebooks; free guided walks once in a month in summer; also offers classes, eg yoga, dancing, karate-do and has excercise bikes. The winter-sports resorts along R3 (see below) are an excellent base for summer trekking and many arrange excursions.
Nunatak, 25 de Mayo 296, T02901-430329, www.nunatakadventure.com. Organizes treks, canoeing, mountain biking and 4WD trips to Lagos Escondido and Fagnano.

Horse riding
Centro Hípico, R3, Km 3021, T02901-443996, T02901-1556 9099 (mob), www.centro hipicoushuaia.com.ar. Rides through woods, on Monte Susana, along coast and through river, 2 hrs, US$40; 4-hr ride with light lunch, US$80; 7-hr ride with *asado*, US$105. Gentle horses, well-cared for, all guides have first-aid training. Very friendly and helpful. All rides include transfer from town and insurance. Hats provided for children; work with handicapped children. They can arrange long-distance rides of several days, eg on Península Mitre.

Winter sports

Ushuaia is becoming popular as a winter resort with 11 centres for skiing, snowboarding and husky sledging. **Cerro Castor Complex**, R3, Km 27, T02901-499301, www.cerrocastor.com. The only centre for Alpine skiing, with 24 km of pistes, a vertical drop of 800 m and powder snow. Attractive centre with complete equipment rental, also for snowboarding and snow-shoeing. The other centres along R3 at 18-36 km east of Ushuaia offer excellent cross-country skiing (and alternative activities in summer).

Kawi Shiken at Las Cotorras, R3, Km 26, T02901-444152, T02901-1551 9497 (mob), www.tierradelfuego.org.ar/hugoflores. Specializes in sled dogs, with 100 Alaskan and Siberian huskies: 2-km ride on snow US$25, 2-hr trips with meal US$60. In summer, offers 2-km rides in a dog cart, US$15.

Tierra Mayor, 20 km from town, T02901-423240, or T02901-1551 3463, www.tierramayor.co. The largest and is recommended. In a beautiful wide valley between steep-sided mountains, offering ½- and full-day excursions on sledges with huskies, as well as cross-country skiing and snow-shoeing. Equipment hire available.

Tour operators

Lots of companies offer imaginative adventure tourism expeditions. All agencies charge the same fees for excursions; ask tourist office for a complete list: Tierra del Fuego National Park, 4 hrs, US$35 (entry fee extra); Lagos Escondido and Fagnano, 7 hrs, US$48 without lunch. With 3 or 4 people it might be worth hiring a *remise* taxi.

All Patagonia, Juana Fadul 40, T02901-433 622, www.allpatagonia.com. Trekking, ice climbing and tours; trips to Cabo de Hornos and Antarctica.

Canal, 9 de Julio 118, loc 1, T02901-437395, www.canalfun.com. Huge range of activities; trekking, canoeing, riding and 4WD excursions. Recommended.

Comapa, San Martín 245, T02901-430727, www.comapa.com. Conventional tours and adventure tourism, bus tickets to Punta Arenas and Puerto Natales, trips to Antarctica, agents for **Cruceros Australis** and for **Navimag** ferries for Puerto Natales–Puerto Montt (10% ISIC discount for Navimag tickets). Hertz also at this office.

Compañía de Guías de Patagonia, San Martín 628, T02901-437753, T02901-1549 3288 (mob), www.companiadeguias.com.ar. Best agency for walking guides, expeditions for all levels, rock and ice climbing (training provided), also diving, sailing, riding, 7-day crossing of Tierra del Fuego on foot and conventional tours. Recommended.

Límite Vertical, T02901-1560 0868, www.limiteverticaltdf.com.ar. 4WD adventures off-road to the shores of Lagos Escondido and Fagnano, taking logging trails and *ripio* roads, seeing beaver damage in the forests, etc. Lunch is an *asado* at an old sawmill; similar tours by other companies stop for lunch on shore of Fagnano. Good fun.

Rumbo Sur, San Martín 350, T02901-422275, www.rumbosur.com.ar. Flights, buses, conventional tours on land and sea, plus Antarctic expeditions, mid-Nov to mid-Mar, English spoken.

Tolkar, Roca 157, T02901-431412, www.tolkarturismo.com.ar. Flights, bus tickets to Argentina and Chile, conventional and adventure tourism, canoeing and mountain biking to Lago Fagnano.

Tolkeyen, San Martín 1267, T02901-437073, www.tolkeyenpatagonia.com. Bus and flight tickets, catamaran trips (50-300 passengers), including to Harberton (Mon, Wed, Fri, US$66) and Parque Nacional, large company.

Travel Lab, San Martín 1444, T02901-436555, www.travellab.com.ar. Conventional and unconventional tours, mountain biking, trekking, etc. English and French spoken, helpful.

Turismo de Campo, Fuegia Basket 414, T02901-437351, www.turismodecampo. com. Adventure tourism, English and French speaking guides, boat and trekking trips in the National Park, birdwatching, sailing and trips to Antarctica.

⊖ Transport

Río Grande *p646*

Book ahead in summer as buses and planes fill up fast. Take passport when buying ticket.

Air

For airport information, see page 646.

To **Buenos Aires**, Aerolíneas Argentinas daily, 3½ hrs direct. To **Ushuaia**, LADE once a week to **Ushuaia** and Patagonian towns.

Airline offices Aerolíneas Argentinas, San Martín 607, T02964-424467; LADE, Lasserre 445, T02901-422968.

Bus

Buses leave from terminal at Elcano and Güemes, T02964-420997, or from **Tecni Austral**'s office Moyano 516, T02964-432885. To **Río Gallegos**, 3 times a week, US$37. To **Ushuaia**, Tecni Austral, 2 daily (heavily booked in summer), 3-4 hrs; US$18, also **Tolkeyen**.

To **Chile** To **Porvenir**, Wed, Sun 0800, 5 hrs, US$14, **Gesell**, passport and luggage control at San Sebastián. To **Punta Arenas**, 8 hrs, US$8 with Tecni Austral.

Car hire

Europcar, Av Belgrano 423, T02901-430365, www.europcar.com; Localiza, San Martín 642, T02901-430191, www.localiza.com.ar.

Ushuaia *p647, map p648*

Air

Book ahead in summer, as flights fill up fast. In winter, poor weather often delays flights. For airport informtion, see page 648.

Schedules tend to change from season to season, so call offices for times and prices, T02901-423970. To **Buenos Aires**, 3½ hrs, **El Calafate**, in summer, 1 hr, both with Aerolíneas and LADE. Flights are also available daily to **Río Gallegos**, 1 hr, and **Río Grande**, several a week, but check with agents, 1 hr. To **Punta Arenas**, 1 hr, Aerovías DAP. The Aeroclub de Ushuaia flies Mon, Wed, Fri to **Puerto Williams**, from the downtown airport.

Airline offices Aerolíneas Argentinas, Maipú 823, T02901-436338; LADE, San Martín 542, p 5, T02901-421123, Lan Chile at the airport, T02901-424244.

Bus

To **Río Grande**, 3½-4 hrs, Mon-Sat 0530, US$18 with bus, **Tecni Austral**. Book through Tolkar, Roca 157, T02901-431412.

To **Río Gallegos**, Tecni Austral, 11½ hrs, US$51. To **Punta Arenas**, Mon, Wed, Fri 0530, 0600, US$49, **Tecni Austral**, and twice a week, **Buses Pacheco**, San Martín 245 (at Comapa agency), T02901-430727, www.buses pacheco.com. From Río Gallegos, several buses daily to **El Calafate**, 4 hrs, US$16.

Urban buses from west to east across town, most stops along Maipú, US$0.55. Tourist office provides a list of minibus companies that run daily from town (stops along Maipú) to nearby attractions.

In summer, buses and minibuses to the **National Park** leave from the bus stop on Maipú at the bottom of Fadul.

To **Lapataia**, 9 a day from 0800, last back 1900, US$12, US$14 (return), with Pasarella, and 8 a day from 0830, last back 2000, with Eben Ezer. From same bus stop, many other *colectivos* go to the **Tren del Fin del Mundo**, **Lago Escondido**, **Lago Fagnano** and **Glaciar Martial**, leave when full. For **Harberton**, check the notice boards at the station at Maipú y Fadul.

Combis Líder, Gob Paz 921, T02901-436421, and Montiel, Marcos Zar 330, T02901-421366.

Car hire

Most companies charge around US$60 per day including insurance and 200 km per day, promotional rates are usually available. Note that hiring a car in Tierra del Fuego is 21% cheaper than anywhere else in the current tax régime.

Hertz, airport, T02901-432429; Wagen, San Martín 1222, T02901-430739.

Taxi

Call T02901-422007 or T02901-440225.

Bahía Hermosa, T02901-422233, and Remise Carlitos, T02901-422222, both are reliable.

Train

For **Tren del Fin del Mundo**, see page 650.

❶ Directory

Río Grande *p646*

Banks 4 banks on San Martín between 100 and 300 have ATMs. **Banco de la Nación Argentina**, San Martín 219; **Bansud**, Rosales 241, cash advance on Visa. **Currency exchange** Thaler Rosales 259. **Post office** Rivadavia 968. **Supermarkets** Norte, San Martín and Piedrabuena, good selection; **La Anónima** on San Martín near Belgrano. **Telephone** *Locutorio*, San Martín at 170 and 458.

Ushuaia *p647, map p648*

Banks Open 1000-1500 (in summer). ATMs are plentiful all along San Martín, using credit cards is by far the easiest, as changing TCs is difficult and expensive. **Currency exchange** Agencia de Cambio Thaler, San Martín 788, daily 1000-1300, 1700-2030; Banco de Tierra del Fuego, San Martín 396. **Embassies and consulates** Chile, Jainén 50, T02901-430909. **Internet** Many broadband cyber cafés and *locutorios* along San Martín. Another at Paz and 25 de Mayo. Gigabyte, Deloqui 395, has Skype. They are often full. **Library** Biblioteca Popular Sarmiento, San Martín 1589, T02901-423103, Mon-Fri 0830-2000, Sat 1000-1300, library with a good range of books about the area. **Post office** San Martín and Godoy, Mon-Fri 1000-1800, Sat 1000-1300. **Telephone** *Locutorios* all along San Martín. **Visas and immigration** Dirección Nacional de Migraciones, Fuegia Basket 87

Contents

Footprint features

Background

History

Much of Argentina's fascinating history is visible on a visit to the country today, not only in colonial architecture and the 19th-century artefacts which fill the museums but in the culture and customs of everyday life. Many towns in the Pampas of Buenos Aires province are just as they were in the 19th century, such as San Antonio de Areco and Chascomús, where the traditions of a lively gaucho culture are still maintained. The lives of early pioneers can be explored in the Welsh towns of Gaiman and Trevelin in Patagonia and in the more remote *estancias* throughout the country. Córdoba's history of Jesuit occupation is visible in many buildings in the city itself and *estancias* in the province. And in the northwest of Argentina you'll find the richest evidence of the country's history. This is where the Spanish first arrived in the 16th century and before them the Incas in the early 15th century, and both have left their mark in colonial architecture and intriguing archaeological evidence. Long before these invasions, the present day provinces of Salta, Catamarca, Tucumán and Jujuy were inhabited by many sophisticated indigenous cultures whose ruined cities can be visited at Santa Rosa de Tastil, Tilcara and Quilmes, and whose beautiful ceramics fill the area's many museums. This is the most rewarding part of the country to visit if you're interested in exploring Argentina's past.

Archaeology and prehistory

Earliest origins

The first people crossed the land bridge spanning Asia and America, and the Bering Strait, between 50,000 and 60,000 years ago, and began a long migration southwards, reaching South America about 30,000 years ago and Tierra del Fuego around 12,000 years ago. Hunters and foragers, they followed in the path of huge herds of now extinct animals, such as mammoths, giant ground sloths, mastodons and wild horses, adapting to fishing along the Chilean coasts. In the northeast of Argentina, these people adopted a more sedentary lifestyle, pausing in their semi-nomadic travels long enough to plant and harvest crops of maize and manioc, and domesticate animals.

Northwest Argentina

Argentina has a rich history of pre-Hispanic indigenous civilizations, with the most important archaeological sites situated in the northwest and west areas of the most highly developed cultures south of the central Andes. Along a migratory path which followed the Andes, this region became a meeting place for established settlers from northern Chile, the central Andes, the Chaco and the hunter-gatherers of the south. Cave paintings and petroglyphs engraved on rocks remain from 13,000 to 10,000 years ago, made by cave dwellers who lived by hunting vizcacha, guanaco, vicuña and birds, some painted with pigments derived from minerals mixed with gesso. Their lines, dots and geometrical forms belong to a symbolic system impossible to interpret today. The extraordinary quantity of handprints visible in the Cueva de las Manos in Patagonia were made as long ago as 10,000 years, and again, their purpose and origin remains a mystery.

By about 1000 to 500 BC, the nomadic groups had grown in size and were too large to subsist on hunting alone. So they started early attempts at agriculture, growing potatoes and maize, among other staples. A mummy found from this period (displayed in Cachi's archaeological museum) with a few artefacts and belongings suggests that these peoples had a developed system of beliefs. By 2000 years ago, small communities had started to gather on the alluvial plains, living on agriculture and herding llamas. In many of the area's museums, you'll see large grinding stones made of granite used to grind maize, as well as arrowheads and pipes used for smoking tobacco. Weaving began around this time, and there are some fine fabrics found at Santa Rosa Tastil.

There were three distinct periods in the cultural development of the northwest. The Early Period (500 BC to AD 650) witnessed the beginnings of agriculture, as well as pottery and metalworking, with the remains of terraces near Humahuaca in Jujuy. The Middle Period (AD 650-850) was marked by the influence of the great culture of Tiahuanaco in present-day Bolivia. Fine metal objects, some of them of gold and silver, were made and new plant varieties were introduced. You'll find stone vessels, anthropomorphic clay pieces, and ornate ceramics from this period all over the Northwest.

In the Later Period (AD 850-1480), known as the Period of Regional Development, small groups of settlers formed communities with individual dwellings, usually based on circular stone walls, next to water sources. Both ritual and functional ceramics were made by people known as the Santamariana or Diaguita culture. Although there was no system of writing, their language, Kakán, survived until the Inca invasion in the late 15th century. These cultures made large, beautifully painted funerary urns, thought to bury the bones of children, since the infant mortality rate was high. The predominant religious beliefs centred around worship of the mother earth goddess, the *Pachamama*, and she's still worshipped in rural communities all over the Northwest today, with lively festivals on 1 August.

The Incas first arrived in the Calchaquíes valleys area between 1410 and 1430, incorporating the area into the part of their empire known as Kollasuyo. They built two parallel roads along the length of the Andes and along the Pacific shore: busy trade routes linking their communities with the rest of the Inca Empire. The Incas made Quechua the official language, punished the chiefs of any groups whose members transgressed, and absorbed the local cult of the earth goddess *Pachamama* into their own system of worship of the sun. The Incas also brought with them their own sacrificial burial customs. The bodies of three children found at the summit of Cerro Llullaillaco on the Salta/Chile border indicate young humans were killed as offerings. These three, aged between seven and 15, were taken to the summit, dressed in special garments, adorned with feather headdresses and jewellery, and put to sleep forever using strong local liquor *chichi*. It's thought that they were offered as a sacrifice to the gods in the belief that to gain life, life has also to be sacrificed. It's also possible that their death sealed some kind of political alliance between the Inca and the chief of a new colony. The children's peaceful faces show no sign of distress so it's likely that they died painlessly within minutes. Salta's MAAM museum (see page 287) has a fascinating display of photographs and an extraordinary array of the artefacts buried with the children. The Calchaquíes valleys were the site of bloody battles when the Spanish attempted to dominate in the 16th century and many indigenous groups were wiped out, but fortunately, in the northwest of Argentina, there are living descendants from many of the original inhabitants, keeping their customs and beliefs alive.

Central and southern Argentina

The Comechingones, who inhabited what are now the provinces of Córdoba and San Luis, lived in settlements of pit-dwellings and used irrigation to produce a range of crops. In the far northeast on the eastern edge of the Chaco were the Guaraní; organized into loose confederations, they lived in rudimentary villages and practised slash-and-burn agriculture to grow maize, sweet potatoes, manioc and beans. They also produced textiles and ceramics.

Further south, the Pampas and Patagonia were much more sparsely populated than the northwest and most groups were nomadic long after the arrival of the Spanish. One of the most important groups were the Querandí, who eked out a living by hunting guanaco and rheas with *boleadoras*, three balls of stone tied with thong and hurled at the legs of a running animal. Patagonia was inhabited by scattered nomadic groups, including the Pampa, the Chonik and the Kaingang, who managed to avoid contact with white settlers until the 19th century. In the steppes of Patagonia, the Tehuelche and Puelche lived as nomadic hunters living off guanaco, foxes and game. In the far south, in southern Patagonia and Tierra del Fuego, there were four indigenous groups: the land-based Ona and Haush, who hunted foxes and guanaco, wearing their hides and constructing temporary dwellings of branches covered loosely with skins; and the sea-based Yaghanes and Alacaluf, who made canoes, paddles, bailers and mooring rope, catching fish with spears or by hand, though seals were their main source of food. These peoples survived until the late 19th century and were befriended and protected by the son of Tierra del Fuego's first settler and missionary. Lucas Bridges' account in the book *Uttermost Part of the Earth* gives an extraordinary insight into the customs and hunting practices of the Ona and Yaghanes. Within 50 years of the arrival of white sheep-farmers, many had been shot or coerced into religious missions where they could be controlled. President Roca's genocidal Conquest of the Wilderness (1879-1880) exterminated any indigenous tribes who resisted the influence of the new settlers in the Pampas and Patagonia. Today no single descendant remains of these tribes, which is why you may see that every statue of Roca is permanently disfigured and has graffiti.

European exploration and settlement

At the time of the arrival of the first Europeans, the land that is now Argentina was sparsely populated with about two-thirds of the indigenous population living in the northwest. European exploration began in the Río de la Plata estuary when in 1516 Juan de Solís, a Portuguese navigator employed by the Spanish crown, landed on the shore – though his men were soon killed by indigenous Querandí. Four years later he was followed by Ferdinand Magellan who explored the Río de la Plata, before turning south to make his way into the Pacific via the straits north of Tierra del Fuego, now named after him. In 1527 both Sebastián Cabot and his rival Diego García sailed into the estuary and up the Río Paraná and the Río Paraguay. Cabot founded a small fort, Sancti Spiritus, not far from the modern city of Rosario, but it was wiped out by indigenous inhabitants about two years later. Despite these difficulties Cabot took back to Spain stories of a great Indian kingdom beyond the Plata estuary, rich in precious metals, giving the Río de la Plata its misleading name: a translation would be 'river of silver'. A Portuguese expedition to the estuary, led by Affonso de Souza, returned with similar tales, and this led to a race between the two Iberian powers. In 1535, Pedro de Mendoza set out with 16 ships and a well-equipped force of 1600 men and founded a settlement at Buenos Aires (actually he settled closer to San Isidro along the coast), which he gave its present name, originally Puerto Nuestra Señora Santa María de Buen Ayre. The indigenous inhabitants soon made life too difficult; the settlement was abandoned and Mendoza returned home but not before sending Juan de Ayolas with a small force up the Río Paraná in search of the Indian kingdom. In 1537 this force founded Asunción, in Paraguay, where the locals were friendly.

After 1535 the attention of the Spanish crown switched to Peru, where Pizarro was engaged in the successful conquest of the Inca Empire, where there was instant wealth in gold and silver and a malleable workforce in the enormous indigenous population. The small settlement at Asunción remained an isolated outpost until 1573, when a force from there travelled south to establish the city of Santa Fe. Seven years later Juan de Garay refounded Buenos Aires (the city's first ever street bares his name, it is in San Telmo), but it was only under his successor, Hernando Arias de Saavedra (1592-1614), that the new settlement became secure, benefiting both from back-up in Asunción and from the many cattle brought over by Mendoza which had increased and multiplied meanwhile.

However, before the time of Mendoza's expedition to the Plata estuary, Spanish expeditions were already exploring northern parts of present-day Argentina. In 1535 Diego de Almagro led a party from Peru, which crossed northwest into Argentina, and in 1543 the Spanish Viceroyalty of Peru was made administrative capital of southern South America. There was greatly increased motivation for exploring the region, however, when silver deposits were found in Potosí (now in Bolivia), and the Governorship of Tucumán was set up as an administrative centre as a halfway point between Bolivia and the port of Buenos Aires. Explorations set forth from Chile and Peru to find trade routes and a source of cheap labour to work the mines, and so the oldest towns in Argentina were founded: Santiago del Egstero (1553), Mendoza (1561), San Juan (1562), Córdoba (1573), Salta (1582), La Rioja (1591), and Jujuy (1593). A total of 25 cities were founded in present-day Argentina in the 16th century, 15 of which survived, at a time when the total Spanish population was under 2000.

Colonial rule

Throughout the colonial period the Argentine territories were an outlying part of the Spanish Empire and of minor importance since Spanish colonial settlement and government was based in Peru, busy exploiting the vast mineral wealth of Potosí in Alto Peru (and large supplies of forced indigenous labour). Argentine lands offered only sparse population and little mineral wealth by comparison. Also, the nomadic nature of many indigenous groups made any attempt at control difficult, whereas in Peru, Spanish rule was more readily superimposed on the centralized administration of the defeated Incas.

Buenos Aires failed to become an important port because apart from the fact that the port wasn't deep enough to welcome large ships, from 1543 all the Spanish territories in South America were governed from Lima, the Vice-Regal capital, and trade with Spain was routed via Lima, Panama and the Caribbean. Trading through Buenos Aires was prohibited, however, the Paraná delta north of the city near Tigre provided ample opportunity for smuggling British and Portuguese goods into the city, and it rapidly expanded as a centre for contraband. By 1776 the city's population was 24,000, double the size of any of the cities of the interior. However, the Governorship of Tucumán was more important as a centre, due to the success of the *encomienda* system, in which lands belonging to indigenous peoples were seized and redistributed to Spanish settlers. The idea was that the *encomenderos* in charge would exchange work done for religious education, but in reality the majority of these men were ruthless exploiters of slave labour and offered little in the way of spiritual enlightenment or even food. In the Valles Cachaquíes the substantial indigenous population resisted conversion by Jesuit missionaries, and was effectively almost wiped out when they rose up against the Spanish landowners. Settlers in the northeast of the country also had their conflicts with the indigenous population. The Pampas and Buenos Aires province were dangerous areas for white settlement, since in these lands wild cattle had long been hunted for their hides by Tehuelches and Mapuches. They drove cattle to Chile over the Andes for trade, and their violent armies, or *malones,* clashed regularly with newly arrived settlers. Around the early 18th century, the figure of the gaucho emerged, nomadic men of mixed *criollo* (early Argentine settlers) and indigenous origin, who roamed free on horseback, living off cattle. Once the Argentine state started to control land boundaries, these characters became emblematic of freedom and romanticized in important fictional works, *Martín Fierro* and *Don Segundo de los Sombras.* The gaucho is still a much admired figure all over Argentina today, though less wild and certainly no longer an outcast.

Jesuits came to 'civilize' the indigenous population under the protection of the Spanish crown in the late 16th century. They quickly set up missions, which employed the reasonably pliant Guaraní residents of the upper Paraná in highly organized societies, with a militant component, equipped to resist the frequent raids by Portuguese in search of slaves. The Guaraní were compelled to comply with their educators since this exempted them from working in the silver mines, and as many as 4000 Guaraní lived in some missions, also producing *yerba mate* and tobacco as successful Jesuit businesses. The Jesuits and their faith were, however, expelled from Argentina by King Charles III of Spain in 1767, as they had grown rich and powerful. The remains of their handsome architecture can be admired in Córdoba city and province, as well as at San Ignacio Mini in Misiones.

Buenos Aires at last gained some considerable power when the new viceroyalty of the River Plate was created in 1776, with the rapidly growing city as head of the large area and now able to trade with Spain and her other ports. However, as the trade of contraband into the city increased, flooding the market with cheaper European-produced goods, conflict increased between those advocating free trade, such as Manuel Belgrano, and those who wanted to retain a monopoly. The population of Buenos Aires increased enormously with the viceroyalty, along with its economy, as *estancias* sprang up to farm and export cattle, instead of rounding up the wild beasts, with great success.

The Wars of Independence

The drive for independence in Argentina was partly a response to events in Europe, where Spain was initially allied to Napoleonic France. In 1806 and 1807 the British, at war with Napoleon and attracted by what they thought were revolutionary tensions in Buenos Aires, made two attempts to seize the city but were defeated. In 1808 Napoleon invaded Spain, deposing King Ferdinand VII, and provoking widespread resistance from Spanish guerrilla armies. Throughout Spanish America the colonial elites debated where their loyalties lay: with Napoleon's brother Joseph, now officially king; with Ferdinand, now in a French prison; with the Viceroy; or with the Spanish resistance parliament in Cadiz.

On 25 May 1810, the *cabildo* of Buenos Aires deposed the viceroy and established a *junta* to govern on behalf of King Ferdinand VII, when the city's people gathered in front of the *cabildo* (which you can still see today) wearing pale blue and white ribbons, soon to become the colours of the Argentine flag. This move provoked resistance in outlying areas of the viceroyalty, Paraguay, Uruguay and Upper Peru (Bolivia) breaking away from the rule of Buenos Aires. Factional rivalry within the junta between supporters of independence and their opponents added to the confusion and instability. Six years later in July 1816, when Buenos Aires was threatened by invasion from Peru and blockaded by a Spanish fleet in the Río de la Plata, a national congress held at Tucumán declared independence. The declaration was given reality by the genius and devotion of José de San Martín, who boldly marched an Argentine army across the Andes to free Chile, and embarked his forces for Peru, where he captured Lima, the first step towards liberation. San Martín was aided by an extraordinary feat from a local *caudillo* in the north, Martín Miguel de Güemes, whose army of gauchos was later to liberate Salta. *Caudillos* were local warlords who governed areas far larger than today's provinces, organizing their own armies of local indigenous groups and gauchos. The *caudillos* did not recognize the Tucumán declaration, but so it was on 9 July 1816 that the United Provinces of the River Plate came into being.

Since independence

The 19th century
Much of the current rift between Buenos Aires and the rest of Argentina has its roots in a long-standing conflict, which emerged in the early 19th century. The achievement of independence brought neither stability nor unity, since the new junta was divided between Federalists and Unitarists, a conflict that was to rage for over 40 years. The Unitarists, found mainly in the city of Buenos Aires, advocated strong central government, free trade, education and white immigration, looking to Europe for their inspiration. The Federalists, backed by the provincial elites and many of the great *estancieros* of Buenos Aires province, resisted, defending local autonomy and traditional values. Behind the struggle were also economic interests: Buenos Aires and the coastal areas benefited from trade with Europe; the interior provinces did not. As the conflict raged, the territory, known officially as the United Provinces of the Río de la Plata, had none of the features of a modern state: there was no central government, nor an army, capital city or constitution.

Order, of a sort, was established after 1829 by Juan Manuel de Rosas, a powerful *caudillo* and governor of Buenos Aires. In 1833, he attempted to gain widespread support from local *caudillos* with his Campaign of the Desert, which claimed vast areas of land from indigenous groups, granted to Rosas' allies. However, his overthrow in 1852 unleashed another round of battles between Unitarists and Federalists and between Buenos Aires and the provinces. In 1853 a constitution establishing a federal system of government was finally drafted but the Buenos Aires province refused to join the new Argentine Confederation, which had its capital at Paraná, and set up its own separate republic. Conflict between the two states erupted over the attempt by Buenos Aires to control and tax commerce on the Río Paraná but the victory of Buenos Aires at Pavón (1861) opened the way to a solution: the city became the seat of the federal government. Bartolomé Mitre, former governor of Buenos Aires became the first president of Argentina. There was another political flare-up of the old quarrel in 1880, ending in the humiliation of the city of Buenos Aires, which was separated from its province and made into a special federal territory.

Although there was resistance to the new constitution from some of the western provinces, the institutions of a modern state were created in the two decades after 1861 by Mitre's important period of government. He set up a national bank, bureaucracy, a postal service and an army. The building of railways across the Pampas did most to create national unity, breaking the power of the *caudillos* by enabling the federal government to send in troops quickly. The new army was quickly employed to defeat Francisco Solano López of Paraguay in the War of the Triple Alliance (1865-1870). They were used again in

President Roca's genocidal Conquest of the Wilderness (1879-1880), which exterminated the indigenous tribes of the Pampas and Patagonia.

In the last quarter of the 19th century Argentina was transformed: the newly acquired stability encouraged foreign investment; the Pampas were fenced, ploughed up and turned over to commercial export agriculture; railways and port facilities were built. The presidency of Domingo Sarmiento had been keen on widespread immigration from Europe, which transformed the character of Buenos Aires and other cities around the Plata estuary, where the population grew from 200,000 in 1870 to two million in 1920. Sarmiento also sought to Europeanize the country, and his impressive educational policy included the importing of teachers from North America. Political power, however, remained in the hands of a small group of large landowners, who had been granted territories after the Conquest of the Desert, and their urban allies. Few Argentines had the vote, and the opposition Unión Cívica Radical, excluded from power, conspired with dissidents in the army in attempts to overthrow the government.

The 20th century

As the British-built railways stretched across the country, the sheep industry flourished, making Argentina's fortune through exporting both wool and meat. Refrigerator ships were invented in the 1870s, enabling meat to be shipped in bulk to the expanding industrial countries of Britain and Europe. One of the landmarks of modern Argentine history was the 1912 Sáenz Peña law, which established universal manhood suffrage, since until then power had been centralized in the hands of the elite, with no votes for the working classes. Sáenz Peña, president between 1910 and 1916, sought to bring the middle and working classes into politics, gambling that the Conservatives could reorganize themselves and attract their votes. The gamble failed: the Conservatives failed to gain a mass following and the Radicals came to power. The Radical Civic Union was created in 1890, but Radical presidents Hipólito Yrigoyen (1916-1922 and 1928-1930) and Marcelo T. de Alvear (1922-1928) found themselves trapped between the demands of an increasingly militant urban labour movement and the opposition of the Conservatives, still powerful in the provinces and with allies in the armed forces. Through the 1920s, Argentina was the 'breadbasket of the world' and its sixth richest nation. Fifty years later, the country had become practically Third World, a fall from grace that still haunts the Argentine consciousness. The world depression following the Wall Street Crash of 1929 devastated export markets, but the military coup that overthrew Yrigoyen in 1930 was a significant turning point: the armed forces returned to government for the first time in over 50 years and were to continue to play a major political role until 1983. Through the 1930s a series of military backed governments, dominated by the Conservatives, held power. The Radicals were outlawed and elections were so fraudulent that frequently more people voted than were on the register. Yet the armed forces themselves were disunited: while most officers supported the Conservatives and the landholding elites, a minority of ultra-nationalist officers, inspired by developments in Europe, supported industrialization and the creation of a one-party dictatorship along Fascist lines. The outbreak of war in Europe increased these tensions and a series of military coups in 1943-1944 led to the rise of Colonel Juan Domingo Perón. When the military allowed a return to civilian rule in 1946, Perón swept into power winning the presidential elections. His government is chiefly remembered by many Argentines for improving the living conditions of the workers through the introduction of paid holidays and welfare measures in his *justicialismo:* social justice. Perón was an authoritarian and charismatic leader, and especially in its early years the government was strongly nationalistic, taking control over the British-owned railways in 1948 by buying them back at a staggering £150 million. Opposition parties were harassed and independent newspapers taken over since Perón wasn't at all interested in free press. Perón is also well known for his famous second-wife, Eva (Evita) Perón, who became the darling of the country, helping her husband's popularity no-end. Although Perón was easily re-elected in 1951, his government soon ran into trouble when economic problems led to the introduction of a wage freeze which upset the labour unions which were the heart of Peronist support. The early and tragic death of Evita in 1952 was another blow; and a dispute with the church in 1954-1955 also added to Perón's problems. In September 1955 a military coup unseated Perón who went into exile, in Paraguay, Panama, Venezuela, the Dominican Republic and, from 1961 to 1973, in Spain.

Perón's legacy dominated Argentina for the next two decades. No attempt was made to destroy his social and economic reforms but the armed forces determined to exclude the Peronists from power. Argentine society was bitterly divided between Peronists and anti-Peronists and the economy struggled, partly as a result of Perón's measures against the economic elite and in favour of the workers. Between 1955 and 1966 there was an uneasy alternation of military and civilian regimes. The military officers who seized power in 1966 announced their intention to carry out a Nationalist Revolution, with austerity measures to try to gain control of a spiralling economy, but they were quickly discredited by a deteriorating economic situation. The Cordobazo, a left-wing student and workers uprising in Córdoba in 1969, was followed by the emergence of several guerrilla groups such as the Montoneros and the People's Revolutionary Army (ERP), as well as the growth of political violence. As Argentina became more ungovernable, Perón, from his exile, refused to denounce those guerrilla groups, which called themselves Peronist.

In 1971 General Alejandro Lanusse seized power, promising a return to civilian rule and calculating that the only way to control the situation was to allow Perón to return. When the military bowed out in 1973, elections were won by the Peronist candidate, Hector Campora. Perón returned from exile in Madrid to resume as president in October 1973, but died on 1 July 1974, leaving the presidency to his widow, Vice-President María Estela Martínez de Perón, his third wife, known as 'Isabelita'. Perón's death unleashed chaos: hyperinflation, resumed guerrilla warfare and the operation of right-wing death squads who abducted people suspected of left-wing sympathies. In March 1976, to nobody's surprise, the military overthrew Isabelita and replaced her with a Junta led by General Jorge Videla.

The new government closed Congress, outlawed political parties, placed trade unions and universities under military control and unleashed the so-called 'Dirty War', a brutal assault on the guerrilla groups and anyone else who manifested opposition. The military leaders were not at all interested in trying to convict those they suspected of being dissidents. They started a campaign of violence against anyone remotely troublesome as well as anyone Jewish or Marxist, and journalists, intellectuals, psychologists and anyone, according to President General Videla, who was 'spreading ideas contrary to Western Christian civilization'. As many as 30,000 people are thought to have 'disappeared' during this period, removed by violent squads who would take them to clandestine detention centres to be raped, tortured or brutally killed. This is one of Argentina's bleakest memories. In order that the disappeared should never be forgotten, the *Madres de la Plaza de Mayo* still parade around the plaza in Buenos Aires with photographs of their lost children pinned to their chests (see box, page 674) looking for answers.

Dirty War

The 'Dirty War', unleashed by the armed forces after 1976, is one of the most violent incidents in modern South American history, and hardly a month goes by without this grim episode provoking further controversy in the Argentine press.

Guerrilla groups started emerging in Argentina after 1969, in angry response to military rule, among them the Monteneros and the People's Revolutionary Army (*Ejército Revolucionario del Pueblo* or ERP). The middle-class educated Monteneros, inspired by a mixture of Peronism, Catholicism and Marxism, proclaimed allegiance to the exiled Perón, and wanted to liberate the working classes from the evils of capitalism. The ERP, by contrast drawing their inspiration from Trotsky and Ernesto 'Che' Guevara, argued that political violence would push the military government towards increased repression which would ignite working-class opposition and lead to civil war and socialist revolution.

If Peronists and non-Peronists disagreed over their aims, their methods were similar: kidnappings and bank robberies raised money and gained publicity; army and police officers were assassinated along with right-wing Peronists; and wealthy Argentine families and multinational companies were forced to distribute food and other goods to the poor to obtain the release of kidnap victims. Head of the Argentine military, General Jorge Videla retaliated by quashing any uprising before it had a chance to establish: pop concerts were banned, as was any gathering of young. Far more terrifying, Videla initiated a plan called The Process of National Reorganization, *El Proceso*. The military carried out their own kidnappings of anyone they deemed likely to be dangerous. Anyone with left-wing

Videla's nominated successor, General Roberto Viola, took over for three years in March 1981 but was overthrown by General Leopoldo Galtieri in December 1981, who failed to keep a grasp on a plummeting economy, and an increasingly discontent public. Attempting to win the crowds, Galtieri's decision to invade the Falkland/Malvinas Islands in April 1982 backfired when the British retaliated by sending a fleet to the south Atlantic, subsequently forcing the Argentines to flee. This loss is still felt in every town in Argentina today. There are monuments to the dead and parades every year commemorating the battles. Many Argentines still consider the Malvinas as Argentine property. After the war was lost in June 1982 General Reynaldo Bignone took over, and promptly created a law giving amnesty to all human-rights abusers in the military (see box, page 676).

Elections in October 1983 were won by Raúl Alfonsín and his Unión Cívica Radical (UCR) and during 1985 Generals Videla, Viola and Galtieri were sentenced to long terms of imprisonment for their parts in the dictatorship. While Alfonsín's government struggled to deal with the legacy of the past, it was overwhelmed by continuing economic problems, the most obvious of which was hyperinflation. Workers rushed to the shops once they'd been paid to spend their earnings before prices rose, and supermarkets announced price increases over the loudspeaker since they were so unstable. When the Radicals were defeated by Carlos Menem, the Peronist (*Justicialist*) presidential candidate, Alfonsín, stepped down early because of economic instability. Strained relations between the Peronist government and the military led to several rebellions, tendencies might be taken without warning, tortured in one of over 340 detention centres, and then, mysteriously, 'disappeared'. All three armed services operated their own death squads and camps in a campaign of indiscriminate violence. By 1978-1979 both the ERP and the Monteneros had ceased to function, and in the process, tens of thousands of people disappeared: although an official report produced after the return to civilian rule put their number at 8960, some 15,000 cases have now been documented and human rights groups now estimate the total at some 30,000. They are still remembered by the *Madres de la Plaza de Mayo* (Mothers of the Plaza de Mayo), a human-rights group made up of relatives, who march anti-clockwise around the Plaza de Mayo in central Buenos Aires every Thursday at 1530, with photos of their 'disappeared' loved ones pinned to their chests, demanding information.

On 24 March 2006, the 30th anniversary of the military junta was marked with a national day of awareness and demonstrations in Buenos Aires, suggesting that the scars of the Dirty War have yet to heal. Videla, along with other military leaders, has been charged with human rights abuse. After serving only five years in prison, he was pardoned by Argentine President Carlos Menem in 1990, but was arrested again in 1998 and found guilty of kidnapping children. He was transferred to house arrest, but in 2009 was sent back to prison when the 1999 ruling was found to be 'unconstitutional'. He now has an international arrest warrant against him, issued by Germany who is seeking to try him for murdering a German citizen in the 1970s.

For more information see www.madres.org, and www.abuelas.org.ar. For a clear explanation in English, see www.desaparecidos.org/arg, and www.yendor.com/vanished.

which Menem attempted to appease by pardoning the imprisoned generals. His popularity among civilians declined, but from 1991 to 1992 the economy minister, Domingo Cavallo, succeeded in restoring economic confidence and the government as a whole with his *Plan de Convertabilidad*. This, the symbol of his stability, was the introduction of a new currency pegged to the United States dollar, and preventing the central bank from printing money that could not be backed up by the cash in reserve. After triumphing in the October 1993 congressional elections at the expense of the UCR, the Peronists themselves lost some ground in the April 1994 elections to a constituent assembly. The party to gain most, especially in Buenos Aires, was Frente Grande, a broad coalition of left-wing groups and disaffected Peronists. Behind the loss of confidence of these dissident Peronists was unrestrained corruption and a pact in December 1993 between Menem and Alfonsín pledging UCR support for constitutional changes, which included re-election of the president for a second term of four years.

By the 1995 elections, the majority of the electorate favoured stability over constitutional concerns and returned President Menem.

In November 1998 Alianza Democrática chose the Radical Fernando de la Rua as its candidate for the October 1999 presidential election. Moves from Menem supporters to put forward Menem for a further (constitutionally dubious) term of office helped delay the Peronist choice of candidate until July 1999 when Eduardo Duhalde received the backing of Menem. Although Alianza Democrática offered little change in economic

The Falklands/Malvinas conflict

The dispute between Britain and Argentina over the Falkland Islands/Islas Malvinas has a long history. Dutch sailor Sebald de Weert made the first generally acknowledged sighting of the islands in 1598. In 1764, France established a small colony there, while the British built an outpost on the northern tip. But when the French government sold Port Louis to Spain in 1766, the British were expelled. In 1811, following the outbreak of the Wars of Independence, Spain withdrew her forces from the islands. And after British warships expelled a force from Buenos Aires in 1833, the islands came under British rule, an act that has angered Argentines ever since.

A hundred years or so later, President Juan Perón was quick to exploit the disputed status of the islands as part of an appeal to Argentine nationalism during his first administration (1946-1955). In 1965, the United Nations called on Britain and Argentina to resolve their differences peacefully, and talks took place, but were complicated by the hostility of the islanders themselves towards any change in their status.

In 1982, when the British government reduced its forces in the area, the Argentine military regime seized their chance. Then president General Galtieri had huge economic problems, and thought a successful invasion would unite the population behind him. An Argentine force of 5000 men landed in South Georgia on 2 April 1982, quickly overwhelming the small British garrison without loss of life. The British military and civilian authorities were expelled and the 1700 inhabitants placed under an Argentine military governor. Though most Latin American states sympathized with Argentina over the sovereignty issue, many were unhappy with the use of force. Backed by a United Nations resolution and the crucial logistical

policy, the Peronists were harmed by the corruption scandals surrounding the Menem administration and the continuing rivalry between Menem and Duhalde, enabling De La Rua to win the presidency and take office in December 1999.

The 21st century

Facing recession and impossible debts with the IMF, President De La Rua implemented austerity measures, but these were not enough to save the peso, nor the many jobs which were lost in late 2000. Young people started to leave the country in massive numbers, looking for work elsewhere, taking their savings with them. In an attempt to keep these reserves of cash within the country, De la Rua started the *corralito* (meaning 'little pen'), a law determining that individuals could only withdraw 250 pesos from their accounts per week, and converting savings to government bonds. People literally lost their savings. In December 2001, the people of Buenos Aires and other large cities took to the streets in an unprecedented display both of violent rioting, and peaceful pot bashing by furious middle-class housewives, the *caserolazas*. The country went through five presidents in a period of a couple of months, but nothing could prevent devaluation, and in January 2002 the peso lost its parity with the dollar. Suddenly Argentina plummeted from being a first world nation on a par with the United States, to being a third world state, with a weak currency, and little hope of bolstering the economy. Huge numbers of Argentines lost their jobs, and many were forced into poverty and homelessness. The blow to the support of the United States, the British government launched a naval force to regain the islands.

The British reoccupation of the islands began on 21 May, attacking Argentine defensive positions around Port Stanley. They met stiff resistance, but most of the Argentine troops were conscripts, poorly trained, ill-equipped, and in the end no match for British forces. On 14 June Argentine forces surrendered. Argentines to this day have never forgotten the fierceness of the fighting. One event is particularly sensitive: the sinking of the *General Belgrano*. The Argentine cruiser had apparently drifted accidently into enemy waters, and while retreating, British forces attacked and sank the cruiser with a huge loss of life. It resulted in nearly half of the deaths of the entire conflict.

Casualties in the war outnumbered the small island population: 746 Argentines (over 300 on the *General Belgrano*) and 256 British soldiers were killed. The consequences of the war for Argentina were that the military government was discredited: perhaps less by defeat than by its obvious misjudgement, and by the accounts given by returning troops of incompetent leadership and lack of supplies. General Galtieri was replaced as president, and in 1983, Argentina returned to civilian rule. It was such a traumatic event in Argentina's recent history that almost every town and village has a monument to the war, and every year in Rosario the war is remembered in a large parade of veterans. In Buenos Aires the Malvinas monument is located at the base of Parque San Martín, almost at Retiro. In 2010, President Cristina Kirchner spoke of reclaiming the Malvinas, even going as far as seeking 'support' from China and other nations. There have been no new developments, although the 2011 Argentine Election may bring this issue to the fore once again.

Argentine psyche has been severe. Duhalde was the last of the quick succession of presidents, and he attempted to impose some order, appeasing the IMF by sacking a large number of public employees who were a considerable drain on public spending. However, corruption remained and street crime increased, with an alarming fashion for express kidnappings among the wealthier Buenos Aires families. Elections held in May 2003 threatened to return Menem to power, in a brief rush of nostalgia for the days of apparent prosperity. But fearing defeat, before a second election could be held Menem stepped down, and ex-governor of Santa Cruz province, Nestor Kirchner, came to power with a meagre 24% of the country's votes. He was not much liked throughout the country, particularly by landowners and farmers, since he raised taxes on exports to an absurd degree. While unemployment remained rife in Argentina, many criticized Kirchner for maintaining a dependency on Plan Trabajar, the government handout to the unemployed, which some feared was eroding the culture of work. In late 2007, elections were held and Nestor Kichner's wife Cristina Fernández de Kirchner ran for the presidency. She won with 41% of the country's vote. As Argentine presidents can only stand for two terms much like the US system, many people see the move as a way of extending Nestor's chance of holding on to power. In certain media outlets, Cristina has been labelled a puppet; a continuation of her husband's presidency. In any rate, she is the first elected female president in Argentina, and she even has her own webpage, www.cristina.com.ar. Since being elected, Christina has fallen in popularity due to increased taxes on the farming sector, and she has been unable to curb the worrying inflation or the apparent instability within the government. During the upcoming election it will be interesting to see the next political step that the country takes.

Population

With an estimated population of 36,000,000, the third largest in South America after Brazil and Colombia, Argentina is one of the least densely populated countries on the continent. Thirty six per cent of the population lives in the urban area of Gran Buenos Aires, leaving most of Patagonia, for example, with 2 sq km per inhabitant. In the province of Buenos Aires, people are mainly of European origin and the classic Argentine background is of Spanish and Italian immigrants. In Patagonia and the Lake District there's a considerable number of Scottish, Welsh, French, German and Swiss inhabitants, with Eastern Europeans to be found in the northeast of the country. In the northwestern provinces, at least half the population are indigenous, or of indigenous descent, mixed with a long line of *criollo* stock. Although *mestizos* (of mixed blood) form about 15% of the population of the whole country, the existence of different ethnic groups wasn't recognized until the mid-1990s. There are 13 indigenous groups, totalling about 500,000 people, 3% of the total population, many living in communities in the northwest, and scattered throughout the country. The largest minorities are the Toba (20%), the Wichi or Mataco (10%), the Mapuche (10%) and the Guaraní (10%). Several of the smaller groups are in danger of extinction: in 1987 the Minority Rights Group reported the death of the last Ona in Tierra del Fuego and noted that the 100 remaining Tehuelches were living on a reservation in southern Patagonia.

Immigration

The city of Buenos Aires and the surrounding province was transformed through immigration in the 19th century into a society of predominantly European origin. White immigration was encouraged by the 1853 Constitution and the new political stability after 1862 encouraged a great wave of settlers from Europe. Between 1857 and 1930 total immigration was over 6,000,000, almost all from Europe. About 55% of these were Italians, followed by Spaniards (26%), and then, far behind, groups of other Europeans and Latin Americans. British and North Americans generally came as stockbreeders, technicians and business executives. By 1895, 25% of the population of 4,000,000 were immigrants. Over 1,300,000 Italians settled in Argentina between 1876 and 1914. Their influence can be seen in the country's food, its urban architecture and its language, especially in Buenos Aires where the local vocabulary has incorporated *lunfardo,* a colourful slang of largely Italian origin, which started out as the language of thieves. Today it is estimated that 12.8% of the population are foreign born. The large influence on immigration nowadays comes from Bolivia and Paraguay.

Culture

Religion

Throughout Spanish America the Catholic Church played an important role in the conquest. From the start of the colonial period, Spanish control in South America was authorized by the Papacy; in return the colonial powers were to support the conversion of the indigenous population to Catholicism. This close identification of Church and state helps to explain why the main centres of Church power and activity were usually (though not always) close to the main centres of Spanish settlement. While present-day Argentina, a border territory on the outskirts of empire, was therefore of relatively minor importance to the Church hierarchy, it became a focus for work by missionary orders, particularly the Jesuits. Jesuit activity in Argentina was centred in two areas: around Córdoba, where they established a training college for the priesthood, and in Misiones and adjoining areas of present-day Paraguay and Brazil, where an extensive network of *reducciones* was set up to convert and 'protect' the indigenous population.

As in much of Spanish America, the Church lost most of its formal political power at independence. Although today over 90% of Argentines are officially Roman Catholics, the Church's political and social influence is much less significant than in neighbouring Chile or in most other South American countries. One reason for this is the introduction of a system of non-religious state schools in the 19th century. The great waves of immigration in the late 19th and early 20th centuries also affected the position of the Church; while the majority of immigrants were Catholics, significant minorities were not, including the large numbers of East European Jews and the Arab immigrants from Lebanon and Syria. Both of these communities have a strong presence especially in Buenos Aires; the largest mosque in South America was opened in the capital in September 2000 and there are estimated to be 800,000 Muslims in the country. Buenos Aires also has the eighth largest Jewish population in the world.

Yet the Catholic Church's power and influence should not be underestimated. The support of the Church hierarchy was important in bringing Perón to power in 1946 and the rift with the Church played a key role in the overthrow of the latter in 1955. The strongly conservative nature of the Catholic hierarchy became particularly apparent during the 1976-1983 military dictatorship; unlike its Chilean counterpart, the Argentine hierarchy was silent on the issue of human-rights violations and gave little support to relatives of the disappeared. According to *Nunca Más*, the official report on the disappeared, military chaplains attended some torture sessions and even assisted in the torture.

The lingering influence of the Church can be seen in several ways: the continuing legal ban on abortion (divorce was finally legalized in 1986) and gay marriage, and in the constitutional provision (removed in the 1994 amendments) that required the president to be a Catholic (and which necessitated President Carlos Menem's conversion).

As in some other parts of Latin America, this close identification of the Catholic Church with the state has, in recent years, provided opportunities for evangelical churches, including the Baptists and Mormons, to recruit followers, particularly among newcomers to the large cities.

Arts and crafts

All over Argentina you'll find fine handicrafts made by local indigenous groups, which vary widely all over the country, or by the continuing tradition of gaucho craftsmen, who make fine pieces associated with rural life.

Gaucho crafts

There's a strong tradition of working precious metals, such as silver, into fine belts and buckles, since the gaucho's way of carrying his wealth with him was originally in the ornate silver *rastras* and buckles which are still used today over leather belts, or to tie *fajas* (woven cloth belts). Silver spurs, stirrups and the fine silver decoration on saddles are all extraordinary examples of traditions dating from the early 18th century. The gaucho *facón*, an all-purpose knife used especially for cutting his *asado*, is made with an elaborately wrought silver handle, and the *mate* (the vessel itself, rather than the drink) which is often just a hollowed-out gourd, can also be an exquisitely worked piece of silver which you'd probably rather display than use. Associated objects with the same fine silverwork today include earrings, belt buckles and scarf rings. Leather was always important for making all the items associated with horses, and obviously widely available, and the complexity of the traditional bridles, belts and straps is impressive. Long thin strips of leather are woven into wide plaits, or *trensas*, and used still for all parts of horse bridlery, as well as more decorative pieces. The *mate* itself is made most traditionally from the gourd, but also from wood, tin, llama (a type of material that looks like silver) or silver, with attractive examples made by artisans in the Lake District at El Bolsón, for example.

Indigenous crafts

Argentina's many indigenous groups produce fine handicrafts, and in the northeast, the Guaraní produce woodwork, much of it inspired by the rich animal and bird life all around them. Delicate fabric for bags is woven from the tough fibrous strands of tree creepers, and there are necklaces made from seeds.

Handicrafts are richest in the northwest, particularly the Valles Calchaquíes, near the *puna* and along the Quebrada de Humahuaca, where there is abundant llama wool and vicuña, which is woven into *ponchos*, or knitted into jumpers, socks, scarves and hats. Brightly coloured woven textiles from Bolivia can also be found at many markets. The ubiquitous pan pipes are the most available examples of instruments from the rich Andean musical tradition, and can be found in abundance at Tilcara and Purmamarca markets. Ponchos are woven throughout the northwest but particularly fine examples can be found in the Valles Calchaquíes and around Salta, where the red ponchos of Güemes are made, and in western Catamarca province, where the finest ponchos of woven vicuña are made. You can also find beautiful woven wall hangings in the Valles Calchaquíes, often depicting scenes of churches in the valleys, and the local symbol, the ostrich-like *suri*. Wood from the giant *cardón* cactus is used for carving distinctive small objects and furniture, with the spines of the cactus leaving attractive slits in the wood.

In the Chaco region, bags are made from textile woven from *chaguar* fibre by Wichí, Toba, and other indigenous groups of the area, as they have done for hundreds of years. The Wichí also make fine wooden objects, animals mainly, from *palo santo*, a greenish scented wood, also used extensively in wood carving by communities that live along the Río Pilcomayo, which forms the border with Paraguay. In northeastern Salta, painted wooden masks are made by the Chané culture for use in traditional agricultural ceremonies. Isolated indigenous groups of Toba, Chané and Mataco in the lowlands to the east of the province produce exquisite carvings of birds and animals, using a variety of local woods. Cow bones are used to make the beaks and feet, as well as an inlay to decorate spoons and other utilitarian items. And *Palo santo* is also used for *mate* vessels, replacing the traditional gourd. Throughout the south, there are superb Mapuche weavings in natural wool colours with bold geometric designs.

Fine art and sculpture

Colonial art

Argentina (along with neighbouring Uruguay) is arguably the most European of Latin American cultures. Mass immigration and the 19th-century extermination of the few remaining indigenous people have created a mainstream culture, which defines itself largely in relation to Europe. The exception to this is in the northwest of the country, where Andean civilizations struggle to retain their identity against the irresistible tide of westernization and the tourist industry.

As the region, which is now Argentina, was initially of little importance to the Spanish, there is relatively little colonial art or architecture in most of the country. However, in the northern regions of Salta, Jujuy and Misiones, there are some impressive colonial buildings and some good examples of colonial painting, especially the remarkable portraits of archangels in military uniform in the churches at Uquía and Casabindo, as well as some exquisite golden retables and pulpits in the churches of the Quebrada de Humahuaca. Yavi, at the very north, is the most remarkable of all these, with a golden sculpture of an angel in military uniform, and beautiful ceramic cherubs on the golden pulpit. Fine colonial art can be seen at the Museo de Arte Hispanoamericano Isaac Fernández Blanco in Buenos Aires. In Misiones, there are several sites with remains of Jesuits missions – particularly impressive is that at San Ignacio. Córdoba province too has remains of Jesuit churches and residences at Santa Catalina and Jesús María.

The 19th century

In the 19th century, as Argentina gained independence and consolidated itself as a modern nation, the ruling elite of the country were determined to make Argentine culture as close to European as possible, against what they saw as the 'barbarism' of indigenous customs. The prosperous Buenos Aires bourgeoisie commissioned European architects to build their mansions and collected European fine and decorative arts to decorate them. Rich Argentines travelled to Europe to buy paintings, and gradually began to demand that European painters come to Argentina to depict the wealth and elegance of the ruling class through portraits and landscapes. The most famous foreign artist was Carlos Enrique Pellegrini, whose fine society portraits can be seen in the Museo Nacional de Bellas Artes in Buenos Aires.

By the middle of the century, as Argentina became more politically stable, a new generation of Argentine-trained artists appeared in Buenos Aires. They absorbed some of the techniques and interests of the European artists who were the first to depict their country, but they also discovered a new interest in Romanticism and Realism. Most famous in this period was Prilidiano Pueyrredón (1823-1870), whom many Argentines consider to be their first national painter. Of more obvious appeal is the rather eccentric Cándido López (1839-1902) whose work has only recently been re-evaluated. López followed the Argentine army to the north of the country during the wars with Paraguay and Uruguay, where he depicted the great battles in a characteristic naïve style. López left behind a remarkable series of paintings, which are often displayed in the Museo Nacional de Bellas Artes in Buenos Aires. By the end of the century, many artists who had been through the National Art School were working in Argentina. Generally speaking, they absorbed European movements decades after they appeared in their original forms. Benito Quinquela Martín's work celebrated the workers in the dockyards of La Boca, in a colourful naïve style, and his paintings can be seen in the gallery bearing his name in La Boca.

The 20th century

In the 20th century, Argentina really found its artistic expression; the dynamism, size and mix of nationalities in the capital created a complex urban society in which artists and intellectuals have prospered. Some of the Bohemian attraction of Buenos Aires can still be felt in its more intellectual cafés and districts. This cultural effervescence has been at the expense of the regions; the capital totally dominates the country, and most artists are forced to move there to have any chance of success.

The first avant-garde artistic movement in Buenos Aires emerged in 1924 with the formation of a group which called itself 'Martín Fierro', in homage to the national epic poem of the same name. This group brought together a small number of upper-class intellectuals, the most famous of which was the writer Jorge Luis Borges. The most important visual artist was Xul Solar (1887-1963), who illustrated many of Borges' texts. Solar was one of the 20th century's most eccentric and engaging artists. He had a great interest in mysticism and the occult, and tried to create an artistic system to express his complex beliefs, mostly small-scale watercolours in which a sometimes-bizarre visionary world is depicted. Many of them are covered in inscriptions in one of the languages he himself created: Neo-Creole or Pan-Lengua. During the final decades of his life Solar lived in a house on the Paraná Delta near Tigre, where he created a total environment in accordance with his fantastic world, even inventing a new game of chess with rules based on astrology. There is now a Xul Solar Museum in the house where he was born in Buenos Aires and where many of his watercolours and objects are displayed.

Intellectual life in the 1920s was divided into two factions, each named after districts in the city. The elegant Calle Florida gave its name to the Martín Fierro set, which belonged to the elite. Several blocks away, the working-class Boedo district gave its name to a school of working-class socialist artists who rejected the rarefied atmosphere of Florida in favour of socially critical paintings in a grim realistic style. Possibly the most important artist associated with this group was Antonio Berni (1905-1981), whose colourful paintings give a vivid impression of Buenos Aires working-class life, and are in the Museo de Bellas Artes and MALBA in Buenos Aires.

In the 1940s, with the political crisis provoked by the Second World War, a new avant-garde movement emerged to overtake the Martín Fierro group. In the mid-1940s, a group of young artists founded an abstract art movement called 'Madí' which attempted to combine sophisticated abstract art inspired by Russian Constructivism with a more chaotic sense of fun. Madí works are characterized by blocks of bright colours within an irregular frame often incorporating physical movement within the structure of the work. As such, they are somewhere between painting and sculpture. For the first time in Argentina, Madí developed artistic principles (such as the irregular frame, or the use of neon gas) before the rest of the world.

Madí was a short-lived adventure plagued by infighting amongst its members and political divisions. The cultural climate under Perón (1946-1955) rejected this type of 'decadent' art in favour of a form of watered-down populism. It was not until the 1960s that cultural life regained its momentum.

The 1960s were a golden age for the arts in Argentina. As in many countries, the decade brought new freedom to young people, and the art scene responded vigorously. Artistic activity was focused around the centre of Buenos Aires between Plaza San Martín and Avenida Córdoba, an area known as the 'manzana loca' (crazy block). This area contained a huge number of galleries and cafés, and most importantly the Di Tella Institute, a privately funded art centre that was at the cutting edge of visual arts. Artistic movements of the time ranged from a raw expressionism called 'Nueva Figuración' to very sophisticated conceptual art. The most provocative form of art during this period took the form of 'happenings', one of the most famous of which (by Marta MinuJln) consisted of a replica of the Buenos Aires obelisk made in sweet bread, which was then eaten by passers-by.

After the military coup of 1966 the authorities began to question the activities of these young artists and even tried to censor some exhibitions. The Di Tella Institute closed, leaving the 'manzana loca' without a heart, and making it more dangerous for alternative young artists to live without harassment (often for little more than having long hair). During the 'leaden years' of the military government during the 1970s, there was little space for alternative art and many left-wing artists abandoned art in favour of direct political action. However, one space in Buenos Aires continued to show politically challenging art: the Centro de Arte y Comunicación (or CAYC), often through works that were so heavily coded that the authorities would not pick up the message.

Since the restoration of democracy in 1983, Argentina has been coming to terms with the destruction or inefficiency of many of its cultural institutions over recent decades. The last few years have seen a rebirth of activity, with improvements in the National Museum of Fine Arts and the creation of the important Centro Cultural Recoleta and more recently the Centro Cultural Jorge Luis Borges and many others. There are important alternative art centres, especially the Ricardo Rojas Centre and the Klemm Foundation, which show some of the most interesting young artists. The art scene in Buenos Aires is very vibrant, with a myriad of conflicting and apparently contradictory styles and tendencies. For information on exhibitions and local artists see http://artistasdebuenosaires.blogspot.com, an arts blog which started in 2004 (in Spanish) and www.whatsupbuenosaires.com (in English).

Literature

Modern Argentina has an extremely high literacy rate, around 95%, and even in small country towns there are good bookshops, and some really splendid librerías in Buenos Aires. Correspondingly, the country has produced some great writers, quite apart from the wonderful Borges, and it is well worth reading some of their work before you come, or seeking out a few novels to bring on your travels.

With an urban culture derived almost entirely from European immigrants, Argentina's literary development was heavily influenced by European writers in the 19th century, the works of Smith, Locke, Voltaire and Rousseau among others being inspiration for the small literate elite of young intellectuals, such as Mariano Moreno (1778-1811), one of the architects of the independence movement. The great theme was how to adapt

European forms to American realities, first in the form of political tracts and later in early nationalist poetry. Outside the cities, popular culture thrived on storytelling and the music of the gauchos, whose famous *payadores* are superbly evocative. They recount lively and dramatic stories of love, death and the land, in poetic couplets to a musical background, with an ornate and inventive use of words (see Music, below). Gaucho poets, like medieval *troubadours*, would travel from settlement to settlement, to country fairs and cattle round-ups, singing of the events of the day and of the encroaching political constraints that would soon bring restrictions to their traditional way of life.

The theme of Argentine identity has been a constant through the country's development and remains a burning issue today. While many writers looked to Europe for inspiration, others were keen to distance themselves from the lands they had come from and to create a new literature, reflecting Argentina's own concerns. The extremes within the country further challenge attempts at creating a single unified identity: the vast stretches of inhospitable and uninhabited land, the vast variety of landscapes and peoples, and the huge concentration of population in a capital that little resembles any other part of the country. These conflicts were clearly expressed in 1845 by politician Domingo Faustino Sarmiento (1811-1888): *Facundo: Civilization and Barbarism*. This was the most important tract of the generation, and became one of the key texts of Argentine cultural history. Strongly opposed to the Federalist Rosas, Sarmiento's allegorical biography of gaucho *Facundo* laments the ungovernably large size of the country which allows *caudillos* like Quiroga and Rosas to dominate. For Sarmiento, the only solution was education and he looked to what he perceived to be the democracy of North America for inspiration.

With the attempt to consolidate the nation state in the aftermath of independence Esteban Echeverría (1805-1851) played a leading role in these debates through literary salons, in poetry and in short fiction. Other memorable protest literature against the Rosas regime included Echeverría's *El Matadero* (The Slaughterhouse, published posthumously in 1871) and José Mármol's melodramatic novel of star-crossed lovers battling against the cut-throat hordes of Rosas, *Amalia* (1855).

The consolidation of Argentina along the lines advocated by Sarmiento and the growth of the export economy in alliance with British capital and technology may have benefited the great landowners of the Littoral provinces. But those who did not fit into this dream of modernity – in particular the gaucho groups turned off the land and forced to work as rural labourers – found their protest articulated by a provincial landowner, José Hernández (1834-1886). He wrote the famous gaucho epic poems *El Gaucho Martín Fierro* (1872) and its sequel, *La Vuelta de Martín Fierro* (The Return of Martín Fierro, 1879). The first part of *Martín Fierro* is most definitely the most famous Argentine literary work and is a genuine shout of rage against the despotic *caudillos* and corrupt authorities, which disrupt local communities and traditional ways of life. Framed as a gauchesque song, chanted by the appealing hero and dispossessed outlaw, it became one of the most popular works of literature, and *Martín Fierro* came to symbolize the spirit of the Argentine nation.

As a small group of families led the great export boom, the 'gentleman' politicians of the 'Generation of 1880' wrote their memoirs, none better than Sarmiento's *Recuerdos de Provincia* (Memoirs of Provincial Life, 1850). As Buenos Aires grew into a dynamic modern city, the gentleman memorialist soon gave way to the professional writer. The key poet in this respect was the Nicaraguan Rubén Darío (1867-1916), who lived for an important period of his creative life in Buenos Aires and led a movement called *modernismo* which asserted the separateness of poetry as a craft, removed from the dictates of national panegyric or political necessity. It was Darío who would give inspiration to the poet Leopoldo Lugones (1874-1938), famous also for his prose writings on nationalist gauchesque themes. Lugones's evocation of the gaucho as a national symbol would be developed in the novel *Don Segundo Sombra* by Ricardo Güiraldes (1886-1927), the story of a boy taught the skills for life by a gaucho mentor.

The early 20th century

The complex urban societies evolving in Argentina by the turn of the century created a rich cultural life. In the 1920s a strong vanguard movement developed which questioned the dominant literary orthodoxies of the day. Little magazines such as *Martín Fierro* (another appropriation of the ubiquitous national symbol) proclaimed novelty in poetry and attacked the dull social-realist writings of their rivals the Boedo group. Argentina's most famous writer, Jorge Luis Borges (1899-1986) began his literary life as an avant-garde poet in the company of writers such as Oliverio Girondo (1891-1967) and Norah Lange (1906-1972). Many of these poets were interested in expressing the dynamism and changing shape of their urban landscape, Buenos Aires, this Paris on the periphery. You can explore Borges' haunts in Buenos Aires with a free tour organized by the tourist office: ask in their information centres for dates and times. Roberto Arlt also caught the dreams and nightmares of the urban underclasses in novels such as *El Juguete Rabioso* (The Rabid Toy, 1926) and *Los Siete Locos* (The Seven Madmen, 1929).

Much of the most interesting literature of the 1930s and 1940s was first published in the literary journal *Sur*, founded by the aristocratic writer, Victoria Ocampo. By far the most important group to publish in its pages were Borges and his close friends Silvina Ocampo (1903-1993), Victoria's sister, and Silvina's husband, Adolfo Bioy Casares (1914-1999) who, from the late 1930s, in a series of short fictions and essays, transformed the literary world. They had recurrent concerns: an indirect style, a rejection of realism and nationalist symbols, the use of the purified motifs and techniques of detective fiction and fantastic literature, the quest for knowledge to be found in elusive books, the acknowledgement of literary criticism as the purest form of detective fiction and the emphasis on the importance of the reader rather than the writer.

Peronism and literature

In the 10-year period of Perón's first two presidencies, 1946-1955, there was a deliberate assault on the aristocratic, liberal values that had guided Argentina since 1800. Claiming to be a new synthesis of democracy, nationalism, anti-imperialism and industrial development, Peronism attacked the undemocratic, dependent Argentine elite (personified in such literary figures as Victoria Ocampo or Adolfo Bioy Casares). This period was seen by most intellectuals and writers as an era of cultural darkness. Some writers such as Julio Cortázar (1914-1984) – a writer of elegant fantastic and realist stories – chose voluntary exile rather than remain in Perón's Argentina. The much-loved novelist, Ernesto Sábato (1911-) who later confronted the *Proceso*, set his best novel *Sobre Héroes y Tumbas* (On Heroes and Tombs, 1961) partly in the final moments of the Peronist regime, when the tensions of the populist alliance were beginning to become manifest. (His novella *El Túnel* is also an interesting read). But Perón was not much interested in the small circulation of literature and concentrated his attention on mass forms of communication such as radio and cinema. This period saw further mature work from the poets Enrique Molina (1910-1997), Olga Orozco (1922-1999) and Alberto Girri (1919-1991), whose austere, introspective verse was an antidote to the populist abuse of language in the public sphere. The literary field was to be further stimulated after the downfall of Perón with the development of publishing houses and the 'boom' of Latin American literature of the 1960s.

The 1960s
In Argentina the 1960s was a decade of great literary and cultural effervescence. The novel to capture this mood was Cortázar's *Rayuela* (Hopscotch, 1963), which served as a Baedeker of the new, with its comments on literature, philosophy, new sexual freedoms and its open, experimental structure. It was promoted in a weekly journal *Primera Plana*, which also acted as a guide to expansive modernity. Thousands of copies of *Rayuela* were sold to an expanded middle-class readership in Argentina and throughout Latin America. Other novelists and writers benefited from these conditions, the most significant being the Colombian Gabriel García Márquez (1928-), who published what would later become one of the best-selling novels of the 20th century, *Cien Años de Soledad* (One Hundred Years of Solitude, 1967), with an Argentine publishing house. Significant numbers of women writers helped to break the male monopoly of literary production, including the novelists Beatriz Guido (1922-1988) and Marta Lynch (1925-1985) and the poet Alejandra Pizarnik (1936-1972).

Literature and dictatorship
The 'swinging' sixties were curtailed by a military coup in 1966. In the years that followed, Argentine political life descended into anarchy, violence and repression. As a result, virtually all forms of cultural activity were silenced and well known writers, including Haroldo Conti (1925-1976) and Rodolfo Walsh (1927-1977), 'disappeared'. Many more had to seek exile including the poet Juan Gelman, whose son and daughter-in-law counted among the disappeared.

Understandably this nightmare world provided the dominant themes of the literary output of these years. The return in old age of Perón, acclaimed by all shades of the political spectrum, was savagely lampooned in Osvaldo Soriano's (1943-1998) novel *No Habrá Más Penas ni Olvido* (A Funny, Dirty Little War, completed in 1975 but only published in 1982). The world of the sombre designs of the ultra right-wing López Rega, Isabel Perón's Minister of Social Welfare, is portrayed in Luisa Valenzuela's (1938-) terrifying, grotesque novel *Cola de lagartija* (The Lizard's Tail, 1983). Of the narrative accounts of those black years, none is more harrowing than Miguel Bonasso's (1940-) fictional documentary of the treatment of the Montoneros guerrilla group in prison and in exile: *Recuerdo de la Muerte* (Memory of Death, 1984). Other writers in exile chose more indirect ways of dealing with the terror and dislocation of those years. Daniel Moyano (1928-1992), in exile for many years in Spain, wrote elegant allegories such as *El Vuelo del Tigre* (The Flight of the Tiger, 1981), which tells of the military-style takeover of an Andean village by a group of percussionists who bring cacophony.

Within Argentina, critical discussion was kept alive in literary journals such as *Punto de Vista* (1978) and certain novels alluded to the current political climate within densely structured narratives. Ricardo Piglia's (1941-) *Respiración Artificial* (Artificial Respiration, 1980) has disappearance and exile as central themes, alongside bravura discussions of the links between fiction and history and between Argentina and Europe.

The return to civilian rule

Following Alfonsín's election victory in 1983, the whole intellectual and cultural field responded to the new freedoms. Certain narratives depicted in harsh realism the brutalities of the 'Dirty War' waged by the military and it was the novelist, Ernesto Sábato, who headed the Commission set up to investigate the disappearances. He wrote in the prologue to the Commission's report *Nunca más* (Never Again, 1984): "We are convinced that the recent military dictatorship brought about the greatest and most savage tragedy in the history of Argentina".

Current literature echoes the famous lines by Borges in the essay *The Argentine Writer and Tradition* (1951): "I believe that we Argentines ... can handle all European themes, handle them without superstition, with an irreverence which can have, and already does have, fortunate consequences." While many of the writers that first brought modernity to Argentine letters have died – Borges, Victoria and Silvina Ocampo, Girri, Cortázar, Puig – the later generations have assimilated their lessons. Juan Carlos Martini (1944-) wrote stylish thrillers, blending high and low culture. Juan José Saer (1937-2005), from his self-imposed exile in Paris, recreated his fictional world, Colastiné, in the city of Santa Fe, in narratives that are complex, poetic discussions on memory and language. The most successful novel of recent years is Tomás Eloy Martínez's (1934-2010) *Santa Evita* (1995) which tells/reinvents the macabre story of what happened to Evita's embalmed body between 1952 and the mid-1970s. The narrative skilfully discusses themes that are at the heart of all writing and critical activity. The critic, like the embalmer of Evita's body, "seeks to fix a life or a body in the pose that eternity should remember it by". But what this critic, like the narrator of Eloy Martínez's novel, realizes is that a corpus of literature cannot be fixed in that way, for literature escapes such neat pigeonholes. Instead, glossing Oscar Wilde, the narrator states "that the only duty that we have to history is to rewrite it". The ending of the novel makes the point about the impossibility of endings: "Since then, I have rowed with words, carrying Santa Evita in my boat, from one shore of the blind world to the other. I don't know where in the story I am. In the middle, I believe, I've been here in the middle for a long time. Now I must write again". (*Santa Evita*, New York and London, 1996, page 369.) See Books, page 700, for recommended reading.

Music

Tango is the country's most prominent and most exported musical form, but by no means its only means of musical expression. The traditional music which binds almost the whole country is *folclore* (pronounced *folc-LAW-ray*), whose stirring rhythms and passionate singing can be found in varying forms throughout the northern half of the country. Superb music is produced in the north, in the Andean region of Salta and Jujuy. And home-grown Rock Nacional is the country's main strand of pop music, successfully fending off North American and European competition throughout the 1980s and 1990s to form a distinctive sound.

Tango

If your trip to Argentina includes any time in Buenos Aires, you'll undoubtedly see some tango – probably danced on the streets of Florida or San Telmo, though it's much more than a tourist attraction. Testimony to the enduring success of the music among Argentines are the radio stations that only play tango, and the *milongas* (dance clubs) filled with young people learning the old steps.

Although also sung and played, the tango was born as a dance just before the turn of the 20th century. The exact moment of birth was not recorded by any contemporary observer and continues to be a matter of debate, though the roots can be traced. The name 'Tango' predates the dance and was given to the carnivals (and dances) of the local inhabitants of the Río de la Plata in the early 19th century, elements of this tradition being taken over by settlers as the local population declined. However, the name 'Tango Americano' was also given to the Habanera (a Cuban descendant of the English country dance) which became all the rage in Spain and bounced back into the Río de la Plata in the middle of the 19th century, not only as a fashionable dance together with the polka, mazurka, waltz and cuadrille but also as a song form in the very popular 'Zarzuelas', or Spanish operettas. However, the Habanera led not a double, but a triple life, by also infiltrating the lowest levels of society directly from Cuba via sailors who arrived in the ports of Montevideo and Buenos Aires. Here it encountered the Milonga, originally a gaucho song style, but by 1880 a dance, especially popular with the so-called 'Compadritos' and 'Orilleros', who frequented the port area and its brothels, whence the Argentine Tango emerged around the turn of the century to dazzle the populace with its brilliant, personalized footwork, which could not be accomplished without the partners staying glued together.

As a dance tango became exceedingly popular and, as the infant recording industry grew in leaps and bounds, it also became popular as a song and an instrumental genre, with the original violins and flutes being eclipsed by the *bandoneón* button accordion, then being imported from Germany. In 1911 the new dance took Paris by storm, thanks to the performance of the dance in a Paris salon by Argentine writer Ricardo Güiraldes, one of a group of aristocrats who enjoyed frequenting the dives where tango was popular. As soon as it was the fashion in Paris, it returned triumphant to Buenos Aires, achieving both respectability and notoriety, and becoming a global phenomenon after the First World War. Actor Rudolph Valentino helped the image of the dance, when his 1926 movie *The Four Horsemen of the Apocalypse* included a tango scene.

But it was Carlos Gardel (1887-1935), Argentina's most loved tango legend, whose mellifluous voice brought popularity to the music of tango, and whose poor background made him a hero for the working classes too. Tango has always been an expression of the poor and of social and political developments in the country. Incredibly, Gardel recorded over 900 songs and was a huge success in many movies. *The Tango on Broadway* (1934) was his biggest success. Today you will still see his image on everything from posters to ice-cream shops, and people still dance to his voice. After Gardel's tragic death in 1935, tango slumped a little, frowned upon by the military regime who considered it subversive. Its resurgence in the 1940s was assisted by Perón's decree that 50% of all music played on the radio must be Argentine. Great stars of this era include the brilliant *bandoneón* player Aníbal Troilo, whose passionate and tender playing made him much loved among a wide audience. In the 1950s, tango again declined, replaced in popularity by rock'n'roll. It had become increasingly the preserve of middle class and intellectual circles, with the emphasis on nostalgia in its themes. But its next innovator and star was Astor Piazzolla (1921-1992), who had played with Troilo's orchestra, and who went on to fuse tango with jazz to create a tango for listening, as well as dancing. Threatened by the military government in the 1970s Piazzollla escaped to Paris, but his success was already international, and his experimental arrangements opened up the possibilities for other fusions. However, in the past thirty years it has made a resurgence and is once again popular with young people in Argentine bars and cafés and it has become a popular dance throughout the rest of the world. A new genre of tango music has arisen which mixes traditional themes with electronica, and groups like The Gotan Project are now world-renowned. All over Buenos Aires, and all over the province, you can find dance classes where the classic moves are taught, followed by a dance or *milonga* where couples, young and old, breathe life into the steps. Part of its attraction, perhaps, is that in the world of tango, men are allowed to be macho and seductive, while their women are required to be sensitive to the subtlety of their next move. Unlike salsa, for example, tango is a dance of repressed passion. Try a class, at least once, while you're in Argentina, to get a feel for the dance from the inside. And then, if you can afford it, see the expert dancers' dextrous footwork at a show such as *El Viejo Almácen* in San Telmo.

Folclore

Beyond Buenos Aires, the dominant musical traditions can be broadly described as *folclore*. This takes various forms over the north of the country, with the finest examples in Salta, but all the northern provinces have a very rich and attractive heritage of folk dances, mainly for couples, with arms held out and fingers clicked or handkerchiefs waved, with the '*Paso Valseado*' as the basic step. The slow and stately Zamba is descended from the Zamacueca, and therefore a cousin of the Chilean Cueca and Peruvian Marinera, where the handkerchief is used to greatest effect. Equally popular throughout most of the country are the faster Gato, Chacarera and Escondido. These are the dances of the gaucho and their rhythm evokes that of a cantering horse with wonderfully stirring syncopation. Guitar and the *bombo* drum provide the accompaniment. Particularly spectacular is the Malambo, where the gaucho shows off his dextrous footwork, creating a complex rhythm using the heels of his boots, alternating with percussion created by whirling the hard balls of the *boleadoras* into the ground, with the spurs of his boots adding a steely note to the rhythm.

Different regions of the country have their own specialities. The music of Cuyo in the west is sentimental and very similar to that of neighbouring Chile, with its Cuecas for dance and Tonadas for song. The northwest on the other hand is Andean, with its musical culture closer to that of Bolivia, particularly on the *puna*, where the indigenous groups play haunting wind instruments, the *quena*, and sound mournful notes on the great long *erke*, evocative of huge mountain landscapes. Here the dances are Bailecitos and Carnavalitos, depending on the time of year. Exquisitely beautiful and mournful songs – the extraordinary high-pitched *Bayualas* – are sung to the banging of a simple drum. And everyone, from children to grandmothers, can quote you a *copla*: two lines of rhymed verse expressing love or a witty joke. Tomás Lipan's music is worth seeking out, especially his *Cautivo de Amor*. Andean bands use the *sikus* (pan pipes) and *charango* (miniature guitar) to create ethereal and festive music which reflects the seasons of the rural calendar. In the northeast provinces of Corrientes and Misiones, the music shares cultural similarities with Paraguay. The *Polca* and *Galopa* are danced and the local *Chamamé* is sung, to the accordion or the harp, in sentimental style. Santiago del Estero has exerted the strongest influence on Argentine folk music as a result of the work of Andres Chazarreta: it is the heartland of the Chacarera and the lyrics are often part-Spanish and part-Quichua, a local dialect of the Andean Quechua language. Listen, too, to Los Caravajal, and Los Hermanos Abalos. Down in the province of Buenos Aires you are more likely to hear the gauchos singing their Milongas, Estilos and Cifras and challenging each other to a Payada or rhymed duel – protest songs and wonderfully romantic and witty stories to guitar accompaniment. Seek out Atahualpa Yupangui's *El Payador Persguido*.

Argentina experienced a great *folclore* revival in the 1950s and 1960s and some of the most celebrated groups are still drawing enthusiastic audiences today. These groups include Los Chalchaleros and Los Fronterizos, the perennial virtuoso singer and guitarist, Eduardo Falú and, more recently, León Gieco from Santa Fe. Most famous of all, though, is the superb Mercedes Sosa, whose rich voice articulated much of the sorrow and joy of the last 30 years in a brilliant series of albums, which also include the most popular *folclore* songs. Start with *The Best of Mercedes Sosa*. Also listen to Ariel Ramírez, a famous singer and pianist whose moving *Misa Criolla* is among his best known work. The *cuartetos* of Córdoba, popular since the 1940s with the characteristic dance in a huge circle, can best be sampled in the much-loved records of Carlos 'La Mona' Jiménez.

Rock Nacional

The great stars of Rock Nacional are still much listened to. The movement started in the 1960s with successful bands Los Gatos and Almendra, whose songwriter Luis Alberto Spinetta later became a successful solo artist. But the Rock Nacional found its real strength in expressing unspeakable protests during the military dictatorship from 1976-1983. Charly García, who was a member of the enormously successful band Sui Generis, captured popular feeling with his song *No Te Dejes Desanimar* (Don't be Discouraged), which roused mass opposition amongst young people against the atrocities of the *Proceso*. Inevitably, the military regime cottoned on to this form of subversive behaviour and stopped rock concerts, so that many bands had given up performing by the end of the 1970s. However, the rock movement survived, and the cynical lyrics of Fito Páez in *Tiempos Difíciles* and Charly García in *Dinosaurios* remain as testimonies to that time, and guaranteed them subsequent success. Once democracy had returned, music became more lightweight with likeable output from Los Abuelos de la Nada and Patricio Rey y sus Redonditos de Ricota, Soda Stereo (one of the most significant bands of the 1980s and they are still popular today) and also the work of Fito Páez who has continued to record and whose album *El Amor Después del Amor* was a success across Latin America. Los Fabulosis Cadillacs and Andrés Calamaro also made some great records, and Charly García continues, undiminished in popularity.

Cinema

Argentina's cinema is one of its liveliest art forms and it has enjoyed a recent renaissance with some brilliant films being made, more in the European or *auteur* tradition, than in Hollywood style. With a couple of worldwide successes and most recently an Oscar for Best Foreign Film with *El Secreto de Tus Ojos* (The Secret of Your Eyes, 2009), Argentine cinema is making its mark on the world stage. Watching a couple of Argentine films is certainly one of the best ways of tapping into the country's culture before you arrive.

In 1922, Buenos Aires had some 27,000,000 film-goers each year and 128 movie theatres, the largest being the Grand Splendid which seated 1350 people. By 1933 there were 1608 cinemas throughout Argentina, with 199 in the capital. However, the taste of the cinema-going public was for Hollywood movies. Hollywood has dominated the screens in Latin America for the first hundred years of film history, averaging some 90% of viewing time in Argentina.

However, in the 1950s, New Argentine Cinema started as a movement of independent films which offered a far more honest and accurate reflection of life in the country. Film clubs and journals created a climate of awareness of film as an art form and the tenets of Italian neo-realism and the *'politique des auteurs'* of *Cahiers du Cinéma* provided alternatives to the studio-based Hollywood system. In Argentina, Leopoldo Torre Nilsson (1924-1978) explored aristocratic decadence and his early film *La Casa del Angel* (The House of the Angel, 1957) was greeted with praise all over the world. Fernando Birri (1925-) used neo-realist principles to explore the hidden realities of Argentina. His film school in Santa Fe made an important documentary about young shanty town children, *Tire Dié* (Throw us a Dime, 1957) and helped pioneer a more flexible, socially committed, cinema.

Younger film makers of the 1960s like Manuel Antín (1926-), David Kohon (1929-2004) and Leonardo Favio (1938-) explored themes such as middle-class alienation or the sexual rites of the youth, set in the cafés and streets of Buenos Aires. Meanwhile, the growing climate of revolutionary sentiment of the late 1960s was reflected in Solanas's *La Hora de los Hornos* (The Hour of the Furnaces, 1966-1968), a key work of populist radicalism.

After a brief spell of radical optimism in the late 1960s and early 1970s, reflected in a number of other nationalist-populist movies, the dream of the second coming of Perón turned into the nightmare that led to the brutal military takeover in March 1976. The spiralling violence affected film-makers as much as artists in any other sector and saw key industry figures threatened and, in some cases, forced into exile. Heavily censored imports, limp comedies and musicals became the norm, the only beneficiaries being foreign producers and distributors. Film-makers such as Solanas, who went into exile, found it difficult to adapt to the new conditions and remained in a cultural wilderness. Within Argentina, the tight military control began to slacken in the early 1980s and some important films were made, including María Luisa Bemberg's (1922-1995) *Señora de Nadie* (Nobody's Woman, 1982) which premiered the day before the invasion of the Falklands/Malvinas.

With the return to civilian rule in 1983, the Radical government abolished censorship and put two well known film-makers in charge of the National Film Institute, Manuel Antín and Ricardo Wullicher (1948-). Antín's granting of credits to young and established directors and his internationalist strategy had an immediate effect. For several years there was a great flowering of talent, a development that would only be halted temporarily by the economic difficulties of the late 1980s. The trade paper *Variety* (25 March 1987) commented on this new effervescence, "Never before has there been such a mass of tangible approval as in the years since democratic rule returned at the end of 1983". In 1986, the Hollywood Academy granted the first Oscar for an Argentine picture, *La Historia Oficial* (The Official History) directed by Luis Puenzo (1946-), which dealt with the recent traumas of the disappearances of the 'Dirty War', but in rather sentimental Hollywood terms. This followed the massive box office success of Bemberg's *Camila*, which commented by analogy on the same subject. Solanas' two films about exile and the return to democracy, *Tangos, el Exilio de Gardel* (Tangos: the Exile of Gardel, 1985) and *Sur* (South, 1988), both offer interesting insights in Solanas' idiosyncratic poetic style. Puenzo, Bemberg and Solanas remained the most visible directors in the 1980s and 1990s, but dozens of other directors made movies in a range of different styles. Lita Stantic made perhaps the most complex film about the 'Dirty War' of the military regime, the superb *Un Muro de Silencio* (A Wall of Silence, 1993). This was a success with the critics, but was ignored by the public who preferred to view politics and repression through a gauze of melodrama and rock music, as in Marcelo Piñeyro's *Tango Feroz* (1993).

Argentine cinema has undergone a revival in the last few years, but the hard economic fact remains that by far the vast majority of screens in the country show Hollywood films, and home-grown movies have to compete in very commercial terms. However, the Oscar nomination of Argentine film *El Hijo de la Novia* (Son of the Bride) in 2002 boosted national self confidence, and was a big success within Argentina. Its anti-hero Ricardo Darín also starred in Fabiano Belinski's sophisticated heist movie *Neuve Reinas* (Nine Queens, 2000), which through a labyrinth of tricks and scams neatly articulates a Buenos Aires where no one can trust anyone. It was a huge success worldwide as well as in the country, and the death of Bielinsky following his second film, *El Aura*, was a tragic loss to Argentine cinema.

Successes of the new Argentine cinema included a return to cinema with a social conscience in Adrián Gaetano's *Bolivia*, addressing the sorry plight of an illegal Bolivian worker in urban Argentina, and his *Un Oso Rojo* (Red Bear, 2002) charting the fate of a newly released prisoner trying to reclaim the affection of his daughter from his wife's new boyfriend. Pablo Trapero's *Mundo Grua* (1999) is a stark but touching portrayal of the life of a crane driver, while Lisandro Alonso's astonishing *Libertad* shows with utter honesty the life of a peon on an *estancia*. In Luis Ortega's charming *Caja Negra* (2004) a young woman's relationship with her outcast father and eccentric ancient grandmother is explored with great humour and compassion. Two of the most striking films of recent years are *Pizza, Birra, Faso* (Pizza, Beer, Cigarettes, 1998) by Stagnaro and Gaetano, and *No Quiero Volver a Casa* (I Don't Want to Return Home, 2001) by Albertina Carri. Lucrecia Martel showed an original voice in her disturbing *La Cienaga* (The Swamp, 2001), a vivid portrayal of a divided family's unhappy summer in their country house. Highly allegorical and rich in atmospheric detail, it's a wonderful contemporary portrait. Her *La Niña Santa* (Holy Girl, 2004) was less successful. The fact is that even now Argentine cinema continues to perform better abroad than it does at home. Remembering the stuffy films of yesteryear, the cinema-going public opts now for the Hollywood fare that dominates the multiplexes up and down the country. Despite state subsidies and a cinema law that levies a 10% tax on every cinema ticket sold, there is still not a big enough domestic market for the films to break even and film-makers are increasingly forced to look abroad for investors. The hope is that other home-grown titles can have such a broad popular appeal, if only to sustain the talent that lies beneath.

Most cinemas in the country show Hollywood movies, but the larger cities have an art house cinema, and if you happen to be around during any of the film festivals, you can usually catch a few recent Argentine releases: Mar del Plata Film Festival in mid-March; Buenos Aires film festival in mid-April; and Salta's film festival in the first week of December.

Spectator sports

It is said that sport came to Argentina through the port of Buenos Aires, brought first by British sailors, who played football on vacant lots near the port watched by curious locals who would later make it their national passion.

Football is out on its own, both in terms of participation and as a spectator sport, with the country being passionately divided between fans of River Plate and Boca Juniors. In second place comes motor racing. The legend of Juan Manuel Fangio in the 1950s is still very much alive and well. Tennis is increasingly popular, especially since there are several successful Argentine tennis players, headed up by Cordobian David Nalbandian and Juan del Potro from Tandil. Basketball and volleyball are both popular participation

The Greatest Gardener in Buenos Aires

Next time you look up at the trees along Buenos Aires' streets, or the next time enjoy the parks of some of Argentina's most important towns, spare a thought for French architect and landscaper Jean Charles Thays. Known as the 'greatest gardener in Buenos Aires', Thays played a large role in 'greening' Argentina by designing botanical gardens, parks and the odd estancia all around the country. Born in France in 1849, he had a successful career as principal assistant to leading landscape architect Édouard André until, on his master's advice, he set sail for Argentina for a short visit at the age of 40. He never left and spent the rest of his life designing and remodelling most of Argentina's green spaces, including the botanical gardens and most of the parks. He also built stylized gardens in local hospitals and other public buildings, and planted over 150,000 trees in the streets of Buenos Aires. Not satisfied with just the capital, Thays also worked throughout Argentina, and you will see his name all over the place. He is remembered for combining the romantic English informality with the French formal garden, as well as his use of open and closed curved roads, lakes with islands, ornamental buildings, sculptures and monuments. He received several awards including the Légion d'Honneur in France, and when he died in 1934 he was revered for his life's work throughout Argentina and Europe.

sports among young people, with strong teams in many sizeable towns, and basketball attracts fans since Argentine players play for the NBA in the States.

Although the best polo in the world is played in Argentina, it's only accessible to an elite class, due to its cost (although you can watch it without it costing you an arm and a leg). Despite being played throughout the country and all year round, the top Argentine players, who now play all over the world, return only for the high handicap season between September and November. This consists of tournaments, played on the outskirts of Buenos Aires, followed by the Argentine Open, which takes place on Palermo's polo field, known as the 'cathedral of polo'.

Rugby was brought to Argentina by the British over a hundred years ago and is played throughout the country. The national team, Los Pumas, reached the semi-finals of the last Rugby World Cup in 2007, and they have recently been accepted to play the Tri Nations. Locally, the most popular teams both come from San Isidro, north of the capital.

Argentina's native sports include the squash-like *pelota paleta* and *pato*, a cross between polo and basketball. Originally played between large bands of gauchos, today, it is played by teams of four horsemen and a football with handles, and is one sport which is unique to Argentina.

Land and environment

Argentina is the second largest country in South America in area, extending across the continent some 1580 km from east to west and 3460 km from north to south. Its northern-most point is at latitude 22°S (just within the tropics); at Tierra del Fuego and Isla de los Estados it extends south of 54°S (the latitude of Scotland or Labrador). The coast of this territory, which extends over 2000 km, runs wholly along the Atlantic apart from the north coast of the Beagle Channel linking the Atlantic and the Pacific. The western border with Chile follows the crest of the Andes, but below 46°S, the drainage is complex and border disputes have arisen ever since the Treaty of 1881 when the principle that the border should follow the watershed was established.

Geology and landscape

Together with Brazil, Paraguay and Uruguay, Argentina is the visible part of the South American Plate which has been moving for the past 125 million years away from its former union with Africa. The submerged part of this plate forms a broad continental shelf under the Atlantic Ocean; in the south this extends over 1000 km east and includes the Falkland Islands/Islas Malvinas. Since the 'break' between the plates, there have been numerous invasions and withdrawals of the sea over this part of the South American continent, but the Andean mountain building from the end of the Cretaceous period (65 million years ago) to the present day dominates the surface geology. Of the many climatic fluctuations, the Pleistocene Ice Age up to 10,000 BC has done most to mould the current landscape. At its maximum, ice covered all the land over 2000 m and most of Patagonia. In the mountains, ice created virtually all the present-day lakes and glaciers, and moraine deposits can be found everywhere. However, the special feature of the heartland of Argentina is the fine soil of the Pampas, the result of ice and water erosion and the unique wind systems of the southern cone of the continent.

The Northwest

Northern and western Argentina are dominated by the satellite ranges of the Andes. Between the mountains of the far northwest is the *puna*, a high plateau rising to 3400-4000 m, on which are situated salt flats or *salares*, some of which are of interest for their wildlife. East of this is the *prepuna*, the gorges and slopes ranging in altitude from 1700 m to 3400 m which connect the *puna* with the plains. On the fringe of the Andes are a string of important settlements including Salta, Tucumán and Mendoza. Though the climate of this region is hot and dry, there is sufficient water to support maize and pasture and a thriving wine industry, mostly relying on irrigation. East of the Andes lies several ranges of hills, the most important of which are the Sierras de Córdoba and the Sierras de San Luis. These are mostly of ancient Precambrian rocks.

The Paraná Basin

The vast Paraná Basin stretches from the borders with Brazil and Paraguay to the Atlantic at Buenos Aires. In the northeast it mainly consists of geologically recent deposits. The easternmost part of this basin, between the Ríos Paraná and Uruguay, is the wettest part of the country. Known as Mesopotamia and consisting of the provinces of Entre Ríos, Corrientes and Misiones, it is structurally part of the Brazilian plateau of old crystalline rocks, the 'heart' of the South American Plate. Here there are undulating grassy hills and marshy or forested lowlands, among them the Esteros del Iberá, an extensive area of flooded forest similar to the Pantanal in Brazil. The horizontal stratum of the rocks in this area is dramatically evident in the river gorges to the north and the spectacular Iguazú Falls shared with Brazil.

The Chaco
Northwest of Mesopotamia and stretching from the Paraná and Paraguay rivers west to the Andean foothills and north into Paraguay and Bolivia lies the Gran Chaco, a vast plain that covers the provinces of Formosa, Chaco and Santiago del Estero, as well as parts of Santa Fe and Córdoba. It is crossed from west to east by three rivers, the Teuco-Bermejo, the Salado and the Pilcomayo. Annual rainfall ranges from 400 mm in the western or Dry Chaco, a semi-desert mainly used for cattle ranching, to 800-1200 mm in the eastern or Wet Chaco, where periodic floods alternate with long periods of drought.

The Pampas
South of 33°S, the latitude of Mendoza and Rosario, is a great flat plain known as the Pampas. Extending almost 1000 km from north to south and a similar distance from east to west, the Pampas cover some 650,000 sq km, including most of Buenos Aires province, southern Córdoba, Santa Fe and Entre Ríos, north eastern La Pampa and a small part of San Luís. This area is crossed by meandering rivers and streams, and there are many lakes, lagoons and marshes. Geologically the Pampas are similar to the Chaco, basic crystalline and granite rocks almost completely overlain with recent deposits, often hundreds of metres thick. Prevailing winds from the southeast and southwest help to create the fine loess-type soils which make this one of the richest farming areas in the world, ideal for grasslands and cattle ranching. Being comparatively close to the ocean, extremes of temperature are rare, another favourable feature.

A distinction is often made between the 'wet' Pampa and the 'dry' Pampa. The former, inland from Rosario and Buenos Aires, is the centre of wheat, maize and other cereal production; the latter, west of 64°W, is where cattle ranching predominates.

The Patagonian steppe
Patagonia extends from the Río Colorado (39°S) south to the Straits of Magellan and covers some 780,000 sq km. Most of this area consists of a series of tablelands and terraces, which drop in altitude from west to east. The basic rocks are ancient, some classified as Precambrian, but the surface has been subjected to endless erosion. Rainfall is lighter and the winds stronger than in the Pampas frequently stripping the surface of cover and filling the air with dust. Only where rivers have scored deep valleys in the rock base can soil accumulate, allowing more than extensive sheep farming.

From the Straits of Magellan north to Lago Argentino (46°S) and beyond, a geological depression separates the edge of the South American Plate from the Andes. Most of Patagonia was under ice during the Quaternary Ice Age and has been rising since the ice receded. This area was presumably the last to be uncovered. However, considerable volcanic activity associated with the uplift of the Andes has taken place along the depression which is transversely divided into basins by lava flows. Alluvial and glacial deposits have created relatively fertile soils in some areas, useful for sheep and producing attractive wooded landscapes in the lake regions in contrast to the general desolation of Patagonia.

The Andes

Geographically the Isla de los Estados forms the southernmost extent of the Andes, which then swing north to become the border between Chile and Argentina just north of the Paine mountains. The 350-km section north of Paine is one of the most dramatic stretches of the Andes. The crest lies under the Southern Patagonian ice cap, with glaciers reaching down to the valleys on both the Argentine and Chilean sides. On the Argentine side this has created the spectacular range of glaciers found in the Parque Nacional Los Glaciares, the most famous of which, the Perito Moreno Glacier, is one of the highlights for many travellers to Argentina. The northern end of this section is Cerro Fitz Roy, which, along with the Torres del Paine (in Chile) at the southern end, is among the most spectacular hiking and climbing centres in South America.

Further north between 46°S and 47°S there is another ice cap, the North Patagonian ice cap, centred on Monte San Valentín on the Chilean side of the border. North of this lies 1500 km of mountain ranges rarely exceeding 4000 m; on the east side of these are a series of attractive lakes, formed by a mixture of glacial and volcanic activity. The high section of the Andes begins at 35°S and includes Aconcagua (6960 m), the highest peak outside the Himalayas. For a further 1000 km northwards, the ranges continue to the border with Bolivia with many peaks over 6000 m, the Argentine side becoming progressively drier and more inhospitable.

Climate

Climate ranges from subtropical in the northeast to cold temperate in Tierra del Fuego, but is temperate and quite healthy for much of the year in the densely populated central zone. Between December and the end of February, Buenos Aires can be oppressively hot and humid. The Andes have a dramatic effect on the climate of the south: although on the Chilean side of the mountains there is adequate rainfall from Santiago southwards, very little of this moisture reaches the Argentine side. Furthermore, the prevailing winds in Patagonia are southwest to northeast from the Pacific. The result is a temperate climate with some mist and fog near the coast, but not much rain. Further inland, the westerlies, having deposited their moisture on the Andes, add strength to the southerly airstream, creating the strong dry wind (*El Pampero*) characteristic of the Pampas. Only when these systems meet humid maritime air in the northeast of the country does rainfall significantly increase, often with violent thunderstorms, and the heaviest precipitation is in Mesopotamia where the summer months are particularly wet.

The highest temperatures are found in the northeast where the distance from the sea and the continuous daytime sunshine produce the only frequently recorded air temperatures over 45°C anywhere in South America. The northwest is cooler due to the effects of altitude, rainfall here occurring largely in the summer months.

Vegetation

Few countries offer as wide a range of natural environments as Argentina; its varied vegetation supports equally diverse wildlife. The main types of vegetation are described below. Details of some of the animals to be seen are given where appropriate in the text; to avoid repetition they are not described. There are 10 main vegetation types:

Llanura pampeana

Extensive cattle grazing and arable farming have altered the original vegetation of the Pampas, notably through the introduction of tree species such as the eucalyptus for shelter. The least altered areas of the Pampas are the coastal lowlands, the Paraná delta and the southern sierras. The sandy soils of the coastal lowlands, including marshes and estuaries, are home to pampas grass or *cortadera*. In the marshy parts of the Paraná delta there are tall grasses with *espinillo* and *ñandubay* (*Prosopis*) woods in the higher areas. Willows and alisos grow along the riverbanks while the ceibo, the national flower of Argentina, grows in the nearby woodlands.

Espinal

These are open woodlands and savannahs which extend in an arc around the Pampas covering southern Corrientes, northern Entre Ríos, central Santa Fe, large parts of Córdoba and San Luis and the centre-west of La Pampa. In these areas xerophitic and thorny woods of prosopis and acacia predominate. The major prosopis species are the *ñandubay*; the white algarrobo; the black algarrobo and the caldén. The *ñandubay* is found in Entre Ríos and parts of Corrientes, along with the white *quebracho*, *tala*, *espinillo* and, on sandy soils, *yatay* palms. The white algarrobo and black algarrobo are found in areas of Santa Fe, Córdoba and San Luis which have been heavily affected by farming. The caldén appears across large areas of La Pampa, southern San Luis and southern Buenos Aires, along with bushes such as the alpataco and the creosote bush (*Larrea*).

Monte

Monte is a bushy steppe with a few patches of trees, in areas with rainfall from 80 mm to 250 mm. Covering large areas of San Juan, Mendoza, La Pampa and Río Negro, it can be found as far north as Salta and as far south as Chubut. Vegetation includes different species of the creosote bush, which have small resinous leaves and yellow flowers, as well as thorny bushes from the cacti family and bushes such as *brea*, *retamo* and *jume*. In the northern areas of *monte* the white algarrobo and sweet algarrobo can be found, while the native willow grows along the riverbanks as far south as the Río Chubut.

Puna and prepuna

Low rainfall, intense radiation and poor soils inhibit vegetation in the *puna*, the major species being adapted by having deep root systems and small leaves; many plants have thorny leaves to deter herbivores. These include species of cacti, which store water in their tissue, and the *yareta*, a cushion-shaped plant, which has been over-exploited for firewood, as well as the *tolilla*, the *chijua* and the *tola*. The *queñoa*, which grows to over 5 m high in the sheltered gorges and valleys of the *prepuna*, is the highest growing tree in Argentina. These valleys also support bushes from the Leguminosae family such as the *churqui*, and species of cacti, such as the cardoon and the *airampu*, with its colourful blossom.

High Andean grasslands

Extending from Jujuy to Neuquén, and then in discontinuous fashion south to Tierra del Fuego, these areas range in altitude from 4200 m in Jujuy to 500 m in Tierra del Fuego. Grasses adapted to the cold include *iros*, *poa* and *stipa* as well as some endemic species.

Subtropical cloudforest

Often known as *yungas*, this extends into Argentina from Bolivia and covers parts of the sub-Andean sierras. It is found in eastern Jujuy, central Salta and Tucumán and eastern Catamarca. Its eastern sides receive the humidity of the winds which cross the Chaco from the Atlantic. Winters are dry but temperature, rainfall and humidity vary with changes in latitude and altitude. These forests are important regulators of the water cycle, preventing erosion and floods. It is best seen in three national parks: Baritú, Calilegua and El Rey.

Vegetation changes with altitude. Along the edge of the Chaco at the foot of the hills and rising to 500 m, where there is annual rainfall up to 1000 m, is a transition zone with mainly deciduous trees such as the *palo blanco*, the *lapacho rosado* and *lapacho amarillo* (pink and yellow tabebuia); the *palo borracho* (Chorisia bottle tree), the *tipa blanca* and the huge *timbo colorado* or black eared tree. Higher and reaching from 500 to 800 m in altitude, where there is greater humidity, are montane or laurel forests. Predominant tree species here are the laurel, the jacaranda and the *tipa;* epiphytes (orchids, bromeliads, ferns, lichens, mosses) and climbers are abundant. Above 800 m and rising to 1300-1700 m annual rainfall reaches some 3000 mm, concentrated between November and March. Here myrtle forest predominates, with a great diversity of species, including great trees such as the *horco molle*, a wide range of epiphytes, and, in some areas such as Baritu, tree ferns. Higher still, the evergreen trees are replaced by deciduous species including the mountain pine (*Podocarpus*), the only conifer native to the northwest, the walnut and the alder. Above these are clumps of *queñoa* and, higher still, mountain meadow grasslands.

The Chaco

The eastern or Wet Chaco is covered by marshlands and ponds with savannah and caranday palm groves, as well as the characteristic red *quebracho,* a hardwood tree overexploited in the past for tannin. The Dry Chaco, further west, is the land of the white *quebracho* as well as cacti such as the quimil (*opuntia*) and the palo borracho (*Chorisia*). Similar climatic conditions and vegetation to those in the Dry Chaco are also found in northern San Luis, Córdoba and Santa Fe and eastern Tucumán, Catamarca, Salta, Jujuy, La Rioja and San Juan.

Subtropical rainforest

This is found mainly in Misiones, extending southwards along the banks of the Ríos Paraná and Uruguay. The wet climate, with annual rainfall of up to 2000 mm, and high temperatures produce rapid decomposition of organic material. The red soils of this area contain a thin fertile soil layer which is easily eroded.

This area offers the widest variety of flora in Argentina. There of over 2000 known species of vascular plants, about 10% of which are trees. Forest vegetation rises to different strata: the giant trees such as the *palo rosa*, the Misiones cedar, *incienso* and the *guatambú* rise to over 30 m high. The forest canopy includes species such as strangler figs and the pindo palm, while the intermediate strata includes the fast growing *ambay* (*Cecropia*), tree-ferns, the *yerba mate* and bamboos. Llianas, vines and epiphytes such as orchids and bromeliads as well as ferns and even cacti compete in the struggle for sunlight.

In the hills of northwestern Misiones there are remnants of forests of Paraná pine (*Araucaria angustifolia*).

Sub-Antarctic forest

This grows along the eastern edges of the southern Andes, from Neuquén in the north to Tierra del Fuego and Isla de los Estados in the south. These are cool temperate forests including evergreen and deciduous trees. Species of *nothofagus* predominate, the most common being *lenga* (low deciduous beech), *ñire* (high deciduous beech), *coihue* and *guindo*. The Pehuen or Monkey puzzle tree (*Araucaria araucana*), is found in northwestern and northcentral Neuquén. The fungus *llao llao* and the hemiparasitic *Misodendron* are also frequent. Flowering bushes include the *notro* (firebush), the *calafate* (*Burberis boxifolis*) and the *chaura* (prickly heath).

Areas of the Lake District with annual rainfall of over 1500 mm are covered by Valdivian forest and a wider range of species. The *coihue* (southern beech) is the predominant species of *nothofagus*, reaching as far south as Lago Buenos Aires. Below colihue canes form a dense undergrowth; flowers include the *amancay* (alstromeria), *mutisias*, and near streams, the fuschia. *Arrayán* trees also grow near water, while the Andean Cypress and the *Maiten* grow in the transition zone with the Patagonian steppe. In areas where annual rainfall reaches over 3000 mm, there is a wider range of trees as well as epyphites, ferns, and lichens such as Old Man's Beard. The *alerce* (larch) is the giant of these forests, rising to over 60 m and, in some cases over 3000 years old.

Magallanic forest, found from Lago Buenos Aires south to Tierra del Fuego, is dominated by the *guindo* (evergreen beech) as well as the *lenga*, the *ñire* and the *canelo* (winter bark). There are also large areas of peatbog with sphagnum mosses, and even the carnivorous *Drosera uniflora*.

Patagonian steppe

Plant life in this area has adapted to severe climatic conditions: strong westerly winds, the heavy winter snowfall that occurs in some years, high evaporation in summer, low annual rainfall and sandy soils with a thin fertile layer on top. The northwest of this area is covered by bushy scrublands: species include the *quilembai*, *molle*, the *algarrobo patagónico*, the *colpiche*, as well as *coiron* grasses. Further south are shrubs such as the *mata negra* and species of *calafate*. Nearer the mountain ranges the climate is less severe and the soil more fertile: here there is a herbaceous steppe that includes *coiron blanco* and shrubs such as the *neneo*. Overgrazing by sheep has produced serious desertification in many parts of the Patagonian steppe.

National parks → www.parquesnacionales.gov.ar.

Fortunately in a country so rich in natural beauty, Argentina has an extensive network of reserves and protected areas, the most important of which are designated as national parks. The history of Argentine national parks is a long one, dating from the donation by Francisco 'Perito' Moreno of 7500 ha of land in the Lake District to the state. This grant formed the basis for the establishment of the first national park, Nahuel Huapi, in 1934.

There are 19 national parks stretching from Parque Nacional Baritú on the northern border with Bolivia to Parque Nacional Tierra del Fuego in the far south. Additional areas have been designated as natural monuments and natural reserves and there are also provincial parks and reserves. The largest national parks are all in western Argentina; these include a string of eight parks in the Andean foothills in the Lake District and Patagonia. These make ideal bases for trekking, with *guardaparque* (rangers) offices at main entrances where you can get advice and maps. Argentina has poor maps for trekking and climbing. Those available from the Instituto Geografico Militar in Buenos Aires are badly out of date and do not show all paths and refuges. Before you travel, therefore, it's a good idea to buy a good basic map of the land you want to explore and to search the national parks website for more information (sadly only available in Spanish). Access to the more remote national parks can be tricky without your own transport and you should allow a couple of extra days, especially for the cloudforest parks in the northwest, and for Parque Nacional Perito Moreno (not the one with the Glaciar Perito Moreno in it). Once you reach the parks, you'll find *guardaparques* very knowledgeable and helpful, and many are happy to take time to explain the wildlife and recommend good walks. The main national parks and other protected areas are shown on the map and further details of all of these are given in the text.

The main administration office of the Argentine National Parks authority is at Santa Fe 680, near the Plaza San Martín in central Buenos Aires. Leaflets are available on some of the parks. For more information, see Essentials A-Z, page 55.

Books

Borges, Jorge Luis, *Collected Fiction*, Penguin, UK. Strange, wonderful and sometimes a little off-the-wall, Argentina's most celebrated modern author still captivates.
Chatwin, Bruce, *In Patagonia*, Vintage/Penguin. The classic travel book. A little outdated and old fashioned but this book inspired a generation of travellers to head to Argentina.
Fernández, José, *El Gaucho Martín Fierro*, Longseller, Argentina. The ulltimate gaucho poem. Long and a little difficult to read, this poem from 1872 was the first work of literature to glorify gauchos and their lives.
Guevara, Ernesto 'Che', *The Motorcycle Diaries*, Verso, UK. Funny, thoughtful and a

ripping read, Guevara's diaries are great to sink into whilst travelling in Argentina.
Granado, Alberto, *Travelling with Che: The Making of a Revolutionary*, Newmarket Press, US. Ernesto Guevara's travelling partner tells his version of their journey together.
McEwan, Colin, ed, *Patagonia: Natural History, Prehistory and Ethnography at the Uttermost Part of the Earth*, British Museum Press. The indigenous cultures of Patagonia and their destruction in the early 20th century. Illustrated, well-written essays.
Palmer, Marina, *Kiss and Tell*, William Morrow, US. The story of a girl falling in love with tango and a tango dancer in the *milongas* of Buenos Aires.

Contents

Footnotes

Basic Spanish for travellers

Learning Spanish is a useful part of the preparation for a trip to Latin America and no volumes of dictionaries, phrase books or word lists will provide the same enjoyment as being able to communicate directly with the people of the country you are visiting. It is a good idea to make an effort to grasp the basics before you go. As you travel you will pick up more of the language and the more you know, the more you will benefit from your stay.

General pronunciation

Whether you have been taught the 'Castilian' pronunciation (*z* and *c* followed by *i* or *e* are pronounced as the *th* in think) or the 'American' pronunciation (they are pronounced as *s*), you will encounter little difficulty in understanding either. Regional accents and usages vary, but the basic language is essentially the same everywhere. In Argentina, the accent is distinctly different to the rest of Latin America in one crucial area. The letters *ll* in all other Spanish-speaking countries are pronounced like the *y* in yellow, in Argentina they are pronounced similar to the *sh* in she. The letter *y* in Argentina is also pronounced like the *sh* in she, instead of the *ee* in feet. Another change is that Argentines tend to use *vos* instead of *tú*.

Vowels

a	as in English *cat*
e	as in English *best*
i	as the *ee* in English *feet*
o	as in English *shop*
u	as the *oo* in English *food*
ai	as the *i* in English *ride*
ei	as *ey* in English *they*
oi	as *oy* in English *toy*

Consonants

Most consonants can be pronounced more or less as they are in English. The exceptions are:

g	before *e* or *i* is the same as *j*
h	is always silent (except in *ch* as in *chair*)
j	as the *ch* in Scottish *loch*
ll	as the *y* in *yellow*
ñ	as the *ni* in English *onion*
rr	trilled much more than in English
x	depending on its location, pronounced *x*, *s*, *sh* or *j*

Spanish words and phrases

Greetings, courtesies

hello	*hola*	yes/no	*sí/no*
good morning	*buenos días*	please	*por favor*
good afternoon/		thank you (very much)	*(muchas) gracias*
evening/night	*buenas*	I speak Spanish	*hablo español*
	tardes/noches	I don't speak Spanish	*no hablo español*
goodbye	*adiós/chao*	do you speak English?	*¿habla inglés?*
pleased to meet you	*mucho gusto*	I don't understand	*no entiendo/*
see you later	*hasta luego*		*no comprendo*
how are you?	*¿cómo está?*		
	¿cómo estás?	please speak slowly	*hable despacio por*
I'm fine, thanks	*estoy muy bien, gracias*		*favor*
I'm called...	*me llamo...*	I am very sorry	*lo siento mucho/*
			disculpe
what is your name?	*¿cómo se llama?*	what do you want?	*¿qué quiere?*
	¿cómo te llamas?		*¿qué quieres?*

I want	*quiero*	leave me alone	*déjeme en paz/*
I don't want it	*no lo quiero*		*no me moleste*
		good/bad	*bueno/malo*

Questions and requests

Have you got a room for two people?
¿Tiene una habitación para dos personas?

How do I get to_? *¿Cómo llego a_?*

How much does it cost?
¿Cuánto cuesta? ¿cuánto es?

I'd like to make a long-distance phone call
Quisiera hacer una llamada de larga distancia

Is service included? *¿Está incluido el servicio?*

Is tax included? *¿Están incluidos los impuestos?*

When does the bus leave (arrive)?
¿A qué hora sale (llega) el autobús?

When? *¿cuándo?*

Where is _? *¿dónde está_?*

Where can I buy tickets?
¿Dónde puedo comprar boletos?

Where is the nearest petrol station?
¿Dónde está la gasolinera más cercana?

Why? *¿por qué?*

Basics

bank	*el banco*	market	*el mercado*
bathroom/toilet	*el baño*	note/coin	*le billete/la moneda*
bill	*la factura/la cuenta*	police (policeman)	*la policía (el policía)*
cash	*el efectivo*	post office	*el correo*
cheap	*barato/a*	public telephone	*el teléfono público*
credit card	*la tarjeta de crédito*	supermarket	*el supermercado*
exchange house	*la casa de cambio*	ticket office	*la taquilla*
exchange rate	*el tipo de cambio*	traveller's cheques	*los cheques de viajero/*
expensive	*caro/a*		*los travelers*

Getting around

aeroplane	*el avión*	immigration	*la inmigración*
airport	*el aeropuerto*	insurance	*el seguro*
arrival/departure	*la llegada/salida*	insured person	*el/la asegurado/a*
avenue	*la avenida*	to insure yourself against	*asegurarse contra*
block	*la cuadra*	luggage	*el equipaje*
border	*la frontera*	motorway, freeway	*el autopista/la*
bus station	*la terminal de*		*carretera*
	autobuses/camiones	north, south, west, east	*norte, sur, oeste*
bus	*el bus/el autobús/*		*(occidente), este*
	el camión		*(oriente)*
collective/		oil	*el aceite*
fixed-route taxi	*el colectivo*	to park	*estacionarse*
corner	*la esquina*	passport	*el pasaporte*
customs	*la aduana*	petrol/gasoline	*la gasolina*
first/second class	*primera/segunda clase*	puncture	*el pinchazo/*
left/right	*izquierda/derecha*		*la ponchadura*
ticket	*el boleto*	street	*la calle*
empty/full	*vacío/lleno*	that way	*por allí/por allá*
highway, main road	*la carretera*	this way	*por aquí/por acá*

tourist card/visa	*la tarjeta de turista*	unleaded	*sin plomo*
tyre	*la llanta*	to walk	*caminar/andar*

Accommodation

air conditioning	*el aire acondicionado*	power cut	*el apagón/corte*
all-inclusive	*todo incluido*	restaurant	*el restaurante*
bathroom, private	*el baño privado*	room/bedroom	*el cuarto/la habitación*
bed, double/single	*la cama matrimonial/ sencilla*	sheets	*las sábanas*
		shower	*la ducha/regadera*
blankets	*las cobijas/mantas*	soap	*el jabón*
to clean	*limpiar*	toilet	*el sanitario/excusado*
dining room	*el comedor*	toilet paper	*el papel higiénico*
guesthouse	*la casa de huéspedes*	towels, clean/dirty	*las toallas limpias/ sucias*
hotel	*el hotel*		
noisy	*ruidoso*	water, hot/cold	*el agua caliente/fría*
pillows	*las almohadas*		

Health

aspirin	*la aspirina*	diarrhoea	*la diarrea*
blood	*la sangre*	doctor	*el médico*
chemist	*la farmacia*	fever/sweat	*la fiebre/el sudor*
condoms	*los preservativos, los condones*	pain	*el dolor*
		head	*la cabeza*
contact lenses	*los lentes de contacto*	period/sanitary towels	*la regla/ las toallas femeninas*
contraceptives	*los anticonceptivos*		
contraceptive pill	*la píldora anti- conceptiva*	stomach	*el estómago*
		altitude sickness	*el soroche*

Family

family	*la familia*	boyfriend/girlfriend	*el novio/la novia*
brother/sister	*el hermano/la hermana*	friend	*el amigo/la amiga*
daughter/son	*la hija/el hijo*	married	*casado/a*
father/mother	*el padre/la madre*	single/unmarried	*soltero/a*
husband/wife	*el esposo (marido)/ la esposa*		

Months, days and time

January	*enero*	November	*noviembre*
February	*febrero*	December	*diciembre*
March	*marzo*	Monday	*lunes*
April	*abril*	Tuesday	*martes*
May	*mayo*	Wednesday	*miércoles*
June	*junio*	Thursday	*jueves*
July	*julio*	Friday	*viernes*
August	*agosto*	Saturday	*sábado*
September	*septiembre*	Sunday	*domingo*
October	*octubre*		

at one o'clock	*a la una*	it's six twenty	*son las seis y veinte*
at half past two	*a las dos y media*	it's five to nine	*son las nueve menos*
at a quarter to three	*a cuarto para las tres/*		*cinco*
	a las tres menos quince	in ten minutes	*en diez minutos*
it's one o'clock	*es la una*	five hours	*cinco horas*
it's seven o'clock	*son las siete*	does it take long?	*¿tarda mucho?*

Numbers

one	*uno/una*	sixteen	*dieciséis*
two	*dos*	seventeen	*diecisiete*
three	*tres*	eighteen	*dieciocho*
four	*cuatro*	nineteen	*diecinueve*
five	*cinco*	twenty	*veinte*
six	*seis*	twenty-one	*veintiuno*
seven	*siete*	thirty	*treinta*
eight	*ocho*	forty	*cuarenta*
nine	*nueve*	fifty	*cincuenta*
ten	*diez*	sixty	*sesenta*
eleven	*once*	seventy	*setenta*
twelve	*doce*	eighty	*ochenta*
thirteen	*trece*	ninety	*noventa*
fourteen	*catorce*	hundred	*cien/ciento*
fifteen	*quince*	thousand	*mil*

Food

avocado	*la palta*	fried	*frito*
baked	*al horno*	garlic	*el ajo*
bakery	*la panadería*	goat	*el chivo*
banana	*la banana*	grapefruit	*la toronja/el pomelo*
beans	*los frijoles/*	grill	*la parrilla*
	las habichuelas	grilled/griddled	*a la plancha*
beef	*la carne de res*	guava	*la guayaba*
beef steak	*el lomo*	ham	*el jamón*
boiled rice	*el arroz blanco*	hamburger	*la hamburguesa*
bread	*el pan*	hot, spicy	*picante*
breakfast	*el desayuno*	ice cream	*el helado*
butter	*la manteca*	jam	*la mermelada*
cake	*la torta*	knife	*el cuchillo*
chewing gum	*el chicle*	lemon	*el limón*
chicken	*el pollo*	lobster	*la langosta*
chilli or green pepper	*el ají/pimiento*	lunch	*el almuerzo/la comida*
clear soup, stock	*el caldo*	meal	*la comida*
cooked	*cocido*	meat	*la carne*
dining room	*el comedor*	minced meat	*la carne picada*
egg	*el huevo*	onion	*la cebolla*
fish	*el pescado*	orange	*la naranja*
fork	*el tenedor*	pepper	*el pimiento*

pasty, turnover	la empanada/ el pastelito	seafood	los mariscos
		soup	la sopa
pork	el cerdo	spoon	la cuchara
potato	la papa	squash	la calabaza
prawns	los camarones	squid	los calamares
raw	crudo	supper	la cena
restaurant	el restaurante	sweet	dulce
salad	la ensalada	to eat	comer
salt	la sal	toasted	tostado
sandwich	el bocadillo	turkey	el pavo
sauce	la salsa	vegetables	los legumbres/vegetales
sausage	la longaniza/el chorizo	without meat	sin carne
scrambled eggs	los huevos revueltos	yam	el camote

Drink

beer	la cerveza	ice/without ice	el hielo/sin hielo
boiled	hervido/a	juice	el jugo
bottled	en botella	lemonade	la limonada
camomile tea	la manzanilla	milk	la leche
canned	en lata	mint	la menta
coffee	el café	rum	el ron
coffee, white	el café con leche	soft drink	el refresco
cold	frío	sugar	el azúcar
cup	la taza	tea	el té
drink	la bebida	to drink	beber/tomar
drunk	borracho/a	water	el agua
firewater	el aguardiente	water, carbonated	el agua mineral con gas
fruit milkshake	el batido/licuado	water, still mineral	el agua mineral sin gas
glass	el vaso	wine, red	el vino tinto
hot	caliente	wine, white	el vino blanco

Key verbs

to go	**ir**	**to be**	**ser** (permanent state) **estar** (positional or temporary state)
I go	voy	I am	soy	estoy
you go (familiar)	vas	you are	eres	estás
he, she, it goes,		he, she, it is,		
you (formal) go	va	you (formal) are	es	está
we go	vamos	we are	somos	estamos
they, you (plural) go	van	they, you (plural) are	son	están

to have (possess)	**tener**
I have	tengo
you (familiar) have	tienes
he, she, it,	
you (formal) have	tiene
we have	tenemos
they, you (plural) have	tienen
there is/are	hay
there isn't/aren't	no hay

This section has been assembled on the basis of glossaries compiled by André de Mendonça and David Gilmour of South American Experience, London, and the Latin American Travel Advisor, No 9, March 1996.

Menu reader

This is a list of Argentine specialities; for translations of basic food terms, see page 33.

Parrilla and asado

The most important vocabulary is for the various cuts of meat in the *asado*, or barbecue, which you can eat at any *parrilla* or steakhouse.

achuras offal
chinchulines entrails
molleja sweetbread
chorizos beef sausages
morcilla blood sausage
tira de asado ribs
bife ancho entrecôte steak
bife angosto sirloin
bife de chorizo or cuadril rumpsteak
lomo fillet steak
chivito kid
cerdo pork
costilla pork chop
cordero lamb
riñón kidney
pollo chicken
cocina criolla typical Argentine food
empanadas small pasties, traditionally meat, but often made with cheese or other fillings

humitas a puree of sweetcorn, onions and cheese, wrapped in corn cob husks, steamed
tamales corn-flour balls with meat and onion, wrapped in corn cob husks and boiled
locro stew made with corn, onions, beans, and various cuts of meat, chicken or sausage
ciervo venison
jabalí wild boar
bife a caballo steak with a fried egg on top
guiso meat and vegetable stew
matambre stuffed flank steak with vegetables and hard-boiled eggs
horipán hot dog, made with meat sausage
lomito sandwich of thin slice of steak in a bread roll, lomito completo comes with tomato, cheese, ham and egg
fiambre cold meats, hams, salami
picada a selection of fiambre, cheeses and olives to accompany a drink

Fish and seafood

cazuela de marisco seafood stew
merluza hake
manduví river fish with pale flesh
pejerrey inland water fish
pacú river fish with firm meaty flesh

surubí a kind of catfish, tender flesh
camarones prawns
cangrejo crab
centolla king crab

Puddings (*postre*), cakes and pastries

dulce de leche the Argentine obsession – a sweet caramel made from boiling milk spread on toast, cakes and inside pastries
budín de pan a gooey dense bread pudding, often with dried fruit
flan crème caramel, an Argentine favourite
helados ice cream, served piled high in tiny cones

media luna croissant (*dulce or salado* – sweet or savoury)
facturas pastries in general, bought by the dozen
tortilla dry crumbly layered breakfast pastry (in northwest)
torta cake (not to be confused with *tarte*: vegetable pie)

Index → *Entries in bold refer to maps*

Advertisers' index

Acknowledgements

I would like to thank the many people who helped me along the way to finishing this book. Firstly I would like to thank Ben Box for his help in actually convincing Alan to take a chance on an unknown Australian and for helping me with various sections of this book. I would also like to thank Alan for thinking I did an OK job on the previous edition, sending me off into the wilderness again and trusting me to come back with a book. And to the ever patient and flexible Felicity, who has been wonderful pulling everything together.

People to thank are Shanie Matthews, for all her help with Bariloche and surrounds, Tracey Chandler for her work on Mar del Plata, Will Massa for his research on the Argentine film industry, and Andre Vltchek for his invaluable Patagonia knowledge.

Throughout Argentina there have been many helpful people who also deserve a thank you: the wonderful guys at Bloom Brunch and Breakfast in Salta, the lovely Rodolfo from Misiones Excursions Turismo in San Ignacio and Macacha Wayar and the friendly staff at the gorgeous Azur Real Hotel Boutique in Córdoba.

And finally I would like to thank my fantastic husband Gabriel García Isola for his endless patience, support, invaluable advice and the many cups of tea, delicious dinners and yummy lunches he made me while I was neck-high in research.

About the author

Australian-born Lucy E Cousins started travelling at the age of 18 months when she crawled across the road in front of her house - much to her mother's horror. Since then she hasn't stopped. She has visited over 30 countries from Jordan to Venezuela, travelled by bus, bicycle, canoe, Amazon ferry and on foot, and has lived in London, Bolivia and Argentina. In 2004, while backpacking for a year around South America, she fell in love with Buenos Aires. Two years later she moved there to start an English-language newspaper with fellow journalist Kristie, called *The Argentina Independent* (www.argentinaindependent.com), previously known as *The Argentimes*. She has since worked as the editor of the *South American Explorers Magazine* (www.saexplorers.org/magazine), was the director of their Buenos Aires office for two years, and has been published in magazines and books in the UK, Argentina, Australia and Bolivia. She met her Argentine husband, Gabriel, late one night in San Telmo, and they spend their time together speaking a mixture of Spanish and English, eating *dulce de leche* and exploring the fascinating country of Argentina.

Credits

Footprint credits

Project Editor: Felicity Laughton
Layout and production: Emma Bryers
Maps: Kevin Feeney
Colour section: Pepi Bluck
Series design: Mytton Williams
Proofreader: Tim Jollands
Cover design: Robert Lunn
Managing Director: Andy Riddle
Commercial Director: Patrick Dawson
Publisher: Alan Murphy
Publishing Managers: Felicity Laughton,
Jo Williams, Jen Haddington
Marketing and PR: Liz Harper
Sales: Jeremy Parr
Advertising: Renu Sibal
Finance and administration: Elizabeth Taylor

Photography credits

Front cover: Cornelia Doerr/photolibrary.com
Back cover: Hervé Hughes/hemis.fr
Page 1: Hugh Sitton/photolibrary.com.
Pages 2-3: David R Frazier Photolibrary Inc./Alamy.
Pages 6-9: Franck Guiziou/hemis.fr; NB Photos/
Alamy; Chad Ehlers/Alamy; Andrew Newey/
Alamy; Luciano Lepre; Marc Verin/photolibrary.
com; Pete Oxford/Nature Picture Library; Jordi
Cami/photolibrary.com; Christian Guy/hemis.fr;
Jose Fuste Raga/mauritius images; Mariana
Eliano/Getty Images; Sylvia Cordaiy Photolibrary
Ltd/Alamay. Pages 10-12: Ryan Bird; Javier
Etcheverry/Alamy; Marion Morrison/South
American Pictures; Bertrand Gardel/hemis.fr

Manufactured in India by Nutech
Pulp from sustainable forests

Footprint feedback

We try as hard as we can to make each
Footprint guide as up to date as possible
but, of course, things always change.
If you want to let us know about your
experiences – good, bad or ugly – then
don't delay, go to **footprinttravelguides.com**
and send in your comments.

Publishing information

Footprint Argentina
6th edition
© Footprint Handbooks Ltd
October 2010

ISBN: 9781907263132
CIP DATA: A catalogue record for this book
is available from the British Library

® Footprint Handbooks and the Footprint
mark are a registered trademark of Footprint
Handbooks Ltd

Published by Footprint
6 Riverside Court
Lower Bristol Road
Bath BA2 3DZ, UK
T +44 (0)1225 469141
F +44 (0)1225 469461
footprinttravelguides.com

Distributed in the USA by Globe Pequot Press,
Guilford, Connecticut

Every effort has been made to ensure that
the facts in this guidebook are accurate.
However, travellers should still obtain
advice from consulates, airlines, etc about
travel and visa requirements before travelling.
The authors and publishers cannot accept
responsibility for any loss, injury or
inconvenience however caused.

Footprint Mini Atlas
Argentina

Pacific Ocean

PARAGUAY

❶ ❷

Jujuy
Salta
Cafayate
Tucumán
Santiago del Estero
Catamarca
La Rioja

Formosa
Resistencia
Corrientes
Posadas
Mercedes

Puerto Iguazú

BRAZIL

❸

San Juan
Córdoba *Mar Chiquito*
Santa Fe Paraná
Mendoza
San Luis Río Cuarto
Rosario
URUGUAY
San Rafael

BUENOS AIRES □
La Plata

CHILE

Santa Rosa
Tandil
Bahía Blanca
Mar del Plata ❹
Neuquén

200 km
200 miles

San Martín de los Andes
Lago Nahuel Huapi
Bariloche
El Bolsón
Puerto Madryn
Península Valdés
Esquel
Trelew

Viedma

Atlantic Ocean

Lago Buenos Aires
Comodoro Rivadavia ❺
Perito Moreno

Puerto Deseado

Puerto San Julián

Falkland Islands/ Islas Malvinas
Darwin

El Chaltén
Lago Viedma
Lago Argentino
El Calafate

West Falkland/ Gran Malvina
East Falkland/ Isla Soledad

Puerto Natales

Río Gallegos

Punta Arenas
Río Grande
Tierra del Fuego
CHILE | ARGENTINA ❻
Ushuaia

Altitude in metres
4000
3000
2000
1000
500
200
0

Neighbouring Country

National highway including Pan-American Highway

Paved road

Unpaved all weather road

Seasonal unpaved road, track

Rail

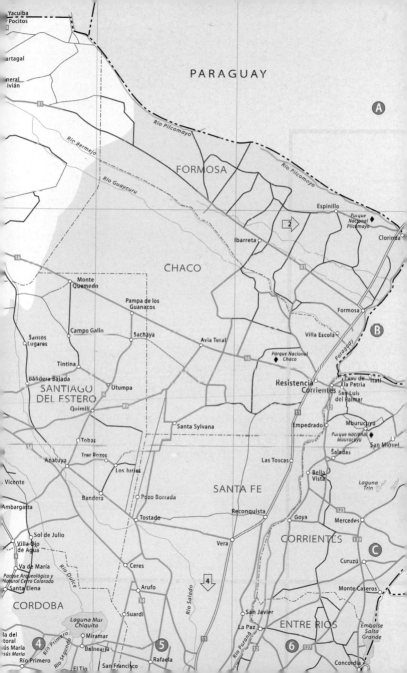

Map 2

PARAGUAY

BRAZIL

Río Pilcomayo

Espinillo

Parque Nacional Pilcomayo

Ibarreta

FORMOSA

Clorinda

(A)

Paraguay

Formosa

Va Escola

Parque Nacional Chaco

Resistencia
Corrientes

Paso de la Patria
San Luís del Palmar

Posadas

Foz do Iguaçu
Iguazú Falls

Ciudad del Este
Puerto Iguazú

Parque Nacional Foz do Iguaçu

Parque Nacional Iguazú

Wanda
Esperanza

Bernardo de Irigoyen

Eldorado
San Pedro

Tobuna

MISIONES

Puerto Rico

Jesús   Jesús
Trinidad
San Cosmé y Damián
Encarnación   San Ignacio
Santa Ana   Santa Ana
LN Alem   Campo Viera
Candelaria   Oberá
San Ignacio Miní
Jardín América

Capiovi

Reserva Natural San Antonio

Dos de Mayo

Mocoá Falls

Empedrado
Mburucuyá

Parque Nacional Mburucuyá   San Miguel

Saladas

Las Toscas

Bella Vista

(B)

Ituzaingó

Laguna de Luna

Esteros del Iberá

Laguna Iberá

Laguna Trín

Laguna Fernández

CORRIENTES

Reconquista

Goya

Mercedes

Colonia Carlos Pellegrini

Santo Tomé

San Javier

Apóstoles

Azara
Garruchos

Alba Posé

Río Uruguay

BRAZIL

Yapeyú

Paso de los Libres

Curuzú

Monte Caseros

La Paz

ENTRE RÍOS

Embalse Salto Grande

Concordia

San Salvador

Ubajay
Parque Nacional El Palmar

Villaguay

Colón

Paysandú

Concepción del Uruguay

URUGUAY

Gualeguay   Gualeguaychú

Fray Bentos

Río Alto Paraná

Río Uruguay

N

50 km
50 miles

(1)   (2)   (3)

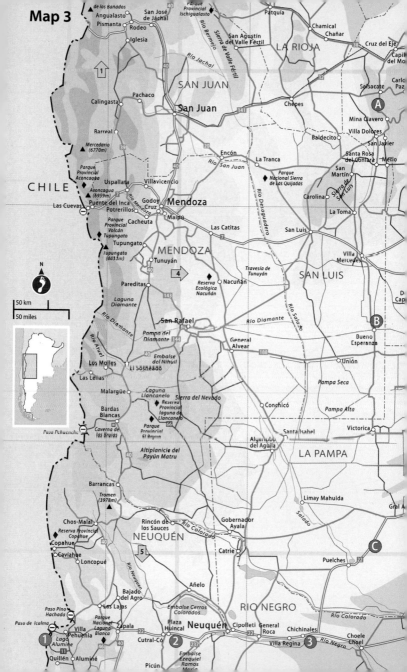

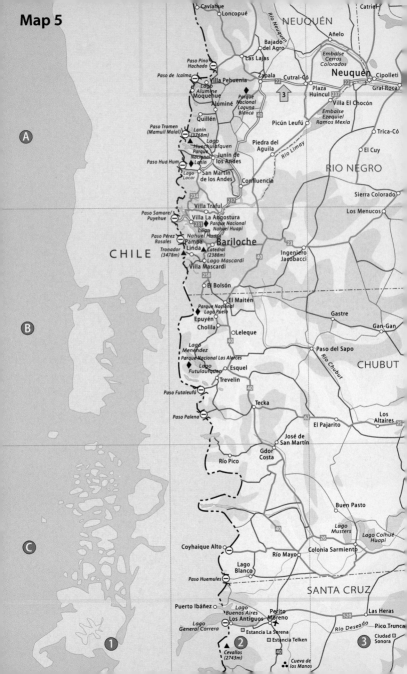

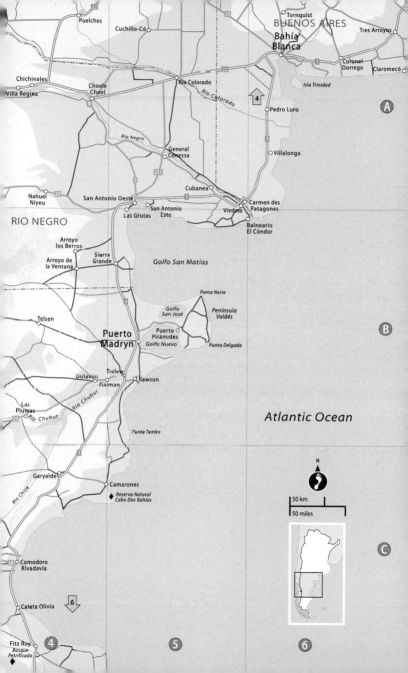

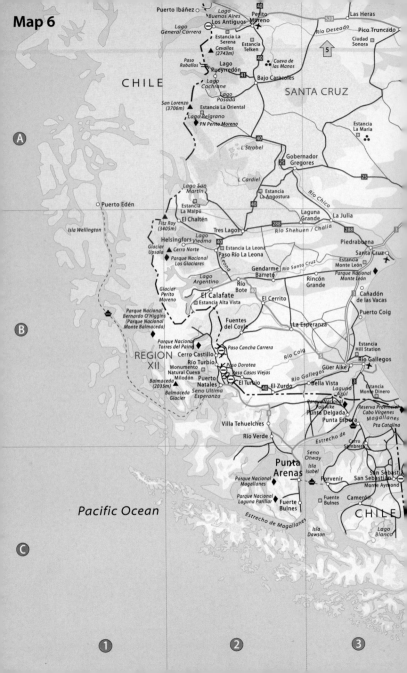

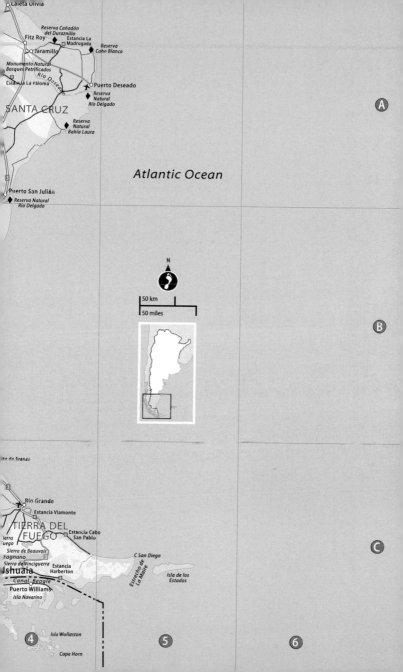

Caleta Olivia

Reserva Cañadón
del Duraznillo
Fitz Roy
Estancia La
Madrugada
Reserva
Jaramillo
Cabo Blanco
Monumento Natural
Bosques Petrificados
Río Deseado
Estancia La Paloma
Puerto Deseado
Reserva
Natural
Río Delgado
SANTA CRUZ
Reserva
Natural
Bahía Laura

Atlantic Ocean

Puerto San Julián
Reserva Natural
Río Delgado

A

B

N

50 km
50 miles

o de Arenas

Río Grande
Estancia Viamonte
TIERRA DEL
Estancia Cabo
FUEGO
San Pablo
Sierra
Fuego
Sierra de Beauvoir
C San Diego
Fagnano
Sierra de Vinciguerra
Estancia
Ushuaia
Harberton
Canal Beagle
Isla de los
Puerto Williams
Estados
Isla Navarino

C

Estrecho de
La Maire

Isla Wollaston

4   **5**   **6**

Cape Horn

Index

Distance chart

	Buenos Aires	Catamarca	Córdoba	Corrientes	Jujuy	La Rioja	Mendoza	Neuquén	Posadas	Resistencia	Río Gallegos	Salta	San Juan	San Luis	Santa Fe	Trelew	Tucumán	Ushuaia	Viedma
Catamarca	1121																		
Córdoba	689	432																	
Corrientes	939	836	894																
Jujuy	1525	565	878	873															
La Rioja	1142	156	453	992	721														
Mendoza	1042	730	675	1443	1296	580													
Neuquén	1161	1469	1167	1911	2045	1319	834												
Posadas	1005	1158	1207	322	1175	1314	1759	2085											
Resistencia	1019	820	874	19	857	970	1436	1896	341										
Río Gallegos	2504	3015	2583	3326	3461	3036	2728	1874	3476	3292									
Salta	1497	537	850	845	120	693	1268	2017	1147	829	3419								
San Juan	1110	623	585	1435	1164	449	168	1002	1763	1419	2799	1136							
San Luis	791	685	412	1192	1229	535	255	784	1510	1185	2461	1201	323						
Santa Fe	485	773	342	557	1105	795	903	1357	866	537	2773	1069	927	652					
Trelew	1352	1863	1431	2174	2319	1884	1576	722	2338	2154	1140	2281	1647	1313	1621				
Tucumán	1193	233	546	748	332	389	964	1713	1070	732	3129	304	832	918	743	1977			
Ushuaia	3090	3601	3169	3912	4047	3622	3314	2460	4062	3878	586	4019	3385	3061	3359	1726	3715		
Viedma	911	1621	1191	1802	2069	1644	1336	567	1897	1717	1640	2041	1407	1083	1184	508	1737	2226	

Distances in kilometres   1 kilometre = 0.62 miles

Map symbols

- ▢ Capital city
- ○ Other city, town
- International border
- Regional border
- ⊖ Customs
- Contours (approx)
- ▲ Mountain, volcano
- ⇌ Mountain pass
- Escarpment
- Glacier
- Salt flat
- Rocks
- Seasonal marshland
- Beach, sandbank
- Waterfall
- Reef
- Motorway
- Main road
- Minor road
- Track
- Footpath
- Railway
- Railway with station
- ✈ Airport
- 🚌 Bus station
- Ⓜ Metro station

- Cable car
- Funicular
- Ferry
- Pedestrianized street
- Tunnel
- One way-street
- Steps
- Bridge
- Fortified wall
- Park, garden, stadium
- Sleeping
- Eating
- Bars & clubs
- Building
- Sight
- Cathedral, church
- Chinese temple
- Hindu temple
- Meru
- Mosque
- Stupa
- Synagogue
- Tourist office
- 🏛 Museum
- Post office
- Police

- ⑤ Bank
- Internet
- Telephone
- Market
- Medical services
- P Parking
- Petrol
- Golf
- Archaeological site
- National park, wildlife reserve
- Viewing point
- Campsite
- Refuge, lodge
- Castle, fort
- Diving
- Deciduous, coniferous, palm trees
- Hide
- Vineyard, winery
- Distillery
- Shipwreck
- Historic battlefield
- Detail map
- Related map